Advances in Business Statistics, Methods and Data Collection

Advances in Business Statistics, Methods and Data Collection

Edited by

Ger Snijkers
Statistics Netherlands

Mojca Bavdaž
University of Ljubljana

Stefan Bender
Deutsche Bundesbank and University of Mannheim

Jacqui Jones
Australian Bureau of Statistics

Steve MacFeely
World Health Organization and University College Cork

Joseph W. Sakshaug
Institute for Employment Research and Ludwig Maximilian University of Munich

Katherine J. Thompson
U.S. Census Bureau

Arnout van Delden
Statistics Netherlands

Registered Office
John Wiley & Sons, Inc., 111 River Street, Hoboken, NJ 07030, USA

Editorial Office
111 River Street, Hoboken, NJ 07030, USA

For details of our global editorial offices, customer services, and more information about Wiley products visit us at www.wiley.com.

Wiley also publishes its books in a variety of electronic formats and by print-on-demand. Some content that appears in standard print versions of this book may not be available in other formats.

Library of Congress Cataloging-in-Publication Data Applied for

Hardback ISBN: 9781119672302

Cover Design: Wiley
Cover Image: © Denphumi/Shutterstock

Set in 9.5/12.5pt STIXTwoText by Straive, Chennai, India

SKY10040859_010523

Contents

List of Contributors

Jessica Andrews
Statistics Canada
Ottawa
Ontario
Canada

Rebecca Andridge
Division of Biostatistics
The Ohio State University
Columbus
OH
USA

Marie Apostolou
Australian Bureau of Statistics
Melbourne
Victoria
Australia

Helen Baird
Australian Bureau of Statistics
Hobart
Tasmania
Australia

Mojca Bavdaž
Academic Unit for Mathematics, Statistics, and
Operations Research
School of Economics and Business
University of Ljubljana
Ljubljana
Slovenia

Laura Bechtel
Economic Statistical Methods Division
US Census Bureau
Washington
DC
USA

Stefan Bender
Data Service Center
Deutsche Bundesbank
Frankfurt
Germany

and

School of Social Science
University of Mannheim
Mannheim
Germany

Jannick Blaschke
Data Service Center
Deutsche Bundesbank
Frankfurt
Germany

Ahmed Bounfour
RITM & European Chair on Intangibles
Université Paris-Saclay
Sceaux
France

Charles F. Brady, Jr.
US Census Bureau
Washington
DC
USA

Melissa Cidade
U.S. Census Bureau
Washington
DC
USA

Gavin Corral
USDA National Agricultural Statistics Service
Washington
DC
USA

Nicholas Cox
Statistics NZ
Wellington
New Zealand

Irene Csorba
Vrije Universiteit Amsterdam
Amsterdam
The Netherlands

Karen CyBulski
Mathematica
Princeton
NJ
USA

Nicole Czaplicki
Economic Statistical Methods Division
US Census Bureau
Washington
DC
USA

Arnout van Delden
Department of Research and Development
(Methodology)
Statistics Netherlands
Heerlen/the Hague
The Netherlands

Susan Demedash
Statistics Canada
Ottawa
Ontario
Canada

Fred Demollin
Department of Business Statistics (Heerlen)
Division of Economic and Business Statistics
and National Accounts
Statistics Netherlands
Heerlen
The Netherlands

Jill A. Dever
RTI International
Washington
DC
USA

Florian Dumpert
Federal Statistical Office of Germany
Wiesbaden
Germany

Marie-Claude Duval
Statistics Canada
Ottawa
ON
Canada

Duncan Elliott
Office for National Statistics
Newport
Wales
UK

Willem Erasmus
ABS – Australian Bureau of Statistics
Business Register Unit
Melbourne
Australia

Johan Erikson
Statistics Sweden
Örebro
Sweden

and

School of Social Science
University of Mannheim
Mannheim
Germany

Deirdre Giesen
Statistics Netherlands
Heerlen
The Netherlands

Colin Hanley
Central Statistics Office
Cork City
Ireland

Gustav Haraldsen
Division for Methods
Statistics Norway
Oslo/Kongsvinger
Norway

Alan Herning
Data Strategy, Integration and Services
Division
Australian Bureau of Statistics
Canberra
Australia

Christian Hirsch
Data Service Center
Deutsche Bundesbank
Frankfurt
Germany

Scott H. Holan
Department of Statistics
University of Missouri
Columbia
MO
USA

and

Office of the Associate Director for Research
and Methodology
U.S. Census Bureau
Washington
DC
USA

Bente Hole
Statistics Norway
Kongsvinger
Norway

Leanne Houben
Department of Innovation
Development and Functional Management
(Innovation Data Services)
Division of Data Services, Research and
Innovation, Statistics Netherlands
Heerlen
The Netherlands

Thomas F. Howells III
Chief, Industry Economics Division
Bureau of Economic Analysis
USA

Rebecca Hutchinson
US Census Bureau
Washington
DC
USA

Jacqui Jones
Macroeconomic Statistics Division
Australian Bureau of Statistics
Canberra
ACT
Australia

Ryan Janicki
Center for Statistical Research and
Methodology
U. S. Census Bureau
Washington
DC
USA

Stephen Kaputa
Economic Statistical Methods Division
US Census Bureau
Washington
DC
USA

Doug Kilburg
U.S. National Agricultural Statistics Service
Washington
DC
USA

Jae Kwang Kim
Department of Statistics
Iowa State University
Ames
IA
USA

Kari L. Klinedinst
US Census Bureau
Washington
DC
USA

Corinna König
Institute for Employment Research
Nuremberg
Germany

Timo Koskimäki
Statistics Finland
Helsinki
Finland

Melissa Krakowiecki
Mathematica
Princeton
NJ
USA

Benjamin Küfner
German Institute for Employment Research
Nuremberg
Germany

Sébastien Landry
Statistics Canada
Ottawa
ON
Canada

Josh Langeland
U.S. Bureau of Labor Statistics
Washington
DC
USA

A.J. Lanyon
Australian Bureau of Statistics
Brisbane
Queensland
Australia

Richard Laroche
Statistics Canada
Ottawa
ON
Canada

Michael D. Larsen
Department of Mathematics and Statistics
Saint Michael's College
Colchester
VT
USA

Danni Lewis
Office for National Statistics
Newport
UK

Dan Liao
RTI International
Washington
DC
USA

Steve MacFeely
Director of Data and Analytics
Department of Data and Analytics
World Health Organization
Geneva
Switzerland

Imam Machdi
BPS – Statistics Indonesia
Deputy of Methodology and Statistical
Information
Jakarta
Indonesia

Josh Martin
Office for National Statistics
Newport
UK

Alina Matei
Institute of Statistics
University of Neuchâtel
Neuchâtel
Switzerland

Jaki McCarthy
U.S. National Agricultural Statistics Service
Washington
DC
USA

Craig H. McLaren
Office for National Statistics
Newport
Wales
UK

Dane Mead
Australian Bureau of Statistics
Brisbane
Queensland
Australia

Alexander Measure
U.S. Bureau of Labor Statistics
Washington
DC
USA

Christian Moscardi
U.S. Census Bureau
Economic Reimbursable Surveys Division
Business Development Staff
Washington
DC
USA

Rr. Nefriana
BPS – Statistics Indonesia
Deputy of Methodology and Statistical
Information
Jakarta
Indonesia

Jessica R. Nicholson
Research Economist
Bureau of Economic Analysis
USA

Alberto Nonnis
RITM & European Chair on Intangibles
Université Paris-Saclay
Sceaux
France

Holly O'Byrne
Statistics Canada
Ottawa
Ontario
Canada

Sorcha O'Callaghan
Central Statistics Office
Cork City
Ireland

Kathy Ott
USDA/National Agricultural Statistics Service
Washington
DC
USA

Paul A. Parker
Department of Statistics
University of Missouri
Columbia
MO
USA

Ratih Putri Pertiwi
BPS – Statistics Indonesia
Deputy of Methodology and Statistical
Information
Jakarta
Indonesia

Giulio Perani
ISTAT
Rome
Italy

Matt Potts
Mathematica
Princeton
NJ
USA

Mahesh C. Pradhan
Economic Census Section
Central Bureau of Statistics
Kathmandu
Nepal

Tanya Price
Australian Bureau of Statistics
Canberra
ACT
Australia

Tjaša Redek
School of Economics and Business
University of Ljubljana
Ljubljana
Slovenia

Heather Ridolfo
U.S. Energy Information Administration
Washington
DC
USA

Heather Ridolfo
U.S. Energy Information Administration
Washington
DC
USA

Amy Anderson Riemer
U.S. Census Bureau
Washington
DC
USA

Joseph B. Rodhouse
USDA National Agricultural Statistics Service
Washington
DC
USA

Luisa Ryan
Australian Bureau of Statistics
Melbourne
Victoria
Australia

Tom Tarling
Office for National Statistics
Newport
Wales
UK

Joseph W. Sakshaug
German Institute for Employment Research
Nuremberg
Germany

and

Ludwig Maximilian University of Munich
Department of Statistics
Munich
Germany

and

University of Mannheim
Department of Sociology
Mannheim
Germany

Joseph W. Sakshau
Statistical Methods Research Department
Institute for Employment Research
Nuremberg
Germany

Paulo Saraiva
Statistics Portugal
Lisbon
Portugal

Scott Scheleur
US Census Bureau
Washington
DC
USA

Sander Scholtus
Statistics Netherlands
The Hague
The Netherlands

Benjamin Schultz
U.S. Census Bureau
Economic Management Division
Washington
DC
USA

Claire Shenton
Office for National Statistics
Newport
Wales
UK

and

Department of Statistics
Ludwig Maximilian University of Munich
Munich
Germany

Paul A. Smith
S3RI and Department of Social Statistics &
Demography
University of Southampton
Southampton
UK

Ger Snijkers
Department of Research and Development
(Methodology)
Division of Data Services, Research and
Innovation, Statistics Netherlands
Heerlen
The Netherlands

and

Centre for Policy Studies
University College Cork
Cork
Ireland

Kristian Taskinen
Statistics Finland
Helsinki
Finland

Zachary Terner
USDA National Agricultural Statistics Service
Washington
DC
USA

and

National Institute of Statistical Sciences
Washington
DC
USA

Katherine J. Thompson
Associate Directorate for Economic Programs
U.S. Census Bureau
Washington
DC
USA

Peter van de Ven
Inter-Secretariat Working Group on National
Accounts
New York
USA

Larry Vittoriano
Mathematica
Princeton
NJ
USA

Marieke Volkert
Institute for Employment Research
Nuremberg
Germany

Ton de Waal
Statistics Netherlands
The Hague
The Netherlands

and

Tilburg University
Tilburg
The Netherlands

David B. Wasshausen
Chief, Expenditure and Income Division
Bureau of Economic Analysis
USA

Deanna Weidenhamer
US Census Bureau
Washington
DC
USA

Diane K. Willimack
U.S. Census Bureau
Washington
DC
USA

Linda J. Young
USDA National Agricultural Statistics Service
Washington
DC
USA

Wesley Yung
Statistics Canada
Ottawa
Canada

Stefan Zins
German Institute for Employment Research
Nuremberg
Germany

Section 1

Introduction to New Measures/Indicators for the Economy

1

Advances in Business Statistics, Methods and Data Collection: Introduction

Ger Snijkers[1], Mojca Bavdaž[2], Stefan Bender[3,4], Jacqui Jones[5], Steve MacFeely[6,7], Joseph W. Sakshaug[8,9], Katherine J. Thompson[10], and Arnout van Delden[1]

[1] Department of Research and Development (Methodology), Statistics Netherlands, Heerlen/the Hague, The Netherlands
[2] Academic Unit for Mathematics, Statistics, and Operations Research, School of Economics and Business, University of Ljubljana, Ljubljana, Slovenia
[3] Data Service Center, Deutsche Bundesbank, Frankfurt, Germany
[4] School of Social Science, University of Mannheim, Mannheim, Germany
[5] Macroeconomic Statistics Division, Australian Bureau of Statistics, Canberra, ACT, Australia
[6] Department of Data and Analytics, World Health Organization, Geneva, Switzerland
[7] Centre for Policy Studies, University College Cork, Cork, Ireland
[8] Statistical Methods Research Department, Institute for Employment Research, Nuremberg, Germany
[9] Department of Statistics, Ludwig Maximilian University of Munich, Munich, Germany
[10] Associate Directorate for Economic Programs, U.S. Census Bureau, Washington, DC, USA

1.1 The ICES-VI Edited Volume: A New Book on Establishment Statistics Methodology

In 2021, when ICES-VI took place, almost 30 years had passed since ICES-I, which yielded the edited volume *"Business Survey Methods"* (Cox et al. 1995), the first reference book covering this topic. During these three decades much has changed with regard to establishment statistics, methods, and data collection. Clearly, it is time for a new volume, discussing these advances.

At the beginning of the 1990s, a group of practitioners working on establishment surveys recognized that the "lack of published methods and communication among researchers was a stumbling block for progress in solving business surveys' unique problems" (Cox et al. 1995: xiii) and concluded that "an international conference was needed to (1) provide a forum to describe methods in current use, (2) present new or improved technologies, and (3) promote international interchange of ideas" (ibid: xiii). In June 1993, practitioners, researchers, and methodologists from around the world met in Buffalo, New York (USA), at the International Conference on Establishment Surveys (ICES) to develop a community based entirely around establishment statistics. Rather than narrowly focus on business surveys, the conference organizers broadened the scope to include all establishment surveys, whose target populations include businesses (establishments, firms), farms, and institutions (schools, jails, governments) – basically, any unit other than a household or a person. This conference created a recurring forum for networking and innovation in an often-overlooked area of survey research methods and became the first in a series of international conferences.

As this community solidified, and the pace of developments in establishment surveys quickened, ICES progressed from a seven-year conference cycle to a four-year cycle, with conferences in 2000 (II), 2007 (III), 2012 (IV), and 2016 (V), with the latest conference (ICES-VI) held virtually in

2021, and ICES-VII being scheduled for 2024. Along the way, the conference title changed, from "establishment surveys" to "establishment statistics," reflecting the increased prevalence of other data sources, such as censuses, registers, big data, and blended data applications in economic measurements. This series of conferences has become a well-respected international platform whose participants include practitioners, researchers, and methodologists in government, central banks, academia, international organizations, and the private sector from around the globe.

The ICES-I edited volume "*Business Survey Methods*" (Cox et al. 1995) stood for almost 20 years as the only comprehensive *overview* reference book dedicated to establishment programs. Featuring chapters drawn from conference presentations, this volume laid the groundwork for other important references. "*Designing and Conducting Business Surveys*" (Snijkers et al. 2013) was published in 2013. This textbook provides detailed guidelines of the entire process of designing and conducting a business survey, ranging from constructs to be measured using a survey, through collection and post-collection processing to dissemination of the results. "*The Unit Problem and Other Current Topics in Business Survey Methodology*" (Lorenc et al. 2018) was published in 2018. In addition to these monographs, the Journal of Official Statistics published a selection of 2007 ICES-III papers in a special section (JOS 2010), and subsequently published dedicated special issues featuring papers from the 2012 ICES-IV (Smith and Phipps 2014) and 2016 ICES-V (Thompson et al. 2018) conferences.

While the topics covered in that first edited volume remain relevant, much has changed over the passing decades. As economies change and sciences evolve, methodologists around the world have worked actively on the development, conduct, and evaluation of modern establishment statistics programs. Furthermore, emerging data sources and new technologies are used in modern applications; some of these were not discussed in the monographs noted above, simply because they did not yet exist or were used on a small scale. These topics include new developments in establishment surveys (such as nonprobability sampling, sophisticated developments in web surveys, applications of adaptive and responsive data collection designs), improvements in statistical process control applications, advanced data visualization methods and software, widespread use of alternative/secondary data sources like registers and big data along with improved methodologies and increased production of multi-source statistics, Internet of Things possibilities (smart farming data, smart industries data), new computer technologies (such as web scraping, text mining), and new indicators for the economy (like Sustainable Development Goals). It is time for a new monograph on establishment statistics methodology! The ICES-VI conference provides an excellent source of material for such a new volume.

ICES-VI was originally planned for June 2020 in New Orleans, but postponed because of the COVID-19 pandemic, and was held as an online conference from 14–17 June 2021. Close to 425 participants from 32 countries representing over 160 organizations, met online to listen to and discuss nearly 100 presentations, dealing with a wide variety of topics germane to establishment statistics. In addition, 17 invited pre-recorded Introductory Overview Lectures (IOL) provided a comprehensive overview of all key topics in establishment statistics (see Appendix). Book contributions from conference authors were solicited via an open call to presenters; in some cases, chapters present consolidated session content. Taken collectively, this edited volume presents materials and reflects discussions on every aspect of the establishment statistics production life cycle.

This volume is entirely new; it is neither an update of the Cox et al. book (1995) nor an update of the Snijkers et al. (2013) textbook. Its scope is broader, containing comprehensive review papers drawn from IOLs and cutting-edge applications of methods and data collection as applied to establishment statistics programs, and thoughtful discussions on both previously existing and new economic measures for economies that are increasingly global. The next section of this introductory chapter discusses the importance of establishment statistics (Section 1.2), followed by trends in establishment statistics research based on the ICES conference programs (Section 1.3), the organization of this volume (Section 1.4), and a conclusion (Section 1.5).

1.2 The Importance of Establishment Statistics

Establishment statistics provide information on businesses, farms, or institutions (Cox and Chinnappa 1995). These statistics not only explain the structure and evolution of economies around the world but they also provide many of the input data required by the System of National Accounts (SNA) and the calculation of gross domestic product (GDP) and contribute to some of the most important policy questions of our age – for example, how globalization and digitalization are impacting national economies, societies, and environments.

Establishment statistics come in many "shapes and sizes," ranging from statistics on a single industry like agricultural statistics or a single topic like research and development (R&D) statistics to all-encompassing statistics like structural business statistics (Jones et al. 2013):

- Agricultural statistics help inform business decisions on plants to crop and policy decisions on subsidies.
- School surveys provide valuable data on the current state of public and private education.
- Government finance statistics provide useful snapshots of spending at the level of local and federal governments, measure hidden and visible public tax collection, and demonstrate accessibility to common utilities.
- Structural business statistics (SBS) answer key policy questions regarding wealth and employment creation in different industries and sectors of the business economy and whether these are growing or declining. They show the costs of doing business in a country, the structure of earnings, and provide critical information on the specialization of national economies, the profitability of industries, sectors and countries, and changes to productivity and competitiveness. They offer insights into structure, performance, and dynamics by industry, region, and size.
- Short-term statistics (STS) provide a wide range of sub-annual statistics (typically quarterly or monthly) to support policy interventions by providing up-to-date statistics on the business economy. Often published as indices, short-term statistics typically include prices (e.g. consumer, producer, and residential property inflation), retail sales, manufacturing and services production, and income statistics.
- International goods and services trade statistics, provide a wealth of information on the volume and value of tangible and intangible bilateral trade flows. With increased intensity of cross-border activities, other statistics have also become relevant:
  - o Foreign affiliates statistics (FATS), which describe the structure and activity of enterprises resident in one country but controlled from another – these statistics are of crucial importance to understand the globalization puzzle.
  - o Foreign direct investment (FDI) statistics, often collected as part of the Balance of Payments, supplement the FATS perspective, and reveal the real impact investment when pass-through or phantom investment and reversable investment are excluded.
  - o The complexity of international trade and the location of value-added activities have been explored with the development of global value chains (GVCs). GVCs can be analyzed from a macro perspective, through the use of global input–output (IO) tables, or from a micro perspective by examining business function statistics. Linking business registers and trade statistics (noted above) also contributes to these analyses.

Taken together, these establishment statistics provide a detailed and comprehensive picture of the economy. They are essential for the compilation of the National Accounts, Input–Output, and Supply–Use tables. The SNA framework, which is frequently used by policymakers, business communities, and economists, is discussed in Sections 1 and 2 of this book. Advances in measurement on phenomena like globalization, climate change, e-commerce, and informal sector of the economy are needed. These topics are discussed in Section 1. While traditional establishment statistics are produced using surveys and administrative data, resulting in multisource statistics (as discussed in Sections 2–4, 6, and 7), the production of these new statistics may profit from new data sources and new technologies, like big data, web scraping, and text mining (Bender and Sakshaug 2022; Hill et al. 2021), as we will see in Sections 5 and 7.

Whatever data sources used, statistics that target organizations must deal with unique features that present entirely different challenges from their household statistics counterparts (Cox and Chinnappa 1995; Snijkers et al. 2013; Snijkers 2016). Even though establishment survey methodology borrows from social survey methodology, blindly applying the same survey methods, collection, and statistical models to establishment statistics can yield disastrous results. A typical – and longstanding – problem in business statistics is the mapping of unit types that are found in secondary data sources (like administrative data sources) and the statistical units that are economically meaningful and comparable over time and across countries, as is shown in Figure 1.1. The ICES-I edited volume (Cox et al. 1995) devoted a chapter to the construction of statistical unit types held in a statistical business register (SBR) (Nijhowne 1995), and a chapter on changes of those unit types over time (Struijs and Willeboordse 1995).

To reduce respondent burden on surveyed establishments or to validate survey collections, establishment programs often utilize administrative data collected from the same (or nearly the same) organizations about their operations, such as Value Added Tax (VAT) or tax data. Linkages

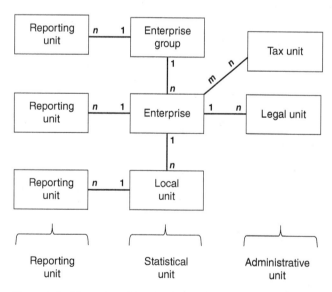

Figure 1.1 The unit problem in establishment statistics: A schematic representation of reporting, statistical, and administrative unit types. Lines represent relations between the unit types: $(1 : n)$, $(n : 1)$, and $(m : n)$, with m, n ≥ 1. The exact situation and terminology may differ between countries. Source: Inspired by Figure 13.1 in Chapter 13 by Cox et al. 2023.

to the corresponding administrative entities are not always straightforward. Governmental administrative data often contain unit types that are combinations of legal units, e.g. tax units that may have a many-to-many relationship with statistical units, as is shown in Figure 1.1 (right side; Cox et al. 2023 [Chapter 13]). In practice, errors may arise when identifying, characterizing, and delineating statistical units, which are referred to as unit errors in van Delden et al. (2018) i.e. errors in the relation (and subsequent linkage) between administrative and statistical units. Van Delden et al. emphasize the importance of assessing the impact of unit errors on the quality of the output establishment statistics, as they affect accuracy and inference.

A related unit problem exists in surveys where the collected data should match the statistical unit. Many establishment surveys have differing survey (sample) units and reporting units: "A survey unit is a business selected from the underlying statistical population of similarly constructed units (i.e. from the sampling frame). A reporting unit is an entity from which data are collected." (Thompson et al. 2015: 774; Haraldsen 2013). Within the same survey, the reporting unit can be the unit sampled from the frame or another entity entirely and can provide information for itself or for other units. While survey samples are mostly based on statistical unit types depending on the sample frame used, sampled units may be split into multiple reporting units (see Figure 1.1, left side). That typically occurs for large complex businesses that have multiple administration systems, as is illustrated in Chapter 16 by Snijkers et al. (2023: Figures 16.5 and 16.6). This has major consequences for the survey design as discussed in Chapter 15 by Haraldsen (2023). Unit errors in surveys, i.e. failure to report on all subunits or errors on the subunit reporting, can lead to inadvertent bias in the produced statistics (Snijkers 2016; Zhang 2012).

Household surveys rely on master address files, requiring up-to-date information on whether a structure is a personal dwelling or an out-of-scope establishment. Establishment surveys develop a register, merging statistical and administrative data to create complete listings in real time (Smith and Yung 2023 [Chapter 27]; Machdi et al. 2023 [Chapter 9]). Registers track changes in survey unit composition as well as additions (births) and deletions (deaths). For example, a business structure might change because of mergers, acquisitions, or divestitures, a business could change its economic activity, a farm could grow new crops, or a local school building could become an administration building. Maintaining these linkages and updates is paramount, as perhaps the most basic or fundamentally important establishment statistics are business register and business demographic statistics. These kinds of information are the backbone of economic statistics, providing the statistical infrastructure upon which almost all other business statistics rely. Not least, business registers provide the enterprise population from which other business survey samples are drawn and extrapolated to. Business register and business demographic statistics provide information on the active enterprise population, and their churn (births, deaths, life expectancy and survival) as well as identify high-growth enterprises/sectors and recently formed high-growth enterprises, poetically referred to as *gazelles*. They also form the basis for small and medium-size enterprises (SME) and entrepreneurial statistics. By mapping the legal and geographic structure of enterprises, business registers hold the key to understanding the operations of multinational enterprises, and by extension globalization. By linking business registers with trade statistics, further light is shed on globalization by also allowing policy makers to understand the role of companies in international goods and services trade.

As establishments modernize and innovate, establishment statistics must likewise continuously evolve; and as economies develop and change, establishment statistics and their production life cycle must change to reflect well the reality. These changes over time are clearly reflected in the ICES series conference programs.

1.3 ICES Trends

The ICES series of conferences is a rich source of information providing insights in the production of the abovementioned statistics, and the changes therein. While much of the survey research methods literature focuses on household surveys and statistics, and social survey methodology has a long-standing history of more than 100 years (Moser and Kalton 1971, Bethlehem 2009, Groves 2011), we can state that the first milestone in the history of establishment survey methodology was ICES-I (note that official establishment statistics go back much longer; Jones et al. 2013, Jones and O'Byrne 2023 [Chapter 8]). The ICES website (hosted by the American Statistical Association, ASA 1993–2021) has become a rich and irreplaceable repository of papers on many topics related to establishment statistics.

This section highlights some of the fascinating developments in establishment statistics in the last three decades. Since the first conference, the goal of the ICES series to present and exchange information and ideas on current and new methods, data sources, and technologies has not changed: each conference features (for the time) state-of-the-art methods applied to produce establishment statistics. However, the scope of the ICES conference programs, the breadth of the methods and topics covered, and the methods themselves have indeed advanced. In these developments, there is one common trend: *integration*. The ICES programs have evolved to provide holistic views of the entire establishment statistics production life cycle, moving from production centered stove pipe approaches (or silos) toward integrated statistics programs with integrated production processes, applying generalized methodologies and alternative data sources, and involving statistics-user and data-provider perspectives.

At the beginning of the ICES series, data collection in establishment statistics (as produced by National Statistical Institutes, NSIs) was simple: many NSIs conducted (often mandatory) mail-out/mail-back sample surveys with paper forms or questionnaires. These forms were characterized by detailed items with lengthy definitions containing technical terms often unfamiliar to the respondent. These definitions stemmed from government or (in Europe) Eurostat regulations and were often not in line with the record keeping information available from the surveyed unit, resulting in high response burden and requiring extensive post-field data cleaning. Economy-wide programs were essentially nonexistent. Instead, establishment surveys were designed to collect data for a specific set of statistics (as discussed in Section 1.2 above), for a specific branch of industry, with surveys designed and executed independently of each other in stove pipes or silos. Survey-specific solutions were developed, essentially in a vacuum, with the exceptions of the sample units and definitions of classifications (e.g. size class and economic activity; Jones and O'Byrne 2023 [Chapter 8]). The focus was on the NSIs internal production process; what happened *within* businesses was a black box. The majority of ICES-I papers (ASA 1993; Snijkers 2009) addressed issues dealing with surveying specific branches of industry, like agriculture, energy, health care, trade, finance, education, manufacturing, and the construction industry. Topics revolved around business frames, sampling and business registers, classification systems, data editing/cleaning, analysis, and estimation. Scant attention was given to general data collection methodology issues like questionnaire design, data quality, and nonresponse.

By the second ICES, a slow shift in establishment statistics research emerged, beginning to trend toward more generalized methodology, integrated statistics programs, and data integration. That said, Linacre (2000: 1) noted that "When you first compare the ICES2 program with the ICES1 program, the first thing that is striking is the amount in common. The overall survey process has not changed much in 5 years, or indeed 25 years, and in many areas, it is a case of slow progress in continuing directions." The trend toward integration and the development of a holistic view has accelerated since ICES-II. While the conference series deserves some credit for providing a forum for collaboration, the drivers for these changes are, as ever, reducing production costs, reducing response burden (i.e. reporting costs), improving data quality, and – above all – meeting emerging and increasing user demands for more timely, detailed, and coherent statistics (Linacre 2000; Edwards 2007; Jones and O'Byrne 2023 [Chapter 8]).

An important integration trend is the need for harmonized and coordinated statistics programs and integrated processes. At ICES-II, Smith (2000: 23) stated that "the most effective road to improved statistical quality and minimum response burden lies through greater unification, harmonization, and integration of statistical programs." Indeed, many NSIs have been integrating their statistics programs and production processes with the objective of maximizing production efficiency, as well as addressing new user demands, both with regard to established economic statistics and new statistics that adequately measure new economic developments like globalization, e-commerce, or the informal economy. Since ICES-II, many of them have presented their plans and experiences at subsequent ICES conferences.

This push to integrated business statistics production processes certainly accelerated the development of standardized business survey methods. The ICES-III, IV, V, and VI programs feature presentations on coordinated sampling designs, integrated business registers, coordinated data collection, questionnaire design tailored to the business context, electronic questionnaires, enhanced survey communication tools, generalized data editing and imputation programs, canned estimation programs, and standardized platforms developed for dissemination of statistics.

Fundamental to this progress is the integration of the establishment perspective into the survey design, yielding a deeper understanding of the business response process. This was first discussed at ICES-I and elaborated upon at every subsequent ICES conference. Opening this "black box" has proved to be instrumental in questionnaire design and pre-testing, in improving survey participation, implementing electronic data collection instruments, and executing mixed-mode designs, thus reducing costs and response burden, and improving data quality.

The use of alternative data sources and data integration is another ICES integration trend. From ICES-I onward, the expanded use of administrative data in establishment statistics has been discussed. As Linacre mentions at ICES-II (2000: 3): "This area is receiving a lot of attention by methodologists and good advances are being made in a number of countries." Historically, administrative data were used to construct sampling frames and business registers. However, methodologists and NSIs systematically promoted exploitation of administrative data to supplement or even replace survey collection, with an on-going objective to reduce response burden.

By ICES-V, the data integration presentations expanded to include big data and other non-traditional (organic) data, with an IOL as well as presentations featuring creative small area estimation applications and investigations of satellite photography data and purchased third-party registers. ICES-VI featured an even larger percentage of presentations on data integration, with applications often involving sophisticated machine learning methods, emphasizing the production of multisource statistics with linked data.

A final integration trend ICES has contributed to, concerns the increased networking and collaboration between experts from different areas, yielding synergy between these areas. Every ICES program retains "traditional" topics like respondent contact strategies, questionnaire design practices, business frames and sampling, weighting, outlier detection, data editing and imputation, data analysis, estimation, and variance estimation. By blending of standard survey methodology and survey statistics topics – applied exclusively to establishment data – and emerging methods and technologies, the ICES conference series has increased what was once a small pool of specialists to a large and international group of multidisciplinary scientists. After six conferences, we can conclude that the goal of the founding group (Cox et al. 1995) has been achieved.

These trends in integration at various levels, which are also seen in other international platforms discussing establishment statistics (see e.g. SJIAOS 2020), will surely continue to be seen at the next ICES conferences, since the basic challenges remain the same. Over the ICES years, the user quality criteria for official statistics have been fully developed, as described by Marker (2017; Jones and O'Byrne 2023 [Chapter 8]). In the future, criteria like timely, relevant, accurate, and coherent statistics will remain to be critical drivers for innovating production procedures and methods. In addition, production efficiency considerations, like costs, time, capacity, and response burden, as well as data quality issues as defined by the total survey error framework (Haraldsen 2013; Snijkers 2016) and other data quality frameworks (for administrative data and big data: van Delden and Lewis 2023 [Chapter 12], Biemer and Amaya 2021; Amaya et al. 2020) will define the production conditions (Jones and O'Byrne 2023 [Chapter 8], Bender et al. 2023 [Chapter 22]).

At ICES-I Ryten (1995: 706) concluded, when discussing "Business Surveys in Ten Years from now," that "national statistical agencies must adjust today's structure of surveys, censuses, and administrative registers as well as today's capabilities." We have seen this trend during the ICES years. However, moving away from siloed statistics production took time, and even today many NSIs are still organized along traditional statistics outputs. The 2020 COVID pandemic demonstrated the fluidity of procedures and methods in NSIs under pressure, producing concurrent measures of generally good quality and yielding new and important statistics at the same time (see Chapter 11 by Jones et al. 2023). We expect this pandemic to be a tipping point, and that in the future NSIs will be more flexible in producing more timely and relevant statistics, using and integrating various data sources, and applying a number of statistical and data collection methods. (For additional discussions on the impact of the COVID-19 pandemic on official statistics, see the Statistical Journal of the IAOS special issues on this topic [SJIAOS 2021a]).

The advantage of today, as compared to the times of ICES-I, is that our methods have developed, more data sources can be used and better exploited, and IT technology has improved, as we have seen above. Now we need to make sure that all these methods, technologies, and data sources come together. Integrating new IT technologies in our methods is a next step we need to take (Bavdaž et al. 2020).

Looking to the future we expect surveys to be better integrated and coordinated, using more sophisticated sample designs and sophisticated estimation methods that benefit from AI (artificial intelligence) and machine learning technologies. Instead of using questionnaires, to a large extent the data will be gathered using System-to-System data communication methods (or Electronic Data Interchange, EDI methods; Buiten et al. 2018) applying for example eXtened Business Reporting Language (XBRL) protocols or Application Programming Interfaces (API). In the next decade, we expect businesses themselves to be ready for this technology, having implemented smart industry technologies (or Industry 4.0; Chakravarti 2021; Haverkort and Zimmermann 2017) using sensor technology and the Internet of Things yielding an integrated business information chain (Bharosa et al. 2015), and having developed harmonized data definitions. As Snijkers et al. (2021) concluded from an exploratory study with precision farming data: "The fruit is not hanging as low as we thought": wide-scale adoption of smart industry technologies and data harmonization between various platforms is inevitable, even if not widely adopted in June 2021. Like with administrative registers, NSIs should work closely together with other parties like software developers of business systems to implement EDI systems, making system-to-system data communication possible, and having the required data stored in the business systems. Also, web scraping and text mining may be used to collect data directly from the internet. An example of the use of web scraping in the field of establishment statistics is the ADIMA database on multinational enterprises as developed by the OECD (Ahmed et al. 2019; see also https://www.oecd.org/sdd/its/statistical-insights-the-adima-database-on-multinational-enterprises.htm). Another example is climate change, where new IT technologies, new data sources and their integration can help to produce the requested statistics, although "in the short- and medium term such data have to be extracted and collected from mostly unstructured data sources." (Bender and Sakshaug 2022: 15). With all these new IT technologies, we need to keep in mind that it is the technology that makes new developments possible, but it is the methodology that makes it work. Ultimately, IT technology is a mere tool to an end, while methodological assessments are needed to evaluate and improve new data collection methods, new data sources, and new estimation methods according to cost requirements and quality frameworks.

A final future integration trend is improved collaboration at the international level, among countries in the developed world but also with developing countries. Again, we can quote Ryten (1995: 706), who states: "The days of strictly national development of business surveys [read: establishment statistics] may be over. Instead, we may be entering an era of joint ventures involving groups of countries organized within supranational entities or motivated by cultural similarities and trading relations." International organizations (see Section 2), like the United Nations (UN), the Organisation for Economic Co-operation and Development (OECD), the World Bank Group, and the European Union (EU), among others, are trying to establish this, but we still have a long way to go. Today, we even see some counter developments, considering e.g. the exit of the UK from the EU. For developing countries, international cooperation is critical to set up intensive programs in capacity building to achieve good working systems of national statistics (see SJIAOS, 2021b, for a discussion on training in statistics).

Producing establishment statistics has developed into a multidisciplinary science, closely related to what nowadays is called Data Science, needing highly educated staff, and it will – or even should – continue to do so. This book reflects the integration trends discussed above and shows the multidisciplinary character of this science. It gives the reader a flavor of the richness, complexities, and variety of facets involved in the production of establishment statistics.

1.4   Organization of This Book

"Advances in Business Statistics, Methods and Data Collection" provides a broad overview of currently available methods, new developments, and challenges for establishment statistics, with manuscripts prepared by practitioners and methodologists from across the globe.

This book is divided into seven sections, each section discussing a major theme related to the production of establishment statistics:

- Section 1: Introduction to New Measures/Indicators for the Economy
- Section 2: Topics in the Production of Official Establishment Statistics and Organizational Frameworks
- Section 3: Topics in the Use of Administrative Data
- Section 4: Topics in Business Survey Data Collection
- Section 5: Topics in the Use of New Data Sources and New Technologies
- Section 6: Topics in Sampling and Estimation
- Section 7: Topics in Data Integration, Linking and Matching.

The first two sections set the overall framework for this volume: Section 1 discusses topics from the user perspective – the demand side, whereas Section 2 discusses topics related to the production side of statistics – the supply side. Sections 3–5 discuss the three broad data sources used in establishment statistics: administrative data, business surveys (in particular data collection), and big data and related IT techniques. Section 6 presents applications with (new) sampling and estimation methods based on these data sources. Finally, Section 7 discusses the integration of the data sources resulting in multisource statistics.

Almost every section starts with one or two introductory chapters, discussing the current status of the section theme, and providing a general overview. Section 4 is one of the exceptions as the order of chapters generally follows the survey life cycle development process: questionnaire design, (pre-)testing, questionnaire evaluation, and survey communication. These introductory chapters are based on the IOLs as presented at ICES-VI (see Appendix).

1.4.1 Section 1: Introduction to New Measures/Indicators for the Economy

This section introduces readers to important macroeconomic issues that are, and will further, impact establishment statistics in the years to come. The section begins with two introductory chapters (Chapters 2 and 3) that provide broad context for what follows in subsequent chapters. These two introductory chapters outline the history and current framework of the SNA before then discussing critical measurement challenges facing that system, such as globalization, digitalization, and sustainability. Thereafter, specific aspects of these broad issues are discussed in more detail.

Chapter 4 outlines how fragmented production chains arising from globally decentralized multinational enterprises (MNEs) complicate the concepts of nationality and economic ownership and make the consistent measurement of national production more difficult. Chapter 5 develops this story further by examining the challenges of measuring intangible assets, which owing to an absence of corporate accounting rules, are often invisible within accounting systems. Their mobility adds an extra dimension of complexity and volatility to the global value chain narrative discussed in Chapter 4, as does the fluid valuation or pricing of these assets. Chapter 6 investigates an emerging measurement challenge highlighted in Chapter 3 – the measurement of the digital economy, i.e. the value of domestic production of digital goods and services and the value of digital trade. Examining developments in the United States as an example, new developments in measuring the digital economy by extending the supply-use framework, are looked at. The challenges of pricing free digital services, data assets, and digital trade are also discussed.

The final chapter (Chapter 7) in this section addresses a critical issue for many developing countries – the measurement of the informal economy and understanding its contribution to the economy. Using Nepal as an example, the chapter examines the different data sources that can contribute to estimating this difficulty to measure phenomena and highlights the foundational importance of business registers for establishment statistics, discussed in more detail in Section 2.

1.4.2 Section 2: Topics in the Production of Official Establishment Statistics and Organizational Frameworks

Section 2 presents an overview of the resources and tools available to help statistical producers. Issues, such as, quality, costs, and response burden are also discussed. Producers of economic statistics face many challenges in balancing the different dimensions of statistical quality (e.g. accuracy, relevance, and timeliness), while simultaneously reducing response burden and maintaining core statistical infrastructure, such as, business registers. This section provides an overview of some of these challenges and examples of how different organizations have managed them.

The first chapter in this section (Chapter 8) is an introductory overview chapter. It starts with a brief historical overview of the evolution of economic statistics, including the establishment of

NSIs. It then looks at the challenges and international guidance available to statistical ecosystems in the form of frameworks of international governance and quality assurance, statistical principles, models and frameworks, classifications, statistical tools, and formal and informal guidelines. The chapter concludes with the case of Statistics Canada's Integrated Business Statistics Program (IBPS). This program aims at improving data quality, reducing response burden, modernizing data processing infrastructure, integrating economic surveys, simplifying, and standardizing processes and reducing costs.

The focus of Chapter 9 is SBRs, the backbone for producing survey-based economic statistics and an important element of an NSIs statistical infrastructure. The chapter provides an overview of the development and maintenance of SBRs in Statistics Indonesia and the Australian Bureau of Statistics, and concludes with an examination of the benefits, opportunities, and challenges associated with SBRs.

With high volumes of data still being collected directly from sampled units, understanding and managing response burden is a high priority for many NSIs. Chapter 10 looks at experiences and recent developments in managing response burden at Statistics Netherlands, Statistics Portugal, and Statistics Sweden, with the aim of increasing awareness and knowledge about official statistics burden-reduction activities.

The final chapter in Section 2 (Chapter 11) provides some international case studies (from Australia, Germany, and the United Kingdom) of how conducting business surveys and compiling economic statistics had to adapt in response to the COVID-19 pandemic. The chapter includes changes to the Australian Bureau of Statistics SBR, changes to maintain response rates, classification changes to implement COVID-19 Government policies, and changes to seasonal adjustment and trend estimation.

1.4.3   Section 3: Topics in the Use of Administrative Data

The three chapters in Section 3 discuss topics related to the use of administrative data in official statistics (also see Sections 6 and 7). In the context of establishment statistics, administrative data have been used already for decades by NSIs for the creation and maintenance of business registers from which samples are selected. Since the 1970's, other types of administrative data have been used to support the production of statistics, such as, data editing and imputation. Since then, administrative data have been used more and more to reduce survey sample sizes, to replace existing sample surveys altogether, or to create new outputs (European Commission 2019).

When administrative data are directly used for population estimates adaptations are often needed because the unit types, population coverage, variable definitions, and periodicity of the administrative data do not always comply with the intended statistic. Furthermore, the data may contain typical and systematic reporting errors that require correction before reliable outputs can be produced. Chapter 12 provides an introductory overview of typical issues that occur when using administrative data for direct use in business statistics, including data acquisition, data processing, and evaluating output quality, among others. For each of these issues, the current state-of-the-art methods are summarized. The chapter ends by discussing unresolved issues in the field.

Although validated methods for processing administrative data have been developed, an internationally accepted set of methods for processing administrative data is not yet available. Chapter 13 describes an administrative data methods research (ADMR) program at the UK Office of National Statistics (ONS) that aims to develop such an internationally accepted methods framework. The ADMR program started with the development of a quality framework, building on existing frameworks that have been developed further by Statistics New Zealand (SNZ). In addition to reviewing existing frameworks, this chapter presents two case studies of administrative data use, one from ONS and one from SNZ.

The final chapter in this section, Chapter 14, continues with examples on the use of administrative data. Two examples of administrative data linkage with survey data to achieve more granular and more timely data from the Central Statistical Office (CSO) in Ireland are outlined. Three key factors for the successful use of administrative data are discussed: handling differences between the unit type observed in the data set versus the actual statistical units, the skewed distribution of the data, and the control (or lack thereof) of the data collection process. The importance of being honest and transparent with data users concerning the limitations of the statistics is also emphasized.

1.4.4 Section 4: Topics in Business Survey Data Collection

Although alternative data sources are commonly used in establishment statistics nowadays (as discussed in Sections 3 and 5), many business (establishment) sample surveys are still being conducted by NSIs, universities, and research organizations. For some of these organizations, sample surveys remain the primary method of collecting business data.

Establishment surveys have evolved and undergone many changes since ICES-I (noted above). The most visible change has been the transition from paper based to electronic questionnaires. Chapter 15 deals with this transition, noting that while computerization does not automatically improve questionnaires, it can help specify concepts, delineate relevant units, and determine required time periods by incorporating dialogues and dynamic features that would be challenging (or next to impossible) to offer on paper. In follow-up, Chapter 16 deals with the challenges of designing a complex survey questionnaire that combines surveys from two Dutch institutes into one new survey with the aim of producing coherent statistics. The importance of early communication with businesses to understand data availability (in terms of data location, access, and timing), and to adequately frame desired concepts and reporting units is stressed. The chapter covers the entire survey process from a redesign perspective.

Technological advances have also influenced questionnaire development, pretesting, and evaluation. Case studies presented in Chapter 17 illustrate how adaptation of cognitive and other qualitative research methods to the measurement of emergent topics was enabled by and benefited from technology, as indeed have research methods. Computerization has also allowed automatic generation of rich process data that shed light on how an electronic questionnaire works in practice, thus supporting real-time fieldwork monitoring and post-field analysis. How these paradata can be used for evaluating and redesigning the questionnaire and the communication strategy is described in Chapter 18, and illustrated with examples from the Netherlands and Canada.

Both qualitative research data and quantitative paradata offer useful insights into the error sources of surveys, but they rarely tell whether suggested solutions actually would diminish or eliminate those errors in practice. This would require experimental research. While experimental research in household surveys is very common, the specificities of businesses and establishment surveys prevent direct application. Chapter 19 presents several experiments (from the United States and Germany), involving recruitment strategies and questionnaire design aimed at reducing nonresponse. These studies show how experiments can successfully be applied in establishment/business surveys.

The final two chapters of this section discuss aspects of establishment survey communication strategies. Chapter 20 discusses the use of web portals for reporting businesses. Web portals offer a single point of access to survey questionnaires, and may also support the response process within businesses, such as delegation and authorization, or offer extra features, such as feeding data back to the respondents. The results of an international survey on the use of web portals are presented for 25 participating NSIs. Chapter 21 describes a promotion campaign among small businesses for the 2017 US Economic Census. This nonconventional campaign aimed at raising awareness among small businesses of the upcoming census, persuading them to participate and to respond electronically.

1.4.5   Section 5: Topics in the Use of New Data Sources and New Technologies

Apart from register data (Section 3) and survey data (Section 4), so-called big data or organic data sources (e.g. web sites, log files, sensor data, satellite images, scanner data) are now potentially available, and are increasingly becoming a key success factor for the work of statisticians, analysts, and researchers as well as for political decision-making. These alternative data sources have received increasing attention and are playing an increasingly important role in the production of establishment statistics. The use of these data sources make new methods for data collection (e.g. web scraping), data processing (e.g. text mining, machine learning techniques, data cleaning), and data visualization indispensable. This section discusses these new data sources, new technologies, and new methods, along with some important challenges (e.g. measurement error, data sharing/access, privacy risks).

Even though more and more available, access to these timely and high-quality granular organic data is not self-evident. A surprisingly large amount of these data remain hidden in tightly regulated silos and other data vaults (MacFeely 2020), resulting in their underexploitation. One reason lies in the nature of the data themselves, which may disclose private information such as a company's business model or total revenue. Chapter 22 presents a framework to enable access to and broader exploitation of granular data. The framework is organized around three building blocks: (i) Laying the technical and procedural foundations; (ii) Generating safe results; and (iii) Generating value for all stakeholders.

Chapters 23–25 of this section are dedicated to the rapid progress in the fields of machine learning (teaching computers to learn from data) and natural language processing (using computers to understand language) for business data. Chapter 23 provides a general introduction to machine learning along with an overview of these techniques in the context of official statistics. The use of machine learning in the Federal German Statistical Office to enable or support fully automated classification and coding, imputations, and editing is outlined. The chapter also explains how tasks are often not implemented using machine learning alone, but are supplemented by other methods. Important questions regarding the use of automation and "new" methods of data processing and the implications for data quality and appropriate quality measurement are discussed.

Chapter 24 discusses the US Bureau of Labor Statistics' (BLS) experiences with using machine learning algorithms to transition from manual to (mostly automated) coding of the Survey of Occupational Injuries and Illnesses (SOII) and demonstrates that although modern machine learning and natural language processing techniques introduce new maintenance challenges, these challenges are surmountable, and the benefits can be significant. The chapter also highlights that the BLS is increasingly applying machine learning and natural language processing techniques to a wide variety of noncoding tasks including record matching, information extraction, and error detection.

Chapter 25 describes the transition to machine learning for product classification in order to reduce response burden and improve data quality in the US Commodity Flow Survey (CFS). The process and results of developing a Machine Learning (ML) model to classify product codes based on free-text descriptions are described, as are the applications to improve the quality of the CFS data and the resulting estimates.

In the final chapter in Section 5, new data sources are combined with existing sources, touching on data integration, a theme that is further discussed in Sections 6 and 7. Chapter 26 discusses how alternative data sources were combined with a national survey to produce subnational estimates of retail sales, yielding the US Census Bureau's Monthly State Retail Sales (MSRS) experimental data product. The MSRS was created without any new data collection and without any additional respondent burden; the focus was on blending available survey and administrative data as well as available alternative data sources to compile a composite estimator.

1.4.6 Section 6: Topics in Sampling and Estimation

There are several elements in establishment survey design that have remained unchanged since ICES-I. Establishment survey populations are generally skewed, with the largest units having the most influence on the estimated totals, with many smaller units contributing little to the survey totals while being relatively more burdened by survey collections. Consequently, stratified one-stage sample designs are frequently used, with the largest units sampled at much higher rates than smaller units. On the other hand, in the decades since ICES-I, the availability of auxiliary data beyond business registers has greatly increased, rendering sophisticated methodology, such as calibration estimation and small area estimation more accessible and enhancing the usage of models in the survey process. The six chapters in this section provide broad overviews of these topics, in addition to two practical case studies.

Chapter 27 provides a comprehensive introductory overview of sampling and estimation in business surveys, focusing on probability sampling and remaining cognizant of selected response burden issues that can be controlled through the sample design or compensated for via the estimation process. The challenges associated with *stratum jumpers* (units sampled that have small sampling weights and unexpectedly large totals) are also discussed. Chapter 28 extends the discussion of balancing respondent burden and estimation accuracy via sample coordination methods; a suite of such methods is discussed along with information on systems in which these methods are implemented.

Chapter 29 reviews variance estimation methods used in business surveys, bringing together discussions on design-based and model-assisted techniques for probability samples as well as replication methods in contrast with the entirely model-based methods required with nonprobability samples. Chapter 30 extends the topic of model-based estimation for establishment surveys via small area estimation. The topic of variance estimation is revisited in Chapter 31 where a design-based/model-assisted variance estimator and a multiple-imputation variance estimator to multinomial data collected in the US Service Annual Survey are described and evaluated in the context of a nearest neighbor hot deck ratio imputation. This section concludes with Chapter 32 with a description and evaluation of research designed to improve the accuracy of an advance economic indicator survey collection's estimator, imputation methodology, and analyst review practices.

1.4.7 Section 7: Topics in Data Integration, Linking and Matching

The final section in this volume discusses data integration, bringing together all data sources and related methods discussed thus far. With the wide array of data sources becoming available, statistics are no longer based on one data source, but a combination of sources. It has been said that the twentieth century was the era of survey sampling; the twenty-first century may be the era of data integration (Zhang 2012; UNECE 2016). Not only does data integration increase research opportunities by broadening the scope of substantive information available for a given unit, it also comes with the promise of many methodological advantages, such as reducing respondent burden, producing more granular data, and improving data and estimation quality. The four chapters in this section provide broad overviews of these topics, in addition to several case studies.

The promise of data integration hinges on performing high-quality linkages between various data sources. This topic is addressed in Chapter 33, where an introductory overview of linkage processes (e.g. linking variables, pre-processing, blocking) and matching algorithms (e.g. deterministic, probabilistic) is presented, along with how they can be applied to linking establishments. An example of linking establishment data at the Australian Bureau of Statistics to produce a statistical data product, illustrates the process and potential for linkage.

As official establishment statistics are increasingly based on multiple data sources, assessing the quality of multisource statistics is an important topic. Chapter 34 delves into this issue by providing a framework for identifying specific error sources in multisource statistics, including representation errors, linkage errors, and measurement errors. A number of recently developed methods to estimate the bias and variance of multisource outputs affected by these different error sources are presented, as are case studies from Statistics Netherlands.

The remaining two chapters of this section present applications evaluating the methodological potentials of data integration. Chapter 35 evaluates the impact of providing previously reported data (PRD) to respondents of the US National Agricultural Statistics Service's 2020 September Agricultural Survey to reduce response burden. Using an experimental design, the extent of discrepancies between the PRD and reported values when the PRD values are shown to respondents are evaluated, as is the frequency of cases requiring post-survey editing. Chapter 36 presents several applications of integrating alternative and administrative data into Statistics Canada's monthly business statistics programs to reduce respondent burden, provide more granular data, and reduce data collection costs without compromising on data quality. The applications include replacing survey data with administrative data, using scanner data to replace survey commodity data, and the use of small area estimation techniques that integrate both survey and administrative data. The impact of the COVID-19 pandemic is revisited, and future initiatives are discussed.

1.5 To Conclude …

"We live in interesting times, in which new developments bring new challenges for statistical agencies. This requires new methods and new skills. We have work to do." This is what Robert Groves concluded in his Keynote speech "Official Statistics and big data," presented at the 2013 European Conference on New Techniques and Technologies (Brussels, Belgium) (Groves 2013). This surely applies to the production of establishment statistics. Like the conference from which these chapters are drawn, this new edited volume highlights new developments and challenges, and showcases new skills and emerging methods.

We, the editors, hope that this new edited volume *"Advances in Business Statistics, Methods and Data Collection"* will earn a place in the toolkit of researchers and practitioners working – with data – in industries across a variety of fields, like survey researchers, government statisticians, National Bank employees, economists, and undergraduate and graduate students in survey research and economics.

Last, but certainly not least, we would like to thank the authors for accepting our invitation to contribute to this volume, and their efforts and perseverance while writing the chapters. Without their contributions, we would not have had a new ICES edited volume.

Disclaimer

U.S. Census Bureau: Any opinions and conclusions expressed in this publication are those of the author(s) and do not reflect the views of the U.S. Census Bureau.

Other institutes: The views expressed in this paper are those of the authors and do not necessarily reflect the policies of their institutes.

References

Ahmed, N., Doyle, D., and Pilgrim, G. (2019). Measuring MNEs using big data: the OECD analytical database on individual multinationals and their affiliates (ADIMA). *Presentation at the European conference on New Techniques and Technologies for official Statistics (NTTS)*, Brussels, Belgium (12–14 March 2019).

Amaya, A., Biemer, P.P., and Kinyon, D. (2020). Total error in a big data world: adapting the TSE framework to big data. *Journal of Survey Statistics and Methodology* 8 (1): 89–119.

ASA (1993, 2000, 2007, 2000, 2012, 2016, 2020/21). *Programs of the International Conference on Establishment Surveys I, II, II, IV, V and VI*. https://www.amstat.org/ASA/Meetings/ICES.aspx. American Statistical Association, Alexandria (Virginia).

Bavdaž, M., Snijkers, G., Sakshaug, J.W., Brand, T., Haraldsen, G., Kurban, B., Saraiva, P., and Willimack, D.K. (2020). Business data collection methodology: current state and future outlook statistical. *Statistical Journal of the IAOS* 36 (3): 741–756. https://doi.org/10.3233/SJI-200623.

Bender, S., Blaschke, J., and Hirsch, C. (2023). Statistical data production in a digitized age: the need to establish successful workflows for micro data access. In: *Advances in Business Statistics, Methods and Data Collection* (ed. G. Snijkers, M. Bavdaž, S. Bender, J. Jones, S. MacFeely, J.W. Sakshaug, K.J. Thompson, and A. van Delden), Chapter 22. Hoboken: Wiley.

Bender, S. and Sakshaug, J.W. (2022). Data sources for business statistics: what has changed? *The Survey Statistician* 85: 10–18.

Bethlehem, J. (2009). *Applied Survey Methods: A Statistical Perspective*. Hoboken: Wiley.

Biemer, P.P. and Amaya, A. (2021). Total error framework for found data. In: *Big Data Meet Survey Science: A Collection of Innovative Methods* (ed. C.A. Hill, P.P. Biemer, T.D. Buskirk, L. Japec, A. Kirchner, S. Kolenikov, and L.E. Lyberg), 133–162. Hoboken: Wiley.

Bharosa, N., van Wijk, R., de Winne, N., and Janssen, M. (ed.) (2015). *Challenging the Chain: Governing the Automated Exchange and Processing of Business Information*. Amsterdam, the Netherlands: IOS Press www.iospress.nl/book/challenging-the-chain/.

Buiten, G., Snijkers, G., Saraiva, P., Erikson, J., Erikson, A.-G., and Born, A. (2018). Business data collection: toward electronic data interchange. Experiences in Portugal, Canada, Sweden, and the Netherlands with EDI. *Journal of Official Statistics* 34 (2): 419–443. (ICES-5 special issue). http://dx .doi.org/10.2478/JOS-2018-0019.

Chakravarti, V.S. (2021). *Internet of Things and M2M Communication Technologies: Architecture and Practical Design Approach to IoT in Industry 4.0*. Cham, Switzerland: Springer.

Cox, B.G., Binder, D.A., Chinnappa, B.N., Christianson, A., Colledge, M.J., and Kott, P.S. (ed.) (1995). *Business Survey Methods*. New York: Wiley.

Cox, B.G. and Chinnappa, B.N. (1995). Unique features of business surveys. In: *Business Survey Methods* (ed. B.G. Cox, D.A. Binder, B.N. Chinnappa, A. Christianson, M.J. Colledge, and P.S. Kott), 1–17. New York: Wiley.

Cox, N., McLaren, C.H., Shenton, C., Tarling, T., and Davies, E.W. (2023). Developing statistical frameworks for administrative data and integrating it into business statistics. Experiences from the UK and New Zealand. In: *Advances in Business Statistics, Methods and Data Collection* (ed. G. Snijkers, M. Bavdaž, S. Bender, J. Jones, S. MacFeely, J.W. Sakshaug, K.J. Thompson, and A. van Delden), Chapter 13. Hoboken: Wiley.

Edwards, R.W. (2007). Business surveys: past, present, and challenges for the future. In: *ICES-III Proceedings: 1-13*. Alexandria (Virginia): American Statistical Association https://ww2.amstat.org/ meetings/ices/2007/proceedings/TOC.pdf.

European Commission (2019). ESS (European Statistical System) Workshop on the use of administrative data for business, agriculture and fisheries statistics, Bucharest, Rumania (October

17–18 2019). https://ec.europa.eu/eurostat/cros/content/ess-workshop-use-administrative-data-business-agriculture-and-fisheries-statistics_en.

Groves, R.M. (2011), Three eras of survey research. *Public Opinion Quarterly*, 75(5):861–871. https://doi .org/10.1093/poq/nfr057.

Groves, R.M. (2013). Official statistics and "big data". *Key note at the 2013 European Conference on New Techniques and Technologies in Statistics (NTTS)*, Brussels, Belgium (5–7 March 2013). https://ec .europa.eu/eurostat/cros/content/keynote-address-robert-m-groves-slides_en.

Haraldsen, G. (2013). Quality issues in business surveys. In: *Designing and Conducting Business Surveys* (ed. G. Snijkers, G. Haraldsen, J. Jones and D.K. Willimack), 83–125. Hoboken: Wiley.

Haraldsen, G. (2023). What computerized business questionnaires and questionnaire management tools can offer. In: *Advances in Business Statistics, Methods and Data Collection* (ed. G. Snijkers, M. Bavdaž, S. Bender, J. Jones, S. MacFeely, J.W. Sakshaug, K.J. Thompson, and A. van Delden), Chapter 15. Hoboken: Wiley.

Haverkort, B.R. and Zimmermann, A. (2017). Smart industry: how ICT will change the game! *IEEE Internet Computing* 21 (1): 8–10. https://doi.org/10.1109/MIC.2017.22.

Hill, C.A., Biemer, P.P., Buskirk, T.D., Japec, L., Kirchner, A., Kolenikov, S., and Lyberg, L.E. (ed.) (2021). *Big Data Meet Survey Science: A Collection of Innovative Methods*. Hoboken: Wiley.

Jones, J. and O'Byrne, H. (2023). Statistical producers challenges and help. In: *Advances in Business Statistics, Methods and Data Collection* (ed. G. Snijkers, M. Bavdaž, S. Bender, J. Jones, S. MacFeely, J.W. Sakshaug, K.J. Thompson, and A. van Delden), Chapter 8. Hoboken: Wiley.

Jones, J., Ryan, L., Lanyon, A.J., Apostolou, M., Price, T., König, C., Volkert, M., Sakshaug, J.W., Mead, D., Baird, H., Elliott, D., and McLaren, C.H. (2023). Producing Official Statistics During the COVID-19 Pandemic. In: *Advances in Business Statistics, Methods and Data Collection* (ed. G. Snijkers, M. Bavdaž, S. Bender, J. Jones, S. MacFeely, J.W. Sakshaug, K.J. Thompson, and A. van Delden), Chapter 11. Wiley, Hoboken.

Jones, J., Snijkers, G., and Haraldsen, G. (2013). Surveys and business surveys. In: *Designing and Conducting Business Surveys* (ed. G. Snijkers, G. Haraldsen, J. Jones, and D.K. Willimack), 1–38. Hoboken: Wiley.

JOS (2010). Special section with articles based on papers from the Third International Conference on Establishment Surveys – preface. *Journal of Official Statistics* 26 (1): 1. www.scb.se/dokumentation/ statistiska-metoder/JOS-archive/.

Linacre, S. (2000). What has and hasn't changed and what are the issues for the future. In: *ICES-II Proceedings: 1–18*. Alexandria (Virginia): American Statistical Association.

Lorenc, B., Smith, P.A., Bavdaž, M., Haraldsen, G., Nedyalkova, D., Zhang, L.C., and Zimmerman, T. (ed.) (2018). *The Unit Problem and Other Current Topics in Business Survey Methodology*. Newcastle upon Tyne, UK: Cambridge Scholars Publishing.

MacFeely, S. (2020). In search of the data revolution: has the official statistics paradigm shifted? *Statistical Journal of the IAOS* 36 (4): 1075–1094. https://doi.org/10.3222/SJI-200662.

Machdi, I., Pertiwi, R.P., Nefriana, R., and Erasmus, W. (2023). The development and maintenance of statistical business registers as statistical infrastructure in Statistics Indonesia and the Australian Bureau of Statistics. In: *Advances in Business Statistics, Methods and Data Collection* (ed. G. Snijkers, M. Bavdaž, S. Bender, J. Jones, S. MacFeely, J.W. Sakshaug, K.J. Thompson, and A. van Delden), Chapter 9. Hoboken: Wiley.

Marker, D. (2017). How have National Statistical Institutes improved quality in the last 25 years? *Statistical Journal of the IAOS* 33 (4): 951–961.

Moser, C.A. and Kalton, K. (1971). *Survey Methods in Social Investigation*. Aldershot (UK): Gower.

Nijhowne, S. (1995). Defining and classifying statistical units. In: *Business Survey Methods* (ed. B.G. Cox, D.A. Binder, B.N. Chinnappa, A. Christianson, M.J. Colledge, and P.S. Kott), 49–64. New York: Wiley.

Ryten, J. (1995). Business surveys in ten years' time. In: *Business Survey Methods* (ed. B.G. Cox, D.A. Binder, B.N. Chinnappa, A. Christianson, M.J. Colledge, and P.S. Kott), 691–709. New York: Wiley.

SJIAOS (2020). Special issue on the future of establishment statistics. *Statistical Journal of the IAOS* 36 (3).

SJIAOS (2021a). Special issues on the impact of COVID-19. *Statistical Journal of the IAOS* 37 (2): 453–522, and 37(4): 1063–1084.

SJIAOS (2021b). Special issue on new developments in the training on statistics. *Statistical Journal of the IAOS* 37 (3).

Smith, P.A. and Phipps, P. (2014). Special issue on establishment surveys (IVES-IV) - preface. *Journal of Official Statistics* 30 (4): 575–577. https://doi.org/10.2478/JOS-2014-0038.

Smith, P.A. and Yung, W. (2023). Introduction to sampling and estimation for business surveys. In: *Advances in Business Statistics, Methods and Data Collection* (ed. G. Snijkers, M. Bavdaž, S. Bender, J. Jones, S. MacFeely, J.W. Sakshaug, K.J. Thompson, and A. van Delden), Chapter 27. Hoboken: Wiley.

Smith, Ph. (2000). Statistics Canada's Broad Strategy for Business Statistics. In: *ICES-II Proceedings: 19-28*. Alexandria (Virginia): American Statistical Association.

Snijkers, G. (2009). Getting data for (Business) statistics: what's new? what's next?. Paper presented at the 2009 NTTS conference, February 18–20, Brussels, Belgium.

Snijkers, G. (2016). Achieving quality in organizational surveys: a holistic approach. In: *Methodische Probleme in der empirischen Organisationsforschung* (ed. S. Liebig and W. Matiaske), 33–59. Wiesbaden: Springer.

Snijkers, G., Haraldsen, G., Jones, J., and Willimack, D.K. (ed.) (2013). *Designing and Conducting Business Surveys*. Hoboken: Wiley.

Snijkers, G., Houben, L., and Demollin, F. (2023). Tailoring the design of a new combined business survey: process, methods, and lessons learned. In: *Advances in Business Statistics, Methods and Data Collection* (ed. G. Snijkers, M. Bavdaž, S. Bender, J. Jones, S. MacFeely, J.W. Sakshaug, K.J. Thompson, and A. van Delden), Chapter 16. Hoboken: Wiley.

Snijkers, G., Punt, T., De Broe, S., and Gómez Pérez, J. (2021). Exploring sensor data for agricultural statistics: the fruit is not hanging as low as we thought. *Statistical Journal of the IAOS* 37 (4): 1301–1314. https://doi.org/10.3233/SJI-200728.

Struijs, P. and Willeboordse, A. (1995). Changes in populations of statistical units. In: *Business Survey Methods* (ed. B.G. Cox, D.A. Binder, B.N. Chinnappa, A. Christianson, M.J. Colledge, P.S. Kott), 65–84. New York: Wiley.

Thompson, K.J., Oliver, B., and Beck, J. (2015). An analysis of the mixed collection modes for two business surveys conducted by the US Census Bureau. *Public Opinion Quarterly* 79 (3): 769–789. https://doi.org/10.1093/poq/nfv013.

Thompson, K.J., Phipps, P., Miller, D., and Snijkers, G. (2018). Preface – overview of the special issue from the Fifth International Conference on Establishment Surveys (IVES-V). *Journal of Official Statistics* 34 (2): 303–307. https://doi.org/10.2478/JOS-2018-0013.

UNECE (2016). Outcomes of the UNECE project on using big data for official statistics. United Nations Economic Commission for Europe, Geneva, Switzerland. https://statswiki.unece.org/display/bigdata/Big+Data+in+Official+Statistics(Big Data in Official Statistics) (accessed 5 February 2022).

van Delden, A. and Lewis, D. (2023). Methodology for the use of administrative data in business statistics. In: *Advances in Business Statistics, Methods and Data Collection* (ed. G. Snijkers, M. Bavdaž, S. Bender, J. Jones, S. MacFeely, J.W. Sakshaug, K.J. Thompson, and A. van Delden), Chapter 12. Hoboken: Wiley.

van Delden, A., Lorenc, B., Struijs, P., and Zhang, L.C. (2018). On statistical unit errors in business statistics. Letter to the Editor. *Journal of Official Statistics* 34 (2): 573–580.

Zhang, L.C. (2012). Topics in statistical theory for register-based statistics and data integration. *Statistica Neerlandica* 66 (1): 41–63. https://doi.org/10.1111/j.1467-9574.2011.00508.x.

Appendix: Available ICES-VI Introductory Overview Lecture (IOL) Videos[1]

Section 2: Introduction to the Production of Official Establishment Statistics – the Supply Side

- Statistical (Economic) producers challenges and help (Jacqui Jones, Australian Bureau of Statistics): https://www.youtube.com/watch?v=aLUAiNQWC_0
- Standardization leads to efficiency (Holly O'Byrne, Statistics Canada): https://www.youtube.com/watch?v=2wsKGsgTG3A

Section 3: Introduction to the Use of Administrative Data

- Methodological aspects of the use of administrative data in business statistics: understanding your data source (Arnout van Delden, Statistics Netherlands): https://www.youtube.com/watch?v=QNnZdfBnK8c
- Use of administrative data in business statistics: approaches for dealing with data issues (Danni Lewis, UK Office for National Statistics): https://www.youtube.com/watch?v=JiHHfs4loo0

Section 4: Introduction to Business Surveys: Questionnaire Design

- Computerized business questionnaires (Gustav Haraldsen, Statistics Norway): https://www.youtube.com/watch?v=uOCRGOYqecI
- Questionnaire completion paradata in business surveys (Ger Snijkers, Statistics Netherlands, and Susan Demedash, Statistics Canada): https://www.youtube.com/watch?v=OYBfd7yYf3Q

Section 5: Introduction to New Data Sources, New Technologies, and New Methods

- Statistical data-production in a digitized age: potentials for statistics, research and society (Stefan Bender, Jannick Blaschke, and Christian Hirsch, Deutsche Bundesbank, Germany): https://www.youtube.com/watch?v=7Bct1583Yfg
- Data, algorithms and data governance (Sofia Olhede, École Polytechnique Fédérale de Lausanne, Switzerland): https://www.youtube.com/watch?v=B8HVD1mRVkY

Section 6: Introduction to Sampling and Estimation

- Introduction to sampling for business surveys (Paul A. Smith, University of Southampton, UK, and Wesley Yung, Statistics Canada):
  - Statistical business registers: https://www.youtube.com/watch?v=he_cD0zhons
  - Sampling in business surveys: https://www.youtube.com/watch?v=r2h98QfxLRM
- Introduction to estimation for business surveys ((Paul A. Smith, University of Southampton, UK, and Wesley Yung, Statistics Canada):
  - Design-based estimation: https://www.youtube.com/watch?v=H6VjHBmt1L4
  - Outliers and model-based estimation: https://www.youtube.com/watch?v=zpp4V2W20jo

Section 6: Introduction to Coordinated Sampling and to Bayesian Methods Applied to Small Area Estimation for Establishment Statistics

- Sample coordination methods and systems for establishment surveys (Alina Matei, Université de Neuchâtel, Switzerland, and Paul A. Smith, University of Southampton, UK): https://www.youtube.com/watch?v=it8e6iF6sSw
- Some thoughts about sample coordination in repeated surveys (Yves Tillé, Université de Neuchâtel, Switzerland): https://www.youtube.com/watch?v=3hgEBNibtSU

---

1 IOL videos for Section 1 (Introduction to New Measures/Indicators for the Economy - the Demand Side) are not available.

- Bayesian methods applied to small area estimation for establishment statistics (Scott H. Holan, Paul A. Parker, University of Missouri and Ryan Janicki, US Census Bureau): https://www.youtube.com/watch?v=l2W0av-2xmc

Section 6: Introduction to Variance Estimation for Probability and Nonprobability Surveys

- Variance estimation for probability surveys (Dan Liao, RTI International, USA): https://www.youtube.com/watch?v=HxQlzNxu1pk
- Variance estimation for nonprobability surveys (Jill A. Dever, RTI International, USA): https://www.youtube.com/watch?v=-fUqH_QFaxY

Section 7: Introduction to Data Integration, Linking and Matching

- Record linkage: background and challenges for linkage of persons and establishments (Michael D. Larsen, Saint Michael's College, Vermont, US): https://www.youtube.com/watch?v=sbdN2LhZhxs
- Business longitudinal analysis data environment (Alan Herning, Australian Bureau of Statistics): https://www.youtube.com/watch?v=yFzCLG4Uzms

2

GDP and the SNA: Past and Present

Steve MacFeely[1] and Peter van de Ven[2]

[1] *Director of Data and Analytics, World Health Organization, Geneva, Switzerland*
[2] *Inter-Secretariat Working Group on National Accounts, New York, USA*

2.1   Introduction

Gross domestic product (GDP) has been described as one of the greatest inventions of the twentieth century (Landefeld 2000). It is unquestionably one of the most powerful and influential statistical indicators in history. No other measure has ever had such an impact on our lives (Masood 2016). GDP is more than a statistic – it not only measures the global economy but also defines it. So important is GDP today, that Karabell (2014, p. 50) describes it as the "the Zeus of the statistical pantheon."

Before the invention of the System of National Accounts (SNA) and GDP, one could argue that the concept of "the economy" did not exist (Karabell 2014) and so, their creation marked a seminal moment in the evolution of economic thinking and policy making (Fioramonti 2013). This chapter summarizes the origins of the SNA and GDP and some of the crucial events and thinking that helped shape what is arguably the most important statistical framework in history. It also illustrates how the concepts and measurement framework are not fixed or static but continue to evolve in parallel with the economy it is measuring.

The chapter begins by outlining the origins of national accounts and GDP – Section 2.2 details how the SNA are compiled today and notes, in Section 2.4, some of the most important revisions or updates to the SNA, along with the implications for business statistics and for users. The article is concluded in Section 2.5.

2.2   The Origins of National Income Statistics – A Brief History

2.2.1   Early Developments

The SNA as we know it today and the most recognizable indicators associated with those accounts, such as GDP and gross national income (GNI), are progeny of the great depression and World War 2. Forged in the fires of these seismic events, they emerged to become global standards (Masood 2016). But the origins of national accounting, or what began as national income statistics, can be traced back much further, to the seventeenth century.

Advances in Business Statistics, Methods and Data Collection. Edited by Ger Snijkers, Mojca Bavdaž, Stefan Bender, Jacqui Jones, Steve MacFeely, Joseph W. Sakshaug, Katherine J. Thompson, and Arnout van Delden.
© 2023 John Wiley & Sons, Inc. Published 2023 by John Wiley & Sons, Inc.

William Petty is usually credited with conceiving national income.[1,2] In his 1665 paper[3] *Verbum Sapienti*, Petty detailed the first systematic integrated set of national income accounts for England and Wales, comprising measures of population, income, expenditure, stock of land, other physical assets, and human capital (Lepenies 2016; Maddison 2003). In his 1676[4] essay *Political Arithmetick*, Petty provided a comparative study of the economic performance of the Netherlands and France. Although some criticized his calculations, arguing his approach was simplistic (Studenski 1958; Stone 1997) and that his imputation methods often employed "dubious assumptions," he was credited by Marx and Engels as the "founder of modern political economics" (Lepenies 2016, p. 15). Mitra-Khan (2011) also asserts, in an argument reminiscent of Desrosières (2003), that Petty, by measuring the economy, also defined it. Other, less well known, contributions were also made in England by Gregory King in 1695, and in France by Boisguilbert in 1697 and Vauban in 1707 (Vanoli 2016).

Maddison (2003) notes that between the eighteenth century and the 1930s, there were about thirty attempts to measure national income in Britain. These attempts were characterized by significant differences in coverage and methodology, with most concentrating on point estimates of income, without any crosschecks to expenditure or production approaches. Despite this proliferation "there was little improvement in their quality or comparability" (Maddison 2003, p. 7). There were of course important developments also being made elsewhere. One notable contribution to national accounting came in 1758 when Francois Quesnay published his "*Tableau Economique*" – the spiritual parent of today's input–output tables.[5]

After Quesnay, the arithmetic approach largely fell out of fashion and did not resurface in any serious way until the twentieth century. During that long hiatus, the great strides made in economics were theoretical but with profound implications for national accounting. From this perspective, Smith's great intellectual contribution was the production boundary and the distinction between productive and unproductive labor (Coyle 2014). Other important arguments, notably between wealth (Marshall) and welfare (Pigou) continue to reverberate today.

2.2.2 Invention of Gross National Product (GNP)

The Great Depression highlighted the need for reliable economic evidence and focused minds on both sides of the Atlantic. Neither economists nor governments had any real grasp of what was happening and consequently they did not know how to manage the worsening global economic crisis. By this time, only around 20 countries had ever attempted to measure their national income (Studenski 1958). Arising from this crisis, two great pioneers of national accounting picked up Petty's baton. In the United Kingdom, a lone academic, Colin Clark, began working on national income estimates. Meanwhile, in the United States, the man perhaps most associated with the invention of GDP, Simon Kuznets, was sponsored by the US government to undertake parallel work.

Colin Clark has been described by Lepenies (2016, p. 31) as "one of the important modern pioneers of gross domestic product" and by Maddison (2003, p. 7) as "a leading figure in the history of macroeconomic measurement." He published "*The National Income, 1924–1931*." His analyses

---

1 Although some credit the Irish economist Richard Cantillon as having "estimated the first real national income accounts" (Warsh, 2006, pp. 35).

2 As an aside, in 1662, Petty also assisted John Graunt in writing "*Natural and Political Observations Made upon the Bills of Mortality*", considered a seminal work of statistics and historical demography (Fox 2009).

3 But not published until 1691.

4 Again, not published until 1690.

5 P.J. O'Rourke (2007, pp. 39) described the *Tableau Economique* as "a minutely labeled, densely zigzagging chart – part cat's cradle, part crossword puzzle, part backgammon board."

from 1932 were based almost entirely on empirical data and accompanied by pages and pages of metadata. Described as "an obsessive collector of data" (Masood 2016, p. 25), he introduced "a new degree of care and thoroughness" (Coyle 2014, p. 12) to the measurement of national income. His work presented, for the first time, consistent estimates of British national income. In doing so, Clark "made pioneering methodological observations on the recording and definition of the national income" (Lepenies 2016, p. 34).

"*National Income and Outlay*," published by Clark in 1937, measured aggregate economic activity, or what he called "national income," from three perspectives: income, expenditure, and production. He provided estimates in both current and constant prices, and factored in depreciation of fixed capital. Hence, Clark is considered the inventor of gross national product (GNP). Of relevance, to Section 2.5 of this chapter, Clark realized from the outset that this measure should not be used as a measure of welfare or wellbeing. In 1940, he published "*Conditions of Economic Progress*." Considered his most important contribution to macroeconomic measurement (Maddison 2003), this study presented comparable estimates of real income across countries adjusted for differences in the purchasing power of currencies. In doing so, he pioneered comparative analysis of economic performance across space and time, including prototype purchasing power parity (PPP) exchange rates. This "was to revolutionise the possibilities for comparative economic history, and analysis of problems of growth and development" (Maddison 2003, p. 14).

On the other side of the Atlantic, prompted by the economic myopia of the great depression, the US Congress demanded better statistics on economic activity. The depression had self-evidently wrought economic chaos, but it also brought into sharp focus the realization that no one understood what had happened to the economy since 1929; there were no reliable or up to date statistics to describe the overall economic situation in the United States. In June 1932, "reeling from the prolonged recession" (Fogel et al. 2013, p. 53), the US Senate passed resolution 220 which required the Secretary of Commerce to submit estimates of the total national income of the United States for each of the calendar years 1929, 1930, and 1931. This was an important moment, not just in the birth of national accounting, but for official statistics more generally, as the resolution made explicit the role of government in providing statistical information to support public policy.

Simon Kuznets, who was working at the National Bureau of Economic Research (NBER), was appointed by Roosevelt and seconded to the Department of Commerce in 1933 to create a set of national accounts. Although the first comprehensive set of accounts were not completed until 1942, his 1933 article "*National Income*" in the Encyclopaedia of the Social Sciences and his study "*National Income, 1929–1932*," presented to Congress in 1934, were pivotal. Duncan and Shelton (1978, pp. 78–79) note "the detail in the 1934 report is remarkable" and that "both in accuracy and in wealth of detail, this report was far ahead of anything yet produced on national income in the United States and perhaps in any country." Kuznets's analyses revealed a 50% drop in national income, providing the authoritative justification for the public investment measures implemented as part of the New Deal (Lacey 2011; Fioramonti 2013). The speed at which national income acquired a prominent place in political debate was remarkable. Well before the Department of Commerce published the final report in 1942, national income statistics had already become the most cited macroeconomic statistics in the United States. In fact, as early as 1936, national income had become a policy objective (rather than just a tool to support policy) with Roosevelt declaring "we must start again on a long, steady, upward incline in national income" in his presidential campaign speeches (Lepenies 2016, p. 74).

Elsewhere, notable developments were made in Sweden with the publication of *National Income in Sweden 1861–1930* in 1937 by Erik Lindahl, Einar Dahlgren and Karin Koch, and in the

Netherlands by Jan Tinbergen and Ed van Cleeff in 1941, and in Denmark by Viggo Kampmann (Vanoli 2016).

2.2.3 The Debate on Including Government

According to Duncan and Shelton (1978) the first reference to GNP in the literature was an article published by Brookings Institution statistician, Clark Warburton in 1934, entitled *"Value of gross national product and its components 1919–1929"* in the Journal of the American Statistical Association. Warburton's concept of GNP was much broader than that suggested by Kuznets, and importantly included government spending.

   While the great depression played a central role in the birth of national accounting, it was World War 2 and Keynesian economics that played a determining role in what was included. In particular, Keynes' (1940) pamphlet *"How to Pay for the War,"* where government spending was included in national income, profoundly affected thinking at the US Office of Price Administration and Civilian Supply (OPACS). The British approach was attractive as it could be used to demonstrate that an increase in government spending on defense did not necessarily entail a prohibitive fall in national income. Crucially Keynes brought the role of the state front and center as a final, rather than only an intermediate, consumer. The realities of wartime economics were consistent with the Keynesian theory of government stimulus. Reflecting the realities of an economy preparing for war, the role of production was also increasingly emphasized. Consequently, Vanoli (2005, p. 20) views the World War 2 as the real "birth of National Accounts." Others too note the importance of Keynes' role in the development of modern national accounts (Coyle 2014; Karabell 2014; Lepenies 2016; Masood 2016). Influenced by Keynesian logic, the OPACS moved away from the Kuznets approach in 1941 and produced an estimate of GNP that includes public expenditure (including defense spending). The following year, Richard V. Gilbert (1942), in an article *"Measuring national income as affected by the war"* published in the Journal of the American Statistical Association, set out the now familiar identity: $GNP = C + I + G + X - M$.

   Kuznets opposed the inclusion of government spending in GNP. In his papers *"National Product, War and Prewar"* (1944) and *"National Product in Wartime"* (1945) he argued against this approach. In a 1948 article *"Review of Economic Statistics,"* Kuznets again reiterated these arguments and also objected to production being the end goal. As a concession he drew a distinction between short-term crises like war, and long-term peacetime. He suggested that during wartime the role of the state and the economy is fundamentally changed – to increase spending on defense. In peacetime, the objective should be to provide goods and services for its citizens. Consequently, he proposed two approaches: (i) a wartime measure where it would be logical to include government spending as final product; and (ii) a peacetime measure, where government spending would not be considered final consumption and where depreciation of capital would be taken into account.

   The British "war-time" definition of the economy won the day. Toward the end of the war, GNP, that included government spending, replaced what was then referred to as national income as the main statistic for assessing economic health. By 1945 Roosevelt was using the term GNP in his speeches. Lepenies (2016) argues that in the USA, GNP was associated with victory. Given the massive military spending that comprised Roosevelt's Victory Program, Weigley (1973, p. 146) has argued that World War 2 was a "gross national product war.[6]"

---

6 Hastings (2011) notes that between 1939 and 1945 GNP in the United States increased from US\$91 to US\$166 billion.

2.2.4 Toward a System of National Accounts

The idea of an interdependent set (or system) of national accounts emerged as early as 1941. It was proposed by two Cambridge economists Richard Stone and James Meade, under Keynes' watchful eye, in a white paper *"An analysis of the sources of war finance and estimate of the national income and expenditure in 1938 and 1940"* (Stone and Meade 1941a) and an accompanying technical article *"The Construction of Tables of National Income, Expenditure, Saving and Investment,"* published in the Economic Journal (Stone and Meade 1941b). This was a landmark in national accounting, as it not only presented a set of interconnected accounts but also because they applied the double-entry bookkeeping method to national accounts. Stone and Meade effectively systematized Clark's approach, but within a Keynesian conceptual framework (in particular, formalizing the relationships between income, output, consumption, investment, and savings). Thus, the SNA was given a theoretical basis it had previously lacked (Lepenies 2016). Critically, this system did not focus on any particular indicator but rather measured the overall economy from a set of different but integrated perspectives. Although these first tables were incomplete, they are nevertheless considered the first SNA, providing a framework linking a coherent set of macroeconomic totals (Vanoli 2016).

Before the end of the war, in 1944, the US, UK, and Canadian administrations began the process of negotiating a harmonized methodology for calculating their national accounts. The result was that the Keynesian model, including government spending, was adopted. Meanwhile Stone, as the Director of the UK Central Statistical Office, also chaired the League of Nations Sub-Committee on National Income Statistics of the Committee of Statistical Experts that adopted, in 1947, the report *"Definition and Measurement of the National Income and Related Totals."* This was the immediate predecessor of the first edition of worldwide standards for SNA, that was subsequently published in 1953 (the Expert Group convened to develop the SNA was also chaired by Stone). It is for this reason that Stone is regarded as the father of the international SNA for which he was awarded the Nobel Prize in Economics in 1984.

2.2.5 Global Proliferation of GDP

In the aftermath of World War 2, a number of developments helped to propagate the SNA, and GNP in particular, into globally accepted standards. Firstly, reconstruction aid, known as the Marshall Plan was not unconditional – to receive aid, European states had to reach growth and development targets. This, in turn, made it necessary to evaluate the effects of aid on economic activity. The Organisation for European Economic Cooperation (OEEC), established to distribute aid and monitor effectiveness, used GNP as the benchmark measure. This, Masood (2016) argues, contributed to mainstreaming the idea that GNP and national prosperity are one and the same. He argues that the cold war that followed also contributed, as that war was defined by statistics, rather than battle, and was designed to demonstrate the superiority of capitalism and its ability to provide "prosperity" and even "happiness." Fioramonti (2013, p. 37) concurs, describing the cold war as a "full-blown 'stats war'." The Bretton Woods agreement, including the creation of the International Monetary Fund (IMF) and World Bank also contributed to the international predominance of GDP. The creation of the UN also played a role, as membership dues were based on member states' GDP (Philipsen 2015). Of course, the adoption in 1953 of the SNA sealed the deal.

In time, these indicators went global, both to meet the needs of the emerging international community for whom common standards and common metrics were needed "to assess whether or not the world was on a constructive economic trajectory" (Karabell 2014, p. 78). As the concept of development economics emerged and the UN began to elaborate development policy, many of the early leading experts came from the OEEC, bringing with them their experiences of the Marshall Plan. But early development policy "had a strong political component from the very beginning" (Lepenies 2016, p. 137) as GDP was used as a tool in the armory against communism. Today, GDP is the best known of all economic indicators. It underpins virtually all of our economic and political systems – it has "colonized the very lexicon of global governance" (Fioramonti 2013, p. 42). Everything from membership fees of the UN (United Nations 2018) to contributions to the EU budget (Eurostat 2020) relies on GDP or GNI statistics. Even the last great bastion of Communism, China, began measuring GDP in 1992 (Pilling 2018).

2.3 SNA and GDP Today

2.3.1 The System at Large

Before addressing the main challenges around the SNA in Section 2.5, it is useful to discuss the basic components of the central framework of national accounts as it stands now. This will be followed, in Section 2.4, by a quick recap of developments that have led to the latest international standards for compiling national accounts: the System of National Accounts 2008 (SNA 2008), and its European equivalent, the European System of Accounts 2010 (ESA 2010). The latter standards are almost fully consistent with the SNA 2008, with a couple of minor exceptions, such as the treatment of services provided by central banks. The main difference between the two standards is that ESA 2010 tends to be slightly more prescriptive, not surprisingly given the administrative use of national accounts data within the European Union.

From a compilation perspective, the central framework of national accounts consists of two main building blocks: (i) the supply and use tables and (ii) the institutional sector accounts. The latter accounts provide a full-fledged overview of all economic flows and positions. In this respect, one can look upon the supply and use framework as a subsystem of institutional sector accounts, as it provides substantially more detail on the production of goods and services, the inputs needed to generate this output, and the transactions in goods and services. But there are more differences, especially when it comes to the unit of observation, the establishment versus the institutional unit, and the grouping of units, activities, or industries versus institutional sectors. More about this further below.

2.3.2 Supply and Use Tables

The framework of supply and use tables can be considered as the starting point for compiling national accounts. Often this framework is perceived as esoteric and difficult to understand, probably because of some of the more detailed intricacies that are being applied to deal with certain phenomena. Another reason may be the sheer magnitude of the tables. In some countries both the supply and use table are as large as 250 columns, representing the various industries according to the International Standard Industrial Classification (ISIC), and up to 2000 rows, representing the products according to Central Product Classification (CPC), and then one does not even take into account the different layers of valuation, first and foremost the distinction between current prices and constant prices (i.e. adjusted for price changes). The main principles of supply and use tables however are quite simple and straightforward. The framework is an example of elegance for the description of the domestic production process and the transactions in goods and services, including imports from and exports to the rest of the world. Below these main principles are described. For more details, reference is made to Chapter 14 of SNA 2008.

The main underlying idea of supply and use tables is its description, for each product, of total supply and total use. The supply and use per product are represented in the rows of the supply table and use table, respectively.

Total supply of a product *i* equals domestic production, usually referred to as *output*, by economic activity, plus imports:

$$\text{Total supply}_i = \sum_{j=1}^{n} O_{i,j} + M_i \tag{2.1}$$

in which:

$O_{i,j}$ = Output of product *i* produced by domestic economic activity *j*

M_i = Imports of product *i*

On the other hand, total use consists of the goods and services that are being used up in the production of other goods and services, referred to as *intermediate consumption*, by domestic economic activity; domestic final use, consisting of final consumption by households (and nonprofit institutions serving households [NPISHs]), final consumption by government, and investments or *gross capital formation* (including changes in inventories); and exports. The following formula presents the total use for product *i*:[7]

$$\text{Total use}_i = \sum_{j=1}^{n} IC_{i,j} + C_i + I_i + X_i \tag{2.2}$$

in which:

$IC_{i,j}$ = Intermediate Consumption of product *i*, used in production by domestic economic activity *j*

C_i = Final consumption of product *i*

I_i = Investments (including changes in inventories) of product *i*

X_i = Exports of product *i*

If one aggregates the above equations for all products (*m*), and combines the two equations representing the identity of total supply being equal to total use by definition, one arrives at what can be considered as the most famous macroeconomic equation, as follows:

$$\text{Total supply} = \text{Total use} \tag{2.3}$$

$$\sum_{i=1}^{m}\sum_{j=1}^{n} O_{i,j} + \sum_{i=1}^{m} M_i = \sum_{i=1}^{m}\sum_{j=1}^{n} IC_{i,j} + \sum_{i=1}^{m} C_i + \sum_{i=1}^{m} I_i + \sum_{i=1}^{m} X_i \tag{2.4}$$

$$\sum_{i=1}^{m}\sum_{j=1}^{n} O_{i,j} - \sum_{i=1}^{m}\sum_{j=1}^{n} IC_{i,j} = \sum_{i=1}^{m} C_i + \sum_{i=1}^{m} I_i + \sum_{i=1}^{m} X_y - \sum_{i=1}^{m} M_i \tag{2.5}$$

$$\text{Output} - \text{Intermediate consumption} = \text{GDP} = C + I + X - M \tag{2.6}$$

Taking a step back, let us use a concrete example of a two-product economy: apples and apple-cider. In the example, it is assumed that 50 units of apples are produced domestically and 20 units are imported. Of this total of 70 units, 40 are directly consumed by households, while 30

---

7 Please note that in this equation, the G of Government is included in final consumption (C) and gross capital formation (I).

are processed by local manufacturers to produce cider. The producer of cider sells his product for the value of 80, of which 60 is consumed by households, and 20 is exported. The simplified supply and use table would then look as presented in Table 2.1 below.

To complete the use table in this example, as presented at the bottom of Table 2.1, the columns of the domestic activities are supplemented with total output (equal to the total output in the supply table) of each domestic economic activity. The difference between output and intermediate consumption equals *value added*, whereas the sum of all value added equals GDP.

Table 2.1 Supply and use tables.

		Supply table				
		Output by domestic industry			Imports	Total supply
		Agriculture	Manufacturing	Total		
Supply by product	Apples	50		50	20	70
	Apple-cider		80	80		80
	Total output/ imports	50	80	130	20	150

		Use table					
		Intermediate consumption by domestic industry			Final expenditures		Total use
					Final		
		Agriculture	Manufacturing	Total	consumption	Investments	Exports	
Use by product	Apples		30	30	40			70
	Apple-cider			0	60		20	80
	Total intermediate consumption/ final uses	0	30	30	100	0	20	150

		Use table (including output and value added by economic activity)					
		Intermediate consumption by domestic industry			Final expenditures		Total use
					Final		
		Agriculture	Manufacturing	Total	consumption	Investments	Exports	
Use by product	Apples		30	30	40			70
	Apple-cider			0	60		20	80
	Total intermediate consumption/ final uses	0	30	30	100	0	20	150
	Value added (gross)	50	50	100				
	Output	50	80	130				

Source: van de Ven (2021).

2.3.3 Institutional Sector Accounts

While supply and use tables provide a more detailed description of the production process and related transactions in goods and services, the institutional sector accounts provide a full overview of incomes, expenditures, and finance for institutional sectors. The following main sectors are distinguished: nonfinancial corporations, financial corporations, general government, households, and NPISHs. In addition, transactions and positions with the rest of the world are recorded separately. The institutional sector accounts have much in common with the profit and loss account and the balance sheet of a corporation. However, while the balance sheets are quite similar, the sector accounts group transactions in a different way. A condensed overview of institutional sector accounts is provided in Figure 2.1 below.

This sequence of accounts can be broken down into *current accounts* and *accumulation accounts*. The current accounts provide information on production, income generated by production, the subsequent distribution and redistribution of incomes, and the use of income for consumption and saving purposes. These concern the upper part of Figure 2.1. The accumulation accounts record flows that affect the balance sheets and consist of the capital and financial account, which primarily record transactions (purchases less disposals of assets and net incurrence of liabilities), and the other changes in assets account, which consists of a separate account for revaluations and one for other changes in the volume of assets. Together these accounts represent the changes in the stock accounts, i.e. the balance sheets. All of this is presented in the lower part of Figure 2.1.

Each of the accounts distinguished in the institutional sector accounts ends with a *balancing item* which is usually the starting item for the subsequent account. The balancing item typically represents the net result of the flows (or positions) recorded in the account in question and is calculated as the difference between the total resources and total uses recorded in the relevant account. Examples of balancing items are gross value added on the production account and saving on the use of income account. The national totals of these balancing items often represent important macroeconomic aggregates. For example, the sum of gross value added generated in the various domestic sectors equals GDP, while the sum of (gross/net) primary income, the balancing item of the primary distribution of income account, represents (Gross/Net) National Income.

The institutional sectors accounts start off with a simplified overview of the production of goods and services, in the production account. It shows the output from production, the goods and services used up in the production process, i.e. intermediate consumption, and the resulting income generated through the production of goods and services: *value added*. The following set of accounts shows the *distribution of income*, i.e. what types of income have been generated by

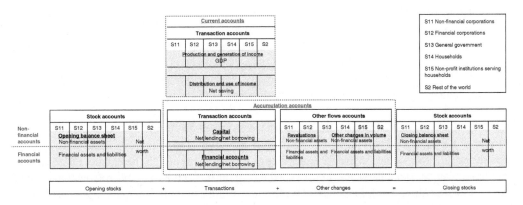

Figure 2.1 Sequence of accounts in the 2008 SNA. Source: van de Ven and Fano (2017).

production, how this income is allocated across sectors, and how other primary income flows (interest, dividends, etc.) affect the level of income. The impact of government interventions through taxes, social contributions and benefits, and the impact of other types of current transfers are presented in the *redistribution of income accounts*. The resulting balancing item is *disposable income*, the income available for final consumption purposes. The use of income account records the latter, together with the resulting *saving*. This balancing item is the linking pin between the current accounts and the accumulation accounts.

The capital account constitutes the first part of the accumulation accounts. From the perspective of balance sheets, it provides two important pieces of information in linking current and capital accounts. First of all, it shows, for each sector, the balancing item *changes in net worth due to saving and capital transfers*, which equals saving *plus* net capital transfers received. The latter transfers often relate to lump sum payments by governments to corporations (e.g. investment grants and payments to save banks in financial distress). It may also include, for example, capital taxes or legacies. The balancing item *changes in net worth due to saving and capital transfers* is a crucial link in the SNA. It represents not only the excess available for investing in nonfinancial or financial assets, or, in the case of a negative balance, the need to borrow funds, it also equals – as the term already suggests – the change in net wealth due to receiving incomes that exceeds expenditures. Other changes in net wealth, due to revaluations and other changes in the volume of assets, are recorded on separate accounts; see below.

The second piece of information that can be derived from the capital accounts concerns the purchases, less disposals, of nonfinancial assets. The resulting balancing item of *changes in net worth due to saving* and capital transfers minus the net purchases of nonfinancial assets, is called *net lending/net borrowing*. If this balancing item is positive, i.e. the sum of saving and net capital transfers exceeds the net accumulation of nonfinancial assets, the remaining funds are available to purchase financial assets, which *ceteris paribus* lead to an increase of the financial wealth of the relevant unit or sector. This is recorded as net lending. If it falls short, it is recorded as net borrowing. In the latter case, the unit or sector would need to borrow funds to cover the shortfall.

The net lending/net borrowing amount from the capital account has its counterpart in the balancing item of the financial account, in which the transactions in financial assets and liabilities are recorded. Conceptually the two balancing items are the same; see also the quadruple accounting principle below. In practice, however, due to the different data sources and methods used to compile the production, income and capital accounts versus those used for the compilation of financial accounts, the items often differ from each other. These differences are referred to as *statistical discrepancies*.

As noted before, balance sheet items are also affected by revaluations and other changes in the volume of assets. The relevant flows are recorded on two separate accumulation accounts, where the balancing item of the revaluations account is called *changes in net worth due to revaluations*, and the balance of the other changes in the volume of assets account is called the *changes in net worth due to other changes in the volume of assets*. These two balancing items, together with the *changes in net worth due to saving and capital transfers*, add up to the changes in *net worth* as recorded on the balance sheet.

Finally, the balance sheets show the values of the stocks of assets and liabilities at the start and the end of the recording period. They also provide insight into the financial status of a sector by illustrating how that sector finances its activities or invests its funds. On the balance sheets, a clear distinction can be made between nonfinancial assets on the one hand, and financial assets and liabilities on the other hand. Examples of nonfinancial assets include produced assets like houses, infrastructure, machinery and equipment, and inventories, but they also comprise non-produced assets such as land, mineral and energy resources, and water resources. Deposits, shares, loans, and bonds are examples of financial assets (and liabilities). The value of the assets and liabilities at the start of a period is referred to as *opening stock* and at the end of the period as *closing stock*.

Net worth, the balancing item from the balance sheet, is defined as the value of all assets owned by an institutional unit or sector less the value of all its outstanding liabilities, and it provides insight into the financial health of a unit or sector. It is recorded, together with the liabilities, on the right-hand side of the balance sheet. In this respect, it should be noted that equity is also considered as a liability in the national accounts.

2.3.4 The Link Between Supply and Use Tables and the Institutional Sector Accounts

In the supply and use tables, the statistical unit for measurement is the *establishment*. An establishment is an enterprise, or a part of an enterprise, that predominantly produces a certain type of good or service, and for which data on the production process (output, intermediate consumption, compensation of employees, consumption of fixed capital and operating surplus) are available. The statistical unit for the institutional sector accounts is the *institutional unit*. This unit can be characterized as "… an economic entity that is capable, in its own right, of owning assets, incurring liabilities and engaging in economic activities and in transactions with other entities" (United Nations et al. 2009, Section 4.2). Typically, for such units having autonomy of decision, full profit and loss accounts and balance sheets are available, or it is feasible to compile them. An institutional unit consists of one or more establishments. Due to this unit issue, it may thus be possible that an institutional unit, or in this case an enterprise, is involved in multiple economic activities.

One should also be aware of the fact that not all establishments recorded under a particular economic activity end up in the same institutional sector. In addition to unincorporated enterprises being recorded as part of the population of the households' sector, other establishments may be recorded either as part of (non)financial corporations, or as part of general government (or nonprofit institutions serving households), depending on whether they produce market goods and services or non-market services. The distinction between market and non-market is based on whether or not the products are sold at "economically significant prices, i.e. … prices that have a significant effect on the amounts that producers are willing to supply and on the amounts purchasers wish to buy" (United Nations et al. 2009, Section 6.95). In practice, this distinction is often based on the so-called 50%-criterion, i.e. whether the sales are more/less than 50% of the production costs.

A more general point relates to the fungible character of income and especially finance. It may not be possible to make a direct relationship between income and finance on the one hand, and the production activities on the other hand. It may show not to be possible, for example, to fully disentangle an unincorporated enterprise (establishment) from the household owning this enterprise, and thus arrive at a clear separation of transactions and positions related to the enterprise and those related to other household activities. How to allocate, for example, the mortgage debt and the saving deposits that are used to purchase a combined dwelling/office space and/or to purchase consumer durables? The same problems may arise when dealing with multi-establishment enterprises. This is one of the reasons for distinguishing institutional units, and not directly linking income and finance to establishments.

2.3.5 Consistency and Coherence

The beauty and elegance of the SNA lies in its consistency and coherence, as represented by the quadruple-entry bookkeeping principle. This latter principle comes down to the point that for a single transaction, four simultaneous entries are recorded in the national accounts. Firstly, the national accounts respect the double-entry bookkeeping, as applied in traditional business accounting. From an accounting system's perspective, one can look upon national accounts as a further extension of business accounting; see e.g. Gleeson-White (2011). In national accounts terminology, each income or capital transaction recorded on the current or capital account has a counterpart entry in the financial account. In the case of the purchase/sale of a financial asset, or in the case of the incurrence of a liability, both entries appear in the financial account. Secondly, as the goal of national accounts is to arrive at exhaustive estimates for all economic agents on the domestic territory of a country, including the engagements of residents with nonresidents, the system does not only reflect the transactions (and financial positions) of a particular unit but also the transactions (and financial positions) of the counterparty unit. As a result, each transaction leads to four entries: the quadruple entry bookkeeping system.

In summary, three basic identities can be distinguished:

- *Budget identity*: This identity represents the traditional double-entry rules. In the SNA, it becomes visible in the (conceptual) equality of the balance of nonfinancial (current and capital) transactions and the balance of financial transactions.
- *Transaction identity*: For each transaction, the sum of all receipts is by definition equal to the sum of payments; and for each financial instrument, the sum of assets is by definition equal to the sum of liabilities. In the supply and use tables, this identity is represented by total supply of good and services being equal to total use.
- *Balance sheet identity*: In addition to the above identities, resulting from the quadruple entry method, one can distinguish a third identity, which is here referred to as the balance sheet identity. For each balance sheet item, the opening stock *plus* the net purchases of the relevant item *plus* revaluations *plus* other changes in the volume of assets is equal to the closing stock. Related to this identity is the conceptual consistency between the change in net worth of a sector and the sum of the following balancing items: *changes in net worth due to saving and capital transfer*, *changes in net worth due to nominal holding gains and losses* (i.e. revaluations), and *changes in net worth due to other changes in the volume of assets*.

Together, these identities not only result in a closed and, at least from a conceptual point of view, fully consistent system. They also provide a powerful tool to check the exhaustiveness, the quality and the reliability of the various source data feeding into the SNA. In compiling national accounts, consistency is often accomplished by changing the original source data which are considered to be lowest quality. It can also be used to fill data gaps, whereby estimates for certain (sub)sectors are compiled as a residual. It should be acknowledged however that usually not all identities are fully respected. In practice, it shows to be quite problematic to arrive at a balance of nonfinancial transactions that matches the balance of financial transactions, for all or at least for some sectors. The difference is typically presented as a *statistical discrepancy*, which is preferable to hiding the discrepancy by, for example, allocating it to accounts receivable/payable.

2.3.6   The Relationship Between National Accounts and Business Statistics

The numbers from national accounts often differ from the original source statistics feeding into the system. The same holds for production statistics and structural business statistics. It is often a source of misunderstanding and frustration between the compilers of source statistics and national accountants. In this respect, one could add that having clear and transparent information on these adjustments may certainly help to mitigate the tensions between the various areas of expertise. It would also support the compilation of more granular data, including the understanding of the micro–macro link, and the communication with users. Here, a more general overview is provided of the usual adjustments made for national accounts purposes.

2.3.6.1   Definitional Adjustments

As noted before, national accounts are compiled according to the concepts and definitions of the SNA (2008) and, for European countries, the European System of Accounts (ESA). The definitional adjustments to source statistics can relate to a variety of cases. An example is the treatment of expenditures on intellectual property products (IPPs) (R&D, software, databases, artistic originals, etc.), which is treated in the national accounts as investments, while in business accounting these expenditures may be recorded as current costs. Other examples relate to the definition of compensation of employees, where national accounts include certain employers' social contributions, tips, and the provision of in-kind compensation (e.g. allowances for transport to and from work, and the provision of meals). The inclusion of production of goods for own final use, such as the case for self-subsistence farming, is another example. Also the time of recording of transactions in national accounts may differ from the one used in source statistics. An example of the latter concerns the recording of output (and intermediate consumption) at the time the product has been produced (used in the production process), instead of recording it at the time of sale (purchase).

2.3.6.2   Adjustments for Exhaustiveness

National accounts aim to arrive at a full coverage of economic activities, thus including informal, hidden, and illegal activities. Adjustments may be made explicitly, especially in cases where data on both supply and use are lacking, or implicitly, by adjusting supply to use or vice versa, depending on what type of information is available. An example of the latter is the estimation of total construction of dwellings based on the number of new dwellings realized in a year and adjusting the output of the relevant construction activities to this total. Examples of the former relate to illegal activities (e.g. the production and consumption of drugs) and paid household activities such taking care of children or house cleaning.

2.3.6.3   Adjustments for Time Consistency

The primary goal of national accounts is to arrive at results which are consistent over time. For many outsiders, this may be one of the more problematic types of adjustments to comprehend. If, for example, improvements are made to source statistics, the improvements in the level estimates usually will not be taken on board in the SNA, until a new benchmark revision is being introduced, to avoid breaks in the series, as a consequence of which developments in the level estimates over time would not only reflect economic developments but also changes in sources and/or methods. The benchmark revisions, which involve a complete overhaul of the level estimates based on new and improved source data, new and revised methodologies and/or the introduction of new international standards, usually take place once every five to ten years. After the benchmark revision the national accounts data for past years are revised to bring them in line with the latest benchmark level estimates. These time series compilations may go back to as much as 70–80 years, but usually they concern a time period of say 20–30 years. The recalculated time series will also result in an additional layer of differences with the underlying source statistics.

2.3.6.4   Balancing Adjustments

After the previous adjustments have been made to the source statistics, the adjusted and completed data are entered into the SNA. As can be expected, total receipts (supply) and total payments (use) for each transaction (product) will not match initially. The matching of the initial estimates, to arrive at a consistent set of data, is referred to as the *balancing process*. As a consequence of this balancing, dependent on the magnitude of the initial imbalances, significant adjustments may be made to the source statistics. These balancing decisions are often based on explicit but sometimes rather implicit assessments of the quality of the underlying source statistics, or they rely on quite typical and well-founded reasons for underreporting such as the underreporting of consumption of cigarettes and alcohol in consumer surveys, or – in the case of institutional sector accounts – the underreporting of receipts of property income (i.e. interest, dividends, etc.).

2.4 Most Recent and Important Revisions to SNA (Implications for Business Statistics)

2.4.1 International Standards Not Set in Stone

International statistical standards are an important tool to arrive at internationally comparable statistics. As noted before, the first set of what can be looked upon as international standards for compiling national accounts was the SNA 1953. Since then, three updates have been agreed upon by the international statistical community: the SNA 1968, the SNA 1993, and the latest version, the SNA 2008. One important characteristic of this update process: each time the standards get more and more extensive and contain more and more details, with the result of having a 2008 version of more than 700 double column pages. To compare with, the SNA 1953 contained, in total, 53 pages. While the latter consisted of a set of six standard accounts and 12 standard tables presenting details and alternative classifications of the flows in the economy, the SNA 2008 includes a complete and very detailed set of integrated accounts and tables for production, income, finance, and wealth accumulation. It also includes quite specific recommendations on the various flows and positions distinguished.

Source: From Historic Versions of the System of National Accounts, by Department of Economic and Social Affairs, © 2022 United Nations. Reprinted with the permission of the United Nations.

International standards are updated for a variety of reasons. The SNA is no different. Most importantly, the standards may need to be updated to keep track of new economic developments. Coping with changes in an economy where production of goods transforms to an economy predominantly producing services; dealing with digitalization, financialization, and (new forms of) globalization; movement to a knowledge economy; etc. all require a further deepening and extension of the standards. Also user demands, among which new areas of economic research in academia and a refocusing of policy, may require a change of emphasis in the international standards. Here, one can think of, for example, environmental-economic issues and the discussion on wellbeing and sustainability more generally. Also new developments in source statistics and statistical methodologies can open new avenues for producing new and/or more granular national accounts. Chapter 3 in this volume (MacFeely and van de Ven 2023). Will deal with the three priority areas for the update of the current SNA 2008: (i) digitalization; (ii) globalization; and (iii) wellbeing and sustainability.

In this section, a short historic overview is provided of the main changes leading up to the updates of SNA 1968 and SNA 1993, in the end resulting in the current standards, SNA 2008. The section concludes with some general observation on the link with source statistics for enterprises.

2.4.2 From SNA 1968 to SNA 1993

Perhaps the single most important new feature of the SNA 1993 was the introduction of a full-fledged set of institutional sector accounts: "In the 1993 SNA the overall sequence of accounts of institutional units and sectors is now subdivided into current accounts, accumulation accounts and balance sheets. Thus, the accounting structure of the System integrates the balance sheets as an additional group. The 1968 SNA did not specify balance sheets in detail" (United Nations et al. 1993). This major change was accompanied with a distinction of new (sub)accounts. For example, the SNA 1993 divided the capital account of the SNA 1968 into an account for the recording of nonfinancial assets, and the financial account for the recording of acquisitions and disposals of financial assets and liabilities, which also led to the introduction of a new balancing item: net lending/net borrowing. The reconciliation account of the 1968 SNA was also integrated into a new set of accumulation accounts, on which all changes in balance sheets were recorded. In addition to accounts for the acquisitions and disposals of assets and liabilities, separate accounts were introduced for revaluations and other changes in the volume of assets. All in all, one could say that the SNA 1993 presented, for the first time, a fully consistent and closed system of accounts.

Obviously, the above also led to the introduction of much more detailed guidance on balance sheets, including the distinction and classification of the various types of assets (and liabilities). In this respect, a significant extension of the asset boundary was also introduced. More expenditures from which benefits can be derived beyond one year were to be treated as investments, leading to the build-up of stocks of nonfinancial assets. As intangible assets in the form of IPPs had become a far more important feature in the economy, three main types of IPPs were introduced in the SNA 1993: (i) mineral exploration; (ii) computer software; and (iii) entertainment, literary, or artistic originals. Another extension of the asset boundary related to the recognition of military expenditures on buildings and equipment as investments. However, expenditures on military weapons, and vehicles and equipment whose sole purpose is to launch or deliver such weapons, were not yet included, even though they may have a service life of more than one year. The recording of the latter expenditures would only change with the following update of the SNA. These changes in the asset boundary are considered quite fundamental, as they lead, almost one to one, to an increase of GDP. On the other hand, however, net domestic product (NDP), i.e. GDP adjusted for depreciation of capital, is far less affected. Many have argued that the latter indicator is by far preferable to using GDP. From a conceptual point of view, this is undisputed. It was, and up to this date still is, not possible to dethrone GDP, for reasons of compilation, many countries not being able to adequately account for depreciation, as well as for reasons of communication, many producers and users feeling uncomfortable to make such a dramatic switch in the principal indicator.

The financialization of the economy, and also the interest and involvement of central bankers in the SNA, resulted into substantial changes from the SNA 1968 to the SNA 1993. One of the results was a revised sub-sectoring of the financial corporations' sector. In addition, the definition and treatment of financial instruments was substantially refined. Examples are the distinction between financial leasing and operational leasing, and the identification of new financial instruments, such as repurchase agreements, derivatives, and secondary instruments, and deep discounted bonds. Most importantly, from a perspective of the impact on GDP was the allocation of financial intermediation services indirectly measured (FISIM), i.e. the services not directly charged by banks, but implicitly charged by receiving a higher interest rate on loans and paying a lower interest rate on deposits. The SNA 1968 already included FISIM as part of the output of banks,[8] but the use of these services was fully allocated to intermediate consumption of a nominal sector, with the recording of FISIM thus having no impact on GDP. The SNA 1993 recommended to allocate FISIM to the actual users, leading to a positive impact on GDP in the case of an allocation to final consumption and exports. The whole concept of FISIM and its allocation to users has been discussed since the start of setting up international standards for national accounts, and also was one of the most controversial issues in recent debates after the financial crisis in 2008–2010.

Furthermore, developments in globalization started to find their way into the SNA. The SNA 1993, for example, introduced a distinction between public corporations, national private corporations, and foreign-controlled corporations. A change in the treatment of earnings from foreign direct investment is another example.

Many other changes could be listed here, such as the introduction of the concept of actual consumption and adjusted disposable income, related to the treatment of services provided for free or at significantly reduced prices by government and other nonprofit institutions to households (e.g. education and health). The SNA 1993 can truly be considered as a major overhaul of the SNA 1968. For reasons not to overburden this paper, reference is made to Annex 1 of the SNA 1993, which contains a very nice overview of all conceptual changes introduced during this update.

2.4.3   From SNA 1993 to SNA 2008

The changeover from SNA 1993 to SNA 2008 was less dramatic. But then again, it was only 15 years later. Knowledge economy, globalization, and – although the financial crisis still had to hit the world – financialization were the key words. In relation to the latter, further improvements and refinements of the financial corporate sector were introduced. Financial "innovations" also had their impact on the guidance for the distinction and recording of financial instruments. The recording of pensions, especially defined benefit schemes, was further elaborated, although no agreement could be reached on the recognition of pension entitlements related to unfunded pension schemes sponsored by government. FISIM was again subject of further refinements, although the main controversy started after the financial crisis, when the increased interest margins on loans and deposits led to a substantial (nominal) growth of financial services. This was looked upon as an anomaly, and the debate centered around the inclusion/exclusion of risk premiums in the calculation of FISIM. All of this has not yet had an effect on the international standards.

When it comes to globalization, the SNA 2008 provides more guidance on the recording of special purpose entities (SPEs), head offices, holding companies and subsidiaries of multinational enterprises (MNE). Most importantly, however, was the improved clarity on the change of economic ownership as the principle for the determination and the timing of recording transactions. This led to a quite significant change in the recording of processing of goods and, although the SNA 1993 did not provide any explicit guidance, also the recording of merchanting. The determination of a change in economic ownership has been on the research agenda ever since, especially concerning the recording of cross-border transactions within MNE, which have become more and more complicated, mainly because of the increased "intangibilitization" and digitalization of the worldwide organization of production, income and finance within multinationals, to which the minimization of the global tax burden added another layer of complexity.

Looking at the knowledge economy, a further extension of the asset boundary was introduced. Expenditures on research and development (R&D) were now also to be recorded as investments in

---

8 Here, it is ignored that the calculation of total FISIM was also slightly revised.

IPPs, while the category software was extended with expenditures on databases, although excluding the knowledge content of data. The change in the recording of military weapons systems, from intermediate consumption to investments, was quite controversial. Some people were dead against looking upon these weapon systems, intended for destruction, as something adding to GDP. Others argued that these expenditures had a service life of more than one year, and provided capital services to the production of defense services, in the sense of protecting a country by way of deterrence.

Finally, something that already started with the update of the SNA 1993 was the growing alignment of the SNA with other international manuals, first and foremost the Balance of Payments Manual and the Government Finance Statistics Manual. With the update of the SNA 2008, this alignment was fully achieved, although differences in wording can still lead to slightly diverging interpretations. But the whole idea of arriving at full conceptual consistency is without discussion and advocated by all.

More details on all changes from the SNA 1993 to the SNA 2008 can be found in Annex 3 of United Nations et al. (2009).

2.4.4 The SNA and Source Statistics for Enterprises

International standards for national accounts always struggle to find an appropriate balance between analytical usefulness of the national accounts results and the availability of relevant source data. In this context, source data for enterprises play a major role. Obviously, one could design surveys in a way that information on transactions and positions can be derived according to the relevant definitions and concepts. However, in a world governed by the wish to minimize the response burden for enterprises, households, governments and nonprofit institutions, and an increasing availability of administrative data and private source data, alignment with business accounting standards play a growing role.

In the area of government statistics, a close connection between national accountants, government statisticians and people responsible for setting the International Public Sector Accounting Standards (IPSAS) has resulted in a close alignment, although well-defined differences still remain. The situation is less favorable when it comes to business accounting standards for corporations. But then again, the latter world is substantially larger and far more diverse. The goals of business accounting are also more divergent from those of statistics, certainly as compared to government statistics where one can observe that government statistics and related national accounts statistics are leading, such as the case in the European Union. Having said that, building an alliance between the statistical world and the business accounting world, including a direct participation in the drafting of new accounting standards, is worthwhile to explore further, and to which more energy and resources could, or should, be allocated.

Leaving apart the recent discussions on the recording of operational and financial leasing, and the very awkward inconsistency introduced in the business accounting standards, according to which the recording for the lessor can differ from the recording for the lessee, most inconsistencies between business accounting standards and the SNA may arise from differences in the recognition of assets and underlying investments. Examples do not only relate to the recognition of expenses on the development of IPPs as investments. They may also involve differences in, for example, the valuation of stocks of assets, where national accounts apply current replacement costs, instead of historic costs often applied in business accounting. Differences in the application of service lives and related depreciation pattern, which in business accounting are often governed by tax rules, may add another layer.

Importantly, especially in the case of IPPs which are often produced in-house, is the impact of treating expenditures on IPPs as investments on the production boundary of national accounts.

To put it simply, in these cases, it is assumed that the enterprise produces a capital good which is delivered to/used by the enterprise itself. Such a recording is irrelevant for an individual enterprise, but in the circular flow of income, consumption and positions applied in national accounts, it is conditional for arriving at a consistent set of accounts.

Although in relation to knowledge assets the SNA has clearly pushed the boundaries, it is good to realize that the discussions on the standards often take into account the feasibility of practical implementation. An example is the allocation of activities of MNE to countries. We will come back to this topic in Chapter 3 (MacFeely and van de Ven 2023). But here, we would like to add that, from a theoretical perspective, one may prefer an allocation which is more in line with "real" economic activity across countries. However, in a world driven by minimization of global tax burden, it is hardly impossible to generate an alternative and more appropriate recording of economic activities in a consistent way across countries. How much we may prefer it, there seems to be no alternative to "follow the money flows." What can be done, to allow for an improved accounting of domestic economic activity, is to clearly distinguish flows and positions related to activities of MNEs.

2.5 Conclusions and Implications for Business Statistics

GDP and the SNA emerged from the great Depression and World War 2. The construction of today's system still reflects issues of that time. But the SNA has not remained static, as noted above, it has evolved considerably over the past 70 years. Continued development is anticipated, driven mainly by evolving user demands and development in the economy. Accordingly, each new generation of the SNA has also placed new demands on business and household statistics. While this will be true in the future also, the anticipated changes will have profound implications for the organization of national and international statistical systems. These issues are explored in Chapter 3 (MacFeely and van de Ven 2023).

The SNA is much more than GDP. It is an elegant system from which a variety of macroeconomic indicators can be derived, not only GDP but also including, GNI, household (adjusted) disposable income, household final consumption and saving, corporate profits and balance sheets (van de Ven 2019). So, while GDP may be the best known and most widely used indicator, it is not necessarily the most important indicator from the SNA.

The main overarching frameworks within the SNA are (i) the institutional sector accounts, providing a complete and internally fully consistent overview of income, expenditure and wealth accumulation by institutional sector and (ii) the supply and use tables, which can be regarded as a much more detailed representation of the process of producing goods and services, including transactions in goods and services between economic actors, and the income (value added) generated by producing goods and services. A major advantage of the SNA is its internal consistency, exemplified by the quadruple entry method, with three types of consistency checks: (i) budget identity, (ii) transaction identity, and (iii) balance sheet identity. The system does not only have a very solid foundation in economic theory but also provides various checks and balances in confronting the various source data used for compiling national accounts, and allows for estimating data for missing (sub)sectors.

For a number of reasons, the original source data will be adjusted in the process of compiling national accounts. An important difference between national accounts and source data will result from definitional divergences. But also requirements of exhaustiveness and time-consistency will lead to adjustments of source data. Last but certainly not least, based on an assessment of quality and reliability of source data, adjustments will be made to arrive at a consistent set of national accounts. It is important to keep track of the relationship between the original source data and the final results of national accounts, even more so in a time of growing user demands for more granular statistics which are linked and aligned with the set of macroeconomic statistics.

As noted before, the international standards for national accounts are not static. They continuously evolve. At this stage, four iterations can be distinguished. Starting with the SNA 1953, three updates have been agreed, resulting in the 1968, the 1993, and the 2008 version of the SNA. Currently, a new update is underway, scheduled to be finalized in 2025. Important themes for the two last updates were globalization, the knowledge economy, and financialization. For the ongoing update, three priority areas have been defined: (i) digitalization; (ii) globalization; and (iii) wellbeing and sustainability. Especially, the latter priority can be considered as a response to the growing unease about the dominance of GDP as a catch-all indicator for progress. All of this will also be further elaborated in Chapter 3 (MacFeely and van de Ven 2023).

References

Coyle, D. (2014). *GDP: A Brief But Affectionate History*. Princeton and Oxford: Princeton University Press.

Desrosières, A. (2003). Managing the economy. In: *The Cambridge History of Science – Vol 7: The Modern Social Sciences* (ed. T.M. Porter and D. Ross). Cambridge: Cambridge University Press.

Duncan, J.W. and Shelton, W.C. (1978). *Revolution in United States Government Statistics 1926 – 1976: Volume 1*. Washington DC: Office of Federal Statistical Policy and Standards, US Department of Commerce. US Government Printing Office.

Eurostat (2020). Monitoring GNI for own resource purposes Monitoring GNI for own resource purposes. Eurostat – Statistics Explained. 22 December, 2020. https://ec.europa.eu/eurostat/statistics-explained/index.php/Monitoring_GNI_for_own_resource_purposes (accessed 09 February 2021).

Fioramonti, L. (2013). *Gross Domestic Problem: The Politics Behind the World's Most Powerful Number*. New York and London: Zed Books.

Fogel, R.W., Fogel, E.M., Guglielmo, M., and Grotte, N. (2013). *Political Arithmetic: Simon Kuznets and the Empirical Tradition in Economics*. Chicago: The University of Chicago Press.

Fox, A. (2009). Sir William Petty, Ireland, and the making of a political economist, 1653–87. *Economic History Review* 62 (2): 388–404.

Gilbert, M. (1942). Measuring national income as affected by the war. *Journal of the American Statistical Association* 37 (218): 186–198.

Gleeson-White, J. (2011). *Double Entry: How the Merchants of Venice Shaped the Modern World – and How Their Invention Could Make or Break the Planet*. Sydney: Allen and Unwin.

Hastings, M. (2011). *Inferno – The World at War, 1939–1945*. New York: Alfred A. Knopf.

Karabell, Z. (2014). *The Leading Indicators – A Short History of the Numbers that Rule Our World*. New York: Simon and Schuster.

Keynes, J. M. (1940). How to Pay for the War: A Radical Plan for the Chancellor of the Exchequer. Macmillan & Co., Limited, London. https://archive.org/details/in.ernet.dli.2015.499597/page/n1/mode/2up (accessed 14 August 2020).

Lacey, J. (2011). *Keep From All Thoughtful Men – How U.S. Economists Won World War II*. Annapolis, Maryland: Naval Institute Press.

Landefeld, S. J. (2000). GDP: one of the great inventions of the 20th century. BEA Survey of Current Business, January 2000. https://apps.bea.gov/scb/account_articles/general/0100od/maintext.htm (accessed 22 January 2021).

Lepenies, P. (2016). *The Power of a Single Number: A Political History of GDP*. New York: Columbia University Press.

MacFeely, S. and van de Ven, P. (2023). GDP and the SNA: future challenges. In: *Advances in Establishment Statistics, Methods and Data Collection*, Chapter 3 (ed. G. Snijkers, M. Bavdaž, S. Bender, J. Jones, S. MacFeely, J.W. Sakshaug, K.J. Thompson, and A. van Delden). Hoboken: Wiley.

Maddison, A. (2003). Macromeasurement before and after Colin Clark. Colin Clark Lecture. delivered at the University of Queensland, 22nd August 2003. http://www.ggdc.net/maddison/articles/colin_clark.pdf (accessed 01 July 2020).

Masood, E. (2016). *The Great Invention: The Story of GDP and the Making and Unmaking of the Modern World*. New York and London: Pegusus Books.

Mitra-Khan, B.H. (2011). Redefining the economy: how the 'economy' was invented in 1620, and has been redefined ever since. Unpublished Doctoral thesis, City University London. https://openaccess.city.ac.uk/id/eprint/1276/1/Mitra-Kahn%2C_Benjamin.pdf (accessed 03 July 2020).

O'Rourke, P.J. (2007). *On the Wealth of Nations*. London: Atlantic Books.

Philipsen, D. (2015). *The Little Big Number*. Princeton: Princeton University Press.

Pilling, D. (2018). *The Growth Delusion: Wealth, Poverty and the Well-being of Nations*. New York: Tim Duggan Books.

Stone, R. (1997). *Some British Empiricists in the Social Sciences*. Cambridge, UK: Cambridge University Press.

Stone, R. and Meade, J.E. (1941a). *An Analysis of the Sources of War Finance and Estimate of the National Income and Expenditure in 1938 and 1940*. London: H.M. Treasury Stationery Office.

Stone, R. and Meade, J.E. (1941b). The construction of tables of national income, expenditure, savings and investment. *The Economic Journal* 51: 216–231. (Reprinted in *Readings in the Concepts and Measurement of Income*. (eds. R.H. Parker and G.C. Harcourt. Cambridge: Cambridge University Press, 1969.).

Studenski, P. (1958). *The Income of Nations: Theory, Measurement, and Analysis: Past and Present: A Study in Applied Economics and Statistics*. New York: New York University Press.

United Nations, European Commission, International Monetary Fund, Organisation for Economic Co-operation and Development, and World Bank (1993). *System of National Accounts 1993*. New York: United Nations. https://unstats.un.org/unsd/nationalaccount/docs/1993sna.pdf.

United Nations, European Commission, International Monetary Fund, Organisation for Economic Cooperation and Development, World Bank (2009). *System of National Accounts 2008*. New York: United Nations. https://unstats.un.org/unsd/nationalaccount/docs/SNA2008.pdf (accessed 19 May 2021).

United Nations (2018). Scale of assessments for the apportionment of the expenses of the United Nations. Resolution 73/271 adopted by the General Assembly on 22 December 2018. A/RES/73/271A/RES/73/271. https://undocs.org/en/A/RES/73/271 (accessed 09 February 2021).

van de Ven, P. and Fano, D. (2017). *Understanding Financial Accounts*. Paris: OECD.

van de Ven, P. (2019). Eurostat Review on National Accounts and Macroeconomic Indicators. Eurona 1/2019. Available at: a2f269a5-80eb-4b18-a6b4-41a20011d7cd (europa.eu) (accessed 28 February 2022).

van de Ven, P. (2021). Developing thematic satellite accounts: the example of a thematic satellite account for transport. OECD Statistics Working Papers 2021/02. ISSN: 18152031. https://doi.org/10.1787/18152031.

Vanoli, A. (2005). *A History of National Accounting*. Amsterdam, Netherlands: IOS Press.

Vanoli, A. (2016). National accounting at the beginning of the 21st century: Wherefrom? Whereto?. Eurostat Review on National Accounts and Macroeconomic Indicators, Eurostat/CROS/EURONA. Issue No 1/2014. ISSN 1977-978X. https://ec.europa.eu/eurostat/cros/system/files/p1-national_accounting_at_the_beginning_of_the_21st_century.pdf (accessed 14 August 2020).

Warburton, C. (1934). Value of the gross national product and its components, 1919–1929. *Journal of the American Statistical Association* 29 (188): 383–388.

Weigley, R.F. (1973). *The American Way of War: A History of United States Military Strategy and Policy*. London: Macmillan.

3

GDP and the SNA: Future Challenges

Steve MacFeely[1] and Peter van de Ven[2]

[1] *Director of Data and Analytics, World Health Organization, Geneva, Switzerland*
[2] *Inter-Secretariat Working Group on National Accounts, New York, USA*

3.1 Introduction

Gross domestic product (GDP), the world's principal measure of economic growth is frequently used as a proxy for prosperity and well-being. Palmer (1966) described GDP as the "chief criterion for national welfare or progress." Throughout its life, GDP has had its share of critics. From the outset, Simon Kuznets, the economist most commonly associated with the creation of GDP, cautioned it could unwittingly act as a "statistical laundry" concealing inequality and would be an unreliable or inappropriate measure of well-being (Kuznets 1962).

Today there are a growing number of commentators arguing that GDP has outlived its usefulness. Their criticisms can be broadly categorized into two classes. The first are measurement problems within the existing framework arising from changes in the economy and society – most notably globalization and digitalization. The second set of criticisms deal with the limits of the SNA framework itself and are sometimes described by the catchall "Beyond GDP" and center on questions as to whether the SNA can or should measure well-being and sustainability.

This chapter summarizes the most important of these criticisms and challenges that will shape the future development of the SNA (and by extension business and social statistics) in the coming years. The challenges posed by globalization for the measurement of national accounts are discussed in Section 3.3, and those posed by digitalization in Section 3.4. In a way they constitute issues which are internal to the system of national accounts, directly affecting the measurement of GDP and national accounts more generally. In Sections 3.5–3.7, the debate surrounding how best to capture well-being and sustainability is outlined. Both well-being and sustainability go well beyond traditional measurement of the economy, although it is also possible to address at least some of the challenges in capturing well-being and sustainability within the system of national accounts, either in the central framework of national accounts, or by broadening the set of accounts.

In a single chapter, it is only possible to give a taste of the challenges that are being faced and the ways in which these are being addressed. For more detailed information on the ongoing work regarding the update of the SNA 2008 see the Supplement to the report of the Intersecretariat Working Group on National Accounts (ISWGNA).[1] Some of the issues detailed in that report, such as measuring the treatment of intangible assets, and the informal economy are discussed by Bavdaž et al. (2023) in Chapter 5 and Pradhan (2023) in Chapter 7. The measurement challenges posed

---

1 https://unstats.un.org/unsd/nationalaccount/iswgna.asp.

Advances in Business Statistics, Methods and Data Collection. Edited by Ger Snijkers, Mojca Bavdaž, Stefan Bender, Jacqui Jones, Steve MacFeely, Joseph W. Sakshaug, Katherine J. Thompson, and Arnout van Delden.

by globalization and the digital economy are also dealt with in more detail, in Chapters 4 (by Koskimäki and Taskinen 2023) and 6 (by Nicholson et al. 2023).

3.2 An Agenda for the Future

Vanoli (2016) identified three main challenges facing national accounting in the near future: how to measure welfare; how to adapt to the complexities of globalization; and how to account for environmental issues and the interaction between economy and nature, and the demands of sustainability. The ISWGNA, in 2020, set out a similar research agenda for updating the SNA 2008, prioritizing: globalization; digitalization; and well-being and sustainability (ISWGNA 2020). In relation to sustainability, environmental issues are primarily addressed by the System of Environmental-Economic Accounting Central Framework (SEEA CF), and the System of Environmental-Economic Accounting—Ecosystem Accounting (SEEA EA), that was recently adopted, at the fifty-second session of the UN Statistical Commission in 2021 (CEEA 2021). The SEEA CF and SEEA EA are fully compatible with the SNA 2008, in the sense that the same principles for valuation of assets are being applied, although in the case of ecosystem accounting the asset (and production) boundary has been broadened substantially. At the fiftieth session of the UN Statistical Commission in 2019, a Friends of the Chair Group on Economic Statistics was established to review the system of economic statistics (UN 2019). The result was a recommendation to develop the interrelationships between economy, society, and environment and address the pressing global trends and underlying risks of inequality, climate change, technological change, demographic shift, and urbanization (Havinga 2020). Any future revision of the SNA will need to frame all of these demands under the umbrella or chapeau of sustainable development.

3.3 The Tangled Web of Globalization

Few words invoke such contrasting feelings as "globalization." For some it is a pejorative term, and expression of contempt. For others it is the ultimate dream. Irrespective of where one might stand, it is, as President Clinton described it, the "central reality of our time" (Lewis 2000). For economic statisticians, it has posed an array of challenges.

There has been considerable debate as to whether globalization is a new phenomenon or not. Philipsen (2015, p. 261) says: "we have always lived in a globalized world, even when we did not know or understand it." Frankopan (2015, p. 242) argues that globalization can be traced back at least 2000 years[2] and, discussing the credit crisis of the seventeenth century, he notes "globalization was no less problematic five centuries ago than it is today." Mayer-Schonberger and Ramge (2018) identify the opening of the Suez Canal in 1869 as the defining moment for globalization. Landes (1998) and Wadsworth and Mann (1931) note also the challenges posed by globalization in medieval times where mercantile innovation led to concerns over "putting out" (outsourcing) and exporting jobs. Clydesdale (2016) argues that the Dutch East India Company, formed in the seventeenth century, the first multinational enterprise, signaled a new age of globalization.

Others, such as Sturgeon (2013) and Ferguson (2006), have argued that there is a clear distinction between what can be termed internationalization and today's more complex and integrated

---

2 International trade, and the geopolitics associated with it, can be traced back even further. Romantics like to believe that it was Agamemnon's love for Helen that caused King Menelaus of Sparta to launch the fabled 1000 ships and trigger a ten-year war with Troy. Economic historians know Helen was a convenient excuse to declare war on Troy as they controlled the Dardanelles (or Hellespont as it was known then) and access to copper and tin – the Spartans were forced to pay exorbitant import tariffs on metals (McCollough 2010).

globalization. Sachs (2012) and Yergin (2012) make similar distinctions, referring respectively to "new globalization" or "the new age of globalization." These distinctions reflect changes in the geopolitical landscape, such as the expansion of the world economy following the collapse of the Berlin Wall in 1989 and China joining the WTO in 2001. It also captures major economic changes, such as privatization and deregulation in the 1980s, the technological and digital revolutions beginning with the World Wide Web (www) in the early 1990s, which facilitated reduced international communications and transactions costs, the financialization of commodities and a blurring of the distinction between tradable and non-tradable services. Baldwin (2018) called these developments the "second unbundling" of globalization[3] which radically changed the nature of international commerce and gave rise to what he calls the trade-investment-service nexus. Others argue these revolutions led to the "death of distance," a "frictionless economy," a "flattened world" and a fourth industrial revolution (Friedman 2006; Warsh 2006; Schwab 2017).

Globalization has profoundly influenced the way enterprises, particularly multi- or transnational enterprises/corporations (MNEs/TNCs), organize their activities. National borders no longer offer barriers or constraints to their modern globalized production processes. As a consequence, understanding MNE activity is a priority activity for many statistical offices, as "the share of MNEs in business statistics represents roughly 40–60% of the added value of the business economy in most countries" (Demollin and Hermans 2020). From a measurement perspective, this poses considerable challenges, and has led to concerns and criticism that business and macroeconomic statistics may not be measuring price, production, trade, and GDP correctly (Sturgeon 2013; Houseman et al. 2014). The difficulty stems from increasingly varied, convoluted and volatile organizational structures and operations adopted by MNEs that constantly shift to aggressively exploit the opportunities presented by global supply or value chains; and tax avoidance mechanisms, such as transfer pricing manipulation, strategic location of debt and intellectual property/intangible assets, tax treaty shopping, and the use of hybrid entities (OECD 2013a; UNCTAD and UNODC 2020). Koskimäki and Peltola (2020, p. 785), discussing MNEs, summarize the problem neatly, explaining "their innovative and agile global production arrangements challenge statisticians, often in unexpected ways." This in turn makes real economic activity at the national level more difficult to estimate but also brings into question whether traditional measures are still meaningful.

In July 2016, the impact of globalization, and how meaningful GDP as the primary barometer of economic progress in a small open economy like Ireland is, came into sharp focus when 2015 real GDP growth was estimated at 26.3% (CSO, 2016). These results graphically illustrated the limits of GDP in a highly globalized economy (Connolly 2017; Deen and Doyle 2016; OECD 2016) and led to Ireland estimating and disseminating a new indicator GNI*, in addition to GDP (Economic Statistics Review Group 2016). The limits of GDP were of course understood before this point. MacFeely et al. (2011) had noted the limitations of GDP for understanding real output and most especially when attempting regional comparisons. Fitzgerald (2014) too had expressed the need for significant additional data to supplement the SNA in order to understand globalized economies.

To compile robust GDP estimates one must understand the legal, operational and accounting structures of MNEs, both at national and global level. A key challenge in this respect is assigning output and value added to the national economies. Decisions regarding "economic ownership" will have important implications for this allocation.[4] Another key challenge is unraveling MNE cross-border transactions so that activities can be properly assigned or proportioned within

---

3 The first unbundling was steam, which drastically reduced transport costs and helped to unbundle the geography of production and consumption.
4 MacFeely (2016) queried whether "nationality" is still a meaningful concept with regard to enterprise ownership, as many large MNEs are effectively super-national, defying geo-spatial classification.

business statistics and the national accounts. Intra-enterprise trade poses particular problems, as ownership does not necessarily change when goods are exported for processing, raw materials can be delivered to subcontractors in foreign countries, transfer prices that bear no relationship to market prices can be calculated when goods move within a MNE, royalties can be due to other group entities for the use of special processing methods or technical support. All these actions have a specific effect on the estimation of GDP for a national economy. Thus, to properly measure these flows, a statistical office must understand both the material and their corresponding financial flows.

In response, international organizations have begun a number of workstreams to try and better capture these activities. Here, one can make a distinction between workstreams which try to disentangle activities of MNEs and arrive at an appropriate allocation of value added according to the international standards of national accounts. These also include providing more granularity in the system, by separately distinguishing transactions and positions of MNEs. Other workstreams try to provide analytical tools to grasp the direct and indirect impact of multinational activities.

Regarding the first workstream, UNECE hosted in 2007 a conference on the challenges for official statistics posed by economic globalization (UNECE 2008). On foot of this, the UNECE established a Group of Experts to examine the impact of globalization on national accounts. In 2011 they published *The Impact of Globalization on National Accounts* (UNECE et al. 2011) and in 2015 the *Guide to Measuring Global Production* (UNECE 2015). The OECD also started the compilation of extended supply and use tables, with the primary goal of singling out activities of MNEs. More and more countries are seeing the value added of breaking down the corporate sector into public corporations, foreign-controlled corporations, corporations belonging to domestic MNEs, and national private corporations. This was also one of the measures taken by Ireland in view of the problems faced in 2015 and afterwards. Importantly, Eurostat is developing a Euro Groups Register (EGR) to develop a unique identification of legal units, global groups and global enterprises. Similarly, OECD is developing a freely accessible Analytical Database on Individual Multinationals and Affiliates (ADIMA)[5];

An example of the second set of workstreams concerns the development, in 2010, of a conceptual and methodological framework on how to measure the impact of economic globalization, culminating in the publication of the *OECD Handbook on Economic Globalization Indicators* (OECD 2010). In cooperation with the WTO, the OECD also launched their Trade in Value Added (*TiVA*)[6] database to facilitate macro analyses of the value added generated in each country in the production of globally traded goods and services. At the time of writing, this database includes input–output tables for 61 countries – it will take many years before a robust global input–output table is available that includes data for developing countries. In 2013, Eurostat commissioned a study *Global Value Chains and Economic Globalization - Towards a new measurement framework* (Sturgeon 2013) to try and understand how to better measure these phenomena and the implications for business statistics. Finally, in 2015 the UN Statistical Commission agreed (Decision 46/107) to establish two expert groups to look at these and other related issues, namely an *Expert Group on the Handbook for a System of Extended International and Global Accounts* (EG-SEIGA) and an *Inter-Secretariat Working Group on International Trade and Economic Globalization Statistics* (ISWG-ITEGS).

---

5 See OECD Statistical Insights: the ADIMA database on Multinational Enterprises. https://www.oecd.org/sdd/its/statistical-insights-the-adima-database-on-multinational-enterprises.htm.
6 https://www.oecd.org/sti/ind/measuring-trade-in-value-added.htm. A limitation of the TiVA database is that they are based on the OECD Inter-Country Input-Output (ICIO). The latest tables, 2018, include tables for 64 countries only.

3.4   The Digital Revolution

The digital and technological revolutions have completely transformed our world. Ubiquitous in their reach, these revolutions have affected everything from production, consumption, investment, international trade, and finance. Artificial intelligence, cryptocurrencies, and 3-D printing are just the tip of the iceberg. These rapid developments pose significant challenges for policy makers, and by extension, for statisticians. Governments trying to formulate ICT-related policies, e-commerce and digital transformation strategies want to know the size of the digital economy, how quickly is it growing and what is the contribution to GDP. What will the digital revolution mean for the labor market (including potential job creation and destruction), education and skills development, innovation, sectoral development, competition, consumer protection, taxation, trade, environmental protection and energy efficiency, as well as regulation related to security, privacy and data protection (UNCTAD 2021). More broadly, can the digital economy be harnessed to reduce economic, social and gender inequalities and what are the regulatory challenges associated with trying to supervise, what is essentially a globalized phenomenon (MacFeely 2018).

A first challenge has been to agree on how the digital economy can be defined and measured. Following the World Summit on the Information Society, held at Geneva in December 2003, the global *Partnership on Measuring Information and Communication Technologies for Development* was established to address these questions during the eleventh session of the United Nations Conference on Trade and Development (UNCTAD XI) in 2004[7] (ECOSOC 2004). One of the key achievements of this partnership has been to develop a core list of ICT indicators for the production of internationally comparable statistics. This list was first endorsed at the thirty-eight session of the UN Statistical Commission in 2007. The core list now includes more than 60 indicators, covering ICT infrastructure and access, ICT access and use by households and businesses, the ICT (producing) sector, trade in ICT goods and services, ICT in education, e-government and electronic waste.

A first version of the *Manual for the Production of Statistics on the Information Economy* was published that same year. This manual was updated in 2009 and again in 2021 as the *Manual for the Production of Statistics on the Digital Economy* (UNCTAD 2021). Other notable methodological manuals include ICT use by households and individuals (ITU 2020), e-government (UNECA 2014), e-waste, and use of ICT in education (UNESCO-UIS 2009). OECD (2011) and Eurostat (2015) have also published manuals on broader areas of information society measurement. The OECD, WTO, and IMF jointly published a *Handbook on Measuring Digital Trade* (OECD et al. 2020) which set out a conceptual framework for measuring the digital economy component of trade. Most recently the 2020 report of the G20 Digital Economy Task Force (OECD 2020a) sets out developments and challenges to date. Unsurprisingly, it recommends the adoption of proposed definitions, indicators, methodologies and data collection, so that institutional capacity can be developed and information on the digital economy can be disseminated and used.

In recent years, several statistical organizations, but most notably the Bureau of Economic Analysis (BEA) in the United States (BEA 2020; Nicholson 2020) and Statistics Canada (2021) have begun developing and publishing prototype digital economy statistics, including digital economy satellite accounts, based on the OECD *Guidelines for Supply-Use tables for the Digital Economy* (OECD

---

7 Current partners (2020) include International Telecommunication Union (ITU), the Organisation of Economic Co-operation and Development (OECD), Eurostat, UNCTAD, UNESCO Institute of Statistics (UIS), ILO, four UN Regional Commissions (UNECLAC, UNESCWA, UNESCAP, UNECA), the World Bank, UNDESA, UNEP/Secretariat of the Basel Convention, and the United Nations University Institute for Sustainability and Peace (UNU-ISP).

2020b) Conceptually, these accounts include all goods and services relating to both ICT and digital economy. But a number of knotty conceptual and measurement challenges remain, not least how to record and value "free" digital services and media, especially when households are exchanging personal data for those services, or how to treat peer-to-peer transactions, such as AirBnB.

A further challenge is that the SNA does not record the stocks and flows of "data" as assets, unless explicitly purchased on the market. Databases are recognized as assets, but the value related to the information content of data is yet to be addressed. Whereas data, or knowledge more generally, always had their role in economic activities, the explosion of electronic data, including business models based on the access to these data, can no longer be ignored.

Other questions remain regarding the best treatment of goods and services that combine both digital and non-digital elements i.e. partially digital. Strassner and Nicholson (2020) have identified some emerging issues that require further work, including the measurement of high-tech goods and services prices, especially for internet and wireless services, cloud computing and ride hailing. They also note that more work is required on digital trade, digital ordering (or e-commerce) and digitally delivered or enabled services. Ahmad and Schreyer (2016), discussing the measurement challenges of digitalization, note the underlying issues are not new, but rather it is the scale that is new. They also note that mismeasurement of digitalization may be contributing to, but does not explain, the productivity puzzle, where rapid technological change has been accompanied by a slowdown in productivity.

3.5 Moving Beyond GDP: GDP Impeached

Despite being the leading economic indicator, GDP has never been universally accepted. From its very inception there have been contested elements – both in its construction and in its application. From the outset, Kuznets himself flagged various concerns with GDP, not least the inclusion of illegal activities, socially harmful industries, defense spending and most government spending. He cautioned that GDP would be an unreliable or inappropriate measure of well-being, noting "the welfare of a nation can scarcely be inferred from a measure of national income" (Kuznets 1962, p. 29). Such was his dissatisfaction with the final formulation of GDP that Mitra-Khan (2011, p. 14) states that "Kuznets, far from being the progenitor of GDP, was its biggest opponent." Prophetically he worried that GDP would become one of the most used but most misunderstood indicators (Masood 2016).

As the negative implications of economic growth for the environment and well-being began to emerge in the 1970s, a number of attempts to challenge the primacy of GDP as the definitive measure of progress surfaced.[8] These initiatives stemmed from a recognition that the existing measurement system had created a "growth trap" where progress was dependent on continual consumption and unsustainable replacement (Slade 2006). Years later, Richard Layard (2011) would quip "anyone who believes in indefinite growth on a physically finite planet is either mad, or an economist." The essence or spirit of these alternatives was perhaps best encapsulated by Robert F. Kennedy's reference to GDP during a 1968 campaign speech in the University of Kansas:

---

8 Exemplified by works, such as, Silent Spring (Carson 1962), The Economics of the Coming Spaceship Earth (Boulding 1966); The Limits to Growth (Meadows et al. 1972), Small is Beautiful (Schumacher 1973); Steady State Economics (Daly 1977) and events, such as, the United Nations Conference on the Human Environment in Stockholm (United Nations 1973). And as climate change emerged as a serious issue, reports such as Climate Change: The 1990 and 1992 IPCC Assessments (WMO and UNEP, 1992); the Stern Review (Stern 2006); and the book and movie An Inconvenient Truth (Gore 2006).

"it measures everything in short, except that which makes life worthwhile" (Kennedy 1968). The gauntlet was laid down in 1972 when King Jigme Singye Wangchuck of Bhutan declared, "Gross National Happiness is more important than Gross Domestic Product." This concept promulgated a more holistic approach toward progress, one that balanced material and non-material values. This concept was not actually translated into an index until 2008 (Alkire 2008).

One of the first actual alternate measures, the measure of economic welfare (MEW) expounded by Nordhaus and Tobin (1972) attempted to measure economic welfare. This was followed by the Index of Social Health, launched in 1987 by the Fordham Institute for Innovation in Social Policy (now the Institute for Innovation in Social Policy[9]). This index is a composite of social indicators and attempts to provide a comprehensive view of "social health." Reflecting a broadening of the concept of development, the Human Development Index (HDI) was launched in 1990 by United Nations Development Programme economist Mahbub Ul Haq. This index was designed to address functional inequality, based on the "capabilities approach" proposed by Amartya Sen who argued "in judging economic development it is not adequate to look only at the growth of GNP or some other indicators of overall economic expansion. We have to look also at the impact of democracy and political freedoms on the lives and capabilities of the citizens" (Sen 1999, p. 150). The next notable development was the Genuine Progress Index (GPI), a variant of the Index of Sustainable Economic Welfare (ISEW), first proposed by Daly and Cobb (1989). It was launched in 1995 by the *Redefining Progress Organization* (Talberth et al. 2007). This approach supplements and "greens" GDP by adding measures to account for various socially productive activities not accounted for (e.g. "psychic income" from unpaid household or volunteer work) and making deductions to account for the negative costs of the undesirable side effects of economic progress (e.g. pollution) and for costs associated with the degradation and depletion of natural capital (e.g. ozone depletion).

The beginning of the twenty-first century witnessed a renewal in the debate on the limitations of the SNA as a tool to provide adequate measures of economic performance, social progress and sustainable development. Talberth et al. (2007) argued that the "nation's most trusted measure of economic performance is … woefully out of sync with people's everyday experiences." The Great Financial Crisis of 2008 only fueled this fire (MacFeely 2016), but so too did concerns regarding the inability of the SNA to satisfactorily capture services activities. The Economist (2016, p. 22) declared that GDP was "a relic of a period dominated by manufacturing" struggling to capture the impact of myriad intangible innovations. Karabell (2014, p. 7) reached a similar conclusion, saying "our statistical map, …, is showing signs of age." There has been a flurry of activity in the past decade attempting to address these issues.

Perhaps the best known of these initiatives was the Commission on the Measurement of Economic Performance and Social Progress (better known as the Stiglitz-Sen-Fitoussi Commission). It was established in 2008 by the then president of France, Nicolas Sarkozy, to determine whether a better or more comprehensive measure of economic and social progress could be established. Their report, *Mis-Measuring Our Lives*, published in 2010 (Stiglitz et al. 2010), emphasized the need to decouple GDP from well-being. Arguing that GDP provides an overly optimistic mirage, the authors proposed a shift in emphasis away from production toward well-being, with greater prominence being given to households, including distribution of income, consumption and wealth, and other aspects affecting well-being and sustainability. They highlighted the need to include unpaid household activities; better adjust for quality changes, especially in services; account for environmental damage and depletion; and measure both objective and subjective well-being. The authors also recommended moving away from a single index toward a dashboard of indicators.

---

9 See http://iisp.vassar.edu/ish.html.

Later that same year the OECD launched their *Better Life Index* (BLI),[10] combining 80 indicators across 15 dimensions to address similar questions. Almost simultaneously, the European Commission, published their roadmap *GDP and Beyond: Measuring progress in a changing world* (European Commission 2009). In an approach similar to that proposed by Stiglitz-Sen-Fitoussi, the European roadmap recognized the need for a broader benchmark of development or progress than just purely economic. The report proposed to complement GDP with additional indicators, such as indicators on quality of life, well-being, and environmental sustainability. It also included actions for more accurate reporting on distribution and inequalities and on extending national accounts to environmental and social issues (Radermacher 2015). Very quickly, this approach became the accepted approach. In 2012, Ban Ki-Moon, the then Secretary-General of the UN, speaking at a meeting on "Happiness and Wellbeing: Defining a New Economic Paradigm," noted the importance of establishing "a Sustainable Development Index, or a set of indicators to measure progress towards sustainable development" (United Nations 2012). The same year, the United Nations University International Human Dimensions Programme on Global Environmental Change (UNU-IHDP), in collaboration with the United Nations Environment Programme (UNEP), launched an Inclusive Wealth Index (IWI). By measuring wealth using countries' natural, manufactured, human and social capital, this index was intended to replace not only GDP but also the Human Development Index (UNU-IHDP and UNEP 2012). Others too have contributed to this endeavor. For example, in 2019, the Eurasian Economic Community launched their Inclusive Growth Index to guide the policy objective of stable economic development and improved living standards in the region (Eurasian Economic Commission and United Nations Conference on Trade and Development 2019).

In Sections 3.6 and 3.7, the two key aspects of the beyond GDP debate, i.e. how to measure well-being and (environmental) sustainability, are discussed.

3.6   Including a Measure of Well-being

As noted above, some of the founding fathers of national accounts statistics, not least Clark and Kuznets, understood from the beginning that GNP or GDP was not an appropriate or reliable measure of welfare or well-being. Hayak (1944, p. 64) summarized the situation well, when he wrote "The welfare and the happiness of millions cannot be measured on a single scale of less and more." Yet today, despite protests from many of our most eminent economists that GDP is not a good measure of welfare (e.g. Deaton 2013; Stiglitz 2014), it has been adopted as the barometer for our collective success and well-being (Talberth et al. 2007; David 2018; Hoekstra 2020). This is all the more curious, for just as Kuznets had warned Congress in 1934 that the welfare of a nation could not be inferred from a measure of national income, compilers today caution that "GDP is often taken as a measure of welfare, but the SNA makes no claim that this is so and indeed there are several conventions in the SNA that argue against the welfare interpretation of the accounts" (United Nations et al. 2009, p. 12).

Nevertheless, GDP has garnered considerable criticism for giving a distorted view of social progress. Kuznets had argued that the purpose of national income should be to measure welfare.[11] In his view, many of the non-market activities excluded today from GDP, such as domestic services performed by households for themselves, should be included. He also argued that activities not

---

10 http://www.oecd.org/newsroom/hows-life-reveals-improvements-in-well-being-but-persistent-inequalities .htm.

11 Welfare in this context is closer to the narrower concept of material or economic wellbeing and should not be confused with the broader or more general concept of wellbeing (and sustainability).

"used directly for the satisfaction of consumers" should be excluded (Vanoli 2016). This implied also that activities, like defense spending, should be excluded. But as noted above, and in MacFeely and van de Ven, 2023 (Chapter 2), that is not how GDP is currently configured.

Measuring well-being is complex. Material well-being – income and wealth – falls within the scope of economic measurement, but emotional, physical and psychological health or well-being do not. Well-being, which incorporates broader developments in society, including health and justice, cannot be measured by living standards of income alone. Furthermore, any measure of well-being must incorporate, at the very least, measures of inequality. Nor is happiness the same as life satisfaction. Not only are there disagreements on how to measure well-being, there are many economists and philosophers who have expressed reservations about the validity and usefulness of measuring self-reported well-being at all (Deaton 2013).

For the above reasons, the ISWGNA established a subgroup in 2020 to investigate the issues relating to the measurement of well-being and sustainability, and how these could potentially be addressed within the system of national accounts. Following a quite pragmatic approach, they identified the following areas where progress could be made relatively quickly: (i) unpaid household work; (ii) distribution of household income, consumption, saving and wealth; (iii) environmental-economic accounting (see Section 3.7); (iv) education and human capital; and (v) health and social conditions. These areas would then be represented in a broader framework of an internally consistent set of accounts, in which the traditional framework for measuring economic activities would be supplemented by extended accounts dealing with some of the aspects which are considered important for capturing well-being and sustainability (ISWGNA 2020). The connection between well-being and sustainability is important and reflects a central message from the Stiglitz-Sen-Fitoussi report that "measures of wellbeing should be put in the context of sustainability" (2010, p. 10).

The multidimensionality of well-being, despite the attempts noted above (Measure of Economic Welfare, Index of Social Health or the Genuine Progress Index as so on), that must reflect present-day losses (or gains) for opportunities to generate future well-being, do not lend themselves easily to being condensed or composited into a single indicator. It is for this reason that Stiglitz-Sen-Fitoussi (2010, p. 11), reminiscent of Hayak, recommended using a dashboard, saying "no single measure can summarize something as complex as the wellbeing of the members of society." They suggested that well-being should comprise the following dimensions: material living standards; health; education; personal activities including work; political voice and governance; social connections and relationships; environment (present and future); and insecurity (economic and physical). They also emphasized that both objective and subjective well-being or quality of life is important.

As noted before, perhaps the best known attempt to measure well-being is the OECD Better Life Index, which is comprised of indicators for housing, income, employment, community, education, environment, civic engagement, health, life satisfaction, safety and work-life balance (OECD 2013b).[12] Van de Ven (2019) argues that a broader system of national accounts, as taken on board by the ISWGNA (see above), could complement such a dashboard of indicators, by providing a set of interconnected accounts which provide further information on (the links between) the most important aspects of well-being and sustainability.

---

12 At his keynote address to the ICES6 conference in June 2021, Roberto Rigobon, summarised the dimensions of Social Wellbeing with the catchy acronym PROMISE: Personal; Relationships; Organisations, Firms, and jobs; Markets and Economy; Institutions; Social and Political; and Environment. He noted, that in many cases, we do not measure these dimensions at all, and where we do, it tends to be the extreme (and often negative) cases e.g. relationships defined by marriages and divorces.

3.7 Putting a Value on the Environment

A longstanding criticism of GDP stems from the fact that it is first and foremost focusing on monetary transactions and therefore does not appropriately account for the impact on the environment, including depletion and degradation of natural resources and ecosystems. In 1989, then President of the World Bank, Barber Conable, reflecting this unsustainable nature of GDP and income noted: "Current calculations ignore the degradation of the natural resource base and view the sales of non-renewable resources entirely as income. A better way must be found to measure the prosperity and progress of mankind" (Conable 1989). Or as Thicke (quoted in Shaxon 2018) colorfully put it: "we have been deficit spending our ecological capital." In 1992, at the Rio Earth Summit, 170 countries adopted *Agenda 21*, which among other things included a provision to overhaul the SNA to properly account for environmental assets and costs of pollution and depletion (United Nations 1993).

Reflecting the Bruntland Commission's (United Nations 1987) concept of "inter-temporal" sustainability, where sustainable development was defined as development that meets the needs of the present without compromising the ability of future generations to meet their own needs, and in recognition that the framework underpinning GDP, the SNA, "does not support a broader assessment of the sustainable use of resources, the impacts of economic production and consumption on the environment" (Obst et al. 2020, p. 629), environmental specialists and national accountants have been working to develop methodologies to include environmental damages, resource depletion and biodiversity loss into the macroeconomic statistics. This is a complex task but steady progress is being made. A first *Handbook of National Accounting: Integrated Environmental and Economic Accounting* was published in 1993 (United Nations 1993). These accounts focused originally on extensions and adjustments to GDP, such as measures of GDP adjusted for depletion and degradation, and how to value and incorporate environmental expenditures into the SNA. This was followed by revisions in 2003 (United Nations 2003) and more recently by the *System of Environmental-Economic Accounting 2012* (SEEA), which was adopted by the UN Statistical Commission as the international standard for environmental-economic accounting. This revision was comprised of two separate volumes: the SEEA 2012 Central Framework or SEEA-CF (United Nations et al. 2014a), focusing on emissions to air and water, material flows, the delineation of environmental activities and transactions, and stocks and flows of natural resources; and the SEEA 2012 Experimental Ecosystem Accounting or SEEA-EEA (United Nations et al. 2014b), with a focus on incorporating physical and monetary data on ecosystem services and ecosystem assets. In March 2021, the UN Statistical Commission endorsed a revised set of international standards on accounting for ecosystem (CEEA 2021). The experimental status of these standards was removed, although some issues remain to be resolved in relation to the monetary estimates for (changes in) ecosystem assets in line with national accounts principles. Whereas the SEEA-CF retains the same production boundary as the SNA but recognizes a broader set of environmental assets including all land and water resources, the SEEA-EA clearly extends the production (and asset) boundary of the SNA using however the same accounting principles (Obst et al. 2020). Accounting for natural capital is a complex task that must grapple with a variety of definitional challenges and requires the valuation of non-market phenomena and assets. Obst et al. (2020) note that the SEEA-EA offers the first real progress in this area of environmental accounting.

Accounting for environmental assets, or natural capital, is important, not only to be able to put a value on these assets, but also to provide a basis for the calculation of Net Domestic Product adjusted for depletion and degradation. In the SEEA-CF, the latter was still limited to (depletion of) natural resources, such as mineral and energy resources, water resources, and biological resources.

SEEA-EA however provides guidance on a further extension to (degradation of) ecosystem assets, distinguishing three types of benefits that can be derived from these assets: provisioning services, regulating and maintenance services, and cultural services. The capital approach is also used in the UNEP IWI mentioned above.

The monetization of nature remains somewhat controversial and has also attracted some criticism (Unmüßig 2014; Victor April 2020; Wolf 2020), and hence the Stiglitz-Sen-Fitoussi Commission recommended developing physical measures and, where considered feasible, monetary measures. Monetary accounts only include assets, which have defined ownership rights and be "capable of bringing economic benefits to their owners, given the technology, scientific knowledge, economic infrastructure, available resources and set of relative prices prevailing on the dates to which the balance sheet relates or expected to do in the near future" (United Nations et al. 2009). In this sense, the valuation is compatible with the exchange values used in national accounts. This also means that the values may not be consistent with sustainable levels of use, while externalities may also not be accounted for. Despite the good conceptual progress made, Lucas (2020, p. 602) notes that the "flexible and modular approach" adopted by the SEEA has resulted in "slow, uneven or inexistent" progress in compiling the required statistics. But Obst et al. (2020) estimate that as of 2020 about 92 countries were already implementing the SEEA-CF. Since a broad consensus started to be reached with the compilation and endorsement of SEEA-EA, significant progress has been made, with the expectation that a true momentum has been created for further enhancements in the availability of statistical results.

In a link between environment and well-being, Stiglitz-Sen-Fitoussi recommended creating two dashboards, one that reflected current well-being and another that dealt with future sustainability (Hoekstra 2020). Lucas (2020) warns that environmental accounting should not focus exclusively on aggregates but should also incorporate a distributional dimension, illustrating how all of these issues are interconnected. Perhaps, most importantly, the development of SEEA highlights the acknowledgement of our dependence on the environment and natural capital. Havinga (2020, p. 588) summarizes progress well, noting that the SEEA "demonstrates not only the theoretical advances but also the feasibility and relevance of SEEA based accounts." Critically, this progress demonstrates the "clear support from the official statistics community and a clear role for national statistical offices in using the SEEA to go 'beyond GDP'."

3.8 Challenges Replacing GDP

Despite the drawbacks and alternatives outlined above, GDP remains the prominent general-purpose barometer for our collective well-being and economic progress. Counterintuitively, the glut of alternatives challenging GDP's hegemony seems only to have cemented the dominant position it enjoys. The abundance of rival indicators illustrates the lack of consensus on a suitable replacement and has arguably undermined the credibility of each individual challenger. So, while many of these new indicators may in fact represent real technical progress, their sheer number can also be viewed as a metric of failure (MacFeely 2016). Despite all the criticisms and shortcomings of GDP, it still enjoys economic hegemony and massive cultural authority. For example, 17 of the SDG indicators rely on GDP[13] and a further 3 on GNI.[14] In Europe, 5 of the core, and 10 of the

---

13 1.5.2; 7.3.1; 8.1.1; 8.2.1; 8.4.1; 8.4.2; 8.9.1; 9.2.1; 9.5.1; 10.4.1; 11.5.2; 12.2.1; 12.2.2; 12.c.1; 14.7.1; 17.1.1; and 17.3.1.
14 1.a.1; 17.2.1; 17.3.1.

auxiliary indicators used in the macroeconomic imbalance procedure scoreboard[15] are dependent on GDP, either as a nominator or denominator. Many other indictors and composite indices include and are weighted by GDP.

So, how might GDP, an indicator so deeply embedded, be replaced or complemented? One approach continues to recognize the importance of GDP as a key economic indicator, but also recognizes its limitations, and consequently attempts to complement it with other economic, environmental, and social indicators to provide a comprehensive assessment of the conditions and progress (Radermacher 2015). Other considerations, where there seems to be little agreement, include whether to adopt a dashboard of metrics or to develop a single replacement aggregate index. Masood (2016, p. 10) argues for a middle path, noting "if it is true that GDP remains the only number that influential politicians, the markets, the banks, the media, and the commentators pay attention to, then the solution cannot be more alternative indicators; nor can it be a dashboard. The solution has to be to value the things that matter and then incorporate this value into the GDP accounts." In other words, if we cannot wean the world off GDP, then GDP must be adapted.

To complicate matters, many of the debates suggest that the SNA is not well understood. This manifests itself in two ways. Firstly, the SNA, and GDP in particular, is criticized for not adequately measuring things it was never designed to measure. Even Stiglitz-Sen-Fitoussi, noted that "GDP is not wrong *as such*, but wrongly used" (Stiglitz et al. 2010, p. 3). It is not clear that any GDP 4.0 will be used more appropriately that its predecessors. A further challenge is that apparently the mechanics and intricacies of the SNA and GDP as such are not well understood by anyone other than compilers. Perhaps in the past, no-one else needed to understand all the details, but now, if we are to move beyond GDP, the strengths and weaknesses of the alternatives must be comprehended. In 2016, MacFeely likened GDP to $E = MC^2$, noting that while both enjoy considerable celebrity and cultural authority, very few really understand either one of them. Thus, the "pathetic paradox" (Chambers 1989, p. 128) that both intellectual landmarks are taken on faith. But that is where the similarity between the two ends. $E = MC^2$, a scientific axiom, is universal and unchanging across time and space,[16] whereas GDP, a manmade concept not found organically in nature, continues to evolve.[17] It is not clear that users fully understand recent revisions to the SNA.[18] Practical experience shows that even specialist users of national accounts data hardly know the intricacies of the system, what and the reason why something is included/excluded, the relationships between the various indicators that can be derived from the system of national accounts, etc.

3.9 Conclusions and Implications for Business Statistics

"Throughout the world, GDP has become a proxy for success and for failure, for sentiment about the future and sense of well-being in the present" (Karabell 2014, p. 50). It is now buried deep within our collective consciousness and will prove difficult to replace. The "genius of GDP is that it somehow manages to squeeze all human activity into a single number" (Pilling 2018, p. 285).

---

15 https://ec.europa.eu/info/business-economy-euro/economic-and-fiscal-policy-coordination/eu-economic-governance-monitoring-prevention-correction/macroeconomic-imbalances-procedure/scoreboard_en.

16 The complications of quantum mechanics are ignored here.

17 The current 2008 SNA is the 4th generation, following the 1953, 1968, and 1993 editions. Global consultations are presently underway in preparation for a 5th generation. See https://unstats.un.org/Unsd/nationalaccount/raconList.asp.

18 MacFeely (2017) surmises that this might explain Paul Krugman's "leprechaun economics" outburst (2016), in reaction to Ireland's reported real GDP growth of 26.3% in 2016 (Central Statistics Office 2016).

The question is whether it is realistic to try and squeeze even more issues into that number? But something must be done. There is a growing consensus that it no longer meets the needs of today, and that GDP "is showing signs of age" (Karabell 2014, p. 7). The criticisms of GDP and the SNA today, largely reflect or mirror many of the debates and concerns expressed about GDP from the outset (see Chapter 2 by MacFeely and van de Ven (2023)).

The Stiglitz-Sen-Fitoussi Commission probably best encapsulates or summarizes the criticisms of GDP. More must be done to incorporate social and environmental issues. More must also be done to better capture the impacts of globalization and digitalization. However, it is also clear that considerable progress has been made, and continues to be done, to address these issues. In relation to digitalization, for example, Ahmad and Schreyer (2016, p. 26) assessed that "on balance the accounting framework used for GDP looks to be up to the challenges posed by digitalization. Certainly, from a conceptual perspective GDP does not look to be deficient." Arguably, the same could be said for the challenges posed by globalization.

Outlined in this chapter, substantial progress has also been made in relation to the challenges posed by accounting for the environment, first and foremost in the context of SEEA, the standards for environmental-economic accounting which are fully compatible with the standards for national accounts. However, more still needs to be done. In this respect, the work initiated by the ISWGNA to develop a broader system of accounts that also reflect well-being and sustainability, may not signal the end of our journey, but it would most certainly be a major step forward.

The development of the SNA will have implications for national statistical systems (NSSs), not just national statistical offices, as many of the developments discussed above cannot be compiled by statistical offices without recourse to administrative data held by other government departments, or in some cases, such as the SEEA-EA, without access to commercial data, big data, citizen science statistics, and subject matter expertise. This will raise a number of challenges for NSSs, not least securing access, managing data instability and a more complex governance environment (MacFeely 2018). It will also require more careful consideration of data infrastructural issues, such as the use of unique identifiers and common classifications across public datasets (MacFeely and Barnat 2017). Developing and broadening the SNA also provides an incentive to rethink the production architecture currently being used for official statistics, to consider for example, accrediting unofficial statistics (MacFeely and Nastav 2019).

Furthermore, data sharing and greater collaboration between statistical offices will be essential to profile and measure MNE activities in a coherent and internationally consistent way. This in turn will be key to addressing the measurement challenges of globalization (UNECE 2021). Koskimäki and Peltola (2020) argue that, in order to facilitate this, the UN Fundamental Principles of Official Statistics may need to be updated to address, among other things, concerns regarding confidentiality. MacFeely (2020, p. 1088) has queried "whether it is sustainable to offer the same level of confidentiality to persons and enterprises; in particular, multinational enterprises" and that perhaps "differential confidentiality" is required where "a distinction can legitimately be made, most especially, when the masking of multinational enterprise activity inhibits the publication of other statistics that are of vital national interest and importance."

The work done to date on developing a unique comprehensive, consistent business register, such as the EGR, will be critical to understanding the structure and role of MNEs and the role of Foreign Direct Investment (FDI) in countries. In 2015, the United Nations Statistical Commission, learning lessons from the EGR, agreed to develop Global Group Register (GGR). Koskimäki and Peltola (2020) note the importance of having a proper legal framework to operationalize the exchange of data between statistical offices to support this work, as this is a prerequisite for the accurate profiling of MNEs. The OECD's ADIMA also points the way to the future, showing what can be done by reusing and organizing publicly available information.

More generally, as also recommended by The *Friends of the Chair Group on Economic Statistics* (UN 2021), a broader framework of accounts for measuring the relationship between the economy, nature and society is needed. In this regard, they recommended that the SNA be updated (and better implemented) and that the SEEA be further developed, so that the various dimensions of well-being and sustainability be captured, also in support of the capital approach for measuring the various forms of capital (economic capital, natural capital, human capital and social capital. Of relevance to business statistics and other domains, the need for better consistency of concepts and data sources between the economy, society, and the environment has been highlighted. As noted above, this may result in more granularity of data, improved linkages to and use of administrative data and other secondary data, and also to household surveys, such as the ones on time use and income and living conditions.

References

Ahmad, N. and Schreyer, P. (2016). Measuring GDP in a digitalised economy. OECD Statistics Working Papers 2016/07. https://www.oecd-ilibrary.org/docserver/5jlwqd81d09r-en.pdf?expires= 1619443977&id=id&accname=guest&checksum=D704D9527476F613CCECBD7744CAD8A1 (accessed 26 April 2021).

Alkire, S. (2008). Bhutan's gross national happiness index 2008. *OPHI Research in Progress Series*. Oxford Poverty & Human Development Initiative (OPHI). University of Oxford. https://www.ophi .org.uk/wp-content/uploads/Alkire_Bhutan_GNH_index_2008_OPHIRP5a.pdf (accessed 29 January 2021).

Baldwin, R. (2018). A long view of globalisation in short: the new globalisation, part 5 of 5. *VoxEU*, 5 December, 2018. https://voxeu.org/content/long-view-globalisation-short-new-globalisation-part-5-5 (accessed 12 June 2021).

Bavdaž, M., Bounfour, A., Martin, J., Nonnis, A., Perani, G., and Redek, T. (2023). Measuring investment in intangible assets. In: *Advances in Establishment Statistics, Methods and Data Collection*, Chapter 5 (ed. G. Snijkers, M. Bavdaž, S. Bender, J. Jones, S. MacFeely, J.W. Sakshaug, K.J. Thompson, and A. van Delden). Hoboken: Wiley.

Bureau of Economic Analysis (2020). New digital economy estimates 2005–2018. https://www.bea.gov/ data/special-topics/digital-economy (accessed 20 April 2021).

Boulding, K.E. (1966). The economics of the coming spaceship Earth. http://www.ub.edu/ prometheus21/articulos/obsprometheus/BOULDING.pdf (accessed 04 February 2021).

Carson, R. (1962). *Silent Spring*. Boston, USA: Houghton Mifflin.

CEEA (2021). System of environmental-economic accounting—ecosystem accounting: final draft. *Prepared by the Committee of Experts on Environmental-Economic Accounting*. Adopted by the 52nd UN Statistical Commission, 1–3 and 5 March 2021. https://unstats.un.org/unsd/statcom/52nd-session/documents/BG-3f-SEEA-EA_Final_draft-E.pdf (accessed 10 April 2021).

Central Statistics Office (2016). *National Income and Expenditure Annual Results*. https://www.cso.ie/ en/releasesandpublications/er/nie/nationalincomeandexpenditureannualresults2015/ (accessed 05 February 2021).

Chambers, W. (1989). *Ghosts on the Roof – Selected Journalism of Whitaker Chambers 1931–1959*. Washington, DC: Regnery Publishing.

Clydesdale, G. (2016). *Waves of Prosperity – India, China and the West: How Global Trade Transformed the World*. London: Robinson.

Conable, B.B. (1989). Foreword. In: *Environmental Accounting for Sustainable Development. A UNEP World Bank Symposium* (ed. Y.J. Ahmad, S. El Serafy and E. Lutz). Washington, DC: The World Bank https://www.cbd.int/financial/values/g-accounting-worldbank.pdf (accessed 16 April 2021).

Connolly, M. (2017). The expected and unexpected consequences of ESA 2010 – an Irish perspective. *Journal of the Statistical and Social Inquiry Society of Ireland* XLVII: 39–64.

Daly, H. (1977). *Steady-State Economics*. San Francisco: Freeman and Co.

Daly, H. and Cobb, J.B. (1989). *For the Common Good: Redirecting the Economy Toward Community, the Environment, and a Sustainable Future*. Boston: Beacon Press.

David, D. (2018). *The Almighty Dollar*. London: Elliot and Thompson Ltd.

Deen, M. and Doyle, D. (2016). 'Leprechaun economics' earn Ireland ridicule, $443 million bill. *Bloomberg*. https://www.bloombergquint.com/global-economics/-leprechaun-economics-earn-ireland-ridicule-443-million-bill (accessed 11 April 2021).

Deaton, A. (2013). *The Great Escape: Health, Wealth and the Origins of Inequality*. New Jersey: Princeton University Press.

Demollin, F. and Hermans, H. (2020). Advancing new collaborative mechanisms for the profiling of MNEs in national, regional and global group registers. *Statistical Journal of the IAOS* 36 (3): 775–783.

Economic Statistics Review Group (2016). Report of the Economic Statistics Review Group (ESRG) – December 2016. https://www.cso.ie/en/media/csoie/newsevents/documents/reportoftheeconomicstatisticsreviewgroup/Economic_Statistics_Review_(ESRG)_Report_Dec_2016.pdf (accessed 11 April 2021).

ECOSOC (2004). Report of the partnership on measuring information and communication technologies for development. *Note by the Secretary-General to the 36th session of the UN Statistical Commission*. E/CN.3/2005/23. https://undocs.org/en/E/CN.3/2005/23 (accessed 20 April 2021).

Eurasian Economic Commission and United Nations Conference on Trade and Development (2019). Inclusive Growth of the Eurasian Economic Union Member States: Assessments and Opportunities. http://www.eurasiancommission.org/ru/act/integr_i_makroec/dep_makroec_pol/Documents/Inclusive_growth_in_EAEU_Member.pdf (accessed 05 February 2021).

European Commission (2009). GDP and beyond measuring progress in a changing world. *Communication from the Commission to the Council and the European Parliament*. Brussels, 20.8.2009 COM(2009) 433 final. https://ec.europa.eu/eurostat/cros/system/files/06_GDP%20and%20beyond.pdf (accessed 05 February 2021).

Eurostat (2015). Methodological manual for statistics on the information society – version 1.0. https://circabc.europa.eu/faces/jsp/extension/wai/navigation/container.jsp (accessed 04 August 2021).

Ferguson, N. (2006). *The War of the World*. New York: The Penguin Press.

FitzGerald, J. (2014). Additional data needed to understand developments in the economy. ESRI Quarterly Economic Commentary, Spring 2014, pp. 34–25.

Frankopan, P. (2015). *The Silk Roads – A New History of the World*, 12. London: Bloomsbury.

Friedman, T. (2006). *The World is Flat: The Globalized World in the Twenty-First Century*. London: Penguin Books.

Gore, A. (2006). *An Inconvenient Truth: The Planetary Emergency of Global Warming and What We Can Do About It*. Emmaus PA: Rodale Press.

Hayak, F.A. (1944). *The Road to Serfdom*. Chicago: The University of Chicago Press.

Havinga, I. (2020). Guest editorial – the future of economic statistics. *Statistical Journal of the IAOS* 36 (3): 585–593.

Hoekstra, R. (2020). SNA and beyond: towards a broader accounting framework that links the SNA, SDGs and other global initiatives. *Statistical Journal of the IAOS* 36 (3): 657–675.

Houseman, S.N., Bartik, T.J., and Sturgeon, T.J. (2014). Measuring manufacturing: how the computer and semiconductor industries affect the numbers and perceptions. Upjohn Institute Working Paper

14-209. http://research.upjohn.org/cgi/viewcontent.cgi?article=1226&context=up_workingpapers (accessed 26 March 2021).

International Telecommunication Union (2020). Manual for Measuring ICT Access and Use by Households and Individuals – 2020 Edition. https://www.itu.int/en/ITU-D/Statistics/Documents/publications/manual/ITUManualHouseholds2020_E.pdf (accessed 20 April 2021).

ISWGNA (2020). Supplement to the report of the Intersecretariat Working Group on national accounts. *prepared by the Intersecretariat Working Group on National Accounts.* Presented at the 51st UN Statistical Commission, 3–6 March 2020. https://unstats.un.org/unsd/statcom/51st-session/documents/BG-Item3d-NationalAccounts-E.pdf (accessed 10 April 2021).

Karabell, Z. (2014). *The Leading Indicators – A Short History of the Numbers that Rule Our World.* New York: Simon and Schuster.

Kennedy, R. 1968. Remarks at the University of Kansas, March 18, 1968. John F. Kennedy Library, Presidential Library and Museum. https://www.jfklibrary.org/Research/Research-Aids/Ready-Reference/RFK-Speeches/Remarks-of-Robert-F-Kennedy-at-the-University-of-Kansas-March-18-1968.aspx (accessed 29 January 2021).

Koskimäki, T. and Peltola, R. (2020). Sharing data on the activities of multinational enterprise groups: innovations to redesign statistical practices and processes. *Statistical Journal of the IAOS* 36 (3): 785–796.

Koskimäki, T. and Taskinen, K. (2023). Bridging the gap between business and macroeconomic statistics: methodological considerations and practical solutions. In: *Advances in Establishment Statistics, Methods and Data Collection*, Chapter 4 (ed. G. Snijkers, M. Bavdaž, S. Bender, J. Jones, S. MacFeely, J.W. Sakshaug, K.J. Thompson, and A. van Delden). Hoboken: Wiley.

Krugman, P. (2016). Leprechaun economics: Ireland reports 26 percent growth! But it doesn't make sense. Why are these in GDP? *Tweet.* https://twitter.com/paulkrugman/status/752841032870551552 (accessed 05 February 2021).

Kuznets, S. 1962. How to Judge Quality. New Republic 1962 issue, October 2029–31. http://www.unz.org/Pub/NewRepublic-1962oct20-00029 (accessed 22 January 2021).

Landes, D. (1998). *The Wealth and Poverty of Nations' Abacus.* New York and London: W.W. Norton & Company.

Layard, R. (2011). 'Happiness: new lessons' in interview with Andrew Marr. https://www.youtube.com/watch?v=4VkQsL73SgE (accessed 05 February 2021).

Lewis, N.A. (2000). The China trade wrangle: the Clinton speech; seeing threats beyond arms, President Urges Cooperation. *New York Times*, U.S. edition, 8 May 2000. https://www.nytimes.com/2000/05/18/world/china-trade-wrangle-clinton-speech-seeing-threats-beyond-arms-president-urges.html (accessed 26 March 2016)

Lucas, C. (2020). Towards distributional national and environmental accounts. *Statistical Journal of the International Association of Official Statistics* 36 (3): 597–605.

MacFeely, S., Moloney, R., and Kenneally, M. (2011). A study of the NUTS 2 administrative regions using input-output analysis. *Journal of the Social and Statistical Inquiry Society of Ireland* 40: 60–111.

MacFeely, S. (2016). The continuing evolution of official statistics: some challenges and opportunities. *Journal of Official Statistics* 32 (4): 789–810.

MacFeely, S. (2017). Measuring the sustainable development goals: what does it mean for Ireland? *Administration* 65 (4): 41–71.

MacFeely, S. and Barnat, N. (2017). Statistical capacity building for sustainable development: developing the fundamental pillars necessary for modern national statistical systems. *Statistical Journal of the International Association of Official Statistics* 33 (4): 895–909.

MacFeely, S. (2018). Big data and official statistics. In: *Big Data Governance and Perspectives in Knowledge Management* (ed. S.K. Strydom and M. Strydom), 25–54. Hershey, PA: IGI Global.

MacFeely, S. and Nastav, B. (2019). You say you want a (data) revolution? A proposal to use unofficial statistics for the SDG global indicator framework. *Statistical Journal of the International Association of Official Statistics* 35 (3): 309–327.

MacFeely, S. (2020). In search of the data revolution: has the official statistics paradigm shifted? *Statistical Journal of the IAOS* 36 (4): 1075–1094.

MacFeely, S. and van de Ven, P. (2023). GDP and the SNA: past and present. In: *Advances in Establishment Statistics, Methods and Data Collection*, Chapter 2 (ed. G. Snijkers, M. Bavdaž, S. Bender, J. Jones, S. MacFeely, J.W. Sakshaug, K.J. Thompson, and A. van Delden). Hoboken: Wiley.

Masood, E. (2016). *The Great Invention: The Story of GDP and the Making and Unmaking of the Modern World*. New York and London: Pegasus Books.

Mayer-Schonberger, V. and Ramge, T. (2018). *Reinventing Capitalism in the Age of Big Data*. New York: Basic Books.

McCollough, C. (2010). *The Song of Troy*. London: Orion.

Meadows, D.H., Meadows, D.L., Randers, J., and Behrens, W.W. (1972). *The Limits to Growth – A Report for the Club of Rome Project on the Predicament of Man*. New York: Potomac Associates – Universe Books.

Mitra-Khan, B.H. (2011). Redefining the economy: how the 'economy; was invented in 1620, and has been redefined ever since'. Unpublished Doctoral thesis. City University London. https://openaccess .city.ac.uk/id/eprint/1276/1/Mitra-Kahn%2C_Benjamin.pdf (accessed 03 July 2020).

Nicholson, J.R. (2020). New digital economy estimates. Bureau of Economic Analysis Working Paper – August 2020. https://www.bea.gov/data/special-topics/digital-economy (accessed 20 April 2021).

Nicholson, J.R., Howells, T.F., and Wasshausen, D.B. (2023). Measuring the US digital economy. In: *Advances in Establishment Statistics, Methods and Data Collection*, Chapter 6 (ed. G. Snijkers, M. Bavdaž, S. Bender, J. Jones, S. MacFeely, J.W. Sakshaug, K.J. Thompson, and A. van Delden). Hoboken: Wiley.

Nordhaus, W.D. and Tobin, J. (1972). Is growth obsolete? In: *Economic Research: Retrospect and Prospect*, Economic Growth, vol. 5 (ed. W.D. Nordhaus and J. Tobin). NBER. e ISBN: 0-87014-254-2. https://www.nber.org/system/files/chapters/c7620/c7620.pdf.

Obst, C., Alfierib, A., and Kroese, B. (2020). Advancing environmental-economic accounting in the context of the system of economic statistics. *Statistical Journal of the International Association of Official Statistics* 36 (3): 629–645.

OECD (2010). OECD Handbook on Economic Globalisation Indicators. https://www.oecd.org/sti/ind/ measuringglobalisationoecdeconomicglobalisationindicators2010.htm (accessed 01 April 2021).

OECD (2011). OECD Guide to Measuring the Information Society. https://www.oecd.org/sti/ ieconomy/oecdguidetomeasuringtheinformationsociety2011.htm (accessed 04 August 2021).

OECD (2013a). Action Plan on Base Erosion and Profit Shifting. https://www.oecd.org/ctp/ BEPSActionPlan.pdf (accessed 26 March 2021).

OECD (2013b). OECD Guidelines on Measuring Subjective Well-being. https://www.oecd.org/ statistics/oecd-guidelines-on-measuring-subjective-well-being-9789264191655-en.htm (accessed 15 April 2021).

OECD (2016). Are the Irish 26.3% better off? *OECD Insights*. http://oecdinsights.org/2016/10/05/are-the-irish-26-3-better-off/ (accessed 11 April 2021).

OECD (2020a). A roadmap toward a common framework for measuring the digital economy. Report for the G20 Digital Economy Task Force, Saudi Arabia 2020. https://www.oecd.org/sti/roadmap-toward-a-common-framework-for-measuring-the-digital-economy.pdf (accessed 27 April 2021).

OECD (2020b). Guidelines for supply-use tables for the digital economy. *Prepared for the meeting of the Informal Advisory Group on Measuring GDP in a Digitalised Economy*. Document:

SDD/CSSP/WPNA(2019)1/REV1. https://www.oecd.org/officialdocuments/publicdisplaydocumentpdf/?cote=SDD/CSSP/WPNA(2019)1/REV1&docLanguage=En (accessed 27 April 2020).

OECD – WTO – IMF (2020). Handbook on Measuring Digital Trade – Version 1. https://www.oecd.org/sdd/its/Handbook-on-Measuring-Digital-Trade-Version-1.pdf (accessed 27 April 2021).

Palmer, E.Z. (1966). *The Meaning and Measurement of the National Income*. Lincoln, NE: University of Nebraska Press.

Philipsen, D. (2015). *The Little Big Number*. Princeton: Princeton University Press.

Pilling, D. (2018). *The Growth Delusion: Wealth, Poverty and the Nations*. New York: Tim Duggan Books.

Pradhan, M.C. (2023). Establishment of base informal sector statistics: an endeavor of measurement from Economic Census 2018 of Nepal. In: *Advances in Establishment Statistics, Methods and Data Collection*, Chapter 7 (ed. G. Snijkers, M. Bavdaž, S. Bender, J. Jones, S. MacFeely, J.W. Sakshaug, K.J. Thompson, and A. van Delden). Hoboken: Wiley.

Radermacher, W.J. (2015). Recent and future developments related to "GDP and Beyond". *Review of Income and Wealth* 61 (1): 18–24.

Sachs, J. (2012). *The Price of Civilization: Reawakening Virtue and Prosperity After the Economic Fall*. London: Vintage, Random House.

Schumacher, E.F. (1973). *Small is Beautiful: A Study of Economics As If People Mattered*. London: Blond and Briggs.

Schwab, K. (2017). *The Fourth Industrial Revolution*. New York: Random House.

Sen, A. (1999). *Development as Freedom*. New York: Anchor Books.

Shaxon, N. (2018). *The Finance Curse*. New York: Grove Press.

Slade, G. (2006). *Made to Break: Technology and Obsolescence in America*. Cambridge, MA: Harvard University Press.

Statistics Canada (2021). Digital Economy and Society Statistics. Last updated 10 February, 2021. https://www.statcan.gc.ca/eng/subjects-start/digital_economy_and_society (accessed 20 April 2021).

Stern, N. (2006). The stern review –final report. HM Treasury – The National Archives. Archived 7 April, 2010. https://webarchive.nationalarchives.gov.uk/20100407172811/http://www.hm-treasury.gov.uk/stern_review_report.htm (accessed 09 February 2021).

Stiglitz, J.E., Sen, A., and Fitoussi, J.-P. (2010). *Mismeasuring Our Lives: Why GDP Doesn't Add Up*. The Report by the Commission on the Measurement of Economic Performance and Social Progress. London: The New York Press.

Stiglitz, J.E. (2014). America's GDP fetishism is a rare luxury in an age of vulnerability. *The Guardian*, 13 October 2014. https://www.theguardian.com/business/2014/oct/13/gdp-fetishism-luxury-vulnerability-economic-measures (accessed 13 April 2021).

Sturgeon, T.J. (2013). Global value chains and economic globalization – towards a new measurement framework. Report to Eurostat. https://ec.europa.eu/eurostat/documents/54610/4463793/Sturgeon-report-Eurostat (accessed 06 March 2021).

Strassner, E.H. and Nicholson, J.R. (2020). Measuring the digital economy in the United States. *Statistical Journal of the IAOS* 36 (3): 647–655.

Talberth, J., Cobb, C. and Slattery, N. (2007). The genuine progress indicator 2006: a tool for sustainable development. *Redefining Progress*. http://web.pdx.edu/~kub/publicfiles/MeasuringWellBeing/Talberth_2006_GPI.pdf (accessed 29 January 2021).

The Economist (2016). The trouble with GDP. *Briefing*. 30 April 2016. https://www.economist.com/briefing/2016/04/30/the-trouble-with-gdp (accessed 05 February 2021).

Unmüßig, B. (2014). Monetizing nature: taking precaution on a slippery slope. *Great Transition Initiative*. https://greattransition.org/publication/monetizing-nature-taking-precaution-on-a-slippery-slope (accessed 05 August 2021).

United Nations (1973). Report of the United Nations Conference on the Human Environment. Stockholm, 5–16 June 1972. A/CONF.48/14/Rev.1. https://www.un.org/ga/search/view_doc.asp?symbol=A/CONF.48/14/REV.1 (accessed 05 August 2021).

United Nations (1987). Report of the World Commission on environment and development. Report to the 42nd Session of the United Nations General Assembly. A/42/427. https://digitallibrary.un.org/record/139811?ln=en (accessed 04 August 2021).

United Nations, European Commission, International Monetary Fund, Organisation for Economic Co-operation and Development, and World Bank (1993). *System of National Accounts 1993*. New York: United Nations. https://unstats.un.org/unsd/nationalaccount/docs/1993sna.pdf.

United Nations (1993). Handbook of national accounting: integrated environmental and economic accounting –interim version. *Studies in Methods*, Series F, No. 61. https://unstats.un.org/unsd/publication/SeriesF/SeriesF_61E.pdf (accessed 04 August 2021).

United Nations (2003). Handbook of national accounting: integrated environmental and economic accounting 2003. *Studies in Methods*, ST/ESA/STAT/SER.F/61/Rev.1. https://seea.un.org/content/handbook-national-accounting-integrated-environmental-and-economic-accounting-2003 (accessed 04 August 2021).

United Nations et al. (2009). System of National Accounts 2008. United Nations, European Commission, IMF, OECD, World Bank. https://unstats.un.org/unsd/nationalaccount/docs/SNA2008.pdf (accessed 19 May 2021).

United Nations (2012). Secretary-general, in message to meeting on 'happiness and well-being' calls for 'Rio+20' outcome that measures more than gross national income. SG/SM/14204, Department of Public Information, New York, 2 April 2012. https://www.un.org/press/en/2012/sgsm14204.doc.htm (accessed 05 February 2021).

United Nations European Union, Food and Agriculture Organization of the United Nations, International Monetary Fund, Organisation for Economic Co-operation and Development and The World Bank (2014a). System of Environmental Economic Accounting 2012 – Central Framework. New York: United Nations. https://seea.un.org/sites/seea.un.org/files/seea_cf_final_en.pdf (accessed 04 August 2021).

United Nations European Union, Food and Agriculture Organization of the United Nations, Organisation for Economic Co-operation and Development and World Bank Group (2014b). System of Environmental-Economic Accounting – Experimental Ecosystem Accounting. New York: United Nations. https://seea.un.org/sites/seea.un.org/files/seea_eea_final_en_1.pdf (accessed 28 February 2022).

United Nations (2019). Summary on the update of the system of economic statistics. *Friday Seminar on Emerging Issues – The Future of Economic Statistics*. I March, 2019, UN New York. https://unstats.un.org/unsd/statcom/50th-session/documents/BG-Item3f-Summary_Friday-Seminar-The-Future-of-Economic-Statistics-E.pdf (accessed 15 April 2021).

United Nations (2021). Report of the friends of the chair group on economic statistics - note by the Secretary-General. UN Economic and Social Council. *Presented to the 52nd session of the UN Statistical Commission*. E/CN.3/2021/7. https://unstats.un.org/unsd/statcom/52nd-session/documents/2021-7-EconomicStats-E.pdf (accessed 26 March 2021).

United Nations on Conference on Trade and Development and United Nations Office on Drugs and Crime (2020). Conceptual Framework for the Statistical Measurement of Illicit Financial Flows – October 2020. https://www.unodc.org/documents/data-and-analysis/statistics/IFF/IFF_Conceptual_Framework_for_publication_15Oct.pdf (accessed 26 March 2021).

United Nations on Conference on Trade and Development (2021). Manual for the Production of Statistics on the Digital Economy: 2020 – Revised Edition. https://unctad.org/system/files/official-document/dtlstict2021d2_en.pdf (accessed 13 June 2021).

United Nations Economic Commission for Africa (2014). Manual for Measuring e-government. United Nations, Addis Ababa. https://repository.uneca.org/bitstream/handle/10855/22774/%20b11524364 .pdf?sequence=1&isAllowed=y (accessed 20 April 2021).

United Nations Economic Commission for Europe (2008). Economic globalisation: a challenge for official statistics. *Proceedings of the 2007 Joint EFTA/UNECE/SSCU Seminar*. United Nations, New York and Geneva. https://unece.org/DAM/stats/publications/Economic%20globalization.pdf (accessed 01 April 2021).

United Nations Economic Commission for Europe Eurostat and Organisation for economic co-operation and development (2011). The Impact of Globalisation on National Accounts. United Nations, New York and Geneva. https://unece.org/DAM/stats/publications/Guide_on_Impact_of_ globalization_on_national_accounts__web_.pdf (accessed 01 April 2021).

United Nations Economic Commission for Europe (2015). Guide to Measuring Global Production. United Nations, New York and Geneva. https://unece.org/DAM/stats/publications/2015/Guide_to_ Measuring_Global_Production__2015_.pdf (accessed 01 April 2021).

United Nations Economic Commission for Europe (2021). Guide to Sharing Economic Data in Official Statistics. United Nations, Geneva. https://unece.org/sites/default/files/2021-02/Data%20sharing %20guide%20on%20web_1.pdf (accessed 19 April 2021).

United Nations Educational, Scientific and Cultural Organizations - Institute for Statistics (2009). Guide to measuring information and communication technologies (ICT) in education. Technical Paper No. 2 Montreal. http://uis.unesco.org/sites/default/files/documents/guide-to-measuring-information-and-communication-technologies-ict-in-education-en_0.pdf (accessed 20 April 2021).

United Nations University International Human Dimensions Programme on Global Environmental Change and United Nations Environment Programme (2012). *Inclusive Wealth Index 2012: Measuring Progress Towards Sustainability*. Cambridge: Cambridge University Press.

Van de Ven, P. (2019). Measuring economic well-being and sustainability: a practical agenda for the present and the future. In: *Eurona – Eurostat Review on National Accounts and Macroeconomic Indicators* (ed. P. Konijn, N. Massarelli and G. Amerini). Eurostat 1/2019.

Vanoli, A. (2016). National accounting at the beginning of the 21st century: wherefrom? whereto? Eurostat Review on National Accounts and Macroeconomic Indicators, Eurostat/CROS/EURONA. Issue No 1/2014. ISSN 1977-978X. https://ec.europa.eu/eurostat/cros/system/files/p1-national_ accounting_at_the_beginning_of_the_21st_century.pdf (accessed 14 April 2020).

Victor, P. A. (April 2020). Cents and nonsense: a critical appraisal of the monetary valuation of nature. *Ecosystem Services*. Vol. 42, 101076. https://doi.org/10.1016/j.ecoser.2020.101076

Wadsworth, A.P. and Mann, J.d.L. (1931). *The Cotton Trade and Industrial Lancashire*. Manchester University Press.

Warsh, D. (2006). *Knowledge and the Wealth of Nations: A Story of Economic Discovery*. New York and London: W.W. Norton & Company.

Wolf, A. (2020). Should Nature Be Monetized? https://medium.com/@anu.garcha12/should-nature-be-monetized-646ff80f1e7b (accessed 05 August 2021).

World Meteorological Organisation and United Nations Environment Programme (1992). Climate change: the 1990 and 1992 IPCC assessments. IPCC First Assessment – Report Overview and Policymaker Summaries and 1992 IPPC Supplement. June 1992. https://www.ipcc.ch/report/ climate-change-the-ipcc-1990-and-1992-assessments/ (accessed 09 February 2021).

Yergin, D. (2012). *The Quest – Energy, Security and the Remaking of the Modern World*. London: Penguin Books.

4

Bridging the Gap Between Business and Macroeconomic Statistics: Methodological Considerations and Practical Solutions

Timo Koskimäki and Kristian Taskinen

Statistics Finland, Helsinki, Finland

4.1 Introduction

As regards economic statistics, there is an ongoing professional discussion on the quality of economic statistics, "The future of economic statistics." This discussion has quite a practical driver: Economic statistics, as they are produced by National Statistical Offices (NSOs) today, clearly face difficulties in describing the national and global economies in a relevant and coherent manner. This is not only our perception as statisticians, there is also a growing distrust to traditional economic statistics among researchers, policymakers, and other users of economic statistics.

In this article, we attempt to bring the discussion on more practical level by first describing and reflecting how the global phenomena we observe in economic statistics emerge in the statistical practices when dealing with the compilation of business statistics. We also propose solutions to improve the coherence between business and macroeconomic statistics, stressing the importance of data sharing internationally between statistical offices and nationally between statistical units of national central banks and statistical offices. Statisticians should work together across national and institutional borders.

4.2 Global Production and Statistics

The traditional economic statistics face well-known difficulties in describing the national economy in a situation where the activities of the enterprises are global and only a section of the value-generating process takes place within a single nation.

One consequence of production chain fragmentation is that goods and cash flows have partially separated from each other. This is particularly visible in global production, where a company manufactures the product in another country from where it is directly exported to a third country, while the invoices travel another route. Producing national statistics on globally decentralized production by multinational enterprises (MNE) include difficult questions: How to identify enterprises involved in global production? What is included in national production? Is the unit we observe domestic or foreign? In which country is the economic ownership of factors of production located and where is the income accumulated?

In general, global production refers to splitting activities and production stages, part of which the enterprise has transferred or outsourced abroad. The transfer can apply to both goods and services,

Advances in Business Statistics, Methods and Data Collection. Edited by Ger Snijkers, Mojca Bavdaž, Stefan Bender, Jacqui Jones, Steve MacFeely, Joseph W. Sakshaug, Katherine J. Thompson, and Arnout van Delden.

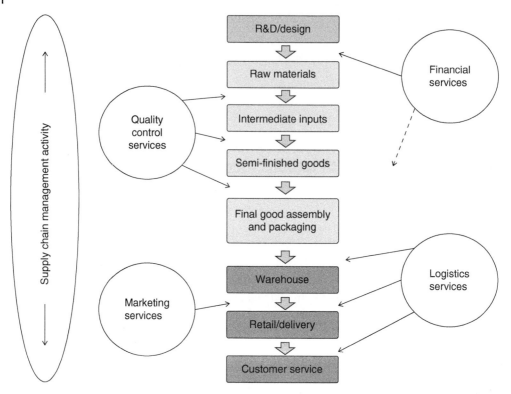

Figure 4.1 Example of fragmentation of the production chain. Source: UNECE (2015, p. 3).

as in the example in the Figure 4.1 above. The stages and activities in the middle of the figure describe the actual production process, starting from product design and purchasing raw materials, and ending with retail trade of the final product and customer service. The stages shown beside actual production process depict activities related to managing the production process, such as quality control, marketing, financial, and transport services. Either the parent enterprise manages the entire chain, as in the Figure 4.1 above, or affiliates manage part of the chain.

Production abroad can be included in domestic production when the statistics applies the economic ownership principle (e.g. national accounts and balance of payments). Production on behalf of affiliates located abroad is, however, always included in the gross national product of the country of location. Nowadays there is a need to include global production, in addition to macroeconomic statistics, also in some business statistics since they do try to follow the guidelines of national accounts to ensure consistency of the national statistics. A discussion is also ongoing on international statistical forums on whether production that takes place in the home country of the enterprises and global production should be distinguished in statistics. Extensive inclusion of global production in, for example, the volume index of a particular industry would make comparison with domestic employment development difficult, but, on the other hand, this would mean that production concept would be uniform with gross domestic product (GDP) calculations.

4.2.1 Concepts of Nationality and Economic Ownership

Key questions in statistics production in general and, especially in statistics on multinational enterprise groups, are the statistical unit and its nationality, and following changes in economic ownership when recoding statistical data. The concepts of nationality and economic ownership are defined, for example, in the manuals that guide the compilation of national accounts and balance of payments like System of National Accounts 2008 (United Nations 2009) and sixth edition of Balance of Payments and International Investment Position Manual (2009).

The statistical unit affects both the production process and interpretation of the statistics. The statistical unit varies between statistics, which causes comparability problems between different statistics. For example, the statistical unit for annual business statistics might be the enterprise, while statistics on economic trends are quite often based on the more detailed kind-of-activity unit. National accounts, in turn, use either the enterprise or establishment depending on the account.

When defining the nationality of the statistical unit, one should consider the scope and duration of the activity, in addition to the location of the activity. For example, enterprises' foreign branches and value added tax (VAT) units are in the grey area and more attention than currently should be paid to them in different statistics, and effort should be made to handle them uniformly throughout economic statistics.

Economic ownership is difficult concept and causes interpretation problems. Economic ownership belongs to the institutional unit that decides, for example, on the use of a commodity, natural resource or intangible right and thus carries the risks and income related to the activity. Recording of global production is in many statistics based on changes in economic ownership in order for income from activities to be visible in the countries where the institutional unit that collects the income is located. Recordings made like this are also better in line with enterprises' national financial statement data and to some extent make data acquisition easier. The downside is, e.g. the need to revise conventional statistics on international trade that are based on crossing national borders.

Economic ownership usually follows legal ownership, but, especially in transactions between multinational groups and their foreign affiliates, the change is not evident – particularly in case of intangible capital. Intangible capital, like various patents, original works and brands are nowadays increasingly important factors of production in the production of both goods and services, and, as a result of technological development, transferring them from one country to another is becoming ever easier. Income collected from intangible rights is, therefore, difficult to allocate correctly based on economic ownership. Recording them in a timely manner is particularly hard when a multinational enterprise group is reorganizing its activities.

4.2.2 Case Finland: Global Production in Economic Statistics

Statistics Finland has improved the processing of global production in economic statistics (Statistics Finland 2019). Currently, global production adjustments in national accounts are conducted already when the preliminary quarterly figures are produced. Economic ownership concept has also been introduced in some business statistics to provide consistent economic statistics. In this chapter we provide examples of the key practices.

4.2.2.1 Identification of Enterprises Involved in Global Production

Recognition of global production is based on enterprise analysis that is carried out in cooperation between business statistics and national accounts experts. Enterprises' financial statements are key background material in enterprise analysis and media also provides essential information on enterprises' activities. Company visits and communication with companies also provide information on global production arrangements and help the enterprise report global production correctly to different statistics.

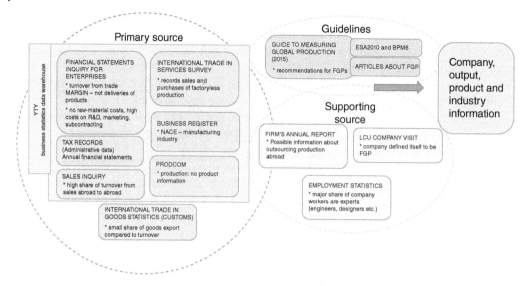

Figure 4.2 Identification and analysis of Factoryless Goods Producers. Source: Adapted from Statistics Finland (2019, p. 42).

In Finland around 90 enterprises that have significant global production arrangements have been identified. They can be divided into the following categories: processing abroad, processing in Finland, merchanting, and factoryless goods production (FGP). Data sources and guidelines used in this work are presented in Figure 4.2. The high share of FGPs is due to the dominance of intellectual property product (IPP) emphasized electronics industry in the past.

The European Task Force on Factoryless Goods Producers (FGPs) led by Eurostat has worked on indicators with which factoryless production could be recognized and found following indicators that best allows for identification of enterprises with global production (UNECE 2017):

– High purchases of services and high sales of goods
– High purchases of services and low purchases of goods for resale
– High production associated with low employment

4.2.2.2 Case on Automotive Industry

One example on global production is the manufacture of cars in Finland. According to Customs' international trade in goods statistics, number of cars exported from Finland has grown remarkably during the last decade (Table 4.1), even though Finnish enterprises do not own any well-known car brands or sell them abroad.

According to the international trade in goods statistics, cars are exported from Finland when national borders are crossed, even though the economic ownership remains with the foreign car manufacturer throughout the production process. By contrast, in statistics based on economic ownership (e.g. national accounts and balance of payments), export and import items relate to car production where ownership is not changed. Thus, cars reported as exports by the trade in goods statistics are removed from economic statistics describing Finland's imports and exports. Only the manufacturing fee received for car assembly and the raw material purchases from Finland needed in the assembly are recorded as Finnish export; likewise, if a car assembled in Finland is sold in Finland, this is added to Finnish imports in economic statistics. These recordings better correspond with the income flow of the Finnish enterprise and the nature of the activities.

Table 4.1 Foreign trade of cars in Finland 2010–2020, number of cars.

Year	Exports	Imports
2010	28,991	141,251
2011	30,068	155,895
2012	30,302	124,774
2013	38,305	126,949
2014	74,066	125,684
2015	104,941	135,407
2016	71,581	143,023
2017	117,047	151,445
2018	142,717	153,914
2019	143,496	150,557
2020	106,871	129,978

Source: International trade in goods statistics, Finnish Customs.

4.2.2.3 Foreign Trade of Goods Based on Economic Ownership

On aggregate level foreign trade of goods based on change of economic ownership does not differ so much from international trade in goods statistics (ITGS) statistics, which is based on cross-border movements of goods. The difference in 2019 was negligible in exports and only 5% in imports (Tables 4.2 and 4.3). Although the effects are not that significant on aggregate level because of

Table 4.2 Summary of adjustments made for ITGS exports, million euros in 2019.

	Phenomenon	Specification	Value 2019	% of total exports (NA) (%)
	ITGS export – Finnish Customs		**65,054**	100
Added	Goods sent abroad for processing; "outward processing" (Finnish principal)	Sales of finished goods to abroad	4,732	7
Excluded	Goods sent abroad for processing; "outward processing" (Finnish principal)	Raw-materials sent for processing purchased from Finland	−544	−1
Added	Goods sent abroad for processing; "inward processing" (Finnish supplier)	Raw-materials for processing purchased from Finland	910	1
Excluded	Goods sent abroad for processing; "inward processing" (Finnish supplier)	Finished goods delivered to abroad	−7,132	−11
Added	Factoryless goods production	Marginal (sales-purchases)	578	1
Added	Goods under merchanting	Marginal (sales-purchases)	1,300	2
	National accounts export – Statistics Finland		**64,898**	100

Source: Statistics Finland, Balance of Payments and International Investment Position. Licensed under CC-BY 4.0.

Table 4.3 Summary of adjustments made for ITGS imports, million euros in 2019.

	Phenomenon	Specification	Value 2019	% of total imports (NA) (%)
	ITGS imports – Finnish Customs		**65,851**	105
	CIF/FOB-adjustment		−3,958	−6
Added	Goods sent abroad for processing; Finnish principal	Raw-materials purchased from abroad	2,343	4
Excluded	Goods sent abroad for processing; Finnish principal	Output of manufuctured goods, sales to Finland	−284	0
Added	Goods sent abroad for processing; Finnish supplier	Finished goods, sales to Finland	1,258	2
Excluded	Goods sent abroad for processing; Finnish supplier	Raw-materials for processing in Finland, purchased abroad	−4,674	−7
Added/exluded	Other adjustments	Classifications, Smuggling, E-commerce etc.	2,076	3
	National accounts import – Statistics Finland		**62,612**	100

Source: Statistics Finland, Balance of Payments and International Investment Position. Licensed under CC-BY 4.0.

adjustments with opposite signs, the more granular data show that these phenomena are indeed significant. For example, goods for processing adjustments are billions of euros on annual level. Inward processing in Finland includes mainly car manufacturing, metal processing and chemical products. On the other hand, Finnish enterprises are sending machines, equipment, textile products and chemicals to be processed abroad.

To help users in interpreting different figures on foreign trade, Statistics Finland publishes quarterly table on adjustments made for Customs' data as part of its Foreign trade of goods and services statistics.

4.2.2.4 Challenges Related to Global Production Recordings

Guide to measuring global production (UNECE 2017) presents typology for global production and defines three main categories: Goods sent abroad for processing, Merchanting and Factoryless goods manufacturing. In practice, MNE structures and value chains are complicated and quite often a kind of mixture of these, which makes it difficult to select only one and follow the recommended recording rules.

Also question on when merchantor becomes factoryless goods producer (FGP), i.e. how large share of IPPs related revenues are needed is a tricky one. Also correct activity classification for FGPs is difficult to define with existing classification manuals – industry, trade, or services? National accounts also need price indexes (deflators) for global production revenues in GDP calculation, and these are difficult to construct and the use of proxy indicators is frequent.

Communication with MNEs and users of statistics also cause challenges since concepts are quite theoretical and partly old-fashioned. For the MNEs, the concepts as they are expressed in statistics manuals are not identifiable in their business practices. In addition to these issues, at least small countries with only a few significant global producers encounter major confidentiality problems when publishing statistics.

4.3 Co-operation Between National Statistical Offices and National Central Bank Statistics Functions Tackling Globalization Problems

Increasing economic globalization call for close collaboration of NSOs, central banks and other producers of key economic statistics, such as the ministry of finance and customs. In Europe, the European Central Bank has a statistics division and national central banks typically have units to produce statistics. The statistical bodies of the central bank system are to some extent independent from the monetary policy- and fiscal functions of the system of the European Central Banks. European Central Bank statistics division and statistics units of the national central banks form a structure system that in many respects resembles the ordinary European Statistical System (ESS) where NSOs are the main actors. European level coordination body for these two systems is the European Statistical Forum where the top management of the both systems convene. As a forum for practical co-operation, there is, within the ESS governance structure, the Committee on Monetary, Financial and Balance of Payments Statistics CMFB

The division of work between central banks and NSOs varies in countries. While NSOs most often compile national accounts and price statistics, in some countries, those are compiled by the central bank. Central banks often, but not always, produce the balance of payments statistics.

According to the UNECE Guide to Sharing Economic Data in Official Statistics (UNECE 2021) inter-agency collaboration is important for the quality of key economic statistics, such as international trade statistics, balance of payments, and sector accounts and the rest-of-the-world accounts compiled as part of the national accounts. Three main factors influence the conditions for successful cooperation between central banks and statistical offices:

– Division of tasks between the producers of official statistics
– Structure and governance of the national statistical system
– Collaboration and regular sharing of expertise

Whatever the formal setting is in each country, good coordination of statistical activities with the entity producing official statistics in the central bank is necessary to ensure the quality and consistency of key macroeconomic statistics and streamline work. Furthermore, the use of common definitions, classifications and methodologies is important in the key macroeconomic statistics.

The current legal frameworks typically do not allow the NSO and entity producing official statistics in the central bank to exchange individual data to produce their statistics. Following European level data sharing solutions have been launched during the last decade.

4.3.1 Foreign Direct Investment Network as an Example of Co-operation

Between the ESS and the European System of European Central Banks (ESCB), the foreign direct investment (FDI) Network is a long-standing mode of collaboration. It was established in 2009 and aims at the reconciliation of singular large financial transactions and positions in FDI. This exchange of information and data sharing involves the compilers of the FDI, mostly national central banks but also some NSOs, and Eurostat that provides secure infrastructure for a confidential exchange of information between the FDI compilers, without regard whether they are Central banks or NSOs. This mechanism has recently been scaled up to allow the compiling institutions

Table 4.4   Transactions and positions exchanged in the FDI Network 2013–2018.

	2013	2014	2015	2016	2017	2018
Transactions No. of cases	143	81	83	157	122	166
Transactions Amounts (EUR Billion)	478	336	808	1448	1078	1302
Positions No. of cases	195	67	292	393	253	256
Positions Amounts (EUR Billion)	1462	822	2490	2787	1565	1343

Source: UNECE Guide to Sharing Economic Data in Official Statistics (UNECE 2021, p. 16).

Table 4.5   Reasons expressed to justify a failure in 2017 reconciliation process on FDI positions.

Reason	No. of cases	Amounts (EUR Billion)
Different valuation method	33	266
Entity not covered	18	92
Corresponding positions not found	6	29
Not classified as FDI	3	11
Other reasons	56	373
Total	116	771

Source: UNECE Guide to Sharing Economic Data in Official Statistics (UNECE 2021, p. 16).

to address the largest asymmetries occurring each quarter and undertakes to address them in the context of the asymmetry resolution meeting.

In the FDI Network system, the initiator EU Member State sends via Eurostat's secure data transmission channel a reconciliation request to the counterpart Member State. The request is detailed with several transaction or position specific data fields, including the names of the enterprises involved and the euro amounts in question.

The number and total value of transactions and positions exchanged via the FDI Network 2013–2018 are presented in Table 4.4. Table 4.5 indicates how the data sharing within the FDI Network is helping developing methodology for statistics

4.3.2   Early-Warning System (EWS)

The early-warning system (EWS) provides a platform for occasional data sharing among statistical authorities as needed. It aims to identify possible restructuring cases for important MNEs and to agree on a common recording, preferably before the changes materialize or need to be incorporated into business statistics, balance of payments or national accounts. The purpose is to ensure consistency of applied methods, statistical treatment and communication of statistics involving MNEs across EU Member States. The EWS provides a light procedure for voluntary cooperation between national statistical authorities and Eurostat, and between business statisticians and national accounts. EWS is developed as an ESS-system for NSOs, but NCBs are involved in discussions depending on the case and national practicalities.

4.3.3 A Roadmap for Solving the Globalization-Related Issues in Monetary, Financial, and Balance of Payments – Statistics

Issues related to globalization typically break the boundaries between the statistical systems of NSOs and national central banks and therefore cooperation is needed. In September 2020 the Committee on Monetary, Financial and Balance of Payments Statistics published a vision paper on globalization and statistics. The vision identified key areas of joint work between central statistical offices and central banks. The main objective is better measurement of globalized economies through enhanced statistical collaboration.

Goals of this globalization vision are:

– The methodologies for monetary, financial and balance of payments statistics will be developed so that the globalization-related national inconsistencies or international asymmetries will be cured
– The role of MNEs is made visible in the macroeconomic accounting framework
– User satisfaction on monetary, financial and balance of payments statistics is measurably improved
– An appropriate framework for statistical information flow between national central banks and NSOs is in place.

Strategies to achieve these goals in the coming years include following MNE related actions:

– Consistent recording of MNE activities in economic statistics by studying all significant European asymmetries related to direct investment and trade statistics, by increasing the number of resolution meetings.
– Organizational measures (e.g. large cases units [LCUs] or similar structures) should be adopted to enable to continuously work on recording of MNE activities.
– European network of statistical business registers
  National and European statistical registers are connected within a European network. These registers include globally unique identifiers (in particular the legal entity identifier – [LEI]), at least for MNEs and their subsidiaries and branches, that are also linked to national identifiers. Within the register, legal and statistical units are identified consistently across countries.
– Exchange of register data and statistical information on MNEs and special purpose entities (SPEs) with non-EU countries.
– European and national central banks and statistical offices foster international work on a micro data sharing standard for statistical purposes. European and national central banks and statistical offices also foster international work on a database on large MNEs and their structure, specifically on SPEs.
– Sharing and protecting micro data:
  Both statistical systems will work on the appropriate compulsory legal basis for sharing micro data between all national and European statistical offices and central banks to the extent necessary for the production of high-quality data, including the high confidentiality standards for the data exchange and the statistical production in these institutions.
– Elimination of globalization-related gaps in source data:
  ESS and ESCB amend their data collections so as to identify intra-MNE transactions and positions (e.g. trade, income, loans).
– Initiative to get better access to administrative sources, including recommended actions to open the appropriate legal gateways exists and possibilities for MNE group reporting will be studied.

- Methodology for sub-sectoring and globalization-relevant breakdowns.
- Separate identification of globalization-relevant statistical units, including factory-less goods producers, enterprises engaged in manufacturing services and merchants is needed.
- Foreign controlled nonfinancial and financial corporations will be identified separately in balance of payments and sector accounts statistics.

4.4 Bridging the Gap Between Business and Economic Statistics Through Global Data Sharing

Above, we have described the issue mainly from the European Union perspective. In the EU, there are structural arrangements like harmonized statistical and data protection legislation, that make data sharing among the NSOs and co-operation between the NSOs and Central Banks somewhat easier than in the rest of the world. Also, so far our examples have been mainly on monetary, financial and balance of payments statistics.

The UNECE task force on the Sharing of Economic Data delivered their recommendations in June 2021, also providing suggestions that do not require EU-type institutional and legal environment. The key message of the report targeted to NSOs was, that instead of being solely national institutions, dealing with national data only, NSOs should exploit the possibilities of global statistical data, collected by statistical authorities of other countries, to produce better quality economic statistics. The recommendations in the guidance apply in principle to any statistics describing cross-border flows, not only economic statistics.

The Guide to Sharing Economic Data (UNECE 2021) makes recommendations for a phased approach to international data sharing for economic and business statistics. Data sharing can involve the exchange of non-confidential aggregates, and only if needed, the exchange of confidential microdata. It can be either continuous, or one-off exchange to address a particular issue. The sensitivity of the shared information increases in a continuum of sharing aggregated data, sharing publicly available data on individual units, sharing metadata on the treatment of individual units, or sharing confidential individual data.

Koskimäki and Peltola (2020) elaborate the ways to share data for better statistics using organizational innovation -framework. The case studies they provide are intended to make statistical innovation visible and promote the application and development of similar solutions to advance data sharing in the future.

4.4.1 Product Innovation – One-Off or Regular Data Sharing for Better Quality

In recent years, several statistical offices have engaged in data sharing exercises with statistical offices of important trading partner countries. They have come to realize the pivotal importance of data sharing to producing relevant and reliable economic statistics, and the exercises have led to product innovation, i.e. significantly improved quality and consistency of statistics. For instance, in 2016, the bilateral trade asymmetry between Canada and China was 21.3 billion USD of which 20.3 billion USD was then explained by in a one-off exercise to share aggregate level data and metadata on compilation methods.

Bilateral agreements between statistical organizations are an effective way of engaging in regular microdata sharing, while differences in legal set-ups can bring challenges. Statistics Canada and the United States Census Bureau have a long-lasting set-up for the sharing of customs import transactions data since 1990. The exchanged data are used to compile export statistics and to ensure their high quality. The simplicity and the lasting nature of this Memorandum of Understanding shows that international data sharing can be operationalized to serve as a regular part of statistical production.

4.4.2   Service Innovation – Improving Respondent Service for MNEs

The EU has been long monitoring and measuring the statistical response burden on businesses. The idea of producing EU trade statistics based on a single flow system within the EU was long debated – intra-EU export data would be exchanged to calculate intra-EU imports. This would bring a massive reduction in response burden for businesses since intra-EU imports would not need to be reported, but it would also improve quality by reducing significantly the asymmetries of trade statistics within the EU. An experimental project first investigated the statistical reusability and quality of the exchanged data and the technical feasibility of exchanging large volumes of data in a secure and timely manner so that it could be integrated to monthly statistical production. The main challenges are the dependency on data from other countries, timing of data exchange and ensuring data confidentiality and security. This exchange of microdata on intra-EU trade in goods just became mandatory among member states. Similar kind of arrangement is also being used in monitoring trade between the United States and Canada.

When MNEs are significant players in the economy of a country, and thus in statistics, it makes sense to establish solid working procedures for dealing with respondent relations and MNE data. Many NSOs have set up large and complex cases units (LCUs) to deal with these tasks, often including MNE relations. Statistics Canada (2016) has developed a respondent relations management program with strategic pillars, such as promoting the agency's positive image and credibility, protecting the confidentiality of respondent information, working continuously to reduce the response burden as much as possible and encouraging respondents to participate in surveys. These strategic goals are particularly important when engaging in data sharing and communicating about it with respondents, since one of the MNEs' key concerns relates to the confidentiality of their data.

Further collaboration of statisticians and MNE representatives could be pursued also internationally at the meetings of the Organisation for Economic Co-operation and Development (OECD) (Business and Industry Advisory Committee [BIAC]) and the UN Standing Intergovernmental Working Group of Experts on International Standards of Accounting and Reporting. Closer alignment of statistical reporting and accounting standards, at least a mapping of concepts, would enable better service for business respondents e.g. in the form of automated data extraction for statistics.

4.4.3   Process Innovation to Statistical Production by Data Sharing

A great example of an innovation that shows how much can be done by reusing and organizing publicly available data better, is the OECD's Analytical Database on Individual Multinationals and their Affiliates (ADIMA). It leverages new and traditional data sources by web scraping and innovative Big Data techniques to compile a harmonized and blended dataset of publicly available data on the scale and scope of the international activities of MNEs. ADIMA draws on MNEs' financial and nonfinancial variables from annual company reports and corporate sustainability reports, the Global Legal Entity Identifier Foundation's (GLEIF) LEI database, MNEs' websites and attributed Internet page rank. In addition, it receives digital inputs from Wikipedia and the Global Database of Events, Language and Tone (GDELT) news services. As a result, ADIMA provides a series of economic indicators by MNE and country, a register of MNE parent-affiliate structures, a register of MNE websites and early warnings on potential restructurings of MNEs with significant impacts on trade, GDP and FDI.

4.4.4   Innovating User Experience – Better Relevance and Consistency for Users

In recent years, several statistical offices have engaged in data sharing with statistical offices of important trading partner countries to improve their trade statistics. This work has been of pivotal importance to users and analysts of trade statistics. For instance, various analysts estimate illicit financial flows and trade misinvoicing applying the partner country trade data comparison method. However, this method assumes that the asymmetries of trade statistics between partner countries would exhibit illicit financial flows. In reality, however, the statistical reasons for asymmetries can be surprisingly large. For instance, the bilateral trade asymmetry between Canada and China was 21.3 billion USD in 2016, but after the sharing of aggregate level data and metadata the countries were able to explain 20.3 billion USD of the asymmetry with different statistical treatment between the countries and then correct it. In March of 2018, Romania undertook a similar exercise with a number of EU countries and significantly reduced asymmetries in both trade inflows and outflows. This type of quality improvement is very important for the users of statistics.

Fundamentally, all data sharing exercises between statistical authorities aim at improving the quality of statistics compiled and published for users. Inter-agency collaboration is important for ensuring the quality of key economic statistics, such as international trade statistics, balance of payments, and sector accounts and the rest-of-the-world accounts compiled as part of the national accounts. Users of statistics benefit from the provision of more consistent and coherent statistics, and from a better understanding and analyses of how MNEs' activity affects the measures of economic activity. Heavy users of statistics benefit most, e.g. those preparing macroeconomic projections and simulations and carrying out economic research can provide more accurate insight and policy advice.

4.4.5   Organizational Innovation – Changing the Business Model of Official Statistics

In recent years, statistical offices have developed ways of dealing with global production arrangements and treating MNEs in statistical production. Some have established specialized organizational units, often called LCUs, to deal with large and complex businesses. In early 2019, the NSOs of Canada, Denmark, Finland, France, Hungary, Ireland, Italy, Luxembourg, Netherlands, and Sweden had established a LCU, while the United Kingdom was carrying out a pilot to develop an International Business Unit. In Belgium, the central bank, and the statistical office of Norway are considering setting up permanent LCUs. Many countries have dedicated programs to perform similar activities as LCUs, for example, profiling of MNEs and other complex cases. The major benefit of a LCU is the collection of timely and accurate data on MNEs enabling a prompt reaction to data changes and the resolution of anomalies and inconsistencies before they are processed by individual statistical domains. Therefore, the Guide to Sharing Economic Data recommends to every country with a significant number of MNEs the establishment of such a unit.

MNEs are global and we need to develop a modern global statistical system within which we can exchange confidential data while ensuring that they will not leave the statistical system and that data privacy and statistical confidentiality are fully protected as well as the use for statistical purposes only guaranteed. Safeguarding statistical confidentiality is essential to maintaining the trust of users and stakeholders and ensuring the sustainability of official statistics. The key element to building trust among MNEs and other respondents is having a proper legal framework for national and international data sharing for statistics.

4.4.6 Cultural Innovation – Key to Making it Happen

Discussion often focuses on legal barriers and technical issues that need to be solved, even though engaging in data sharing requires, more than anything, a profound cultural change in statistical systems. International organizations are key players in promoting this cultural change and providing discussion fora to share country experiences. The UNECE/Eurostat/OECD Group of Experts on National Accounts and the CES Bureau have been fundamental in this regard. One of the key roles of a LCU is to facilitate the necessary cultural change within the organization and/or across organizations.

The one office, perhaps ahead of others in embracing the cultural change, is Statistics Canada. They decided to review the legal, technical, and financial frameworks for data sharing. The review helped overcome many cultural constraints and maximize the amount of information which can be shared for statistical purposes in the current conditions. Furthermore, as previously discussed Statistics Canada has developed an enterprise portfolio management program, following the model of customer relationships management programs that are common in the private sector. This is also changing the service attitude from seeing MNEs as objects of mandatory surveys to understanding their strategic importance as stakeholders of the statistical office and enablers of the production of official statistics in high quality. It has introduced a new culture of looking at surveying from the respondents' perspective.

Effective communication is key to overcoming cultural barriers and trust issues. In the United Kingdom,[1] the statistical confidentiality principles have been summarized into what is commonly called the "Five Safes": Safe people; Safe projects; Safe settings; Safe outputs; Safe data. When summarized for the data sharing context, the following conditions of data sharing apply:

- Only recognized statistical authorities and their staff who have been accredited are involved;
- Data will be used exclusively for statistical purposes to deliver high-quality official statistics;
- Data will reside in a secure setting where it is impossible for unauthorized people to access data;
- All statistical outputs are checked and confirmed as non-disclosive; and
- Only the minimum amount of data to fulfil the mandate of statistical authorities is exchanged.

4.4.7 Innovation in Other Industries to Learn From

Important progress has been made by the OECD/G20 Inclusive Framework on base erosion and profit shifting (BEPS), where over 135 countries are collaborating to put an end to tax avoidance strategies that exploit gaps and mismatches in tax rules to avoid paying tax. The BEPS initiative has increased transparency by establishing a new reporting mechanism in the form of a dashboard of BEPS indicators and launching a new BEPS Action 13 on country-by-country reporting among tax authorities. Under this action, jurisdictions commit to requesting the largest MNEs, i.e. MNEs with more than 750 million euros in consolidated revenues to provide the global allocation of their income, taxes and other indicators of the location of economic activity. Information to be compiled by MNEs includes the amount of revenue reported, profit before income tax, income tax paid and accrued, the stated capital, accumulated earnings, number of employees and tangible assets, broken down by jurisdiction. MNEs are required to provide the report annually for each tax jurisdiction in which they do business. Several NSOs have already requested access to the country-by-country reporting data held by their local tax authorities. This may provide an important source of information for validating MNE data within and across EU countries.

---

1 The "Five Safes" – Data Privacy at ONS: blog.ons.gov.uk/2017/01/27/the-five-safes-data-privacy-at-ons/.

According to United Nations Office on Drugs and Crime (UNODC) every year criminals launder some US$1.6 trillion in illicit funds across the globe. Toughening data privacy regulation, like the EU General Data Protection Regulation (GDPR) impose strict limits on the processing and sharing of personal information, which also poses a barrier to authorities' efforts at curbing money laundering. Data sharing is key for pattern spotting. Banks have, therefore, embarked on techniques relying to artificial intelligence and machine learning to help identify and thwart illicit transactions. Banks simply cannot rely on their own data only. It would deny them the full picture of potentially suspicious activities. International data sharing using innovative technologies designed to preserve data privacy is key to combatting money laundering. Leading authorities, like the United Kingdom's Financial Conduct Authority (FCA) have developed new solutions using privacy-enhancing technologies (PETs) to allow such data sharing.

Customs authorities have long engaged in international data sharing to facilitate legitimate border crossing of goods and services by means of secure electronic exchange of information between Customs authorities of other countries. This data exchange is intended to mitigate the many obstacles, costs, and difficulties international transport faces at borders. In view of the large volumes of cross-border transport, Customs authorities cannot control every vehicle or container anymore. Instead, they have had to adjust their business model to engage in risk management and identify high risk consignments by exchanging and analyzing data available through a common Electronic Data Interchange system. This data exchange also enables the analysis of trade flows, and prevention of illegal activities, such as trade misinvoicing, tariff, duty, and revenue offences.

Private businesses are increasingly aware of the value of data and are striving for innovation to utilize data to improve productive and feed economic growth. For instance, some businesses have extended their activities to new areas just to get access to data on consumer behavior. Now companies are discussing how to create a common data market place for data exchange, where the owners of the data, i.e. private people, could provide their data for purposes they select, for instance medical or environmental research, and would get a compensation when their data are used.

References

International Monetary Fund (2009). *Balance of Payments and International Investment Position Manual*, Sixth Edition. https://www.imf.org/external/pubs/ft/bop/2007/pdf/bpm6.pdf.

Koskimäki, T. and Peltola, R. (2020). Sharing data on the activities of multinational enterprise groups: innovations to redesign statistical practices and processes. https://doi.org/10.3233/SJI-200646. *Statistical Journal of the IAOS*, vol. 36, no. 3, pp. 785–796.

Statistics Finland (2019). Globalisation and economic statistics. Working Papers 3/2019. http://www.stat.fi/tup/julkaisut/tiedostot/julkaisuluettelo/ywrp3_201900_2019_21530_net.pdf (accessed 6 September 2019).

Statistics Canada (2016). Compendium of Management Practices for Statistical Organizations from Statistics Canada's International Statistical Fellowship Program. Available at: https://www150.statcan.gc.ca/n1/en/pub/11-634-x/11-634-x2016001-eng.pdf.

United Nations, European Commission, International Monetary Fund, Organisation for Economic Co-operation and Development, and World Bank (1993). *System of National Accounts 2008*. https://unstats.un.org/unsd/nationalaccount/docs/sna2008.pdf. New York: United Nations. https://unstats.un.org/unsd/nationalaccount/docs/1993sna.pdf.

UNECE (2015). Guide to Measuring Global Production. https://unece.org/fileadmin/DAM/stats/publications/2015/Guide_to_Measuring_Global_Production__2015_.pdf (accessed 28 December 2015).

UNECE (2017). Economic Commission for Europe. *Conference of European Statisticians, Group of Experts on National Accounts*, Sixteenth session (31 May–2 June 2017). ECE/CES/GE.20/2017/6. https://unece.org/fileadmin/DAM/stats/documents/ece/ces/ge.20/2017/6_-_EU_Task_Force.pdf (accessed 30 April 2017).

UNECE (2021). *Guide to Sharing Data in Official Statistics*. https://unece.org/statistics/publications/guide-sharing-economic-data-official-statistics (accessed 1 February 2021).

5

Measuring Investment in Intangible Assets

Mojca Bavdaž[1], Ahmed Bounfour[2], Josh Martin[3], Alberto Nonnis[2], Giulio Perani[4], and Tjaša Redek[1]

[1] School of Economics and Business, University of Ljubljana, Ljubljana, Slovenia
[2] RITM & European Chair on Intangibles, Université Paris-Saclay, Sceaux, France
[3] Office for National Statistics, Newport, UK
[4] ISTAT, Rome, Italy

5.1 Introduction

Investment in intangible assets is nowadays recognized as a major source of growth, innovation, and value creation (Corrado et al. 2005; Gu and Lev 2011; Bounfour and Miyagawa 2015; Roth 2020). Over a century ago, Veblen (1908) defined intangible assets as "immaterial items of wealth, immaterial facts owned, valued, and capitalized on an appraisement of the gain to be derived from their possession" (p. 105). The concept developed gradually and appeared in many streams of research. Empirical work by Kendrick, Denison, Jorgenson and others first exposed how a significant share of productivity growth cannot be explained by standard productivity growth elements (tangible capital and labor), but rather with other factors, such as education, skills, R&D, health and know-how (Ducharme 1998). Research on patents or brands and value creation also underlined the contribution of these assets to value creation (Hall et al. 2005; Sandner and Block 2011). At the firm level, the resource-based view (Barney 1991; Wernerfelt 1984) and the dynamic capabilities approach (Bounfour 2003; Teece et al. 1997; Teece 2015) underlined the heterogeneity of firms and the critical role of intangibles for firms' performance. Others highlighted instead their impact in communities, such as nations, regions and cities (Bounfour and Edvinsson 2005).

The methodological and empirical approach to measuring intangible assets and investment was most profoundly marked by Corrado et al. (2005, 2006) building on the work of Nakamura (2001). Intangible assets were classified into computerized information, innovative property and economic competencies (Table 5.1). *Computerized information* reflects knowledge embedded in computer programs and computerized databases, either created by firms for their own use or purchased. *Innovative property* encompasses both "scientific R&D" and "nonscientific R&D". It reflects the scientific knowledge embedded in patents and licenses, non-patented know-how, mining R&D, innovative and artistic content in commercial copyrights, licenses, and designs. *Economic competencies* represent the value of brand names and other knowledge embedded in firm-specific human and structural resources. This conceptualization of intangible assets is nowadays prevalent in economic literature (Corrado et al. 2006). However, further extensions or redefinitions of existing categories may be needed to incorporate the relevant aspects of new

Advances in Business Statistics, Methods and Data Collection. Edited by Ger Snijkers, Mojca Bavdaž, Stefan Bender, Jacqui Jones, Steve MacFeely, Joseph W. Sakshaug, Katherine J. Thompson, and Arnout van Delden.
© 2023 John Wiley & Sons, Inc. Published 2023 by John Wiley & Sons, Inc.

Table 5.1 Intangible assets classification.

Type of intangible asset		SNA introduction
Computerized information	Computer software	SNA 1993
	Computerized databases	SNA 1993[a]
Innovative property	R&D, including social sciences and humanities	SNA 2008
	Mineral exploration and evaluation[b]	SNA 1993
	Entertainment, literary, and artistic originals[c]	SNA 1993
	Development costs	/
	New architectural and engineering designs	/
Economic competencies	Branding	/
	Firm-specific human capital	/
	Organizational structure	/

a) "Large databases" were included as part of software in SNA 1993; databases (regardless of size) introduced as a separate subcategory in SNA 2008 (Ahmad 2004).
b) The term used in SNA 2008 to match the International Accounting Standards. Originally referred to as Mineral exploration in SNA 1993.
c) Originally referred to as Copyright and license costs.
Sources: Corrado et al. (2005, 2006), SNA 1993 (United Nations et al. 1993), and SNA 2008 (United Nations et al. 2009).

technologies (Industry 4.0), population ageing and the impact on competence structure, market power of firms, firm size and global value chains (GVCs) position (Redek et al. 2019).

Concerted international effort to measure intangible investment began with the revision of the System of National Accounts (SNAs) in 1993 (United Nations et al. 1993), when intangible fixed assets (AN.112) were defined as nonfinancial produced fixed assets that mainly consisted of mineral exploration (AN.1121), computer software (AN.1122), and entertainment, literary and artistic originals (AN.1123) intended to be used for more than one year. The SNA revision of 2008 (United Nations et al. 2009) added R&D as another class of intangibles, refined the definition of the others, and renamed intangible fixed assets into intellectual property products. The capitalization of R&D came as a result of growing pressure from the academic community to recognize a wider set of intangibles as assets. Such pressure continues for other types of intangible assets, especially economic competencies, currently treated as intermediate consumption.

The chapter will first review data sources with the emphasis on experience achieved at the international level by surveying businesses' investment in intangible assets (Section 5.2) and the measurement challenges in surveys (Section 5.3). Then, it will highlight the value of intangible assets, with the focus on their contribution to productivity (Section 5.4). The chapter concludes with some guiding principles to be adopted in designing future surveys (Section 5.5) and recommendations for future action (Section 5.6).

5.2 Data Sources on Intangibles

There is so far no standardized approach to measuring intangibles. Nevertheless, many data sources exist that can be useful in (partially) shedding light on intangibles. Several EU projects, e.g. COINVEST, INNODRIVE (www.innodrive.org), SPINTAN (www.spintan.net) and GLOBALINTO (www.globalinto.eu), and research collaborations, e.g. INTAN-Invest (www.intaninvest.net), have used existing macro and industry-level data or developed firm-level microdata. The latest outcome is the GLOBALINTO input–output intangibles database for the EU-28 (Tsakanikas et al. 2020). The main sources for **industry-level data** include the EUKLEMS database, official national accounts data, the use tables from the supply and use framework, Eurostat's BERD (Business Expenditure on Research and Development) data, the OECD's ANBERD (Analytical Business Enterprise Research and Development) database, and results from various surveys (e.g. Community Innovation Survey [CIS]). These sources are freely accessible as the data represent various indicators from official statistics. Additional sources are sometimes used to fill the white spots (e.g. in INNODRIVE, data from FEACO, the European Federation of Management Consultancies Associations). The development of methodology was typically led by exhaustiveness, reproducibility, comparability across countries and time, and consistency with the national accounts' definitions (Corrado et al. 2018).

Firm-level microdata were mainly created by combining available survey data related to intangible investment, but this approach also suffers from problems of approximations (e.g. Piekkola et al. 2011). In very rare cases, firm-level data sources covering a large part of the target population were used for estimating a part of intangible investment (e.g. linked employee-employer datasets (LEED) in Finland, Denmark, Slovenia and Norway as part of the GLOBALINTO project). Access to firm-level microdata is also very restricted, and mainly limited to registered researchers.

Gathering firm-level microdata on intangibles from firms directly through **surveys** should reduce uncertainty stemming from approximations but has its own challenges.

5.2.1 Past Surveys on Intangibles

Several surveys have been used to measure intangibles (Table 5.2). The *Investment in Intangible Assets Survey* (IIA Survey) in the United Kingdom paved the road to measurement of intangible investment at the micro level using a survey as compared to, at that time, prevailing macro-work (Awano et al. 2010). Developed by Imperial College London and the UK National Statistical Institute Office for National Statistics (ONS) as part of the UK NESTA's Innovation Index, it was conducted twice, in 2008/2009 and 2011, and targeted firms in industrial and service sectors with 10 or more employees. Before the IIA Survey, the Isreali National Statistical Institute explored the service lives of R&D (Awano et al. 2010) and the French National Statistical Institute led a pilot survey in 2005 on selected activities related to intangibles, namely marketing, R&D, innovation and intellectual property (Kremp and Tessier 2006).

The IIA Survey was the first to include both purchased intangibles and intangibles developed in-house, it included a broad range of intangible assets, and it attempted to estimate depreciation rates from the expected duration of benefits from different intangibles (Awano et al. 2010; Office for National Statistics and Imperial College London 2016). Based on the UK experience, the INAPP (Italian National Institute for the Analysis of the Public Policies) and the Italian National Statistical Institute (ISTAT) carried out the first full-scale *Statistical Survey on Intangible Investment* (in Italian: *Rilevazione statistica sugli investimenti intangibili*) in 2013, targeting industrial and service firms with 10 or more employees (Angotti 2017).

In academia, a team of researchers led by Prašnikar from the University of Ljubljana, Slovenia, conducted several surveys of intangibles targeting larger firms: the largest manufacturing and service firms in Slovenia with 100 or more employees (in 2010 and 2011 respectively), the largest manufacturing firms in Bosnia and Herzegovina, and firms with 50 or more employees in Albania (in 2012), and public sector firms in Slovenia (in 2015). Also outside of official statistics, the

Table 5.2 Main characteristics of surveys on intangibles.

Survey characteristic	French survey	UK survey	Italian survey	Surveys by University of Ljubljana	Eurobarometer survey	GLOBALINTO survey
Country coverage and time of data collection	France (2005)	UK (2008/2009 and 2011)	Italy (2013)	Slovenia (2010–2011, 2015), Bosnia and Herzegovina (2012), Albania (2012)	27 EU countries, Croatia, Iceland, Japan, Norway, Serbia, Switzerland, Turkey, FYRM, US (2013)	Denmark, Finland, France, Germany, Greece, Slovenia, UK (2020/2021)
Sponsor	French National Institute of Statistics and Economic Studies (INSEE) and relevant ministries	UK National Endowment for Science Technology and the Arts (NESTA)	Italian National Institute for the Analysis of the Public Policies (INAPP). In cooperation with the Italian National Statistical Institute (ISTAT)	Slovenian Research Agency (partly)	European Commission	European Commission
Design and administration	INSEE and Sessi.	Imperial College London and UK National Statistical Institute (ONS)		University of Ljubljana	European Commission, DG Joint Research Centre. Conducted by TNS Opinion and Social	Partners of Horizon 2020 GLOBALINTO project (work led by University of Ljubljana, Slovenia, and NTUA, Greece). Conducted by GDCC
Survey mode	CATI	Postal survey	Mixed mode (principal mode: web survey)	CAPI	CATI	CATI (email used in some cases for recruiting and/or data collection)

Targeted firm size, sector coverage and achieved sample size	Firms (independent units and groups) of all sizes. Industry and Services. N = 7,040, of which 831 groups and the rest are independent units	Firms with 10+ employees. Market economy. IIA 2009: N = 838. IIA 2010: N = 1,180	Firms with 10+ employees. Industry and Services. N = 10,631	Firms with 50+ employees (100+ for Slovenia). Manufacturing (service sector only in Slovenia). *Slovenia 2010: N = 100. BiH 2012: N = 58. Albania 2012: N = 40. Slovenia 2015: N = 177*	Firms with at least one employee. Industry and Services. N = 11,317	Firms with 20+ employees. Industry and knowledge intensive services. N = 1796
Questionnaire structure	46 questions in four sections	28 questions, of which 26 questions on intangibles in six sections	46 questions in six sections	Seven sections with a total close to 50 questions with several items	8 general questions about the firm and 10 questions with several items on intangibles	51 questions, most with several items. 5 general questions about the firm
Core components of intangibles covered (in order of appearance)	– Marketing and advertising communication – Innovation – R&D – Intellectual property assets (brands, copyright, patents design)	– Employer funded training – Software – Reputation and branding – R&D – Design – Organization or business process improvement	– Employer funded training – Software – Reputation and branding – R&D – Design – Organization or business process improvement	– Computerized information – Innovative capital – Economic competencies	– Training – Software development – Company reputation and branding – R&D – Design of products and services – Organization or business process improvement	– R&D – Employer funded training – Organization or business process improvement – Software and databases – Design – Reputation and branding

(Continued)

Table 5.2 (Continued)

Survey characteristic	French survey	UK survey	Italian survey	Surveys by University of Ljubljana	Eurobarometer survey	GLOBALINTO survey
Types of questions on core components of intangibles	For each component: a filter Yes/No question, several questions on objective and effectiveness of investment, and questions on the amount of investment as percentage of turnover	For each component: a filter Yes/No question, a pound amount of investment, separately for internal resources and external providers, and duration in years and months	For each component: a filter Yes/No question, a euro amount of investment, separately for internal resources and external providers, and duration in years and months	For each component, four Yes/No ladder questions, expressing increasing use of the component	For each component: questions asking for investment as percentage of turnover (separately for internal resources and external providers) and asset life, offering predefined value brackets	For each component: a filter Yes/No question, a question asking for investment as percentage of turnover, separately for internal resources and external providers, question on impact of COVID-19
Additional components and aspects covered	– General information (firm characteristics, group, turnover, etc.) – Investment strategy – Perceived effects – IPR policy	/	Mineral exploration Effect of the crisis on intangibles and mitigation of the crisis effect	– Informational capital – Social capital – Relational capital – Eco-capital – Determinants of investments – Firm strategy – Firm characteristics (target markets, value chains, etc.)	– General information (group, employment, establishment, turnover, M&A, percentage structure by market) – Strategy (priorities) – Drivers and barriers (multiple answers) – Impact and Innovation	– General information (activity, group, employment, turnover) – Strategy (priorities, percentage structure by market, competition, FDI) – Human and technological resources – Organizational capabilities – Firm performance – Questions on policy – COVID-19 questions

Source: Adapted and expanded from Redek and Bavdaž (2019).

European Commission commissioned a Eurobarometer study *Investing in intangibles: Economic assets and innovation drivers for growth* conducted in 2013 to investigate the corporate investment in intangible assets (Eurobarometer 2013; Montresor et al. 2014). The survey targeted firms with at least one employee in industrial and service sectors in 27 EU countries and nine other countries. The most recent international survey, part of the GLOBALINTO project, measured corporate investments in intangible assets and their impact on firm performance in firms with at least 20 employees in industry and knowledge intensive service sectors in Denmark, Finland, France, Germany, Greece, Slovenia and the United Kingdom (Bavdaž and Redek 2020; Caloghirou et al. 2021).

5.2.2 Comparison of Past Surveys on Intangibles

The surveys had a few **things in common**: they all covered manufacturing, included at least large firms, and distinguished (at least implicitly) between purchased intangible assets and investment developed within firms. The coverage was the broadest in the French survey and Eurobarometer. The French survey distinguished between independent firms and groups, and asked questions about location of investment and decision-making. Prašnikar and his team followed the three broad types of intangibles proposed by Corrado et al. (2005, 2006; see Table 5.1), but also added: *eco-capital* that addresses corporate social responsibility with regards to the environment, *relationship capital* that builds on the value chain relationships and *social capital* that builds on the relations between in-house stakeholders (workers, owners, managers). Others used subtypes of intangibles that were essentially the same with slight differences in wording (software and databases as Computerized information; R&D and design as Innovative property; branding, training and organizational improvement as Economic competencies) except for the French survey that covered just some subtypes (see Table 5.2).

The surveys **differed** most importantly in what **kind of data they collected about intangible investment**, which is closely linked to the survey mode, length, and topics covered. The self-administered UK and the Italian surveys asked for monetary amounts of expenditure. The French survey, the Eurobarometer and GLOBALINTO surveys (conducted as computer-aided telephone interviews, CATIs) asked for percentages with respect to the business' turnover. The Eurobarometer made the answering easier as the survey offered seven response options (*0%, Less than 1%, 1–5%, 5–15%, 15–25%, 25–50%, More than 50%*). Prašnikar (2010) also offered response options but with much narrower intervals for most of the intangible types. In addition, they relied on a series of three yes–no questions where each further question represented a higher degree of development (cascading or laddering questions as introduced by Miyagawa et al. 2010).

The Eurobarometer does not offer any definitions or explanations. Other surveys offer some definitions, typical examples, costs to be included/excluded etc. Still, it can be claimed that broad definitions and a few examples are hardly sufficient for the multitude of practical situations in which firms make investments. The terminology was often left to the interpretation of the respondent.

The UK, the Italian and the Eurobarometer surveys also asked for the typical asset life as an approximation for depreciation rates; the UK and the Italian surveys sought years and months while Eurobarometer eased the survey task by offering four different time spans ranging from *Less than 2 years* to *More than 10 years*. Prašnikar and the GLOBALINTO survey added questions that shed more light on specific types of intangible investment (e.g. types of design). The largest difference among the surveys concerns questions related to (potentially) relevant business aspects like strategy, motivations, competition, barriers, risks, innovation, expected benefits and impact, impact of policy, and impact of crises (e.g. the Italian survey – the 2008 financial crisis, the GLOBALINTO survey – the COVID-19 pandemic). Such additional questions were present in academic surveys and, to a certain extent, in the French survey and the Eurobarometer, enabling the analysis of determinants and/or impact of intangibles that goes beyond the numerical estimation which is also possible at the macro level.

Although some questionnaires were long, the repetition of the same battery of questions (e.g. for each type of intangible investment) simplified the **response task** as did the use of the same scales or question types throughout the questionnaire. Selecting from a range of response options should also be easier than providing a specific number.

CATI surveys were conducted on the premise that it was possible to answer the questions on the spot, without engaging in time-consuming detailed search for data. **Respondent selection** was thus of utmost importance as the respondent had to be knowledgeable of very diverse areas. For this reason, the GLOBALINTO survey asked for a respondent from the firm's top management, including the financial director, who should be in the position of estimating diverse intangible investments. Even when the mode of data collection allowed firms to prepare the data, firms had difficulties gathering such data. The Eurobarometer asked about data availability and results showed that only 20% of firms reported R&D as intangible assets in their balance sheets, 17% reported software development and 29% reported other categories (training, design, reputation, branding, etc.). Prašnikar (2010) sought several respondents among managers of each business for their field interviews to cover relevant parts of the questionnaire, which ensured higher data quality and also allowed for a longer questionnaire but made the data collection significantly more demanding.

Another important difference comes from very different achieved **sample sizes**. The Italian survey achieved by far the largest sample per country, with more than 10,000 responses, which enabled detailed analysis of subgroups within the target population. The Eurobarometer collected the largest sample overall with more than 11,000 responses though samples for some countries were small. Prašnikar (2010) collected only 100 responses in Slovenia, however, this represented a good coverage of leading firms with a significant contribution to the national economy. Information about the target population and the sampling design is very important to correctly interpret the results. Targeting or oversampling industries or firms that are expected to invest (more) in intangible assets increases the chances of finding relevant firms, but conclusions might not be representative of the whole business population.

5.3 Measurement Challenges in Surveys

Problems in collecting data on intangible assets and intangible investment are a consequence of the characteristics of intangibles (Corrado et al. 2005; Goodridge et al. 2014; Haskel and Westlake 2018).

5.3.1 Intangibles Are Intangible and Mobile

First, intangibles do not have a physical or financial embodiment. As such, they are not as easily counted or physically measured, as tangible assets are. You can count the number of cars, but you cannot weigh software. Especially when intangibles do not exist on asset registers, they may be overlooked. Physical presence may help the business to conceptualize the assets when responding and reduce the risk of omission. As noted in Snijkers et al. (2013), the "awareness" of data is important for respondents to business surveys, and the visibility of a physical asset related to that data will help with awareness. The same is not true of intangibles.

The intangible nature makes intangible assets highly mobile. Consequently, in today's connected world, these assets are easily movable across connected businesses and across borders, which makes them also fit to play a major role in shifting profits across businesses and countries, thus minimizing global tax burden of multinationals (see also the point on pricing in the continuation).

5.3.2 Own-Account Investment Prevails

Second, intangible assets are often created by the business for own use – so called own-account investment, or "output for own final use" in the National Accounting jargon. As the business does not purchase the asset on the market, there is no "transaction" associated with the investment and the data may not be recorded in the business. But a business can only respond effectively when the data actually exists in the business (Bavdaž 2010; Snijkers et al. 2013), and a business will only retain data in order to manage business operations, or because it has to for legal or regulatory reasons. While the value of transactions in purchased assets must be kept for annual financing accounting purposes, the "value of own-account investment" is not required, and so is unlikely to be kept.

Own-account investment is far more common for intangibles. For instance, even if a retail business could choose to build a new retail premise itself, it is much more likely to purchase an existing building or pay a construction company to build one for them. The same usually goes for machinery and equipment and other tangible assets.

While purchased investments – transactions on the market for assets, or services leading to the creation of assets – are also an important source of intangible investments, businesses are much more likely to create such assets themselves. Data from the e-commerce survey (Eurostat 2021) shows that in 2019 20% of enterprises (10+ employees) employ information and communication technology specialists (capable of creating a software asset for use by the business), rising to 75% in large enterprises (250+ employees) – surely much higher than the equivalent figures for builders or machinery makers. Branding assets are readily created by in-house marketing departments, and although there is a significant industry that sells advertising services, Martin (2019) estimates that own-account investment in branding is many multiples of the value of purchased branding investments in the United Kingdom. Indeed, based on existing macro estimates of intangible investment (e.g. Office for National Statistics 2018) almost all types of intangibles are mostly created by the investing business.

As such, the measurement of investment in intangible assets is inherently the measurement of two distinct concepts: the purchase of intangible assets (akin to the purchase of tangible assets), and the creation of intangible assets in-house. Own-account creation of tangible assets is generally an afterthought in business surveys: the Annual Business Survey (ABS) in the United Kingdom asks a single question of businesses covering "the value of work carried out by own staff for business use," which accounts for around 5% of total investment (Martin and Baybutt 2021). While surveys about intangible investment do often make the distinction, the questions are often asked in the same way, asking businesses to simply "state a value" for the total value of the investments. Since that data is unlikely to exist in the business, the response is likely to be at best a rough estimate, and more likely missing.

5.3.3 Pricing of Intangibles Is Difficult

When intangible assets are created within national groups or multinational enterprises, they are often "purchased" at discretionary high prices by the subsidiaries to move profits back to the parent. In a highly digitized world, such a process creates challenges for governments, especially due to revenue location. The high intangibility of Ireland's economy in Europe is often mentioned as an illustrative case (Connolly 2018). More globally, the location of intangibles is to be underlined in relationship to GVC strategies. According to the principle of the smiling curve (Shin et al. 2012), value is located upstream and downstream the value chain, therefore leaving a minor share for the production part. Naturally, such a scheme might be revised due to supply disruptions caused by the COVID-19 pandemic.

5.3.4   In Search of the Most Suitable Respondent for Intangibles

The most suitable respondent in the business for questions on purchased investment and own-account investment may be different. Whittard et al. (2009) concluded from the pilot survey before the 2008/2009 UK survey that different people in the business would be needed to complete different parts: specifically, "R&D managers" (technical staff) are appropriate for the section on "technical R&D" and "finance managers" or "directors" are appropriate for the section on "non-technical R&D". The two UK surveys, and other past surveys following a similar design, allow for this delineation by combining all questions relating to each type of intangible spending into a single section, as described in Section 5.2.2. Hence, distinct parts of the questionnaire could be completed by different individuals or departments within the business, independently of each other (e.g. section on training by a HR representative, section on software by the IT department etc.), though care should be taken to avoid any overlap (e.g. software within R&D, design within software etc.).

While this makes some intuitive sense, it runs counter to the recommendations in Snijkers et al. (2013) to group together questions that require similar data, or from the same respondent. Take the software section: the IT department may be the location of the software professionals who create software in-house, but the purchases of software (through licenses) may be handled by (and, crucially, recorded by) the finance department. Further, the service lives of software might well be answered by the IT department, or a more senior manager with oversight of the business more broadly.

In fact, three different people in the business could be most suitable for the three questions in each section of the UK surveys. As such, the arrangement by asset type may be counterproductive. Following Snijkers et al. (2013), an arrangement by "location of data in the business" might be more fruitful – for instance, grouping all questions on purchased investment together (to be answered by the finance department) and then all staff/time-based questions (to be answered by the HR, or function-specialist departments). A response coordinator would be useful to ensure consistency of reporting.

5.3.5   Investments in Intangibles Take Time

Another important characteristic of intangibles is the pattern of the investment: given that much intangible asset creation is in-house, the creation (and investment) can take multiple periods (quarters or years). The purchase of a machine or building on the market is easily dated as the date on which payment is made, or construction completed, or asset received (depending on the accounting system). By contrast, the iterative creation of a computer program, film or prototype may take many months or even years to complete. The appropriate time to record this may be far less clear for a business. This problem may be even greater when the investment is made as part of normal business processes, as is often the case for branding and organizational capital, for instance. Allocating effort and expense to different accounting periods for such an ongoing process is likely to be extremely challenging for businesses: for instance, a multi-year R&D project may only be assessed/accounted for at the end of the process, so businesses may find annual or sub-annual surveys difficult to respond to. So, while Willeboordse (1997) advises that business surveys should be "specific about the reference frame," that may be ineffective in the case of intangibles, and more leniency might be more effective (in extreme case, allowing the business to choose a relevant timeframe for their reporting).

5.3.6 Data Existence Questioned

One of the properties of intangible assets described in Haskel and Westlake (2018) is "sunkenness". Intangibles can rarely be re-sold, since they are often specific to the business and embodied within the business. The brand or organizational structure of a business cannot easily be sold on, and as such the investments, once made, are sunk costs. This contrasts with tangible assets, where the physical asset itself can often be re-sold or re-purposed. As a result, the recording of intangible assets on company ledgers and balance sheets (or even on internal records) is often poor. While international business accounting standards require a careful account of tangible assets, intangibles are rarely included. The inability to re-sell many intangibles, and the lack of a requirement to record them in public accounts, leaves businesses with limited incentive to record their values.

In sum, the salient characteristics of intangible investment for business survey collection are:

- They cannot be counted or similarly measured in a physical sense, such that they may be overlooked, and businesses may find it difficult to conceptualize them.
- They are often the result of "own-account investment" which means there is no transaction associated with the investment, which may further lead to the assets being overlooked. The likelihood of data being held on own-account investment is far lower than for "purchased investment," and the approach to collecting data might therefore need to be different. "Purchased" intangibles might suffer from bias in transfer prices if sold within multinational enterprises or groups.
- Own-account investments in intangibles may take place over multiple periods, or iteratively over many periods. As such, the allocation of an investment to an accounting period may be more challenging than for purchased investments.
- Since most intangibles are not recognized in business accounting rules, and since they cannot readily be re-sold, businesses may not capture information on these assets.

5.3.7 Evidence of Inconsistent Respondent Behavior

Using survey data on intangible investments from the United Kingdom, Martin and Baybutt (2021) test the degree to which these characteristics manifest themselves in the business responses. As well as the two UK IIA surveys (see Section 5.2.1), some elements of intangible investment are also captured in the United Kingdom Innovation Survey (UKIS) (the UK implementation of the CIS), the official quarterly capital investment survey in the UK (QCAS), the UK ABS, and the business R&D survey (BERD).

Awano et al. (2010) linked IIA (data for 2008) with UKIS from 2007 (data for 2006), and found a large degree of discrepancy – less than half of the matched sample ($n = 81$) consistently reported positive spending on each intangible investment category across the surveys. They note that this could partially be due to the non-contemporaneous nature of the match, so Martin and Baybutt (2021) updates this to compare data for 2008 and 2010 from both sources. This results in a larger number of matches, but a similar level of disagreement, as shown in Table 5.3. Note that while

Table 5.3 Inconsistency between responses to UK Investment in Intangible Asset surveys (IIA 2009 and IIA 2010) and the UK Innovation Survey (UKIS 2009 and UKIS 2011).

	Proportion inconsistent	
	IIA 2009 – UKIS 2009 $n = 126$ (%)	IIA 2010 – UKIS 2011 $n = 1042$ (%)
R&D	29	8
Branding	36	14
Training	59	21
Business process improvement	25	7
Design	18	10

Notes: The assets compared differ to those in Awano et al. (2010) following a review of the differences in question wording between the UK Innovation Survey and the Investment in Intangible Asset surveys.
Source: Adapted from Martin and Baybutt (2021).

consistency appears higher for 2010 data, this is entirely due to a far larger number of agreements on the lack of investment – considering only businesses that responded positively to either of the surveys, the inconsistency rate is far higher, and in line with the previous comparison.

Inconsistency is generally a little lower for R&D than for the other intangible assets, perhaps because R&D is an established concept and data is more often retained by businesses. Inconsistency on training is highest, likely due to confusion as to which training costs to include, especially staff costs and on-the-job training. Consistency is generally higher between surveys for tangible assets than for intangible assets, although even in this case there are still frequent examples of disagreement. Similar findings come from other comparisons, e.g. about own-account software investment on QCAS versus ABS in 2015 and 2016 (see Martin and Baybutt 2021, for a full account).

5.3.8 Summarizing the Challenges in Intangible Surveys: The 4 "F" Words

The challenges of collecting data from businesses on intangibles investment can be characterized by four "F words" (Martin and Baybutt 2021):

- *Fuzzy*: Definitions of different intangible assets vary from researcher to researcher and can often overlap or be unclear. While assets included in the National Accounts have precise definitions, those measured outside the boundary do not. These terms, for businesses and researchers, are *fuzzy*. Whittard et al. (2009) report that interviewees required precise definitions to be able to respond effectively.
- *Forgotten*: Data on intangibles are difficult to collect from businesses, as business accounting poses high hurdles for these assets to be recorded – as a result, businesses rarely have the information available to respond to business surveys. Businesses often appear to give "inconsistent responses" to survey questions – most starkly, *forgetting* whether they did any investment in a particular asset or not between surveys.
- *Framing*: Surveys about intangibles are often carried out under the auspices of a research project, or through surveys about "innovation," rather than standard "official statistics" surveys by National Statistical Institutes. The question wording and context can be leading businesses to respond in an unusual way, so *framing* of questions may be key to understanding responses.
- *Frequency*: In the case of intangibles, especially the common own-account investment in intangibles, the production process can be gradual over many periods. Asking business to provide

investments in any given period can thus cause problems, and evidence shows greater discrepancy between quarterly and annual returns for intangibles than for tangibles. The *frequency* of surveys could therefore be key.

5.4 Intangibles and the Productivity Puzzle

Despite the progress in value recognition of intangibles (Thum-Thysen et al. 2017), measurement issues and data availability are still an open issue on the agenda. We still need data to understand the productivity puzzle – how intangibles contribute individually or jointly to innovation and productivity growth; and evaluate the growing impact of organizational design – including globalization, platforms and digital transformation.

5.4.1 Analytical Considerations

An important consideration when analyzing intangibles is their **complementarity**. Since intangibles are heterogeneous and combinatory in nature, they should be analyzed jointly rather than separately (Athey and Roberts 2001; Milgrom and Roberts 1995; Roberts 2004). For intellectual property rights, the discussion has focused on firm practices and their related impact on firms' performance (Guo-Fitoussi et al. 2019). Several authors also analyzed the complementarities of intangible types. Crass and Peters (2014) examined complementarity between innovative capital, human capital, branding capital and organizational capital. Their results are mixed: while the introduction of organizational innovation enhances productivity, modification of workplace practices slows it. Others analyzed the complementarity between IT, organizational processes and new products and services (Bresnahan et al. 2002) or between process innovation and product innovation (Martínez-Ros and Labeaga 2009), and ICT, organizational capital and other intangibles (Brynjolfsson et al. 2002; Corrado et al. 2012). Understanding the complementarities between intangibles is an interesting perspective to embrace further, for understanding innovation growth and productivity (Bounfour and Miyagawa 2015; Delbecque et al. 2015).

Another important consideration when analyzing intangibles is the **impact of digital transformation** on productivity due to the ubiquity of digital technology. Understanding this impact is a key issue for research and policy making. Brynjolfsson et al. (2021) underlined that the "standard" measure of total factor productivity growth (without accounting for intangibles) is low during the boom of investment in IT and digital, as the installed capital prepares for the next productivity growth, hence the productivity growth in the form of a 'J'-curve. For Japan, Miyagawa et al. (2020) observed low productivity growth in the late 1990s and high productivity growth in the 2010s, while capital formation was larger in the 1990s than in the 2010s. Based on their analysis, the "revised" total factor productivity growth rate (accounting for intangibles) from 1995 to 2017 is higher than the standard one. So the lag in productivity growth, due to digital, is an important aspect that can explain at least partially the productivity slowdown experienced by many economies in recent times.

5.4.2 Role of Global Value Chains

Intangibles play an important role in value creation in GVCs, and these sophisticated business models can be seen as partly the result of organizational capital investment. As both GVC and intangibles enhance productivity, it is interesting to explore further the mechanism that link them to productivity. Few papers consider the contribution of intangibles and participation into GVCs

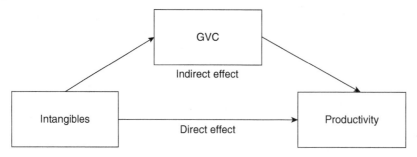

Figure 5.1 Potential links between GVCs, intangibles and productivity. Source: Bounfour et al. (2019).

jointly (Jona-Lasinio et al. 2016). To highlight the complexity of the issue, we use some of our econometric results based on network centrality measures calculated from World Input–Output Database (WIOD) (Timmer et al. 2015) to proxy for GVC participation levels, while estimation of intangible investment is from the INTAN-Invest database (Corrado et al. 2016). Additionally, the EUKLEMS database is used for production factors (labor and mainly tangible capital stock). Using industry level data, a comprehensive dataset consisting of 17 countries and 16 sectors observed for the period 2000–2014 is considered (Nonnis et al. 2021).

Following Baron and Kenny (1986), a mediating effect of GVC is hypothesized between intangibles and productivity (Figure 5.1): both intangibles and GVC are expected to enhance productivity directly, but intangibles also favor GVC participation. Therefore, intangibles enhance productivity also through a second channel. The indirect effect is expressed as the product of the intangible effect on GVC and the GVC effect on total factor productivity.

GVC participation is measured using network scores. Three measures are identified: *strength centrality*, calculated as the sum of all transactions involving a node; *eigenvalue centrality score*, calculated by counting the number of ties that a node has with others and *betweenness centrality*, which measures each node's importance in linking other nodes (Brandes 2001; Freeman 1978). Details about the econometric estimation are provided in (Nonnis et al. 2021).

When studying direct effects, results show that all considered intangible types (R&D, software and databases, design, branding and organizational capital) have positive and significant effects on total factor productivity, and so do the first two GVC participation proxies used, node strength centrality and eigenvalue centrality. Instead, betweenness centrality does not have a significant effect on total factor productivity. Therefore, our results suggest that GVC enhances productivity, but the mere role as bridges for other industries is not relevant in this sense.

The mediating effect of GVC participation through which intangibles impact productivity is analyzed by the multilevel data technique of Krull and MacKinnon (2001). An econometric evaluation of the system of simultaneous equations showed that for all cases except organizational capital, evidence is found for the mediating effect of GVC integration (see Table 5.4). The indirect effect of brand and design accounts for around 60% of the total effect on total factor productivity, R&D for 45%, while software and computers only about 16% of the total effect on total factor productivity. The indirect effect is bigger than the direct effect for brand and design, both indirect and direct effects are close for R&D, while the indirect effect is smaller for software and nonsignificant for organizational capital.

Therefore, besides the well-known direct effect on productivity, results highlight another mechanism with a second-round effect through which intangibles enhance productivity: the indirect effect arises because intangibles encourage GVC participation, that in turn improves production efficiency.

Table 5.4 Mediation analysis results.

	(1) R&D	**(2) Software**	**(3) Design**	**(4) Org. capital**	**(5) Brand**
Indirect effect	0.0332***	0.0161**	0.0501***	−0.00113	0.0527***
	(0.00406)	(0.00532)	(0.00419)	(0.00613)	(0.00626)
Direct effect	0.0406***	0.0839***	0.0339***	0.113***	0.0290**
	(0.00547)	(0.00652)	(0.00545)	(0.00787)	(0.00908)
Total effect	0.0737***	0.0999***	0.0839***	0.112***	0.0817***
	(0.00356)	(0.00371)	(0.00402)	(0.00435)	(0.00464)
Proportion total effect mediated	0.4504	0.1612	0.5971	—	0.6450
Observations	2385	2633	2606	2680	2666

Note: Bootstrapped standard errors in parentheses.
$*p < 0.05$, $**p < 0.01$, $***p < 0.001$.
Source: Bounfour et al. (2019).

5.5 Collecting Data on Intangibles: The Way Ahead

A decade is not a long time from the perspective of official statistics. As an example, a flagship of EU business surveys like the CIS was developed during the 1980s, first launched in 1992 and continues to change frequency and coverage even after its inclusion in an EU statistical law in 2004 (Perani 2021a). Better linkages could be established between existing surveys on innovation, R&D and ICT, and data collection for structural business statistics. Further evolution of surveying on intangibles could be seen under two complementary perspectives: (i) continuous methodological improvement of the current approach to intangible asset measurement (see the review of past surveys in Section 5.2.1); (ii) serving current and identifying potential additional needs, methods and data uses even beyond the realm of official statistics. Regardless of the evolutionary path, ensuring data availability will be the key ingredient for its success.

5.5.1 Methodological Improvements

Good measurement starts with clear *conceptual definitions*. The concept of intangibles continues to evolve, which makes its operationalization an uneasy task. Similarly demanding concepts such as R&D and innovation solved this first step through the development of international manuals (Frascati and Oslo, respectively) that now inform questionnaire design.

Questionnaire design should support the response process at the organizational level to assign the task to (most) knowledgeable respondent(s), as well as at the individual level to help individual cognitive processes (Bavdaž 2010; Willimack and Nichols 2010). Such support is not easy to design because of the spread of relevant information across the business (Lorenc 2006; Snijkers et al. 2013). Two solutions are to organize survey questions: (i) by type of questions (e.g. put all financial questions together) or (ii) by type of intangible asset (e.g. put together all questions on design together, e.g. on the types of design used, the financial amount invested, the financial amount of internal resources used, and its strategic value). Far greater guidance could be given on both the best respondent for each question and on relations between questions. Visual aids like color coding could be used to indicate the likely location of the necessary data within the business.

The identification of the best respondent for each question would require further research, but could draw from Whittard et al. (2009) and other similar studies. It is important to have this vary by industry and/or size band, since the appropriate person may vary across those dimensions (as highlighted in Snijkers et al. 2013).

Another important aspect is how to design specific *survey questions*. As the types of intangible assets might appear vague and/or prone to misinterpretation, the comprehension processes could be supported by transforming the key elements of definitions in several survey questions (Haraldsen 2013), which would increase the number of questions but is also expected to improve data quality. Even when a respondent correctly understands what is being asked (e.g. about own-account investment), the relevant figures are likely to have never existed in the business and would require a large computational effort from the respondent to estimate. Instead, breaking the request into "manageable data chunks" (Snijkers et al. 2013) may improve the response outcome, e.g. from a rough estimate to a good estimate (Bavdaž 2010), which again adds to the number of questions for improved data quality. A respondent may be much more able to report the number of software developers, the fraction of their working time spent developing new software assets for internal use, and any direct non-labor costs associated with that activity, than estimate (through a complex sum-of-costs method) the sum of own-account investment in software. In the end, the key questions to answer are: how much accuracy is needed and who (businesses with their knowledge and data, or the National Statistical Institute with alternative sources and computational knowledge) is in a better position to provide it, considering also the cost.

Additional issues to be tackled include the *target population and the unit of observation*. A legal unit can be the easiest to delineate in practice and typically holds a lot of data for legal or regulatory reasons, but in today's connected world is rarely sufficiently autonomous to be treated as an independent unit. An enterprise (in the European Statistical System as defined by Council Regulation 696/93) has autonomy in decision-making, especially for the allocation of its current resources, but may consist of several legal units, which complicates data collection and record linkage. The CIS, for instance, uses the enterprise as the unit of observation. However, businesses go beyond the national borders and may undertake activities at the global level. The choice of the unit of observation may have an impact on the distinction between own-account and purchased intangibles (e.g. if purchased from a dependent legal unit), the size of IA investment (e.g. transfer prices might inflate/deflate purchases of IA between dependent legal units) and conclusions we can draw from productivity and innovation studies (e.g. when decisions about IA investment are made globally the links between determinants and IA investment at the level of a legal unit might not be causal).

5.5.2 Data Needs Today and Tomorrow

The current approach to IA measurement stems directly from the SNA theoretical framework. In the future, a specific target group of users should be identified who could support development of IA surveys by making available the resources needed and providing useful feedback for their quality improvement. Thus, it will be essential to focus on (i) who the key users of IA surveys will be; (ii) what output they could expect from IA surveys; (iii) why they should have a preference for IA surveys compared to other data sources; and (iv) when such a process could be finalized.

5.5.2.1 Current and Potential Users

Ideally, the *main users* of IA survey data should be the national accountants who could use them as a key source for calculation of capital investment (without excluding the option to keep relying on a combination of statistical and administrative sources). So far, the leading users of IA surveys data have been macroeconomists, mostly those dealing with growth accounting. Microeconomists could be increasingly interested in exploiting the potential of IA survey data to shed light on firms' strategies and innovation practices (e.g. Riley and Bondibene 2018). Policymakers, on the other hand, need processed and interpreted information for policy use. Involving further groups of users (businesses and their associations, consulting services, etc.) would be relevant, but hard to achieve.

Given the importance of regional policy at subnational levels, it is worth mentioning recent efforts toward modeling the impact of intangibles on regional growth and innovation in Europe (Beliaeva et al. 2021), and disseminating data and related indices around the Intan-Reg database by the European chair on intangibles (www.chairedelimmateriel.universite-paris-saclay.fr).

5.5.2.2 A (Single) IA Survey or a Bundle of Data Sources?

The leading users of IA surveys have also heavily relied on various separate sources. When deciding about the best *data sourcing strategy*, the main issue is whether to integrate existing sources or replace them with a single source. The key comparative value of a single source is generated in their production process. Metadata and paradata created in the production process can provide users with detailed information about the conceptual background of IA surveys and, more importantly, about the response process. Asking questions with a single instrument also increases the chances of collecting consistent data about the observed unit. This leads to less cleaning, checking and cross-validation, which is a clear advantage for data users: both when using data as inputs of statistical data processing and empirical evidence to test economic models.

The flexibility of IA surveys, i.e. the possibility to broaden or focus their scope (especially, IA investments surveys) according to the needs of users, is an important feature that could facilitate its integration in the existing statistical systems. Such integration would start with testing (first pilot, then full scale), continue with increasingly challenging tests of robustness of the results (i.e. comparative tests with other data sources for statistical production or econometric modelling) and close with a regular data production in a selected number of countries adopting the same survey model. Based on past experiences with large business surveys, to achieve such a standard of adoption could take at least a further decade.

Many other data sources can also be useful, either as a replacement of some survey items or as a complement to the survey. In this latter case, these sources could be used for sample selection or quality assurance, as well as for analysis. Variables might include R&D tax relief or costs offsetting tax liabilities, subsidies for R&D, ICT or training, registered patents and copyrights, etc.

5.5.2.3 A Parallel Development Path: Assessing Intangible Asset Stocks

The measurement of intangible assets at enterprise level was mostly a business for management consultants and accountants (Cohen 2011). The most used concept was that of *intellectual capital*, as a component of the overall value of an enterprise, and for its measurement several methods and schemes were developed (for reviews, see Radjenović and Krstić 2017, and Jurczak 2008) but the issue of properly quantifying the value of a business (including the stock of both tangible and intangible assets) has not yet been settled.

Current IA surveys mostly focus on intangible investments, that is IA flows. An option to make IA surveys more attractive for users and easier to answer for businesses is that of broadening their scope by also incorporating *qualitative questions* of nominal or ordinal nature that address additional IA-related and relevant aspects, e.g. assets produced internally, stock of intangible assets, business strategy, motivation, barriers, impact etc.

These aspects would first need conceptualization. So far, economic theory has focused on the macroeconomic effects of IA investments and growth accounting, and less on the IA investments at firm level and their contribution to firm growth. Marr and Spender (2004) and Marzo (2011) offer a review within evolutionary economics, Molloy et al. (2011) suggest an approach to measurement inspired by the resource-based theory. The approach used by management professionals is that of running an "expert survey", i.e. an internal audit (de Homont and Voegele 2016) but this approach is not applicable in statistical surveys. A growing literature is arguing that regular reporting of IA investments and related asset evaluation could, or even should, become a standard practice in businesses. A primary need is that of improving firms' self-awareness of the potential, and value, of their own assets but the disclosure of such information could generate benefits to both the firm and the economic system (National Research Council 2009; Kang and Gray 2011; Castilla-Polo and Gallardo-Vázquez 2016).

A diffused practice of "voluntary disclosure" of IA-related information and data is a condition to allow for the development of a self-administered IA statistical survey. One option could be to calculate, for a sample of enterprises, a ROI of intangible assets similarly as for tangible ones (Murray 2012) and to use the results for estimating the value of the IA stock in a whole industry or industrial system while considering heterogeneity by industry and size.

A pilot exercise was undertaken by the Italian Statistical Systems (as a joint venture between the Italian Statistical Institute and the National Institute for Public Policy analysis) with the testing of a mix of quantitative and qualitative questions (Perani 2021b). The new qualitative module is aimed at collecting information on the firms' organization, their internal processes, and their performances with reference to a range of nonfinancial goals: from environmental concerns to industrial relations, and scientific and technical achievements.

5.6 Conclusion

To give IA surveys (essentially those collecting investments data) a relevant role in official statistics, some recommendations about the actions to be implemented can be given as follows.

- Develop an *international manual on intangibles* that would harmonize existing concepts and their operationalization so as to collect relevant information and make IA statistics comparable internationally, in time and with other domains. More effort is needed for conceptually defining those IA components that have not yet become part of National Accounting, e.g. organizational capital. Operationalization also calls for a systematic inquiry into business data availability that then feeds into questionnaire design. Primarily, further research should shed more light on what business data constitutes the best basis for distinguishing between current and investment costs, and asset lives to better estimate own-account IA production and its impact.
- Develop *questionnaire design* further by incorporating the latest methodological recommendations (see also Chapter 15 by Haraldsen (2023)), e.g. question structure that supports the response process in the business, terminology that is familiar to businesses, questions that support cognitive processes especially in the absence of readily available data and any other action aimed at ensuring a high level of consistency between the conceptual background and the survey's methodology (the core value of IA surveys).
- Ensure the use of relevant *units of observation* while considering characteristics of business networks (especially ownership and decision-making structures) and purposes of IA statistics. Different solutions might be needed when preparing national versus global statistics. National

Statistical Institutes have access to good sampling frames, possess know-how in profiling of complex businesses at national level and increasingly collaborate on profiling at international level.

- Focus on *user needs* by monitoring current and potential users and uses. The key strategy is that of understanding current demand – mostly, by extending the cooperation between producers and users, as it is common in official statistics. Such cooperation may also be internal to official statistics with Business Statistics as producers and National Accounting as users. Data for National Accounts needs to be high-quality, timely and frequent, and fully capture the relevant concepts (once they have been precisely defined), cover all parts of the economy, and align to appropriate national accounting principles, such as economic ownership. This is a high bar, and as such the requirements for National Accountants are somewhat circular. Without good quality data, and near-readiness for more intangible assets to be incorporated into the National Accounting frameworks, practitioners likely will not be interested in the topic. But without a requirement to include intangibles in the National Accounts, they might not have an interest in investing in developing the data. Pressure from economists to explore this topic, especially those interested in productivity, the digital economy, and GVCs will likely continue to drive the work.
- Furthermore, the aim is to *generate new demand* by identifying and testing original analytical models (and matching with other data sources). Several studies of growth accounting could be replicated by dramatically reducing the number of data sources used (Gil and Haskel 2008; Giovannetti and Piga 2014; Baldwin et al. 2012; Crass et al. 2015).
- Encourage businesses to *monitor investment in intangible assets* and disclose more information about it to ensure better data availability for both management and statistical purposes, and strive for a *change in the corporate accounting rules* (Lev 2018, 2019). Marked progress can only be made if the corporate accounting rules are changed along two complementary lines: (i) the structure of income statements is changed so as to allow the identification and measurement of the fundamental and non-ambiguous intangibles (e.g. R&D, software, data, training, advertising); (ii) these intangibles can be more broadly capitalized so as to allow firms, especially organic growth ones, to build assets and to finance them from external sources. By so doing, intangibles would have a better chance to be leveraged as collateral.

Inclusion of intangibles measurement in official statistics in Europe or other developed countries would likely be beneficial to the rest of the world as it would set a benchmark for others. Currently, studies of intangibles are conducted *ad hoc*, infrequently and at irregular intervals even in countries that have researchers pursuing this economic topic and data that allows estimation of intangibles (e.g. data from innovation surveys, registers of employees with occupations and employers, or other combinations of data sources). Given that the SNA 1993 already required inclusion of mineral exploration, computer software, and entertainment, literary or artistic originals, and the SNA 2008 added R&D, countries around the world should be able to offer at least some aggregate estimates on these categories. However, this is a very limited perspective on intangibles themselves, not to mention the limitations on productivity analysis.

In sum, to systematically capture a holistic view of intangibles, more than just sporadic research initiatives are needed as open questions and challenges are numerous and would be best addressed with a concerted effort. A markedly improved measurement of intangibles can only happen if concept definitions become clearly defined, preferably as a new international standard, and more relevant data becomes available at the business level, preferably in response to adjusted accounting rules.

Acknowledgment

The views expressed in this chapter are those of the authors and do not necessarily reflect the policies of their employers. The authors would like to thank Peter van de Ven (OECD) and Sanjiv Mahajan (Office for National Statistics) for excellent discussions in the ICES-VI session that was the basis for this chapter as well as to session participants. A special thanks to Steve MacFeely (previously UNCTAD, now WHO) for reviewing earlier versions and for chairing the session. Some parts of the text are based on research project GLOBALINTO that received funding from the European Union's Horizon 2020 under grant agreement No 822259.

References

Ahmad, N. (2004). The measurement of databases in the national accounts. https://unstats.un.org/UNSD/nationalaccount/aeg/papers/m2databases.PDF (accessed 11 January 2021).

Angotti, R. (2017). Intangible asset survey: i risultati della Rilevazione statistica sugli investimenti intangibili delle imprese. INAPP Report 3.

Athey, S. and Roberts, J. (2001). Organizational design: decision rights and incentive contracts. *American Economic Review* 91 (2): 200–205.

Awano, G., Franklin, M., Haskel, J., and Kastrinaki, Z. (2010). Measuring investment in intangible assets in the UK: results from a new survey. *Economic & Labour Market Review* 4 (7): 66–71. https://doi.org/10.1057/elmr.2010.98.

Baldwin, J.R., Gu, W., and Macdonald, R. (2012). Intangible capital and productivity growth in Canada. *The Canadian Productivity Review* 29: 1–44.

Barney, J. (1991). Firm resources and sustained competitive advantage. *Journal of Management* 17: 99–120.

Baron, R.M. and Kenny, D.A. (1986). The moderator–mediator variable distinction in social psychological research: conceptual, strategic, and statistical considerations. *Journal of Personality and Social Psychology* 51 (6): 1173.

Bavdaž, M. (2010). The multidimensional integral business survey response model. *Survey Methodology* 36 (1): 81–93.

Bavdaž, M. and Redek, T. (2020). *Set-up of subcontracted survey – monitoring and assessment for quality control* [H2020 GLOBALINTO WP4]. Ljubljana: School of Economics and Business, University of Ljubljana. https://globalinto.eu/wp-content/uploads/2020/03/D-4_2-Set-up-of-subcontracted-survey-and-quality_FINAL_corrected-status.pdf.

Beliaeva, T., Bounfour, A., and Nonnis, A. (2021). Modelling intangibles at the regional level in Europe: what lessons from a multidimensional approach? *Knowledge Management Research & Practice*, https://doi.org/10.1080/14778238.2021.1941359 1–14.

Bounfour, A. (2003). *The Management of Intangibles: The Organisation's Most Valuable Assets. Routledge Advances in Management and Business Studies*. London, New York: Routledge.

Bounfour, A. and Edvinsson, L. (2005). A public policy perspective on intellectual capital. In: *Perspectives on Intellectual Capital* (ed. B. Marr), 170–182. London, New York: Rutledge.

Bounfour, A. and Miyagawa, T. (ed.) (2015). *Intangibles, Market Failure and Innovation Performance*. Cham: Springer.

Bounfour, A., Nonnis, A., Ozaygen, A., Kim, K., and Beliaeva, T. (2019). *The Productivity Contribution of Intangible Assets and Participation in Global Value Chains* . [H2020 GLOBALINTO WP2]. Paris:

Université Paris-Saclay. https://globalinto.eu/wp-content/uploads/2020/03/GLOBALINTO_D_2_2
.pdf.

Brandes, U. (2001). A faster algorithm for betweenness centrality. *Journal of Mathematical Sociology* 25
(2): 163–177.

Bresnahan, T.F., Brynjolfsson, E., and Hitt, L.M. (2002). Information technology, workplace
organization, and the demand for skilled labor: firm-level evidence. *The Quarterly Journal of
Economics* 117 (1): 339–376.

Brynjolfsson, E., Hitt, L.M., and Yang, S. (2002). Intangible assets: computers and organizational
capital. *Brookings Papers on Economic Activity* 2002 (1): 137–181.

Brynjolfsson, E., Rock, D., and Syverson, C. (2021). The productivity J-curve: how intangibles
complement general purpose technologies. *American Economic Journal: Macroeconomics* 13 (1):
333–372.

Caloghirou, Y., Protogerou, A., Panagiotopoulos, P., and Tsakanikas, A. (2021). *Final report describing
the survey results and methodology* [H2020 GLOBALINTO WP4]. Athens: National Technical
University of Athens (NTUA), Laboratory of Industrial and Energy Economics (LIEE). https://
globalinto.eu/wp-content/uploads/2022/02/D4.4_Globalinto-Survey-Report_Final.pdf.

Castilla-Polo, F. and Gallardo-Vázquez, D. (2016). The main topics of research on disclosures of
intangible assets: a critical review. *Accounting, Auditing & Accountability Journal* 29 (2): 323–356.

Cohen, J.A. (2011). *Intangible Assets: Valuation and Economic Benefit*. Hoboken: Wiley.

Connolly, M. (2018). The expected and unexpected consequences of ESA 2010 - an Irish perspective.
Journal of the Statistical and Social Inquiry Society of Ireland 47 (2017–2018): 39–70.

Corrado, C., Haskel, J., Iommi, M., Jona-Lasinio, C., Mas, M., and O'Mahony, M. (2018).
Advancements in measuring intangibles for European economies. *EURONA* 2017 (2): 89–106.

Corrado, C., Haskel, J., and Jona-Lasinio, C. (2016). Intangibles, ICT and industry productivity growth:
evidence from the EU. In: *The World Economy* (ed. D.W. Jorgenson, K. Fukao and M.P. Timmer),
319–346. Cambridge: Cambridge University Press.

Corrado, C., Haskel, J., Jona-Lasinio, C., and Iommi, M. (2012). Intangible capital and growth in
advanced economies: measurement methods and comparative results. No. 6733. IZA Discussion
Papers, 2012.

Corrado, C., Hulten, C., and Sichel, D. (2005). Measuring capital and technology: an expanded
framework. In: *Measuring Capital in the New Economy*, Studies in Income and Wealth, vol. 65
(ed. C. Corrado, J. Haltiwanger and D. Sichel), 11–46. Chicago: The University of Chicago Press.

Corrado, C., Hulten, C., and Sichel, D. (2006). *Intangible Capital and Economic Growth* (No. 2006–24).
https://www.federalreserve.gov/pubs/feds/2006/200624/200624pap.pdf (accessed 1 August 2019).

EUR-Lex (1993). Council Regulation (EEC) No 696/93 of 15 March 1993 on the statistical units for the
observation and analysis of the production system in the Community OJ L 76, 30.3.1993, 1–11.

Crass, D., Licht, G., and Peters, B. (2015). Intangible assets and investments at the sector level:
empirical evidence for Germany. In: *Intangibles, Market Failure and Innovation Performance*
(ed. A. Bounfour and T. Miyagawa), 57–111. Cham: Springer.

Crass, D. and Peters, B. (2014). Intangible assets and firm-level productivity. ZEW Discussion Papers 14.

de Homont, P. and Voegele, A. (2016). Separating intangible value by surveys. *International Tax Review*,
31 August 2016.

Delbecque, V., Bounfour, A., and Barreneche, A. (2015). Intangibles and value creation at the industrial
level: delineating their complementarities. In: *Intangibles, Market Failure and Innovation
Performance* (ed. A. Bounfour and T. Miyagawa), 27–56. Cham: Springer.

Ducharme, L.-M. (1998). *Measuring Intangible Investment Introduction: Main Theories and Concepts*.
OECD. https://www.oecd.org/sti/ind/1943178.pdf.

Eurobarometer (2013). Flash Eurobarometer 369: investing in intangibles: economic assets and innovation drivers for growth. https://europa.eu/eurobarometer/api/deliverable/download/file?deliverableId=43738 (accessed 5 June 2021).

Eurostat (2021). Enterprises that employ ICT specialists (isoc_ske_itspen2). Eurostat data explorer. https://appsso.eurostat.ec.europa.eu/nui/show.do?dataset=isoc_ske_itspen2 (accessed 5 October 2021).

Freeman, L.C. (1978). Centrality in social networks conceptual clarification. *Social Networks* 1 (3): 215–239.

Goodridge, P., Haskel, J., and Wallis, G. (2014). Estimating UK investment in intangible assets and Intellectual Property Rights, Intellectual Property Office Report 2014/36. https://assets.publishing.service.gov.uk/government/uploads/system/uploads/attachment_data/file/561709/Estimating-UK-Investment-intangible-assets-IP-Rights.pdf (accessed 3 September 2021).

Gil, V. and Haskel, J. (2008). Industry-level expenditure on intangible assets in the UK. http://citeseerx.ist.psu.edu/viewdoc/download?doi=10.1.1.467.9444&rep=rep1&type=pdf (accessed 20 August 2021).

Giovannetti, E. and Piga, C.A. (2014). Private and external benefits from investment in intangible assets. BIS Research Paper 203. https://doi.org/10.2139/ssrn.2548913.

Gu, F. and Lev, B. (2011). Intangible assets: measurement, drivers, and usefulness. In: *Managing Knowledge Assets and Business Value Creation in Organizations: Measures and Dynamics* (ed. G. Schiuma), 110–124. IGI Global.

Guo-Fitoussi, L., Bounfour, A., and Rekik, S. (2019). Intellectual property rights, complementarity and the firm's economic performance. *International Journal of Intellectual Property Management* 9 (2): 136–165.

Hall, B.H., Jaffe, A., and Trajtenberg, M. (2005). Market value and patent citations. *RAND Journal of Economics* 36 (1): 16–38.

Haraldsen, G. (2013). Questionnaire communication in business surveys. In: *Designing and Conducting Business Surveys* (ed. G. Snijkers, G. Haraldsen, J. Jones and D. Willimack), 303–357. Hoboken: Wiley.

Haraldsen, G. (2023). What computerized business questionnaires and questionnaire management tools can offer. In: *Advances in Business Statistics, Methods and Data Collection* (ed. G. Snijkers, M. Bavdaž, S. Bender, J. Jones, S. MacFeely, J.W. Sakshaug, K.J. Thompson, and A. van Delden) Chapter 15. Hoboken: Wiley.

Haskel, J. and Westlake, S. (2018). *Capitalism Without Capital: The Rise of the Intangible Economy*. Princeton University Press.

Jona-Lasinio, C.S., Manzocchi, S., and Meliciani, V. (2016). Intangible assets and participation in global value chains: an analysis on a sample of European countries. *Rivista di Politica Economica* 7 (9): 65–95.

Jurczak, J. (2008). Intellectual capital measurement methods. *Economics and Organization of Enterprise* 1 (1): 37–45.

Kang, H.H. and Gray, S.J. (2011). Reporting intangible assets: voluntary disclosure practices of top emerging market companies. *The International Journal of Accounting* 46 (4): 402–423.

Kremp, E. and Tessier, L. (2006). L'immatériel, au coeur de la stratégie des entreprises. *Le 4 Pages des statistiques industrielles*. N° 217- mai 2006. Sessi, Ministère de l'Économie, des Finances et de l'Industrie. https://www.bnsp.insee.fr/ark:/12148/bc6p070sr5t/f1.pdf (accessed 03 March 2022).

Krull, J.L. and MacKinnon, D.P. (2001). Multilevel modeling of individual and group level mediated effects. *Multivariate Behavioral Research* 36 (2): 249–277.

Lev, B. (2018). The deteriorating usefulness of financial report information and how to reverse it. *Accounting and Business Research* 48: 465–493. https://doi.org/10.1080/00014788.2018.1470138.

Lev, B. (2019). Ending the accounting-for-intangibles status quo. *European Accounting Review* 28 (4): 713–736. https://doi.org/10.1080/09638180.2018.1521614.

Lorenc, B. (2006). Two topics in survey methodology: modelling the response process in establishment surveys; inference from nonprobability samples using the double samples setup. Doctoral dissertation. Stockholm University, Stockholm.

Marr, B. and Spender, J. (2004). Measuring knowledge assets – implications of the knowledge economy for performance measurement. *Measuring Business Excellence* 8 (1): 18–27.

Martínez-Ros, E. and Labeaga, J.M. (2009). Product and process innovation: persistence and complementarities. *European Management Review* 6 (1): 64–75.

Marzo, G. (2011). Accounting for intangibles and the theories of the firm. Available at SSRN: https://doi.org/10.2139/ssrn.1926641.

Martin, J. and Baybutt, C. (2021). The F words: why surveying businesses about intangibles is so hard. *Proceedings of the IARIW-ESCoE Conference on Intangible Assets*, London (11–12 November 2021). https://iariw.org/wp-content/uploads/2021/10/baybut-paper.pdf (accessed 12 November 2021).

Martin, J. (2019). Measuring the other half: new measures of intangible investment from the ONS. *National Institute Economic Review* 249 (1): R17–R29.

Milgrom, P. and Roberts, J. (1995). Complementarities and fit strategy, structure, and organizational change in manufacturing. *Journal of Accounting and Economics* 19 (2–3): 179–208.

Miyagawa, T., Lee, K., Kabe, S., Lee, S., Kim, H., Kim, Y., and Edamura, K. (2010). Management practices and firm performance in Japanese and Korean firms – an empirical study using interview surveys. RIETI Discussion Paper 10-E-013.

Miyagawa, T., Tonogi, K., and Ishikawa, T. (2020). Does the productivity J-curve exist in Japan?: empirical studies based on the multiple q theory. RES Discussion Paper Series. No. 6, Rissho University.

Molloy, J.C., Chadwick, C., Ployhart, R.E., and Golden, S.J. (2011). Making intangibles "tangible" in tests of resource-based theory: a multidisciplinary construct validation approach. *Journal of Management* 37 (5): 1496–1518.

Montresor, S., Perani, G., and Vezzani, A. (2014). How do companies 'perceive' their intangibles? New statistical evidence from the INNOBAROMETER 2013. JRC Technical Reports. http://publications.jrc.ec.europa.eu/repository/bitstream/JRC88865/innobarometer_report.pdf (accessed 26 April 2019).

Murray, A. (2012). Rethinking ROI: the metrics of intangible assets. *KM World* (30 October 2012). https://www.kmworld.com/Articles/Columns/The-Future-of-the-Future/Rethinking-ROI-The-Metrics-of-Intangible-Assets-85810.aspx (accessed 20 August 2021).

Nakamura, L. (2001). What is the US gross investment in intangibles? (at least) one trillion dollars a year! Working Paper No. 01-15, Federal Reserve Bank of Philadelphia, Philadelphia, PA.

National Research Council (2009). *Intangible Assets: Measuring and Enhancing Their Contribution to Corporate Value and Economic Growth*. Washington, DC: The National Academies Press https://doi.org/10.17226/12745.

Nonnis, A., Bounfour, A., and Özaygen, A. (2021). The combined contribution of intangible capital and global value chain participation to productivity. *International Journal of Intellectual Property Management* 11 (1): 21–37.

Office for National Statistics (2018). Developing experimental estimates of investment in intangible assets in the UK: 2016. https://www.ons.gov.uk/economy/economicoutputandproductivity/productivitymeasures/articles/experimentalestimatesofinvestmentinintangibleassetsintheuk2015/2016 (accessed 05 October 2021).

Office for National Statistics and Imperial College London (2016). Investment in Intangible Assets Survey, 2009-2010: Secure Access. [data collection]. 3rd Edition. UK Data Service. SN: 6701. https://doi.org/10.5255/UKDA-SN-6701-3.

Perani, G. (2021a). Business innovation measurement: history and evolution. In: *Handbook on Alternative Theories of Innovation* (ed. B. Godin, G. Gaglio and D. Vinck). Edward Elgar Publishing.

Perani, G. (2021b). Measuring intangibles in firms: past experiences and future prospects of voluntary surveys. *Presentation at the Conference on New Techniques and Technologies for Statistics NTTS2021*, Brussels, Belgium.

Piekkola, H., Lintamo, M., Riley, R., Robinson, C., Geppert, K., Görzig, B., Neumann, A., Henningsen, M., Skjerpen, T., Jurajda, S., Stancik, J., and Verbič, M. (2011). Firm-level intangible capital in six countries: Finland, Norway, the UK, Germany, the Czech Republic and Slovenia. In: *Intangible Capital–Driver of Growth in Europe* (ed. H. Piekkola), 63–95. Vaasa: University of Vaasa.

Prašnikar, J. (ed.) (2010). *The Role of Intangible Assets in Exiting the Crisis*. Ljubljana: Časnik Finance.

Radjenović, T. and Krstić, B. (2017). The microeconomic perspectives of intellectual capital measurement. *Facta Universitatis, Series: Economics and Organization* 14 (3): 189–202.

Redek, T. and Bavdaž, M. (2019). *Measuring the Intangibles Using Survey Data* [H2020 GLOBALINTO WP1]. Ljubljana: School of Economics and Business, University of Ljubljana. https://globalinto.eu/wp-content/uploads/2019/11/GLOBALINTO_D_1_3.pdf.

Redek, T., Domadenik, P., Farčnik, D., Istenič, T., Koman, M., Kostevc, Č., and Žabkar, V. (2019). *A Survey on Challenges to Growth: The Productivity Puzzle in the Context of (New) Growth Determinants* [H2020 GLOBALINTO WP1]. Ljubljana: School of Economics and Business, University of Ljubljana. https://globalinto.eu/wp-content/uploads/2019/09/GLOBALINTO_D_1_1.pdf.

Riley, R. and Bondibene, C.R. (2018). Winners and losers in the knowledge economy: the role of intangible capital. *Paper prepared for the 35th IARIW General Conference*, Copenhagen, Denmark (20–25 August 2018).

Roberts, J. (2004). *The Modern Firm: Organizational Design for Performance and Growth*. Oxford: Oxford University Press.

Roth, F. (2020). Revisiting intangible capital and labour productivity growth, 2000–2015: accounting for the crisis and economic recovery in the EU. *Journal of Intellectual Capital* 21 (5): 671–690.

Sandner, P.G. and Block, J. (2011). The market value of R&D, patents, and trademarks. *Research Policy* 7 (40): 969–985.

Shin, N., Kraemer, K.L., and Dedrick, J. (2012). Value capture in the global electronics industry: empirical evidence for the "smiling curve" concept. *Industry and Innovation* 19 (2): 89–107. https://doi.org/10.1080/13662716.2012.650883.

Snijkers, G., Haraldsen, G., Jones, J., and Willimack, D. (2013). *Designing and Conducting Business Surveys*. Hoboken: Wiley.

Teece, D.J. (2015). Intangible assets and a theory of heterogeneous firms. In: *Intangibles, Market Failure and Innovation Performance* (ed. A. Bounfour and T. Miyagawa), 217–239. Cham: Springer.

Teece, D., Pisano, G., and Shuen, A. (1997). Dynamic capabilities and strategic management. *Strategic Management Journal* 18 (7): 509–533.

Thum-Thysen, A., Voigt, P., Maier, C., Bilbao-Osorio, B., and Ognyanova, D. (2017). Unlocking investment in intangible assets in Europe. *Quarterly Report on the Euro Area (QREA)* 16 (1): 23–35.

Timmer, M.P., Dietzenbacher, E., Los, B., Stehrer, R., and De Vries, G.J. (2015). An illustrated user guide to the world input–output database: the case of global automotive production. *Review of International Economics* 23 (3): 575–605.

Tsakanikas, A., Roth, F., Caliò, S., Caloghirou, Y., and Dimas, P. (2020). The contribution of intangible inputs and participation in global value chains to productivity performance–evidence from the EU-28, 2000-2014 (No. 5). Hamburg Discussion Papers in International Economics.

United Nations, European Commission, International Monetary Fund, Organisation for Economic Co-operation and Development, and World Bank (1993). *System of National Accounts 1993*. New York: United Nations. https://unstats.un.org/unsd/nationalaccount/docs/1993sna.pdf.

United Nations, European Commission, International Monetary Fund, Organisation for Economic Co-operation and Development, and World Bank (2009). *System of National Accounts 2008*. New York: United Nations. https://unstats.un.org/unsd/nationalaccount/docs/SNA2008.pdf.

Veblen, T. (1908). On the nature of capital: investment, intangible assets, and the pecuniary magnate. *Quarterly Journal of Economics* 23 (1): 104–136. https://doi.org/10.2307/1883967.

Wernerfelt, B. (1984). A resource-based view of the firm. *Strategic Management Journal* 5: 171–180. https://doi.org/10.1002/smj.4250050207.

Whittard, D., Stam, P., Franklin, M., and Clayton, T. (2009). Testing an extended R&D survey: interviews with firms on innovation investment and depreciation. NESTA Innovation Index Working Paper.

Willeboordse, A. (ed.) (1997). *Handbook on Design and Implementation of Business Surveys*. Luxembourg: Eurostat.

Willimack, D.K. and Nichols, E. (2010). A hybrid response process model for business surveys. *Journal of Official Statistics* 26 (1): 3–24.

6

Measuring the US Digital Economy

Jessica R. Nicholson[1], Thomas F. Howells III[2], and David B. Wasshausen[3]

[1] *Research Economist, Bureau of Economic Analysis, USA*
[2] *Chief, Industry Economics Division, Bureau of Economic Analysis, USA*
[3] *Chief, Expenditure and Income Division, Bureau of Economic Analysis, USA*

6.1 Introduction

The US Bureau of Economic Analysis (BEA) is committed to advancing measurement of the digital economy. The rapid pace of technological change has required statistical agencies to develop new methodologies that capture newly emerging products, changes in consumer and business behavior, and novel ways to produce and deliver goods and services.

BEA has developed statistics on the domestic production of digital goods and services and on the value of digital trade. Digital goods are goods that rely on or enable digital technology; this includes goods that are transformed into a digital format, like a book or musical recording, and goods that individuals use to access these goods such as computers and smartphones. Digital services are services that are transmitted electronically or that support the development and maintenance of digital infrastructure. Digital trade relates to goods and services that are ordered or delivered remotely. The BEA statistics relating to digital goods and services were developed in the spirit of aligning with evolving international guidelines on digital economy measurement.

This chapter shares recent trends in digital economic activity as measured by BEA statistics. It will describe the current methods BEA uses to measure the digital economy as well as the ongoing research efforts to further develop and refine the estimates.

6.2 Experimental Digital Economy Measures

In March 2018, the BEA, for the first time, published preliminary estimates of US digital economy gross output, value added, employment, and compensation (Barefoot et al. 2018). BEA has

* Jessica R. Nicholson is a Senior Economist in the National Economic Accounts Directorate at the US Bureau of Economic Analysis (BEA). Thomas F. Howells III is Chief of the Industry Economics Division and David B. Wasshausen is Chief of the Expenditure and Income Division, both in the National Economic Accounts Directorate at BEA. The authors would like to thank the following individuals at BEA who contributed to the content of this report: Ana M. Aizcorbe, Senior Research Economist; Jennifer Bruner, Economist in the International Economic Accounts Directorate; Alexis N. Grimm, Senior Economist in the International Economic Accounts Directorate; William A. Jolliff, Mining, Manufacturing, and Fixed Assets Branch Chief in the National Economic Accounts Directorate; Ricardo Limés, Chief, Multinational Operations Branch in the International Directorate; and Dylan Rassier, Chief of the National Economic Accounts Research Group.

Advances in Business Statistics, Methods and Data Collection. Edited by Ger Snijkers, Mojca Bavdaž, Stefan Bender, Jacqui Jones, Steve MacFeely, Joseph W. Sakshaug, Katherine J. Thompson, and Arnout van Delden.
© 2023 John Wiley & Sons, Inc. Published 2023 by John Wiley & Sons, Inc.

since updated those estimates with expanded coverage, more recent data, and better alignment with international guidance.

The estimates are BEA's initial efforts to lay the foundation for a digital economy satellite account, which when initially published, were the first set of estimates within the framework of the national accounts. Since the initial publication of BEA's digital economy statistics in March 2018, other organizations have published their own estimates of the digital economy's economic impact. International organizations, such as the Organisation for Economic Co-operation and Development (OECD), the United Nations, and G20, are continuing to develop guidance on how to consistently and accurately measure the digital economy across countries.

BEA's measures will continue to evolve as ongoing research uncovers opportunities to better measure prices for high-tech goods and services like ride hailing and other digitally intermediated services. Some of these efforts are described in this chapter.

6.2.1 Methodology

BEA constructed the estimates within a supply-use framework following the same methodology developed for the initial estimates published in the March 2018 report. The methodology is the same as is used for other special estimates, or satellite accounts, that BEA produces on arts and culture, travel and tourism, and outdoor recreation.

A satellite account is a supplemental set of statistics that focuses on one aspect of the economy. They are fully consistent with BEA's core statistics, such as gross domestic product (GDP). The digital economy estimates are still considered experimental and are not yet an official BEA satellite account because of data constraints that prevent the estimates from capturing the full breadth of economic activity related to the digital economy. These data constraints are described later in more detail.

The supply-use table (SUT) framework is an integral and essential element of the US economic accounts (Young et al. 2015). The supply table presents the total domestic supply of commodities, or goods and services, from both domestic and foreign producers that are available for use in the domestic economy. The use table shows the use of these commodities by domestic industries as intermediate inputs and by final users as well as value added by industry. The SUTs are a complete, balanced set of economic statistics, and they present a full accounting of industry and final-use transactions. BEA publishes SUTs at three levels of detail: sector (21 industry groups), summary (71 industry groups), and detail (405 industry groups).

The SUTs are built up from more detailed unpublished information that include approximately 800 domestic industries, 450 final users, and 5000 goods and services classified using the North American Industrial Classification System (NAICS) (United States Census Bureau 2021c). The NAICS codes comprise six digits, which reading from left to right, indicate the general sector down to a detailed industry. The US statistical system does not currently have a separate classification system for commodities, which are groups of similar products defined by the characteristics of the product (commodity) itself rather than by the production process. At present, BEA uses its own commodity classification system to assign each commodity the code of the industry in which the commodity is the primary product. The foundation for this commodity classification system is the six-digit NAICS code. The NAICS structure is updated every five years with the latest incorporated version being the 2012 NAICS.

BEA constructed the estimates presented in this chapter following a three-step process. First, BEA developed a conceptual definition of the digital economy. When BEA first undertook the task of measuring the digital economy, there was no agreed definition or framework for estimating the economic contribution of the digital economy. Second, BEA identified specific goods and services categories within BEA's supply-use framework relevant to measuring the digital economy. Third, BEA used the supply-use framework to identify the industries responsible for producing these goods and services, and estimated output, value added, employment, compensation, and other variables for these industries.

In the second step of the process, over 300 goods and services were chosen to be included in the digital economy estimates. The decision to include an item was based on BEA analyst expertise and on outside information and research. The appendix of the BEA's working paper "Updated Digital Economy Estimates-June 2021" lists all the goods and services included in the estimates (Nicholson 2021). Conceptually, a digital economy satellite account should include all goods and services related to the digital economy. However, because many goods and services are only partially digital and because of the emergence of new goods and services that previously did not exist, additional data and research are needed to complete the coverage of the digital economy in the BEA estimates.

Since the initial publication of digital economy estimates in March 2018, BEA has expanded the coverage of the estimates to include a wider coverage of e-commerce as described in Section 6.2.1.1.2 of this chapter. BEA will continue to expand the coverage of the estimates with new data and methodologies as they become available. For example, some BEA goods and services categories contain a mix of both digital and nondigital products; the BEA goods category "watches" includes both traditional and Internet-enabled watches. BEA needs additional data to separately identify the portion of output associated with this item that is relevant to the digital economy estimates and has therefore excluded the item from the current estimates. Inclusion of this commodity fully would overestimate the item's contribution to the digital economy. Data gaps and measurement challenges for specific digital economy categories are described in the next section.

6.2.1.1 Defining the Digital Economy

BEA's information and communications technology (ICT) sector served as a starting point for the definition of the digital economy. The BEA ICT sector consists of computer and electronic product manufacturing (excluding navigational, measuring, electromedical, and control instruments manufacturing); software publishers; broadcasting and telecommunications; data processing, hosting and related services; Internet publishing and broadcasting and web search portals; and computer systems design and related services. BEA's definition is generally consistent with the internationally accepted definition of the ICT sector used and developed by the statistical offices of the OECD and UN.

While not all ICT goods and services are fully in scope, the ICT sector and the digital economy largely overlap. The BEA estimates include the entire ICT sector as well as additional goods and services determined to be in scope for the digital economy.

As noted in the tables below, the digital economy estimates currently include near-comprehensive coverage of digital economy hardware (Table 6.1), software (Table 6.1), business-to-business (B2B) e-commerce (Table 6.2), and business-to-consumer (B2C) e-commerce (Table 6.2). Additionally, many purchased digital services are included with the exceptions noted in Table 6.3.

6.2.1.1.1 *Infrastructure*

Infrastructure is comprised of the basic physical materials and organizational arrangements that support the existence and use of computer networks and the digital economy; primarily ICT goods and services. Table 6.1 describes the subcomponents included in infrastructure and

Table 6.1 Infrastructure.

Infrastructure subcomponent	Subcomponent description	Status of inclusion in BEA estimates
Hardware	The manufactured physical elements that constitute a computer system including, but not limited to, monitors, hard drives, and semiconductors. Also includes communications products and audio and visual equipment products	Included almost comprehensively
Software	The programs and other operating information used by devices such as personal computers and commercial servers, including both commercial software and software developed in-house by firms for their own use	Included almost comprehensively
Structures	The construction of buildings where digital economy producers create digital economy goods or supply digital economy services. The structures category also includes buildings that provide support services to digital products. This includes the construction of data centers, semiconductor fabrication plants, the installations of fiber optic cables, switches, repeaters, etc.	Not yet included; part of ongoing work

Table 6.2 E-commerce.

E-commerce subcomponent	Subcomponent description	Status of inclusion in BEA estimates
Business-to-business (B2B) e-commerce	Purchasing of goods and services between businesses using the internet or other electronic means. Manufacturers, wholesalers, and other industries engage in both interfirm and intrafirm e-commerce (when one establishment electronically orders goods or services from another establishment in the same firm) to produce goods and services for final consumption	Goods included almost comprehensively; inclusion of services is part of ongoing work
Business-to-consumer (B2C) e-commerce	The sale of goods and services by businesses to consumers, or retail e-commerce, using the internet or other electronic means	Goods included almost comprehensively; inclusion of services is part of ongoing work

indicates BEA's coverage of each subcomponent in the current digital economy estimates. BEA does not currently calculate the value of digital economy structures but is working to include this component. Data from the US Census Bureau's Value of Construction Put in Place survey will help inform the estimate.

6.2.1.1.2 E-commerce

E-commerce is the remote sale of goods and services over computer networks by methods specifically designed for the purpose of receiving or placing orders. Products purchased through e-commerce are also referred to as "digitally ordered."

E-commerce output is measured as the wholesale or retail trade margin on digitally ordered goods and services sold over the Internet or through some other electronic market such as

Table 6.3 Priced digital services.

Priced digital services sub-component	Sub-component description	Status of inclusion in BEA estimates
Cloud services	Computing services based on a set of computing resources that can be accessed on-demand with low management effort, including remote and distributed hosting, storage, computing, and security services	Included almost comprehensively; Estimate is derived using additional source data including the Economic Census and Statista's Technology Market Outlook
Telecommunications services	Services related to telephony, cable and satellite television, and radio broadcasting. Internet is excluded	Included almost comprehensively
Internet and data services	Services related to providing internet access and to hosting, searching, retrieving, and streaming content and information on the web	Partially included; part of ongoing work
Digital intermediary services	The service of providing information on and successfully matching two independent parties to a transaction via a digital platform in return for an explicit fee. The output of these platforms typically consists of the fees paid by the producer and/or the consumer of the product being intermediated	Not separately identified; part of ongoing work
All other priced digital services	All other purchased digital services (excluding cloud services, telecommunications services, internet and data services, and digital intermediation services)	Included, but work is ongoing to expand coverage

electronic data interchange. The margin is equal to total revenue earned from online sales less the cost of goods sold. In the earliest digital economy estimates, there was limited coverage of e-commerce only the margins for B2B wholesale and B2C retail transactions from electronic market establishments were included.

In the digital economy estimates published in August 2020, BEA used survey data from the US Census Bureau to introduce expanded e-commerce coverage by including margins from both B2C and B2B e-commerce from traditional brick and mortar establishments in addition to the electronic market establishments (Table 6.2) (Nicholson 2020). BEA used data from the Annual Retail Trade Survey (ARTS; www.census.gov/programs-surveys/arts.html) to expand the coverage of B2C e-commerce in the digital economy estimates to include retail e-commerce across all types of outlets, or stores, in the economy (United States Census Bureau 2021a). The proportion of online sales to total sales for each type of retail outlet was used to partially include retail margins for traditional retail establishments. For B2B e-commerce, BEA followed the same methodology for each type of wholesaler using data from the Annual Wholesale Trade Survey (AWTS; www.census .gov/programs-surveys/awts.html) (United States Census Bureau 2021b). These methodological improvements have been carried through to the latest update of the digital economy estimates in June 2021.

6.2.1.1.3 Priced Digital Services
Priced digital services relate to computing and communication and are performed for a fee charged to the consumer. Additionally, this category includes services that support the digital economy such

as computer repair services and digital consulting services. Some data gaps still exist. For example, the estimates do not include an estimate of online learning services which are in scope for the digital economy.

Table 6.3 describes how priced digital services are captured in the BEA digital economy estimates. BEA is engaged in ongoing research efforts to estimate the value of digital intermediary services.

6.2.1.2 Calculating Results

BEA estimated nominal value added, output, compensation, and employment by industry for the digital economy. After identifying the goods and services included in the digital economy, BEA identified the industries that produce these goods and services using the supply table. Digital economy gross output by industry represents the total value of in-scope gross output produced by each industry across all digital economy goods and services. Value added for the digital economy is derived by industry as digital economy gross output less the corresponding consumption of intermediate inputs. Direct measures of the consumption of intermediate inputs associated with the production of digital economy output are not available and instead the ratio of intermediate consumption associated with digital output for an industry is assumed to be the same as the ratio of intermediate consumption to total output for that industry.

Compensation and employment for the digital economy are derived through the same procedure as value added. Specifically, the ratio of an industry's digital economy output to total output is applied to total employment and compensation for the industry.

Next, price and quantity indexes for digital economy gross output and value added were prepared in three steps. First, gross output indexes are derived by deflating each digital good and service produced by an industry that is included as part of its gross output from the supply table. Second, BEA derived indexes for intermediate inputs by deflating all commodities from the use table that are consumed by the industry as intermediate inputs in the production of digital goods and services. Imported inputs were identified using the import proportionality assumption, and domestically produce and imported intermediate inputs are deflated separately. Third, using the double-deflation method, the separate estimates of gross output and intermediate inputs by industry are combined in a Fisher index-number formula to generate price and quantity indexes for value added by Industry.

6.2.2 Domestic Trends

The results presented in this section are based on BEA's most recent SUTs published in September 2020 (BEA 2020).

6.2.2.1 Value Added

GDP is the value of the goods and services produced by the nation's economy less than the value of the goods and services used up in production. GDP by industry, or value added, is a measure of an industry's contribution to overall GDP. The digital economy accounted for 9.6% (US$2051.6 billion) of US current-dollar GDP (US$21,433.2 billion) in 2019. When compared with traditional US industries or sectors, the digital economy ranked just below the manufacturing sector, which accounted for 10.9% (US$2345.8 billion) of current-dollar GDP, and ranked above finance and insurance, which accounted for 7.8% (US$1665.8 billion) of current-dollar GDP (Chart 6.1).

Digital economy real value added grew at an average annual rate of 6.5% per year from 2005 to 2019, compared to 1.8% growth in the overall economy (Chart 6.2). Within the digital economy, the fastest growing component was B2C e-commerce, which experienced average annual growth of 12.2%.

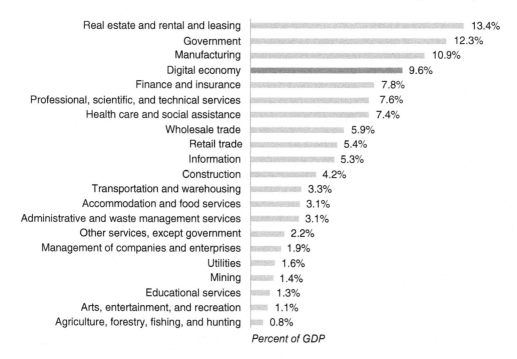

U.S. Bureau of Economic Analysis

Chart 6.1 Digital economy and industry share of total gross domestic products, 2019.

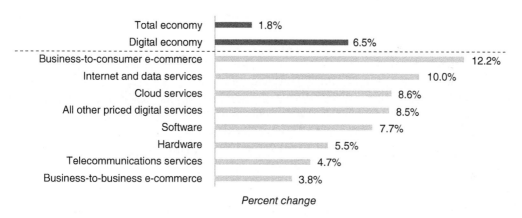

U.S. Bureau of Economic Analysis

Chart 6.2 Components of the digital economy: real value–added average annual growth from 2005 to 2009.

In most industries across the US economy, the digital portion of the industry's economy grew faster than the total industry overall during the same period as measured by real value added average annual growth (Chart 6.3). The digital portion of the arts, entertainment, and recreation industry grew the fastest at an average annual rate of 12.1%. In retail trade, the nondigital portion of the industry grew at only 0.2% at an average annual rate while the digital portion of the industry grew at a rate of 11.6%.

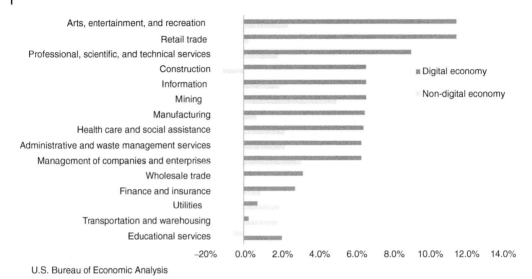

U.S. Bureau of Economic Analysis

Chart 6.3 Average annual growth rate of real value added by industry, digital and non-digital, from 2005 to 2019.

One caveat to the industry growth rates is that data gaps may impact the growth rates in certain industries. For example, the only industry that experienced a contraction of the digital economy was educational services. However, as noted above, the contraction of digital activity in this industry is due to data gaps that currently prevent the inclusion of online learning in the digital economy estimates.

6.2.2.2 Gross Output

Gross output is a measure of sales or revenue from production for most industries; gross output for a given industry is equal to the sum of the industry's value added plus intermediate inputs. Real gross output for the digital economy grew at an annual rate of 5.1% from 2005 to 2019, faster than the total economy, which grew at an average annual rate of 1.5%. When output is indexed to a base year, the compound effect of the faster output growth in the digital economy relative to the overall economy is clearly seen by the divergence of the two lines in Chart 6.4. The fastest growing components of digital economy output were B2C e-commerce (12.5% at an average annual rate) and Internet and data services (10.9%). Hardware grew the slowest at 2.3%.

6.2.2.3 Prices

During this period, prices for digital economy goods and services decreased at an average annual rate of 0.4% (Chart 6.5). Prices for all goods and services in the economy increased at an average annual rate of 1.9%. As the digital economy matures and technology improves, prices for hardware, software, and some services have declined, as reflected in the gross output price index for the digital economy. The gross output price index for the digital economy is based primarily on consumer and producer price indexes published by the US Bureau of Labor Statistics. BEA has prioritized research on prices for emerging technologies as described later in this chapter.

6.2.3 International Collaboration and Alignment

In today's global economy, it is imperative that national statistics across countries rely on similar methods to facilitate comparisons and aggregation. BEA is committed to international efforts

Index level (2005 = 100)

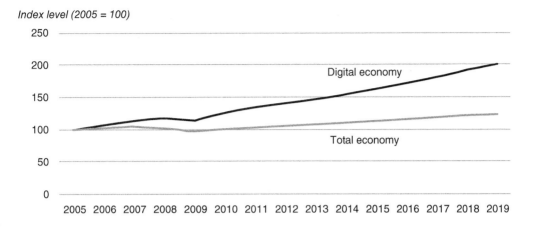

U.S. Bureau of Economic Analysis

Chart 6.4 Real gross output index.

Index level (2005 = 100)

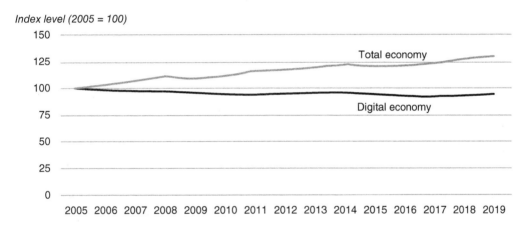

U.S. Bureau of Economic Analysis

Chart 6.5 Gross output prices index.

to develop comparable statistics and actively participates in several working groups within international organizations. BEA also collaborates with other statistical agencies informally to share ideas and research to continually improve the availability of information to measure the digital economy.

6.2.3.1 The Organization for Economic Co-operation and Development Working Party on National Accounts

In 2017, the OECD Working Party on National Accounts (WPNA) formed an Informal Advisory Group on Measuring GDP in the Digital Economy (the advisory group). Under the leadership of Erich Strassner, Associate Director for National Economic Accounts at BEA, the advisory group has defined a framework and template for digital SUTs that will help countries develop internationally comparable statistics on the digital economy (OECD 2019). The creation of this template allows for digital SUTs prepared by different countries to consistently and systematically capture information on the most important aspects of the digital economy. This type of information is defined as a key priority by the OECD Committee on Statistics and Statistical Policy and in the System of National Accounts research agenda.

In December 2019, the OECD invited all members of the WPNA to provide estimates, where possible, for the high priority indicators identified within the Digital SUTs. The OECD is looking to make progress on developing methodologies and obtaining feedback for populating the Digital SUTs, even when the methods are experimental or produce incomplete statistics. The BEA in the United States, and several other OECD member states are currently working to determine the extent to which official national statistics can be used to populate these tables.

BEA's digital economy estimates presented in this chapter use terminology recommended by the OECD, and BEA continually strives to align with international guidance on digital economy measurement.

6.2.3.2 International Comparisons

Statistics Canada released their first set of digital economy estimates in May 2019 (Sinclair 2019). The digital economy estimates for Canada align closely with BEA's initial estimates before the BEA included expanded coverage of B2C and B2B e-commerce. BEA and Statistics Canada consulted with each other throughout the process of creating the measures and continue to do so as the measures evolve. Both BEA and Statistics Canada also continue to work to employ the latest guidance from the OECD on measuring GDP in a digitalized economy, which both the United States and Canada are actively involved in developing (OECD 2018, 2019).

The Australian Bureau of Statistics (ABS) has also developed estimates of the digital economy within the supply-use framework that are consistent with the original BEA methodology (Zhao 2019). ABS estimates are on a financial year basis that runs from July through June. To facilitate comparisons between the United States and Canada for this study, these estimates are converted to a calendar year basis by splitting a financial year values in half and adding the resulting value to the split value for the adjacent year (ABS 2019).

Chart 6.6 displays the share of the digital economy of current-dollar GDP for the United States, Canada, and Australia. In 2016, the latest year for which data are available for each country, the digital economy with expanded e-commerce coverage accounted for 9.0% of US GDP, 5.6% of Canadian GDP, and 5.7% of Australian GDP. When the US estimates are limited to only primarily digital products, the digital economy accounted for 6.8% of US GDP. Coverage differences exist because of data availability by country and country-level decisions about what to include and exclude in the digital economy measures.

Digital economy estimates are available for all three countries from 2012 to 2016. Over this period, the digital economy, valued at current prices, grew the fastest in the United States at an average annual rate of 5.7% (note that this growth rate is calculated using the expanded coverage measures). Corresponding growth rates for Canada and Australia were 5.4% and 3.1%, respectively.

Finland has also published an estimate of the digital economy based on the BEA methodology (Ali-Yrkkö et al. 2020). Replicating the original BEA measures which only accounted for primarily digital products, the Finnish measures estimate that the digital economy accounted for 6.4% of Finland's GDP in 2017 (compared to 6.9% in the United States and 5.5% in Canada that year). With expanded coverage – including partially digital goods and services – the digital economy accounted for 9.6% of GDP (compared to 9.3% in the United States in 2017 when the digital economy estimates include expanded coverage of e-commerce). Again, coverage varies between the US estimates and the Finnish estimates.

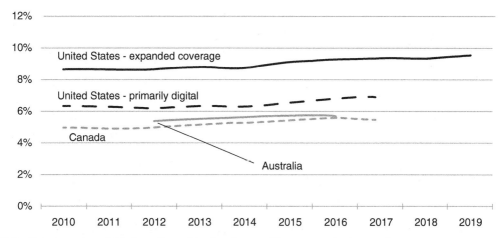

Note: Data are not available for call countries for all years. Coverage varies by country.
U.S. Bureau of Economic Analysis

Chart 6.6 Digital economy share of total gross domestic product, by country. Note: Data not available for all countries for all years. Coverage varies by country. Source: US Bureau of Economic Analysis.

6.2.4 Other Areas of Research

The current digital economy estimates provide insight into the impact of the digital economy on the overall US economy. However, there are opportunities for BEA to expand these statistics into a comprehensive digital economy satellite account to reflect more completely the digital economy's contribution to economic growth. There is also value in measuring the impact of items that fall outside of the national accounts production boundary, like services provided for free and data. The research efforts described below are all ongoing and will enhance BEA's measurement of the digital economy.

6.2.4.1 "Free" Digital Media

A growing development in the digital economy is the provision of "free" digital media that is supported by advertising and marketing. Advertising refers to cases where a content provider sells ad space to a third party, while marketing refers to cases where there is no third party. The concept of advertising- or marketing-supported media content is not new, but the contribution of digitalization has generated a proliferation of professional and amateur content through online platforms such as social media and streaming services in addition to more traditional outlets such as newspapers.

In the past, households were subject to advertising and marketing messages in exchange for nondigital content provided through outlets such as television and radio – all households had to do was consent to messages by either watching them or otherwise occupying their time during the break in content. A household's contribution to the exchange was limited to paying attention or tolerating the break in content. With digitalization, households are still subject to advertising and marketing messages, but now the exchange for content takes place online and generally requires households – either knowingly or unknowingly – to submit personal data that can be used to design messages that more effectively target specific households and match specific preferences and needs. A household's contribution to the exchange is expanded by the submission of personal data.

The current treatment of "free" media in national accounts is to treat advertising and marketing expenditures as inputs into production. In the case of advertising, a transaction is recognized between media content providers and advertising firms, but no transaction is recognized between households and media content providers or advertising firms. In the case of marketing, the function takes place entirely in-house, and no transaction is recognized between households and the marketing firms. In each case, values of final products sold to households reflect the costs of advertising or marketing.

The current treatment for "free" media in national accounts was sufficient in the past when a household's only contribution to the exchange was their mere consent for viewing or avoiding messages. However, with households now contributing personal data to the exchange, interest has surfaced to better understand and measure the household's role. The most likely treatment is some sort of barter transaction between the media content provider and households.

One option is to recognize "free" media content in exchange for households' attention services for advertising and marketing messages (Nakamura et al. 2017). In this case, the transaction could be valued by the content provider's cost of producing the content. Another option is to recognize capital services that underlie the "free" media content in exchange for households' personal data as demonstrated (Heys 2019). In this case, the transaction could be valued by the content provider's cost of producing the capital services. Each of these options results in an increase in value-added for the household sector – production of attention services with the first option and production of own-account services with the second option. For the US economy, Nakamura et al. (2017) find that the explosion in "free" digital content is partially offset by the decrease in "free" print content, resulting in a modest average annual increase in real GDP of 0.1% point for the period 2005–2015.

6.2.4.2 Measurement and Treatment of Data

Consistent with international guidelines, the US national accounts do not currently include stocks and flows of data as an asset. The US accounts include purchased software and own-account software as categories of intellectual property products, and those measures include databases to the extent that databases are a type of software. The value of the information content – i.e. the embedded *data* – is included in the market price of purchased databases. However, the value of the information content is excluded from the measured value of own-account databases – only the cost of preparing own-account data in a format that conforms to the database is included, not the cost of acquiring or producing own-account data.

Recent global conversations among national accountants have focused on the treatment of data as an asset in response to the rapid increase in the collection and use of data among businesses, governments, nonprofits, and households. Anecdotal evidence on the value of data as a business asset or commodity is abundant in popular media articles and other outlets. At the end of 2018, two of the largest global data firms – Google and Facebook – had a combined market capitalization of US$1.1 trillion and net income before tax of US$60.3 billion. The two firms amounted to 5.3% of the market capitalization of all S&P 500 firms and 3.6% of US domestic corporate profits before tax.

Data that can be used in production over multiple periods generally appear to fit within the asset boundary of the national accounts as a fixed asset because they result from a production process, they are subject to economic ownership, and they provide benefits to their economic owner.

Purchased data products – those that have been sold or licensed – are presumably already reflected in national accounts because they result from market transactions. However, most data products are not transacted in active markets; they are built and maintained in-house. The most likely treatment for own-account data in national accounts is to expand the scope of own-account databases to include the cost of acquiring or producing the embedded data. The most likely valuation method for own-account data is a sum of costs, which could include the cost of collecting, recording, organizing, and storing own-account data.

Under international standards, a sum of costs valuation method includes labor costs, economic depreciation, intermediate consumption, other taxes less subsidies on production, and a net return to fixed capital. When measured correctly, these components should result in a value that is comparable to a market value. In practice, statistical compilers generally estimate own-account measures based on labor costs for relevant occupations plus a markup for the other components. Identifying relevant occupations for data as an asset may be less straightforward than identifying relevant occupations for software and databases because data activities are presumably spread over a broad range of occupations. BEA is currently developing a methodology based on unsupervised machine learning as one way to identify data activities based on the task content of occupations. Very preliminary findings suggest that wage spending alone by private US businesses on just collection activities increased from US$50 billion in 2005 to US$75 billion in 2018 – an average annual increase of 3.8%. However, of the spending amounts estimated, a sizable portion – about 30% – is related to R&D activity that may already be included as capital formation in the US National Income and Product Accounts.

6.2.4.3 Prices

BEA has embarked on several initiatives with external partners to leverage alternative data sources to improve the measurement of high-tech goods and services prices. So far, new deflators for software and medical equipment were developed and introduced in the 2018 Comprehensive Update of the National Income and Product Accounts (Kelly et al. 2018). Improved price indexes for smartphones and feature phones were similarly implemented in the 2019 annual update (BEA 2019). Research continues in three important areas: Internet and wireless services, cloud services, and ride hailing.

6.2.4.3.1 Internet and Wireless Services

BEA, in collaboration with outside partners, conducted research to develop a methodology to disentangle purchases of phones and wireless services when they are bundled together as part of a long-term service contract (Byrne et al. 2019). Getting the allocation right is especially important for real personal consumption expenditures (PCE) because the price deflators for phones and wireless services exhibit very different trends. The adjusted estimates suggest that real PCE spending currently captured in the category Cellular Phone Services increased 4% points faster than is reflected in published data.

The current effort is to improve the deflators for Internet and wireless services. To that end, BEA has obtained survey data that can potentially be used to construct price indexes for these types of services; the data contain information on households' annual payments to wireless and Internet providers and features of the plans, including features of the phones that are potentially bundled with the services.

6.2.4.3.2 Cloud Services

Cloud services – the practice of using a network of remote servers hosted on the Internet to store, manage, and process data – allows small business to access and use computing capabilities without the expense associated with purchasing a local server or a personal computer. BEA has contracted with 451 Research, an organization that tracks the cloud services sector, to provide a set of price indexes for cloud services. BEA is exploring using the 451 Research indexes for deflating spending on cloud services in the national accounts. BEA has also contracted with an academic expert to provide an assessment of the potential usefulness and limitations of the resulting indexes (451 Research 2021).

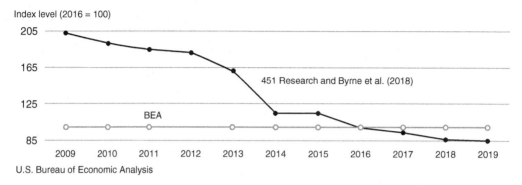

Index level (2016 = 100)

U.S. Bureau of Economic Analysis

Chart 6.7 Cloud services prices indexes. US Bureau of Economic Analysis.

Expert analysis of the 451 Research price indexes suggests that the price deflators currently used in the national accounts are problematic. After expert review of the 451 Research Cloud Prices Index (Sichel, D., Wellesley College, unpublished results), BEA combined the index data for 2016 through 2019 with cloud price index data from Byrne et al. (2018) for 2009 through 2016 to develop an experimental cloud service price index. Chart 6.7 displays this index, labeled 451 Research and Byrne et al. (ibid) next to the official cloud services price index currently in use at BEA (Chart 6.7). The results clearly show that the official price index is not capturing the apparent price declines for these services for this sector and is therefore likely understating the growth of real output. Based on these findings, BEA is currently considering implementing these new deflators in the national accounts and in the digital economy estimates in updates planned for calendar year 2021.

6.2.4.3.3 Ride-hailing Services

The rapid growth in platform-enabled services has raised questions about the ability of standard data sources and methods to keep up. For nominal spending, the concern is that new providers of these services may be missing from the establishment surveys typically used to collect revenue data. There is a similar issue for price indexes. At the same time, the digital revolution has brought novel data sources that could supplement the data underlying the national accounts.

BEA has obtained from Rakuten Intelligence ride-level data for ride-hailing services and taxi services in New York City as part of a case study on these issues. In a pilot project, preliminary results suggest that price indexes constructed under different assumptions can show very different patterns. Specifically, if ride-hailing services are excluded from the sample, the resulting price index shows appreciably faster growth than an index that includes it. Moreover, there is a potential substitution bias problem: indexes that treat ride-sharing services and taxi services as the same service show slower price increases than those that treat them as different services. In particular, the now-common practice of dynamic pricing raises challenges to standard price index techniques and suggests new methods will be required for ride-hailing services as well as other platform-enabled services.

To complete this research on rides-hailing services, BEA has purchased data for three additional cities (Washington, DC, Los Angeles, and Chicago). At the same time, BEA is exploring alternative data sources for other types of platform-enabled services such as Airbnb.

6.3 Measuring Digital Services Trade

Digital technology has enabled seamless transmittal of services around the globe. Remote purchase and delivery of some services can occur in seconds thanks to the internet, fiber optics, mobile devices, and other technologies. Services are a growing share of US exports; in 1980, services accounted for 17.5% of the value of US exports and in 2019, they accounted for 34.6%. Additionally, the United States has historically run an international trade deficit, but since 1971 has run a growing surplus on international services trade.

The ability to quickly and easily transmit services over the Internet has undoubtedly contributed to the growth of services trade. Traditional measures of international services trade do not provide information on whether services are delivered digitally. BEA collects data on trade in services by category based on the Extended Balance of Payments Services classification (EBOPS 2010), which is based on the type of service traded and not on the mode of delivery. The EBOPS guidelines were established by the Manual on Statistics of International Trade in Services (United Nations Department of Economic and Social Affairs 2010) and Balance of Payments and International Investment Position Manual, Sixth Edition (International Monetary Fund 2009).

BEA was a pioneer in measuring digital trade and first published estimates related to trade in digital services in a 2012 research paper (Borga and Koncz-Bruner 2012). In 2016, BEA officially began publishing annual statistics on ICT and potentially ICT-enabled services using concepts defined by the United Nations Conference on Trade and Development's Task Group on Measuring Trade in ICT Services and ICT-Enabled Services (Sturgeon et al. 2015).

6.3.1 Defining Digital Services for International Trade

ICT services are those services that are used to facilitate information processing and communication. BEA's trade in ICT services statistics include three categories of services from BEA's statistics on international trade in services: telecommunications services, computer services, and charges for the use of intellectual property for licenses to reproduce and/or distribute computer software.

ICT-enabled services are services with outputs delivered remotely over ICT networks. Because for many types of services, the actual mode of delivery is unknown, BEA uses the concept of *potentially* ICT-enabled services. Potentially ICT-enabled services include service types that can predominantly be delivered remotely over ICT networks, a subset of which are *actually* delivered via that method.

Potentially ICT-enabled services include ICT services and also BEA's published statistics on international trade in six major service types: insurance services; financial services; charges for the use of intellectual property; telecommunications, computer, and information services; certain other services included in other business services (research and development services; professional and management consulting services; architectural, engineering, scientific, and other technical services; and trade-related services), and certain other services included in personal, cultural, and recreational services (audiovisual services and other personal, cultural, and recreational services).

BEA's international services statistics include measures of international trade in ICT and potentially ICT enabled services by type of service, by type of service and affiliation, and by country or affiliation.

6.3.2 Trends in ICT and ICT-enabled Services

In 2019, US services exports totaled US$875.8 billion (Chart 6.8). Of this total, 59.1%, or US$517.5 billion, were potentially ICT-enabled services. The share of potentially ICT-enabled services exports in total services exports has been growing since 1999 when they accounted for 43.0% of the total value of US services exports. Although the value of ICT services exports has grown over time, they have been accounting for a declining share of the total value of potentially ICT-enabled services. In 1999, ICT services exports accounted for 19.0% of the total

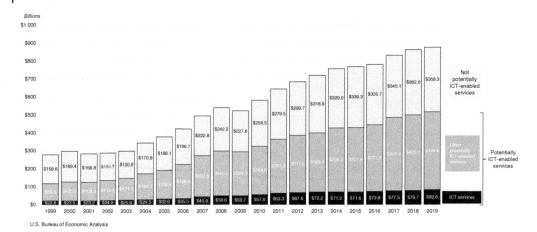

Chart 6.8 Exports of ICT and potentially ICT-enabled services in total exports of services. Source: US Bureau of Economic Analysis.

value of potentially ICT-enabled services exports compared to 16.0% in 2019. In other words, "other" potentially ICT-enabled services have grown faster as digital trade capabilities expand over time.

Similar trends have occurred with imports of these services (Chart 6.9). Potentially ICT-enabled services accounted for 50.6% of the US$588.4 billion services imports in 2019 compared to 34.0% in 1999 when services imports totaled US$196.7 billion. ICT services accounted for 23.9% of potentially ICT-enabled services imports in 1999. This share fell to less than 16% from 2006 through 2009 but has since slowly trended back up and was 17.3 in 2019.

In 2019, potentially ICT-enabled services in other business services, primarily professional and management consulting services and research and development services, accounted for the largest shares of exports (33%) and imports (33%) by service type (Chart 6.10). Exports in five of the six major categories exceeded imports, with the largest surplus occurring in financial services. The combined surpluses in these five categories more than offset a deficit in insurance services.

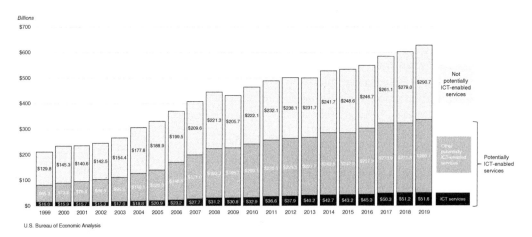

Chart 6.9 Imports of ICT and potentially ICT-enabled services in total imports of services. Source: US Bureau of Economic Analysis.

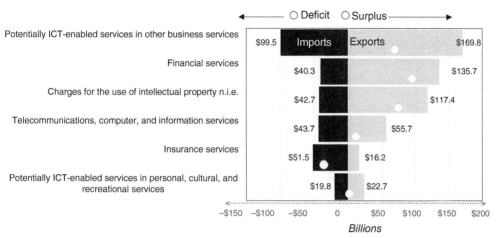

U.S. Bureau of Economic Analysis

Chart 6.10 Trade in potentially ICT enabled services by service type, 2019. Note: ◯ denotes trade balance.

6.3.3 Areas of Research

Research on digital trade at BEA is ongoing and has focused on three main areas: coordination with international working groups, expansion of existing survey instruments, and research on survey coverage of digital economy firms.

BEA has been actively engaged in multilateral efforts, along with other national statistical offices, the OECD, World Trade Organization (WTO), and International Monetary Fund (IMF) under the auspices of the Working Party for Trade in Goods and Services, to define a conceptual framework for the measurement of digital trade. New international guidance has defined digital trade as trade that involves digital ordering or digital delivery. That is, the concept of digital trade is defined based on the nature of the transaction rather than the nature of the product itself.

A digitally ordered transaction is one that is conducted remotely over computer networks by methods specifically designed for the purpose of receiving or placing orders. Digital ordering is also known as e-commerce, and it may involve orders of goods or services. Digital delivery involves services provided remotely, in an electronic format, using computer networks specifically designed for the purpose of delivering the service. The concept of digitally delivered services broadly aligns with the concept of ICT-enabled services, with some key differences in covered products and methods of delivery. For example, transactions via phone are covered by the concept of ICT-enabled services but are not considered to be digitally delivered. Digital ordering and digital delivery are not mutually exclusive; many, but not all, digitally ordered services are also digitally delivered. For more details on the definition and measurement of digital trade, see the *Handbook on Measuring Digital Trade, Version 1,* a joint publication by the OECD, WTO, and the IMF (World Trade Organization, and International Monetary Fund 2020).

With emerging digital trade measurement guidelines in focus, BEA has collected new detail on certain benchmark international trade in services surveys that will enable the compilation of statistics on digitally delivered services. BEA included the questions on its 2017 Benchmark Survey of Transactions in Selected Services and Intellectual Property with Foreign Persons (BE-120) and its 2019 Benchmark Survey of Financial Services Transactions between US Financial Services Providers and Foreign Persons (BE-180) (Bureau of Economic Analysis 2021b). The new detail requested that survey respondents identify, for certain services categories collected on the form, the percentage of services exports that were performed remotely (from a domestic US office) for a foreign customer located outside of the United States via computer, e-mail, phone, etc.; likewise, respondents were asked to identify the percentage of their purchased services that were performed remotely by the foreign seller. The new questions were originally designed to measure trade in services by mode of supply as defined in the General Agreement on Tariffs and Trade (GATT), but the results will be repurposed by BEA for measuring digitally delivered trade (Mann 2019). Although digitally delivered services exclude those services delivered by phone, fax, physical mail, and manually typed e-mails or texts, which would be considered "remotely performed," it is expected that such transactions compose a small part of remotely performed services, so the new measures should be a good proxy for digitally delivered services.

In addition to collecting new details on international trade in services, BEA also added new questions to its 2019 Benchmark Survey of US Direct Investment Abroad (BE-10) to assist in measuring US multinational enterprises' digital economy activities. New questions asked respondents to separately identify sales that were digitally ordered or digitally delivered as well as those that are derived from the operation of digital intermediary platforms, provision of cloud computing services, or advertising sales, which includes placement in digital media. New questions were added to collect the percentage of the respondent's sales of services that were delivered remotely, sales of services that were digitally ordered, and sales of goods that were digitally ordered, along with checkboxes to identify if this information was sourced from accounting records or from recall/general knowledge. The survey asks respondents to select a range for the sales figures because the expectation is that many firms may not know exactly what percentage of their sales falls into each of these categories. The hope is that firms may be able to provide approximations of these values to inform future sets of BEA digital economy statistics.

In addition, questions requesting the sales derived from the operation of digital intermediary platforms and the provision of cloud computing services, for both US parent companies and their foreign affiliates, and from advertising, which includes placement in digital media, for foreign affiliates were added. Employment and certain costs and expenses were also collected for US parent companies' cloud computing and digital intermediation services activities.

Initial feedback from BE-10 survey respondents led BEA to publish additional guidance for answering the new questions (Bureau of Economic Analysis 2021a). The additional guidance draws out definitions of digitally delivered services and digitally ordered good and services and provides examples for respondents. The guidance also addresses questions related to intermediary platforms and distinction of ownership of the services or goods sold on the platforms.

Finally, BEA continues to evaluate its mailing lists to ensure that its survey coverage adequately captures newly emerging and rapidly growing digital firms. Research will be ongoing to study how firms engaged in digital trade structure their activities to serve foreign markets, including whether they serve international markets from the United States or via foreign affiliates located in regional headquarters or in the local markets that they serve.

6.4 Conclusion and Way Forward

There are many other emerging technologies that are creating a profound impact on the production and consumption of goods and services around the world. The use of digital inputs to produce products, artificial intelligence, cryptocurrencies, and 3-D printing are just a few of these emergent technologies. The US statistical system, including BEA, are continuously working to modernize national statistics and to conduct research to capture the penetration and impact of these technologies.

Moving forward, BEA will continue efforts to produce digital economy estimates on a regular basis. Through this effort, BEA hopes to identify novel datasets to continue to expand the coverage of the estimates toward the development of a full satellite account. Focused research on aspects of the digital economy such as free digital media, cloud computing, and international trade in services will help BEA to accurately measure today's changing economy. BEA regularly engages with the international community on how to best measure and record digital economic activity. This work is consistent with BEA's strategy to produce statistics that are timely, accurate, and relevant to the public.

References

451 Research (2021). Cloud price index. 451research.com/services/price-indexing-benchmarking/cloud-price-index (accessed 1 March 2021).

Ali-Yrkkö, J., Koski, H., Kässi, O., Pajarinen, M., Valkonen, T., Hokkanen, M., Hyvönen, N., Koivusalo, E., Laaksonen, J., Laitinen, J., and Nyström, E., (2020). The size of the digital economy in Finland and its impact on taxation. ETLA Reports 106. https://pub.etla.fi/ETLA-Raportit-Reports-106.pdf.

Australian Bureau of Statistics (ABS) (2019). Digital activity in the Australian economy. https://www.abs.gov.au/articles/digital-activity-australian-economy.

Barefoot, K., Curtis, D., Jolliff, W.A., Nicholson, J.R., and Omohundro, R. (2018). Defining and measuring the digital economy. Bureau of Economic Analysis. https://www.bea.gov/research/papers/2018/defining-and-measuring-digital-economy.

Borga, M. and Koncz-Bruner, J. (2012). Trends in digitally enabled trade in services, 1998–2010. Bureau of Economic Analysis. https://www.bea.gov/research/papers/2012/trends-digitally-enabled-trade-services.

Bureau of Economic Analysis (BEA) (2019). The 2019 annual update of the national income and product accounts. *Survey of Current Business* 99 (8): https://apps.bea.gov/scb/2019/08-august/pdf/0819-nipa-update.pdf.

Bureau of Economic Analysis (BEA) (2020). The 2020 annual update of the industry economic accounts. *Survey of Current Business* 100 (10): https://apps.bea.gov/scb/2020/10-october/pdf/1020-industry-annual-update.pdf.

Bureau of Economic Analysis (BEA) (2021a). Benchmark Survey of US Direct Investment Abroad (BE-10). https://www.bea.gov/be10 (accessed 1 March 2021).

Bureau of Economic Analysis (BEA) (2021b). International Surveys: US International Services Transactions. https://www.bea.gov/international-surveys-us-international-services-transactions (accessed 1 March 2021).

Byrne, D., Corrado, C., and Sichel, D.E. (2018). The rise of cloud computing: minding your P's, Q's and K's. National Bureau of Economic Research. Working paper 25188. https://www.doi.org/10.3386/w25188.

Byrne, D.M., Sichel, D.E., and Aizcorbe, A. (2019). *Getting Smart About Phones: New Price Indexes and the Allocation of Spending Between Devices and Services Plans in Personal Consumption Expenditures*, Finance and Economics Discussion Series 2019–012. Washington: Board of Governors of the Federal Reserve System https://doi.org/10.17016/FEDS.2019.012.

Heys, R. (2019) The impact of digitalization on the national accounts and the satellite accounts. Unpublished paper prepared for the Intersecretariat Working Group on National Accounts Subgroup on Digitalization.

International Monetary Fund (2009). *Balance of Payments and International Investment Position Manual*, 6e. International Monetary Fund.

Kelly, P.A., McCulla, S.H., and Wasshausen, D.A. (2018). Improved estimates of the national income and product accounts: results of the 2018 comprehensive update. Bureau of Economic Analysis. *Survey of Current Business* 98 (9): https://apps.bea.gov/scb/2018/09-september/pdf/0918-nipa-update.pdf.

Mann, M. (2019). Measuring trade in services by mode of supply. Bureau of Economic Analysis. Working Paper Series. WP2019–7. https://www.bea.gov/system/files/papers/WP2019-7_2.pdf.

Nakamura, L., Samuels, J.D., and Soloveichik, R. (2017). Measuring the 'free' digital economy within the GDP and productivity accounts. Bureau of Economic Analysis. https://www.bea.gov/system/files/papers/WP2017-9.pdf.

Nicholson, J.R. (2021). Updated digital economy estimates – June 2021. Bureau of Economic Analysis.

Nicholson, J.R. (2020). New digital economy estimates. Bureau of Economic Analysis. https://www.bea.gov/system/files/2020-08/New-Digital-Economy-Estimates-August-2020.pdf.

Organisation for Economic Co-operation and Development (OECD) (2018). Guidelines for supply-use tables for the digital economy. OECD Statistics and Data Directorate, Committee on Statistics and Statistical Policy, Working Party on National Accounts. SDD/CSSP/WPNA(2018)3. https://www.oecd.org/officialdocuments/publicdisplaydocumentpdf/?cote=SDD/CSSP/WPNA(2018)3&docLanguage=En.

Organisation for Economic Co-operation and Development (OECD) (2019). Guidelines for supply-use tables for the digital economy. OECD Statistics and Data Directorate, Committee on Statistics and Statistical Policy, Working Party on National Accounts. SDD/CSSP/WPNA(2019)3.

Organisation for Economic Co-operation and Development, World Trade Organization, and International Monetary Fund. (2020). *Handbook on Measuring Digital Trade.* Version 1. http://www.oecd.org/sdd/its/Handbook-on-Measuring-Digital-Trade-Version-1.pdf.

Sinclair, A. (2019). *Measuring Digital Economic Activities in Canada: Initial Estimates.* Statistics Canada https://www150.statcan.gc.ca/n1/pub/13-605-x/2019001/article/00002-eng.htm.

Sturgeon, T.J., Fredriksson, T., Fondeur, S. and Korka, D. (2015). International trade in ICT services and ICT-enabled services: proposed indicators from the partnership on measuring ICT for development. *United Nations Conference on Trade and Development (UNCTAD) Division on Technology and Logistics, Science, Technology and ICT Branch, ICT Analysis Section.* https://unctad.org/system/files/official-document/tn_unctad_ict4d03_en.pdf.

United States Census Bureau (2021a). Annual Retail Trade Survey. www.census.gov/programs-surveys/arts.html (accessed 16 February 2021).

United States Census Bureau (2021b). Annual Wholesale Trade Survey. www.census.gov/programs-surveys/awts.html (accessed 16 February 2021).

United States Census Bureau (2021c). North American Industrial Classification System. www.census.gov/naics/ (accessed 1 March 2021).

United Nations Department of Economic and Social Affairs. (2010). Manual on statistics of international trade in services 2010. ST/ESA/M.86/Rev. 1. https://unstats.un.org/unsd/publication/Seriesm/seriesM_86Rev1e.pdf.

Young, J.A., Howells III, T.F., Strassner, E.H., and Wasshausen, D.B. (2015). Supply-use tables for the United States. Bureau of Economic Analysis. https://apps.bea.gov/scb/pdf/2015/09%20September/0915_supply_use_tables_for_the_united_states.pdf.

Zhao, P. (2019). Measuring digital activities in the Australian economy. Australian Bureau of Statistics. https://www.abs.gov.au/statistics/research/measuring-digital-activities-australian-economy.

7

Establishment Based Informal Sector Statistics: An Endeavor of Measurement from Economic Census 2018 of Nepal

Mahesh C. Pradhan

Economic Census Section, Central Bureau of Statistics, Kathmandu, Nepal

7.1 Introduction

Nepal is committed to achieving the Sustainable Development Goals (SDGs) by 2030 Government of Nepal, National Planning Commission, (2017). The global ambitions have also been aligned with the constitution of Nepal, periodic plans and annual budgets with social, economic, and environmental development aspirations. SDGs can only be achieved by setting quantitative benchmarks for sectoral development indicators as a starting point. The Government of Nepal has given a space in their plans and programs for enhancing the national statistical system.

Nepal has a large informal economy, and proper measurement of that economy is essential. Before the informal economy can be measured and official statistics produced, an official definition for the informal and formal economies must be agreed. Although the informal economy is often discussed in Nepal, as yet no official definition of the "informal sector" is set out in legislation or policy documents. In common practice however, economic transactions or activities associated with enterprise or employment, outside of the formal boundary are understood as informal.

The Central Bureau of Statistics (CBS) is the government agency in Nepal authorized to compile various kinds of official statistics, using different data sources, including census, surveys and administrative records, to inform government policies and decision-making. CBS has adopted contemporary definitions of "formal" and "informal sector" as outlined in international statistical guidelines for the compilation of labor force statistics. The results of regular statistical operations, such as, population census, manufacturing establishment census, labor force surveys, living standard surveys, and other thematic economic surveys generally identify, at least partially, statistics on informal activity in respect of employment and nonagricultural enterprise activity.

In this chapter, the current legal status and policy issues regarding informal sectors, as well as efforts to measure those sectors, especially in economic census, are discussed.

7.2 Issues of Informal Sector in Legislation and Policies in Nepal

In recent years, the Government of Nepal has made clear their ambition to formalize economic activities outside the formal economy in different legal, policy documents, and programs. These actions, as outlined in policies, plans, and programs are briefly detailed below.

Advances in Business Statistics, Methods and Data Collection. Edited by Ger Snijkers, Mojca Bavdaž, Stefan Bender, Jacqui Jones, Steve MacFeely, Joseph W. Sakshaug, Katherine J. Thompson, and Arnout van Delden.

7.2.1 Constitution 2015

The *Constitution of Nepal*, promulgated in 2015, envisions a set of labor and employment policies that aim to formalize employment in the national economy Nepal Law Commission (2015). The policy intends to nurture a competent and professional labor force and enhance employment within the country. State policies anticipate guaranteeing social security and protecting workers basic rights, in accordance with the concept of decent labor. These constitutional policies aim to formalize all informal employment in the long run.

7.2.2 Labor Act 2017

The 2017 *Labor Act* includes basic provisions related to labor, such as, prohibition of bonded labor, child labor, and unequal remuneration; trade union rights; and facility of treatment Nepal Law Commission (2017a). The act has categorized employment in five categories, namely: regular; specific; time based; casual; and partial. This legal document details obligations regarding the formalization of kinds of employment in respect of the provisions of social security, employment only with contractual agreement, leave arrangements, etc. These provisions are clear indications of the state's aspiration to formalize the economy.

7.2.3 Contribution Based Social Security Act 2017

The 2017 *Social Security Act* was enacted to secure the rights of labor with respect to social security. The act defines own account workers and labor. Labor is defined as a worker or staff engaged with pay by an employer Nepal Law Commission (2017b). It also includes labor working in designated informal sectors. However, the government has yet to define the informal sector in any published state decree.

7.2.4 Fifteenth Periodic Plan (2019/20–2023/24)

The *Fifteenth Periodic Plan* envisions to create a foundation for economic prosperity, helping Nepal to graduate to an upper-middle-income country. This plan also focuses on programs aiming to fulfill the SDGs by 2030. The plan also intends to achieve equitable economic growth with employment creation by mobilizing the public, private, and cooperative sectors. The long-term vision envisions formalizing the informal economy to increase production and productivity. It has targeted the ratio of unregistered (informal) establishments over total establishments, aiming to reduce that ratio from 50% in 2018/19 to 10% in 2023/24 Government of Nepal, National Planning Commission, (2021). Despite the challenges, the government emphasizes the importance of formalizing the informal sectors for achieving various sectoral goals, such as, the expansion of financial services and revenues, enhancing private and cooperative sectors, and implementing social security and protection systems.

7.2.5 National Employment Policy 2014

The 2014 *National Employment Policy* also aims to transform employment from informal to formal in order to improve the quality of employment Ministry of Labour and employment of Nepal (2014). The legislation and policy documents all address the necessity of formalizing the informal economy. However, these policies lack any strategies to develop informal sector statistics to measure informal economy levels. Furthermore, the basic concept and definition of informal sector have not been agreed from a national perspective. In this respect, the prevailing policies require an agreed definition for the informal sector, to facilitate both policy implementation and measurement.

7.3   Concept and Definition of Informal Sector

The fifteenth International Conference of Labour Statisticians (ICLS), 1993, and the System of National Accounts (SNA), 1993, set out statistical definitions of the informal sector for the purposes of data collection and data analyses. The SNA (1993) defines the informal sector as units engaged in the production of goods and services that form part of the household sector as household enterprises or unincorporated enterprises owned by households with the primary objective of generating employment and income for the persons concerned United Nations (1993) p 135. These household enterprises do not have a legal status independent of the households or household members owing them.

Similarly, the fifteenth ICLS, 1993, adopted an operational definition of the informal sector. Accordingly, the informal sector comprises "informal own-account enterprises" and "enterprises of informal employers." These informal own-account enterprises are unregistered under national legislation. Similarly, enterprises of informal employers are household enterprises owned and operated by employers employing at least one employee on a regular basis where the enterprise or its employees are unregistered under national legislation. The informal employers, employees in the enterprises of informal employers, own-account workers, and unpaid family members contributing to the enterprises are all engaged in the informal sector.

For the purposes of this study, the informal sector is restricted to nonagricultural activities. The aforementioned concepts and definitions have been adopted in full survey life cycle of labor force surveys in Nepal.

In defining the informal sector, the concept and definition must distinguish between the informal sector enterprise and informal employment. According to fifteenth ICLS, informal sector enterprises are units that do not have legal status independent of households or the household members that own them and are located in households United Nations (2009) p 475. Hence, enterprises that are not registered to government agencies must be considered as informal sector enterprises. Furthermore, in the economic census of Nepal, unregistered establishments are assumed to be informal sector establishments.

7.3.1   Definition of Informal Sector from Statistical Perspective

The 2002 International Labour Organization (ILO) *Resolution and Conclusions on Decent Work and Informal Economy* was a milestone in the efforts to address the "informal economy" which it referred to as "all economic activities by workers and economic units that are – in law or in practice – not covered or insufficiently covered by formal arrangements." From a statistical perspective, fifteenth and seventeenth ICLS concepts and definitions are key for application in statistical operations. The fifteenth ICLS defined employment in the informal sector as comprising all jobs in informal sector enterprises, or all persons who, during a given reference period, were employed in at least one informal sector enterprise, irrespective of their status in employment, and whether it was their main or a secondary job. However, the fifteenth ICLS definition of the informal sector did not include households producing goods exclusively for their own final use which was addressed by seventeenth ICLS. This framework disaggregates total employment according to two dimensions: type of production unit and type of job. Production units are categorized into three groups namely formal sector enterprises, informal sector enterprises, and households (Hussmann 2004, p. 4).

Regarding measurement aspects of the informal sector, labor force surveys in Nepal have solely followed the prevailing concepts of ICLS from data collection to data analysis. The Nepal Labour

Force Survey (NLFS) 1998 defined the informal sector in terms of current economic status Central Bureau of Statistics/UNDP/ILO, NEPAL (1999) p.16. An individual whose main job was not in the agriculture sector was counted as working in the informal sector if his or her prevailing job satisfied each of the conditions below:

a. If employment status of an individual was a paid employee, the institutional sector was an unregistered private firm and number of employees in the establishment was less than 10, then, it was considered informal.
b. If individual operated their own business with no employees, then, it was also considered informal.
c. If individual operated their own business with regular employees or contributing family members without pay or other, and number of employees in the establishment was less than 10, then, it was considered informal.

The NLFS 2008 defined the informal sector for enterprises where the number of regular paid employees was less than 10. Establishments with no regular paid employees were also considered to be in the informal sector Central Bureau of Statistics/UNDP/ILO, NEPAL (2009).

The NLFS 2017/18 followed the concept agreed at the seventeenth ICLS. The informal sector (nonagriculture) comprised of those employed in enterprises that are neither incorporated nor registered with authorities. Persons employed in private households were regarded to be in the informal sector. While defining informal sector employment, the production units are classified mainly in three sectors: formal sector enterprises, informal sector enterprises, and households Central Bureau of Statistics/ILO, (2019) p.25. Similarly, the status of employment is categorized as own account workers, employers, contributing family members, employees. Regarding employment, *informal employment* comprises contributing family members in both formal and informal sector enterprises; informal employees in both formal and informal sector enterprises; own account workers in the informal sector enterprises; employers of informal sector enterprises; and employees of households.

Other operations, including the census of population, living standard survey, census of establishments, and other thematic surveys have not explicitly conceptualized or defined the informal sector, either in their data collection instruments or statistical results.

7.4 Endeavors of Measuring Informal Economic Activities in Nepal

The general data sources used for official economic statistics in Nepal are censuses, surveys, and administrative records. Economic activity data for individuals have been collected via population censuses, agriculture censuses, economic census, and household surveys namely living standard surveys, and labor force surveys. However, there are no targeted data collections on informal sector activity. Informal sector data has been derived from the same sources noted above, such as, labor force and living standards surveys, and population censuses. The Economic Census in Nepal supplied statistics on informal sector establishments for the first time.

Efforts to include informal sector activities in each statistical operation is discussed below.

7.4.1 Nepal Labor Force Survey

Over the past 20 years, CBS has conducted three labor force surveys: 1998, 2008, and 2017/2018. The third labor force survey 2017/18 produced labor-related statistics on current employment, unemployment, underemployment, and labor utilization. The main objectives of the survey were to determine the size, status, and structure of the labor force, and objectively to measure the changes in the labor force. The NLFSs also made effort to breakdown employment between the formal and informal sector.

Variables that are relevant to identify statistics on informal sector employment are the following:

- Identification of Main Paid Job/Business Activity: Individuals aged 15 years and above were asked about work for salary or wage, operation of any business for income generation, and contribution to household owned business for without receiving salary/wage.
- Characteristics of main paid job/business activity: Individuals were asked about occupation (kinds of usual activity performed), status of employment, type of contract (permanent, temporary) and contract period, status of social security, paid leave, sick leave, or compensation for illness or injury; place of work; main economic activity (produced goods or services) of the business where the individual was engaged (industry); and the sector of the industry.

7.4.2 Nepal Living Standard Surveys (NLSS)

CBS also conducted three nationwide household Living Standard Surveys in 1995/96, 2003/04, and 2010/11; each was year-round and consisted of multiple topics related to household welfare. Living standards surveys were conducted with the primary objective of measuring living standards and determining poverty levels Central Bureau of Statistics (2011); p 4. These surveys covered a wide range of topics related to "household welfare," including work and time use, employment, unemployment, and nonagricultural activities. Informal employment and informal sector activity can be determined from questions on jobs and time use (engagement status in paid employment in agriculture or nonagriculture; self-employment in agriculture; or nonagriculture), paid work (industrial sector in which work was performed, contributions to employee provident fund, security of pension, medical care, and number of employees); and engagement in nonagriculture enterprises/activities. Though the data on informal activities were collected in living standards surveys, the surveys did not publish any informal sector characteristics. Nevertheless, limited informal sector statistics can be derived from the Nepal Living Standard Surveys (NLSS) microdata.

7.4.3 Population Censuses

CBS has extensive experience of conducting population censuses. The 2011 population census was the eleventh undertaken. It was conducted in two phases: household listing followed by individual enumeration. Regarding informal economic activity, the census posed two questions, "usual activity status of individual of age 10 years and above" during individual enumeration, and "involvement of households in non-agriculture small scale industry during household listing operation."

Although the censuses collected data on the economic activity of the population, employment by occupation, industry and status of employment, and no statistics on informal sector employment were published. However, status of employment can provide partial informal sector statistics. For example, unpaid family workers can be considered as informal employment irrespective of whether they worked in for a formal or an informal enterprise.

The 2001 and 2011 censuses of population collected information on the status of households operating small-scale nonagricultural enterprises. This, to some extent, provided status of informal sector industries around the country. Small-scale nonagricultural industry or own account nonagricultural enterprises were defined as those which were unincorporated/nonregistered, having no regular paid employees, and operated by a household which are conducive to the household's economic benefit. Output produced by these small-scale economic activities may be either for sale or home use; however, if the product is service oriented, it should be sold and not retained for home use Central Bureau of Statistics/ICIMOD (2003). Farm households were also asked whether the household operated small-scale enterprises or businesses other than agriculture. Although the census did not collect employment for nonagriculture business, it nevertheless provided an indication of the status of household-level informal sector businesses operated in the country.

7.5 Economic Census 2018

Economic Statistics is one of the most important components of official statistics. Regular censuses, surveys, and administrative record systems provide the basic statistical infrastructure for producing official statistics. Various approaches exist to estimate the volume of formal and informal employment and its contribution to the economy. Economic Census conducted at regular intervals is considered as one of the principal sources for quantifying the number of informal sector enterprises or establishments.

An economic census is the complete enumeration of all establishments belonging to a given population at a particular time with respect to well-defined characteristics located within geographical boundaries of a country. CBS conducted economic census (named the National Economic Census) in Nepal for the first time in 2018 with technical assistance from the Government of Japan. The enumeration unit of census was the establishment as defined by the International Standard Industrial Classification (ISIC) of all economic activities – Revision 4. The census covered all establishments for a range of different industry sectors (but excluding *agriculture, forestry and fisheries* [not registered Section A], *public administration, defense and compulsory social security* [Section O], *Activities of households as employers; undifferentiated goods- and services-producing activities of households for own use* [Section T] *and Activities of extraterritorial organizations and bodies* [Section U][1]) in order to determine the composition of the establishment-based economy. According to the ICLS definition, unregistered units do not have legal status, so these establishments were assumed to be informal sector establishments.

The main objective of the 2018 economic census was to provide basic statistics on the status of establishments and enterprises in Nepal, to inform central and local government with the information necessary to inform policy-making and support the SNA and academic research. It would also provide a population universe to be used as a sampling frame to support various surveys, and act as a benchmark in the establishment of a statistical business register.

7.5.1 Contents of Economic Census 2018

Important variables included in the census were location information of the establishment, registration status at government offices, characteristics of manager or owner, business characteristics (business hours, business period, year of starting the business; tenure, kind of business, and area of business place), employment status (number of persons engaged in establishment by type of engagement (*working proprietors/partners, managers, unpaid family workers, regular employees, temporary workers*), main economic activity, single or multiunit status, number of branches, account-keeping status, average monthly revenues/sales and operating expenses, access for credit (financial Institutions and others). The results derived from the question on registration status and account-keeping status are key variables for deriving informal sector statistics from the census.

---

1 As detailed in ISIC rev.4.

A number of economic and business characteristics were derived including both dimensions of registered (formal) and unregistered (informal) sector in terms of establishment and employment. The census revealed new insights for economic sectors which were not covered by other statistical operations. The census was successful in providing official figures on informal establishments, and their characteristics, disaggregated by ISIC sections to local level.

7.6 Status of the Informal Sector Statistics

Informal sector statistics are derived from different sources like Nepalese labor force surveys, population, and economic censuses. The status of informal statistics for each source is briefly discussed as below.

7.6.1 Informal Sector Statistics from Nepal Labor Force Survey 1998 and 2008

The 2008 NLFS estimated that about 2142 thousand people aged 15 years and over were currently employed in the nonagricultural informal sector (accounting for about 70% of total nonagricultural employment) compared with 1657 thousand in 1998/99 (73% of current nonagricultural employment). Between 1998 and 2008 employment in the nonagricultural informal sector grew by 29.3% (NLFS 1998, 2008). The NLFS 2008 revealed a total of 2655 thousand informally employed persons, of which, the share of employees without formal condition was 39.7%, employers, and others in informal sector 4%, self-employed without employees 36.5%, and contributing family workers (19.8%). Central Bureau of Statistics/UNDP/ILO, NEPAL (2009).

7.6.2 Informal Sector Statistics from Nepal Labor Force Survey 2017/18

Table 7.1 presents employment by formal and informal sector. NLFS results show that approximately 7.1 million persons were employed and 908,000 were unemployed (unemployment rate of 11.4%) out of a working age population of approximately 20.7 million. Further, survey results reveal that the informal sector accounted for roughly 62% of employment. The main contributor to total employment was informal nonagriculture employment, accounting for 41% of all jobs. Out of the total, approximately, 4.5 million males employed, almost 46% were employed in the nonagriculture informal sector. The equivalent share for female employment was almost 33%.

Table 7.2 presents the distribution of employment for each sector. Total employment in the informal sector was about 4.4 million, out of which, males accounted for a bigger share – approximately 60%. Out of the total 2.9 million persons employed in the informal nonagriculture sector; males accounted for about 70%. The proportion of females employed in the informal agriculture sector is quite high at about 59% – see Table 7.2.

Analyses of employment by occupation in the informal sector shows that a larger proportion of employment in informal nonagriculture are concentrated in Service and sales workers, Elementary occupations, craft and related trades workers, and skilled agricultural, forestry and fishery workers, accounting for almost 94% of the total 4.4 million employed Central Bureau of Statistics/ILO, (2019); (NLFS 2017/18).

7.6.3 Informal Sector Statistics from National Population Census 2011

As part of the enumeration for the 2011 National Population Census, the usual activities of enumerated individuals (10 years and above) during the last 12 months in selected households was

Table 7.1   Employment by sector.

Sn	Sector	Total employed		Male		Female	
		In 1000	Percent	In 1000	Percent	In 1000	Percent
A	Formal	2675	37.8	1792	40.3	884	33.5
A.1	Agriculture	90	1.3	58	1.3	32	1.2
A.2	Nonagriculture	2586	36.5	1734	39.0	852	32.3
B	Informal	4411	62.2	2655	59.7	1756	66.5
B.1	Agriculture	1434	20.2	595	13.4	839	31.8
B.2	Nonagriculture	2904	41.0	2035	45.8	869	32.9
C	Private households	73	1.0	25	0.6	48	1.8
	Total	7086	100.0	4447	100.0	2640	100.0

Source: Data from NLFS 2017/18. Central Bureau of Statistics/ILO, (2019);

Table 7.2   Employment by sector.

SN	Sector	Total employed		Male		Female	
		In 1000	Percent	In 1000	Percent	In 1000	Percent
A	Formal	2675	100.0	1792	67.0	884	33.0
A.1	Agriculture	90	100.0	58	64.4	32	35.6
A.2	Nonagriculture	2586	100.0	1734	67.1	852	32.9
B	Informal	4411	100.0	2655	60.2	1756	39.8
B.1	Agriculture	1434	100.0	595	41.5	839	58.5
B.2	Nonagriculture	2904	100.0	2035	70.1	869	29.9
C	Private households	73	100.0	25	34.2	48	65.8
	Total	7086	100.0	4447	62.8	2640	37.2

Source: Data from NLFS 2017/18. Central Bureau of Statistics/ILO, (2019);

collected. This comprised questions on activity status, occupation, industry, employment status, and reasons for not doing any economic activity. These results do not give the precise status of informal employment as there was insufficient information on whether persons were engaged in the formal or informal sectors. However, for unpaid family workers engaged in formal or informal sector, they were assumed to be informal employment. On this assumption, about 1.3% of the total economically active population can said to be partially in informal employment Central Bureau of Statistics, Nepal (2013) (Population Census 2011).

In 2001 Population Census, a total of 840,128 households, or 20% of all households reported operating nonagriculture, small-scale economic industries Central Bureau of Statistics 2002. For the 2011 census, the proportion of households engaged in small-scale nonagriculture industries was 14% (Population Census 2001 (Central Bureau of Statistics 2002) and 2011 (Central Bureau of Statistics 2014b)), illustrating the reduction of household participation in informal nonagriculture economic activities over the decade.

7.6.4   Informal Sector Statistics from National Economic Census 2018

The 2018 Economic Census is also a major source of informal sector official statistics in terms of establishment statistics. It is the primary source of economic data, providing important statistics on the composition and functioning of the national economy, including both the formal and informal sectors. The variables used to identify informality were "registration status" and "account keeping status" for reporting establishments.

The Census found 923,356 establishments, with 3,228,457 persons engaged. The census revealed some interesting facts, such as about half of all total establishments enumerated were operating without registration in any government agency (see Table 7.3). This was the first official estimate on the number of informal establishments operating in the country. Table 7.3 shows the registration status of establishments for each ISIC sector. The share of unregistered establishments was higher for industries like Accommodation and food service activities (63.3% of that sector), Wholesale and retail trade, repair of motor vehicles and motorcycles (56% of that sector), Other service activities (52.7% of that sector), and Manufacturing (51.4% of that sector).

Of the 460,422 unregistered establishments, proportions of unregistered establishments were notably concentrated in Wholesale and retail trade, repair of motor vehicles and motorcycles industry (60.5%) followed by Accommodation and food service activities (17.9%), Manufacturing (11.6%), Other service activities (6.6%), and Human health and social work activities (1.1%).

A total of roughly 3.23 million persons were engaged by 923 thousand establishments yielding an average of 3.5 persons engaged per establishment. Although the proportion of registered to unregistered establishments were nearly equal, accounting for about 50% each in each sector, only 26% of total persons were engaged by unregistered establishments (Figure 7.1), i.e. three quarters of persons are engaged by formal or registered establishments.

Across the ISIC industries (Table 7.4), the share of persons engaged working in unregistered establishments was highest in Accommodation and food service activities (46%) followed by Wholesale and retail trade, repair of motor vehicles and motorcycles (45%), Other service activities industry (34%), Arts, entertainment and recreation (21%), and Manufacturing (21%).

Of the 832,187 persons engaged in unregistered establishments, almost 93% were employed in a handful of sectors: Wholesale and retail trade, repair of motor vehicles and motorcycles; Accommodation and food service activities; Manufacturing and Other services.

7.6.5   Status of Keeping Accounting Record

The 2018 Economic Census also collected information from entities which consisted of a single unit or a head office only. There are altogether 900,924 entities,[2] for which the "status of preparing accounting record" was collected. 472,350 entities did not keep accounting records. Thus, from the perspective of accounting practices, 52.4% of entities were considered informal. Accommodation and food service activities; Wholesale and retail trade, repair of motor vehicles and motorcycles; Manufacturing; and Other services industries with no accounting records were the highest (see Table 7.5).

7.6.6   Informality in Micro Small and Medium Establishments (MSME)

Micro-, small-, and medium-sized enterprises (MSMEs) are the backbone of a growing economy. They play a substantial role in generating employment, sustaining livelihoods, particularly in

---

2   The residual 22,432 units were branches or subbranches of head office establishments.

Table 7.3 Registration status of establishments by industry.

ISIC sections	ISIC industry	Total	Registered	Unregistered	Registered	Unregistered	Not stated
			Establishments		Percent		
	Total	923,356	462,605	460,422	50.1	49.9	0
A	Agriculture, forestry, and fishing[a]	24,229	24,229		100	0	0
B	Mining and quarrying	663	481	182	72.5	27.5	0
C	Manufacturing	104,058	50,566	53,458	48.6	51.4	0
D	Electricity, gas, steam, and air conditioning supply	1,242	1,242		100	0	0
E	Water supply; sewerage, waste management, and remediation activities	2,525	1,916	609	75.9	24.1	0
F	Construction	1,608	1,265	342	78.7	21.3	0.1
G	Wholesale and retail trade, repair of motor vehicles, and motorcycles	498,069	219,253	278,747	44	56	0
H	Transportation and storage	3,182	2,847	334	89.5	10.5	0
I	Accommodation and food service activities	130,540	47,931	82,590	36.7	63.3	0
J	Information and communication	2,796	2,487	308	88.9	11	0
K	Financial and insurance activities	17,996	16,524	1,462	91.8	8.1	0.1
L	Real estate activities	207	166	40	80.2	19.3	0.5
M	Professional, scientific, and technical activities	8,204	5,673	2,417	69.1	29.5	1.4
N	Administrative and support service activities	6,873	4,931	1,940	71.7	28.2	0
P	Education	40,839	39,174	1,634	95.9	4	0.1
Q	Human health and social work activities	19,990	14,934	5,047	74.7	25.2	0
R	Arts, entertainment, and recreation	2,821	1,800	1,021	63.8	36.2	0
S	Other service activities	57,514	27,186	30,291	47.3	52.7	0.1

a) Surveyed only registered.
Source: Data from National Economic Census 2018. Central Bureau of Statistics (2019a).

Figure 7.1 Share of number of persons engaged by registered and unregistered establishments.

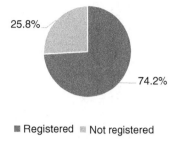

25.8%

74.2%

■ Registered ■ Not registered

less-developed countries. MSMEs in Nepal emerged as a major contributor to employment creation, regional development, and economic growth.

Although most countries use three criteria: assets, employment, and annual turnover to categorize establishments by size, in Nepal categorizes industries into five groups (micro, cottage, small, medium, and large) largely based on the investment of fixed capital as defined in the Industrial Enterprise Act 2020 (IEA 2020) Nepal Law Commission (2020). However, in the absence of other information, CBS classifies establishments as follows:

- Micro establishment – engage up to 9 persons
- Small establishment – engage between 10 and 49 persons
- Medium establishment – engage between 50 and 99 persons
- Large establishment – engage 100 persons or more

The 2018 Economic Census showed that MSMEs accounted for 99.8% of the 923,356 establishments (Table 7.6). With a total of 3,228,457 persons engaged, MSMEs accounted for almost 85% of total establishment employment. Of the 460,422 unregistered establishments, micro establishments accounted for 99.5%, with small, medium, and large establishments making up the balance (See Figure 7.2 and Table 7.6).

Table 7.6 shows the number of MSMEs by industry. Of the 880,254 micro establishments, 52% were unregistered. Similarly, of the 38,737 small establishments, 5% were unregistered; of the 2253 medium-sized establishments, just less than 4% were unregistered. Across unregistered establishments, most sectors were dominated by microscale industries.

Of the 832,187 persons engaged by unregistered establishments, micro establishments accounted for almost 94%; unregistered small establishments accounted for around 4%, unregistered medium establishments almost 1%, and unregistered large establishments a little over 1%, respectively.

7.6.7 Street Business Situation

The economic census also collected information on kind of business, using seven categories, namely: (i) street business; (ii) home business; (iii) business in building with sturdy construction for shop or office (business place and owner's residence are separate); (iv) business in traditional market; (v) business in modern shopping mall; (vi) business occupying one block or one building; and (vii) others. A street business means any business that offers goods or services for production or sale without having a permanently built building or structure but only a temporary address, mobile stall or booth, runs from a sidewalk or roadside, or around but outside a market. In the 2018 economic census, only street business establishments with a fixed location were enumerated.

Table 7.4 Persons engaged in establishments by registration status and industry.

ISIC sections	ISIC industries	Total	Registered	Not registered	Registered	Not Registered	Not stated
			(Persons engaged)			Percent	
	Total	**3,228,457**	**2,394,097**	**832,187**	**74.2**	**25.8**	**0.1**
A	Agriculture, forestry, and fishing[a]	106,410	106,410		100	0	0
B	Mining and quarrying	7,726	7,186	540	93	7	0
C	Manufacturing	510,523	405,315	104,514	79.4	20.5	0.1
D	Electricity, gas, steam, and air conditioning supply	20,170	20,170		100	0	0
E	Water supply; sewerage, waste management, and remediation activities	15,312	12,511	2,801	81.7	18.3	0
F	Construction	14,750	13,729	972	93.1	6.6	0.3
G	Wholesale and retail trade, repair of motor vehicles, and motorcycles	988,346	539,867	448,321	54.6	45.4	0
H	Transportation and storage	20,027	18,952	1,072	94.6	5.4	0
I	Accommodation and food service activities	346,273	186,001	160,200	53.7	46.3	0
J	Information and communication	39,789	39,064	722	98.2	1.8	0
K	Financial and insurance activities	206,979	200,529	6,437	96.9	3.1	0
L	Real estate activities	1,977	1,918	58	97	2.9	0.1
M	Professional, scientific, and technical activities	33,254	28,560	4,544	85.9	13.7	0.5
N	Administrative and support service activities	45,999	40,829	5,166	88.8	11.2	0
P	Education	513,336	500,166	12,270	97.4	2.4	0.2
Q	Human health and social work activities	164,498	143,547	20,924	87.3	12.7	0
R	Arts, entertainment, and recreation	16,062	12,637	3,425	78.7	21.3	0
S	Other service activities	177,026	116,706	60,221	65.9	34	0.1

a) Surveyed only registered.
Source: Data from National Economic Census 2018. Central Bureau of Statistics (2019a).

Table 7.5 Status of keeping account records by industry.

ISIC section	Total entities	Keeping account record status					
		Entities			Percent		
		Yes	No	Not stated	Yes	No	Not stated
A[a)]	23,899	17,333	6,500	66	72.5	27.2	0.3
B	638	385	252	1	60.3	39.5	0.2
C	103,112	46,261	56,696	155	44.9	55.0	0.2
D	942	880	58	4	93.4	6.2	0.4
E	2,442	1,697	739	6	69.5	30.3	0.2
F	1,489	1,129	358	2	75.8	24.0	0.1
G	495,199	206,568	288,103	528	41.7	58.2	0.1
H	1,479	1,119	356	4	75.7	24.1	0.3
I	130,044	50,861	79,030	153	39.1	60.8	0.1
J	2,285	1,776	504	5	77.7	22.1	0.2
K	11,093	10,637	429	27	95.9	3.9	0.2
L	187	141	45	1	75.4	24.1	0.5
M	7,976	4,208	3,644	124	52.8	45.7	1.6
N	5,815	3,870	1,942	3	66.6	33.4	0.1
P	39,996	38,112	1,820	64	95.3	4.6	0.2
Q	16,372	13,312	3,003	57	81.3	18.3	0.3
R	2,722	1,614	1,095	13	59.3	40.2	0.5
S	55,234	27,338	27,776	120	49.5	50.3	0.2
Total	900,924	427,241	472,350	1,333	47.4	52.4	0.1

a)   Surveyed only registered.
Source: Data from National Economic Census 2018. Central Bureau of Statistics (2019a).

The total number of establishments identified as street businesses was 34,101, accounting almost 4% of establishments. The number of persons engaged in street business was 45,330 or roughly 1% of persons engaged. Street businesses were predominantly unregistered establishments (95%) – see Table 7.7.

Out of the enumerated 18 ISIC industry groups, there were street businesses operating in nine of them. Most of the 34,101 street business establishments were classified to "Wholesale and retail trade, repair of motor vehicles and motorcycles sector" (78%); followed by "Accommodation and food service activities sector" (15%) and "Other Services" (4%). About 18% of these street businesses reported keeping accounts while the remaining four-fifths did not.

7.7   Annual Revenues/Sales, Operating Expenses in Not-Registered Establishments

Information on average monthly revenues/sales and operating expenses were collected from establishments for the fiscal year 2017/18. All revenues or income received from operating economic

Table 7.6 Establishments by scale of industry.

ISIC section	Total	Net total	Both (registered and not) Establishments				MSM[a] %	Not registered Establishments			
			Micro	Small	Medium	Large		Micro	Small	Medium	Large
Total	923,356	923,027	880,254	38,737	2,253	1783	99.8	458,258	2,032	88	44
A	24,229	24,229	21,972	2,112	74	71	99.7	0	0	0	0
B	663	663	394	255	8	0	99.1	176	6	0	
C	104,058	104,024	98,960	3,878	457	0	99.3	53,199	244	8	
D	1,242	1,242	898	263	57	31	98.1	0	0	0	7
E	2,525	2,525	2,129	383	11	0	99.9	557	50	1	
F	1,608	1,607	1,285	281	21	21	98.7	322	20	0	1
G	498,069	498,000	494,555	3,274	108	0	99.97	278,648	97	2	
H	3,182	3,181	2,919	217	27	0	99.4	322	10	2	
I	130,540	130,521	127,751	2,634	97	0	99.96	82,412	176	1	
J	2,796	2,795	1,968	686	84	58	97.9	300	7	1	1
K	17,996	17,986	14,096	3,631	93	0	99.0	1,309	142	9	
L	207	206	162	34	10	2	99.5	40	0	0	2
M	8,204	8,090	7,731	320	24	0	98.4	2,399	17	1	
N	6,873	6,871	6,195	630	27	0	99.7	1,903	37	0	
P	40,839	40,808	24,306	15,395	842	0	99.3	1,298	313	14	
Q	19,990	19,981	17,562	2,068	160	193	99.0	4,632	386	22	9
R	2,821	2,821	2,527	273	11	17	99.6	938	82	1	7
S	57,514	57,477	54,844	2,403	142	0	99.8	29,803	445	26	

a) MSM means Micro, Small, Medium.
Source: Data from National Economic Census 2018. Central Bureau of Statistics (2019b) & Central Bureau of Statistics (2020a).

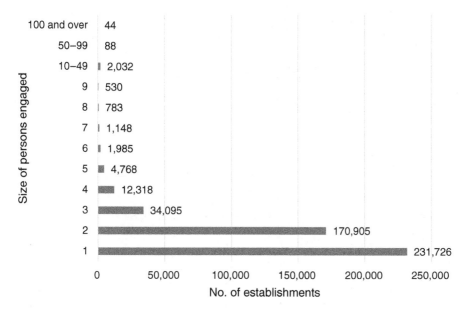

Figure 7.2 Number of unregistered establishments by size of persons engaged.

Table 7.7 Establishments and persons engaged by registration status for street business.

Sn	Variables	Registered	Not registered	Not stated	Total
1	Establishments	1,763	32,335	3	34,101
	Share in %	5.2	94.8	0.0	100.0
2	Persons engaged	2,859	42,467	4	45,330
	Share in %	6.3	93.7	0.0	100.0

Source: Data from National Economic Census 2018. Central Bureau of Statistics (2019a).

activities, such as selling goods or providing services, interest and noninterest income from banks, insurance premiums, and fees were all included in revenues or sales. Similarly, operating expenses, including all expenses being paid to operate economic activities. This included operating costs, such as costs of raw materials, other operating costs, such as fuels, gas, electricity, and water expenses, transportation expenses, rental expenses, commissions, tax expenses, and so forth. To derive average annual revenues or sales, average monthly revenues or sales were multiplied by 12. Similarly, for average annual operating expenses. The profit/loss was computed as the difference between annual sales and expenses, which is assumed to be conceptually close to operating surplus/mixed income in gross domestic product (GDP). The concept of the annual revenues/sales is close to that of gross output in the SNA.

The census results show that annual sales/revenues were 2916 billion rupees (US$ 28.6 billion) and annual profits were 853 billion rupees (US$ 8.4 billion) in Nepal in 2017/18 (the year 2074 in Nepalese calendar). While the annual sales and profits for unregistered entities were 233 billion rupees (US$ 2.3 billion) and 72 billion rupees (US$ 0.7 billion), respectively (see Figure 7.3 and Table 7.8). Unregistered establishments accounted for 8% of total annual sales (Table 7.8). In the

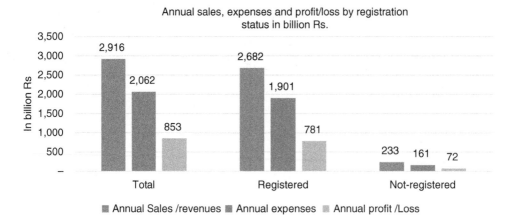

Figure 7.3 Annual sales, expenses, and profit/loss.

Table 7.8 Annual sales, expenses, and profit/loss by registration status.

Type of entities	Annual sales/revenues	Annual expenses	Annual profit /loss
		In billion Rs.	
Total	2,916	2,062	853
Registered	2,682	1,901	781
Not-registered	233	161	72
		Percent	
Total	100	100	100
Registered	92.0	92.2	91.5
Not-registered	8.0	7.8	8.4

Source: Data from National Economic Census 2018. Central Bureau of Statistics, (2020b).

absence of a contribution of the informal sector to total GDP, this figure can be used as an approximation of the contribution of unregistered establishments to total annual sales and gross output. However, as the economic census did not cover all ISIC industry groups, this approximation is most likely an underestimate.

7.8   Need of Regular Measurement Informal Sector

Large informal sectors are prevalent in most developing countries, especially in low-income countries. Measuring informal sector activities is important not only to quantify and understand the contribution of the informal activities to the total economy and employment but also to understand potential tax leakages, and the proportion of the working population not covered by social insurance and other state-sponsored welfare schemes. The informal economy plays an important role in production, employment, and income generation, and there is growing interest in this topic, accompanied by an acceptance of the need to measure informal sector activities either in terms of employment or enterprises, or both. In order to plan for the introduction of social security schemes, the size of the informal economy must be quantified.

Informal sector enterprises or establishments generate informal employment, production, and income. These entities are unincorporated, market-oriented, and unregistered. Regular surveys, such as economic census and labor force surveys are probably the most reliable data sources for capturing information on informal enterprises or establishments and for deriving indicators relating to informal activities. The results from these statistical operations are critical in assisting policy makers to formulate policies on the informal economy, including the creation of decent work and productive employment to promote sustained economic growth.

If the informal sector activities are not considered in the measurement of economy, estimates of the GDP will be underestimated, as will employment estimates. Additionally, if the informal sector is unmeasured within the national statistical system, it will undermine efforts to formulate policies to improve the working conditions and social protection of persons engaged in the informal sector. Furthermore, attempts to increase productivity in the informal sector, develop capacity in informal sector, or implement formalization and reform programs will all be weakened owing to a lack of statistical information. Hence, statistics on the informal sector are essential.

Measuring the informal economy is complex. Producing robust informal sector statistics that include the volumes and characteristics of that sector is essential to have a full understanding of the labor and business economies. It is also essential for a fully developed set of national accounts.

7.9 Conclusion

Nepal, as a developing country, has made significant efforts in to measuring the size of informal economy via surveys and censuses. Three editions of the labor force survey have provided informal sector statistics in terms of employment, using ICLS concepts and definitions. Likewise, the first economic census, conducted in 2018, also produced official estimates on the number of informal establishments for the first time in Nepal. In addition, population censuses and other surveys have also collected partial information on informal activities. The 2018 economic census highlighted for the first time that about half of all establishments are unregistered – a statistic that attracted a lot of attention. This result had immediate policy implications for the fifteenth periodic plan, which aims to reduce the proportion of unregistered establishments significantly. The census also shed light on several important business characteristics, such as the number of street businesses, the scale of industry in terms of the number of persons engaged, the number of businesses that keep formal accounts, and their estimates revenues/sales, expenses, and profits or losses.

The statistical facts from censuses and surveys have revealed the importance of the informal economy in Nepal, highlighting the role it plays in employment creation, income generation, and economic production. These findings and patterns will no doubt be replicated in many other developing countries. It is imperative that the size of informal sector is systematically measured by regular statistical operations like economic censuses and/or labor force surveys. The measurement of the informal sector is critically important for the formulation and evaluation of effective policies to support the transformation from informal to formal economies, and the creation of decent work, social security programs, and sustainable economic growth.

It is desirable to measure the contribution of the informal sector to GDP. Although the labor force surveys and economic census has supplied size of informal employment and number of informal establishments by ISIC, the available data may be insufficient to compute robust estimates for gross value added (GVA). For example, labor force surveys do not provide informal production by sector, which is essential for estimating GVA. Although the economic census provided average annual sales/revenues by ISIC sections, which gives a close approximation of gross output, it remains difficult to estimate intermediate consumptions.

The basic requirements to understand the informal economy are gross output, intermediate consumption, compensation of employees, and gross value added so that the contribution of the informal sector to GDP can be properly estimated. As noted above, these variables are still missing or incomplete from the existing data sources. Hence, thematic establishment surveys of the informal sector or mixed household-enterprise surveys are required to measure value added of the informal sector and other features of informal economic units. A mixed household-enterprise survey is desirable as it would also reveal enterprise and household production.

References

Central Bureau of Statistics (2002). Population Census 2001-National Report Table 7: Households Operating Small Scale Non-Agricultural Activities by Type of Activity for Regions and Districts.

Central Bureau of Statistics (2019a). National Economic Census 2018. National Report, Report No. 1-1 by Industry.

Central Bureau of Statistics (2019b). National Economic Census 2018. National Report, Report No. 1-2 by Size of Persons Engaged.

Central Bureau of Statistics, (2020a). National Economic Census 2018, National Profile, Profile No. 1 by Province.

Central Bureau of Statistics, (2020b). National Economic Census 2018, National Report on Revenues/Sales, Expenses, and Profit and Loss, Report No. 2-1 by Industry.

Central Bureau of Statistics/ICIMOD (2003). Mapping Nepal Census Indicators 2001 and Trends. http://lib.icimod.org/record/21217. pp. 84–87.

Central Bureau of Statistics, Nepal (2017). Labour statistics. A Compendium of National Statistical System of Nepal. pp. 170–184.

Central Bureau of Statistics (2011). Nepal Living Standards Survey 2010/11.

Central Bureau of Statistics/ILO (2019). Report on the Nepal Labour Force Survey 2017/18.

Central Bureau of Statistics/UNDP/ILO, NEPAL (2009). Report on the Nepal Labour Force Survey 2008.

Central Bureau of Statistics/UNDP/ILO, NEPAL (1999). Report on the Nepal Labour Force Survey 1998.

Central Bureau of Statistics (2014a). Chapter 1: Economically active population: dimensions and dynamics. *Population Monograph of Nepal Volume III (Economic Demography)*.

Central Bureau of Statistics (2014b) Chapter 2: Own account economic activities of Nepalese households. *Population Monograph of Nepal Volume III (Economic Demography)*.

Central Bureau of Statistics, Nepal (2013). National Population and Housing Census 2011 (Tables from Form-II) Volume 03.

Central Bureau of Statistics, Nepal (2014). National Census of Manufacturing Establishments, 2011/12 National Level.

Government of Nepal, National Planning Commission (2017). Sustainable Development Goals – Status and Roadmap: 2016–2030.

Government of Nepal, National Planning Commission (2021). The Fifteenth Plan (Fiscal Year 2019/20–2023/24). www.npc.gov.np/images/category/15th_plan_English_Version.pdf.

Government of Nepal, Ministry of Finance (2017). Economic Survey Fiscal Year 2016/17. https://new .mof.gov.np/site/publication-detail/1292 (accessed 30 June 2021).

Nepal Law Commission (2015). The Constitution of Nepal, published in Nepal Gazette. https://www
.lawcommission.gov.np/en/wp-content/uploads/2021/01/Constitution-of-Nepal.pdf.

Nepal Law Commission (2017a). The Labour Act 2017, published in Nepal Gazette. https://www
.lawcommission.gov.np/en/wp-content/uploads/2021/03/The-Labor-Act-2017-2074.pdf.

Nepal Law Commission (2017b). The Contribution based Social Security Act 2017. Date of Publication
in Nepal Gazette 13 August 2017 (2074.4.29). https://www.ilo.org/dyn/natlex/docs/ELECTRONIC/
105433/128933/F582338382/NPL105433%20Npl.pdf.

Ministry of Labour and employment of Nepal (2014). National Employment Policy of Nepal 2014
(unofficial translation). https://www.ilo.org/wcmsp5/groups/public/---asia/---ro-bangkok/---ilo-
kathmandu/documents/policy/wcms_539895.pdf.

ILO (2013). Measuring informality: A statistical manual on the informal sector and informal
employment.

Ralf Hussmann (2004). Measuring the informal economy: From employment in the informal sector to
informal employment. Working Paper No. 53, ILO.

United Nations (1993). *System of National Accounts 1993*, 133–136.

United Nations (2009). *System of National Accounts 2008*, 471–482.

Section 2

Topics in the Production of Official Establishment Statistics and Organizational Frameworks

8

Statistical Producers Challenges and Help

Jacqui Jones[1] and Holly O'Byrne[2]

[1] *Australian Bureau of Statistics, Canberra, ACT, Australia*
[2] *Statistics Canada, Ottawa, Ontario, Canada*

8.1 Introduction

Across the world, National Statistical Institutes (NSIs), and often Central Banks, produce economic statistics. Statistics produced by NSIs are regarded as "official" statistics, a brand representing specific professional principles aligned with the UN Fundamental Principles of Official Statistics. These official statistics are used for monitoring the health of domestic economies, to inform policy making, and for international comparisons.

The chapter starts with a brief historical overview of the evolution of economic statistics, including the establishment of NSIs. It then looks at the challenges and help in our statistical ecosystem. The international statistical system provides enormous help for us, including informally learning from one another. To illustrate this, Statistic Canada's integrated business statistics program is provided as a case study. This program is aimed at improving data quality, reducing response burden, modernizing data processing infrastructure, integrating economic surveys, simplifying, and standardizing processes and reducing costs.

8.2 A Brief Overview of the Evolution of Economic Statistics, and the Establishment of National Statistical Institutes

Throughout history, good quality economic data has been needed to inform decision-making and monitor the health of economies. Today, despite major developments in business surveys and statistical methods, and increased access to nonsurvey data, many of the challenges remain. For example, acquiring good quality timely data, response burden, up-to-date coherent and consistent classifications, creating and maintaining time series, keeping pace with economic developments, and demand outweighing supply.

Economists such as Adam Smith (1723–1790), Karl Marx (1818–1883), Alfred Marshal (1842–1924), and John Maynard Keynes (1883–1946) did not have the luxury of accessible comprehensive economic data to analyze. Both Marshal and Keynes noted that there was a need for more quantitative information for economic theory (Persons 1925, p. 180). There were moves to more systematically collect data but developments were slow. For example, in 1834, Charles Babbage, Thomas Malthus, and Richard Jones formed the United Kingdom (UK) Royal Statistical

Advances in Business Statistics, Methods and Data Collection. Edited by Ger Snijkers, Mojca Bavdaž, Stefan Bender, Jacqui Jones, Steve MacFeely, Joseph W. Sakshaug, Katherine J. Thompson, and Arnout van Delden.

Society. The objectives of the Society were *the collection and classification of all facts illustrative of the present condition and prospects of Society, especially as it exists in the British Dominions* (Royal Statistical Society 2021). Then in 1839, the American Statistical Association was formed.

Up to the early 1930s economic data remained patchy (Persons 1925 provides a good overview of how statistics in the United States [US] increased between 1919 and 1925). The patchy data was often focused on specific areas such as production, stock numbers, and freight handling data (United States and U.S. Census Bureau, Statistical Abstracts of the United States 1878 provide a good overview of available statistics). This created enormous issues in understanding economic impacts, especially during the Great Depression of the 1920s and 1930s when there was the 1929 stock market crash, banking panics, monetary contraction, and the sterilization of gold (gold inflows not included in the monetary base). The impacts were extreme with estimates of industrial production falling by 32% and unemployment hitting 20% in the United States (Bordo and Haubrich 2012). Something had to be done to improve measurement of the economy.

In 1934, Simon Kuznets (US, National Bureau of Economic Research) produced the first US national income accounts for the period 1929–1932[1].

Kuznets in a 1941 paper notes that "available data were often limited to inaccurate administrative data that was not categorized in any useful way or widely accessible" (p. 27). He stresses throughout his paper the importance of time series data. Then in 1937, Colin Clark published National Income and Outlay, with current price and constant price estimates for 1924 and 1929–1936. Clark was also the first person to produce quarterly estimates (from 1929 to 1936). This work was the foundation for the first official British National Accounts in 1941. In his work Clark encouraged the use of estimation, which would eventually change Government's use of statistics (Cairncross 1988).

With increased interest in Keynesian economics after World War II, many governments around the world started to manage the economy more directly and increase their focus on the need for statistics to help them. In 1945 in Australia, the government released the White Paper on Full Employment. Later that year, the Director-General of the Department for Post–War Reconstruction wrote to the then Acting National Statistician "requesting that major improvements be made to economic statistics to facilitate national economic planning" (ABS 2005, p. 38). This paved the way for further development of Australian Balance of Payments and National Accounts.

In the United Kingdom, the 1942 report "Social Insurance and Allied Services" (often referred to as the Beveridge report) posed the establishment of the UK welfare system. The Beverage report looked at how the five giants of idleness, ignorance, disease, squalor, and want, could be abolished (Beveridge, paras 6–16). It proposed a social program setting the foundation of the UK welfare system that would require statistics to monitor it.

The establishment of centralized NSIs generally coincided with the increased need for comprehensive, coherent, and timely statistics. Prior to 1941, individual government departments in the United Kingdom had their own statistical units (Pullinger 1997). This often resulted in incoherent statistics, which was a particular frustration of Sir Winston Churchill in his war-time efforts. When he was appointed to Prime Minister in 1940, he took the opportunity to establish the Central Statistical Office (1941) in the War Cabinet Office *for the purpose of collecting a regular series of statistics from government departments covering the development of the War effort. These statistics were to be accepted and used as authoritative in interdepartmental discussions* (The National Archives' Catalogue 1934–1987).

The development of National Accounts was pivotal in establishing more frequent comprehensive economic data to monitor the health of an economy (see Chapter 2 by MacFeely and van de

---

1 https://apps.bea.gov/scb/2020/08-august/0820-influencer-kuznets.htm

Table 8.1 Illustrative overview of the development of UK Economic Censuses and Surveys.

1864	First mines and quarries employment information.
1866	First Agriculture Census (took 10 yrs to achieve a satisfactory response rate).
1886	First Census of Wages (achieved a 75% response rate).
1907	First Economic Census.
1913	Census of Production established on a five-yearly basis (but did not occur as planned due to budgets and war).
1924	Voluntary survey of wages and hours.
1941	Establishment of the Central Statistical Office and more frequent monthly and quarterly data collected from businesses.
1948	Census of Production moved to annual and used the first Standard Industrial Classification.
1950	First Census of Distribution established on a five-yearly basis.
1951	Voluntary capital expenditure survey as information excluded from the Census of Production.
1952	Sampling and estimation introduced for the Census of Production. The sample frame was the 1950 Census responses.
1958	Census of Production returned to five-yearly and the 1958 Standard Industrial Classification introduced. Monthly and quarterly surveys continued to collect data for use in National Accounts (e.g. sales, stocks, and capital expenditure).
1960s	Review of statistics. Resulted in major changes to increase the frequency and detail of data, reduce processing times, and harmonize concepts. Business Statistics Office was set-up to run the surveys and produce the statistics.
1968	Census of Production introduced the 1968 Standard Industrial Classification, and the 1963 data was reclassified to the 1968 industrial classification.
1998	Annual Business Inquiry replaced and integrated many surveys.

Source: Adapted from information in Smith and Pennick (2009).

Ven (2023a) for more information). As already outlined, prior to this, only aspects of an economy were measured. Table 8.1 provides an illustrative overview (not comprehensive) of the development of UK Economic Censuses and surveys. As you can see, the data were patchy up to the first Economic Census in 1907 and remained infrequent until the early 1940s. One of the issues with the Economic Census was the inconsistency between census years, e.g. coverage of industries and small businesses, making comparisons difficult. In Smith and Pennick's 100-year review of the UK Census of Production, consistent challenges are noted in relation to response burden, consistent concepts and questions, classifications, and length of time to produce the statistics.

Simon Kuznets (USA), Colin Clark (UK), and later Richard Stone (UK) were National Accounts pioneers paving the way for an international Accounts Framework. Stone's 1952 work (A standardized System of National Accounts [SNA]) was revised and published the following year, as the 1953 System of National Accounts (SNA53), however, only one aspect of Stone's work (measuring national income) was included in the 46 pages (Lequiller and Blades 2014).

Although limited in content, countries implementing SNA53 quickly realized its utility for economic monitoring and policy making, even with relative short time series. The SNA53 definitions and concepts were also useful for other statistical themes such as prices and labor force data.

The SNA was subsequently revised in 1968 (to 250 pages), 1993 (to 700 pages), and 2008 (to a two column per page format to prevent more pages). The increase in page numbers acts as a proxy for the increasing detail contained in each revision.

Producing National Accounts requires large volumes of data. Assets and transactions for each sector of the economy (government, households, nonfinancial corporations, financial corporations, nonprofit institutions serving households, and the rest of the world) must be collected or estimated from monthly, quarterly, and annual surveys as well as administrative data, e.g. tax data, and other nonsurvey sources. NSIs face ongoing challenges to maintain the suite of surveys (e.g. budgets, systems, and response burden).

In many NSIs, as well as feeding into National Accounts, business surveys, and administrative data are produced as publications in their own rights. For example, monthly the Australian Bureau of Statistics publishes:

- retail sales estimates from the retail sales survey;
- merchandise trade in goods estimates from the Customs and Excise data;
- labor force estimates from the monthly population survey; and
- lending indicators from regulatory data.

All of these are also used in the compilation of the Australian National Accounts (for further information see ABS 2021).

Increasingly, there are more opportunities for using nonsurvey data (e.g. bank transaction data, tax data, mobile phone data), and for many countries, these opportunities sped up in response to COVID-19 (for example, De Broe et al. 2021). These nonsurvey data sources can often be used to partially or fully replace existing survey data, provide new insights and/or be used in validation (for example, Honchar et al. 2021, Peisker et al. 2021, and ONS 2018).

8.3 Our Statistical Ecosystem

Today, our statistical ecosystem includes statistical suppliers (e.g. NSIs, Central Banks, international statistical organization (e.g. United Nations [UN], International Monetary Fund [IMF], and Organization for Economic Co-operation and Development [OECD])), data providers (e.g. survey respondents and nonsurvey providers), users, and domestic and global economies.

Despite advancements over the decades there remain challenges for:

- acquiring good quality timely data;
- response burden;
- maintaining up-to-date classifications;
- creating and maintaining time series;
- keeping pace with economic developments; and
- demand outweighing supply with often reduced budgets.

In addition to these there are challenges in data collection and statistical compilation. The challenges here have moved from taking sometimes years to collect data and produce statistics (see Table 8.1) to maintaining up-to-date and adaptive data collection and compilation systems (see Section 8.5).

As evidenced by NSIs' responses to the COVID-19 pandemic, there is an increasing expectation and need for statistical producers to pivot and respond quickly. The balance of timeliness versus accuracy tipped more in the direction of timeliness during the pandemic with many NSIs setting-up rapid surveys and using new data sources to produce near real-time information.

These challenges are very interwoven, for example:

Up-to-date coherent and consistent classifications: Are time-consuming to update and implement. Given the importance of preserving time series, when they are updated, it requires NSIs to re-classify existing time series often going back decades. Over the years, as economies become more complex, so to do the classifications. An example of this is the International Standard Industrial Classification (ISIC). Table 8.2 shows not only the frequency of updates to the ISIC but also how the classification has increased in complexity and size.

Keeping pace with economic developments: Often means having to measure new or transformed "things," requiring new or expanded data. As economies become more complex and inter-related, acquiring this data on the basis you need (e.g. definitions and concepts, see Chapters 5 (Bavdaž et al. 2023) and 6 (Nicholson et al. 2023)) becomes more difficult and, if a survey, burdensome to provide. Often, the need to measure "new things" comes before the periodic updating of economic standards (Chapter 3, by MacFeely and Van de ven (2023b), provides an overview of the future direction of the SNA). In contrast, accounting standards (used by businesses) are more regularly revised and can lead to discrepancies with economic standards. An example of this is the 2016 International Accounting Standards Board's (IASB) revision to the treatment of leases in financial statements. In the SNA 2008 there is a distinction between assets used under operating leases and those under financial leases. The IASB revision creates divergence with this. The most significant change is for businesses with nonfinancial

Table 8.2 International Standard Industrial Classification of All Economic Activities (ISIC) Classification structures 1948–2006.

Version	Levels	Level names	Code format	Number of items
1948	1–3	Division	1	9
		Major group	11	44
		Group	111	113
1958 (rev 1)	1–3	Division	1	10
		Major group	11	44
		Group	111	124
1968 (rev 2)	1–4	Major division	0	10
		Division	01	34
		Major group	012	72
		Group	0123	160
1989 (rev 3)	1–4	Tabulation category	One letter code	17
		Division	01	60
		Group	012	159
		Class	0123	292
2006 (rev 4)	1–4	Section	One letter code	21
		Division	01	88
		Group	012	238
		Class	0123	419

Source: Adapted from United Nations UNSD — Classification Detail.

assets under an operating lease, who are now required to bring the value of those assets onto the balance sheet because of "right of use." For the lessor there is no change in the accounting standard change. This means that survey respondents will have difficulties (and possibly unable) to supply lease data on an SNA basis (for further information see Lay 2018).

Demand outweighing supply: The need to monitor increasingly complex economies, inform fiscal and monetary policy, and provide data for modeling and forecasting, results in an increasing demand for more timely and detailed statistics (the digital economy is an example of this see Chapter 6 by Nicholson et al. 2023). This is then set in the context of NSIs often facing reduced budget, aging infrastructure, and increased competition for the necessary skill sets (Seyb et al. 2013).

8.4 Help Available to Us

Our international statistical eco-system provides help in meeting the challenges of supplying good quality economic statistics, but the volume of help is immense and can be difficult to navigate. The following sections provide an overview of that help: international governance, statistical principles, models and frameworks, statistical manuals and handbooks, classifications, statistical tools, and formal and informal help (see Figure 8.1).

8.4.1 International Governance

Although NSIs are dispersed across the world there is an international statistical system that binds them together and there to support them.

In the United Nations, the United Nations Statistical Commission (UNSC) brings together Chief Statisticians from around the world. Established in 1947, it "unites us in our common goal: promoting the development of statistical information as an essential instrument for development and as a substantive contribution to public policy and private action" (United Nations 2017). Over the years the UNSC has established: city groups, task forces, expert groups, working groups, friends of the

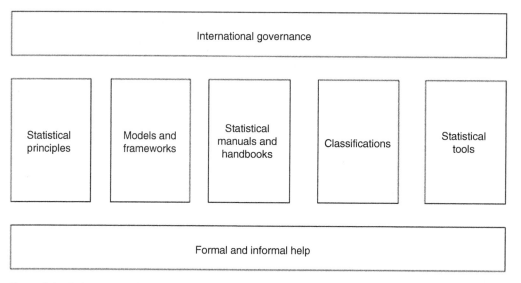

Figure 8.1 Help available in our international statistical eco-system.

Table 8.3 The role of United Nations Statistical Commission groups and committees.

Type of group			Role
City groups (long-standing)			Focus on **advancing methodologies** toward the development of statistical standards.
Task force (short-term)	**Expert group** (medium-term)	**Working group** (long standing)	Focus on **methodology to develop a statistical standard** including updates to manuals/handbooks. Sometimes do technical research and development with data.
Friends of the Chair groups (short-term)			Focus on **coordination, with stakeholders and statistical activities**. Occasionally work on methodology.
Committees			Focus on **coordination and strategic vision**, including liaising with stakeholders to coordinate statistical activities in the relevant theme.
Inter-agency and expert groups			Twin focus: **methodology and coordination**. Primary role is the development of a statistical standard including updates to manuals/handbooks, and stakeholder liaison to coordinate statistical activities in the relevant theme.

Business and trade

Committee of experts on business statistics

Intersecretariat **Working group** on International trade and economic Globalisation statistics

Expert group on international trade and economic globalisation statistics

Interagency **task force** on International trade statistics

City groups
Voorburg group on service statistics
Wiesbaden group on business registers
Delhi group on informal sector statistics

Figure 8.2 UN groups in the Business and Trade theme.

chair groups, committees and inter-agency and expert groups, to carry out specific co-ordination, developments, and/or develop visions. The role of each is summarized in Table 8.3.

Over the years the UN statistical system has developed on a theme basis, such as Business and Trade; National Accounts; Prices; Energy; Environment; and Agriculture. Figure 8.2 shows the UN groups for the Business and Trade theme. Other international organizations such as the OECD, IMF, and International Labor Organisation (ILO) also have theme-based groups.

In 2019, partly in response to the high volume of groups, at the UNSC fiftieth session it was "requested that a Friends of the Chair group be established for a period of not more than two years to undertake an assessment of the efficiency, effectiveness and responsiveness of the governance of the current system of economic statistics, without creating more bureaucracy or adding undue burden on national statistical organizations and international organizations" (UNSC 2021, p. 2). The group reported to the UNSC in 2020 and 2021. The 2021 report made "recommendations for an agile and more responsive system of economic statistics based on four themes: (a) networking collaboration and user consultation; (b) transforming and challenging the system: statistical infrastructure and operations, and data solutions; (c) enabling: institutional arrangements and governance; and (d) experimenting, integrating and documenting: statistical frameworks and methods" (UNSC 2021, p. 1). This included improved coordination and collaboration between group. All these improvements would very much help and support NSIs in producing official economic statistics.

8.4.2   Statistical Principles to Produce and Disseminate Official Statistics

There are international statistical principles and standards for producing and disseminating official statistics. For example:

- The UN Fundamental Principles of Official Statistics (UNSC 2014), which broadly outlines professional standards for official statistics; and
- The IMF Special Dissemination Data Standards (SDDSs), which commits countries to the dissemination of a minimum set of economic and financial statistics.[2]

Official statistics is a brand that represents specific professional principles. In 1994, the UNSC endorsed the UN Fundamental Principles of Official Statistics, which were subsequently amended and adopted in 2014 (UNSC 2014).

> The Fundamental Principles of Official Statistics (FPOS) are a pillar of the Global Statistical System. By enshrining our profound conviction and commitment that official statistics have to adhere to well-defined professional and scientific standards, they define us as a professional community, reaching across political, economic and cultural borders.
>
> (United Nations 2015, p. 3).

In the European Statistical System (ESS), for Latin America and the Caribbean, and in some countries, e.g. United Kingdom, specific codes of practice (CoP) for official statistics have been developed, broadly aligned to the UN Fundamental Principles of Official Statistics. The European Statistics Code of Practice (Eurostat 2017a, b) contains the high-level principles listed in Table 8.4. Compliance with the CoP is periodically assessed via peer reviews with strict follow-up for countries not fully compliant. The third round of peer reviews commenced in 2021 using a combination of self-assessment and peer review visits (Eurostat 2020).

---

2 IMF Standards for Data Dissemination: https://www.imf.org/en/About/Factsheets/Sheets/2016/07/27/15/45/Standards-for-Data-Dissemination.

Table 8.4 European Statistics Code of Practice Principles.

Principle 1	Professional independence
Principle 2	Mandate for data collection and access to data
Principle 3	Adequacy of resources
Principle 4	Commitment to quality
Principle 5	Statistical confidentiality and data protection
Principle 6	Impartiality and objectivity
Principle 7	Sound methodology
Principle 8	Appropriate statistical procedures
Principle 9	Nonexcessive burden on respondents
Principle 10	Cost effectiveness
Principle 11	Relevance
Principle 12	Accuracy and reliability
Principle 13	Timeliness and punctuality
Principle 14	Coherence and comparability
Principle 15	Accessibility and clarity

Source: Adapted from Eurostat (2017a).

8.4.3 Statistical Production Models and Frameworks

Models to help statistical producers include the Generic Statistical Business Process Model (GSBPM),[3] the Generic Statistical Data Editing Model (GSDEM),[4] and the Generic Statistical Information Model (GSIM). The GSBPM provides an overview of the statistical production processes: specify need, design, build, collect, process, analyze, disseminate, archive, and evaluate. It was developed to give an overview of the processes and areas that need to be managed but also to assist with specifying statistical production metadata (Section 8.7 lists the metadata-driven model used at Statistics Canada, which facilitates the creation and storage of production metadata).

Sitting above the statistical production processes are the following:

- Quality management;
- Metadata management;
- Statistical framework management;
- Statistical programme management;
- Knowledge management;
- Data management;
- Process data management;
- Provider management; and
- Customer management (UNECE Secretariat 2009).

The GSDEM looks in more detail at the editing processes. While the GSIM looks at information needed for the statistical production process, related to the GSBPM, or any other business process

---

3 Generic Statistical Business Process Model – Generic Statistical Business Process Model – UNECE Statswiki: https://statswiki.unece.org/display/GSBPM.
4 2 Introducing the GSDEM – 2 Introducing the GSDEM – UNECE Statswiki: https://statswiki.unece.org/display/sde/2+Introducing+the+GSDEM.

model.[5] GSIM was then extended to include the statistical classifications model, focusing on the development of a classification database to improve the accessibility, maintenance, and common use of classifications across an NSI's statistics (UN DESA 2015). Section 8.5 provides an example of the GSBPM in practice.

8.4.3.1 Quality Assurance Frameworks

There are several quality assurance frameworks (QAFs) available to help us evaluate the quality of our statistics, processes, and environments. For example the IMF's Data Quality Assessment Framework (DQAF),[6] the OECD Good Statistical Practice (OECD 2015), and the ESS QAF (ESS 2019), which aligns with the European Codes of Practice (see Figure 8.2). These can be used for self-assessments and some international organizations (e.g. IMF, OECD, and ESS) also carry out periodic external reviews.

The IMF's DQAF includes a generic high-level framework and seven specific frameworks (e.g National Accounts Statistics, Consumer Prices Index and Balance of Payments and International Investment Position Statistics). In contrast, the OECD and European quality assurance frameworks have just one framework.

8.4.4 Statistical Manuals and Handbooks

With the multitude of things that need to be measured, classified, and compiled; and the number of international groups focused on developing methods and guidance it is unsurprising that there are numerous manuals and handbooks available. They broadly fall into three high level groupings: themes, methods and quality/managing national statistical systems. Themes include: National Accounts, International Trade and Balance of Payments, Labor, Productivity, and Wellbeing. The OECD provides an overview of manuals and handbooks by theme.[7] These manuals and handbooks generally provide concepts, definitions, and guidance on producing statistics relevant to the theme. From a methods perspective there is for example, the Eurostat Handbook on Methodology of Modern Business Statistics (Eurostat 2017b). Then there are handbooks more about managing and organizing national statistical systems (for example, United Nations 2021). Table 8.5 provides some more examples.

These manuals and handbooks take time to develop and, where relevant, update. This means that the measurement and production of statistics on "new" or changing things are often undertaken without international agreement on concepts, definitions and methods. There are several examples of this in this book (e.g. Chapters 2–7: MacFeely and van de Ven 2023a,b; Koskimäki and Taskinen 2023; Bavdaž et al. 2023; Nicholson et al. 2023; Pradhan 2023). In these circumstances, discussions at international meetings, presentations at conferences and journal articles become essential sources of information.

8.4.5 Classifications

Classifying businesses, products, employment, workers, transactions and flows is an essential part of producing official statistics. Internationally there are classifications and guidance available to help us and ensure international comparability. The United Nations Statistics Division maintains "The International Family of Classifications," which includes, for example economic, demographic, labor, education, and geography classifications.

---

5 Clickable GSIM – Clickable GSIM – UNECE Statswiki: https://statswiki.unece.org/display/clickablegsim.
6 IMF -Introduction to the Data Quality Reference Site: https://dsbb.imf.org/dqrs/DQAF.
7 Statistical manuals and guidelines by topic – OECD: https://www.oecd.org/statistics/statisticalmanualsandguidelinesbytopic.htm.

Table 8.5 Examples of international manual and handbooks.

Themes	Methods	Quality and managing national Statistical systems
Compilation of National Accounts	Handbook of methodology of modern business statistics	National Quality Assurance Frameworks manual for official statistics
Supply and Use and Input/Output tables	European business statistics methodological manual for statistical business registers	Handbook on improving quality by analysis of process variables
Compilation of satellite accounts	Handbook on seasonal adjustment	The Handbook on Management and Organization of National Statistical Systems
Compilation of illegal activity statistics	Handbook for monitoring and evaluating business surveys response burdens	
Short-term economic statistics		
Advancements in measuring intangibles		

8.4.5.1 Classifying Businesses

The first step in classifying a business is determining whether it is an institutional unit "capable of owning goods and assets, incurring liabilities and engaging in economic activities and transactions with other units in its own rights" (United Nations et al. 2009, para 1.9.). Once this is established, the unit needs to be classified as either market or nonmarket and allocated to a sector (e.g. nonfinancial corporation, financial corporation, General Government, or nonprofit institutions serving households). Figure 4.1 in the 2008 SNAs provides a flow diagram of the steps for allocating institutional units to sectors and subsectors (United Nations et al. 2009, p. 64).

Institutional units then need to be analyzed in terms of structure (see Chapter 9 by Machdi et al. 2023, Figure 9.2, and Section 9.5.1.1) and activities to determine an industry classification. The ISIC, or country adaptions of ISIC, are generally used to classify economic units by their principal activity, secondary activities, and ancillary activities (United Nations et al. 2009, paras 5.8–5.10).

8.4.5.2 Classifying Employment and Workers

People employed or working for themselves (e.g. own account workers) can be classified to, for example, occupation, type of employment (e.g. full-time/part-time), type of employment contract (e.g. permanent/casual). To ensure international comparability there is, for example, the

- International classification of status in employment[8];
- International standard classification of occupations[9]; and
- International Classification of Status at Work[10].

---

8 https://unstats.un.org/unsd/classifications/Family/Detail/222.

9 https://www.ilo.org/wcmsp5/groups/public/@dgreports/@dcomm/@publ/documents/publication/wcms_172572.pdf.

10 https://ilostat.ilo.org/resources/concepts-and-definitions/classification-status-at-work/ (accessed 6 March 2022).

8.4.5.3 Classifications Overview

There are also classifications for products, consumption, and trade. Table 8.6 provides an overview of some of the available international classifications.

8.4.6 Statistical Tools

To produce statistics NSIs need to collect, clean, process, and disseminate data (further details can be seen in the GSBPM). These common needs provide opportunities for tools to be developed and shared. Part of the aim of the High-Level Group for the Modernization of Official Statistics (HLG-MOS) is to do just that:

> The mission of the HLG-MOS is to oversee development of frameworks, and sharing of information, tools and methods, which support the modernisation of statistical organisations. The aim is to improve the efficiency of statistical production processes, and the ability to produce outputs that better meet user needs.[11]

There is also the OECD Statistical Information System – Collaboration Community (SIS-CC) The SIS-CC is an open source community for official statistics, focusing on product excellence, and delivering concrete solutions to common problems through co-investment and co-innovation. Table 8.7 provides some examples of statistical tools available in the statistical ecosystem.[12]

8.4.7 International Collaboration and Support

Our statistical ecosystem also provides formal and informal collaboration and support. Many countries have government-funded formal agreements to provide statistical assistance and capability building. For example, the ABS, has traditionally supported the Melanesian countries (e.g. Fiji, Solomon Islands, Vanuatu, and Papua New Guinea). Statistics New Zealand has similar arrangements supporting the Polynesian and Realm countries (e.g. Samoa, Tonga, Tokelau, Cook

Table 8.6 Overview of some international classifications.

Businesses and products	Employment and workers	Consumption in different institutional sectors	Trade
Institutional units Institutional sectors International Standard Industry Classification (ISIC) Central Product Classification (CPC)	International classification of status in employment (ICSE) International standard classification of occupations (ISCO) International Classification of Status at Work (ICSaW)	Classification of the outlays of producers according to purpose (COPP) Classification of individual consumption according to purpose (COICOP) Classifications of Functions of Government (COFOG) Classification of the purposes of nonprofit institutions serving households (COPNI)	Standard international trade classification (SITC) Harmonized commodity description and coding systems (HS)

---

11 HLG-MOS Terms of Reference 2020-2022 – HLG-MOS Terms of Reference 2020-2022 – UNECE Statswiki: https://statswiki.unece.org/pages/viewpageattachments.action?pageId=285212803&metadataLink=true.
12 Further information on tools available across the GSBPM can be found at: www.statswiki.unece.org/display/cpa

Table 8.7 Examples of statistical tools available in the statistical eco-system.

Collection tools	Cleaning and coding tools	Seasonal adjustment tools[d]	Statistical disclosure control[e]	Dissemination
Blaise[a]	BANFF[b] Jasper[c]	X-Arima J-Demetra SEATS	Tau-argus (for tabular data) mu-argus (for microdata)	Statistical Data and Metadata eXchange (SDMX)

a) Produced and maintained by Statistics Netherlands. Blaise can be used to describe survey questions in a data model, be used across different modes, and for editing data. Further information at https://blaise.com/.
b) see Section 8.10 and (Thomas 2017).
c) (see Mohl 2007).
d) see Section 11.6.2.
e) (see Hundepool 2003).

Islands, and Nuie). The ABS and Statistics New Zealand meet regularly to discuss and harmonize regional work and work closely with the Secretariat of the Pacific Community and other regional donors/technical partners (e.g. IMF). The UK Office for National Statistics has partnerships with Ghana, Kenya, Rwanda, and the UN Economic Commission for Africa.

In terms of informal collaboration, this can take many forms such as bilateral discussions, research projects, workshops, and conference attendance.

8.5 Summary Before the Case Study

Our statistical ecosystem provides us with immense amounts of help but finding and navigating what is available can be challenging. As discussed, many of the challenges faced by NSIs have remained the same across the decades, e.g. acquiring good quality timely data; response burden; maintaining up-to-date classifications; creating and maintaining time series; keeping pace with economic developments; and demand outweighing supply with often reduced budgets. The next part of this chapter provides an overview of how Statistics Canada approached some of the challenges by developing the Integrated Business Statistics Program, to deal with the challenges of: improving data quality, reducing response burden, modernizing data processing infrastructure, and integrating business surveys to reduce costs. There is much that can be learnt from this to help statistical producers.

8.6 Standardization Leads to Efficiency: Canada's Integrated Business Statistics Program

In 2010, Statistics Canada launched the Corporate Business Architecture (CBA) initiative. At the time, growing financial pressures in the organization led to a thorough review of business methods, statistical processes, and systems infrastructure. The main objectives were to identify opportunities for efficiencies, determine methods for enhancing quality assurance, and finding ways to improve responsiveness in the delivery of statistical programs. This resulted in numerous recommendations including the development and mandatory use of shared and generic corporate services for collecting, processing, storing, and disseminating statistical information. To achieve these goals, Statistics

Canada initiated several projects including a major transformation project for its economic statistics surveys, the Integrated Business Statistics Program (IBSP).

The IBSP is a continuation of an effort to build a harmonized business surveying approach that began in the late 1990s with the Unified Enterprise Statistics (UES) program (Brodeur et al. 2006). Over time, the UES infrastructure became antiquated and substantial resources would have been required for systems maintenance. Given that the model was not easily adaptable to changing requirements, it was an opportune time to redesign the model.

The IBSP now provides a standardized framework for economic surveys conducted at Statistics Canada. The survey process itself incorporates the structure of the UNECE GSBPM (see Section 8.4.3), which provides focus on the following phases: design, build, collect, process, analyze, disseminate, and evaluate. IBSP surveys use Statistics Canada's Business Register (BR) as a common frame. Questionnaires are based on harmonized concepts and content. Surveys share common sampling, collection, and processing methodologies that are driven by metadata. In addition, common tools are in place to edit, correct, and analyze data. The resulting system is flexible and adaptable to new survey processing requirements. As such, the use of IBSP is approached from a corporate perspective when reviewing most economic survey redesigns and system enhancements. More surveys are taking advantage of this fully developed processing system as a way of eliminating, or reducing, the costs associated with large program redesigns.

Today, over 130 of Statistics Canada's economic surveys are processed within the IBSP infrastructure. This accounts for approximately 70% of all economic surveys.

8.7 IBSP Objectives

In constructing the IBSP model, the team focused on six core objectives. These were the following:

- improving data quality by applying standardized methods and processes, implementing harmonized content, and facilitating coherence analysis;
- reducing response burden;
- modernizing the data processing infrastructure;
- integrating the majority of economic surveys into the new model;
- simplifying and standardizing processes to reduce learning curves and improve timeliness; and
- reducing ongoing costs associated with operational aspects of surveys to realize efficiencies.

To attain these objectives, survey programs have to adapt to specific requirements of the IBSP model. At the same time, the model had to be designed with flexibility to respond to unique program requirements. Achieving the right balance between developing a standardized, coherent model, while retaining flexibility for program specific requirements was the greatest challenge faced in implementing IBSP.

Over time, the requirements for IBSP inclusion have been adapted, as have the methods and standards. However, the original framework provides the necessary consistency for incorporating new integration procedures. The overall goal remains to achieve higher quality while gaining efficiencies.

8.8 Cornerstones of an Integrated Infrastructure System

The IBSP was envisioned to be a scalable and efficient infrastructure for business surveys. The system was designed to incorporate many different surveys while limiting processing constraints.

At the time of development of IBSP, the first set of surveys to be incorporated, and their processing needs, were known. However, ongoing processing requirements of new and existing surveys needed to be incorporated with minimal strain on processing and support staff. The scalability and efficiency were achieved by designing a system that is driven by metadata. That is, all steps required for processing a survey are understood based on metadata that is captured in the system and there is no manual intervention between the different survey processes.

8.9 Metadata-Driven Model

Statistics Canada developed corporate metadata repositories for managing publications, services, and statistical holdings. However, prior to the IBSP, there were relatively few survey programs that had well-developed metadata for managing survey processes. The IBSP metadata framework is expansive and covers all aspects of survey processing (Hostetter 2013). This adds to the increase in efficiency, robustness, and responsiveness in delivering survey processing services for IBSP programs.

Metadata are stored in easily modifiable tables that are used to drive system programs. The system programs are not hard-coded to run specific tasks. Instead, the system programs simply access information from the metadata tables to direct their execution.

IBSP meets general metadata guidelines of being active, being created for a purpose, and being used in downstream processes by creating descriptive metadata for final data output but also creating processing metadata. A variable created for IBSP processing is tagged with descriptive elements such as name and origin, but metadata also indicate how validation, editing, imputation, and estimation must be done and will track a variable's passage through the various survey processing steps.

Since metadata are integrated into all processing steps, there is a single point of entry for IBSP users when accessing and entering metadata required for the management of processing requirements. A desktop application allows for entry, modification, and review of all survey metadata, as well as the point of access to run the survey processes. This enables a seamless integration within the system to instantly validate that metadata meets the run conditions of each process and identify related metadata that are required.

The use of a metadata-driven system minimizes rework and facilitates reuse. This enables the production management team to easily update processing metadata as survey requirements change and adapt over time. An equally important outcome is the improvement of quality and coherence over time. The metadata allow invaluable management information to aid the monitoring process as much of these metadata are output for users in the data repository.

8.10 Integrated Infrastructure

The IBSP infrastructure incorporates components of the Statistics Canada suite of generalized systems for sampling (G-SAM), edit and imputation (BANFF), estimation (G-Est), and seasonal adjustment (TSPS). The IBSP also accesses Statistics Canada repositories for different types of data, paradata, and metadata that act as Data Service Centres.

The main Data Service Centres are the following: the BR, which serves as the frame; Tax warehouse, which contains all tax files; the Integrated Metadata Base (IMDB), which contains metadata related to survey processes, content, classifications, and code sets; and the Collection warehouse, which contains raw data from respondents and paradata from collection.

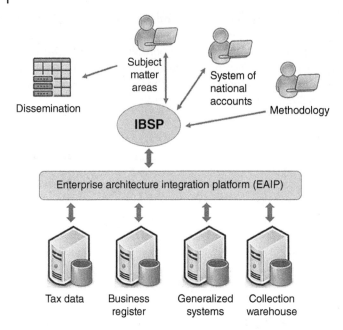

Figure 8.3 IBSP infrastructure on EAIP. Source: Enterprise Statistics Division (2015) updated.

The Enterprise Architecture Integration Platform (EAIP) allows seamless data transformations between the Data Service Centres and the generalized systems for processing. One important benefit to using the EAIP is increased stability and reliability of the system since any modification to a Data Service Centre does not require matching changes to the IBSP interfaces. See Figure 8.3 for a visual representation of the EAIP.

8.11 Information Management

The information management principles within IBSP are based on both legislative requirements and internal Statistics Canada directives. It is integral to provide Canadians with access to a trusted source of information while minimizing the overall storage footprint.

The bulk of IBSP documentation required to meet the information management objectives will be created, maintained, and retained in the metadata framework or the IBSP data mart where files reside.

Internal IBSP information management guidelines include the deletion of information that has no business value. Development is currently underway to automate the existing manual deletion process.

8.12 Standardization and Cooperation Within IBSP

As mentioned above, one of the key objectives of the IBSP was to improve data quality by applying standardized methods and processes, implementing harmonized content, and facilitating coherence analysis. In using standardized methods and processes, the IBSP is able to take advantage of robust systems already in place at Statistics Canada. This creates an environment in which a single entity is not required to produce and maintain all the inputs for processing. There are checks and balances within the different areas at Statistics Canada to ensure the highest quality is available to users. IBSP takes advantage of this guaranteed quality to maintain a high standard of survey processing and generate outputs that are timely and relevant to its own data users.

8.13 The Business Register

The BR is a data service center identifying all businesses operating in Canada and foreign businesses with links to Canadian companies. It includes information about how businesses are organized, the industries they operate in, their size in terms of revenues and number of employees, and their location. The BR is updated through several administrative sources and profiling practices. Using the BR ensures quality, while being able to manage survey overlap.

There are four statistical attributes derived for businesses on the BR. The highest level is the statistical enterprise (usually the legal unit, except in some very complex businesses). The second highest level is the statistical company (the lowest level to measure investment). The next level is the statistical establishment (usually equivalent to a profit center). The lowest level is the statistical location (employment and/or revenue data is available).

8.13.1 The BR as the Common Frame

As the common frame for IBSP surveys, the IBSP sampling system can ingest the standard file format of the BR and apply the steps to generate the necessary sample and population files for processing within IBSP. The BR systems use these standard sample files to generate the outputs for managing collection, which include questionnaire identifiers and contact information. The sampling unit level and collection unit level could be the same or different, depending on the requirements the survey.

8.13.2 Allocation Factors on the BR

Another standard use of the BR within the IBSP is as an input to the allocation process. The allocation process may be required to produce survey estimates at the most detailed level of a business's structure. Since the BR stores data on businesses operating across Canada at all statistical levels of operations, it was decided that the BR would store the allocation factors based on revenues and employment factors (salaries and wages). Where surveys had previously created their allocation factors and processes, the standardization of these inputs on the BR has improved coherence between survey and administrative data and allowed for a simplified integration of allocation into the survey processing framework.

The use of allocation varies across survey programs and is dependent on the structure of a given industry (specifically the number of complex businesses in the population), the breadth of the data reported by respondents, the collection strategy employed, and the level of estimates required. For example, if business data is collected for national operations, the impact of allocation will be greater. If data is collected at provincial and territorial levels, there would be no need for allocation processes to be run.

8.13.3 Commodities and Activities on the BR

Surveys that produce commodity estimates have indicated that the ability to store and sample based on known commodity activities would improve the efficiency of sampling and the quality of commodity estimates. To respond to this request, the BR implemented a new feature to store commodity or activity information. Subject matter divisions are responsible for populating and updating the field.

8.13.4 Robust Methodologies and Generalized Systems

The use of the generalized systems in IBSP means that stable and reliable methods are available to IBSP. There is an existing process of research and approval for development of the most appropriate and useful methods. The systems are well documented and the IBSP is able to create the required inputs from stored data and metadata. As updates are made to the generalized systems, the IBSP is insulated from these changes until related updates can be made to the IBSP system. However, if methods are improved or bugs are fixed, the IBSP can take advantage of those improvements without modifying the existing metadata.

The IBSP has become one of the largest users of the generalized systems G-Sam (sampling), Banff (edit and information), G-Est (estimation), and TSPS (time series) at Statistics Canada (Further information on statistical tools see Section 8.4.6). This allows for a relationship between the two development areas. IBSP provides input to required changes and error resolution, along with requests for new development to meet ongoing processing needs. The IBSP is also involved in the testing and certification of new versions of the generalized systems.

Similar to the process of research and development for the generalized systems, all methodology principles and processes used in the IBSP have gone through an approval process whereby a steering committee reviewed the recommendations prior to approving the method for inclusion in the IBSP. The process for making changes to the existing survey methods is the same. The development cost of the change and the impact on other surveys are included in the approval process. Solutions that are less resource-intensive may be proposed for inclusion in IBSP or external processes may be set up to meet the survey's needs instead.

8.14 Standard Tools for Developing EQ

Though not unusual in questionnaire design, the IBSP uses a modular design for developing electronic questionnaires (EQ). There are standard business modules that are required for collecting and confirming business and industry information, changes in business structure, contact information, and general comments. Survey-specific modules are created to collect the main survey content. This allows for easier compilation of required modules and rendering of the full questionnaire. It also allows for consistent design of the standard modules since they will always use the same variable cell codes and flow.

Incorporating EQ as the main mode of collection in IBSP, with a reduction on paper questionnaire usage, meant that standard practices for developing the EQ needed to be developed. A set of standard templates was created to provide the EQ development team question text and flow, variable cell codes and formats, edits, auxiliary, and prefill information. The standard process allows for fewer errors in the transfer of information.

The IBSP EQ design framework also considers the processing requirements of a survey. Certain fields that will make processing more efficient (checkboxes, flow conditions, totals, etc.), will usually be incorporated into the design. In addition to the design, a review of the EQ outputs is done for processing purposes. Depending on the type of information being collected, the output may be in a flat file or a rostered file, or both. Additional processing constraints may need to be resolved related to the output format. Being involved at the design stage allows for earlier mitigation of theses constraints.

8.15   Developing a Harmonized Content Model

The full benefits of developing an integrated infrastructure can only be obtained by also integrating a harmonized conceptual framework. For IBSP, this began with the application of standards. All IBSP surveys must apply statistical standards including:

- The North American Industrial Classification System (NAICS);
- The North American Product Classification System (NAPCS); and
- The chart of accounts (COA) (Martineau 2012) as the reference taxonomy for organizing business financial information.

Many financial variables are common across economic surveys. By harmonizing the definitions of these variables and systematically applying standards, common content has been developed and implemented across programs. This is critical in creating coherence across programs and minimizing the effort required to build, test, and implement questionnaires.

The objective of utilizing tax information to its fullest potential guided the development of questionnaire content related to revenue and expense variables. The mapping of the IBSP revenue and expense variables to their tax concepts creates a direct link between the survey content and the administrative data which allows for the direct replacement of the financial variables for specific units in sample. The COA was reviewed and revised to ensure that the COA variables met the conceptual needs of the Canadian SNA.

Harmonized content does not simply link the financial components between surveys and the SNA. Considerable effort is made to ensure that the true concept of the question is reflected in the metadata variable model so that future surveys integrating into the IBSP can take advantage of similar variable naming conventions and, where appropriate, use the same variable cell code. This makes the analytical process easier for all parties and allows for easier coherence analysis of survey content.

8.16   The IBSP Data Mart and Analytical Tools

IBSP data and metadata are all stored within the IBSP databases; however, a set of specific outputs from the many operational processes are stored within the IBSP data mart. The format of the data files is standard, and the contents can be interpreted based on the additional metadata outputs that are also stored on the data mart.

This process facilitates the integration of IBSP with Statistics Canada dissemination systems. Due to the standard nature and structure of the outputs, the SNA can directly extract the data required for their programs. Similarly, the Economic Disclosure Control and Dissemination System (EDCDS), which is the Statistics Canada corporate tool used to ensure appropriate levels of quality and disclosure risk for statistical data releases, is able to extract survey data to be applied within their system. IBSP changes that may impact the format of outputs and structure of the data mart are coordinated with all data users.

The IBSP also offers users a comprehensive analytical tool, which not only allows users to view microdata and macro estimates but also provides a suite of diagnostic reports. Users also create their own analytical products based on files from the data mart.

8.17 Managing Response Burden

Response burden has always been a concern for Statistics Canada. Data that can be provided by respondents is a highly important part of being able to distribute useful and relevant statistical products to Canadian citizens. However, as the needs for data grow and the desire to measure new and changing areas of the economy arise, finding additional ways to reduce the response burden allows a broader package of statistical products to be developed. The methods of reducing response burden usually focus on the use of administrative data in place of survey data, as the sources are growing richer in many areas of economic and auxiliary industry information. On top of that, the IBSP has incorporated some general collection improvements.

8.18 Electronic Questionnaires

In the previous section, the creation of electronic questionnaires was highlighted for the standardization of the creation process. However, implementing EQ instead of a paper questionnaire helps respondents interpret reporting concepts. Fitting survey questions on paper questionnaires meant sometimes showing compact tables, small print, directional areas for conditional input, and various other aspects that may have been confusing to respondents. The EQ built-in features reduce these challenges while allowing customization of text for different types of respondents.

Automated questionnaire flows can direct respondents to the next relevant section based on their own previous responses and based on frame information accessible from auxiliary files. This allows survey organizers to collect specific information from specific units. It also supports an integrated data replacement strategy as sample units known to have good quality administrative data can be directed past the related part of the questionnaire while other units are not. The addition of flow-based questionnaires to the survey process also improves the processing of survey data since the path of response for each respondent could be different but is always known. This reduces the time required to develop a processing strategy since it can be done prior to the start of collection and doesn't require a review of the response data for patterns.

Other features of the EQ design allow for more consistent data while reducing the burden of respondents. For example, automated total calculations can be done on screen and data relationship edits can also be programmed to alert respondents when there are data inconsistencies.

8.19 Large and Complex Enterprises

Business and agriculture surveys frequently try to manage response burden by selecting samples instead of carrying out a census of the target population. While this minimizes burden on smaller units, the largest units are always selected in sample. This is because the largest businesses and farms have a significant impact on the statistical estimates. For this to be an effective sampling strategy, the large units need to consistently report their information despite being selected in a substantial number of surveys with varying reporting and reference periods.

Statistics Canada has developed and implemented two programs to enhance the relationships with these large firms and coordinate survey reporting, which IBSP is able to take advantage of.

8.19.1 EPM/LAOS Programs

The Enterprise Portfolio Management Program (EPM) is mandated to work with Canada's largest and most complex businesses to keep frame profiles of their operations up to date, negotiate reporting arrangements, ensure coherent data reporting across surveys, and provide a single point of contact to rapidly respond to concerns raised by businesses or industry analysts.

The Large Agricultural Operations Statistics Program (LAOS) is like the EPM program but maintains the profiles for large farming operations in Canada to reflect their current farming operations. The LAOS program is also responsible for data collection and developing custom reporting arrangements.

8.19.2 Customized Collection

A mostly manual process had existed at Statistics Canada for managing the collection of data from the large and complex businesses. A reporting spreadsheet of necessary content would be designed based on the needs of the surveys and sent to respondents; however, the process of receiving the data and manually transferring it to the necessary survey programs caused delays in the analysis.

A new tool was developed at Statistics Canada that is similar to the EQ used for regular collection and can be targeted to the large and complex businesses. Determining the common content is similar to the previous process; however, the tool is built using metadata which can easily adapt to changes. The information from respondents can be seamlessly incorporated into the existing collection infrastructure which reduces the time required in obtaining the data, the amount of manual intervention, and potential errors in the data.

8.20 Tax Replacement Strategy

Over time at Statistics Canada, the tax data imputation process and overall data quality has improved. With this reliable source of administrative data available, the IBSP was able to implement a tax replacement strategy that maximized use of administrative financial data. It also allowed surveys to focus more effort on measuring information on commodities, business practices, research and development, and capital expenditures.

At the time of sample selection, the population is divided into two parts: very complex enterprises (approximately 2000) which are difficult to incorporate tax replacement, and small and medium enterprises for which tax replacement of all financial variables is used.

A major paradigm shift in the use of tax replacement was implemented in IBSP with the Smart Tax Replacement Strategy. This process acknowledges that several complex enterprises on the BR can also take advantage of tax replacement if they meet conditions of availability, accuracy, coherence (Martineau 2013), and stability over the most recent three years.

Since all this information relating to the tax replacement is managed at the time of sampling, this information is seamlessly transferred to the collection service as well as the processing system for implementation.

8.21 Active Collection Management

Active collection management is used to indicate that collection efforts are dynamically adjusted based on data already received. This provides efficiency in follow-up efforts, reduces response burden, and provides a coherent strategy for maintaining quality for all required estimates.

The iterative approach in the IBSP Rolling Estimate (RE) model (Mills et al. 2013), which produces estimates and quality indicators, is the driving force in active collective management for IBSP. Follow-up of outstanding sample units (nonrespondents) is based on two important pieces of information: quality indicators for key variables by domain of estimation; and measures of impact for each unit (see Figure 8.4).

If all quality indicators are met, active collection will be closed and follow-up can be stopped. If not, resources will be allocated to units that are deemed influential to key estimates and their quality. The list of priority units for collection follow-up is generated directly within the IBSP process and automatically provided to collection services for incorporation in their tools for interviewers. The process of halting collection (complete or by domain of estimation) is done via manual redirection of follow-up efforts.

8.22 Rolling Estimate Model

The conceptual change to processing and analysis in IBSP was an enormous change within Statistics Canada, comparable to the development of the survey processing infrastructure. The usual processing strategy is linear where collection would be nearly complete prior to initiating survey processing and analysis. As demonstrated in Figure 8.5, the IBSP implements a Rolling Estimate (RE) model, which is iterative and allows processing and analysis to continue simultaneously with collection efforts. As seen with the active collection management strategy, this iterative model not only allows more real-time analysis of individual respondent data but also facilitates a top-down approach to data analysis, which focuses on estimates and quality rather than the microdata editing. Although previous work spent on manual microdata correction was believed to result in much higher-quality estimates, studies indicated that some of the effort did not impact estimates (Saint-Pierre and Bricault 2011; Godbout et al. 2011).

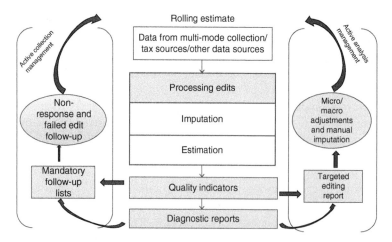

Figure 8.4 Active Collection Management cycle. Source: Enterprise Statistics Division (2015).

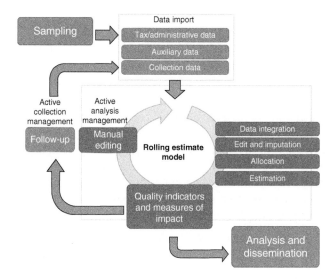

Figure 8.5   The Rolling Estimate model. Source: Enterprise Statistics Division (2015).

To produce successful rolling estimates, all processing and estimation needs are known prior to the start of collection. This is the metadata that drives the system. The system also uses all available information for each sampled unit including collection, historical, and administrative data. This process proceeds, without manual prevention, to impute for all nonresponse, carry out allocation and estimation, and generate updated collection priority lists.

Changes to the microdata are still permitted within the IBSP; however, due to the iterative approach of the RE model, these changes are applied directly to the collected data in the next iteration. This ensures consistency in the data as all edit and imputation rules are easily maintained. Similarly, adjustments to the estimates are permitted to account for industry changes not noted on the frame. These are applied in the next iteration within the estimation process.

8.23   IBSP Growth and Adaptation

Since its inception, the IBSP has been continuously growing and adapting to new programs and processes. The IBSP has two major releases each year. These contain new functionalities required for survey programs that are integrating into IBSP, as well as improvements to existing functionalities. The IT management at Statistics Canada also requires specific infrastructure upgrades which improve the efficiency and stability of the overall system.

This continual improvement to the IBSP application allows for more surveys to integrate, but more importantly, increases the breadth of surveys that can be processed within IBSP. Complex surveys that had once been deemed inappropriate for IBSP are now being integrated.

As IBSP becomes more and more attractive as the survey processing option at Statistics Canada, entire survey programs are being transferred into the family of IBSP surveys. Some of these survey programs have their own infrastructure systems that work outside of the IBSP. These systems might be for frame and sample management or for generating specific dissemination requirements. Due to the standard nature of the IBSP system, the separate systems can be designed to function symbiotically without interrupting the flow of information to analysts, program managers, and users.

The infrastructure and current usage of IBSP makes it a prime location to test proposals by different subject matter areas. The IBSP has been involved in several different tests related to full use of administrative and tax data. Similar tests were carried out to investigate whether a census of financial administrative data with frequent samples for characteristic information would yield estimates with appropriate levels of quality.

Discussions surrounding big data processing at Statistics Canada have used the standard infrastructure and metadata-driven properties of the IBSP as a starting point in development of a new system.

One large advancement coming to the IBSP in the near future is cloud computing. Statistics Canada is undertaking the transfer of most survey processes to a cloud computing environment. This might require modifications to the application and transfer points that already exist within the EAIP; however, the expectation is that it can only come with advancements in the ability to process data. It will also present various different tools for self-serve reporting features that are based on the standard data repositories.

8.24 Efficiencies Gained and Learned

In this case study, there have been many areas highlighted that are proof of efficiencies gained in creating the standard process.

Two separate, yet important, areas to show efficiencies are related to analytical and methodological staff working on each survey and the IT staff required to support each project. IBSP survey programs have noted a decrease in staff, or similarly an increase in surveys managed by the same staff. The IBSP IT support and development resources can be used to demonstrate measurable resource savings. All programs, prior to integrating into IBSP, contain their own IT support teams. IT resources available for IBSP mean that most of those survey-specific IT staff can be transitioned to different programs. The IBSP IT support staff is approximately 13 people. By comparison, the IT resources to run 130 separate survey programs using different systems would be immense.

The impact of IBSP efficiencies on timeliness of data releases has been noted across many of the IBSP surveys. In the past few years, data releases have been moving closer to the start of the reference period than ever before. As innovations surrounding administrative data sources are explored, it is expected that preliminary data release can be facilitated by IBSP.

The initial objective related to collection solely via EQ is one area where the IBSP needed to re-evaluate. Some smaller programs that integrated into the IBSP were structured around manual processes of spreadsheet reporting. The cost–benefit analysis of developing EQ for these surveys identified a new need within the Operations Field at Statistics Canada. There is now a self-contained team dedicated to developing spreadsheet reporting templates with automated extraction that can be accessed by the IBSP application.

8.25 Conclusion

The development of the IBSP system was a challenging endeavor that is ever evolving. As a Statistics Canada generic processing system, the IBSP has transitioned from an innovative tool to manage the Corporate Business Architecture needs of the time to a viable alternate to the redevelopment of antiquated processing systems. The standardized framework, integrated infrastructure, and metadata-driven technologies have born witness to the scalability of functionalities and expanded usage. Efficiencies via the reduction of resources required, collection costs, response burden, and analytical time required to produce high-quality estimates have been witnessed over the course of the many production cycles.

The use of the IBSP will only grow in the future and the intense planning that was undertaken at the start of the program will be able to fully support the expected growth.

References

ABS (2005). *Informing a Nation: The Evolution of the Australian Bureau of Statistics, 1905–2005*. Australian Bureau of Statistics. Catalogue No. 1382.

ABS (2021). *Australian System of National Accounts, Concepts, Sources and Methods*. Australian Bureau of Statistics. 5216.0 - Australian System of National Accounts: Concepts, Sources and Methods, 2020-21 (https://www.abs.gov.au/statistics/detailed-methodology-information/concepts-sources-methods/australian-system-national-accounts-concepts-sources-and-methods/latest-release).

Bavdaž, M., Bounfour, A., Martin, J., Nonnis, A., Perani, G., and Redek, T. (2023). Measuring investment in intangible assets. In: *Advances in Establishment Statistics, Methods and Data Collection*, Chapter 5 (ed. G. Snijkers, M. Bavdaž, S. Bender, J. Jones, S. MacFeely, J.W. Sakshaug, K.J. Thompson, and A. van Delden). Hoboken: Wiley.

Beveridge, W. (1942). *Beveridge Report: Social Insurance and Allied Services*. HMSO. Cmd 6404.

Bordo, M.D. and Haubrich, J.G. (2012). Deep Recessions, Fast Recoveries, and Financial Crises: Evidence from the American Record. *NBER Working Paper 18194*, Cambridge, MA: National Bureau of Economic Research.

Brodeur, M., Koumanakos, P., Leduc, J., Rancourt, E., and Wilson, K. (2006). *The Integrated Approach to Economic Surveys in Canada*. Statistics Canada. Catalogue 68-514.

Cairncross, A. (1988). The development of economic statistics as an influence on theory and policy. In: *National Income and Economic Progress* (ed. J.O.N. Perkins, T. Van Hoa and D. Irononger), 11–20. Palgrave Macmillan.

De Broe, S., Boscha, O., Daasa, P., Omitted authors: Buiten, G., Laevensa, B., and Kroesea, B. (2021). The need for timely official statistics. The COVID-19 pandemic as a driver for innovation. *Statistical Journal of the IAOS* Pre-press (Pre-press): 1–7.

Enterprise Statistics Division (2010). *Integrated Business Statistics Program Blueprint*. Statistics Canada internal document.

Enterprise Statistics Division (2015). *Integrated Business Statistics Program Overview*. Statistics Canada. Catalogue 68-515.

ESS (2019). *Quality Assurance Framework of the European Statistical System*, Version 2.0.

Eurostat (2017a). *European Statistics Code of Practice*. Eurostat. https://ec.europa.eu/eurostat/web/products-catalogues/-/KS-02-18-142#:~:text=The%20Code%20aims%20to%20ensure,professional%20independence%2C%20impartiality%20and%20objectivity.

Eurostat (2017b). *Handbook on Methodology of Modern Business Statistics*. Eurostat. Handbook on Methodology of Modern Business Statistics | CROS (https://ec.europa.eu/eurostat/cros/content/handbook-methodology-modern-business-statistics_en).

Eurostat (2020). *European Statistical System Peer Reviews, Third Round: 2021-2023, Overall Methodology for the Third Round of Peer Reviews*, Eurostat.

Godbout, S., Beaucage, Y., and Turmelle, C. (2011). Achieving quality and efficiency using a top-down approach in the Canadian Integrated Business Statistics Program. *Presented at the Conference of European Statistics*, Slovenia, 2011.

Honchar, O., McIntosh, K., and Zheng, S. (2021). *A Monthly Indicator of Turnover Using Business Activity Statement Data*. Australian Bureau of Statistics. A Monthly Indicator of Turnover using Business Activity Statement Data | Australian Bureau of Statistics (https://www.abs.gov.au/statistics/research/monthly-indicator-turnover-using-business-activity-statement-data).

Hostetter, E. (2013). *IBSP Conceptual Framework*, Statistics Canada internal document.

Hundepool, A. (2003). The ARGUS-software. In: *Monographs of Official Statistics, Work Session on Statistical Data Confidentiality Luxembourg, 7 to 9 April 2003*, 347–363. Luxembourg: European Commission.

Koskimäki, T. and Taskinen, K. (2023). Bridging the gap between business and macroeconomic statistics: methodological considerations and practical solutions. In: *Advances in Establishment Statistics, Methods and Data Collection*, Chapter 4 (ed. G. Snijkers, M. Bavdaž, S. Bender, J. Jones, S. MacFeely, J.W. Sakshaug, K.J. Thompson, and A. van Delden). Hoboken: Wiley.

Kuznets, S. (1941). Statistics and economic history. *The Journal of Economic History* 1 (1): 26–41, Cambridge University Press.

Lay, T. (2018). International accounting standard board changes to treatment of leases – potential impacts to Australian macroeconomic statistics, *Joint Meeting of the Working Party on Financial Statistics and the Working Party on National Accounts* (6–7 November 2018). OECD conference centre Paris.

MacFeely, S. and van de Ven, P. (2023a). GDP and the SNA: past and present. In: *Advances in Establishment Statistics, Methods and Data Collection*, Chapter 2 (ed. G. Snijkers, M. Bavdaž, S. Bender, J. Jones, S. MacFeely, J.W. Sakshaug, K.J. Thompson, and A. van Delden). Hoboken: Wiley.

MacFeely, S. and van de Ven, P. (2023b). GDP and the SNA: future challenges. In: *Advances in Establishment Statistics, Methods and Data Collection*, Chapter 3 (ed. G. Snijkers, M. Bavdaž, S. Bender, J. Jones, S. MacFeely, J.W. Sakshaug, K.J. Thompson, and A. van Delden). Hoboken: Wiley.

Machdi, I., Pertiwi, R.P., Nefriana, Rr., and Erasmus, W. (2023). The development and maintenance of statistical business registers as statistical infrastructure in Statistics Indonesia and the Australian Bureau of Statistics. In: *Advances in Establishment Statistics, Methods and Data Collection*, Chapter 9 (ed. G. Snijkers, M. Bavdaž, S. Bender, J. Jones, S. MacFeely, J.W. Sakshaug, K.J. Thompson, and A. van Delden). Hoboken: Wiley.

Lequiller, F. and Blades, D. (2014). *Understanding National Accounts*. OECD.

Martineau, P. (2012). *Use of the Chart of Accounts in Determining the Content of Statistics Canada Business Surveys*, Statistics Canada internal document.

Martineau, P. (2013). *Smart Tax Replacement*, Statistics Canada internal document.

Mills, F., Godbout, S., Bosa, K., and Turmelle, C. (2013). Multivariate selective editing in the Integrated Business Statistics Program. *Joint Statistical Meeting*, Montreal Quebec, Canada (3–8 August 2013).

Mohl, C. (2007). The continuing evolution of generalized systems at Statistics Canada for Business Survey Processing. *Paper presented at the Third International Conference of Establishment Surveys*, Montreal, Quebec, Canada (18–21 June 2007).

Nicholson, J.R., Howells, T.F., and Wasshausen, D.B. (2023). Measuring the US digital economy. In: *Advances in Establishment Statistics, Methods and Data Collection*, Chapter 6 (ed. G. Snijkers, M. Bavdaž, S. Bender, J. Jones, S. MacFeely, J.W. Sakshaug, K.J. Thompson, and A. van Delden). Hoboken: Wiley.

OECD (2015). Recommendation of the Council on Good Statistical Practice, OECD/LEGAL/0417, https://legalinstruments.oecd.org/en/instruments/OECD-LEGAL-0417 (accessed 8 March 2022).

ONS (2018). *VAT Turnover Data in National Accounts: Background and Methodology*. Office for National Statistics. VAT turnover data in National Accounts: background and methodology - Office for National Statistics. https://www.ons.gov.uk/economy/grossdomesticproductgdp/methodologies/vatturnoverdatainnationalaccountsbackgroundandmethodology (accessed 8 March 2022).

Peisker, A., Lay, T., and Smedes, M. (2021). *Recent Applications of Supermarket Scanner Data in the National Accounts*. Australian Bureau of Statistics. Recent applications of supermarket scanner data in the National Accounts | Australian Bureau of Statistics. https://www.abs.gov.au/statistics/research/recent-applications-supermarket-scanner-data-national-accounts (accessed 8 March 2022).

Persons, W.M. (1925). Statistics and economic theory. *The Review of Economics and Statistics* 7 (3): 179–197.

Pradhan, M.C. (2023). Establishment of base informal sector statistics: an endeavor of measurement from Economic Census 2018 of Nepal. In: *Advances in Establishment Statistics, Methods and Data Collection*, Chapter 7 (ed. G. Snijkers, M. Bavdaž, S. Bender, J. Jones, S. MacFeely, J.W. Sakshaug, K.J. Thompson, and A. van Delden). Hoboken: Wiley.

Pullinger, J. (1997). The creation of the office for National Statistics. *International Statistical Review* 65 (3): 291–308.

Royal Statistical Society (2021). *History*, RSS – History. https://rss.org.uk/about/history/ (accessed 8 March 2022).

Saint-Pierre, É. and Bricault, M. (2011). The common editing strategy and data processing of business statistics surveys. *Paper presented at the Conference of European Statistics*, Slovenia.

Seyb, A., McKenzie, R., and Skerrett, A. (2013). Innovative production systems at Statistics New Zealand: overcoming the design and build bottleneck. *Journal of Official Statistics* 29 (1): 73–97.

Smith, P. and Pennick, S. (2009). 100 years of the Census of Production in the UK. GSS Methodological Series, No. 38. Office for National Statistics. https://webarchive.nationalarchives.gov.uk/20160107223300/http://www.ons.gov.uk/ons/guide-method/method-quality/specific/gss-methodology-series/index.html; https://gss.civilservice.gov.uk/guidance/methodology/methodology-publications/.

The National Archives' Catalogue (1934–1987). Records of the Cabinet Office, Records of the Central Statistical Office. Records of the Central Statistical Office | The National Archives. https://discovery.nationalarchives.gov.uk/details/r/C703 (accessed 31 October 2021).

Thomas, S. (2017). Future Development of Statistics Canada's Edit and Imputation System Banff, Work Session on Statistical Data Editing, *Conference of European Statisticians*, The Hague, Netherlands (24–26 April 2017). https://unece.org/fileadmin/DAM/stats/documents/ece/ces/ge.44/2017/mtg2/Paper_20_Canada.pdf (accessed 18 March 2022).

UN DESA (2015). Generic Statistical Information Model (GSIM): statistical classifications model reprint of UNECE document. *Meeting of the Expert Group on International Statistical Classifications*, New York (19–22 May 2015), ESA/STAT/AC.289/22. Microsoft Word - 0-Cover.doc. https://unstats.un.org/unsd/classifications/expertgroup/egm2015/ac289-22.PDF.

UNECE Secretariat (2009). Generic Statistical Business Process Model Version 4.0. *Paper prepared for the Joint UNECE/Eurostat/OECD Working Session on Statistical Metadata* (April 2009).

United Nations (2015). UN Fundamental Principles of Official Statistics – Implementation guidelines. Microsoft Word - Implementation Guidelines_complete draft without cover2.FINAL.doc. https://unstats.un.org/unsd/dnss/gp/Implementation_Guidelines_FINAL_without_edit.pdf (accessed 31 October 2021).

United Nations (2017). *The United Nations Statistical Commission at 70 Years*. United Nations. https://unstats.un.org/unsd/statcom/70th-anniversary/documents/UN_Statistical_Chairs_booklet_WEB.pdf.

United Nations (2021). *The Handbook on Management and Organization of National Statistical Systems*, 4the. https://unstats.un.org/capacity-development/handbook/index.cshtml#:~:text=The%20fourth%20edition%20of%20the,that%20is%20fit%20for%20purpose.

United Nations, European Commission, International Monetary Fund, Organisation for Economic Co-operation and Development, and World Bank (2009). *System of National Accounts 2008*. New York: United Nations.

United States and U.S. Census Bureau (1878–2012). *Statistical abstract of the United States*. U.S. G.P.O.: Washington https://www.worldcat.org/title/statistical-abstract-of-the-united-states/oclc/1193890?page=citation.

UNSC (2014). Resolution adopted by the General Assembly on 29 January 2014 68/261. Fundamental Principles of Official Statistics, A/RES/68/261. Microsoft Word - N1345511.doc. https://unstats.un.org/unsd/dnss/gp/fp-new-e.pdf.

UNSC (2021). Report of the Friends of the Chair Group on Economic Statistics, E/CN.3/2021/1. https://documents-dds-ny.un.org/doc/UNDOC/GEN/N20/378/21/PDF/N2037821.pdf?OpenElement.

9

The Development and Maintenance of Statistical Business Registers as Statistical Infrastructure in Statistics Indonesia and the Australian Bureau of Statistics

Imam Machdi[1], Ratih Putri Pertiwi[1], Rr. Nefriana[1], and Willem Erasmus[2]

[1] BPS – Statistics Indonesia, Deputy of Methodology and Statistical Information, Jakarta, Indonesia
[2] ABS – Australian Bureau of Statistics, Business Register Unit, Melbourne, Australia

9.1 Introduction

An inclusive and exhaustive Statistical Business Registers (SBRs) is the backbone for producing survey based economic statistics and an important element of a National Statistical Institutes (NSIs) statistical infrastructure. It provides the populations and characteristics of statistical units. It also serves as a central data source for querying legal units, enterprises, and enterprise groups.

Additionally, the SBR can provide links to administrative units and registers, as a central data source, enabling the use of administrative data for statistical purposes. It can provide unique identifiers enabling linkages at the microlevel across statistical domains as needed for producing national and international statistics.

This chapter provides an overview of SBRs in Statistics Indonesia and the Australian Bureau of Statistics (ABS). It starts by looking at the Indonesian and Australian context (Section 9.2) and then proceeds to definitions of a SBR (Section 9.3). Section 9.4 provides an overview of the evolution of the SBRs, moving onto looking at SBR design (Section 9.5), benefits (Section 9.6), challenges (Section 9.7), and opportunities (Section 9.8). The chapter concludes with an overview of the future spine concept (Section 9.9).

9.2 The Indonesian and Australian Context

In 2020, Indonesia had a population of more than 270.2 million (BPS 2021b) and the estimated population of Australia was 25.6 million (ABS 2020). According to the results of the 2016 Indonesia Economic Census, the business population in Indonesia was 26.7 million economic units engaged in various economic activities other than agriculture (BPS 2017b). In contrast, in June 2020, Australia had 2.4 million actively trading businesses, contributing to the Australian economy (ABS 2021).

The Indonesian business population has diverse business characteristics that may be different from many other countries. Micro and small businesses dominate the number of economic units (98.33%) compared to the remaining medium and large businesses (BPS 2017b). Looking further into their formality, the majority (93.15%) of Indonesia's businesses were informal (not legal entity) and recognized as households with unregistered business. In terms of business networks, most

Advances in Business Statistics, Methods and Data Collection. Edited by Ger Snijkers, Mojca Bavdaž, Stefan Bender, Jacqui Jones, Steve MacFeely, Joseph W. Sakshaug, Katherine J. Thompson, and Arnout van Delden.
© 2023 John Wiley & Sons, Inc. Published 2023 by John Wiley & Sons, Inc.

businesses (98.18%) in Indonesia were sole proprietorships. Meanwhile, wholesale and retail trade, repair of motor vehicles and motorcycles, accommodation and food service activities, and manufacturing were the first, second, and third-biggest economic industries in terms of the number of establishments, respectively, covering 80% of total businesses (BPS 2017b). In the last three years (2018–2020), the contribution of the economic growth in terms of gross domestic product (GDP) was dominated by manufacturing, agriculture, wholesale and retail trade, vehicle repair, construction, and mining sectors, about 63.66% in total (BPS 2021a). In addition to traditional economic arrangements, the emergence of the industrial revolution 4.0 in Indonesia, has seen many economic activities extensively using digital platforms. Micro and small businesses use these digital platforms to sell goods, participate in the sharing economy, and provide many different services in transportation, food, banking, travel, hotel, health, and others.

In Australia, the 2.4 million actively trading businesses are legally registered with an Australian Business Number (ABN) and therefore considered formal businesses. They are almost equally split between corporations (financial and nonfinancial) and household-based businesses, with the split being 47.5% and 52.3%, respectively. Unknowns represent 0.2% (ABS 2021). A total of 97.5% of Australian businesses employ less than 20 employees, and only 2.5% employ 20 or more employees (ABS 2021). Similarly, 97.0% of these businesses contribute an annualized turnover of less than five million Australian Dollars (AU$), and only 3.0% of these businesses deliver an annualized turnover of five million or more AU$ (ABS 2021). Companies represent 38.3% of actively trading businesses in Australia, sole proprietors 28.4%, partnerships 9.9%, trusts 23.4%, and the public sector less than 0.02% (ABS 2021).

The 2.4 million Australian businesses are classified using the Australia and New Zealand Standard Industrial Classification (ANZSIC). In June 2020, the three largest industries with a combined number of business contribution of 39.8% were: Construction (16.4%); Professional, Scientific and Technical Services (12.5%); and Rental, Hiring and Real Estate Services (10.9%) (ABS 2021).

9.3 The Definition of a Statistical Business Register

The "Guidelines on Statistical Business Register" define a SBR as a "regularly updated, structured database of economic units in a territorial area, maintained by an NSI, and used for statistical purposes" (UN/UNECE 2015, p. 1).

The ABS overlay a broader purpose description over this definition to make it more practical: SBRs are foundational statistical infrastructure for compiling high quality economic statistics as they provide economy wide coverage of economic units, using consistent unit structures and classifications. This enables various economic survey frames that are inputs to the National Accounts (NA) and business demography to be consistently compiled on the same basis. (Ryan et al. 2020, p. 767).

From these definitions, the purpose of a SBR is to function as foundational statistical infrastructure for high-quality economic statistics. In most NSIs, including the ABS, the SBR identifies the scope of the economy to be measured (the production boundary), while the National Accounts (NA) measure the performance of units within the scope of the production boundary.

9.4 The Evolution of SBRs in Statistics Indonesia and the Australian Bureau of Statistics

Badan Pusat Statistik – Statistics Indonesia (BPS for short) is the Indonesian National Statistical Institute (NSI). Its role was mandated by the Statistics Act Number 16 Year 1997. One of its main duties is to capture the economic portrait of the country and provide evidence of economy-wide coverage for policy makers. To ameliorate the production of high-quality official economic statistics, the SBR plays the fundamental role of a backbone in providing basic information for conducting economic surveys, enabling the use of administrative and statistical data sources for efficiency, increasing the harmonization of surveys and integration of survey data, and serving as the coordinating mechanism for economic statistics.

The ABS is Australia's independent NSI with its functions and responsibilities laid out in the Census and Statistics Act 1905 and the Australian Bureau of Statistics Act 1975. It provides reliable information to tell the story of Australia.

The ABS is responsible for developing, compiling, analyzing, and disseminating statistical information across a range of sectors, including Agriculture, Environment, Building and Construction, Transport, Tourism, Financial Institutions, and Innovation and Technology. It also produces Main Economic Indicators including Private New Capital Expenditure, Retail Trade, Business Indicators, Building Approvals, Job Vacancies, New Motor Vehicle Sales, and Housing and Lending Finance.

Within the ABS there is a Statistical Standards and Infrastructure section, which includes the ABS Business Register Unit (ABS BRU) and the Address Register Unit. The ABS BRU is responsible for delivering the ABS SBR, as the main statistical infrastructure underpinning most of these economic products, and then downstream for the National Accounts. It ensures coherence and consistency in the populations that is used to deliver these statistical information and products.

9.4.1 Development of the Statistical Business Register in Statistics Indonesia

The development of the SBR has evolved through several phases since BPS adopted computerization in 1970 and maintained databases electronically. Each phase addresses a particular development stage of the SBR.

9.4.1.1 Phase 1 (1970–2012): Business Directory

The SBR embryo was based on a business directory. In the 1970s, BPS maintained business directories of limited industries in manufacturing and transportation. As the economy grew over time in Indonesia, the business directories covered more complete industries as captured by the 2006 Economic Census. For ease of data maintenance, the business directory was classified according to industry and maintained by Subject Matter Areas (SMAs), which are industry-based organizational units at BPS. Each SMA had its procedure to validate, modify, and store its business directory, including industry-specific variables. Some SMAs updated their business directories periodically through their surveys, for instance, an annual large- and medium-scale manufacturing survey. Nevertheless, other areas such as information and communication, rice mills, and transportation performed the update on an ad hoc basis. Business frames were constructed by integrating the updated business directories maintained by SMAs. In terms of the IT environment, business frames, and business directories were managed by different databases and applications for maintenance, updating, and dissemination purposes.

9.4.1.2 Phase 2 (2013–2015): Integrated Business Register

The Integrated Business Register (IBR) development aimed to integrate the siloed business processes for maintaining the business directories by SMAs. Aligned to the System of National Accounts (SNA), the common concept of statistical units in the IBR covered enterprise groups, enterprises, and establishments for capturing business characteristics in Indonesia. In addition, standard procedures for validating, modifying, and storing the business register information were established to be carried out by the SMAs (see Section 9.5.1.4). The IBR system provided a database and a portal for implementing the maintenance procedures and dissemination of the business register. The business register database was mainly derived from the existing business directories and profiling information using the internet. With some tools, the portal facilitated SMAs to perform matching, profiling, and updating activities upon the business register database (see Section 9.5.1.4).

9.4.1.3 Phase 3 (2015–2021): The Statistical Business Register

The SBR was developed with an enhanced feature of administrative data integration. In the 2016 Economic Census preparations, the SBR was updated with administrative data collected from local government institutions, ministries, and other related government institutions. The updated SBR generated the initial business lists along with prefilled questionnaires which were, then verified in the field by enumerators when conducting the 2016 Economic Census. In the case that a new business was found in the field within a census block, a questionnaire was completed for the new business, and the business list updated. As part of the BPS transformation program, the SBR was designed to be an integral part of the Corporate Statistical Infrastructure (CSI). Also, under the transformation program, BPS designed the SBR governance to have a dedicated SBR unit for managing integration, updating the comprehensive economic information, and coordinating administrative data exchange with other government agencies. The opportunity to improve the SBR data accuracy, and its comprehensive coverage was widely opened by data exchange with the Directorate General of Tax, the Indonesian Investment Coordinating Board, and the National Public Procurement Agency. However, it required establishing formal cooperation with each agency and working through the technical capability of data exchange.

9.4.2 Development of the Statistical Business Register in the Australia Bureau of Statistics

NSIs collect substantial amounts of data via surveys. Business sample surveys are based on frames that need to reflect the current business population as accurately as possible. The need to deliver survey frames resulted in the evolution of the ABS SBR (see Figure 9.1).

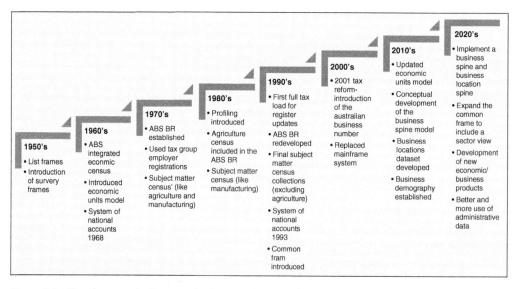

Figure 9.1 Timeframe and milestones in the evolution of the ABS SBR.

Before 1969 ABS list frames were compiled for each population of interest, such as a list of manufacturing businesses, or a list of retailers. Before the arrival of computers, these list frames were predominantly maintained in siloed, paper-based formats and compiled using information from periodic industry-based censuses. Over time the list frames became dated, of impaired quality, and coherence between different frames was heavily compromised. Siloed maintenance of these lists frames significantly jeopardized the consistency between them. This made it difficult to reconcile survey results into national products, such as the compilation of Australian National Accounts.

ABS ran a full economic census in 1968. This census was used as the foundation for the first ABS SBR and the establishment of a more cost-effective ABS survey program.

With the integration of the list frames into the ABS SBR, coherence between the frames was possible as a standard set of statistical units was available for use in the different surveys. Standard classifications were also applied and an Economic Units Model, broadly aligned with the SNAs, was introduced.

The ABS Economic Units Model was last updated in 2013 (see Figure 9.2). It identifies four main units: Enterprise Group (EG), Legal Entity (LE), Type of Activity Unit (TAU), and Location (Figure 9.2). These units are described in the ABS SESCA (2008).

The unit definitions in the ABS Economic Units Model defines the scope or coverage of the population, as well as the characteristics or contents of the units in scope.

Following the 1968 Economic Census, regular updates of the Australian Taxation Office (ATO) Group Employer Registrations were used to maintain the ABS SBR, supplemented by ABS subject matter economic census', e.g. manufacturing, agriculture. In 2021, the agriculture census is the only economic census left.

In the mid-1970s, the ABS introduced taxation data as the first comprehensive administrative data source to update the ABS SBR. Specific legislation was introduced to enable the ATO to provide ABS with these records. In the 1980s, a clerical profiling program was established to accommodate the maintenance of the larges businesses in Australia that could not be maintained through tax records alone.

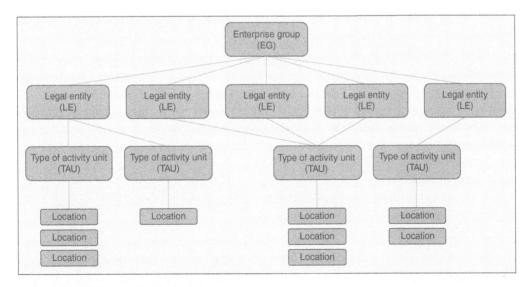

Figure 9.2 ABS Economic Units Model.

In 2001, a significant advance was made possible when the Australian Government introduced a single registration number, the ABN, for all Australian businesses, to register as a legal business. This put the ABS in the privileged position to have a complete list of legal entities operating in Australia, enhanced with other registration information such as industry and sector classification. It also expanded the scope of ABS SBR to include nonemployers as well as employers.

By integrating the individual list frames, adopting the ABS Economic Units Model, and using a consistent administrative source (from the Australian Tax Office), the ABS SBR became an established part of the ABS statistical foundational infrastructure and been a single source of truth for economic statistics for over 50 years.

9.5 Statistical Business Register Designs

9.5.1 The Design of the BPS SBR

The BPS SBR was designed aligned to the UNECE Guidelines on Statistical Business Registers (2015). These guidelines define an SBR as a regularly updated, structured database of economic units in a territorial area, maintained by an NSI, and used for statistical purposes. According to the SBR design document (BPS 2017a), the design covers essential elements of: the statistical unit model, unit coverage, data sources, main processes, and SBR integration. The SBR databases are designed to store information on updated data sources, a master frame, survey frames, and SBR-based statistical outputs.

9.5.1.1 Statistical Unit Model

The BPS statistical unit model is aligned to international standards about the concept of enterprise group, enterprise, and establishment (UNECE 2015; United Nations et al. 1993). The statistical unit model provides the notion of structural statistics based on the relationships between an enterprise group, an enterprise, and an establishment. It provides the basis for delineating and recording the enterprise group, the enterprise, and the establishment and performing statistical aggregates and tabulated data. According to the SNA 2008, an enterprise group is formed from a large group of corporations (conglomerate), whereby a parent corporation controls several subsidiaries (United Nations et al. 1993). A subsidiary is recognized in the form of an enterprise within an enterprise group. An enterprise is viewed as an institutional unit as a producer of goods and services, for instance, a corporation, a household, a government institution, and a nonprofit institution serving households (United Nations et al. 1993). An enterprise may have one or more establishments. An establishment is defined as an enterprise, or part of an enterprise, that is situated in a single location and in which only a single productive activity is carried out or in which the principal productive activity accounts for most of the value added (United Nations et al. 1993).

9.5.1.2 Unit Coverage

An SBR should capture the productive activities undertaken by all institutional units. In the current BPS SBR design, the institutional units are those which engage in production activity as nonfinancial corporations, financial corporations, and households with registered business, illustrated in Figure 9.3. It is planned to include government units and nonprofit institutions serving households in the near future once the current institutional units reach their maturity in the SBR development and maintenance. In the Indonesian context, households with unregistered business are very challenging, especially given their dominance in the economy, approximately 93.15% of the business

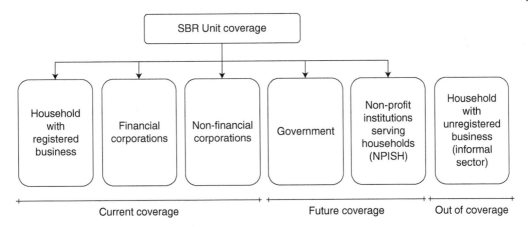

Figure 9.3 BPS SBR Unit Coverage.

population (BPS 2017b). These production activities are volatile and rapidly change in terms of births and deaths. Given these issues and the maturity of the SBR, households with unregistered business are currently excluded.

9.5.1.3 Data Sources

The current BPS SBR design uses administrative sources and statistical sources. The ultimate design recommends having only one primary source to create new units in the SBR to avoid unnecessary duplications from sources and additional integration tasks. To determine the primary source, an assessment study of administrative sources was conducted. This found that administrative tax data has the best coverage, content, and access (Suharni and Pertiwi 2016). The secondary sources, derived from the Indonesian Investment Coordinating Board and the National Public Procurement Agency, are best used to improve the content of the SBR but not increase unit coverage, for example, updating the contents on address, contact person, business activity, and product fields. On the other hand, statistical sources derived from the economic census, the agricultural census, business surveys, large business profiling, and SBR quality improvement surveys are used both as the primary source to create new units in the SBR and the secondary source to improve the content of the SBR.

9.5.1.4 Main Processes

The SBR data management life cycle is designed with six main processes (see Figure 9.4).

- Process 1: Acquire data sources
  This process acquires administrative and statistical sources for the SBR update, to increase the SBR unit coverage and improve the SBR content. The SBR live database, as the output of this process, comprises the Administrative Data Table, the Statistical Data Table, and the Statistical Unit Data Table. The process starts with merging records from administrative and statistical sources to the Administrative Data Table and the Statistical Data Table, respectively. It performs a content-based similarity function to match new records with the existing records within the Administrative Data Table and the Statistical Data Table for the SBR update applied in the Statistical Unit Data Table. Records in the Statistical Units Data Table have linkage to records in the Administrative Data Table and the Statistical Data Table through their identifiers to ensure data integrity.

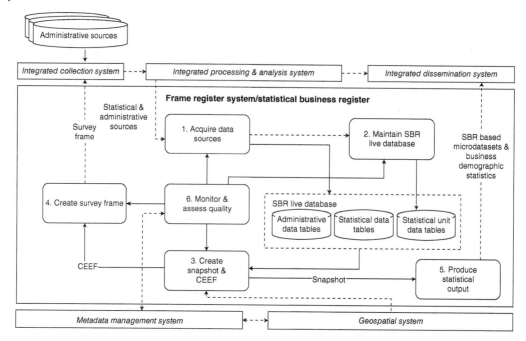

Figure 9.4 BPS SBR Main Processes and Integration.

- Process 2: Maintaining the SBR live database
  This process maintains the statistical unit information by performing manual updates. Profiling is a process of delineating the statistical units within an enterprise group (UNECE 2015). It takes information from annual business reports, financial statements, official websites, business news, or other online sources to manually identify the statistical units, make relationships with an enterprise group and apply the update. Some missing or questionable data values can also be manually updated from undertaking a quality improvement survey. In other cases, query execution is frequently used for unresolved cases on the Process 1 or ad hoc requests from manual resolution information such as phone query, Internet search, on-site visit, and interview.
- Process 3: Create snapshot and Common Enterprise Establishment Frame (CEEF)
  This process takes the population statistical units to create a snapshot and produces the CEEF based on the snapshot. The purpose of having a snapshot is to create valid and unchanging statistical units for a particular time reference for use by all surveys and dissemination of business demographic statistics. The CEEF is part of a snapshot that contains only active statistical units and their characteristics for survey sample selection and other statistical purposes.
- Process 4: Create survey frame
  This process creates a survey frame as a subset of CEEF that matches the specification of the survey target population and the survey reference period. The benefits of this process are harmonization of the surveys, increased potential for integration of survey data, reduction of costs, and more coherence in the resulting statistics (UNECE 2015).
- Process 5: Produce statistical outputs
  This process produces demographic statistics of businesses based on the snapshot data for dissemination purposes. The dissemination outputs are in the form of microdata and publication by providing statistical information on a business directory, births and deaths of enterprises and

establishments, their survival rate, and their contribution to economic growth and productivity (UNECE 2015).

- Process 6: Monitor and assess quality
This process measures the SBR quality through monitoring and assessment activities of whether SBR information can identify statistical units, generate snapshots, CEEF and survey frames, and provide SBR-based statistics with specified quality dimensions.

9.5.1.5 SBR Integration

Through a transformation program, the BPS has been developing CSI, which is a set of systems and tools to support the operations of the Indonesian statistical system. The transformation program aims to obtain efficiency, coherence, interoperability, and cooperation in the production of official statistics. As stated in Statistical Business Framework and Architecture (SBFA), the SBR is one of CSI components designed to be integrated with other CSI components such as the geospatial system, metadata system, integrated collection system, integrated processing and analysis system, and dissemination system (BPS 2016). The integration of SBR with other CSI components is shown in Figure 9.4.

9.5.2 The Design of the ABS Statistical Business Register

The current ABS SBR is based on the traditional integrated register concept and implemented in the form of a structured database. This works on the principle that data are maintained in a tightly integrated data holding. Administrative data sources aligned to specific ABS SBR specifications, are governed by external providers. To supplement this, ABS clerically collects (profiling) data that is integrated into the ABS SBR. The ABS SBR reflects and contains all the key unit level characteristics. Predefined standardized point in time outputs are extracted on a regular basis from the ABS SBR integrated holdings. Details of the ABS SBR structure are shown in Figure 9.5.

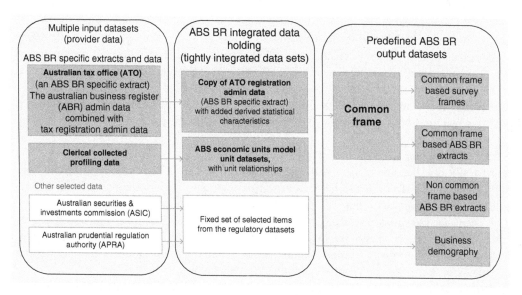

Figure 9.5 ABS SBR Structure.

The tightly integrated ABS SBR structure delivers improved quality, coherence, consistency, efficiency, and the standard use of methodologies and classifications for business/economic surveys, based on a single source of truth.

A constraint of an inflexible tightly integrated register structure is that it does not accommodate the use of unintegrated data into the ABS SBR, and therefore cannot produce outputs beyond the predefined standardized point in time outputs.

The ABS is currently looking at a future more adaptive structure. The final Section 9.9 reflects on the evolutionary steps to the next generation of the ABS SBR and potentially other SBRs.

9.5.2.1 Centralized Maintenance

To ensure consistency over time and coherence between survey outputs, it was important that the ABS SBR centralizes maintenance with regular updates.

Although the ABS SBR represents a complete population of all registered businesses in Australia, the characteristics of ABNs are based on a legal registration process. ABNs are a good representation of the Legal Entity and can be used to capture simple units in the economy. For businesses with complex structures, other units in the ABS Economic Units Model are created through clerical maintenance processes called profiling.

While not common practice by other NSIs, for efficiency purposes, the ABS adopted a two-population model for the ABS SBR. The purpose of this approach is to simplify the maintenance of most units and focus resources on maintaining the accuracy of the smaller population of complex units. The units that have simple structures are maintained by administrative sources and are known as the ABS nonprofiled population, while the units that are profiled are included in the ABS profiled population.

The stock of Legal Entities in the nonprofiled population is updated with the flow of ABN births and deaths and enhanced by applying monthly maintenance algorithms that derive statistical content, e.g. sector classifications. This ensures consistency over time.

For the profiled population, an ABS profiler investigates the Legal Entities in each complex business and establishes the structure and content of the Enterprise Group and Type of Activity Unit. It is a clerical process that uses the ABS Economic Unit Model definitions and characteristics to establish the structures. Information collected through the normal survey program responses are fed back to the ABS SBR maintenance processes. This is governed through strict survey frame maintenance procedure rules to ensure feedback is treated consistently. Although it is a clerical process, maintenance is centralized to enhance efficiency in contrast to each survey area undertaking the work.

The regular maintenance ensures that the ABR SBR reflects the Australian economy as close as possible to real time, while continuing to maintain coherence in the end statistical products.

9.5.2.2 Dissemination

The ABS SBR is a dynamic register with regular monthly updates of both the profiled and nonprofiled populations. To ensure coherence in statistical products, every quarter a "snapshot" is produced, which is a point in time view of the ABS SBR. This is known as the Common Frame.

Consistent derivation rules (e.g. algorithms to derive sector classifications, and size measures such as employment and turnover) are applied to the ABS SBR information to create the Common Frame, including survey stratification information. The Common Frame is then used as the comprehensive source for truth for individual ABS Survey Frames.

A further advantage of the Common Frame is that comprehensive and consistent quality assurance can be performed, described, and communicated to all ABS internal users, such as outlier detection and treatment or longitudinal comparisons. Anomalies are identified and homogeneously addressed. Each quarter, documentation is compiled including analysis on births, deaths, and resurrections movements from the previous period; reclassification changes; and any market intelligence relevant to this. The Common Frame is cleared as fit for purpose by an ABS internal stakeholder and internal user group. Following clearance, the Common Frame is used to create business survey frames.

9.5.2.3 Uses

The Common Frame is used for around twenty different ABS economic survey frames. These surveys are conducted at different frequencies, including nine quarterly, four biannually, five annually, and one quinquennially. Ad hoc survey frames are also requested. Each year, the annual surveys always use the same Common Frame quarter as the quarterly surveys, e.g. the ABS Annual Industry Statistics (AIS) survey frame is always based on the June Common Frame. This has the benefit of maintaining the coherence between the surveyed units from the same Common Frame. It also creates the opportunity to manage overlaps between selected survey units to reduce provider burden.

Feedback received from survey areas is fed back to the ABS SBR maintenance processes, and where sample frame maintenance procedures permit, updates to the ABS SBR can flow through to the Common Frame for use by all surveys.

The ABS SBR is also used to produce an annual business demography publication: *Counts of Businesses Entries and Exits* (CABEE) publication. This includes the longitudinal changes in Australian domestic businesses counts and characteristics (e.g. industry, sector, and size). When individual list frames were used, it was not possible to create these views.

Ad hoc extracts from the ABS SBR are also used to feed into one-off analysis, such as to support COVID-19 impact analysis on Australian business behaviors, or analysis of research and development activity.

9.6   Statistical Business Register Benefits

The main reason for an NSI to adopt an integrated SBR is to ensure high-quality, efficiently produced, and cost-effective statistical products.

Benefits from the integrated ABS SBR approach can be grouped into three groups: statistical production, operational benefits, and cost saving benefits. These benefits are not mutually exclusive.

These benefits can be summarized as follows:

- Statistical benefits including coherence between statistical outputs, consistency over time, and improved quality.
- Operational benefits including: greater efficiency in production of the statistics, improved client responsiveness through real-time updated unit information, reduced provider burden from overlap control of selected units, centralized maintenance with one subject matter expert group, and consistency in both input data as well as maintenance methodologies.
- Cost-saving benefits including lower operating costs from a once do, many use process approach. The upfront costs in the SBR have downstream efficiency savings.

The integrated SBR reduces statistical risk compared to other approaches and supports the earliest possible delivery of statistical products to market.

9.7 Statistical Business Register Challenges

The BPS SBR, as the solution to modern statistical infrastructure, faces multifaceted challenges of governance, policy, statistical business integration, and system development, which may inhibit SBR implementation. During the SBR implementation, BPS faced three key challenges: SBR governance and policy; business process integration; and system development.

9.7.1 SBR Governance and Policy

With currently 2.4 million formal businesses and more to come from administrative data, it is a challenge to see the governance of BPS having enough capacity to perform its functions. With this complexity, based on the SBR design document (BPS 2017a), the SBR will be centrally managed by the Business Register Unit (BRU) at a directorate level that performs the following functions:

- to manage the profiling program and procedures for large businesses;
- to perform data quality assurance;
- to generate business frames for surveys; and
- to produce business demographics.

In the future state, the SBR organizational arrangements must meet specific requirements. It must adhere to the organizational vision and mission, business strategy and agility, the size of organizational structure, and organizational function coherence. In addition to this, any organization changes must follow procedures for obtaining a recommended organization from the Ministry of Administrative and Bureaucratic Reform and approval via a Presidential Regulation. Currently, SBR functions are performed by the Methodology unit as an ex-officio SBR unit in collaboration with other units/divisions such as SMAs, national account, IT, and public relation units. As a result, this introduces problems of enterprises/establishments being overlooked or recorded twice, risks around prioritization as it is not the core business, limited resources, and coordination with other BPS areas.

At the national level, SBR governance for coordinating data acquisition needs to be established on a legal basis. Although the awareness of government institutions to share their data is growing, it faces the challenge of sharing administrative data while having data protection regulations that stipulate exclusive rights to certain government institutions to protect their data. It requires efforts to establish a cooperation agreement between BPS and the intended government institution. The negotiation is often very delicate to reach an agreement because of different treatment toward their data protection regulation. Due to confidentiality, some variables are not allowed to be obtained, and other variables may only be obtained without actual values, but the values masked with a classification of value ranges. Also, the delicacy of negotiation to reflect mutual benefits for both sides often occurs and delays the cooperation agreement. The understanding of common objectives is currently discussed thoroughly from technical to high-level meetings for reaching an agreement.

In addition, administrative data acquisition faces different concepts of business units among government institutions according to their interests. For instance, the Directorate General of Tax identifies a business using a tax identification number, disregards types of business units, and classifies business sizes based on tax values. In contrast, the Indonesian Investment Coordinating Board devises a business identification number, differentiates enterprise and establishment, and classifies business sizes according to the investment/capital values. Thus, the use of administrative data from different government institutions without common business identification leads to a technical complexity in profiling, linking, and matching business information, performing data integration with SBR databases, and examining SBR data quality.

9.7.2 Business Process Integration

In the absence of the intended SBR governance at BPS, establishing a business process for SBR development and maintenance in an integrated and coherent way is quite challenging. BPS must diminish problems of overlapping sampling business units among business surveys, respondent burden, and the tendency of low response rates in business surveys. A standard operating procedure (SOP) for SBR operations has been developed to build an integrated and coherent SBR business process to be carried out by SMAs. The SBR quality is still the primary issue. Under the current SBR governance, the Methodology Unit, with limited staff, manages the SBR and has difficulties supervising and controlling SBR operations toward SOP compliance. Further effort is required to conduct business process reengineering for integrated statistics on business surveys. Currently, the Economic Wide Survey (EWS) is being developed as a prototype of business survey integration by exercising the reengineered business process and the use of the SBR as the single source for the survey frame. Future implementation of EWS is desirable, although it requires common understanding by SMAs and setting up regulation for implementation enforcement.

9.7.3 System Development

The SBR as part of the Frame Register System (FRS) is not a single system but an integrated system with other systems and tools in CSI developed by procured IT consultants. To achieve service excellence in SBR operations, SBR development must cope with the CSI development and critical challenges in project management, system architecture, and system requirement specification (SRS).

Implementing the project management for CSI development requires a strategy to consider the size, complexity, and risk of the project in association with IT procurement, resource allocation, and performance measurement. The CSI project is highly complex consisting of 32 large systems with complex dependency and requires a high government budget. The government budget is reviewed on an annual basis, with the project management strategy sliced into 17 packages. Each package is constructed from several related main functional requirements of CSI components and represents a complete stack of a fully functioning systems to support a specific business process. Once it is delivered, stakeholders should quickly see the system's value, and the contribution of the government budget can be broken down per system. This makes it more manageable to execute the procurement process, human resource allocation, and government budget accountability according to the defined packages. However, the project will take a long time to accomplish. Within the project management strategy, the FRS is treated as one package consisting of the SBR, Administrative Area Frame, Census Block Master Frame, and Household Master Frame.

The project management allocates human resources into working groups with IT consultants to develop the system packages. BPS adopts an agile system development methodology, where building system architecture, SRS, and system solutions evolve through collaboration between self-organizing cross-functional working groups and IT consultants. A working group handles one system package. A specific working group as an integrator is designated to ensure the integrity among system packages and to measure the progress and quality of the overall system packages. It is also crucial for each working group, including the FRS working group, to assign competent persons from SMAs and IT staff and to provide sufficient continuous time working with IT consultants, especially in developing system architecture and SRS.

Developing system architecture and the SRS are the fundamental steps in system development for CSI, including SBR. System architecture is defined as a high-level design of system solutions, while the SRS is a more detailed description derived from the system architecture. In the case of the FRS package development, business analysts and IT architects often cope with difficulty communicating the value of system architecture and convincing the working groups that the system architecture will perform effectively and efficiently to satisfy user requirements. The quality of SRS is profoundly reliant on the complexity of the SRS and the ability of the working group to validate the SRS built by system analysts. Both the working groups and IT consultants must have a big-picture viewpoint, detailed requirements competence, and communicate well about transforming notions from a statistical perspective to the perspective of system architecture and SRS, and vice versa. Otherwise, they may fail to specify important user needs on system architecture and SRS under contractual and time limitations. The risks are that the system solution is incomplete, unacceptable, and leads to a legal dispute.

9.8 Opportunities in SBR Implementation

Despite the many challenges, there are opportunities for SBR development in BPS. Opportunities allow SBR to have bargaining points and to overcome the challenges strategically. Besides this, BPS gains opportunities to accelerate SBR implementation from the internal transformation program to modernize statistical production, Indonesia One Data Policy to improve national data governance and data exchange among government agencies, and the improvement of administrative data on tax, business investment, and procurement.

9.8.1 Transformation Program

BPS has implemented the statistical transformation program called the Statistical Capacity Building – Change and Reform for the Development of Statistics (STATCAP – CERDAS) since 2014. The main objective is to modernize the production of high-quality official statistics by improving effectivity, efficiency, and integration of the statistical business process supported by effective ICT systems and human resource management. The transformation program has key principles as guidance for its output and outcome. One of the key principles is the use of the SBR managed by the BRU for integrated business surveys. Other key principles include National Account and macro statistics as the primary beneficiaries of integrated statistical business process, the use of administrative data and registers as data sources for statistics, survey management for the conduction of optimally integrated surveys, centralized IT infrastructure and management, and the implementation of paperless data collection.

Under this transformation program, SBR gains executive commitment as it is purposely designed in the SBFA (BPS, 2016). SMA's awareness is also significantly improved in relation to the importance of SBR and the understanding of their roles and responsibilities in updating and utilizing the SBR. Business directories and IBR data provide an opportunity to establish the initial SBR data, which delivered the initial list of businesses and updated frames to support the Economic Census 2016. Having a complete and updated SBR encourages SMAs to put more effort into SBR improvement through data cleansing, matching, and validation. Moreover, change management in the transformation program plays a significant role in engaging change agents to improve collaboration for achieving shared objectives of SBR use. The regular meeting attended by change agents establishes good communication among them, removes a silo mindset, and sets an obligation toward statistical modernization.

Due to the Covid-19 pandemic, the transformation program needed to be accelerated due to the value chain disruption of an increase in data demand and a deficit in data and resource supply (CCSA 2020). The pandemic forced the BPS to prioritize survey programs, optimize the use of administrative, and accelerate digital innovation and technology adoption. In response to these, BPS cut some less impactful operational activities to serve stakeholders' data needs and focus more resources on the modernization of statistics business process, including the transition from the conventional approach of siloed updating to the integrated internal and external data updating approach.

9.8.2 National Policy and Initiative

The Indonesia One Data initiative is the government data policy signified by Presidential Regulation Number 39 Year 2019 to establish national data governance enabling government data sharing and exchange among government institutions, improving data quality and transparency, and strengthening the national statistical system. It has four data principles: data standard compliance, metadata support, data interoperability facility, and the use of data reference. In this policy, the BPS chief statistician is a member of the National Data Steering Committee that has the main tasks of providing direction, setting up data policy, and evaluating the implementation of Indonesia one data initiative. In supporting the implementation, BPS has the key responsibility for setting data standards and metadata structure, examining data prioritization, providing a recommendation for data collection, and building the statistical capacity in all government institutions.

Indonesia one data initiative provides benefits for SBR development in Indonesia. It urges government institutions to share their data, including administrative data related to registered business. Various government initiatives such as tax reform, ease of doing business (EODB), and e-commerce improve the quality of registered business data which is utilized as data sources for updating the SBR live database. It significantly reduces efforts and costs of conducting registered business data collection and improves the SBR data quality.

The tax reform initiative led by the Directorate General of Tax, Ministry of Finance implemented a variety of programs on tax policy and administration reform since 2015, such as tax amnesty, tax stimulus for micro, small, medium enterprises, online services to taxpayers in the form of easy reporting, payment and easy access to tax information, and financial information disclosure for tax purposes. The tax programs improve administrative tax data collected by the Directorate General of Tax in terms of more businesses reporting as taxpayers. It increases coverage of statistical units with enhanced data quality in terms of accuracy, completeness, and timeliness and allows further use of tax data for statistics purposes. The tax reform initiative continues and made adjustments to tax administration service procedures related to COVID-19. This has seen the development of digital-based tax services focusing on user experience, and increasing tax compliance, specifically businesses engaged in the digital economy. This should bring promising opportunities for tax data as the SBR's primary updating data source in the longer term.

Under the Government Regulation Number 24 Year 2018 on Integrated Electronic Based Service of Business License, another initiative launched by the government in 2018 is the EODB by simplifying the procedures of business license attainment through an online submission system (OSS). It is a government breakthrough to overcome the problems of fragmented data due to different procedures and systems across the central government and local governments through OSS. The OSS implementation provides benefits to the BPS in that the OSS data is used as the primary SBR data source in addition to tax data. OSS data has superiority in linking business entities across agencies. This is achieved via a unique business identification number named *Nomor Induk Berusaha* (NIB) that applies across agencies in the OSS registration system allowing easier integration of administrative data with less data matching effort and reducing redundancy. In the future, it will maintain consistent and coherent business data across government agencies.

In 2019, the government introduced the Government Regulation Number 80 Year 2019 on electronic-based trading, which is the legal guidelines for the country's e-commerce industry. The regulation aims to improve the governance of Internet-based and electronic trading activities and ensure tax compliance among e-commerce businesses. It defines the type of entities that can engage in e-commerce, such as business practitioners, consumers, and government agencies, where the business practitioners are categorized into sellers, e-commerce providers, and intermediary service providers. Businesses and individuals (domestic or foreign) engaging in e-commerce activities must adhere to several new requirements of attaining a business license obtained through OSS, a tax identification number, a technical license, and a business identification number. The regulation creates an opportunity in that BPS is mandated to collect data from e-commerce providers and intermediary service providers to provide regular reports about business entities and transactions with specific confidentiality measures. This data, in turn, will be integrated with the SBR to improve compliance with standard SNA 2008 and the International Standard Industrial Classification (ISIC) of All Economic Activities Revision 4 concepts and definitions. The regular reports also bring the opportunity to support the national account with more comprehensive information concerning digital economy growth in Indonesia and its indicators.

9.9 The Future Spine Concept

The Integrated ABS SBR has served the ABS well for around 50 years. An Integrated SBR approach works well where the main purpose of the SBR is to deliver populations for statistical surveys, and where the structure of the economy remains relatively stable.

In rapidly changing economic environments (e.g. the COVID-19 pandemic), an inflexible highly integrated SBR model design creates constraints. An example could be using administrative data to produce statistical products beyond the Common Frame or Survey Frames or supporting data substitution in survey collections.

To overcome these constraints, the Spine Concept was born.

A spine is the minimum set of information needed to combine statistical units from multiple information sources, e.g. administrative, survey, and operational information. The spine is particularly beneficial where relationships are manually established and maintained, e.g. using the ABS Economic Units Model. Figure 9.6 provides an overview of the Spine concept using the ABS Business Spine as an example.

In the conceptual model, all input information sets exist and are maintained as stand-alone sources of truth for the purpose for which they are created. This purpose might be the traditional ABS SBR core input information sets such as ATO administrative registration data, or information that is created for a totally different purpose such as survey collected information. These information sets are not associated or integrated with each other. To facilitate the creation of user-driven integrated outputs (e.g. existing Common Frame) from the core register data sets or new solutions using administrative information directly from the input information sets, a business spine is created. This spine contains the minimum information needed to associate or integrate individual sets of information of businesses.

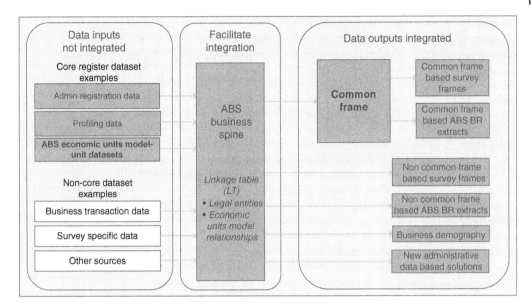

Figure 9.6 ABS Business Spine Concept.

Under this model, the ABS BRU would be the custodian of the Business Spine and core input datasets, such as the ABS Economic Units Model, profiling maintenance, and taxation registration data. Other input datasets may be maintained by other teams, including survey data external to the ABS SBR.

All existing ABS SBR outputs, e.g. Common Frame, Survey Frames, and CABEE can still be reproduced using the Spine. The spine can also be used by other teams to support data substitution and to develop new statistical solutions.

The intention is to create an ABS Business Spine as broader Statistical Infrastructure, maintained through the same standard consistent processes used for the existing ABS SBR.

Further information on the Spine concepts can be found in Ryan et al. (2020, pp. 767–774).

9.10 Conclusion

The SBR is not just an updated database but also allows for data integration, business process transformation, and coordination with internal and external stakeholders. SBR is the core infrastructure in the statistical integration process. With the SBR construction, data integration is expected to be seamless. SBR development requires strategic-level commitment and technical competence to tackle challenges and to grasp opportunities. SBR governance, policy, business process transformation, and IT systems are the key factors in an NSI to improve the SBR as part of the modernized statistical production. In association with external stakeholders, the national governance, and policy in administrative data acquisition can accelerate the SBR maturity and quality.

Over a 50-year period, the ABS SBR has evolved to: integrate list frames, use administrative source in a consistent maintenance process, and produce a quarterly Common Frame. The ABS SBR has been adopted by the ABS business survey program as the single source of truth for survey populations. This ensures that the ABS SBR delivers value and benefits that would not have been possible otherwise. These include statistical benefits, as well as operational and cost savings benefits for the organization.

It is envisaged that the next generation of the ABS SBR will use a business spine approach. This will open up expanded and additional opportunities, including the ability to use more administrative information in statistical products, user-driven outputs and better support of collection operations.

Acknowledgment

The work of the BPS SBR development has been supported under the cooperation between the BPS – Statistics Indonesia and the Australian Bureau of Statistics since 2013.

References

ABS SESCA (2008). ABS business register and the ABS units model, version 1.1. Australian Bureau of Statistics. https://www.abs.gov.au/statistics/classifications/standard-economic-sector-classifications-australia-sesca/2008-version-1-1 (accessed 30 August 2021).

ABS (2020). National, state and territory population. Australian Bureau of Statistics. https://www.abs.gov.au/statistics/people/population/national-state-and-territory-population/dec-2020 (accessed 30 August 2021).

ABS (2021). Counts of Australian businesses, including entries and exits. Australian Bureau of Statistics. https://www.abs.gov.au/statistics/economy/business-indicators/counts-australian-businesses-including-entries-and-exits/jul2016-jun2020 (accessed 30 August 2021).

BPS (2016). Statistical Business Framework Architecture Version 4.5, Jakarta.

BPS (2017a). Statistical Business Register and Large Business Unit Design Document Version 9, Jakarta.

BPS (2017b). Result of Establishment Listing of Economic Census 2016 Indonesia, Jakarta.

BPS (2021a). Pertumbuhan Ekonomi Indonesia Triwulan IV Tahun 2020, Berita Resmi Statistik. Jakarta.

BPS (2021b). Potret Sensus Penduduk 2020 Menuju Satu Data Kependudukan Indonesia, Jakarta.

CCSA (2020). How COVID-19 is Changing the World: A Statistical Perspective, Technical Report.

Ryan, L., Thompson, C., and Jones, J. (2020). A Statistical Business Register spine as a new approach to support data integration and firm-level data linking: an ABS perspective. *Statistical Journal of the International Association for Official Statistics* 36: 767–774.

Suharni, L. and Pertiwi, R.P. (2016). The selection of administrative data sources for Statistical Business Register updating in BPS. *Proceedings of the 25th Meeting of the Wiesbaden Group on Business Registers – International Roundtable on Business Survey Frames*, Tokyo.

UNECE (2015). Guidelines on Statistical Business Register, Number ECE/CES/39. United Nations. Geneva. https://unstats.un.org/unsd/business-stat/SBR/Documents/UN_Guidelines_on_SBR.pdf (accessed 30 August 2021).

United Nations, European Commission, International Monetary Fund, Organisation for Economic Co-operation and Development, and World Bank (1993). *System of National Accounts 1993*. New York: United Nations. https://unstats.un.org/unsd/nationalaccount/docs/1993sna.pdf.

10

Managing Response Burden for Official Statistics Business Surveys – Experiences and Recent Developments at Statistics Netherlands, Statistics Portugal, and Statistics Sweden

Johan Erikson[1], Deirdre Giesen[2], Leanne Houben[2], and Paulo Saraiva[3]

[1] Statistics Sweden, Örebro, Sweden
[2] Statistics Netherlands, Heerlen, The Netherlands
[3] Statistics Portugal, Lisbon, Portugal

10.1 Introduction

Much of the data required for official statistics is still collected directly from businesses. Some businesses, especially – but not exclusively – the larger ones, receive frequent and recurring mandatory data requests from National Statistical Institutes (NSIs). The time and effort required to comply with these data requests can be a real burden for businesses. This burden may appear in terms of time and/or money spent on reporting and/or in terms of a more subjective "irritation burden," if respondents do not find the reporting user friendly or do not see the usefulness of data requests.

Survey organizations are well aware of the importance of managing response burden. They know that if burden is considered too high by respondents, it may impact unit and item nonresponse, measurement errors (e.g. Bavdaž 2010), and statistical agency costs (e.g. need for more reminders or data cleaning, Giesen 2012; Berglund et al. 2013). Also, governments around the world are concerned with capping regulatory costs (Renda et al. 2019; OECD 2014), and the costs of mandatory reporting to NSIs are part of these costs. However, the costs of official statistics reporting are negligibly small compared to the overall administrative costs of government reporting. For example, the European Union (EU) Project on Baseline Measurement (2009) estimated that less than 0.5% of the total costs for businesses of meeting obligations to provide information to the government were caused by statistical regulations. However, the European Commission (EC) High Level Group of Independent Stakeholders on Administrative Burdens (2009, p. 1) concluded that "…statistics is an area of great concern for businesses, mainly due to the high perceived burden."

Various international and national guidelines on the production of statistics highlight the importance of managing response burden. Principle 5 of the United Nations Fundamental Principles of Official Statistics (2014) states that statistical agencies should take burden into account: "Data for statistical purposes may be drawn from all types of sources, be they statistical surveys or administrative records. Statistical agencies are to choose the source with regard to quality, timeliness, costs and the burden on respondents." The European Statistics Code of Practices takes this a step further, and states in principle 9: "The response burden is proportionate to the needs of the users and is not excessive for respondents. The statistical authorities monitor the response burden and set targets for its reduction over time."

Thus, understanding and managing response burden is an important topic for NSIs (e.g. Giesen et al. 2018) and in business survey methodology (e.g. Bavdaž et al. 2020). Many governments and

Advances in Business Statistics, Methods and Data Collection. Edited by Ger Snijkers, Mojca Bavdaž, Stefan Bender, Jacqui Jones, Steve MacFeely, Joseph W. Sakshaug, Katherine J. Thompson, and Arnout van Delden.

statistical agencies have policies to minimize the response burden placed on businesses. However, awareness and knowledge about official statistics burden reduction activities often remain behind the walls of NSIs: implementation and effects of these actions might be known internally and to a handful of experts. In this chapter, we provide an overview of the recent developments in response burden management strategies for business surveys in three NSIs: Statistics Netherlands, Statistics Portugal, and Statistics Sweden.

In this chapter, the terms "business surveys" and "businesses" are used, but most of the response burden concerns and the actions discussed to manage burden are relevant for surveys of all types of organizations.

In Section 10.2, we first discuss the concept of response burden and its measurement. In Section 10.3, we look at the organization of response burden management. In Section 10.4, we discuss methods to reduce the response burden and the practices and experiences of the three NSIs. Finally, Section 10.5 provides a short discussion of the expected and desired future developments regarding response burden management.

10.2 Understanding and Measuring Response Burden

10.2.1 The Concept of Response Burden

The literature on business survey response burden usually distinguishes actual and perceived response burden (PRB) (e.g. Haraldsen et al. 2013, also called objective and subjective burden, e.g. by Willeboordse 1997). With actual burden being the time and/or money spent on survey reporting, whereas perceived burden describes the respondent's perception of responding to the data request. Several studies have shown that although perceived burden and actual burden are related, they are not the same. Moreover, both are relevant for understanding response behavior (e.g. Hak et al. 2003; Hedlin et al. 2005; Giesen 2012; Berglund et al. 2013; Yan et al. 2019).

The Total Business Survey Burden model (Jones et al. 2005; Dale et al. 2007; Haraldsen et al. 2013) provides a very useful overview of the causes and consequences of response burden in business surveys. As shown in Figure 10.1, response burden starts in the first part of the model when data needs are transformed into survey requirements in an interaction between stakeholders and the survey organization. Next, in the second part of the model, survey design characteristics, such as sampling and communication, determine the actual data collection. In the third part of the model, PRB is generated in an interaction of characteristics of the survey design, the respondent, and the response context. The PRB affects the response behavior. The four arrows in the model symbolize the four steps of the cognitive response model (e.g. Tourangeau et al. 2000). The response behavior determines the quality of the data released to the survey agency, as indicated by the traffic light. Finally, the model shows that data may need to be edited or checked with the respondent before it can be used for statistical production.

10.2.2 Measuring and Monitoring Response Burden

NSIs operationalize response burden measurement and monitoring in different ways (Bavdaž et al. 2015). These differences may partly reflect different purposes of burden measurement. For example, as discussed by Haraldsen et al. (2013), an annual estimate of money spent by all businesses on statistical reporting may be a relevant measure for politicians who want to monitor administrative burden. However, for NSIs that want to monitor and improve the quality of their

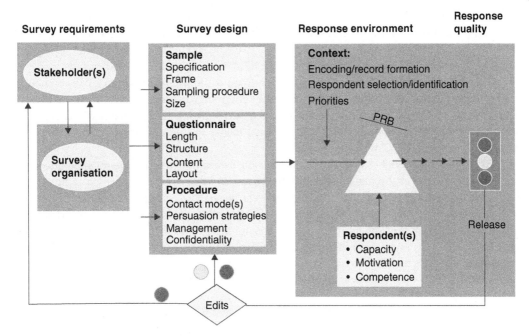

Figure 10.1 The Total Business Survey Burden model. Source: Adapted from Jones et al. 2005.

data collection, more insight is needed in actual and perceived burden at the level of the data collection instrument.

Statistics Netherlands has monitored response burden since the 1990s. Initially, following Dutch government practices, response burden was measured in monetary terms based on the total annual time spent on completing surveys by businesses multiplied by an average wage. This figure is still monitored annually. The time spent on a survey is measured using a short question periodically added to questionnaires. It asks for the total time spent on providing data (including internal data collection and reporting by the respondent and others). See Appendix 10.A for the exact presentation of this question. The wage rate is based on wage statistics for administrative staff. More recently, next to burden based on response, a gross burden indicator has been calculated and monitored, based on the total sample sizes. This latter indicator is one of the key performance indicators of Statistics Netherlands.

Measuring and monitoring burden at the survey level and the total business population level remains important for response burden management at Statistics Netherlands. However, for individual businesses, national total burden reduction is not relevant. On the contrary, businesses that hear about overall burden reduction but do not experience that themselves may become even more irritated. Overall burden reductions are only meaningful for respondents to the extent they actually notice them. For this reason Statistics Netherlands started to analyze and monitor response burden at the business level (Vaasen-Otten et al. 2018). These analyses show that on the one hand response burden was nonexistent or only small for most businesses. Of all businesses in the Netherlands, 92% did not spend any time on Statistics Netherlands' surveys. Of those that had responded to one or more surveys in 2016, 65% spent less than two hours per year. On the other hand, there were clearly hotspots of disproportionally high-burdened businesses: 4% of all responding businesses submitted more than 20 questionnaires in a year and almost 2% spent more than 40 hours per year completing Statistics Netherlands' questionnaires. As expected, based on the data needs and sampling strategies, most of the businesses with a high response burden were large businesses. However, some small- and medium-sized businesses were also found in the hotspots of disproportionally high-burdened businesses.

Another indicator used to monitor respondent burden is the number and types of complaints made by respondents. All complaints that businesses communicate directly via e-mail, webforms, or phone calls are registered and reported regularly. Also complaints made about Statistics Netherlands' questionnaires or approach strategy via social media are monitored (and if needed acted upon via social media support).

In 2017, Statistics Portugal started an initiative using a voluntary questionnaire, as an attached module after the end of the main survey questionnaire, inviting units that participate in one or more of 75 surveys, covering a total of 60,000 different businesses, to respond. The survey results provided an overview image of how the statistical reporting obligations were seen by data providers. This initiative had another version in 2019 (see Appendix 10.A for the exact wording of the questions). Although voluntary, the response burden module achieved high response rates indicating widespread acceptance of this measurement approach. These questions collect data on the difficulty in answering a questionnaire, the number of people involved, the total time spent, and also the perception of the relevance of the statistics produced by Statistics Portugal. This measurement is largely in line with the recommendations of the *Handbook for Monitoring and Evaluating Business Survey Response Burdens* (Dale et al. 2007), as it captures Perceived burden, Actual Burden, and Motivation. The only recommended dimension not addressed explicitly yet in the Portuguese Burden module is "Perceived causes of Burden." Questions on this will be considered for future versions.

When combining these burden data with other indicators, businesses are plotted, identifying priority surveys to be simplified. These analyses help to establish priorities, especially when dealing with small- and medium-size businesses. Some examples of simplification are clarifying the exact wording of questions, and the implementation and the improvement of help boxes.

The burden question module in now planned to be used every two years (in 2021 a new edition was conducted for all infrannual surveys, and in 2022 annual surveys will be covered). Thus, it is possible to monitor the evolution of burden as well as the perception of the usefulness of statistics for society and own business. The results of this measurement process are communicated to all businesses that participate in surveys in the reference year, using personalized feedback, comparing the most recent results with previous years. This approach improves the relevance of the process and respondent motivation. Although this personalized feedback report uses a very simple template, it is followed by some context notes to explain differences between years, for instance, changes in the questionnaire or in the survey methodology.

The management of respondents' complaints and suggestions is another important source for initiatives to contain burden. Statistics Portugal has a system that centralizes all respondent complaints through an area of the data collection portal (WebInq), using an electronic form with classifications of subjects. All complaints and suggestions are analyzed, with a response to respondents within a defined period. Many of these interactions result in improvements in surveys and services provided.

Since 2009, Statistics Sweden has kept a register of business participation in official statistics. This register contains information on all direct business data collections by Statistics Sweden, with the purpose of gaining an overview of a business's total response burden. The register also contains estimates of the time it takes to provide data (see Lorenc et al. 2013 for a more detailed description). Statistics Sweden also measures actual burden by adding a question to business survey questionnaires. The question measures the time taken to find and provide the information, as well as the time to complete the questionnaire (see Appendix 10.A). Total burden over time is published in Statistics Sweden's annual report.

10.3 Organization of Response Burden Management

As implicated by the Total Business Survey Burden model, the organization of response burden management by NSIs involves various actors and activities, both inside and outside of the NSI. Requirements and possibilities vary over NSIs, as they depend on the national context and legal framework, and also vary over time with changes in data requirements, technology, data sources, policy agendas, etc.

10.3.1 Legal Context and Cooperation with Other Government Bodies

As shown in the Total Business Survey Burden model, response burden originates with stakeholders' data needs. Obviously, a crucial step in the organization of burden management is to have procedures to assess if and how requests for new data lead to new data collection from businesses and how response burden is taken into account in these assessments.

Many countries have such procedures in place today. For example, in Finland, the Statistics Act states that statistical authorities must consult with respondents or their representatives (e.g. trade organization) before a new data collection can be started (UNECE 2018). In the Netherlands, the statistical law dictates that new data can only be collected if these data are not already available elsewhere in governments registers. By the same law, Statistics Netherlands has been granted access to these registers. Data already collected by other government agencies are reused, enriched, and combined for statistical purposes. Sweden has a similar regulation that requires that the government should only collect data once. With a few exceptions, there is no external regulatory pressure to limit the statistical burden in Portugal. The Portuguese measures to contain statistical burden are internal initiatives, of a proactive nature.

In the Netherlands, in a regular intergovernmental meeting of the Administrative Burden Coordinators, representatives of all governmental departments discuss the progress of burden reduction and share best practices and lessons learned. The intergovernmental meeting jointly reports to the Ministry of Economic Affairs on the actions taken to reduce regulatory burden. One of the common tools used is to discuss the workability and feasibility of new policy and legislative proposals with entrepreneurs and their representatives. This means that the businesses perspective is involved early on in the process of developing or changing regulations.

Sharing experiences in burden reductions between government bodies is valuable and important. However, the main opportunities for reducing business response burden in society as a whole lies in moving beyond thinking about data provision for statistics as something separated from other data provision requests put on businesses. It is not a trivial solution, mainly because of the proliferation of nonharmonized metadata, and/or barriers to working together toward broad objectives and minimizing individual agendas. Reusing data from other government agencies is also only efficiently possible if there is information on existing or potential data, including references of its quality level and metadata. Changes in registers provide opportunities and threats to NSIs use of these registers, the availability and quality of registers should be continuously monitored and where possible coordinated.

One way of facilitating the cooperation of public entities is through the provision of financing programs for administrative modernization projects. Portugal has the Simplex program (https://www.simplex.gov.pt/) which was launched in 2006 as an administrative modernization strategy transversal to the government and central and local public administration services. Several examples of how NSIs can reduce response burden by cooperation with other organizations are discussed in Section 10.4.

10.3.2 Organization of Burden Management Within the NSI

Various disciplines and departments within an NSI affect response burden (e.g. sampling, communication, and questionnaire design). It may be challenging to ensure that respondents' interests are always taken into account and that various initiatives for response burden reduction are shared and coordinated. For this reason, some NSIs have organized a form of coordination of representing the respondents' interests and sharing knowledge about response burden within the NSI. For example Statistics Canada has an Ombudsman for Businesses and Statistics New Zealand a Respondent Advocate (see also Giesen et al. 2018).

Statistics Netherlands has established an organizational structure to manage response burden strategically, tactically, and operationally. A program steering group consisting of senior managers of all divisions involved in producing and communicating statistics acts as a forum to discuss and coordinate all main policies and activities focused on response burden. A delegation from the program steering group regularly discusses response burden-reducing initiatives with the Respondents' Advisory Board. This advisory board consists of chairs of trade organizations and directors of companies. A program coordinator for reducing response burden acts as a secretary to both the program steering group and the Respondents' Advisory Board. The coordinator closely monitors all response burden developments within Statistics Netherlands and, together with the program steering group, endorses initiatives and innovations, aimed at reducing burden on businesses.

Since 2005, statistical burden in Statistics Portugal has been governed mainly via a central data collection department. Internally, this department was formally mandated to measure and contain statistical burden, in conjunction with subject matter, methodology, and information systems departments. Data collection is involved in the design of statistical operations (not in the compilation of statistics), and it also has a strong role in the management of administrative data.

At Statistics Sweden, there was a strong governmental pressure to reduce burden in the early 2000s. One of the results of this was that Statistics Sweden introduced an initiative whereby businesses that felt overburdened can contact the data collection department and ask for burden reductions (extensions or being excluded). There is no explicit right to be excluded from a mandatory survey due to burden, but the situation of the individual business is always assessed if such a request is received, and in some cases, it is possible to grant an exemption. This is done in contact with survey managers and methodologists. There is no guarantee that a business will always get burden reduction actions, as it also depends on how burdened the business is compared to similar businesses of a similar size with similar activities.

10.4 Burden Reduction Measures

As burden is affected by many different factors, burden reduction measures involve many different types of measures. In this section, we discuss the main types of actions that the NSIs of Sweden, Portugal, and the Netherlands are currently using or exploring. These include more traditional measures, such as improving questionnaires through testing, and more innovative measures such as exploring system-to-system solutions for data collection. Burden reduction through cooperation with other institutions is also described.

10.4.1   Using Alternative Sources

One way is to reduce the amount of data collected from businesses is to use alternative data sources (secondary sources). Traditionally, the main alternative data source has been administrative registers, which is data collected by other agencies or private data holders that can also be used for statistics. One example is data reported for taxation purposes. Administrative data have been used in statistics for a long time, but from time to time new or improved administrative sources emerge. Some factors to consider when using administrative sources are coverage, completeness, and data quality (e.g. Wallgren and Wallgren 2014).

But with the digitalization of society, new possibilities arise. This so-called data revolution generates a lot of data, and the question is whether it is possible to retrieve and use these data. Three examples of such new possibilities are (i) to use web scraping to retrieve data from the internet; (ii) the use of scanner data, which is detailed data on sales of consumer goods obtained by "scanning" the bar codes for individual products at electronic points of sale in retail outlets, providing detailed information about quantities, characteristics and values of goods sold as well as their prices; and (iii) to tap into new digital data sources that can be large in volume, less structured, and more volatile than the sources we as statisticians are used to working with, so-called "Big Data." Both web scraping and scanner data constitute a rapidly expanding source of data with considerable potential (see e.g. Kalisch 2017; Ten Bosch et al. 2018; Daas and van der Doef 2020).

According to Organization for Economic Co-operation and Development (OECD), the exponential growth of the digital economy has enabled the rise of business models based on the collection and processing of Big Data. The use of this kind of large volume data has the potential to generate substantial efficiency and productivity gains. However, acquiring the infrastructure and knowledge to benefit from economies of scale and scope and network effects related to Big Data brings new challenges. Transaction data from cash registers, credit cards, etc., and the so-called "Internet of things," from mobile phones and various kinds of sensors are examples of this. These data are characterized by large volumes, volatility, and/or lack of structure. With modern computing techniques, these data sources can be used for statistics. Some factors to consider are how useable the data really are for statistics, coverage, the possibility for the statistical office to get access to the data, and stability over time (e.g. Daas et al. 2015; Braaksma et al. 2020).

10.4.2   Improving Primary Data Collection

It is not always possible to build statistics on existing data sources collected by others. Therefore, direct data collection will still be necessary in the future. Designing respondent-friendly questionnaires is an important means to enhance data quality and reduce response burden (e.g. Giesen 2013; Lund et al. 2013). To gain insights into how data collection design affects response burden and data quality, it is important to collect feedback from respondents in the various stages of the survey design process (e.g. Willimack 2013; Bavdaž et al. 2019). Two examples illustrate the importance of involving respondents in the (re)design of questionnaires. Statistics Portugal found that, in some cases, removing a variable in a questionnaire is not always a burden reduction. Sometimes respondents need some variables to provide the data for other variables, i.e. as an indirect variable to calculate another requested data item. In the Netherlands, a comparable experience was made when redesigning the data collection for the survey on International Trade in Goods Statistics. One of the changes, aimed at reducing burden, was to reduce the reporting frequency from monthly to annually for businesses with trading values below a certain threshold. Interviews with businesses revealed that while annual reporting would indeed be a burden reduction for some businesses, others would prefer to keep their monthly reporting routine, for example to prevent being faced with many missing or inconsistent data items at the end of the year (Geurden-Slis et al. 2016). This finding led to the decision to leave it up to the eligible businesses to decide if they wanted to report monthly or annually.

10.4.2.1 Redesigning Content to Fit Data Provision Capacities

Instead of asking how we could make it as easy as possible for the respondent to answer our questions, we should also ask ourselves what available data do respondents have, and how we capture that data. This means we need to know and understand the administrative systems that businesses use for bookkeeping, wages and salaries, sales and other operations, and which information these systems hold. Businesses have had such systems for a long time (Erikson et al. 2016).

A further step in tailoring to business capacities is to change the survey boundaries. Traditionally, each statistical program has decided what data it needs and set up a survey to collect that information. A different way would be to take the data provision capacities rather than the data needs as the starting point. That would mean basing the collection on which systems the information is available from rather than on the needs of different statistical programs. This would, if you go all the way, mean one collection per business system (accounting, wages, etc.), and period (month, quarter, year). Consolidation of surveys has been introduced in several countries (Born 2016; Statistics Canada 2015; Saraiva 2016a, 2016b).

Of course, basing the data collection on data availability in business systems comes with some challenges.

First, not all businesses use the same systems, so the system content can vary between different systems. We can try to influence system content, but not through the businesses themselves, but rather system providers, and they need a business case for further development, as they need to be able to sell the system to businesses. For businesses to be willing to purchase this, they in turn need to see the value of the purchase.

Second, business systems may not fulfill all data needs of the statistics, especially not in a standardized manner. For example, the accounting systems are built on a country's chart of accounts, but that chart may not be standardized or contain parts that can be used more freely based on the needs of each company. For example, in the Swedish chart of accounts, the division of turnover by type of income is free to use as deemed appropriate by each business. This means that the same account number can be used for different types of income by different businesses.

Third, the concepts and definitions used in business systems might not be exactly aligned with the definitions of the target variables in the statistics.

These challenges do not mean that statistical agencies should not strive to adapt to the data provision capacities of businesses, rather that the challenges need to be addressed. Collecting data based on what is available in business systems could mean a large reduction of response burden. It will also open the door for easier or even automated data transfer.

10.4.2.2 Sample Coordination

Another way to reduce burden is reducing the annual number of sampled units. Without alternative sources or new methods this will however come at the cost of a lower-data quality. In the late 1990s, Statistics Netherlands achieved large burden reductions by using administrative sources and new methodologies. These enabled less-frequent data collections and a reduction in sample sizes for several surveys.

As discussed in Section 10.2, Statistics Netherlands recently started to monitor burden on the business level to detect small- and medium-sized business that had more than a proportionate share of the survey obligations. In the sampling system, an indicator has been added that shows how often a business was in Statistics Netherlands' samples in the last 12 months. Currently policies are being developed on how to deal with overburdened small businesses. If and where it is possible, these businesses will be excluded from samples. Where sampling exclusion is not possible, it is explored how actual and perceived burden can be reduced by tailored communication and business support. For example, a personal instruction on how to use a more efficient method for reporting where possible (e.g. data upload instead of manual completion of questionnaires) may provide burden reduction for certain businesses.

10.4.2.3 Business Survey Communication

Features of business survey communication include establishing contact with sampled businesses, bypassing gatekeepers, informing respondents about the survey, dispatching the questionnaire to the right person at the right moment in time, reminding and nonresponse follow-ups, and dealing with questions from businesses (Snijkers and Jones 2013). The distribution of surveys to businesses and respondents can be divided into two phases. One concerns how the business survey is distributed to businesses; the other is the internal distribution that takes place within businesses. Response burden can be reduced by designing communication in a way that makes the distribution of surveys and the response task as easy as possible, e.g. by clearly communicating how to login to a web survey or by having a competent helpdesk that can be easily reached.

Statistics Portugal has the WebInq service (https://webinq.ine.pt/), which is a data collection portal for business and social surveys, including communication with respondents. Virtually, all business survey data are collected using electronic questionnaires, and a file upload feature is also available for many surveys. When survey data are uploaded using a structured file, the data are automatically available in an electronic form for reviewing and editing. As soon as the data are finalized, a pdf image of the completed questionnaire is available, which may be used for archiving or proof of data delivery by the respondent. This data collection cycle gives businesses control, as they can have an integrated view of the surveys they have to respond to: those with a delayed response; those in progress or already delivered; and also offers an electronic means of contact. These factors contribute to a perception of ease of response, which is regularly assessed. As part of this process, respondent suggestions and comments are reviewed, by the development team and changes often implemented. Other features of WebInq are also important to help reduce burden. For instance, it is possible to have one or more respondents per business, which helps the internal distribution of surveys. This functionality also allows the creation of a completion chain so several people within a business can complete a single questionnaire. Another relevant resource is the provision of personalized reports, which are made available in the area reserved for the respondent accredited by the business (see the next section for more information on these feedback reports). Through two-yearly satisfaction surveys, to assess the quality of service with users, it is noted that these features significantly help the management of the burden.

Statistics Portugal essentially uses electronic communication with data providers, and this fact is highly appreciated by respondents. The use of traditional postal mail is residual, being used only for businesses that participate in a survey for the first time.

One of the Statistics Netherlands' actions to improve perceived response burden has been to standardize the communication with respondents, among others by centralizing the handling of questions and complaints (Giesen and Berkenbosch 2013). These measures focus on the large bulk of the respondents. For large and complex businesses Statistics Netherlands has had a special Large Case Unit since 2010. This unit specifically maintains contact with the largest enterprise groups, both improving the quality of the data and the service for this important group of respondents (Demollin 2019).

Currently, Statistics Netherlands is investigating the possibility of building a portal for businesses so that data exchange takes place in accordance with the latest security standards, communication with the respondent is as smooth as possible and information can also be delivered back to the respondent. In 2020, the first mock-up version of the portal (a clickable design without underlying technical facilities) was discussed with several businesses respondents in video interviews and well received. An important next step is exploring EU compatible authorization and identification techniques (eHerkenning).

Statistics Sweden is also developing a new portal for communication with businesses. In this portal, businesses will be able to sign up for delivering data through machine-to-machine solutions, name their authorized representatives and more. The possibility of communicating digitally without using e-mail will also be investigated.

A different communication development at Statistics Netherlands involves rolling out a stricter enforcement policy. The core of the strategy is that, on the one hand, timely response is facilitated as much as possible via various communication actions. For example by timely contact with new sample units, preferably by phone, to inform them in a friendly manner what is expected of them. On the other hand, enforcement is stricter and quicker: in the case of nonresponse, fewer reminders are sent, nonrespondents receive a strict warning letter and practically all businesses that finally fail to comply are confronted with enforcement (which may ultimately result in a penalty for which the amount, among others, is based on the size of the businesses). The main goal of this new policy is to both speed up and increase response. In time, this should allow for smaller samples, which will also decrease response burden.

This new enforcement strategy and the accompanying communication materials were developed with input from the Respondent Advisory Board and respondents and tested in a pilot project for the Quarterly Statistics on Car Trade in Quarters 3 and 4 2018. The pilot resulted in faster response on key moments for publication, only caused criticism from a few businesses and did not have any detrimental effect on the quality of the response. However, enforcement for small companies proved to be rather time-intensive. Based on the pilot, it was decided to implement this policy in a stepwise approach, developing and adjusting it with "learning by doing." The implementation was suspended due to the COVID-19 pandemic, but will be rolled out in 2021. See Appendix 10.B for an example of an extra card that is added to the letters to inform respondents about the faster and stricter enforcement (the legal obligation and deadlines are – as is standard – also communicated in the letter).

During the COVID-19-pandemic, to be as attentive as possible to the circumstances of the businesses, Statistics Netherlands adapted all letters, and switched to e-mail whenever possible. During the first months, a small card was added to the letters, to acknowledge that responding may be challenging, but on other hand explain the importance of responding. A similar text is placed on the websites for respondents (see Appendix 10.C).

10.4.2.4 Feedback

When businesses complain about responding to surveys, they often mention that they do not see the value of participation, they are unaware of the purpose of the survey, they do not receive any feedback on the data they have made available, and they do not know what happens with these data. These feelings may significantly decrease the motivation of businesses and respondents in the data collection process. Using a well-designed communication strategy offers an opportunity to motivate the businesses and the respondents to participate in the survey (Snijkers and Jones 2013). Considering that the motivation of respondents is one of the factors affecting perceived burden, one way of raising motivation is to give something back.

Statistics Portugal conducted a study in 2013 in which it was found that the majority of businesses consider official statistics useful or very useful for society (75%), but fewer found it useful for their own business (45%). As a result of these findings, Statistics Portugal introduced regular and personalized feedback for businesses participating in their business surveys (see Appendices 10.D and 10.E for examples). This significantly improved the relationship with data providers. For example, tourism is one of the themes in which the perception of the usefulness of information for the business itself has significantly improved. Comparing the data from the last completed questionnaires, there is a positive difference of 6 pp (an increase from 57% to 65% on the perception of the usefulness of statistical information for hotels).

The initiative started with the launch of pdf feedback reports. Initially reports were static but are now customized, using data held in the dissemination data warehouse integrated with the individual indicators of the specific company. At the start of 2021, this service covered more than 60,000 businesses and had a high level of value recognition, which is measured by the ad hoc burden survey. Having started with survey data, these feedback reports now also cover statistical burden reduction measures, as is the case with the effect of taking advantage of administrative data in simplifying a given survey. Although the main target of the feedback reports are the respondents, the next step is to target senior managers of the businesses to be also regularly informed about these results.

Statistics Netherlands developed several initiatives to promote the awareness and use of relevant statistics to the business world. For example, a dedicated Internet site was developed for businesses where information for participating in surveys and links to outcomes are integrated (https://www.cbs.nl/nl-nl/deelnemers-enquetes/deelnemers-enquetes/bedrijven). Also, for several surveys, dedicated leaflets were developed to highlight the usefulness of the statistics the data are requested for. In 2018, an experiment was conducted with a leaflet for the information and communications technology (ICT) survey for businesses to study if the leaflet affected response behavior. The experimental group received a leaflet with examples of findings of the ICT survey and information on where to find more statistics. The control group did not receive a leaflet. No differences in response rates were found (Houben et al. 2018). Unfortunately, the experiment did not measure if the leaflet may have affected the perceived usefulness of the survey or the perceived burden. These findings are in line with other studies that show it is not easy to develop communication materials that generate significant effects in response behavior or perceptions (e.g. Hedlin et al. 2008; Bavdaž and Bolko 2013; Tuttle et al. 2018).

10.4.2.5 File Transfer and Other Techniques (Hybrid Data Collection)

For a long time, data collection has gradually moved to the Internet, but to reduce response burden significantly, a higher degree of automation is necessary. In Erikson et al. (2016), a step-wise approach to digitalized data collection is described, going from web questionnaires through semiautomated file transfer solutions to fully automated "machine to machine" (a.k.a. "system to system") solutions. For the last step to be possible, a full adaptation to what data is available in business systems as described above is necessary, and the same holds for a semiautomated solution where a file is extracted from a system by the business and then transferred to the statistical office. But there is also the possibility to have hybrid solutions, for example allowing businesses to upload a data file from a system into a web questionnaire, fill in the information not included in the file, and send the web questionnaire to the statistical office. Successful implementations of such solutions are in place in several countries, including Sweden (Erikson 2012; Erikson et al. 2016), Portugal (Saraiva 2018), and The Netherlands (Buiten et al. 2018).

In 2013, Statistics Portugal developed an Automatic Data Transmission (TAD) solution by uploading eXtensible Markup Language (XML) files or by web services. The XML file allows the response to be used in one or more survey questionnaires, or even different units within the business to submit data for the same survey questionnaire, which simplifies data provision from more complex businesses. This alternative collection mode is available for 14 surveys (2021), of which approximately 8000 questionnaires were received in 2020. After uploading the data through TAD, the respondent can access and edit the data through an electronic form on the data collection portal.

10.4.3 Survey-assisted Modeling with Mixed Sources

To reduce burden further, it is possible to use a combination of the methods described above to combine sources to create a more efficient survey design. One way is to use an administrative source like tax data as the starting point for the main variables and to use direct collection from a sample for specific details. That way, since you already have known totals for some main indicators, you can use that information to tailor the sample design from current real data, resulting in smaller targeted samples either to target businesses that have values for certain indicators (e.g. businesses that have tangible assets according to balance sheet data could be asked for investment data) or make a small sample to get details on how a main variable is divided by different dimensions (e.g. only businesses with a large turnover could be asked for data on turnover by type of customer).

One example is the Statistics Portugal National Data Infrastructure (IND), where administrative and survey data are stored and prepared for statistical production. Covering both businesses and individual data, IND is a multipurpose solution providing data for statistical production. It adopts specific data models to analyze and edit the data, especially in terms of outliers and suspicious values. For instance, IND stores businesses issued electronic receipt data, which is being used to replace variables collected by several surveys, simplifying them and having the potential to completely replace these surveys by administrative data. In Portugal, all businesses have to issue an electronic receipt for transactions with individual consumers or another client company, and this kind of data are been integrated into IND, with high potential value for statistical production.

The use of administrative and other data sources offers other opportunities to reduce the burden (actual or perceived). One example is the prefilling of items in an electronic questionnaire with administrative data, either for confirmation or just for information. Prefilling items makes burden reduction really noticeable for respondents and informs them about what the NSI already knows about a certain business. Prefilling can have risks too, for example conserving errors over time or from other sources into statistics and confidentiality, but from a strict burden reduction perspective it is a useful tool.

Another example comes from Sweden. The Swedish Structural Business Statistics Survey uses a hybrid design with tax data as the base for several different sample surveys that collect additional details. The sample design for these surveys involves current data from the tax returns to target relevant businesses. Modeling is also used to combine administrative data and survey data. The direct data collection also uses a hybrid design as described above, where the main variables from the tax material is preprinted in the questionnaire, and only further details are collected. To reduce burden, since 2010, businesses can also upload a file from their accounting system into the web questionnaire (Erikson 2012). The data from the file is transformed into variables in the questionnaire and filled in automatically, leaving only those variables not covered by the content in the file to fill in manually.

10.4.4 Reducing Burden Through Cooperation

There are many data-sharing initiatives to limit the burden on businesses. While there are many positive effects of data sharing, there are also some challenges, for example.

Deciding which institution can collect which information? Dealing with time lapses between collection at one agency and availability for others? And framing additional collection at other agencies that need more detail than a main indicator collected by somebody else?

There are also many more specific regulations that require information to be included in various reports, so it will probably take quite some time to reach these goals. Therefore, it is also good to look at possibilities to cooperate in various ways between agencies to simplify data provision for businesses.

For instance, Statistics Portugal, Visit Portugal, Central Bank of Portugal, and Portuguese immigration and borders service are currently developing a joint solution for the registration of guests in hotel establishments, in order to build a unique solution for the collection of tourism data (hotels and other accommodations) for these four entities.

10.4.4.1 Coordination of Metadata

To enable efficient coordinated collections between agencies and allow for effective technical cooperation, the first and most important step is to work with shared metadata. Without coordinated concepts and classifications, for example, built on what is used in legislation, statistical standards and standards used in society, further coordination will be much harder or even impossible. One way of approaching this cooperation is to start with the terms and concepts that are widely used in several agencies, and then for agencies to align their additional concepts and needs to these basic terms and concepts.

In some cases, the concepts used by businesses are not completely aligned with the target variables for statistics, in such cases, it is worth exploring whether data can be collected using business concepts, and then transformed into the target variables by the Statistical offices using modeling or other measures.

In Sweden, the Tax Authority, the statistical office, and the Swedish Businesses Registration Office have agreed to harmonize concepts based on the terms used in the annual reports reported to the Businesses Registrations Office, and build at least some of the reporting to the statistical office and the Tax Authority on those concepts, adding specific needs of the other two agencies within the same framework (Erikson et al. 2016). The government agency responsible for developing generally accepted accounting principles, the Swedish Accounting Standards Board Bokföringsnämnden (BFN), is also an active and important partner in this work.

The Swedish taxonomy for reporting economic statistics was published in a first final version in December 2020, covering monthly and quarterly reporting. A final version covering annual reporting will follow in 2021. The possibility to report data based on the taxonomy will start in the second quarter of 2021. The taxonomy has been built in XBRL (eXtensible Business Reporting Language) and has been built on existing taxonomies for annual reports to the Businesses Registration Office. The taxonomy for reporting economic statistics reuses as many concepts as possible but adds the specific details only necessary for statistical purposes. The maximum reuse of existing annual reports and concepts also means that the content of the taxonomy differs from previous surveys, but it is possible to match the variables in the taxonomy with the variables in the surveys. Businesses can sign up for automated flows of XBRL file based on the taxonomy and create system to system data provision of data that cover the information needs of several current surveys. Data will be sent automatically from the business system through an application programming interface (API) to the statistical office once a month, once a quarter, or both. The surveys covered by the taxonomy will no longer request data from businesses that report according to the taxonomy but will instead have their relevant data transferred from the taxonomy survey to be combined with the additional data collected from other businesses.

As this type of coordination encompasses more than just concepts, Statistics Portugal has developed an Integrated Metadata System (https://smi.ine.pt/), which consists of a repository of concepts, classifications, variables, data collection supports, and methodological documentation. This system covers all the statistical operations carried out in the national statistical system (NSS) and the data disseminated in the Statistics Portugal Portal. Its various components are related, so its management follows strict rules of harmonization and integration. The main objectives of this system are to support statistical production in the design phase of statistical operations and support the dissemination of data, enabling the documentation of indicators whose data are disseminated through the Dissemination database. It is intended that this system constitutes an instrument of coordination and harmonization within the National Statistical System, also covering metadata related to administrative data.

10.4.4.2   Technical Cooperation and Standards

To reduce burden for businesses, even if common concepts and definitions are used, cooperation on a technical level is also necessary. For example, system developers prefer not to build separate technical solutions for reporting data to different authorities, so for them, a common technical approach is preferred. This can involve both techniques for data transfer, like programming against API interfaces, and formats for files and data to be transferred.

A format that is widely used for data transfer on many levels, both within a business, between businesses (B2B, business to business solutions) and for reporting to government agencies is XBRL, which is not only built on XML but also includes a number of layers for definitions, validation, presentation, etc. XBRL is a global de facto standard adopted by the European Security and Markets Authority (ESMA) as the European Single Electronic Format for reporting of annual reports. Businesses registered on the stock exchange already report data in XBRL to supervisory authorities in many countries. Using XBRL as a file format for reporting data to government agencies means that there is a common ground to build on, one that is also working well in combination with modern techniques for data transfer. XBRL is built on the concept of taxonomies, which is a way to describe data needs in detail, with all layers and validation rules included. Data providers create instance documents built on the taxonomies including all data that they have based on the taxonomies, these instance documents can be automatically generated from business systems (if system providers have programmed that possibility) and transferred to government agencies.

Sometimes the best option is to adopt a standard used by a large number of businesses and other stakeholders, even if this standard was not created for statistical purposes. This is the case of the international standard for electronic exchange SAF-T (Standard Audit File for Tax), which is defined by the OECD for the exchange of accounting data from organizations to a national tax authority or external auditors. SAF-T was adopted in 2008 by Portugal and since spread to other European countries, e.g. Luxembourg, Austria, Germany, France, and Norway. Portugal established a technical requirement for national information through a legal act in 2006, making it mandatory for all businesses. By law, all company accounts must be organized according to this standard to allow the production of SAF-T files whenever requested by the tax authorities. Due to the universality of its adoption in businesses, this standard also created a significant technical advantage for the exchange of data for statistical purposes.

10.4.4.3   Standard Business Reporting

If you have both coordinated concepts and coordinated technical solutions, it is possible to have what is called Standard Business Reporting (SBR). This combines the use of standardized data definitions, the structure of the digital reports, the hierarchical relationship of the data, the process through which data is transferred, and the technology used for the transfer (Karper 2019). SBR means that it is possible for a business to report data to several agencies in one single reporting process, it does not have to mean that all data is reported to all agencies, but rather that the reporting process delivers the relevant data to the relevant agencies based on which agency is allowed to access which information. The coordination can be built into the business system, making it possible for a business to do all reporting at the same time.

If you implement a SBR process, it could also be possible to make data sharing more efficient. For example, if today there is agreement that the statistical office receives value added tax (VAT) data from the tax authority as an administrative source, implementing SBR would make it possible for a business to report the VAT data to the tax authority and the statistical office simultaneously. Resulting in the statistical office no longer having to wait for the tax authority to process and share data, at least for those businesses applying the SBR process.

Portugal developed a SBR system in 2006. The Simplified Business Information (IES) was created under the government program Simplex, for the simplification and modernization of Public Administration. This initiative was a joint effort of four public administration entities (Ministry of Finance, Ministry of Justice, Statistics Portugal, and Central Bank of Portugal). IES fulfills several information obligations by businesses in a single annual act, which were previously dispersed, and results in the availability of identical data to different Public Administration bodies through different channels. With the IES, the various information obligations are met electronically on a single occasion and totally digitalized.

IES had a significant impact, covering all businesses in Portugal, as well as in the different Public Administration entities responsible for collecting this data.

For Statistics Portugal, the main advantages were the following complete coverage of the business population (400,000 businesses); reduced availability of main statistical structural information from 12 to 6.5 months; information received automatically by electronic means; and a significant increase in the information detail. With the implementation of the IES, it was possible to eliminate one of the most expensive surveys carried out by Statistics Portugal (sample of 50,000 businesses).

New IES developments are underway, highlighting a new simplification to prepopulate the IES Financial Statements with data extracted from the OECD Standardized Audit File for Tax Purposes (SAF-T). This file is mandatory for all businesses and contains all their annual accounts data, according to a national Accounting Harmonization System (approved by Decree-Law n° 158/2009 of 13 July). With the implementation of this new system, all businesses must produce a SAF-T (PT) file and send annually. With these new developments, a reduction of more than 50% of the information required through the IES is expected. The creation of this file is fully automated; therefore, the development of monthly and quarterly files will only require a small investment. In this way, it will be possible to sustain the production of infra-annual statistics, leading to the elimination of several business surveys.

Additionally, in the scope of cooperation with other entities, Statistics Portugal started in 2020 joint work with Central Bank of Portugal regarding the analysis of data collected through one of our main administrative business sources.

Another example from Statistics Portugal is the 2018 development of a National Data Infrastructure (IND). This is an integrated system for the appropriation and use of administrative data and other sources, designed for statistical production, and increasing the economic and social value of the statistical information as a public good. Covering both businesses and individual data, IND is a multi-purpose solution providing statistical data to Statistics Portugal and other stakeholders. The recent developments are the register-based Census, dwellings and geospatial information, electronic receipts (Tax Authority), and monthly income registers (Tax Authority and Social Security).

In the Netherlands, a group of private-sector bodies, software companies, and government agencies have developed a standard to integrate and automate the chain of administrative processes: the Reference Classification System of Financial Information (RCSFI). From April 2021 onwards, Dutch business can import their RCSFI-data to the Structural Business Survey Questionnaire at the push of a button (see Appendix 10.F for screenshots with examples of how this option is presented in the questionnaire). Prefilling questionnaire items clearly shows respondents how their burden is reduced, shows the other items that still need to completed, and still allows respondents to make manual edits to the prefilled data. Businesses from three selected industries (accountancy, retail, and hospitality) will be the first for which this option is enabled. The ultimate aim is to implement this working method for the other industries and for other statistics for which financial accounting data is requested. The gradual implementation is chosen for reasons of manageability.

10.5 Discussion

As described earlier, new ways to move beyond traditional techniques to reduce burden on businesses and modernize data collection are opening, from using alternative data sources, redesigning surveys, consolidating surveys and hybrid collection in cross-agency cooperation, and SBR and possibly in the future no additional reporting. But possibilities vary across different domains, and some new possibilities will not be possible to implement across all areas, it will be necessary to allow businesses different ways of providing data at least over a long transitional period. This means that to minimize the burden placed on businesses, statistical offices need to be flexible and use a smart combination of possibilities, moving as far as possible in different areas based on the different conditions. The more traditional ways of reducing burden will still be important. The toolbox has become bigger, but just like a hammer is not the best tool for all house building activities, the different burden-reduction tools will need to be used in an efficient combination to achieve the best results. It is important to remember that burden reduction activities do not stand on their own in the statistical production process, and that they are in reality one part of the whole survey design. This means that response burden reduction activities can have an impact on the whole production process. For example, using alternative data sources and hybrid data collection designs will impact other parts of the production process, such as integrating different data sources with potentially different coverage, a transformation of units (from administrative units in the data collection to statistical units in the final statistics), and a transformation of concepts (from business concepts in the data collection to statistical concepts in the final statistics). The survey design process needs to take all these matters into account, and balance the criteria of quality, cost, and burden in the most optimal way. This will probably mean that while we put less burden and work on businesses, we put more work on ourselves as statisticians. That said, using alternative data sources and tailoring data collection to available data in businesses is not only a burden reduction activity, but it can have both positive and negative effects, sometimes simultaneously, on both quality and cost. Our point is that burden needs to be an important factor in survey design, and that tailoring to data availability makes it easier for businesses to provide data.

While the toolbox of burden reduction activities has grown, there are still challenges and future areas for improvement. One of the most important is that statistical offices still need to improve in working with the businesses and their representatives. The imperative is not to think for businesses, but actually work together in finding what makes life easiest for them regarding data provision. One of the challenges here is to find the best way to get knowledge such as talking directly with businesses or talking to other parties like accounting consultants and system providers. The answer is probably both. Smaller businesses that use off-the-shelf book-keeping software and let accounting consultants provide data for them are very different to big businesses that have their own accounting departments with tailored business systems. Also, businesses give data to many government agencies, and want an easy way to provide all requested information, so statistical offices need to compromise and harmonize with other agencies as well. But the key to burden reduction is to know businesses and their needs, and let businesses influence how they are allowed to provide data. Adapting our data collection to the data availability and capacity of businesses was pointed out by several attendees at the ICES VI session on Response burden management as the activity that has the biggest potential of reducing burden.

Another thing that statistical offices should improve is to be more data driven to empirically test how our actions actually affect actual and perceived burden, response behavior, costs of producing statistics, and quality. We still have some way to go in evaluating what we are doing in a consistent way. And we need to evaluate the survey design as a whole, again striving for a balance between quality, cost, and burden.

One aspect of burden that should be analyzed and discussed more is the perspective of the respondent rather than just the business. Respondents are persons, and they are in very different situations. Some respondents in big businesses have data provision as their job, while for other respondents, it's just an additional obligatory (and for many, deemed as unnecessary) task placed on top of their job (owners of small businesses, for example). Some respondents provide data for only one business, while others such as accounting consultants can provide data for many businesses and for many surveys. Due to these differences, the burden reduction activities with the best impacts will vary. For example, feedback of business statistics may be of great importance to respondents who run their own business as it may help them understand the position of their business in the market. In contrast, feedback of business statistics may not be at all important to accounting consultants and for bigger businesses it might be of value to someone other than the actual respondent. Here, a flexible tailored approach is necessary, taking into account both the respondent and the business perspective.

Finally, the need to work together with other government agencies on data collection from businesses is something that we are certain will grow in importance in the future. It can be a difficult task, harmonizing concepts and compromising on what, how, and when to collect. We also need to harmonize technical solutions across agencies and use both data-sharing possibilities between agencies and simultaneous transmission of data through SBR designs. This adds to the complexity of the statistical production process, and requires development of both technical solutions and processes, as well as continuous cooperation between many parties; government agencies, businesses, system providers, etc. But this is an endeavor that is expected by stakeholders – governments expect their agencies to cooperate and place as little burden as possible on businesses, and businesses expect that data provided to one agency will be reused by other government agencies instead of having to provide it again.

In summary, we have in recent years expanded the toolbox for burden reduction, and there is good potential to reduce burden on businesses. There is also a potential to use the tools better, to combine tools in a flexible way, and to work better together with businesses. Burden reduction issues will need to continue to be a priority for statistical offices around the world.

Disclaimer and Acknowledgments

The views expressed in this chapter are those of the authors and do not necessarily reflect the policies of their employers. The authors would like to thank Anita Vaasen-Otten, Statistics Netherlands, for helping to organize and for chairing the invited ICES VI session that was the basis of this chapter. Our sincere thanks also go to Mojca Bavdaž, University of Ljubljana, for acting as a discussant at this session and giving valuable input in thinking about common themes and specific challenges. Finally, we would like to express our gratitude to Jacqui Jones, Australian Bureau of Statistics, for reviewing various versions of this chapter and helping us to improve it.

References

Bavdaž, M. (2010). Sources of measurement errors in business surveys. *Journal of Official Statistics* 26 (1): 25–42. www.scb.se/contentassets/ca21efb41fee47d293bbee5bf7be7fb3/sources-of-measurement-errors-in-business-surveys.pdf.

Bavdaž, M. and Bolko, I. (2013). Two slovenian experiments to increase motivation. In: *Comparative Report on Integration of Case Study Results Related to Reduction of Response Burden and Motivation of Businesses for Accurate Reporting* (ed. D. Giesen, M. Bavdaž and I. Bolko), 47–58. BLUE-Enterprise and Trade Statistics, BLUE-ETS, European Commission, European Research Area, 7th Framework Programme https://www.researchgate.net/publication/350581227_Comparative_report_on_integration_of_case_study_results_related_to_reduction_of_response_burden_and_motivation_of_businesses_for_accurate_reporting_Deliverable_81_of_the_BLUE-ETS_project.

Bavdaž, M., Giesen, D., Korenjak Černe, S., Löfgren, T., and Raymond-Blaess, B. (2015). Response burden in official business surveys: measurement and reduction practices of National Statistical Institutes. *Journal of Official Statistics* 31 (4): 559–588. https://doi.org/10.1515/jos-2015-0035.

Bavdaž, M., Giesen, D., Moore, D.L., Smith, P.A., and Jones, J. (2019). Qualitative testing for official establishment survey questionnaires. *Survey Research Methods* 13 (3): 267–288. https://doi.org/10.18148/srm/2019.v13i3.7366.

Bavdaž, M., Snijkers, G., Sakshaug, J.W., Brand, T., Haraldsen, G., Kurban, B., Saraiva, P., and Willimack, D.K. (2020). Business data collection methodology: current state and future outlook. *Statistical Journal of the IAOS* 36 (2020): 741–756. https://content.iospress.com/download/statistical-journal-of-the-iaos/sji200623?id=statistical-journal-of-the-iaos%2Fsji200623.

Berglund, F., Haraldsen, G., and Kleven, Ø. (2013). Causes and consequences of actual and perceived response burden based on Norwegian data. In: *Comparative Report on Integration of Case Study Results Related to Reduction of Response Burden and Motivation of Businesses for Accurate Reporting* (ed. D. Giesen, M. Bavdaž and I. Bolko), 29–35. BLUE-Enterprise and Trade Statistics, BLUE-ETS, European Commission, European Research Area, 7th Framework Programme https://researchgate.net/publication/350581227_Comparative_report_on_integration_of_case_study_results_related_to_reduction_of_response_burden_and_motivation_of_businesses_for_accurate_reporting_Deliverable_81_of_the_BLUE-ETS_project.

Born, A. (2016). Harmonizing financial information from Businesses at Statistics Canada. *Proceedings of the Fifth International Conference of Establishment Surveys (ICESV)*, Geneva, Switzerland (20–23 June 2016). https://ww2.amstat.org/meetings/ices/2016/proceedings/146_ices15Final00226.pdf (accessed 30 July 2021).

Braaksma, B., Zeelenberg, K., and De Broe, S. (2020). Big data in official statistics: a perspective from Statistics Netherlands. In: *Big Data Meets Survey Science: A Collection of Innovative Methods* (ed. C.A. Hill, P.P. Biemer, T. Buskirk, L. Japec, A. Kirchner, S. Kolenikov, and L. Lyberg), 303–338. New York: Wiley.

Buiten, G., Snijkers, G., Saraiva, P., Erikson, J., Erikson, A.-G., and Born, A. (2018). Business data collection: toward electronic data interchange. Experiences in Portugal, Canada, Sweden, and the

Netherlands with EDI. *Journal of Official Statistics* 34 (2): 419–443. https://doi.org/10.2478/JOS-2018-0019.

Daas, P.J.H. and van der Doef, S. (2020). Detecting innovative companies via their website. *Statistical Journal of IAOS* 36 (4): 1239–1251. https://doi.org/10.3233/SJI-200627.

Daas, P.J.H., Puts, M.J., Buelens, B., and van den Hurk, P.A.M. (2015). Big data as a source for official statistics. *Journal of Official Statistics* 31 (2): 249–262. https://doi.org/10.1515/jos-2015-0016.

Dale, T., Erikson, J., Fosen, J., Haraldsen, G., Jones, J., and Kleven, Ø. (2007). *Handbook for Monitoring and Evaluating Business Survey Response Burdens*. European Commission https://ec.europa.eu/eurostat/documents/64157/4374310/12-HANDBOOK-FOR-MONITORING-AND-EVALUATING-BUSINESS-SURVEY-RESONSE-BURDEN.pdf/600e3c6d-8e8d-44f7-a8f5-0931c71d9920.

Demollin, F. (2019). Systematic approach to addressing MNEs and the impact on national processes. *Proceedings of the 2019 Directors General of the National Statistical Institutes (DGINS) Conference*, Bratislava, Slovakia (9–10 October 2019). https://dgins2019.sk/wp-content/uploads/2019/10/DGINS-2019-Session-2-Kroese-Final.docx.pdf (accessed 30 July 2021).

Erikson. J. (2012). Mixed mode by importing accounting data into Structural Business Statistics web questionnaires. *Proceedings of the Conference of European Statisticians, Seminar on New Frontiers for Statistical Data Collection*, Geneva, Switzerland (31 October–2 November 2012). https://unece.org/fileadmin/DAM/stats/documents/ece/ces/ge.44/2012/mtg2/WP24.pdf (accessed 30 July 2021).

Erikson, A.-G., Erikson, J., and Hertzman, C. (2016). Automated data collection and reuse of concepts in order to minimise the burden. *Proceedings of the Fifth International Conference of Establishment Surveys (ICESV)*, Geneva, Switzerland (20–23 June 2016). https://ww2.amstat.org/meetings/ices/2016/proceedings/147_ices15Final00184.pdf (accessed 30 July 2021).

European Commission High Level Group of Independent Stakeholders on Administrative Burdens (2009). *Opinion of the High Level Group. Subject: Priority Area Statistics*. Brussels, July 7, 2009.

Geurden-Slis, M., Giesen, D., and Houben, L. (2016) Using the respondents' perspective in redesigning the survey on international trade in goods statistics. *Proceedings of the Fifth International Conference of Establishment Surveys (ICESV)*, Geneva, Switzerland (20–23 June 2016). https://ww2.amstat.org/meetings/ices/2016/proceedings/065_ices15Final00102.pdf (accessed 30 July 2021).

Giesen, D. (2012). Exploring causes and effects of perceived response burden. International Conference on Establishment Surveys. *Proceedings of the Fourth International Conference of Establishment Surveys (ICESIV)*, Montreal, Canada (11–14 June 2012). https://ww2.amstat.org/meetings/ices/2012/papers/302171.pdf (accessed 30 July 2021).

Giesen, D. (2013). Reducing response burden by questionnaire redesign. In: *Comparative Report on Integration of Case Study Results Related to Reduction of Response Burden and Motivation of Businesses for Accurate Reporting* (ed. D. Giesen, M. Bavdaž and I. Bolko), 71–77. BLUE-Enterprise and Trade Statistics, BLUE-ETS, European Commission, European Research Area, 7th Framework Programme https://researchgate.net/publication/350581227_Comparative_report_on_integration_of_case_study_results_related_to_reduction_of_response_burden_and_motivation_of_businesses_for_accurate_reporting_Deliverable_81_of_the_BLUE-ETS_project.

Giesen, D. and Berkenbosch, B. (2013). Managing perceived response burden: why and how – experiences from the Netherlands. *Proceedings of the UNECE Seminar on Statistical Data Collection*, Geneva, Switzerland (25–27 September 2013). https://unece.org/fileadmin/DAM/stats/documents/ece/ces/ge.44/2013/mgt1/WP15.pdf (accessed 30 July 2021).

Giesen D., Vella M., Brady C.F., Brown P., Ravindra D., and Vaasen-Otten A. (2018). Response burden management for establishment surveys at four National Statistical Institutes. *Journal of Official Statistics* 34(2): 397-418. https://doi.org/10.2478/jos-2018-0018.

Hak, T., Willimack, D., and Anderson, A. (2003). Response process and burden in establishment surveys. *Proceedings of the Joint Statistical Meetings – Section on Government Statistics)*. Alexandria, VA. American Statistical Association. pp. 1724–1730. http://www.asasrms.org/Proceedings/y2003/Files/JSM2003-000457.pdf (accessed 30 July 2021).

Haraldsen, G., Jones, J., Giesen, D., and Zhang, L. (2013). Understanding and coping with response burden. In: *Designing and Conducting Business Surveys* (ed. G. Snijkers, G. Haraldsen, J. Jones and D. Willimack), 219–251. Hoboken: Wiley.

Hedlin, D., Dale, T., Haraldsen, G. and Jones, J. (eds.) (2005). *Developing Methods for Assessing Perceived Response Burden*. Research report, Stockholm: Statistics Sweden, Oslo: Statistics Norway, and London: Office for National Statistics. https://ec.europa.eu/eurostat/documents/64157/4374310/10-DEVELOPING-METHODS-FOR-ASSESSING-PERCEIVED-RESPONSE-BURDEN.pdf/1900efc8-1a07-4482-b3c9-be88ee71df3b (accessed 30 July 2021).

Hedlin, D., Lindkvist, H., Bäckström, H., and Erikson, J. (2008). An experiment on perceived survey response burden among businesses. *Journal of Official Statistics* 24 (2): 301–318. https://scb.se/contentassets/ca21efb41fee47d293bbee5bf7be7fb3/an-experiment-on-perceived-survey-response-burden-among-businesses.pdf.

Houben, L., Groot, W., Debie, D., Goris, G., Opreij, A., Geers, X., and Snijkers, G. (2018). A continuous search to improve targeted communication in business surveys. *Paper presented at the 5th International Business Data Collection Methodology Workshop*, Lisbon, Portugal (19–21 September 2018).

Jones, J., Rushbrooke, J., Haraldsen, G., Dale, T., and Hedlin, D. (2005). Conceptualising total business survey burden. *Survey Methodology Bulletin*, UK Office for National Statistics, No. 55, pp. 1–10.

Kalisch, D.W. (2017). An implementation plan to maximise the use of transactions data in the CPI. Information Paper. ABS Catalogue No. 6401.0.60.004. Australian Bureau of Statistics. https://www.abs.gov.au/ausstats/abs@.nsf/mf/6401.0.60.004 (accessed 30 July 2021).

Karper, E. (2019). Standard Business Reporting: what is it and how can you benefit? https://info.vismaconnect.nl/blog/standard-business-reporting-what-is-it (accessed 30 July 2021).

Lorenc, B., Kloek, W., Abrahamson, L., and Eckman, S. (2013). An analysis of business response burden and response behaviour using a register of data provision. *Proceedings of the Conferences on New Techniques and Technologies for Statistics*, Brussels, Belgium (5–7 March 2013). https://ec.europa.eu/eurostat/cros/system/files/NTTS2013fullPaper_121.pdf (accessed 30 July 2021).

Lund, K., Haraldsen, G., Kleven, Ø., and Berglund, F. (2013). The usability of web functionality. In: *Comparative Report on Integration of Case Study Results Related to Reduction of Response Burden and Motivation of Businesses for Accurate Reporting* (ed. D. Giesen, M. Bavdaž and I. Bolko), 79–89. BLUE-Enterprise and Trade Statistics, BLUE-ETS, European Commission, European Research Area, 7th Framework Programme. https://researchgate.net/publication/350581227_Comparative_report_on_integration_of_case_study_results_related_to_reduction_of_response_burden_and_motivation_of_businesses_for_accurate_reporting_Deliverable_81_of_the_BLUE-ETS_project.

OECD (2014). *OECD Regulatory Compliance Cost Assessment Guidance*. OECD Publishing https://doi.org/10.1787/9789264209657-en.

Renda, A., Laurer, M., Modzelewska, A., and Zarra, A. (2019). Feasibility study: introducing "one-in-one-out" in the European Commission. Final Report for the German Ministry for Economic Affairs and Energy Center of European Policy Studies CEPS. https://ceps.eu/download/publication/?id=25815&pdf=Feasibility-Study.pdf (accessed 30 July 2021).

Saraiva, P. (2016a). Integrated Survey Management System: Statistics Portugal experience. *Presentation at the Fifth International Conference of Establishment Surveys (ICESV)* (20–23 June 2016). Geneva, Switzerland: Statistics Switzerland.

Saraiva, P. (2016b). *Integrating data collection: wins and challenges. Presentation at the UNECE Workshop on Statistical Data Collection, 'Visions on Future Surveying'*, Statistics Netherlands, The Hague (1–5 October 2016). Geneva: United Nations Economic Commission for Europe (UNECE).

Saraiva, P. (2018). Survey only as a last resort – automated business data interchange, please. *Keynote speak at the Fifth International Workshop on Business Data Collection Methodology (BDCM)*. Lisbon, Portugal

Snijkers, G. and Jones, J. (2013). Business survey communication. In: *Designing and Conducting Business Surveys* (ed. G. Snijkers, G. Haraldsen, J. Jones and D. Willimack), 359–430. Hoboken: Wiley.

Statistics Canada (2015). *Integrated Business Statistics Program Overview*. Catalogue No. 68-515-X. Ottawa: Statistics Canada, https://www150.statcan.gc.ca/n1/en/catalogue/68-515-X (accessed 30 July 2021).

Ten Bosch, O., Windmeijer, D., van Delden, A., and van den Heuvel, G. (2018). Web scraping meets survey design: combining forces. *Proceedings of the Big Surv18 Conference*, Barcelona, Spain (25–27 October 2018). https://bigsurv18.org/conf18/uploads/73/61/20180820_BigSurv_WebscrapingMeetsSurveyDesign.pdf (accessed 30 July 2021).

Tourangeau, R., Rips, L., and Rasinski, K. (2000). *The Psychology of Survey Response*. Cambridge, UK: Cambridge University Press.

Tuttle, A.D., Beck, J.L., Willimack, D.K., Tolliver, K.P., Hernandez, A., and Fan, C.-C. (2018). Experimenting with contact strategies in business surveys. *Journal of Official Statistics* 34 (2): 365–395. https://doi.org/10.2478/jos-2018-0017.

UNECE (2018). *Guidance on Modernizing Statistical Legislation*. Geneva, Switzerland: United Nations. https://digitallibrary.un.org/record/3829988.

United Nations (2014). Fundamental principles of official statistics. https://unstats.un.org/unsd/dnss/gp/FP-New-E.pdf (accessed 30 July 2021).

Vaasen-Otten, A., Geurden-Slis, M., and Giesen, D. (2018). Towards Response Burden Management across surveys. *Proceedings of the UNECE Conference of European Statisticians Workshop on Statistical Data Collection*, Geneva, Switzerland (10–12 October 2018). https://unece.org/fileadmin/DAM/stats/documents/ece/ces/ge.58/2018/mtg7/DC2018_S4_Vaasens_etal_Netherlands_AD.pdf (accessed 30 July 2021).

Wallgren, A. and Wallgren, B. (2014). *Register-based Statistics: Statistical Methods for Administrative Data*, 2nde. Chichester: Wiley.

Willeboordse, A. (1997). Minimizing response burden. In: *Handbook on Design and Implementation of Business Surveys* (ed. A. Willeboordse), 111–118. Luxembourg: Eurostat. https://ec.europa.eu/eurostat/ramon/statmanuals/files/Handbook%20on%20surveys.pdf.

Willimack, D.K. (2013). Methods for the development, testing, and evaluation of data collection instruments. In: *Designing and Conducting Business Surveys* (ed. G. Snijkers, G. Haraldsen, J. Jones and D. Willimack), 253–301. Hoboken: Wiley.

Yan, T., Fricker, S., and Tsai, S. (2019). Response burden: what is it and what predicts it? In: *Advances in Questionnaire Design, Development, Evaluation and Testing* (ed. P. Beatty, D. Collins, L. Kaye, J.L. Padilla, G. Willis, and A. Wilmot), 193–212. Hoboken: Wiley.

Appendix 10.A: Burden Measurement Questions

Statistics Netherlands – Time Measurement in Dutch and English

---

Benodigde tijd

Het CBS werkt aan het verbeteren van het verzamelen van gegevens. Om na te gaan in welke mate dit lukt, meten wij periodiek de tijd die nodig is voor het verzamelen en rapporteren van de benodigde informatie aan het CBS.

Hoeveel tijd is besteed aan het verzamelen en rapporteren van de benodigde informatie voor dit onderzoek?

Reken a.u.b. alle tijd die het uzelf en/of anderen heeft gekost om de gevraagde informatie aan het CBS te leveren.

[   ] uren   minuten

Time needed

CBS is working to improve the way information is collected. To see how well we are doing this, we periodically measure the time it takes to collect the required information and report it to CBS.

How much time did it take you to collect and report the information required for this survey?

Please include all the time you and/or others have spent in order to submit the requested information to CBS.

hours   [   ] minutes

Statistics Portugal – Burden Questionnaire

Burden questionnaire last edition occurred from 2017 to 2019, covering the main surveys.

Source: Instituto Nacional de Estatística.

Statistics Portugal Burden Questionnaire Translation

Statistics Portugal is committed in the continuous improvement of the quality of services provided to society. Therefore, we would like to know your opinion concerning our services. The confidentiality of your answer is, as always, guaranteed by Statistics Portugal. Help us to improve! Please answer to the following questionnaire. Its completion does not take more than two minutes.

1. **In your company, how many persons (including you) were involved in this answer to Survey X?**
   Note: In a Combo Box the following eight items are displayed: 1 person/2 persons/3 persons/4 persons/5 persons/6–10 persons/More than 10 persons/Do not Know or No opinion
2. **How much time do you spent, in total, to provide the answer to the Survey X?**
   Note: In a Combo Box the following nine items are displayed: 0–10 minutes/11–30 minutes/31–60 minutes/1–5 hours/6–8 hours/1 day/2–4 days/5 or more days/Do not Know or No opinion
3. **How do you rank the level of difficulty to provide the answer to the Survey X?**
   Note: In a Combo Box the following six items are displayed: Very easy/Easy/Neither Easy nor Difficult/Difficult/Very difficult/Do not Know or No opinion
4. **In your opinion, could the required information in the Survey X be obtained through another source of information?**
   Note: In a Combo Box the following three items are displayed: Yes/No/Do not Know or No opinion
   1. **If Yes, indicate which:**
   Note: Free Text
5. **How do you rank the usefulness, of the information**
   1. **To society:**
   2. **To your company:**
   Note: In a Combo Box the following five items are displayed in both questions: Very useful/Useful/Little Useful/Useless/Do not Know or No opinion
   With your opinion, Statistics Portugal can better know its respondents and provide a service with increasing quality. This space is yours; give us your opinion about:

- Statistics Portugal surveys
- What kind of information would you like to get in return for your collaboration?
- Other subjects that you consider relevant
  Note: Free Text

Statistics Sweden

Source: Statistics Sweden (SCB).

Translation: "How long time did it take to find and provided the requested information?" (answer in hours and minutes) and the extra instruction translates as "Statistics Sweden works on lowering the time that business and organizations spend on providing information. Therefore we are grateful if you answer this voluntary question."

Appendix 10.B: Example of Statistics Netherlands' Communication About Mandatory Reporting

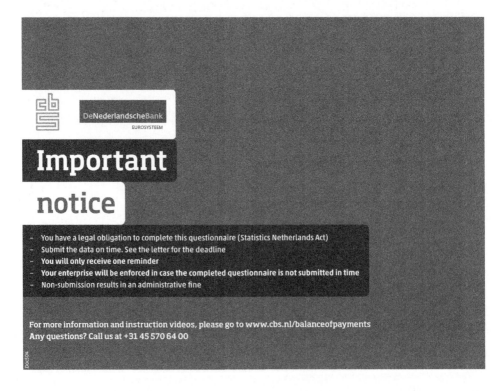

Appendix 10.C: Example of Adaptation Communication to Data Providers due to COVID-19 Crises – Website Statistics Netherlands 2021

Share this page

Annual / Production statistics

Data delivery in times of coronavirus

We understand that providing data to Statistics Netherlands is not easy in these challenging times. However, reliable figures on the current state of the country are of vital importance. It is precisely in times like these that public authorities, scientists, enterprises and citizens want to know how the country and its inhabitants are doing. Just think of data on health, care and the economy, for example. That is why the collection of data continues as usual at CBS. We hope you continue to submit important data to us, even in these times and we thank you for understanding.

Appendix 10.D: Personalized Feedback to Business Data Provider – Monthly Report

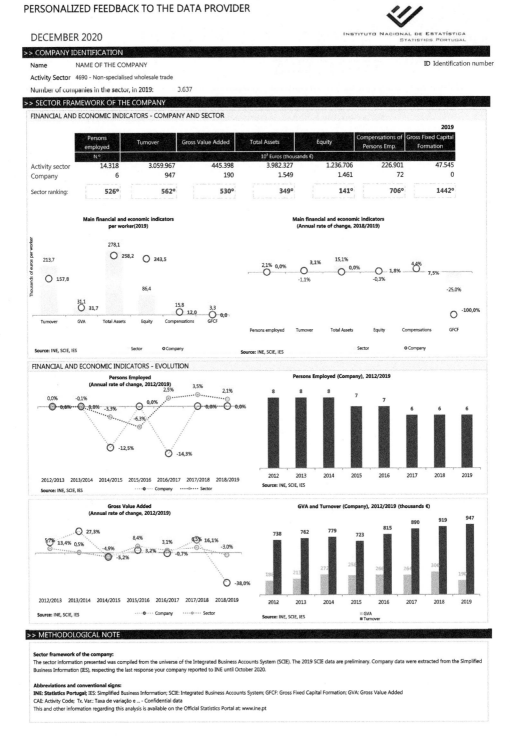

Source: Instituto Nacional de Estatística.

Appendix 10.E: Personalized Feedback to Business Data Provider – Yearly Report

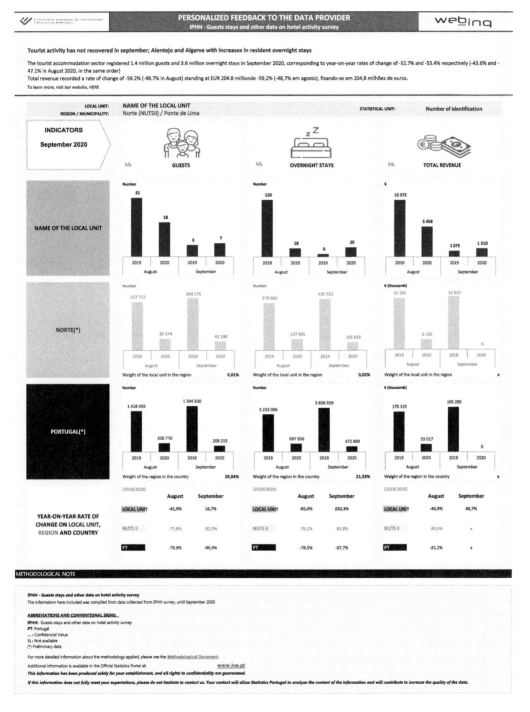

Source: Instituto Nacional de Estatística.

Appendix 10.F: Example of RCSFI Import in Statistics Netherlands Structural Business Statistics Questionnaire

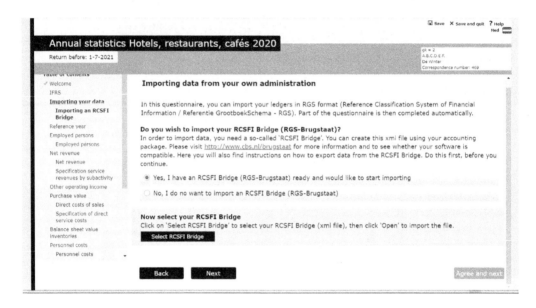

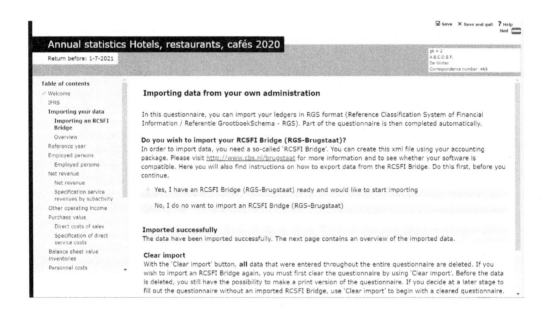

Source: CBS.

11

Producing Official Statistics During the COVID-19 Pandemic

Jacqui Jones[1], Luisa Ryan[2], A.J. Lanyon[3], Marie Apostolou[2], Tanya Price[1], Corinna König[5], Marieke Volkert[5], Joseph W. Sakshaug[5], Dane Mead[3], Helen Baird[4], Duncan Elliott[6], and Craig H. McLaren[6]

[1] *Australian Bureau of Statistics, Canberra, ACT, Australia*
[2] *Australian Bureau of Statistics, Melbourne, Victoria, Australia*
[3] *Australian Bureau of Statistics, Brisbane, Queensland, Australia*
[4] *Australian Bureau of Statistics, Hobart, Tasmania, Australia*
[5] *Institute for Employment Research, Nuremberg, Germany*
[6] *Office for National Statistics, Newport, Wales, United Kingdom*

11.1 Introduction

In January 2020, many countries started to record a small number of COVID-19 cases and by the end of January the World Health Organization (WHO) declared a global health emergency. Then on 11 March, WHO declared COVID-19 a pandemic. In response, many countries introduced lockdowns and nonessential services were shut, which heavily impacted many aspects of the economy. For example, in Australia, between 14 March and 4 April, payroll jobs decreased by 6.3% with the heaviest impacts in accommodation and food services (27.2% of payroll jobs lost) and arts and recreation services (20.6% of payroll jobs lost) (ABS 2020a). Many governments responded by introducing subsidy programs. Figure 11.1 shows the Australian timeline of COVID-19 cases and associated events in quarter one, 2020. Globally by the end of 2020, there had been around 82 million confirmed cases of COVID-19 with approximately 1.8 million deaths (ABS 2021a).

More than ever, economic statistics were essential for monitoring the impacts of COVID-19 and for assisting governments to develop and monitor responsive policies. At the same time, the COVID-19 pandemic stress tested the production of official statistics.

As businesses moved to working at home, where they could, hibernated or ceased trading National Statistical Institutes (NSIs) and other survey organizations had to be innovative and respond quickly to preserve the quality of economic statistics. There were rapid changes to the business population (e.g. industry, size, and turnover), which increased the risk to the quality of statistical business registers. Collecting data became increasing difficult and many of our statistical methods were challenged, such as seasonal adjustment, and re-weighting the Consumer Price Index (CPI).

At the Australian Bureau of Statistics (ABS), for example, the high volume of methods to be reviewed and adapted meant that the monthly Economic Statistics Methods Board (ESMB) (that endorses changes to methods that will or potentially will change the numbers) had to be moved to weekly. International organizations (e.g. OECD, IMF, and Eurostat) worked with NSIs to rapidly

Advances in Business Statistics, Methods and Data Collection. Edited by Ger Snijkers, Mojca Bavdaž, Stefan Bender, Jacqui Jones, Steve MacFeely, Joseph W. Sakshaug, Katherine J. Thompson, and Arnout van Delden.

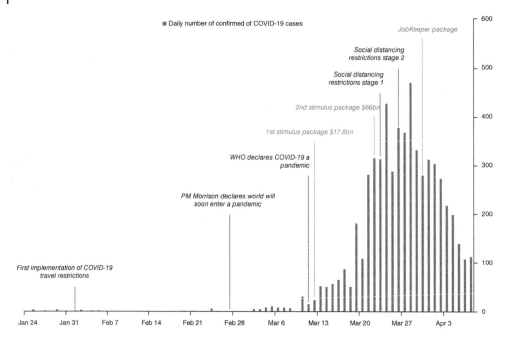

Figure 11.1 The Australian timeline of COVID-19 cases and associated events in quarter one, 2020. Source: ABS (2020a).

produce new methods guidance (e.g. UNECE guidance on producing a CPI during a lockdown (UNECE 2021), and Eurostat guidance on seasonal adjustment (Eurostat 2020)). In the ABS, a new team was set-up to review and classify, in near real-time, the hundreds of government COVID-19 policies, and ensure appropriate changes were made to survey questions, response categories, and/or instructions. From March 2020 to June 2021, the ABS classified just over 1200 COVID-19 related policies.

From a user perspective, people needed to know what was happening in near real-time. Many NSIs introduced rapid surveys (e.g. Rodrigues et al. 2021), new and/or more frequent releases (e.g. ABS Weekly Payroll Jobs and Wages) and gained access to new nonsurvey data, as private sector organizations realized that their data could help in these unprecedented times (e.g. McIlroy and Cranston 4 May 2020).

To assess some of the impacts of the pandemic on the production of official statistics, this chapter provides some international case studies of business survey and economic statistics responses to COVID-19, from the perspectives of the statistical business register (Section 11.2), maintaining response rates (Section 11.3 and 11.4), classification and statistical implementation of COVID-19 Government policies (Section 11.5), and seasonal adjustment and trend estimation (Section 11.6).

11.2 Managing the Australian Statistical Business Register During COVID-19[1]

The COVID-19 pandemic and associated government support and stimulus packages led to some businesses changing their business reporting behavior to the Australian Tax Office (ATO). This

1 Contributed by Luisa Ryan and AJ Lanyon. Thanks to Richard Mumford, Nick Skondreas and Julie Cole for their management of the ABS BR administrative data during this period, and for Justin Farrow, Jack Steel, Melanie Black and Anthony Russo for methods support.

included changes to business details, businesses reactivating their taxation reporting, and fewer businesses canceling their registrations. To understand, and manage, the potential impacts on the ABS survey frames, and economic statistics, a number of interventions were made to June and September 2020 ABS Business Register (ABS BR) "snapshots" (the Common Frame) from which the majority of ABS survey sample frames are taken. This section describes the investigations undertaken, the impacts on the ABS Business Register Common Frame and Survey Frames used to support the production of business statistics, and the ABS response.

11.2.1 ABS Business Register and COVID-19

Most ABS economic survey sampling frames are sourced from the ABS BR via a point in time snapshot known as the Common Frame. Business structures and characteristics are maintained on the ABS BR using Australian Business Number (ABN) registrations data from the ATO's Australian Business Register (ABR)[2] and other ATO data (e.g. business roles and employees). Data on the structures of Australia's largest and most complex businesses are also collected by ABS and applied using the ABS Economic Units Model.[3]

The advent of COVID-19 led to government-imposed restrictions on business operations in some industries to limit the spread of the virus, as well as an unprecedented range of business support packages by the Australian and state governments. The key Australian government support packages for businesses included the following:

- The "Boosting Cash Flow for Employers" announced on March 12, 2020, as temporary support to small and medium businesses and not-for-profit organizations. It was delivered as tax credits via quarterly Business Activity Statement (BAS) reporting to the ATO.
- Temporary changes to insolvency safe harbor rules announced on March 25, 2020, providing Company Directors protection from The Corporations Act 2001 if they continued to trade while insolvent during the COIVD-19 period. The initial period of six months (April 3 to September 30, 2020) was subsequently extended to March 31, 2021.
- The Australian government "JobKeeper" scheme announced on March 30, 2020, initially providing a $1,500 fortnightly payment for eligible employers to maintain employment relationships for businesses significantly affected by COVID-19. The initial period of six months (to September 27, 2020) was subsequently extended to March 28, 2021. This extension had two phases: September 28, 2020, to January 3, 2021 (Tier 1 AU$1200/Tier 2 AU$750) and January 4, 2021 to March 28, 2021 (Tier 1 AU$1000/Tier 2 AU$650). Tier 1 employees or business participants were those who worked for 80 hours or more in the specified periods. Tier 2 were all other eligible employees or business participants.

Figure 11.2 shows the key dates relating to the major Australian government COVID-19 support packages for businesses. The significance of the JobKeeper and Boosting Cash Flow for Employers packages is highlighted in Figure 11.3.

An outcome of the government restrictions and support packages was an observable change in business reporting behavior to the ATO. This section outlines the key changes to business reporting behavior, the impacts on the ABS BR and associated frames, and the ABS response during the June and September 2020 quarters. In 2020, these quarters had the biggest impact in terms of restrictions and economic activity in Australia.

---

2 The ABR is maintained by the Australian Taxation Office.
3 The Economic Units Model links administrative units (e.g. ABNs) with the statistical units (e.g. Type of Activity Unit) used to collect, analyse and disseminate ABS data.

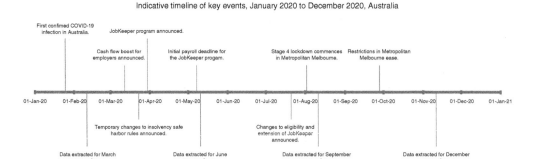

Figure 11.2 2020 timeline of key COVID-19 events in Australia. Source: Australian Bureau of Statistics/CC BY 4.0.

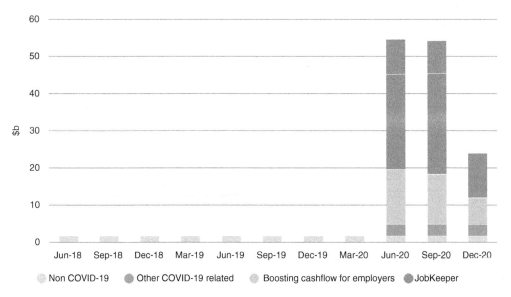

Figure 11.3 Australian Government Support for Business in Response to COVID-19. Source: ABS (2021b)/Australian Bureau of Statistics/CC BY 4.0.

11.2.2 Changes to Business Reporting

A by-product of Australian and State government COVID-19 restrictions and support programs (see Section 11.5) were changes to aspects of business reporting to the ATO. ATO business reporting obligations can differ depending on the status of the business. However, there is a general obligation for businesses to update the ATO of any business changes within 28 days (e.g. contacts, activity). All businesses (both employers and nonemployers) with over AU$75,000 turnover (or AU$150,000 turnover for not for profit organizations) are required to submit at least an annual BAS.

In 2020, during the COVID-19 pandemic, a series of reporting changes were observed in ATO data:

- In the early stages of COVID-19, there was an increase in the number of businesses identifying as employers (as defined by the ABS) and an increase in employers who re-commenced BAS taxation reporting to access the Australian government "JobKeeper" payment for their employees.

- Across multiple months, there was an increase in the level of industry re-coding as businesses updated ABN details in the process of accessing Commonwealth and State government support programs.
- Ongoing there were fewer business cancelations (businesses formally deregistering) as businesses negatively impacted by COVID-19 accessed government support programs. A business exit is when a business is no longer in scope of the Common Frame for any reason, including a cancelation, a lack of reporting activity, or no longer having an in-scope tax-role. A business birth is the registration of a new business, while a business entry includes business births, or an existing unit recommencing reporting activity or receiving an in-scope tax role.

11.2.3   Potential Impacts to the ABS BR

To maintain the accuracy of the ABS BR, and the quality of the Common Frame and Survey Frames, the ABS needs to understand and manage changes recorded in administrative data in the quarters after they happen in the real world. This was particularly important during the COVID-19 period. Ideally, real-world changes, such as a change in employing status or primary activity, should be reflected on the ABS BR in the quarter of the event. Where this is not possible, the change may be picked up in a subsequent period as a correction by either the businessowner, the ATO or ABS. It should be noted that the number of businesses included in ABS statistics may differ to business counts produced by the ATO given that the ABS scope is restricted to active businesses undertaking production-based activity in line with the System of National Accounts.

The ABS BR is a dynamic statistical business register including business entries and exits, plus key details such as the business and trading names, contact details, industry, sector, type of legal organization, and employment. Large, complex enterprises that operate in the Australian economy account for 1% of businesses, but more than 50% of turnover. They are maintained on the ABS BR via direct profiling contact with the business. The details for the other 99% of businesses are sourced from administrative data and referred to as the nonprofiled population. The number of business entries and exits vary over the course of the year. For instance, exits are usually lower in the September and December quarters as businesses winding down finalize taxation obligations during these periods (see Figure 11.4). In June, September, and December quarters of 2020, there were higher entries and fewer exits than in previous years.

11.2.4   Increasing Number of Employers

ABS considers a business to be employing when it has an ATO Income Tax Withholding (ITW) payee role. In the early stages of COVID-19 (April and May 2020), there were significant increases in the number of employing businesses in scope of ABS frames due to

- approximately 31,000 nonemploying businesses requesting an ITW role, thus identifying as new employers for the purposes of the ABS BR. The "normal" average per quarter is approximately 10,000 (see Figure 11.5); and
- an additional 23,000 employing businesses re-commencing taxation reporting therefore coming back into the scope of ABS frames. Previously, these were considered long-term nonremitters and out of scope.

Figure 11.5 shows how these changes aligned with the announcement of the JobKeeper program. When changes to business births, cancellations, and resurrections were first observed, the reasons for these changes were not available within the Common Frame processing timeframes. Given the

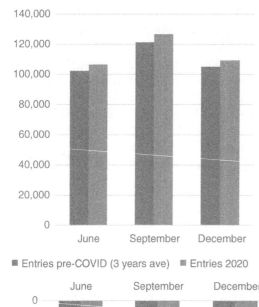

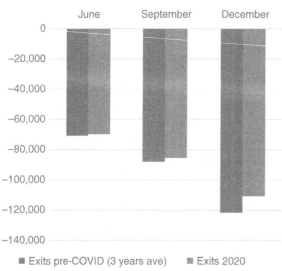

Figure 11.4 Entries and exit to the ABS Common Frame Pre-COVID and during 2020. Source: Australian Bureau of Statistics (Unpublished)/CC BY 4.0.

economic environment, it was questionable whether these changes were genuinely due to businesses becoming employers during the early stages of COVID-19.

To provide time to better understand the situation, as well as manage sample rotation, it was decided to retain approximately 54,000 of the new "employing" businesses as nonemployers on the June 2020 Common Frame (covering the period mid-February to mid-May); in effect treating these units as frozen units. This effectively stopped reported changes by these businesses flowing through to the Common Frame until the data could be validated.

Subsequent analysis confirmed that 78% of these businesses were genuine employers with 97% of the employers having four or less employees, though they did not necessarily become employers during the June 2020 Common Frame period. Compared with previous state and territory business distributions, there was a higher proportion of new employer frozen units in the states (New South Wales and Victoria) most impacted by COVID-19 lockdowns. The industry with the largest business changes, based on the Australian and New Zealand Standard Industry Classification (ANZSIC) was

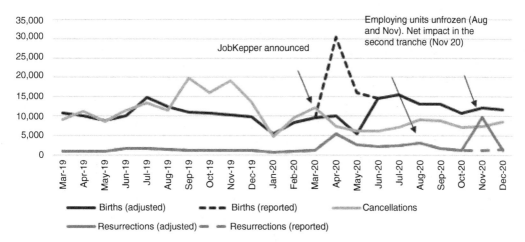

Figure 11.5 Births, Cancellations, and Resurrections of Active employing ABNs on the ABS BR. Source: Australian Bureau of Statistics (Unpublished)/CC BY 4.0.

Professional, Scientific, and Technical Services. This Industry Division had 5.9% of the frozen units compared with 3.4% of all the units in the overall June 2020 Common Frame. The Management Advice and Related Consulting Services class was a key contributor.

The turnover and wage impacts of freezing the units was analyzed using ATO administrative data. As the frozen units were mainly small employers (four employees or less), the aggregate impact to turnover under-coverage was 0%. The wages under-coverage in the June 2020 Common Frame was 0.35%. Wages had a higher under-coverage rate as more of the frozen units reported wages than turnover. The high wage reporting was also a result of the administrative requirement for employees receiving JobKeeper to have been on the business books as at March 1, 2020 (leading to an increase in applications for an ITW role); the reporting of wages can often precede the reporting of turnover; and the distribution of turnover in the total business population is more skewed than for wages. A smaller number of units report turnover and small units contribute more to wages than to turnover.

The Professional, Scientific, and Technical Services Division accounted for 21% of the total value of wages under-coverage in the June 2020 Common Frame. The industry with the highest wages under-coverage rate was the Rental Hiring and Real Estate Division (0.98%).

Overall, the analysis showed that there was minimal statistical impact from freezing the units on the Common Frame. From a practical perspective freezing the units was important, as including all the additional employing units in one quarter would have made it harder to manage sample rotation, changes in weights, and editing and imputing data, which may have led to impacts on survey estimate quality in an already volatile period.

The preliminary impacts on survey frames were also analyzed. For both annual and quarterly surveys, the impacts (turnover and wages) were broadly similar to the Common Frame, although the under-coverage impact on the annual surveys was smaller as the frozen units were limited to only three months of the financial year. The monthly Retail Survey was more heavily impacted due to its narrower industry scope and inclusion of employing units only.

Generally, events that occur outside the reference period are phased into the statistical business register over multiple quarters to avoid spikes in survey frame changes and survey estimates of movement. The phasing in of the units "frozen" in the June 2020 Common Frame commenced in the September 2020 Common Frame. However, as the levels of both new employer births and employers recommencing reporting were still high, it was important to manage the rate at which units were unfrozen. To preserve an overall outcome in line with the natural increase for this period, the largest units from the June 2020 Common Frame were unfrozen. These were offset by freezing some of the units that recorded changes from nonemploying to employing status in the September 2020 Common Frame to achieve a zero net impact from the unfreezing action. New births started to return to more normal levels in the December 2020 Common Frame, so a larger number of units were unfrozen (see Figure 11.5 – resurrections in November 2020) for this period based on reported wages. The unfreezing process will continue over subsequent quarters.

11.2.5 Industry Recoding

In Australia, industry coding is applied using the ANZSIC, and each quarter there are industry recodes as businesses change their production activities. The number of quarterly recodes had been increasing over the last few years; however, June and September 2020 industry recodes were higher than normal. Prior to 2019, industry recodes were approximately two to three thousand per quarter. In the June and September 2019 Common Frames, industry recodes were approximately three to four thousand each quarter. In the June and September 2020 Common Frames the number of recodes at the industry Division level were 4838 and 6371. At the four-digit class level, the number of recodes for the June and September 2020 Common Frames were 6077 (0.24% of all units on the Common Frame) and 8196 (0.33%).

Investigations found that the increased recodes were due to businesses updating their industry details on the ABR prior to applying for both Australian and state government-support packages. Industry coding was not a criterion for any of the Australian government-support programs. However, for some state government packages, the eligibility criteria included having an up-to-date and/or specific industry code. The industries most impacted by COVID-19 had the highest levels of recodes, e.g. cafes and restaurants and retail. The recodes were also higher in the states most impacted by COVID-19 and associated restrictions. Desktop (Internet) checks on a sample of businesses whose codes had been updated indicated that these changes in these quarters were generally quality improvements to the stock rather than a short-term activity change.

While the level of industry recoding reached higher levels during COVID-19, the overall impact on the June and September 2020 Common Frames was not considered large enough to warrant further adjustment. For the Retail Survey frames drawn from the June and September 2020 Common Frames, some recodes were not accepted where they increased the frame size as this did not align with the economic narrative during this period. These changes will be phased into the Retail Survey Frame over a longer timeframe due to the sensitivity in this frame.

11.2.6 Business Cancellations

Business cancellations are businesses that formally deregister. This typically happens when a business closes, a business is sold, a business changes structure, or a business no longer operates in Australia. Generally, the business cancellation occurs sometime after the business ceases or changes operations. For example, before a business is able to cancel its ABN, it is required to submit any outstanding activity and tax statements and settle any remaining tax debts. In Australia, the financial year finishes on 30 June, resulting in higher business cancellations generally in the December Common Frame.

Lower levels of business cancelations were observed during the COVID-19 period (Figure 11.4 – cancellations) as businesses with activities impacted by restrictions and the general economic environment accessed government support packages to remain viable. This included the temporary changes to the insolvency safe harbor rules that provided company directors protection from *The Corporations Act 2001* if they continued to trade while insolvent during the COVID-19 period. The lower business cancelations in 2020 inflated the number of businesses on the June and September 2020 Common Frames as there were fewer offsets to business entries (see Figure 11.4).

11.2.7 The New Normal?

In terms of gross domestic product (GDP), in 2020, the Australian economy contracted in the March and June quarters and grew in the September and December quarters as COVID-19 restrictions were lifted in most states, and the safety net of government support (e.g. JobKeeper) continued (see Figure 11.6).

By the end of 2020, some aspects of business reporting behavior begun to settle. However, by mid-2021, COVID-19 cases were increasing again in Australia and extended, and short-term lockdowns were reinstated in many states. This led to an unprecedented number of ABNs changing their ANZSIC class on the ABR in response to government support programs.

Going forward, it will be interesting to see if businesses continue to have higher levels of engagement with ATO registration information, including higher rates of industry recoding. The ABS will continue to closely monitor ATO data, and apply adjustments as appropriate, in order to produce Common Frames and Survey Frames to support the collection of high-quality economic data. The potential impact of business cancellations and exits will also be monitored as COVID-19 government support programs are unwound.

The year 2020 was an unprecedented year for both businesses and statisticians measuring business behavior. A key reflection from this period is that government programs can impact how

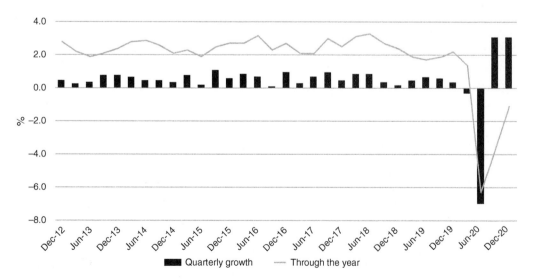

Figure 11.6 Australia Gross Domestic Product, chain volume measures, seasonally adjusted. Source: Australian Bureau of Statistics (2021c).

businesses report administratively. To ensure downstream statistics reflect real-world activity for the period, it is critical that such changes are understood and managed in the statistical business register.

11.3 Mitigating COVID-19 Response Rate Risks in the Collection of the ABS Producer and International Trade Price Indexes[4]

Prior to the COVID-19 pandemic, the ABS used paper questionnaires and respondent communication to collect prices for the Producer and International Trade Price Indexes (PITPI). Work was in train to move to web collection in 2021. As the COVID-19 lockdowns and social distancing restrictions were introduced from March 2020, many businesses moved to working at home or temporarily closed. Continuing paper collection and communications posed too high a risk to PITPI data collection, as respondents would increasingly not be at their normal business address to receive mail and complete questionnaires. In the space of a month, an interim collection approach was designed and implemented using e-mail communications and PDFs of questionnaires. This section provides an overview of the approach, outcomes, and lessons learned.

11.3.1 Overview of ABS Producer and International Trade Price Indexes

ABS PITPI measure the changes in the prices of goods and services as they either leave the place of production (as outputs) or as they enter the production process (as inputs). These indexes are indicators of industry price changes in the economy and used by the public and private sectors for a variety of purposes, including the following:

- as a key input to the derivation of deflators in the Australian National Accounts;
- as a short-term indicator of inflationary trends;
- to inform business and government policy decisions (including indexation of legal contracts in both the public and private sectors); and
- by international organizations such as the Organization for Economic Co-operation and Development and the International Monetary Fund for economic monitoring and comparison.

The Survey of Producer Prices has a purposive sample of 2500 businesses and collects prices for almost 15,000 product specifications. The collected data is used to produce 782 PITPI. The PITPI program also produces 2053 indexes for National Accounts and Balance of Payments deflators.

From early March 2020, the COVID-19 pandemic quickly disrupted business operating conditions across Australia in myriad ways, and it became increasingly clear that the disruptions were bringing collection risks to all ABS business surveys. For the Survey of Producer Prices, the use of paper-based questionnaires posed a high risk to the PITPI response rate, sample, and product frame. These changes in turn posed significant statistical risk to PITPI statistical outputs and National Accounts and Balance of Payments deflators. At the same time, government needed these

4 Contributed by Marie Apostolou and Tanya Price. Thanks to Andrew Tomadini, Robert Villani, and Darryl Malam for their open, adaptive leadership of statistical production through this challenging time. Many analysts in the Producer Prices and International Trade Price Indexes made implementation of the strategy possible. We acknowledge our colleagues in Policy & Legislation, Information Security, and the National Data Acquisition Centre for their willingness to adapt existing policy paradigms and support innovative solutions. A special thanks to Kylie Patman for her excellent project management and execution of the strategy, creative wrangling of management information for the statistics presented in this chapter and her positive resilience throughout.

high-quality statistics to inform decision-making in a complex environment. In response, the prices management team rapidly developed a strategy to mitigate these high statistical risks.

11.3.2 ABS Producer and International Trade Prices Data Collection

For over two decades, the Survey of Producer Prices had primarily used paper questionnaires posted quarterly to businesses. Each business questionnaire is customized to contain unique descriptions of goods and services and specify a date or period for which price information is requested. Respondents use the questionnaire to provide price information and note if a product is out of stock or changed in nature. Response is compulsory under the Census and Statistics Act 1905. If a business does not respond within two weeks, a contact center agent telephones to encourage response either by returning the questionnaire or providing answers over the telephone.

In 2018, the Prices Modernization team started developing an online questionnaire to replace the paper questionnaires by 2021. The team investigated PITPI collection processes and systems, developed questionnaire prototypes, and conducted cognitive testing with businesses. In the testing interviews, respondents stated a strong preference for receiving the questionnaires via e-mail. Common themes from the interviews were that businesses receive most business communication by e-mail and no longer check post boxes daily. Businesses reported that their irregular post collection and internal mail delivery meant that they often first learned of ABS requests when contacted to query nonresponse and had become accustomed to providing data by phone.

In March 2020, when COVID-19 was declared a pandemic, it quickly became clear that many businesses were moving their employees to work from home, hibernating, or shutting down. ABS surveys sent to business addresses were unlikely to be received. In addition, Australia's national postal service advised that deliveries would be less frequent, meaning that if business respondents were still working from their usual business address, it would take even longer for the survey questionnaire to reach them and be returned by post.

The PITPI statistical production teams were increasingly concerned about maintaining data quality during a time of rapid change in the business environment and potential change in the products, services, imports, and exports measured through the Survey of Producer Prices. In price indexes, it is essential to understand the smallest changes in the characteristics of a good or service and if they are actively traded. Prices analysts frequently need to obtain supplementary information on business activity to explain movements. In March 2020, media sources indicated that some businesses might downsize or reallocate employees to different roles. Since PITPI respondents have unique knowledge of sourcing accurate pricing information, personnel changes could reduce data quality, response rates, and timeliness. By the end of the month, ABS contact center agents reported that known business respondents were hard to contact, and this was already impacting other ABS survey response rates. Facing a high likelihood of reduced and delayed response and change in products, the production teams recognized the need to urgently develop alternative ways to collect PITPI data.

11.3.3 Developing the COVID-19 Response

The development of an effective, timely response strategy required the expertise of a wide range of ABS people. A multidisciplinary Prices Rapid Response (PRR) team was created bringing together Prices Modernization, PITPI statistical production, data collection, ABS legal, and IT security experts to develop and implement a response optimization strategy. The PRR team quickly canvassed and evaluated a range of options. Pre-COVID business processes, policy, and security positions were challenged and shifted. For example, although earlier research found that businesses wanted to receive and send questionnaires by e-mail, this did not comply with established ABS legal and IT security protocols. The PRR team used a collaborative, multidisciplinary approach to explore and overcome these and other design, policy, legal, and security issues to enable rapid development of an innovative, effective response strategy.

11.3.4   The Optimizing Response Strategy

The PRR's Optimizing Response Strategy (hereafter, the strategy) centered on continuing traditional pre-COVID-19 postal questionnaire delivery and respondent engagement activities and supplementing these with e-mail contact and questionnaire delivery. The strategy aimed to

- maximize the probability of reaching business respondents by using both post and e-mail;
- enable respondents to return their completed questionnaires and business conditions information by e-mail or over the telephone; and
- tailor communication to conditions and needs as the pandemic unfolded.

11.3.5   Prefield Preparation

Once the strategy was approved, the PRR had one week to work through how to introduce e-mail communication, begin essential prefield preparatory work (Snijkers and Jones 2013) and meet unchanged questionnaire dispatch deadlines. An assessment of existing respondent e-mail addresses found that less than 40% of businesses records contained accurate e-mail addresses. The team worked with the ABS business contact center and Prices statistical production teams to telephone the 2500 businesses to collect e-mail addresses within a few weeks. After intense effort to contact ongoing and new respondents, the teams obtained e-mail addresses for almost 90% of businesses. Existing Prices statistical and data collection systems were not designed to store, send, receive, and monitor e-mail communication to the extent needed for the new approach strategy so this was also changed.

As this was the first time that businesses would be contacted by e-mail, the PRR team developed a two-stage e-mail approach that would meet credibility, data quality, and security concerns. In Stage 1, businesses would be sent a "broadcast e-mail" acknowledging the difficult situation, asking how the ABS could help them to respond, and offering to e-mail pdf versions of the questionnaires. In Stage 2, personalized e-mails would be sent to respondents who requested a pdf questionnaire.

By enabling businesses to provide quick replies in an easy mode, it was anticipated that respondent burden would decrease and response would likely increase (Willimack and Snijkers 2013). Once respondents returned their completed questionnaire, their contribution would be personally acknowledged by return e-mail, a factor that we expected would build confidence in the efficacy of e-mail response in the June and subsequent quarters. The strategy and two-stage plan would be tested and, if needed, adapted throughout the June quarter.

11.3.6   Field Development and Operations

Letters and e-mail content had to be quickly developed. Since early March 2020, the team had followed business and social media to understand how major businesses were communicating with customers about changed business practices. Major businesses were using e-mail to communicate directly with their customers on topics such as in-store conditions, product availability, and purchasing options. Their e-mails were informative, helpful, warmly direct, and frequently sent. There were obvious similarities between these e-mails and established principles of persuasion used to increase survey response (Snijkers and Jones 2013) that could be used in new PITPI letters and e-mails.

In addition to this, businesses and their representative organizations were publicly calling on government for support and key government decision-making agencies were looking to ABS statistics to inform decisions about that support. These provided an opportunity to develop content articulating that respected, legitimate authorities (Snijkers and Jones 2013) including the Reserve Bank of Australia and the Treasury were relying on businesses to provide essential information. This message provided positive reinforcement of the survey benefits, another factor to motivate response (Dillman et al. 2014).

In contrast to previous ABS letters, the new letters and e-mails reflected the context of the pandemic, were more direct, and offered more help. For example, the letters and e-mails included the following:

> We recognise that many businesses are impacted by unprecedented events, including COVID-19. Responding to ABS surveys is an essential way to get high quality evidence to the Reserve Bank of Australia, Treasury and other economic decision makers so they can help businesses to manage through the impact of COVID-19.

Typically, businesses have two weeks to respond to the Survey of Producer Prices. To maximize the probability of respondents understanding that response was needed soon, letters and e-mails asked, *how can we help you to complete the form by Tuesday, 21 April 2020* and then provided suggestions for making response easier, including e-mail and telephone. This approach invoked the heuristic of reciprocity (Cialdini 2001) to motivate reciprocal respondent action and used previous ABS research, which found that respondents wanted to use different modes.

To reduce reading time, all messages were presented in short sentences and paragraphs with bold headings. The layout of letters and e-mails was simple and clean. The Stage 1 broadcast e-mail is a good illustration of this (see Figure 11.7).

The Stage 2 e-mails were longer and included more content. A standard e-mail template was developed, which was then customized with the respondent's name, due date, and a pdf of their unique questionnaire. Included in this e-mail was a pdf guide to responding by e-mail that aimed to address ABS and business security and confidentiality concerns. The guide outlined the IT security implications of sharing files, encouraged respondents to check their businesses' policy on sharing confidential information by e-mail and suggested the most secure file formats for returning completed questionnaires.

With the rapidly changing business environment, the statistical production team needed to know more about specific goods or services and overall business operations. For example, was a product not traded because of port or other supply chain restrictions rather than a drop in demand? It would save time and be easier for respondents and the ABS if this information was provided within questionnaires rather than requested later by telephone. Therefore, in letters and e-mails, respondents were asked to

> ***Use the survey to tell us how the business is doing***
> *We are **keen to understand your business** operating environment and **how that may impact the prices** we ask you about. Please tell us about these impacts when you provide your answers.*

Subject line: Urgent advice regarding Survey of Producer Prices – due Wednesday 6 May 2020

Good afternoon,

I am emailing on behalf of the Australian Bureau of Statistics (ABS) to you as a current contact for the Survey of Producer Prices.

Answers to the survey are due by Wednesday, 6 May but do you have the survey form?

With the challenging conditions related to COVID-19, mail delivery delays and working from home may mean that the paper form that we mailed on 22 April is yet to arrive.

The ABS is meeting the needs of businesses now by delivering a copy of the survey form through email and enabling response through ways other than mail.

Can we help by emailing a copy of the form?

If you would like us to email a copy of the form, **Reply All to this email** (please ensure survey.email@abs.gov.au is included).

Or, would you like to provide your answers by phone?

Please telephone us on 1800 010 XXX within Australia or +61 2 6252 XXX between 9am and 5pm.

If you **already have paper form** or expect it soon and are using it to respond, you **do not need to reply** to this email to let us know.

If there is a **new contact** for the survey, we would appreciate your forwarding this email to them so they can **get in touch** with us.

Your answers to the survey are very much needed at this time

Responding to ABS surveys is an essential way to get high quality evidence to the Reserve Bank of Australia, Treasury and other economic decision makers so they can help businesses to manage through the impact of COVID-19.

Thank you very much for your important contribution always and particularly at this difficult time.
Yours sincerely,

Name Name
Assistant Director
Producer Prices and International Trade Indexes
Prices Branch | Macroeconomic Statistics Division | Australian Bureau of Statistics

Figure 11.7 Broadcast e-mail content, June quarter 2020. Source: ABS (2020).

In reminder e-mails and letters to nonresponding businesses, this message was reinforced by asking respondents to respond even if *prices had not changed*. Businesses interpreted this message as enabling them to reply by e-mail with a simple statement of "no change on price of product." Together these messages resulted in more data and explanatory information coming back within questionnaires and reduced some of the need for statistical production analysts to contact businesses to validate data in postfield (Snijkers and Jones 2013) telephone or e-mail discussions.

The strategy was implemented for the June quarter 2020, with collection from April to the end of June. Throughout the June quarter, the strategy was reviewed for effectiveness and impacts on ABS staff workloads. Small adjustments to content messaging were made to meet changing external conditions and to streamline ABS operations. From the September quarter 2020 onwards, businesses that provided data by e-mail were deemed to prefer e-mail dispatch and were directly e-mailed questionnaires.

11.3.7 Outcomes of the Optimizing Response Strategy

The strategy successfully delivered the target response rate of 97%. Despite unprecedented and challenging business conditions, the response rate was higher than the previous quarter and the June quarters of 2018 and 2019 (see Table 11.1). Businesses also responded sooner, improving timeliness, and easing statistical production pressures.

Response rates decomposed by response mode are shown in Table 11.2. The share of paper and postal responses fell from 68.2% in the March quarter 2020 to 37.3% when the strategy was introduced in the June quarter 2020. Conversely, the share of e-mail response increased from 1.7% in the March quarter 2020 to 27.9% in the June quarter 2020. Response timeliness was also much faster for businesses that responded by e-mail resulting in the target response rate being met earlier.

As the Strategy was extended beyond the June quarter 2020, this response pattern expanded further to the point of the share of e-mail response overtaking paper/postal response in the September quarter 2020. Figure 11.8 shows how e-mail became the highest response mode in the September and December quarters 2020.

Despite challenging conditions, respondents provided good quality price information. E-mailing nonresponding businesses obtained immediate response, sometimes containing data within e-mail text. As requested in e-mails and letters, respondents provided information on business conditions and product changes. This enabled analysts to immediately understand data and reduce editing calls. Respondents provided positive feedback on the use of e-mail, saying it was consistent with

Table 11.1 Survey of Producer Prices Final Response Rates, by Quarter, 2018–2020.

	March Qtr (%)	June Qtr[a] (%)	Sept Qtr[a] (%)	Dec Qtr[a] (%)
2020	96.0	98.0	97.2	96.9
2019	95.1	96.8	96.0	94.2
2018	96.6	96.5	97.3	96.2

a) Optimizing response strategy implemented from June Quarter 2020.

Table 11.2 Survey of Producer Prices, response rate share by response mode, 2020.

Mode	March Qtr 2020 (%)	June Qtr[a] 2020 (%)	Sept Qtr[a] 2020 (%)	Dec Qtr[a] 2020 (%)
Paper/Postal response	68.2	37.3	32.7	29.5
E-mail response	1.7	27.9	35.3	40.4
Phone response	24.2	29.6	25.0	23.5
Online repository[b]	5.9	5.2	7.0	6.5
Total	100.0	100.0	100.0	100.0

a) Optimizing response strategy implemented from June Quarter 2020.
b) A small proportion of PITPI establishments provide data by a secure online repository.

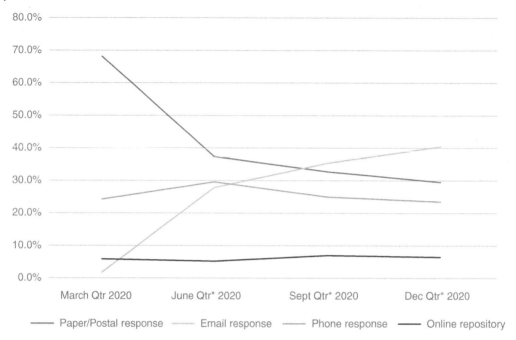

Figure 11.8 Survey of Producer Prices, Response share by mode, 2020 quarters.

preferred business practice and helped them to work from home. Of the 1000 businesses that responded by e-mail, 400 requested and were moved to permanent contact by e-mail.

Most importantly, the Strategy enabled the production of high-quality PPIs, ITPIs, and deflators for the National Accounts and Balance of Payments. At the end of the June quarter 2020, a comprehensive review of the results showed the effectiveness of the strategy. Given the effectiveness and ongoing COVID-19 disruption, the strategy was maintained.

11.3.8 Lessons Learned

The COVID-19 pandemic created unprecedented risks to the collection of business survey data, which required innovative responses and collaboration. As this case study highlights, to respond rapidly to these risks, the ABS fast-tracked innovation and reset policy, business processes, systems, and respondent communication modes.

Some of the key lessons learned from implementing the Optimizing Response Strategy included the following:

- Good corporate governance and responsive decision-making are critical. ABS senior managers trusted the multidisciplinary team to uncover problems, scope solutions, troubleshoot potential barriers, and implement rapidly.
- Small, multidisciplinary teams enable rapid development of effective solutions. The PRR team comprised a small number of experts that used agile and collaborative practices.
- To mitigate statistical risk, we must be willing to take risks. Since usual paper collection practices would not work, the ABS had to take a risk on e-mail. The team scoped the risks associated with e-mail and designed safe implementation strategies.
- Innovation requires initial investment, but returns can be high. Implementing personalized e-mail in a secure statistical environment required additional resources. This investment was

worth it in a high-risk situation. The benefits of innovation can be extended by using this case as a pathfinder for further research and development.

- Innovations require benchmarking, management information, and monitoring. Because e-mail was new, there was no preexisting monitoring system. An existing system was enhanced to capture response by mode and provide real-time status reports.
- Having a good stock of knowledge on business characteristics, behaviors, and needs is essential. Previous research and expertise enabled rapid development of effective solutions that met ABS and respondent needs.
- Business respondents need to know why their data is needed even more during busy, uncertain times. The teams' messages explained how providing data helped decision-makers to make informed decisions that affect businesses.
- E-mail works for data collection from businesses. PITPI's high response rate was achieved because of two-way e-mail communication; without e-mail, response rates would have been significantly lower.
- In the future, as businesses formalize new working arrangements, paper, and postal communication for data collection will be become less viable. E-mail and other online solutions are essential.

11.4 The Impact of Changing Data Collection Modes in the IAB Establishment Panel in Response to the COVID-19 Pandemic[5]

This section provides an overview of the mode changes implemented in the Institute for Employment Research (IAB) Establishment Panel in Germany in response to the COVID-19 pandemic. Two impacts of the mode changes are reported. First, the effects of the change from face-to-face to telephone interviewing on the panel response rates; and second, an assessment of whether take-up rates for self-completion (either via web or mail) were higher in 2020 compared to 2019 for the newly recruited establishments in the refreshment samples.

Since 1993, the IAB has annually conducted the IAB Establishment Panel, which is a voluntary longitudinal employer survey. The survey collects comprehensive data from establishments such as detailed information on the employment structure and its development, and operational investments and innovations. The survey results support the advisory activities of the Federal Employment Agency of Germany and is used for decision-making by politicians and various associations.

The target population consists of every establishment in Germany with at least one employee liable for social security contributions on 30 June of the previous year. The survey is based on a complex sampling design where establishment size classes, industries, and federal states serve as stratification variables. On average, about 16,000 establishments participate each year. The annual sample has two subsamples: repeatedly surveyed establishments that have participated in at least one of the last two waves and a newly recruited refreshment sample to compensate for panel attrition. The new subsample includes both existing and newly founded establishments.

Until 2020, most interviews were conducted face to face with an interviewer using either a paper questionnaire (PAPI) or, since 2018, an electronic questionnaire (CAPI). Before 2018, self-completion of the paper questionnaire was only possible if the establishment requested it. In 2018, IAB researchers conducted a large-scale methodological experiment with a sequential mixed-mode (web to face to face) design in the refreshment sample of the IAB Establishment Panel

---

5 Contributed by Corinna König, Marieke Volkert, and Joseph W. Sakshaug.

alongside a parallel single-mode (face to face) design control group. In the experimental group, a self-completion web questionnaire was initially offered followed by a face-to-face interview for those who did not respond to the web questionnaire. This experiment was carried out to gain knowledge and experience on whether establishments in Germany would participate via the web mode, as this mode offered substantial cost savings relative to face-to-face interviewing. In 2019, the web-first sequential mixed-mode design continued for a part of the refreshment sample. In 2020, as the COVID-19 pandemic hit, the acquired experience of using the web mode in the previous two waves provided an essential option for maintaining response rates.

Until 2020, the majority of interviews were still conducted face to face. However, as COVID-19 restrictions came into place in Germany, face-to-face interviews were no longer feasible. At the same time, the importance of the panel data increased in providing insights into the impacts of the pandemic. Skipping a wave of data collection was therefore not an option. To protect both the representatives of the establishments and the interviewers from COVID-19, a different data collection design was implemented. The data collection design changed from primarily face-to-face interviewing to telephone interviewing and web and paper self-completion. This shift in data collection design was a major challenge in the short time available (about two and a half months), since the original 2020 wave planning was almost complete when the effects of COVID-19 reached Germany.

In regular weekly meetings with the survey organization, the new data collection design was devised. Of course, this decision faced challenges as switching from face-to-face to telephone interviews had never been done before in the panel and many establishments had only been interviewed face to face in previous rounds of the panel. To minimize response risks, it was decided that it is more important that establishments were contacted by the same interviewer as the year before, although that interviewer had no experience of conducting telephone interviews. In addition, as fieldwork planning was already at an advanced stage, there were no capacities to switch to interviews conducted in a telephone center. Instead, face-to-face interviewers were trained to conduct interviews from home using their private telephones with the positive effect of avoiding infection in a telephone center. Finally, the use of the web mode was clearly facilitated by the introduction of the web questionnaire since 2018.

During the planning stage, there were questions regarding the accessibility and willingness of establishments to participate in the survey during the pandemic. The reduction of external contacts, temporary (forced) closures, quarantine orders, and insolvencies may have worsened accessibility. Additionally, it would be more challenging for interviewers to determine the reasons for nonresponse if contact with the establishment could not be made. There were a number of identified risks, including the following:

- Changing stress levels impacting the willingness of establishments to respond.
- Poor accessibility and unwillingness to participate leading to selectivity in the sample, as these two nonresponse reasons are unlikely to be randomly distributed across all establishments in times of a pandemic.
- Selectivity occurring between the self-completion modes (paper and web questionnaire) and the interviewer-administered mode (telephone interviewing), depending on which is offered to the establishments.

To better understand the likelihood of these risks materializing a mode design experiment was conducted in the refreshment sample. The experiment was designed to study selection effects by mode and investigate mode effects, a highly relevant issue given the introduction of the new telephone mode in the panel.

Before describing the details of the 2020 data collection design, other changes in the survey that may have had an impact on unit nonresponse are described. The first change from previous years was that the survey advance letter, which was always sent in the name of the Federal Employment Agency (BA) chairperson, was not sponsored by the Confederation of German Employers' Associations (BDA). Presumably this decision was motivated by concerns not to additionally burden establishments during an economic crisis. However, we can only speculate on this regard. There was reason to believe that this lack of support might have had a negative impact on the willingness of the establishments to participate in the survey. The second change concerned the questionnaire content. Usually, the interview begins with a question on employment size, asking for the number of people employed in different employment groups and compares it with the numbers from the previous year. Concerns about reduced willingness to respond prompted the study team to revise the questionnaire and start with questions about the impact of COVID-19 on the establishment to underline the importance of this year's participation in the survey.

The data collection design of the IAB Establishment Panel is always implemented differently for establishments that already belong to the panel and the newly recruited refreshment sample. For the purposes of this analyses we defined panel establishments in 2020 as those who successfully responded to the survey in 2019, resulting in 14,630 cases in total. The refreshment sample in 2020 consisted of 37,991 newly selected establishments.

Figure 11.9 provides a schematic overview of the data collection mode designs used for the 2020 subsamples but gives no details about the timing of the mode sequences or the number of reminders. This information is included in the following descriptions of the subsamples. Among the panel establishments, two subsamples are differentiated: P:Web and P:Mixed.

The first panel establishment subgroup, P:Web (694 cases), had responded in the web mode in the previous year (2019), and was initially invited to complete a web questionnaire in 2020. Up to two reminders were sent approximately two weeks apart. Both reminders included the web link but only the second reminder offered the option of completing a self-enclosed paper questionnaire with a stamped-return envelope. Two weeks after the last reminder (or 6.5 weeks after the initial invitation), a telephone (CATI) nonresponse follow-up was conducted.

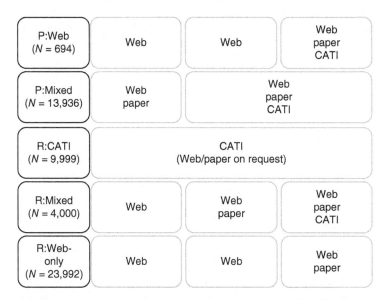

Figure 11.9 Overview of the Data Collection Mode Designs for the 2020 Subsamples.

The second subgroup of panel establishments, P:Mixed (13,936 cases), had previously responded by a face-to-face interview in 2019 and were informed in the invitation letter about the different data collection approach in 2020. Self-completion modes (paper with a stamped-return envelope and web) were initially offered for two weeks, before interviewers began calling establishments that had not yet participated.

We now turn to the mode design for the refreshment sample in 2020. A mode design experiment was implemented for the refreshment sample as selection effects and effects on data quality were expected with the introduction of the telephone mode. Establishments were randomly assigned across three groups of different sizes. Group sizes were oriented toward managing the fieldwork of interviewers in an optimal manner and delivering data on time.

The first refreshment subgroup, R:CATI (9999 cases), received an invitation letter with a paper questionnaire but no stamped-return envelope and was immediately contacted by interviewers via telephone. The enclosed paper questionnaire was provided as a guide to facilitate the telephone interview, although respondents who refused the telephone interview were offered the option of self-completing a paper or web questionnaire.

The second refreshment subgroup, R:Mixed (4000 cases), was initially invited to complete the web questionnaire. After 20 days, a reminder letter was sent along with the paper questionnaire and stamped-return envelope. The reminder mentioned that a telephone interviewer would be contacting the establishment shortly if self-completion was not possible.

The third refreshment subgroup, R:Web-only (23,992 cases), was initially invited to complete the web questionnaire and received two reminder letters approximately two weeks apart, with the last one including a paper questionnaire and a stamped-return envelope as a nonresponse follow-up.

Using the 2020 unweighted cross-sectional data, response rates were calculated according to AAPOR standards (AAPOR 2016). In total, 31.3% of the surveyed establishments participated in the survey, but the proportion varied greatly between the subsamples (see Table 11.3). For the panel establishments, which participated in 2019, 72.2% participated in 2020. In the refreshment sample, 15.5% of the establishments took part.

Table 11.3 shows that the individual subsamples differed in their response rates. P:Mixed, containing the previously face-to-face interviewed establishments from 2019, had the highest response of 72.5% in 2020, even with the primary mode being CATI. In comparison, establishments in P:Web, who answered online in the previous year, yielded a slightly lower response rate of 66.7% in 2020. Among the refreshment sample there was clearly a difference between R:Web-only and the other two refreshment subsamples, whose response rates hardly differed. The establishments in R:Web-only, who were only contacted by mail and asked to participate via paper or web, yielded the lowest response rate of 13.1%.

Table 11.3 2020 Response rates by subsamples.

2020	Subsample	Response rate (in %)	N
Panel sample	P:Web	66.7	694
	P:Mixed	72.5	13,936
	Total	72.2	14,630
Refreshment sample	R:CATI	19.8	9,999
	R:Mixed	19.2	4,000
	R:Web-only	13.1	23,992
	Total	15.5	37,991

Apart from different levels of commitment to the panel as well as different modes offered, systematic differences in group composition might have affected the response rates. Regarding the establishment size there was little variation between the refreshment and the panel samples as smaller establishments with less than 20 employees were represented more frequently in the panel sample. P:Web and P:Mixed differ to the extent that P:Web included a higher percentage of establishments with more than 50 employees. The three refreshment subsamples were nearly identical in their distribution across establishment size. Among the participating establishments in the refreshment and panel samples, the distribution of those with 1–19 employees was higher than in their respective full samples. Especially for R:CATI and R:Mixed, these establishments were more represented among the respondents, whereas establishments with more than 200 employees were less represented. For P:Web and P:Mixed it was also true that establishments with 1–19 employees were overrepresented among the pool of respondents.

The difference in distributions across industry between the overall refreshment and panel samples was small and varied by about 2% points. Between the three refreshment samples no differences in industry distribution were seen. In comparison, the industry distribution differences between P:Web and P:Mixed were a little larger as establishments in "manufacturing of capital and consumer goods," "liberal professions," and "health and social work" were more frequently included in the P:Web group. Focusing on the respondents in the refreshment sample, establishments in "manufacturing of capital and consumer goods" were overrepresented compared to the full sample whereas establishments in "retail" and "transport, storage" were underrepresented. Among the panel respondents, differences in the distributions across industries were generally smaller. A slight decline in representativity can be seen for establishments in "liberal professions" and "manufacturing of capital and consumer goods," whereas the percentage of establishments in "construction" was slightly higher.

To assess how successful the transition to telephone surveys was and whether establishments were more willing to complete a self-completion questionnaire during the pandemic, the 2020 subsample response rates were compared with the corresponding subsamples of 2019. Figure 11A.1 in the Appendix presents the mode design for every subsample in 2019; however, it must be emphasized that no experiment was conducted. In 2019, the refreshment sample response rate was lower than expected, which is why two additional groups, R:CAPI2 and R:Web-only,[6] were later added to the sample.

Table 11.4 displays the share of respondents in 2019. Focusing on the panel sample and comparing the overall response rates of 2019 and 2020, the rate in 2020 (72.2%) was more than 10%-points lower than in 2019 (83.6%). In contrast, among the refreshment sample, the response rate increased in 2020 (15.5%) by about 2.7%-points compared to 2019 (12.8%).

To assess the change from face-to-face to telephone interviews, subsamples with similar mode designs were compared:

- Web-first panel establishments (P:Web in 2020 and 2019) participated online in the previous wave and were offered the web mode first in 2019 and 2020. Only the nonresponse follow-up was different with CAPI follow-ups used in 2019 and CATI follow-ups in 2020. The response rates show that participation increased in 2020 (66.7%) by about 10%-points compared to 2019 (56.9%).
- The largest panel subsamples (P:PAPI in 2019 and P:Mixed in 2020) were interviewed face to face in 2019 and by telephone in 2020. The response rate for these subsamples decreases by about

---

6 In 2019, there were 911 cases from R:CAPI1 and R:CAPI2 that were moved to R:Web-only at the end of the field period because of too few available interviewers. These establishments were excluded from the analysis as they were contacted multiple times with various mode designs, and can therefore not be assigned to a particular subsample.

Table 11.4 2019 Response rates by subsamples.

2019	Subsample	2019 Response rate (in %)	N	Comparable 2020 response rates (in%)
Panel sample	P:PAPI	84.6	14,031	P:Mixed: 72.5
	P:CAPI	68.9	260	
	P:Web	56.9	167	P:Web: 66.7
	Total	83.6	14,525	
Refreshment sample	R:CAPI1	15.6	11,362	R:CATI: 19.8
	R:PAPI	28.4	975	
	R:Mixed	10.3	1,330	R:Mixed: 19.2
	R:CAPI2	20.7	2,630	
	R:Web-only	12.1	14,613	R:Web-only: 13.1
	Total	12.8	29,999	

12%-points between 2019 and 2020. At this point, it is unclear why the 2020 response rate was lower for these groups. Given that these establishments previously participated in the survey via face to face, perhaps one explanation is that they perceived telephone interviews as a more burdensome mode or that they would not receive the same level of interviewer support via the telephone. It is reasonable to wonder if apart from the different offered modes, the COVID-19 crisis particularly affected establishments in this group. At this point, we can only speculate about the reasons for the response rate decline, and we are continuing to inspect the data for further insights.

Next, we compare the response rates of the refreshment samples in 2019 and 2020.

- R:CATI in 2020 and both R:CAPI1 and R:PAPI in 2019 were contacted by interviewers either by telephone (2020) or face to face (2019). The comparison shows that the 2020 R:CATI response rate (19.8%) was slightly higher than the combined R:CAPI1 and R:PAPI response rate (16.6%) in 2019. Only the individual comparison reveals that telephone interviewing in 2020 achieved a higher response rate than CAPI face-to-face (15.6%) in 2019 but a lower response rate than PAPI face to face (28.4%) in 2019.
- The evaluation of subsamples using a sequential mixed-mode design, starting with web followed by interviewer contact is made by comparing R:Mixed in 2020 and R:Mixed in 2019. Here, we see a significant increase in the response rate in 2020 (19.2%) by almost 9%-points compared to 2019 (10.3%).
- The last comparison consists of the self-administered only groups of R:Web-only in 2019 and 2020. Both groups do not reveal a difference in the response rate as the response rate was just 1%-points larger in 2020 (13.1%) than in 2019 (12.1%).

In summary, replacing face-to-face interviewing with telephone interviewing in 2020 yielded seemingly mixed results in terms of response rates compared to the previous year. Panel establishments previously interviewed face-to-face exhibited a lower response rate in 2020 when they were first offered the web mode followed by telephone follow-ups. In contrast, panel establishments that completed a web interview in the previous year yielded a higher response rate in 2020 under the sequential mixed-mode design. It is not possible to ascertain if only the mode change was responsible for the decrease in response rate for the former group since it is reasonable to assume that the economic situation due to COVID-19 also had an impact on willingness to participate among these panel establishments. For the refreshment sample, it can be concluded that the introduction of telephone data collection performed well, as the response rates of the single-mode telephone and sequential mixed-mode (paper/web followed by telephone) groups were higher than their corresponding face-to-face groups from the previous year. Lastly, there was no evidence that establishments in 2020 were more willing to participate via self-completion compared to 2019, as the self-completion response rates were similar in both years. Further analyses may reveal possible explanations for these findings.

11.5 Classification and Statistical Implementation of Australian COVID-19 Government Policies[7]

In response to the COVID-19 pandemic that began in early 2020, various parts of Australia were temporarily locked down to limit the spread of the virus, with travel restrictions and social distancing introduced. The economic impact of the pandemic led to the fastest and largest fiscal stimulus program in modern Australian history, with over AU$130 billion spent on the two largest response programs (JobKeeper and Boosting Cashflow for Employers) (see Figure 11.3). This compared to the total amount of AU$53 billion spent in response to the 2008–2009 Global Financial Crisis. Hundreds of other individual policy interventions were also announced by the Australian Commonwealth, state and territory governments to support households and businesses through the pandemic. This section provides an insight into the ABS organizational response to ensure that these COVID-19 policy interventions were appropriately classified and measured in economic statistics.

11.5.1 Building a New Work Program

Prior to the COVID-19 pandemic, the ABS maintained an informal process to review the conceptual classification of new government policies and manage their implementation across economic statistics. At the point of a new policy being announced, typically as part of budget measures or machinery of government changes, relevant subject matter experts would engage internally to discuss the policy and agree on a review process. This would typically lead to a conceptual paper being taken to the ABS Conceptual Classification Committee (CCC) and/or a methodological paper being taken to the ABS ESMB, depending on the nature of the policy and its impact across the concepts, sources, and methods used in compiling Australia's economic statistics.

As the government's pandemic response ramped up through March and April 2020, it was clear that the existing process would be inadequate in dealing with the large volume of policy announcements. In response to this, within a couple of weeks, a newly formed COVID-19 Response team was established to manage the conceptual analysis of these policies. This allowed data statistical processing staff to focus on other statistical issues and priorities during the pandemic, including the provision of innovative new data outputs for users and managing the impact of remote working arrangements for staff and data providers (ABS 2020b).

---

7 Contributed by Dane Mead and Helen Baird.

From April 2020, the COVID-19 Response team worked through a range of new and existing forums to progress the policy analysis. Internally, extensive engagement was undertaken with subject matter experts to seek agreement on the appropriate conceptual classification of policies. To support the timeliness of decision-making, the monthly CCC and ESMB were combined into a single forum that met on a weekly and then a fortnightly basis to endorse conceptual and methodological papers as the pandemic evolved. Externally, the team met regularly with data providers in the public sector, including the Commonwealth Department of Finance and state and territory treasuries, to discuss the classification of policies in Government Finance Statistics (GFS) source data.

11.5.2 Changes to Business Surveys

Once the classification of a government policy was agreed for the compilation of GFS, the ABS needed to ensure that data from businesses receiving the support was also collected and treated consistently. A group of experts from statistical production areas across the ABS was brought together to discuss how government policies would interact with business activities and hence how to guide business survey reporting. The group considered the range of businesses who would engage with a policy (across the economy or only within targeted industries, for example), and how they were likely to record the support in their business accounts.

The group first met in late April 2020, as the first data collection activity, following the announcement of COVID-19 policies, would be reported in the Average Weekly Earnings survey. This was then followed by the need to ensure consistent collection in the Quarterly Economy Wide survey and subsequently in the annual Economic Activity survey.

For each COVID-19 support policy, the expert group considered what types of businesses were impacted, which surveys these businesses were in scope of and the relative size of the policy within aggregate statistics. The group then considered whether a change to question wording or survey guidance material was warranted, with targeted changes then implemented. The level of detail needed in editing notes was also considered to assist the compilation activities of data processing staff.

11.5.3 Policy Case Study – JobKeeper

This section uses Australia's JobKeeper policy as a case study to outline the end-to-end ABS process to classify COVID-19 policy interventions and then implement the determinations across economic statistics.

In September 2020, the Australian Statistician released an analytical article on the economic impacts of COVID-19 to that point (ABS 2020c). The article highlighted that as lockdowns, travel restrictions, and social distancing came into force across Australia, the domestic economy contracted in the March quarter 2020. By the end of the June quarter, Australia had experienced the first two consecutive quarters of GDP falls in almost 29 years. The June quarter GDP fall of 7.0% (quarter-on-quarter) was also the largest fall in quarterly GDP since records began in 1959. Many people experienced working reduced hours or being stood down. Employment fell between March and June with the highest proportion of payroll job losses in Accommodation and food services (20.3%) and Arts and recreation services (18.6%). These two industries also had sharp decreases in job vacancies (65.9% and 95.2%).

As one of the policy responses, the Australian Commonwealth Government implemented the JobKeeper payment. By the end of the policy, JobKeeper had provided over A$100 billion in support to achieve three broad objectives: to support businesses affected by the economic downturn; to preserve the employment relationship between employers and employees; and to provide income support for households (The Treasury, 2020).

JobKeeper payments were made by the ATO directly to eligible employers. Under the first round of JobKeeper, these employers were directly responsible for ensuring that eligible employees received a wage of at least A$1500 per fortnight for a maximum period of six months from March 30, 2020. These wages were delivered through their payroll and within the conditions of their existing employer–employee relationships.

11.5.3.1 Classification of the Policy

Referring to international statistical manuals (e.g. the System of National Accounts) and conceptual guidance, the ABS considered how JobKeeper payments should be treated in ABS official economic statistics. They were subsequently determined as an "other subsidies on production" paid from government to eligible employers (SNA 2008 2009, para 7.106). In addition, employees whose employers were receiving the JobKeeper payment were classified as employed and in receipt of a wage.

In making this classification determination, the ABS also reviewed the International Monetary Fund's Special Series on COVID-19, which included a note discussing "Government Support to Businesses and Households" (IMF 2020, p. 2):

> substance over form may call for looking beyond the specific scheme's details, in order to capture the real economic effects at play. This in turn implies trying to identify the primary intent of the scheme, such as primarily helping households or primarily helping businesses. In this evaluation, while the decision should generally not be, unduly, influenced by cash flow arrangements, the latter may become important where these provide valid indicators of the underlying policy intent.

The economic substance of this Australian policy was for JobKeeper to primarily target employers, incentivizing them to keep employees on the payroll and to quickly resume production when COVID-19 restrictions eased. The ABS classification therefore aligned with the IMF guidance on the appropriate classification of comparable government support in other countries (IMF 2020, p. 3):

> When the support is mainly to support employers and self-employed maintaining their business, and in case of the employers to keep their employees on the payroll, with a view to having a quick return to production, support should be recorded as other subsidies on production, with the continued payments of remuneration by the employer to its employees recorded as wages and salaries.

11.5.3.2 Implementation of Policy Classification

Following internal endorsement of this classification determination through the joint ESMB-CCC forum, the ABS published a paper on the conceptual decision. This classification was also discussed directly with key stakeholders including the Department of Finance and Commonwealth Treasury who agreed with the determination. The COVID-19 Response team then engaged across ABS economic statistical areas to ensure consistent and coherent implementation of the determination (ABS 2020d).

The GFS and National Accounts work programs worked together to ensure alignment on both the classification and timing recognition of expenditure linked to the policy. Through this engagement, it was agreed that JobKeeper expenditure would be recognized based on daily accrued wage subsidies applicable to each quarterly period. This timing recognition method was consistent with other wage subsidies. In addition, the National Accounts also implemented industry splits of Job-keeper by deriving industry proportions from a new ATO JobKeeper dataset.

The ABS also anticipated that business survey respondents receiving JobKeeper payments would query how to report data on the number of employees, their wages and salaries, and the classification of JobKeeper receipts in their survey responses.

In response to this, the Average Weekly Earnings survey questionnaire was updated to provide specific guidance:

1. The "Number of employees" question (asking respondents to record the number of employees on all payrolls of the organization who received pay for any part of the last pay period) had a new instruction to include "Employees paid using wage subsidies such as the JobKeeper payment."
2. The "Taxable gross weekly earnings, including overtime" question had a new instruction to include "Payments made using wage subsidies such as the JobKeeper payment."

With the Jobkeeper payments, there were three main outcomes for employees (ABS 2020e):

1. No change in earnings for full-time employees whose job and regular hours worked were largely unaffected by the pandemic;
2. A reduction in earnings for full-time employee's that had a significant drop in hours worked (in some cases down to zero) in businesses that were heavily impacted by the pandemic. These employees experienced a reduction in earnings, to the JobKeeper rate of A$750 per week; or
3. An increase in earnings for part-time and junior employees' jobs, where pre-pandemic earnings were less than the JobKeeper rate of A$750 per week.

Labor and wage statistics were other areas that needed to be reviewed in relation to the JobKeeper policy.

In Labor Statistics, it was agreed that people receiving payroll payments supported by JobKeeper through an existing employer–employee relationship, for which they have a job attachment, would be treated as employed (ABS 2020f). It was also confirmed that payroll payments supported by JobKeeper would be treated as wage and salary payments and were included in earnings statistics (ABS 2020g).

The headline Wage Price Index (WPI) estimates excluded JobKeeper payments, which were treated as a reduction in the cost of labor for employers (ABS 2020h). This was because the principle purpose of the WPI is to measure changes in the cost of labor (in hourly terms) for employers in the Australian Labour Market, with wage subsidies outside the conceptual boundary for WPI (see Figure 11.10). To support analysis of income growth, two experimental series including wage subsidies were introduced alongside the headline WPI estimates.

11.5.4 Lessons for the Organization

The ABS response to the COVID-19 pandemic was received positively by a range of external stakeholders and key data users. Stakeholders and users provided comments on the timeliness, accuracy, and relevance of new products, and praised the collaborative and flexible approach to which the organization responded to the pandemic.

The importance of monitoring and classifying new government policies, as well as accurately measuring their impact on the economy, will continue to be a key data quality priority beyond the pandemic. In particular, the high-quality outcomes of ABS COVID-19 policy analysis highlighted the value of mobilizing subject matter experts during a period of rapid economic or fiscal

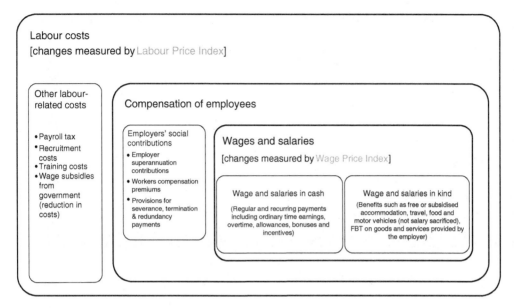

Figure 11.10 Labor costs conceptual framework. Source: ABS (2020h).

disruption. This allowed staff taken offline to resolve a high volume of complex conceptual issues in a relatively short period of time, without the operational distraction of statistical compilation activities.

In addition, regular engagement with affected stakeholders will continue to be prioritized to ensure that the statistical community has a clear understanding of how Australian government policies are being classified, measured, and reported in economic statistics produced by the ABS. This includes leveraging a range of existing meetings and seminars to inform stakeholders on the conceptual outcomes, as well as publishing papers so they are made accessible to the broader community.

It is also an enduring outcome for the ABS that clearer processes are now in place to ensure that individual conceptual decisions are consistently implemented across the suite of economic statistics for Australia.

11.6 Seasonal Adjustment and Trend During and Post–COVID-19[8]

Seasonally adjusted time series are often lead indicators in monthly and quarterly economic statistics published by NSIs. Seasonally adjusted estimates help users interpret time series movements by estimating and removing systematic variations associated with the time of year and arrangement of the calendar (for example regular seasonal peaks in sales because of Christmas and Easter holidays). Trend estimates are also published by some NSIs (Australian Bureau of Statistics, 2018; Fortier et al. 2019) and can provide information on the underlying level of a time series to help

8 Contributed by Duncan Elliott, Jacqui Jones and Craig H. McLaren. We would like to thank the following country participants that provided information on their NSIs approach to seasonal adjustment and trend estimates during COVID-19: Jennie Davies and Julian Whiting (Australian Bureau of Statistics); Jan van den Brakel (Statistics Netherlands/Maastricht University); Steve Matthews (Statistics Canada); Andrew Richens, Steve White, Ben Brodie, Richard Penny (Statistics New Zealand).

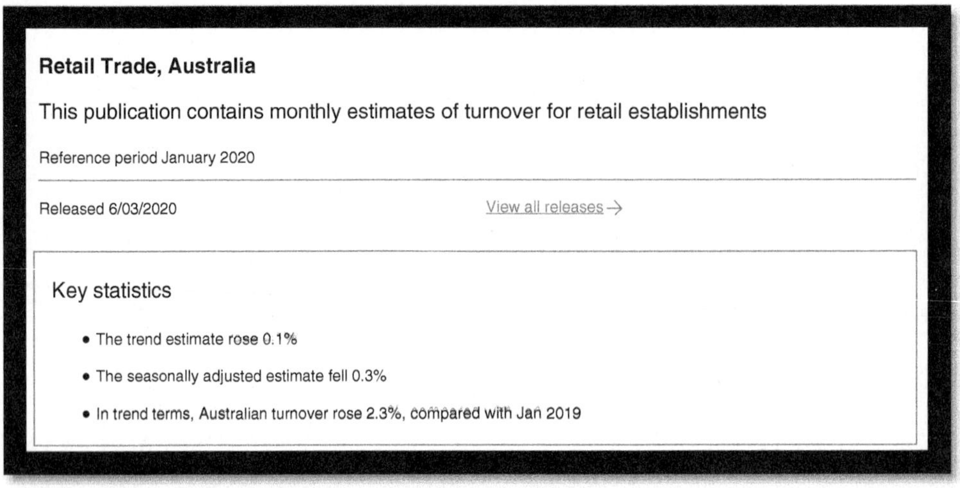

Retail Trade, Australia

This publication contains monthly estimates of turnover for retail establishments

Reference period January 2020

Released 6/03/2020   View all releases →

Key statistics

- The trend estimate rose 0.1%
- The seasonally adjusted estimate fell 0.3%
- In trend terms, Australian turnover rose 2.3%, compared with Jan 2019

Figure 11.11 Australian Bureau of Statistics Retail Trade Publication, reference period January 2020.

detect turning points. For more detailed discussions on the purpose of seasonal adjustment and trend estimation see Granger (1978), Dagum and Luati (2009), Wyman (2010), Quenneville and Findley (2012).

COVID-19 challenged many elements of the generic statistical business process model,[9] including seasonal adjustment and trend estimation. This section outlines the challenges of producing seasonally adjusted and trend estimates during the COVID-19 pandemic, with an overview of interventions made by NSIs.

11.6.1   Pre-COVID Publication and Presentation of Data

To help interpret movements in time series, monthly and quarterly data are often seasonally adjusted, and in some cases trend estimates are calculated. Headline statistics typically include month-on-month (or quarter-on-quarter) change, or change from the previous year, using the seasonally adjusted and trend estimates. To illustrate this, Figure 11.11 shows the headline Retail Sales statistics published by the Australian Bureau of Statistics (ABS 2020i) and Figure 11.12 Retail Sales headline statistics published by the Office for National Statistics (ONS 2020a).

11.6.2   Seasonal Adjustment and Trend Estimation in Practice

The variation in an observed times series can be decomposed into trend-cycle, seasonal and irregular components. X-11 variants (e.g. X-13-ARIMA-SEATS) and SEATS are the main methods of seasonal adjustment used by NSIs (Eurostat 2015) often combined with time series models (ARIMA models with regression effects) to extend the series and address effects that do not conform to trend-cycle, seasonal and noise. Official statistics trend estimates typically use either the trend-cycle component from seasonal adjustment, or filtered versions of the seasonally adjusted time series to track the short-term trend, see for example (Dagum 2018).

NSIs use a variety of software to undertake seasonal adjustment but two commonly used are JDemetra+ (National Bank of Belgium 2020) and X-13ARIMA-SEATS (US Census Bureau 2017).

---

9 https://ec.europa.eu/eurostat/cros/content/gsbpm-generic-statistical-business-process-model-theme_en.

Table 1: Main retail figures

Seasonally adjusted, percentage change, Great Britain, January 2020

	Most recent month on a year earlier	Most recent 3 months on a year earlier	Most recent month on previous month	Most recent 3 months on previous 3 months
Value (amount spent)	2.1	1.5	1.2	−0.5
Value (quantity bought)	0.8	0.8	0.9	−0.8
Value (excluding automotive fuel)	2.2	1.5	1.9	−0.5
Volume (excluding automotive fuel)	1.2	0.9	1.6	−0.8

Source: Office for National Statistics – Monthly Business Survey – Retail Sales Inquiry

Figure 11.12 Office for National Statistics, Retail Trade Publication, reference period January 2020.

Common practice is to fix certain parameters and update these on an annual basis, or when there are significant revisions to the original data (Eurostat 2015). Different countries and publications may have different policies on which parameters are fixed or revised and when they are revised. For example, Retail Sales for Great Britain are seasonally adjusted using X-13ARIMA-SEATS and parameters are usually revised annually. This is referred to as partial concurrent adjustment as there will be some revisions to estimated seasonal factors and the coefficients in the time series model when additional time points are added. Section 4.2 of the European Statistical System Guidelines on Seasonal adjustment recommends partial concurrent adjustment (Eurostat 2015).

Partial concurrent adjustment allows some revisions as new data becomes available, while not causing unnecessary revisions. If a "current" adjustment (sometimes referred to as forward factor adjustment) is used, seasonal factors and calendar effects are estimated at a specific period for the year ahead. These "fixed" forward factors are used to seasonally adjust new data points each period. This results in revisions only occurring when forward factors are reviewed and re-estimated. Full "concurrent" adjustment on the other hand can cause more frequent revisions as the specification of models and filter lengths can change as additional data become available. The issue of revisions for seasonal adjustment is covered in more detail in (Elliott et al. 2018). An example of how overall revisions may be reduced by moving from current (forward factors) to concurrent adjustment is discussed by (Trewin 1999). Similar arguments for updating and revising trend estimates can also be made.

11.6.3 Publication and Presentation During COVID-19

The COVID-19 pandemic has had a significant impact on economies across the world. As governments restricted travel and business operations, introduced policy responses (see Section 11.5), and people responded to the restrictions and pandemic, economic time series experienced very large movements. The standard decomposition of a time series is not designed to deal with such large movements and can cause problems for estimation if not correctly treated, e.g. through the use of the standard regression-ARIMA framework for prior corrections in timeseries (Maravall and Gomez 1996) and (Findley et al. 1998).

11.6.4 Options for Time Series Publications During COVID-19

To address the seasonal adjustment and trend estimation problems caused by large time series movements, there are at least four different options:

1. Model outliers using a regression-ARIMA framework
2. Use forward factors for seasonal and calendar components
3. Suspend the seasonally adjusted and/or trend estimates
4. Publish higher frequency data, such as daily or weekly information.

In early 2020, as the pandemic unfolded, Eurostat published guidance for seasonal adjustment practitioners (Eurostat 2020). The main recommendation was to model outliers at the end of time series, but it also notes the use of current adjustment (forward factors) as a valid alternative. It should be noted that the forward factor approach assumes there is no significant change to seasonal patterns. An alternative, discussed in Whiting and Zhang (2021), is to suspend the publication of seasonally adjusted estimates for a set period. Another consideration for time series is publishing higher-frequency time series, with the aim of earlier detection of turning points (Eurostat 2020). Note that this option, if used in addition to continuing monthly or quarterly publications, should mean that one of options one to three will still be required.

Examples of these different approaches, in response to COVID-19 time series impacts, can be found across different statistical outputs and NSIs.

11.6.5 Modeling Outliers

During COVID-19 many countries adopted the modelling outliers approach, such as the Irish Central Statistical Office (Foley 2021), Central Statistical Bureau of Latvia (Central Statistical Bureau of Latvia 2020), Statistics Norway (Statistics Norway 2020), ONS (Elliott et al. 2021), Statistics Canada, Statistics New Zealand, and the US Census Bureau (Government Statistics Section, American Statistical Association 2021). As the example in Figure 11.13 shows, modeling outliers can significantly improve estimation of the components of a time series. See (Mehrhoff 2018) for further details. There are variations on the way in which modelling of outliers at the end of the series can be handled:

- review alternative types of outliers and implement with each new publication;
- use automatic modelling routines for outlier adjustment; and
- specify every period that may be affected by COVID-19 as an outlier.

The approach taken in the UK was to review seasonally adjusted outputs prior to each publication and use statistical evidence and subject matter expertise for each output to decide on the most appropriate interventions. This was a radical departure from the usual set of annual seasonal adjustment reviews. The main principles that governed this rapid intervention strategy included:

1. prioritizing important time series within each statistical domain;
2. maintaining the quality of seasonally adjusted outputs;

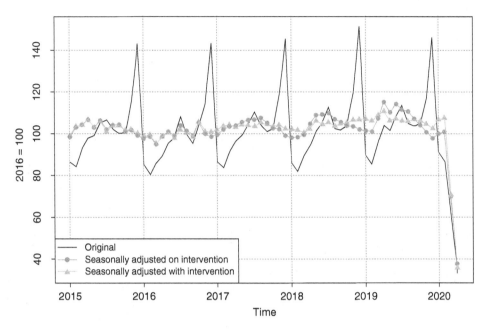

Figure 11.13 Retail Sales of Clothing in Great Britain, chain volume measure 2016 = 100, January 2015 to April 2020. The intervention includes additive outliers for March and April 2020 (used in publication). Calculations provided for purpose of illustration as published data may be different.

3. minimizing revisions so long as the quality of the seasonally adjusted estimates were maintained;
4. conducting rapid and timely reviews, as there was usually a matter of only a day in which to complete detailed analysis before publishing; and
5. regular communication with subject matter experts on proposed interventions and impacts.

Figure 11.13 compares seasonally adjusted estimates with (what was published) and without an intervention for outliers at the end of the series for Retail Sales of Clothing in Great Britain (ONS 2020a, 2020b). Trend estimates do not form part of the publication, but to illustrate the impact, Figure 11.14 shows trend components with and without an intervention. Seasonally adjusted and trend estimates are both distorted with what looks like a residual seasonal pattern. The practical intervention in this case included additive outliers for March and April 2020. The inclusion of additive outliers was justified as restrictions on movement and the opening of certain types of retail outlets started in March 2020. The seasonally adjusted series with analytical intervention clearly shows the sudden fall in sales and does not cause excessive revisions to the past time points.

Figure 11.15 provides an illustrative example of revisions performance of alternative approaches to deal with the impact of the COVID-19 pandemic, using the Retail Sales of clothing time series for Great Britain. Revisions to the seasonally adjusted estimates were caused in part by revisions to the original time series, and then dependent on the intervention approach used. The "modelling outliers" approach has revisions caused by the partial concurrent update including any changes to outliers specified by the analyst reviewing the series, while the automatic outliers approach has revisions due to the automatic outlier detection used in X-13ARIMA-SEATS (Findley et al. 1998), and the forward factors revisions only revise the seasonal factors at March 2021 (the simulated point of an annual review). The median and maximum revisions were calculated over subsequent vintages of the data ending in the period March 2020 to March 2021.

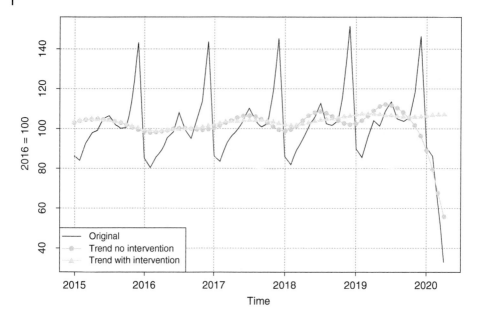

Figure 11.14 Illustrative impact of no intervention on the trend component. Retail Sales of Clothing in Great Britain, chain volume measure 2016 = 100, January 2015 to April 2020. The intervention includes additive outliers for March and April 2020. Calculations provided for purpose of illustration as published data may be different.

The modeling outliers approach had a slightly lower median revision to growth rates at lag 1, but at longer lags forward factors tend to have a lower median revision, which is to be expected as forward factors only causes revisions when seasonal factors are revised (except revisions caused by revisions to the original data). If a forward factors approach had been used, this would have caused larger revisions further back in the series. Automatic outliers would have caused larger revisions in general.

The "modelling outlier" approach adopted for Retails Sales in Great Britain initially used additive outliers at the current end of the time series, with more parsimonious models being implemented as more COVID-19 affected data became available, replacing successive additive outliers with combinations of level shifts, additive outliers and ramp-type variables for the discontinuity ((Foley 2021) provides more details on Ireland's approach).

11.6.6   Forward Factors

During COVID-19, the ABS suspended the publication of trend estimates and moved time series that were anticipated to have significant and prolonged impacts from COVID-19 from a partial concurrent approach to forward factors (Whiting and Zhang 2021). On a new COVID-19 methods webpage,[10] the ABS listed all series moved to forward factors and updated as series were returned to partial concurrent seasonal adjustment or forward factors maintained following an annual review. Examples of other countries that moved to forward factors for all or some series were: Germany, Croatia (most monthly series), France, Italy, UK (just the weekly labor market stats) (TSAUG 2021).

In the ABS, it is a standard practice to undertake annual seasonal adjustment reviews to examine changing seasonal and trading day factors, trend and seasonal breaks, and outliers. For series

---

10 https://www.abs.gov.au/articles/methods-changes-during-covid-19-period.

Median absolute revision

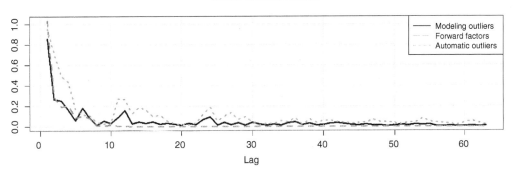

Maximum absolute revision

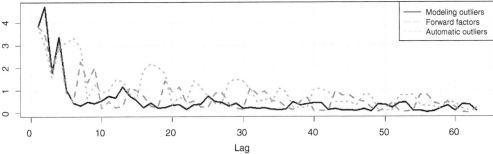

Figure 11.15 Median and maximum absolute revisions to the month-on-month growth rate of the seasonally adjusted series for Retail Sales of Clothing in Great Britain, chain volume measure 2016 = 100 by lag from the last available time point calculated over 12 publication periods March 2020 to February 2021. The "modeling outliers" approach was used in practice, while forward factors is shown for comparison (assuming an annual review in March 2021). Note that this also includes some revisions to the unadjusted data, as part of the regular production process.

moved to forward factors, it was critical to do annual reviews within a year of introduction. Annual reviews included an assessment of unusual behavior and the need for prior adjustments to maintain quality. A decision was then made on whether to maintain forward factors or switch back to partial concurrent adjustment. As with the original decision to move a series to forward factors, this was based on whether it was still anticipated that the series would have a significant and prolonged impact from the COVID-19 pandemic.

11.6.7 Option to Suspend Series

The suspension of a seasonally adjusted or trend series should be based on an overall quality assessment (Whiting and Zhang 2021). The suspension of trend estimates should happen when abrupt changes in the level of the series are likely, and insufficient time points after the break are available to reliably measure the size of the break. Such abrupt changes may come from abrupt falls and recoveries. In the ABS trend, estimates for all statistical outputs were suspended from February 2020 because of COVID-19 (ABS 2020j).

A similar argument can be made for suspending seasonally adjusted estimates in cases where it is likely that there is a sudden structural change in the seasonal component. Assessing sudden structural changes in the seasonal component is challenging to do in a timely way, because of the way in which seasonality is defined. In these cases, it is important to think about the causes and nature of seasonality and whether and how these are likely to be affected by COVID-19. Whiting and Zhang (2021) explore the potential to use Bayesian structural time series models using covariate time series to help identify seasonal breaks. One challenge with this approach is finding covariates to use in the model that are not affected by COVID-19 but are correlated with the series for which a seasonal break is suspected. This sort of approach may be useful for high-profile seasonally adjusted series but may not be practical to implement in large sets of detailed National Accounts series for example.

Statistics Canada published some trend estimates during the COVID-19 pandemic such as wholesale trade where they are used as a visual indication of the trend in time series charts, while the main commentary and analysis focuses on the seasonally adjusted series. See for example (Statistics Canada 2020a) and (Statistics Canada 2021), which also include a warning about possible large revisions during times of economic disruption. Figure 11.16 shows the vintages of the trend estimate for Canadian wholesale trade measured in current prices, with the level in the top panel and monthly growth rates in the bottom. The most notable revision occurs in the first period when COVID-19 impacts the April 2020 publication.

Statistics Canada suspended other trend estimates, such as the Labor Force Survey from March 2020 (Statistics Canada 2020b).

Statistics New Zealand noted that following the suspension of trend estimates in their International Travel publication (Statistics New Zealand 2020), they would be reintroduced when

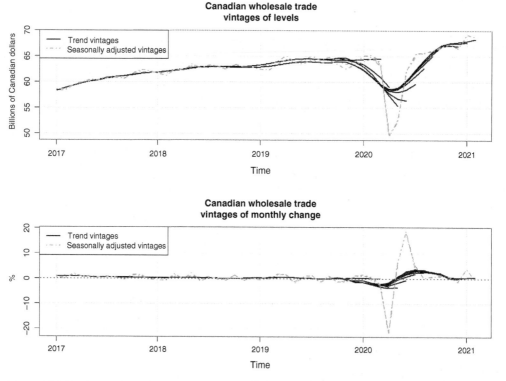

Figure 11.16 Vintages of trend and seasonally adjusted estimates for Canadian wholesale trade in current prices from monthly publications from March 2020 through to February 2021. Top panel: levels in billions of Canadian dollars. Bottom panel: month-on-month percentage change in the levels.

underlying travel patterns stabilize. Re-introduction of trend estimates will require trend breaks to be applied. Principles around the number of time periods required for estimation of different types of breaks are discussed in (Whiting and Zhang 2021), with the recommendation that three periods of a sustained change in the level for a level shift, and three years for a seasonal change of regime are needed. However, it will depend on the nature of the series and intervention required, with other types of interventions considered such as ramp type variables discussed, for example in Lytras and Bell (2013) and Foley (2021). Other considerations include consistency across different series within publications, where from a statistical point of view some series may have stabilized and others not.

The decision to reinstate seasonally adjusted or trend estimates will depend on the reliability and accuracy of the estimates and their utility for the user.

11.6.8 Use of High-Frequency Estimates

Throughout the COVID-19 pandemic, there has been a consistently high demand for timely information to help policy makers in unprecedented times. This poses challenges for seasonal adjustment and trend estimation. For example Elliott et al. (2021) discusses the introduction of weekly estimates for some variables in the UK Labour Force Survey, where a modified version of SEATS was used for seasonal adjustment and trend estimation using an experimental method developed by Palate (2020) and discussed in more detail in Ladiray et al. (2018). Within the publication (ONS 2020c), time series with large structural changes, such as average hours worked, required the use of forward factors, whereas series without a significant structural change (e.g. total employment) used partial concurrent adjustment and trend estimates. These data were published as experimental data to meet specific user requests for timely data. ONS also published a suite of other higher-frequency data in a direct response to the COVID-19 pandemic with a faster economic indicators publication (ONS 2021), including weekly seasonally adjusted outputs for selected variables.

The Deutsche Bundesbank also has examples of higher-frequency data (Deutsche Bundesbank 2020), with seasonal adjustment being performed using an extension of the STL method (Ollech 2020). The pandemic has increased the demand for methods to decompose daily and weekly time series into trend, seasonal, and other calendar-related components.

11.6.9 Other Time Series Challenges

The COVID-19 pandemic raised significant challenges for time series analysis in official statistics. For example, revisions due to benchmarking, or where nowcasting methods are needed to be used for data that is not sufficiently timely. Univariate time series models now cast data based on historical patterns, whereas many time series were unlikely to follow these historical patterns during the COVID-19 period. In some instances, surveys stopped collecting data because of COVID-19. For example, in the UK, the International Passenger Survey stopped data collection in mid-March 2020 and estimates for travel and tourism and international migration produced using time series models combining administrative data and sample surveys, see ONS (2020d) and Rogers et al. (2021).

11.6.10 Conclusion

The COVID-19 pandemic caused significant challenges for time series analysis in official statistics, particularly for production of seasonally adjusted and trend estimates. Government restrictions on movement, policy responses, and business and peoples' responses to the pandemic caused significant movements in economic time series, as well as challenges for accurate estimation. Seasonally adjusted and trend estimates derived by decomposing time series can easily be distorted by such large movements, requiring changes to standard practices. This can include interventions using outliers in time series models, the use of forward factors for seasonal adjustment, or the suspension of outputs until structural changes can be estimated reliably.

Producers of official statistics not only continued to provide important economic time series and appropriate interpretation of movements in these series throughout the COVID-19 pandemic but also responded by developing new outputs such as data at higher frequencies than the standard monthly or quarterly data.

Appendix

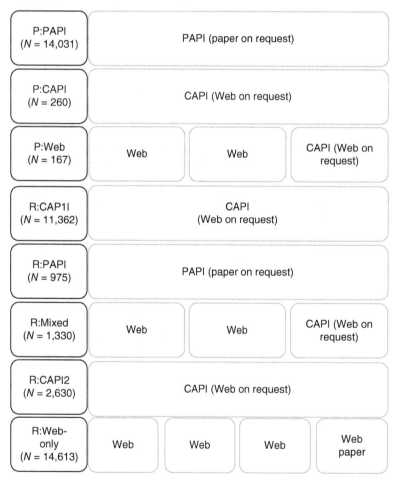

Figure 11A.1 Overview of the 2019 Data Collection Mode Designs for every Subsample.

References

ABS (2018). Improvements to trend estimation. Australian Bureau of Statistics. https://www.abs.gov .au/ausstats/abs@.nsf/Lookup/6291.0.55.001Main%20Features7March%202018 (accessed 4 August 2021).

ABS (2020a). Droughts, fire, cyclones, hailstorms and a pandemic – the March quarter 2020. *The Australian Statistician's Analytical Series*. Australian Bureau of Statistics, 15 June 2020. https://www .abs.gov.au/articles/droughts-fires-cyclones-hailstorms-and-pandemic-march-quarter-2020 (accessed 15 August 2021).

ABS (2020b). Measuring the impacts of COVID-19 in Australia. Australian Bureau of Statistics. http:// www.abs.gov.au/covid-19 (accessed 21 January 2021).

ABS (2020c). A series of unprecedented events – the June quarter 2020. *The Australian Statistician's Analytical Series*. Australian Bureau of Statistics. http://www.abs.gov.au/articles/series-unprecedented-events-june-quarter-2020 (accessed 27 February 2021).

ABS (2020d). Economic measurement during COVID-19: selected issues in the Economic Accounts. Classifying JobKeeper payments in ABS economic accounts. Australian Bureau of Statistics. http:// www.abs.gov.au/statistics/economy/business-indicators/economic-measurement-during-covid-19-selected-issues-economic-accounts/may-2020 (accessed 21 January 2021).

ABS (2020e). Average weekly earnings, Australia. May 2020, Spotlight – *Compositional changes during the COVID-19 period*. Australian Bureau of Statistics. http://www.abs.gov.au/statistics/labour/ earnings-and-work-hours/average-weekly-earnings-australia/may-2020#spotlight-increases-in-average-weekly-earnings-compositional-changes-during-the-covid-19-period (accessed 13 March 2021).

ABS (2020f). Classifying people in the Labour Force Survey during the COVID-19 period. Australian Bureau of Statistics. http://www.abs.gov.au/articles/classifying-people-labour-force-survey-during-covid-19-period (accessed 13 March 2021).

ABS (2020g). Average weekly earnings, Australia. May 2020, Spotlight – *Average weekly earnings survey methods during COVID-19*. Australian Bureau of Statistics. http://www.abs.gov.au/statistics/labour/ earnings-and-work-hours/average-weekly-earnings-australia/may-2020#spotlight-average-weekly-earnings-survey-methods-during-covid-19 (accessed 13 March 2021).

ABS (2020h). Methods changes during the COVID-19 period. Measuring the Wage Price Index during the COVID-19 pandemic. Australian Bureau of Statistics. http://www.abs.gov.au/articles/methods-changes-during-covid-19-period#measuring-the-wage-price-index-during-the-covid-19-pandemic (accessed 13 March 2021).

ABS (2020i). Retail Trade, Australia. https://www.abs.gov.au/statistics/industry/retail-and-wholesale-trade/retail-trade-australia/jan-2020 (accessed 5 September 2021).

ABS (2020j). Retail Trade, Australia. https://www.abs.gov.au/statistics/industry/retail-and-wholesale-trade/retail-trade-australia/mar-2020 (accessed 5 September 2021).

ABS (2021a). A second quarter of strong recovery – the December quarter 2020. *The Australian Statistician's Analytical Series*. Australian Bureau of Statistics, 29 March 2021. https://www.abs.gov .au/articles/second-quarter-strong-recovery-december-quarter-2020 (accessed 6 July 2021).

ABS (2021b). Government Support for Business, December quarter 2020, Australian National Accounts: National Income, Expenditure and Product, December 2020. Australian Bureau of Statistics. https://www.abs.gov.au/articles/government-support-business-december-quarter-2020 (accessed 6 July 2021).

ABS (2021c). Australian National Accounts: National Income, Expenditure and Product, December quarter 2020. Australian Bureau of Statistics. https://www.abs.gov.au/statistics/economy/national-accounts/australian-national-accounts-national-income-expenditure-and-product/dec-2020 (accessed 10 July 2021).

American Association for Public Opinion Research (AAPOR) (2016). *Standard Definitions: Final Dispositions of Case Codes and Outcome Rates for Surveys*. AAPOR.

Cialdini, R.B. (2001). *Influence, Science and Practice*. Boston: Allyn & Bacon.

Central Statistical Bureau of Latvia (2020). Seasonal adjustment of time series during COVID-19 crisis. https://github.com/CSBLatvia/SA-COVID-19-public/blob/master/SA-COVID-19-EN.md (accessed 10 July 2021).

Dagum, E.B. and Luati, A. (2009). A cascade linear filter to reduce revisions and false turning points for real time trend-cycle estimation. *Econometric Reviews* 28 (1–3): 40–59.

Dagum, E.B. (2018). Trend-Cycle Estimation. In: *Handbook on Seasonal Adjustment* (ed. G.L. Mazzi, D. Ladiray and D.A. Rieser), 365–390. Luxembourg: Publications Office of the European Union.

Deutsche Bundesbank (2020). Deutsche Bundesbank monthly report August 2020. https://www.bundesbank.de/resource/blob/841054/fafb2bd0e26d8dae55268d5cd1d6bc38/mL/2020-08-monatsbericht-data.pdf (accessed 10 July 2021).

Dillman, D.A., Smyth, J.D., and Melani Christian, L. (2014). *Internet, Phone, Mail, and Mixed-Mode Surveys; The Tailored Design Method*, 4e. Hoboken: Wiley.

Elliott, D., Kirchner, R., and McLaren, C.H. (2018). Revisions. In: *Handbook on Seasonal Adjustment* (ed. G.L. Mazzi, L. Dominique and D.A. Rieser), 516–566. Luxembour: Publications Office of the European Union.

Elliott, D., McLaren, C.H. and Nikolova, A. (2021). Rapid Intervention for Seasonal Adjustment Reviews in UK Short Term Statistics and High Frequency Seasonal Adjustment. Office for National Statistics. https://coms.events/NTTS2021/data/abstracts/en/abstract_0058.html.

Eurostat (2015). ESS Guidelines on seasonal adjustment. https://ec.europa.eu/eurostat/documents/3859598/6830795/KS-GQ-15-001-EN-N.pdf (accessed 5 June 2021).

Eurostat (2020). Guidance on time series treatment in the context of the COVID-19 crisis. https://ec.europa.eu/eurostat/documents/10186/10693286/Time_series_treatment_guidance.pdf (accessed 5 June 2021).

Findley, D.F., Monsell, B.C., Bell, W.R., Otto, M.C., and Chen, B.-C. (1998). New capabilities and methods of the X-12-ARIMA seasonal-adjustment program. *Journal of Business & Economic Statistics* 16 (2): 127–152.

Foley, P. (2021). Seasonal adjustment of Irish official statistics during the COVID-19 crisis. *Statistical Journal of the IAOS* 37 (1): 57–66.

Fortier, S., Matthews, S. and Gellatly, G. (2019). Trend-cycle estimates – Frequently asked questions. Statistics Canada. https://www.statcan.gc.ca/eng/dai/btd/tce-faq (accessed 5 June 2021).

Government Statistics Section, American Statistical Association (2021). *Virtual roundtable discussion on time series and seasonal adjustment estimation during the COVID-19 pandemic*.

Granger, C.W.J. (1978). Seasonality: causation, interpretation and implications. US Census Bureau. https://www.census.gov/ts/papers/Conference1978/Granger1978.pdf (accessed 6 June 2021).

IMF (2020). *The International Monetary Fund's Special Series on COVID-19, Government Support to Businesses and Households*, 6 May 2020. http://www.imf.org/en/Publications/SPROLLs/covid19-special-notes (accessed 21 January 2021).

Ladiray, D., Palate, J., Mazzi, G.L., and Proietti, T. (2018). Seasonal adjustment of daily and weekly data. In: *Handbook on Seasonal Adjustment* (ed. G.L. Mazzi, D. Ladiray and D.A. Rieser), 757–785. Publications Office of the European Union.

Lytras, D. and Bell, W.R. (2013). Modelling recession effects and the consequences on seasonal adjustment. US Census Bureau. https://www.census.gov/content/dam/Census/library/working-papers/2013/adrm/jsm2013lytrasfinal.pdf (accessed 6 June 2021).

Maravall, A. and Gomez, V. (1996). Programs TRAMO and SEATS. Spanish National Central Bank. https://www.bde.es/f/webbde/SES/Secciones/Publicaciones/PublicacionesSeriadas/DocumentosTrabajo/96/Fich/dt9628e.pdf (accessed 7 June 2021).

McIlroy, T. and Cranston, M. (4 May, 2020). ABS seek alternative data to chart recovery. Australian Financial Review. https://www.afr.com/politics/federal/abs-seeks-alternative-data-to-chart-recovery-20200502-p54p93 (accessed 7 June 2021).

Mehrhoff, J. (2018). Outlier detection and correction. In: *Handbook on Seasonal Adjustment* (ed. G.L. Mazzi, D. Ladiray and D.A. Rieser), 137–168.

National Bank of Belgium (2020). JDemetra+. https://github.com/jdemetra (accessed 8 June 2021).

ONS (2020a). Retail sales, Great Britain: January 2020. Office for National Statistics. https://www.ons.gov.uk/businessindustryandtrade/retailindustry/bulletins/retailsales/january2020#main-points (accessed 10 June 2021).

ONS (2020b). Retail sales, Great Britain: April 2020. Office for National Statistics. https://www.ons.gov.uk/businessindustryandtrade/retailindustry/bulletins/retailsales/april2020 (accessed 10 June 2021).

ONS (2020c). Single-month and weekly Labour Force Survey estimates: December 2020. Office for National Statistics. https://www.ons.gov.uk/employmentandlabourmarket/peopleinwork/employmentandemployeetypes/articles/singlemonthlabourforcesurveyestimates/december2020 (accessed 10 June 2021).

ONS (2020d). Overseas travel and tourism, provisional: April to June 2020. Office for National Statistics. https://www.ons.gov.uk/peoplepopulationandcommunity/leisureandtourism/bulletins/overseastravelandtourism/apriltojune2020 (accessed 11 June 2021).

ONS (2021). Coronavirus and the latest indicators for the UK economy and society: 22 April 2021. Office for National Statistics. https://www.ons.gov.uk/peoplepopulationandcommunity/healthandsocialcare/conditionsanddiseases/bulletins/coronavirustheukeconomyandsocietyfasterindicators/22april2021 (accessed 11 June 2021).

Ollech, D. (2020). dsa: Seasonal Adjustment of Daily Time Series. R package version 0.74.18. https://CRAN.R-project.org/package=dsa (accessed 2 July 2021).

Palate, J. (2020). Routines for modelling and seasonal adjustment of high frequency series. https://github.com/palatej/rjdhighfreq (accessed 7 June 2021).

Quenneville, B. and Findley, D.F. (2012). The timing and magnitude relationships between month-to-month changes and year-to-year changes that make comparing them difficult. *Taiwan Economic Forecast and Policy* 43 (1): 119–138.

Rodrigues, S., Moreira, A. and Saraiva, P. (2021). The creations of the fast and exceptional enterprise survey in COVID times. *UNECE, Conference of European Statisticians, Expert Meeting on Statistical Data Collection*, 27–30 September, 2021.

Rogers, N., Blackwell, L., Elliott, D., Large, A., Ridden, S., and Wu, M. (2021). Using statistical modelling to estimate UK international migration. Office for National Statistics. https://www.ons.gov.uk/methodology/methodologicalpublications/generalmethodology/onsworkingpaperseries/usingstatisticalmodellingtoestimateukinternationalmigration (accessed 5 July 2021).

SNA 2008 (2009). *System of National Accounts 2008*. New York: United Nations.

Snijkers, G. and Jones, J. (2013). Business survey communication. In: *Designing and Conducting Business Surveys* (ed. G. Snijkers, G. Haraldsen, J. Jones and D.K. Willimack), 359–430. Hoboken: Wiley.

Statistics Canada (2020a). Wholesale trade, March 2020. https://www150.statcan.gc.ca/n1/daily-quotidien/200520/dq200520b-eng.htm (accessed 15 July 2021).

Statistics Canada (2020b). Labor Force Survey, March 2020. https://www150.statcan.gc.ca/n1/daily-quotidien/200409/dq200409a-eng.htm (accessed 15 July 2021).

Statistics Canada (2021). Wholesale trade, February 2021. https://www150.statcan.gc.ca/n1/daily-quotidien/210416/dq210416a-eng.htm (accessed 15 July 2021).

Statistics New Zealand (2020). International Travel, March 2020. https://www.stats.govt.nz/information-releases/international-travel-march-2020 (accessed 16 July 2021).

Statistics Norway (2020). Seasonal adjustment during the Corona crisis – continuation in 2021. https://github.com/statisticsnorway/SeasonalAdjustmentCorona (accessed 20 July 2021).

The Treasury (2020). Commonwealth Treasury JobKeeper Payment overview. http://treasury.gov.au/coronavirus/jobkeeper (accessed 27 February 2021).

Trewin, D. (1999). Introduction of concurrent seasonal adjustment into the retail trade series. Australian Bureau of Statistics. https://www.ausstats.abs.gov.au/ausstats/free.nsf/0/0F728F17D917FDF5CA256ADA000631E0/$File/85140_1999.pdf.

TSAUG (2021). Statistical methods and tools for time series, seasonal adjustment and statistical disclosure control. *Time Series Analysis User Group report on the different approached used for the treatment of the COVID-19*.

UNECE (2021). Guide on producing CPI under lockdown. https://unece.org/sites/default/files/2021-06/Guide%20on%20producing%20CPI%20under%20lockdown_2021.05.14_0.pdf (accessed 10 June 2021).

US Census Bureau (2017). X-13ARIMA-SEATS. https://www.census.gov/srd/www/x13as/ (accessed 14 July 2021).

Whiting, J. and Zhang, M. (2021). Seasonal adjustment throughout periods of significant disruption and uncertainty. Australian Bureau of Statistics. https://www.abs.gov.au/statistics/research/seasonal-adjustment-throughout-periods-significant-disruption-and-uncertainty (accessed 2 June 2021).

Willimack, D.K. and Snijkers, G. (2013). The business context and its implications for the survey response process. In: *Designing and Conducting Business Surveys* (ed. G. Snijkers, G. Haraldsen, J. Jones and D.K. Willimack), 39–82. Hoboken: Wiley.

Wyman, D. (2010). Seasonal adjustment and identifying economic trends. Statistics Canada. http://www.statcan.gc.ca/pub/11-010-x/2010003/part-partie3-eng.htm (accessed 19 July 2021).

Section 3

Topics in the Use of Administrative Data

12

Methodology for the Use of Administrative Data in Business Statistics

Arnout van Delden[1] and Danni Lewis[2]

[1] *Statistics Netherlands, The Hague, The Netherlands*
[2] *Office for National Statistics, Newport, United Kingdom*

12.1   Introduction

Traditionally, official business statistics have been produced as single-source statistics based on surveys in which a coherent set of variables is observed. The advantage of this approach is that units, population, variables, and timing can be defined by the National Statistical Institute (NSI). Nowadays, a wide variety of sources other than surveys are available, such as public administrative data, data from business administrations, and big data sources. These new data sources offer the possibility to increase the information richness of the outputs, reduce data collection costs and response burden, increase output granularity, and achieve more up to date and more frequent outputs. Since these new sources were generally designed for purposes other than official statistics, their units, populations, variables, and frequencies often differ from those of the intended target population. The secondary use of these alternative data sources implies that specific methodology is needed that is aimed to yield "best," i.e. unbiased and accurate, population estimates.

Our focus is on administrative data, which we define as data collected by an organization external to the statistical office for administrative purposes, thus not targeted for use in official statistics (UNECE 2011). Administrative data can be used in different ways in the statistical production process, see de Waal et al. (2016) and Kloek and Vaju (2013). First of all, we distinguish direct from indirect use. With direct use, the values in the administrative data source are directly used for output estimates, while with indirect use, the data has an auxiliary role in the production process. Direct use can be further split up into the case where administrative data is used as the only data source, or the situation where it is combined with other sources (most often a survey). Forms of indirect use are the use of administrative data as a source to impute missing data, as a benchmark upon which survey data are calibrated, and as an external source to validate estimates. In the remainder of this chapter, we focus on the direct use of administrative data, although we also make some remarks about their indirect use. We will give examples of the use of administrative data in both single source and multisource statistics.

Administrative data is a relatively well defined and structured data source and is therefore an attractive secondary source for business statistics. Though, it is necessary to be cautious and not view administrative data as a panacea. It is easy for one to view administrative data as a perfect data source, covering the whole population and providing data from official administrative records that must surely be correct. If that would be the case, one could use the data to directly compute

Advances in Business Statistics, Methods and Data Collection. Edited by Ger Snijkers, Mojca Bavdaž, Stefan Bender, Jacqui Jones, Steve MacFeely, Joseph W. Sakshaug, Katherine J. Thompson, and Arnout van Delden.

the population parameter of interest; for instance, a total would be obtained by simply summing all the relevant micro data values. However, in practice, the estimation of a population parameter of interest is usually more complicated, due to one or more sources of error in the data set. In this chapter, we aim to highlight key areas to be aware of when using administrative data for business statistics.

As a starting point for those key areas, we have looked into the various error types that may occur in the primary production process when using administrative data as a secondary source. A systematic overview of those error types can be found in Brancato and Ascari (2019), Reid et al. (2017), and Zhang (2012) providing quality frameworks for administrative data, and Amaya et al. (2020), Japec et al. (2015), and National Academies of Sciences, Engineering, and Medicine (2017) describing quality frameworks for big data including administrative data. We grouped the errors that occur with secondary use of administrative data into four aims to achieve when using administrative data in official statistics: "link to a population frame," "from actual to target population," "from observed to targeted variables," and "from observed to targeted periods" (see the middle four rows in Figure 12.1). These four aims are to be achieved as part of the main "Process" step in the generic statistical business model (UNECE 2019).

Furthermore, Bakker and Daas (2012) and Hand (2018) describe some additional challenges when using administrative data for statistical output. We have grouped those issues into the aims "receive the data," "inspect the data," and "assess data quality" (see Figure 12.1). The first two aims need to be tackled before the data can actually be processed and are connected to good "provider management," see UNECE (2019, p. 6). The final aim needs to be tackled after the data has been processed and relates to the "Analyse" step in UNECE (2019).

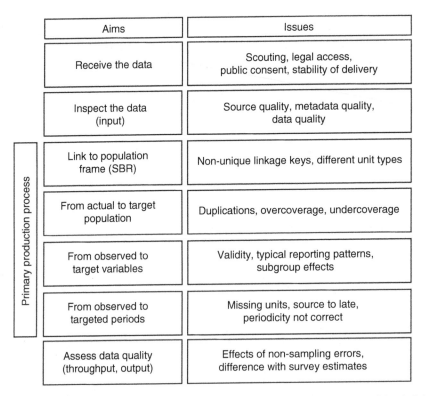

Aims	Issues
Receive the data	Scouting, legal access, public consent, stability of delivery
Inspect the data (input)	Source quality, metadata quality, data quality
Link to population frame (SBR)	Non-unique linkage keys, different unit types
From actual to target population	Duplications, overcoverage, undercoverage
From observed to target variables	Validity, typical reporting patterns, subgroup effects
From observed to targeted periods	Missing units, source to late, periodicity not correct
Assess data quality (throughput, output)	Effects of non-sampling errors, difference with survey estimates

(Rows "Link to population frame (SBR)" through "From observed to targeted periods" are bracketed as "Primary production process")

Figure 12.1 Overview of aims to achieve when producing official statistics with administrative data and some typical issues associated with those aims.

The remainder of this chapter summarizes the current state-of-the-art methods for dealing with these issues. Section 12.2 describes the steps that are essential to enable access and delivery of administrative data. The following sections discuss methodologies relating to receiving the data (Section 12.2), inspecting the data (Section 12.3), data linkage (Section 12.4), moving from actual to target population (Section 12.5), moving from observed to target variables (Section 12.6), moving from observed to targeted periods (Section 12.7), and assessing data quality (Section 12.8). Section 12.9 discusses unsolved issues and Section 12.10 concludes the chapter.

12.2 Receive the Data

A number of elements are essential to enable access to and delivery of administrative data:

- *Data scouting*: It is useful to actively search for potentially useful administrative data sources. This could be online or by regular contact with data owners, such as government organizations or commercial vendors.
- *Legal access to data*: A crucial element for an NSI to use administrative sources is legislation covering legal access to the data and guaranteeing provision of that data. It's important that the variables included allow for linking to other datasets. Železnik Gorjan and Božič Verbič (2019) and Şahinler et al. (2019) report that data holders are often initially hesitant to deliver administrative data because they want to avoid releasing personal data or breaking the General Data Protection Regulation law.
- *Public consent*: The general public should have trust in the NSI that privacy is assured in any administrative data they are using, and that the NSI is allowed to link data sources. For example, ensuring that the NSI does not report outlying values to agencies responsible for identifying fraud. In some countries, legal regulations require explicit consent from business respondents before their survey data can be linked to administrative data (Sakshaug and Vicari 2018). For other NSIs, for instance at Statistics Netherlands (in Dutch: Centraal Bureau voor de Statistiek, CBS), the data linkage is separately regulated in a special national legislation and informed consent is not necessary. Still, CBS needs to inform the users when sending them a questionnaire and when publishing output that their survey data can be combined with other data.
- *Stability of delivery*: Stable and timely delivery of the administrative data is needed to guarantee timely publication of official statistics. The NSI should be informed immediately by the data holder about any event that may hinder a correct data delivery, such as network problems, erroneous data processing, or cessation of the administrative data source; see for instance van Delden et al. (2011). A risk analysis should be completed, and mitigations are needed for important statistical outputs that rely on external data sources.
- *Relation with data suppliers*: The NSI should invest in their contacts with the data holder (GSS 2014), for instance by appointing contact persons at the NSI and ask the same from the data holding organization. It is a good practice to have regular meetings between both parties to discuss quality issues and changes in the data source. Most data holders appreciate it when quality issues that are found are reported back to them, that way they know that the NSI aims to make best use of their data.

For administrative datasets that are fundamental for statistical outputs, it is useful for someone from the NSI to work regularly at the data holder's office, to enable informal exchange of experiences about the data. The core purpose of contact management is to *prevent* the occurrence of errors rather than to correct them.

12.3 Inspect the Data

When a new administrative data source is first received, it is important to assess its fitness for purpose – is the data source suitable for producing statistical outputs and does it meet the quality required by users. Since data are often used in combination with other sources and for multiple purposes, it may not be possible to completely define the intended output beforehand.

Following Karr et al. (2006) and Daas et al. (2009), three (hyper)dimensions can be used to judge whether the source is fit for purpose: source, metadata, and data. The source dimension captures the data supplier information, source relevance, data confidentiality issues, and security of data delivery. The metadata dimension judges clarity of the metadata accompanying the data source, the comparability between the metadata of the administrative data relative to those of the intended output, the presence of unique identifiers, and data storage and data manipulations by the data source holder. For instance, the metadata may clarify whether the data holder stores dumps of the full data set or stores updates. Daas et al. (2009) developed checklists for the source and metadata dimensions.

The data dimension concerns the data units and measurements. Numerous frameworks that judge the data quality of an administrative source have been developed (see Reinert and Stoltze 2014 and references therein). Additionally, various general data quality frameworks are available; examples are frameworks from the Australian Bureau of Statistics (ABS 2009), Statistics New Zealand (Reid et al. 2017), and Statistics Canada (2002). Data quality of administrative sources is on the one hand determined by the difference between what the data intends to capture (the original purpose) versus its realization; and on the other hand, by the difference between its original versus its secondary purpose. Understanding the interests of the data holder with the data at hand sheds light on the relative quality within an administrative data source: subpopulations and variables that are of higher priority to the data holder tend to be of higher quality than those supplemented to the data source on request of an NSI.

In order to get more insight into the usefulness of the data in a new administrative data source, the ESSnet on the use of administrative and accounts data in business statistics (Verschaeren et al. 2013) mentions three types of exploratory methods:

- data profiling methods to check admissible ranges of variables, missing data, and extreme values;
- data mining methods, also referred to as unsupervised machine learning, which are used to find typical reporting patterns in the data (see Section 6.2). Most of these methods use clustering techniques;
- visualization methods that can be used to investigate the data distributions and data patterns. Examples of such methods are the table plot and the heat map.

12.4 Link to Population Frame

If the values in the administrative data source are directly used for output estimates, one of the first processing steps is usually its linkage to a population frame. With linkage, we mean that records in the administrative data set are matched with records in the population frame. In business statistics, it is common to have a frame with an enumeration of statistical units, further referred to as a statistical business register (SBR), see for instance UNECE (2015) for international guidelines on SBRs. An SBR offers the opportunity to investigate coverage problems with administrative data (see Section 12.5). Besides the statistical units, an SBR usually also contains a few background variables of those statistical units, such as number of employees and economic activity. The presence of an SBR is a means to coordinate and standardize outputs of business statistics, within one country and to ameliorate comparability of business statistics over different countries. The statistical units are often composites of legal units, and those relations are also maintained in the SBR. In practice, besides the legal and statistical units, also various other administrative unit types may occur in data sets with economic data, which complicates their linkage to the SBR (van Delden et al. 2018). In countries where an SBR is not available and in countries where relations between statistical unit types and administrative unit types are not in the SBR or elsewhere (see e.g. UNSD 2014), it is very hard to be certain about the coverage of the administrative data.

One practical constraint to linking can occur when the administrative data owner is only willing or able to provide hashed data. This provides major complications for linking data at the unit level – it may be necessary to accept a lower-quality linkage or possibly find a trusted third party to do the linking. In the remainder of this section, we will first provide an overview of basic linkage methods (Section 4.1) followed by some methods to deal with linkage of administrative data to the SBR when the unit types in the administrative data differ from the statistical units (Section 4.2). The linkage errors that may occur during the linkage process may result in biased estimates when left uncorrected (Sakshaug and Antoni 2017). The evaluation of the quality of linkages and methods to correct for them are treated by Larsen and Herning (2023: Chapter 33 in this volume).

12.4.1 Basic Linkage Methods

Most countries provide unique identification numbers for legal units. These numbers are required for legal issues such as tax payments. The presence of these unique identification numbers in principle accommodates the use of deterministic linkage. Unfortunately, not all data sets will contain those identification numbers. Some data sets may contain only nonunique information such as legal or trade name, address, and postal codes. For example, Andics et al. (2019) had to link administrative data on shops (establishments) to their SBR, on the basis of address information. First of all, linkage of two data sets on characteristics such as name and address usually implies that the spelling needs to be harmonized. Second, the linkage is not unique, so it is helpful to estimate a probability of correct linkage. In such a case, probabilistic record linkage methods can be used (see, e.g. Fellegi and Sunter 1969; Larsen and Herning, 2023: Chapter 33 in this volume). In probabilistic record linkage, the level of agreement between nonunique identifiers of each pair of records in two data sets is determined. This agreement is used to estimate the ratio of the probability that the pair is a match to the probability that the pair is not a match. When this ratio is above a specific upper threshold, it is assumed that the pair is a true match, below a lower threshold signifies no match, and in between, manual inspection is needed. The estimation of these probabilities can be improved by manually inspecting a number of candidate pairs followed by supervised machine-learning (see, e.g. Christen 2012). Finally, we mention that some data sets may be linked by using geographical location as the linkage key (see, for instance Šuštar and Eremita 2021).

12.4.2 Linkage of Data Sets in the Presence of Different Unit Types

In practice, administrative business data may contain unit types that differ from the statistical units that are used to compile official statistics. What is minimally necessary in this situation, is to know the relations between administrative unit types, such as tax units, and the statistical units that are derived from them. These kinds of relations are often contained within the SBR. More specifically, one could just extract the set of relations between different unit types and store these as a separate spine that can be used to link data sets (see Ryan et al. 2020).

Perko (2019) describes the situation of building a population register with tourist accommodation establishments. Perko uses an administrative data set in which the main focus was the accommodation *provider* and developed an algorithm that recognizes the difference between a unit in the administrative data source and statistical unit in the targeted Statistical Register. Dima and Clipcea (2019) tried to link administrative data in agricultural statistics to a farm register, both containing agricultural holdings. Although the definition of an agricultural holding was the same in both data sets, a holding in the farm register could sometimes be linked to multiple holdings in the administrative data, and their relation was not entirely clear.

Another situation that might occur is that the unit types in administrative business data are a composite of the targeted statistical unit. Two approaches are used to handle this situation. The first approach is to estimate a model that relates the target variable to one or more auxiliary variables that are available for the statistical units (Enderer 2008; Jang 2016; Lewis and Woods 2013). For example, Lewis and Woods (2013) apportioned value added tax (VAT) data based on the proportion of employees belonging to each statistical unit. The second approach is to use the administrative data only for those statistical units where the administrative units have a one-to-one or many-to-one relation with the statistical units, and use survey data otherwise (Chen et al. 2016; van Delden 2010).

12.5 From Actual to Target Population

Since administrative data sources are collected for purposes different to statistical uses, it is natural that they tend not to cover the exact population of interest for business statistics. This means that just using the available records for a target population estimate may lead to bias. It is useful to consider the representativity of the administrative data. Lothian et al. (2019) suggest understanding representativity issues by creating well-maintained registers and using them to measure and adjust for coverage errors in less-representative administrative data sources. This could be done using calibration or Bayesian priors.

There may be units that are in administrative data populations, which are not required for statistics (overcoverage). A bigger concern are the businesses that are in the statistics population but not available in the administrative data (undercoverage). This could either be due to those businesses not being in scope of the administrative source or because they are reported to that source with less frequency than we require for statistical outputs.

Figure 12.2, from Lewis and Woods (2013), shows the coverage situation for a particular administrative source.

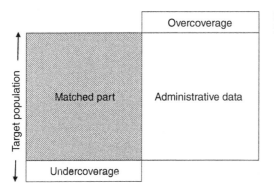

Figure 12.2 Coverage of administrative data. Source: Lewis and Woods (2013).

For overcoverage, the challenge here is to identify the units that are out of scope for statistics. Assuming this is straightforward to do, we can then remove those ineligible units from the datasets. There could also be duplication or different versions of the same record. In this case, it is necessary to identify and remove the duplicates. Where there are different values, we will need a rule to determine which one to retain – for example the most recent. Information from the data provider should help in understanding which version is likely to be most suitable.

For undercoverage, we could decide to employ a mixed approach, using administrative data where it is available and survey data to cover the rest of the population. If a full microdata set is required, we could consider imputation for businesses not available – but given their likely different characteristics, this is not expected to produce good results in most circumstances. Moreover, when there are multiple target variables, it is very difficult to develop an imputation model that maintains all relations between those target variables. If only aggregate level outputs are required, we may aim to address this problem in the estimation of the targeted parameters.

12.5.1 Estimation Methods to Adjust for Undercoverage

We treat two types of estimation methods here. If besides the administrative data, also a sample with known inclusion probabilities of the population is available, one may try to use that sample to correct for selectivity by estimating pseudo weights. That approach is treated by van Delden et al. (Chapter 34 in this volume) on multisource statistics. Alternatively, when auxiliary variables are available for the whole target population that correlate with the variable of interest, and these auxiliary variables are also available for the administrative data, then these could be used to compute a correction. Examples of such variables are the number of employees, the number of legal units, and economic activity that are available in an SBR. By linking the administrative data to the SBR, one can simply add those auxiliary variables to the administrative data. In practice, the choice between using administrative data complemented with survey data (the mixed approach) or using estimation methods will depend on which parts of the statistical population have good coverage in the administrative data and on the costs of surveying and the estimated accuracy of the different options.

We will now further explain the estimation methods using auxiliary variables. The simple ratio adjustment for estimating the administrative data part of the population is given in Särndal et al. (1992)

$$\hat{Y}_c = X_c \frac{\hat{Y}_m}{\hat{X}_m}$$

where X_c is the total of the auxiliary variable, $\hat{X}_m$ is an estimate of the total of the auxiliary variable in the part of the target population for which we have administrative data, and $\hat{Y}_m$ is an estimate of the target variable in that part of the target population for which we have administrative data.

As the name suggests, the simple ratio adjustment method is based on an implied ratio model. It may be possible to make better use of available auxiliary variables by using unit-level linear regression models. A logarithmic transformation may be needed to deal with the positively skewed nature of many typical economic variables. In these cases, the model can only be fitted to businesses with positive values because zero is undefined on the log scale. If there are any zero values in the data, a logistic regression can be fitted initially to predict the probability of a zero value. These probabilities are then multiplied by the predictions from the linear model. A back transformation must be applied to return the predictions to the original scale. For some variables, it may be necessary to use robust linear regression methods to deal with outliers in the data.

12.5.2 Temporary Coverage Issues

Apart from under- and overcoverage of parts of the population, some of the administrative data sets are gradually completed over time, thus causing temporary coverage issues. For this situation, Ouwehand and Schouten (2014) consider representativeness indicators, or R-indicators, looking at the representativeness of available data. The R-indicators have originally been developed in the context of survey sampling, but Ouwehand and Schouten (2014) apply them to administrative data. In a survey context, the indicators are based on the estimated variation in the probability to respond for different groups in the population; these probabilities are referred to as response propensities. In the context of administrative data units "report" the data rather than "respond" to survey questions, the computation of the R-indicator follows the same formulae. According to Schouten et al. (2009), the set of units that have reported their values are defined as being representative when "response" propensities are equal for all population units. The R-indicator ranges between 0 (fully nonrepresentative) and 1 (fully representative). Ouwehand and Schouten (2014) investigated R-indicators with VAT data and found that even when the reporting rate was relatively low, the R-indicator could still be quite high. The set of data that is available at a certain moment in a big data source is referred to in Meng (2018) and other literature as being a nonprobability sample. Some more information on estimating and correcting for selectivity in the case of a nonprobability sample can be found in van Delden, Scholtus, and de Waal (Chapter 34 in this volume).

12.6 From Observed to Targeted Variables

We define an error on the measurement side as the difference between the obtained value for a variable in the source and the true value according to the targeted concept. This difference is due to validity error, measurement error (in the obtained value), and data processing error. Validity error is the difference in the value of the variable measured according to the definition of the variable of interest versus and the definition of the administrative variable. This error can be mitigated or corrected by harmonization methods. The measurement error is the difference between the hypothetical "true" value of the administrative variable and the captured value. Processing errors concern the difference between the captured values and the final values.

12.6.1 Harmonization Methods

Even perfectly accurate data values may be useless for certain intended outputs (Hand 2018), due to differences between the variable definitions in the administrative data and the statistical population of interest. It is therefore important to carefully look into those differences in definitions. In some situations, the variable of interest can be obtained directly by adding up (or subtracting) values of variables from the administrative source.

If the variable of interest has already been measured in another source, for example in a survey, then it is worthwhile to link the two sources at the microlevel and investigate to what extent the actual recorded values agree with each other. For such a situation, van Delden et al. (2016) used a harmonization approach that distinguishes among different domains for which the data are published. They applied their method to the estimation of yearly turnover by industry. They divided the industries into four groups based on the analysis of the definitions and by applying a robust linear regression analysis. A "Control" group which consists of industries without any differences in constructs and an "Accept" group which consists of industries with conceptual differences but with small numerical differences. For those two groups, no harmonization step is needed. Further, there is a "Reject" group that consists of industries with conceptual differences and substantial nonsystematic numerical differences; for those industries, the administrative data source cannot be used. The fourth group "Adjust" consists of industries with conceptual differences and substantial systematic numerical differences: those are the industries which can be corrected (harmonized). The results of the correction factors for 2012 data based on the methods in van Delden et al. (2016) are shown in Table 12.1. The approach is similar to Lewis and Woods (2013) who use a ratio to correct for differences between the turnover definition of administrative data and the turnover variable of interest. Also, Rudys (2019) uses a linear relation between survey and VAT turnover, but in their case, it is used for small area estimation.

An alternative approach is to derive a correction factor which accounts for measurement errors in both data sources. This can be done using latent variable models. In the case of classification variables, latent class models can be used, in the case of numerical variables, one can use structural equation models. Latent variable models describe the relationship between a true, latent variable, and a number of observations which are referred to as indicators. In a latent variable model, all sources are considered to contain errors. A gold standard set can be included in the model, for instance based on a small subsample of either source used that is edited thoroughly, which should then coincide with the latent variable. Scholtus et al. (2015) has applied this methodology to exactly the same 2012 data set as was used in Table 12.1; results are shown in Table 12.2. One can see that the standard errors are larger when both sources are allowed to contain errors. The slopes of the regression analyses are sometimes different from those obtained by the robust regression, see also the results in Scholtus et al. (2015).

Sometimes the population of units consists of subgroups that show different behavior in the administrative data compared to the population of interest. For such a situation, one can use finite mixture models, see Di Zio and Guarnera (2013). With a mixture model, one can describe different

Table 12.1 Intercept and slope of a correction formula for VAT turnover in four car trade industries (NACE codes) estimated by robust regression (with standard errors).

Parameter	45112		45190		45200		45400	
	Estim.	s.e.	Estim.	s.e.	Estim.	s.e.	Estim.	s.e.
Intercept	0.01	0.00	−0.00	0.00	0.00	0.00	0.00	0.00
Slope	1.27	0.01	1.06	0.01	0.97	0.01	1.17	0.04
R^2	0.98		0.97		0.99		0.96	

Source: Scholtus et al. (2015).

Table 12.2 Intercept and slope of a correction formula for VAT turnover in four car trade industries (NACE codes) estimated by a structural equation model (with standard errors).

Parameter	45112		45190		45200		45400	
	Estim.	s.e.	Estim.	s.e.	Estim.	s.e.	Estim.	s.e.
Intercept	0.11	0.05	0.07	0.06	0.04	0.06	0.01	0.03
Slope	1.22	0.02	1.07	0.04	0.76	0.12	1.18	0.06

Source: Scholtus et al. (2015).

error patterns/structures and model the probability that a unit belongs to a group. Using a mixture model approach, van Delden et al. (2020) found that the relation between quarterly survey and administrative turnover within an economic sector differed for groups within the population, this is further treated in Section 8.3. Mixture models can sometimes also be useful to achieve a better understanding of the data. For instance, Hand and Blunt (2001) modeled the distribution of size of credit card purchases at petrol stations in the United Kingdom (UK) as a mixture of subpopulations. They found that some people always fill the tank at each purchase, while others aimed to achieve round numbers such as £20 and £30.

12.6.2   Editing Methods for Measurement Errors

Measurement errors in individual records of administrative data typically occur with variables that are of less importance to the register holder. There are a number of typical measurement error types in administrative data. Examples of such error types are summarized in Table 12.3 and based upon Hoogland (2016), Lewis and Woods (2013), McLennan (2018), Țîru et al. (2019), and the experience of the authors.

Editing of administrative data is most efficiently done with a sequence of deductive editing, macroediting, and selective editing. Deductive editing concerns the application of rule-based methods to automatically detect and correct common errors. These rules use the sequence of values over time, similar entities within the same data set, or background variables such as industry code and size class. For instance, to detect systematic unit errors, one may use a rule that checks whether the ratio of the current value to a previous value is outside a lower and upper threshold value (Lewis and Woods 2013; Țîru et al. 2019). Examples of rules to detect entities that report values that refer to the wrong period can be found in Hoogland (2016). A large proportion of errors typically come

Table 12.3   Typical error types in administrative data.

Error type	Explanation
Zero errors	A value of 0 is filled in rather than the true value. This may especially occur when the variable is not important for the register holder or when it has no consequence for the reporter.
Systematic unit error	The value differs by a factor of 100 or 1000 from the true value.
Values referring to the wrong period	For instance: the value refers to a monthly period according to the definition, but a four-week value is reported.
Reporting patterns	For instance: identical monthly values are reported from January till November and a large balancing value is reported in December.
Values referring to the wrong unit	The set of units to which the reported value refers differs from the units that are registered in the data set. This may for instance occur in tax data, which can be due to time delays in the registration of the business structure.
Errors by applying an administrative rule wrongly	For some administrative data many rules apply and they may be applied wrongly. For instance: turnover should be reported including the part with 0% taxes, but the latter part may be omitted.
Random errors	For instance: a typing error made by a reporter who fills in data for the register manually.

Table 12.4 Analysis of measurement errors (% of units) in VAT data for monthly (M) and quarterly (Q) reporters.

| Year | Monthly reporters (M) | | | Quarterly reporters (Q) | | |
| | Systematic unit errors (avg.) | Random errors (avg.) | | Reporting patterns | | |
		Quartile distances	Previous periods	Equal values[a]	One zero[b]	Other[c]
2015	0.01	0.25		10.54	3.32	4.44
2016	0.03	0.25	0.25	10.86	3.81	4.43
2017	0.02	0.25	0.25	11.25	4.32	4.84
2018	0.02	0.25	0.33	12.03	3.56	4.59

a) The value for all quarters within a year is identical.
b) For one of the quarter, the value is zero.
c) Other systematic patterns: three quarters have an identical value whereas one value differs, one of the quarterly values is negative, all quarterly values are zero except one.
Source: Țîru et al. (2019).

from a small number of error types (Hand 2018) so that relatively little effort will lead to substantial initial improvement in overall quality. An example of a measurement error analysis of VAT is given in Țîru et al. (2019). For entities that report on a monthly basis, they analyzed "systematic unit errors" and "random errors" (Table 12.4). Systematic unit errors within monthly reporters were found in 0.01–0.03% of the units, random errors based on quantiles in 0.25% of the units, and random errors based on historical data of the same unit in 0.25–0.33% of the units. For units reporting on a quarterly basis, units with "reporting patterns" were counted. A large proportion of those units, 10–12%, report the same value all quarters of a year, 3–4% report one quarterly value that is zero, and 4–5% have another quarterly pattern. Detected measurement errors are replaced by corrected values using imputation methods, for instance ratio imputation.

After all, commonly occurring errors are removed automatically, and macroediting can be applied. This concerns the analysis of time series of domain estimates, distributional characteristics, and quality indicators for domains. When the estimate of a domain is considered to be suspicious, this domain is inspected further by means of selective editing. Selective editing concerns the use of quality indicators within a domain and use of score functions that aim to filter influential records. After selection, these records are edited manually. An overview of the literature on indicators for macro- and selective editing administrative data can be found in Goorden and Hoogland (2020) with a focus on short-term statistics. Manual editing can also be used to correct processing errors, such as erroneous imputations.

12.6.3 Correcting for Bias Due to Decentralized and Autonomous Organizations

A specific situation occurs when an administrative source is filled by several decentralized, autonomous organizations. For instance, institutes, municipalities, or regions within a country (Feuerhake 2007; National Academies of Sciences, Engineering, and Medicine 2017) collect administrative data on a certain topic, which are thereafter combined into a national administrative data set. Each of those decentralized organizations can have their own local systems, with different interpretations and different local administrative reporting behavior (McLennan 2018).

For instance, in the Netherlands, hospitals have different reporting behavior in reporting comorbidities, which may lead to biased estimates of the Harmonized Standardized Mortality

Rates. van Delden et al. (2018) developed an automatic procedure to detect which decentralized data suppliers are likely to have shifts in reporting behavior. Manzi et al. (2011) describes a situation in which estimates are based on combinations of surveys from multiple regions. They use a hierarchical Bayesian model in which the bias per survey (organization) is explicitly modeled. Their method requires that one (unbiased) benchmark level estimate is available, which is similar to van Delden et al. (2018) who use reference groups.

12.7 From Observed to Targeted Periods

For short-term statistical outputs in particular, administrative data may not always be available quickly enough to feed into publications. Another time-related issue arises when the administrative data are available in a different periodicity to that required – for example quarterly rather than monthly. For both cases, it is necessary to use estimation or time-series techniques to be able to produce statistical outputs.

12.7.1 Estimation Methods When Data Are Not Available on Time

We can consider two separate cases. In the first case, it may be that a large proportion of the administrative data is available on time, but a small portion is not. In this case, imputation can be used to fill the gaps. As the proportion of unavailable data increases, this ceases to be a sensible strategy. In Maasing et al. (2013), it was observed that having 80% of data being available would be an appropriate threshold. Where there is less than 80%, it is necessary to use aggregate estimation or time-series methods.

When imputation can be used, the aim is to ideally take advantage of both data from similar businesses that are present in the administrative data, and previous period information for those businesses which are not yet available. In this case, we can use the classic ratio imputation, where missing value y_i^t for unit i in period t is imputed by multiplying the previous period value by the average growth in the imputation class h between the current and previous periods:

$$y_i^t = \left(\frac{\sum_{j \in h} y_j^t}{\sum_{j \in h} y_j^{t-1}} \right) y_i^{t-1}$$

The imputation class is a grouping of businesses with similar characteristics, often defined according to industry and size. For the case of highly seasonal data, the method may work better using growths from the period 12 months before, rather than from the month before. When there is no previous value available, it will be necessary to use an alternative method, such as a trimmed mean or median value from within a well-defined imputation class.

In the second case, when limited administrative data are available, we need to consider aggregate level estimation methods. Here we consider three specific examples.

12.7.1.1 Benchmarking

Benchmarking is a method for combining a series of high-frequency data with a series of less frequent data to create a consistent time series. The series of less frequent data is used to benchmark the high-frequency series. Benchmarking aims to preserve the movements in the high-frequency series, while keeping consistency with the less-frequent data.

Benchmarking may be used to improve the quality of monthly estimates derived from incomplete administrative data, using quarterly estimates derived from almost complete data. In order to apply this in real time, we need to apply a benchmark forecast. This relies on the adjustments between the monthly and quarterly series being fairly limited and consistent. We then calculate the benchmark forecast total, denoted by $\widehat{Y}^m$ for month m, based on a factor C_1 which summarizes the previous period adjustments, and the incomplete total for month m based on available data, denoted by $\widetilde{Y}^m$:

$$\widehat{Y}^m = \widetilde{Y}^m C_1$$

There are various methods for calculating C_1. One simple option is to calculate mean adjustments from a set number of previous periods. For more complex methods see Fortier and Quenneville (2007) and Brown (2012). Vlag et al. (2013) found that the choice of method is less important than ensuring the conditions for using benchmarking are met. It is necessary that the quarterly series is of good quality and not affected by level shifts.

12.7.1.2 Forecasting from Previous Complete Data

Another option to deal with incomplete administrative data is to use time series methods to forecast from previous complete data. A range of methods were evaluated in Parkin (2010) and Parkin and Brown (2012):

- *Simple forecast*: applying the growth between the last two periods to the last level.
- *Holt–Winters*: fitting a model with seasonal factors and either a linear or a quadratic trend.
- *Univariate ARIMA*: fitting a standard ARIMA forecasting model.
- *Singular spectrum analysis (SSA)*: a method which attempts to uncover the structure of a process that generated a time series by decomposing it into a set of components. Some of these components are then combined to construct a representative time series. The idea is to choose a representative series that contains the essential behavior of the original series, but with less noise or irregularity. The representative series is then used to forecast monthly turnover.

In Parkin and Brown (2012), the Holt–Winters method showed the most promising results. In general, more complex forecasting methods were not found to offer any improvement over the classic Holt–Winters approach.

12.7.1.3 Estimation Techniques

Rather than using specific time series forecasting or benchmarking techniques, we can consider simpler estimation methods based on historic data. We might seek to maintain a fully enumerated survey of the largest businesses due to their overwhelming influence on the accuracy of economic outputs. The goal is then to use estimation techniques for small and medium businesses, based on either historic or forecast administrative data. In Broad (2012) the following estimator is proposed in the context of estimating monthly turnover utilizing VAT data:

$$\widehat{Y}^t = \widehat{Y}^t_{\text{SURV}} + R \times \widehat{Y}^{t-a}_{\text{VAT}}$$

where $\widehat{Y}^t$ is the monthly estimate at time t, $\widehat{Y}^t_{\text{SURV}}$ is the survey estimate for large businesses, R is a ratio adjustment, and $\widehat{Y}^{t-a}_{\text{VAT}}$ is the VAT Turnover value from small and medium businesses at a number of months a before time t. The following three types of method were tested:

- The simple case of adding (forecast or mature) VAT data for small and medium businesses to the sampled large businesses ($R = 1$).

- Modeling VAT turnover data for small and medium businesses using the relationship between VAT and survey data for large businesses (R is based on the ratio of survey to VAT data for large businesses).
- Maintaining a small survey of small and medium businesses and using the relationship between VAT and survey data for those businesses to model the rest (R is based on the ratio of survey to VAT data based on the sampled small and medium businesses).

The performance of the methods was largely determined by the quality of the VAT data and relationship between businesses being used to fit the model. For more details, see Broad (2012).

12.7.2 Estimation Methods to Adjust for Periodicity

In some cases, administrative data are not available in the periodicity required for short-term statistics. A common example is VAT turnover data, which for some countries may largely be available on a quarterly rather than monthly basis. Lewis and Woods (2013) discuss the complex system of staggers in the UK VAT data, whereby VAT data are not only quarterly for the vast majority of businesses but also that a quarter could start in any month.

This makes it difficult to make direct use of the administrative data for monthly statistics. One possible solution is the cubic spline – a polynomial is fitted to the quarterly data and the monthly points in between can then be derived. The method can provide reasonable results, although it is important to check that the fitted line behaves within the feasible range of the variable of interest. For example, to ensure that it does not produce negative values for positive valued variables.

Parkin (2010) compares the cubic spline method to a simple base method of dividing quarterly values by three. The cubic spline was implemented using the expand procedure in SAS, which calculates the spline so that its integral over a quarter is equal to the total turnover in that quarter. The surprising result was that the cubic spline offered no significant improvement over the simpler method. Labonne and Weale (2018) investigate state space models to address the same problem. They find that the state space model approach works well as long as the VAT data are clean.

12.8 Assess Data Quality

12.8.1 Throughput Quality

In Sections 12.4–12.7, we have described how to deal with linkage, coverage, measurement, and time-related issues. We described treated methods and processes aimed at improving the quality of the final output. Throughput quality concerns the amount of processing errors that are made during these steps. In most cases, the errors that are made in a processing step can be evaluated with a small audit sample in which the results of a step are checked carefully. For instance, a small audit sample for linkage errors is used to check which linkages are correct or not, or an audit sample is taken to check for errors in automatic editing. The outcomes of the audit samples are subsequently used to try to improve the processes, for instance information on linkage errors might be used to correct estimators for bias due to linkage error. Of course, these correction steps themselves are likely to be imperfect and have their own errors. Information about the accuracy of correction methods is usually only evaluated during the design of such a method and not regularly checked during each production cycle.

There are some processing steps whose quality can be evaluated at each production cycle. For instance, one could measure the fraction of automatic imputations that have been adjusted in manual editing. Also, the difference between early and later estimates (when imputed values are replaced by observations) is a measure of the imputation errors that are made.

12.8.2 Output Quality

Output quality in the broad sense is determined by different dimensions. Following Eurostat terminology, it concerns relevance, accuracy and reliability, timeliness and punctuality, coherence and comparability, accessibility and clarity. So far, we have described various error types and methods to correct for them.

As part of the ESSnet on Quality of multisource statistics (KOMUSO), Brancato and Ascari (2019) described the relation between error types and output quality dimensions, Figure 12.3. Validity error denotes the difference between the variable definition in the administrative source and the definition of the target variable. Validity error influences output relevance. Accuracy and reliability are influenced by errors on the representation side: frame and source errors (under- and overcoverage and duplicates), by errors on the measurement side (measurement error, missingness, and

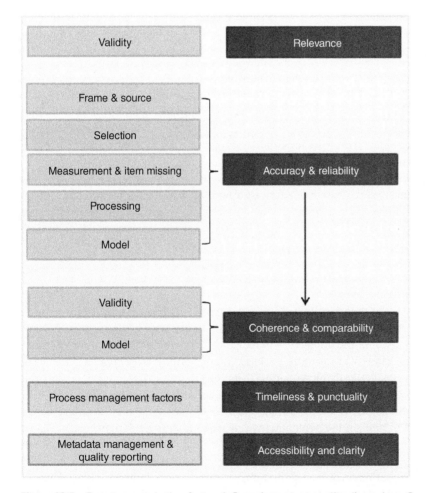

Figure 12.3 Error types and other factors influencing output quality dimensions. Source: Based on Brancato and Ascari (2019).

processing error), and by model assumption errors (when models are used). Coherence refers to the similarity between different input data sources that relate to the same variable. Comparability refers to the use of the same methods and sources for different domains. Not only timeliness and punctuality are determined by the steps to process the data source, but also sometimes model-based estimates are used when there are many missing values. Finally, accessibility and clarity are aided by having documentation that describes the metadata (population, unit, and variable definitions) and reporting of the quality.

The ESSnet KOMUSO gave some quantitative measures for accuracy, coherence, relevance, and timeliness that refer to both sampling and nonsampling errors (de Waal et al. 2019). Part of that work is also useful for administrative data. Under certain conditions and for some error types, measures for bias and variance can be given. A general framework to estimate accuracy has been proposed by Meng (2018) for representation errors followed by Biemer and Amaya (2018) for representation and measurement errors. The question remains how the components of the formulas that they propose can be estimated.

In addition to this, de Waal et al. (2021) give an overview of methods to compute output quality. They vary from semiquantitative general quality frameworks to numerical methods (bootstrap techniques) and analytical formulae.

12.8.3 Analysis of Differences Between Survey and Administrative Data Estimates

When analyzing or implementing estimates based on administrative data for the first time, one may be confronted with (significant) differences between the estimates produced by the administrative data and those that would have resulted from using the existing survey approach. Understanding the causes of those differences can help determine whether it is acceptable to replace the survey with administrative data and also provides important information to users of the statistics in understanding any discontinuity.

Also of interest is when an NSI publishes two series of data: a high-frequency series based on a survey and a low-frequency series based on administrative data or the other way around. In that situation one might be interested to investigate whether there are systematic differences between the two sources and what are the causes thereof. In that case, one can decompose the differences between the two outputs into its components: population differences, response differences, imputation differences, and so on. Groen (2012) provides an example of how this can be achieved. van Bemmel (2018) has extended this approach. This approach can be a good means to discover which error types affect each of the estimates.

van Delden et al. (2020) analyzed why there were systematic differences in quarterly turnover from monthly survey data (high-frequency series) compared to quarterly turnover from VAT, the lower-frequency series, because the differences hindered benchmarking survey to the VAT data. The problem was that quarterly VAT turnover was larger than quarterly survey turnover in the last quarter of the year, and smaller in the first quarter. The problem was analyzed for four economic sectors (manufacturing, retail trade, construction, and job placement) and for the years 2014–2016. They used a mixture model, in which the population was allowed to be divided into different groups, where each set of units in the population was allowed to have a different linear relation between survey data (response variable) and VAT data. They found the data for job placement was described best by a population with six groups (Figure 12.4). For 2016, group 1 (4.8% of the units) consisted of enterprises that reported nearly the same turnover values in both sources. Group 2 (0.0% of the units) consisted of enterprises that erroneously included a VAT rate into their reported turnover. Group 3 (14.7% of the units) concerned enterprises with a larger variance than group

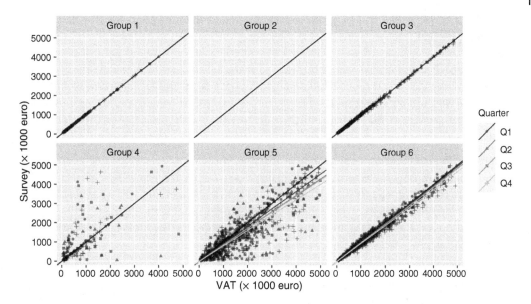

Figure 12.4 Six groups fitted for Job placement in 2016. Source: van Delden et al. (2020).

1 but have the same slope. Group 4 (6.9% of the units) were enterprises with very large outliers. Groups 5 (34.0% of the units) and 6 (39.6% of the units) were sets of enterprises with quarterly effects. The quarterly effects in group 5 were larger than in group 6, their slopes in quarters 2–4 are smaller while the variance is larger.

When the estimated quarterly linear relations between survey and VAT data of the different groups were combined, van Delden et al. (2020) indeed found that the overall quarterly slope between survey and VAT data was smaller in the fourth quarter than in the first quarter.

In the analysis above, van Delden et al. (2020) just compared the relationship between the values in the two sources. They did not make an assumption beforehand that one of the sources is correct, because any difference between estimates produced by administrative and survey data does not necessarily imply that one source is better than the other, or that there isn't value in both sources. Hand (2018) comments that it is important to realize that economic measures, such as gross domestic product, can be measured in different ways. The estimates from different administrative data could be equally valid, even if they disagree. Insight is needed into the quality and representativity of those estimates. Hand (2018) suggests that an important question to ask is whether the new estimates have changed the underlying message.

12.9 Unsolved Issues

The field of statistics concerning the use of administrative data for economic outputs is still in development. In this section, we outline some of the key unsolved and challenging issues.

- *Using and accessing data*: A key step in using administrative data is having ongoing availability of the data and a system to store and process it. In practice, there can often be a lag between agreeing to switch from survey to administrative data and creating the necessary IT systems. This is why it is important to not stop the survey before the IT system is built and functions properly. Longer term, once the survey has been stopped, it is possible that the administrative source may cease to exist, for example due to a change in legislation. Good communication with the data owner can help here, but it is also wise to have a backup plan in case the data supply unexpectedly stops.

- *Data linkage*: It is not always straightforward to make a clear link between the unit types on the business register, and those in administrative datasets. For example, in the case of data from businesses with complex structures, where it may be unclear for which specific legal units the data are obtained. The challenge here is to try to derive the correct units, based on the information available.

Furthermore, following Harron et al. (2017), we mention three ongoing research topics with respect to data linkage: how can we evaluate linkage quality?; how can we mitigate bias or correct for bias due to linkage errors?; and how can we link two data sets while preserving privacy issues? We may need to consider informed consent to deal with privacy. A final issue is considering how to optimize the linkage process for multiple sources, for instance with respect to the timing of the sources and thresholds within probabilistic linkage methods.

- *Coverage*: There is more work to be done in general on understanding the best approaches for mitigating coverage issues and understanding their effect on representativity. A particular unsolved issue is in estimating overcoverage. The simplest approach is to identify and remove administrative data units that are out of scope or duplicates. Di Cecco et al. (2018) note that additional studies may be made to understand the nature of these units and identify deterministic rules for removing them. They suggest that coverage estimates could be derived using Dual System Estimation and propose a latent model with capture–recapture techniques to deal with overcoverage in the scenario where data are available from multiple sources.
- *Errors on the measurement side*: With respect to errors on the measurement side, a key question is how can we effectively analyze differences between measurement error in the administrative source and definitional differences between the administrative and statistical target variables? Other outstanding issues are the following: how can we detect and correct reporting patterns that originate from decentralized, autonomous organizations?; and how can we keep harmonization methods up to date?
- *Time-related issues*: Research continues to find a satisfactory solution to the problem of administrative data that are not available in the correct periodicity. In addition to that, a major concern when relying on administrative data over time is discontinuities. If the tax regulations change, for example this can have an unanticipated effect on statistics that are based on those data. In some circumstances, it could happen that administrative data are not delivered at all, perhaps due to system issues. When the administrative data are used for a crucial output, then one should have a mitigation strategy to be prepared in case of problems with the data delivery. This could include modelling the data in some way or in the extreme case, deciding to stop the statistical publication.
- *Quality*: A key unsolved issue is estimating the bias and variance of statistical outputs based on administrative data. For estimates based on sample surveys, it is often straightforward to calculate estimates of sampling variance, which can be published alongside outputs to give a simple indication of their accuracy. Zhang (2012) is one example of relatively recent attempts to begin to develop a quality framework of inference for statistics based on administrative or register data. But there is still much progress to be made in order to quantify the bias and variance of estimates derived from those sources.
- *Survey versus administrative data*: A common method for understanding something about the quality of statistics based on administrative data is to compare them with the estimates that would

have been produced from traditional surveys. This can provide a reassuring message when the estimates from both sources are similar. But when those estimates diverge, it is not necessarily clear which estimate is the most accurate – both are subject to errors, many of which cannot be easily quantified.

12.10 Conclusion

Administrative data are a valuable data source for business statistics and a means to reduce the administrative burden of businesses and explore information that would not usually be available from surveys. The design of a process to obtain reliable estimates from administrative data can be quite cumbersome, mainly because they were not intended to be used for official statistics. Differences between the target population, variables, and periods and their observed counterparts may require a large number of processing steps. Although one aims to apply automatic processing steps, business statistics based on administrative data usually still require significant manual effort to analyze the outcomes and to make adjustments where needed. One of the reasons may be because data in business statistics tend to be very skewed. Another reason might be because there can be serious differences between administrative and statistical units and those administrative units can be very dynamic.

In addition to the practical efforts and drawbacks, a key challenge is the development of a set of methods to deal with the issues that occur with the secondary use of administrative data. Despite this, there are many examples of administrative data being used to enhance the production of business statistics and considerable work continues to further the research and practical applications in this field.

References

ABS (2009). 1520.0: ABS data quality framework. https://www.abs.gov.au/ausstats/abs@.nsf/lookup/1520.0Main+Features1May+2009 (accessed April 2022).

Amaya, A., Biemer, P.P., and Kinyon, D. (2020). Total error in a big data world: adapting the TSE framework to big data. *Journal of Survey Statistics and Methodology* 8: 89–119.

Andics, A., Macsári, I., and Takács, I. (2019). Challenges in using administrative cash register data in Hungarian retail trade statistics. *Paper presented at the European Establishment Statistics Workshop 2019*, Bilbao, Spain (24–27 September 2019).

Bakker, B.F.M. and Daas, P.J.H. (2012). Methodological challenges of register-based research. *Statistica Neerlandica* 66 (1): 2–7.

van Bemmel, K.J.H. (2018). *Verschillen DRT-KICR Uitzendbranche. Analyseverslag*. Version 2.0. CBS rapport, 04-04-2018. (in Dutch)

Biemer, P.P. and Amaya, A. (2018). A total error framework for hybrid estimation. *Presentation given at BIGSURV18*, Barcelona, Spain, (26 October, 2018).

Brancato, G. and Ascari G. (2019). *Quality Guidelines for Multisource Statistics – QGMSS*. Deliverable of grant agreement 3 of the ESSnet of Quality of multi-source statistics. https://ec.europa.eu/eurostat/cros/content/essnet-quality-multisource-statistics-komuso_en (accessed April 2022).

Broad, P. (2012). *Use of administrative VAT data in the Monthly Business Survey*. ONS internal report.

Brown, I. (2012). An empirical comparison of benchmarking methods for economic stock time series. *Proceedings of the Fourth International Conference on Establishment Surveys (ICES- IV)*, Montreal, Canada.

Chen, C., Page, M.J., and Stewart, J.M. (2016). Creating new and improved business statistics by maximising the use of administrative data. *Paper presented at the Fifth International Conference on Established Surveys (ICES-V)*, Geneva, Switzerland.

Christen, P. (2012). *Data Matching: Concepts and Techniques for Record Linkage, Entity Resolution, and Duplicate Detection. Data-Centric Systems and Applications.* Berlin Heidelberg: Springer-Verlag.

Daas, P.J.H., Ossen, S.J.L., Vis-Vischers, R., and Arends-Tóth, J. (2009). *Checklist for the Quality evaluation of Administrative Data Sources.* CBS Discussion Paper. https://ec.europa.eu/eurostat/documents/64157/4374310/45-Checklist-quality-evaluation-administrative-data-sources-2009.pdf/24ffb3dd-5509-4f7e-9683-4477be82ee60 (accessed April 2022).

van Delden, A., Scholtus, S., and de Wolf, P.P. (2011). The case of the missing tax data. *The Statistics Newsletter for the extended OECD Statistical Network* 53: 6–8.

van Delden, A., Pannekoek, J., Banning, R., and de Boer, A. (2016). Analysing correspondence between administrative and survey data. *Statistical Journal of the IAOS* 32: 569–584.

van Delden, A., van der Laan, J.A., and Prins, A. (2018). Detecting reporting errors in data from decentralised autonomous administrations with an application to hospital data. *Journal of Official Statistics* 34 (4): 863–888.

van Delden, A., Lorenc, B., Struijs, P., and Zhang, L.-C. (2018). On statistical unit errors in business statistics. *Journal of Official Statistics* 34 (2): 573–580.

van Delden, A. Scholtus, S., and Ostlund N. (2020). Modelling measurement errors to enable consistency between monthly and quarterly turnover growth rates. *Proceedings of the Statistics Canada Symposium 2018*, Ottawa, Canada (7–9 November 2018).

van Delden, A., Scholtus, S., de Waal, T., and Czorba, I. (2023). Methods for estimating the quality of multisource statistics. In: *Advances in Establishment Statistics, Methods and Data Collection*, Chapter 34 (ed. G. Snijkers, M. Bavdaž, S. Bender, J. Jones, S. MacFeely, J.W. Sakshaug, K.J. Thompson, and A. van Delden). Hoboken: Wiley.

De Waal, T., Scholtus, S., van Delden, A., Di Zio, M., Cibella, N., Tuoto, T., and Scanu, M. (2016). Estimation methods for the integration of administrative sources. Task 1: identification of main types of usages of administrative sources. Deliverable D1 for Eurostat Grant. https://ec.europa.eu/eurostat/cros/system/files/d1_20161223.pdf (accessed April 2022).

Di Cecco, D., Di Zio, M., Filipponi, D., and Rocchetti, I. (2018). Population size estimation using multiple incomplete lists with overcoverage. *Journal of Official Statistics* 34 (2): 557–572.

Di Zio, M. and Guarnera, U. (2013). A contamination model for selective editing. *Journal of Official Statistics* 29 (4): 539–555.

Dima, I. and Clipcea, M. (2019). Testing the possibility of using administrative data in agricultural statistics. *ESS Workshop on the Use of Administrative Data for Business, Agriculture and Fisheries Statistics in Bucharest.* Romania (17–18 October 2019).

Enderer, J. (2008). Is the utilization of administrative data in short term statistics an ideal standard in the conflicting priorities of user demands, response burden and budget restrictions? *Proceedings of the IAOS Conference 'Reshaping Official Statistics'*, Shanghai, China (14–16 October 2008).

Fellegi, I.P. and Sunter, A.B. (1969). A theory for record linkage. *Journal of the American Statistical Association* 64: 1183–1210.

Feuerhake, J. (2007). Replacement of existing Surveys using Alternative Data Sources. *Seminar on Reengineering of Business Statistics.* Lisbon, Spain (11/12 October 2007).

Fortier, S. and Quenneville, B. (2007). Theory and application of benchmarking in Business Surveys. *Proceedings of the Third International Conference on Establishment Surveys (ICES- III)*, Montreal, Canada.

Goorden, M. and Hoogland, J.J. (2020). *Assessing quality of administrative data used for STS: a literature inventory.* Workpackage 8 of EU Grant Development and quality improvement of the short term statistics (STS).

Groen, J. (2012). Sources of error in survey and administrative aata: the importance of reporting procedures. *Journal of Official Statistics* 28 (2): 173–198.

GSS, Government Statistical Service (2014). *Using administrative data: good practice guidance for statisticians.* https://gss.civilservice.gov.uk/wp-content/uploads/2018/03/Using-admin-data-good-practice-guidance-for-statisticians-6.pdf (accessed April 2022).

Hand, D.J. (2018). Statistical challenges of administrative and transaction data. *Journal of the Royal Statistical Society Series A* 181 (3): 555–605.

Hand, D.J. and Blunt, G. (2001). Prospecting for gems in credit card data. *IMA Journal of Management and Mathematics* 12: 173–200.

Harron, K., Dibben, C., Boyd, J. et al. (2017). Challenges in administrative data linkage for research. *Big data and society* 2017: 1–12.

Hoogland, J. (2016). Editing and imputation of administrative business data. *Presentation at the Fifth International Conference on Establishment Surveys (ICES-V)*, Geneva (20–23 June 2016).

Jang, L. (2016). Resolving differences in statistical units: Statistics Canada's experiences with using administrative data in economic programs. *Paper presented at the Fifth International Conference on Establishment Surveys (ICES-V)*, Geneva, Switzerland (20–23 June 2016).

Japec, L., Kreuter, F., Berg, M., Biemer, P.P., Decker, P., Lampe, C., Lane, J., O'Neil, C., and Usher, A. (2015). *AAPOR Task Force Report on Big Data.* Oakpark Terrace, IL: American Association for Public Opinion Research; 2015. http://www.aapor.org/Education-Resources/Reports/Big-Data.aspx (accessed April 2022).

Karr, A.F., Sanil, A.P., and Banks, D.L. (2006). Data quality: A statistical perspective. *Statistical Methodology* 3: 137–173.

Kloek, W. and Vaju, S. (2013). The use of administrative data in integrated statistics. *Paper presented at the New Techniques and Technologies for Statistics (NTTS) Conference*, Brussels, Belgium, 2013, 128–138.

Labonne, P. and Weale, M. (2018). Temporal disaggregation of overlapping noisy quarterly data using state space models: estimation of monthly business sector output from Value Added Tax data in the UK. Economic Statistics Centre of Excellence (ESCoE) Discussion Papers ESCoE DP-2018-18, Economic Statistics Centre of Excellence (ESCoE).

Larsen, M.L. and Herning, A. (2023). Record linkage for establishments: background, challenges, and an example. In: *Advances in Establishment Statistics, Methods and Data Collection*, Chapter 33 (ed. G. Snijkers, M. Bavdaž, S. Bender, J. Jones, S. MacFeely, J.W. Sakshaug, K.J. Thompson, and A. van Delden). Hoboken: Wiley.

Lewis, D. and Woods, J. (2013). Issues to consider when turning to the use of administrative data: the UK experience. *Paper presented at the New Techniques and Technologies for Statistics (NTTS) Conference*, Brussels, Belgium, 2013. https://ec.europa.eu/eurostat/cros/system/files/NTTS2013fullPaper_142.pdf (accessed April 2022).

Lothian, J., Holmberg, A., and Seyb, A. (2019). An evolutionary schema for using "it-is-what-it-is" data in official statistics. *Journal of Official Statistics* 35 (1): 137–165.

Maasing, E., Remes, T., Baldi, C., and Vlag, P. (2013). *STS estimates based solely on administrative data.* Deliverable 4.1 of the ESSnet Admin Data. https://ec.europa.eu/eurostat/cros/system/files/SGA %202011_Deliverable_4.1.pdf (accessed April 2022).

Manzi, G., Spiegelhalter, D.J., Turner, R.M., Flowers, J., and Thompson, S.G. (2011). Modelling bias in combining small area prevalence estimates from multiple surveys. *Journal of the Royal Statistical Society Series A* 174: 31–50.

McLennan, D. (2018). *Data Quality Issues in Administrative Data* (ed. E. Mackey and M. Elliot). Published with a Series of the Administrative Data Research Network.

Meng, X.-L. (2018). Statistical paradises and paradoxes in big data (I): law of large populations, big data paradox, and the 2016 US presidential election. *The Annals of Applied Statistics* 12 (2): 685–725.

National Academies of Sciences, Engineering, and Medicine (2017). *Innovations in Federal Statistics: Combining Data Sources While Protecting Privacy*. Washington, DC: The National Academies Press. https://www.ncbi.nlm.nih.gov/books/NBK425873/ (accessed April 2022).

Ouwehand, P. and Schouten, B. (2014). Measuring representativeness of short-term business statistics. *Journal of Official Statistics* 30 (4): 623–649.

Parkin, N. (2010). *Interpolation and Extrapolation from Value Added Tax Returns*. ONS internal report.

Parkin, N. and Brown, G. (2012). *Comparison of Singular Spectrum Analysis and Holt–Winters Forecasts of Quarterly VAT*. ONS internal report.

Perko, J. (2019). Administrative data source in tourism statistics. *Paper presented at the ESS Workshop on Administrative Data for Business, Agriculture and Fisheries Statistics, Bucharest*, Romania (17–18 October 2019).

Reid, G., Zabala, F., and Holmberg, A. (2017). Extending TSE to administrative data: a quality framework and case studies from Stats NZ. *Journal of Official Statistics* 33 (2): 477–511.

Reinert R. and Stoltze, P.T. (2014). *Checklist for evaluating the quality of input data*. Work package 1 of Specific Grant Agreement 1 of ESSnet KOMUSO, Quality in multisource statistics. https://ec.europa.eu/eurostat/cros/system/files/essnet_wp1_report_final_version4.pdf (accessed April 2022).

Rudys, T. (2019). The use of VAT declaration data in Survey on Service enterprises. *ESS Workshop on the Use of Administrative Data for Business, Agriculture and Fisheries Statistics,* Bucharest, Romania (17–18 October 2019).

Ryan, L., Thompson, C., and Jones, J. (2020). A Statistical Business Register spine as a new approach to support data integration and firm-level data linking: an ABS perspective. *Statistical Journal of the IAOS* 36: 767–774.

Şahinler, H.E., Öztürk, M., Kurban, B., Koçak, H.B., Tüzen, M.F., and Arslanoğlu, S. (2019). Lessons learnt and experiences along the way: centralized admin data collection in TurkStat. *Paper presented at the ESS Workshop on Administrative Data for Business, Agriculture and Fisheries Statistics,* Bucharest, Romania (17–18 October 2019).

Sakshaug, J.W. and Antoni, M. (2017). Errors in linking survey and administrative data. Chapter 25 in: *Total Survey Error in Practice* (ed. P.P. Biemer, E. de Leeuw, S. Eckman, B. Edwards, F. Kreuter, L.E. Lyberg, N.C. Tucker, and B.T. West). https://doi.org/10.1002/9781119041702.ch25 (accessed April 2022).

Sakshaug, J.W. and Vicari, B.J. (2018). Obtaining record linkage consent from establishments: the impact of question placement on consent rates and bias. *Journal of Survey Statistics and Methodology* 6: 46–71.

Särndal, C.-E., Swensson, B., and Wretman, J. (1992). *Model Assisted Survey Sampling*. New York: Springer-Verlag.

Scholtus, S., Bakker, B.F.M., and van Delden, A. (2015). Modelling measurement error to estimate bias in administrative and survey variables. Discussion Paper, The Hague: Statistics Netherlands. https://www.cbs.nl/nl-nl/achtergrond/2015/46/modelling-measurement-error-to-estimate-bias-in-administrative-and-survey-variables (accessed April 2022).

Schouten, B., Cobben, F., and Bethlehem, J. (2009). Indicators for the representativeness of survey response. *Survey Methodology* 35: 101–113.

Statistics Canada (2002). *Statistics Canada's Quality Assurance Framework*. Catalogue no.12-586-XIE. https://www150.statcan.gc.ca/n1/pub/12-586-x/12-586-x2002001-eng.pdf (accessed April 2022).

Šuštar, C. and Eremita, M. (2021). The integration of administrative data for the identification of the ownership of agricultural land. *Paper presented at the virtual conference on New Techniques and Technologies for Statistics (NTTS)*, Brussels, Belgium (9–11 March 2021).

Țîru, A.M., Pop, I., and Oancea, B. (2019). Error detection and data imputation methods for administrative data sources used in business statistics. *Paper presented at the ESS Workshop on Administrative Data for Business, Agriculture and Fisheries Statistics,* Bucharest, Romania (17–18 October 2019).

UNECE, United Nations Economic Commission for Europe (2011). *Using Administrative and Secondary Sources for Official Statistics: A Handbook of Principles and Practices.* New York and Geneva: United Nations. http://www.unece.org/fileadmin/DAM/stats/publications/Using_Administrative_Sources_Final_for_web.pdf (accessed April 2022).

UNECE, United Nations Economic Commission for Europe (2015). *Guidelines on statistical business registers.* http://www.unece.org:8080/fileadmin/DAM/stats/publications/2015/ECE_CES_39_WEB.pdf (accessed April 2022).

UNECE, United Nations Economic Commission for Europe (2019). *Generic Statistical Business Process Model version 5.1.* https://statswiki.unece.org/display/GSBPM/GSBPM+v5.1 (accessed April 2022).

UNSD, United Nations Department of Economic and Social Affairs Statistics Division (2014). Report of global status of statistical business register programmes. https://unstats.un.org/unsd/economic_stat/Economic_Census/globalSbrAssessmentReport.pdf (accessed April 2022).

Van Delden, A. (2010). Methodological challenges using VAT for turnover estimates at Statistics Netherlands. *Paper presented at the Conference on Administrative Simplification in Official Statistics, Simply 2010*, Ghent, Belgium (2–3 December 2010).

Verschaeren, F., Lewis, D., Lewis, P., Benedikt, L., Putz, C., Miltiadou, M., and Vekeman, G. (2013). *Checking for errors and cleaning the incoming data.* Deliverable 2.3 of the ESSnet use of administrative and accounts data in business statistics. https://ec.europa.eu/eurostat/cros/system/files/SGA%202011_Deliverable_2.3_1.pdf (accessed April 2022).

Vlag, P., Bikker, R., de Waal, T., Toivanen, E., and Teneva, M. (2013). *Extrapolating admin data for early estimation: some findings and recommendations for the ESS.* Deliverable 4.3 of the ESSnet Admin Data. https://ec.europa.eu/eurostat/cros/system/files/SGA%202011_Deliverable_4.3.pdf (accessed April 2022).

de Waal, T., van Delden, A., and Scholtus, S. (2019). *Complete overview of Quality Measures and Calculation Methods (QMCMs).* Deliverable of workpackage 3 of specific grant agreement 3 of the ESSnet of Quality of multi-source statistics. https://ec.europa.eu/eurostat/cros/content/essnet-quality-multisource-statistics-komuso_en (accessed April 2022).

de Waal, T., van Delden, A., and Scholtus, S. (2021). Commonly used approaches and methods for measuring output quality. *Spanish Journal of Statistics* 2: 79–107.

Železnik Gorjan, N and Božič Verbič, A. (2019). Use of administrative data for statistical production at SURS. *Presentation given at the ESS Workshop on the Use of Administrative Data and Social Statistics*, Valencia, Spain (4 and 5 June 2019).

Zhang, L.-C. (2012). Topics of statistical theory for register-based statistics and data integration. *Statistica Neerlandica* 66 (1): 41–63.

13

Developing Statistical Frameworks for Administrative Data and Integrating It into Business Statistics. Experiences from the UK and New Zealand

Nicholas Cox[1], Craig H. McLaren[2], Claire Shenton[2], Tom Tarling[2], and Ella W. Davies[2]

[1] *Statistics NZ, Wellington, New Zealand*
[2] *Office for National Statistics, Newport, Wales*

13.1 Introduction

13.1.1 Background

The quantity of administrative data that are created, stored, and processed in the world has grown exponentially over recent years. There are several definitions of administrative data but for the purposes of this chapter, the UNECE (2011) definition "Administrative sources are data holdings containing information which is not collected for statistical purposes" is used. This also includes transactional sources such as credit card or store card data. National Statistical Institutes (NSIs) have been repurposing administrative data for decades. The Nordic countries in particular were among the first to use administrative data in the form of population registers for the large-scale production of official statistics, replacing surveys as the primary data source, and the Danish 1980 Population Census being the first of its kind (Nordbotten 2010).

Administrative data are key to the creation and maintenance of registers (for example, population registers and statistical business registers) and sample frames, and this type of data can be used to better target sample allocation, reduce the required size of samples, or feed directly into key statistics. Statistical producers are under pressure to reduce the costs of producing statistical outputs while maintaining or even improving the quality of the outputs produced. With survey response rates declining (Luiten et al. 2020), countries are increasingly moving toward exploring the use of administrative and alternative (that is, nonsurvey) data sources for statistical production. There will always be a need for surveys although these are increasingly moving over to self-administered online modes where the number of questions will be tightly constrained. But complementing these with extra data, and where possible reducing the burden on survey respondents by reducing or replacing samples, is the key to transformation. Combining new administrative and alternative sources with surveys will allow NSIs to meet the ever-increasing user demand for improved and more detailed statistics. As such, many NSIs have, or are working toward, putting administrative and alternative data sources at the core of their statistics, including the UK's Office for National Statistics (ONS) and Statistics New Zealand (StatsNZ) among others.

The UK Statistics Authority has strongly encouraged public bodies to fully utilize administrative data for statistical purposes (UK Statistics Authority 2020). As part of the ONS transformation process, there are ambitious plans to put administrative data at the core of statistical production and consequently, ONS is increasing their use (ONS 2020a).

Advances in Business Statistics, Methods and Data Collection. Edited by Ger Snijkers, Mojca Bavdaž, Stefan Bender, Jacqui Jones, Steve MacFeely, Joseph W. Sakshaug, Katherine J. Thompson, and Arnout van Delden.
© 2023 John Wiley & Sons, Inc. Published 2023 by John Wiley & Sons, Inc.

As administrative data are not typically collected for statistical purposes, they pose a number of challenges if they are to be used in the production of official statistics (Hand 2018; Bakker and Daas 2012). Hand (2018) presented what he considers to be the main statistical challenges arising from administrative data that cover issues including but not limited to

- data quality,
- representativity of administrative data,
- changes in definitions between survey and administrative data,
- the development of principles and robust methods for linkage.

With survey data, there is well established theory and a coherent framework for the methods used (Groves and Lyberg 2010). While the amount of administrative data available for statistical usage has increased, the development of statistical theory to support its use in official statistics has not increased at the same rate with a considerable amount of work still to do. That's not to say that within the statistical community, we are not using or investigating a wide variety of statistical sources, but the methods used are not based on widely standardized theory like we have for surveys. Indeed, Bakker and Daas (2012) highlighted that there is no consensus even on the basic terminology. Much of the current theory and knowledge is based on best practices developed by countries such as the Nordic countries and the Netherlands who have been using administrative data for statistical outputs for some time. While registers of personal data in these countries are not developed primarily for the purpose of statistical use, the Statistics Act in Norway gives unlimited access to such registers meaning that statistics can be produced using administrative data rather than needing to augment with survey data (Statistics Norway 2007). However, with varying degrees of development for administrative data sources across different countries, there has been limited work toward a unified international approach to developing a theoretical framework.

13.1.2   Administrative Data Methods Research Program

In response to David Hand's (2018) paper, the UK Government Statistical Service Methodological Advisory Committee (GSS MAC – a service that provides government departments with methodological advice and access to a pool of subject matter experts), facilitated workshops with leading experts to discuss the challenges and set the strategic direction for the future development of administrative data methods across the GSS. Following these initial discussions, ONS carried out an evaluation into current methodological work into administrative data and completed an initial high-level review of published research into this topic. The Administrative Data Methods Research Program (ADMR), a methodological research program, was initiated by ONS to address the challenges by developing a statistical framework for using and integrating administrative and transactional data to produce official statistics and analysis.

The specific aims of the ADMR are to

- Address the key methodological and statistical challenges of using administrative and transactional data
- Collaborate on the cross cutting methodological challenge across the GSS, academia, and internationally
- Create a framework of methods to effectively utilize administrative data, maximizing its potential
- Catalogue and share best practice
- Ensure the Administrative Data Methods Research Programme has a clear impact and application on official statistics within the ONS, GSS, and beyond

By meeting these aims, the ONS will help to ensure robustness of statistical outputs more widely, in addition to helping put administrative data at the core of statistics within ONS.

The program seeks to encourage collaboration and engagement, sharing of research and best practices. Gaps in research will be identified and addressed, to provide a coherent statistical framework for the use of administrative data.

In practice, the ADMR program of work is still in initial development within the UK. While the challenges and a number of key projects to address the challenges have been identified, it will take time to complete all of these projects. Consequently, it will be some time before ONS is in a position to propose a framework based on the culmination of the work of the ADMR program.

While the ADMR program is still in the early stages, there are still examples where administrative data is already being incorporated into statistical outputs. Furthermore, research programs have been commissioned to improve the quality of statistical outputs through development of quality frameworks and using knowledge gained to make the best use of administrative data. These are examined in Section 13.2.

Within the ONS population, migration and social statistics system examples of using administrative data for statistical outputs include creating population estimates by anonymously linking person records on such data sources to create administrative-based population estimates (ABPEs), as the current population statistics system relies heavily on the decennial census, where the quality of our population estimates declines as we move further away from census year. This work also includes developing quality frameworks to ensure ONS is able to understand how changes in units' interactions with administrative data sources affect outputs (ONS 2020a). Another strand of this program involves improving the estimation processes for international migration statistics using a range of administrative data sources. This research focuses on linked longitudinal administrative data, which has its own unique types of errors due to the incorporation of measurements over time. As part of this work ONS has built on the quality framework developed by Statistics New Zealand (2016) developing further into two generalizable tools; one for use with any single longitudinal data source, and another for multiple sources that are longitudinally linked (Blackwell and Rogers 2021). While the framework was developed in the context of population and migration statistics, it is generalizable and also useful for understanding and improving business statistics.

Elsewhere within the ONS, economic statistics are also undergoing transformation by including value added tax (VAT) turnover in the production of economic statistics. More specifically, for the production of short-term indicators, including the Index of Services (IoS), Index of Production (IoP), and Construction estimates. This is explored further in Section 13.3.3.

The first purpose of the remainder of this chapter is to give an overview of quality frameworks that are currently available, which is a key focus of the ADMR program (Section 13.2). The second purpose is to pass through two case studies of administrative data use: within the ONS in the UK (Section 13.3) and StatsNZ (Section 13.4) to examine practical, methodological, and quality issues that were encountered and how they were dealt with. The chapter ends with a final conclusion (Section 13.5).

13.2 Quality Frameworks for Administrative Data

There is a requirement to assess the quality of administrative data sources for statistical production. However, one complication is the multiple ways new sources can be integrated into the statistical production process, introducing uncertainty along the way (de Waal et al. 2020b). Many NSIs have already done substantial work on composing administrative data quality frameworks (ABS 2009;

Daas et al. 2009a, b; Laitila et al. 2011; Statistics New Zealand 2016), and this section will highlight some of these, in addition to outlining the research ONS has contributed to this area. It will conclude with how the ADMR program is working toward a quality framework for administrative data which will feed into the wider theoretical framework for administrative data.

Quality management is central to the production of official statistics and covers the process of identifying quality concerns and managing them within outputs. The Code of Practice for Official Statistics (OSR 2018) states that "quality means statistics fit their intended uses, are based on appropriate data and methods, and are not materially misleading." Therefore, the quality of statistics is inherently complex and should be broken down into different quality dimensions. The importance of each dimension can be prioritized to meet the user requirements of a specific output, producing a tailored quality approach for each of these based on the final user needs. As part of a quality management process, there should be a set of indicators to detect and measure potential areas of concern. These indicators can be mapped to the stages of the production process model. The Generic Statistical Business Process Model (GSBPM 2019) has quality management as a central principle that underpins all stages of the process, from design to output evaluation.

Statistical quality frameworks provide guidance on best practices and act as a safeguard to ensure public confidence in official statistics. Quality frameworks should look beyond the final output to address the requirements of a statistical system at all stages of the production process. In the development of a framework, the interaction with stages of the GSBPM is key to ensure the robustness of the framework and applicability within an NSI. Throughout the GSBPM, there will be steps likely to affect various quality aspects and identifying these is key to ensuring the fitness for purpose of an output.

One of the first projects to be initiated as part of the ADMR Program was a project on Quality Frameworks with the aim to investigate existing examples in use worldwide to review and establish best practices. This project is being led by the Government Data Quality Hub which sits within ONS. The remit of the Hub is much broader than the production of statistics alone, with the aim of improving the quality of data and analysis across government and promoting good practice in data quality across wider society.

In December 2020, the Government Data Quality Hub launched a new data quality framework "Toward a data quality culture" (GDQ Hub 2020). This framework focuses primarily on assessing and improving the quality of input data, whereas the quality framework that the ADMR are working toward will focus more on general quality assurance of administrative data, for the purpose of statistical production. The GDQ quality framework covers both operational and statistical data. In contrast, the ADMR quality framework will focus primarily on administrative data with a view to addressing all methodological aspects for each stage of the statistical process.

Quality as a concept is inherently difficult to measure. There are several dimensions that can be applied to make quality assessment easier. The core dimensions have been defined by the European Statistical System (ESS), with NSIs able to add in additional ones to fit their needs. These core dimensions are the following: relevance; accuracy and reliability; timeliness and punctuality; accessibility and clarity; and coherence and comparability (ESS 2019).

While these dimensions have proven sufficient within the traditional survey processing pathway, they can fall short of meeting the needs of administrative data-based statistics, which tend to require a more detailed consideration of the various error types that can occur throughout the administrative data journey. Existing quality frameworks in this area revise the list of dimensions to account for this (Cerroni et al. 2014). Often, they extend from looking at output quality to the sources of uncertainty that can occur in the underlying data and statistical processes, and mapping these to specific error types.

In the following subsections, we discuss three frameworks that have been examined within ONS as part of this quality framework theme.

13.2.1 Statistics Netherlands and UNECE Framework

The UNECE Big Data Quality Framework (BDQF) (UNECE 2014) works around the principles of fitness for use, flexibility, and effort versus gain. These are to ensure the framework is as applicable as possible and maintains usability. The use of a data source is evaluated against its fitness for use. Flexibility allows the framework to be applied throughout the production process and with different source types. Finally, the principle of effort versus gain looks to set minimum requirements that should be met in order to balance effort for assessing data quality against added value of using the data.

The BDQF focuses on three areas, which align to the stages of the GSBPM. These are

- *Input*: The process(es) of acquiring the data for analysis.
- *Throughput*: Points within the business process where the data is transformed in some way.
- *Output*: Assessment and reporting of quality from the data sources.

Under each of these areas, there are three hyper-dimensions of quality (Karr et al. 2006); Source, Metadata, and Data, with quality dimensions and indicators sitting beneath them. This concept was adapted from the Statistics Netherlands administrative data quality framework (Daas et al. 2009a, b). It allows for different stages of the process to be judged against quality dimensions that are most relevant at that point. This supports the flexible criteria of the BDQF.

The Source hyper-dimension looks at risks from the type of data, the characteristics of the organization that supplies the data, and the governance relating to the collection and storage of the original source. Metadata examines the completeness of the meta information accompanying the dataset, as well as exploring the identifiers associated with the data. The treatment of the data is explored here to ensure the data supplier has performed checks on the data or modified the source for use. Checklists have been developed to help evaluate the source and metadata hyper-dimensions by guiding the user through the different quality indicators (Daas et al. 2009b).

The Data hyper-dimension examines the quality of the data within the data source. It mainly focuses on accuracy with some consideration of technical checks provided. When assessing the Data hyper-dimension, Statistics Netherlands have developed a Representativity Index (Schouten and Cobben 2007). The index aims to measure how the values of the units in the data source are (dis)similar to the those in the population at a certain point in time.

13.2.2 Stats New Zealand and Zhang Framework

These frameworks are based on the identification of error throughout the processing of multisource statistics. The original framework was proposed by Zhang (2012) with two main phases to statistical processing. The framework was expanded on by StatsNZ (Reid et al. 2017) to include a third phase in order to develop their quality framework for administrative data-based statistics.

Phase 1 of the Zhang framework concerns the processing of a single source for its primary use by its source holder. The concepts in here are consistent between survey and administrative sources to ensure applicability across source types. This phase can be broken down further to look at measurement errors (associated to variables) and representation errors (unit errors). Errors in measurements include validity errors – differences between the source concept and the target measurement concept – and processing errors, which may introduce errors into the dataset. Errors in the units look to assess the units in a source against the target population.

Phase 2 refers to the secondary use of data collected by others and looks at where errors can arise from the integration of sources to create a statistical output. The concepts within Phase 2 can also be applied to statistics derived from a single administrative source, not just linked datasets. Within the Measurements concepts of Phase 2, errors include mapping errors and comparability errors. This phase ends with an integrated microdata set.

The third phase was included by StatsNZ (Reid et al. 2017) as an estimation and evaluation phase to account for errors that arise in the creation of the final outputs. The purpose of this stage is to identify and measure any biases that may be introduced into the final estimate through processes such as weighting, seasonal adjustments, and model-based errors. The third phase is a documentation of next steps of controlling, measuring, and reducing errors.

13.2.3 The ESSnet Komuso Project

The ESSnet Komuso project ran from 2016 to 2019 and included many participating NSIs. Extensive work into quality frameworks, indicators, measures, and recommendations were produced relating to multisource statistics. Here, multisource statistics are defined as statistics produced from the combination of several data sources, which include nonsurvey datasets. The project produced a number of reports including reports on quality measures and computation methods (De Waal et al. 2020a). The quality measures follow Zhang's error framework and are aligned to the ESS dimensions of statistical quality, defined earlier. The Komuso project also mapped established error categories to more specific error types, and puts more focus on modeling errors (errors arising during any modeling processes) than previous frameworks.

13.2.4 The Southampton University Error Project

These error classifications have been expanded upon in a review as part of a project commissioned by the ADMR program. In order to investigate this issue in depth, the ONS ADMR program commissioned the Southampton University's Statistical Sciences Research Institute. The aim of the project was to describe and classify different methods to measure errors in nonsurvey sources as a framework. As part of this work, the researchers developed statistical methods to quantify error in administrative data sources, which the ADMR program is currently trying to apply to more case studies within ONS. This complements and builds on work that is already being developed by ONS on error frameworks for longitudinal data (ONS 2020b), that in turn built on the StatsNZ quality framework for administrative data.

In the absence of a sampling design, the use of administrative data in official statistics relies on model-based, rather than design-based approaches. These model-based approaches aim to ensure that the data used from the administrative sources produce or contribute toward accurate estimates and inference. While design-based approaches typically ensure unbiased estimates in theory (so long as the assumption of random missingness of nonresponse holds), model-based approaches rely on strong assumptions and bias adjustments to ensure unbiased estimates. In some cases, the model may trade off bias with variance. The types of models may vary depending on the application but often the modeling will provide substantial challenges if the data quality is not very good. When administrative data quality cannot be assured to be high, additional data sources are required to either assess the quality or to be used in conjunction to augment the quality of estimation. For quality assessment, structural equation models (SEMs) were investigated to estimate errors of measurement.

SEMs are versatile types of models that essentially combine linear regression and confirmatory factor analysis. They are mostly used for continuous variables and are useful for assessing data quality with multiple data sources because the model assumes latent variables that are free of measurement error. A latent variable is assumed to be a "perfect" measure of the target construct and is not observed, but rather inferred from other, observed variables. The model can then assess how closely correlated the measured variables are to this latent variable, where a higher correlation indicates less measurement error. SEMs were fitted to clothing prices data using survey data alongside web-scraped data; however, a lack of available data meant results were not clear. This highlighted a significant, but common limitation of SEMs, that they are not very stable with small data sets. Nevertheless, with applications allowing for more data, these models could potentially offer an effective way of assessing administrative data quality.

The project highlights the challenges involved with nonsurvey data sources, and that in the absence of statistical theory to guide inference, models must be used that capture the complexity of the problem. This often requires additional survey data sources to help verify the quality of the administrative data sources.

The case studies which follow examine the usage of administrative data in production of business statistics, and the impact their usage has on survey redesign, frequency of statistical publications, and production of short-term indicators. The quality concerns of using such data are considered and methods to address them. Both StatsNZ and the ONS examine implementation of new statistical pipelines to allow for administrative data ingestion, and the implications on timeliness and periodicity quality concerns. Similar approaches for statistical method redesign are used, through different forms, with the ONS using a partition approach for blending administrative and survey data, and StatsNZ using "managed collection" to address handling of complex units.

With both the ONS and StatsNZ seeking to produce higher-frequency subannual business statistics, administrative data, and the associated quality frameworks will be key areas for methodological work. Subsequent to the work done in the areas covered by these case studies, the impact of coronavirus (COVID-19) has driven statisticians toward higher usage of administrative data. As such the quality dimensions of timeliness and punctuality, accuracy and reliability, coherence and comparability, accessibility and clarity, and relevance will continue to be examined and addressed, building on the identified challenges from these case studies.

13.3 Case Study One – The Use of Value Added Tax Data in the United Kingdom

13.3.1 Organizational Context Within the Office for National Statistics

ONS has an ongoing commitment to utilize data from VAT returns obtained from the UK's tax office, Her Majesty's Revenue and Customs (HMRC). Businesses provide this information directly to the HMRC as part of their regular reporting requirements. The use of this dataset provides an opportunity for ONS to reduce the dependency on sample surveys while also reducing respondent burden on the business. The VAT dataset has significantly greater coverage than sample surveys, which can reduce the variance of the final estimates and allows the publication of increased detail such as regional breakdowns.

The intricacies of the VAT dataset pose methodological and practical challenges, such as the processing of large datasets, the timing and periodicity of the returns, treatment of returns for large complex tax units which can be different to those units used in a traditional sample survey, validation of high-frequency estimates, dealing with different return dates due to the tax system requirements, and combining the use of survey data returns with administrative data in a production context. These issues, and a high-level assessment of the VAT data source, are discussed in detail in ONS (2019).

Statistical pipelines can be developed to streamline and process both the data ingestion, and statistical processing. Organizationally, this can be managed with both centralized processing for common tasks, and localized processing for specific outputs. Within the ONS, a central team manages the external client relationship. This can help coordinate data deliveries and legal requirements. For the data usage, the organizational approach can depend on both the methods required to process the data, and the use then of the transformed data in different outputs. For example, for the use of the VAT dataset in economic statistics outputs, it is desirable to use consistent and coherent methods, so a team based in economic statistics processes and creates the outputs required.

The strategic use of the VAT data source within the ONS has been an important step in transforming data sources but has provided some challenging methodological issues which are discussed in Sections 13.3.1–13.3.4.

13.3.1.1 Administrative Data in Practice

The content of administrative data tax records will vary by country. Often, there is a vast amount of information available to be used, although the level of detail can be dependent on user requirements and data sharing arrangements.

Within the United Kingdom, agreements to use the VAT administrative data for statistical purposes ensure there is a provision of a regular data feed which gives turnover returns at the individual tax unit level. The VAT turnover in the tax form (and hence the dataset) is not the amount of VAT a business pays, it is the "total value of sales and all other outputs excluding VAT" which is collected as part of the VAT return. This information is only to be used in the statistical compilation process, where this data are used to create aggregate totals. McLaren and Whipple (2019) and McLaren et al. (2021) discussed issues from a broader conceptual and UK context, including statistical pipelines, dealing with the different frequency of returns, analysis for time series, and timeliness of the VAT returns.

13.3.1.2 Dealing with the Data

In the United Kingdom, VAT turnover data are primarily 3-monthly in profile, but some are monthly, or 12-monthly, which can begin or end on any month of the year. For example, enterprises can submit their VAT return at different frequencies, e.g. on a monthly, quarterly, or annual basis, and also provide updated information in later periods. VAT returns can also be submitted on a variety of different staggers, i.e. the dates for which the return refers to. The treatment of the staggers poses challenges to assign a monthly path to the data. The complexity of dealing with staggers makes this a challenging dataset for processing. If the VAT returns were uniformly divided over the period they refer to, then any real underlying seasonal signal would be smoothed. Short-term indicators require monthly data to be available, particularly when assessing short-term signals. Methods, referred to as calenderization (Quenneville et al. 2013), have needed to be developed using seasonal and trading day data from short-term monthly indicator surveys.

As with any data source, cleaning methods will need to be applied. The use of cleaning methods for input data is a standard methodological approach used in the production process and is applied for both sample survey data and VAT data. However, the parameter setting needs to be tailored given the nature of the VAT data.

The timeliness of the VAT data in relation to the reference period required for publication necessitates estimation or nowcasting for the most recent period for the VAT data. There is a need to internally nowcast data for those small businesses which may have a delay in the availability of their VAT data. The nowcasted data is only used in internal processing and is then discarded. In the context of the UK processing approach, this can lead to the situation where the VAT data is not timely enough to be used for higher-frequency outputs (e.g. monthly), as it may require significant nowcasted data. One approach currently used is to first publish data based on the existing monthly sample survey and replace selected sample survey information with VAT data once greater coverage (e.g. in turnover in comparison to the population) is achieved on the VAT returns.

There is also a different treatment based on the employment size of the reporting unit, where the survey collection is retained for larger-sized businesses, whereas VAT data will be used for the smaller-sized businesses. Retaining survey data for selected reporting unit based on their larger employment size will deliver quick, monthly data, and allow these (typical influential) businesses to be contacted to discover the reasoning behind fluctuations.

13.3.1.3 Complex Units in UK Tax Data

One of the more challenging considerations is the mapping between administrative tax units and the reporting unit. Van Delden et al. (2018) discusses the issue of different unit types in business statistics. For example, when an enterprise consists of more than one reporting unit the VAT turnover must be apportioned to each reporting unit (see later sections for the impact this can have on regional estimates). The proportion of registered employment of each reporting unit can be used to apportion or distribute the turnover. However, this assumes a direct relationship between VAT turnover and employment that is not appropriate for all industries. This can typically impact the largest reporting units, which means it can be advantageous to continue to use sample survey data in these cases.

Figure 13.1 describes a representation and relationships between different observation, statistical, and administrative units in the context of the UK VAT dataset and the separate statistical and reporting units, where reporting units are those in the sample survey.

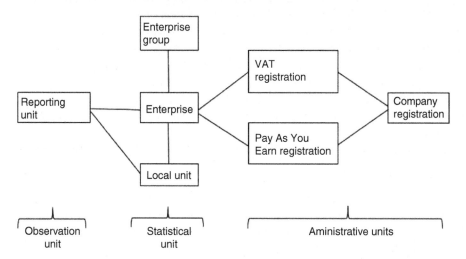

Figure 13.1 Diagrammatical representation of the relationship between different units in the context of sample surveys (e.g. reporting units and statistical units) and VAT administrative data within the United Kingdom.

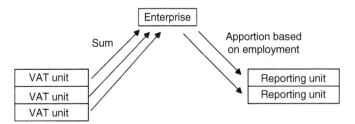

Figure 13.2 Diagrammatical representation of how an enterprise can be apportioned back to a number of reporting units.

Related to this is the concept of complex units which can be represented as a number of individual VAT units (Figure 13.2), which are then summed to the enterprise level. In complex cases, this data can then be apportioned back out based on employment to a reporting unit level (e.g. aligned to the sample survey).

The complexity of the administrative dataset will obviously differ by country but will need to be considered in the context of statistical pipelines and processing.

13.3.2 Developing Statistical Pipelines for Processing

Processing both administrative data (VAT) and survey data has required different methods as the underlying data will display different properties, e.g. in terms of timeliness, and parameter settings for different methods such as forecasting and editing. Consistent and reproducible methods are important, so that the steps involved are designed to follow a standard production pipeline.

The following processing steps summarize the existing pipeline which is already used in practice, although it is continually being reviewed and adapted.

Structural editing and VAT return cleaning:

- Duplicate processing check to determine if there is a duplicate row of data
- Thousand-pound rule check which uses the rule if $0.0065 <$ Current turnover/Previous turnover < 0.00135, then New current turnover = Current turnover $\times 1000$
- Quarterly pattern rule which excludes firms which may be estimating their returns. The rule used is where the quarterly returns within a year (e.g. quarter 1, quarter 2, quarter 3, and quarter 4) meet a pattern of repeating data, e.g. the same value four times (x,x,x,x), or the same value three times followed by data which likely reflects a residual to sum to an annual total, e.g. (x,x,x,y), or nil returns for three consecutive periods followed by data which will equal an annual return, e.g. (0,0,0,y). Checks can also be applied where the returns x or y are not equal to zero. In these cases the industry median value is then used.
- Identifying first returns, which then flags the 5% largest first returns for further investigation.

Matching, linking, and apportionment:

- Data is joined with business register records.
- In practice, more than 99% of the VAT data (in terms of individual administrative VAT units) can be matched each month to the separate business register. This is achieved by using a unique identifier for each business.
- In practice, VAT units are not always identical to ONS reporting units. VAT units are matched to enterprises using a matching and linking module, and then aggregated up.
- VAT units can report on different staggers (e.g. the time of reporting and length of period).

Calendarization:

- For where the VAT data is used, a consistent series over time is calculated where the 3-month and 12-month returns are converted onto a monthly basis.
- Monthly seasonal factors of each cell are calculated (sample-level industry stratified by employment), by using a seasonal adjustment approach (e.g. the use of Signal Extraction in Arima Time Series as described in https://www.census.gov/srd/www/x13as/).

Estimation and aggregation:

- Standard ratio estimation is used, which is based on historical annual turnover for each reporting unit.
- Aggregates are created by industry and size band, to output to the aggregation processing system.
- VAT data is then aggregated along with survey data using a partition approach, which allows user input into choosing data based on VAT for selected reporting units and data separately based on the survey. This partition approach can control where VAT data is used, e.g. the use of VAT data to replace survey information for smaller-sized employment businesses, while keeping the survey information for large-sized employment businesses. The flexibility that the partition approach provides enables the expansion of the use of VAT data to targeted industries to manage the introduction of source data changes.
- Deflate (where needed), apply seasonal adjustment and publish.

13.3.3 The Use of Administrative Data in UK Monthly Short-term Indicators

Table 13.1 shows how VAT turnover data has been used to replace responses from survey units with varying percentages depending on the appropriateness of the data (table current as of April 2021).

In practice, UK monthly outputs still initially use survey data until it is replaced with VAT data as it becomes available. Survey data for the targeted units (e.g. Table 13.1) is replaced typically after three months, as the VAT data feed is not comprehensive enough for the requirements of the outputs, as businesses can choose to remit information over a longer timeframe. The VAT source can be used earlier, provided there is the accepted trade off with the revision properties of the aggregate output.

13.3.4 The Use of Administrative Data for Regional Estimation

Within the UK, there is user demand for increased detail on economic activity for the subnational estimates. This includes estimates for economic activity for England, Northern Ireland, Scotland,

Table 13.1 Illustration of how sampling individual units are replaced with administrative VAT records for different economic sectors.

	Production	Services		Construction	Total
Total sample size	30,000 in a combined Monthly Business Survey			8,000	N/A
Survey units replaced	1,800	5,800		2,400	10,000
VAT units	88,000	562,000		100,000	750,000
% of Gross Value Added for each sector which is calculated by VAT returns	12.4%	6.4%		14.3%	7.7%

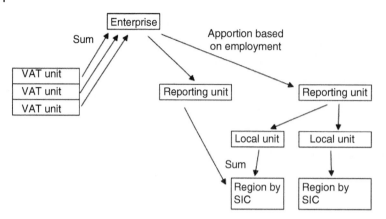

Figure 13.3 Example of the complexities involved when apportioning to regions for a particular standard industry classification (SIC).

and specific regions within England. The UK total is then calculated as the sum of these estimates. In practice, due to the arrangement for the Devolved Administrations, some of these estimates are calculated separately. For example, Scotland[1] and Northern Ireland[2] calculate their own estimates for some key variables.

Regional estimates of gross domestic product (GDP) (ONS approach) are based on the economic activity of the site, as it is believed to capture the economic activity actually taking place in the region. The same approach is taken within our annual regional accounts estimates, but differs slightly to short-term estimates of economic activity published by Scotland (Quarterly Scottish GDP) and Northern Ireland (composite economic index). These are based on an industry classification that is a hybrid between the site-level activity and the overall business activity. For most businesses, the overall business and the site are the same, so while the actual difference between the estimates based on the two different classifications is not known, it is believed to be small.

In the context of administrative data, the complex relationships between the different types of units (VAT, reporting and local) also need to be taken into account. An example of the complexities involving the reporting unit (cf. Figure 13.1) and local unit is summarized in Figure 13.3. In this example, reporting units (e.g. with the sample survey) may be comprised of different numbers of local units, and this illustrates how a regional estimate by standard industrial classification (SIC) could be created.

From a practical perspective, Figure 13.4 explains how the turnover can also be allocated to Local Units by using the employment variable. The Local Unit's location determines the region where the turnover is allocated to. Note that the employment variable can thus be used twice to allocate turnover: first from enterprise to reporting units (for complex enterprises) and second from reporting unit to local units.

In this example, to calculate the turnover for one region (e.g. Wales), the turnover from each UK reporting unit is apportioned by employment into the local units. The sum is then calculated using the value of each local unit within each industry grouping, to get the total value for the region within that industry.

However, there are industries where this approach is not optimal as the relationship between turnover and employment does not hold. For example, businesses in certain industries may have

1 https://www.gov.scot/publications/gdp-quarterly-national-accounts-for-scotland-2019-q3/
2 https://www.nisra.gov.uk/statistics/economic-output-statistics/ni-composite-economic-index

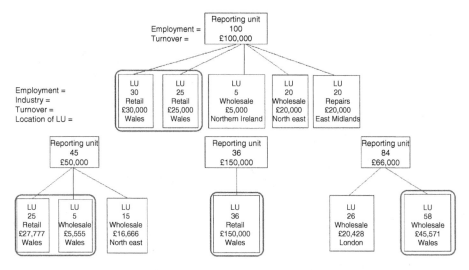

Figure 13.4 Example allocation of a reporting unit to local unit based on selected UK regions (Wales, Northern Ireland, North East, East Midlands, and London).

large turnover and relatively low employment, so apportioning the turnover based on employment may lead to inaccurate results. To overcome, this issue these industries can be treated separately with bespoke solutions.

13.3.5 Example: Comparison of VAT Data to Survey Data

An example of the comparison between administrative data usage, and estimates obtained from sample surveys is captured by McLaren et al. (2021). The different independent approaches can be used to compare and validate both the magnitude and the direction of the growth rates. Relevant information is reproduced here to illustrate the differences.

Figures 13.5 and 13.6 show comparisons for two selected series, between seasonally adjusted growth rates estimated following two different methods: (i) the regional gross domestic product (RGDP) approach for Wales which uses Gross Value Added as a proxy for GDP (solid line); and (ii) the Welsh Short-Term Indicators (WSTIs) survey-based estimate (dashed line).

The main differences between the different types of estimates are attributable to the underlying data sources and methods.

RGDP's data sources are split in two, comprising VAT data and external administrative data sources (ONS 2021). VAT data forms approximately 70% of the total data for the publication leaving approximately 30% to external data sources. Using VAT enables RGDP to make the most of data which cover millions of records available for use for official statistics. VAT data acts like a business census covering UK businesses with a turnover of £85,000 and over. Using VAT data overcomes many sampling issues we observe with business surveys, i.e. low sampling rates for smaller businesses. WSTI's uses a wide and diverse range of data sources (17 unique data sources go into creating WSTI outputs). The principle data source for production and service industries is the UK's Monthly Business Survey (MBS). This UK-wide survey collects information on turnover and on employee numbers. Since the survey was not designed with any explicit regional breakdown element, Welsh coverage can vary over time as smaller businesses are selected via a rotational sampling scheme. The principle data source is complemented with the top up survey that collects wholly Welsh turnover from UK companies who have a significant presence in Wales.

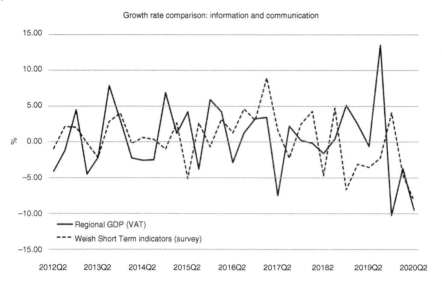

Figure 13.5 Comparison between seasonally adjusted growth rates for selected industry: "Information and Communication," on both VAT administrative data and sample survey for Wales.

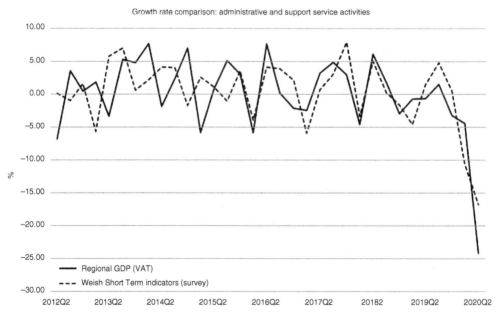

Figure 13.6 Comparison between seasonally adjusted growth rates for selected industry "Administrative and support service activities," on both VAT administrative data and sample survey for Wales.

Both approaches cover processing of current prices and volume data, deflation, indexation, seasonal adjustment, weighting, and chain-linking, but these processes are not identical when calculating each estimate. For example, seasonal adjustment in WSTI occurs at a lower level (SIC 2 digits) rather than at the SIC 1 digit level when calculating RGDP, and constraining to a UK total does not take place when calculating WSTI. These differences mean that the two series are unlikely to be identical due to those processing steps. However, this comparison demonstrates how the administrative data source is a viable option to replace a dedicated sample survey provided any differences can be explained.

13.4 Case Study 2 – A Greater Use of Administrative Data in New Zealand's Labor Market Statistics

13.4.1 Organizational Context

The statistical methods group of Stats NZ produced the *Guide to reporting on administrative data quality*[3] in 2016. This guide embedded the error framework of Li-Chun Zhang (2012) as part of organizational thinking when statistical areas examine the quality of administrative data. The framework is embedded as part of the discovery phase when examining whether an administrative source can be utilized for official statistics.

Like the case study from the United Kingdom, Stats NZ has invested in ensuring our subannual financial indicators have made extensive use of VAT data. But would the frameworks that were established as part of our organizational thinking for maximizing our use of administrative data in our financial statistics be reused? Would it work for our subannual labor market statistics?

Significant transformation occurred in the New Zealand tax system that enabled Stats NZ to rethink the use of administrative data in our subannual labor market statistics. From April 2019 most New Zealand employers are now required to electronically file payroll information, known as payday filing. Payday filing is timelier and has more information about employees' pay period, making it a more flexible and useful data source. Larger employing enterprises are required to file their return to Inland Revenue within two working days of each payday. All other enterprises have 10 working days to file a return. While most enterprises file electronically, it is still possible for some smaller employers to file by paper which have slightly longer timeframes to be processed.

Stats NZ and Inland Revenue have formal agreements for sharing data in place and data are transferred daily to Stats NZ. As the transformation at Inland Revenue was wider than just labor market statistics, Stats NZ set up a dedicated team to ensure that the impacts from this transformation did not negatively impact the statistical pipelines for the many uses of administrative data from Inland Revenue across Stats NZ.

Stats NZ started to use the error framework as part of the discovery phase to assess whether the future Stats NZ quarterly employment survey could benefit from this transformation at Inland Revenue. This framework was used to critically evaluate this new data, particularly looking at where this data may still need to be supplemented by a Stats NZ business survey. For example, applying this framework highlighted the representation errors (unit errors). The administrative data were linked to the Stats NZ business register to compare our statistical unit model against the tax collection units. This work was critical to inform where Stats NZ needed to continue a direct collection.

This discovery phase generated what would become the first official monthly statistics on employment in New Zealand. Prior to this, the Stats NZ quarterly employment survey results were the first indicator of what was happening in the New Zealand labor market.

---

3 Guide to reporting on administrative data quality in 2016: https://www.stats.govt.nz/methods/guide-to-reporting-on-administrative-data-quality-2.

Table 13.2 The Stats NZ sub-annual suite of demand-side labor statistics.

	Monthly employment indicator	Quarterly employment survey	Quarterly business employment data
New to Stats NZ	Yes	Updating a survey which has a long history at Stats NZ	Yes
Timeliness	Four weeks after the end of the month	Five weeks after the end of the quarter	Nine weeks after the end of the quarter
Reference period	Covers all activity in the month	The pay week ending on, or before the 20th of the middle month of the quarter	Covers all activity in the quarter
Key variables	Average weekly filled jobs	Average weekly paid hours for FTE's	
		Average hourly earnings	
		Total weekly earnings	Filled jobs
		Total weekly paid hours	Gross earnings
Key dimensions		Industry of employer	
	Industry of employer	Full or part time	Industry of employer
	Age	Age	Age
	Sex	Sex	Sex
	Regional council	Regional council	Regional council
Use of administrative data from Inland Revenue	Uses payroll information for almost all employing businesses in New Zealand	In phase two the QES will use payroll data for all employing businesses, except the largest and complex group structures	Uses payroll information for almost all employing businesses in New Zealand
Direct survey collection by Stats NZ	No	Yes. 4000 enterprises including all large and complex units.	No. However, it uses data from the quarterly surveys as part of the modeling
Alignment with sub-annual financial collections	No	Yes	Yes
Used in New Zealand's national accounts	No	Yes	Yes
Development	Implemented in November 2019	Phase one implemented in March 2021	Implemented December 2020

The research developed from the monthly employment indicator development was then used to assist in the redesign of our quarterly employment survey. Also, a lot of the statistical pipeline created for the monthly employment indicator were able to be reused to develop the new quarterly business employment data collection. These changes created a new landscape for our sub-annual labor market statistics in New Zealand in 2021. Table 13.2 provides a summary of each of the three collections and how they fit together.

The following sections will discuss the development of each of these three statistical collections, starting with the development of the monthly employment indicator.

13.4.2   Stats NZ's New Monthly Employment Indicator

First published in November 2019, the monthly employment indicator is a new statistical collection produced by Stats NZ. It has been developed using a combination of data from two different sources from Inland Revenue: the employer monthly schedule and payday filing. This data has been utilized to produce information about two key dynamics in the labor market. The number of filled jobs in the economy and gross earnings paid by enterprises to employees.

It is now Stats NZ's most timely release of information on the labor market for New Zealand. It is published four weeks after the end of the reference month.

The monthly employment indicator collection includes data on filled jobs and gross earnings belonging to both full-time and part-time employees (as these are not distinguished in the administrative data) foreign residents and members of the permanent armed forces with wages and salaries of self-employed people who pay themselves a wage or salary. Excluded are workers with scheduler payments, self-employment income not taxed at source, employees on unpaid leave, and unpaid employees.

Figure 13.7 shows one of the key high-level series that the monthly employment indicator was designed to produce using only administrative data, the monthly number of filled jobs in New Zealand.

Developing the new monthly employment indicator required building a completely new pipeline to use this new payday filing from Inland Revenue. As per the case study from the United Kingdom, this involves some very simple checks at the business level, as well as checks for duplicates or tax codes that shouldn't be included or don't exist. A small but challenging issue was the need for a small amount of imputation. This is because there still are a small number of businesses that are late to file with Inland Revenue when Stats NZ close off the collection window to begin our analysis phase. While this impacts less than 1.5% of total filled jobs measured in the most recent month, our key concerns were whether there may be seasonal reasons for variance in late filing that we don't yet understand. However, as this payday filing source was new, we have accepted that

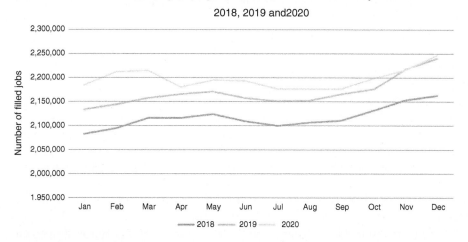

Figure 13.7   Number of filled jobs 2018–2020. Source: Stats NZ/CC BY 4.0.

this is something that will have to be evaluated when we have longer time series-data available to analyze.

When the monthly employment indicator was first released by Stats NZ in November 2019 Stats NZ produced only high-level industry summary statistics. This was partly due to resourcing and partly due to the new nature of the administrative data source. No one was to know that an employment shock was just around the corner.

From early in 2020 a variety of government agencies, the Reserve Bank, and bank economists were pushing hard for more granular information about the New Zealand labor market.

This included demand for

- more detailed industry analysis – which industries were being impacted the most?
- gender splits – were females more likely than males to lose jobs?
- age breakdowns – were younger age groups impacted more?
- regional breakdowns – we knew our tourism regions would be harder hit, how much harder?

Due to the quick turnaround cycle between each monthly release, these expansions were introduced in phases throughout 2020.

The ability to react quickly to user demand was always one of the key aspirations behind our organizational drive to increase the use of administrative data. Our traditional stratified random sample designs utilized for surveys were often optimized to minimize the number of respondents that needed to be surveyed. While the key positive of this was the reduction of burden on respondents, a consequence was that we would often lose the ability to dig deeper into the data to explain what was driving changes below the survey design level which was often at a high level of industry aggregation.

13.4.3   Redesigning the Quarterly Employment Survey

The Stats NZ quarterly employment survey (see Table 13.2, middle column) collects information about employment, earnings, and hours paid at industry and national levels. A key difference of this collection is that the reference period is the pay week ending on, or before the 20th of the middle month of the quarter.

This survey has a history dating back to the 1960s in New Zealand. The sample design for this survey had remained relatively unchanged since the 1990s utilizing a stratified random sample designed using two dimensions for the stratification (i) high-level industry classification, and (ii) the number of employees the business has from the Stats NZ business register. Even now, the quarterly employment survey is still Stats NZ's largest subannual survey collection with nearly 4000 enterprises surveyed each quarter.

The quarterly employment survey has a pivotal role in the New Zealand government. It is utilized as a key benchmark for social transfers paid by the government such as the New Zealand pension which are administered by New Zealand's Ministry for Social Development. For this reason, Stats NZ needed to invest heavily in the development stage to make sure we understood the implications of the change in design.

Figure 13.8 highlights one of the most important outputs of the quarterly employment survey, average ordinary time weekly earnings. It also highlights that Stats NZ has over 30 years of time-series data for this collection, which is one of the reasons why implementing any changes in methodologies is challenging.

Prior to 2019, the quarterly employment survey was the only source of information on the amount of hours enterprises were paying employees for in New Zealand. However, in 2019, New Zealand's

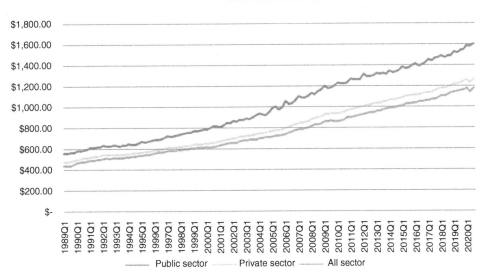

Average ordinary time weekly earnings (FTEs) by sector
1989 Q1 to 2020 Q3

Figure 13.8 Key results from the quarterly employment survey. Source: Stats NZ/CC BY 4.0.

tax agency also started to collect information from employers on the number of hours paid for the first time.

With the new monthly employment indicator proving that a greater use of administrative data in our labor market statistics was possible, it was now time to redesign a quarterly employment survey for the future. The new design for the quarterly employment survey will be introduced in two different phases.

13.4.3.1 Phase One

The first phase is to introduce the "managed collection" of large and complex enterprises in the New Zealand economy into the sample design of the new quarterly employment survey. These are the same enterprises that Stats NZ have selected for our quarterly subannual financial collection.

There are two key reasons behind this need for a "managed collection" of large and complex enterprises for employment information for the quarterly employment survey.

- For some large enterprises in the New Zealand economy which span multiple industrial activities, Stats NZ develops dedicated activity units on the business register. For these units, we will require a direct response from the unit as the administrative data is at a more consolidated level.
- There are some large enterprises that report their tax data through as group returns to our Inland Revenue organization.

Due to their significance, many of the largest enterprises in the New Zealand economy have always been in the historic quarterly employment survey. The information collected in this survey for these large enterprises is utilized to help ensure that the Stats NZ business register maintains up to date information on the size of enterprises geographic locations. At the same time, Stats NZ have optimized the sample design so that in the first phase we have a similar sample size to the past quarterly employment survey of approximately 4000 enterprises. Stats NZ has also invested in moving the new quarterly employment survey to becoming an online survey collection, as well as using this opportunity to move it off legacy software.

After this "managed collection" design is in place for large and complex enterprises, Stats NZ will then start making greater use of the new information on hours worked collected from Inland Revenue.

13.4.3.2 Phase Two

Stats NZ then intends to remove the enterprises that were still randomly sampled in phase one so that the new design of the quarterly employment survey replicates the design of our subannual financial collections. The future design of the quarterly employment survey will be a dedicated direct survey collection of just the largest and complex enterprises in New Zealand with administrative data being used sourced for every other enterprise in scope in the population. This will approximately halve the number of enterprises that are required in the survey collection to 2000 enterprises.

There were two key reasons for this phasing. The first reason was that it will allow Stats NZ to have several quarters of survey data from these new managed collection enterprises to ensure that our researched design can be proven. Given the importance of the quarterly employment survey results in the adjustment of social transfers, this was critical. Second, as the administrative data on hours paid is new for New Zealand it allows more administrative data to be used as part of the seasonal adjustment series development.

13.4.4 Introducing Stats NZ's New Quarterly Business Employment Data

After developing the new monthly employment indicator, and redesigning the quarterly employment survey, the next targeted development was the production of another new statistical output for Stats NZ. This is known as the business employment data release (see Table 13.2, last column). It provides customers with a quarterly measure of labor demand. The purpose of this measure is to provide a new range of labor market insights to complement the point-in-time (or "payweek") needed in the quarterly employment survey.

As the entire quarter is covered, the business employment data help measure the impacts of seasonal or "one-off" events. To ensure this new employment data can be easily associated with our existing financial collections, it was built to reuse the exact same population frame as our existing quarterly financial measures. This will allow a chance for greater inferences to be made between our labor market demand statistics and financial variables, for example in productivity studies.

From the March quarter in 2021, the quarterly employment survey design will be aligned with the subannual financial collections that Stats NZ conducts. Stats NZ will then utilize the information collected in the redesigned quarterly employment survey for the large and complex enterprises collected in our Stats NZ survey in our modeling of administrative data.

A lot of the challenges creating the quarterly business employment data collection were resolved by developing the monthly employment indicator first. Particularly the ingestion of data from Inland Revenue into our statistical pipelines. However, introducing this new business employment data had a few unique challenges.

Introducing a new quarterly statistical collection into our labor market statistics meant that Stats NZ had to provide advice to our customers that this new collection should now be considered for use instead of the quarterly employment survey. This is because customers, including our National Accounts area, had developed customized data requests from the quarterly employment survey well below the targeted sample design of the survey because it was the only option available.

As Stats NZ did not have historic survey information about all large and complex enterprises in the New Zealand economy this meant that there are limitations in the production of the historical series. For this reason, the historic series has been published as a provisional series only.

13.5 Concluding Remarks

Both the United Kingdom and New Zealand have in recent years been focused on ensuring a greater use of administrative data in subannual economic statistics. The approaches taken for both countries have many similarities, both in terms of subject matter, frameworks, and the methodological decisions taken. Importantly, they both have resulted in a decrease in burden on business respondents, particularly on the smaller- and medium-sized businesses. Both case studies have also highlighted that as part of confronting historic survey results, it is important to understand the sorts of errors that are introduced by the new administrative data approach and compare that to the types of errors that are traditionally accepted from historic sample designs.

In both Stats NZ and the ONS, methodological experts have had key roles in ensuring that the approaches that are taken to increasing the use of administrative data in economic statistics is done in a systematic and integrated manner. This is because there is almost always an important balancing act that economic statisticians need to make when considering a greater use of administrative data. What can seem like an obvious decision to use administrative data can often be found to pose challenges in some areas when evaluated methodically. We find this in many cases where targeted business surveys are still required as part of our new collections, which recognize we often need to utilize a combination of traditional business surveys combined with administrative data as the preferred approach.

References

ABS 2009. 1520.0: ABS Data Quality Framework. https://www.abs.gov.au/ausstats/abs@.nsf/lookup/ 1520.0Main+Features1May+2009 (accessed November 2020).

Bakker, B.F.M. and Daas, P.J.H. (2012). Methodological challenges of register-based research. *Statistica Neerlandica* 66 (1): 2–7.

Blackwell, L. and Rogers, N.J. (2021). A longitudinal error framework to support the design and use of integrated datasets. In: *Measurement Error in Longitudinal Data* (ed. A. Cernat and J.W. Sakshaug). Oxford: Oxford University Press.

Cerroni, F., Di Bella, G., and Galie, L. (2014). Evaluating administrative data quality as input of the statistical production process. *Rivista di Statistica Ufficiale* 1–2: 117–146.

Daas, P.H.J., Ossen, S.J.L., and Arend-Toth, J. (2009a). Framework of quality assurance for administrative data sources. *Statistics Netherlands, Division of Methodology and Quality*.

Daas, P.J.H., Ossen, S.J.L., Vis-Visschers, R.J.W.M, and Arend-Toth, J. (2009b). Checklist for the quality evaluation of AD sources. Discussion paper 09042. *Statistics Netherlands*.

de Waal, T., van Delden, A., and Scholtus, S. (2020a). Commonly used methods for measuring output quality of multisource statistics. *Spanish Journal of Statistics* 2 (1): 79–107.

de Waal, T., van Delden, A., and Scholtus, S. (2020b). Multi-source statistics: basic situations and methods. *International Statistical Review* 88 (1): 203–228.

van Delden, A., Lorenc, B., Struijs, P., and Zhang, L.-C. (2018). On statistical unit errors in business statistics. *Journal of Official Statistics* 34: 573–580.

GDQ Hub (2020). The Government Data Quality Framework. www.gov.uk/government/publications/ the-government-data-quality-framework (accessed December 2020).

Groves, R.M. and Lyberg, L. (2010). Total survey error: past, present, and future. *Public Opinion Quarterly* 74 (5): 849–879.

Hand, D. (2018). Statistical challenges of administrative and transaction data. *Journal of the Royal Statistical Society Series A* 181 (3): 555–605.

Karr, A.F., Sanil, A.P., and Banks, D.L. (2006). Data quality: a statistical perspective. *Statistical Methodology* 3: 137–173.

Laitila, T., Wallgren, A., and Wallgren, B. (2011). Quality assessment of administrative data. *Statistics Sweden Methodology Reports* 2011: 2.

Luiten, A., Hox, J., and de Leeuw, E. (2020). Survey nonresponse trends and fieldwork effort in the 21st century: results of an international study across countries and surveys. *Journal of Official Statistics* 36 (3): 469–487.

McLaren, C.H. and Whipple, M. (2019). Use of administrative data in the production of short-term economic indicators. *Proceedings of the European Network for Better Establishment Statistics Conference*, Bilbao, the Basque Country, Spain. https://statswiki.unece.org/display/ENBES/EESW19+Programme (accessed July 2021).

McLaren, C.H, Lo Presti, A., Requena L, Ryall, E., Whipple, M., and White H. (2021). Sub-national GDP estimates in the United Kingdom using administrative data. *Office for National Statistics* (Internal document, pre-print available on request.)

Nordbotten, S. (2010). Use of administrative data in official statistics – past, present and future – with special reference to the Nordic countries. In: *Official Statistics – Methodology and Applications in Honour of Daniel Thorburn* (ed. Carlson, Nyquist and Villani), 15–28. https://officialstatistics.wordpress.com (accessed July 2021).

Office for National Statistics (2019). Quality assurance of administrative data (QAAD) report for Value Added Tax turnover data. https://www.ons.gov.uk/economy/economicoutputand productivity/output/methodologies/qualityassuranceofadministrativedataqaadreportfor valueaddedtaxturnoverdata (accessed February 2021).

Office for National Statistics (2020a). Population and migration statistics system transformation – overview. *Office for National Statistics*. https://www.ons.gov.uk/peoplepopulationandcommunity/populationandmigration/internationalmigration/articles/transformationofthepopulationand migrationstatisticssystemoverview/2019-06-21 (accessed February 2021).

Office for National Statistics (2020b). Working paper series no 19 – an error framework for longitudinal administrative sources; its use for understanding the statistical properties of data for international migration. *Office for National Statistics*. https://www.ons.gov.uk/methodology/ methodologicalpublications/generalmethodology/onsworkingpaperseries/onsworkingpaperseries no19anerrorframeworkforlongitudinaladministrativesourcesitsuseforunderstandingthestatistical propertiesofdataforinternationalmigration (accessed February 2021).

Office for National Statistics (2021). Data source catalogue for regional GDP. https://cy.ons.gov.uk/ economy/grossdomesticproductgdp/datasets/quarterlycountryandregionalgdpdatasourcecatalogue?: uri=economy/grossdomesticproductgdp/datasets/quarterlycountryandregionalgdpdatasourcecatalogue (accessed May 2021).

Office for Statistics Regulation (2018). *Code of Practice for Statistics*, 24. London: Office for Statistics Regulation. https://code.statisticsauthority.gov.uk/wp-content/uploads/2018/02/Code-of-Practice- for-Statistics.pdf (accessed February 2021).

European Statistical System (2019). Quality assurance framework of the European Statistical System Version 2.0. https://ec.europa.eu/eurostat/documents/64157/4392716/ESS-QAF-V1-2final.pdf/ bbf5970c-1adf-46c8-afc3-58ce177a0646 (accessed March 2021).

Quenneville, B., Picard, F., and Fortier, S. (2013). Calendarization with interpolating splines and state space models. *Journal of the Royal Statistical Society. Series C (Applied Statistics)* 62 (3): 371–399. http://www.jstor.org/stable/24771811.

Reid, G., Zabala, F., and Holmberg, A. (2017). Extending TSE to administrative data: a quality framework and case studies from Stats NZ. *Journal of Official Statistics* 33 (2): 477–511.

Schouten, B. and Cobben, F. (2007). R-indexes for the comparison of different fieldwork strategies and data collection modes. Discussion paper 07002. *Statistics Netherlands*. https://www.researchgate .net/publication/238096269_R-indexes_for_the_comparison_of_different_fieldword_strategies_ and_data_collection_modes (accessed July 2021).

Statistics Norway (2007). The evolution of the statistical system of Norway. p. 3. https://unstats.un.org/ unsd/dnss/docViewer.aspx?docID=1599 (accessed July 2021).

Statistics New Zealand (2016). Guide to reporting on administrative data quality. https://www.stats .govt.nz/methods/guide-to-reporting-on-administrative-data-quality-2 (accessed July 2021).

UK Statistics Authority (2020). Statistics for the public good: informing the UK. Improving lives. Building the future. https://uksa.statisticsauthority.gov.uk/statistics-for-the-public-good/ (accessed July 2021).

UNECE, United Nations Economic Commission for Europe (2011). *Using Administrative and Secondary Sources for Official Statistics: A Handbook of Principles and Practices.* New York and Geneva: United Nations. http://www.unece.org/fileadmin/DAM/stats/publications/Using_ Administrative_Sources_Final_for_web.pdf (accessed July 2021).

UNECE, United Nations Economic Commission for Europe (2014). Big data quality framework: a suggested framework for the quality of big data. Version 4.01. https://statswiki.unece.org/download/ attachments/108102944/Big%20Data%20Quality%20Framework%20-%20final-%20Jan08-2015.pdf? version=1&modificationDate=1420725063663&api=v2 (accessed July 2021).

UNECE, United Nations Economic Commission for Europe (2019). Generic statistical business process model. Version 5.1. https://statswiki.unece.org/display/GSBPM/GSBPM+v5.1 (accessed July 2021).

Zhang, L.-C. (2012). Topics of statistical theory for register-based statistics and data integration. *Statistica Neerlandica* 66: 41–63.

14

The Evolution of Integrating Administrative Data in Business Statistics in Ireland

Colin Hanley and Sorcha O'Callaghan

Central Statistics Office, Cork City, Ireland

14.1 Introduction

There has been a growing demand from users and policymakers for more granular and relevant information on businesses in Ireland. The increase in demand poses a challenge for compilers of business statistics in the Central Statistics Office (CSO). Traditional data collection methods are resource-intensive and increasing the scope of survey data collection would increase pressure on those resources while also increasing the burden on survey respondents. An alternative way to meet this demand is to utilize administrative data.

Administrative data are collected by other government bodies for the purposes of providing public services. National Statistical Institutes (NSIs) have increasingly utilized these available data sources for statistical purposes. Nearly all members of the European Statistical System (ESS) have moved toward increased use of administrative data. ESS members have used administrative sources in business statistics (Costanzo 2011) and as part of the "new data sources" area, administrative data was included among the five key areas of the ESS Vision 2020. Like other NSIs, the CSO expanded the use of administrative data to develop more outputs.

Under the legal mandate provided by the Statistics Act 1993a, the CSO can get access to administrative data to assess its potential for statistical work. For business statistics, the data was initially used as a core resource in the development of the annual business register for which it could collect primary data through surveys. Since then, business statistics has increasingly integrated administrative data into the statistical production process.

Administrative data can be used by the NSI in different ways depending on the quality of the source. Using the data sources in the creation of outputs, we need to consider the input, process, and output quality (Laitila et al. 2011). This determines whether the data are used to improve the production system, used in combination with other sources, or used directly in the statistical product. In this chapter, we will illustrate how we have used administrative data as an input resource in the development of the business register, a process resource when producing Structural Business Statistics (SBS) product as well as both an input and output resource in microdata linking outputs.

The statistical business register records information on all businesses active in the state. It is derived from administrative data sources from the Revenue Commissioners of Ireland and the Companies Registration Office (CRO). The information from employer, corporation, and income

Advances in Business Statistics, Methods and Data Collection. Edited by Ger Snijkers, Mojca Bavdaž, Stefan Bender, Jacqui Jones, Steve MacFeely, Joseph W. Sakshaug, Katherine J. Thompson, and Arnout van Delden.
© 2023 John Wiley & Sons, Inc. Published 2023 by John Wiley & Sons, Inc.

tax registrations are used to identify businesses. These businesses identified from the administrative data are then used to form samples for the various business surveys collected by the CSO. Administrative data was then integrated into the processing of survey data such as SBS.

The CSO produces SBS from three surveys, the Census of Industrial Production (CIP), the Building and Construction Inquiry (BCI), and the Annual Services Inquiry (ASI). The requirement is for a census of enterprises in the Irish Business economy. To reduce burden on respondents, the CSO uses a split population approach. Returns for part of the population are covered by the sample, while tax returns are used for the remaining enterprises creating census dataset with values for each enterprise in the population.

Of course, government agencies who collect this data can produce statistics from their own resources as well. Where the CSO can add value to the resource is through data linkage. Linking different sources of administrative data and survey data together provides an opportunity to develop new outputs that meet the growing demand from users. In this chapter, we will give two examples of where business statistics in the CSO have done so. The first example links export data with business data to produce a publication on exporting enterprises in Ireland. The second links administrative data with the business register to produce timely indicators of the impact of COVID-19 on businesses in Ireland.

The digital transformation of government services has and will continue to provide compilers of business statistics with additional data resources. Previously, there was an 18-month lag in receiving employee payment data that has since been modernized to allow near real time provision of this data. Further data sources on employee wages and enterprises value added tax (VAT) data could be leveraged to provide more timely estimates on trends in business statistics. As more services are digitalized, more data sources will be available to business statisticians. This provides endless opportunities to not only delivery on their current mandate but also to produce more informative indicators.

14.2 Administrative Data

Government departments and agencies need to collect information from individuals and businesses to provide public services. For example, a tax office will collect information on taxes paid by individuals and businesses. The data collected from this is essentially a by-product of the main goal of these departments in providing the public service. While this data is not primarily collected for statistical purposes, it can be supplied to the CSO under Section 30(1) of the Statistics Act 1993a (see Section 14.3.1). This allows the CSO to assess its potential for improving the data operations in business statistics.

When evaluating the data sources for statistical potential, the statistical usability of the data needs to be considered from different aspects. As an input resource, is the data of sufficient quality to be used in the statistical operations, either in combination with other sources or to improve the production process. The data can also be evaluated as an output resources where the data is of high enough quality to directly produce a statistical process. Daas et al. (2009) has proposed different indicators to assess the statistical usability of the data which can help the NSI decide how the data can be used in the statistical process.

14.2.1 Benefits

Administrative data can be used in many ways within the statistical process depending on the type and quality of the data. It can be used to validate, impute for nonresponse, or even used directly in the statistical product (see van Delden and Lewis 2023 [Chapter 12]). Administrative records can give clear insights into an enterprise which might help explain some otherwise unexpected survey returns. It can be used as an auxiliary variable for imputation in a statistical product or directly in the statistical product. A core function administrative sources have in business statistics is in creating and maintaining the population frame. As well as the benefits within the statistical process, administrative data have many additionally practical benefits.

14.2.1.1 Resources

Collecting primary statistical data through surveys can be resource intensive. Questionnaires need to be designed, samples created, respondents contacted (either electronically or manually), reminders issued to respondents to encourage participation, and in some cases, contacted after collection to verify the response. All this can be resource-intensive and still deliver a less than ideal response rate. Acquiring administrative data from another public sector body can be more cost-effective as the data is already being collected. While there might be some cost to the NSI, such as purchasing access or paying to facilitate the transmission of the data, the overall cost will likely be much smaller than the cost of primary data collection.

14.2.1.2 Coverage

One of the ways to limit cost in primary data collection is to take a sample of the population and make inferences about that population. This method comes with a degree of uncertainty. Since administrative data is the by-product of providing public services, it can often provide close to full coverage of the population. This reduces the uncertainty inherent with sampling and reduces the burden of nonresponse on the compiler of business statistics. The greater coverage allows for more detailed analysis of subpopulations which give more insight into specific sectors or geographic locations.

14.2.1.3 Timeliness

In some cases, administrative data can be utilized to provide more timelier statistics. This is dependent on the administrative data source itself. Different data sources are subject to different rules established by the body that collects the data. For example, annual business statistics in the CSO are published about 18 months after the reference year. The reason for the delay is that the figures on active enterprises depend on processed corporation and income tax return data supplied by the Irish Revenue Commissioners, which businesses have 11 months after the reference year to submit. However, the digitalization of government services is starting to provide more current data. Data sources, such as VAT data and data on wages are collected in a timelier manner. This can then be used to provide outputs with similar timeliness as short-term surveys but with the added granularity provided from the administrative data.

14.2.1.4 Response Burden

Reducing cost and increasing coverage, timeliness, and frequency are benefits that administrative data has for the compiler, but it also benefits the businesses responding to the surveys. Businesses in general prefer a less regulatory burden. While they acknowledge the need for some level of bureaucracy some might view statistical surveys as an unnecessary burden. This is particularly true if the respondent has already provided the same information to another public sector body. A more joined up approach will allow for a more efficient extraction of information from businesses. If the business provides information to one public sector body and that information is available to the statistical body, then the NSI could provide added value by collecting data not otherwise available.

14.2.2 Challenges

The advantages of using administrative data are substantial. However, there are challenges of using secondary data for statistical purposes that the complier of business statistic must be aware of (see Chapter 12 by van Delden and Lewis (2023) and Chapter 13 by Cox et al. (2023) in this volume for more information on the issues of using administrative data). This section briefly looks at some of those challenges and what the user can do to minimize its impact (For a more comprehensive look at the issues of using administrative data see Chapters 12 and 13 in this volume).

14.2.2.1 Access

First and foremost is getting access to the administrative data as it might not be a priority for the data holders. Ideally, it would be beneficial for the NSI to have a legal mandate that allows them access to administrative data (see Section 14.3.1).

14.2.2.2 Quality

When collecting primary data, the statistician can design the collection to meet their specified needs. This is not the case with administrative data which is collected by another body external from the NSI and will likely be collected without statistical considerations. The quality of the data is dependent on the effectiveness of the body collecting the data and can be subject to change without consultation with the NSI. Another aspect that needs to be considered is the definition of the variables collected. Since administrative data is collected for a specific purpose, it might not align with the desired variable of the NSI. For example, the tax office might collect an enterprise's turnover that is subject to tax while the NSI needs all turnover produced from the enterprise. It is therefore critical for the business statistics compiler to have a good understanding of the data that they are using. To achieve this, means the NSI should develop and maintain good relations with the provider of administrative data. Continuing communications with the data providers will allow the statistician to understand the data they are using, know its limitations, and how those limitations can be corrected for in a way that will allow them to meet their specific needs. This enables the government departments to consult with the NSI on future developments and new data sources which enhances the statistical process. In the CSO, we have liaison groups with the key data providers who update us on new data sources and review the specifications of current data provision arrangements.

14.2.2.3 Statistical Units

In business statistics, primary data is often collected and processed at the enterprise statistical unit. Conversely, administrative data is not collected at the enterprises level but a separate administrative level, often the legal unit. The enterprise is defined as "the smallest combination of legal units that is an organisational unit producing goods or services, which benefit from a certain degree of autonomy" (UN 2007, p. 11). The enterprise may also consist of one or more legal units as well as kind of activity units (KAUs) and local units. This can present challenges to the business statistics compiler when using administrative data.

In many cases, the legal unit is equal to the enterprise unit and the process of linking the two units is straightforward. However, for larger enterprises, the structure is often more complex with the enterprise unit encompassing many legal units. Misidentification of the relationships between units can lead to errors in the statistical output, known as unit error (Van Delden et al. 2018).

Another important aspect to consider is that variable distributions in business statistics are often skewed. Larger enterprises, despite their small share of the demography count, can contribute a much larger share of the total value of performance variables, such as turnover or gross value added (GVA) compared to the smaller counterparts. This means that it is vital for the statistician to have the larger enterprises correct to ensure that accurate indicators are being produced. As already mentioned, larger enterprises can comprise many legal units so significant work will need to be done to better understand the unit structure of enterprises and avoid unit error.

Modeling the structure of the enterprise, known in business statistics as profiling, is used to identify the relationship between the different units and the enterprise. This can involve looking at company reports, accounting details, or even contacting the enterprise itself to determine the structure. This can be a resource intensive exercise which might involve the creation of specific areas in the statistical office who will profile large- or medium-sized cases. The CSO has a large cases unit who examine the largest enterprises in Ireland and a medium cases unit who profile other key enterprises based on several criteria. In the next section, we will illustrate how administrative data has been incorporated into data operations in the CSO.

14.3 Administrative Data in CSO Business Statistics

14.3.1 Legal Mandate

The Statistics Act 1993a gives the CSO authority to evaluate records from other public authorities for its statistical potential. Section 30 of the act, on the use of records of public authorities for statistical purposes state:

30.- (1) For the purpose of assisting the Office in the exercise of its function under this Act, the Director General may by delivery of a notice request any public authority to-

(a) Allow officers of statistics at all reasonable times to have access to, inspect and take copies of or extracts from any records in its charge, and
(b) Provide the Office, if any such officer so requires, with copies or extracts from any such record,

and the public authority shall, subject to subsection (2) of this section, comply with any such request free of charge (Statistics Act 1993a).

Data supplied by other public authorities are received by the CSO's Administrative Data Centre (ADC). In the ADC, the data is pseudonymized prior to any statistical analysis. This involves replacing identifying fields with Protected Identifier Keys (PIKs) to ensure privacy. Administrative data that is collected by the CSO is not shared with other government departments and agencies under Section 33 of the Statistics Act (1993b). The CSO can then use the data in its statistical process as an aid or even a replacement to surveys. This helps to improve the efficiency of statistical operations while also developing new products or insights.

14.3.2 Business Register

The CSO maintains a business register as a source of information on enterprises. This information is then used to develop business surveys, create sampling frames, and aid with production of statistical outputs. The register is compiled of all enterprises in Ireland that contribute to gross domestic product (GDP), the legal units of that enterprise, as well as local units and KAUs.

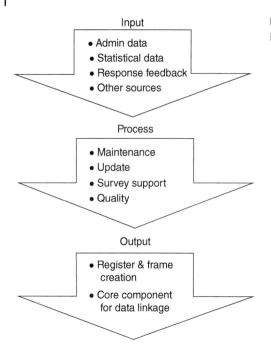

Figure 14.1 CSO Business Register production process.

The register also outlines the structure of the enterprise and its relationship to other enterprises in an enterprise group if applicable. It is also a core component for integrating and maximizing the use of administrative data through microdata linking. The foundation of this information is provided from administrative data sources.

The business register team in the CSO use administrative data as an input resource to birth enterprises onto the register, see Figure 14.1. Data on activity and registrations from employee, corporation tax, and income tax are used to birth new enterprises into the business register. The information derived from these sources include the business characteristics, such as the economic activity of the enterprise. The following administrative data sources are used for the business register:

(1) Quarterly Revenue registration and "Pay as you Earn" (PAYE) Remittance activity data
(2) Monthly PAYE Modernisation data (PMOD)
(3) Annual Corporation Tax and Income Tax returns
(4) CRO registration data

A business is active and is on the register if the above data sources show that it generates turnover, employs staff, or makes investments over a specified period. Validation checks are made throughout this process to ensure that there is no duplication or errors.

The dataset of all active enterprises is then combined with a snap shot of the business register to create the business register frame for the required reference year. The frame is then used by the survey areas to draw their samples to collect primary statistical data. As well as the core statistical functions that the business register aids in, it is also a core instrument for integrating administrative sources with survey data by the legal unit to produce further insights into businesses in Ireland. The development of the business register is an example of using administrative data as an input resource. The administrative data is used along with other resources to produce the output, in this case the business register. The next section looks at using administrative data as process resource when producing the SBS series.

14.3.3 Structural Business Statistics (SBS)

The CSO is required under Council Regulation (EC) (No 295/2008) to produce annual SBS. In practice, the CSO uses data from three annual censuses to compile the SBS series. These are:

(i) The **CIP** covers all enterprises which are wholly or principally involved in industrial production. This survey is carried out on an annual basis. Administrative data are used for some microenterprises which are not surveyed as well as nonrespondents across all case sizes. The scope of the CIP extends to NACE Rev. 2 sections B, C, D, and E.

(ii) The **BCI** was introduced in 2009 for reference year 2008 onwards and replaced the Census of Building and Construction (CBC). The CBC covered all private firms with 20 or more persons engaged whose main activity was building, construction, or civil engineering (i.e. Section F of NACE Rev. 2). The BCI extended this coverage to also include a sample of private firms with less than 20 persons engaged. Administrative data are used for some microenterprises which are not surveyed as well as nonrespondents across all case sizes. The Business Register is used as the sampling frame for the BCI.

(iii) The **ASI** has been conducted as an annual survey of both distributive and nondistributive services since 1991. Results are published aggregated by the type of activity (NACE), region, size class, etc. All enterprises with one or more persons engaged are included. The survey covers all enterprises in the Retail, Wholesale, Transport & Storage, Accommodation & Food, Information & Communication, Real Estate, Professional, Scientific & Technical Activities, Administrative & Support Activities, and Other Selected Services sectors (NACE Rev. 2 sectors G, H, I, J, L, M, N, R, and S).

The above surveys are designed to provide estimates of the principal trading aggregates for all enterprises in the relevant sectors. The "enterprise" is the unit used for survey purposes, i.e. one return is sought in respect of each enterprise covering all constituent branches, local units, or subsidiaries. They are based on sample surveys, and the sample is stratified based on number of persons engaged in the enterprise. A census of enterprises with 20 or more persons engaged is selected. In addition, a stratified random sample is selected for the enterprises with less than 20 persons engaged, with decreasing sampling proportions taken in the lower persons engaged ranges. All enterprises with one or more persons engaged are included in the survey frame.

Instead of weighting the sample units to produce results, the CSO uses corporation and income tax data to create a return for every nonrespondent or nonsurveyed enterprise. The primary financial value the survey uses is profit/loss data with estimates for labor costs added to arrive at a value for GVA. Other financial variables normally received from the survey form are estimated using actual survey returns as the data is not available from the administrative data. This is done using standard ratio-estimation. A basic example would be the ration of turnover to GVA. If for a particular NACE the ratio of turnover to GVA is 4:1, we would simple multiply the derived administrative GVA by 4 to give us a turnover value. This is an example of using process quality administrative data to aid with the production of the SBS series. We can also use other administrative data sources in combination with the SBS to produce more insights.

14.4 Data Linkage Using Administrative Data

One area where administrative data can be most effectively utilized is data linking. Demand from users for more timely and granular data is becoming greater than what traditional methods can meet in any practical sense. As already discussed, primary statistical data collection is costly and increases burden on businesses. However, linking administrative data, with both survey data and other sources of data presents an opportunity to create new statistical products that meet user needs without increasing burden.

Data linking projects that include administrative sources can be challenging, and we need to be aware of the risk associated with it. Some of the risks are those already discussed around administrative data such as data acquisition and asymmetries between statistical units and administrative units, but there is also no formal methodological framework for linking administrative data in business statistics (for more information on record linkage see Larsen and Herning 2023: Chapter 33 in this volume). Here we give two examples of microdata linking projects we have conducted and share our experiences and lessons learned.

14.4.1 Exporting Enterprises in Ireland

Exporting Enterprises in Ireland (CSO 2019) was created with a view to providing a more detailed insight into the relationship between exports by enterprises in Ireland and their turnover. The United Kingdom's (UK) decision to leave the European Union (EU) led to queries from users about enterprises that exported to the UK. These included questions such as

- Number of enterprises that exported to the UK
- Number of personnel engaged in those enterprises
- The turnover of enterprises in Ireland that engage in exporting
- The percentage of turnover dependent on exports to the UK or another country

These questions seem straightforward. Business Statistics had the data on enterprise turnover and personnel while Trade Statistics had data on exports. However, they were not linked together so we could not provide the answer. Linking the data allowed us to create the publication that helps address many of those relevant questions.

14.4.1.1 Trade Data Sources

The underlying data used in the project was based on amalgamating trade data with the Central Business Register (CBR) and SBS surveys. The trade data is a combination of the following:

(i) **International Trade in Goods Statistics (ITGS)** is data on exports of goods collected by a branch of the Irish Revenue Commissioners via the Intrastat survey for Intra-EU trade. External EU trade is collected via Extrastat.

(ii) **Balance of Payments Data (BOP).** Various Balance of Payments and National Accounts quarterly and annual surveys have been used to provide data for this publication. These effectively provide all of the services data in use, as well as merchanting of goods trade and goods for processing adjustments.

(iii) **VAT Information Exchange System (VIES)** system was also used to increase the levels of microdata available for this publication. VIES was designed to prevent VAT zero-rating provisions for goods traded in the EU. In the VIES system, enterprises report the VAT number of the partner company with whom they are trading in the EU. These VAT numbers can then be linked with the CSO's Business Register to increase coverage of exporting enterprises.

14.4.1.2 Linking
Initially, the linkage work focused on incorporating ITGS data with the Business Register and SBS survey data. However, preliminary results did not capture the importance of globalization to enterprises in Ireland. Therefore, the scope of the project was expanded to include exports in services, as well as goods for processing and merchanting trade data. This added increased complexity to the project.

The primary tool for micro-data linking throughout the creation of this product was the CSO Business Register. The statistical unit types that need to be linked included the legal, enterprise, and enterprise group.

The unique identifiers used in the data linking process were the following:

- Enterprise number from the business register
- Administrative VAT number
- BOP number derived from enterprise group number on the business register

14.4.1.3 Linking Trade to Business Register
The three main sources of trade data are the BoPFacts database, the VIES administrative data source and the ITGS. Each source has a unique identifier for matching to the Business Register.

The companies surveyed by BOP have their own unique identifier on the BoPFacts database. This BOP number is derived from the enterprise group number and can be matched back to the business register. VIES reporting is required for VAT purposes and each entry having a corresponding VAT number. Likewise, both the Intrastat and Extrastat data collection systems are closely interlinked with the VAT system and use the VAT number as the unique identifier. Data with a VAT number as a unique identifier are linked to the business register which contains both the VAT number and the corresponding enterprise number.

Once the trade data has linked the enterprise number it is matched to the Business Register Frame. From this we can identify the following sets:

- Match with SBS population
- Enterprises with NACE outside coverage of SBS population
- Enterprises with NACE in SBS population but not matched
- Remaining legal units

The first two sets are straightforward. For most enterprises in Ireland, there is a one-to-one relationship between the legal unit and the enterprise unit. In the case of linking the trade data from administrative sources to the business register, the legal units match with enterprises on the population frame. The complexity of the project comes from matching the remaining legal units.

The unmatched legal units are profiled to identify relationships between these units and the enterprises in Business Demography. Profiling of these enterprises tend to reveal two possibilities. The first is where an enterprise has many legal units identified in its structure. In the situation where one enterprise is in Business Demography, the corresponding unmatched legal units are rolled up into the enterprise unit that is already present in the Business Demography.

The second is where there are many enterprises in the Business Demography where the trade data in the ancillary units are split out among the active enterprises. This is done using the turnover as a proxy for size of the enterprise. For example, we have an ancillary unit with trade data of 100. There are three active enterprises in the group each with ENT A having 300 turnover, ENT B 200 and ENT C 500. In this case, the trade would be distributed in proportion to turnover, so ENT A would get 30, ENT B 20, and ENT C 50.

The data from BopFacts is a combination of survey returns and dummy entities which store aggregated estimates from SBS returns. The BOP survey returns are reported for the enterprise group and is split out among the enterprises in that group. To maximize the availability of microdata for the project, we used the VIES data to identify additional enterprises that are not currently surveyed. VIES statements are required on the supply of goods and services to VAT registered traders to other EU member states. The VIES dataset therefore contains information on services exports to the EU. By matching the enterprises that completed BoP surveys with the VIES dataset and removing them we identified additional enterprises engaged in exporting of services. This helps increase insights into the business characteristics of service exporters. Using various sources of data and profiling different units allowed us to maximize coverage and overcome some of the challenges imposed by linking administrative data with survey data.

14.4.1.4 Results

The results presented in the release include only enterprises whose value of exports exceeded €5,000 in the reference year. The results also created a new indicator, export intensity, which is the ratio of exports to turnover. Only enterprises with an export intensity of greater than 5% in the reference year are classified as an exporting enterprise. This 5% threshold is chosen based on emerging European standards (Eurostat 2019, p. 34). The effect of this is that some classifications may be volatile year-on-year because only those enterprises which meet this condition were included. However, if the threshold criteria were not imposed, then the numbers of exporting enterprises would be significantly inflated.

The export intensity of an enterprise is bounded by zero and one, with an export intensity of zero meaning that the enterprise does not export and an export intensity of one meaning that the enterprise is completely reliant on exports, i.e. does not sell domestically. When publishing the results, all export intensity values are provided on an aggregate level, with classifications described by trading destination, sector, country of ownership, enterprise age, and region. The results of the data-matching project (see Table 14.1) show that in 2017, there were 10,516 exporting enterprises in Ireland with 358,525 persons engaged with these enterprises. The total value of exports for these enterprises was €337.3 billion, of which €189.3 billion was exported goods and €148.0 billion was exported services. The turnover for these exporting enterprises for 2017 was €435.7% billion meaning that 77.4% of their turnover was accounted for by exports.

The destination with the most enterprises exporting to it was the United Kingdom with 8885. This was followed by Germany, Netherlands, and France.

Table 14.1 Sources of turnover for exporting enterprises, 2015–2017.

		2015	2016	2017
Exporting enterprises	No.	10,114	10,071	10,516
Persons engaged	No.	334,686	343,650	358,525
Exports	**€m**	**292,593**	**301,964**	**337,311**
Goods	€m	189,418	184,173	189,304
Services	€m	103,176	117,791	148,006
Remaining turnover	€m	93,164	97,227	98,416
Total turnover	**€m**	**385,758**	**399,191**	**435,726**
Export intensity	%	75.8	75.6	77.4

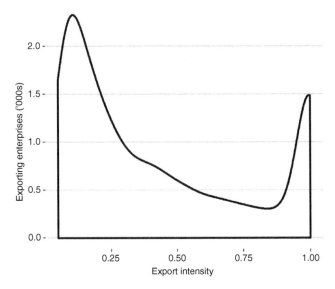

Figure 14.2 Distribution of Export Intensity 2017.

There were 368,525 personnel engaged with an exporting enterprise. Of those, 124,741 were engaged with an enterprise with an export intensity greater than 75%, meaning that they were predominately an export focused business. More than half of those (70,296) worked for Industrial enterprises while 41,253 worked in Services.

The results of the data-matching project reveal a twin peak distribution of export intensity (see Figure 14.2). This shows that exporters in Ireland were mostly either very reliant on exports or were occasional exporters. Half of the enterprises had an export intensity between 5% and 30%, while one in four exporters had 75% or more of their turnover from exports.

Linking the various sources of trade data enabled us to answer what on the face is some very basic questions. How much turnover comes from exporters? How many enterprises export to a certain destination? How many people work for exporting enterprises? This illustrates how utilizing administrative data, in conjunction with survey data can create new insights and add value for the user of business statistics. The next example shows how we can further utilize administrative to create more timely indicators.

14.4.2 Business Signs of Life

Like many other countries, Ireland had to impose restrictions on business operations to combat the spread of COVID-19 in 2020 and 2021. Doing so resulted in the temporary and permanent closures of many businesses who employed a significant proportion of the adult working population. In response to the restrictions, the government introduced two income support schemes: A Wage Subsidy Scheme (WSS) and a Pandemic Unemployment Payment (PUP). The WSS was implemented by the Revenue Commissioners which subsidizes wages of employees working for businesses impacted by the restrictions. The other was the PUP which was administered by Ireland's Department of Social Protection and was available to any individual let go from their employment during the pandemic. The administrative data from both schemes were made available to the CSO under the Statistics Act 1993a.

The *Business Signs of Life* series (CSO 2021) were created to examine changes in the Irish Business Economy during the COVID-19 pandemic using these available administrative data sources. This could provide more timely indicators than traditional statistical sources since annual statistics on the business population are generally published with a time lag of 18 months. However, changes in business activity have taken place more abruptly in 2020 and 2021 and timelier statistical measures were required. Two "business Signs of Life" series were developed (Series Two will be discussed in Section 14.5.5).

Series One of "Business Signs of Life" reports on the interaction between employment-related payments and business activity. It examines the enterprise sectors which have been most impacted by the pandemic and its associated restrictions. The results represent exploratory data matching and analysis by the CSO based on data from the following sources:

- The **CBR** is a register of all active enterprises in the State. There is a time lag of 18 months when determining enterprise activity
- Revenue's real-time **PMOD** has been operational for all employers in the state since the beginning of 2019. Under the system, employers are required to report their employee's pay and deductions in real-time to Revenue each time they operate payroll.
- **PUP** is a support for employees and self-employed who have lost their employment because of the COVID-19 pandemic. The data is made available by the Department of Social Protection.
- **Temporary Wage Subsidy Scheme (TWSS)** and its successor the **Employee Wage Subsidy Scheme (EWSS)** are available to employers who kept their employees on the payroll during the COVID-19 pandemic. The data for both schemes is at an individual level with a unique identifier for both enterprise and employee.

The initial base population of enterprises used for linking was the 2018 SBS population. However, since the analysis is of employment-related payments, enterprises with zero persons engaged were excluded from the analysis. As a result, all proportions in the release relate to a base population of 242,681 enterprises.

As mentioned in Section 14.2.1, annual business statistics are published about 18 months after the reference year due to the tax return data from the Irish revenue Commissioners. Therefore, some intrinsic timing issues influence the base population. Since the enterprise population is based on the reference year 2018, some enterprises may have ceased trading and new enterprises commenced over the period January 1, 2019–March 15, 2020. Due to these time-lag differences the usual demographic changes in the business population have not been measured in establishing a baseline for the report. The extent to which this has occurred cannot be accurately assessed until source data becomes available. For comparison, the most up-to-date number of enterprise deaths for a one-year period refers to reference year 2016, when there were 14,629 enterprise deaths as per the CSO's Business Demography release (CSO 2020b). Given this limitation, it is likely that the proportional estimates of use of the State schemes, i.e. the WSS and the PUP, due to COVID-19 are underestimated because of these previously ceased companies.

14.4.2.1 Linking

There were two different types of working personnel that needed to be considered in this project: those that get a wage or salary and those that do not. The PMOD dataset shows in near real time all the enterprises who have paid a wage or salary to an employee or a self-employed individual who paid themselves a wage or salary. The data is available in pseudonymized form to the business statistics compiler. This allowed for the creation of a prepandemic snapshot of employment in Ireland. With the snapshot in place, the WSS data is then linked by the employee and enterprise and the PUP for the first month of the scheme. It then goes through an iterative process each month to update the movement between employees to and from different support schemes and employers.

The second type of working personnel that need to be identified is the self-employed who do not pay themselves a wage or salary and therefore do not show up on the PMOD dataset. Self-employed who lost work due to the pandemic could avail of the PUP payment and those that did so could be matched to the business register using a unique identifier.

The data is checked to ensure that any outliers are not missed, and that employment data is in line with expectation. In the case of misalignment then profiling is used to match the legal unit with the appropriate enterprise.

14.4.2.2 Results

The results of this project show that of the 242,681 enterprises in the analysis, over 149,710 had personnel availing of COVID-19 income support. Linking the administrative data together allowed us to observe movements of individuals from PUP to WSS and to different enterprises. This allowed us to give insights into the enterprises most adversely affected by the pandemic. For example, the results showed that almost 7% of enterprises let all their personnel go at the beginning of the pandemic restrictions in March /April 2020 and as of January 2021 had not had anyone back on the payroll. This gives an indication of the enterprises that have closed and remained closed throughout the pandemic. The coverage that administrative data has is illustrated by the level of detail in the analysis. Figure 14.3 shows the NACE Rev.2 activities with the highest proportion of enterprises

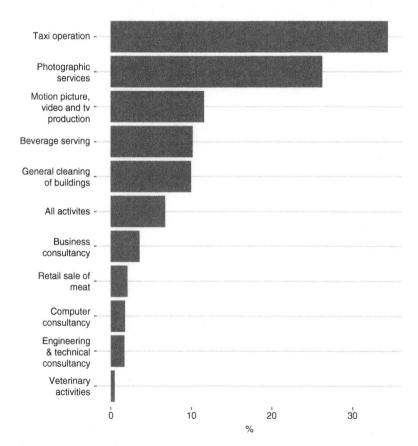

Figure 14.3 Percentage (%) of enterprises with all personnel continuously on Pandemic Unemployment Payment by selected NACE Rev.2 activities, April 2020–January 2021.

with all personnel on PUP. More than a third (34.4%) of enterprises in the Taxi operation sector fall into this category followed by Photographic activities. Conversely, vets and engineering activities had among the lowest proportion of enterprises with all personnel continuously on PUP.

The results also give timely feedback on policy-making decisions. During the first wave of the virus in Ireland in March and April 2020, the government implemented restrictions on business operations. As the first wave of infections declined there was an easing of restrictions over the summer. As infections increase again in the autumn and winter new restrictions were implemented. Figure 14.4 shows how the implementation and easing of restrictions impacted enterprises in different activities.

For example, high levels of enterprises in *Building completion and finishing activities*, which includes plasterers, painters, and fitters, etc., availed of the PUP during the first lockdown. This decreased following the Phase 1 easing of government restrictions and remained low during the second wave as restrictions were limited for the construction sector. However, as case numbers increased over Christmas new restrictions for the sector were implemented leading to a large increase in the number of enterprises availing of PUP.

Similarly, following Phase 3 easing of restrictions on 29 June there was a sharp decline in PUP uptake in *Hairdressing and other beauty treatment* businesses as they were allowed to reopen. Enterprises in this activity which had associated persons on PUP decreased over the summer. This increased again during the October lockdown and fell in December before increasing to 77.9% by January 12, 2021 following the re-introduction of Level 5 restrictions.

The results from the Business Signs of Life release illustrate just how administrative data can be utilized to meet the demand from timely and detailed information. The COVID-19 restrictions impacted businesses across Ireland; however, the impact was not equal, and policymakers needed timely and detailed information on the impact of businesses to navigate the crisis. Using traditional

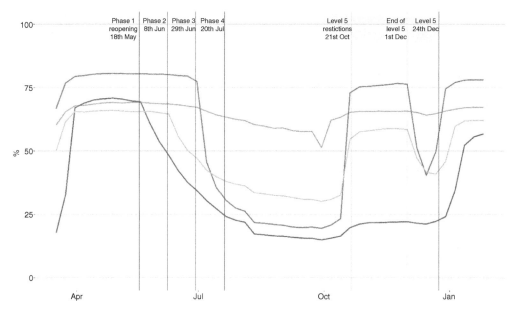

Figure 14.4 Percentage (%) of enterprises which had personnel on Pandemic Unemployment Payment by selected NACE Rev.2 activity, March 2020–January 2021.

data collection methods, we could produce timely indicators or detailed indicators, but it would be difficult to produce both. Linking the available administrative data sources allowed for the creation and publication that offered detailed insights with a quick turnaround.

14.4.3 Lessons Learned

The previous two projects highlight some of the potential that administrative data and data linking presents. However, it should be noted that these projects are just the foundation from which we can build institutional knowledge in business statistics on data linking in the CSO. With that said here are some of the main takeaways from our experience that might be helpful for future projects.

14.4.3.1 Quality
It is important to assess the quality of the administrative data used in any data linking project. Determining the statistical usability of the data source, whether it is used as an input, output, or process resource, will allow you to effectively maximize its potential while maintaining quality outputs.

14.4.3.2 Profiling
It's crucial that the compiler of business statistics is aware of the different statistical units used in each data source. Survey data is often at the enterprise or group level while administrative data will be at the admin/legal unit level. Furthermore, in business statistics the data can often be skewed with the larger enterprises accounting for a larger portion of the variable. Therefore, to ensure that the new product is robust, it is vital that the legal units of the enterprise are identified. In the CSO, there are dedicated units for the largest enterprises in Ireland. Data linking projects can lead to indirect profiling where previously unidentified relations between units are revealed, particularly of small and medium enterprises (SME) not under the remit of the dedicated profiling units. This information on enterprise structures can then be fed back into the business register.

14.4.3.3 Coverage
When linking data sources, it is important to be aware that the output from the data linking is very much dependent on the data sources. Linking survey data with a small sample will limit the scope of the output. Using administrative data, in conjunction to survey data will allow for greater coverage and therefore greater insight. Therefore, linking administrative data might be preferable if the aim is to provide more detail, particularly on SMEs and regional statistics.

14.4.3.4 Transparency
As discussed earlier in the chapter, there are limitations to using administrative data and microdata linking projects. For example, in some instances there can be a trade-off between timeliness and quality. You may not get 100% matches, or 100% coverage and the compiler will need to use their own judgment on how best to deal with the limitations. In the Business Signs of Life release for example, there is the time-lag asymmetries between data sources which leads to a potential underestimation. The limitations of the project should be made clear to the users, transparency is key in explaining the challenges of delivering more timely data. In the CSO, we have created a new publishing format called a "Frontier Series" for publications that use "new methods which are under development and/or data sources which may be incomplete, for example new administrative data sources" (CSO 2020a). Using the publishing format allows us to provide useful insights while also making sure the limitations are clear to the user.

14.5   The Use of VAT Data in Business Statistics

14.5.1   The Current Situation

VAT data is a very rich source of information and has many applications for use in business statistics. The Office for National Statistics (ONS) in the United Kingdom (UK) uses VAT turnover data from more than half a million enterprises in the generation of GDP estimates and short-term statistics (ONS 2018).

In Ireland, the use of administrative data sources in Short-term Business Statistics is currently very limited. The only available administrative data source suitable for short-term statistics regarding financial turnover in Ireland is VAT data, which is available on a bi-monthly basis from the Irish Revenue Commissioners. We also have access to the enterprise's annual VAT return from the previous year.

14.5.2   VAT Data Available in Ireland

In Ireland, the default filing time for VAT is bi-monthly. However, depending on a firm's VAT liability or based on some firm's arrangements with the Revenue Commissioners, this can vary. Businesses that have a VAT liability between €3001 and €14,400 file every four months and those with a VAT liability less than €3000 may file every six months. Some traders are also permitted to file annually and make payments in equal instalments. Companies are required to file a VAT3 return on the 19th day of the month after the end of the reporting period. The VAT3 return records the VAT payable or reclaimable by the trader in the taxable period. There are different rates of VAT currently applicable to goods and services in Ireland. These are, the standard rate, the reduced rate, the second reduced rate, the zero rate, and the livestock rate. Traders are required to complete a Return of Trading Details (RTD) form annually. The RTD form details the total purchases and sales for the year, broken down by the VAT rate. Because the VAT3 returns filed every two months (or four or six months in some cases) contain only the VAT due for the reporting period and neither the VAT rate nor the cost of the good or service, we will need to build a model that can predict a sales/turnover value from this short-term information. The annual RTD return does contain the total sales and the VAT rate, so the model will be built using the RTD data, the VAT3 returns for the year associated with the RTD return, the NACE and size of the business and also information regarding whether the enterprise is an importer or an exporter.

14.5.3   VAT Data for Short-Term Business Statistics

There is a constant requirement for more timely short-term statistics, however, survey response rates continue to fall. There are many reasons for this, including survey apathy. The Central Statistics Office is considering using VAT data in the future to generate quarterly short-term indices. Other European countries, such as the Netherlands (Ouwehand and Schouten 2014) currently use VAT data in this manner. Currently, all of the short-term business statistics in Ireland are based on survey data, with surveys being conducted in a traditional way by using paper or electronic questionnaire. Most short-term statistics are generated from monthly surveys with some being quarterly. VAT data from the Irish Revenue Commissioners can easily be linked to enterprises on the Central Business Register.

Neither survey data, with falling response rates, nor VAT data, with varied return patterns, on their own are likely to give the best solution to generating short-term statistics. However, a blend of the two has the potential to decrease administrative burden for the enterprise and increase quality.

In terms of accessing the VAT data for its statistical usability, there will be a number of stages. First, a model will have to be built to predict the sales/turnover value from the VAT3 return as discussed in the previous section. Second, both the VAT data and the survey data will have to be analyzed to assess how representative it is of all enterprises (not just those for whom we have survey data). To do this, we can use auxiliary variables that can be linked to both responding and nonresponding enterprises. For example, previous VAT returns for the same period, wages data, business size and NACE classification, previous survey returns, etc. Another issue to consider is the zero rate of VAT which applies to certain goods and services including exports, intra-Community supplies of goods to VAT-registered persons in other EU Member States, certain food and drink, certain oral medicine, certain books and booklets, certain animal feeding stuffs, certain fertilizers, seeds and plants used to produce food, clothing and footwear appropriate to children under 11 years of age, and supplies to VAT-registered persons authorized by Revenue under the zero-rating scheme for qualifying businesses.

14.5.4 VAT Data as a Timely Indicator of Business Signs of Life

VAT data can also be used for Business Signs of Life. Currently business demography statistics incur a lag of 18–20 months when recording business births and deaths. However, business births and deaths are very important indicators of the health of an economy and hence more timely indicators of business demography would prove very useful. A change in VAT activity or a significant change in VAT liability would be an early indicator that a business is experiencing difficulties. This business could then be monitored more closely to see if activity stops or pauses for a long time potentially indicating the business is no longer trading. In this case, the company could probably not be taken off the CSO's central business register until it was officially liquidated or shutdown however, that would not stop some short-term indicators being generated. Statistics based on early indicators of enterprise deaths and births would provide useful metrics to policymakers regarding the health of different economic sectors, particularly as COVID-19 supports are phased out. Measuring business births is also an interesting indicator of a country's economic health. This has led to the CSO developing the "Business Signs of Life" series.

14.5.5 Business Signs of Life Series

For Series Two of the *Business Signs of Life*, the CSO are planning to use a combination of official dissolution data along with VAT data and data on government support payments to monitor levels of activity in businesses in Ireland. Certain criteria will be used to decide the degree to which enterprise activities are curtailed during the COVID period. An activity barometer will be generated based on criteria such as the degree of dependency of an enterprise on state wage supports and the extent to which VAT activity or liability is decreasing. We are also attempting to source other data relating to government grants for businesses during the pandemic. The above analysis attempts to give a more real time view of enterprises whose activities are significantly curtailed and heading toward closure than business demography.

14.6 Summary

The digital transformation of government services will continue to provide business statistics with additional data resources. These data sources could be effectively utilized to provide more business insights demanded from our users. Primary data collection is resource intensive and can be viewed as an unnecessary burden on business. Administrative data provides opportunities to not only deliver on their current mandate but also to produce new, more timely and informative indicators without increasing cost and burden.

To get the most out of administrative data, it is important to identify its statistical usability. For a significant period of time, the CSO has used administrative data as an input to produce the Central Business Register. We have also shown how we use administrative data as part of the process when producing the SBS series. Finally, we gave two examples of data linking projects that used administrative data: as an input resource in *Exporting Enterprises in Ireland* to produce more relevant insights while the *Business Signs of Life* illustrate how we can use an output resource to produce timely indicators of the impact of COVID-19 on businesses in Ireland.

However, administrative data does present some challenges. How and what data are collected might not be aligned with your specified needs. This can be overcome by working collaboratively across government departments. This enables data providers to consult with the CSO on future developments and new data sources which improve the statistical potential of the administrative data over time.

The benefits of using administrative data for business statistics in the CSO is clear. It is a core component of the business register and used to enhance the data operations in business statistics in the CSO. Data linking projects demonstrate to ourselves and data providers the improvements to our operations which enhance the information we provide for evidence-based policy making. Integrating and maximizing administrative data into the data operations of the CSO will be crucial if we are to meet the demand for new and more granular insights on businesses in Ireland.

References

CSO (2020a). Our publishing formats, Cork. https://www.cso.ie/en/methods/ourpublishingformats/ (accessed 24 July 2020).

CSO (2020b). Business demography 2018, Cork. https://www.cso.ie/en/releasesandpublications/er/bd/businessdemography2018/ (accessed 24 July 2020).

CSO (2021). Business signs of life series one: state supports March 2020 to January 2021, Cork. https://www.cso.ie/en/releasesandpublications/fp/fp-bslss/businesssignsoflifeseriesonestatesupportmarch2020tojanuary2021/ (accessed 28 April 2021).

CSO (2019). Exporting enterprises in Ireland 2017, Cork, viewed 13 November 2019. https://www.cso.ie/en/releasesandpublications/ep/p-eeii/exportingenterprisesinireland2017/ (accessed 13 November 2019).

Costanzo, L. (ed.) (2011). *Main Findings of the Information Collection on the Use of Admin Data for Business Statistics in EU and EFTA Countries*, Deliverable 1.1 of the ESSnet Admin Data, 2011.

Council Regulation (EC) No 295/2008 of 11 March 2008 concerning structural business statistics. https://eurlex.europa.eu/LexUriServ/LexUriServ.do?uri=OJ:L:2008:097:0013:0059:EN:PDF (accessed 01 June 2020).

Cox, N., McLaren, C.H., Shenton, C., Tarling, T, and Davies, E.W. (2023). Developing statistical frameworks for administrative data and integrating it into business statistics: experiences from the UK and New Zealand. In: *Advances in Establishment Statistics, Methods and Data Collection*, Chapter 13 (ed. G. Snijkers, M. Bavdaž, S. Bender, J. Jones, S. MacFeely, J.W. Sakshaug, K.J. Thompson, and A. van Delden). Hoboken: Wiley.

Daas, P.J.H, Ossen, S.J.L, Vis-Visschers, R.J.W.M and Arends-Toth, J. (2009). Checklist for the Quality evaluation of Administrative Data Sources. Discussion paper 09042, Statistics Netherlands.

van Delden, A. and Lewis, D. (2023). Methodology for the use of administrative data in business statistics. In: *Advances in Establishment Statistics, Methods and Data Collection*, Chapter 12 (ed. G. Snijkers, M. Bavdaž, S. Bender, J. Jones, S. MacFeely, J.W. Sakshaug, K.J. Thompson, and A. van Delden). Hoboken: Wiley.

van Delden, A., Lorenc, B., Struijs, P., and Zhang, L.C. (2018). Letter to the editor. *Journal of Official Statistics* 34: 573–580.

Eurostat (2019). Micro data linking, Luxembourg. https://ec.europa.eu/eurostat/documents/3859598/10295208/KS-GQ-19-013-EN-N.pdf/5e2fdf0a-2bf9-7430-309a-3565fc1d329f?t=1575968597000 (accessed 12 February 2020).

Laitila, T., Wallgren, A. and Wallgren B. (2011). Statistics Sweden, Research and Development – Methodology Reports from Statistics Sweden, Quality Assessment of Administrative Data.

Larsen, M.L. and Herning, A. (2023). Record linkage for establishments: background, challenges, and an example. In: *Advances in Establishment Statistics, Methods and Data Collection*, Chapter 33 (ed. G. Snijkers, M. Bavdaž, S. Bender, J. Jones, S. MacFeely, J.W. Sakshaug, K.J. Thompson, and A. van Delden). Hoboken: Wiley.

ONS (2018). VAT turnover data in National Accounts: background and methodology. https://www.ons.gov.uk/economy/grossdomesticproductgdp/methodologies/vatturnoverdatainnationalaccountsbackgroundandmethodology (accessed 14 June 2020).

Ouwehand, P. and Schouten, B. (2014). Measuring representativeness of short-term business statistics. *Journal of Official Statistics* 30 (4): 623–649.

Statistics Act 1993a, No.21/1993, s.30, Dublin: Stationery Office. http://www.irishstatutebook.ie/eli/1993/act/21/section/30/enacted/en/html#sec30 (accessed 05 May 2021).

Statistics Act 1993b, No.21/1993, s.33, Dublin: Stationery Office. http://www.irishstatutebook.ie/eli/1993/act/21/section/33/enacted/en/html#sec33 (accessed 05 May 2021).

Section 4

Topics in Business Survey Data Collection

15

What Computerized Business Questionnaires and Questionnaire Management Tools Can Offer

Gustav Haraldsen

Division for Methods, Statistics Norway, Oslo/Kongsvinger, Norway

15.1   Introduction

Business questionnaires are like any other questionnaires in that they contain the same elements as any other questionnaire. Hence, common wording tips, visual principles, and question order recommendations apply (see, e.g. Bradburn et al. 2004, Martin et al. 2007, or Dillman et al. 2009). At the same time, business questionnaires are also different in that they ask about the businesses, while social survey questionnaires ask about the survey respondents (Haraldsen 2013a; see Jones et al. 2013, and Snijkers 2016, for an overview of business survey characteristics).

The same kind of duality applies to respondents. Business respondents are human beings who, when at office, read, interpret, and relate to the requests communicated in questionnaires in the same way as in any other survey. The cognitive four-step process, with comprehension, data retrieval tasks, judgements, and response, still applies (Tourangeau 1984; Tourangeau et al. 2000). But because business respondents do not report about themselves, but inform about business matters, their access to information sources outside themselves becomes more important than what is normally the case in social surveys. In social surveys, we usually try to isolate the respondent from his or her social environment (Foddy 1993; Krosnick and Presser 2010). In business surveys, however, environmental properties are an important part of the data collection design (Edwards and Cantor 1991; Sudman et al. 2000; Willimack and Nichols 2010; Bavdaž 2010; Lorenc 2006). To complete a questionnaire, the respondent in charge is expected to take contact with other employees and look up information in internal administration systems. Collecting data which are needed to answer the questions typically takes more time than filling in the questionnaire. (Haraldsen and Jones 2007; Willimack and Snijkers 2013; for a description of the data retrieval tasks and the internal business response process see Chapter 16 by Snijkers et al. (2023))

Also, while being selected to social surveys is an exceptional event, this is common routine in businesses. Businesses often receive several surveys at the same time, and business surveys are often panels (Bavdaž 2010). Hence, for those who respond to business survey requests, this is a regular job task. This probably makes business respondents more professional than social survey participants. On the other hand, keeping track of different response deadlines and looking up previously reported data are all demanding tasks. Because these tasks take so much time and have so much impact on the response quality, they are as important to the business survey as the questionnaire itself and should therefore be designed so that they play together with the questionnaire (Haraldsen 2013a; for an example see Chapter 16 by Snijkers et al. (2023)).

Advances in Business Statistics, Methods and Data Collection. Edited by Ger Snijkers, Mojca Bavdaž, Stefan Bender, Jacqui Jones, Steve MacFeely, Joseph W. Sakshaug, Katherine J. Thompson, and Arnout van Delden.

The dominant mode in business surveys has been paper-based, self-administrated, postal surveys. With this design, contacts between surveyor and those surveyed are a series of one-way distributions: a prenotice followed by a questionnaire and followed up with reminders from the surveyor. Questionnaires that are completed and posted by survey respondents. The questionnaires are standardized. There might be different versions, but no individual adjustments. Neither do respondents get any immediate feedback on how they read and answer the questions.

In contrast, **computerization** opens the possibility for real or synthetic dialogues at every step of the data collection (Couper 2008; Tourangeau et al. 2013). Much of the survey communication between the surveyor and the sampled businesses can be done using email or chat services. A computerized dialogue, or even a virtual interviewer, which mimics an interview can be implemented in the questionnaire. Chat services, inside the questionnaires can also bring respondents in direct contact with the survey help desk. In this way, the difference between self-administrated surveys and interview surveys narrows (Conrad et al. 2007; Conrad and Schober 2010).

In interview surveys the interviewer both acts as a *motivator*, a *mediator* who reads the questions and records the answers, and an *administrator* who collects and returns completed questionnaires to the surveyor. Hence, in self-administrated surveys, the respondents are not only left with a self-completion questionnaire. They are also left with motivating arguments and administrative tasks.

In this chapter, we will first point at some key challenges related to concept-, unit- and time delineations in business questionnaires and make some general recommendation concerning these. Next, we will highlight differences between social and business surveys when it comes to motivation strategies and administrative tasks during the response process. Based on these reflections, we will discuss how computerized management tools can motivate and help with administrative tasks and how computerization can contribute to improved measurement instruments. Finally, we will conclude with some critical reflections and a call for research which can back up or question the proposed improvements.

15.2 Business Survey Challenges

Generally, there are three kinds of question clarifications which may be relevant in survey questionnaires; specifications of what belongs and does not belong to the *concepts* used in the questions, delineations of the *relevant unit(s)* (i.e. the observational unit), and delineations of the *time period* respondents should report for (see Figure 3.7 in Haraldsen 2013b).

15.2.1 Concepts

Business questionnaires are very much about facts. They ask about the number of employees, hours worked, amount invested in equipment, volume produced and sold, and product prices. Because facts are given in concrete numbers, we tend to believe that this kind of questions are straightforward to understand and answer. This is probably even more so in business surveys because the facts asked for typically refer to common business terms. But common terms may not have common definitions. In business questionnaires, this is evident because of separate instruction documents that often have more pages than the questionnaire itself or by questions with long lists about what should be included and excluded in the answers. Research has shown that respondents often skip instructions (Peytchev et al. 2010). Because responding to surveys is part of business respondents' working tasks, one should perhaps expect that they read instructions more conscientiously than social survey respondents. On the other hand, what first tends to be skipped are definitions of terms respondents find familiar. Therefore, we think the safest strategy is to minimize the need for supplementary clarifications.

Original version:

Investments in fixed assets. With fixed assets, we refer to machinery, constructions, transport equipment or other tangible assets. Include only assets with a minimum cost of 1500 Euros and minimum estimated durability of 3 years.
[   ] 00 Euro

Alternative version:

How much was invested in machinery, constructions, transport equipment or other tangible assets?
[   ] 00 Euro

Did any of these assets cost less than 1500 Euro or had an estimated durability below 3 years?
○ Yes → How much did these minor purchases add up to?   [   ] 00 Euro
○ No

Figure 15.1   Minimizing the need for supplementary clarifications and definitions.

How much was invested in machinery, constructions, transport equipment or other tangible assets?
☐ None   [   ] 00 Euro

Figure 15.2   Avoiding implicit expectations.

For many business questionnaires, this strategy breaks with a tradition where questions are not questions, but just *keywords followed by lengthy definitions*. One and the same question may also include several sub-questions. Two question tips that are highly relevant to business surveys is therefore to *move definitions into the questions* and *split complex questions into individual questions*. The example in Figure 15.1 is an illustration of both these tips.

One of the subtler pitfalls in questionnaires are errors caused by *implicit expectations* (Yan 2005). In the present example, the response box calls for an amount given in hundred euros. Even if it is possible to put in a zero or leave the response box open, the response format still conveys an expectation saying that businesses normally have something to report. This kind of implicit expectations may lead to over-reporting. If the respondent leaves the response box unfilled, it may also be interpreted as an item nonresponse rather than a "nothing invested" answer. Hence, *nothing to report should be clearly included*, e.g. like is shown in Figure 15.2.

Transform instructions into questions, ask for one thing at a time and beware of implicit expectations – these are our three main tips for how to improve communication of concepts in business questionnaires.

15.2.2   Units

Unit delineations are particularly challenging in business survey. The observational unit, i.e. the unit to observe and report from, is often defined by kind of activity by locations or kind of activity across locations (Haraldsen 2013a). Such units may, however, not coincide with how the company's budgets are set up and accounts are kept. Moreover, questions about different units are commonly presented in a spreadsheet format, which generally is considered a challenging question format.

Business respondents are often accountants or others who are familiar with spreadsheets. Thus, when asked, they may prefer matrix questions above individual questions repeated for each unit. This is particularly true when the number of units is high, and the same questions are asked again and again, which is boring and burdensome. However, being the preferred question format does not mean being the format which produces the best response quality. Spreadsheets leave little space for more than just keyword questions. When units or data requests are similar, but still different from those readily available in existing spreadsheets, there is also a risk of copy-and-paste errors. In addition, not all questions may be equally relevant to all units. If so, we are also faced with the same risks of errors caused by implicit assumptions or empty cells misinterpreted as item nonresponse, as we discussed in Section 15.2.1.

To avoid *misinterpretations of keywords* used in matrices, we recommend *replacing the first matrix line with complete questions* that can explain the terms in full sentences. We call this a hybrid format. Figure 15.3 shows an example on how this could be done on paper. Later we will discuss which functionalities can be built into a computerized version.

Even if this way of presenting makes it easier to understand what the questions ask for, the completion task may still be challenging. Given that the respondent realizes that the answers cannot be directly copied from their book-keeping system, it follows that some adjustments or calculations are needed before the survey questions can be answered. Invoices, investments, and different kinds of production expenses are all normally filed by events which need to be summarized and categorized according to the specifications given in the questionnaire. Mismatch between requests and information sources is usually reported as the heaviest response burden in business surveys (Dale and Haraldsen 2007; Haraldsen et al. 2013; Haraldsen 2018; see also Chapter 10 by Erikson et al. (2023)).

15.2.3 Time References

Business statistics is about supervising status and change in the economy. It is of utmost importance, both for commercial and political stakeholders, to detect instabilities even if they do not yet show in gross figures, to distinguish between different causes of change, and to facilitate different

- **What was the total revenue of Establishment_1 in 2020?**   [　　　] 00 Euro

- **What was the operating costs of Establishement_1 in 2020?**   [　　　] 00 Euro
- **How much of these costs were salaries?**   [　　　] 00 Euro

- **How much did Establishment_1 invest in machinery, construction, transport equipment and other tangible fixed assets in 2020?**   [　　　] 00 Euro
- **How much did Establishment_1 earn from sale of fixed assets in 2020?**   [　　　] 00 Euro

- In the table below, we have listed all known establishments in the enterprise. **Please give the same information for these establishments as you just did for Establishment_1**
    - All numbers should be given in 100 euros
    - If not, all establishments are listed, use the blank lines to add new establishments.

Establishments	Revenue	Operating costs	Salaries	Invested assets	Sold assets
Establishments_2					
Establishments_3					
Establishments_4					

Figure 15.3 Combining individual questions and a matrix in a hybrid format.

kinds of forecast analyses. For all these purposes, panel design is a preferable sampling procedure. The economy also changes faster than cultural and social conditions. Hence, recurring surveys based on panels are common (Smith 2013; see also Chapter 27 by Smith and Yung (2023)). While having many analytical advantages, this design also opens for two quality risks: conditioning and telescoping (terms introduced by Neter and Waksberg 1964).

Conditioning is when present responses are colored by previous participation and reports (for a discussion, see Sturgis et al. 2009). Companies usually carefully file documentation, including copies of completed questionnaires. When the same questions are repeated periodically, one easy way out is therefore to look up what was reported last time and make rough estimates of what has changed since then. This is especially unfortunate if there are errors in the previous report or when definitions are slightly changed, for instance because of changes in public regulations.

Telescoping is when events that took place outside the reference period are included in the survey answers. In social surveys, this is a common problem when respondents are asked to recall events long back in time (Touranageau and Bradburn, 2010). In business surveys, the main reason for telescoping may rather be that the time between reports is so short that it is hard to keep different periods apart. Another source of telescoping is when there is a mismatch between the reference period used in the questionnaire and the reference period used in available business records, e.g. when the fiscal year used in bookkeeping does not match with calendar year used in the questionnaire.

A common way to avoid telescoping is to *preload results from previous reports* together with questions asking for updated data. Showing what has already been reported, should prevent double reporting. On the other hand, showing previous results may also invite to conditioning, in particular if looking up new data takes time or giving an updated answer involves calculations. Hence, the risk of telescoping needs to be balanced against the risk of conditioning (for a discussion on the relationships between availability and likely outcomes, see Bavdaž 2010, and Haraldsen 2013b). Moreover, preloading should always go *together with soft error checks* which flag answers which claim no change, break with trends in earlier reports, differ much from what is reported by similar enterprises, or in other ways seems unlikely. With paper questionnaires checks like these need to be done during postsurvey editing. In computerized questionnaires, they can be done during the response process.

15.3 The Path to Competent and Motivated Respondents

Figure 15.4 describes the processes taking place in businesses during survey completion (Haraldsen et al. 2015, Haraldsen 2018).

The response quality depends on the respondent's motivation, competence, and access to relevant information. These factors are affected both by the survey procedure and measurement instrument and by the context the respondent operates in (Willimack and Snijkers 2013). When data have to be gathered from different sources, different respondents may be involved and one of them may act as a response coordinator (Snijkers and Jones 2013; Bavdaž 2010).

One important difference between social surveys and business surveys is also that the business management, by selecting who should be the responsible respondent or response coordinator and by giving this task high or low priority, affects how competent and motivated the selected persons(s) will be. Moreover, by being responsible for the company's documentation system, the management also have an influence on the accessibility and quality of the information sources the respondent should use. Finally, if the information requested is considered market-sensitive, the management may censor what is reported.

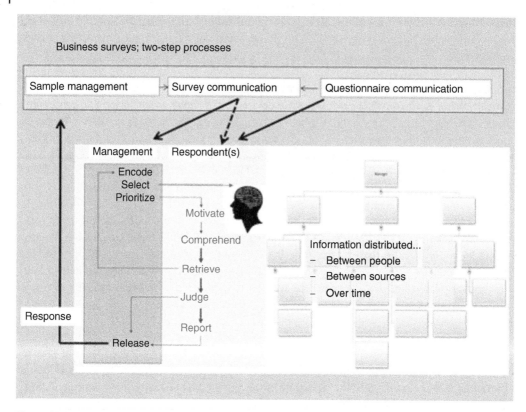

Figure 15.4 Business survey response processes. Source: Haraldsen 2018.

Hence, the path to competent and motivated business respondents goes through a *benevolent business management*. What we should expect from this management is that their main concern is about the relationship between financial costs and benefits. From this perspective, it is easy to understand that completing questionnaires initially appears as a waste of time which does not deserve to be prioritized (Willimack and Snijkers 2013). Vague claims about the usefulness of business statistics hardly change this (Torres van Grinsven et al. 2014). Instead, two other concrete strategies are often recommended (Haraldsen et al. 2013; Bavdaž et al. 2015). To reduce the cost, surveyors are urged to implement measures that reduce the time it takes to complete the questionnaires. To increase the benefits, they are urged to offer instant, tailored statistical products which the management consider useful in their efforts to improve products and services.

Even if these are good ideas, neither of them are easy to implement. Business questionnaires can obviously be improved. Still, the time it takes to complete business questionnaires is already relatively low and making it even lower may harm the response quality. Instead of trying to reduce questionnaire completion time even more, a better idea may be to offer efficient administrative tools, both to the business management who needs to delegate completion tasks, and to response coordinators who need to run internal data collections and keep track of deadlines and the completing status of different questionnaires (see, e.g. Chapter 16 by Snijkers et al. (2023)).

Businesses are very different. Offering tailored statistics that are considered useful to participating businesses may therefore be a complicated and costly task (as follows, e.g. from evaluation studies in the Netherlands: Houben et al. 2018; Bavdaž et al. 2020). This becomes even more complicated because the statistics businesses would most of all welcome statistics that strengthen their market position. Unfortunately, this is the same statistics that national statistical offices are prevented to offer. One way of avoiding this conflict, is to offer a self-service application where the user can create their own statistical tables and compare results with their own figures. In this way, we leave the tailoring to the businesses themselves (as is done, e.g. in Portugal: Saraiva 2016, Buiten et al. 2018).

15.4   What Computerization Can Offer

Computerization does not automatically change business questionnaires to the better but can be used to address some of the challenges we have described in Section 15.2. In our opinion, computerization should focus on three topics which will be discussed under the headings «Source-Oriented Instruments», «Combined Communication Means», and «Designed Dialogues».

15.4.1   Source-Oriented Instruments

Electronic questionnaires can be presented on different devices. For respondents completing questionnaires in office, however, a desktop computer will normally be the standard equipment, and consequently, this is the device we design for. Still, two kinds of exceptions are worth mentioning. One is when all or most of the respondents have little or nothing to report. Examples of surveys with a few questions to everybody are when we ask businesses to update their number of employees or report their expected revenues for the next month. So-called «Needle in a haystack» surveys are surveys where the majority must answer just one or a few filter questions, while an unknown minority will have more questions. Examples are surveys about R&D activities, rare investments, or services only offered to certain customers. While, with a few questions to everybody, the whole questionnaire can be easily presented on a smartphone or similar device, when we are looking for needles in the haystack, a better solution will probably be to combine a short smartphone screening survey with a longer web questionnaire designed for a «proper» desktop computer.

The other kind of exception are surveys aimed at mobile respondents, such as truck drivers, business travelers, or respondents working on construction sites. In such surveys, some questions may come closer to the information source if they are posed in the field. Like with «Needle in a haystack» surveys, this calls for mixed-device designs. In several of these cases, a highly relevant mix is to combine a smartphone or laptop diary where the respondent reports about actions as they happen, with a follow-up questionnaire for desktop completion of supplementary information. In transport surveys, the smartphone part of the survey can also include GPS information about traveling routes.

The reasoning behind these examples is a source-oriented approach saying that the carrier of the questionnaire should facilitate completion as close to the information source as possible: «You fish where the fish is». The same source-oriented approach should be applied when deciding the content of questionnaires and the services offered in a questionnaire administration system.

There is a tradition to name business questionnaires after the statistics they contribute to and to fill the questionnaire with questions about every topic that goes into those particular statistics. This is what we call a "stove-pipe" approach. By contrast, from a source-oriented approach, it will be better to have sets of homogenous questionnaires that are targeted at respondents with different competence and access to different information sources.

To put such a design into practice and ensure that all questionnaires that go into the same statistics are completed and returned together, the management need to name a response coordinator, and the coordinator needs a questionnaire administration tool. Computerized business questionnaires should therefore be distributed together with a computerized administration system, preferably a web portal. Again, taking a source-oriented approach, the administration system should both make it easier for the business management to assign survey responsibilities to employees and make it easier for those selected to perform information retrieval tasks and keeping track of internally distributed questionnaires. Figure 15.5 lists web portal functionalities that need to be discussed in this respect. In our opinion, those listed in the right column are better tailored to business surveys and thus more user friendly than those listed in the left column (for a more detailed discussion on web portals see Chapter 20 by Hole and Houben (2023)).

Questionnaire specific access credentials, typically pin codes (Functionality 1 in Figure 15.5) is a login procedure tailored for single surveys, but rather inconvenient for businesses that receive a mixture of monthly, quarterly, and annual questionnaires. Hence, some National Statistical Institutes (NSIs) have established dedicated web portals where businesses will *find all questionnaires* they are requested to complete (Chapter 20 by Hole and Houben (2023)). Such a web portal should not only be a postbox for questionnaires. It should rather be considered as a virtual workplace for those who are selected to perform survey tasks. In the Norwegian Altinn system, the business survey portal is even placed inside a common portal serving all kinds of contacts between businesses and public authorities (https://www.altinn.no/en/). In this way, business surveys are made available inside a work environment already known and used in the businesses' daily work. As in ordinary workplaces, the communication between the surveyor and those surveyed should be two-way (Functionality 10 in Figure 15.5), e.g. with a chat service or a link to a social media site in addition to e-mail contacts.

Because it is enterprises or establishments, and not the respondents, that are sampled in business surveys, it is normally left to the business management to decide who should handle incoming questionnaires. We cannot control their choice, but can still try to influence it. One way is to apply the source-oriented approach and point out to the management what kind of people we want to fill in what questionnaires (see, e.g. Chapter 5 by Bavdaž et al. (2023)). In addition, to encourage the management to follow our guidelines, we should offer *a delegation tool* which makes it easy to assign read and write access to different questionnaires to different people (Functionality 4 in Figure 15.5). Many companies use contracted firms to keep their accounts or perform various

	Not tailored	Tailored
1	Questionnaire specific access credentials	One common login procedure to all relevant questionnaire
2	List all questionnaires	List of relevant questionnaires only
3	Fixed list	Search and sorting tools
4	Predetermined respondent(s)	Delegation possible
5	Fixed questionnaire	Splittable questionnaire
6	Online completion only	Offline completion possible
7	No status information	Status information
8	No preview	Preview facilities
9	No archive	Archive
10	One-way communication	Two-way communication

Figure 15.5 Web portal functionalities.

services. It is important that the delegation system also enables the business management to outsource questionnaires covering these topics to those running external services.

When the survey is split into different questionnaires or call for inputs from different sources (e.g. Chapter 16 by Snijkers et al. (2023)), it should be the responsibility of the response coordinator to collect the requested information, complete the questionnaire(s), and report back to the surveyor within the deadline. Consequently, the coordinator will be the most important user of the administration tools offered at the web portal.

To decide where relevant information is found, the coordinator may need *a preview of the questionnaire content* (Functionality 8 in Figure 15.5). A pdf-version is therefore often offered. If the questionnaire has a complicated structure with many filter questions and alternative paths; however, a simple reproduction of what is in the questionnaire will be a messy document. The preview version should therefore have its own design governed by the purpose of giving an overview. For this purpose, a questionnaire flowchart and the information requests should probably be presented separately.

The coordinator will often have to run an internal data collection process to gather the information needed. For this he or she will need the same delegation rights as the company management. When the questionnaire contains different kinds of questions, it would even be useful if the coordinator can *split questionnaires* into several parts which are completed by different respondents and then imported back to the master questionnaire (Functionality 5 in Figure 15.5).

To take full advantage of web services, the questionnaire needs to be online. To download questionnaires for offline completion involves additional work, error risks, and security issues (Functionality 6 in Figure 15.5). Still, *offline versions* can sometimes be a way to bring the questionnaire or parts of the questionnaire closer to the information source, e.g. in surveys aimed at mobile respondents. Another example is when enterprises with numerous establishments, instead of filling in large matrices, can attach predefined spreadsheets to the questionnaire. If the questionnaire allows for attached spreadsheets, it of course also allows for attaching any other kind of offline applications.

Other useful portal functionalities are filters which show only relevant questionnaires and allow their selection according to deadlines, responsible reporter, or completion status (Functionalities 2, 3, and 7 in Figure 15.5) and an archive where previous reports are stored (Functionality 9 in Figure 15.5).

15.4.2 Combined Communication Means

Texts are the main communication form in questionnaires. We know, however, that respondents focus on initial words at the beginning of the questions and tend to leave out later texts and sentences (Graesser et al. 2006). Questions should therefore be kept short. No matter how big the PC screen is, it is also important to acknowledge that it is harder to read long texts on the screen than on paper (Snijkers et al. 2007; Eskenazi 2011). Moreover, a computerized questionnaire screen contains more information than a paper questionnaire page. Action buttons are needed to go from page to page, and in longer questionnaires, there might either be progress indicators or a navigation pane which informs the respondents where they are in the questionnaire. In addition come links to supplementary instructions, and presentations of activated error messages. This adds up to a lot of texts. Thus, whatever electronic device we are using, we should look for ways to simplify or even replace texts.

The first alternative that comes to mind is visualization. Visualization is also used in paper questionnaires, but there is a wider range of visual tools in computerized questionnaires. The visual elements can be turned on and off, be still or animated and can be tailored to different parts of the sample or to different response patterns.

Another media alternative that we are less familiar with in self-completion questionnaires, are sound clips. Hence, with computerization the tool box becomes larger, but so becomes also the risk of causing noise and confusion. When wording questions, we are advised to use different fonts or font sizes in a consistent way to distinguish between different kinds of text, and to choose fonts and font sizes which mirror the importance of different text elements. Likewise, visual and auditory tools should be used for particular purposes that are different from the purpose of other questionnaire elements, and be designed in a way which correspond to the importance of its purpose.

The purpose of visual tools are to guide the respondent through the questionnaire. The visual design should be guided by how the surveyor wants the respondents to focus and move between different parts of the questionnaire screen.

Each screen page of the questionnaire should hold one, and only one topic. In business surveys, the length and content of the questionnaire will often differ by the number of establishments within the enterprise or by the number of goods or services produced. Therefore, the surveyor first needs answers to some initial questions before the table of questionnaire content is decided. The first step will be to decide what version of the questionnaire the respondent should have. Then there is time to draw the respondent's attention to the action button that brings up the next page and topic. In Figure 15.6, we illustrate how the respondent can be guided through these steps by changing the degrees of visibility.

In this example, the initial screen starts with just one topic listed in the left pane and only three bullet points in the questionnaire pane. Note also that the "forward" and "back" buttons at the bottom of the screen are shaded. They are shown in a discrete way, but not yet operative. This is all done to catch the respondent's attention to the three bullet points. The first bullet point simply states which enterprise the questionnaire applies to. The next two pose the first questions, which are about the establishment composition during the reporting year. Enterprises which only had one establishment operating in the reporting year, do not need to split enterprise figures between establishments, and will have a simpler version of the questionnaire than enterprises with several, operative establishments.

There are four *levels of visibility* on this dynamic page. Some elements are hidden, one element is shaded, the first two questions are fully visible, and the bullet points and actual questions are highlighted. The table of contents is not shown until it is decided if the enterprise had more than one establishment operative, and therefore needs to give revenue, cost, and investment figures per establishment. The table of contents and other topics which are common to enterprises with one or more establishments, could have been shown from the start but that could have taken the focus away from the questions. Their subsequent appearance after the initial questions are answered grabs attention at the right time. When it comes to the action buttons at the bottom of the screen, however, we found it important to show from the start that they were there, even if they were not operative until all questions at the first page were completed. Also, because the respondent is on the first page, only the "Forward" button is activated.

In paper questionnaires, it is recommended to number the questions and use arrows to lead the respondent past nonapplicable questions. In a computerized version, hiding or showing applicable follow-up questions replaces directive arrows and, to a certain degree, also makes numbering unnecessary or even confusing. Another reason why numbering is dropped, is that different paths for different respondents may cause complicated numbering structures.

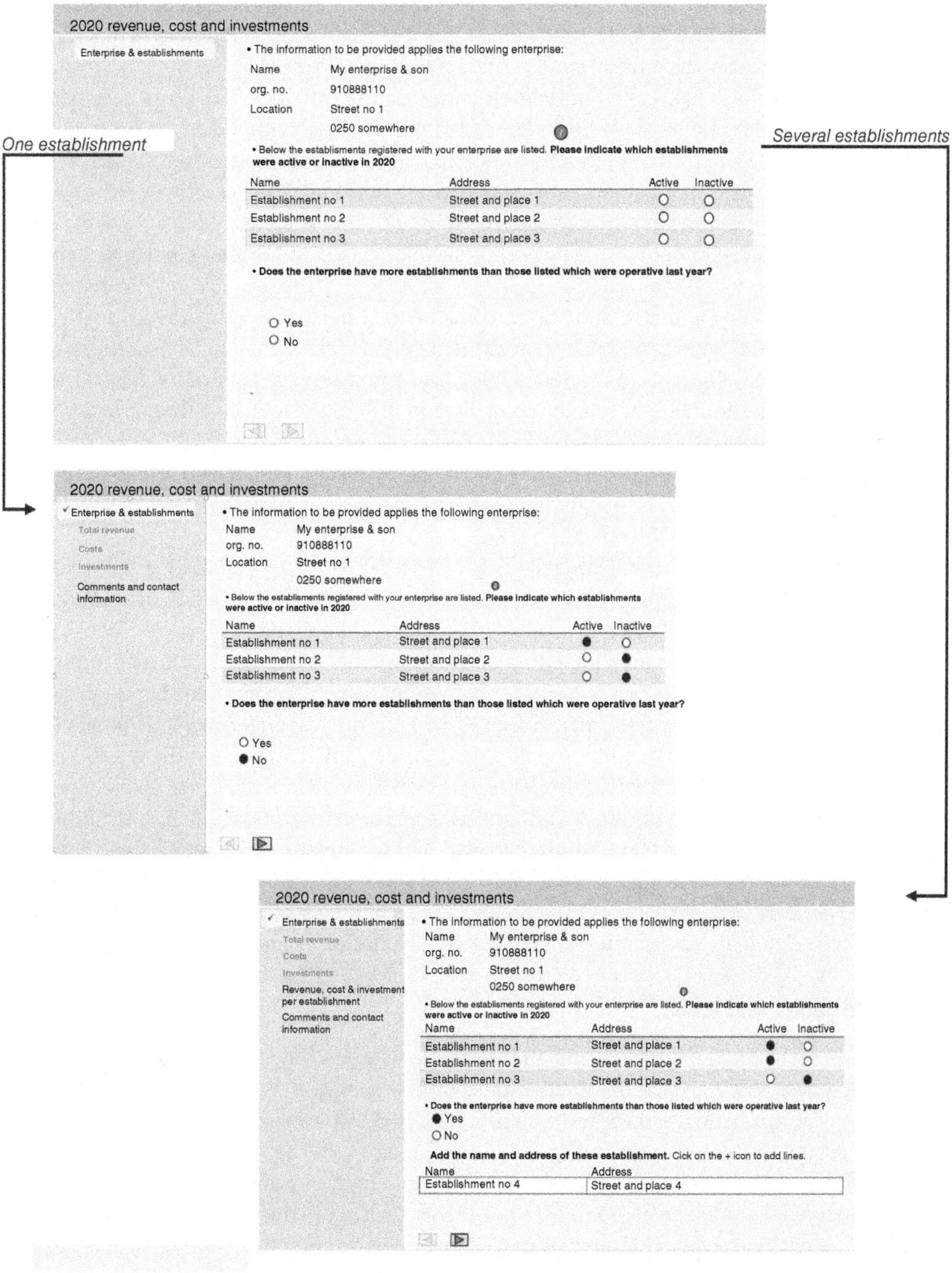

Figure 15.6 Guiding by visibility.

In this example, the list of topics is presented in a pane along the left margin of the screen. An alternative is to give each topic a folder at the top of the screen. We do not recommend this solution because we think it makes the table of contents less visible and flexible.

The table of contents is also called navigation pane because the titles may serve as hyperlinks that can be used to navigate between topics instead of page by page with the action buttons at the bottom of the screen. Hyperlinks are usually indicated in gray and/or underscored texts. We prefer colors, which stand out well on computer screens. In Figure 15.6, «Total revenue», «Costs», and «Investments» are hyperlinks that can be clicked on in any order the business respondents want. Information that the respondent will enter on these three pages about total enterprise revenue, costs, and investments will be preloaded on the page where the enterprise totals are to be distributed between establishments. For this reason, the respondents are hindered to jump directly to this page by making the hyperlink «Revenue, cost, & investment per establishment» inactive until the enterprise totals are entered. The same reasoning applies to the first and last page of the questionnaire. These parts of the questionnaire need to be completed in the order decided by the surveyor.

Gray texts indicating hyperlinks are one out of several meaningful symbols at the questionnaire page. Most of them give meaning because they follow the W3C standard and are also used in other web sites. The only one we have found necessary to explain is the + icon used if one needs to specify more than one additional establishment.

In the question where the establishment list is introduced, an *"i"* inside a blue ball indicates a hyperlink leading to the definition of an establishment. This kind of clickable instructions are seldom used by respondents (Peytchev et al. 2010), and should only be used for additional information that is not vital for the understanding of the questions. When used, it is also a question where instructions should be presented to catch the respondent's attention. The common recommendation is that it should be presented as close to where the respondent look as possible, e.g. inserted between the question and the response field. Anyway, that add text to the questionnaire. Therefore, we should look for alternatives. Those who click on such an icon are actively looking for help. They may look for definitions of unfamiliar terms or perhaps more often, instructions on how available information should be adjusted to give a correct answer. Mismatch between what is asked for and what is readily available is one of the main source of response burden in business surveys (Haraldsen 2018). In particular when complicated response tasks are explained, audio-visual means might be a suitable communication mode (see Chapter 16 by Snijkers et al. (2023)).

15.4.3 Designed Dialogues

The dialogue between the surveyor and the respondent follows a planned path of questions, responses, probes, and clarifications predesigned by the surveyor. With computerization, it is possible to make this dialogue flow fairly natural, but to do so it needs to be carefully planned. *Flowcharts* are more than ever an indispensable planning tool. The flow chart in Figure 15.7, which describes a computerized version of the investment question from Figure 15.1, contains the most used elements: squares which indicate questions, decision diamonds which refer to visible or hidden (dotted) filter questions, arrows describing paths through the question sequence, and finally a double square which links the present sequence to the next one. Individual question flows are the smallest unit in a higher-level flowchart which describes the question flow on different pages and, taken altogether, the page flow of the questionnaire. Each of the flow charts may be simple, linked together they form a complex structure.

Figure 15.8 suggests how the hybrid matrix from Figure 15.3 could be changed into a computerized dialogue. Behind this example there is a complex network of flowcharts. Moreover, different levels of visibility are used to guide the respondent through the question and answering process.

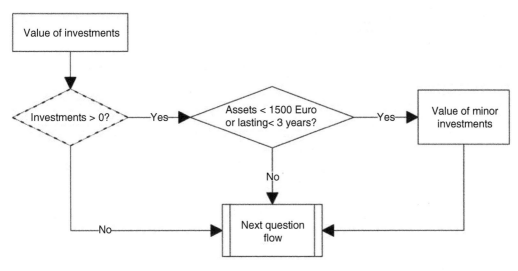

Figure 15.7 Question flowchart.

- According to what you have reported to the National Tax Authorities, the total revenue of your enterprise in 2020 was 467 462 000 Euro. **How much of this was revenue from Establishment_1?**

  28 475 6 | 00 Euro

- **What was the operating costs of Establishment_1 in 2020?**

  19 820 0 | 00 Euro
- **How much of these costs were salaries?**

  5 529 6 | 00 Euro

- On the previous page you reported that 8 863 500 euro was invested in machinery, construction, transport equipment and other tangible fixed assets in 2020. **How much did Establishment_1 invest in fixed assets?**

  806 7 | 00 Euro

- **How much did Establishment_1 earn from sale of fixed assets in 2020**

  1 571 9 | 00 Euro

- In the table below, we have listed all known establishments in the enterprise. **Please give the same information for these establishments as you just did for establishement_1**

Establishments	Revenue	Operating costs	Salaries	Invested assets	Sold assets
Establishment_1	28 475 600	19 820 000	5 529 600	806 700	1 571 900
Establishment_2	12 670 100	9 960 900	8 964 800	1 126 400	00
Establishment_4	426 316 300	239 602 900	35 297 700	6 910 400	4 978 600
Not yet specified	0			20 000	
Enterprise total	467 462 000	269 383 800	49 792 100	8 863 500	6550 500

Invested assets of 20 000 euro is not yet specified. **Please specify**

Figure 15.8 Matrix dialogue.

Note first that Establishment_3 is missing in the table list in Figure 15.8, while Establishment_4 is added. This is because the initial questions described in Figure 15.6 revealed that Establishment_3 was inactive in 2020, while an establishment which was not on the preloaded list was added. By *preloading* relevant units to other parts of the questionnaire (that is leaving out Establishment_3), a source of noise and irritation is avoided.

There are two other examples of preloads in the matrix example. In the first question, data from an external source, in this case the National Tax Office, is referred to. In the question about investments made by Establishment_1, information that the respondent previously entered for the enterprise is now included in the question. Such preloads anchor the establishment questions to enterprise information.

The enterprise totals are also listed in the last row of the table together with a row which subtracts the amounts from "Not yet specified" as they are entered in the table. This countdown ensures consistency between the enterprise total and distribution between establishments. When there is no enterprise anchor, there is still a running tally which will expose obvious summation errors. Other highly relevant question anchors in business questionnaires, are numbers reported in previous surveys and extracts from the companies' business records or personnel and administration systems.

Finally, a small, but important detail. Note that there are no empty cells in the matrix. Cells where there is no information are prefilled with 00, telling the respondents that no answer will be counted as "None."

A question flow based on flowcharts and supported by visualizations, anchors to internal or external sources and running feedback as the questions are answered should form the frontline of a computerized questionnaire. Next, these features can be backed up by error checks and help services.

Error checks are microedits built into the questionnaires (Lorenc et al. 2018). We normally distinguish between hard checks which require corrections, and soft checks which are warning that can be taken into account or be disregarded. Generally, one should carefully consider which edits can be outsourced from the surveyor to the respondent and be particularly careful with hard checks. The one highlighted and followed up by a stop sign and request for correction in Figure 15.8 is a rather obvious miscalculation. Often, however, errors are often not so obvious. In these cases, the computerized error controls can mimic the telephone call we might have taken during in-house editing. Figure 15.9 gives an example on how such a computerized dialogue could look like.

Help services can be integrated into the questionnaire in different ways. Help may be part of the questions given to everybody. This is what we do when we move instructions into the question wording or add bullet points defining terms or adding clarifications. In computerized questionnaires we can take this a step further by integrating information and services available on electronic devices. One example is GPS data. This is a kind of information that could be used on maps presented together with questions about the truck load and traveling conditions.

The clickable "*i*" that led to supplementary information in Figure 15.6 is an example of look-up services. In the previous section, we suggested that help with complicated response tasks could be presented by audio-visual means. For even more comprehensive help, help icons could even lead to help centers. But whether such clickable icons lead to texts, speaking voices, video clips, or service desks, they are still just computerized versions of the old separate instructions. Consequently, they run the same risk of being overlooked and should not be used for crucial information.

Another way of activating help service is by paradata; i.e. process data collected behind the scene while the respondent is completing the questionnaire. In social surveys, probing sessions have been activated when respondents wait too long to answer certain questions (Conrad et al. 2007). This is generally not a good idea in business surveys where we rather want the respondent to take the time needed to look up relevant information. In business surveys, paradata which detect responses which have been changed several times or which are missing at the end of a session may work better as help activators.

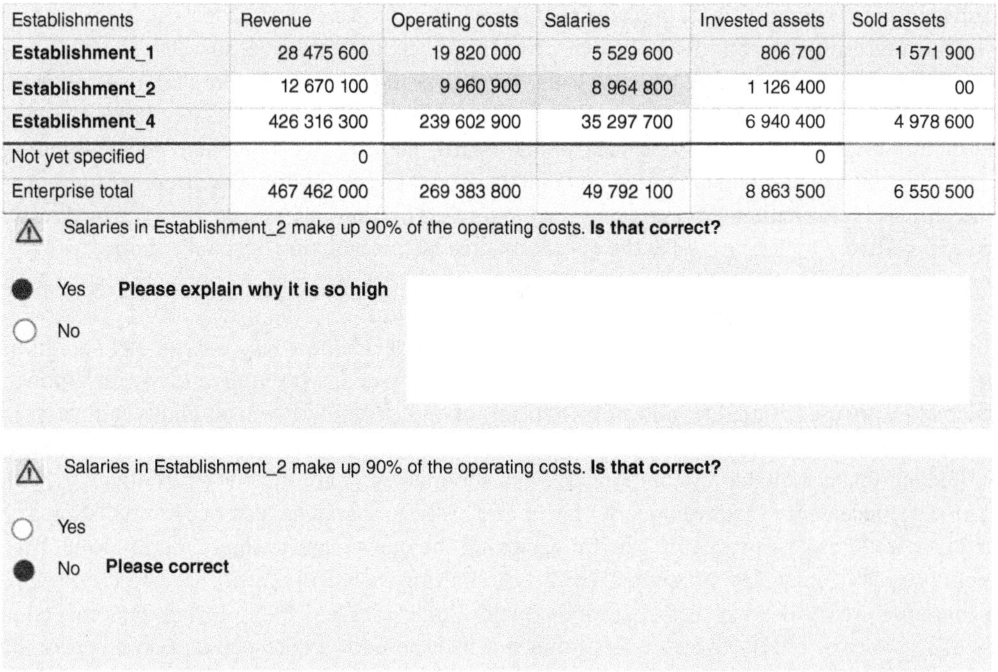

Establishments	Revenue	Operating costs	Salaries	Invested assets	Sold assets
Establishment_1	28 475 600	19 820 000	5 529 600	806 700	1 571 900
Establishment_2	12 670 100	9 960 900	8 964 800	1 126 400	00
Establishment_4	426 316 300	239 602 900	35 297 700	6 940 400	4 978 600
Not yet specified	0			0	
Enterprise total	467 462 000	269 383 800	49 792 100	8 863 500	6 550 500

⚠ Salaries in Establishment_2 make up 90% of the operating costs. **Is that correct?**

● Yes   **Please explain why it is so high**

○ No

⚠ Salaries in Establishment_2 make up 90% of the operating costs. **Is that correct?**

○ Yes

● No   **Please correct**

Figure 15.9   Correction dialogue.

Like with guiding visualization, the questionnaire designer needs to decide how prominent different kinds of help should be. In addition, help can be mediated in different ways. Hence, the designer must also decide what kind of communication fits what kind of message. With what means and how strong different questionnaire elements should be mediated is what makes designing questionnaires so challenging, and with more assorted tools, comes a greater challenge.

15.5   What We Know That We Don't Know

In this chapter, we have argued that computerization opens for a change from linear survey instruments to digitized communication forms and have discussed how this could be done in a way that takes characteristics of business surveys into account. Strictly speaking, however, it is not given that utilizing the functionalities computerization offer, will work better than the traditional requests backed up by separate instructions. Even if there are numerous observational studies of how business surveys work, scientific evidence of what works best in business surveys are still sparse. What we have tried to do is to define and link three kinds of functionalities to specific business survey challenges. We think that is a good starting point for future research.

At several places in this chapter, we have discussed the impact of business respondents being more experienced and professional than social survey respondents. We have asked if the fact that surveys are part of business respondents' daily work leads to more careful reading and serious considerations than what is the case in social surveys, or if the number of questionnaires and repetitions rather lead to lazy routines and lower response quality. Furthermore, we have asked if familiarity with reports in a different format than questionnaires make information requests followed by instructions and the spreadsheet format both a preferred and better way to collect data from businesses than questionnaire design based on principles from social surveys.

These are quite fundamental questions that need to be studied. But before doing so, it is even more fundamental to question the premise for this discussion. The fact that businesses receive more questionnaires than private persons does not necessarily mean that it is the same persons who are repeatedly filling in the questionnaires, and that these persons are as familiar with spreadsheets and other kinds of information requests as we tend to think. This may at least vary between businesses and with different topics covered in the questionnaires. Before studying the quality impact of experience and professionalism we need to know more about *how experienced* business respondents actually are and *what kind of competence* they actually possess.

At the other end of a research model, we also need to decide how response quality should be measured. Because responding to business surveys usually is obligatory, unit or item nonresponse, which often are used as quality indicators in social surveys, generally are poor quality indicators in business surveys.

Paradata, made available in computerized questionnaires, is an obvious alternative. As with other survey elements, however, quality indicators based on paradata also need to be tailored to the purpose. The same procedure as with designing the questionnaire should be followed; first, carefully specify some key questions which are vital for the survey, next, use these questions to construct error rules which can serve as quality indicators and then, during data collection use activated error checks, which may or may not be exposed to the respondent, to measure the response quality. A longer discussion on how paradata can be used for different purposes is in Chapter 18 by Snijkers et al. (2023).

Acknowledgments

Thanks to Mojca Bavdaž and Jacqui Jones who read and commented on different drafts of this manuscript. And thanks to Ger Snijkers who has not only been an important peer reviewer during this writing process, but with whom I have had lots of discussions during a long row of courses in business survey methodology that we have held together. These courses and discussions have been my main source of inspiration.

References

Bavdaž, M. (2010). The multidimensional integral business survey response model. *Survey Methodology* 36 (1): 81–93.

Bavdaž, M., Bounfour, A., Martin, J., Nonnis, A., Perani, G., and Redek, T. (2023). Measuring Investment in Intangible Assests. In: *Advances in Business Statistics, Methods and Data Collection*, Chapter 5 (ed. G. Snijkers, M. Bavdaž, S. Bender, J. Jones, S. MacFeely, J.W. Sakshaug, K.J. Thompson, and A. van Delden). Hoboken: Wiley.

Bavdaž, M., Giesen, D., Korenjak Černe, S., Löfgren, T., and Raymond-Blaess, V. (2015). Response burden in official business surveys: measurement and reduction practices of National Statistical Institutes. *Journal of Official Statistics* 31 (4): 559–588.

Bavdaž, M., Snijkers, G., Sakshaug, J.W., Brand, T., Haraldsen, G., Kurban, B., Saraiva, P., and Willimack, D.K. (2020). Business data collection methodology: current state and future outlook. *Statistical Journal of the IAOS* 36 (2020): 741–756. https://doi.org/10.3233/SJI-200623.

Bradburn, N.M., Sudman, S., and Wansink, B. (2004). *Asking Questions: The Definitive Guide to Questionnaire Design – For Market Research, Political Polls, and Social and Health Questionnaires.* San Francisco: Jossey-Bass.

Buiten, G., Snijkers, G., Saraiva, P., Erikson, J., Erikson, A.-G., and Born, A. (2018). Business data collection: towards electronic data Interchange. Experiences in Portugal, Canada, Sweden, and the Netherlands with EDI. *Journal of Official Statistics* 34 (2): 419–443.

Conrad, G., Schober, M.F., and Coiner, T. (2007). Bringing features of human dialogue to web surveys. *Applied Cognitive Psychology* 21: 165–187.

Conrad, G. and Schober, M.F. (2010). New frontiers in standardized survey interviewing. In: *Handbook of Emergent Methods* (ed. S.N. Hesse-Biber and P. Leavy), 173–188. New York: Guilford Press.

Couper, M.P. (2008). *Designing Effective Web Surveys.* Cambridge: Cambridge University Press.

Dale, T. and Haraldsen, G. (ed.) (2007). *Handbook for Monitoring and Evaluating Business Response Burdens.* Luxembourg: Eurostat.

Dillman, D.A., Smyth, J.D., and Christian, L.M. (2009). *Internet, Mail, and Mixed-Mode Surveys: The Tailored Design Method*, 3rde. Hoboken, NJ: Wiley.

Edwards, W.S. and Cantor, D. (1991). Toward a response model in establishment surveys. In: *Measurement Error in Surveys* (ed. P. Biemer, R.M. Groves, L.E. Lyberg, N.A. Mathiowetz, and S. Sudman), 211–233. New York: Wiley.

Erikson, J., Giesen, D., Houben, L., and Saraiva, P. (2023). Managing Response Burden for Official Statistics Business Survey – Experiences and recent Developments at Statistics Netherlands, Statistics Portugal, and Statistics Sweden. In: *Advances in Business Statistics, Methods and Data Collection*, Chapter 10 (ed. G. Snijkers, M. Bavdaž, S. Bender, J. Jones, S. MacFeely, J.W. Sakshaug, K.J. Thompson, and A. van Delden). Hoboken: Wiley.

Eskenazi, J. (2011). iPad vs newspaper: what the eyes tell us. Paper presented at the Tobii Eye Tracking Conference on User Experience, London (9–10 June).

Foddy, W. (1993). *Constructing Questions for Interviews and Questionnaires: Theory and Practice in Social Research.* Cambridge: Cambridge University Press.

Graesser, A.C., Zhiqioang, C., Lowerse, M.M., and Daniel, F. (2006). Question Understanding Aid (QUAID): a web facility that tests question comprehensibility. *Public Opinion Quarterly* 70 (1): 3–22.

Haraldsen (2018). Response processes and response quality in business surveys. In: *The Unit Problem and Other Current Topics in Business Survey Methodology* (ed. B. Lorenc, P.A. Smith, M. Bavdaz, G. Haraldsen, D. Nedyalkova, L.C. Zhang, and T. Zimmerman). Cambridge: Cambridge Scholars Publishing.

Haraldsen, G. (2013a). Questionnaire communication in business surveys. In: *Designing and Conducting Business Surveys* (ed. G. Snijkers, G. Haraldsen, J. Jones, and D.K. Willimack), 303–357. Wiley, Hoboken, NJ.

Haraldsen, G. (2013b). Quality issues business surveys. In: *Designing and Conducting Business Surveys* (ed. G. Snijkers, G. Haraldsen, J. Jones, and D.K. Willimack), 83–125. NJ: Wiley, Hoboken.

Haraldsen, G. and Jones, J. (2007). Paper and web questionnaires seen from the business respondent's perspective. In: *Proceedings of the 3rd International Conference on Establishment Surveys (ICES III), Montreal (18–21 June)*, 1040–1047. Alexandria, VA: American Statistical Association.

Haraldsen, G., Jones, J., Giesen, D., and Zhang, L.-Z. (2013). Understanding and coping with response burden. In: *Designing and Conducting Business Surveys* (ed. G. Snijkers, G. Haraldsen, J. Jones, and D.K. Willimack), 219–252. Hoboken, NJ: Wiley.

Haraldsen, G., Snijkers, G., and Zhang, L.-Zh. (2015). A total survey approach to business surveys. Presentation at the International Total Survey Error Conference, Baltimore, US (19–22 September 2015).

Hole, B. and Houben, L. (2023). Web Portals for Business Data Collection. In: *Advances in Business Statistics, Methods and Data Collection*, Chapter 20 (ed. G. Snijkers, M. Bavdaž, S. Bender, J. Jones, S. MacFeely, J.W. Sakshaug, K.J. Thompson, and A. van Delden). Hoboken: Wiley

Houben, L., Groot, W., Debie, D., Goris, G., Opreij, A., Geers, X., and Snijkers, G. (2018). A continuous search to improve targeted communication in business surveys. Paper presented at the 5th International Workshop Business Data Collection Methodology, Lisbon (19–21 September).

Jones, J., Snijkers, G., and Haraldsen, G. (2013). Surveys and business surveys. In: *Designing and Conducting Business Surveys* (ed. G. Snijkers, G. Haraldsen, J. Jones, and D.K. Willimack), 1–38. Hoboken, NJ: Wiley.

Krosnick, J.A. and Presser, S. (2010). Questions and questionnaire design. In: *Handbook of Survey Research*, 2nde (ed. P.V. Marsden and J.D. Wright). Bingley, UK: Emerald.

Lorenc, B. (2006). Two topics in survey methodology: modelling the response process in establishment surveys; inference from nonprobability samples using the double samples setup. Doctoral thesis. Department of Statistics, Stockholm University.

Lorenc, B., Norberg, A., and Ohlsson, M. (2018). Studying the impact of embedded validation on response burden, data quality and costs. In: *The Unit Problem and Other Current Topics in Business Survey Methodology* (ed. B. Lorenc, P.A. Smith, M. Bavdaž, G. Haraldsen, D. Nedyalkova, L.C. Zhang, and T. Zimmerman), 199–211.

Martin, E., Hunter Childs, J., DeMaio, T., Hill, J., Reiser, C., Gerber, E., Styles, K., and Dillman, D. (2007). *Guidelines for Designing Questionnaires for Administration in Different Modes*. Washington, DC: U.S. Census Bureau https://www.census.gov/srd/mode-guidelines.pdf.

Neter, J. and Waksberg, J. (1964). A study of response errors in expenditure data from household interviews. *Journal of the American Statistical Association* 59 (305): 18–55.

Peytchev, A., Conrad, F.G., Couper, M.P., and Torangeau, R. (2010). Increasing Respondents' use of definitions in web surveys. *Journal of Official Statistics* 28 (49): 633–650.

Saraiva, P. (2016). Integrated survey management system: statistics Portugal experience. Paper presented at the 5th International Conference on Establishment Surveys (ICES-V), Geneva, Switzerland (20–23 June 2016), Statistics Switzerland.

Smith, P. (2013). Sampling and estimation for business surveys. In: *Designing and Conducting Business Surveys* (ed. G. Snijkers, G. Haraldsen, J. Jones, and D.K. Willimack), 165–218. Hoboken, NJ: Wiley.

Smith, P. and Yung, W. (2023). Introduction to Sampling and Estimation for Business Surveys. In: *Advances in Business Statistics, Methods and Data Collection*, Chapter 27 (ed. G. Snijkers, M. Bavdaž, S. Bender, J. Jones, S. MacFeely, J.W. Sakshaug, K.J. Thompson, and A. van Delden). Hoboken: Wiley.

Snijkers, G. (2016). Achieving quality in organizational surveys: a holistic approach. In: *Methodische Probleme in der empirischen Organisationsforschung* (ed. S. Liebig and W. Matiaske), 33–59. Wiesbaden, Germany: Springer Gabler.

Snijkers, G., Demedash, S., and Andrews, J. (2023). Using Paradata in Electronic Business Survey Questionnaires. In: *Advances in Business Statistics, Methods and Data Collection*, Chapter 18 (ed. G. Snijkers, M. Bavdaž, S. Bender, J. Jones, S. MacFeely, J.W. Sakshaug, K.J. Thompson, and A. van Delden). Hoboken: Wiley.

Snijkers, G., Houben, L., and Demollin, F. (2023). Tailoring the Design of a New Combined Business Survey: Process, methods, and Lessons Learned. In: *Advances in Business Statistics, Methods and Data Collection*, Chapter 16 (ed. G. Snijkers, M. Bavdaž, S. Bender, J. Jones, S. MacFeely, J.W. Sakshaug, K.J. Thompson, and A. van Delden). Hoboken: Wiley.

Snijkers, G. and Jones, J. (2013). Business survey communication. In: *Designing and Conducting Business Surveys* (ed. G. Snijkers, G. Haraldsen, J. Jones, and D.K. Willimack), 359–430. Hoboken, NJ: Wiley.

Snijkers, G., Onat, E., and Vis-Visschers, R. (2007). The annual structural business survey: developing and testing an electronic form. Proceedings of the 3rd International Conference on Establishment Surveys (ICES-III), Montreal, American Statistical Association, Alexandria, VA (18–21 June), pp. 456–463.

Sturgis, P., Allum, N., and Brunton-Smith, I. (2009). Attitudes over time: the psychology of panel conditioning. In: *Methodology of Longitudinal Surveys* (ed. P. Lynn), 113–126. West Sussex, UK: Wiley.

Sudman, S., Willimack, D.K., Nichols, E., and Mesenbourg, T.L. (2000). Exploratory research at the U.S. Census Bureau on the survey response process in large companies. In: *Proceedings of the Second International Conference on Establishment Surveys (ICES-II)*, 327–337. American Statistical Association.

Torres van Grinsven, V., Bolko, I., and Bavdaž, M. (2014). In search of motivation for the business survey response task. *Journal of Official Statistics* 30 (4): 579–606.

Tourangeau, R. (1984). Cognitive sciences and survey methods. In: *Cognitive Aspects of Survey Methodology: Building a Bridge Between Disciplines* (ed. T.B. Jabine, M.L. Straf, J.M. Tanur, and R. Tourangeau), 73–100. Washington, DC: National Academy of Science.

Tourangeau, R. and Bradburn, N.M. (2010). The psychology of survey response. In: *Handbook of Survey Research*, 2nde (ed. P.V. Marsden and J.D. Wright). Bingley, UK: Emerald.

Tourangeau, R., Conrad, F.G., and Couper, M.P. (2013). *The Science of Web Surveys*. Oxford: Oxford University Press.

Tourangeau, R., Rips, L.J., and Rasinski, K. (2000). *The Psychology of Survey Response*. New York: Cambridge University Press.

Willimack, D.K. and Nichols, E. (2010). A hybrid response process model for business surveys. *Journal of Official Statistics* 26 (1): 3–24.

Willimack, D.K. and Snijkers, G. (2013). The business context and its implications for the survey response process. In: *Designing and Conducting Business Surveys* (ed. G. Snijkers, G. Haraldsen, J. Jones, and D.K. Willimack), 39–82. Hoboken, NJ: Wiley.

Yan, T. (2005). Gricean effects in self-administrated surveys. Dissertation, Faculty of the Graduate School of the University of Maryland College Park, MD.

16

Tailoring the Design of a New Combined Business Survey: Process, Methods, and Lessons Learned

Ger Snijkers[1], Leanne Houben[2], and Fred Demollin[3]

[1] *Department of Research and Development (Methodology), Division of Data Services, Research and Innovation, Statistics Netherlands, Heerlen, The Netherlands*
[2] *Department of Innovation, Development and Functional Management (Innovation Data Services), Division of Data Services, Research and Innovation, Statistics Netherlands, Heerlen, The Netherlands*
[3] *Department of Business Statistics (Heerlen), Division of Economic and Business Statistics and National Accounts, Statistics Netherlands, Heerlen, The Netherlands*

16.1 Introduction

Official business surveys, conducted by National Statistical Institutes (NSIs), usually are being conducted for years or even decades, using approximately the same design (Snijkers et al. 2013). Minor changes may happen from year to year, but a major redesign, to the extent that we in fact end up with a new survey, is quite rare because recurring surveys produce time series. However, in the current era, major redesigns of business surveys may be expected more.

One driver for a redesign is efficiency improvement by integrating several similar surveys using comparable processes into one production process. In 2000, Statistics Netherlands started the IMPlementation EConomic Transformation (IMPECT) program (Snijkers et al. 2011) to redesign its Annual Structural Business Surveys (SBSs). The individual SBS surveys were designed after World War II (Atsma 1999), following a stove-pipe (or silo) approach, with each industry sector survey having its own production process. The IMPECT program was mainly aimed at reducing production costs by integrating the stove-pipe processes, and resulted in a new combined annual SBS survey, with one harmonized production process. In 2010, Statistics Canada launched the Integrated Business Statistics Program (IBPS) (see Jones and O'Byrne 2023 [Chapter 8]; Ravindra 2016). Except for efficiency improvement, the IBPS objectives were quality considerations (like coherence, timeliness, and relevance) and response burden reduction. Nowadays major redesigns may also be initiated because of the use of secondary data sources like administrative and big data (see van Delden and Lewis 2023 [Chapter 12], Bender et al. 2023 [Chapter 22]). At country level, a driver to redesign surveys is the need for aligned statistics on the same topics across institutes. The COVID-19 pandemic showed this need (see Jones et al. 2023 [Chapter 11]). Bender (2021) stresses the need for harmonized measurements for large enterprises, for which differences may result from different conceptualizations and measurement procedures across institutes.

Redesigns involve many, often complex steps to get coherent statistics (NAS 2018). This chapter discusses combining several financial surveys for the very large enterprises conducted by Statistics Netherlands (CBS) and the Dutch National Bank (DNB) into one single new business survey: *The CBS-DNB Finances of Enterprises and Balance of Payments Survey.* We will discuss the survey

Advances in Business Statistics, Methods and Data Collection. Edited by Ger Snijkers, Mojca Bavdaž, Stefan Bender, Jacqui Jones, Steve MacFeely, Joseph W. Sakshaug, Katherine J. Thompson, and Arnout van Delden.

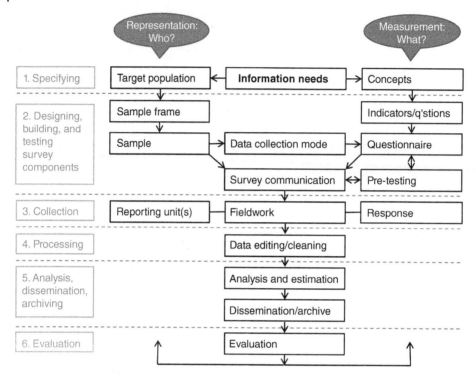

Figure 16.1 The total survey error process-quality framework.

components involved in this redesign process, the steps taken, methods used, and the lessons learned with a focus on data collection. Apart from efficiency improvement, the main driver for this redesign were quality considerations: statistics on the same concepts from the original surveys were not consistent, even though in theory they should be equal at the aggregated level. Both institutes had to go back to the original definitions of the target concepts and target population of the individual surveys as well as consider various error sources as described in the Total Survey Error (TSE) framework to find the causes for these differences.

The TSE framework provides a structured overview of steps in the survey process, and related error sources. Groves et al. (2004/2009) discuss this process-quality framework in general, Haraldsen (2013a) and Snijkers (2016) adapted it to business surveys. Instead of the TSE framework, NSIs often use the Generic Statistical Business Process Model (GSBPM) as a reference process framework (Jones and O'Byrne 2023 [Chapter 8], UNECE 2019, Memobust 2014). Both frameworks identify the same high-level stages in the survey process: 1. specifying and planning the survey, 2. designing, building, and testing the survey components, 3. collecting the data, 4. processing the data (including data cleaning), 5. analysis, dissemination, and archiving, and 6. process evaluation. In this chapter, we will use the TSE process-quality framework (see Figure 16.1). The redesign process shows that every step and every error source in the TSE framework matter, and all error sources need to be considered carefully to achieve coherent statistics.

In the next two sections, we describe the background (Section 16.2) and the development process of the new survey (Section 16.3). Section 16.4 discusses the questionnaire development, and Section 16.5 presents the communication strategy developed to inform and prepare the targeted population for the new survey and evaluates its effectiveness. Section 16.6 wraps up by discussing survey design insights and lessons learned.

16.2 Toward the New "CBS-DNB Finances of Enterprises and Balance of Payments" Survey

In the Netherlands, both Statistics Netherlands (CBS) and the DNB have a statutory function in producing financial business statistics in the Dutch and European Statistical System, but with a different foundation: CBS statistics are regulated by Eurostat, the European Statistical Institute, while DNB statistics are regulated by the European Central Bank (ECB).

Until the early 2000s, both institutes operated as two independent institutes, producing their own statutory statistics based on their own processes, e.g. having their own business registers, and conducting their own data collections, according to their own procedures. CBS conducted the quarterly and annual Statistics of Finances of Enterprises (SFE) surveys to collect, among others, Balance-of-Payment (BoP) data from the largest nonfinancial corporations (NFCs) groups (with more than 23 million euros aggregated balance sheet) as input for the Quarterly Sector Accounts, National Accounts, and the gross domestic product (GDP). DNB collected monthly and annual BoP reports from these NFCs to prepare the BoP statistics and the International Investment Position (IIP) statistics.

Even though the same populations were targeted, and data on comparable variables were collected, substantial differences between the CBS and DNB statistics were seen. Extensive post-field data cleaning efforts (stage 4 in Figure 16.1), in a first attempt to eliminate the differences, did not yield consistent statistics. As a result, the focus shifted to methods, procedures, and processes of both institutes. At first sight, this showed a lot of similarities. However, when zooming-in on the survey procedures, illogical differences surfaced. It was concluded that these macroeconomic statistics were produced at high production costs, with comparable processes running in both institutes, but with different procedures, and needing a lot of post-field data editing, at high costs (response burden) for the sampled enterprises.

As a result, it was decided to intensify the cooperation between both institutes. The first priority was to find the causes for inconsistencies (see Section 16.3) in order to eliminate them. It turned out that the differences could not be solved without harmonization of unit and variable definitions, methods, and processes, i.e. evaluating the original conceptualizations and operationalizations of these surveys (see stages 1 and 2 in Figure 16.1). In the end, in 2014, it was concluded that coherent statistics could only be achieved by combining the individual surveys into one quarterly survey: *The CBS-DNB Finances of Enterprises and Balance of Payments Survey.* The first statistics based on this new survey were published by CBS in June 2019.

16.3 Achieving Coherent Statistics

When studying the survey procedures as implemented by both institutes, multiple potential causes for the differences in the data collected with the original surveys were found. The main factors to concentrate on to harmonize data were identified as:

- definition of Special Purpose Entities (SPEs, or Special Purpose Vehicles, VHCs), and the implementation of the definition when specifying legal units,
- composition of the target population (observation units) and differences in the structure of legal units within individual enterprise groups, and
- timing of sending out the questionnaires and periodicity.

The first actions were taken in the field of SPEs. SPEs mostly are legal units constructed for tax optimization, having no or few nonfinancial assets and employees, and little or no production

(Eurostat 2019a). Teams of DNB and CBS started comparing their definitions. Although conceptual definitions were similar, differences were discovered at the operational level in the implementation and judgment of individual cases. This led to differences in the observed structure of enterprise groups.

In multiple collaborative sessions, first SPEs were defined on the conceptual level, considering three main characteristics: (i) balance sheet totals (total assets and liabilities) are mainly coming from a foreign country, (ii) the balance sheet totals are almost completely invested in foreign enterprise groups, and (iii) limited domestic activities or presence. The main discussions were on the exact percentages in order to quantify the definition. It was agreed that at least 90% of the balance sheet totals in SPEs should come from abroad and its domestic workforce should have a maximum of five full-time equivalents.

Furthermore, it was agreed to maintain one SPE database for both institutes. The database was located at CBS, and both institutes could add or delete legal units based on mutually shared information flows. The database was a first attempt to achieve harmonization of the operationalized target populations.

As a result, the differences in the statistics became smaller, but there was still room for improvement. A team was assigned to compare the observation structures of the entities in both statistics. To this end, a group of large enterprises, present in both target populations, were selected. Again, it were the details that made the difference. Due to the use of different sources leading to both target populations, differences in the periodicity of maintaining the populations, and differences in starting dates of applying changes in group structures, the operationalization of the populations was not equal. After exhaustive comparison of both populations and the underlying methods and processes, it was concluded that the differences would never disappear completely unless all surveys would be based on one register. As CBS had just revised its Business Register and had fully aligned the register with the Tax Office and the National Trade Register, it was decided that this Business Register would become the standard for surveying Enterprise Groups (Coenen and van Brummelen 2018). In addition, it was decided to take the enterprise group structures as defined by the Business Register, as the observation units, which also defines the consolidation clusters in the data collection.

Again, an improvement could be seen in aligning CBS and DNB statistics, however a full alignment was still not achieved. In the third step, the comparison of the data collection procedures of both institutes identified misalignments caused by differences in periodicity in the data collection: DNB conducted a monthly survey, while CBS sent out questionnaires on a quarterly basis.

In addition, the majority of the differences was found for enterprises with different contact persons for DNB and CBS. It appeared that DNB respondents were generally found in the Treasury Department (responsible for the enterprise cashflow and financial management), while the CBS respondents mainly were found in the Group-Accounting Department (responsible for the Balance of Payment and Profit-and-Loss Statement at enterprise group level). Trying to solve the differences in the data for individual enterprises often lead to discussions between treasury and accounting respondents, with DNB and CBS staff as neutral observers in the middle. This showed that reporting data by an enterprise representative is depending on the accounting systems used, time lags in system updates, and interpretations of the respondent. An extra dimension is the recurring reporting over time: as long as the data are retrieved in exactly the same manner, the reports are comparable. However, due to maintenance and technical upgrades of IT systems, the reporting procedures have to be updated frequently. In addition, changes in respondents can make comparability with earlier reports problematic. It was concluded that these internal enterprise factors affect the reported data.

In the quest for a full-proof solution, the involved DNB and CBS staff concluded that nearly all possible causes for potential differences had been fixed. Still, with every subsequent data collection cycle, differences occurred in the individual enterprise data. Human behavior was often discovered as a cause for these differences, e.g. ad hoc decisions made by people involved in the reporting processes within the enterprises, as well as within CBS and DNB. The effect of this human behavior factor on the data could not be ignored, since we were dealing with the largest enterprises in the Netherlands, but was very hard to control.

In the end, it was concluded that all possible harmonizing actions had been taken without a satisfactory result. The logical question that followed was "why are there two data collection processes anyway?" Following this analysis phase, in 2014 a joint program was started aimed at producing coherent macroeconomic statistics of high quality across both institutes by the integration of the surveys into one combined production chain. This could only be achieved by combining the expertise from both institutes, the alignment of responsibilities, tasks, methods, processes and working procedures, and integrating business registers (Bieleveldt et al. 2014, Eding 2017). This would also reduce production costs, as well as response burden for enterprises. It was agreed that CBS would focus on nonfinancial sectors, while DNB would focus on the financial sector and securities. In September 2017, CBS and DNB signed a unique cooperation agreement, marking their collaborative relationship.

In the first step, CBS and DNB staff collaboratively discussed the integration of the surveys into one combined survey and one combined set of required variables. It took some time to compare the data needs of both institutes; in 2014, the new combined conceptual data model (stage 1 in Figure 16.1) was ready (Bieleveldt et al. 2014, Demollin 2014). As no secondary sources were adequate, this model served as input for the development of the new joint mandatory quarterly CBS-DNB survey: *The CBS-DNB Finances of Enterprises and Balance of Payments Survey* (stage 2 in Figure 16.1).

In the years 2014–2018, four project teams worked on the design of the new combined survey (Bieleveldt et al. 2014, Hermans 2015, Eding 2017). These projects were focused on the development of:

- a single, jointly-used Business Register, aimed at harmonization of the unit definitions (Coenen and van Brummelen 2018),
- a new, combined questionnaire (Göttgens 2016),
- a new data management and editing system, aimed at efficient case/response management and post-field data cleaning (based on the questionnaire) (Baart et al. 2017); and
- a communication strategy with the enterprises, aimed at introducing the survey, informing them, and ultimately getting response (Houben and Snijkers 2016, Houben 2016).

In the remainder of this chapter, we will focus on the questionnaire development and the communication strategy.

16.4 Questionnaire Communication: Tailoring the Design

This section focuses on the questionnaire design and development methodology. We applied two design principles to tailor the questionnaire to the business context:

- Questionnaire design = communication design. The questionnaire is a communication instrument, and should be user-friendly for respondents without needing any user instructions: it

should be self-explaining (Snijkers et al. 2007, van der Geest 2001, for a discussion on this principle see Haraldsen (2013b, 2023 [Chapter 15])).
- Take the respondent's position. The questionnaire should follow as much as possible the business context, and facilitate the completion process (for a discussion on the business context and the business's response process, see Willimack and Snijkers (2013)).

16.4.1 Steps in the Questionnaire Development Process

The questionnaire development process started in 2015, and consisted of several steps (Snijkers 2017, 2019):

1. A feasibility study, conducted in 2015, consisted of visits to five enterprises in order to study the availability of the requested data and the internal business response process (Snijkers et al. 2015, Snijkers and Arentsen 2015, Snijkers 2017). This study provided requirements (see Section 16.4.2) for the questionnaire design and tailoring to the enterprises' response process.
2. The questionnaire architecture was developed in 2015–2016 (Göttgens 2016). This included an overview of all variables in the questionnaire, a questionnaire schedule (i.e. the location of the variables in the questionnaire), and the user-interface design. The same five enterprises were visited again to test the user-interface for usability issues, showing positive results.
3. The questionnaire was gradually developed in 2017. The first draft (version 1) in early 2017 included only a few major modules, and was pre-tested (Giesen and Visschers 2017). Having positive results from the pre-tests, an extended draft with all modules (version 2) was developed in the fall of 2017, which was reviewed by all project members and discussed with the question-naire programmers (Section 16.4.6). The fully developed questionnaire (version 3) was ready before the end of 2017. Originally, the new survey was to be fielded in 2018 but it was decided that 2018 was a pilot year, in which businesses were given the opportunity to get prepared for the new survey in 2019 (Section 16.5).
4. In early 2018, the questionnaire was tested again without the option of making major changes: nine enterprises were visited (Snijkers 2018). These enterprises were carefully selected based on their response behavior for the original surveys, and their internal data structures. The focus was on identifying risks of working with the new questionnaire, so the main results concerned the business survey communication strategy (instructing and helping enterprises to work with the questionnaire), and post-field data editing. The final questionnaire (version 4) is shown in Figures 16.3 and 16.4.
5. In March 2019, the questionnaire (version 4) was finalized and implemented, including all additional instruction materials (manuals, instruction videos, background information, etc.; see www.cbs.nl/balanceofpayments). The fieldwork started in April 2019.

Even though the data model is quite complex, the structure of the questionnaire is simple. The core of the questionnaire is structured around the BoP items (assets and liabilities), and the Profit and loss statement (originally collected by CBS) as represented in the Index panel at the left side of the questionnaire (see Figure 16.2). For some balance sheet items, more detailed information is requested in a matrix of cross-border financial transactions (reconciliations or movements) (orig-inally collected by DNB). By clicking the "Movements" buttons to the right, or the active items in the Index, a screen with this table will be opened (see Figure 16.3).

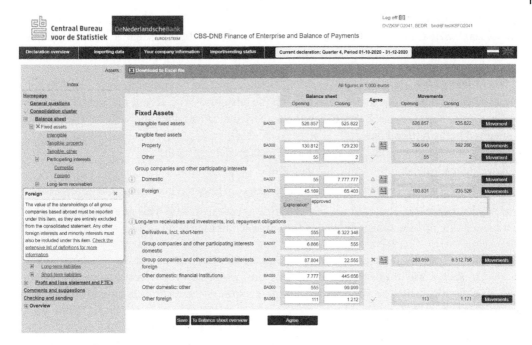

Figure 16.2 One screen of the final questionnaire (core).

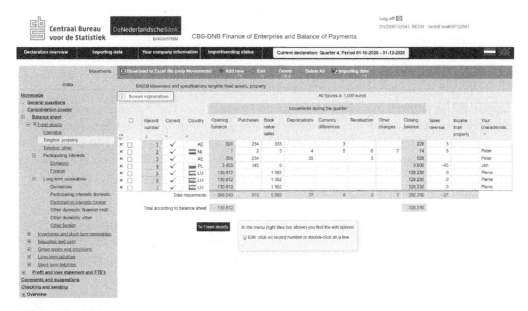

Figure 16.3 Movements Table (Tangible: property).

16.4.2 The Feasibility Study

Instead of moving directly from the data model to the development of the new questionnaire, first the feasibility of the data model was investigated (Snijkers et al. 2015, Snijkers and Arentsen 2015, Snijkers 2017). This study asked the following research questions to get more insights into data availability and the internal response process (Willimack and Nichols 2001, 2010, Lorenc 2007, Bavdaž 2007, 2010a, 2010b, Willimack and Snijkers 2013, Haraldsen 2013a, 2018, 2023 [chapter 15], Haraldsen et al. 2015):

1. *What (data)*: What data do businesses have? Do they have the requested data, are the data definitions clear, and do they match or differ with the businesses own accounting definitions?
2. *Where (people and sources)*: Where can the requested data be found and what business staff is involved in the retrieval process?
3. *Who (units)*: Do we get the data about the correct (predefined) units?
4. *When (time)*: When are the requested data available?

From the findings to these four questions, a fifth, and core research question could be answered:

5. *How (questionnaire)*: How can we best collect the requested data? This refers to the design of the questionnaire, the timing, as well as the survey communication strategy.

In April/May 2015, five large nonfinancial enterprises were visited on-site. The enterprises were selected in such a way that a variety of internal business data structures was covered: ranging from an enterprise with a centralized accounting department to a complex enterprise structure consisting of several independent units. Among several methods to be used in a feasibility study (Willimack et al. 2023 [Chapter 17], Willimack 2013, Snijkers and Willimack 2011, Bavdaž 2009), we used in-depth interviews including probing (also called concept testing at the Australian Bureau of Statistics, Price 2021): a topic list for a two-hour discussion on the data model was prepared based on the research questions. As for the "how" question, we looked for spontaneous reactions throughout the discussions, and used probes like: "What would work for you?", and "What would help you with regard to reporting these data?"

At the same time, an independent study was carried out by PricewaterhouseCoopers (PWC 2015) with the same focus. This study consisted of two parts: an accounting expert review, and on-site visits with four enterprises.

Both studies resulted in the same general conclusion about the new proposed survey: combining the CBS and DNB surveys into one survey seems logical for both organizations, but offers no synergy to the enterprises, because of the different internal response processes within businesses (see Section 16.3). Consequently, they do not perceive the new data requirements as a reduction in response burden. This conclusion made a tailored design even more important.

The feasibility study gave the following answers to the research questions:

- *What*: Most required data are available, however differences between survey data definitions and definitions used by enterprises can be expected. Thus, definitions should preferably be integrated in the questionnaire (not using hidden instructions). However, because of long and detailed definitions, this was hard to achieve.
- *Where*: Even though most of the data are available, not all of them are easy to collect. The data can be divided into three groups regarding the retrieval process: easy, doable, and hard to get. With the increase of internal data sources, the related response process becomes more complex (see next Sections 16.4.3 and 16.4.4).
- *Who*: With increasing complexity of the enterprises structure, consolidated reporting may cause problems. The observational unit for which the data should be reported, should be clear to all respondents involved in the response process.
- *When*: Enterprises should be able to report the data on a quarterly basis.

16.4.3 What Data and Where Are the Data?

The findings about the data availability were translated onto the data model and presented as a color-coded overview of the data model (a simplified model is presented in Figure 16.4). The coding is based upon the ease of retrieving the required data and their sources:

- *(G in Figure* 16.4*)*: The data are readily available from the Group Accounts at the highest enterprise group level. This includes the BoP items, the Profit and Loss Statement, as well as the opening and closing positions for the movement tables.
- *(Y in Figure* 16.4*)*: Some high-level data are also available at a central location (the Treasury), but not in the Group Accounts. This requires more effort as CBS contacts usually were in the Group-Accounting Department, while DNB contacts were in the Treasury Department.
- *(O in Figure* 16.4*)*: The data are available, but in decentralized ledgers. This includes the detailed movement data, which require considerable effort to retrieve. This holds especially for enterprises with a significant presence abroad, having many cross-border transactions.
- *(R in Figure* 16.4*)*: These data are not available.

These results were confirmed when the final questionnaire was pretested in 2018 (Snijkers 2018): the data asked for in Figure 16.2 are easy to retrieve (G), while the movements tables (Figure 16.3) are coded orange (O).

The color-coded overview presented management and researchers with a clear overview of potential risks in the data collection and processing stages: the more steps and the more sources are involved in the response process, and the deeper within the business data have to be retrieved, the higher the risks of survey errors like measurement errors, item nonresponse, and unit errors. Based on these results several items were deleted from the conceptual data model. Still, the movement tables (Figure 16.3) remained a risky part of the questionnaire.

Assets		Movements characteristics					Movements during quarter							
							Receivables							
								Movements during quarter						
								Receivables		Revaluation				
	Assets Main item	Country	Sector	Original maturity	Remaining maturity	Counter-party	Opening balance	Increase receiva-ble	Decrease receiva-ble	Currency differen-ces	Revalu-ation	Depreci-ations	Other changes	Closing balance
Intanglible fixed assets	G						G	G	G	O	O	G	G	G
Tangible - property	O	O					O	O	O	O	O	O	O	O
Tangible - other	Y	O					Y	Y	Y	Y	Y	Y	Y	Y
Consumer Credit Supplied	G	R		R			G							G
Loan Supplied	G	G	G	O		O	G	O	O	O	O		O	G
Debtors and Advances	G	O					G	O	O	O	O		O	G
Transferable Deposits (Bank accounts)	G	Y					G	O	O	O	O		O	G
Cash	G						G	O	O	O			O	G
Other Deposits	G	Y		Y			G	O	O	O	O		O	G

Figure 16.4 Color-coded data model: Business Information Accessibility Scale.

16.4.4 The Business Response Process

Behind this color-coded overview, a response process in a business takes place. Depending on the business administration/data structure, this process can have various levels of complexity as is shown in Figure 16.5. For businesses with a centralized accounting system, the internal process is straightforward: the observation unit (or statistical unit) is represented by one reporting unit, within which one respondent (the contact person) has access to the central Group Accounts, which houses all requested data. For more complex data structures, the retrieval process can become increasingly complex, involving more data sources at various locations and more respondents/data providers. It turned out that for some enterprises the data were not even located in the Netherlands, but in another European country, or even outside of Europe. This applied e.g. to enterprises with decentralized general ledgers, like enterprises consisting of several units (each owning their own ledger), and foreign-owned multinationals. For a small number (8) of enterprises, it was decided that the data collection was deconsolidated: the individual reporting units could report for themselves, and CBS would consolidate them into the designated observation unit.

Again, the 2018 pretest (with the final questionnaire) revealed how complex and non-transparent these processes could be (Snijkers 2018, 2019). In one enterprise, visualized in Figure 16.6, three

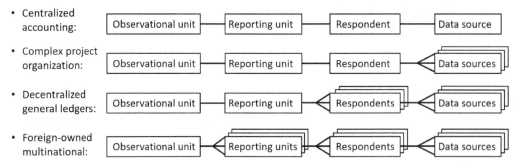

Figure 16.5 Various response processes.

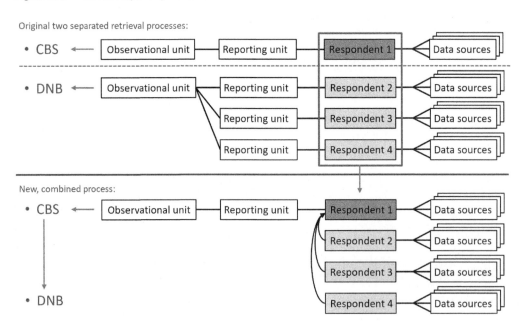

Figure 16.6 A complex internal business response process.

different respondents reported to DNB for three different sub-units, while another respondent reported to CBS for the entire consolidated enterprise. These four respondents were located in different units of the enterprise, and were unaware of each other's reporting to DNB and CBS. For the new combined survey, these four respondents had to work together and integrate their response processes into one: the CBS respondent became the central response coordinator, while the other three respondents had to report to this coordinator.

16.4.5 How: Questionnaire Design Requirements

The feasibility study identified three groups of questionnaire design requirements:

1. Questionnaire content issues:
   - The terminology in the questionnaire should be clear because of the difference between statistical and accounting definitions.
   - As a starting point, the enterprises wanted to have an overview of the requested data.
   - The structure of the questionnaire should be clear and follow the generally used business accounting classifications. In particular, this concerns the relationship between the variables in the core of the questionnaire (Figure 16.2) and the movement tables (Figures 16.3).
   - The questionnaire should clarify the consolidated unit the survey addresses.
2. User interface and usability issues:
   - A clear overview of the content of the questionnaire should be presented, using an index, which also can be used for navigation and progress control.
   - It should be possible to complete the questionnaire in every possible order, including top–down and bottom–up completion.
   - The questionnaire should be accessible from various locations and completed by various respondents.
   - Consequently, the questionnaire should be available in Dutch and English.
   - Data entry should not only be possible manually but also by uploading/importing data (csv) files.
   - A data export option or print option should be available.
   - The questionnaire should contain some intelligence, consistency checks, and validation rules as respondents expect them.
   - To facilitate the internal data retrieval process, it should be possible to indicate where the data come from. In this way internal coordinators can contact the right internal respondents when needed.
   - Working with matrixes/grids is not a problem.
3. Communication strategy:
   - The visited businesses asked to introduce the new questionnaire in advance to prepare internal response processes.

These requirements could only be met with an electronic questionnaire, which was in line with CBS policy to only use electronic business questionnaires. In the final questionnaire (see Figures 16.2 and 16.3), the following features are included:

1. Questionnaire content features:
   - Data definitions can be accessed by clicking the information button (i) (see Figure 16.2), but also by downloading a definition document from the questionnaire welcome page as well as from the information website (www.cbs.nl/balanceofpayments).
   - An Excel template providing an overview of the requested data, can be downloaded from the questionnaire and from the information website.

- The consolidation cluster is shown in one of the first screens in the questionnaire, and has to be approved before a respondent can move on. (Still, when several respondents/data providers are involved in the internal response process, the data reported may not match this cluster, leading to unit errors (Snijkers et al. 2023a [Chapter 1].)

2. User-interface and usability features:

- The final questionnaire includes all of the above mentioned features (Snijkers et al. 2023b [Chapter 18]). For an overview, we refer to the information website where a user manual with completion instructions can be downloaded, and two instruction videos can be watched.

3. Communication strategy:

- In response to the get-prepared request, the fielding of the survey was postponed for one year; instead a pilot was conducted (Section 16.5).

16.4.6 Questionnaire Development

Following the feasibility study, in early 2016, a project team started with the design and development of the questionnaire. Apart from a project leader, this multidisciplinary team existed of six people: a questionnaire designer from the Data Collection Division (who is owner of the questionnaire, and developed the questionnaire content sheet, Figure 16.7a), a content matter expert from the CBS statistical department (previously involved in the data model developments, and in contact with DNB and the CBS National Accounts department), an expert from the CBS large case unit (where most businesses in the target population are), a former field staff officer (knowledgeable about the response processes in businesses), and a methodologist (with expertise in business questionnaire design, business response processes, and business survey communication).

The questionnaire development was cyclical and included two aspects: operationalization of the content, and development of the user interface. As for the content, the data model was translated into an overview of the entire questionnaire content using Excel (Figure 16.7a): (i) each individual data item is represented by a data entry box (meaning that if a box was missing here, the variable would not be in the final data file) and (ii) each tab represents a screen in the questionnaire (thus serving as input for the user interface). When we started developing the questionnaire, we thought that the data model was finalized, but going into the details required going back and forth to the data model, as the model needed additional specifications.

An initial visualization of the user interface was designed in PowerPoint (Figure 16.7b). A draft version of the user interface was first pretested in the spring of 2016 with the businesses who had participated in the feasibility study (Snijkers 2017, 2018). As the navigation using the index worked well, we proceeded with confidence.

In addition, a list of usability issues and functions was prepared, taking the business requirements into account. Each issue was rated according to the Must, Should, Could, Would (MoSCoW) principles, which was used as input for the external software developer. The fully developed questionnaire had to be ready by the end of 2017, as it was to be used in the pilot year 2018.

After this long period of development, we had one remaining question: how would the final questionnaire (Figures 16.2 and 16.3) work in practice? To answer this question, we analyzed a set of paradata, in particular questionnaire completion data: see Chapter 18 (Snijkers et al. 2023b).

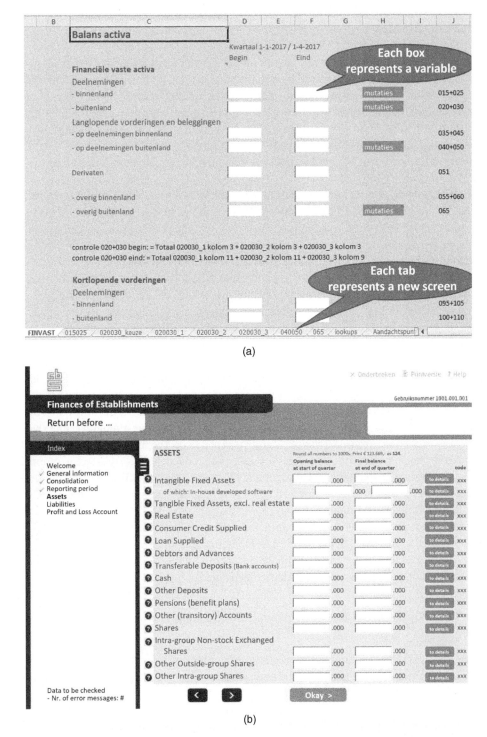

(a)

(b)

Figure 16.7 (a) Translation of data model into an Excel questionnaire schedule. (b) Visualization of the user interface in Powerpoint.

16.5 Introducing the Survey in the Field: The Survey Communication Strategy

The discussions with businesses during the questionnaire development stage showed that the introduction of this new questionnaire would have major implications for businesses, particularly those with a significant presence abroad (with many movements to report) and/or a complex response process. Since they indicated that they needed up to a year to get prepared, the fielding of the survey was postponed for one year (from 2018 to 2019), and 2018 was used for a pilot. An information campaign was started at the end of 2017, one-and-a-half year before the survey would be fielded in early 2019, to inform businesses about the upcoming new, mandatory survey, and the pilot year.

We started developing this strategy in 2016 after the feasibility study (Houben and Snijkers 2016, Houben 2016). To tailor the communication strategy better and get support for this new survey, this strategy was developed in close collaboration with representatives of the private sector: The Confederation of Netherlands Industry and Employers.

We identified three phases in the survey communication strategy: (i) the pre-field phase, (ii) the field phase, and (iii) the post-field phase (Snijkers and Jones 2013). The general principle behind our communication strategy is the *commitment principle*, one of Cialdini's compliance principles (2009). As research showed that past response behavior is a very strong predictor of survey participation (Willimack and Snijkers 2013, Davis and Pihama 2009), we hypothesized that building a relationship and getting enterprises to take the first steps in the pilot year (the pre-field phase), would positively affect their response behavior in the first quarter of the field phase, and consequently in the next quarters. Also, an intensive information campaign (to be continued in the field phase) would signal that their survey participation is important. In this way, we tried to train businesses to be good respondents, instead of nonrespondents. We expected to see a learning effect in the first survey year (2019): businesses would be more accustomed to the questionnaires, and the internal processes would have been established. Thus, we hoped to get the responses earlier in the subsequent quarters, having more time to process the data and produce the statistics. Acceleration of the response was desired by the statistical department. Of course, this was still dependent on the moment in time when the data would become available in the business, among other factors which we cannot influence (Snijkers and Jones 2013).

We monitored and evaluated this strategy thoroughly: whether businesses exploited our outreaches to get prepared in the pre-field phase, the development of response rates in the field phase, and the effects of enforcement in the post-field phase. Section 16.5.1 discusses the communication strategy in greater detail, Section 16.5.2 discusses its effectiveness.

16.5.1 The Three Phases in the Survey Communication Strategy

16.5.1.1 Pre-field Phase

The goal of the pre-field phase (pilot in 2018) was to inform enterprises about the upcoming new survey, and to nudge them to get prepared for the new questionnaire (Houben and Snijkers 2016). The sample consisted of 362 units from the largest enterprises in the Netherlands, among which special communication subgroups were identified, based on cruciality (relevance of an enterprise), discrepancies in previously reported CBS and DNB data, different contact persons for the original CBS and the DNB questionnaires (Section 16.3), and newly selected enterprises.

This phase consisted of the following steps and communication instruments:

- *12 December 2017*: Notification letters with an information folder of the new upcoming survey with login credentials were sent to both DNB and CBS contact persons; DNB informed their contacts separately that CBS will contact them for the new survey. Simultaneously, our new website www.cbs.nl/balanceofpayments with video clips and short instructions was launched. The letter informed businesses about the possibility to get prepared for the new survey, but it was made clear that they still had to complete the original surveys until early 2019. Also, the CBS help-desk phone number was listed, in case of questions.
- *16 March to 12 April 2018*: All businesses with different contact persons for the original CBS and DNB surveys received individual telephone calls to inform them about the new survey, to encourage them to login on the questionnaire, and get themselves prepared as this group was considered risky (Section 16.3).
- *6 April 2018*: First reminder letters were sent to all businesses, again with the login credentials. The letter emphasized that CBS will enforce nonrespondents from the beginning of the field phase onwards.
- *30 April 2018*: Invitation letters were sent to all contact persons from CBS and DNB to participate in an information meeting about the new survey at DNB in Amsterdam.
- *25 June 2018*: The information meeting at DNB, Amsterdam.
- *4 July 2018*: Feedback was sent to all businesses about the information meeting, with tailored messages to the businesses that did and did not attend this meeting.
- *28 September to 13 November 2018*: Telephone calls to businesses that had not yet logged in, to stress once again the importance of preparing for the new questionnaire.
- *12 November 2018*: Final reminder letters to get prepared. In this letter, we also mentioned that the original CBS and DBN questionnaires would stop from the reporting year 2019 onward.
- *Between May 2018 and February 2019*: Tailored instructions to businesses that were new to the sample. Because of business demography (births, deaths, mergers, and acquisitions) 35 new businesses were added to the sample. As soon as these new businesses were identified, they were contacted and informed about the new questionnaire. Unfortunately, because of the late entry they did not have the same opportunities to get prepared as the businesses that were included in the pre-field phase from the beginning.
- *February 2019*: General instructions for our help-desk to get prepared for the field phase.
- *12 April 2019*: End of the pre-field phase (login to the pilot questionnaire closed), and start of the field phase.

During the pre-field phase, we meticulously registered our actions and business activities: businesses called, business reactions, businesses attending the information meeting, and all logins on the pilot questionnaire. We could determine the first-time login, and the total number of logins for each enterprise as is shown in Figure 16.8 (Punt et al. 2019).

Figure 16.8 shows the development of businesses' first-time logins during the pilot year, with the communication actions superimposed. Gradually, more businesses logged in. At the end of the pre-field phase, 75% of the 362 contacted enterprises had logged in at least once. After some of the actions (like the notification letter, telephone contacts, the reminder letter in April, as well as the information meeting), we see a steep increase in the number of enterprises logging-in for the first time, indicating that these actions had an effect.

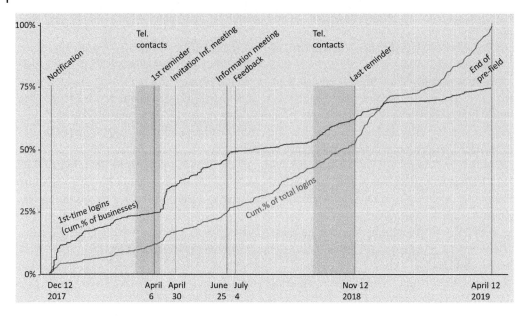

Figure 16.8   First-time logins (cumulative percentage of businesses) and total number of logins (cumulative percentage of total logins) in the pre-field phase.

A second line in Figure 16.8 shows the development of all logins for all enterprises during the pilot year. By setting the total number of logins to 100%, we see a steady increase in activity during 2018, but about 50% of all logins occurred at the end of the pilot year, after the final reminder letter in mid-November. At the time of the invitation for the information meeting (end of April 2018), about 35% of all enterprises had logged in at least once, but the relative share to the total activity at that moment is only around 15%. These percentages are strong indications that enterprises are merely exploring during the start of the pilot period, while most of the preparation work is done at later stages. Not all businesses logged in equally often: in total 153 businesses logged-in three times or more, 119 businesses logged-in once or twice, and 90 businesses did not log-in at all. The actual level of activity, however, could be higher since we do not know what businesses did offline.

16.5.1.2   Field Phase of the First Wave of the Survey

We hoped that our efforts in the pre-field phase had sufficiently raised businesses' awareness about the new survey. In fact, the message from businesses in the October-2018 phone calls was: "You've done enough, now it is time for us to get ready." So, in the field-phase we could build on the pre-field communications except for businesses newly added to the target population. The sample now counted 397 enterprises. Figure 16.9 shows the development of the response rate in the field-phase (Punt et al. 2019):

- *12 April 2019*: An advance letter was sent to all 397 sampled enterprises. The due date, indicated in the letter, was 13 May 2019.
- *30 April 2019*: A pre-due date reminder was sent to 369 enterprises. At that date, 7% (28) of the sampled businesses had already responded.
- *8 May to 27 May 2019*: The CBS help-desk called nonresponding enterprises by telephone for motivating and reminding. During the field phase our help-desk got 441 requests. Two thirds of the questions were in these weeks, with a peak just before the initial due date. Many ques-

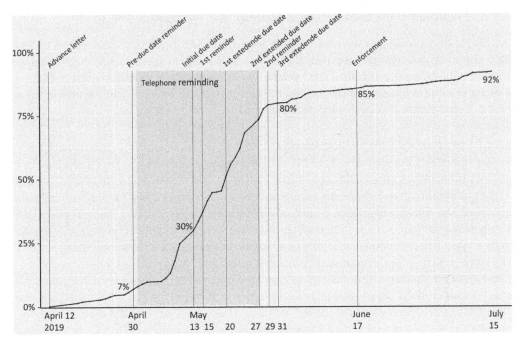

Figure 16.9 Development of the response rate during the field phase (first wave of the survey in 2019).

tions concerned extension of the deadline ($n = 177$), as well as general questions about filling in the new questionnaire ($n = 119$). Furthermore, businesses asked for a copy of the advance letter ($n = 67$), or a new login password ($n = 18$).

- *13 May 2019*: The initial due date. At this moment in time 30% of the businesses had responded, which was well below the targeted response rate of 85%.
- *15 May 2019*: A reminder letter was sent, indicating an extended deadline. By now, the total response rate had increased to 37%, while 177 enterprises (45%) had asked for extension.
- *20, 27, and 31 May 2019*: Extended deadlines. In consultation with individual businesses, the deadline could be extended to 20, 27, or 31 May 2019 at the latest. At the time of the final extended deadline, the total response rate had increased to 80%.
- *Two days after the (extended) deadline*: a reminder letter was sent to all nonresponding enterprises. This reminder was strictly phrased, and referred explicitly to the enforcement steps in the post-field phase.
- *17 June 2019*: Transfer of 60 nonresponding enterprises to the Enforcement Department, and start of the post-field phase. At this time, the response rate had increased to 85%, the targeted response rate.

16.5.1.3 Post-field Phase of the First Wave of the Survey

At the beginning of the post-field phase, the files of all 60 nonresponding businesses were checked thoroughly. These 60 businesses were contacted again, and asked to respond as soon as possible. This resulted in 14 businesses responding, with 46 enterprises being actually enforced. By mid-July 2019, the response rate had increased to 92% ($n = 365$), and continued increasing to a final 97% (n=385) in mid-August (Punt et al. 2019).

16.5.2 Evaluation of the Communication Strategy: Was the Strategy Effective?

Given the energy invested in the pilot year, we were interested in whether these efforts had an effect. Our main research question was: did the intensive pre-field approach affect the response behavior in the first quarter of 2019? Furthermore, we examined the response progress in the next quarters: how fast did businesses respond in the next waves? Do we see a learning effect? These research questions are discussed in the next Sections 16.5.2.1 and 16.5.2.2.

16.5.2.1 Effectiveness of the Pre-field Strategy

In order to evaluate the effectiveness of the pre-field strategy, we tested the hypothesis based on Cialdini's commitment principle that businesses that were more active in the pre-field phase, had a higher probability to respond in the field phase. The analysis was based on pre-field and field login dates, the duration of a login session, as well as response dates during the field phase (the completed questionnaire can be submitted several times) (Punt et al. 2019). Unfortunately, we did not have questionnaire completion paradata, so we did not have data on what businesses actually did when completing the questionnaire (Snijkers et al. 2023b [Chapter 18]).

We divided the businesses into different groups, based on their participation level in the pre-field phase. We assumed that businesses that weren't active at all in the pre-field phase, would not be committed to participate in the field phase. We expected that businesses that had checked the questionnaire just briefly during the pre-field phase, and didn't get prepared well, would also show low levels of commitment. As for businesses that were active in the pre-field phase, indicated by several logins, we assumed that they were committed to participate in the survey, since they already had invested in their own response process. To determine the cutoff levels of these groups, we did a box-plot analysis on the login distribution for the pre-field phase, resulting in three groups as shown in Table 16.1. In addition to these three groups, we had the group of 35 businesses that entered the pre-field phase at a later stage. Based on the applied commitment theory, we assumed that this "New" group is not committed to participate in the survey, and consequently will show low or very low effort levels.

To explore the groups' response behavior, we checked their first-time login development during the field phase (see Figure 16.10). The pre-field high-activity group is faster in opening the questionnaire, and reaches the highest final first-time login rate. (Some of these enterprises had already logged in before the advance letter was sent.) The low and no-activity groups are slow starters, with the "No" group doing a little better in the first weeks, but the "Low" group is improving when the due date approaches. At the end, the "Low" group performed better than the "No" group, where this "No" group needed some enforcement to get started. The businesses in group "New" show a

Table 16.1 The pre-field activity groups, their assumed field effort levels, and number of enterprises.

Pre-field group	Login frequency during pre-field	Effort during pre-field phase	Assumed effort in field phase	Number of enterprises
High	3 or more	High	High	153
Low	1 or 2	Low	Low	119
No	0	None	Very low	90
New	Partly pre-field phase	Not applicable	(Very) low	35
Total				**397**

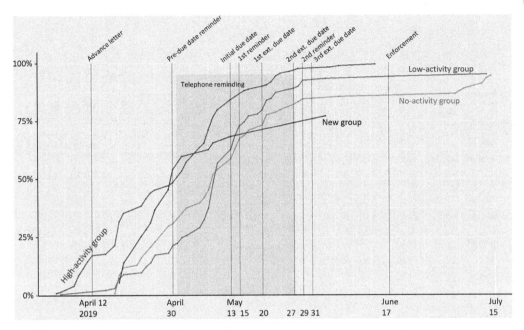

Figure 16.10 Development of first logins in the field phase (first wave of the survey in 2019) for the four pre-field groups (cumulative percentages of businesses in each group).

totally different first-login pattern: there is a fast increase in businesses opening the questionnaire early in the quarter, but this slows down after the pre-due date reminder. In the end, this group performed worst of all groups.

The response rate development for these groups during the first wave in 2019 (see Figure 16.11) suggests a similar pattern: groups "No," "Low," and "High" show similar response behaviors, but the high-activity group is faster than the low-activity group, which in turn is faster than the no-activity group. Groups "High" and "Low" reach the same high final response rate (of 95%), while the "No" group finishes a little lower (90%), showing a clear enforcement effect. Group "New" again, shows a different pattern: starting fast, but then falls back, and reaches only 71%.

These patterns indicate the assumed positive relationship between pre-field and field response behavior. To test whether the difference in response behavior between the four groups is significant, we applied the χ^2-test to Table 16.2. In this table, the groups "No" and "New" seem to be overrepresented in the Nonresponse column under the hypothesis that the pre-field and field behavior are independent of each other. This χ^2-test shows that the pre-field and field behavior are not independent, which confirms our assumption.

An additional variable that was available to further test this hypothesis, was the number of times a questionnaire was submitted. This variable might be an indicator of data quality, regarding complete and accurate response: the more times submitted, the better. E.g. respondents in enterprises might have discovered errors or missings, and resubmitted to correct the reported data. This variable was cut into three distinct categories (Table 16.3). The χ^2-tests has a p-value much lower than 0.05; therefore, the null-hypothesis of independence is rejected. We may assume that the quality of the submitted data is higher for businesses that were more active in the pilot: they resubmitted more often. To get an even better understanding of this relationship, a paradata analysis of the post-field data editing process would be needed (stage 4 in Figure 16.1).

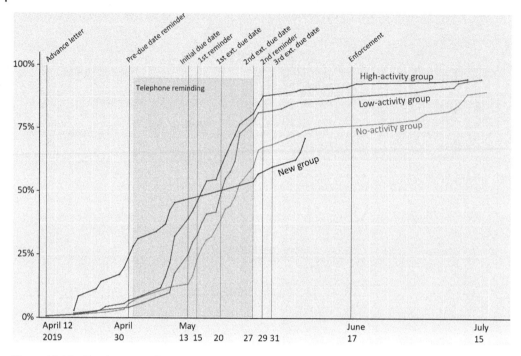

Figure 16.11 Development of the response rate in the field phase (first wave of the survey in 2019) for the four pre-field activity groups (cumulative percentages of businesses in each group).

Table 16.2 Number of responding and nonresponding enterprises in the first wave of the survey in 2019 for the four pre-field activity groups.

Pre-field activity group	Response (n)	Nonresponse (n)	Total (n)	Response rate (%)
High	145	8	**153**	95%
Low	113	6	**119**	95%
No	81	9	**90**	90%
New	25	10	**35**	71%
Total	**364**	**33**	**397**	**92%**

$\chi^2 = 22.76, df = 3, p = 4.52\text{e-}5.$

Finally, we looked at the activity levels during the field phase for the four pre-field activity groups: the number of logins and the login duration during the field phase. Again, we assumed a positive relationship: the businesses that already invested in this, would be more committed. However, this relationship might not be as strong as the ones discussed above, because businesses could have been working off-line with the questionnaire, using the import function. And when they had prepared well during the pilot year, the completion in the first wave of the survey might not take that long anymore. Tables 16.4 and 16.5 show the statistically significant differences between the four pre-field activity groups for the number of logins and login duration, respectively.

To conclude, all χ^2-tests give statistical evidence that the level of effort during the field phase (measured with four different indicators) is positively associated with the pre-field effort level. We did not find a significant difference between the two groups with high and low pre-field activity,

Table 16.3 Number of enterprises for number of times the questionnaire was submitted for the four pre-field activity groups.

Pre-field activity group	Number of times the questionnaire was submitted			Total
	No submissions (nonresponse)	1 submission	2 or more submissions	
High	8	57	88	**153**
Low	6	59	54	**119**
No	9	39	42	**90**
New	10	15	10	**35**
Total	**33**	**170**	**194**	**397**

$\chi^2 = 28.93, df = 6, p = 6.27\text{e-}5.$

Table 16.4 The number of enterprises divided by number of login times (quartiles) for the four pre-field activity groups.

Pre-field activity group	Number of times logged in (quartiles)				Total
	0–5	6–10	11–17	18–81	
High	22	45	30	56	**153**
Low	39	28	28	24	**119**
No	25	27	23	15	**90**
New	14	13	5	3	**35**
Total	**100**	**113**	**86**	**98**	**397**

$\chi^2 = 32.98, df = 9, p = 0.0001.$

Table 16.5 The number of businesses per login duration (quartiles) for the four pre-field activity groups.

Pre-field activity group	Login duration (quartiles)				Total
	0 s–4 h11 min	4 h12 min–7 h43 min	7 h44 min–14 h12 min	14 h13 mins–2 days7 h	
High	26	33	41	53	**153**
Low	33	31	27	28	**119**
No	26	25	25	14	**90**
New	15	10	6	4	**35**
Total	**100**	**99**	**99**	**99**	**397**

$\chi^2 = 23.65, df = 9, p = 0.0049$

however, meaning that enterprises that were active in the pre-field phase in any way, were more likely to show more effort during the field phase, responded quicker and better. We concluded that the pre-field communication strategy has been effective, and successful in stimulating businesses to get prepared and to be good respondents in the field phase. A more detailed analysis, including background characteristics of enterprises, would have been appropriate to confirm this finding, and to check for spurious associations.

Based on these results, it was decided to implement a pre-field phase for new enterprises for the next survey year: enterprises that were new to the 2020 sample, received a pre-notification letter in early-March 2020 giving them access to the – for them new – questionnaire one month before the start of fieldwork in order to get prepared. This was considered sufficient time regarding the fact that half of all activities in the pilot year (2018) took place in the last months (see Figure 16.8). Also, giving them more time ahead might not work because December is a busy month for businesses. A practical consideration was that the sample was not yet drawn.

16.5.2.2 The Response Rate Development in the Next Quarters of 2019

We also hoped for a learning effect in the first year of the survey as enterprises would get experienced with completing the questionnaire, and had established a completion process. We hypothesized an accelerated response for subsequent quarters. This indeed happened: Figure 16.12 shows that for subsequent quarters in 2019, the responses were coming in sooner, and the final response rates reached a higher level.

This pattern continued in the next years, 2020 and 2021. In addition, the number of businesses that needed enforcement declined in these years. A more detailed analysis focusing only on enterprises that had participated in all waves, and taking into account changes in contact persons, would have been appropriate, but we concluded that the communication strategy was effective for a longer period of time, and had helped to speed up the production process, as was desired by the statistical department at the start of the process.

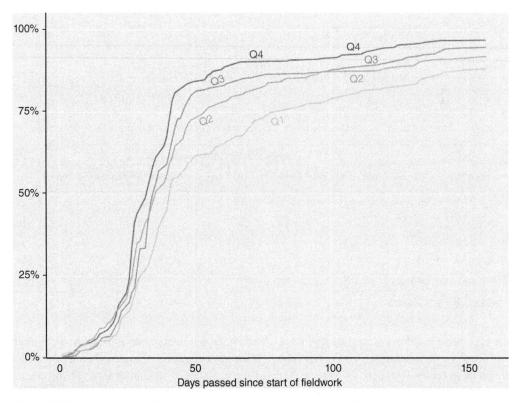

Figure 16.12 Development of the response rate in the four quarters in 2019 (cumulative percentages of enterprises).

16.6 Lessons Learned

Every step in the survey design process, as defined in the TSE process-quality framework (Figure 16.1), is of importance to achieve coherent statistics across different institutions. Repairing the design afterward, by extensive data editing and cleaning, does not always lead to the desired results, is very costly, and involves a lot of staff. Therefore, it is important to carefully think about a good design right from the beginning, which is the first stage in the TSE framework (the conceptualization stage): the detailed specification of the concepts (the required output at variable level) and the target population.

Lesson 1: The first stage in the design process, the specification of the concepts to be measured and the target population, has an impact on the data quality. When (re)designing a survey, this stage should be addressed with care.

Next, we have seen that ad-hoc decisions on individual level, both within CBS and DNB, and the sampled businesses (e.g. diverging procedures between the two institutes and ad-hoc decisions about the consolidation of businesses), had an impact on the final survey data. So, the implementation of variable and population definitions also needs to be specified in great detail, e.g. specification of profiling criteria for inclusion or exclusion of units. Variable definitions are implemented in a questionnaire. This refers to stage two in the TSE model: the operationalization of the survey components.

Lesson 2: In the second stage of the survey process, the development of the survey components, all definitions need to be implemented in great detail, leaving no room for ad-hoc judgment. In case ad-hoc decisions still need to be made during the data collection stage, these need to be documented and shared with the survey staff to ensure that in the same situations the same decisions are made. This requires careful monitoring of the data collection process.

When moving to the business context, we have seen that changes in the internal business response processes, like updates of IT systems and changing contact persons, have an effect on the survey outcomes. Since statistical reporting is of no priority to businesses' contact persons, they may not transfer their established procedures to a next colleague. This may especially be the case when the internal response process within a business is complicated, as for our survey. Also changes in the structure of enterprises, and consolidated reporting, affects the data when the observational unit is not clearly defined for the respondent.

Lesson 3: Changes in business internal response process can have a major impact on the survey outcomes, especially when surveying the very large enterprises. However, NSIs cannot control these changes. Therefore, these are considered a risk and need to be monitored and followed up carefully. At CBS, a Large Case Unit was established for this reason (Vennix 2012, Demollin 2019a). The staff in this department maintains a good relationship with large enterprises and monitors changes. In addition, profiling is important to keep the structures of these large enterprises up-to-date (Demollin 2019b, Demollin and Hermans 2020, Eurostat 2019b).

General methodology of social surveys recommends first developing a draft of the questionnaire, followed by pre-testing (see e.g. Groves et al. 2004/2009, Blair et al. 2013); these steps can be iterated when needed. For business survey questionnaire development, we recommend a three-step approach:

1. Conduct a feasibility study based on specified information needs, and explore the business context (the internal data collection process and internal data structures in the target population),
2. Develop a draft questionnaire based on the feasibility study results,
3. Pre-test the draft questionnaire. Again, steps 2 and 3 can be iterated if needed.

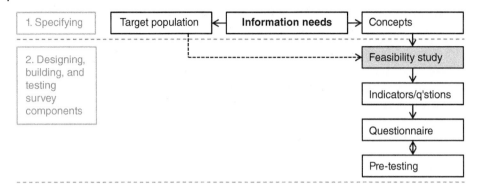

Figure 16.13 Recommended questionnaire development process in business surveys.

Such a feasibility study is an investment in the final survey data, reducing measurement errors, nonresponse errors, and response burden. A comparable approach is practiced by the Australian Bureau of Statistics (Price, 2021), in which very early in the development process conversations are held with businesses to understand their needs, pain-points, opportunities, and challenges in relation to statistical needs. A similar approach is discussed in Chapter 17 by Willimack et al. (2023).

Lesson 4: Development of a business questionnaire should start as early in the process as possible by conducting a feasibility study in order to properly tailor the design to the business context, as is indicated in Figure 16.13 (based on Figure 16.1). Discussing the requested data for a first time with businesses when pretesting an already drafted questionnaire comes too late in the process.

The feasibility study showed how important the internal response process within businesses is to get good data in time: even a well-designed questionnaire requires from businesses to do their job and get ready, i.e. establish a new internal process, and get everybody involved at the table. Businesses wanted to get an overview of the changes and their consequences, and have an overview of the requested data. Consequently, businesses should be offered the chance to get prepared, e.g. by prenotifications.

Lesson 5: For businesses, a new questionnaire may need a new internal business response process. In case of major redesigns that affect this process, businesses want to be pre-notified about changes. To have to-the-point pre-notifications and a smooth transition, it is important to have good insights in this internal process.

Lesson 6: To estimate the workload, and establish a new internal response process, businesses want to know upfront what data they have to report, i.e. an overview or a list of variables and their definitions. Completing the questionnaire itself is the final step in the response process, after all the data-retrieval work has been done.

Pre-notifying businesses is part of the communication strategy. The basic principle behind our strategy was the commitment principle (Cialdini 2009): once businesses started working with the questionnaire, they had taken the first steps. As such, we trained and helped them to become good respondents, instead of becoming nonrespondents. In a recurring survey, like ours and most businesses surveys, initial completion should pay off.

The analysis showed that our approach worked: businesses who were active in the pilot, performed better in the field stage than businesses who did not get prepared. Also, we saw an ongoing effect: for each successive quarter, the responses came in earlier and reached a higher rate. This confirms the conclusions of other studies on past response behavior and the effectiveness of pre-field measures (Snijkers and Jones, 2013): past response behavior is a very strong predictor for future behavior.

This brings us to three lessons learned regarding the survey communication and responding to the survey:

Lesson 7: In a major redesign, which in fact is the design of a new survey, the questionnaire and survey communication go together, and need to be designed jointly.

Lesson 8: The commitment principle achieves better survey participation and can be implemented in several pre-field measures which assist businesses in establishing their role and responsibilities from the very start. This strategy can also be implemented for new waves of the survey and new enterprises.

Lesson 9: It takes time for businesses to learn the process. In recurring surveys, this has implications for the assistance and support. It is not just a one-time action, but assistance should be provided whenever needed. New enterprises may be defined as a separate target group that may need special attention.

A concluding lesson from this exercise is that it is important to invest in the business survey design. To achieve coherent statistics on the same topic for the same target population, for which the data are collected by various surveys conducted by two institutes, post-field repairing and additional actions did not have the desired effect; individual survey effects remained while being very costly for both institutes, as well as for the reporting enterprises. Even though at the start of this redesign process, it was concluded that a combined survey would not seem to reduce response burden for these enterprises, we are convinced that after having established a new internal response process, this redesign is less costly to them (on enterprise level). Anecdotal comments about this new combined survey by business' contact persons to our large case unit officers support this conclusion.

Lesson 10: Investing in your survey design, which comes down to investing in your data, is worthwhile. Prevention is better than repairing. Even if in the short-term it may increase costs both for the survey organizations and the reporting businesses, at longer run it is more cost-efficient.

Acknowledgment

In the projects discussed in this chapter a large number of colleagues from CBS and DNB have participated. Here, we would like to mention especially those who have participated in the questionnaire design and survey communication projects. They are in alphabetical order, from CBS: Ken Arentsen, Patrick Baart, Michelle Creemers, Daisy Debie, Stefan de Kok, Ger Emmerink, Robert Göttgens, Michel Hayen, Casper Hueting, Ton Hooijmans, Meindert Kappe, Peter Muyrers, Cyrille Pluijmen, Tim Punt (intern), Hen Pustjens, and Patricia Smeets; and from DNB: Eva Hagendoorn and Rini Hillebrand. The electronic questionnaire was developed by Revolux S.àR.L. ®, a software house, located in Luxembourg, that is specialized in the development in data collection instruments.

The authors are grateful to Mojca Bavdaž (University of Ljubljana, Slovenia), Stefan Bender (Bundesbank, Germany), Eva Hagendoorn (DNB), and Hank Hermans (CBS) for reviewing the manuscript.

Disclaimer

The views expressed in this paper are those of the authors and do not necessarily reflect the policies of Statistics Netherlands nor the Dutch National Bank.

References

Atsma, J. (1999). A statistical description of economic life in the Netherlands (in Dutch: Een statistische beschrijving van het economisch leven in Nederland). In: *Counted for one Century (in Dutch: Welgeteld een eeuw)* (ed. J. van Maarseveen and R. Schreijnders), 137–150. Voorburg: Statistics Netherlands.

Baart. P., Göttgens, R., Houben, L., Kok de, S., and Pustjens, H. (2017). Project plan joint project CBS-DNB Finances of Enterprises and Balance of Payments, CBS 2017-2019 (in Dutch). Internal document, Statistics Netherlands, Heerlen, The Netherlands.

Bavdaž, M. (2007). Measurement errors and the response process in business surveys. Ph.D. Dissertation. University of Ljubljana, Slovenia.

Bavdaž, M. (2009), Conducting research on the response process in business surveys. *Statistical Journal of the IAOS* 26 (1): 1-14. https://doi.org/10.3233/SJI-2009-0692.

Bavdaž, M. (2010a). Sources of measurement errors in business surveys. *Journal of Official Statistics* 26 (1): 25–42. https://www.scb.se/dokumentation/statistiska-metoder/JOS-archive/.

Bavdaž, M. (2010b). The multidimensional integral business survey response model. *Survey Methodology* 36 (1): 81–93.

Bender, S. (2021). The design of a new complex survey for the very large non-financial enterprises in the Netherlands: discussion. Discussion in Session CS01 at ICES-VI, 6th International Conference of Establishment Statistics, 15 June 2021. On-line Conference 14–17 June 2021, American Statistical Association.

Bender, S., Blaschke, J., and Hirsch, C. (2023). Statistical data production in a digitized age: the need to establish successful workflows for micro data access. In: *Advances in Business Statistics, Methods and Data Collection*, Chapter 22 (ed. G. Snijkers, M. Bavdaž, S. Bender, J. Jones, S. MacFeeley, J.W. Sakshaug, K.J. Thompson, and A. van Delden). Hoboken: Wiley.

Bieleveldt, E., Hoekstra, R., and Pustjens, H. (2014). Towards a new collaboration between Statistics Netherlands and the Dutch National Bank with regard to Balance of Payments and Sector Accounts (in Dutch: Vernieuwing samenwerking CBS-DNB op het gebied van betalingsbalans en sectorrekeningen). Project Initiation Document, Statistics Netherlands, Heerlen, and Dutch Central Bank, Amsterdam, The Netherlands.

Blair, J., Czaja, R.F., and Blair, E.A. (2013). *Designing Surveys: A Guide to Decisions and Procedures*, 3rde. Thousand Oaks, CA: Sage.

Cialdini, R.B. (2009). *Influence: Science and Practice*, 5e. Boston: Allyn and Bacon.

Coenen, B. and van Brummelen, M. (2018). One statistical business register for Statistics Netherlands and the Dutch Central Bank. Paper presented at 26th Meeting of the Wiesbaden Group on Business Registers, Neuchâtel, Switzerland (24–27 September 2018).

Davis, W.R. and Pihama, N. (2009). Survey response as organisational behaviour: An analysis of the annual enterprise survey, 2003–2007. Paper presented at New Zealand Association of Economists Conference, Wellington, New Zealand (1–3 July 2009).

Demollin, F. (2014). *Joint data model Quarterly Statistics on Finances of Enterprises (in Dutch: Gezamenlijk datamodel KSFO-kwartaalkubus)*. Internal memorandum, Statistics Netherlands, Heerlen, The Netherlands.

Demollin, F. (2019a), Congo: consistency activities within CBS. Presentation at the 2019 UNECE Meeting of the Group of Experts on National Accounts: Measuring Global Production, Geneva, Switzerland (10–12 April 2019). https://unece.org/info/events/event/18004.

Demollin, F. (2019b). Profiling and data collection. Presentation at the 2019 UNECE Meeting of the Group of Experts on National Accounts: Measuring Global Production, Geneva, Switzerland (10–12 April 2019). https://unece.org/info/events/event/18004.

Demollin, F. and Hermans, H. (2020). Advancing new collaborative mechanisms for the profiling of MNEs in national, regional and global group registers. *Statistical Journal of the IAOS* 36 (3): 775–783. https://doi.org/10.3233/SJI-200670.

Eding, G.J. (2017). Integrating balance of payments and sector accounts in the Netherlands. Presentation at the UNECE Meeting of the Group of Experts on National Accounts: Measuring Global Production, Geneva, Switzerland (31 May–2 June 2017) https://unece.org/info/events/event/19176.

Eurostat (2019a). Glossary: Special-purpose entity (SPE). Eurostat Statistics Explained. Eurostat, Luxembourg. https://ec.europa.eu/eurostat/statistics-explained/index.php?title=Glossary:Special-purpose_entity_(SPE) (accessed 19 July 2021).

Eurostat (2019b). European Profiling to better measure Multinational Enterprise Groups' activities. Presentation at the 2019 UNECE Meeting of the Group of Experts on National Accounts: Measuring Global Production, Geneva, Switzerland (10–12 April 2019). https://unece.org/info/events/event/18004.

Giesen, D. and Vis-Visschers, R. (2017). Design and results of usability tests with the new quarterly CBS/DNB questionnaire, February–May 2017 (in Dutch). Internal report, Statistics Netherlands, Heerlen, the Netherlands.

Göttgens, R. (2016). Project plan for developing the new CBS/DNB questionnaire (in Dutch). Internal document, Statistics Netherlands, Heerlen, The Netherlands.

Groves, R.M., Fowler, F.J. Jr., Couper, M.P., Lepkowski, J.M., Singer, E., and Tourangeau, R. (2004/2009). *Survey Methodology*. Hoboken: Wiley.

Haraldsen, G. (2013a). Quality Issues in business surveys. In: *Designing and Conducting Business Surveys* (ed. G. Snijkers, G. Haraldsen, J. Jones and D.K. Willimack), 83–125. Hoboken: Wiley.

Haraldsen, G. (2013b). Questionnaire communication in business surveys. In: *Designing and Conducting Business Surveys* (ed. G. Snijkers, G. Haraldsen, J. Jones and D.K. Willimack), 303–357. Hoboken: Wiley.

Haraldsen, G. (2018). Response processes and response quality in business surveys. In: *The Unit Problem and Other Current Topics in Business Survey Methodology* (ed. B. Lorenc, P.A. Smith, M. Bavdaž, G. Haraldsen, D. Nedyalkova, L.-Ch. Zhang, and Th. Zimmerman), 157–177. Newcastle upon Tyne, UK: Cambridge Scholars Publishing.

Haraldsen, G. (2023). What computerized business questionnaires and questionnaire management tools can offer. In: *Advances in Business Statistics, Methods and Data Collection*, Chapter 15 (ed. G. Snijkers, M. Bavdaž, S. Bender, J. Jones, S. MacFeely, J.W. Sakshaug, K.J. Thompson, and A. van Delden). Hoboken: Wiley.

Haraldsen, G., Snijkers, G., and Zhang, L.-Ch. (2015). A total survey error approach to business surveys. Presentation at the International Total Survey Error conference (TSE15), Baltimore, USA (19–22 September 2015).

Hermans, H. (2015). Approach for the new quarterly survey on finances of enterprises (in Dutch: Aanpak SGOII). Internal memorandum, Statistics Netherlands, Heerlen, The Netherlands.

Houben, L. (2016). Project plan for the Development of the Communication Strategy for the new quarterly CBS-DNB Survey (in Dutch). Internal document, Statistics Netherlands, Heerlen, The Netherlands.

Houben, L., and Snijkers, G. (2016). Business Survey Communication Strategy for the new quarterly CBS-DNB survey (in Dutch: Communicatiestrategie DRA-SFO). Internal report, Statistics Netherlands, Heerlen, The Netherlands.

Jones, J. and O'Byrne, H. (2023). Statistical producers challenges and help. In: *Advances in Business Statistics, Methods and Data Collection*, Chapter 8 (ed. G. Snijkers, M. Bavdaž, S. Bender, J. Jones, S. MacFeely, J.W. Sakshaug, K.J. Thompson, and A. van Delden). Hoboken: Wiley.

Jones, J., Ryan, L., Lanyon, A.J., Apostolou, M., Price, T., König, C., Volkert, M., Sakshaug, J.W., Mead, D., Baird, H., Elliott, D., and McLaren, C.H. (2023). Producing official statistics during the COVID-19 pandemic. In: *Advances in Business Statistics, Methods and Data Collection*, Chapter 11 (ed. G. Snijkers, M. Bavdaž, S. Bender, J. Jones, S. MacFeely, J.W. Sakshaug, K.J. Thompson, and A. van Delden). Hoboken: Wiley.

Lorenc, B. (2007). Using the theory of socially distributed cognition to study the establishment survey response process. *ICES3 Proceedings. International Conference on Establishment Statistics III*, Montreal, pp. 881–891. http://ww2.amstat.org/meetings/ices/2007/proceedings/ICES2007-000247 .PDF.

Memobust (2014). *Theme: GSBPM: Generic Statistical Business Process Model. Module in the Memobust Handbook on Methodology of Modern Business Statistics*. Luxembourg: Eurostat. https://ec.europa .eu/eurostat/cros/content/handbook-methodology-modern-business-statistics_en.

NAS (2018). *Reengineering the Census Bureau's Annual Economic Surveys*. Washington, DC: National Academies of Sciences, Engineering, and Medicine, The National Academies Press. https://doi.org/ 10.17226/25098.

Price, T. (2021). ABS early-stage survey development research techniques: Exploratory research and concept testing. Methodology Memorandum (July 16, 2021), Australian Bureau of Statistics, Canberra.

Punt, T., Snijkers, G., and Houben, L. (2019). Informing large enterprises to get prepared for a new survey: some analysis results. Presentation at the 2019 UNECE workshop on statistical data collection 'new sources and new technologies', Geneva, Switzerland (14–16 October 2019). https://statswiki.unece.org/display/Collection/Documents+2019+Data+Collection+Workshop.

PWC (2015). Results of the study on the Data Model for Non-financial Enterprises (in Dutch: Resultaten analyse datamodel niet-financiële ondernemingen). Confidential PWC report, commissioned by Statistics Netherlands. PricewaterhouseCoopers Advisory NV, Amsterdam, the Netherlands.

Ravindra, D. (2016). Challenges and benefits of producing business statistics within a highly centralized model. In: *Proceedings of the 5th International Conference on Establishment Surveys*. Alexandria, VA: American Statistical Association. http://ww2.amstat.org/meetings/ices/2016/ proceedings/153_ices15Final00050.pdf.

Snijkers, G. (2016). Achieving quality in organizational surveys: a holistic approach. In: *Methodische Probleme in der empirischen Organisationsforschung* (ed. S. Liebig and W. Matiaske), 33–59. Wiesbaden: Springer.

Snijkers, G. (2017). Questionnaire communication to collect financial data from large non-financial enterprises. Paper presented at the 2017 European Establishment Statistics Workshop (EESW2017), Southampton, UK (30 August–1 September 2017).

Snijkers, G. (2018). Evaluation of the new combined CBS-DNB questionnaire: on-site business visits, business information day, and evaluation meeting (in Dutch: Evaluatie van de nieuwe gecombineerde SFO-DRA vragenlijst: bedrijfsbezoeken, bedrijvendag en evaluatiebijeenkomsten). Internal report (unfinished), Statistics Netherlands, Heerlen, the Netherlands.

Snijkers, G. (2019). Questionnaire communication to collect financial data from large non-financial enterprises – 2: the Field Experience. Paper presented at the 2019 European Establishment Statistics Workshop (EESW2019), Bilbao, Basque Country, Spain (24–27 September 2019).

Snijkers, G., and Arentsen, K. (2015). Collecting financial data from large non-financial enterprises: a feasibility study. Paper presented at the 4th International Workshop on Business Data Collection Methodology, Washington DC, USA (14–16 September 2015).

Snijkers, G., Arentsen, K., and Hillebrand, R. (2015). Feasibility study new combined CBS-DNB survey: implementation and results (in Dutch: Haalbaarheidsstudie DRA-SFO: opzet en resultaten). Internal report Statistics Netherlands, Heerlen, in collaboration with Dutch National Bank, Amsterdam, the Netherlands.

Snijkers, G., Bavdaž, M., Bender, S., Jones, J., MacFeely, S., Sakshaug, J.W., Thompson, K.J., and van Delden, A. (2023a). Advances in business statistics, methods and data collection: introduction. In: *Advances in Business Statistics, Methods and Data Collection*, Chapter 1 (ed. G. Snijkers, M. Bavdaž, S. Bender, J. Jones, S. MacFeely, J.W. Sakshaug, K.J. Thompson, and A. van Delden). Hoboken: Wiley.

Snijkers, G., Demedash, S., and Andrews, J. (2023b). Using paradata in electronic business survey questionnaires. In: *Advances in Business Statistics, Methods and Data Collection*, Chapter 18 (ed. G. Snijkers, M. Bavdaž, S. Bender, J. Jones, S. MacFeely, J.W. Sakshaug, K.J. Thompson, and A. van Delden). Hoboken: Wiley.

Snijkers, G., Göttgens, R., and Hermans, H. (2011). Data collection and data sharing at Statistics Netherlands: Yesterday, today, tomorrow. Paper presented at the 59th Plenary Session of the Conference of European Statisticians (CES), United Nations Economic Commission for Europe (UNECE), Geneva (14–16 June 2011). www.unece.org/fileadmin/DAM/stats/documents/ece/ces/2011/20.e.pdf.

Snijkers, G., Haraldsen, G., Jones, J., and Willimack, D.K. (2013). *Designing and Conducting Business Surveys*. Hoboken: Wiley.

Snijkers, G. and Jones, J. (2013). Business survey communication. In: *Designing and Conducting Business Surveys* (ed. G. Snijkers, G. Haraldsen, J. Jones and D.K. Willimack), 359–430. Hoboken: Wiley.

Snijkers, G., Onat, E., and Vis-Visschers, R. (2007). The annual structural business survey: developing and testing an electronic form. Proceedings of the 3rd International Conference on Establishment Surveys (ICES-III), Montreal (18–21 June 2007), American Statistical Association, Alexandria, VA, pp.456–463.

Snijkers, G. and Willimack, D.K. (2011). The missing link: from concepts to questions in economic surveys. Paper presented at the 2nd European Establishment Statistics Workshop (EESW11), Neuchâtel, Switzerland (12–14 September 2011).

UNECE (2019). Generic Statistical Business Process Model: GSBPM (version 5.1). United Nations Economic Commission for Europe, Geneva, Switzerland. https://statswiki.unece.org/display/GSBPM/GSBPM+v5.1).

van Delden, A. and Lewis, D. (2023). Methodology for the use of administrative data in business statistics. In: *Advances in Business Statistics, Methods and Data Collection*, Chapter 12 (ed. G. Snijkers, M. Bavdaž, S. Bender, J. Jones, S. MacFeely, J.W. Sakshaug, K.J. Thompson, and A. van Delden). Hoboken: Wiley.

van der Geest, T.M. (2001). *Web Site Design is Communication Design*. Amsterdam, Netherlands: John Benjamins.

Vennix K. (2012). The treatment of large enterprise groups within Statistics Netherlands. *Proceedings of the Fourth International Conference on Establishment Surveys (ICES-IV)*, Montreal (June 2012). https://ww2.amstat.org/meetings/ices/2012/papers/301992.pdf.

Willimack, D.K. (2013). Methods for the development, testing and evaluation of data collection instruments. In: *Designing and Conducting Business Surveys* (ed. G. Snijkers, G. Haraldsen, J. Jones and D.K. Willimack), 253–301. Hoboken: Wiley.

Willimack, D. K. and Nichols, E. (2001). Building an alternative response process model for business surveys. Paper presented at the 56th Annual Conference of the American Association for Public Opinion Research (AAPOR), Montreal (17–20 May 2001), also in Proceedings of the Joint Statistical Meetings, American Statistical Association, Alexandria, VA, CD-ROM.

Willimack, D. and Nichols, E. (2010). A hybrid response process model for business surveys. *Journal of Official Statistics* 26 (1): 3–24.

Willimack, D.K. and Snijkers, G. (2013). The business context and its implications for the survey response process. In: *Designing and Conducting Business Surveys* (ed. G. Snijkers, G. Haraldsen, J. Jones and D.K. Willimack), 39–82. Hoboken.

Willimack, D.K., Ridolfo, H., Anderson Riemer, A., Cidade, M., and Ott, K. (2023). Advances in question(naire) development, pretesting, and evaluation. In: *Advances in Business Statistics, Methods and Data Collection*, Chapter 17 (ed. G. Snijkers, M. Bavdaž, S. Bender, J. Jones, S. MacFeely, J.W. Sakshaug, K.J. Thompson, and A. van Delden). Hoboken: Wiley.

17

Advances in Question(naire) Development, Pretesting, and Evaluation*

Diane K. Willimack[1], Heather Ridolfo[2], Amy Anderson Riemer[1], Melissa Cidade[1], and Kathy Ott[3]

[1] U.S. Census Bureau, Washington, DC, USA
[2] U.S. Energy Information Administration, Washington, DC, USA
[3] USDA/National Agricultural Statistics Service, Washington, DC, USA

17.1 Introduction

Since their introduction to establishment surveys at the First International Conference on Establishment Surveys (ICES) (Dippo et al. 1995), cognitive research methods have become widely accepted for questionnaire development and pretesting in surveys of businesses, organizations, and farms. Their application was further demonstrated at subsequent ICES's and associated special issues of the *Journal of Official Statistics* (2010, 2014, 2018). The adoption of these and other qualitative research methods has relied on effectively adapting household pretesting methodologies to the establishment survey environment (Willimack et al. 2004). As new, improved, or alternative pretesting methodologies have emerged over the past 25 years, establishment survey researchers have embraced their use as well, particularly as an evolving US and worldwide economy demands timely and relevant statistics on emerging topics to better inform decision-making by economists and policy makers (Bavdaž et al. 2019; Foundations for Evidence-Based Policymaking Act of 2018).

As new technologies and business models change how businesses produce or finance goods and services, economic measurements along with their underlying concepts may also require re-definition. For instance, advancements like robotics and telemedicine overtly impact production functions; factoryless goods production based on contract arrangements and outsourcing shifts production risks; telework and e-commerce disrupt basic economic constructs associated with traditional geographic delineation of labor markets and consumer behavior; and digital innovation alters value creation and disrupts typical revenue streams.

Changes in our economic environment may thus require changes in economic measurement, acceptance of survey and non-survey data, and adaptation of our methods for data collection. To ensure that survey data are of high quality, development and pretesting of survey question(naire)s and other data collection instruments retain a significant role in the survey life cycle. However, these new and emergent economic topics and their measurement requirements also call for further

---

* The analysis, findings, and conclusions, or any views expressed in this publication are those of the authors and should not be construed to represent the policies of the U.S. Government agencies that employ them. The U.S. Census Bureau has reviewed this paper for unauthorized disclosure of confidential information and has approved the disclosure avoidance practices applied (Approval ID: CBDRB-FY22-ESMD005-001).

adaptation of methods for questionnaire and instrument development and pretesting. Moreover, technology itself has contributed to creation of or advancement in pretesting methodologies, driven by necessity to remain viable among the disruptions and limitations imposed by the coronavirus pandemic.

The purpose of this chapter is to offer a flavor of the creative and innovative manner in which establishment survey researchers currently approach question(naire) and instrument development, pretesting and evaluation to address new data needs stemming from our ever-evolving economy. These data needs must often be addressed before international research and guidance provide conceptual frameworks to inform operationalization, as was demonstrated in Chapter 5's description of researchers striving to collect useful data on intangible assets in the absence of a well-defined conceptual framework (see Bavdaž et al. 2023, Snijkers and Willimack 2011).

In Section 17.2, we use several case studies from our statistical agencies to demonstrate current approaches to pretesting. Despite the variation in techniques and the breadth of subject matter to which they may be applied, we discern several common themes that characterize the advancements in methods for developing, pretesting, and evaluating establishment survey question(naire)s and data collection instruments. These themes are summarized in Section 17.3, along with discussion of how remaining challenges may be addressed, continuing to refine and enhance pretesting methodologies for establishment surveys and the economic statistics they support. (Note that the words "pretesting" or "testing" shall be used to refer to any of the three steps "development, pretesting, and evaluation.")

17.2 Adaptation and Innovation in Pretesting Methods

In this section, six case studies illustrate how the establishment survey target population motivated the selection and/or adaptation of, and its impact on, a number of qualitative pretesting methodologies applied to investigate emerging or resurgent economic topics:

- *Case Study #1*: Collaborative partnerships between stakeholders and researchers aided the development and pretesting of questions on the emerging technology of robotics.
- *Case Study #2*: Using multiple methods was critical for examining detailed attributes of labor costs across multiple collection modes amongst a geographically dispersed target population.
- *Case Study #3*: Methodologies for studying businesses' record-keeping practices were re-invented to investigate alignment of accounts with industry classifications, as well as availability and accessibility of data relative to various organizational structures and geographic divisions.
- *Case Study #4*: As early adopters of electronic data collection modes, establishment surveys are well-positioned to generate advancements in usability testing methods, which benefit from technological development, while also being challenged by instrument designs enabled by emerging technical methodologies.
- *Case Study #5*: Cross-cutting adaptation and implementation of pretesting methodologies in an online environment was required due to the coronavirus pandemic.
- *Case Study #6*: Electronic instruments capture not only data entered by respondents but also respondents' interactions with the computer, known as paradata, or data about the collection process, which can augment results from other pretesting methods.

We note that our exposition of pretesting methods in these case studies is not exhaustive, as a rich literature describes the application of a wide variety of qualitative and quantitative research methods in the field of question(naire) development, pretesting, and evaluation, e.g. *Evaluating Survey Questions: An Inventory of Methods* (FCSM 2016; https://nces.ed.gov/FCSM/pdf/spwp47.pdf; see also Willimack 2013 for specific applications in establishment surveys).

17.2.1 Case Study #1: Emerging Topic of Robotics – *it takes a village*

17.2.1.1 Background

The proliferation of robotics throughout a variety of industries, along with its effects on labor distributions, productivity measures, and the US gross domestic product, prompted economists and decision makers to attempt measuring its influence on the national economy (Buffington et al. 2018).

Census Bureau researchers carried out qualitative research on two ongoing surveys to evaluate the ability of companies to report information related to robotics. This case study highlights the roles of stakeholders, such as subject matter experts, survey sponsors, data users, or other interested parties, forming collaborative partnerships with researchers to effectively investigate this new topic (Anderson Riemer 2021).

The Annual Survey of Manufactures (ASM) is a mandatory annual Web-administered survey of approximately 50,000 manufacturing establishments with one or more employees. It collects a variety of financial information, such as revenues and value of shipments, employment and payroll, cost of materials consumed, operating expenses, and capital expenditures, and provides associated summary statistics monitoring the industry's position in the US economy (see www.census.gov/programs-surveys/asm).

The Annual Capital Expenditure Survey (ACES) is a mandatory annual Web-administered survey collecting data at the enterprise level for approximately 50,000 companies with employees and 20,000 companies without employees. The survey provides estimates of business spending by US businesses for new and used structures and equipment. The data are used to improve estimates of capital stocks, analyze trends of depreciation, and monitor and evaluate healthcare expenditures (see www.census.gov/programs-surveys/aces).

ASM robotics questions are asked at the establishment level and request the gross value of current robotics equipment and capital expenditures during the previous year for new or used robotics equipment. Also tested were questions about the number of robots at the establishment, the average purchase price of already owned robots, and the number and average purchase price of new or used robotics equipment acquired during the reference year (Buffington et al. 2018). The ACES robotics questions asked about enterprise-level capital expenditures for new and used robots during the reference year.

17.2.1.2 Pretesting Methodology

17.2.1.2.1 Developing the Recruiting Sample and Screening

Two rounds of cognitive testing were conducted for both the ASM and ACES surveys to evaluate the proposed robotics questions. Although the sampling frame for pretesting both surveys consisted of prior year respondents, topics such as robotics, that are relatively rare and not easily observed outside the company, may benefit from collaboration with subject matter experts to aid sample selection. Thus, to increase the number of successful contacts, researchers relied on them heavily for developing and prioritizing recruiting lists based on their industry knowledge.

ASM subject matter experts examined research journals, news articles, and reviewed previously reported capital expenditures data to identify sub-industries or companies likely to have robotics equipment. High monetary values in the "Other Capital Expenditures" category reported on the prior year's ASM in certain sub-industries indicated a potential robotics acquisition (Buffington et al. 2018).

ACES subject matter experts also reviewed similar information to identify potential companies with robotics in nonmanufacturing industries. However, the amount of publicly available information about nonmanufacturing robotics was limited. The recruiting sample for ACES focused on companies in the healthcare, retail, and wholesale industries because a higher likelihood of having robotics equipment was expected. Manufacturing was in-scope for ACES, but not included in this study because of the preceding ASM robotics research.

Although these collaborative efforts helped to identify companies and/or industries that were likely to operate robotics, screening remained critical to ensure interviews were completed with cases that actually possessed this type of equipment. Most ASM respondents who were screened for robotics were eligible to be interviewed, while only about half of the screening interviews conducted with ACES non-manufacturers successfully identified enterprises with robotics equipment. This was likely due to limited information available about robotics in nonmanufacturing industries.

17.2.1.2.2 Preparing for Interviews

Subject matter experts for both surveys developed the first draft of survey questions. They were invited to review and provide feedback on interview protocols and other materials, working closely with researchers to make necessary adjustments prior to testing. Feedback from subject matter experts helped ensure that the researchers correctly understood and interpreted the questions' measurement objectives.

17.2.1.2.3 Early Stage Scoping Interviews

Researchers employed a combination of early stage scoping (ESS) and cognitive testing probes during the first rounds of testing because use of robotics had not been measured previously. ESS is an exploratory method where researchers discuss proposed survey topics and underlying concepts with respondents to discern the response process and identify early issues related to reporting the proposed content. The intent of ESS research is to aid development of survey questions prior to conducting cognitive testing (Stettler and Featherston 2012). However, schedule and resource constraints did not allow for such a dedicated round of testing.

To compensate, interviews started with a dialogue about robotics at a broad level and then funneled down to more specific ESS probes before moving on to the cognitive interview. ESS probes enabled researchers to gain a deeper awareness about the respondents' use and understanding of robotics, along with information about how these data were stored and accessed within enterprise accounting systems. This detailed information led to more coherent question revisions.

17.2.1.2.4 Cognitive Interviews

Twenty interviews were planned for each of two rounds of testing, providing a total of 40 interviews for each survey. Despite efforts described earlier, researchers were unable to reach these targets, with a total of 32 interviews completed for ASM and 26 interviews for ACES.

All interviews were conducted in person for the ASM robotics research. While typical procedures call for travel to conduct interviews at a business's location, targeting 8–10 interviews per trip, most of the robotics trips achieved only 3–5 interviews because of the challenge identifying enough eligible respondents in the same geographic area. The ACES project was challenged further to identify geographically concentrated nonmanufacturing companies with robotics. To accommodate this, approximately two-thirds of the interviews in each round were conducted by telephone to supplement in-person interviews.

Subject matter experts observed most interviews and were able to hear firsthand how respondents reacted to the proposed robotics questions. Time permitting, subject matter experts were invited to ask additional questions outside of the protocol to further probe on information the respondent shared. Subject matter expert involvement in the interviews often led to closer collaboration with researchers.

Where possible, subject matter experts and researchers discussed interview results while still in the field. This helped deepen the researcher's understanding of the robotics concept, resolved misunderstandings, and facilitated discussions about modifications to the testing methodology for subsequent rounds of testing, as well as for changes to the final questions. Subject matter experts benefited from these discussions by gaining insight into the respondent's capability to answer proposed questions and the quality of data being provided.

Subject matter experts were asked to summarize their findings from observing interviews. Researchers produced a final report that summarized major findings from testing and researcher recommendations. Researchers reviewed the final report with subject matter experts, and decisions about content changes were documented in the report.

17.2.1.2.5 *Post-Collection Evaluation*
Because of the challenges in identifying respondents and obtaining a robust number of interviews during pretesting for each survey, along with continued concerns on respondents' understanding highlighted in the research findings, researchers conducted debriefing interviews with respondents following data collection. Respondent debriefings focused on evaluating survey responses and respondents' understanding of the robotics terminology.

Although the robotics questions had been improved due to cognitive testing, the limitations experienced during recruiting and interviewing meant that there was still a knowledge gap about robotics for non-manufacturers. Researchers recommended that ACES included an open-ended question asking respondents to describe their robotics during data collection. Although not published, this information gave subject matter experts more insight into the types of robots being used and provided opportunities for researchers and subject matter experts to conduct additional studies that would help further refine the robotics questions.

17.2.1.3 Summary
For the research on robotics, involvement of subject matter experts differed substantially compared to typical cognitive testing research for establishment surveys at the Census Bureau. While the process is led by cognitive researchers, subject matter experts usually contribute input for preparing testing materials and some guidance on sample selection criteria (e.g. size, geography, and industry), and they may also be present during pretesting interviews. The emerging topic of robotics with many unknowns required a much closer and extensive collaboration, constituting a more active role that benefited both groups. In addition, final results from the ASM and ACES testing were incorporated into externally available working papers from the Census Bureau's Center for Economic Studies (Buffington et al. 2018) and discussed during a workshop hosted by academia (Miranda and Seamans 2020), thus spreading question(naire) development research broadly.

17.2.2 Case Study #2: Multiple Modes and Methods – *different strokes for different folks*

17.2.2.1 Background
The U.S. National Agricultural Statistics Service (NASS) conducts the voluntary Agricultural Labor Survey (ALS) biannually. Data from the survey are used to produce national and regional employment and wage estimates for all agricultural workers directly employed by US farms and ranches for four reference weeks in a calendar year. These estimates are used by federal, state, and local governments, educational institutions, private companies, and farm operators (see https://www.nass.usda.gov/Surveys/Guide_to_NASS_Surveys/Farm_Labor/index.php).

In 2017, stakeholders requested enhancement of the ALS to provide a more reflective measure of wages paid (Ridolfo and Ott 2020a). Previously collected data on gross wages paid did not account for varying pay structures. The most common pay structures for agricultural workers in the United States are base wages and piece-rate pay. Base wages are the minimum amount paid, not including bonuses, overtime pay, or commissions. Piece-rate pay is pay based on the number of units harvested. Two forms of employment prevail, where farm workers can be hired directly by farm operations or through third-party contractors. Since the ALS only measures gross wages paid to workers hired directly by the farm operation, stakeholders wanted NASS to explore the feasibility of measuring wages paid to contract workers. NASS survey research methodologists were tasked with developing new questions for the ALS and evaluating their impact on response rates and overall data quality, as well as developing a new Contractor Labor Survey (CLS) to measure wages paid via third-party contractors. This was a high priority project with a short timeframe and limited resources.

The ALS uses multiple data collection modes. Respondents are mailed a paper questionnaire and have the option of responding via web. Nonresponse follow-up is conducted using computer-assisted telephone interviewing (CATI) and limited in-person interviewing. Most responses are collected via mail and CATI. It was imperative to test these questionnaire changes in each mode of data collection. However, conducting pretesting with farm operators is challenging given their locations in rural, geographically distant areas across the United States, requiring researchers to travel to respondents to conduct pretesting in person, which is costly and time-consuming.

For the CLS, it was expected that it would be more efficient to obtain wages paid to contract workers directly from the third-party contractors, and thus a new survey with a new target population had to be developed and tested. With a limited timeframe and resources, NASS developed a research plan to evaluate the new measures using multiple testing methods – iterative rounds of cognitive interviews, exploratory interviews, embedded experiments, and behavior coding.

17.2.2.2 Pretesting Methodology

17.2.2.2.1 Cognitive Testing

NASS only had sufficient resources to conduct cognitive testing on the paper questionnaires for the ALS and the proposed CLS. Cognitive testing of the ALS was conducted with farm operators and covered new questions on base, bonus, and overtime wages and piece-rate pay. The interviews were done in-person and remotely, that is, using virtual connections over the internet, enabling NASS to evaluate the surveys with a variety of farm types across the country.

Given the complexity of pay structures, and the amount of effort required to convert records into survey responses, many iterations of the new questions were needed. The ability to conduct interviews remotely permitted NASS researchers to modify the questionnaire and get feedback from respondents more quickly. Early cognitive testing allowed NASS to understand the types of information respondents were able to report (Ridolfo and Ott 2020a). Additional cognitive testing was conducted after carrying out embedded experiments and behavior coding, which will be described next, enabling NASS to test questionnaire revisions based on those research results (Ridolfo and Ott 2021a; Ridolfo and Ott 2021b).

Multiple rounds of cognitive testing were also conducted for the CLS (Ott and Ridolfo 2018). NASS identified respondents for this testing through a list of farm contractors publicly available from the US Department of Labor. These interviews were conducted in person in two geographic regions of the United States. They not only informed researchers about respondents' comprehension of the survey questions and ability/willingness to report information on their workers but also the feasibility of tracking down and surveying this transient population. After two rounds of cognitive testing, NASS concluded that this population was very hard to survey. They lacked knowledge of surveys, were reluctant to report information, and were very difficult to contact. It was determined that the costs needed to properly survey this population outweighed the benefits.

17.2.2.2.2 Exploratory Interviews

In lieu of conducting the CLS, NASS explored whether farm operators could answer ALS questions about workers hired through third-party contractors (Ridolfo and Ott 2020b). These exploratory interviews were conducted over the telephone with farm operators. This was a quick and efficient way to determine if farm operators had knowledge or records of detailed payroll information for workers hired through third-party contractors. Results showed that farm operators did not have sufficient knowledge to report wages and associated information for these workers on the ALS. Given the results from the earlier cognitive testing with third-party contractors and from the exploratory interviews with farm operators, NASS decided not to pursue measuring wages paid to contract workers.

17.2.2.2.3 Experiments

Although cognitive testing is useful in learning sources of measurement error, it cannot determine the extent of that error. Therefore, conducting randomized experiments was high priority for NASS stakeholders who were primarily concerned with how the new ALS questions on base, bonus, and overtime wages and piece-rate pay may affect unit and item nonresponse. Since there was insufficient time to conduct standalone experiments, they were embedded in production data collection. NASS had two opportunities to embed experiments in the production survey before finalizing the instrument. In April and October of 2018, NASS conducted split sample experiments, where a portion of the sample received the original ALS and a portion received the revised ALS containing the new questions (Reist et al. 2018). These experiments found that survey version had no significant impact on response rates at the national level. Item nonresponse for gross and base wages was also at an acceptable level.

17.2.2.2.4 Behavior Coding

CATI is one of the primary modes of data collection for the ALS. Although time was not sufficient for additional cognitive testing of the CATI instrument, NASS felt it was important to evaluate this mode. Cognitive testing and behavior coding had recently been conducted on the CATI instrument prior to the addition of the new questions. The behavior coding found interviewers were having difficulty administering survey questions as worded (Ridolfo et al. 2020a).

When the new questions were added to ALS, the CATI instrument was also revised to improve readability, and it was further evaluated using behavior coding conducted after each experiment. Although this method cannot determine why issues arise, it was a useful low-cost method to see how the questions in the CATI instrument performed in a production setting. The behavior coding studies revealed that the CATI interviewers were making major changes and skipping survey questions at high rates, including the revised and new questions. These results informed further revisions to the CATI instrument and highlighted the need for additional interviewer training and monitoring, as well as the importance of examining mode differences in the analysis of the embedded experiments (Ridolfo et al. 2021; Rodhouse et al. 2021).

17.2.2.3 Summary

Using a mixed-methods approach allowed for a more complete understanding of questionnaire design flaws and data collection procedures affecting data quality. NASS maximized the evaluation of the new ALS questions by harnessing the benefits of each method. Cognitive testing provided an avenue for developing questions about the new constructs for all modes of data collection. However, it only evaluated the performance of those questions in the paper mode. The cognitive testing and exploratory interviews allowed NASS to determine that it would not be feasible to measure wages paid by third-party contractors. The embedded experiments enabled comparisons between questionnaire versions under actual production conditions. Behavior coding revealed critical information about the effectiveness of interviewers' administration of the CATI instrument, and also alerted researchers to examine mode effects in the results of the experiments.

This mixed-methods approach not only enabled NASS researchers to pretest proposed new survey questions across modes and with different target populations, it was also a prudent strategy for question(naire) pretesting under limited time and resources. Results from the various testing methods augmented one another, while also building on strengths and compensating for weaknesses. Along with providing evidence upon which to base production decisions, combining results culminated with NASS implementing a revised ALS that included the new questions requesting base wages and base hours.

17.2.3 Case Study #3: Record-Keeping Study – "*I don't keep my records that way*"

17.2.3.1 Background
After reviewing the Census Bureau's annual economic survey programs, an external expert panel recommended streamlining data collection efforts by integrating surveys, to ease respondent burden and improve operational efficiency (National Academies of Sciences, Engineering, and Medicine 2018). Accomplishing these goals required harmonization of content and statistical units across these annual surveys. Research began with a record-keeping study to aid understanding of data accessibility associated with businesses' organizational structures. This study was carried out in two phases designed to examine factors associated with structure and/or accessibility of data.

17.2.3.2 Pretesting Methodology for Phase I
Phase I consisted of 29 interviews with respondents from middle-sized companies having between 50 and 4999 employees and at least 10 establishments. Nearly all interviews were conducted in person at the company's business location. The protocol was built around a generic chart of accounts, providing a roadmap for the interview:

1. Using the chart of accounts for context, respondents were asked to link their financial records to their company's organizational structure and management objectives. This provided researchers with insights into how records were kept for businesses' purposes which could later be compared to survey questions designed to meet statistical needs.
2. Respondents were asked to describe in their own words what their business does, and then to indicate their North American Industry Classification System (NAICS) sector. Next, respondents selected their company's revenue-producing goods and services from a list used in the 2017 Economic Census. Researchers later compared this information with the Census Bureau's "official" industry classification for the company, and they were able to detect some notable mismatches.
3. Researchers then delved into companies' reporting of four key variables:
   o Sales/receipts/revenues (typically referred to as "turnover" in Europe)
   o Inventory
   o Expenses, focusing on payroll and employment
   o Capital expenditures

Respondents were shown specific question(naire)s for Census Bureau surveys they participated in. They were asked to explain generally how they gathered data from multiple sources, and whether they needed to manipulate data to provide answers to the survey questions. Researchers probed discrepancies between respondents' reporting practices and the question's intent.

This approach to querying respondents' record-keeping practices netted three critical findings that set the stage for Phase II research:

1. Industry classification is artificial. As a standardized classification system, the NAICS infrastructure is unnatural, imposed upon respondents from their external environment, and businesses must grapple with aligning themselves accordingly to report data for statistical purposes.
2. Operating units to which businesses tracked data depended on management's objectives, such as cost controls for budgeting purposes, maximizing revenues versus profit, or maintaining a competitive advantage versus a business presence. That is, different data may be tracked for different operating units, depending on managers' goals.
3. Consolidated financial reports are the mainstay for all businesses or organizations, providing reliable and reportable data for the specific topics we queried. Beyond this, there were disparities between data that respondents could report and data they did report, and they were forthright in expressing their distress over having to decide for themselves how to map their data to the survey questions. Respondents could "break out" their data in different ways, depending on what factors managers were trying to control. It was critical, however, that "break-outs" could be rolled back up to a "top-line" consolidated figure that traced back to their financial reports. These consolidated figures were their anchors.

17.2.3.3 Pretesting Methodology for Phase II

The second phase focused on data accessibility. The research was guided by the larger question: what data do businesses have available, at what "level," and by what topic? This question constitutes the so-called "unit problem," the nature of which lies in discrepancies between statistical units and business units (van Delden et al. 2018). Since, as noted by Bavdaž (2010) and observed in Phase I, businesses establish accounting systems that best support their activities and management priorities, statistical reporting must be retrofitted to that system. Respondents must "create" the target statistical units (van Delden et al. 2018) on their own. Embedded within the determination of the survey collection (statistical) unit is the accessibility of the requested data.

17.2.3.3.1 Data and Methods

Keeping in mind the significance of the choice of unit, researchers undertook a qualitative study to ascertain the accessibility of data at various units by various topics. Research questions included:

1. Can participants reconcile Census Bureau collection unit choices with their own organizational setup?
2. How easy or difficult is it to report the requested data at the lowest collection unit?

To address these research questions, Census Bureau researchers extended the business information accessibility scale framework (Snijkers and Arentsen 2015; Snijkers et al. 2023), which includes the four color-coded categories defined in Table 17.1 for respondents to rank the accessibility of their data at various increments, in terms of both time and organization. The authors hypothesized that "the more steps and the more sources involved in the response process, and the deeper within the business information has to be retrieved, the higher the risks of survey errors like measurement errors and item nonresponse." This builds on Bavdaž (2010) work on accessibility as a contributor to both burden and measurement error.

Table 17.1 Business information accessibility scale.

Color	Concept	Description
Green	Easily accessible	The information is easily and readily available (at group accounts level).
Yellow	Accessible with minor effort	The information is available at a central location, but not in the group accounts (treasury level), which requires more effort.
Orange	Accessible with major effort	The information is available, but decentralized (general ledger level), which requires considerable effort to acquire.
Red	Inaccessible	The information is not available.

Source: Based on Snijkers and Arentsen 2015; (see also Snijkers et al. 2023: Figure 16.4).

The accessibility scale was administered using a card sort methodology, where participants "sort," or assign, items to broadly defined categories, demonstrating their view of associations among items and with categories. Researchers administered a closed card sort (Baxter et al. 2015), where respondents were provided with the accessibility scale (in contrast to an open card sort, where respondents create the categories themselves). While Phase I interviews were face-to-face, COVID-19 travel restrictions meant that researchers needed to adapt and carry out the card sort methodology entirely online, as follows:

1. Researchers showed respondents several terms descriptive of business units – e.g. company, establishment, line of business – along with definitions (see Cidade et al. 2021), and prompted them to name the equivalent used by their company.
2. Researchers asked respondents to describe their "specific industry," which is their six-digit NAICS code(s), as well as their "general industry," which is their four-digit NAICS code(s).
3. Respondents were introduced to the color-coded Accessibility Scale and asked to interpret the categories of accessibility, specifically regarding the differences between yellow, orange, and red, so that researchers would be able to contextualize their responses to the card sorts.
4. The respondent then saw virtual "cards," each listing a different business unit and the equivalent word or phrase that the respondent identified from their own business, as well as four squares, labeled and color-coded to correspond to the Accessibility Scale. See Figure 17.1 for an excerpt of the virtual card sort that asks about revenue.
5. Researchers asked respondents to sort each of the business units into one of the accessibility categories, and to "think aloud" as they engaged in the exercise. As respondents discussed the accessibility of the data at each level, interviewers probed to ascertain the meaning behind the categorization.
6. The card sort exercise included revenue, expenditures, and assets. Respondents could click on the business unit and drag it to the box corresponding with the accessibility they assigned to the data.

In early 2021, researchers interviewed 30 middle-sized firms using this novel method. Respondents understood the various business unit definitions, and, for the most part, related them to the corresponding unit at their business. During the card sort section of the interview, respondents talked about accessibility as they moved through the business units. Preliminary findings suggest that accessibility ratings are tied to dispersion of the data (that is, does the respondent need to "ask" someone at the company to acquire the data?), the amount of aggregation or data cleaning needed to report the data (that is, do the data need to be "rolled up" to a higher unit of analysis?), and

Figure 17.1   Excerpt from the accessibility card sort displaying the question about revenue.

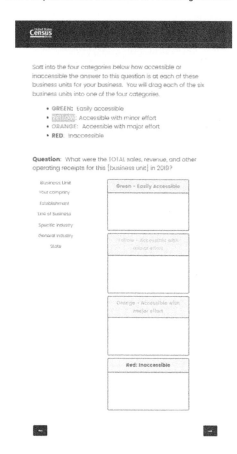

the match or mismatch in data parameters (that is, does their data use the same "includes" and "excludes" definitions as the Census Bureau is asking?).

17.2.3.3.2   *Data Visualization*

A strength of this methodology is that the resultant data can be "mapped" into the various color-coded categories, creating a visual effect that is easier to understand than text alone. Figure 17.2 displays the data visualization of findings for the accessibility of Total Revenue, where each row is a completed interview. Each column is a business unit – company, establishment, line of business, state, specific industry, and general – and each color corresponds to the accessibility of Total Revenue data at that unit. Note that blank spaces denote where respondents were either unable to speak to this topic, this concept did not apply to their business, or the interviewer suspected that the respondent was not clear on the task at hand.

17.2.4   Case Study #4: Usability Testing – *when human meets computer*

17.2.4.1   Background

The Commodity Flow Survey (CFS) is a mandatory survey conducted every five years as a joint collection of the U.S. Census Bureau and the U.S. Bureau of Transportation Statistics (BTS). Detailed data on the movement of commodities in the United States are used by policy makers and transportation planners for a variety of purposes such as evaluating demand for transportation facilities

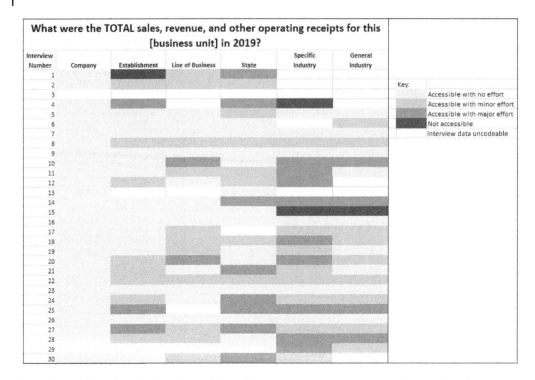

Figure 17.2 Data visualization of accessibility of revenue data, by business unit, by interview. Source: Cidade et al. 2021/American Statistical Association; (see also Snijkers et al. 2023: Figure 16.4).

and services, energy and environmental concerns, and infrastructure and equipment (see https://www.bts.gov/cfs).

During the reference year, respondents answer questions quarterly for a self-selected random sample of shipments. Over the years, respondents expressed concerns about the associated burden (Barnett Thomas et al. 2007), which remained unresolved by development of an electronic instrument. Respondents also struggled with matching descriptions of commodities they shipped with BTS's Standard Classification of Transportation Goods (SCTG).

Respondents from large companies encouraged Census Bureau staff to investigate alternative methods for collecting these data. During the 2017 CFS, an ad-hoc reporting option was offered to selected respondents in an attempt to circumvent the laborious sampling process. A secure depository, referred to as a portal, allowed respondents to upload large amounts of shipment data from their records on a semi-continuous, automatic basis, eliminating the need for respondents to select a quarterly sample of their shipment records. The portal also included machine learning (ML) technology to search for and assign SCTG codes based on respondents' own descriptions (Moscardi 2021b).

17.2.4.2 Pretesting Methodology

In preparation for the 2022 CFS, subject matter specialists planned for improvements to the instrument, leveraging advancements in technology to be integrated into the data collection instrument, easing respondent burden and reducing potential measurement error. Implementation of this technology on a broader scale required usability testing. Application of traditional methods for usability testing was not always straightforward as the complexity of the business survey response process intersected with advancements in information technology and software applications. Researchers were challenged further by conservative survey software development models at the Census Bureau.

To meet these challenges, researchers worked closely with subject matter specialists to develop a multistage research effort that included exploratory ESS interviews, usability testing, a field test, and debriefing interviews with field test respondents (Keegan and Stettler 2021).

17.2.4.2.1 Exploratory ESS Interviews

Researchers conducted exploratory ESS interviews in-person with prior CFS respondents using the CFS portal. Respondents with fully electronic record systems concluded that sending an electronic document with all shipment information, rather than selecting a random sample on their own, would likely reduce burden. The size of the company typically correlated to having fully electronic record systems. Smaller companies were occasionally found to use paper as part of their shipment record process. Overall, respondents that had the capability to share files electronically were supportive of this process. Some companies pointed out that although records were all electronic, the requested shipment data were sometimes stored in separate databases that were not connected.

17.2.4.2.2 CFS Usability Testing

Feedback from ESS interviews was used to build requirements to update the portal. Limited usability testing was conducted prior to the release of a field test. Overall, researchers and subject matter experts wanted to know if the instrument was feasible and desirable to respondents.

Due to resource and time constraints, along with shifting to an all-virtual testing environment owing to the global pandemic, only four respondents participated in usability testing. Each was given eight tasks designed to mimic the steps they would take during actual survey completion.

ML, which looks for patterns in data using efficient modeling techniques that can impute, classify, or predict patterns in data (see https://www.census.gov/topics/research/data-science/about-machine-learning.html), was first incorporated into the portal for usability testing and the field test. For CFS data collection, this feature is being used to assist respondents in searching through long lists of commodities or products to select the associated SCTG code (Moscardi and Hashemipour 2019; Moscardi 2021a).

ML has been used in survey collection instruments that involve questions that require coding or choosing from lists as a means to increase data quality by having respondents resolve issues rather than a subject matter expert intervening post-collection. Prior to the implementation of ML, respondents had to self-code all commodities using SCTG codes.

Data uploaded by respondents includes commodity descriptions that ML reviews and, if possible, assigns the corresponding SCTG code. If a proper SCTG code cannot be assigned, the portal prompts respondents to validate mismatched product descriptions (see Figure 17.3). Subsequently, ML produces up to five most likely matches and respondents are asked to make an appropriate selection (see Figure 17.4). If none of the choices are acceptable, the respondent can choose "None of these" and provide their own description, which is accepted and reviewed later by subject matter experts.

During usability testing, researchers provided a pre-filled spreadsheet rather than requesting live data, allowing researchers to control the upload process and the items displayed by the ML tool. It also reduced unknown variables that could have occurred if the respondent uploaded their own data. During the ML review, a "product validation" screen appeared (see Figure 17.3) after the spreadsheet was uploaded. Respondents needed to select "validate product" for each description that failed the ML review. When respondents click "validate product" on each line, they are asked

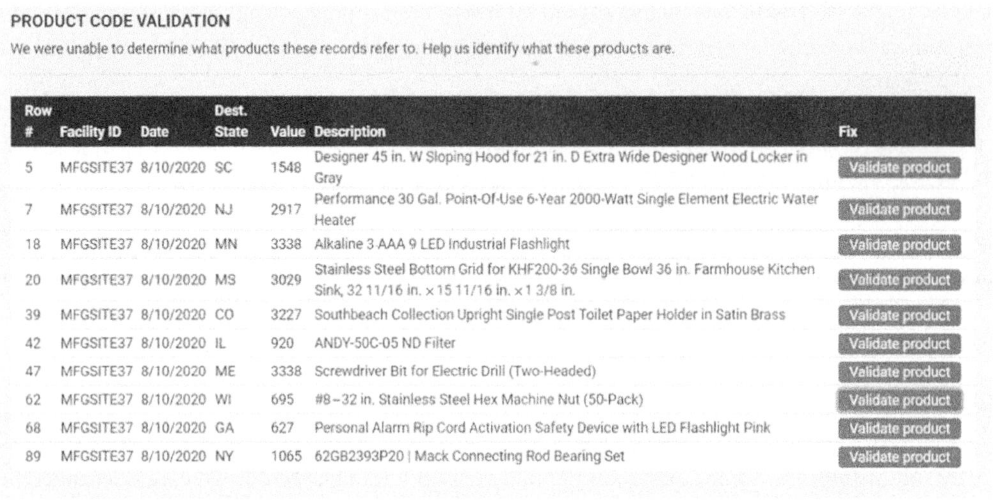

PRODUCT CODE VALIDATION

We were unable to determine what products these records refer to. Help us identify what these products are.

Row #	Facility ID	Date	Dest. State	Value	Description	Fix
5	MFGSITE37	8/10/2020	SC	1548	Designer 45 in. W Sloping Hood for 21 in. D Extra Wide Designer Wood Locker in Gray	Validate product
7	MFGSITE37	8/10/2020	NJ	2917	Performance 30 Gal. Point-Of-Use 6-Year 2000-Watt Single Element Electric Water Heater	Validate product
18	MFGSITE37	8/10/2020	MN	3338	Alkaline 3 AAA 9 LED Industrial Flashlight	Validate product
20	MFGSITE37	8/10/2020	MS	3029	Stainless Steel Bottom Grid for KHF200-36 Single Bowl 36 in. Farmhouse Kitchen Sink, 32 11/16 in. x 15 11/16 in. x 1 3/8 in.	Validate product
39	MFGSITE37	8/10/2020	CO	3227	Southbeach Collection Upright Single Post Toilet Paper Holder in Satin Brass	Validate product
42	MFGSITE37	8/10/2020	IL	920	ANDY-50C-05 ND Filter	Validate product
47	MFGSITE37	8/10/2020	ME	3338	Screwdriver Bit for Electric Drill (Two-Headed)	Validate product
62	MFGSITE37	8/10/2020	WI	695	#8–32 in. Stainless Steel Hex Machine Nut (50-Pack)	Validate product
68	MFGSITE37	8/10/2020	GA	627	Personal Alarm Rip Cord Activation Safety Device with LED Flashlight Pink	Validate product
89	MFGSITE37	8/10/2020	NY	1065	62GB2393P20	Mack Connecting Rod Bearing Set	Validate product

Figure 17.3 Machine learning product validation screen. *Note*: Data are fictional.

Fix Error ✕

Row #	43
Facility ID	AB123
Date	9/1
Dest. City	Springfield
Dest. State	AZ
Dest. ZIP	12345
Value	99
Weight	42
Desc.	Honey

Which of these categories best describes this product?

○ Food
○ Recycling
○ Bees
○ None of these. Please describe.

Submit and Continue

1 of 1

Skip

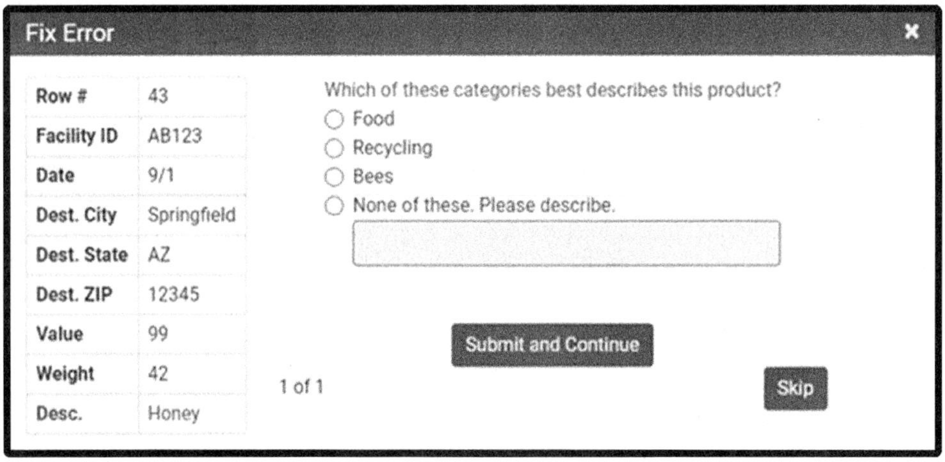

Figure 17.4 Machine learning error screen. *Note*: Data are fictional.

to select a description that best suits how they would describe "Honey" (see Figure 17.4), which was the product description in the test spreadsheet intended to fail the ML review.

Typical usability probes were also asked (e.g. are the key features clear and usable, did the respondent fail or pass the task? Is the layout clear or confusing?). Respondents reacted positively to the ML functionality and overall portal design, and requested clearer confirmation that their changes were accepted during the ML process. The tasks were clear, and respondents completed them successfully.

17.2.4.2.3 CFS Field Test

Feedback from the usability testing was incorporated into the field test instrument. In November 2020, a request was sent to 500 prior CFS respondents to participate in the pilot test. There were 100 respondents that replied to the request, 30 of whom provided a spreadsheet with their shipment data.

17.2.4.2.4   Respondent Debriefings

Twelve post-collection debriefing interviews were conducted with a subset of field test respondents to evaluate their experience with the portal. Researchers asked about response strategies, data sources, and evaluation on the overall instrument/process. Debriefing questions specifically about the ML functionality was limited to the validation process. Researchers did not discuss the ML functionality in depth since its success lies in it being invisible to respondents.

17.2.4.3   Summary

Including research across the various development phases of the portal allowed respondents to have continual input on the design of the instrument. It also helped researchers and subject matter experts learn how to promote portal use to additional CFS respondents for the 2022 CFS data collection.

17.2.5   Case Study #5: Remote Testing, Logistics, and COVID – *reality is virtual*

17.2.5.1   Background

As described in Case Study #4, to effectively pretest web-based electronic data collection instruments, usability testing has traditionally been conducted in person. The traditional laboratory setting was less viable for establishment surveys, because it was infeasible for respondents to travel to locations outside their offices during a typical workday, nor was it reflective of the workplace where survey response took place. Consequently, establishment survey researchers often travelled to the business location and conducted usability testing in situ, using respondents' own computer equipment to observe the response process and the use of records.

17.2.5.2   Remote Testing at NASS

Conducting in-person cognitive interviews and usability testing has long been a challenge for NASS given the costs associated with travelling to farms and ranches in rural, geographically dispersed areas across the United States. NASS researchers located in Washington, DC, supplemented in-person testing by training statisticians in field offices to conduct cognitive interviews (Ridolfo et al. 2020b), as well as conducting limited cognitive testing over the telephone. NASS was also an early adopter of remote cognitive testing for several years, employing a variety of web conferencing software including WebEx, GoToMeeting, and Zoom, to supplement in-person testing when travel funds were limited.

NASS's experience with this methodology facilitated a nearly seamless transition from in-person interviewing to full remote testing when the coronavirus pandemic emerged in spring 2020, and all travel by Federal employees was halted. Unlike NASS, survey researchers at the U.S. Census Bureau and elsewhere were less prepared for a full-scale shift to pretesting methods without meeting respondents in person. Survey researchers were faced with determining how to maintain data collection responsibilities under these circumstances.

17.2.5.3   Remote Testing at the Census Bureau

Given the predominance of online electronic instruments for collecting establishment data at the Census Bureau, usability testing was underway, or about to begin, for several major survey programs. As it became evident that the pandemic would not be short-lived, procedures for remote usability testing needed to be developed, vetted, tested, and implemented quickly to maintain survey production schedules, to the degree possible and practicable.

Together with their counterparts working on household surveys at the Census Bureau, establishment survey researchers began the shift to remote usability testing by creating critical infrastructure, requiring not only a secure telecommunications platform but also compliance with legal and IT security requirements. Researchers then developed training and job aids with tips, troubleshooting, and FAQs for dealing with glitches often experienced with technology. They also prepared documentation for respondents on accessing, downloading, and using the platform.

As experience and familiarity grew, Census Bureau researchers developed a step-by-step routine for remote interviewing including recruitment, sample management, and protocols. Outlined in Figure 17.5, each step was designed to be both adaptive to remote collection and to account for the various uncertainties inherent in an unfolding global pandemic. For example, local lockdowns and stay-at-home orders meant that potential respondents were not necessarily working at their physical offices, and so they would not receive a phone call or letter if those modes were used.

As shown in Figure 17.5, researchers undertook recruitment for a project by sending email to firms meeting inclusion criteria for the study, inviting their participation, and linking them to an online platform where they could select a day and time for their interview appointment. Following this, they were automatically sent three follow-up emails confirming their appointment times, informing them that the study required the use of a specific telecommunications platform to participate, and encouraging them to complete the online consent form. The three confirmation emails were intended to give respondents ample opportunity for re-scheduling or cancelling beforehand,

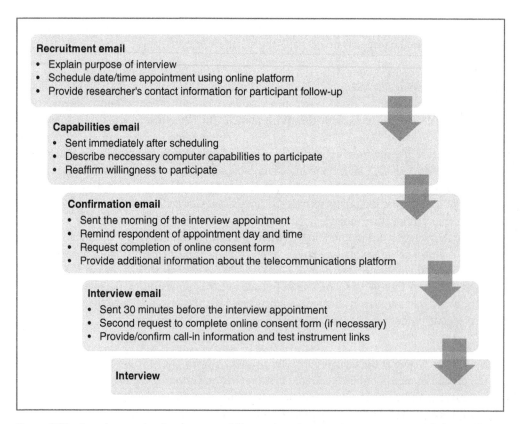

Figure 17.5 Recruitment plan for remote usability testing of economic surveys at the U.S. Census Bureau.

as researchers noted an increase in the number of committed respondents who failed to attend their interview appointment ("no-shows").

17.2.5.4 Summary

As with any methodology, there are benefits and drawbacks. While web conferencing provided cost-effective means to reach a variety of establishment respondents, as well as ensure continuity of research during challenging times, it is not ideal for all research participants, and gaining cooperation and successfully completing interviews is sometimes difficult. For example, older individuals, such as US farmers and ranchers whose average age is 57.5 years, may be less tech savvy and less willing to participate in remote testing. Additionally, some areas, particularly rural areas, may not have sufficient internet connectivity to engage in an interview.

In many ways, using web conferencing software to conduct remote interviews was superior to conducting interviews by telephone or in-person. The web conferencing software facilitated data capture by recording the interviews and producing transcripts available immediately following the interview. Screen sharing ensured researchers and participants were discussing the same questions and visual design features, which may be more challenging over the telephone. The use of this software also allowed multiple stakeholders to observe interviews from any location. In other ways, this method was less superior to in-person interviews. Video capture allowed researchers to observe some nonverbal cues, although behaviors off-screen such as the use of aids (e.g. calculators, records, and support from others) during the response process were not always observable. While web conferenced interviewing may be completed more quickly, lending itself to iterative testing, it is not suitable for employing other concurrent methods during the interview, such as eye tracking. Additional benefits and drawbacks are listed in Table 17.2.

17.2.6 Case Study #6: Pretesting Plus Paradata – *a look underneath the hood*

17.2.6.1 Background

While many pretesting techniques utilize qualitative research methods to attribute meaning, that is, internal validity, to statistical estimates and inferences, quantitative analyses assess external validity by gauging the magnitude, and hence the impact, of qualitative findings. The final case study demonstrates how these research methodologies complement one another by examining process data – in this case, web instrument paradata – to assess the potential impact of qualitative findings.

The mandatory Census of Agriculture (COA) conducted by NASS every five years for reference years ending in "2" and "7," provides a complete count of all US farms and ranches. It is the leading source of information on these types of establishments and the people who run them.

17.2.6.2 Pretesting Methodology

17.2.6.2.1 Usability Testing

The 2017 COA featured a new web instrument that was evaluated through two rounds of usability testing during development. The goals of this testing were to reduce measurement errors that may be associated with poor system design or did not meet standard webpage heuristics, and to make modifications to the instrument so that it more closely matched respondents' expectations. The testing revealed several issues with the design of the instrument that impeded the user's experience. Some of these issues were robust (e.g. occurring with many respondents), while other issues were only observed with a few respondents, although they had the potential of contributing to significant measurement error if they occurred on a larger scale.

Table 17.2 Benefits and drawbacks of remote interviewing.

Testing Component	Benefits	Drawbacks
Recruitment	• Recruitment hosted online enables quicker response to recruitment materials. • Respondents can be recruited nationwide rather than locations being limited by travel costs. • The online scheduler enables tracking the number of interviews along various variables of interest (e.g. industry or size), and automatically curtails recruiting when targets are met.	• The number of "no-shows" may increase. • Less tech-savvy individuals may be disinclined to participate. • Limitations due to internet connectivity remain.
Data	• Quick turnaround of interviews, analysis, and revisions enables greater adaptability and more iterative testing. • With the respondent's permission, interviewers may record the screen sharing, providing additional data for analysis. • Interviewer notes are entered directly into an online protocol, resulting in consolidated notes and more streamlined analysis. • Transcripts and recordings are available directly following the interview.	• Some respondents may be unable to successfully use the telecommunications platform, even with support. • It is not well suited for pretesting paper instruments. • Eye tracking hardware cannot be used with respondents. • Nonverbal cues usually collected during in-person interviews are lost.
Observers	• Additional observers may be present for the interview, as determined by the interviewer. • Interviewers are able to control observer behavior by muting their lines or dismissing them from the interview without interrupting its flow. • Travel becomes unnecessary for both observers and interviewers, reducing costs. • Recorded screen sharing demonstrates respondents' reactions to poor design, which resonates with sponsors, stakeholders, and colleagues.	• Observers are somewhat more likely to interrupt remote interviews with questions than when interviews are conducted in person.

For example, some sections of the 2017 COA questionnaire used an interleafed format, where respondents received additional questions directly following a positive response to a filter question. During usability testing, some respondents commented that they learned if they answered "yes" to certain questions, they would be asked additional follow-up questions (Pick et al. 2017). A few also remarked that they should go back and change their answers to avoid answering additional questions. It was not clear from the usability testing how widespread this issue may be and if design improvements were needed. However, addressing these issues in the design and functionality of the instrument would be costly.

17.2.6.2.2 *Analysis of Web Paradata*

To evaluate the impact on measurement error and to determine whether changes to the instrument were warranted, NASS collected and analyzed paradata from a web field test to assess whether these issues were occurring on a larger scale. Paradata included types of devices, browsers, mobile orientation (e.g. portrait and landscape), and date and time of each web instrument session, as well as response data, including the date and time each question was answered and a flag that indicated whether the answer to the question was changed.

Approximately 15,000 farm establishments were invited to participate in this field test and 2945 responded. NASS examined the paradata from the field test to determine the frequency of answer changing. Results showed that this behavior occurred at low rates, and thus no changes were made to the survey instrument (McGovern and Sirkis 2017).

17.3 Pretesting Methodologies: Current Features and Future Needs

17.3.1 Current Features and Consequences

These case studies illustrate how an evolving economy led to researchers' creativity in developing and/or adapting pretesting methodologies. We discuss several pervasive themes associated with these developments.

17.3.1.1 Finding "the Missing Link": Collaborative Partnerships

A common, persistent impediment to developing effective survey questions has been the disconnect between underlying economic concepts and clear specifications for economic measurement, dubbed the "Missing Link" by Snijkers and Willimack (2011). This gap is being narrowed, according to these case studies, by the emergence of working collaborative partnerships formed between research methodologists and subject matter experts.

To a large degree, collaboration grew out of a common practice among cognitive researchers to include subject matter specialists, survey managers, sponsors, or other stakeholders as observers during cognitive interviews. Upon witnessing respondents grappling with our survey question(naire)s, stakeholders observed notable discrepancies between the intent of a question and the response it garnered, raising concerns about the validity of the data for the intended purpose. Collaboration deepened researchers' understanding of underlying concepts while prompting discussions about question wording, as well as modifications to testing methodologies.

Outcomes of collaborative partnerships include revamping survey questionnaires to improve alignment with business practices and records, reducing respondent burden through streamlining questionnaires, and improved targeting of surveys to appropriate respondents relative to the survey's intent. These collaborations may have also motivated subject matter experts to disseminate pretest findings among their colleagues, furthering their understanding of challenges in economic measurement.

17.3.1.2 The Odyssey: Exploratory Methods

One by-product of these collaborative partnerships is the growth in exploratory research conducted to aid writing survey questions. Exploratory methods, such as ESS or record-keeping studies, are particularly beneficial for establishment surveys because of underlying technical concepts and accounting requirements. Although designed to support development of survey questions prior to pretesting, methodological research has demonstrated how exploratory probing techniques may be effectively incorporated within cognitive interviews (Herrell et al. 2017). These methods have also proven fruitful with subject matter experts for revealing the underlying concepts and measurement goals of draft survey questions (Tuttle et al. 2010).

17.3.1.3 Leave No Stone Unturned: Multiple Methods

The case studies also illustrate different reasons and strategies for applying multiple research methods, demonstrating their value for specifying measurements, pretesting the same survey questions across modes, evaluating the effectiveness of data collection instruments, or investigating the response process. We observe combinations of exploratory methods, cognitive interviews, and respondent debriefings; resource constraints driving creative uses of traditional methods in non-traditional settings; adaptation of research methods to unforeseen circumstances; and application of methods borrowed from other disciplines to discern unique features of business respondents' data retrieval and judgment strategies.

17.3.1.4 Methuselah: The Many Roles of Technology

The case studies demonstrate multiple complementary – and competing – roles of emerging technologies and their measurement. As technological advances change the economic production function, underlying concepts evolve, measurements require redefinition, and emerging technologies become the topic of survey questions. As automation impacts how businesses do business, data systems become integrated, while restricted access may be more readily managed. This likely alters the survey response process, along with respondents' needs and expectations, challenging data collection instruments to employ state-of-the art dynamic functionalities and intuitive interfaces.

Economic measurement, the survey response process, and the design of the data collection instrument intersect under the auspices of survey research methodologists, who represent the respondent as survey question(naire)s are developed and pretested, aiming to improve response quality while minimizing respondent burden. New, improved technologies expand the researchers' toolkit, providing new pretesting and analytical tools/procedures. For instance, eye-tracking hardware and software augment other usability testing tools; remote testing overcomes logistical impediments for conducting cognitive or usability testing; qualitative data analysis software streamlines summary of verbal information; and web paradata aid evaluation of data collection instruments.

17.3.1.5 Trust the Process: The Response Process

Despite diversity in their topics and methodologies, interview protocols used in these case studies share in their explicit attention devoted to portions of the business survey response process *not* encompassed by the traditional four-step cognitive response model (Tourangeau et al. 2000), revealing factors germane to pretesting establishment surveys that differ from pretesting surveys of households/individuals.

Business survey response models explicitly consider the impact of organizational and management requirements on a respondent's cognitive processes (Willimack and Snijkers 2013; Willimack and Nichols 2010; Bavdaž 2010). This includes organizational structures, management's criteria for designating the survey respondent, competing priorities, and procedures and permissions for releasing survey responses. Among the four cognitive steps, while comprehension remains important, the retrieval and judgment steps are predominant, due to reliance on business records for answers to survey questions. Respondents may not have direct access to requested information which may not align with recorded data, further complicating their ability to report.

Giesen (2007) evaluated the business survey response model as a framework for conducting pretest interviews, noting the need for additional exploratory questions. Protocols often ask about the business's structure, size, and industry, the respondents' role and experience with financial reporting, procedures for gathering data, the need for other data sources, and processes for manipulating recorded data to answer survey questions.

17.3.2 Future Needs and Implications

Many potential research projects may be drawn from these case studies, starting with common features and consequences discussed in Section 17.3.1. Rather than continue a litany of research proposals, instead we extrapolate three key points that may take establishment survey pretesting methodology to the "next level," whereby the science is improved, procedures are adaptable and innovative, the utility of results is expansive, and collaborative partnerships between subject matter specialists and methodological researchers are the norm.

First, while establishment surveys and household surveys share a number of attributes – in particular, a person answers the questions because a business cannot "speak" for itself – several intrinsic differences require different directions for data collection instruments and procedures and the research methodologies that support them. The nature of the response process in establishment surveys – the organizational context that impacts respondents' behaviors – adds complexities that must be incorporated into survey research methodologies. Understanding and integrating the role of records and how respondents interact with them should be at the core of establishment survey design and data collection procedures. The case studies demonstrate that emphasis in pretesting should shift from that which is cognitive to understanding business processes, to better align survey procedures.

Secondly, these cases studies show the added value when research methodologists form effective collaborative partnerships with subject matter specialists and those who share a stake in correctly measuring the "right" economic variables. The collaborative approach can be credited with improvements in survey question(naire)s where participating stakeholders have embraced pretest findings.

We observe pretesting results being distributed beyond survey practitioners, as subject matter specialists share reports with colleagues within their scholarly disciplines. In this way, data users will be better informed about the nature – and the limitations – of survey data being used in economic analysis and decision-making. No measurement is perfect. Data users and stakeholders are encouraged to seek in-depth understanding of where data originate, recognize discrepancies revealed through pretesting and other qualitative evaluations, and consider the implications for interpreting their analytical results.

Nevertheless, more can be done toward making these outcomes pervasive. While we commend subject matter experts for sharing qualitative research findings with colleagues, we challenge the ongoing practice whereby they tend to be final decision-makers about survey questions, wording, and design, sometimes despite contrary recommendations based on pretesting results, without disclosing their rationale. Moreover, it is imperative that both researchers and stakeholders understand the impact of discrepancies between measurements and underlying concepts, to ensure that data collected via survey questions align with data needs and are interpreted properly.

Frankly, dissemination of methodological research remains an issue within our field as well, and a dearth of publications is ongoing. We noted that establishment surveys' complexities dictate the need for multiple question(naire) development and pretesting methods, such that research strategies and protocols are flexible, and qualitative researchers can skillfully adapt research methods to a given context. However, without evidence, it is difficult to assess whether utility gained from adding methods in a testing strategy is warranted relative to resource requirements. Thus, documentation and public dissemination of establishment survey research helps advance our field while also benefiting stakeholders as described earlier.

As qualitative research methodologies have become more rigorous, issues of disclosure risk also increase (Pascale et al. 2020). Researchers often use frame data to describe study participants and to guide analysis. Including stakeholders and others in the research process, the rise of remote technology, and use of electronic devices all raise additional privacy issues and data security concerns. Researchers must be aware of these risks and develop contingencies to ensure confidentiality and privacy for their participants.

Lastly, we emphasize the role and needs of establishment survey methodological researchers in measuring this constantly evolving world economy. Production surveys' adoption of pretesting results indicates their value. Collaborative partnerships and knowledge sharing within and across disciplines ensure researchers' preparedness to address emerging topics and their economic impact. Modifying or creating research methodologies to address emerging needs also expands their application and effectiveness.

Our final point is that methodologies for carrying out establishment survey question(naire) pretesting and/or evaluation are indeed adaptable, such that skilled researchers may continue to build and grow the science, regardless of whether it is the topic or the tool that changes. Emerging economic topics requiring reliable measurement have evolved from "e-commerce" in the past to current topics that include "robotics," "key performance indicators," and "intangible assets," to future topics such as "autonomous vehicles," "virtual labor force," "data and information as marketable commodities," and "space travel as leisure/entertainment." At the same time, data collection tools evolve, currently featuring dynamic applications that are built to adapt, in real time, to respondents' answers to survey questions, involving artificial intelligence such as ML or passive data capture from alternative sources. Advancement of establishment survey question(naire) pretesting methodologies to address future emerging economic topics and evolving data collection tools is left to the reader.

Acknowledgments

The authors offer several acknowledgments: Research reported in Case Studies #2, #5, and #6 was carried out by Heather Ridolfo when she was employed at the National Agricultural Statistics Service of the U.S. Department of Agriculture (NASS/USDA), and she thanks them for their support. We also appreciate the generosity of the ICES-VI Publication Committee and helpful feedback from our editors Mojca Bavdaž, Jacqui Jones, along with review comments from Ger Snijkers. We further acknowledge scholarly contributions and/or professional support from Rebecca Keegan, Christian Moscardi, Kristin Stettler, Joseph Barth, and Carol Caldwell (retired) of the U.S. Census Bureau, along with helpful reviews and input from NASS/USDA colleagues Pam McGovern, Robin Sirkis, Emilola Abayomi, David Biagas, and Joseph Rodhouse.

We close by dedicating this chapter in memory of Jennifer Edgar of the U.S. Bureau of Labor Statistics, who was to have been our co-author. We want our readers and colleagues to remember Jennifer's insightful contributions to the field of survey methodology, particularly with respect to advancements in establishment survey research, as well as her pragmatism in ensuring that research and project goals were achieved, her career as a public servant and official statistician, her dedication to our profession, and her personal and professional influence on each of us as friends and colleagues. She is missed.

References

Anderson Riemer, A.E. (2021). Adapting qualitative research techniques to pretest emerging economic topics. Paper presented at the Sixth International Conference on Establishment Surveys, virtual (14–17 June).

Barnett Thomas, L., Morrison, R.L., and O'Neill, G. (2007). Cognitive aspects associated with sample selection conducted by respondents in establishment surveys. Paper presented at the Third International Conference on Establishment Surveys, Montreal, Canada (18–21 June).

Bavdaž, M. (2010). Sources of measurement errors in business surveys. *Journal of Official Statistics* 26: 25–42.

Bavdaž, M., Giesen, D., Moore, D.L., Smith, P.A., and Jones, J. (2019). Qualitative testing for official establishment survey questionnaires. *Survey Research Methods* 13 (3): 267–288. https://doi.org/10 .18148/srm/2019.v13i3.7366.

Bavdaž, M., Bounfour, A., Martin, J., Nonnis, A., Perani, G., and Redek, T. (2023). Measuring Investment in Intangible Assests. In: *Advances in Business Statistics, Methods and Data Collection*, Chapter 5 (ed. G. Snijkers, M. Bavdaž, S. Bender, J. Jones, S. MacFeely, J.W. Sakshaug, K.J. Thompson, and A. van Delden). Hoboken: Wiley.

Baxter, K., Courage, C., and Caine, K. (2015). *Understanding Your Users: A Practical Guide to User Research Methods*, 2nd edition, Waltham: Elsevier Science.

Buffington, C., Miranda, J., and Seamans, R. (2018). Development of survey questions on robotics expenditures and use in US manufacturing establishments. Working paper 18–44, U.S. Census Bureau, Washington, DC. https://www.census.gov/library/working-papers/2018/adrm/ces-wp-18-44.html.

Cidade, M.A., Willimack, D.K., Stettler, K., and Hanna, D.V. (2021). Expanding record-keeping study methodology to assess structure and availability of data in business records. Paper presented at the Sixth International Conference on Establishment Surveys, virtual (14–17 June).

Dippo, C.S., Chun, Y.I., and Sander, J. (1995). Designing the data collection process. In: *Business Survey Methods* (ed. B.G. Cox, D.A. Binder, B.N. Chinnappa, A. Christianson, M.J. Colledge, and P.S. Kott), 283–302. New York: Wiley.

Federal Committee on Statistical Methodology (2016). Evaluating survey questions: an inventory of methods. Statistical policy working paper 47, Washington DC. https://nces.ed.gov/FCSM/pdf/ spwp47.pdf.

Foundations for Evidence-Based Policymaking Act of 2018. Public Law 115-435, H.R. 4174 – 115th Congress (2017–2018), 14 January 2019. https://www.congress.gov/bill/115th-congress/house-bill/ 4174/all-info.

Giesen, D. (2007). The response process model as a tool for evaluating business surveys. Paper presented at the Third International Conference on Establishment Surveys, Montreal, Canada (18–21 June).

Herrell, K., Purcell, M., and Bucci, M.S. (2017). Integrating early stage scoping techniques into traditional pretesting methods: inside the development of a survey on small business lending. Paper presented at the Joint Statistical Meetings, Baltimore, Maryland (July 29–August 3).

Journal of Official Statistics (2010). Special section with articles based on papers from the Third International Conference on Establishment surveys, vol. 26, no. 4.

Journal of Official Statistics (2014). Special issue on establishment surveys, vol. 30, no. 4.

Journal of Official Statistics (2018). Special issue on establishment surveys (ICES-V), vol. 34, no. 2.

Keegan, R. and Stettler, K. (2021). Adapting qualitative pretesting methods to aid development and evaluation of electronic data transfer techniques to augment survey collection. Paper presented at the 2021 Federal Computer Assisted Survey Information Collection Workshop, virtual (13–14 April).

McGovern, P. and Sirkis, R. (2017). Findings from the paradata analysis of the 2016 Census of Agriculture computer-assisted web interview (CAWI) test. Washington, DC: National Agricultural Statistics Service.

Miranda, J. and Seamans, R. (2020). Overview and goals. Remarks presented at the Virtual Robotics Workshop, New York University Leonard N. Stern School of Business, virtual (23 June).

Moscardi, C. (2021a). Modernizing CFS collection and operations with machine learning. Paper presented at the Sixth International Conference on Establishment Surveys, virtual (14–17 June).

Moscardi, C. (2021b). A new way of collecting transactional data for the Commodity Flow Survey. Paper presented at the 2021 Federal Computer Assisted Survey Information Collection Workshop, virtual (13–14 April).

Moscardi, C. and Hashemipour, M. (2019). Using natural language processing to improve the Commodity Flow Survey. Paper presented at the 2019 Federal Computer Assisted Survey Information Collection Workshop, Washington, DC (April).

National Academies of Sciences, Engineering, and Medicine (2018). *Reengineering the Census Bureau's Annual Economic Surveys*. Washington, DC: The National Academies Press https://doi.org/10 .17226/25098.

Ott, K. and Ridolfo, H. (2018). Agricultural labor contractor cognitive testing final report. Washington, DC: National Agricultural Statistics Service.

Pascale, J., Willimack, D.K., Bates, N., Lineback, J.F., and Beatty, P.C. (2020). Issue paper on disclosure review for information products with qualitative research findings. Washington, DC: U.S. Census Bureau. https://www.census.gov/library/working-papers/2020/adrm/rsm2020-01.html.

Pick, K., Ridolfo, H., Lawson, L., and Sloan, R. (2017). Findings and recommendations from usability testing for the 2017 Census of Agriculture computer-assisted web interview (CAWI) system – round 2 with respondents. Washington, DC: National Agricultural Statistics Service.

Reist, B., Wilson, T., Ridolfo, H., and Young, L.J. (2018). Findings for the 2018 Agricultural Labor base wage question experiments. Washington, DC: National Agricultural Statistics Service.

Ridolfo, H., Biagas, D., Abayomi, E.J., and Rodhouse, J. (2020a). Behavior coding of the October 2017 Agricultural Labor Survey. Washington, DC: National Agricultural Statistics Service.

Ridolfo, H., Biagas, D., Abayomi, E.J., and Rodhouse, J. (2021). Behavior coding of the April 2018 Agricultural Labor Survey. Washington, DC: National Agricultural Statistics Service.

Ridolfo, H. and Ott, K. (2021a). 2019 Agricultural Labor base and overtime hours cognitive testing report. Washington, DC: National Agricultural Statistics Service.

Ridolfo, H. and Ott, K. (2021b). 2019 Cognitive testing of the Agricultural Labor Survey. Washington DC: National Agricultural Statistics Service.

Ridolfo, H. and Ott, K. (2020a). Cognitive testing of the April 2018 Agricultural Labor Survey. Washington, DC: National Agricultural Statistics Service.

Ridolfo, H. and Ott, K. (2020b). Reporting contract labor on the Agricultural Labor Survey. Washington, DC: National Agricultural Statistics Service.

Ridolfo, H., Ott, K., Beach, J., and McCarthy, J. (2020b). Pre-testing establishment surveys: moving beyond the lab. *Survey Practice* 13 (1): 11810.

Rodhouse, J., Ridolfo, H., Abayomi, E.J., and Biagas, D. (2021). Behavior coding of the October 2018 Agricultural Labor Survey. Washington, DC: National Agricultural Statistics Service.

Snijkers, G. and Arentsen, K. (2015). Collecting financial data from large non-financial enterprises: a feasibility study. Paper presented at the 4th International Workshop on Business Data Collection Methodology, Washington, DC (14–16 September).

Snijkers, G., Houben, L., and Demollin, F. (2023). Tailoring the design of a new combined business survey: process, methods, and lessons learned. In: *Advances in Business Statistics, Methods and Data Collection*, Chapter 16 (ed. G. Snijkers, M. Bavdaž, S. Bender, J. Jones, S. MacFeely, J.W. Sakshaug, K.J. Thompson, and A. van Delden). Hoboken: Wiley.

Snijkers, G. and Willimack, D.K. (2011). The missing link: from concepts to questions in economic surveys. Paper presented at the 2nd European Establishment Statistics Workshop (EESW11), Neuchâtel, Switzerland (September 12–14).

Stettler, K. and Featherston, F. (2012). Early stage scoping: bridging the gap between survey concepts and survey questions. Paper presented at the Fourth International Conference on Establishment Surveys, Montreal, Canada (11–14 June).

Tourangeau, R., Rips, L.J., and Rasinski, K. (2000). *The Psychology of Survey Response*. New York: Cambridge University Press.

Tuttle, A.D., Morrison, R.L., and Willimack, D.K. (2010). From start to pilot: a multi-method approach to the comprehensive redesign of an economic survey questionnaire. *Journal of Official Statistics* 26 (1): 87–103.

van Delden, A., Lorenc, B., Struijs, P., and Zhang, L.-C. (2018). Letter to the editor: on statistical unit errors in business statistics. *Journal of Official Statistics* 34 (2): 573–580.

Willimack, D.K. (2013). Methods for the development, testing, and evaluation of data collection instruments. In: *Designing and Conducting Business Surveys* (ed. G. Snijkers, G. Haraldsen, J. Jones and D.K. Willimack), 253–301. Hoboken: Wiley.

Willimack, D.K., Lyberg, L., Martin, J., Japec, L., and Whitridge, P. (2004). Evolution and adaption of questionnaire development, evaluation, and testing methods for establishment surveys. In: *Methods for Testing and Evaluating Survey Questionnaires* (ed. S. Presser, J.M. Rothgeb, M.P. Couper, J.T. Lessler, E. Martin, J. Martin, and E. Singer), 385–407. Hoboken: Wiley.

Willimack, D.K. and Snijkers, G. (2013). The business context and its implications for the survey response process. In: *Designing and Conducting Business Surveys* (ed. G. Snijkers, G. Haraldsen, J. Jones and D.K. Willimack), 39–82. Hoboken: Wiley.

Willimack, D.K. and Nichols, E. (2010). A hybrid response process model for business surveys. *Journal of Official Statistics* 26: 3–24.

18

Using Paradata in Electronic Business Survey Questionnaires*

Ger Snijkers[1], Susan Demedash[2], and Jessica Andrews[2]

[1] Department of Research and Development (Methodology), Statistics Netherlands, Heerlen, The Netherlands
[2] Statistics Canada, Ottawa, Ontario, Canada

18.1   Introduction

The questionnaire is the survey data collection instrument, with the role of getting valid, accurate, and complete data. To achieve this goal, questionnaire design needs careful attention taking the business context into consideration (Willimack and Snijkers 2013, Haraldsen 2013a, 2023 [Chapter 15], Snijkers et al. 2023 [Chapter 16]). Even after carefully designing and pretesting the questionnaire (Willimack 2013, Willimack et al. 2023 [Chapter 17]), the question remains: does the questionnaire work as intended? Electronic questionnaires offer the means to answer this question using data on the questionnaire completion process. These process data are an example of paradata.

When the questionnaire does not work as intended, this can lead to unintended consequences: additional costs for businesses (response burden), errors in the data, additional costs for the surveyor such as additional questions and complaints from business respondents, and additional data cleaning costs. A study in the Unites States shows that 40% of the total number of resources needed in the production process for five US Census Bureau Annual Economic Surveys is allocated to post-field data editing and cleaning (NAS 2018); which makes this the costliest step in the production process. We argue that this should be prevented as much as possible, and data quality issues should be solved as early in the process as possible, i.e. when the questionnaire is being completed. As we will see, paradata on the questionnaire completion process can help questionnaire designers to improve the questionnaire, and thus yield data of good quality early in the survey process.

As to the entire survey design, in accordance with Groves et al. (2004/2009, Snijkers 2016), we state that it is the job of a survey designer to minimize errors in survey statistics by making design and estimation choices that minimize the errors in each step of the survey process, within constraints. Figure 16.1 in Chapter 16 (Snijkers et al. 2023) shows an overview of the business survey process. For each step in this process model, we can identify error sources which affect the quality of the final survey statistics. These error sources are defined in the Total Survey Error Framework (Biemer 2010, Lyberg and Stukel 2017). By including the error sources in the process model, we obtain a process-quality approach, which – according to us – is the basic approach for survey designers. Paradata, i.e. data about the processes in each step, can help survey designers to make better (i.e., fact-based) choices, and help to improve the efficiency of these processes. (For a more detailed

---

*This chapter is based on an ICES-VI Introductory Overview Lecture (IOL), which is available at https://www.youtube.com/watch?v=OYBfd7yYf3Q.

Advances in Business Statistics, Methods and Data Collection. Edited by Ger Snijkers, Mojca Bavdaž, Stefan Bender, Jacqui Jones, Steve MacFeely, Joseph W. Sakshaug, Katherine J. Thompson, and Arnout van Delden.

discussion on the process-quality approach in business surveys, we refer to Snijkers (2016), Jones et al. (2013), and Haraldsen (2013b).)

In this chapter, we will discuss the use of paradata in business surveys, in particular with regard to monitoring and evaluating electronic business survey questionnaires. By discussing a number of examples, we will illustrate the usefulness of paradata in business surveys. This chapter starts with a brief discussion on the concept of paradata in general (Section 18.2). Sections 18.3 and 18.4 focus on questionnaire completion paradata: first examining these paradata in more detail, followed by examples from Statistics Netherlands and Statistics Canada. Section 18.5 concludes this chapter.

18.2   Paradata

Often paradata are restricted to data generated from the data collection process (Kunz and Hadler 2020, Wagner 2016, Callegaro 2013, Heerwegh 2011). Having the process-quality approach in mind, in follow up to Kreuter (2013), Kreuter et al. (2010) and Snijkers and Haraldsen (2013), we apply a broader definition of paradata as additional data that cover any aspect of the survey process. In all these processes, paradata describe individual events (Heerwegh 2011, van der Aalst 2016), and may generally be defined as event log data.

Paradata can be used both in process management and in quality management. From a process management perspective, Snijkers and Haraldsen (2013) distinguish between paradata related to (i) production, (ii) the respondent, and (iii) project management. Production-side paradata are data about the survey production processes within the survey organization. This includes paradata on the data collection, such as the dispatching of questionnaires, sending out letters, staff performance, the data capture process (number of questionnaires processed), response rates, as well as paradata on the profiling process and data editing/cleaning process. Respondent-side paradata include questionnaire completion data (such as login data, key stroke data, log data, audit trails, and activated error messages), as well as help desk data (for example, questions and complaints and follow-up questions by respondents). Project-management paradata are a special kind of production-side paradata. These are paradata on a higher level, and include the consumption of money, resources, and time in design projects or fieldwork processes.

In addition to this process management perspective, Snijkers and Haraldsen (2013) relate paradata to a quality management perspective. As suggested by Kreuter and Casas-Coscadero (2010, see also Kreuter 2013), in this perspective, paradata are related to error sources in the survey process, i.e. to the total survey error framework (Snijkers 2016, Groves et al. 2004/2009). As such paradata-based quality indicators can be computed, like the number of times specific error checks have been activated in a questionnaire, or the number of times an answer has been changed (see Snijkers and Haraldsen 2013, and Wagner 2016, for an overview of paradata-based quality indicators).

An example of the application of various kinds of paradata in a combined process-quality management approach in business surveys comes from Statistics Norway (Haraldsen and Stavnes 2021): in a Data Collection Control Panel (Figure 18.1), paradata are used to monitor, analyze, and document the data collection process. The charts in this dashboard have been selected to provide information on two important key evaluation criteria in the data collection process: quality and costs.

The charts in Figure 18.1 show the final results of the data collection process for the 2018 Norwegian Annual Structural Business Survey (SBS), with a sample size of 13,854 business units. The line and pie charts in pane 1 and 2 show the response rate pattern and the response status at each moment during the fieldwork. The line charts in pane 1 show the accumulated

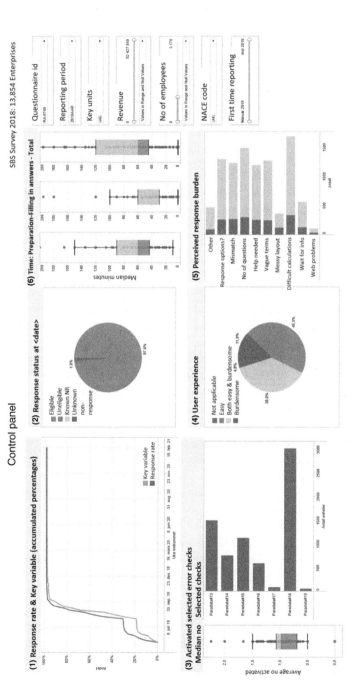

Figure 18.1 Data collection control panel from Statistics Norway (Haraldsen and Stavnes 2021).

unit response rate and a weighted response rate for a selected key variable. In this case, the key variable is the percentage of the total revenue in the sample, which is already known from the Tax Authorities. In the first period of the data collection, we see a gap between these two lines, indicating that low-revenue enterprises were the first to respond. The pie chart in pane 2 shows the response status: the response is broken down into accepted responses, not eligible cases, and the nonresponse cases at a specific date during the fieldwork. The paradata used as input for these charts are automatically generated production-side paradata.

In addition to these charts, response quality is measured by selected error checks and user experience. This is shown in the bar and box plot charts in pane 3. The bar chart shows the number of times seven (for this purpose) selected error checks are automatically activated while respondents completed the questionnaires (i.e., respondent-side paradata). Here, one error check (#18) is activated significantly more than others, which indicates that this variable needs to be looked into. The box plot to the left of the bar chart, describes the activation distribution for all error checks. The user experience is measured by a number of perceived response burden questions that respondents were asked to complete at the end of the questionnaire (Haraldsen 2018). The pie chart in pane 4 shows how respondents felt about filling out the questionnaire: here 4.8% found the questions burdensome, while 45.3% thought the questions were easy, and 38.0% found them both easy and burdensome. For those who found the questions burdensome, the bar chart in pane 5, shows the heaviest burdens. For this survey they are: complicated or lengthy calculations needed, the high number of questions in the questionnaire, unclear and vague terms or instructions used in the questionnaire, difficult to decide what response or response alternative would be the correct one, mismatch between available data and what was asked for, and help from colleagues was needed to find the requested data.

Finally, the box plots in pane 6 show the costs for the respondents measured by the time spent preparing information needed to answer the questions in the questionnaire, the time spent filling out the questionnaire, and their sum, the total time spent (i.e., actual response burden). Both time estimates are based on questions at the end of the questionnaire.

This control panel is interactive. In addition to giving an overview of the data collection process as a whole, the process can be further analyzed in two ways. Using the drop-down lists at the right side of the panel, units with different characteristics can be selected, e.g. high or low revenue enterprises or units with different industry codes (like ISIC, NACE, and NAICS codes[1]), newly added or previously participating units. Alternatively, clicking on different parts of the graphs in the control panel, units with different response patterns can be singled out. As an example, one may compare the quality and cost indicators between those who responded early and those who responded late by marking the first and the last period of the data collection in the line graph in pane 1. Another example would be to click on the "Burdensome slice" in the User experience pie chart (in pane 4) to analyze the response pattern, response quality, and costs for those who found the questions hard to answer.

These charts are used to monitor the data collection process during the fieldwork. Once the data collection is finished, the final control panel picture will serve as a quality-and-cost documentation of the data collection process. A more detailed discussion on the charts in this control panel is given by Haraldsen (2018).

---

1 ISIC, NACE, and NAICS are classification systems to categories businesses according to their main economic activity. ISIC (International Standard Industrial Classification) is the general classification system. Regionally used systems are NACE (Nomenclature statistique des Activités économique dans la Communauté Européenne) as used in the European Union, and NAICS (North American Industry Classification System) as used in the USA and Canada (Jones and O'Bryne 2023 [Chapter 8]; Smith 2013).

Another example of the use of paradata to analyze a business survey process is provided by Lammers (2018). Even though he does not use the term "paradata," this is an example of analyzing process data to improve the survey process. He uses event log data to study the efficiency of the profiling process at Statistics Netherlands. In business surveys, profiling of enterprises is an important step (ibid: 80): "Profiling is a method of analyzing the legal, operational and accounting structure of an enterprise group at national and world level, in order to establish the statistical (observational) unit within that group, their links and the most efficient structures for the collection of statistical data." Lammers used process mining as an analytical technique: a technique to discover, monitor, and improve processes by analyzing event log data (van der Aalst 2016, Fluxicon 2020). The analysis tool he used was Disco: an analysis program for process mining. He concludes that the profiling process was inefficiently conducted, because of overprocessing (including unnecessary steps and loops adding no value), overproduction (profiling that has no statistical impact), and waiting. Based on these results, several improvements were suggested and tested before implementation. The tests showed a 45% increase in efficiency. Consequently, the improvements were implemented.

The Norwegian dashboard shows how paradata can be used to monitor and manage the data collection process, whereas Lammers' study shows how production-side process data can be used to study the efficiency of any survey process. With respondent-side paradata we can go deeper, and look inside the questionnaire completion process itself, i.e. what business respondents actually do when they complete an electronic questionnaire? In the remainder of this chapter we will focus on these questionnaire completion paradata, illustrating its use with examples from Statistics Netherlands and Statistics Canada.

18.3 Questionnaire Completion Paradata

Questionnaire completion paradata are event data, chronologically showing how respondents completed a questionnaire, i.e. what they did, step by step. These paradata are collected automatically by the electronic questionnaire along with the survey data (provided that the system offers this option). Such a data file typically consists of variables like a date and time stamp, a respondent identification, a page or field id, and the action carried out, with one action (event) per record. Also, data on the browser and device used by the respondent may be collected. Examples of paradata files are shown in Figure 18.2: Figure 18.2a shows a data file from Statistics Netherlands (CBS), Figure 18.2b shows data from Statistics Canada (StatCan).

The CBS paradata are about the questionnaire as discussed in Chapter 16 by Snijkers et al. (2023). The example in Figure 18.2a shows that respondent 12345_EX_PROD logged in on February 13th, 2020, at 11:53 a.m., using the Dutch version of the questionnaire (Language:NL), and checked the general questions on page */SGO/General.aspx*. It took this respondent five minutes and 41 seconds to check and confirm the consolidation cluster (i.e., the consolidated observation unit for which the questionnaire needs to be completed) on page */Cluster*. At 12:20 p.m., this respondent logged out, logging in again at 13:30. This second session expired 20 minutes later, at 13:50. He logged in again at 14:02, confirming the consolidation cluster again, and moving to the fixed assets section in the Balance of Payments (*/SFO/Balance/FixedAssets*). He logged out at 14:27 without any other actions carried out.

Similar paradata are shown in Figure 18.2b for the Canadian Job Vacancy and Wage Survey (see Section 18.4.2), with the top showing the original compressed file with records of variable length. These raw data are not yet ready for analysis. The file includes information on date, time, action, page information (including any help pages visited), the user-id (which is anonymized), details

(a) Record layout Statistics Netherlands

Time stamp	Resp. ID	Action	Page/Field	Additional info
13-2-2020 11:53	12345_EX_PROD	LOGIN	LOGIN	Language:NL
13-2-2020 11:53	12345_EX_PROD	/Default.aspx	/Default.aspx	
13-2-2020 11:53	12345_EX_PROD	AGREE	/SFO/General.aspx	AGREE
13-2-2020 11:54	12345_EX_PROD	/Cluster	/Cluster	Fields posted in 5m 41s: ClusterAgree
13-2-2020 12:20	12345_EX_PROD	LOGOUT	LOGOUT	
13-2-2020 13:30	12345_EX_PROD	LOGIN	LOGIN	Language:NL
13-2-2020 13:30	12345_EX_PROD	/Default.aspx	/Default.aspx	
13-2-2020 13:50	12345_EX_PROD	EXPIRED	EXPIRED	expired
13-2-2020 13:50	12345_EX_PROD	LOGOUT	LOGOUT	
13-2-2020 14:02	12345_EX_PROD	LOGIN	LOGIN	Language:NL
13-2-2020 14:02	12345_EX_PROD	/Default.aspx	/Default.aspx	
13-2-2020 14:02	12345_EX_PROD	/SFO/General.aspx	/SFO/General.aspx	
13-2-2020 14:03	12345_EX_PROD	/Cluster	/Cluster	Fields posted in 0m 3s: ClusterAgree
13-2-2020 14:07	12345_EX_PROD	AGREE	/Cluster	AGREE
13-2-2020 14:07	12345_EX_PROD	/Cluster	/Cluster	
13-2-2020 14:07	12345_EX_PROD	/SFO/Balance/Default.aspx	/SFO/Balance/Default.aspx	
13-2-2020 14:07	12345_EX_PROD	/SFO/Balance/FixedAssets	/SFO/Balance/FixedAssets	
13-2-2020 14:27	12345_EX_PROD	LOGOUT	LOGOUT	

(b) Record layout Statistics Canada

Figure 18.2 Questionnaire completion paradata files from (a) Statistics Netherlands and (b) Statistics Canada.

on the device and browser used, the Statistics Canada host website, and finally the time taken for each action. As with regular survey data, a first step in the analysis of paradata, after collection, is inspection and cleaning of the raw data. The bottom picture shows the same data in an easy-to-read format of fixed length. In this example, a respondent signed into the application using Mozilla on Windows NT (User_Agent); the rows describe the actions of this respondent on June 15th, 2015, at around 9:25 a.m. EST: this respondent visited pages 3 and 4 of the questionnaire and then stopped.

These paradata files can become huge. For the entire sample of 426 businesses of the CBS survey (the target population is the largest businesses in the Netherlands), the paradata file in Figure 18.2a counted 176,625 event records. The file for the StatCan Job Vacancy and Wage Survey (Figure 18.2b) counted 8.5 million records for 100,000 business locations, with a file size of 7 Gb. A paradata file that was analyzed for the Dutch Annual Structural Business Survey in 2007 counted 11.5 million event records for 42,902 businesses (Snijkers and Morren 2010).

From these paradata, information about the questionnaire completion process can be extracted, such as:

- date and time the questionnaire was accessed and submitted
- the path taken to complete the questionnaire
- buttons and functionalities used
- error messages activated
- the language used
- the time spent
  - o for each question/on each page
  - o for the entire questionnaire
- browser and device used
- in real time, during data collection: where the respondent is in the questionnaire.

In turn, this provides information on the completion behavior, data quality, and response burden.

The paradata can be used in two ways: (i) to monitor the fieldwork in real time, and (ii) for post-field analysis to evaluate the questionnaire. Both in real-time monitoring and post-field analysis, it is important to think about what paradata are needed: these need to be specified upfront, depending on the research questions. Basically, this is the same as with survey data: in the first step, the required data are specified. Next, the electronic questionnaire should be designed in such a way that the required paradata are collected and saved. Of course, the electronic questionnaire software system should facilitate this. The systems used at CBS are Blaise and the Revolux system® (which is used for the CBS questionnaire in this study); at StatCan the Electronic Questionnaire Generation System (EQGS) is used along with the Business Collection Portal (BCP) and Blaise.

At StatCan, paradata are used to monitor the fieldwork in real time by following nonresponding participants and checking whether they have already started completing the questionnaire, in order to get full response: participants who have not yet started are followed up (see Section 18.4.2). At CBS, these paradata are used during the fieldwork in case respondents have questions about the completion of the questionnaire: the paradata show where they are in the questionnaire and what they have done thus far. With this information, they can be helped adequately.

The second way questionnaire completion paradata can be used is in post-field analysis, studying how a questionnaire actually was completed. In this way we can see whether a questionnaire worked as intended. Thus, we can identify flaws in the questionnaire design as well as the communication strategy, and next improve the design, i.e. better tailor the design to the business context.

18.4 Looking Inside the Questionnaire Completion Process

When preparing this chapter, we searched for studies in business surveys analyzing questionnaire completion paradata. We concluded that these studies are very rare, in contrast to social surveys (see e.g., Kreuter 2013, Kunz and Hadler 2020, Beatty et al. 2020). As far as we know, questionnaire completion paradata in business surveys were discussed for the first time by Snijkers and Morren (2010). They analyzed audit trails for the (then new) 2007 electronic Structural Business Survey questionnaire of Statistics Netherlands (see also Snijkers et al. 2012). They analyzed navigation, completion profiles, the completion time, duration, number of sessions, and session duration for a number of subgroups (size classes and economic activity). They concluded that about 75% of the SBS respondents completed the questionnaire and sent the data in one day, 85% did this in one week. On the other hand, the average response time was 77 days, which suggested that many businesses waited for about 2.5 months before starting with the questionnaire. The completion profiles they identified are: (i) the conscientious respondent (going back and forth in the questionnaire, showing an optimal response strategy), (ii) the "quick-and-dirty" respondent (showing a 'satisficing' completion behavior; Krosnick and Presser 2010), and (iii) the "printer" respondent (who printed the questionnaire, completed it off-line, and then entered the data into the electronic questionnaire).

A further study we found comes from the UK Office of National Statistics: Stewart et al. (2018) analyzed paradata for the electronic Monthly Wages and Salaries survey questionnaire[2]. Like in the examples we will describe in Section 18.4, they looked into completion profiles (ibid: 181): "The aim was to identify how respondents completed the electronic questionnaire; if we could understand respondent behavior we could begin to identify and anticipate where problems might arise in the questionnaire." From this study, analyzing the paradata of 300 businesses, they identified five main response profiles: (i) Completers (who completed the questionnaire linearly, in the order it was designed: 64% of the 300 businesses), (ii) Checkers (completing the questionnaire until the end and then going back using the "previous" buttons: 11%), (iii) Attentive checkers (like the checkers, but going back using the navigation panel at the left side of this questionnaire, moving to specific pages directly: 1%), (iv) Familiarizers (completing the questionnaire in any order, going back and forth: close to 20%), and (v) Learners (these respondents first familiarized themselves with the questionnaire going back and forth, and then progressed by completing the rest linearly: 2.5%).

Furthermore, with the use of paradata, they could identify problems in the questionnaire quickly, and issue a new version. For this purpose, they analyzed the activated error messages. Following Couper (2008), their goal was to prevent errors in the first place, instead of having to show error messages. Based on their analysis, as well as many requests from business respondents during usability testing, they included an overview page at the beginning of the questionnaire, showing the data that is asked for. As a result, paradata analysis for new cycles of the survey showed that Familiarizers and Learners moved to becoming Completers. They stated that this overview page has now become a standard facility in all electronic ONS business surveys.

As to the use of paradata in electronic business questionnaires, Stewart et al. (2018) concluded that paradata are a fast and cheap tool to identify problems in questionnaires, saving time, money, and resources to improve the questionnaire, as well as reducing response burden. In addition, they also concluded that the analysis of paradata may identify questionnaire locations where respondents have problems, but additional, quantitative information is needed to identify what these problems are. A drawback they mention was the processing of the raw paradata. The raw paradata were stored as an Excel spreadsheet, in which for every new respondent action a new row was added, leading to "an unfeasibly large number of rows" (ibid: 188), as we have also seen in Section 18.3. As a more suitable tool to analyze paradata, they chose Google Analytics.

To illustrate the use of questionnaire completion paradata in more detail, the next subsections discuss a number of studies from CBS and StatCan. In 2020 at CBS, paradata have been analyzed (using SPSS) to evaluate the new electronic questionnaire for the Dutch Finances of Enterprises and Balance of Payments Survey (Section 18.4.1). A related example of the use of paradata in order to study the effectiveness of a survey communication strategy for this questionnaire is discussed in Chapter 16.5 (Snijkers et al. 2023): log-in data were analyzed to see whether pre-field communications (like pre-notifications) had an effect on the response behavior during the first cycle in the field. Statistics Canada has been using paradata for a number of business surveys since 2015, both in post-field analysis and real-time monitoring of the fieldwork (using SAS and R), as we will see in Section 18.4.2.

---

2 Yet another study (we found after finalizing this chapter) comes from Germany: Volkert (2022) analyzes questionnaire completion paradata to study questionnaire navigation.

18.4.1 Completing the CBS-DNB Quarterly Survey on Finances of Enterprises and Balance of Payments

In Chapter 16, Snijkers et al. (2023) describe the development process and design features of a new quarterly survey "Finances of Enterprise and Balance of Payments" conducted by CBS in close collaboration with the Dutch National Bank, DNB, aimed at producing coherent statistics. This questionnaire asks for financial data according to the Balance of Payments and the Profit and Loss Statement. For some Balance of Payment items, individual financial transaction data are asked for in movement tables. For each quarter, the balance opening and closing positions are shown: the closing position data have to be entered, while the opening position is pre-filled (from the previous quarter). The questionnaire was sent to 397 enterprises in April 2019 for the first time, asking for data about the first quarter of 2019.

In a feasibility study, a number of design features were identified, which served as input for the electronic questionnaire design. These include:

- The questionnaire should have an Index panel to provide overview of the content, for navigation, and progress control.
- The questionnaire should be accessible from various locations and completed by various respondents.
- It should be possible to complete the questionnaire both top–down and bottom–up, or in any order that is convenient for the respondent.
- The questionnaire should facilitate both manual completion and by uploading/importing data files into the questionnaire; also, a data export option should be available.
- A print option should be available, showing an overview of the data asked for.
- Consistency checks and validation rules should be implemented in the questionnaire.
- The questionnaire should be available in Dutch and in English.

After the questionnaire was fielded in April 2019, we were interested whether these features were actually used, i.e. if the design worked as intended, and where improvements are needed. To answer these questions, the questionnaire completion paradata for this questionnaire were analyzed (Trilsbeek 2020). Unfortunately, the paradata for the first three quarters were deleted when we started this study, meaning that the first quarter that could be analyzed was 2019Q4. These data were collected in the first months of 2020, for a sample of 426 enterprises. We assumed that working with the questionnaire for a number of quarters would show a learning process, which should be present in the paradata. Since the data of the first three quarters had been deleted, we could not study this assumption.

The analysis of the paradata (as presented in Figure 18.2a) focused on the following topics, which will be discussed in the next subsections:

1. How was the questionnaire completed? What completion profiles can be identified?
2. How many enterprises used the import function?
3. How many enterprises used the Dutch and English version?
4. How long did it take to complete the questionnaire?
5. When was the questionnaire completed?

18.4.1.1 Questionnaire Completion Profiles

As for our first research question we looked into the paths respondents took to complete the questionnaire. We identified a number of completion profiles: top–down, bottom–up, section-wise, and imported. These are shown in Figure 18.3.

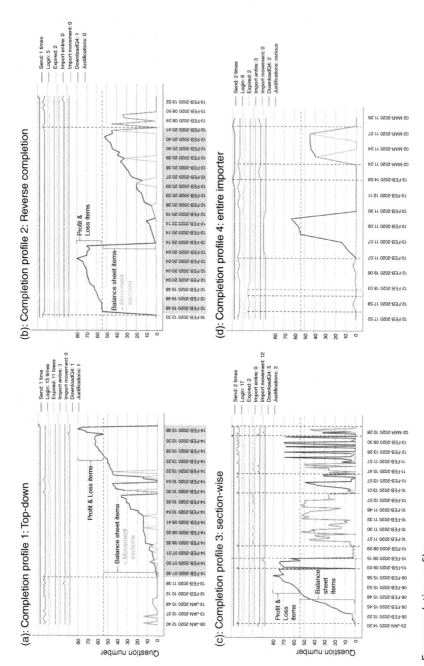

Figure 18.3　Four completion profiles.

In the graphs, in Figures 18.3a-d, the answer boxes were numbered following the order of the Index: questions 1–53 represent the Balance of Payment items, 54–81 represent the Profit and Loss statement items. The *y*-axis shows these question numbers. The *x*-axis is the timeline. The two bottom lines in the graphs show the position in the questionnaire: the dark line represents the Balance of Payments and Profit and Loss Statement items, while the spiked, lighter line represents the movement tables. The lines at the top represent individual actions over time (in order of appearance from top to bottom): Questionnaire Sent, Login, Expired, Import entire questionnaire, Import Movements, Downloaded, Error check activated (justification).

Figure 18.3a shows a respondent working their way through the questionnaire from top to bottom, first completing the Balance of Payment items and the related Movement tables, and then moving on to the Profit and Loss Statement items, following the order the items are presented in the questionnaire (the questions are numbered in this order). This respondent did this in one day, February 14th (after first having explored a few Movement tables on four separate days in January and February), starting at 7:45 a.m., and sending the data at 1:38 pm. At two moments, the questionnaire session expired (this is done automatically after 20 idle minutes), and they had to login again. The respondent in Figure 18.3b shows the reverse completion profile: this respondent started with the Profit and Loss Statement items at the end of the questionnaire, and then moved to the Balance of Payment items (at the beginning of the questionnaire), and the related Movement tables. This was done on February 12th, starting at 7:48 p.m. and ending this session at 8:41 p.m. He continued with the Movement tables the next day, starting at 8:24 a.m. and sending the data at 1:52 p.m. He did this in three sessions, having two expirations. Figure 18.3c shows a section-wise completion profile in which first the Balance of Payment and Profit and Loss Statement items were completed, which is followed by importing the individual Movement tables. After this a number of items were checked, and the data were sent twice. This process started on February 6th, and ended at March 2nd, needing 17 logins. A final profile we will discuss here, is the importer as is shown in Figure 18.3d. This respondent imported the entire questionnaire three times on February 12th, followed by checking the data in various sessions. The data were submitted twice.

Even though we did not count the frequencies for these profiles, they tell us that the questionnaire was completed in various ways. We concluded that the questionnaire design facilitates this, as we hoped for. In addition to these profiles, for 51 enterprises we saw multiple logins in the same sessions, indicating that multiple respondents worked with the questionnaire at the same time. Unfortunately, in our paradata we do not have the respondent's web address, so we cannot distinguish between various respondents from one enterprise.

18.4.1.2 Usage of Download and Import Functions

Next, we were interested in how many enterprises used the Import function. The questionnaire offers the option to import an Excel file, not only for the entire questionnaire but also for the individual Movement tables. To import a file, first an Excel template had to be downloaded from the questionnaire. Again, this can be the entire questionnaire or a single Movement table. In the paradata files, this was indicated by action indicators like: "DOWNLOAD 2019Q4 Full" and "IMPORT_Entire", and "DOWNLOAD 2019Q4 BA009" and "IMPORT_Movement/BA009" for the download and import of Balance-Assets Movement table 009 (tangible fixed assets).

The analysis showed that 224 enterprises (53% of all 426 enterprises) downloaded the entire Q4-questionnaire 359 times, while 24 enterprises (5.6%) used the Download option for Movement tables. Eighty-three Enterprises (20%) used the Import option: 50 enterprises imported the entire questionnaire 206 times; 49 enterprises imported Movement tables 262 times, of which 16 enterprises used both Import options.

The use of the export function was considered satisfactory, but could be higher, since this option can be used to get an empty template at the beginning of the completion process, as well as to store the reported data at the end. The use of the import function is less than we had hoped for, especially when considering that this is the fourth quarter that enterprises completed this questionnaire. We assumed that people working with the questionnaire were not aware of these options. For the next quarter, we added a "tip" in the advance letter pointing at the import option, we highlighted this option in the questionnaire, and we instructed our helpdesk to point enterprises asking for help to this option. To get a better idea of why this function was not used that much, we could have looked into this more closely by checking the number of movements (transactions) enterprises reported, in relation to the use of the import function. Also, we could have re-contacted enterprises who reported many movements manually, and ask why they did not use the import option.

18.4.1.3 Usage of Dutch and English Versions of the Questionnaire

Another result from the feasibility study was that the questionnaire should be available in both Dutch and English. Discussions with the enterprises showed that the English accounting terminology is known better than their Dutch synonyms. Also, we discovered that in some cases the data had to be provided by departments in another country (see Chapter 16, Snijkers et al. 2023). The paradata however showed that the English version of the questionnaire was not used as much as we had anticipated, as can be concluded from Table 18.1: only 60 enterprises (14%) used the English version of the questionnaire, of which 40 enterprises (9.4%) used both languages.

18.4.1.4 Time Needed to Complete the Questionnaire

A fourth issue we were interested in was related to response burden: how long did it take enterprises to complete the questionnaire? Figure 18.4 shows a bar chart with the frequency distribution of the completion time for the 426 enterprises. This graph also includes 41 nonresponding enterprises, which are mainly in the 1-hour group. We also decided to include the minutes when there was no activity, resulting in an expiration after 20 idle minutes. We assumed that during those minutes respondents were still working with the questionnaire, doing tasks such as collecting data or studying the data definitions.

In total, all 426 enterprises worked for 1,994 hours with the questionnaire, resulting in an average completion time of 4.7 hours, and a median of 3.2 hours. For the responding enterprises, the average completion time is 5.1 hours, and a median of 3.6 hours. For those enterprises that used the import function, the median completion time is reduced by half an hour to 3.1 hours. This does not mean that they spent less time on the entire completion process since we do not know how much time is needed to prepare the import files.

Of the 385 responding enterprises, 264 (69%) completed the questionnaire in up to five hours, and 318 (83%) in up to eight hours. However, the interesting part is the tail of the distribution: 33

Table 18.1 Language used to complete the questionnaire.

Language used	Enterprises No.	%
Dutch	366	85.9
English	20	4.7
Both	40	9.4
Total	**426**	**100**

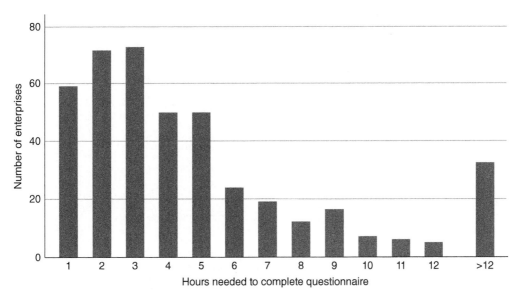

Figure 18.4 Number of hours needed to complete the questionnaire.

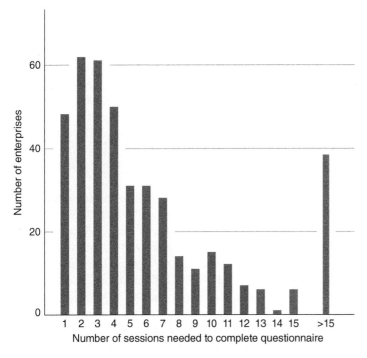

Figure 18.5 Number of sessions needed to complete the questionnaire.

enterprises (8.6%) needed more than 12 hours to finalize this task. It would be interesting to know why this took so long. We did not follow up on this by identifying and contacting these enterprises.

In addition, we also looked into the number of sessions (Figure 18.5). On average, 7 sessions were needed, with a median of 4. The average duration of a session is 41 minutes, and the average time between two consecutive sessions is 2 days. 90% of all responding enterprises (347) finished the job

Table 18.2 Completion duration in number of days.

Number of days	First response		Last response	
	Nr.	Cum.	Nr.	Cum.
1 day	179	179 (47%)	118	118 (31%)
2 days	59	238 (62%)	47	165 (43%)
3–7 (1 week)	49	287 (75%)	52	217 (56%)
8–14 (2 weeks)	40	327 (85%)	56	273 (71%)
15–28 (4 weeks)	35	362 (94%)	54	327 (85%)
29–> (5 weeks>)	23	385	58	385
Total	**385**		**385**	

in 15 sessions or fewer, leaving 38 enterprises needing 16 or more sessions, with a maximum of 81 sessions. Again, the question is who are these enterprises and why did they need so many sessions?

From the paradata, we can also extract the completion duration: the time between the first login and the first and last response. This is shown in Table 18.2. Again, the tails are the most interesting parts considering that this is the fourth quarter enterprises worked with the questionnaire: there were 23 enterprises that needed five weeks or more to submit the data for the first time, and 58 enterprises that needed this much time for a final response.

We concluded that apart from the enterprises in the tail, the response burden seems quite reasonable for this complex questionnaire. These data, however, as already stated above, do not provide information about the time needed to collect the data internally. Thus, we may conclude that this is an underestimation of the total time needed. It would have been interesting to see whether the response burden had dropped over the four quarters in 2019, when enterprises learned to work with this questionnaire. But, as said, when retrieving the data from our system, the data for the first three quarters had been deleted.

18.4.1.5 Effect of the Communication Strategy

So far, we have looked at the questionnaire itself, but we can also include the communication strategy in our paradata analysis, and study the effect of reminders on the completion behavior. For 2019Q4, the fieldwork started with an advance letter sent on January 16th, 2020 (submissions started coming in from January 6th onward), with a due date for February 13th. This was followed by a pre-due date reminder on January 30th, and post-due date reminders on February 14th and 28th, with extended due dates for February 20th and 27th, which was the last extended due date before the start of the enforcement procedure. Next, March 2nd and 9th were offered as final due dates to respond, which was followed by the law enforcement of nonresponding enterprises. Figure 18.6 shows the distribution of the 2,932 logins and 608 submissions during this quarter.

These graphs show the number of logins and submissions on working days in the period between January 6th and March 30th, 2020. Each block represents one working week of five days, from Monday (day 1) to Friday (day 5), for a period of 13 weeks. Weekend days are not included since next to no activity was seen on Saturdays and Sundays; including these activities would distort the pictures.

From Figure 18.6, we can conclude that the pre-due date does not have a large effect: we see a slightly accelerated increase in activity (number of logins) and submissions in the days after this letter. This acceleration results in spikes both for the number of logins and submissions close to the first due data (January 30th). In addition, the paradata analysis showed that 37% of all enterprises

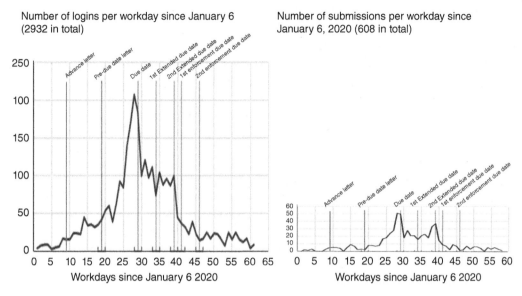

Figure 18.6 Distribution of logins and submissions for 2019Q4 (fieldwork in 2020Q1).

had not yet logged in at all at the time of the first due date. We did not follow up on these enterprises, although it would be interesting to know the reason for this. As we will see in the next subsection, at Statistics Canada, paradata are used to identify these units in real-time fieldwork monitoring.

After the first due date, the activity level drops to a level of about 100 logins each day, with a second spike in the number of submissions at the 2nd extended due data (February 27th). At this due date, 75% of all enterprises had submitted a final response. After this date the activity level and number of submissions dropped. In conclusion, the graphs show a clear effect of these due dates. We assume that businesses schedule these dates and work toward them.

18.4.2 Business Survey Use of Paradata at Statistics Canada

Statistics Canada has multiple business surveys that have used paradata since 2015 (Demedash and Buckley 2016), while the use of paradata in social surveys started some 10 years earlier (Laflamme 2008, Laflamme et al. 2008). These data have been used for a variety of projects such as exploring which questions are difficult for respondents, devices used to complete questionnaires, respondent behavior around questions that split the questionnaire into parts, as well as for modeling response likelihood of different respondents. For the Census of Agriculture, it was also possible to see which edits were triggered, allowing survey managers to determine which questions were problematic, as well as respondent behavior upon experiencing edits. The paradata, available for most Statistics Canada surveys, are limited to data on respondent behavior and not on values entered by respondents. Thus, although it was possible to see that a respondent had returned to a question several times, surveys would only capture the response on submission and not see any previous responses. The paradata (see Figure 18.2b) have chronological details on when and how often questionnaires were accessed, the device and browser used, and in which language each page of a questionnaire was accessed.

The first business survey to use paradata extensively was the Job Vacancy and Wage Survey (JVWS, Demedash and Buckley 2016). This is a long survey with 52 vacancy questions and over 20 wage questions administered quarterly to approximately 100,000 businesses. Survey managers were interested in which questions were difficult for the respondents, as well as those questions where the respondents quit the electronic questionnaire. Paradata log files were used to identify the time spent on each question, including the use of help buttons. As a result, a summary page was identified as being problematic, and was changed by adding an edit to direct the respondent to click on the "Continue" button instead of the "Next" button. This reduced the time spent on this page by almost 45 seconds in the next quarter.

Some of the most useful data was on the path taken by a respondent, which was sometimes surprising. The graph in Figure 18.7 shows the most common types of paths taken by respondents who took 20 steps in the electronic questionnaire, for a given session, during the second quarter of 2015 (the first full quarter of data for the survey). The *x*-axis represents the number of sequential steps taken by the respondent, the *y*-axis is the page number accessed in the electronic questionnaire: each successive page in the questionnaire was numbered. The graph shows the paths taken by four different respondents. The questions on pages 9 and 46 saw jumps between them as two respondents went back and forth. This completion pattern was identified for many respondents: these respondents had answered zero vacancies on page 9, and consequently jumped from page 9 to page 46. The lower dark line shows a partial respondent who stopped in the electronic questionnaire at page 18, while the other three lines show completed questionnaires.

The Job Vacancy and Wage Survey has many edits built into the electronic questionnaire to help validate the respondents' answers. Many of the respondents trigger edits, sometimes multiple edits. An edit is triggered when the respondent provides an atypical response to a given question. For example, an edit would be triggered if a respondent tried to put character data into a numeric field for the number of vacancies. Once an edit is triggered, a text box appears on the screen with

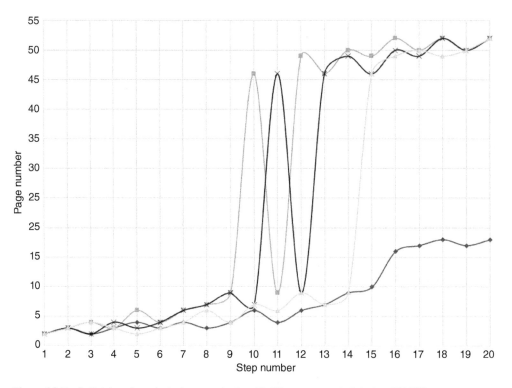

Figure 18.7 Path taken for selected respondents with 20 steps recorded during 2015Q2.

Table 18.3 The number of respondents, hits, and correction rates by edit ID for 2015Q2.

Edit	Hits	Respondents	Correction rate (%)
Q13 Sum of vacancies not equal to vacancies in Q6	26,454	1,615	12.9
Q1 and Q2 Client Information is invalid	16,521	13,083	97.7
Q3 Number of employees is blank or zero	3,901	3,596	60.6
Q13 Number of vacancies is blank	2,851	840	51.6
Q13 Job Title is blank	2,556	671	38.0

information on why the edit was triggered. The respondent then has the option to correct the answer or to ignore the message and move on to the next question. In the collection system, an edit summary report can be created to show which respondents triggered which edits and if they were corrected by the respondent. The edit summary report was combined with the paradata to show more detailed respondent information rather than just a count of edits triggered. The top five edits that triggered during the second quarter of 2015 along with their counts, the number of respondents triggering the edits and correction rates are shown in Table 18.3 (Demedash and Buckley 2016).

The same top five edits triggered in the second quarter and third quarter of 2015, however, the third quarter saw a decrease in the number of edits triggered. Thus, this could possibly indicate that the respondents learned from their errors in the second quarter and did not make the same errors in the third quarter. The edit that had the most triggers was for the sum of the vacancies in question 13. This edit had over 26,400 edits by over 1,600 respondents in the second quarter of 2015. The edit was triggered when the sum of the vacancies did not match the total number of vacancies in question 6. Also, only 13% of the edits of question 13 were corrected by the respondent. The second most commonly triggered edit was that for the question that asked for the respondent to update their information in questions 1 and 2. The edit was triggered if the respondent made any spelling errors or left any fields blank for each of the two questions. However, 98% of the edits for questions 1 and 2 were corrected by the respondent. Question 3 had the third highest number of edits triggered. This question asked the respondent for the number of paid employees. If the respondent did not answer this question or put a zero in the field, the edit was triggered. This question had a respondent correction rate of over 60%. Even though the respondent could have legitimately entered a zero or left it blank, both plausible and acceptable answers, the edit was triggered to ask the respondent to verify the answer. The fourth and fifth most common edits to trigger were for nonresponse to the number of vacancies for a given occupation and job titles for the corresponding vacancies. These edits had a correction rate of 38% and 52%, respectively. During this analysis, there were five edits that were expected to trigger but did not, so corrections were made to the system so that these edits were able to be triggered by incorrect responses. Therefore, looking at the edits triggered and those not triggered at all, allowed us to improve our electronic questionnaire for future cycles.

Analysis of device and length of time to complete questionnaires on each device were done for several other surveys. Differences between types of devices were seen depending on the subject matter of the survey. For instance, a sound recording survey had a majority of respondents using Macintoshes to respond unlike most other surveys. Having the paradata by device and browser also helps surveys to identify what devices should be used for future questionnaire testing, for instance smart televisions or gaming devices. It is also important to consider the type of device used in the design of a survey: respondents for some surveys were slower on tablets and smart phones than those that used desk tops, while for other surveys the opposite was found.

The Census of Agriculture, through using paradata, was able to determine which farm types took longer to fill questionnaires, and also which pages caused the most edits. The information on help page use and time on page, and in particular which help pages were rarely used, can be used in future censuses to improve question clarity and potential implications of question concepts. The Agriculture Frame Update Survey used paradata to look at how length of time would be lengthened for the Census of Agriculture if a section was added as well as looking at pages where respondents frequently abandoned the questionnaire. This information led to a better understanding of which questions are either seen as too difficult or too intrusive by respondents.

Several surveys in Statistics Canada's Integrated Business Survey Platform (IBSP, see Jones and O'Byrne 2023 [Chapter 8]) had their electronic questionnaire paradata analyzed. As mentioned above, one key point of interest was the device type used for different surveys. For some surveys, there were also differences in response times for French versus English. All surveys found that most of their questionnaires were completed in a single session, while several respondents took more than one. For business surveys in particular, this may be due to the fact that data need to be collected from various sources, and multiple people may be involved in this process (see Chapters 15 (Haraldsen 2023), and 16 (Snijkers et al. 2023) for a discussion on the business response process). Most respondents also took one of a few standard routes through each survey questionnaire. It was found, however, that a small group of respondents took extremely long paths through the questionnaire, restarting the questionnaire and revisiting pages tens of times. Understanding the reasons for these paths will be helpful in improving questionnaire design. A Research and Development Survey has concentrated particularly on new respondents' paths to evaluate which questions were causing the most problems and questionnaire exits for respondents unfamiliar with the survey.

Studies were also done for these surveys to evaluate the effectiveness of reminder letters. As expected, all surveys using reminder strategies saw increases in returns in the days closely following a reminder. The questionnaire completion paradata, however, showed that even for questionnaires that were not returned shortly after a reminder, there was an uptick in activity in the questionnaire. This indicated that these reminders still had an effect on the response behavior, even though this was not visible in the response rates.

Real-time data-collection monitoring using paradata was undertaken at Statistics Canada in 2017 for the JVWS. This included looking at partial respondents, those who had not completed the questionnaire during the current cycle and respondents who had never entered the electronic questionnaire. A list of priority respondents was identified using key variables such as business size and economic region, and sent to subject matter staff to follow up. The aim was to convert these businesses into respondents before the collection cycle ended. Unfortunately, no follow-up was done due to other priorities in the collection process.

Real-time analysis was also done on the Annual Survey of Research and Development in Canadian Industry in 2020 and 2021. This questionnaire was sent out to over 8,600 Canadian companies. In order to increase the response rates, key respondents were identified based on business characteristics, such as industry, revenue size and employment size. E-mails were sent out to 104 large nonresponding companies, which had little or no paradata activity in the electronic questionnaire, with the hope that many would complete the questionnaire. Two companies called in their answers and were entered by the Collection, Planning, and Research Division, while 16 responded with completed questionnaires. This resulted in a response rate of 17% for these key respondents. Based on these results, this will be done in future cycles in order to improve response rates for large companies and key components in selected tables.

A final interesting project that has begun with the IBSP surveys is to predict which respondents need follow up and which would likely complete the questionnaire without further interventions.

This would save resources for other respondents and potentially reduce costs. Two different studies have taken place both using modeling with paradata variables, such as number of calls received, total call time and number of problem status codes both in the current and previous year; questionnaire type (short or long) and questionnaire number; time spent both in total and on key pages in the questionnaire, the last day of access and the maximum page accessed, as well as estimated business revenue. The first study tested a range of machine learning methods and had success with random forests at predicting which respondents would respond by a certain date. A second study used survival analysis and principal component analysis to model response propensity. Work continues with these studies to better direct respondent interventions.

18.5 Conclusions

In this chapter, we have discussed paradata in general, and questionnaire completion paradata in detail. Paradata are process data: event log data with one event in each record. These paradata can be collected for every step in the survey process, automatically or manually. We have seen how paradata can be used to monitor, manage, and analyze the business survey data collection process. In addition, we have seen how paradata can be used to study other processes in the production of business statistics. We have also seen examples of how questionnaire completion paradata can be used to monitor the completion process of electronic questionnaires and evaluate the design. In addition, these paradata were shown to be useful in the evaluation of the survey communication strategy. By studying these paradata, we get a better understanding of the completion behavior of respondents. These paradata tell us what we do not know about the design: they can help survey designers to make better, fact-based design decisions, and to improve survey efficiency.

Paradata can be used in real-time monitoring of the data collection, and in post-field analysis to study whether the questionnaire is completed as intended, and identify issues in the completion process. Next, the design can be improved. Paradata identify the issues, but cannot explain why the issue occurred. To get a better understanding of what is actually happening, combining the paradata with the survey data, background characteristics of the survey units, and a follow-up debriefing study with companies about the completion process would be needed.

When preparing for using paradata, the following two steps need to be taken into account:

1. Before collecting and analyzing the paradata, start with specifying your research questions: think about the kind of analysis you would like to do (according to your research questions), and define the paradata accordingly. This specification process is very similar to the specification of survey data (see Figure 16.1 in Chapter 16, Snijkers et al. 2023). Your questionnaire (or in general, your system) needs to facilitate the collection and storing of these paradata (Callegaro (2013) discusses software to collect paradata). Paradata files can become huge in size.
2. Once the raw paradata have been collected, data inspection and cleaning are required in order to get a clean data file that can be analyzed. Again, this is similar to the survey process itself. Analysis tools that can be used are SPSS and Disco (for process mining, van der Aalst 2016, Fluxicon 2020) (as used at CBS), SAS and R (used by Statcan), and Google Analytics (UK ONS).

From the results from the CBS and StatCan studies as well as the UK study (in Section 18.4), we can conclude that completing a questionnaire is not a linear process, and can be quite complex (see Snijkers et al. 2023 [Chapter 16]; Demedash and Buckley 2016). The paradata analysis showed where the questionnaire design can be improved. Facilitating the completion process with an adequate questionnaire design, and monitoring the completion progress can be very helpful to respondents and help agencies to receive more and better quality data from respondents. Note that actions taken off-line are not included in the paradata. So, businesses may work with the questionnaire, without these actions being registered. This means that the results should be reconsidered carefully.

Statistics Canada has been using paradata for business surveys since 2015, as we explained in Section 18.4.2. Paradata have become an integrated part of their survey monitoring methodology: Statistics Canada considers paradata as equally important as survey data. They are particularly useful when combined with survey data and business information to help understand respondent behavior and to identify nonrespondents and partial nonrespondents. Incorporating paradata during post-collection analysis allows survey questions to be improved, and testing of different devices and browsers for the next cycle to be expanded. Analyzing the frequency of help pages accessed enabled question clarity to be improved either by changing the question or adding more information on the questionnaire page thus reducing response burden. Real-time analysis plays an important role in increasing response rates through directly contacting nonrespondents, which could then improve the survey's estimates. Overall, paradata should be used in conjunction with survey data to produce a richer analysis.

We encourage designers and practitioners in business surveys to use paradata in real-time fieldwork monitoring and post-field analysis to evaluate the questionnaire. From the examples discussed in this chapter, it should be clear that these data provide a rich source of information, and can help surveyors to do a better job, i.e. to minimize errors in each step of the survey, and to make better (fact-based) design decisions (Groves et al. 2004/2009, Snijkers 2016). In addition, as Couper suggests (2008), paradata analysis can generate theories and suggest hypotheses for questionnaire testing and respondent de-briefing, identifying issues to focus on in next survey cycles (Willimack et al. 2023 [Chapter 17]; Bavdaž et al. 2019), thus combining quantitative and qualitive methods. Finally, these studies would add to business survey methodology in general: they establish insights in how business survey processes are carried out and could be better tailored to the respondent's completion process, in order to improve data quality and producer as well as respondent cost-efficiency.

Acknowledgment

From Statistics Netherlands, we would like to thank Nika Trilsbeek (intern) who has analyzed the paradata, as well as Michelle Creemers, Casper Hueting, Margreet Geurden-Slis, and Jan van den Brakel for their assistance. The electronic questionnaire was developed by Revolux S.àR.L.®, a software house, located in Luxembourg, that specializes in the development of data collection instruments.

From Statistics Canada, we would like to thank Matthew Buckley, Paul Hunsberger, Joshua Gutoskie, Paul Gilchrist, Ivelina Delahousse, Guillaume Gazil, Nancy Wu, and Loïc Muhirwa for their work on paradata.

We would like to thank Gustav Haraldsen (Statistics Norway) for contributing to this chapter by sharing the data collection control panel (Figure 18.1) with us.

The authors are grateful to Mojca Bavdaž (University of Ljubljana, Slovenia) and Reinoud Stoel (Statistics Netherlands) for reviewing the manuscript.

Disclaimer

The views expressed in this paper are those of the authors and do not necessarily reflect the policies of Statistics Netherlands nor Statistics Canada.

References

Bavdaž, M., Giesen, D., Moore, D.L., Smith, P.A., and Jones, J. (2019). Qualitative testing for official establishment survey questionnaires. *Survey Research Methods* 13 (3): 257–288. https://doi.org/10.18148/srm/2019.v13i3.7366.

Beatty, P.C., Collins, D., Kaye, L., Padilla, J.-L., Willis, G.B., and Wilmot, A. (ed.) (2020). *Advances in Questionnaire Design, Development, Evaluation and Testing*. Hoboken: Wiley.

Biemer, P.P. (2010). Overview of design issues: total survey error. In: *Handbook of Survey Research*, 2nd edition (ed. P.V. Marsden and J.D. Wright), 27–57. Bingley, UK: Emerald Group Publishing Limited.

Callegaro, M. (2013). Paradata in web surveys. In: *Improving Surveys with Paradata: Analytic Uses of Process Information* (ed. F. Kreuter), 261–279. Hoboken: Wiley.

Couper, M. (2008). *Designing Effective Web Surveys*. Cambridge, UK: Cambridge University Press.

Demedash, S. and Buckley, M. (2016). Job vacancy and wage survey paradata log files: a new realm of respondent behavioural analysis. In: *Proceedings of the Survey Methods Section, SSC Annual Meeting, June 2016*. Statistical Society of Canada.

Fluxicon (2020). Process Mining in Practice. https://fluxicon.com/book/read/ (accessed 26 August 2021).

Groves, R.M., Fowler, F.J. Jr., Couper, M.P., Lepkowski, J.M., Singer, E., and Tourangeau, R. (2004/2009). *Survey Methodology*. Hoboken: Wiley.

Haraldsen, G. (2013a). Questionnaire communication in business surveys. In: *Designing and Conducting Business Surveys* (ed. G. Snijkers, G. Haraldsen, J. Jones and D.K. Willimack), 303–357. Hoboken: Wiley.

Haraldsen, G. (2013b). Quality issues in business surveys. In: *Designing and Conducting Business Surveys* (ed. G. Snijkers, G. Haraldsen, J. Jones and D.K. Willimack), 83–125. Hoboken: Wiley.

Haraldsen, G. (2018). Response processes and response quality in business surveys. In: *The Unit Problem and Other Current Topics in Business Survey Methodology* (ed. B. Lorenc, P.A. Smith, M. Bavdaž, G. Haraldsen, D. Nedyalkova, L.-Ch. Zhang, and Th. Zimmerman), 157–177. Newcastle upon Tyne, UK: Cambridge Scholars Publishing.

Haraldsen, G. (2023). What computerized business questionnaires and questionnaire management tools can offer. In: *Advances in Business Statistics, Methods and Data Collection*, Chapter 15 (ed. G. Snijkers, M. Bavdaž, S. Bender, J. Jones, S. MacFeely, J.W. Sakshaug, K.J. Thompson, and A. van Delden). Hoboken: Wiley.

Haraldsen, G. and Stavnes, E.D. (2021). Control panel for self-administered data collections in Altinn (in Norwegian: Styringspanel for selvadministrerte datainnsamlinger i Altinn). Unpublished paper, Statistics Norway.

Heerwegh, D. (2011). Internet survey paradata. In: *Social and Behavioral Research and the Internet: Advances in Applied Methods and Research Strategies* (ed. M. Das, P. Ester and L. Kaczmirek), 325–348. New York: Routledge.

Jones, J. and O'Byrne, H. (2023). Statistical producers challenges and help. In: *Advances in Business Statistics, Methods and Data Collection*, Chapter 8 (ed. G. Snijkers, M. Bavdaž, S. Bender, J. Jones, S. MacFeely, J.W. Sakshaug, K.J. Thompson, and A. van Delden). Hoboken: Wiley.

Jones, J., Snijkers, G., and Haraldsen, G. (2013). Surveys and business surveys. In: *Designing and Conducting Business Surveys* (ed. G. Snijkers, G. Haraldsen, J. Jones and D.K. Willimack), 1–38. Hoboken: Wiley.

Kreuter, F. (2013). Improving surveys with paradata: introduction. In: *Improving Surveys with Paradata: Analytic Uses of Process Information* (ed. F. Kreuter), 1–9. Hoboken: Wiley.

Kreuter, F., and Casas-Cordero, C. (2010). Paradata, working paper 136. Working paper series of the German Council for Social and Economic Data, Berlin, Germany. www.ratswd.de/en.

Kreuter, F., Couper, M., and Lyberg, L. (2010). The use of paradata to monitor and manage survey data collection. *Proceedings of the Survey Research Methods Section: 282–296.* Joint Statistical Meetings, American Statistical Association.

Krosnick, J.A. and Presser, S. (2010). Questions and questionnaire design. In: *Handbook of Survey Research*, 2nd edition (ed. P.V. Marsden and J.D. Wright), 263–313. Bingley, UK: Emerald Group Publishing Limited.

Kunz, T. and Hadler, P. (2020). Web paradata in survey research. GESIS – Leibniz Institute for the Social Sciences (GESIS – Survey Guidelines). Mannheim, Germany. https://doi.org/10.15465/gesis-sg_037.

Laflamme, F. (2008). Data collection research using paradata at Statistics Canada. Paper presented at the 2008 International Statistics Canada Methodology Symposium: Data Collection: Challenges, Achievements and New Directions, Catalog 11-522-X, Statistics Canada, Ottawa (28–31 October).

Laflamme, F., Maydan, M., and Miller, A. (2008). Using paradata to actively manage data collection survey process. *Proceedings of the Survey Research Methods Section: 630–637.* Joint Statistical Meetings, Denver (3–7 August). American Statistical Association, Alexandria, VA.

Lammers, J. (2018). Improving the efficiency of enterprise profiling. In: *The Unit Problem and Other Current Topics in Business Survey Methodology* (ed. B. Lorenc, P.A. Smith, M. Bavdaž, G. Haraldsen, D. Nedyalkova, L.-Ch. Zhang, and Th. Zimmerman), 79–89. Newcastle upon Tyne, UK: Cambridge Scholars Publishing.

Lyberg, L. and Stukel, L.E. (2017). The roots and evolution of the total survey error concept. In: *Total Survey Error in Practice* (ed. P.P. Biemer, E. de Leeuw, S. Eckman, B. Edwards, F. Kreuter, L.E. Lyberg, N.C. Tucker, and B.T. West), 3–22. Hoboken: Wiley.

Snijkers, G. (2016). Achieving quality in organizational surveys: a holistic approach. In: *Methodische Probleme in der empirischen Organisationsforschung* (ed. S. Liebig and W. Matiaske), 33–59. Wiesbaden: Springer.

Snijkers, G. and Haraldsen, G. (2013). Managing the data collection. In: *Designing and Conducting Business Surveys* (ed. G. Snijkers, G. Haraldsen, J. Jones and D.K. Willimack), 431–457. Hoboken: Wiley.

Snijkers, G., Houben, L., and Demollin, F. (2023). Tailoring the design of a new combined business survey: process, methods, and lessons learned. In: *Advances in Business Statistics, Methods and Data Collection*, Chapter 16 (ed. G. Snijkers, M. Bavdaž, S. Bender, J. Jones, S. MacFeely, J.W. Sakshaug, K.J. Thompson, and A. van Delden). Hoboken: Wiley.

Snijkers, G. and Morren, M. (2010). Improving web and electronic questionnaires: the case of audit trails. Paper presented at the 5th European Conference on Quality in Official Statistics , Helsinki (4–5 May 2010). https://q2010.stat.fi/media//presentations/SnijkersMorren-Audit_trails_Q2010-paper-Session4_internet-v20100526_.pdf.

Snijkers, G., Morren, M., and Tries, S. (2012). Tailoring the design of web questionnaires to the completion process in business surveys: about audit trails, eye-tracking and other methods. Introductory Overview Lecture (IOL) at the 4th International Conference on Establishment Surveys (ICES-IV), Montreal, Canada (12–14 June 2012).

Smith, P. (2013). Sampling and estimation for business surveys. In: *Designing and Conducting Business Surveys* (ed. G. Snijkers, G. Haraldsen, J. Jones and D.K. Willimack), 165–218. Hoboken: Wiley.

Stewart, J., Sidney, I., and Timm, E. (2018). Paradata as an aide to questionnaire design. In: *The Unit Problem and Other Current Topics in Business Survey Methodology* (ed. B. Lorenc, P.A. Smith, M. Bavdaž, G. Haraldsen, D. Nedyalkova, L.-Ch. Zhang, and Th. Zimmerman), 177–197. Newcastle upon Tyne, UK: Cambridge Scholars Publishing. https://statswiki.unece.org/display/ENBES/EESW17+Programme.

Trilsbeek, N. (2020). Audit trails: a glance at the "unobservable" completion process of a business survey. Internship report, supervised by Snijkers, G., Geurden-Slis, M., and van den Brakel, J., Statistics Netherlands and Maastricht University, Heerlen/Maastricht.

van der Aalst, W. (2016). *Process Mining: Data Science in Action*, 2nd edition. Heidelberg: Springer-Verlag.

Volkert, M. (2022). How do respondents navigate an establishment survey questionnaire? Evidence from the IAB establishment panel. Paper presented at the 6th International Business Data Collection Methodology Workshop, Olso, Norway (13–15 June 2022).

Wagner, J. (2016). Responsive design and paradata: paradata-based quality indicators. Introductory Overview Lecture (IOL) at the 5th International Conference on Establishment Surveys (ICES-V), Geneva, Switzerland (21–23 June 2016).

Willimack, D.K. (2013). Methods for the development, testing and evaluation of data collection instruments. In: *Designing and Conducting Business Surveys* (ed. G. Snijkers, G. Haraldsen, J. Jones and D.K. Willimack), 253–301. Hoboken: Wiley.

Willimack, D.K., Ridolfo, H., Anderson Riemer, A., Cidade, M., and Ott, K. (2023). Advances in question(naire) development, pretesting, and evaluation. In: *Advances in Business Statistics, Methods and Data Collection*, Chapter 17 (ed. G. Snijkers, M. Bavdaž, S. Bender, J. Jones, S. MacFeely, J.W. Sakshaug, K.J. Thompson, and A. van Delden). Hoboken: Wiley.

Willimack, D.K. and Snijkers, G. (2013). The business context and its implications for the survey response process. In: *Designing and Conducting Business Surveys* (ed. G. Snijkers, G. Haraldsen, J. Jones and D.K. Willimack), 39–82. Hoboken, NJ: Wiley.

19

Recent Findings from Experiments in Establishment Surveys

Josh Langeland[1], Heather Ridolfo[2], Jaki McCarthy[3], Kathy Ott[3], Doug Kilburg[3], Karen CyBulski[4], Melissa Krakowiecki[4], Larry Vittoriano[4], Matt Potts[4], Benjamin Küfner[5], Joseph W. Sakshaug[5,6,7], and Stefan Zins[5]

[1] *U.S. Bureau of Labor Statistics, Washington, DC, USA*
[2] *U.S. Energy Information Administration, Washington, DC, USA*
[3] *U.S. National Agricultural Statistics Service, Washington, DC, USA*
[4] *Mathematica, Princeton, NJ, USA*
[5] *German Institute for Employment Research, Nuremberg, Germany*
[6] *Ludwig Maximilian University of Munich, Department of Statistics, Munich, Germany*
[7] *University of Mannheim, Department of Sociology, Mannheim, Germany*

19.1 Introduction

As survey methodologists continue to grapple with increasing survey costs and decreasing response rates, it becomes more important to monitor and improve the efficiency of current data collection procedures. Experiments are useful tools for evaluating survey methodologies since investigators can isolate the effect of interventions in well controlled experiments. Whether survey managers wish to include a new element of data collection (mode of contact, timing of contacts, questionnaire design, etc.) or would like to evaluate existing methodologies, controlled randomized experiments can be utilized to measure the impact of specific interventions. While a wide assortment of literature exists for experiments in household surveys, the results are not easily transferable to establishment surveys. There is generally a dearth of results for experiments in establishment surveys demonstrating a need for more empirical published research.

Establishments differ from households in numerous ways, and some of these differences may have substantial impacts on the design of experiments and generalizability of findings for these surveys (see Willimack and McCarthy 2019). Several authors expanded on Tourangeau's (1984) cognitive response process model to highlight differences between household surveys and surveys of establishments (Edwards and Cantor 2004; Sudman et al. 2000; Lorenc 2006; Willimack and Nichols 2010; Bavdaž 2010). The additional steps included in the response model for establishments include identification of the respondent (who within the company will have knowledge of the survey topic), assessment of priorities (standard duties are typically addressed prior to survey requests), retrieval of information from company records (is the respondent able to easily access and compile the information being requested), and release of the data (does the respondent have the authority to release the data?). These additional steps often affect the response processes leading to different results for similar experiments in establishment surveys compared to household surveys. Given the unique response process of establishment surveys, it is important to maintain

Advances in Business Statistics, Methods and Data Collection. Edited by Ger Snijkers, Mojca Bavdaž, Stefan Bender, Jacqui Jones, Steve MacFeely, Joseph W. Sakshaug, Katherine J. Thompson, and Arnout van Delden.

a literature of empirical findings from well-designed experiments in establishment surveys. This chapter presents research from four different survey organizations. We will show how key features of establishments affected the design of experiments and the importance of establishment specific research findings (rather than adopting research from household surveys).

This chapter is structured as follows: in Section 19.2, we review a pair of experiments that examined the effects of mailed survey materials on cooperation rates in an establishment computer-assisted telephone interview (CATI) survey conducted by the US Bureau of Labor Statistics (BLS). The first experiment tested the effects of an advance letter and the second experiment examined the usefulness of mailing an information folder. Section 19.3 presents three experiments designed to examine efficiencies in data collection. The United States Department of Agriculture (USDA) National Agricultural Statistics Service (NASS) experimented with different techniques to increase response to subsets of the population for the US Census of Agriculture. The first experiment varied timing and types of contacts, the second experiment examined the effect of tailored messaging and alternative data collection materials on farms that are likely to respond online, and the third tested targeted communications for potential farms. Section 19.4 reviews an experiment that compared nonresponse follow-up sent via US Postal Service and FedEx in a survey of mental health and substance abuse institutions conducted by the US Substance Abuse & Mental Health Services Administration (SAMHSA). Section 19.5 provides an overview of an experiment that altered the level of detail of questionnaire instructions and the impact on item nonresponse in the IAB Job Vacancy Survey (IAB-JVS) conducted by the Institute for Employment Research in Germany. We conclude in Section 19.6 with a summary and discuss how issues specific to establishments impacted these experiments.

Each experiment presented begins by providing the background and motivation for the underlying experiment. The design of the experiment is then described, followed by the presentation of results. Finally, the discussion summarizes the experiment and highlights lessons learned.

19.2 Experiments with Mailed Survey Packets to Improve Recruitment Strategies in a National Establishment Survey (BLS)

19.2.1 Motivation

The US BLS Current Employment Statistics (CES)[1] program is a voluntary monthly panel survey where establishments report data on employment, hours, and earnings of workers. Each month, approximately 5800 new units are sampled and go through an onboarding process called enrollment that consists of the following steps:

1. *Address refinement and respondent identification*: Interviewers use a variety of techniques to update the respondent contact information or identify the correct person (e.g. someone in HR) within the sampled establishment to provide the survey response. Common techniques include calling the establishment and a review of the company's website for contact information.
2. *Send enrollment packet*: After identifying the appropriate respondent in the address refinement step, interviewers then send an enrollment packet through postal mail. The enrollment packet consists of a folder containing an introduction letter and the survey form.

---

1 See https://www.bls.gov/opub/hom/pdf/ces-20110307.pdf for more details on the Current Employment Statistics program.

Table 19.1 Intervention timeline.

Contact method	Time of month
Intervention 1: advance letter	Beginning of panel
Address refinement	Week 1
Send enrollment packet	Week 2–4
Intervention 2: folder type	
Enroll respondent	Week 2–4

3. *Enrollment of respondents*: A few days after sending the enrollment packet, interviewers will begin calling the identified respondents to gain cooperation. Once contacted, the interviewer will introduce themselves, explain the purpose of the survey and answer any questions the respondent may have. At that point, the interviewer may collect data for the current month or schedule a time to call and collect the data.

The BLS conducted a series of experiments intended to determine the effectiveness of various interventions on CES enrollment rates. Enrollment rates refer to the proportion of businesses agreeing to be a part of the survey which are measured in proxy by successful data collection. The first experiment evaluates the impact of an advance letter sent to establishments prior to address refinement (Step 1). Advance letters are used to provide establishments with a positive, timely notification of the upcoming survey request (Lavrakas 2008) and can increase the perceived legitimacy of the survey request. Under these considerations, it was hypothesized that the use of an advance letter may increase enrollment rates and reduce CATI interviewer effort to contact establishments.

The second experiment tests the effect of various folder designs sent with the enrollment package (Step 2). Sending the survey form in a folder is hypothesized to increase the saliency of the survey request; a large envelope is required and will stand out from regular postal mail. Furthermore, if a respondent keeps the folder on her desk, it may remind her of the survey request and encourage response. Table 19.1 shows the data collection process and the point during enrollment when the two interventions occur. The following sections highlight the methods and results of the two experiments.

19.2.2 Advance Letter Study

19.2.2.1 Experiment Design

A subset of businesses sampled for the August, September, and October 2019 panels were randomized into one of three treatment conditions while controlling for establishment size (six size classes based on number of employees) and industry type (based on two-digit North American Industrial Classification System [NAICS]). The treatments varied whether an establishment received an advance letter prior to attempting address refinement or not (No advance letter). The sender for the letter was also randomized as coming from the national office in Washington, DC (DC) or a regional collection office in Kansas City, Missouri (KC). The enrollment patterns for the treatments were tracked across the three panels from August 2019 through December 2019. The sample sizes added each month for the three treatments are listed in Table 19.2.

Table 19.2 Advance letter sample sizes.

Treatment	No advance letter	Advance letter – DC	Advance letter – KC
August (Panel 1) n	483	476	484
September (Panel 2) n	438	431	435
October (Panel 3) n	467	471	454

19.2.2.2 Results

The enrollment rates were captured for the treatment groups every month from August through December 2019. Final response disposition codes were mapped into one of two codes: successfully enrolled and not enrolled. Enrollment rates were then calculated as the number of successfully enrolled units divided by the total number of units in the experiment. Results are presented for each month in Table 19.3. October was the first month that all three panels were in the experiment. At this point, units in Panel 1 are in their third month of being contacted; units in Panel 2 are in their second month of being contacted; and units in Panel 3 are being contacted for their first time. During October, the KC group achieved a response rate of 65.9%. The no advance letter group was slightly lower at 65.3%, and the DC group was lowest at 63.0%. A Chi-square test fails to detect a statistically significant difference in the enrollment rates ($\chi^2_2 = 2.902$, $p = 0.23$) between the three treatment groups. The enrollment rates for the other months are also shown in Table 19.3, and the enrollment rates do not vary significantly across the treatment groups for any month. Since we would expect the advance letter to have a diminishing effect as time elapses, the enrollment rates for October are presented in Table 19.3 by treatment and further broken out by panel. If we want to see the effect on units that are being contacted for the first time and would have just received the advance letter, we must look at enrollment rates for August units (only units from Panel 1) and October units Panel 3. The Chi-square tests fail to find any significant difference for enrollment rates between the treatment groups for these units. If the effect was not seen in the first month, we don't expect to see it in later months.

The results in Table 19.3 suggest that an advance letter did not increase survey cooperation from establishments. While the enrollment rates fail to provide evidence that an advance letter increases survey cooperation, they do not provide any information on the interviewers' effort to successfully enroll a unit. If a respondent is aware of an upcoming survey request, there may be

Table 19.3 Advance letter enrollment rates (ER) by treatment.

Months	No advance letter		Advance letter – DC		Advance letter – KC		ChiSq	Pr > ChiSq
	n	ER (%)	n	ER (%)	n	ER (%)		
August	483	66.5	476	64.1	484	64.0	0.810	0.6669
September	921	67.0	907	63.1	919	64.4	3.197	0.2022
October	1388	65.3	1378	63.0	1373	65.9	2.902	0.2344
October Panel 1	483	72.0	476	67.9	484	69.0	2.134	0.3441
October Panel 2	438	67.8	431	65.9	435	71.2	2.968	0.2267
October Panel 3	467	56.1	471	55.4	454	57.5	0.418	0.8113
November	1388	69.3	1378	68.0	1373	69.4	0.799	0.6707
December	1388	70.2	1378	68.1	1373	69.0	1.539	0.4633

fewer calls required to reach them. To test if there was a difference in the distribution of number of calls (interviewer effort) among the treatment groups, an ANOVA test was performed for each month units were introduced into the sample (August – only Panel 1 units; September – only Panel 2 units; October – only Panel 3 units). The respective p-values for the ANOVA tests are $p = 0.7575$, $p = 0.4226$, and $p = 0.2744$, indicating there is no significant difference in the distribution of number of calls required to gain successful enrollment between the treatment groups.

19.2.3 Folder Design Study

19.2.3.1 Experiment Design
Following the advance letter experiment, BLS experimented with CES survey materials mailed to respondents after contact is made with the establishment and an appropriate contact is identified (see step 2). A subset of businesses sampled for the November 2019 (Panel 4), December (Panel 5), and January 2020 (Panel 6) panels were randomized into one of three treatment groups. The treatments were being mailed the current folder (Old, see Figure 19.1), being mailed the updated folder (New, see Figure 19.2), or having the survey materials mailed in an envelope (No Folder). The sample size added each month for the three treatments are presented in Table 19.4.

19.2.3.2 Results
The enrollment rates for the three treatment groups were captured every month from November 2019 through March 2020. Units were mapped into one of two disposition codes: successfully enrolled or not enrolled. The enrollment rates were then calculated as the number of successfully enrolled units divided by the number of units in the experiment. Successful enrollment is measured in proxy by successful data collection. Results are presented for each month in Table 19.5. January was the first month when all three panels were in the experiment. At this point, Panel 4 has been in the experiment three months, Panel 5 has been in the experiment two months, and Panel 6 is just

Figure 19.1 Old Folder. Source: American Statistical Association.

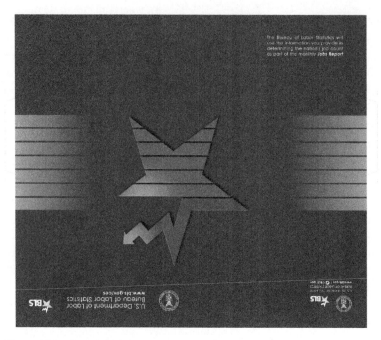

Figure 19.2 New Folder. Source: American Statistical Association.

Table 19.4 Folder design sample sizes.

Treatment	No folder	New folder	Old folder
November (Panel 4) n	516	513	516
December (Panel 5) n	437	443	452
January (Panel 6) n	369	375	371

Table 19.5 Folder design enrollment rates (ER) by treatment.

Months	No folder		New folder		Old folder		ChiSq	Pr > ChiSq
	n	ER (%)	n	ER (%)	n	ER (%)		
November	516	67.1	513	63.4	516	62.2	2.879	0.2370
December	953	62.2	956	60.4	968	59.6	1.460	0.4819
January	1322	67.8	1331	66.0	1,339	66.2	1.027	0.5983
January Panel 4	516	70.9	513	70.0	516	70.3	0.113	0.9449
January Panel 5	437	69.6	443	69.8	452	65.9	1.925	0.3819
January Panel 6	369	61.2	375	56.0	371	60.9	2.672	0.2629
February	1322	70.7	1331	69.5	1,339	70.4	0.565	0.7539
March	1322	65.9	1331	65.1	1,339	66.2	0.228	0.8921

being introduced into the experiment. Since the use of a folder may influence enrollment propensity beyond the first month (e.g. if the respondent leaves the folder on her desk, it may remind her to respond to the survey), the enrollment rates for January are further broken out by panel. Examining the table, we find that neither the use of a folder, nor the design of a folder, has a significant impact on enrollment rates. Whether it be a unit's first month in sample (November and January Panel 6) or if a unit has been in the sample for several months (February and March), the use or design of the folder fails to find a significant impact on enrollment.

While the use of a folder does not appear to impact enrollment propensity, it may reduce the workload for interviewers attempting to enroll units. To determine if the folder decreases workload, we use a Wilcoxon rank-sum test to determine if there is a difference in the distributions of the number of calls placed to successfully enroll a unit. Since a folder may influence enrollment propensity extending past the first month a unit was contacted, the p-values for three ANOVA tests are provided: November (Panel 4 units), December (Panel 4 and 5 units), and January (Panel 4, 5, and 6 units). The respective p-values are the following: $p = 0.4479$, $p = 0.4833$, and $p = 0.9227$. The results of the ANOVA test fail to determine a significant difference in the distribution of number of calls required to enroll units. Thus, it is unlikely that folders have an impact on interviewer effort.

19.2.4 Discussion

The results from the advance letter experiment and the folder experiment were counter to what was hypothesized. In both studies, it is not clear why no effect was found in enrollment rates with the treatments. In studies of households, an advance letter may have a higher chance of reaching the person answering the telephone than it would in an establishment setting. If the advance letter is sent to the frame address of an establishment, there is little guarantee the employee receiving the letter will be the same employee answering the phone, especially as establishment size increases.

The results of the folder experiment also ran contrary to expectations. It was hypothesized that the delivery of a large piece of mail would catch the eye of a respondent and increase the saliency of the survey. It was also thought the folder would have a beneficial impact on enrollment as time elapses by acting as a constant reminder of the survey request. Since we did not find any effect on enrollment rates for either the use of a folder or folder design, it is possible that respondents paid little attention to the folder. Instead of keeping it on their desk or on a shelf, they may have viewed it as junk mail and immediately discarded it.

The results highlight the importance of conducting experiments during data collection. Both the advance letter and the folder cost money to print, package, and post. Results from the experiment suggest that we can eliminate both the advance letter and folder without harming enrollment rates and saving money while doing so. Future qualitative studies would be welcomed to understand why the advance letter and folder had no impact on enrollment rates.

19.3 Experiments Testing Changes to Data Collection Timing and Content of Contacts in the US Census of Agriculture (NASS)

19.3.1 Motivation

The Census of Agriculture (COA[2]) the leading source of information on US farms and ranches. The COA provides a complete count of US farms and ranches and the people who operate them. Taken once every five years, the COA measures land use and ownership, agricultural production,

---

2 For additional details about the COA, see https://www.nass.usda.gov/AgCensus/index.php

operator characteristics, production practices, income, and expenditures. The COA population frame contains over three million units, which consist of known farms and potential farms (i.e. operations). This frame is maintained by NASS and potential farms are added from numerous outside list sources. Information about individual units is updated based on responses to an initial screening survey or other ongoing NASS survey contacts. A unit is defined as a farm if they raised or sold, or normally would have sold, US$ 1000 or more of agricultural products during the Census year. Potential farms are units that may be farms but have never responded to the NASS screening survey. Under the definition of a farm, small production units – whether rural or urban – are considered a farm; however, these units may not consider themselves to be "farming." Traditionally, all units are mailed a paper questionnaire with the option of web response. Nonresponse follow-up is conducted via paper, telephone, and in-person visits. A major challenge is getting these three million units to respond in a timely manner, while minimizing costs.

Prior to each COA, NASS makes changes to the content and data collection procedures based on review of prior censuses, emerging technologies, changing trends in agriculture, agricultural data, and stakeholder feedback. These changes are evaluated using a multimethod approach, which includes data and paradata analyses, cognitive testing, usability testing, and field tests (McCarthy et al. 2018). In 2021, NASS conducted the 2020 Content Test (collecting data for the 2020 reference year), a large-scale field test that served as a dry run for the 2022 COA. The 2020 Content Test followed the same general data collection procedures and timeline as the actual COA and provided an opportunity to test new materials and implement experiments on data collection strategies, which otherwise may be more difficult to conduct in a production setting. The overall sample size of the 2020 Content Test was approximately 36,000. Unlike the 2022 COA, participation in this Content Test was voluntary. Nonresponse follow-up was conducted via CATI for the several of the groups, CATI responses are not included in these analyses because the focus was on increasing mail and web returns.

In this chapter, we focus on three experiments embedded in the 2020 Content Test designed to test new data collection strategies intended to increase response, expedite the response process, and lower costs. In all experiments, the control group followed similar procedures used in the 2017 COA. Each experiment is described in more detail below.

Data for these analyses include records received as of 17 April 2021. Although data collection efforts ended on 17 April, a small number of forms could have been returned after that date, but are not included in these analyses. Some operational systems were not in place for this test, so response rates and out-of-scope status were calculated using the available information and may differ slightly from how they will be calculated in the 2022 COA.

Several factors were considered when creating the universes and samples for these experiments. The universe and subsequent samples included farms covering all farm types and sizes across all geographic areas of the United States. There were several production surveys in the field in the few months before and the first months after this Content Test was fielded. Operations that were in a selected list of such surveys were excluded from the universe. Also, after sampling, regional field offices reviewed the sample and removed any operations that they had special data collection plans with or wanted removed from this survey for other practical data collection reasons. After sorting the universe on state, county, farm type (such as cattle, grains and oilseeds, hogs and pigs), farm value of sales, and total land (continuous variables), three thousand farms and ranches were randomly selected and assigned to each group.

The sample for each treatment and control group was 3000. However, the final N used for each group was slightly lower than 3000 due to mailings returned by the US Postal Service as undeliverable, or individual operations removed from the mailout at the request of NASS field office staff.

Costs and the average days to an in-scope response are shown for each experimental group. The costs include outgoing and return postage, printing, paper/envelopes, and paper processing costs, and an average cost for helpline calls. Statistical testing was not conducted for the average number of days or the costs.

Response rates were calculated by dividing responses (partial and completes) by the number of mailed invitations minus undeliverable as addressed (UAA) returns. For all rates, statistical comparisons were done on the proportions between the experimental group and the control group. The tests were completed using the "N−1" Chi-squared test of independence.

Experiment 1   Alternative Data Collection Materials, Timing, and Procedures

Survey Design

The objective of this test was to improve the overall response rate and percent completed online, obtain responses more quickly and reduce costs. This experiment consisted of four treatment groups and a control group (see Table 19.6). The control group used procedures similar to past COAs. There were five mailings; a web invitation letter, questionnaire package, a pressure sealed web reminder, a second questionnaire package, and a third questionnaire package.

The first treatment included a compressed time between mailings and an emphasis on the COA deadline. For this group, there were five mailings: a web invitation letter, questionnaire package, a pressure sealed web reminder, a second questionnaire package, and a second pressure sealed web reminder.

We theorized that moving mailings closer together in time and making explicit reference to the deadline would increase the salience of COA response for respondents. Similar changes to the schedule have been tested and proven successful by the US Census Bureau for the Economic Census (Tuttle et al. 2018). Initial mailings were intended to push respondents to web response. The schedule and content of the follow-up mailings emphasized that the deadline for responding was approaching, followed by messages that the deadline had been extended, or response was overdue. We expected costs per response to be lowered if the number of responses was increased or if they were received from less-expensive mailings (i.e. those without questionnaires), or were received earlier so later mailings could be reduced.

The second treatment included a change in content and format of the traditional mailings, replacing many of the words in the mailings with infographics highlighting data from the previous COA. We wanted to reduce the cognitive burden with word count reduction and increase motivation by influencing perception of COA usefulness. Experiments conducted in the context of a European project BLUE-ETS showed that it is challenging to impact response behavior with data offerings as data users and respondents are often different people (Giesen 2013). For this group, there were five mailings: a web invitation letter, questionnaire package, a pressure sealed web reminder, a second questionnaire package, and a second pressure sealed web reminder.

The third treatment group replaced all but one questionnaire mailings with web push mailings. For this group, there were five mailings: a web invitation letter, questionnaire package, a pressure sealed web reminder, a web reminder letter, and a second pressure sealed web reminder. The intent of this treatment was to test the impact of replacing some expensive questionnaire package mailings with less-expensive survey invitations on response.

Table 19.6 Experiment 1 treatment groups.

Date	Control group	T1 – changes to timing and emphasis on deadline	T2 – changes to format to reduce words and include COA data	T3 – some questionnaires replaced with web push invitations	T4 – eliminated final mailing, early CATI calling
1 December 2020	Web invitation letter (in envelope)	Web invitation letter (in envelope)	Web invitation letter (in envelope)	Web invitation letter (in envelope)	Web invitation letter (in envelope)
4 January 2021	Questionnaire package	Questionnaire package	Questionnaire package	Questionnaire package	Questionnaire package
25 January 2021	Standard pressure sealed web reminder	"Deadline Approaching" reminder web reminder	Redesigned pressure sealed web reminder	Standard pressure sealed web reminder	Standard pressure sealed web reminder
5 February 2021		"Deadline Extended" Questionnaire package			
12 February 2021		"Response Overdue" web reminder			
16 February 2021	Standard questionnaire package		Redesigned questionnaire package	Web reminder letter (in envelope)	Standard questionnaire package
12 March 2021	Standard questionnaire package		Redesigned questionnaire package	Pressure sealed web reminder	

The fourth treatment group used the same materials as the control group but had a reduction in questionnaire mailings. For this group, there were four mailings: a web invitation letter, questionnaire package, a pressure sealed web reminder, and a second questionnaire package. The last questionnaire mailing was eliminated and CATI calling began earlier.

This experiment had some additional factors considered for the universe and sample. Some questionnaire changes impacted specific commodities such as raspberries, hemp, and mink. These commodities are too rare to have enough operations in sample to report them, so operations with control data for these commodities had a higher chance of selection for the test.

Results

Overall response rates and response rates by mode are shown in Table 19.7 for the control and each treatment group. Responses include in-scope and out-of-scope returns. Nonresponse was significantly reduced in the first treatment group with a compressed schedule and emphasis on the deadline. In contrast, in treatments 3 and 4, where questionnaire mailings were replaced with less-expensive mailings with instructions for responding online, and where the last mailing was eliminated, nonresponse was significantly higher. Treatment 2, which reduced text and included examples of data from past COAs, was not significantly different from the control group.

The average number of days from initial mailout and costs per sample are included in Table 19.7. The average number of days and the cost were not statistically tested.

Experiment 1 Discussion

This experiment showed that simply reducing questionnaire mailings or changing their format by replacing words with graphics did not help increase response. However, more responses were gained when more explicit references to the deadline were included in mailings, even when the schedule was shortened and one less questionnaire packet was used. Costs per sample were also lower for this treatment over the control (no statistical testing conducted).

Table 19.7 Experiment 1 response rates by mode, cost, and average days between mailout and response.

	Control	T1 (compressed schedule, emphasis on deadline)	T2 (reduce words, use of COA data as graphics)	T3 (some questionnaires replaced with web push invitations)	T4 (eliminate last mailing, start CATI calling earlier)
Mail response	996 (34.4%)	948 (32.8%)	975 (33.6%)	696 (24.1%)***	832 (28.6%)***
Web response	579 (20.0%)	692 (23.9%)**	567 (19.6%)	669 (23.1%)**	604 (20.8%)
Helpline response	15 (0.5%)	24 (0.8%)	12 (0.4%)	16 (0.6%)	17 (0.6%)
Nonresponse	1306 (45.1%)	1230 (42.5%)**	1346 (46.4%)	1512 (52.3%)***	1455 (50.0%)**
N	2896	2894	2900	2893	2908
Cost per response	US$ 14.12	US$ 12.69	US$ 14.94	US$ 11.77	US$ 12.79
Cost per sample	US$ 7.52	US$ 7.07	US$ 7.79	US$ 5.44	US$ 6.22
Average days for in-scope response	57	52	56	51	54

Note: ***p-value < 0.001 **p-value = <0.05. Statistical testing not done for cost per response, cost per sample and average days to in-scope response.

Experiment 2   Test of Alternative Procedures for Operations Identified as Likely to Complete Online

Survey Design

The objective of this test was to increase web response and reduce cost by tailoring procedures for operations we hypothesized would be more likely to complete the COA online. Operations that were identified on the NASS list frame as having Internet access were targeted for this experiment. Approximately six thousand operations were selected and randomly assigned to the control and treatment groups. The treatment group did not receive questionnaires. The instructions for reporting online in the web push letters were the same as the control group except for the statement that a questionnaire would be mailed in a later mailing was replaced with a statement that said the respondent may call and request a paper questionnaire (see Table 19.8 for more details).

Results

Overall response rates and response rates by mode are shown in Table 19.9 for the control and treatment group. The treatment group, which did not include questionnaires in the mailings, prompted more online responses, but had a significantly lower overall response rate.

The average number of days from initial mailout and costs per sample are shown in Table 19.9. Costs for the treatment group were lower since almost all responses were on the web (no statistical testing was conducted for the costs or the average days to respond).

Experiment 2 Discussion

Our attempt to push likely online responders to web response by eliminating mailed paper questionnaires did not appear to be successful. While online responses were increased, this was at the expense of the overall response rate. This experiment demonstrated that our criteria for "likely to respond online" (i.e. mere Internet access) was not very effective. Although the control group reported more often online than operations in our first experiment, they were still more likely to respond by mail than online. The type of treatment tested here might be more effective if other criteria such as prior online response or stated willingness to complete online was used to target operations.

Table 19.8   Experiment 2 treatment groups.

Date	Control group	Treatment group (online response requested, no questionnaires mailed)
1 December 2020	Web push invitation; no mailed questionnaire	Web push invitation with new language (in envelope); no mailed questionnaire
4 January 2021	Questionnaire package	Web push reminder (in envelope); no questionnaire
25 January 2021	Pressure sealed web reminder, no questionnaire	Pressure sealed web reminder, no questionnaire
16 February 2021	Questionnaire package	Web push reminder (in envelope); no questionnaire
12 March 2021	Questionnaire package	Pressure sealed web reminder; no questionnaire

Table 19.9 Experiment 2 response rates by mode, cost, and average days between mailout and response.

	Control	Treatment
Mail response	944 (32.1%)	8 (0.3%)***
Web response	802 (27.3%)	1268 (43.5%)***
Helpline response	30 (1.0%)	17 (0.6%)
Nonresponse	1164 (39.6%)	1623 (55.7%)***
N	2940	2916
Cost per response	US$ 12.48	US$ 5.77
Cost per sample	US$ 7.39	US$ 2.50
Average days for in-scope response	53	49

Note: ***p-value < 0.001. Statistical testing not done for cost per response, cost per sample, and average days to in-scope response.

Experiment 3   Targeted Communications for Potential Farms

Survey Design

Outside lists used to add records to the list frame include many records with limited agricultural production and records that may have an affiliation with agriculture but are not producing agricultural products (for example, agricultural suppliers, processors, operations no longer in business). These potential farms may not feel that NASS screening surveys are intended for them and thus may not respond. This experiment included only those potential operations that had not responded to a previous NASS screening survey. Approximately, six thousand potential farms and ranches from the targeted subgroup were selected and randomly assigned to two groups. The control group received mailings similar to prior COAs for all types of operations. The treatment group did not receive any paper COA questionnaires. The content of the web push letters emphasized that all agricultural activity regardless of amount should be reported and that response is needed from both in-scope and out-of-scope records. The treatment group timing was compressed and letters contained "deadline approaching, response required" in the third mailing and "response overdue" in the fourth mailing. The final mailing for the treatment group was a postcard tear-off that only included four agricultural activity-screening questions (see Figure 19.3). This final mailing was intended to be easy to complete and included questions that even those with no activity could answer. See Table 19.10 for more details.

Results

When including the tear-off mailer as responses, overall, the treatment group had significantly lower nonresponse than the control group as shown in Table 19.11. The treatment group prompted more responses from both in scope and out–scope respondents. The treatment group had a total of 373 responses, of which 331 were tear-off responses. The treatment group was also significantly lower in cost and prompted faster responses.

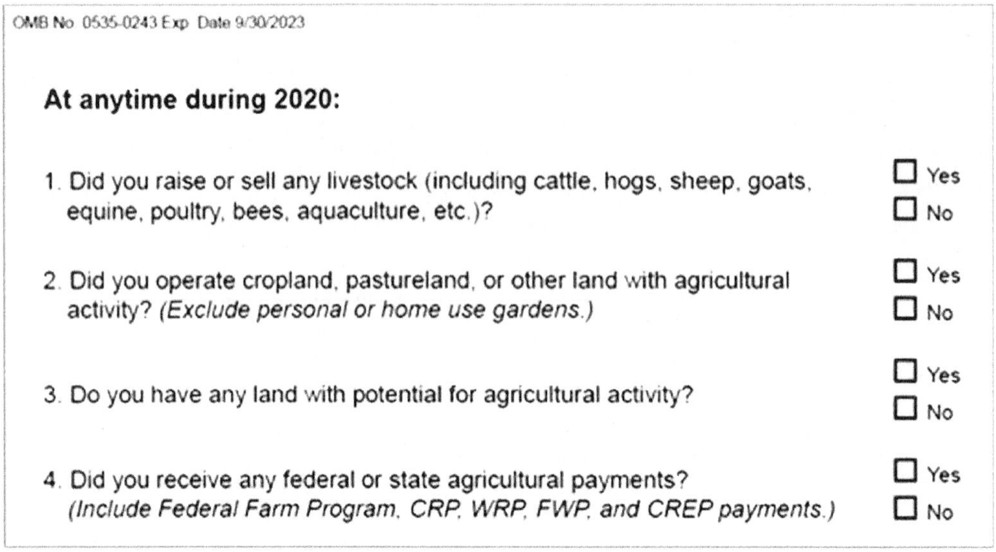

OMB No 0535-0243 Exp Date 9/30/2023

At anytime during 2020:

1. Did you raise or sell any livestock (including cattle, hogs, sheep, goats, equine, poultry, bees, aquaculture, etc.)? ☐ Yes ☐ No

2. Did you operate cropland, pastureland, or other land with agricultural activity? *(Exclude personal or home use gardens.)* ☐ Yes ☐ No

3. Do you have any land with potential for agricultural activity? ☐ Yes ☐ No

4. Did you receive any federal or state agricultural payments? *(Include Federal Farm Program, CRP, WRP, FWP, and CREP payments.)* ☐ Yes ☐ No

Figure 19.3 Tear-off postcard used for experiment 3.

Table 19.10 Experiment 3 treatment groups.

Date	Control group	Treatment group (references to agricultural activity instead of "farms" and response from those with NO agricultural activity)
12 December 2020	Web push invitation; no mailed questionnaire	Web push letter with new language (in envelope); no questionnaire
4 January 2021	Questionnaire package	Pressure sealed web reminder with new language; no questionnaire
25 January 2021	Pressure sealed web reminder, no questionnaire	Pressure sealed web reminder with new language; no questionnaire
5 February 2021		Pressure sealed web reminder with new language; no questionnaire
12 February 2021		Tear-off return postcard with four agricultural activity screening questions
16 February 2021	Questionnaire package	
12 March 2021	Questionnaire package	

The tear-off mailer is shown in Figure 19.3 and was an effective last contact for this group. It was mailed to 2495 records from the treatment group whose responses had not yet been recorded. Of the 2495, 331 were returned by a respondent who had not responded in another mode. Of those 331, 207 answered at least one question on the card as "yes" and were considered as in scope, and 124 came back with no questions answered "yes" and/or notes indicating they were out of scope and were considered out of scope.

Experiment 3 Discussion

Traditionally, NASS has treated units who have not responded to our earlier screening survey the same as those known to be farms. However, the response rates for these units have historically

Table 19.11 Experiment 3 response rates by mode, cost, and average days between mailout and response.

	Control	Treatment
Mail response (including 331 tear-off mailers)	411 (14.7%)	373 (13.1%)
Web response	282 (10.1%)	569 (20.0%)***
Helpline response	48 (1.7%)	36 (1.3%)
Nonresponse	2060 (73.6%)	1873 (65.7%)***
N	2801	2851
Cost per response	US$ 37.99	US$ 13.61
Cost per sample	US$ 6.95	US$ 2.91
Average days for in-scope response	47	43

Note: ***p-value < 0.001. Statistical testing not done for cost per response, cost per sample, and average days to in-scope response.

been much lower, while their costs are high due to repeated mailings of expensive questionnaire packages. By emphasizing that they may not represent "typical" farms or agricultural production of any kind and allowing a much smaller tear-off mailer, more responses can be prompted. The tear-off mailer does not provide the same level of information as the full questionnaire but does allow some scoping to be done. This can allow the list frame to be updated or identify individual respondents who can be followed up to collect additional information. It also allows for identification of units with no agricultural activity who can be removed from any later data collections.

Overall Summary

Taken together, these three experiments illustrate how targeting different subgroups of establishments with different procedures can impact response and which changes are effective. For many units on NASS's list frame, there is sample information available to identify subsets of establishments based on their characteristics. This can be used to tailor procedures for these subsets. However, testing these procedures in experiments is critical, as illustrated here with positive results for only some of our treatments. List frame data for establishments can provide information for targeted tests, something not usually available for household surveys.

19.4 Comparing FedEx to Traditional Postage in a Survey of Substance Abuse and Mental Health Facilities (by Mathematica for SAMHSA)

19.4.1 Motivation

The Behavioral Health Services Information System (BHSIS) is a congressionally mandated data collection on substance abuse and mental health treatment services. Sponsored by the SAMHSA, the BHSIS[3] has numerous interrelated components, including the National Survey

---

3 See www.samhsa.gov/data/data-we-collect for more information.

of Substance Abuse Treatment Services (N-SSATS) and the National Mental Health Services Survey (N-MHSS). These two annual, voluntary surveys of about 20,000 substance abuse facilities and 16,000 specialty mental health facilities are conducted by Mathematica. The surveys collect data about behavioral health treatment services in the United States, including the number of people receiving services, patterns of treatment service, and other important treatment- and policy-related information. The data are used in SAMHSA reports, program administration, decision-making, planning, and policy analysis. Data also inform a widely used, publicly available online facility search tool, the online Behavioral Health Treatment Services Locator. This system compiles and updates data for substance use and mental health treatment facilities throughout the United States. These data are available for any individual seeking treatment services and are also frequently used by industry professionals for locating appropriate facilities for client referrals.

For the Locator to provide the most up-to-date and comprehensive information to the public, the data must be high quality, current, and encompass as many licensed and operating facilities as possible. SAMHSA has set 90% as the response rate threshold to meet this minimum requirement. In the past decade, there has been a steady decline in response rates, leading the study team to continually review and modify the data collection strategies on the N-SSATS and N-MHSS to meet the response rate requirements. Some of these enhancements included initially prefilling question data based on facility responses from the prior round for the respondent to verify, increasing the number of nonresponse follow-up mailings and notifications, creating a worksheet to help facilities respond and reduce respondent burden, and extending the surveys' field periods. In 2017 and early 2018, there was a decrease in the response rate for the N-SSATS, and another strategy was needed to mitigate this decline. It was hypothesized that if the survey packet was more salient to the facility director, they would be more likely to respond. Gasper et al. (2020) presented findings from an establishment survey experiment that showed a trend for United States Postal Service (USPS) Priority Mail to increase response compared to USPS First Class Mail. Since FedEx is regularly used by businesses and has implied urgency to its delivery, we theorized that FedEx would increase response. To test this theory, a FedEx experiment was added to the 2018 data collection cycle.

19.4.2 Experiment Design

Table 19.12 presents the major data collection activities and schedule for the 2018 N-SSATS. As shown, the only difference between the treatment and control groups was that the second packet was mailed via FedEx 2Day shipping instead of USPS First-Class mail to the treatment group. This was done to highlight the perception of the packet's importance and increase the likelihood of it reaching the facility director. Because of FedEx's standard practice of requiring a signature for delivery, a test was designed to determine whether FedEx would yield a positive impact on facility response. Prior to the second packet, facilities had already received three mailings via USPS first-class mail. Traditionally, the second reminder mailing was sent in the fielding process via USPS first-class mail, and it included a cover letter, web login instructions, and 2017 N-SSATS state profiles, which provided a snapshot of national and state estimates of treatment and services.

On 22 May, the nonresponding facilities were evenly divided into two samples: a treatment group ($N = 5013$) and a control group ($N = 5017$). The facilities were evenly distributed between the two groups by state and network size (four classes as presented in Table 19.13). In the survey terminology, a network is a group of administratively connected facilities. Facilities within the same network

Table 19.12 Major data collection activities and schedule.

Activity	Schedule	Control group	Treatment group
Advance letter mailed USPS First Class	15 February 2018	X	X
First N-SSATS packet mailed USPS First Class	30 March 2018	X	X
Web goes live	30 March 2018	X	X
Reminder letter mailed USPS First Class	20 April 2018	X	X
Second N-SSATS packet mailed USPS First Class	30 May 2018	X	
Second N-SSATS packet mailed FedEx 2Day	30 May 2018		X
Begin telephone follow-up	2 July 2018	X	X
Third N-SSATS packet with questionnaire mailed USPS First Class	27 July 2018	X	X
Targeted reminder letters mailed FedEx 2Day	5 October 2018	X	X
Data collection ends	2 November 2018	X	X

Table 19.13 Average days to complete by facility characteristics.

	Substance abuse treatment setting				
	Inpatient	Residential	Outpatient	Mix	Overall
Treatment	62.4	59.5	58.0	60.7	58.5
Control	62.4	70.1	67.6	71.0	68.2
All	62.4	64.7	62.9	65.8	63.4

	Treatment focus				
	Substance abuse	Mental health	Mix	General health care	Overall
Treatment	57.7	59.2	59.5	65.3	58.5
Control	66.3	70.7	69.6	78.0	68.2
All	62.0	65.6	64.6	71.5	63.4

	Network size				
	Stand-alone	Small (2–4)	Medium (5–9)	Large (10 or more)	Overall
Treatment	56.0	61.3	64.2	54.1	58.5
Control	66.5	71.5	67.1	67.1	68.2
All	61.3	66.5	65.7	60.2	63.4

were allocated to the same experimental group. The contents of the second reminder mailing were identical in the two groups. The packets were sent via FedEx 2Day shipping to the treatment group and via USPS First-Class Mail to the control group. The packets went out on 30 May 2018 – nine weeks after data collection began. Other than the method of mailing, the procedures for the treatment and control groups did not differ throughout the field period.

For analysis, all facilities that completed the survey before 2 June – the date the mailings would have begun arriving at the facilities – were excluded. Facilities that closed or otherwise were ineligible to complete the 2018 N-SSATS were also excluded. The final analysis sample included 4312 treatment facilities and 4314 control facilities.

19.4.3 Results

To account for multiple comparisons during the analysis process, the desired alpha for significance was set at 0.01 and the Bonferroni correction was applied. The adjusted alpha used for determining significance was 0.0005. The rate at which facilities responded to the 2018 N-SSATS after receiving the second reminder was examined. As Figure 19.4 shows, facilities that received the FedEx mailing (the treatment group) responded faster than those that received the first-class mailing (the control group). The average time to complete the survey was significantly lower for the treatment group (58 days) than for the control group (68 days). About 30 days after the experimental mailing, the methods to improve response among nonresponding facilities increased in intensity, starting with telephone follow-up. A third reminder mailing, which included a hardcopy questionnaire, was sent 58 days after the experimental mailing, and a final reminder was sent 70 days after the third reminder via FedEx. Although no difference was noted in the number of completed surveys at the end of data collection between the two groups, fewer high-intensity resources were allocated to the treatment group during nonresponse follow-up. This is because about 9% ($n = 397$) more facilities in the treatment group completed their survey prior to the onset of the high-intensity follow-up.

Facilities completed the survey via three modes: web, telephone, and hardcopy. As indicated in Figure 19.5, facilities in the treatment group completed the survey faster by web and overall, at higher numbers. The control group completed more telephone surveys than the treatment group. The number of facilities that mailed back a completed hardcopy survey was comparable between the two groups.

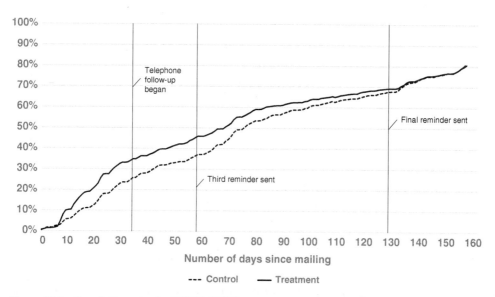

Figure 19.4 Completion rates for 2018 N-SSATS treatment and control groups.

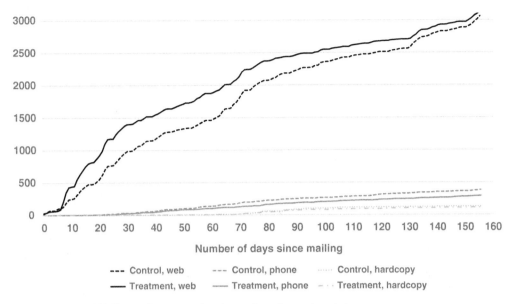

Figure 19.5 N-SSATS completes over time by mode and experimental group.

Various characteristics of facilities that completed the 2018 N-SSATS in the experimental groups were examined to see if any type of facility was more impacted by the FedEx change than others. No significant difference was noted in the response outcomes by these characteristics between groups. The facility characteristics included the following:

- The substance abuse treatment setting (inpatient, residential, outpatient, or a mix of any of those three)
- The facility's treatment focus (substance abuse, mental health, a mix of those two, or general health care)
- The number of associated facilities in the sample (network size: stand-alone, small (2–4 facilities), medium (5–9 facilities), or large (10 facilities or more).

Table 19.13 shows the average days to complete by the noted facility characteristics. Inpatient facilities, facilities with a general health care focus, and facilities in a medium-size network responded at a slightly slower rate. For each of these comparisons, none of these differences were significant.

Although the difference was not significant, stand-alone facilities and large networks (those with 10 or more facilities) had an average number of days to complete that was less than small- (two to four) and medium- (five to nine) size networks. As Figure 19.6 shows, the impact of the FedEx mailing was similar for networks of all sizes. Given that there are more stand-alone facilities in the sample, the effect expressed in the absolute terms (number of completes) is more pronounced.

The next analysis was whether the facility was part of the 2017 N-SSATS sample and, if so, whether the facility completed the survey that year. As Figure 19.7 shows, the FedEx mailing had no impact on facilities that were prior nonrespondents, i.e. those that did not complete the N-SSATS in 2017. The FedEx mailing significantly decreased the average number of days to complete the survey for facilities that completed it in 2017, as well as those that were new to the sample in 2018. Facilities that completed the survey in prior rounds responded at a higher rate than either those that were new to the sample or did not complete in the previous round. This corroborates findings that past behavior is an important predictor of response.

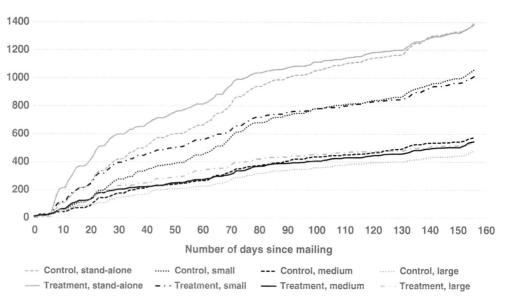

Figure 19.6 N-SSATS completes over time by network size and experimental group.

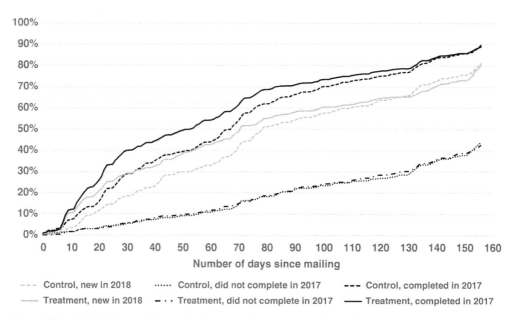

Figure 19.7 N-SSATS completion rates by sample type and experimental group.

Because the results of the FedEx experiment that indicated a positive increase to the rate of response to the N-SSATS, the second packet mailing was sent via FedEx to all nonresponding facilities in 2019. Figure 19.8 shows the completion rate for N-SSATS for: 2017 (the year that the second packet mailing was sent to all facilities via USPS first-class mail), the treatment and control groups for 2018, and 2019 (the year that the second packet was sent to all facilities via FedEx 2Day). An important difference between the 2018 N-SSATS and the 2017 and 2019 N-SSATS was that client count data were not collected in the 2018 fielding process, as it is collected every other year and

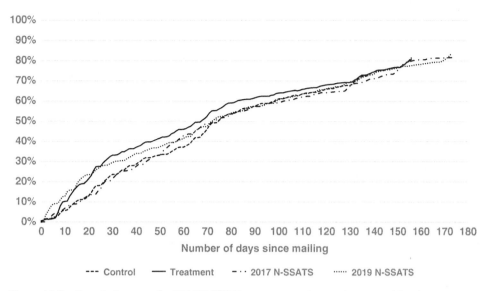

Figure 19.8 Completion rates for 2018 N-SSATS treatment and control groups with other years.

requires increased burden on the participants. Comparing the average number of days to complete, a significant change between 2017 and 2019 was noted, decreasing from 69 to 66 days. The early response by the treatment group in 2018 mirrored the response in 2019. Similarly, the 2017 response was comparable with the control group in 2018.

As noted, the N-MHSS is the mental health equivalent to the N-SSATS. The N-MHSS is fielded one month after N-SSATS begins. The N-MHSS uses similar strategies as the N-SSATS for reducing nonresponse, following the same protocol for fielding reminder mailings, telephone follow-up, and so on. Based on the early positive impact of the FedEx experiment, the second reminder mailing of N-MHSS in 2018 was sent via FedEx to all nonrespondents. Similar to Figure 19.8, Figure 19.9

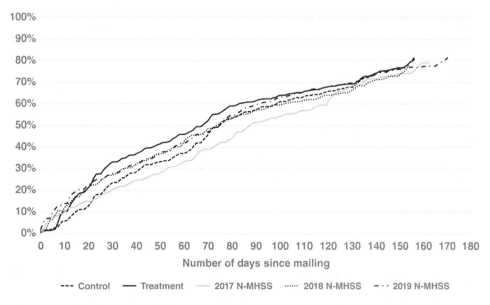

Figure 19.9 Completion rates for 2018 N-SSATS treatment and control groups with N-MHSS years.

shows the completion rates for N-MHSS in 2017, 2018, and 2019 (2017 was the year the second reminder was sent via USPS first-class mail). As with N-SSATS, client count information is collected every other year; for N-MHSS, the 2018 survey collected client count data. Comparing the average number of days to complete between 2017 and 2018, a significant change was also noted, decreasing from 73 to 63 days. The average number of days to complete remained 63 days for the 2019 fielding round when FedEx was also used.

19.4.4   Discussion

Mailing the second reminder mailing via FedEx rather than USPS appeared to be an effective tool to facilitate faster survey response. The impact was generalized across two different samples of facilities: those providing substance abuse treatment and those providing mental health treatment. Encouraging facilities to respond earlier enabled more high-intensity resources to be focused on a smaller set of nonresponding facilities.

Changing the second reminder to FedEx also proved to be successful in improving the response rate for these surveys; the goal of attaining response rates at or above 90% for these surveys was achieved. The final response rate for N-SSATS increased from 90.2% in 2017 to 92.4% in 2018 and remained consistent at 92.3% in 2019. The N-MHSS final response rates followed a consistent pattern: 88.2% in 2017, 90.8% in 2018, and 91.3% in 2019.

Given the common usage of FedEx as an expedited delivery service of high-priority materials, the suggested urgency of a FedEx envelope may have helped to increase its implied importance. This approach seems to have helped get the reminder past the facility's gatekeeper and into the hands of the respondent, leading to faster completion rates.

19.5   Addressing Item Nonresponse with Clarifying Information – Evidence from the IAB Job Vacancy Survey (IAB)

19.5.1   Motivation

In addition to experiments on contact and response enhancement strategies, questionnaire experiments may also aid researchers by providing useful insights on how to improve questionnaire design. Specifically, they can help in identifying factors related to item nonresponse, survey burden, and data quality. The following study conducted using the IAB-JVS by the Institute for Employment Research in Nuremberg, Germany, illustrates such a questionnaire experiment. A more extensive description of this experiment can be found in Küfner et al. (2021).

The IAB-JVS covers topics such as job vacancies, job flows, and search and recruitment processes and is conducted as a voluntary, annual, and nationally representative establishment survey.[4] The vacancy and recruitment questions can be particularly burdensome to answer as establishments may need to look up internal records to provide precise answers. In particular, the IAB-JVS asks three specific date questions concerning when the last successful search and recruitment process occurred: (i) the earliest possible hiring date for the posted position ("At what date should this position be filled at the earliest?"); (ii) the date the search officially started ("When did you start searching for this vacancy?"); and (iii) the date of the decision to hire the applicant ("When did you decide to hire this applicant?"). Historically, these items have suffered from a high level of item nonresponse ranging between 12% and 21%, with the search date item facing a slightly higher

---

4 See Bossler et al. (2020) for more information about the IAB Job Vacancy Survey.

proportion of missing data than the other two items. Item nonresponse compromises the quality and utility of these items, which are often used by substantive researchers to study the efficiency of search and recruitment processes (e.g. Rebien 2019; Gürtzgen and Moczall 2020), and simultaneously indicates how burdensome these items are for establishments to answer.

Referring to theoretical models of cognitive survey response (Tourangeau et al. 2000; Willimack and Nichols 2010; Bavdaž 2010) multiple reasons for this high share of item nonresponse are plausible. The question comprehension could be negatively affected by vague and ambiguous concepts. For example, the applicant decision date could be either the date of the final interview, the date the supervisor decides, or the budget manager agrees to hire the applicant, depending on the establishment-specific hiring process. Data retrieval may also be problematic if these dates are not available in business records or difficult to remember. Additional problems could arise in judging which is the adequate date when multiple dates could be used to answer the question.

As discussed in (establishment) survey guidelines or recommendations (Australian Bureau of Statistics 2010; Morrison et al. 2010; Haraldsen 2013; Redline 2011), providing additional clarifying information and examples next to the question can assist respondents in understanding the survey question in the intended way. In addition, date retrieval from business records or recall could be facilitated by providing this additional information. Providing examples could serve as a guide which aids respondents in selecting the most appropriate date. In summary, providing additional clarifying information and examples could improve multiple stages of the response process, enabling respondents to provide more precise answers with potentially less burden.

This study tested whether item nonresponse in the three aforementioned IAB-JVS search and recruitment date questions could be reduced by providing additional clarifying information and examples. The additional information provided easy-to-look-up events and was experimentally presented to a random half of participants to assist them in the response process. The tested hypothesis was that this additional information would reduce item nonresponse for these items.

Questionnaire design experiments are not very often reported in the establishment survey literature and, to our knowledge, no experiment on providing additional clarifying information has been published. In an experiment on item nonresponse, Ott et al. (2016) showed that placing questions on personal characteristics at the beginning rather than at the end of the questionnaire reduced item nonresponse to these questions. Another example is O'Brien and Levin (2007) who experimented with answer prompts and showed that these can help to reduce item nonresponse in an online establishment survey. However, there is a notable gap in the literature on the provision of clarifying information that is addressed in this study.

19.5.2 Experiment Design

The additional clarifying information provided in each question included two concrete examples of process dates for specific milestone events. These milestone events were intended to help make the concepts more concrete and less vague or ambiguous. The examples also included keywords to facilitate searching business records or internal communications. To identify appropriate milestone events, expert interviews were conducted with substantive and survey methodological researchers. It is important to note that the milestone events provided in the examples were only intended to be used as a guide and did not encompass all possible events that could occur during an establishment's search and recruitment processes. The examples were simply designed to assist respondents in identifying the information sought and facilitate data retrieval and judgment of the most appropriate date to answer the question.

Specifically, the treatment group received the following clarifying information (see the Online Supplemental Material for screenshots of the online questionnaire):

Earliest hiring date item:

Here you could, for example, enter the following events:

> *Date of a possible project start, in which the new employee should participate*
> *For replacements: Day on which the position was vacant.*

Start search date item:

Here you could, for example, enter the following events:

> *Date of publication of the job advertisement (e.g. on the homepage, a newspaper or an online job market)*
> *Date of public posting.*

Applicant decision date item:

Here you could, for example, enter the following events:

> *Date of final approval by the supervisor*
> *Date of the final interview.*

To increase the likelihood that respondents would notice the additional information, it was displayed in italics between the question and the answer box (Couper 2008). Hence, it fits into the reading logic (top to bottom). To test whether respondents actually read the additional information, item durations were evaluated. In addition, a possible spillover effect on the first nontreated item was analyzed. This nontreated item asked for the date the employment relationship began ("When did this employment relationship begin?") and immediately followed the three treated items. This item was not treated with the additional clarifying information because it has less item nonresponse. It also seems to be less burdensome for establishments to answer compared to the previous three items because this date is recorded in employment contracts and therefore should be possible to identify. Nonetheless, this study checked whether the experimental effects (if any) from the three preceding treated items carried over to this item as it had a similar appearance and format to the treated items.

Since the three treated items are important for researchers, it was decided not to experiment with the production survey, but rather with a separate survey that ran parallel to the main survey in 2019. The only difference to the production survey was that the experimental survey was conducted entirely online, as opposed to the concurrent mixed mode (mail/web) design used in the production survey. Except for this difference, the survey design and field organization followed the same principles as in the main IAB-JVS survey. As each item was displayed on a separate screen, time stamps were collected to record the time taken to answer or skip an item.

An optimal allocation was implemented to increase the efficiency of the sampling design and, hence, the power of the planned statistical tests. The allocation procedure was optimized toward the historical distribution of item nonresponse in the treated questions. Using the procedure proposed by Friedrich et al. (2018), the allocation problem was solved to the empirical distribution of the item nonresponse indicators from the previous year's (2018) survey. This resulted in a minor gain in efficiency compared to a proportional (to stratum size) allocation. The average reduction of the expected design effect for item response indicators was only 0.86%. The control and experimental groups were created by splitting each stratum into two approximately equal-sized groups.

19.5.3 Results

19.5.3.1 Item Duration

To check whether respondents likely noticed and read the clarifying information, item durations are examined. Figure 19.10 illustrates the average item duration for each treated item by treatment and control group. This figure additionally differentiates between all eligible respondents (upper panel), item respondents (middle panel), and item nonrespondents (lower panel) to identify different patterns between these groups.

Looking at all eligible respondents, the treated group took on average significantly longer to proceed to the next item than the control group. The largest difference occurred for the first item (earliest hiring date: 56 versus 30 seconds; $p = 0.000$), followed by the second item (start search date: 29 versus 23 seconds; $p = 0.000$), and the third item (applicant decision date: 31 versus 26 seconds; $p = 0.063$). Item respondents showed a very similar pattern with significantly longer item durations in the treatment group than in the control group for each item. These results support the conclusion that item respondents in the treatment group read the additional and clarifying information.

A similar pattern is also observed for the item nonrespondents. Item durations in the treatment group were significantly longer than in the control group. However, item nonrespondents took less time to go forward to the next question compared to the item respondents. All in all, item nonrespondents in the treatment group seemed to have noticed and at least partially read the additional information provided.

19.5.3.2 Item Nonresponse

To test the stated hypothesis that providing additional clarifying information reduces item nonresponse, this study investigates item nonresponse rates. To do this, this study examines each

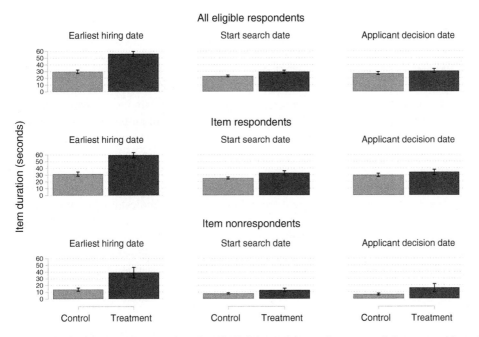

Figure 19.10 Average item durations for all eligible participants (upper panel), item respondents (middle panel), and item nonrespondents (lower panel), by item and treatment and control groups. Error bars indicate 95% confidence intervals. Source: Adapted from Küfner et al. (2021).

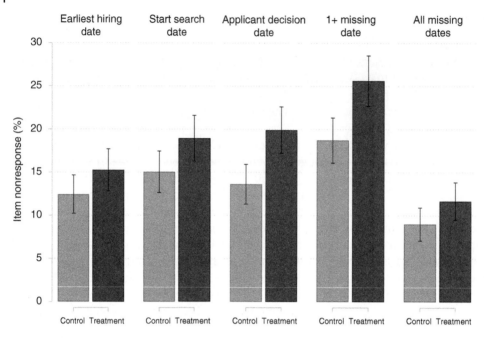

Figure 19.11 Rates of item nonresponse by treatment and control groups by item, at least one missing item, and all missing items. Error bars indicate 95% confidence intervals. Source: Adapted from Küfner et al. (2021).

treated item individually and two summary nonresponse indicators: whether a nonresponse occurred in at least one of the treated items and whether nonresponse occurred in all three treated items for a given establishment. The results are presented in Figure 19.11. In contrast to our expectation, the item nonresponse rate in the treatment group was higher than in the control group. This pattern was consistent across all three items and both summary indicators. The earliest hiring date, start search date, and applicant decision date items had nonresponse rates of 15.3%, 19.0%, and 19.9% in the treatment group, respectively, compared to the corresponding control group values of 12.4%, 15.0%, and 13.6%. Hence, the treatment group produced between 2.9% and 6.6% points higher item nonresponse than the control group. The statistical significance of the difference was at the 10% level for the earliest hiring date item and at the 5% level for the start search date and the applicant decision date items. Further, both summary indicators provided evidence for more item nonresponse in the treatment group. The difference in the item nonresponse rate between the treatment and control groups for the indicator of having at least one missing item was 6.9% points and statistically significant at the 5% level. The all-missing indicator showed a 2.7% point higher item nonresponse rate in the treatment group, which is statistically significant at the 10% level. In summary, the findings illustrated that providing additional clarifying information resulted in more item nonresponse than not providing this information.

19.5.3.3 Spillover Effects
Finally, possible spillover effects of the treatment on the first nontreated item that directly followed the three treated items is analyzed. As this item captured the date and the employment relationship began, it was also a date item with a similar appearance and format to the three preceding treated

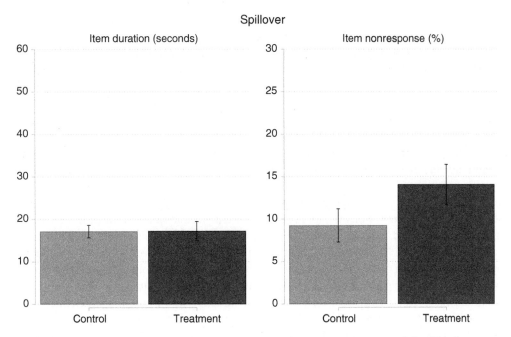

Figure 19.12 Item duration, and item nonresponse for the first non-treated item following the experimental items, by treatment and control groups. Error bars indicate 95% confidence intervals. Source: Adapted from Küfner et al. (2021).

items. Figure 19.12 shows the average item duration and nonresponse rate for this item. First, no statistically significant difference in item duration was observed between the treatment and control groups. This was the expected result as the treatment and the control groups received the identical question without additional information. However, there was a higher item nonresponse rate in the treatment group for this nontreated item. While the item nonresponse rate in the treatment group was 14.1%, the item nonresponse rate in the control group was 9.2%. This difference was statistically significant at the 5% level. This result demonstrated that the negative treatment effect on item nonresponse is carried over to the first nontreated item with the same question appearance.

19.5.4 Discussion

This case study showed that providing additional clarifying information to establishments to facilitate answering job vacancy duration questions did not reduce, and rather exacerbated, item nonresponse. There was also evidence that the negative treatment effect spilled over onto an adjacent nontreated question. Hence, the posited hypothesis was clearly rejected by the empirical results of the experiment. Although the reasons for providing additional clarifying details might be justified for establishment questionnaire items, the implementation, as shown, can potentially backfire.

This study exemplified four special characteristics of experiments in establishment surveys: Establishment heterogeneity, unanticipated results, allocation based on background information, and the potential benefit of qualitative interviews. First, the large heterogeneity among establishments leads to special challenges that increase the need for research on developing adequate questions and instructions that apply to the unique circumstances of all establishments. While small-scale qualitative interviews could provide useful insights into the response process and the question comprehension of individual establishments and inform appropriate questionnaire design, large-scale population-based experiments are still needed to provide evidence on the effect of the newly developed questions and instructions across the full spectrum of establishment types. Addressing establishment heterogeneity, thus, constitutes a major motivation for experimenting with establishment surveys. Second, the present study also showed that the effects of questionnaire changes are hard to predict in establishment surveys. Due to establishment heterogeneity and unobserved establishment response processes, question wording and instruction changes can potentially lead to unintended effects. Without such experiments, however, practitioners might directly implement questionnaire changes that produce unwanted effects without knowing it.

Third, as mentioned in the experiments previously discussed in this chapter, establishment surveys could benefit from utilizing more background data on the sampled units. In this experiment, such background data from previous waves (i.e. item nonresponse in the previous year) and the sampling frame (i.e. establishment size, industry, and region) were exploited to conduct an optimal allocation in order to increase the efficiency of the experimental design. And fourth, questionnaire design experiments embedded within establishment surveys could potentially profit from mixed-method approaches, combining qualitative interviews and debriefings with quantitative experiments. Conducting qualitative interviews before fielding the experiment could aid survey organizations in adjusting the treatment to the needs of the establishments and carrying out qualitative interviews after the experiment could help researchers understand the observed treatment effect. The latter would be especially useful in this case study as it may shed more light on the reasons for the observed backfiring effect.

19.6 Summary

Taken together, this chapter presents new experimental results from four different establishment surveys dealing with recruitment strategies and questionnaire designs. First, an experiment conducted by the BLS revealed that neither an advanced letter nor a folder containing survey materials positively affected enrollment rates to the CES program. Second, NASS experimented with different recruitment strategies demonstrating that emphasizing the response deadline could aid in increasing response rates. In contrast, a reduction of questionnaire mailings or a format change were not effective. While an additional experiment targeting the subgroup of likely web respondents with a push-to-web strategy was not effective, a special recruiting strategy with a light task for establishments with limited agriculture productivity helped increase response. Third, Mathematica experimentally tested whether FedEx mailings that suggest high business importance could help to increase response and revealed a successful strategy to get the survey invitation past the gatekeeper. Fourth, a questionnaire design experiment conducted by the IAB demonstrated that providing additional clarifying information did not reduce item nonresponse, but in fact increased item nonresponse to vacancy duration questions.

These studies illustrate why experiments with establishments can provide useful information to survey researchers. In doing so, they highlighted elements that make experiments with establishments unique. Survey experiments with household surveys often do not have the advantage of extensive auxiliary information that many establishment surveys have. For example, experiments can be tailored to target specific subgroups of establishments based on frame or administrative data (see NASS), samples can be designed accounting for known characteristics of establishments (see IAB) or results can be analyzed with auxiliary data or subsectors of establishment populations in mind (see Mathematica). In addition, establishments may behave differently than households if more complex multistage contact procedures are required or their records do not match question- naire concepts. Hypotheses based on findings from experiments in household surveys may or may not be confirmed with establishments, so continued experimentation in establishment surveys will be important to improve them. Other strands of literature and expertise might be useful to be considered to better integrate knowledge of organizational behavior into formation of hypotheses and interpretation of results.

Further, our experiments have shown that the hypothesized behavior of establishments is merely that – hypotheses. Results from three experiments (BLS, NASS, and IAB) did not confirm the authors' theoretical hypotheses. Hence, experiments are needed to confirm (or disprove) the effi- cacy of these alternative procedures. The unexpected results from the experiments should encour- age survey researchers to conduct more experiments in establishment surveys to empirically test their assumptions. These experiments should be conducted not only to test new procedures in pretests but also to evaluate the effectiveness of the current survey design and questionnaires used. As demonstrated by the BLS, such experiments could show that recruiting strategies used for many years are no longer effective today and therefore financial resources can be spent more efficiently. Even when experiments confirm hypotheses, the generalizability of the findings needs confirma- tion, preferably in an experimental setting. Mathematica's treatment produced expected results that persisted in a nonexperimental setting, which shows strong support for the intervention. But the question remains whether the findings would generalize to other survey topics, survey lengths, establishment sizes, or industries.

In summary, experiments are a powerful and hitherto underutilized strategy in establishment surveys. Experiments can help to inform design choices and allocate resources more efficiently. In addition to the experiments in this chapter that address nonresponse, experiments could also assist survey organizations to gain insights for other survey design aspects like mode effects or data quality.

Acknowledgment

Research reported in Section 19.3 was completed when Heather Ridolfo was employed at the National Agricultural Statistics Service of the U.S. Department of Agriculture, and she thanks them for their support.

References

Australian Bureau of Statistics (2010). *Forms Design Standards Manual*. Canberra: Australian Bureau of Statistics.

Bavdaž, M. (2010). The multidimensional integral business survey response model. *Survey Methodology* 36 (1): 81–102.

Bossler, M., Gürtzgen, N., Kubis, A., Küfner, B., and Lochner, B. (2020). The IAB Job Vacancy Survey: design and research potential. *Journal for Labour Market Research* 54 (13): 1–12.

Couper, M.P. (2008). *Designing Effective Web Surveys*. New York: Cambridge University Press.

Edwards, W.S. and Cantor, D. (2004). Toward a response model in establishment surveys. In: *Measurement Errors in Surveys*, Wiley Series in Probability and Statistics (ed. P.P. Biemer, R.M. Groves, L.E. Lyberg, N.A. Mathiowetz, and S. Sudman), 211–233.

Friedrich, U., Münnich, R., and Rupp, M. (2018). Multivariate optimal allocation with box-constraints. *Austrian Journal of Statistics* 47 (2): 33–52.

Gasper, J., Palan, M., and Muz, B. (2020). Survey of employer policies on the employment of people with disabilities. In: *Report prepared for the Chief Evaluation Office (CEO) and the Office of Disability Employment Policy (ODEP)*. Rockville, MD: Westat.

Giesen, D. (2013). Comparative report on integration of case study results related to reduction of response burden and motivation of businesses for accurate reporting. BLUE-ETS Project. Deliverable 8.1. Grant Agreement Number 244767.

Gürtzgen, N. and Moczall, A. (2020). Sequential versus non-sequential search among German employers–evidence from a job vacancy survey. *Applied Economics Letters* 27 (11): 873–879.

Haraldsen, G. (2013). Questionnaire communication in business surveys. In: *Designing and Conducting Business Surveys* (ed. G. Snijkers, G. Haraldsen, J. Jones, and D.K. Willimack), 303–357. Hoboken, NJ: Wiley.

Küfner, B., Sakshaug, J.W., and Zins, S. (2021). More clarification, less item nonresponse in establishment surveys? A split-ballot experiment. *Survey Research Methods* 15 (2): 195–206.

Lavrakas, P.J. (2008). *Encyclopedia of Survey Research Methods*, vol. 0. Thousand Oaks, CA: Sage Publications, Inc. https://doi.org/10.4135/9781412963947.

Lorenc, B. (2006). Two topics in survey methodology: modelling the response process in establishment surveys; inference from nonprobability samples using the double samples setup. Doctoral dissertation. Department of Statistics. Stockholm, Stockholm University.

McCarthy, J.S., Ott, K., Ridolfo, H., McGovern, P., Sirkis, P., and Moore, D. (2018). Combining multiple methods in establishment questionnaire testing: the 2017 census of agriculture testing bento box. *Journal of Official Statistics* 34 (2): 1–25.

Morrison, R.L., Dillman, D.A., and Christian, L.M. (2010). Questionnaire design guidelines for establishment surveys. *Journal of Official Statistics* 26 (1): 43–85.

O'Brien, J. and Levin, K. (2007). Web design issues in a business establishment panel survey. *Proceedings of the Third International Conference of Establishment Surveys*. Montreal, Canada: American Statistical Association.

Ott, K., McGovern, P., and Sirkis, R. (2016). Using analysis of field test results to evaluate questionnaire performance. *Proceedings of the Fifth International Conference of Establishment Surveys*. Geneva, Switzerland: American Statistical Association.

Rebien, M. (2019). Employers search: are employee referrals effective? *Economics Bulletin* 39 (4): 2499–2506.

Redline, C. D. (2011). Clarifying survey questions. Doctoral dissertation. Joint Program in Survey Methodology. University of Maryland, College Park.

Sudman, S., Willimack, D.K., Nichols, E., and Mesenbourg, T.L. (2000). Exploratory research at the US Census Bureau on the survey response process in large companies. *Proceedings of the Second International Conference on Establishment Surveys*, American Statistical Association, pp. 327–337.

Tourangeau, R. (1984). Cognitive sciences and survey methods. In: *Cognitive Aspects of Survey Methodology: Building a Bridge Between Disciplines*, vol. 15, 73–100. National Academy Press.

Tourangeau, R., Rips, L.J., and Rasinski, K.A. (2000). *The psychology of survey response*. Cambridge, U.K: Cambridge University Press.

Tuttle, A.D., Beck, J.L., Willimack, D.K., Tolliver, K.P., Hernandez, A., and Fan, C. (2018). Experimenting with contact strategies in business surveys. *Journal of Official Statistics* 34 (2): 365–395.

Willimack, D.K. and Nichols, E. (2010). A hybrid response process model for business surveys. *Journal of Official Statistics* 26 (1): 3–24.

Willimack, D.K. and McCarthy, J.S. (2019). Obstacles and opportunities for experiments in establishment surveys supporting official statistics. In: *Experimental Methods in Survey Research: Techniques that Combine Random Sampling with Random Assignment*, Hoboken, NJ: John Wiley & Sons. 309–325.

20

Web Portals for Business Data Collection

Bente Hole[1] and Leanne Houben[2]

[1] *Statistics Norway, Kongsvinger, Norway*
[2] *Statistics Netherlands, Heerlen, The Netherlands*

20.1 Introduction

With increasing digitalization and demands on reducing both response burden and cost, National Statistical Institutes (NSIs) are increasingly interested in portals for collecting business data. In this chapter we provide an overview of portal features and research results that can help NSIs understand the current state of web portals and provide inspiration for their future developments.

Initially, a web portal (or a portal website) was defined as "that part of a website which acts as a gateway, or launch point, through which users navigate the World Wide Web" (OECD 2002). Portals evolved from search engines by adding features and services so that today, a web portal is "a comprehensive internet resource system that provides information services" (Che and Ip 2018, p. 8). Portals not only revolutionized access to information and knowledge, they also support interaction between information users and information providers (see Lee et al. 2010). According to Fuangvut (2005), portals can be classified using different perspectives. We can distinguish between public portals that everyone can visit and private portals that include corporate and enterprise portals. From an information seeking perspective, horizontal portals provide the same offer to all users while vertical portals are user-centric and tailor the offer to the user's role. When considering market segments, types of portals are numerous, e.g. information portals, e-commerce portals, collaborative portals, etc. An even longer list can be composed when thinking of intended users, e.g. patient portals, student portals, employee portals, vendor portals, etc. Enterprise portals usually offer similar features, such as a single point of access with a one-stop shop for all information services, collaboration and communication tools, content and document management, personalization through customization of content and services to user needs, and integration of functions and data from multiple systems into new components (Allan 2009).

Some governmental portals are set up to provide information for businesses. For instance, each country in the European Union is entitled to offer a Point of Single Contact website (PSC), where information can be found on all aspects of doing business in that country, e.g. the rules and formalities for starting and running a business, and users can complete relevant administrative procedures (European Commission 2017). Many e-Government websites in other parts of the world contain similar information (see for instance business.gov.au [Australia], business.gov .om [Oman] and business.mofe.gov.bn [Brunei] for some examples in English and the UN e-Government Knowledge Base United Nations, n.d. for other links).

Advances in Business Statistics, Methods and Data Collection. Edited by Ger Snijkers, Mojca Bavdaž, Stefan Bender, Jacqui Jones, Steve MacFeely, Joseph W. Sakshaug, Katherine J. Thompson, and Arnout van Delden.

In some countries, like the Netherlands and Norway, the NSI is one of the public-sector bodies that contribute and provide information for its country's PSC website (Business.gov.nl 2020; Altinn 2021). Statistics Norway even runs most of its business surveys through Norway's PSC, the Altinn portal.

The transition from paper to electronic questionnaires have led to new challenges and opportunities for NSIs. Electronic reporting requires new procedures, processes, tools and systems. For instance, NSIs need safe and practical ways to make their web questionnaires available and to receive answers/data from the sampled respondents. As many businesses take part in several (recurring) NSI surveys, a single point of access to respond to survey requests is needed. A web portal is often used to cover these needs (see Haraldsen 2013).

We started our research by taking a closer look at a selection of web portals, both NSI-specific and other portals that cover statistical reporting of businesses. This investigation led to a list of features and content that is typically found in such portals. Based on this information we developed a simple questionnaire that we sent to several NSIs around the world. We complemented our research with some in-depth interviews and a further study of selected portals with features of interest.

We will regularly refer to two Norwegian portals for illustration and description purposes. A large amount of experience is gathered with these portals. We will refer to the NSI-specific portal (IDUN) used by Statistics Norway from 2004 to 2014, and the official government portal (Altinn) that is still in use today. Other portals and NSI web content will also be used for specific illustration or for describing a best practice.

The chapter continues with Section 20.2, where we describe our study and survey in more detail, present the results and give examples based both on the responses that we got to our survey and our other investigations. Section 20.3 describes the steps that Statistics Netherlands has taken toward the development of a customized web portal for its business respondents. In Section 20.4 we provide some recommendations and take a brief look at future developments.

20.2 The NSI Web-Portal Study

We started our study by visiting different NSI and eGovernment web sites, focusing on their login and other web portal pages that were available to us, and sporadically collecting information from some of our colleagues from different NSIs in Europe, Australia, the USA and Canada.

To gather information more systematically, we developed a short questionnaire, based on the knowledge gained during the first stage of the study. This way we could ask the same information from more NSIs and hence get a better overview of portals used for business data collection.

20.2.1 More About the Survey

The survey was developed and conducted in the second half of 2020. The International Relations unit at Statistics Netherlands provided us with email addresses to contact persons in all NSIs that are part of the European Statistical System. We also included other countries in the study, where we had already been in touch through our professional network. An email with more information about the study and a link to the questionnaire was sent to 35 countries and 37 NSIs (see Appendix 20.A). 25 NSIs from 23 different countries responded.

The questionnaire consisted of 23 questions (see Appendix 20.B). At the start of the questionnaire, we filtered out NSIs that do not have a portal for business data collection. Those who did not use a portal were asked whether they had plans to build or to start using an existing portal. Those NSIs that used a portal were asked for more information about the following nine attributes:

(1) *Type and size of portal:* To get an idea of how many NSIs share their portal with other organizations, how many business surveys each portal is used for, and how many portals are also used for non-business surveys.

(2) *Common features and status*: To get an overview of the most common features, what features are still under construction and what features are to be implemented in the future.

(3) *Registration and login procedures*: To learn more about how respondents gain access to the surveys, how widespread the use of electronic identification (eID) seems to be, and what security measures different NSIs take.

(4) *Authorization and delegation*: To learn how the reporting task is safely delegated, also when several people are involved in responding to a business survey.

(5) *Data import and transfer*: To understand whether portals enable import of data, machine-to-machine data transfer and/or file transfer as most NSIs aim at collecting data directly from the respondent's computer systems when possible, and on combining this kind of data collection with questionnaires.

(6) *Information about the business unit*: To find out whether the portal is used for delineation of observation unit, e.g. specifying which part of an enterprise the NSI needs data for.

(7) *Feeding data back to the respondents*: To find out whether any portals contain tools that allow the respondents to access and compile relevant resulting statistics.

(8) *Contact options*: To learn about contact and communication options different NSIs offer.

(9) *Strengths and weaknesses:* To gain more knowledge about the pros and cons of today's portals.

20.2.2 Survey Results and Other Findings

In the following, we provide an overview of the results. The survey results are extended with information and examples found through other sources, included in the references. In some cases, we contacted the respondents and requested additional information. We have also studied relevant documentation and logged on to and browsed some portals, both those reported for in the survey and others.

Based on our study, we conclude that there are two types of web portals for reporting businesses:

(I) Access-point portals
   Access points only provide access to a specific questionnaire or survey without any other functionality. Respondents can create a user account and log in to get access to one specific questionnaire or survey.

(II) Integrated portals
   These portals contain a range of different features and functionality and are typically part of, or integrated with, a full electronic reporting and data collection administration system.

NSIs that offer an integrated portal, typically use it to provide businesses with relevant information and to communicate with the business respondents. This way the portal serves as a tool for the NSI to maintain their relationship with the businesses. The portal may contain an overview of the questionnaires relevant to the business, information about the business (as known by the NSI), representation of the business in statistical (unit) terminology, and in some cases even statistical information (output) tailored to each business. Many portals offer options to exchange data in various ways; in addition to filling in questionnaires, the businesses may receive digital notifications and exchange data or data files via the portal.

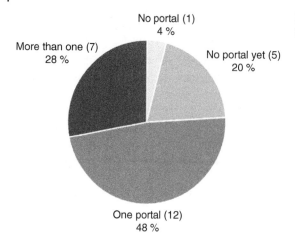

No portal (1)
4 %

More than one (7)
28 %

No portal yet (5)
20 %

One portal (12)
48 %

Figure 20.1 Portal use in the responding NSIs. Source: Own survey.

19 of the 25 NSIs who responded to our survey had a web portal which they used to conduct business surveys. Seven of those 19 reported that they had more than one portal used for business surveys, as can be seen in Figure 20.1.

Five of the six organizations who reported that they had no web portal, indicated that they intend to use a portal in the future, either by building a portal ($N = 3$) or by integrating with or making use of an existing portal ($N = 2$). The one organization that did not intend to build a portal said this was because all their data collection efforts were outsourced; they hire other organizations to collect data on their behalf and the different contractors each have their own data-collection system.

Next, we present the portal attributes studied. We describe quantitative survey results, and then expose specific cases, good practices, and other qualitative data.

20.2.2.1 Type and Size of Portals

More than half ($N = 11$) of the 19 NSIs that use a portal for business data collection reported that they use the portal also for other types of surveys, like social surveys or surveys of other entities or organizations, like municipalities, state entities, colleges and universities. Statistics Sweden mentioned that they plan to use their web portal also for computer-aided telephone interviews (CATIs) in the near future. Their portal's rich functionality has enabled them to implement about 95% of all their web surveys (about 250 altogether, including social surveys and other non-business surveys) in one tool.

The number of business surveys that are run through the 19 NSI portals range from one to 200. Four NSIs reported that they use their portal for 10 or fewer surveys, four use their portal for more than 100 surveys, while the rest ($N = 11$) report a number between 20 and 80 surveys per year.

Some countries, such as Canada, Greece and the Netherlands, currently use an intermediate form of portal: they have several mini portals (i.e. access points) in use, each giving access to one survey. Each respondent who receives a web questionnaire can choose to create a password linked to their name or business name. That password allows them to save and submit their questionnaire later. It also allows them, in case they receive more than one questionnaire for a single survey, to see all the questionnaires that are due for that survey. For instance, an accountant for a large bank where many locations are selected for a single survey would access the survey link and see each of the questionnaires that are due for each location. If the survey is recurring (monthly for example), they would also see past due questionnaires. But this only applies to a single survey; if they also receive questionnaires for another survey, they would see those via a different link.

Statistics Netherlands currently has a similar "portal" solution for four of their most comprehensive business surveys. These solutions include import functions and quality checks in the surveys. One of these surveys is the CBS-DNB Finances of Enterprise and Balance of Payments Survey which was established in 2019 as a collaboration between Statistics Netherlands and the Dutch National Bank (CBS 2020; see also Chapter 16 (Snijkers et al. 2023)).

Only two of the NSIs using a portal, the National Institute of Statistics and Economic Studies (INSEE) in France and Statistics Norway, reported that they share their portal with other organizations. Statistics Portugal do not share their portal as such, but mentioned that they cooperate with Portugal's tourism authorities, among others, on a common solution for data and file transfer. Statistics Liechtenstein reported that their national administration intends to establish a web portal as a single point of contact for all businesses. Statistics Lichtenstein plans to use this portal for their business surveys as soon as it is available.

Governmental portals and other joint portals cover several topics and needs, which may in turn make them more relevant for businesses to use. As we mentioned in the introduction, some portals contain information for start-ups and other information relevant for those running a business. The Estonian governmental portal EESTI.EE and the Norwegian Altinn portal are two examples: Estonia's EESTI portal was recently redesigned and upgraded.

As Figure 20.2 shows, it contains information for the public, as well as for businesses.

The *Accounting and Reporting* menu leads to information about all reporting obligations a company has and links both to the tax authority's website as well as to Statistics Estonia's, among others, as shown in Figure 20.3.

Statistics Estonia offers a separate web-based channel, eSTAT, for completion and submission of statistical questionnaires. The authentication procedure is the same as for the EESTI governmental portal.

During 2014–2017 Statistics Norway went from using their own customized portal IDUN to using the joint governmental portal Altinn to conduct their business surveys because of two main reasons: (i) the IDUN portal was becoming outdated, particularly the questionnaire component and the log-in function. (ii) Norwegian authorities demanded that Altinn should be used for all communication between businesses and the public sector, including Statistics Norway. This meant that digital services for businesses should be made available and all official (digital) letters should be routed through Altinn. The government also demanded that all digital services that require login and authentication should use ID-porten, the common login solution to online public services in Norway, comprising Altinn (Digdir 2017). A service development solution, including a tool for questionnaire development, is also part of the Altinn platform.

Altinn started as a cooperation between the Norwegian Tax Administration, the Brønnøysund Register Center (a government administrative agency responsible for Norway's business register and other state registers) and Statistics Norway in 2002 and was intended to be an alternative reporting channel for financial data. Since the 2003 launch of the Altinn portal, the number of agencies becoming service owners in Altinn has increased steadily. The cooperation now consists of more than 60 different service owners, with the Tax Administration and the Norwegian Labour and Welfare Administration as two of the largest. Being part of such a large constellation is a great advantage for Statistics Norway as the use of the portal has become widespread and common. All businesses registered in Norway have a profile with contact information and their own inbox in Altinn, and they are obliged to use the portal. On the other side, as one of many stakeholders and not among the largest ones, Statistics Norway's needs are not always on top of the priority list.

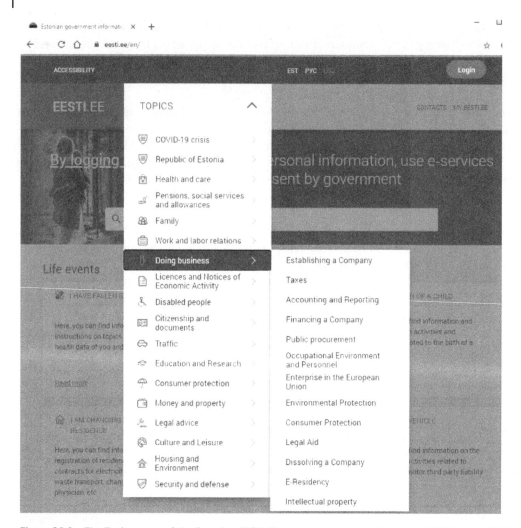

Figure 20.2 The Topics menu of the Estonian EESTI.EE governmental portal (accessed 20 February 2021). Source: EESTI.EE.

20.2.2.2 Common Features and Status

We listed 12 different features in our questionnaire that we considered quite common for portals used for business surveys. Most of the portals covered by our survey were reported to have the following eight:

- Info pages about each survey ($N = 15$)
- Pdf or other printer-friendly version of some or all questionnaires ($N = 15$)
- Separate user instructions (help with filling in), like videos or written guidelines ($N = 15$)
- Frequently asked questions, FAQ ($N = 14$)
- Business/entity information, like name, address, constituent parts of the business, type, contact information ($N = 14$)
- A notification system for important messages, like due date notification ($N = 12$)
- Archive or overview of submitted questionnaires ($N = 12$)
- Overview of the surveys that a certain business is obliged to take part in ($N = 11$)

Figure 20.3 Information about reporting for companies on EESTI.EE (accessed 20 February 2021). Source: EESTI.EE.

Many of the portals have an overview of all surveys that the portal contains ($N = 9$), methodological documentation, like concepts, variables, metadata, etc. ($N = 8$) and a calendar with survey field period ($N = 7$). Only four portals are reported to provide customized feedback reports or statistics relevant for each business (e.g. regional information or sector specific information).

Other features mentioned in the Other-category, were:

- Backoffice management
- XML upload and webservices (for one or more questionnaires and/or business units)
- Self-service options, for checking filing status and applying for time extensions
- Secure email messaging
- A notification system for reminders
- Integrated file upload

One NSI added that some of the mentioned features are placed on its public website, but accessible via the respondent portal. Information about survey concepts, for example, are not specifically located within the portal itself, but this information can be reached via the questionnaire in the portal. This is probably the case also for some of the other portals.

Seven NSIs reported that they considered all their portal's features as complete with no plans to extend or improve its functionality. Two stated that some features were still under construction and nine of the NSIs reported that some features needed further improvement (see Figure 20.4).

Statistics Netherlands is investigating how to build a new, common portal for its business surveys (see Section 20.3).

As for Statistics Norway, the whole platform which the Altinn portal is built on, as well as the questionnaire development tool that goes with it, is being upgraded and modernized; part of this undertaking is a shift from an on-premises to a cloud-based platform.

Statistics Portugal's Webinq is one of the seven portals that contain a calendar that shows when the different surveys are conducted, see Figure 20.5.

The Norwegian Altinn portal provides an example of how business/entity information can be displayed in the portal. Information about the business units, like name, organization number and structure, is taken from the Central Coordinating Register for Legal Entities, Norway's central business register. Figure 20.6 is a screenshot from the test environment in Altinn where test person Niklas Uthus is logged in. Uthus represents Ånneland og Oltedal Regnskap, which is a sub-entity

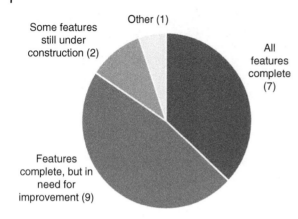

Figure 20.4 Portal status. Source: Own survey.

(i.e. an establishment) belonging to the enterprise (legal unit) Strongfjorden og Lote Regnskap. He is also authorized to represent two other enterprises, Kjerrgarden og Slåstad Regnskap and Tingvoll og Eidså Regnskap, as well as Ånneland og Oltedal Regnskap's two other sub-entities, Ulset og Kollungstveit Regnskap and Mjosundet og Berlevåg Regnskap.

Altinn also provides its users with an archive for storing all submitted questionnaires (see Figure 20.7). This is a new feature compared to Statistics Norway's old portal IDUN, and is a great advantage, both for Statistics Norway and for the businesses, as the respondent can easily go back and find what has been reported, by whom and when. The respondent can create a copy of what has been sent in earlier, update the data and send in a new version of the questionnaire, if needed.

20.2.2.3 Registration, Authentication, and Authorization

Cankaya (2011) defines authentication as the process of verifying an entity's identity, given its credentials. Authentication is the first step in any security process.

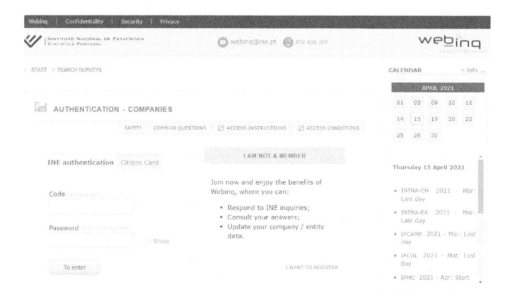

Figure 20.5 Screenshot from Statistics Portugal's Webinq portal (accessed November 2020). Source: Instituto Nacional de Estatística.

Figure 20.6 Screenshot from the Norwegian Altinn portal – display of business information. Source: Altinn.

Authorization is the process of giving an authenticated user permission to access a specific resource or function. This term is often used interchangeably with access control or client privilege. In some instances, systems require the successful verification of more than one factor before granting access. This kind of multi-factor authentication requirement is often deployed to increase security beyond what passwords alone can provide.

The Norwegian Digitalization Agency (2021) describes an eID, as an electronic way of proving one's identity on the internet. An eID can be used for online authentication and login for both citizens and organizations (European Commission 2021).

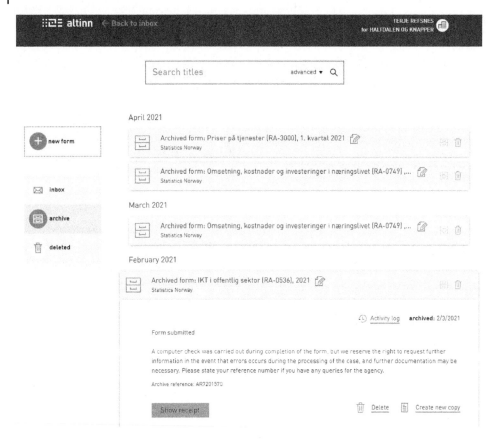

Figure 20.7 Screenshot from the Norwegian Altinn portal – archive (test environment). Source: Altinn.

Most of the surveyed NSIs reported that their portal offers only one way of logging in ($N = 12$). Of these twelve, eight reported that their portal offers a simple username-and-password-based login. In some cases, the respondents register and create a user account in the portal to gain access, in other cases the NSI sends them the required login credentials by post.

Eight NSIs reported that they enable the respondents to log in by using an eID of some sort. For six of the eight portals that offer the use of eID for login, the respondents can also choose to access the portal by using a regular username-and-password combination. Four portals are reported to offer two- or multi-factor authentication; two of them offer only this type of authentication.

In some cases, like for the Norwegian Altinn portal, a portal can offer several different security levels, each with its own set of login requirements, see Figure 20.8.

For most of Statistics Norway's surveys, the respondents can log in using their national identity number (social security number) and single-use codes from Altinn. This corresponds to security level 2. Most Norwegians prefer to use the same eID as they use for accessing their bank online (BankID) to log on to Altinn, which corresponds to security level 4. Businesses can choose to invest in a digital enterprise certificate, like Buypass or Commfides, which can also be used for logging in on security level 4. Figure 20.9 shows an overview of the most used eIDs in Altinn.

Statistics Norway's former portal IDUN offered a simple login procedure, using the responding unit's organization number as a username and a password provided by Statistics Norway. Passwords

Security level 4 – Login with BankID, Buypass, Commfides and BankID on Mobile

If you log on with Commfides, BankID, BankID on Mobile or Buypass, you are logged on with the highest security level. You will need this security level for instance if you wish to sign the form for changing your account number for refunds from NAV or send an official receivers report.

Security level 3 – Login with MinID (via ID-porten) or enterprise certificate

If you choose to log on with PIN codes for MinID, you will access the second highest security level in Altinn, and will have access to most services. Enterprise certificate will also give you access to security level 3.

Security level 2 – Login with Altinn code letter/SMS-code

With one-time code from Altinn, you can log in to security level 2. You can access a range of services.

Security level 1 – Login with only a password

If you log on with only a password, you will have access to a limited number of services in Altinn. You will not be able to change the mobile telephone number in My Profile in this security level.

Security level 0 – Log in without national identity number/D-number

If you do not have a national identity number or a d-number, you can log on with a user name and a password which you have registered. This gives you access to security level 0 in Altinn, and only a few services are available.

Figure 20.8 The different security levels used in Altinn.

were not changed on a regular basis, which constituted a safety risk. The passwords were shared by many different individuals within a business and there was no set procedure for changing passwords as people changed jobs. The passwords were sent to the businesses' official addresses through regular mail each time a new survey or new round of data collection started.

More secure login procedures are recommended, but it may be challenging to get a large population of users to adopt them. For example, as Statistics Norway started using the Altinn portal, the rather strict two-factor login procedure that was required (national ID number + user's own password + PIN code sent by mail) was criticized for being too cumbersome. In the beginning, the pick-up rate was poor; most respondents preferred paper to Altinn if given a choice. Many business respondents were also skeptical since they had to log in using their personal ID to answer a survey on behalf of their employer. If the use of Altinn had not been made mandatory for all Norwegian enterprises, Statistics Norway would probably not have been able to replace IDUN with Altinn. As the use of digital enterprise certificates (Company Digital ID) and eIDs for online banking (Bank-ID) was introduced and became common in Norway, the use of Altinn accelerated. There are still some individuals who are skeptical and hesitant about using their personal eID, but most Norwegian enterprises report that they prefer and save time and money by using Altinn.

Only two NSIs, namely Statistics Portugal and Statistics Estonia, reported that they support an eIDAS-compliant login as a complete authentication and authorization procedure. This is a

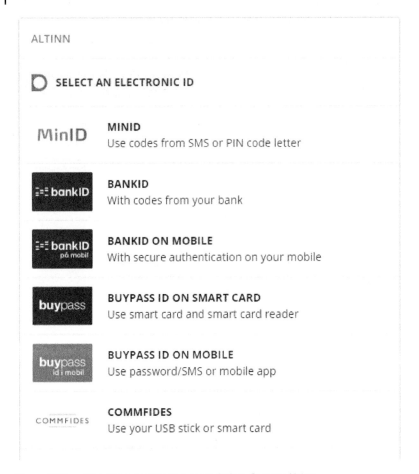

Figure 20.9   eID options for logging on to Altinn. Source: Altinn.

login which enables users from EU countries to use their national eIDs to get access to other EU or EU-associated countries' systems (CEF Digital Home n.d.; European Commission 2021). Figure 20.10 shows a screenshot from Estonia's EESTI portal where for instance people with a Dutch eID can log in.

Nine portals in our study provide the businesses with an authorization tool for access administration, so that they can delegate response tasks.

In Webinq, Statistics Portugal's portal, only one person per business is authorized by the NSI initially. This person has the authority to give other employees access rights to the portal. These access rights range from completing questionnaires, to viewing questionnaires, to viewing detailed benchmark information about the business.

To register in Statistics Estonia's application for electronic reporting, eSTAT, the business needs a username-and-password combination provided in a letter sent to the director of the business, and a valid digital certificate installed. Once the registration is done the business can report electronically for different surveys.

If the business has another unit reporting on its behalf, e.g. an accounting service or another affiliated unit, the business must authorize the reporting unit and the reporting unit must register

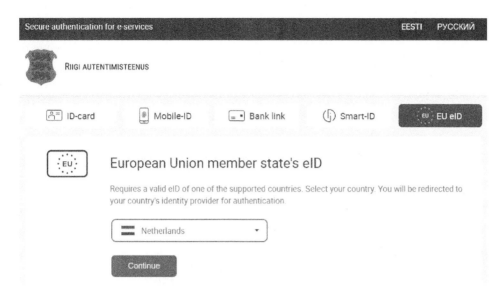

Figure 20.10 Example of the use of eID across European country boarders. Source: EESTI.EE.

to the eSTAT system as well. The pair "observation – reporting unit" has to be designated in the eSTAT system.

Only individuals can log on to eSTAT. One person, e.g. an accountant working at an accounting firm, can submit questionnaires for several businesses and, conversely, the questionnaires of one observational unit may be submitted by several persons (e.g. the accountant, the human resources manager and the executive manager can complete different questionnaires). An official representative of the business must determine who is allowed to submit and correct statistical questionnaires on behalf of that economic entity. To enable the contact persons of an economic entity to submit data via eSTAT, Statistics Estonia create a main user for the economic entity. The main user in turn has the right to create more users and can make sure that each user only can see and access the data needed for their work.

Authentication is based on the use of ID-card, Mobile-ID or Smart-ID, as shown in Figure 20.11.

Foreign citizens who have neither an Estonian ID-card, a mobile-ID or a Smart-ID, can access eSTAT with a password. To get a password, one must access and submit an application electronically via the login page and register as a user. When Statistics Estonia receives the application, the head of the business in question is asked by email for consent to issue a password. When the consent is granted, Statistics Estonia issues a password for data submission, which is sent by mail (Statistics Estonia 2020).

20.2.2.4 Data Import and Transfer

12 of the 19 portals enable the respondents to import data into a questionnaire, while 13 enable file transfer. Files of different extensible markup language (XML) format seem to be common, but also less structured file types, like semi-colon separated values files or other delimited text files, are transferred through many of the portals. Eight of the 19 portals offer both import of data and file transfer. Only three of the 19 portals are reported to offer data transfer machine to machine (M2M), see Figure 20.12.

Three NSIs reported that they have, or are developing, a separate tool or solution for M2M data transfer; these are not included in the three portals counted above. For instance, the U.S.

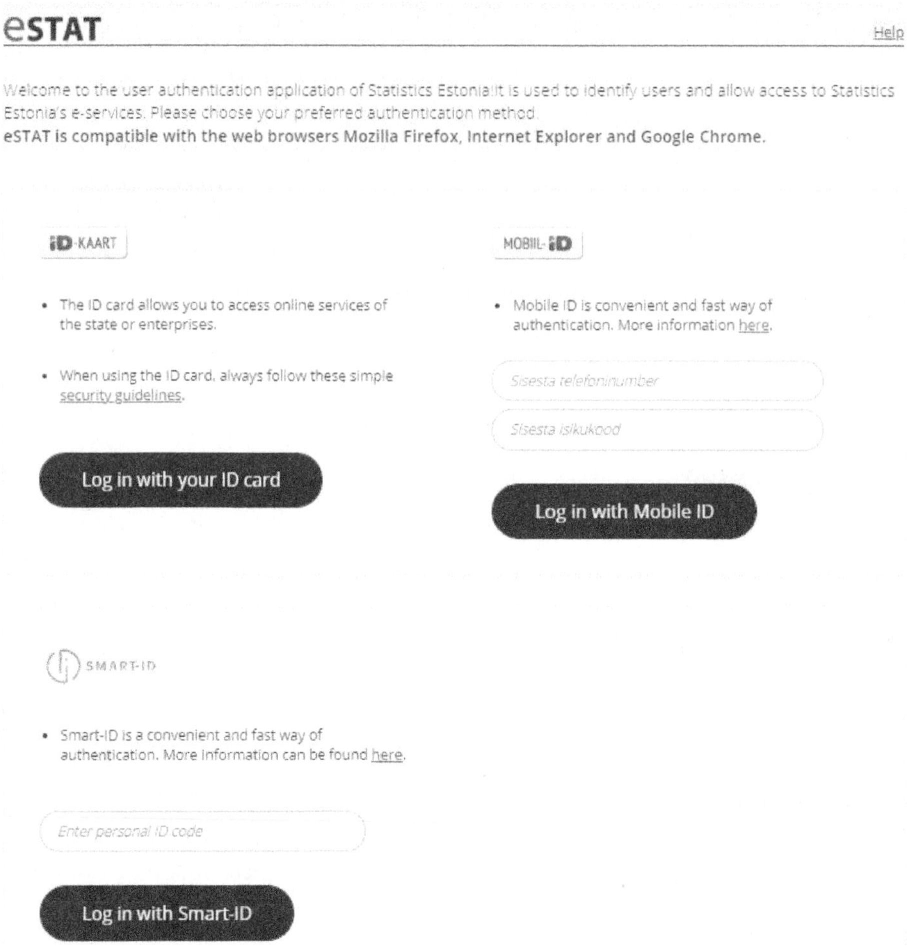

eSTAT

Welcome to the user authentication application of Statistics Estonia. It is used to identify users and allow access to Statistics Estonia's e-services. Please choose your preferred authentication method.
eSTAT is compatible with the web browsers Mozilla Firefox, Internet Explorer and Google Chrome.

ID-KAART

- The ID card allows you to access online services of the state or enterprises.

- When using the ID card, always follow these simple security guidelines.

Log in with your ID card

MOBIIL-ID

- Mobile ID is convenient and fast way of authentication. More information here.

Sisesta telefoninumber

Sisesta isikukood

Log in with Mobile ID

SMART-ID

- Smart-ID is a convenient and fast way of authentication. More information can be found here.

Enter personal ID code

Log in with Smart-ID

Figure 20.11 eSTAT login page (accessed 20 February 2021). Source: Portal Site of Statistics Estonia.

Census Bureau reported that their portal links respondents to an electronic reporting instrument (Centurion) via single sign-on. There is also a secure messaging feature in the portal, where respondents can send them spreadsheets, etc., but the preferred method is that they use Centurion to provide electronic responses.

INSEE in France reported that they have a separate tool (R2D2) that enables file transfer for a few of their surveys.

Slovenia reported that their portal enables uploading xml data files for some surveys, which are developed in Excel.

The Australian Bureau of Statistics explained that their file-transfer capability is very new and was only used for one survey in 2020. Only selected respondents will be enabled to use this functionality. To collect data for the Survey of Job Vacancies, for example, the sample is approximately 5000 businesses. About 25 of those are very large businesses that operate in multiple states and need to report to the NSI their vacancies by state. These 25 businesses are sent a customized excel file for all the state splits and it is those files/forms that are uploaded through the file transfer. The

Figure 20.12 No. of portals that enable import of data, M2M data transfer and/or file transfer.

No. of portals	Import (N = 12)	M2M (N = 3)	File transfer (N = 13)
8	✓	—	✓
4	—	—	✓
2	✓	—	—
2	—	—	—
1	—	✓	—
1	✓	✓	—
1	✓	✓	✓

remainder of businesses are not provided this option and instead either respond through their web form through the portal or provide the data by phone.

Statistics Sweden and the Statistical Office of the Slovak Republic reported that they are developing an M2M solution as part of their portal. The Norwegian Altinn portal offers M2M transfer of data already, as does Statistics Portugal's portal. Statistics Portugal reported that the data- or file-transfer feature is a feature with potential to join more institutions. As we have already mentioned, they are currently working with tourism authorities, Bank of Portugal, Foreign Boarder Control and tourism companies, to build a joint solution covering several information requirements.

20.2.2.5 Identifying the Right Business Unit

Van Delden et al. (2018) state that the notion of "business," and its measurement, are not clear-cut. In fact, several business concepts, so-called (types of) statistical units, are used in business statistics. In some cases, the statistical unit that one wants to measure does not correspond to the business unit as the respondent defines it. Hence, it can sometimes be a challenge to make clear to respondents exactly which unit or part of an enterprise one needs data for, and thus avoid unit errors.

Most of the NSIs ($N = 16$) reported that they try to communicate what unit they need data for through the questionnaire itself. Quite a few ($N = 11$) use the letter that they send out to the business respondents to explain which unit they need information about, most of these ($N = 9$) have unit information in both questionnaire and letter. Five NSIs reported that it is made clear in the portal environment; one of those five uses only the portal environment to provide information about which unit it needs data for.

As mentioned earlier, every enterprise and establishment registered in Norway's national business register have their own inbox in Altinn, based on its register ID, i.e. its organization number. As long as the statistical unit that Statistics Norway needs data for corresponds with the enterprise or establishment registered in the register, and messages and questionnaires from Statistics Norway are distributed to the right inbox, it is usually quite clear for the respondent

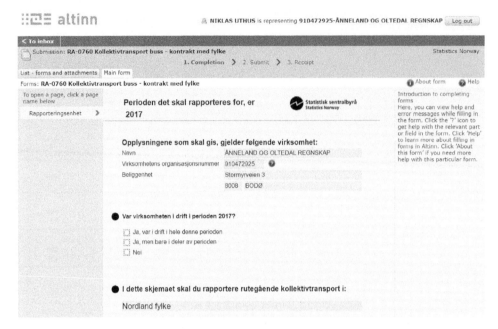

Figure 20.13 Screenshot of one of Statistics Norway's questionnaires in Altinn. Source: Altinn.

what unit the NSI asks for information about. Figure 20.13 shows what it looks like as the respondent Niklas Uthus (test person) has opened a questionnaire from Statistics Norway from Ånneland og Oltedal regnskap's inbox in Altinn. The name, organization number and address of the observation unit is also preprinted initially on the first page of the questionnaire. Conveying the right location is of importance, since sub-entities in some enterprises can have similar or even the same name.

20.2.2.6 Returning Data to the Respondents

As mentioned in Section 20.2.2.2, only four out of the 19 portals are reported to offer customized feedback reports or statistical output tailored to each business. Statistics Portugal's portal Webinq is one of them. Currently, Statistics Portugal offers businesses a PDF with benchmark information, see Figure 20.14 for a sample. However, in the future, they plan to introduce a dashboard that offers interactive data feedback to the businesses.

Two other examples can be found in Statistics Netherlands and in Statistics New Zealand, though neither of these are integrated as a part of their respective reporting portals. Research done by Statistics Netherland showed that businesses are interested in relevant statistical data for their business, but that they struggle to find the right information on the extensive public website or any of the other output channels the NSI has (Houben et al. 2020). Statistics Netherlands therefore created a first version of a dashboard containing a selection of the information that is of interest to businesses. When their new portal is ready, the dashboard will also be made accessible there, automatically presorting the information according to the sector and region that a specific business belongs to. The dashboard provides the users with up-to-date data, such as the number of businesses by industry and by region, turnover, and the latest survey results on expected turnover, employment and investments (Statistics Netherlands 2021).

Statistics New Zealand offers similar tools via their *Data for business* page which is available from https://www.stats.govt.nz/. Through this page businesses can access overviews and detailed

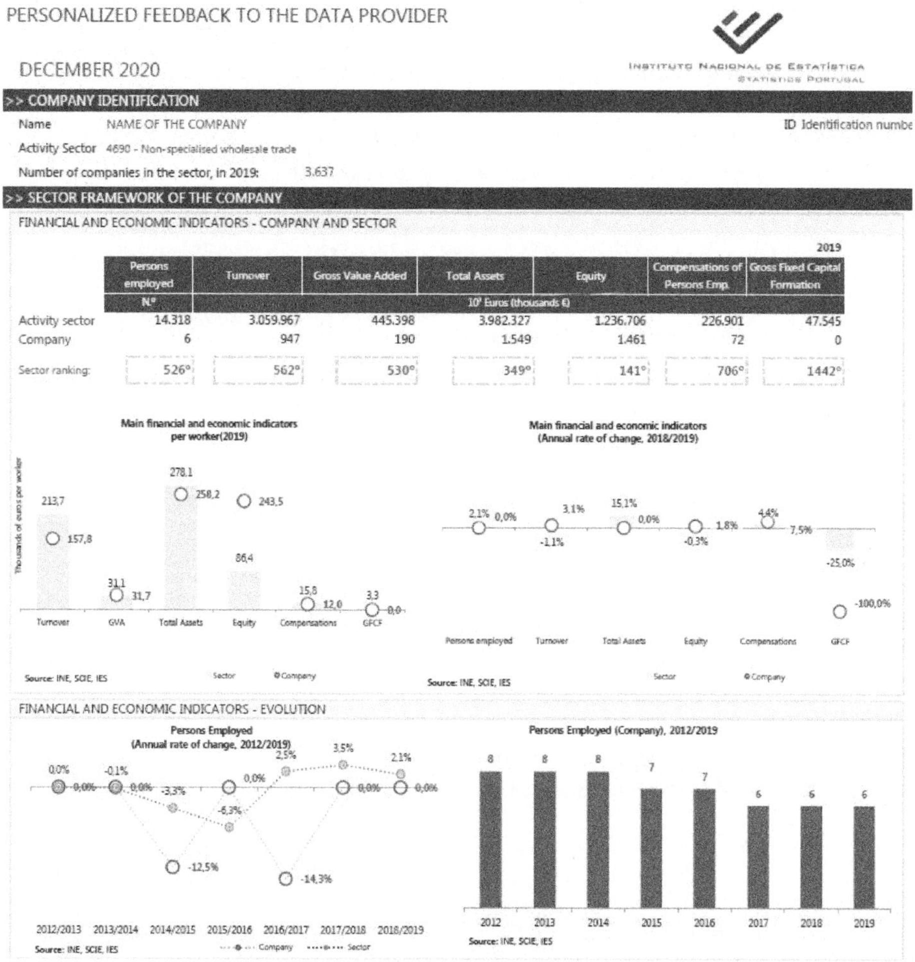

PERSONALIZED FEEDBACK TO THE DATA PROVIDER

DECEMBER 2020

INSTITUTO NACIONAL DE ESTATÍSTICA
STATISTICS PORTUGAL

>> COMPANY IDENTIFICATION

Name NAME OF THE COMPANY ID Identification numbe

Activity Sector 4690 - Non-specialised wholesale trade

Number of companies in the sector, in 2019: 3.637

>> SECTOR FRAMEWORK OF THE COMPANY

FINANCIAL AND ECONOMIC INDICATORS - COMPANY AND SECTOR

2019

	Persons employed	Turnover	Gross Value Added	Total Assets	Equity	Compensations of Persons Emp.	Gross Fixed Capital Formation
	Nº	10³ Euros (thousands €)					
Activity sector	14.318	3.059.967	445.398	3.982.327	1.236.706	226.901	47.545
Company	6	947	190	1.549	1.461	72	0
Sector ranking:	526º	562º	530º	349º	141º	706º	1442º

Figure 20.14 Part of a feedback report from Statistics Portugal's Webinq portal. Source: Instituto Nacional de Estatística.

data on who their potential customers are and where they are located, benchmark their business performance against others, see how many new businesses there are in their region, view business survival rates, and get statistics on the financial performance and position of businesses in their industry (Statistics New Zealand, n.d.).

Statistics Belgium reported that their portal doesn't provide a tool for feeding back data to the respondents, but stress that they prefill all available administrative information in each questionnaire. The same is done by many other NSIs as well.

20.2.2.7 Contact Options and Communication

Most of the portals ($N = 16$) display a phone number which the respondents can use to contact the NSI. Most ($N = 13$) also contain an email address which the NSI can be contacted on, either integrated as part of the portal or simply displayed in the portal. A few portals contain a contact form ($N = 5$), while a chat option is offered only by one NSI.

In cases where the portal is used for sending messages and/or for notifying respondents, the communication tends to be one-way; the NSI may inform and notify the businesses through the portal, but apart from filling in and submitting questionnaires, the businesses are not able to correspond with the NSI directly through the portal itself.

A screenshot from the eSTAT instruction manual shows how all messages that Statistics Estonia has e-mailed to the responding business are also displayed in the system. When a new message is sent, it shows in the upper menu bar (bell icon with a red oval on it), see Figure 20.15 (Statistics Estonia 2020).

In the Norwegian Altinn portal, messages or digital letters from Statistics Norway are put in the businesses' inboxes, along with questionnaires for completion, see Figure 20.16.

The U.S. Census Bureau, on the other hand, offers two-way communication through their Respondent Portal, as shown in Figure 20.17. The *Send message* menu option is connected to a specific survey through a "survey card", which is available for users who have created an account,

Figure 20.15 eSTAT screenshot showing messages sent from Statistics Estonia. Source: Portal Site of Statistics Estonia.

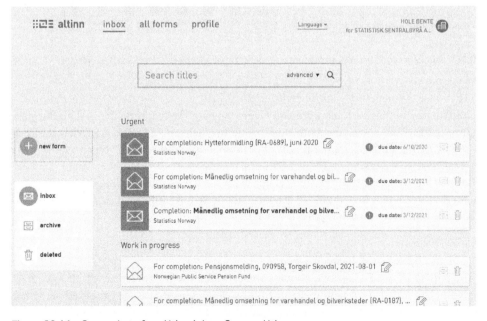

Figure 20.16 Screenshot of an Altinn inbox. Source: Altinn.

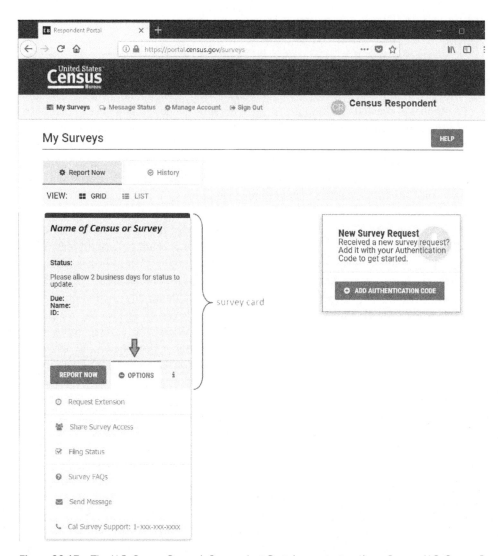

Figure 20.17 The U.S. Census Bureau's Respondent Portal – contact options. Source: U.S. Census Bureau.

logged in and linked themselves to the specific survey using an authentication code provided by the Census Bureau (U.S. Census Bureau 2021).

20.2.2.8 Strengths and Weaknesses

We asked the respondents to mention one or two of their portal's main strengths. Uniformity, standardization, multi-survey access and single sign-on, as well as usability and user-friendliness were mentioned in different terms by several respondents. Otherwise, the responses were quite varied.

We also asked the respondents what they felt should be improved in their portal. Again, the answers varied a great deal. Some of the things mentioned by several respondents was functionality for data transfer machine-to-machine, and performance, i.e. speed and responsiveness of the system.

We will come back to some of the mentioned aspects in Section 20.4.

20.3 Investigating How to Build a Customized Portal at Statistics Netherlands

To improve the response experience for businesses, Statistics Netherlands is exploring how to build a customized portal for business respondents. These developments are tackled agile and make use of a number of previous developments. Most notably, the design and development of a new modular computer-assisted web interviewing (CAWI), CATI and computer-assisted personal interviewing (CAPI) data-collection system. This single system will replace the four previously used, non-linkable data collection applications. If the portal is realized, it will be the entrance to the new data collection system. Important features of the newly built data collection system are the pre-filling of the structural business statistics questionnaires with administrative data, and a new application in which all business data, (non)response data and all communication with the businesses is registered. In addition, Statistics Netherlands examines how the planned portal can provide access to a recently built data collection channel for secondary data sources. With this portal Statistics Netherlands can securely collect data from, and return information to, the business respondents. Furthermore, ideas have been developed to link the portal to the Statistics Netherlands' extensive public website, providing the businesses tailored information on current output and publicly available dashboard information on data published in the past.

In the run-up to the portal's plans, Statistics Netherlands carried out several preliminary investigations and took a wide-scope inventory by interviewing approximately 40 key staff members with different backgrounds, many contacts with the business community, and/or a great deal of affinity with businesses. Qualitative interviews asked what they thought a portal for companies should look like, what they thought was most important and why, what problems they anticipated, and whether they could come up with solutions. As a follow-up, the business needs were formulated. Furthermore, it was examined how the business needs would fit in other portal related developments at Statistics Netherlands and what approach and portal structure of other governmental organizations and NSIs would be interesting for the portal of Statistics Netherlands. The result was a roadmap, in which a minimal viable product (MVP) has been defined, and a planned approach for the follow-up (Lemmens and Houben 2019).

Other portal builders appeared to have paid little attention to user tests, namely pre-testing with businesses, and later regretted this. We decided to pay close attention to the respondents' needs and preferences beforehand, prepared to adjust if needed (Blank 2013; Ries 2011). We set up a qualitative user test for different types of businesses, including multinationals, small and middle-sized businesses, and accountancy companies. Important questions were: what should the portal look like, which functions are really necessary, which functions are desirable, which functions are superfluous, and is there a difference between the wishes of the various types of businesses? All interviews were performed online.

To make the image as concrete as possible for the businesses, the tests were performed using a demo of the portal (mockup) in PowerPoint. The demo was built based on the knowledge gained previously and looked like a real portal on the outside but did not contain any underlying technical functionality. The most important parts of the mockup were:

- *My login*: The part where the business can log in and access the portal.
- *My overview*: The main menu in the portal. From this page the business gets access to the pages My surveys, My company data and My statistical information. In addition, this page shows also what data must be supplied and when, and how the helpdesk can be contacted.

- *My surveys*: Here the business can, among other things, access and submit questionnaires, submit other data, view previously submitted data, and view background information about the surveys for which they have to submit data.
- *My company data*: In this page the business can check how it is registered, who the main contact person is, what contact details of the business the NSI have registered, and how the business can change these if necessary.
- *My statistical information*: This page gives the business access to a dashboard and pre-sorted statistical information.

All interviewees were very positive about the design and thought it made a lot of sense. They said that it would give the businesses a good overview of the information they had to provide, they would get a complete insight in which questionnaires had been completed and which questionnaires had not, they would have a clear overview of the business information, they would have easy access to information that would be of interest to them, and they would be able to contact Statistics Netherlands in an easy way. The first three businesses had some comments on the layout. We registered them and had the mockup reviewed again by a user experience (UX) designer. After the designer had made a few more changes to the design, the mockup was more in line with our website and we did not get any additional negative remarks about the layout. The interviewees stated that they liked the subtle design. There are not too many images on the page, and the dark gray color was said to radiate authority.

The interviewees found the portal very user-friendly. One business representative mentioned that he would prefer the portal to be part of a government-wide portal. In the test version, a breadcrumb trail was included to ease navigation to other web pages, but the interviewees preferred to navigate via the main menu, or via the browser (Back arrows).

After completion of the business tests, the mockup was again discussed with several stakeholders within Statistics Netherlands and the Advisory Council that represents the trade-organizations and the accountancy companies. Their input contributed to a further refinement of the mockup, as input for the Minimum Viable Product to be built (Houben et al. 2020).

20.4   Recommendations and Future Developments

Starting points and conditions for building and using a portal may be quite different across countries and NSIs due to different legislation and varying digital maturity. Additionally, the way an NSI is organized, the role it plays in society (what level of trust it has, for instance), and what IT platforms and systems are available to it, influences what kind of tools and functionalities an NSI can apply and develop, as well as its competence, capacity, economy and priorities. The choice of functionality and design of a portal will also depend on the scope and target population it is intended for.

As Haraldsen states in Chapter 15 (2023), computerized business questionnaires should be distributed together with a computerized administration system, preferably on a web portal. He presents a table of web portal alternatives that should be discussed and considered, especially by those who conduct recurring business surveys.

20.4.1   Recommendations

Based on our experience and study findings, here is some general advice for NSIs that intend to build, improve or expand a web portal intended for collecting data from businesses.

Before building, improving, or expanding:

(1) Be clear on what you want to accomplish and what is most important to your NSI. A web portal should be applied to achieve efficient, low-burden data collection, for the survey organization and for the responding businesses. This can and should be measured, both qualitatively and quantitatively (see point 7–9 below).

(2) Make sure you know the different users and their needs, including both internal (NSI) users and external ones (businesses and respondents). Consult other stakeholders as well, like trade organizations and other business and economic interest groups. Talk to them and test your ideas. What do different users want and need? What is likely to generate value, for the NSI and for the reporting businesses?

   (a) Small businesses that only take part in surveys every now and then will most likely have different needs and preferences than large enterprises that take part in several recurring surveys on a regular basis.

   (b) The fact that much of the reporting is outsourced, for instance to accountancy companies or other third-party organizations, should also be considered.

   (c) Be aware of the different roles involved in business reporting; not just the actual respondent, but management, coordinators and data providers (see Willimack and Snijkers 2013).

   (d) Aim at easing the whole response process within the businesses. To do that, you need to have a clear idea of who needs access to what, and what tools are needed to coordinate, distribute and delegate the reporting tasks.

   (e) Knowledge of what data businesses typically have and what kind of systems they tend to use is also relevant.

If you are starting from scratch:

(3) Check if there are other existing portals or initiatives, like common authentication and authorization functionality, that are worth considering.

(4) Consider using existing open source code and a design system; code, components and patterns that are already tested and quality assured are readily available online, in many cases for free.

(5) Work agile and aim at adjusting and improving your portal's modules and services during use.

(6) Stick to known web standards and conventions. Applying accessibility guidelines will most likely result in simple and easy to use graphical user interfaces for both portal web pages, including log-in pages, and for the surveys they host (see W3C n.d.).

   Note that offering a single sign-on and the use of common log in procedures may be more valuable and effective than having all relevant features and data located in one place. As long as the user can access all relevant data, functionality and services in a simple and seamless fashion, if and when they need it, it does not matter if the different modules, data and features are actually integrated as part of the portal itself or not.

Evaluation:

(7) Use statistics and feedback from your helpdesk or user support and monitor what effect different measures and improvements have on your users.

(8) Monitor the response burden regularly and systematically, for instance by adding a set of standardized questions about actual and perceived response burden to a selection of questionnaires (see Dale and Haraldsen 2007; Haraldsen et al. 2013).

(9) User experience and satisfaction surveys can also be applied to understand how well your portal works (see for instance Graham et al. 2020).

20.4.2   Future Web Portal Developments

– *Tailoring, flexibility, freedom of choice and self-service.*
In the years to come, we think that more portals will offer several ways of granting access, depending on the type of user and intended uses. We may also see more functionality enabling the portal users to choose how they prefer to communicate with the NSI, how they delegate and perform reporting tasks and what feedback or data they would like to have.

Ideally, a web portal should allow businesses and their respondents to select among several notification options. Some may prefer email, others text messages; some might like the notification to be sent to a specific employee, others prefer to be notified through a common or official email address, etc.

Flexibility and choice may be equally important when it comes to the actual reporting and data submission. Since businesses tend to be rather heterogenous in terms of size, systems used, digital maturity, etc., it may be wise to offer several ways of fulfilling their reporting duty. If alternative data sources do not exist and the collection is stable, the best option is to retrieve or import data directly from the business systems, provided that the retrieved data meets the quality requirements.

For some businesses, uploading data files may be the least burdensome way to report. If data needs to be filled in manually, sometimes reporting by use of an app on a cell phone may be practical. The Road Freight Transport survey is an example where such a data collection method may be efficient and more user friendly than a traditional survey. With an app, using Global Positioning System (GPS) data, the truck drivers could report specifics about the goods that they deliver, as they deliver it.

Cross-survey data submission may become more common, especially when it comes to economic or financial data. For example, in Portugal and Sweden businesses can submit data for more than one survey, and/or for more than one observational unit, in the form of a single XML or XBRL (eXtensible Business Reporting Language) file.

"One-stop shop" web pages and content tailored to each business, for instance in the form of a My Page, will probably grow in numbers. Dashboards where the respondents can access relevant statistics and help themselves in putting the statistics together, like the ones that Statistics Portugal and Statistics Netherlands intend to integrate in their portals, may also be relevant for more NSIs.

– *Security and data protection*
Data collectors have to respect laws and regulations concerning data protection and data minimization, like the General Data Protection Regulation (GDPR). Data providers are increasingly aware of the value and hence the need for protection of their data and expect data collectors to offer secure ways of transferring, saving, and using their data. Since businesses are obliged to provide data to NSIs, it is the NSIs' duty to ensure the safety of business data and prevent data leakage. Data leakage can have a major impact on the trust and confidence in the NSI, which in turn may lead to reduced willingness to provide data and respond to surveys. Solid authentication and authorization procedures thus become more important. The use of eID, for persons, businesses and systems/machines, is becoming more widespread and common.

Maintaining a stable multi-entity association between survey, respondent, and business is important. It is also wise to communicate how the NSI ensures that data are safe.

– *Built-in data verification and two-way communication*
Functionality enabling instant data validation and feedback is high up on many NSIs priority list. Quality checks built in as part of the questionnaires can give the NSI the possibility to inform

the respondent immediately if there are logic or suspected errors in the given data. This helps to reduce the number of re-contacts, which in turn lowers the respondent burden. Not everything could or should be checked as data is filled in or imported, but if edits and quality checks must be performed after submission, measures should be taken to speed up this process so that the respondent can be notified as soon as possible. Infrastructure and tools that can provide secure, but functional correspondence between the surveyor and the respondent are sometimes necessary, especially if sensitive data are exchanged during this communication.

– *Use of application programming interfaces (APIs), automation, and integration*
   The use of system-to-system or M2M solutions and APIs are becoming increasingly widespread. Future web portals should facilitate M2M and mixed-mode data collection. Retrieval of data directly from corporate accounting systems is within reach in many countries, due to accounting rules and standards (Buiten et al. 2018). Automated processes, both for the data collector's and the data provider's part, are desirable and more achievable than ever, thanks to new technology and cloud-based platforms.

   Altinn offers APIs both for application owners like Statistics Norway and for end users, allowing them to perform tasks like creating an application instance, uploading form data and attachments and downloading form data, among other things (Altinn n.d.). Since 2015 most payroll and personnel systems in Norway have been integrated with Altinn, much due to the so-called a-ordning. The a-ordning is a coordinated service used by employers to report information about income and employees to the Norwegian Labour and Welfare Administration, Statistics Norway and the Norwegian Tax Administration. The information is submitted electronically, either via the employer's payroll system using Altinn's APIs or manually via a form in Altinn (The Norwegian Tax Administration 2018). In many aspects, Altinn can be considered a hub or distribution point where data are shared between different entities and authorities. Instead of having to deal with a multitude of different APIs offered by different data providers, data collectors like Statistics Norway can in many cases relate to Altinn and its standard APIs to get hold of available data.

   Scholta et al. (2018) propose a transition from a one-stop shop to a no-stop shop, where the citizen does not have to perform any action or fill in any forms to receive government services because the government initiates the service. NSIs could act similarly: If data is readily available and can be accessed by authorized authorities, the authorities – including NSIs – should take advantage of this. For example, the Estonian project "Vision for a single online point of contact for entrepreneurs," completed in November 2020, aimed at developing a vision and identifying the activities necessary for creating a single and reliable web-based point of contact for entrepreneurs for communicating with the public sector. The before mentioned EESTI.EE platform is planned to extend the use of machine-readable data and to establish a framework for providing access to a business's data. This will allow authorized third parties to access and use the data about a business, without the business having to submit the same information again. An entrepreneur will be able to authorize other legal and natural persons to access data about the business in public sector information systems (Ministry of Economic Affairs and Communications, Estonia 2020).

   The Nordic Smart Government initiative constitutes another example. Its vision is to simplify the administration for small and medium-sized enterprises in the Nordic region and create growth by effective and innovative use of data, digitalization, and automation. The ecosystem providing real-time business data for business-to-business and business-to-government, will consist of public and private systems handling financial and economic data used by the enterprises in various enterprise resource planning (ERP) Systems. Business administration such as transactions and reporting to governmental authorities is to be supported by the ecosystem, as well as access to financial information for counterparts. The already existing digital systems and solutions must apply standardized interfaces (APIs), which will enable them to share data automatically (Nordic Smart Government 2020).

Design and features of web portals will most certainly continue to change over time, but we believe that portals will continue to play an important role in business data collection for years to come.

Disclaimer and Acknowledgements

The views expressed in this chapter are those of the authors and do not necessarily reflect the policies of their employers. The authors would like to thank all who responded to our questionnaire. A special thanks to Paulo Saraiva (Statistics Portugal), Ilona Ethla and Marika Korka (Statistics Estonia), Tanya Price (Australian Bureau of Statistics) and Chandra Adolfsson (Statistics Sweden) for their extra input and contributions. Thanks also to Nyree Lemmens (Statistics Netherlands) and Einar D. Stavnes (Statistics Norway) for reviewing this chapter and Carina Franssen (Statistics Netherlands) for distributing the questionnaires. Finally, many thanks to Mojca Bavdaž (University of Ljubljana) and Jacqui Jones (Australian Bureau of Statistics) for reviewing and editing various versions of this chapter.

Appendix 20.A: List of NSIs the Questionnaire was Sent to

1. Australia: Australian Bureau of Statistics
2. Austria: Statistics Austria
3. Belgium: Statistics Belgium
4. Bulgaria: National Statistical Institute
5. Croatia: Croatian Bureau of Statistics
6. Cyprus: Statistical Service of Cyprus
7. Czech Republic: Czech Statistical Office
8. Canada: Statistics Canada
9. Denmark: Statistics Denmark
10. Estonia: Statistics Estonia
11. Finland: Statistics Finland
12. France: National Institute of Statistics and Economic Studies (INSEE)
13. Germany: Federal Statistical Office
14. Greece: National Statistical Service of Greece
15. Hungary: Hungarian Central Statistical Office
16. Iceland: Statistics Iceland
17. Ireland: Central Statistics Office
18. Italy: Italian National Institute of Statistics (ISTAT)
19. Kyrgyzstan: National Statistics Committee of Kyrgyzstan
20. Latvia: Central Statistical Bureau of Latvia
21. Liechtenstein: Office of Statistics
22. Lithuania: Statistics Lithuania
23. Luxemburg: National Institute of statistics and economic studies (STATEC)
24. Malta: National Statistics Office

25. Netherlands: Statistics Netherlands
26. Norway: Statistics Norway
27. Poland: Central Statistical Office
28. Portugal: Statistics Portugal
29. Romania: National Institute of Statistics
30. Slovakia: Statistical Office of the Slovak Republic
31. Slovenia: Statistical Office of the Republic of Slovenia
32. Spain: National Statistics Institute
33. Sweden: Statistics Sweden
34. Switzerland: Swiss Federal Statistical Office
35. United states of America: U.S. Bureau of Labor Statistics
36. United states of America: U.S. Census Bureau
37. United states of America: National Center for Science and Engineering Statistics

Appendix 20.B: Word Copy of Questionnaire

Web Survey Portals

The following questions are about web survey portals used for collecting data from businesses.

Section 1

1 Does your statistical organization use one or more web portal for conducting business surveys?
- Yes, one
- Yes, more than one
- No

Section 2

2 Do you plan to build such a portal or to start using an existing portal?
- Yes, we plan to build a portal
- Yes, we plan to make use of an existing portal
- No
- Maybe

3 Why/why not?

Section 3

If your organization has more than one web portal, please answer for the portal with the most business surveys.

4 Is the portal used by your statistical organization only, or do you share it with other organizations?

- Used only by my statistical organization
- Shared portal
- Other

5 Is the portal also used for other types of surveys, like social surveys (persons) or surveys meant for other units or organizations, like municipalities, state entities, etc.?

- No, only for businesses surveys
- Yes, it is used also for other types of surveys

6 Approximately how many business surveys are run through the portal each year?

7 What kind of login procedures are in use?

☐ Simple, username and password-based
☐ Login by use of an electronic identification, eID
☐ Login that requires two or more distinct forms of ID (2- or multi-factor authentication)
☐ eIDAS compliant login (enables users from other EU countries to use their national eIDs to get access)
☐ Other

8 If there is anything else you would like to add about login procedure, please fill in here:

9 What features does your portal contain?

☐ A notification system for important messages (e.g. due date)
☐ Overview of the surveys that a certain business has to take part in
☐ Overview of all surveys that the portal contains

▫ A calendar that shows which surveys are run when
▫ Archive or overview of submitted questionnaires
▫ Info pages about each survey
▫ Pdf or other printer-friendly version of some or all the questionnaires
▫ Frequently asked questions, FAQs
▫ Separate user instructions (help with filling in), like videos or written guidelines
▫ Methodological documentation (concepts, variables, metadata, etc.)
▫ Customized feedback reports or statistics relevant for each business (e.g. regional information or sector specific information)
▫ Business/entity information like name, address, structure, type, contact information
▫ Other

10 Are all of your portal's features complete, or are some still under construction?
   ○ All portal features are complete
   ○ Some portal features are still under construction
   ○ Features are complete, but some need further improvement
   ○ Other

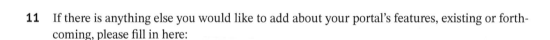

11 If there is anything else you would like to add about your portal's features, existing or forthcoming, please fill in here:

12 Does the portal enable the respondent to import data into a questionnaire?
   ○ Yes
   ○ No
   ○ Don't know

13 Does the portal enable machine to machine data transfer?
   ○ Yes
   ○ No

14 Does the portal enable file transfer?
   ○ Yes
   ○ No

15 If there is anything else you would like to add about data or file transfer, please fill in here:

Section 4

16 In case you want information only about a certain part of an enterprise, how do you make this clear to the respondent?
  □ It is explained in the letter sent to the business
  □ It is made clear in the portal environment
  □ It is made clear in the questionnaire
  □ Other

17 If there is anything you would like to add with regard to describing the observation unit, please fill in here:

18 Does the portal provide an administrative tool which the respondents can use to access and/or compile relevant data and information?
  o No
  o Yes

19 What contact options are available through the portal?
  □ Email (integrated in portal)
  □ Chat
  □ Contact form
  □ Phone (number is displayed in the portal environment)
  □ Other

20 Does the portal provide the businesses with an authorization tool for access administration so that they can delegate response tasks?
  o Yes
  o No

21 What would you say are the main strengths of your portal – what are you most proud of? Name one or two things.

22 What would you say should be improved in your portal? Name one or two things.

Section 5

23 If you have any additional information that you would like to add, please fill in here:

References

Allan, R. (2009). *Virtual Research Environments*. Elsevier, Chandos Publishing https://doi.org/10.1016/B978-1-84334-562-6.50009-8.

Altinn (2021). Statistical obligations. https://www.altinn.no/en/start-and-run-business/running-business/statistical-obligations/ (accessed 24 February 2021).

Altinn (n.d.). Altinn API. https://docs.altinn.studio/teknologi/altinnstudio/altinn-api/ (accessed October 2020).

Blank, S. (2013). *The Four Steps to the Epiphany*. K&S Ranch.

Buiten, G., Snijkers, G., Saraiva, P., Erikson, J., Erikson, A.-G., and Born, A. (2018). Business data collection: toward electronic data interchange. Experiences in Portugal, Canada, Sweden, and the Netherlands with EDI. *Journal of Official Statistics* 34 (2): 419–443. https://doi.org/10.2478/jos-2018-0019.

Business.gov.nl (2020). Partners. https://business.gov.nl/partners/ (accessed 24 February 2021)

Cankaya, E. (2011). Authentication. In: *Encyclopedia of Cryptography and Security* (ed. H.C.A. van Tilborg and S. Jajodia). Boston, MA: Springer https://doi.org/10.1007/978-1-4419-5906-5_772.

CBS (2020). CBS-DNB Finances of Enterprises and Balance of Payments. https://www.cbs.nl/en-gb/participants-survey/overzicht/businesses/onderzoek/cbs-dnb-finances-of-enterprises-and-balance-of-payments (accessed 2 October 2020).

CEF Digital Home (n.d.). eID. https://ec.europa.eu/cefdigital/wiki/display/CEFDIGITAL/eID (accessed 15 January 2021).

Che, X. and Ip, B. (2018). *Social Networks in China*. Elsevier, Chandos Publishing https://doi.org/10.1016/B978-0-08-101934-4.00001-7.

Dale, T. and Haraldsen, G. (ed.) (2007). *Handbook for Monitoring and Evaluating Business Survey Response Burdens*. European Commission, Eurostat.

Digdir (2017). Help and guides for Common ICT solutions. http://eid.difi.no/en/id-porten (accessed 15 January 2021).

European Commission (2017). Internal Market, Industry, Entrepreneurship and SMEs - Points of Single Contact. https://ec.europa.eu/growth/single-market/services/services-directive/in-practice/contact_en (accessed 27 February 2021).

European Commission (2021). Electronic Identification. https://digital-strategy.ec.europa.eu/en/policies/electronic-identification (accessed 30 July 2021).

Fuangvut, T. (2005). Campus portals: a framework for development accommodating end-users' online activities. PhD thesis. School of Economics and Information Systems, University of Wollongong. http://ro.uow.edu.au/theses/431.

Graham, T., Ali, S., Avdagovska, M., and Ballermann, M. (2020). Effects of a web-based patient portal on patient satisfaction and missed appointment rates: survey study. *Journal of medical Internet research* 22 (5): e17955. https://doi.org/10.2196/17955.

Haraldsen, G. (2013). Questionnaire communication in business surveys. In: *Designing and Conducting Business Surveys* (ed. G. Snijkers, G. Haraldsen, J. Jones, and D. Willimack). New Jersey: Wiley.

Haraldsen, G. (2023). What computerized business questionnaires and questionnaire management tools can offer. In: *Advances in Business Statistics, Methods and Data Collection*, Chapter 15 (ed. G. Snijkers, M. Bavdaž, S. Bender, J. Jones, S. MacFeely, J.W. Sakshaug, K.J. Thompson, and A. van Delden). Hoboken: Wiley.

Haraldsen, G., Jones, J., Giesen, D., and Zhang, L. (2013). Understanding and coping with response burden. In: *Designing and Conducting Business Surveys* (ed. G. Snijkers, G. Haraldsen, J. Jones, and D. Willimack). New Jersey: Wiley.

Houben, L., Lemmens, N., and Giesen, D. (2020). Summary of the qualitative test results mock-up portal for business respondents (preliminary study 2). Statistics Netherlands (in Dutch).

Lee, C.S., Goh, D.H., and Chua, A.Y.K. (2010). An analysis of knowledge management mechanisms in healthcare portals. *Journal of Librarianship and Information Science* 42 (1): 20–44. https://doi.org/10.1177/0961000609351371.

Lemmens, N. and Houben, L. (2019). CBS broad Portal (preliminary study 1). Statistics Netherlands (in Dutch).

Ministry of Economic Affairs and Communications, Estonia (2020). Project "Vision for single online point of contact for entreprenueurs". Provided by Statistics Estonia.

Nordic Smart Government (2020). Nordic Smart Government. https://nordicsmartgovernment.org (accessed 10 February 2021).

OECD (2002). Portal. Glossary of statistical terms. https://stats.oecd.org/glossary/detail.asp?ID=4720 (accessed July 2021).

Ries, E. (2011). *The Lean Startup: How Constant Innovation Creates Radically Successful Businesses*. London: Portfolio Penguin.

Scholta, H., Mertens, W., Kowalkiewicz, M., and Becker, J. (2018). From one-stop shop to no-stop shop: an e-government stage model. *Government Information Quarterly* 36 (1), January 2019, 11–26.

Snijkers, G., Houben, L., and Demollin, F. (2023). Tailoring the design of a new combined business survey: process, methods, and lessons learned. In: *Advances in Business Statistics, Methods and Data Collection*, Chapter 16 (ed. G. Snijkers, M. Bavdaž, S. Bender, J. Jones, S. MacFeely, J.W. Sakshaug, K.J. Thompson, and A. van Delden). Hoboken: Wiley.

Statistics Estonia (2020). Instruction manual for data submission in eSTAT environment. https://www .stat.ee/sites/default/files/2020-07/eSTAT-manual.pdf (accessed 2 February 2021).

Statistics Netherlands (2021). Dashboard bedrijven. https://www.cbs.nl/nl-nl/visualisaties/dashboard-bedrijven#A-U. In Dutch (accesses May 2021).

Statistics New Zealand (n.d.). Data for business. https://www.stats.govt.nz/tools/data-for-business (accessed 2 February 2021).

The Norwegian Digitalization Agency (2021). Electronic ID. https://www.norge.no/en/electronic-id (accessed November 2020).

The Norwegian Tax Administration (2018). The a-ordning. https://www.skatteetaten.no/en/business-and-organisation/employer/the-a-melding/about-the-a-ordning/about-a-ordningen (accessed October 2020).

United Nations (n.d.). UN e-Government Knowledgebase website. https://publicadministration.un .org/egovkb/en-us/Resources/Country-URLs (accessed 24 February 2021).

U.S. Census Bureau (2021). How Do I Get Started?. https://www.census.gov/content/census/en/topics/business-economy/information/response/get-started.html#par_textimage_2 (accessed 15 January 2021).

van Delden, A., Lorenc, B., Struijs, P., and Zhang, L. (2018). Letter to the editor. *Journal of Official Statistics* 34 (2): 573–580. https://doi.org/10.2478/jos-2018-0027.

W3C, The World Wide Web Consortium (n.d.). Web Content Accessibility Guidelines (WCAG). https://www.w3.org/WAI/standards-guidelines/wcag/ (accessed October 2020).

Willimack, D.K. and Snijkers, G. (2013). The business context and its implications for the survey response process. In: *Designing and Conducting Business Surveys* (ed. G. Snijkers, G. Haraldsen, J. Jones, and D. Willimack). New Jersey: Wiley.

21

A Creative Approach to Promoting Survey Response[1]

Charles F. Brady, Jr. and Kari L. Klinedinst

US Census Bureau, Washington, DC, USA

21.1 Introduction

Every five years, the US Census Bureau collects extensive statistics about nearly four million businesses that are essential to understanding the American economy. This official count, better known as the Economic Census, serves as the foundation for the measurement of US businesses and their economic impact. As part of the Census Bureau's mission to provide timely information on the health of the US economy, this business census serves as the most extensive collection of data related to business activity.

Foundational to our efforts is understanding how businesses respond to surveys. The primary purpose of the Economic Census is to provide economic benchmarks. In general, business populations are highly skewed, with a small number of businesses contributing the majority of data to the published totals. Obtaining quality response data from the largest companies is crucial and is generally the primary focus of the published research on collection methods and contact strategies (Thompson et al. 2015; Thompson et al. 2018). Using qualitative research findings from a study of 30 large companies, Sudman et al. (2000) present a hybrid establishment survey response process model, reinforced by additional findings (Willimack and Nichols 2010). This model recognizes the organizational behavioral steps that make establishment survey response a combination of both organizational and cognitive factors. An independent study with a larger variety of business sizes presented in Bavdaž (2010) supports this while expanding on the response process model. All these studies determined that the complexity of a business organization needs to be accounted for in the design and collection of a survey and highlighted the unique response burden elements imposed on the largest and most complex firms: for example, a single questionnaire may need to be "farmed out" to different departments to obtain a complete response. Typical of many National Statistics Institutes (NSIs), the Census Bureau has a well-established account manager program, whose primary purpose is to establish and maintain ongoing contact and support with the largest companies surveyed in its economic programs (Giesen et al. 2018).

That said, the largest companies included in the Economic Census only represent a small fraction of the total *number* of businesses surveyed. For the remaining businesses, awareness and critical

1 The Census Bureau has reviewed this paper for unauthorized disclosure of confidential information and has approved the disclosure avoidance practices applied. (Approval ID: CBDRB-FY21-ESMD002-029).
Any opinions and conclusions expressed in this publication are those of the authors and do not reflect the views of the US Census Bureau.

Advances in Business Statistics, Methods and Data Collection. Edited by Ger Snijkers, Mojca Bavdaž, Stefan Bender, Jacqui Jones, Steve MacFeely, Joseph W. Sakshaug, Katherine J. Thompson, and Arnout van Delden.
© 2023 John Wiley & Sons, Inc. Published 2023 by John Wiley & Sons, Inc.

information about the Economic Census had to be provided in a more indirect, cost-effective manner, with nominal supporting research on optimal contact strategies. These businesses had to be convinced not only to participate in the Census but to do so electronically. In parallel with this change, a secure online respondent portal was introduced, designed to make filing easier while improving data quality.

Emphasizing the value of response is theorized to elicit responses, including from the smallest businesses (Torres van Grinsven et al. 2014). Emphasizing the importance of the individual business' contribution to the survey has been shown to positively affect response (Kennedy and Phipps 1995), and perceptions of the usefulness of the survey are improved by the enclosures while there is no evidence of an effect on perceptions of how burdensome the survey is (Hedlin et al. 2008).

The shift from paper to electronic data collection is known to lower collection costs. A previous study among the US businesses found that web response worked quite well regardless of the business size for well-designed questionnaires asking for data with straightforward concepts; when these two conditions do not hold, although valid, voluntary web collection was more confined to larger units (Thompson et al. 2015).

The chapter describes how a team consisting of Census Bureau staff with expertise in outreach, research, subject matter content, and overall communications, as well as a marketing services contractor, created and implemented a promotional campaign that successfully tapped the motivation of small businesses for electronic participation in the Census. The approach built on past experience and findings from a series of focus groups. The chapter first describes the characteristics of the US Economic Census (Section 21.2) and the approach and methods used in setting up the promotion campaign (Section 21.3), then presents the results of focus groups (Section 21.4), development of campaign materials (Section 21.5) and campaign implementation (Section 21.6), and finishes with the look ahead (Section 21.7) and conclusions (Section 21.8).

21.2 Background

Economic Census collects data from nearly four million employer businesses, large, medium, and small, covering most industries and all geographic areas of the United States using questionnaires tailored to their primary business activity. To reduce the burden on American businesses, the Census Bureau does not send Economic Census surveys to most very small firms (Fink et al. 2015). Obtaining timely, complete responses from all other small businesses ensures results are representative and reflect the diversity and dynamic nature of small businesses. At companies with more than one location, surveys are sent to the company headquarters or other company appointed contacts. Only a few industries are not fully covered by the Economic Census such as agriculture, education, and transportation, as they are covered by agencies of the US Departments of Agriculture, Education, and Transportation, respectively.

In the initial survey requests, the US Census Bureau as well as other governmental statistical agencies are required to inform potential respondents of the legal requirements under Title 13 of the US Code, but they also assure them their response is confidential due to another section of the same law. Only persons sworn to uphold the confidentiality may view the information and the data can be used for statistical purposes only. Further, copies retained in respondents' files are immune from legal process.

The overall collection strategy for the 2017 Economic Census is outside of the scope of this chapter but best practices and learnings from data collection informed the work on promotional campaign. There were a variety of experiments that primarily informed changes and updates to the collection strategy. These experiments (Tuttle et al. 2018) were incorporated into the collection of several annual business surveys and one quarterly survey and contained five experiments whose designs are based on business survey decision-making and response processes such as mail sequence, messaging, and envelope appearance. A nonresponse follow-up experiment (Thompson and Kaputa 2017) informed the change to include certified mailings with a selection of small unit businesses.

One of the initiatives that promotes response to the Economic Census is the Account Manager (AM) program. Since 1992, this program has provided 1000 or more of the nation's largest companies with a single point of contact at the Census Bureau to encourage reporting, answer questions, and help companies in any way possible to report. Evidence has shown that large multiple-location companies with an AM have higher response rates for the Census than those without an AM (Marske et al. 2007). For the 2012 Economic Census, this program had grown to include 1648 companies that account for 890,980 business locations and utilized 200 Census Bureau staff.

To guide promotion among the remaining units, the 2017 Economic Census Publicity and Outreach (ECPO) Team was formed. The team consisted of Census Bureau staff with expertise in outreach, research, subject matter content, and overall communications, as well as a marketing services contractor. The Respondent Outreach and Promotion Branch, Economic Management Division, US Census Bureau, led the team. One of the main lessons from conducting outreach for previous Economic Censuses was to rely upon successful partnerships with stakeholders to carry the message. Intermediaries such as trade associations and chambers of commerce, trusted voices in their respective communities, communicate to their constituents (respondents to the US Census Bureau) the importance and relevance of response to economic surveys and the economic census (Brady 2016).

The most significant change to response for the 2017 Economic Census was the shift to all-electronic response. The exception to these changes were small companies located in the US territories that had a paper option available, including a Spanish version for Puerto Rico.

21.3   Approach and Methods

The approach to motivate smaller businesses to respond to fully electronic 2017 Economic Census was rooted in a partnership with a marketing private firm. After setting up the objectives, response information from 2012 Economic Census was analyzed to understand how key challenges in obtaining electronic response differed among industries and locations. Focus groups were planned around critical segments of the target population to better tailor promotion and fine tune the communication. More detail is provided below.

21.3.1   Public Sector – Private Sector Partnership

Developing an effective outreach program for this wide variety of businesses (in terms of size and sector) is a time-consuming and expensive process. Contracting with a private firm leverages dedicated expertise on the current state of the market, quickly building on proven successful marketing strategies. The Census Bureau decided to contract with a private firm to support research, planning, development, and implementation of a broad-spectrum communications campaign targeting high respondent engagement for the 2017 Economic Census. This approach is not confined to the Economic Census: for example, Desouza and Bhagwatwar (2012) describe a similar strategy implemented in the 2010 population census. The Census Bureau selected

Grafik Marketing Communications for the project. Grafik had worked on two previous economic censuses, thus providing critical expertise, and expediting any learning curve. Throughout, Grafik worked alongside the Census Bureau, often aligning with principles long held by staff within the agency, including those ultimately responsible for the project. The result was a dynamic approach to engaging respondents made possible with the addition of private sector vision.

Grafik relied upon the following ideals to guide their contribution:

Personal relationships matter. Developing face-to-face relationships is instrumental, particularly with national business organizations and trade associations. Once the relationship is established, these intermediaries will speak on behalf of the Census Bureau. The 2014 *Harvard Business Review* article entitled, "Unlock the Mysteries of Your Customer Relationships" (Avery et al. 2014), supports this notion, emphasizing that the importance of approaching relationships with a long-term perspective is a more effective approach than overutilization of customer relationship management (CRM) databases monitored solely by technical staff.

More customized and relevant content is impactful. Consumers can be frustrated by ambiguous content which does not fit their needs or interests.

Less is more. We learned through extensive focus group testing and sessions with partner organizations that this adage is critical to effective outreach. "Too long, didn't read" (TL; DR) is a valuable mantra for today's marketing. The title of this *CNET* 2013 article says it all: "When 15 seconds is too long; welcome to the 'TL; DR' world." (Sullivan 2013). Snijkers and Jones (2013) observe that "when people are about to make a decision, they process just enough information (not more and not less), at a minimum level of effort, to ascertain what they need to know to make that decision." Other focus-group based studies and articles support this contention: see Landreth (2002, 2004), Galloway (2017), Feenberg et al. (2017). In short, recipients *scan.*

The first two ideals had been historically put in practice in the Census Bureau's outreach. The last was not; earlier marketing material tended toward full-page narratives. Eventually, these lengthy paragraphs became short lists with the important messages strategically placed at the beginning.

21.3.2 Strategic Objectives

The 2017 Economic Census respondent outreach campaign began in earnest with a series of kickoff sessions, conducted November 2014 through January 2015. The goal was to consider insights and recommendations from the 2012 Economic Census and to plan program milestones for strategy and research. The result was a detailed timetable for 2015 activities. In February and March 2015, the ECPO team defined strategic objectives for response promotion and developed a preliminary three-year timetable.

The following objectives were initially prioritized:

Communicate the transition to 100% electronic response. Strategic objectives included the prioritization of Internet response, which significantly shifted the approach for the 2017 Economic Census, as compared to 2012, thus setting context and direction for research and planning. The elimination of paper forms was a fundamental change that redefined target segmentation and messaging (note that the addition of respondent portal requirements was also a fundamental change, but this aspect was not included in the planning efforts until 2016).

Developing long-term relationships with intermediary partners. This remained a top priority – even more important with changes to reporting methodology.

Reach specific response goals for the 2017 Economic Census by company profile (size, location, industry). Well-defined targets allowed us to identify low responding areas. This helped us to prioritize outreach during the collection phase.

Leverage the 2017 Economic Census outreach and communications as a ramp-up to the 2020 Decennial Census. Although the ECPO team acknowledged the magnitude that association with the 2020 Decennial Census could have, the timing of the 2017 Economic Census was too early for related messaging to be included in decennial messaging. The team did, however, make note of the Decennial Census in Economic Census presentation materials wherever possible. Since membership on the ECPO team included Communications Directorate staff who were responsible for parts of the 2020 promotion, there was consistent awareness as well.

21.3.3 Target Segmentation and Focus Groups

Target segmentation was a very important driver for managing response promotion. This effort became a compass for the program that set a solid strategic foundation for planning and decision-making. It directed the selection of markets for multiple rounds of focus group research designed to investigate barriers to response (specifically electronic) and inform messaging development, and drove city selection guidance for onsite presentations during collection (see Section 21.6.9).

To define target segments for 2017, the Census Bureau's Center for Economic Studies analyzed 2012 Economic Census single-establishment business response data to identify metropolitan areas and industries that had lower-than-average performance. This allowed us to locate trends at geographic levels, as multi-establishment businesses may have locations across wide geographic areas. Because of the shift to all-electronic reporting, we plotted overall response rate (regardless of mode) vs. past electronic response to define four target groupings for research and communications planning: "Challenge", "Opportunity", "Lower Tech" (paper), and "Ready", as outlined in Figure 21.1 below. These target segmentations allowed us to determine which areas needed help with overall response versus those that might struggle with the switch to all-electronic reporting.

The "Challenge" group includes markets and industries that have traditionally low response rates regardless of reporting mode. Running a single establishment in these industries may be the reason

Figure 21.1 Target Segmentation for Metro Areas and Industries (Grafik Marketing, unpublished results).

that such establishments had not yet embraced digitalization. The "Lower-Tech" group includes historically strong respondents, which is probably due to general compliance with rules. This group may need help, however, to switch from the use of paper to all electronic reporting because of low digitalization. The "Ready" segment has the capacity and willingness to respond, thus high compliance, and the "Opportunity" group may be digitized because of their own needs, even if working as a single establishment.

In April and May 2015, the ECPO team, specifically our marketing services contractor, developed a targeted qualitative research strategy. This included three rounds of focus groups with single- and multi-establishment businesses and discussions with intermediary groups in the selected research markets. Research markets were selected from each of the four target segments. The team explored perceptions and messaging for many different target mindsets, including those who historically responded well with paper forms.

In each round, Census Bureau staff met with partners from its closest organizations, such as Small Business Development Centers and Chambers of Commerce, in the markets selected for research. Scheduling the supplemental local meetings with focus yielded travel cost and time efficiencies and set an approach to meetings we followed throughout the program. Discussions covered advance information about the 2017 Economic Census, input from stakeholders about online reporting, preliminary messaging, and communications planning. Overall, this engagement early in the process provided valuable insights for communications planning, including a "temperature check" on respondent mindsets and specific recommendations for online reporting.

21.3.4 Communications Plan

Throughout most of 2016, concurrent with qualitative research efforts, the ECPO team laid groundwork for a communications plan. This included an expanded scope to include more frequently occurring economic surveys, mapping the respondent journey for online reporting, and definition of internal implementation roles for different areas within the Census Bureau.

The 2017 Economic Census and Current Economic Surveys Communications Plan was completed in September 2016. The plan delineated between official, direct correspondence to respondents and our strategy incorporating indirect outreach via intermediary channels, and addressed goals and objectives, target markets, communications strategy, messaging, and a draft timeline.

Based upon our strategy and research foundation, we locked in our approach for targeting and messaging and set the framework for implementation. The plan became our actionable "playbook" as we moved forward with creative development and next-level tactical planning for the campaign.

After presentation of the plan, the ECPO team moved immediately into campaign messaging and preparation for creative development. As stated earlier, the new Census Bureau requirement for online reporting through a respondent portal was a priority. In November 2016, the team received a full briefing on usability studies as key input for campaign development and additional target research.

The changes from 2012 to 2017 went far beyond the elimination of paper forms, as respondents would now be required to provide their email addresses to create online accounts in a multi-step set up process. Official letters would now provide an authentication code to unlock the Economic Census and populate the survey into an online dashboard for access. These changes introduced a more complicated process with several new hurdles for respondents. Promotional efforts needed to set expectations for the new requirements while they drove people to the portal.

21.4 Results from Focus Groups

The main overall result from focus groups is that businesses report being more motivated to respond knowing that the data is available to them and that "less is more" in communication. Details about implementation and specific findings are provided below.

21.4.1 Focus Groups – Round One

In July 2015, in order to gauge opinions of the broader business community, regardless of whether a participant engaged in Census Bureau surveys, we conducted eleven focus groups with single and multi-establishment businesses in four markets, one from each target grouping as reflected in Figure 21.2. Discussion topics included mindsets about government reporting, perceptions about the Census Bureau, messaging themes, and Economic Census program elements.

Findings provided valuable direction and specific recommendations for the 2017 Economic Census, including:

- The small business community was still largely unaware of the Economic Census.
- Online reporting has become the expected norm and was not seen as a barrier for response.
- Even though reactions to messaging themes were mixed, showing samples of Economic Census results (i.e. information is used) was identified as a compelling motivator for response.

Other recommendations were related to timing of the Economic Census mailout and due dates, envelope features, and even a proposed name to change to "US Business Census."

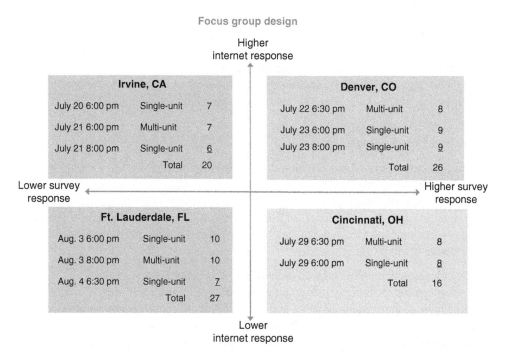

Figure 21.2 Focus Group Round 1 Design – Size and Target Grouping, and Total Participants ($n = 89$) (WBA Market Research, unpublished results).

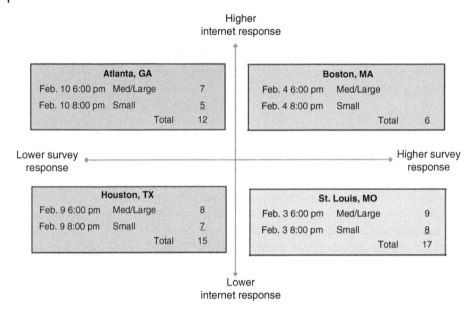

Higher
internet response

Atlanta, GA		
Feb. 10 6:00 pm	Med/Large	7
Feb. 10 8:00 pm	Small	5
	Total	12

Boston, MA		
Feb. 4 6:00 pm	Med/Large	
Feb. 4 8:00 pm	Small	
	Total	6

Lower survey
response ←

→ Higher survey
response

Houston, TX		
Feb. 9 6:00 pm	Med/Large	8
Feb. 9 8:00 pm	Small	7
	Total	15

St. Louis, MO		
Feb. 3 6:00 pm	Med/Large	9
Feb. 3 8:00 pm	Small	8
	Total	17

Lower
internet response

Figure 21.3 Focus Group Round 2 Design – Size & Target Grouping, and Total Participants ($n = 50$) (*Blizzard in Boston) (WBA Market Research, unpublished results).

21.4.2 Focus Groups – Round Two

Additional focus groups were conducted with known respondents in early 2016. This additional research step was taken to confirm receptiveness to Internet reporting, the electronic reporting tool, and messaging with known respondents who had previously taken Census economic surveys. Groups were once again held in four cities, one from each target grouping, with a total of fifty participants, as reflected in Figure 21.3. These fifty participants represented a variety of company types, positions within a company, and company sizes by both number of employees and locations, as shown in Figure 21.4. Findings from Round One were validated – known respondents had a high degree of consistency with earlier groups with the general small business community.

21.4.3 Intermediary Meeting at Census

Our next research step was to solicit the counsel of several intermediary partners, including representatives from the American Payroll Association and America's Small Business Development Centers. In November 2016, the Census Bureau hosted a facilitated session to garner their input on a draft communications plan, feedback on plans for Round Three focus groups, and reactions to preliminary communications materials. The input we received was pivotal to our direction and approach for the campaign:

- The 2017 Communications Plan was well received and supported.
- Overview of upcoming focus group topics and methodology was also approved.
- Recommendation was given to pare down and simplify content for "response motivators" and to make sure communications are respondent-centered, not Census-centered. Tell respondents what is in it for them. Emphasized the need for more relevant messaging about businesses and less messaging about the Census Bureau.
- Simplified efforts should be made to tell the story of the business owner.

Company Type		
Accounting	Healthcare	Orthodontics
Auto quick lube	Home Healthcare	Plumbing
Chemical manufacturing	Hotel	Private equity
Child care	Manufacture test equipment	Real estate management
Fast food restaurants	Non-profit	Retail sporting goods
Food service	Nursing homes	Specialty grocery
Funeral home	Oil & Gas manufacturing	TV production

Title/Position		
Account Coordinator	Director of Finance	Office Manager
Accounting Specialist	Executive Administrator	Owner
CEO	Executive Director	Payroll Director
CEO	Financial Manager	Sr. Accountant
Chairman	HR Director	Sr. Tax Accountant
Controller	HR Manager	VP

# Employees at Location	
5 to 19	14
20 to 149	22
150 to 299	3
300 or more	11

Number of Units	
1 to 2	18
3 to 5	8
6 to 9	3
10 or more	21

Figure 21.4 Focus Group Round 2 – Additional company information ($n = 50$) (WBA Market Research, unpublished results).

21.4.4 Focus Groups Round Three

Round Three focus groups were held in February 2017 to get final input from known respondents on messaging, communications materials, and the new online reporting requirements. Groups were held in four cities, one from each target grouping, with a total of fifty-four participants, as reflected in Figure 21.5. These fifty-four participants represented a variety of company types, positions within a company, company sizes by both number of employees and locations, and data usage, as shown in Figure 21.6.

These groups provided an important confirmation for campaign direction and valuable insights for the 2017 program:

- Response to government requests for information had become a fact of life for the participants.
- Most respondents have no clear idea why they are being asked to provide information.
- Most companies are not aware that economic data from the Census Bureau is available for their use, free, and available online.
- Companies are more motivated to respond once they know that data from the Census Bureau economic surveys is available to them.
- Reporting online is becoming more and more the standard practice.
- In today's fast-paced business world, less is more.

21.4.5 Additional Meetings

In each round, Census Bureau staff met with partners from its closest organizations, in the markets selected for research. These local meetings yielded travel cost and time efficiencies and provided valuable insights for communications planning, including learnings on respondent mindsets and

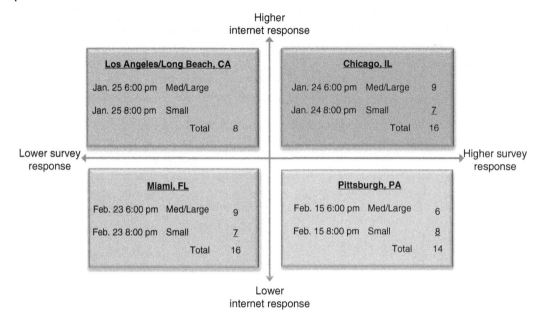

Figure 21.5 Focus Group Round 3 Design – Size and Target Grouping, and Total Participants ($n = 54$) (WBA Market Research, unpublished results).

Company Type		
Aircraft Parts Maint./Repair	Commercial Real Estate	Law Firm
Distilled Beverage Importer	Concrete Manufacturer	Non-Profit Educ. Training
Banquet Hall	Distributor - Engine Parts	Pediatric Medical Care
Biotech	Drug Treatment Facility	Public Library
Chemical/Metal Wholesaler	Engineering Consulting	Record Company
Chocolate Mfg.	Fast Food	Restaurants
CNC Machining	Fitness Classes	Retail Women's Clothing

Title/Position		
Accounting Manager	Dir. Of Finance	Office Manager
Business Manager	Dir. Of Operations	Owner
CEO	Finance Consultant	President
CFO	Finance System Manager	Senior Tax Analyst
Compliance Officer	General Counsel	Tax and Compliance
Controller	General Manager	VP. HR

# Employees at Location		Number of Units	
5 to 19	18	Single	24
20 to 149	27	2	7
150 to 299	4	3 to 5	11
300 or more	5	6 to 9	6
		10 or more	6

Data Usage	
I do not personally use industry statistical data to make business decisions, but others in my company do	25
I personally use industry statistical data to make business decisions	17
My company does not use industry statistical data to make business decisions	6

Figure 21.6 Focus Group Round 3 – Additional company information ($n = 54$) (WBA Market Research, unpublished results).

specific recommendations for online reporting. Organizations indicated strong willingness to assist with future outreach, even offering to provide direct help with response for small businesses.

21.5 Development of Campaign Materials

Creative development for the response promotion ad campaign began in April 2017 and continued throughout the year. Contractors developed a creative brief that summarized final research learnings and set direction for ad concepts and design. Three creative directions were presented in May 2017. The focus for all three was a lighthearted approach, the power of storytelling, and the notion that every business is needed to complete the picture.

Figure 21.7 Core Ad Campaign Image (U.S. Census Bureau 2017). Source: U.S. Census Bureau.

Transforming the draft campaign into the final product required several steps. Once a concept was selected and approved by the ECPO team and leadership in June 2017, a second intermediary meeting to review and discuss the concept solidified our direction. The campaign was fully developed and executed over the next six months with close, multi-disciplinary coordination.

The ECPO team invited Economic and Communications Directorate staff to submit proposals that fit this model. For the versions which included Census Bureau data, staff statisticians provided review to confirm accuracy.

The Communications Directorate provided style guides and color patterns to help determine final font and color scheme. While our contractor's designers recommended the initial black and yellow scheme as striking and universally accepted, the blue and white combination ultimately selected from approved color patterns fit well with other Census branded materials (Figure 21.7).

The "See How It All Adds Up" campaign was first used at the America's Small Business Development Centers conference in September 2017 and our full set of campaign assets (See Figure 21.8 for examples) was completed by the end of 2017 for a January 2018 full launch to support an official shift in the Economic Census response due date to June 12, 2018. Among the key campaign materials were brochures, videos, a website, and partner briefing presentations, each presented briefly below.

21.5.1 Brochures

Despite today's digital age, response to the printed Economic Census brochure was overwhelmingly positive, based upon feedback from intermediaries and response from conference attendees. The six-panel format and succinct content delivered the right amount of information. Nearly 50,000 were distributed to intermediaries and at conferences, including a Spanish language version. Partners in each target market took possession of packets, and sometimes boxes, of brochures for local distribution. An electronic version was also available online.

Figure 21.8 Sample of final promotional campaign content (U.S. Census Bureau 2018). Source: U.S. Census Bureau.

21.5.2 Videos

Eight campaign videos were produced and published (currently archived at Economic Census Videos). This was a collaborative effort, with scripts and creative consultation from our contractor, and direction and production by the Center for New Media and Promotion in the Census Bureau's Communications Directorate. This in-house staff also work on other Census Bureau efforts, including the Decennial Census, and were a valuable resource. While scheduling time with staff to avoid competing projects required advance planning, it was well worth the effort. Production benefited from the use of the existing creative campaign and messaging as the basis for development. Use of the existing material also reinforced branding across all content and stock footage was used to lower costs. Videos were shared both externally to promote survey response and internally for Census Bureau staff on in-house monitors.

The suite of videos was as follows:

- Short targeted videos (6) – Based upon digital and print ads presenting "equation" style messaging. We employed stock footage, graphics, music, and made them twenty seconds long to increase effectiveness (Pressgrove et al. 2021). The industry-based themes were accounting, computers, travel, pets, watch repair, and investments.
- Economic Census and survey videos (2) – In "Meet James," a fictional restaurant owner uses Economic Census data to find a new location to expand his business. "The Data Journey" describes the agency's collection through dissemination processes.

21.5.3 Campaign Website

The goal for the new Economic Census website (www.census.gov/EconomicCensus) was to carry over the look and feel of the campaign while maintaining the standards for Census Bureau survey webpages. The website served as the primary source for learning about the Economic Census and finding promotional materials. Content and wording on the website evolved as more materials were available, as we entered the collection phase.

21.5.4 Partner Briefing Presentation Content

Our Partner Briefing presentation was at the core of the campaign. It contained all key messaging, including content for the website and online presentations, and became the main component for meetings around the country. Additionally, the Partner Briefing was built with the flexibility to continue the conversation beyond Economic Census data collection and into subsequent survey years. Based upon publicly available membership counts for the organizations we visited, our reach may have been 100,000 potential respondents or more.

21.5.5 Island Areas

For the first time, we developed a single brochure to promote the Economic Census of Island Areas and Puerto Rico. The brochure followed the same look and feel as the stateside brochure but required content changes since the island areas and Puerto Rico typically do not participate in intercensus survey programs.

Brochure content was developed by the ECPO team in consultation with the Economic Census of Island Areas staff. Staff translated the brochure to Spanish. Content in both versions (English and Spanish) included links to the campaign website.

The local governments valued the brochure for its insightful qualities. The message was clear and informative.

21.6 Campaign Implementation

The "See How It All Adds Up" campaign launched in January 2018, extending across online and offline media, through internal and external communications, with a consistent look, tone and feel.

The ECPO team coordinated all efforts, fully integrating with many different in-house disciplines. The Census Bureau's Communications Directorate developed a plan and detailed schedule to help guide all activities and deliverables. To finalize implementation plans, we used the target segmentation to prioritize markets and industries for targeted outreach via all channels. Details from each campaign area follow here.

21.6.1 "9-8-7" Campaign

"9-8-7" was a direct marketing email campaign to approximately 3000 intermediaries delivering Economic Census information to build awareness and response promotion materials directly to their membership. The campaign was implemented in three waves in 2018 with requests to forward one email on each of the following dates – 9 April (awareness), 8 May (webinar invitation), and 7 June (due date). "9-8-7" dates focused messaging and simplified the "ask" for intermediaries.

The Communications Directorate distributed the emails, which included videos and links to the website. The campaign was successful with open and click-through rates at least double the Census Bureau average. The metrics were as follows:

- Total emails sent: 36,515
- Total emails delivered: 35,513
- Total unique opens: 7915
- Total unique clicks: 1545
- Average email open rate: 22.5% (twice the Census Bureau benchmark)
- Average click rate: 4.4% (four times the Census Bureau benchmark)

21.6.2 Webinar

As part of the campaign, the ECPO team leads held a webinar for 182 intermediaries and respondents on 17 May 2018. Content included information adapted from the Partner Briefing and covered details about the online reporting process. Timed a few weeks before the due date, the webinar provided guidance for respondents and was well received by attendees. More importantly, it allowed the Census Bureau to send an "invitation" as part of the email series rather than a "promotion" – a tactic that generally has more acceptance and perceived value by recipients. Including the webinar as part of our promotion campaign provided a benefit for intermediaries and their members as we entered the collection phase after mailout. It allowed us to provide response details at the appropriate time and afforded us the opportunity to send three separate email invitations to raise awareness and promote response.

21.6.3 Email Awareness Campaign

The "9-8-7" campaign to intermediaries was coordinated with and supported by a wide-reaching email awareness campaign and included access to cross-promotional marketing efforts that focused on the Economic Census. This included weekly emails to 235,000 Census Bureau email subscribers from February 2018 through early June 2018.

21.6.4 Internal Communications

Prior to and during the data collection period, the Communications Directorate strived to keep employees informed and educated. This included two internal newsletter articles and a Director's blog. This effort profiled employees who work with the data, a proven tactic that not only recognized staff for the work they do, but also provided unique insight into how the Economic Census came together. Developing stories at each stage of the Economic Census was a good way to help employees be ambassadors in their communities.

21.6.5 Economic Census Day for Census Bureau Staff

On 1 May 2018, to coincide with the Economic Census mailout, the ECPO team led an internal awareness event at Census Headquarters. Advertised as Economic Census Day, this three-hour event included presentations by the Census Bureau and the Bureau of Economic Analysis leadership, which reinforced the goals and efforts of the program.

21.6.6 Media Relations

For media relations, the Communications Directorate disseminated clear, timely, and accurate information regarding the Economic Census and its impact on stakeholders while promoting materials to encourage response. Efforts included an all-electronic press kit, an external Director's blog, and releases announcing key phases of the Economic Census.

21.6.7 Congressional and Intergovernmental Affairs

The Communications Directorate worked with the ECPO team and our Respondent Advocate to conduct an education and outreach campaign to 535 federal and 108 state government representatives. Activities included briefings, meetings, webinars, correspondence, and weekly updates.

21.6.8 Social Media

From February through June 2018, the ECPO team and the Communications Directorate sought to leverage the ongoing agency-wide social media plan to find key opportunities to facilitate timely engagement with followers on LinkedIn, Twitter, and Facebook. Note that we did not use resources for paid ads.

Messaging encouraged target audiences and markets to take action by responding to the Economic Census, if received (except for businesses with no employees and very small businesses with employees that were not included in the census).

21.6.9 Meetings and Events

In 2018, the strategy for event participation evolved considerably and included two different kinds of events. Participation in tradeshows and conferences remained a high priority, reaching key intermediary groups and low-response industries, but the program was also expanded to include smaller, in-person meetings with organizations in priority markets, where we went beyond outreach and established relationships for ongoing Census Bureau communications. Our key takeaways were:

- The Census Bureau brand carries weight. Partner organizations were receptive to setting up meetings.
- Engagement level of meeting attendees was very high. Active involvement in discussion, good questions, many requests for follow-up.
- Partner briefings meetings with multiple intermediaries in markets, held independently from those scheduled to coincide with focus group travel, were well received. Leveraging the opportunity to present to several multipliers of our message, hosted by a key partner in each market, resulted in broader outreach and new partnerships. A key to our success was relationships with Data Dissemination Specialists, local area Census staff who provide data dissemination and collection support across the country.
- Attendees offered to provide assistance with outreach to their organization. Brochures were distributed, requests were made for electronic content, and contact info was collected for next steps.
- Meeting in person was key. Our personal attendance demonstrated that the Census Bureau appreciates local market partnerships as a high priority and underscored the importance of our message. This would not have been achieved via telephone or video conference.

21.7 Moving Forward

21.7.1 Respondent Portal Changes

Since the inception of the 2017 Economic Census respondent outreach campaign, the number of surveys using the respondent portal has risen from three to fifteen. The opportunity for broadened outreach will increase as more surveys migrate into portal usage.

Providing information and communications through the respondent portal will open a new avenue for response promotion. To date, the only means of direct communications with actual survey respondents had been official mailings, generic e-blasts, and follow-up phone calls. The opportunity now presents itself to communicate directly on the portal dashboard and via account emails, both before and after survey due dates. We are currently planning for development and testing of options, including testing a preference for industry and survey-specific content. Focus group participant voiced this recommendation. If successful, this would supplement existing efforts, such as ongoing intermediary outreach.

Portal functionality will also give us the chance to identify and track other opportunities, such as providing appropriate support materials to current nonresponse cases who responded in past surveys.

21.7.2 Adaptation for Current Surveys

From the outset, the "See How It All Adds Up" campaign was created to be easily adapted for our more frequently occurring economic surveys. The basic premise remains – the value of response is evident in the value of resulting data. We replaced "Economic Census" with "Economic Surveys" in our materials and direct readers to our new website, entitled "Economic Surveys Response," with appropriately updated materials to address survey response. In implementing this strategy, we are providing information to support current surveys, while solidifying and establishing new intermediary contacts leading up to the 2022 Economic Census.

21.8 Conclusion

This chapter describes the development and execution of a large-scale outreach strategy for small businesses. The cornerstone of this strategy is to make respondents aware of the value of economic census data for their own business decisions, showing the tangible reward and gaining their cooperation. Other NSIs have effectively tested similar strategies (Snijkers et al. 2007; Hedlin et al. 2008), providing prior survey results as a form of positive reciprocity. This concept is not new to surveys: the theme of reward (expected gain) is central in social exchange theory (e.g. Dillman 2007, pp. 14–27).

The lighthearted outreach tone is new, however, as is the recognition that the specific campaigns need to be targeted to the *people* that will answer the business survey. Twenty-second videos replaced three-minute testimonials. Vignettes provided specific examples of how a business owner could use these data now e.g. a restaurant owner deciding to open a second location. This engaging approach worked: emails were read at a higher rate than the US Census Bureau benchmark, more materials were distributed, and there was an increased number of trade organizations that committed to messaging. Future efforts will rely less on anecdotal responses and indirect measurements to assess such campaigns.

The campaign was built upon three principles: (i) personal relationships matter, (ii) more customized and relevant content is impactful and (iii) less is more. The success of the campaign is largely due to the first. The principle applies to the development collaboration as well as the outreach effect. Perhaps the most essential aspect of the project was the team effort it required, both across and outside of the agency. Census staff experts in the diverse areas of marketing, communications, research, and statistics collaborated with private sector expertise to develop a campaign with a tone rarely seen in the U.S. Federal Government. This teamwork fostered strong and lasting partnerships that will prove invaluable in future efforts. The advertisement campaign developments rely heavily on the second two principles. With the presence of the respondent portal, future response promotion efforts could benefit from even more detailed, and potentially more impactful, customization.

References

Avery, J., Fournier, S. and Wittenbraker, J. (2014). Unlock the Mysteries of Your Customer Relationships. *Harvard Business Review,* July–August 2014.

Bavdaž, M. (2010). The multidimensional integral business survey response model. *Survey Methodology* 36: 81–93. *Survey Methodology* June 2010 (publications.gc.ca).

Brady, C. (2016). Respondent outreach practices at the US Census Bureau. *Proceedings of the Fifth Conference on Establishment Surveys, Geneva, Switzerland,* June 2016.

Desouza, K.C. and Bhagwatwar, A. (2012). Leveraging Technologies in public agencies: the case of the U.S. Census Bureau and the 2010 census. *Public Administration Review* 72: 605–614. https://doi.org/10.1111/j.1540-6210.2012.02592.x.

Dillman, D.A. (2007). *Mail and Internet Surveys: The Tailored Design Method*, 2nde. New York: Wiley.

Feenberg, D., Ganguli, I., Gaule, P., and Gruber, J. (2017). It's good to be first: order bias in reading and citing NBER working papers. *The Review of Economics and Statistics* 99 (1): 32–39.

Fink, E.B., Beck, J.L. and Willimack, D.K. (2015). Data-driven decision making and the design of economic census data collection instruments. *Proceedings of the 2015 Federal Committee on Statistical Methodology Research Conference*, Washington D.C., United States, December 2015.

Galloway, C. (2017). Blink and they're gone: PR and the battle for attention. *Public Relations Review* 43 (5): 969–977. https://doi.org/10.1016/j.pubrev.2017.06.010.

Giesen, D., Vella, M., Brady, C.F. Jr., Brown, P., Ravindra, D., and Vaasen-Otten, A. (2018). Establishing and maintaining a relationship with businesses: a comparison of response burden management in official business surveys at the U.S. Census Bureau, Statistics Netherlands, Statistics Canada and Statistics New Zealand. *Journal of Official Statistics* 34 (2): 397–418. https://doi.org/10.2478/jos-2018-0018.

Hedlin, D., Lindkvist, H., Backstrom, H., and Erikson, J. (2008). An experiment on perceived survey response burden among businesses. *Journal of Official Statistics* 24 (2): 301–318.

Kennedy, J. and Phipps, P. (1995). Respondent motivation, response burden, and data quality in the survey of employer-provided training. *In Proceedings of the Annual Meeting of the American Association for Public Opinion Research*, Fort Lauderdale, FL, viewed 25 June 2021. https://www.bls.gov/osmr/research-papers/1995/pdf/st950250.pdf.

Landreth, A. (2002). Results and Recommendations from Cognitive Interviews with Selected Materials from the American Community Survey. Suitland, MD: U.S. Census Bureau. https://www.census.gov/library/working-papers/2003/adrm/ssm2003-10.html (accessed July 2021).

Landreth, A. (2004). Survey Letters: A Respondent's Perspective. Paper presented at the American Association for Public Opinion Research, Phoenix (13–16 May 2004).

Marske, R., Torene, L. and Hartz, M. (2007). Company-Centric Communication Approaches for Business Survey Response Management. *Proceedings of the Third International Conference on Establishment Surveys*, Montreal, Canada, June 2007.

Pressgrove, G., McKeever, R., and Collins, E. (2021). Effectiveness of persuasive frames in advocacy videos. *Public Relations Review* 47 (4): 102060. https://doi.org/10.1016/j.pubrev.2021.102060.

Snijkers, G., Berkenbosch, B., and Luppes, M. (2007). Understanding the Decision to Participate in a Business Survey. *Proceedings of the Third International Conference on Establishment Surveys*, Montreal, Canada, June 2007.

Snijkers, G. and Jones, J. (2013). Business survey communication. In: *Designing and Conducting Business Surveys* (ed. G. Snijkers, G. Haraldsen, J. Jones and D. Willimack), 359–430. Hoboken, NJ: Wiley.

Sudman, S., Willimack, D.K., Nichols, E., and Mesenbourg, T.L. (2000). Exploratory research at the US Census Bureau on the survey response process in large companies. In: *Proceedings of the Second International Conference on Establishment Surveys*, 327–337. *American Statistical Association*.

Sullivan, D. (2013). When 15 seconds is too long; welcome to the 'TL;DR' world. *CNET*, June 2013.

Thompson, K.J., Oliver, B., and Beck, J. (2015). An analysis of the mixed collection modes for two business surveys conducted by the US Census Bureau. *Public Opinion Quarterly* 79 (3): 769–789.

Thompson, K.J. and Kaputa, S. (2017). Investigating adaptive nonresponse follow-up strategies for small businesses through embedded experiments. *Journal of Official Statistics* 33 (3): 1–23.

Thompson, K.J., Phipps, P., Miller, D., and Snijkers, G. (2018). Overview of the special issue from the fifth international conference on establishment surveys (ICES-V). *Journal of Official Statistics* 34 (2): 303–307. http://dx.doi.org/10.2478/JOS-2018-0013.

Torres van Grinsven, V., Bolko, I., and Bavdaž, M. (2014). In search of motivation for the business survey response task. *Journal of Official Statistics* 30 (4): 579–606.

Tuttle, A.D., Beck, J.L., Willimack, D.K., Tolliver, K.P., Hernandez, A., and Fan, C. (2018). Experimenting with contact strategies in business surveys. *Journal of Official Statistics* 34 (2): 365–395.

U.S. Census Bureau (2017). The Economic Census. See How it All Adds Up [Image].

U.S. Census Bureau (2018). The Economic Census. See How it All Adds Up [Brochure].

Willimack, D.K. and Nichols, E. (2010). A hybrid response process model for business surveys. *Journal of Official Statistics* 26: 3–24.

Section 5

Topics in the Use of New Data Sources and New Technologies

22

Statistical Data Production in a Digitized Age: The Need to Establish Successful Workflows for Micro Data Access

Stefan Bender[1,2], Jannick Blaschke[1], and Christian Hirsch[1]

[1] *Data Service Center, Deutsche Bundesbank, Frankfurt, Germany*
[2] *School of Social Science, University of Mannheim, Mannheim, Germany*

22.1 Introduction

Nowadays, empirical researchers and statisticians find themselves in a curious situation. On the one hand, data are everywhere and come from an ever-increasing number of different sources. Researchers use more data they no longer directly collect themselves (e.g. via surveys). Instead, they often analyze organic data (Groves 2011) collected for other purposes that are now being reused, e.g. via ETL[1] or an adapted version of the Total Survey Error Approach (Biemer et al. 2017; Amaya et al. 2020). Many chapters in this book are evidence of how fundamentally the emergence of these new data sources has transformed the practice of social science research.

On the other hand, a surprisingly large amount of relevant data remains hidden in tightly regulated silos, which means they are underexploited by empirical research and statistics (e.g. SVR-Gutachten 2021). One reason lies in the nature of the data themselves, which oftentimes allow the disclosure of information about an individual person's health or a company's business model. Initiatives like the FAIR data principles (Wilkinson et al. 2016; European Commission 2018) or the reproducibility standards of the AEA (Vilhuber 2019; Vilhuber 2021) are a direct reaction to this situation and an attempt to build bridges to these silos by capturing best practices for research data use.

At the same time, there are strong movements for granting access to official micro data for the public good. For example, in the United States, the Foundations for Evidence-Based Policymaking Act requires each statistical agency to produce and disseminate data while ensuring that data are used only for statistical purposes and that the confidentiality of the data is protected (Lane 2020). Germany is heading in a similar direction, as evidenced by the work of the German Data Forum,[2] the activities around the National Research Data Infrastructure,[3] or the recent announcement about opening new institutes to access new administrative data sources such as tax data.

However, providing access to micro data is quite a complex endeavor. The challenge comes from protecting the identity of the reporting entities while simultaneously allowing data users to study distinct features of these entities, e.g. effects on an individual person's health or a company's business model. In order to master this balancing act between increased confidentiality and the

---

1 ETR stands for Extract, Transform, Reload.
2 For more information on the German Data Forum, see https://www.konsortswd.de/en/ratswd/.
3 For more information on the National Research Data Infrastructure, see https://www.nfdi.de/en-gb.

Advances in Business Statistics, Methods and Data Collection. Edited by Ger Snijkers, Mojca Bavdaž, Stefan Bender, Jacqui Jones, Steve MacFeely, Joseph W. Sakshaug, Katherine J. Thompson, and Arnout van Delden.

high analytical value of micro data, data providers need to implement statistical, organizational, or technical measures to prevent the disclosure of sensitive information. However, how can this be done without placing too much of a constraint on the analytical value? In addition, how does the choice of measure interact with other aspects of data access?

To resolve this tension, we present a simple model in Section 22.2 of this paper that provides a guideline for evaluating proposals on how to successfully enable granular data access. The first building block of our model considers the technical and procedural requirements, while the second looks at safe output. Lastly, the third building block represents the value for stakeholders from providing access to granular data. The first two building blocks of our framework mirror existing models of knowledge generation and statistical production (Blanc et al. 2002; Radermacher 2019). However, unlike these models, we introduce "generating value" as an additional and, in our opinion, crucial condition for successful approaches to data access.

This view fits well into recent developments (Ritchie 2016; Lane 2020). Historically, the emphasis has been on avoiding the risk of identification. The "five safes" approach (Desai et al. 2016; Ritchie 2017), which provides an excellent framework for assessing and managing risk, bears testimony to this. Although this approach is widely used, especially in the public sector, the focus has slowly started shifting toward a more balanced approach in recent years.[4] Risk is increasingly perceived as a binding constraint in an optimization problem that aims at maximizing stakeholder value.[5]

According to this view, data providers balance stakeholder value and identification risk by choosing the level of risk that they are willing to tolerate. In this context, a key success story in accessing administrative granular data has been the introduction of research data centers (RDCs) (Ritchie 2021). RDCs are restricted-access facilities, often at the premises of the data owner, that provide accredited researchers with access to sensitive granular data.

This paper is organized as follows. Section 22.2 introduces the three building blocks for successful workflows enabling access to micro data (BUBMIC model), these being: (i) laying the technical and procedural foundations, (ii) generating safe results, and (iii) generating value for all stakeholders. Section 22.3 briefly discusses the concept of FAIR data. Section 22.4 applies the BUBMIC model to RDCs and shows why they are so successful. Section 22.5 concludes our paper.

22.2 Building Blocks for Successful Workflows Enabling Access to Micro Data

In this section, we present a simple model for the main BUilding Blocks for enabling MICro data access (BUBMIC model). Our framework is based on existing models of knowledge generation and statistical production (Blanc et al. 2002; Radermacher 2019). Consistent with this literature, we organize the BUBMIC model's six key components in a circular process chart.

Figure 22.1 depicts these components grouped into the three broader building blocks: (i) laying the technical and procedural foundations, (ii) generating safe results, and (iii) generating value for all stakeholders. Our contribution is to combine existing models from the previous literature (building blocks 1 and 2) with the idea of generating stakeholder value (building block 3). We will now discuss each category in greater detail.

---

4 See Ritchie (2017) for a discussion on the reasons for this.
5 This view should not be mistaken as taking risks lightly. Readers with a background in economics will confirm that binding constraints determine the level of value attainable in the optimization problem.

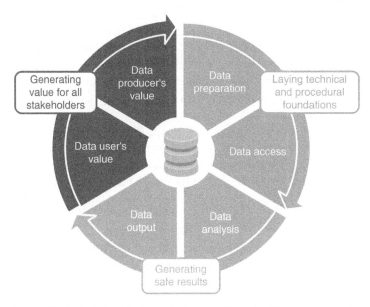

Figure 22.1 Building blocks to design workflows enabling access to micro data in the BUBMIC model.

22.2.1 Building Block 1: Laying the Technical and Procedural Foundations

The first building block concerns the foundation of micro data access and combines data preparation and data access. We find that preparing data for usage usually involves four main decisions. First, the data provider needs to specify how the respective data can be transferred from the production system to the analytical environment in which the user can then access the data. Here, a specific emphasis needs to be placed on the reproducibility of later outputs (Vilhuber 2020).

Second, since micro data are prone to disclosure risk, access is usually only granted to an anonymized version. The decision on the degree of anonymization (e.g. full, formal, or factual[6]) depends on different factors, such as the design of the analytical environment (e.g. remote access vs. secure on-site access[7]) and the risk preferences of the data-providing institution. For establishment data, anonymization may need to go beyond removing direct identifiers such as names and addresses, as other variables in the data may also allow firms to be identified (Lane 2020). For example, simply sorting data by firm size (e.g. total assets) may identify the largest firms in a given sector or region.

Third, unlike macro data, micro data allow information to be linked at the level of the individual entity. As linking data greatly enhances their analytical value for users, data providers should prepare their micro data in a way that facilitates their linkage at a later stage. Note that if linking different micro datasets is allowed, applying further anonymization steps might be needed to ensure that no entity is identified on the basis of the enriched information.

---

6 We use the following definitions from INEXDA Working Group on Data Access (2020): Non-anonymized: no anonymization (i.e. raw data). Formal anonymization: identifiers, names, and addresses deleted. No direct identification possible (i.e. scientific use files). Factual anonymization: data perturbation. Identification possible only with significant effort (i.e. secure use files). Full anonymization: no identification possible (i.e. public use files).
7 We use the following definitions from INEXDA Working Group on Data Access (2020): Secure on-site access: provision at the premises of the institution in a dedicated secure environment. Remote access: researchers can access data remotely from their own institution.

So far, all decisions have involved manipulating the actual data in one way or another. However, preparing data for usage also involves describing the data appropriately. Therefore, as a fourth decision, data providers need to assess which metadata standard best fits their data. In general, metadata standards[8] are often domain-specific or targeted at specific applications, and constitute very granular and semantically rich statements that provide important context to the data. Special emphasis should be placed on an unambiguously and machine-readable taxonomy, e.g. by utilizing controlled vocabulary such as a thesaurus or keywords.

In addition, data providers need to pay particular attention to aspects that are specific to micro data, such as a clear description of entities and identifiers to support data linkage (INEXDA Working Group on Data Access 2020). This involves recording any available identifiers (e.g. country tax number, LEI, ISIN) that help identify the individual firm, bank, or household, for example. In the case of establishment data, this may include drafting a uniform language on how to differentiate individual firms from company groups.

Designing a metadata schema for micro data also requires the documentation of structural breaks in the data that occur over time, e.g. due to changes in underlying rules for data reporting. Consequently, all metadata items should be time-dependent. For example, consider that in 2012 a legislative change altered the reporting population in the data from A to B. Therefore, metadata items providing information on the data's reporting population should cover both time periods: before 2012 the appropriate value is A, after the structural break in 2012 the value is B. Other examples of structural breaks include changes to the set of variables collected and changes in sampling.[9]

Traditional metadata largely describe data from the viewpoint of a data-providing institution (e.g. sampling and population). However, it is also recommended to add metadata on previous data usages as a way of helping users discover new data that might be appropriate for their research or analysis. For example, users could learn how and by whom the data have been used previously, and what other data sources were used in those research or analytical projects. One means of obtaining structured information on data usage could be recommendation systems that take empirical research papers as a source of information (Lane 2020).

In addition, data providers should decide whether to provide standardized datasets to data users. Standardized datasets are characterized by a preselection of variables as well as refined data quality checks and comprehensive documentation. While standardized datasets might limit data users' flexibility when it comes to variable selection, they bring many advantages that cannot be achieved otherwise.

First, standardized datasets allow a perfect match between the actual data and the corresponding documentation, e.g. in the form of metadata on the variables and codes included (e.g. sector, country, or currency codes), best practices for safe usage, or as descriptions of applicable access requirements.

Second, the standardization of datasets enables their unique identification in the final research results. With the help of unique identifiers (e.g. digital object identifiers (DOIs)[10]), data users can reference the exact data cuts, and readers of the research results can find them later and potentially reproduce the results. For this, standard datasets should be fixed snapshots that do not change over

---

8 Examples of commonly used metadata standards are the Data Documentation Initiative (DDI), the Dublin Core Metadata Initiative (DCMI), the DataCite Metadata Schema, the da|ra Metadata Schema, the Metadata Encoding and Transmission Standard (METS), Preservation Metadata Maintenance Activity (PREMIS), and the Statistical Data and Metadata Exchange (SDMX).

9 For a full example of how to account for this, see the INEXDA Metadata Schema (Bender et al., 2019).

10 For more information on DOIs, see https://www.da-ra.de/get-a-doi.

time. This implies that in the event of a data update, e.g. when data become available for a new month, a new standard dataset should be created containing the same information as the previous one plus the new data and potentially some revisions of old data points.

Third, standardization eases data linkages. On the one hand, this refers to the technical feasibility of the linkage, as data providers know exactly which IDs are included in the datasets and can therefore provide consistent mapping tables. On the other hand, data providers can link the corresponding access rules directly to both the individual datasets and the linkage. For instance, it might be allowed to use two datasets individually, while a combination might cause a breach of confidentiality due to an identification of the underlying entities.

Finally, the decision to standardize data really is a decision on the degree of automation in workflows to access micro data. For instance, access procedures could be largely automated if the respective access requirements can be clearly assigned to the requested dataset. We will discuss a specific use case of this in Section 22.4.4.5, where we present the Annodata schema.

Once the data-providing institution has decided on data preparation, it should start designing suitable data access pathways, which brings us to the second part of the first building block in Figure 22.1. This requires decisions on a number of aspects, including paperwork (e.g. applications and contracts), the governance of the approval process, the mode of data access (e.g. secure on-site or remote access), and the degree of data anonymization available to each type of data user (e.g. internal, external). Rules and procedures related to data access should ideally be linked directly to the standard datasets and be "publicly available, transparent, and universally applicable as part of the metadata" (Cabrera et al. 2020).

For example, one generally observes a trade-off between the degree of anonymization and the mode of data access, in that the greater the risk of identifying individual entities in the data, the more restrictive the access mode will be. In Section 22.4, we discuss the example of a research data center (RDC) and its theoretical underpinning of the "five safes" approach (Desai et al. 2016; Ritchie 2017) in greater detail.

22.2.2 Building Block 2: Generating Safe Results

Once access is granted, data users will work with the data and metadata and produce their own results. If data access has only been possible under specific technical or organizational conditions, the data provider will most likely also regulate how results are obtained. For example, if data access has been on-site in a secure environment at the data provider's premises, it may be required that all results leaving the secure environment must be fully anonymized.[11] Usually, data providers equip users with a detailed description of rules (e.g. adherence to minimum sample size) and ways to check compliance of their results.[12] In addition, data providers might conduct an output control for each result that users want to take out of the controlled analytical environment.

We recommend that readers interested in the discussion surrounding the assessment and management of risk use the "five safes" framework like many before them. We note that implementing approaches to micro data access naturally require these components to be discussed from a variety of different perspectives (e.g. legal, technical, and organizational). Readers interested in any of these perspectives are encouraged to refer to Desai et al. (2016), Ritchie (2017) or Schönberg (2019).

---

11 Fully anonymized results can be identified neither directly (e.g. based on a name or address or an officially issued identification code) nor indirectly through deduction, accounting for all the means that might reasonably be used by a third party.

12 See Research Data and Service Centre (2021) for an example of principles and rules applicable to visiting researchers.

22.2.3   Building Block 3: Generating Value for All Stakeholders

The four components we have presented so far – data production, access, analysis, and output control – all describe the knowledge-generating process of micro data (e.g. Blanc et al. 2002; Radermacher 2019). However, the third and final building block adds another very important prerequisite for designing micro data access workflows that goes beyond those classic approaches: the generation of value for all stakeholders involved. For simplification, we will assume that no intermediary such as a data trustee is involved in the provision and process of accessing micro data.

Generating value for data users is generally rather easy to motivate as it correlates strongly with the data's analytical value. Data users generate results in the form of scientific publications or analytical reports that are valuable for themselves, their community, or their employer. For example, the results might provide fundamental insights for policy decisions that in turn will serve the public interest. In the private sector, start-ups might use existing data sources to train algorithms without having to incur the cost of building up a dataset of their own. In the latter case, analytical value also corresponds to business value.

We can conclude that once the value to this data user exceeds their costs of using the data, e.g. the effort involved in applying and actually implementing the data access process, data users will benefit from the opportunity to access the micro data. Also, note how the data provider's decisions described above can affect both the data users' value and cost. For instance, adequate metadata and uniquely identified data reduce the costs of data usage, while requiring (physical) on-site access at the data provider's premises increases them significantly.

Generating value for data providers is far more complex. The usual approach for private sector data provision follows the business model of commercial data vendors (e.g. Bloomberg), where the data user has to purchase access to the data. However, it is questionable whether this business model will also work if the data are of business value to both the data provider and the data user, e.g. a start-up operating in the same sector. If the data provider's data are of sufficient interest that data users are prepared to pay for them, it is likely that they are associated with a direct competitor. Hence, it is unclear whether the data producer would share the data even if they were remunerated for doing so.

In the case of public data providers, value is not usually generated through remuneration but purely through the generated knowledge itself. However, as it remains extremely difficult to measure the additional knowledge generated by data sharing (e.g. in an RDC), a more systematic approach needs to be explored. Figure 22.2 attempts to present different possible outcomes from data sharing and shows the corresponding channels that are organized around the first two building blocks of our model (i.e. knowledge generation or statistical production).

First, providing access to micro data may help enhance the allocation of resources to improve data that are of most value to scientific research and statistics. Second, describing data by their use instead of how they are produced help identify appropriate data for an analytical or research project. Finally, the impact of micro data usage by researchers or statistical agencies on policy decisions should be measured. Note that this latter topic can only be addressed if solutions have already been found for the previous two aspects.

Moreover, the results of data users' work could provide valuable insights into the analytical potential of the data or possible data quality issues. However, although most public data providers grant data access for scientific research purposes, data users seldom report their results back to them. As Lane (2020) observed, this lack of precise information about research outcomes leads to a situation where public data providers are not able to communicate the societal value of their service.

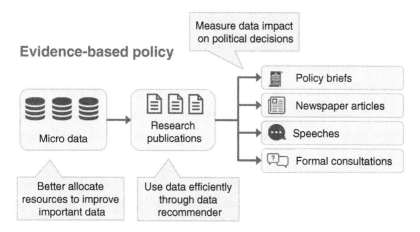

Figure 22.2 The ideal use of (sensitive) micro data for evidence-based policy making.

As a possible way to overcome this, she proposes a data platform on which data providers search for their data and find research results based on them. Specifically, Lane (2020) suggests a knowledge graph that connects results, data, and data users so that one could identify data experts and recommend bundles of datasets that are often used together. Prerequisites for this would include a sufficiently large body of research articles, a common understanding of the datasets included, and user engagement to provide feedback and the validation of suggestions. Importantly, the public, too, would benefit from this approach as they would learn what has been done with the data, increasing public awareness of their true value. Eventually, they could make an informed decision about whether the investment in the data has been worth the cost.

In conclusion, data providers who are not legally obliged to grant access to their data only do so voluntarily if their value exceeds the cost of data provision (data preparation, data access management, and potentially output control) and the expected costs of a breach of confidentiality. As before, all variables in this maximization problem are affected by the choices the data provider made in the other two building blocks in Figure 22.1. For example, the expected costs of a confidentiality breach decrease when stricter data protection measures as described in the "five safes" framework are implemented (e.g. only allowing secure on-site access to anonymized data followed by an output control). Similarly, the progressive automation of tasks related to data provision, such as tools to streamline output control or the generation of contracts, reduces the data provider's costs.

Here, it is important to understand that the cost functions of the data provider and data user are inverse, at least for the most part. For example, stricter access rules and the application of anonymization and data perturbation techniques significantly reduce both the risk of identification as well as the data's analytical value.

22.3 An Alternative Approach to Measuring Value: FAIR Data

One existing and widely used approach to measuring the value of data objects (e.g. data, metadata, code, and the derived results) are the FAIR guiding principles (Wilkinson et al. 2016; European Commission 2018).[13] Findable, Accessible, Interoperable and Reusable (FAIR) data objects

---

13 Many initiatives already focus on the FAIR guiding principles. For more details, see (Cabrera et al., 2020) or https://www.go-fair.org/.

facilitate data management and benefit the entire academic community, supporting knowledge discovery and innovation (Cabrera et al. 2020). We argue that sound implementation of our three building blocks will generate data objects that generally adhere to all four FAIR principles.

The BUBMIC model ensures findability through accompanying and broadly available metadata as well as the use of unique identifiers (e.g. DOIs). This allows not only humans but also machines to find and clearly identify data objects. Moreover, we recommend linking different metadata objects to further support their findability. For example, metadata on a standard dataset could contain relations to previous versions of the same standard dataset or direct links to publications that are based on it (Bender et al. 2019).

The second part of the BUBMIC model's first building block describes the importance of defining and communicating clear rules and prerequisites for data access. How this is implemented in detail very much depends on the data requested, the access modes available and the data user (e.g. internal or external data user). However, one thing that all approaches have in common is that "roles, rights, and responsibilities of all agents involved in data processing and the data access process have to be documented and communicated transparently" (Cabrera et al. 2020).

The third FAIR dimension refers to the interoperability of different data. Enhancing analytical value by linking datasets is becoming more and more crucial, as it is also one of the main reasons to apply for micro data access rather than use what are often publicly available macro data. In Section 22.2.1, we recommend that data providers prepare their data in a way that supports semantic interoperability (e.g. via common identifiers or the provision of matching tables).

Lastly, our module discusses steps to ensure the reusability of data, particularly the importance of standard datasets and comprehensive metadata describing the content of each standard dataset. This is especially important for data that were originally collected for a specific use case (e.g. conducting a survey for a research project) and, therefore, might not have been properly documented in the first place. In addition, we have highlighted the importance of unique identifiers. Used properly, these allow data users to link their results to the respective standard dataset as well as clear and transparent data access rules, which should be linked directly to the relevant standard datasets. This would enable future data users to replicate the results, as they can now comprehend the exact data content as well as possible ways to access the data.

In conclusion, data objects that adhere to the FAIR principles generate significant value for both data users and data providers. While data users can work more easily with the data, data providers benefit above all from increased trust in the data they offer and the results calculated from those data. Stakeholders on both sides can capitalize on a significant transfer of knowledge and on a more efficient data access procedure.

22.4 Applying the BUBMIC Model to Research Data Centers

In this section, we explain how the three building blocks from the BUBMIC model have been applied in the context of RDCs. RDCs are a well-established means of facilitating access to administrative micro data for scientific research purposes in the public sector.[14] The existing literature typically uses the dimensions from the "five safes" framework (safe projects, safe people, safe settings, safe data, and safe output) to describe an RDC's approach to safe data access. This framework has come to be widely recognized as the standard model for implementing data access in the public sector (Ritchie 2021).

---

14 See Ritchie (2021) for more information on RDCs.

The "five safes" framework has a clear emphasis on assessing and managing the risk of confidentiality breaches. However, as described in Section 22.3, data providers balance the costs of expected confidentiality breaches and the effort involved in providing data against their expected value. We therefore introduce the data provider's value as a second counterweight alongside the risk-minimizing measures described in the "five safes" framework, which we will refer to often on account of its paramount importance.

We use the Research Data and Service Centre of the Deutsche Bundesbank (BBk-RDSC) as a concrete real-world example. The BBk-RDSC manages access to confidential economic and financial micro datasets for scientific researchers. It also serves as an intermediary between the Bundesbank's various departments collecting and producing different micro datasets and the data users. It advises researchers on data selection, data access, data content, and appropriate analytical approaches for their micro datasets.

For the purpose of this paper, we focus on the BBk-RDSC's approach to generating stakeholder value while minimizing their costs. Readers interested in a more detailed description of the BBk-RDSC are warmly encouraged to refer to "Data Access to Micro Data of the Deutsche Bundesbank" by Tobias Schönberg (2019).

22.4.1 Building Block 1: Laying the Technical and Procedural Foundations

The first part of the BUBMIC model is "data preparation," which is aligned with the "safe data" dimension of the "five safes" framework. The BBk-RDSC applies different anonymization techniques to its data, ranging from removing direct identifiers such as names and addresses (formal anonymization) to full anonymization that renders it impossible to identify entities. In general, original data are most valuable to data users, followed by the de-identified version of those data (Lane 2020).

Where applicable, the BBk-RDSC refines data to standardized research datasets containing pre-selected variables and comprehensive documentation,[15] including detailed metadata. In comparison to the original data from the Bundesbank's data-producing business units, these data contain additional modifications to improve their usability for research purposes and ensure consistency with other datasets in the BBk-RDSC's portfolio. Each standard research dataset is uniquely identifiable with a DOI,[16] which must be used in all resulting publications. Note how this helps ensure compliance with the FAIR principles.

Moving on to the second part of the first building block, which is "data access," we evaluate the BBk-RDSC along the dimensions "safe people" and "safe projects." Access is only provided to external[17] researchers affiliated with a recognized scientific research institute who plan to use the data in the context of independent and noncommercial research projects.

In order to ensure that this is the case, the BBk-RDSC has established three measures. First, all interested researchers have to submit an application form with a detailed project description explaining why Bundesbank micro data are necessary and how they will be used. Data access may only be granted on a need-to-know basis, which means that if the research question can be answered without the micro data requested, access may not be granted.

---

15 The BBk-RDSC's data report series can be publicly accessed on its website: https://www.bundesbank.de/en/bundesbank/research/rdsc/publications/data-reports.

16 For an overview of all DOIs registered by the BBk-RDSC, see https://www.da-ra.de/dara/search/search_result?v=1&q=defaultSearch%3A%28deutsche+bundesbank%29&fq=publicationAgent_facet%3ADeutsche%5C+Bundesbank&&rtList=&mdlang=en&lang=en&personal=false&widget=&widgetclient.

17 The BBk-RDSC also manages data access for in-house Bundesbank researchers and analysts, but this falls outside the scope of this paper.

Second, researchers must submit a recent version of their CV to demonstrate their affiliation with a recognized research institute and their non-commercial interest in the data. The BBk-RDSC further requires a minimum educational level of a bachelor's degree to ensure that applicants have appropriate statistical expertise to handle micro data.

Lastly, researchers will only be granted authorization to access Bundesbank micro data after being briefed on their legal obligations during and after the project, and signing a contract. The contract contains a detailed description of all access requirements, obligations, and possible penalties in case of misconduct.

22.4.2 Building Block 2: Generating Safe Results

Regarding the "safe settings," the BBk-RDSC generally only provides formally anonymized data to external researchers which furthermore can only be accessed in the secure environment at the BBk-RDSC's premises. For experienced researchers, the BBk-RDSC offers controlled remote execution (CRE), where researchers can send their code to the BBk-RDSC, which runs it on the original data and returns the generated and controlled results.[18] In addition, some survey datasets can also be downloaded as scientific use files (SUFs), while fully anonymized data are available in the form of public use files (PUFs) on the Bundesbank's website.

Although researchers may have access to formally anonymized data for their research project, they can only take fully anonymized data out of the secure environment of the BBk-RDSC. In order to ensure that their calculation results (e.g. descriptive statistics or regression tables) do not contain any directly or indirectly identifiable information on individual entities, researchers have to demonstrate that each observation in their calculation results is based on at least five entities from the underlying Bundesbank dataset and that the largest two entities do not account for more than 85% (dominance rule).[19]

Researchers who believe that their calculation results meet these criteria submit them for clearance to BBk-RDSC staff members, who check and verify adherence to the rules once again (statistical disclosure control (SDC) or output control). With the exception of SUFs and PUFs, all results generated by researchers are subject to an SDC. The BBk-RDSC only releases calculation results that are fully anonymized and therefore considered "safe output" within the meaning of the "five safes" framework.

Once researchers have processed their calculation results for publication (e.g. as a scientific research paper, report, or presentation), they are obliged to submit the publication to the BBk-RDSC for checking whether it only contains calculation results that underwent an SDC and to ensure that any Bundesbank micro datasets used are correctly cited. Results may not be published until the BBk-RDSC checker has given written approval, which may be withheld if the results intended for publication do not comply with the criteria for "safe output" outlined above. The BBk-RDSC does not, however, check the substantive plausibility of the calculation results or the final publication.

---

18 On request, the BBk-RDSC will send the researcher a data structure file which structurally resembles the original data but contains no real values. Together with a prototype program code provided by the BBk-RDSC, this can be used to write the researcher's own program code for performing the desired analyses. This code is then sent to the BBk-RDSC via email and used by staff to generate analytical results. These results are subject to statistical disclosure control. After they are checked, they are sent to the researcher by email. At no point does the researcher have access to the (original) micro dataset. CRE is open for researchers who have demonstrated, in a current or previous research project, that they have sufficient experience in using the micro dataset in question.
19 For more information, see Research Data and Service Centre (2021).

22.4.3 Building Block 3: Generating Value for All Stakeholders

RDCs are widely viewed as a success model for data access in the public sector (Bender et al. 2021), as they create value for all stakeholders involved. First, they provide researchers with access to high-quality administrative micro data. Such data often contain information unavailable in data from commercial data vendors. Second, besides the data's sheer content, RDCs have also established measures to enhance analytical value by providing e.g. comprehensive metadata.

As a national central bank, the Bundesbank provides official statistics serving the public good. Making data accessible generates additional value for the Bundesbank in two ways. First, scientific results such as journal articles generate knowledge that might benefit both evidence-based policy decisions in the ESCB and the scientific community within the Bundesbank. Second, researchers might provide feedback on their experience using the data. This could help improve data quality or lead to a better understanding of how the data can be used.

However, granting external data users access to confidential micro data also comes with the potential risk of data leakage. Despite the BBk-RDSC's precautions ("five safes") and strict penalties in users' contracts, confidential information on individual entities might theoretically still reach the public. The second cost factor that should be carefully weighed against the value generated are the RDC's fixed and variable costs (e.g. staff costs).

For researchers, the value equation remains as described in Section 22.2.3. Their value mainly comes from the results they produce (e.g. publication of a novel article in a prestigious journal), while their costs depend on the amount of effort they need to spend in order to be granted data access (e.g. application process, signing a contract) and to get their research results through the SDC.

In order to make the most of its objective function, i.e. to maximize stakeholder value while minimizing costs, the BBk-RDSC has implemented a number of measures that are targeted at different parts of the first two building blocks in Figure 22.1. The remainder of this section presents some selected examples.[20]

22.4.4 Examples of Generating Value for All Stakeholders

22.4.4.1 Rules for Visiting Researchers at the RDSC[21]

Access to confidential Bundesbank micro data via the BBk-RDSC is subject to strict requirements, in particular concerning output and publication control. To help researchers comply more easily with these requirements, the BBk-RDSC drew up the document "Rules for visiting researchers at the RDSC," which summarizes all the applicable rules regarding guest research visits at the Bundesbank, the release of calculation results, and the approval of publications based on these results.

Inexperienced researchers in particular benefit from the clear and transparent communication of rules, which helps them acclimatize more quickly to working with confidential micro data at the BBk-RDSC. In addition, the document boosts confidence among reporting agents, such as banks and enterprises, and data producers, such as Bundesbank business units, that both researchers and the BBk-RDSC are handling the data properly. This reduces the expected costs in the event of a breach of confidentiality.

---

20 Examples of other value-enhancing measures include sample codes, detailed workflow documentation, email templates, and a concept and R package to archive finished research projects.
21 For more information, see Research Data and Service Centre (2021).

22.4.4.2 SDC Packages in Stata[22] and R[23]

To help users make sure their output complies with the applicable rules, the BBk-RDSC provides software packages for Stata and R. Users can use the commands from the packages after descriptive or regression tables to assess whether publishing tables of that kind would cause a disclosure problem (e.g. in case the results are based on fewer than five different entities). Note that the commands are only semi-automatic, as users still have to use them correctly.

The two packages significantly reduce the workload for both researchers and the BBk-RDSC staff members who have to conduct the SDC. It also helps illuminate why calculation results might be rejected by the BBk-RDSC and reduces the number of interactions that are usually needed with inexperienced researchers wishing to submit their calculation results for SDC in the correct form.

22.4.4.3 Dobby, the BBk-RDSC's High-Performance and Streamlined Data Production Pipeline[24]

The BBk-RDSC recently started developing "dobby," an R package that helps streamline the production of standard research datasets, a process that includes cleaning, quality-testing, and anonymizing micro datasets. An acronym of "Data Orchestration Blueprint Based on YAML," dobby builds on the two well-tested and production-ready R packages drake (Landau 2018) and validate (van der Loo and de Jonge 2021).

dobby is the BBk-RDSC's attempt to unify and further automate the production codes for standard research datasets while maintaining flexibility to account for dataset-specific properties. It increases transparency on how datasets are produced and smooths the transfer of knowledge within the BBk-RDSC. Ultimately, the resulting efficiency gains will reduce the BBk-RDSC's costs for data production and thus boost the value it generates overall.

22.4.4.4 RDSC Contract Generator[25]

Before any research project can begin, researchers have to sign a contract. The BBk-RDSC distinguishes between different contract types and asks researchers to sign a formal undertaking on the first day of their guest researcher visit at the BBk-RDSC. Due to dataset- and researcher-specific legal requirements, the different contract types vary strongly in terms of the information required and the overall level of complexity.

To reduce the time and effort spent on drafting contracts, the BBk-RDSC has developed an application that automates the creation of contracts and helps draft them in significantly less time. This RDSC Contract Generator, as it is known, was programmed in Python and contains a graphical user interface that guides BBk-RDSC staff members through the preparation of each individual contract in the most user-friendly manner possible.

22.4.4.5 Annodata Schema[26]

One of the BBk-RDSC's main responsibilities is to manage access to confidential Bundesbank micro data for scientific research purposes. To do this, it has established procedures designed to ensure ongoing compliance with all legal, technical, organizational, and administrative requirements. These procedures and rules are well documented and aligned with all the affected

---

22 The Stata ado files ("nobsdes5", "nobsreg5" and "maxrdsc") are available on the BBk-RDSC's website: https://www.bundesbank.de/en/bundesbank/research/rdsc/data-access.
23 The R package "sdcLog" is available on GitHub https://github.com/matthiasgomolka/sdcLog/issues.
24 See Gomolka et al. (2021) for more information on dobby.
25 See Blaschke et al. (2020) for more information on the RDSC Contract Generator.
26 See Bender et al. (2021) for more information on the Annodata schema, and INEXDA Working Group on Data Access (2020) for a specific Annodata use case.

stakeholders within the Bundesbank, such as the legal unit, IT security, or the data-producing business units.

Whether or not a researcher is ultimately granted data access very much depends on (i) the data requested (e.g. degree of anonymization or planned linkage), (ii) the characteristics of the researcher (e.g. potential commercial interest or educational background), and (iii) the selected mode of access (e.g. secure on-site access or download). Moreover, the applicable access protocols that are required before the start of a research project (e.g. the contract type a researcher has to sign) may likewise vary, depending on these three dimensions.

As the number of datasets in the BBk-RDSC's portfolio steadily increases, along with the average number of datasets used in a single research project, it becomes more and more complex and cumbersome to keep track of all the rules and how they interact. Therefore, the BBk-RDSC started investigating how it could automate tasks and decisions associated with data access management, which eventually led to the development of the Annodata framework. Annodata (a contraction of "annotation to data") are structured metadata information needed for data access management that previously only existed in an unstructured form, e.g. in legal texts or as tangible expert knowledge. The aim of the Annodata framework is "to complement extant metadata schemas not to supersede them" (Bender et al. 2021).

The BBk-RDSC expects the use of the Annodata framework to yield four main benefits. First, the Annodata framework adheres to the FAIR principles. It creates transparency about where data can be found and how they can be accessed, which in turn facilitates both reusability and the reproducibility of previous outcomes. In addition, the Annodata framework covers linkage possibilities and potential restrictions.

Second, the availability of structured and standardized information on the requested data, the applicable access rules as well as the requesting researcher and their project will ease the automation of data access management at the BBk-RDSC. The Annodata framework places great emphasis on unambiguous, machine-readable information on the basis of which decisions can be derived deterministically.

Third, researchers will benefit from the increase in transparency surrounding the BBk-RDSC's data access management procedures, giving them a better understanding of the applicable access rules, restrictions, and protocols. This improved grasp will speed up the application process and eventually lead to a higher level of trust in the objectivity of the BBk-RDSC.

Fourth, the Annodata schema provides a common taxonomy underpinning the exchange of knowledge between different data-providing institutions. In the context of the international INEXDA[27] network, representatives from different central banks, statistical institutes, and international organizations discussed their approaches to data access for research purposes. As differences in the terminology and legal foundations used complicated the discussion, the INEXDA Working Group on Data Access developed the INEXDA Annodata schema[28] containing mostly controlled keywords with a clear definition. In a next step, the INEXDA Annodata schema will be used for harmonization activities.

Overall, the Annodata framework has the potential to significantly increase the efficiency of data access management procedures and thus to reduce costs for both the BBk-RDSC as well as applying researchers. Moreover, by supporting the FAIR principles, it also boosts the value generated for stakeholders.

---

27 The International Network for Exchanging Experience on Statistical Handling of Granular Data (INEXDA) supports the G20 process by providing a platform for exchanging experiences on statistical handling of granular data for central banks, statistical institutes and international organisations. For more information, see Members of the INEXDA Network (2018).

28 See INEXDA Working Group on Data Access (2020) for the INEXDA Annodata schema.

22.5 Conclusion

In this paper, we introduced the BUBMIC model, an approach that groups the workflow of providing access to, and the analysis of, sensitive micro data into three broader building blocks: (i) laying the technical and procedural foundations, (ii) generating safe results, and (iii) generating value for all stakeholders. By doing this, we are not reinventing the wheel, since building blocks 1 and 2 can be found in existing models from the literature. Our innovation is to combine these existing components with the idea of generating stakeholder value (building block 3), which in our mind is a crucial and often overlooked success factor in micro data access proposals.

To provide tangible examples for building block 3 of the BUBMIC model, we introduced developments that help data providers and data users minimize the cost function and increase the benefit of using sensitive micro data in Section 22.4. One example worth highlighting is the Annodata framework, which introduces structured, machine-readable metadata information that can support the automation of, and communication about, data access management (Bender et al. 2021). However, we also emphasized the need for more comprehensive discussions about all the channels through which RDCs generate value for stakeholders.

By introducing the BUBMIC model, we have clearly not resolved the peculiar situation of being flooded with (too much) data while at the same time still seeing relevant data hidden away in tightly regulated silos where they are underexploited by empirical research and statistics. We do, however, view the BUBMIC model as an important step toward building bridges to these silos to allow sensitive data to be analyzed for the public good. In our mind, the key building block to these bridges is to identify the value that can be unlocked for all the stakeholders involved.

Acknowledgments

The authors would like to thank our colleagues at the Research Data and Service Centre (BBk-RDSC) for their valuable suggestions and feedback. We are particularly grateful to Tobias Schönberg for his detailed description of the BBk-RDSC's workflows, published as "Data Access to Micro Data of the Deutsche Bundesbank" (BBk-RDSC Technical Report 2019-02), which laid the foundations for Section 22.4 of this article. We also thank Julia Lane and her group as well as the INEXDA members for fruitful discussions that helped us sharpen our arguments and ideas. All remaining errors are our own.

Disclaimer

The views expressed in this chapter are those of the authors and do not necessarily reflect the views of the Deutsche Bundesbank or the Eurosystem.

References

Amaya, A., Biemer, P.P., and Kinyon, D. (2020). Total error in a big data world: adapting the TSE framework to big data. *Journal of Survey Statistics and Methodology* 8 (1 February): 89–119.
Bender, S., Hausstein, B., and Hirsch, C. (2019). An introduction to INEXDA's metadata schema. Proceedings from the Ninth IFC Conference in Basel, Switzerland (30–31 August 2018).

Bender, S., Blaschke, J., Doll, H., Hirsch, C., and Ritchie, F. (2021). The annodata framework: putting FAIR data into practice. Deutsche Bundesbank, Research Data and Service Centre.

Biemer, P.P., de Leeuw, E.D., Eckman, S., Edwards, B., Kreuter, F., Lyberg, L.E., Tucker, N.C., and West, B.T. (2017). *Total Survey Error in Practice*, Wiley Series in Survey Methodology. Wiley.

Blanc, M., Radermacher, W. and Körner, T. (2002). Quality and users. Quality in the European Statistical System – The way forward, Luxembourg. pp. 45–60.

Blaschke, J., Hering, F., and Huth, L. (2020). Document automation at the Research Data and Service Centre using the RDSC Contract Generator. *Technical Report 2020-02*, Deutsche Bundesbank, Research Data and Service Centre.

Cabrera, N. B., Bongartz, E. C., Dörrenbächer, N., Goebel, J., Kaluza, H., and Siegers, P. (2020). White paper on implementing the FAIR principles for data in the Social, Behavioural, and Economic Sciences. RatSWD working paper series, no. 274/2020, https://doi.org/10.17620/02671.60.

Desai, T., Ritchie, F., and Welpton, R. (2016). Five Safes: designing data access for research. Economics working paper series no. 1601, UWE Bristol.

European Commission (2018). Turning FAIR into reality. European Commission, Luxembourg, https://ec.europa.eu/info/sites/info/files/turning_fair_into_reality_1.pdf.

Gomolka, M., Blaschke, J., Brîncoveanu, C., Hirsch, C., and Yalcin, E. (2021). Data orchestration blueprint based on YAML {dobby}: research data pipelines in R. *Technical Report 2021-03*. Deutsche Bundesbank, Research Data and Service Centre.

Groves, R.M. (2011). Three eras of survey research. *Public Opinion Quarterly* 75 (5) Special Issue 2011: 861–871. https://doi.org/10.1093/poq/nfr057.

INEXDA Working Group on Data Access (2020). *Final report*. https://www.inexda.org/wp-content/uploads/2020/05/FINAL_INEXDA_WG_DA_Final_Report.pdf.

Landau, W.M. (2018). The drake R package: a pipeline toolkit for reproducibility and high-performance computing. *Journal of Open Source Software* 3 (21): 550. https://doi.org/10.21105/joss.00550.

Lane, J.I. (2020). *Democratizing Our Data – A Manifesto*. MIT Press.

Members of the INEXDA Network (2018). INEXDA – the Granular Data Network. Irving Fisher Committee working paper no. 18.

Radermacher, W. (2019). *Official Statistics 4.0 – Verified Facts for People in the 21st Century*. Springer.

Research Data and Service Centre (2021). Rules for visiting researchers at the RDSC. *Technical Report 2021-02 – version 1-0*, Deutsche Bundesbank, Research Data and Service Centre.

Ritchie, F. (2016). Can a change in attitudes improve effective access to administrative data for research?. Economics working paper series no. 1607, UWE Bristol.

Ritchie, F. (2017). The "five safes": a framework for planning, designing and evaluating data access solutions. In: *Data for Policy 2017: Government by Algorithm? (Data for Policy)*. Zenodo.

Ritchie, F. (2021). Microdata access and privacy: what have we learned over twenty years? *Journal of Privacy and Confidentiality* 11 (1): 1–18. https://doi.org/10.29012/jpc.766.

Schönberg, T. (2019). Data access to micro data of the Deutsche Bundesbank. *Technical Report 2019-02*, Deutsche Bundesbank, Research Data and Service Centre.

SVR-Gutachten (2021). SACHVERSTÄNDIGENRAT zur Begutachtung der Entwicklung im Gesundheitswesen. Digitalisierung für Gesundheit – Ziele und Rahmenbedingungen eines dynamisch lernenden Gesundheitssystems [Digitalisation for health – Aims and framework conditions for a dynamically learning health system (members: Ferdinand Gerlach, Wolfgang Greiner, Beate Jochimsen, Christof von Kalle, Gabriele Meyer, Jonas Schreyögg, Petra A. Thürmann)]. https://www.svr-gesundheit.de/fileadmin/Gutachten/Gutachten_2021/SVR_Gutachten_2021.pdf. English (executive summary only): https://www.svr-gesundheit.de/fileadmin/Gutachten/Gutachten_2021/Executive_Summary_Englisch.pdf.

van der Loo, M.P.J. and de Jonge, E. (2021). Data validation infrastructure for R. *Journal of Statistical Software* 97: 1–31.

Vilhuber, L. (2019). Report by the AEA data editor. *AEA Papers and Proceedings* 109: 718–729.

Vilhuber, L. (2020). Reproducibility and replicability in economics. *Harvard Data Science Review* 2 (4): https://doi.org/10.1162/99608f92.4f6b9e67.

Vilhuber, L. (2021). Report by the AEA data editor. *AEA Papers and Proceedings* 111: 808–817.

Wilkinson, M.D., Dumontier, M., Aalbersberg, I.J., Appleton, G., Axton, M., Baak, A., and Bouwman, J. (2016). The FAIR guiding principles for scientific data management and stewardship. *Scientific Data* 3: 160018. https://doi.org/10.1038/sdata.2016.18.

23

Machine Learning in German Official Statistics[1]

Florian Dumpert

Federal Statistical Office of Germany, Wiesbaden, Germany

23.1   Introduction

While machine learning has been tried and often established in many areas of science and economics for some time, official statistics has only begun to address this issue in the last decade. The origins of machine learning go back well into the twentieth century, see for instance the Dartmouth Summer Research Project on Artificial Intelligence (Samuel 1959), or the theoretical anticipation of the methods, etc. However, many of this field's approaches only gained some applicability outside of research and in official statistics as computing power and large (not necessarily official) data sets became increasingly available and legally accessible.

This chapter aims to provide an overview of the use of machine learning in official statistics, in particular in Germany. However, this goal is not to be achieved by way of a complete list of projects. Rather, the necessary strong link between science and research, national and international exchange and collaboration and specific application shall be revealed and explained by way of examples. The examples are taken from the field of earnings statistics, all of whose data are collected from reporting establishments in the form of samples.

The chapter presents in the second section a short introduction to machine learning, in Section 23.3 an overview of machine learning in official statistics in general, and in Section 23.4, the developments of machine learning in (German) official statistics from a methodological and organizational point of view. Section 23.5 covers the examination of some projects in the Federal Statistical Office of Germany with a slight emphasis toward editing and imputation. The chapter concludes with an outlook.

23.2   Terminology and a Short Introduction to Machine Learning

First, of course, the question arises as to what is actually meant by the term "machine learning" and how it fits into the processes and methods of official statistics. Let us start with a short definition of the term and a differentiation from other terms that are often mentioned in this context.

---

1 This paper represents the author's personal opinion and does not necessarily reflect the view of the Federal Statistical Office of Germany. Joerg Feuerhake, Stefan Bender and Arnout van Delden deserve great thanks for their critical review of the document and their valuable suggestions for improvement.

Advances in Business Statistics, Methods and Data Collection. Edited by Ger Snijkers, Mojca Bavdaž, Stefan Bender, Jacqui Jones, Steve MacFeely, Joseph W. Sakshaug, Katherine J. Thompson, and Arnout van Delden.
© 2023 John Wiley & Sons, Inc. Published 2023 by John Wiley & Sons, Inc.

Here, we only treat statistical machine learning, which learns empirically inductively. Other forms, in particular logical-symbolic machine learning, are not considered. The latter ultimately aim at constructing theorem provers and are not relevant for official statistics. Inevitably, the question arises – not only but also in the field of official statistics – how machine learning fits into the world of statistical methods. Already by asking this question, a first point is set: we consider machine learning (at least such learning that we believe can be usefully applied in official statistics) from a statistical point of view and as a statistical method. This is not necessarily self-evident, since one could also take a more numerical and algorithmically oriented approach, as computer science does. If early sources (Samuel 1959) are consulted, the goal of machine learning can be defined as follows: "The studies reported here have been concerned with the programming of a digital computer to behave in a way which, if done by human beings or animals, would be described as involving the process of learning. [...] Programming computers to learn from experience should eventually eliminate the need for much of this detailed programming effort."

Transferred to the world of statistics, which of course is less about solving board games and more about processing tasks in the statistical production process, this means that when using machine learning, the statistician is relieved of the task of precisely specifying the statistical model underlying a data situation in advance. While the approach without machine learning consists of modeling the relationship between explanatory variables and variables to be explained (target variables) on the basis of prior theoretical or empirical knowledge as well as on the basis of exploratory data analysis, machine learning is – in principle – capable of doing this by itself, provided that a sufficient number of data points are available. This advantage is technically presented by the fact that machine learning approaches provide for larger hypothesis spaces and thus a much higher flexibility than is otherwise common in statistics.

A hypothesis space is the set of all functions that are tested to determine whether they optimally describe the functional relationship between the explanatory variable and the variable to be explained in a suitable sense. To make this more concrete, let us use a linear model. Let us say that the variable y to be explained depends on the explanatory variables x_1 to x_3 presumably as follows: $y = \theta_0 + \theta_1 x_1 + \theta_2 x_1^2 + \theta_3 x_2^2 + \theta_4 x_2 x_3 + \theta_5 x_3$. Then the hypothesis space consists of polynomials of degree 2 due to the modeling. Higher degrees, further interactions or even other functional relationships, e.g. exponential, are not even considered in the optimization. Machine learning is not subject to this restriction. Here, much larger hypothesis spaces are taken into account, e.g. the set of all continuous functions (Steinwart and Christmann 2008, Chapter 4; Christmann et al. 2016) or the set of all integrable functions. Machine learning is also capable of recognizing variables that have no relevance to the task at hand as such, and thus of not incorporating these variables into the model. However, if there is too little data (i.e. too little information) available to learn the optimal function, machine learning does not show its strength in this respect. At least in this case (if not always), it is worthwhile to explicitly model known prior knowledge also in the case of machine learning (see Section 23.5.2 for an example of explicitly modeled information). Also, precisely because of their high flexibility and few to no assumptions on the population and on the data generating process, machine learning approaches provide fewer opportunities for interpretation and inference than other statistical approaches. It should also be taken into account that the use of machine learning places higher demands on the available hardware, usually in the form of cores, graphics cards, and RAM. Additionally, it is highly recommended to check that machine learning is used in a valid way. For example, the performance of a model should not be evaluated using the same data that has already been used for training. Instead, performance is usually assessed using validation and test data sets in different variations (e.g. cross-validation). While the training data can be manipulated if necessary to improve the performance of the machine learning model (e.g. by upsampling or downsampling, see Section 23.5.2), it is important to ensure that the test data sets represent the population well. Furthermore, in machine learning algorithms, care must be taken to ensure that the available hyperparameters are appropriately selected, so-called "tuning." Besides the elementary, but very inefficient grid search, there are different approaches for this. Bischl et al. (2021) provides methodological hints for performance estimation and tuning.

Another aspect must be mentioned here: the machine learning community speaks of a model being trained, and the use of this term is not incorrect. After all, a functional relationship between input and output is learned using a machine learning algorithm. The result, the learned functional relationship, which is then called a model, can refer to (conditional) expected values, quantiles, modes, etc. Nonmachine-learning statistics would often see under a statistical model something more extensive, namely a whole distribution or a set of distributions. Some algorithms used in terms of machine learning also actually provide probability models (e.g. Naïve Bayes, logistic regression), others only provide estimates based on scores.

Typically, four classes of machine learning are commonly distinguished:

- *Supervised learning*: Both observations of the explanatory variables and the corresponding observations of the variable to be explained are available. Examples for machine learning approaches in this field are Naïve Bayes, k-nearest-neighbor, classification and regression trees, boosting, random forest, support vector machines, and neural networks. James et al. (2013) provides a summary of supervised learning and the mentioned approaches.
- *Unsupervised learning*: this class does not have a predefined variable to be explained. Typical tasks in unsupervised learning are variable selection, dimension reduction, outlier detection, and clustering. Examples for machine learning approaches here are the well-known algorithms k-means and principal component analysis but also density-based spatial clustering isolation forest. James et al. (2013) provides a summary of unsupervised learning and some of the mentioned approaches.
- *Semisupervised learning*: values of the explanatory variable and the variable to be explained exist, the latter are given at the time of training (i.e. at the time of learning the model) only for a part of the data; the unsupervised part is used to assist in finding the structure of the supervised part. The author is not aware of any current example from official statistics where semisupervised learning has been used successfully. A worth reading paper on semisupervised learning is given by van Engelen and Hoos (2020).
- *Reinforcement learning*: Here, a strategy is to be learned by means of exploitation and exploration, which optimizes an objective function in a suitable sense. The author is not aware of any successful examples of the use of reinforcement learning in official statistics. However, this type of machine learning has become known worldwide at the latest with AlphaZero (Silver et al. 2018) and recently with MuZero (Schrittwieser et al. 2020). Other areas of application include diabetes research (Tejedor et al. 2020).

A good introduction to machine learning in general from a more applied point of view is given by Schierholz and Ghani (2020).

Let us for this chapter stay in the field of supervised learning, i.e. in the situation where both observations of the explanatory variables and the corresponding observations of the variable to be explained are available. Nonmachine-learning statistics now deals with questions of the type

- What influence does an explanatory variable have on the variable being explained?
- Is there true causality or is there only a correlation?
- Which type of model (which high-dimensional surface/hyperplane, if any) best describes the true underlying phenomenon?

- What variance not accounted for by the model occurs in the data and how can it be modeled?
- Which is the best (type of) model?

If a method is used in the sense of machine learning, these questions initially take a back seat. As mentioned in various places (e.g. Efron 2020, Yung and Turmelle 2019, Shmueli 2010, Breiman 2001), in the current chapter, we too see supervised machine learning less as a class of methods than by its objective of the most accurate point estimate (prediction) possible of the unknown expression of the target variable of a so far not seen observation.

There are statistical methods that have their strengths in one task rather than the other. The classical linear model, which is rather inflexible due to its strong model assumptions per construct, is therefore more suitable for the clarification of the abovementioned questions. A support vector machine or a deep neural network are more suitable for point estimation because of their high flexibility. This does not mean, of course, that there are not approaches to making a support vector machine "interpretable" or "explainable"; nor does it mean that predictions from a linear model must be bad. However, a tendency with respect to the "preferred" task is certainly often apparent. Methods can therefore be examined and optimized under one or the other objective. In the following, we therefore speak of machine learning methods or nonmachine learning methods, depending on the focus.

As explained before, supervised machine learning methods require training data. These are not always available (in sufficient quantity). What "sufficient" means can often not be easily determined in advance. Theoretical estimates exist in the form of concentration inequalities (such as, in particular, Bernstein's inequality in Hilbert spaces) and Oracle inequalities, see Shalev-Shwartz and Ben-David (2014). However, these require assumptions about the underlying data generating process of which one does not want to assume too much when using machine learning. An impression of how much data is needed may be obtained empirically by plotting the number of data used for training against the selected performance measures. If the curve is flat at the right edge, this indicates (as an unproven rule of thumb) that (purely quantitatively) a sufficient amount of data is available.

In addition, if training data are available, questions of its quality regularly arise. Training data that is distorted or otherwise incorrect is, of course, poison for machine learning. In the worst-case, the machine learning process learns all the errors as well and ultimately delivers the dreaded "garbage in, garbage out." Consider, as an example, a classification problem and assume that there is a training data set where the putative true class has been determined manually (e.g. by clerks in a statistical office) for some or many statistical units (e.g. establishments or employees). In this case, there is a possibility that different clerks would arrive at different estimates of what the true class membership is. This fact exposes two problems: On the one hand, it is unclear how to interpret an observed misclassification of a machine learning procedure. Does such a misclassification mean that the machine learning procedure is wrong or that the manually set class membership was wrong (or in the multiclass case, both)? Thinking further, however, machine learning could thus also be useful for identifying units that may have been incorrectly classified manually. On the other hand, there is the question of the uncertainty of the manual classifications used for learning. Different clerks might arrive at different classifications; in official statistical practice, however, there are hardly the resources to measure an interrater reliability, and the uncertainty in the training data is therefore often systematically underestimated. Note that when the concepts to be predicted are not well defined, the interrater reliability will be low. In that case, the question is not whether the machine-learning model gives a better prediction than the manual determined class membership, but then one first has to define the concepts and classes to be predicted more precisely.

Moreover, following Russell and Norvig (2010), we see machine learning as statistical method and only as part of the subject area of artificial intelligence. However, all experiments, studies, and production deployments use only statistical machine learning approaches (sometimes referred to as "weak AI") and no aspects of artificial intelligence beyond that so far. Cases such as incorrect assignment to a reporting group caused by machine learning can easily be noticed and corrected by the statistical unit involved. Thus, from this point of view, the procedure does not differ from, for example, a manual assignment by a clerk. Misestimates or misclassifications in other cases lead, in the worst-case – and of course, to be avoided as far as possible – to a poor estimate of one or more parameters of a population, but have no immediate repercussion on the misclassified or otherwise wrongly estimated statistical unit. In this case, machine learning approaches do not differ from other statistical methods.

Often mentioned together with machine learning is big data, for which we prefer the following timeless definition from Suthaharan (2014): "It means that some point in time, when the volume, variety and velocity of the data are increased, the current techniques and technologies may not be able to handle storage and processing of the data. At that point the data is defined as Big Data." Sometimes also the terminus "new (digital) data" is used (including possible extraction methods such as web scraping). Of course, this is justified in the sense that machine learning approaches are often useful when dealing with a lot of data or data that deviates from the classical survey structure, including selective data from a nonprobability sample. Nevertheless, machine learning is neither sufficient nor necessary for a proper handling of selective data sets. For this reason, this chapter does not discuss big data, new (digital) data or web scraping in detail.

23.3 Machine Learning in Official Statistics – International Overview

Machine learning is playing an increasingly important role in statistical agencies worldwide. This is evident, among other things, in the frequency with which machine learning approaches are presented and discussed in conference presentations and papers, for example at the European Establishment Statistics Workshop 2019, the Conference on New Techniques and Technologies for Official Statistics 2019 and 2021, the BigSurv Conference 2018, 2019 and 2020, or the International Conference on Establishment Statistics 2020/2021. Increasingly, we can also see the development of organizational structures that (partly under the umbrella of "data science") embed machine learning in official statistics or in the overlapping area between science and official statistics. Beck et al. (2018) summarizes the results of a national and international survey on the use of machine learning in statistical institutions. There were positive responses from 21 national statistical offices, some statistical offices of the German Länder, and some other German agencies (such as the Deutsche Bundesbank). Classification and imputation were the most frequently mentioned application areas. Consequently, the majority of machine learning approaches is applied in processes 5.1–5.5 (integrate data; classify & code; review, validate & edit; impute; derive new variables & statistical units) of the Generic Statistical Business Process Model (GSBPM), a model that describes (official) statistics production in a general and process-oriented way (UNECE 2021). More recently, international projects on machine learning in official statistics have also emerged. For example, the Machine Learning Project 2019/2020 of the United Nations Economic Commission for Europe High-Level Group for the Modernization of Official Statistics (UNECE HLG-MOS) (Julien 2020), which continued as ML2021 led by the Office for National Statistics (the British national statistical office) and supported by UNECE. The project covered classification and coding (Sthamer 2020), editing and imputation (Dumpert 2020b), imagery (Coronado and Juárez 2020), quality (Yung et al. 2020), and integration (Measure 2020).

Since this chapter will also focus on editing and imputation issues as well as quality aspects, the main results of the UNECE HLG-MOS Machine Learning Project 2019/2020 in these areas will be summarized in the following.

Several pilot studies took place in the editing and imputation subgroup. Two for editing (UK and Italy), four for imputation (Belgium-VITO, Italy, Poland, and Germany). They provided the following results:

- Learning from former editing results is possible: it is possible to predict whether a unit needs special attention.
- The extraction of rules suffers, however, from the trade-off that good predictions are only achievable with very detailed (i.e. long and complex) rules. This refers to the quality aspect of interpretability and explainability (see the quality framework "QF4SA" described below).
- Machine learning delivers comparable (compared to traditional methods) results in a more automated way.
- Machine learning methods produced often (but not always) plausible predictions.
- Machine learning can produce more timely statistics by skipping some pre-treatment of variables, e.g. being aware of correlations, statistical transformations (like logarithm) of the values, etc., but there is also the experience that a successful use of machine learning in production is possible only after a lot of (successful) experimentation on the topic. So far, it is not possible to state when (in general) data pre-processing beyond technical aspects is necessary or useful when using machine learning.
- Machine learning can reduce human intervention (e.g. when it is doing variable selection automatically).
- Imputation projects with time dependencies in the data (like in time series) can be successful; however, successful at this point means that machine learning did not perform worse. Similar results could be achieved with very simple predictors (like simply previous year's value, etc.).
- It may happen that no single machine learning method works best for a given problem.
- Some machine learning methods (or approaches within them) perform better in terms of distributional aspects than other ones.
- There is a need to shift the interest of stakeholders to accuracy and timeliness of results rather than to the interpretation of the coefficients of a model.
- One should also always consider and check against a baseline method that is simple, well accepted, and reasonably performing; this is to avoid drowning in complexities with only marginal effects.

The quality work package identified five quality dimensions for statistical algorithms (explainability, accuracy, reproducibility, timeliness, and cost-effectiveness) and summarized them in the Quality Framework for Statistical Algorithms (QF4SA). Both machine learning and nonmachine-learning methods are covered. The five quality dimensions and corresponding recommendations are explained briefly below, directly following Yung et al. (2020). All five dimensions of the QF4SA should be considered when deciding on the choice of an algorithm:

- Explainability means the ability to understand the logic underpinning the algorithm used in prediction or analysis, as well as the resulting outputs. Explainability is greatly assisted by depicting the relationship between the input and output variables and providing the necessary information on the methodology underpinning the algorithm. Statistical offices should use methods for explainability to help users understand the relationship between input and output variables.

- Accuracy means the closeness of computations or estimates to the exact or true values that the statistics were intended to measure. The accuracy of statistical information hence refers to the degree to which it correctly describes the phenomena it was designed to measure. Accuracy may refer to (G1) the data elements or (G2) aspects about the distribution, as in the case of imputation. In addition, a common objective of statistical surveys is to estimate a set of parameters of the target finite population. Therefore, within a quality framework, (G3) the accuracy of the estimates of these parameters is generally also considered a key measure of quality. Statistical offices should calculate the expected prediction error, as well as the prediction error, to protect against potentially poor-quality training data; and statistical offices should use the highest-quality training data possible when applying prediction algorithms.
- Reproducibility (at its lowest level) means the ability to replicate results using the same data and algorithm originally used (methods reproducibility; higher levels are included in QF4SA, too). Statistical offices should take action to implement methods reproducibility.
- Timeliness means the time involved in producing a result from conceptualization to algorithm building, processing, and production. A useful distinction may be the timeliness in development and production, with the former generally taking longer than the latter. Statistical offices should add development and processing time to the commonly used concept of timeliness.
- Cost-effectiveness means the degree to which the results are effective in relation to their cost, e.g. the accuracy per unit cost. It is a form of economic analysis that compares the relative merits of different algorithms. Statistical offices should in particular consider two aspects when considering cost-effectiveness: cheaper operating costs and time to recoup fixed costs.

A workstream of ML2021 has the goal to explore some dimensions of QF4SA in a consolidated project to analyze the output based on a set of standard metrics and procedures.

In the remainder of this chapter, we focus on machine learning in official statistics in Germany.

23.4 History and Current Status of Machine Learning in German Official Statistics

23.4.1 Federal Statistical Office of Germany

In 2017, the development of the so-called "Digital Agenda of the Federal Statistical Office" started. One of many topics discussed was machine learning. A "Proof of Concept Machine Learning" was introduced as one of four lighthouse projects of the Digital Agenda. The proof of concept was to conduct a review of the applicability of machine learning in official statistics processes. An overview of potential applications in official statistics should be available. Before starting this work, the Federal Statistical Office already had some experience with the use of machine learning. As of around 2015, some projects were already underway, e.g. in the business register, in craft statistics, and in the structure of earnings survey. A brief overview of early developments is already given by Beck et al. (2018). The proof of concept concluded in 2018 that projects that classify, impute values, and identify units using random forests or similar tree-based methods, support vector machines, or neural networks are widely used. Use cases can be found in almost all specialized statistics. Usually, processes in statistics design, data mining, data analysis, and statistics dissemination and evaluation are supported by machine learning methods. For the realization of projects using machine learning methods, a suitable infrastructure must be available. Regarding necessary software, currently there is no way around R and Python.

From applying machine learning methods, the Federal Statistical Office expected and still expects higher quality of official statistics (for example, through improved or now possible editing, including any necessary corrections), more efficient processes (for example, through faster execution of coding by means of supporting the clerks with suggestions for codes or complete automation in unambiguous cases) as well as more analysis possibilities (for example, through estimation of information to a specialized statistic, if the variable in question was not collected). An inquiry into the topic is also already obvious due to the European Statistics Code of Practice, which requires the use of up-to-date statistical methods (Eurostat 2018). Though machine learning is a very prominent topic, it is not a buzz word, as Julien (2020) states.

As a result of the inquiry into the topic and the proof of concept as well as parallel ongoing preliminary work, a separate (organizational) Section "Machine Learning and Imputation Methods" was established in the Division for Mathematical-Statistical Methods at the Federal Statistical Office, which aims to support the departments in methodological questions and in practical implementation as a competence center on these topics.

As of early 2021, there were approximately 30 completed or ongoing machine learning projects at the Federal Statistical Office. Naturally, not all of them are successful. However, this need not be a disadvantage, because valuable insights for the future can also be gained from failed projects.

In addition to specific technical projects, some of which are described in more detail in Section 23.3, the Federal Statistical Office also participates in collaboration (i) with the statistical offices of other countries and international organizations, (ii) with statistical societies, and (iii) with the scientific community.

An example of (i) is the participation in the UNECE HLG-MOS Machine Learning project 2019/2020 (Julien 2020). The Federal Statistical Office participated in the editing and imputation and quality subprojects.

One example of (ii) is provided by the work of the Deutsche Arbeitsgemeinschaft Statistik (German Consortium in Statistics; a consortium of scientific societies and professional associations that regard the further development of statistical theory and methodology) on the question of how statistics can enrich the field of artificial intelligence. The areas of study design, assessment of data quality and data collection, distinction between causality and associations, evaluating uncertainty, interpretability, and validation as well as education and training were identified and discussed (Friedrich et al. 2021).

The collaboration with the scientific community in the field of machine learning – (iii) – takes place on different levels. Currently, there is no research institute institutionally interwoven with the Federal Statistical Office in German official statistics, so the collaboration is usually case by case. For example, a joint workshop on machine learning was held at the University of Stuttgart in 2019 (Stuttgart Workshop on Statistical Learning). In addition to publications and talks on the methodology used and current issues, research contracts are awarded or joint research projects are carried out. In the area of machine learning, reference is made here, for example, to Thurow et al. (2021a, 2021b) and Bischl et al. (2021).

23.4.2 History and Current Status in the German Official Statistics Network

The federal structure of the Federal Republic of Germany is reflected in the independent existence of the statistical offices of the Länder (i.e., of the federal states). A large part of the specialized statistics is collected and evaluated on a decentralized basis. The Federal Statistical Office is responsible for the methodological and technical preparation of statistics, the coordination of statistical production, questions of standardization, the compilation and dissemination of the federal result, the collection of data for so-called "central surveys," and the international representation of the German statistical system. Since many steps of data processing are located at the statistical offices of the Länder and at the same time many application examples for machine learning in official statistics can be found in GSBPM phase 5 ("process"), an involvement of the Länder in this topic is institutionalized in the form of a joint working group "Machine Learning." In addition, the statistical offices of the Länder also carry out valuable projects in the field of machine learning on their own initiative and independently from the Federal Statistical Office. For example, and by no means to be understood as exhaustive, studies on imputing the number of newborn children used in the German microcensus (Pech 2019), on editing used in the accommodation statistics (Hessisches Statistisches Landesamt 2020, Schömann and Rohde 2021), and on improving the provision of product descriptions used in the consumer price statistics for the research data center (Kaukal and Peters 2019) may be mentioned here.

23.5 Some Current Projects at the Federal Statistical Office

23.5.1 Overview

The fields of application of the about 30 ongoing or already completed projects in the field of machine learning in the Federal Statistical office are widely spread. Exemplary – and again not exhaustive – are the following: Automated use of scanner data in price statistics (and here specifically: assignment of individual products to the corresponding COICOP[2] 10-digit code), a feasibility study for a faster flash estimation of the German gross domestic product, and investigations into the automation of classifications into economic sectors, which were previously carried out manually, on the basis of free-text entries. Some other projects are presented in more detail below. It is clear that not all of the projects started could be successfully completed in the sense that the machine learning methods were finally integrated into statistical production. The reasons for this are manifold. Often, there is not enough training data available with sufficient accuracy. For example, if a variable is to be estimated, a training data set is needed in which this variable to be estimated already exists for other, but comparable statistical units. If such a training data set does not exist or does not exist in sufficient quantity and quality, no supervised machine learning method can be used with good conscience. Difficulties also arise when the number and structure of the explanatory variables or the variable to be explained change at shorter intervals, e.g. due to changes in legislation. Statistical models (including those learned by machine learning) regularly become useless in this case.

The example applications of machine learning sketched below deal with questions about earnings. The related data are reported by employers (at establishment level) to statistical offices, where they are processed in form of various statistics. The first example (Section 23.5.2) is about classification, a typical field for machine learning. The other examples (Section 23.5.3) illustrate machine learning in the context of imputation from different points of view. All examples are based on concrete questions and application cases in German official statistics.

23.5.2 Machine Learning to Increase Analysis Capabilities in the Area of Minimum Wage Using Official Statistics

One of the tasks of the German Minimum Wage Commission is to evaluate the effects of the general statutory minimum wage of EUR 8.50 per hour worked introduced on January 1, 2015, and to report

---

2 Classification of Individual Consumption According to Purpose (UNSTATS 2021).

on this to the German government. The Minimum Wage Commission requires suitable data for this purpose. In its first report, it therefore proposed linking the Structure of Earnings Survey (SES) with the Integrated Employment Biographies (IEB) of the Federal Employment Agency and the Institute for Employment Research.

The SES records data on earnings. They are broken down by economic sector and personal information on employees such as gender, year of birth, length of service with the company, occupation, and training qualification. In addition, information about the employment relationship is collected: number of paid working hours, information on collective agreement, type of employment, and the extent of vacation entitlement. The SES thus enables statements to be made about the distribution of employee earnings and about the influence of important factors that determine individual earnings. Since gross monthly earnings are recorded together with monthly hours worked, gross hourly earnings can be calculated for all employees. For most economic sectors, the SES is a survey of a sample of establishments. For some establishments, several values have to be imputed (missing by design). Finally, parts of the SES are a secondary use of a subset (sample) of the data records of administrative sources. The SES in this form was collected every four years at the time. Further details are given by Statistisches Bundesamt (2016).

The IEB combine complete, historicized, and processed data from different data sources. Using the IEB, it is possible to trace employment histories – consisting of periods of employment, periods of benefit receipt, periods of unemployment and job-seeking, and participation in measures for activation and professional integration (Institut für Arbeitsmarkt- und Berufsforschung 2021). In contrast to the SES, the IEB covers all employees subject to social insurance contributions.

The panel data of the IEB are to be enriched with otherwise missing information on gross hourly earnings or on the minimum wage affectedness from the SES in order to improve the analysis possibilities. In addition to (probabilistic) record linkage, statistical machine learning methods (not only, but also) can be used for this purpose. The Federal Statistical Office has tested statistical machine learning methods with data from the SES 2014. The goal was to learn models that would allow the classification of employees into "affected by the minimum wage" and "not affected by the minimum wage" with sufficient reliability. This information could then be applied to the IEB data by running the classification model there. Only variables that are available in both the SES and the IEB are used as explanatory variables for the models. A generalization of this approach to other source and target statistics is conceivable.

Early investigations already showed that it makes sense to separate the data set into full-time employees (FT), part-time employees (PT), and marginal employed (ME) persons with the aim of learning separate models. This approach was also pursued during the research. The statistical (machine learning) methods that were investigated in all three cases (FT, PT, ME) were – in addition to the Naïve Bayes classifier and logistic regression – various random forest and boosting approaches. Further variations resulted from different strategies (upsampling, downsampling, SMOTE, ROSE) to deal with the imbalance in the occurrence of the two classes ("affected by the minimum wage" and "not affected by the minimum wage") in the data set as well as from the consideration of additional information at the aggregate level on the prevalence of the minimum wage in the stratum to which the considered establishment of an employee belongs. Upsampling in this context simply means to randomly sample (with replacement) the minority class to be the same size as the majority class. Downsampling in this context means to randomly subset all the classes in the training set so that their class frequencies match the least prevalent class. SMOTE (Chawla et al. 2002) generates synthetic units by means of interpolation of closely spaced real minority class units, ROSE (Lunardon et al. 2014) generates synthetic units based on kernel density estimates of the training data.

Since the classification problem is a binary one, the quality of the classification methods was measured using the usual quality measures accuracy, recall, and precision. Accuracy is the proportion of correct predictions among all cases in the test data set; recall is the proportion of employees paid less than 8.50 EUR per hour that were retrieved; precision is the proportion of employees truly paid less than 8.50 EUR per hour among all retrieved employees. It is known that recall and precision are opponents: one of them can easily be increased at the expense of the other. This results in a selection leeway for the users of the classification algorithm. Depending on whether the primary goal is to classify as many employees as possible as affected by the minimum wage (accepting that some employees may also be erroneously classified as affected by the minimum wage) – which could be ensured by high recall values – or whether the primary goal is to classify as few employees as possible as affected by the minimum wage – which could be ensured by high precision values – different models or model specifications must be selected. In all cases, the accuracy should not fall below the respective no-information rate (NIR, i.e. the proportion of the majority class). While in the group of full-time employees accuracies of 99% (with a NIR of 90%), recall values in the range of 95–99.5% and precision values also in the range of 95–99.5% are achieved. That is, the choice of the final model or the final model specification does not play a very decisive role for FT. The results in the area of PT and ME are clearly more variable (see figure below). For example, a random forest for PT (NIR 89%), learned on the basis of an upsampling approach, achieves the following average values (over ten variations of training and test data from the SES 2014): accuracy approx. 92%, recall approx. 47%, precision approx. 71%.

Figure 23.1 is used to visualize the conflict of objectives described above. The figure shows the key figures of various calculated models, namely the accuracy on the abscissa, the precision for "affected by the minimum wage" on the ordinate and the recall for "affected by the minimum wage" by "color coding." An ideal model would be light-colored and "top right" at point (1|1).

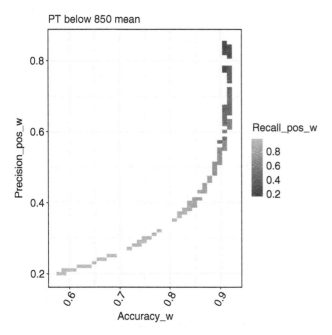

Figure 23.1 Key figures of various calculated classification models (for PT). Source: Florian Dumpert. This graph is also expected to appear in this form in a paper published by Springer.

Due to the constraint that the naïve estimator should be outperformed, models to the left of 89% accuracy are not of interest at all, but are included here to illustrate the results for completeness. The conflict between precision and recall is particularly clear: the higher the precision of a model (i.e., the more trustworthy an assignment to "affected by the minimum wage"; plotted higher up in the graph), the fewer of the interesting cases ("affected by the minimum wage") are recognized as such (represented by darker rectangles in the graph).

Obviously, different methods in different variations deliver a broad band of different results for the three target variables overall accuracy, recall, precision, and thus leave room for setting priorities in the choice of model.

A random forest for ME (NIR 61%), learned on the basis of a downsampling approach, achieves the following average values (over 10 variations of training and test data from the SES 2014): accuracy approximately 76%, recall approximately 57%, precision approximately 75%.

If an infinite number of data points were available for training (i.e. for learning the model), all considered methods would be able to perform the classification in the best possible way. The background to this is consistency proofs that have been conducted for these methods in the scientific community. However, without further assumptions, it is unclear how well the information contained in the data set can already be extracted by the methods based on a given finite number of data points. It may therefore be worthwhile to assist the methods in training by making information explicit (by introducing appropriate additional variables). Such an approach was also explored in the present case. For each employee, the proportion of employees paid the minimum wage in the strata in which the employee's establishment is located was added as an additional variable. The strata are distinguished from each other by a regional component, an industry component, and a size component. Figures 23.2 and 23.3 show (moderately for PT and much stronger for ME) that the information made explicit in this way improves the classification results (as measured by accuracy). Figure 23.2 shows the results for PT, using an upsampling approach, the threshold for the classification scores is 0.5. The abscissa shows the different methods tested, the ordinate contains the respective achieved accuracies (more precisely: the accuracies achieved over 10 repetitions in

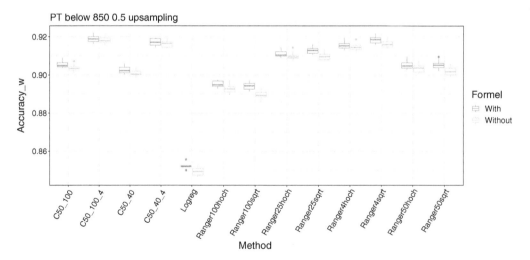

Figure 23.2 Comparing the accuracy for several classification methods (for PT). Source: Florian Dumpert. This graph is also expected to appear in this form in a paper published by Springer.

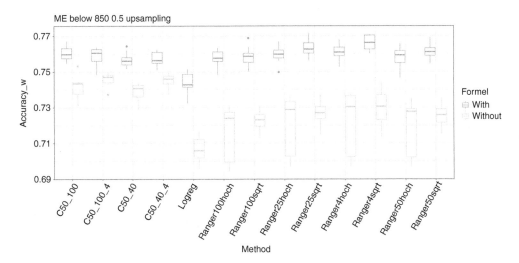

Figure 23.3 Comparing the accuracy for several classification methods (for ME). Source: Florian Dumpert. This graph is also expected to appear in this form in a paper published by Springer.

the form of boxplots). Two boxplots are displayed for each method. The boxplot on the left shows the accuracy when the additional information on the minimum wage share in the strata is used, while the boxplot on the right shows the accuracy when the additional information is not explicitly included. Two aspects are clearly visible: (i) All variants of the tree-based methods (boosting [label: C50_] or random forest [label: ranger], each with different hyperparameter settings) perform significantly better than the logistic regression [label: logreg], which was also calculated as a baseline method. (ii) The explicit inclusion of the additional information is worthwhile in all cases. Figure 23.3 shows the results for ME, using an upsampling approach, the threshold for the classification scores is 0.5. Three aspects are clearly visible for ME: (i) All variants of the tree-based methods (boosting [label: C50_] or random forest [label: ranger], each with different hyperparameter settings) perform better than the baseline logistic regression [label: logreg]. (ii) The explicit inclusion of the additional information is worthwhile in all cases. (iii) Without the explicit inclusion of the additional information, the results for the random forest models are more volatile than when the additional information is explicitly present. The other methods do not show this large increase in volatility.

The results are currently (2021) being examined by the Institute for Employment Research. In a first step, it is necessary to examine on which and for which data basis the models were learned (trained) and tested. The creation of a comparable data situation in the Integrated Employment Biographies with regard to the definitions and delimitations of variables is a prerequisite for the meaningful application of the models learned at the Federal Statistical Office.

Further details on this project can be found in Dumpert and Beck (2021). This project is a good example of how national collaboration can advance (official) statistics. The models that attribute information to the Integrated Employment Biographies are available to the Institute for Employment Research itself, but potentially also to other researchers, opening up new possibilities for analysis and thus potentially providing a better understanding of the impact of the introduction of the minimum wage. A similar, additional project involves estimating the FT/PT label in SES and Integrated Employment Biographies (Schmidt 2020).

23.5.3 Machine Learning for Editing and Imputation

23.5.3.1 Relevance

As stated in Beck et al. (2018), machine learning is mainly used for classification and imputation. At the time of the survey by Beck et al. (2018), there was hardly any experience with machine learning for editing and imputation at the Federal Statistical Office. Initial research on the topic of machine learning for imputation in the Federal Statistical Office is documented in Spies and Lange (2018). This resulted in a particular research interest in this direction. Imputation is one possible approach to deal with missing values in data sets. Missing values occur regularly in the field of official statistics. The reasons for this are manifold and range from simple noncollection of variables (by design) to the deletion of existing but implausible values in the course of editing to nonresponse due to missing reports from the respondents. Imputation is then a way to avoid having to restrict oneself to complete cases, to avoid bias in estimates (e.g. of parameters of a population) due to missing values, or to complete data sets so that algorithms can handle them or complete tables can be made available for science or to produce output. Depending on the goal to be pursued by imputation, the various methods conceivable for this purpose are suitable to different extents. Possible goals of imputation were presented by Chambers (2006) and range from the most exact "recovery" of missing values to the completion of the data in such a way that the key parameters of interest of a population are estimated as well as possible, to a "reproduction" of the distribution of the data. All of these goals also occur in the field of official statistics, as shown, among others, by the work on editing and imputation in the context of the UNECE HLG-MOS project 2019/2020 (Dumpert 2020b). Undoubtedly, editing and imputation contribute to an improvement in the quality of the outputs of official statistics; insofar as they are automated or partially automated, they also increase the efficiency of the processes.

In Sections 23.5.3.2 and 23.5.3.3, we will now describe in more detail two projects that German official statistics are currently working on, one of them of a more theoretical nature, the other more applied. Both studies concern the structure of earnings in establishments, specifically the Structure of Earnings Survey as well as its successor. While the more theoretical project is expected to be generalizable to other statistics, the applied project is, for the time being, specifically designed for the successor of the Structure of Earnings Survey.

23.5.3.2 Editing and Imputation in the New Digital Earnings Survey[3]

The New Digital Earnings Survey is to be conducted for the first time once in April 2021 and monthly from January 2022; from 2022, it will replace the previous earnings surveys: the quadrennial Structure of Earnings Survey and the Quarterly Earnings Survey. Within the scope of the new survey, monthly earnings data are to be collected for all employees of 58,000 establishments. In order to be able to process the resulting volume of data (approx. 7 million records per month), an automated editing and imputation procedure is required. Methods to be used for this purpose must be able to process numerical as well as categorical variables appropriately. In addition, an implementation of the basic algorithm should already exist since some years to avoid problems with teething troubles.

In the run-up to the implementation of the new survey, various systems that seemed prima facie suitable for this purpose were investigated, in particular the CANCEIS software from Statistics Canada (e.g. Guertin et al. 2014), HoloClean (Rekatsinas et al. 2017), and missForest (Stekhoven and Buehlmann 2012).

---

3 The author thanks Natalie Peternell who is carrying out the project for providing texts on which this section is based.

- HoloClean is able to perform rule-based error detection; additionally, it offers imputation through a softmax regression model. At the time of the investigation, HoloClean did not appear suitable for use in the New Digital Earnings Survey: HoloClean could only process categorical variables; numerical variables, therefore, needed to be discretized before being used in the software. In tests, this led to strong distortions in the results. Furthermore, no applications, especially no positive examples of HoloClean in other statistical offices were known at the time of the investigation.

- CANCEIS was originally developed by Statistics Canada for editing and imputation in the Canadian Census. CANCEIS can process edit rules, identify outliers, and perform corrections and imputations (rule-based or donor-based). It shows usable results in tests for the New Digital Earnings Survey. CANCEIS will eventually be implemented for production. However, missForest will also be studied.

- missForest fulfills essential requirements: it is freely available, open source, and can handle both variable types. However, error detection (using predefined edit rules like, e.g. "The age of an employee must be at least 14 and at most 80 years" or "A part-time employee has at most 37 hours of overtime per week") and deletion of erroneous entries must be implemented separately (and outside missForest). missForest is a nonparametric method to impute missing values in data sets with mixed type variables. It is based on the R package randomForest (Breiman et al. 2021). For each variable Y that has missing values, a random forest is learned sequentially. For the training of Y, only the units that have observed values in variable Y are used. Initially, the missing values of these units in the other variables X1, ... are filled by simple mean imputation. The missing values of variable Y are then estimated using the random forest thus trained. After one run, the data set no longer contains any missing values. However, there may still be room for improvement, namely to replace the initial mean imputation of the variables by random-forest-based imputations. This in turn may have implications for the imputations already performed, etc. The entire procedure is therefore repeated until a termination criterion is met. As the final data set has to fulfill certain hard edit rules, another loop outside missForest is necessary. In this outer loop, the entries of the output of missForest (the output is a complete data set) are checked again against the hard editing rules. For each of these editing rules, subject matter experts have specified beforehand which variables of a set of variables where an edit rule is violated should be changed during editing. If there are entries that violate the editing rules, they are deleted. Thus, there is again an incomplete data set and missForest must be restarted to create a new complete data set. The outer loop is iterated until another (outer) termination criterion is met. Ideally, there is then no more record that violates a hard edit rule. missForest calculates per iteration the normalized root mean squared error (NRMSE) for numeric variables and for the categorical variables the proportion of falsely classified (PFC) as imputation error. For the exact definition of NRMSE and PFC see, e.g. Stekhoven and Buehlmann 2012. Thus, imputations with missForest aim rather at a reconstruction of the missing values. As will be shown in the following section, this objective of imputation can lead to distortions in the distribution of the variables; however, without losing its raison d'être. The final implementation is not based on the R package missForest, but on missRanger (Mayer 2019), whose implementation is far more efficient than that of missForest.

Finally, CANCEIS will be implemented for productive operation. The results of CANCEIS are to be used primarily for statistical production; however, missRanger will ideally be further evaluated in parallel by the methodology division, i.e. redundantly at first glance. This would enable comparisons of the performance of CANCEIS and missRanger with respect to processing results and required runtimes in the editing and imputation process.

So far, there are only the simulation studies in advance, i.e. the studies performed based on SES 2018, in the context of which artificially missing or implausible values were set in such data sets that did not violate any edit rules. These studies led to the decision in favor of CANCEIS and miss-Forest/missRanger and to a discarding of HoloClean. A methodological question that still needs to be clarified is, however, how the imputation quality can be measured during operation, i.e. from 2022 on. Besides the use of external sources, it is conceivable to use completely plausible (sub) data sets out of the available data, i.e. in such data sets that fulfill all edit rules. On the latter, the original simulation study (i.e. artificially creating missing or implausible data, imputing, comparing to the true values) could then be carried out again (possibly on a smaller scale) at regular time intervals yet to be determined.

23.5.3.3 Studies on the Preservation of the Distribution under Imputation

If it is unclear a priori which analyses are to be performed on a data set provided by official statistics, imputation aimed at estimating certain targeted population parameters may be unfavorable. Although these particular targeted population parameters could be estimated very reliably in this case, other variables may not. To mitigate this problem, imputation could aim to "reproduce" the (possibly hypothetical) multivariate distribution of the complete data (or even better, of the population). To put it a little more concrete: For this purpose, imagine (as an example only) an establishment statistic that is supposed to collect the costs of companies in their structure and let us assume that imputations are required here. Let us assume that it is known in advance, which evaluations (in order to estimate target parameters of the population) of these statistics are important. These could be, for example, average costs of a certain type in certain strata. If the number of target variables is manageable, imputation procedures can be constructed in a way that these target variables are well estimated (for example, in terms of small, but imputation-appropriate RMSE). This is common practice. However, if the number of target variables is too large or if it can be assumed that not all relevant target variables are known beforehand (e.g. because external institutes will also perform calculations based on micro data of this business statistic), focusing imputation on a few target variables may be the wrong approach. In this case, the goal of imputation is rather to preserve or recover (multivariate) moments, quantiles, extrema, etc., of the (true) distribution, ultimately the true (multivariate) distribution itself, in order to allow more or less arbitrary evaluations on the microdata without bias.

Three questions immediately arise: (i) How should the quality of the reproduction be measured? (ii) Which imputation methods are able to achieve good results? (iii) How does this goal fit with the other goals of imputation already cited above?

First preliminary work in this direction is provided by Dumpert (2020a) on the basis of the German Cost Structure Survey of Enterprises in Manufacturing, Mining, and Quarrying. The stability of higher univariate moments of multivariate distributions was investigated by imputation using various machine learning methods.

In order to further investigate the questions, a simulation study was conducted on the basis of official data, including an anonymized version of the Structure of Earnings Survey (Thurow et al. 2021a, 2021b). This involved artificially generating missing values in the complete data set, then imputing the blanks, and finally comparing the original complete data set and the imputed data set. As a first step, the investigation was restricted to the univariate case, i.e. the marginal distributions of the variables to be imputed were examined. The consideration of multivariate distributions is currently the subject of ongoing research. The procedure and the results of this study will be briefly outlined here.

Without external information, statistical methods can only deal meaningfully with two missing mechanisms: Missingness completely at random (MCAR) and missingness at random (MAR). A variable is missing completely at random if the probability that a value is missing does not depend on the value of the variable to be imputed or on the values of auxiliary variables. If the probability that a value is missing does depend on the values of auxiliary variables, but not on the value of the variable to be imputed, the variable is called missing at random (e.g. de Waal et al. 2011).

The simulation study considered two different missing mechanisms (MCAR and MAR), six different imputation methods – naive imputation with mode or mean, Amelia (Honaker et al. 2011), missRanger (Mayer 2019), MICE with random forest, MICE with predictive mean matching, MICE with normal model (van Buuren and Groothuis-Oudshoorn 2011), and various measures of imputation accuracy. In addition to normalized root mean square error (NRMSE) and proportion of falsely classified (PFC), see Stekhoven and Buehlmann (2012), the Kolmogorov–Smirnov statistic, the Cramer–von Mises statistic (see Shorack and Wellner 2009), Mallow's L^2-distance (see Levina and Bickel 2001), and the Kullback–Leibler divergence (Cover and Thomas 2006) for metric variables as well as a modification of Cramer's V for categorical variables were used for special attention to distribution. In addition to the pure calculation of these measures, permutation tests were – if useful – performed in order to be able to determine p-values regarding the null hypothesis of equal (univariate) distributions (of the imputed versus the original complete distribution) in addition to the purely relative comparison of the methods. In order to investigate the stability of the results, 100 simulation runs were performed for each simulation set-up.

The empirical results indicate a (theoretically not yet shown) discrepancy between the NRMSE or PFC and distance measures. While the latter measure distributional similarities in the microdata, NRMSE and PFC focus on the reproducibility of the microdata. To illustrate this more clearly, let us take a closer look at NRMSE and PFC. Both measures consider in a certain sense the difference between true values and imputed (i.e. estimated) values at the level of microdata, i.e. the differences in the entries of a data set, and average them appropriately. This is particularly important to mention in order to clarify that the determination of the quality measure thus does not take place at the level of target parameters, but at the level of the microdata. Roughly speaking the more accurately a single datum is estimated, the smaller (i.e. better) NRMSE or PFC becomes. At first glance, this also solves the imputation problem. However, it is well known that properties of the distribution (in the simplest case: the variance) are distorted by optimization on the basis of the individual microdata, which is why imputation by means of (conditional) mean is not recommended in almost all cases (van Buuren 2012, p. 45). Empirically, it could be seen that a low NRMSE or PFC does not seem to imply lower distributional discrepancies. Nevertheless, NRMSE and PFC may have their justification in certain situations. This is the case, for example, when an accurate imputation of variables to statistical units is required, such as membership in a particular subgroup, or when filling registers from which individual-level data are later to be obtained. Chambers (2006) describes the goal of such "imputations" as predictive accuracy.

While the NRMSE and PFC measures appear to be appropriate for assessing pointwise differences and thus for point predictions, distribution-preserving imputation procedures are required to obtain correct statistical inference procedures. Therefore, selecting an imputation scheme based solely on the NRMSE and PFC measures is not the right way to go, especially if the data analyst's approach is focused on statistical decisions or testing procedures. This suggests that both classes of accuracy measures, the NRMSE or PFC results and the distribution-based distance measures, recommend different imputation procedures for their use in imputing missing values. For example, the missRanger approach provided low NRMSE and PFC results across different missingness rates

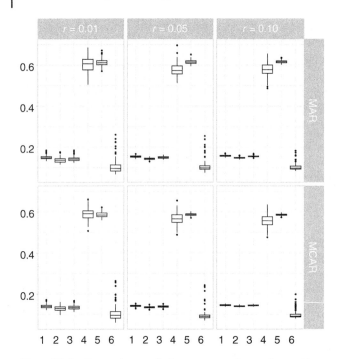

Figure 23.4 Comparing predictive accuracy of some imputation methods. Source: Florian Dumpert. This graphic is already published in this paper: https://content.iospress.com/articles/statistical-journal-of-the-iaos/sji210798.

in the abovementioned study, but the same method performed worse when evaluated with the Kolmogorov–Smirnov statistic or the Cramer–von Mises statistic. Therefore, the results suggest that an imputation scheme may be appropriate for imputation in terms of predictive accuracy, but not for distribution-preserving imputation. This can be seen exemplary in Figures 23.4 and 23.5. Figure 23.4 shows boxplots for NRMSE based on 100 repetitions of artificially creating missing values (in $r \times 100\%$ of the data) and subsequent imputation in the SES data set. The lower the NRMSE, the higher the predictive accuracy (1: Amelia, 2: Mice.Norm, 3: Mice.Pmm, 4: Mice.RF, 5: Naïve, 6: missRanger). Figure 23.5 on the other hand shows boxplots for the p-values of the Kolmogorov–Smirnov statistic based on 100 repetitions of artificially creating missing values (in $r \times 100\%$ of the data) and subsequent imputation in the SES data set. Each boxplot pair corresponds to the following missing mechanism: the left one to the MCAR, and the right one to the MAR mechanism. Smaller values tend to argue against the null hypothesis that original distribution and distribution after imputation match, i.e. roughly spoken, the smaller the value, the lower the distributional accuracy (1: Amelia, 2: Mice.Norm, 3: Mice.Pmm, 4: Mice.RF, 5: Naïve, 6: missRanger). missRanger leads not only to small NRMSE values in all scenarios (high predictive accuracy) but also to low p-values of the Kolmogorov–Smirnov test in many scenarios and for many variables (i.e. roughly spoken, to a low distributional accuracy). MICE with normal model on the other hand indicated higher NRMSE and PFC values (i.e. lower predictive accuracy) while leading to high p-values of the Kolmogorov–Smirnov test (i.e. not indicating any distributional discrepancy). For details on this study, refer to Thurow et al. (2021a, 2021b).

This project is an example of successful cooperation between official statistics and science. With its own resources, official statistics could only provide such research services to a very limited extent.

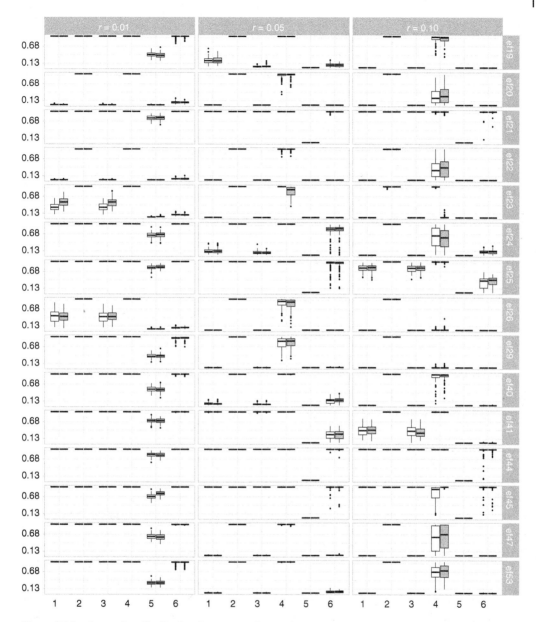

Figure 23.5 Comparing distributional accuracy of some imputation methods. Source: Florian Dumpert. This graphic is already published in this paper: https://content.iospress.com/articles/statistical-journal-of-the-iaos/sji210798.

23.6 Summary and Outlook

This chapter presented an overview of the use of machine learning (while distinguishing it from other fields such as big data) in official statistics. With the increasing availability of computing capacities (and partly also the availability of large data sets on which machine learning can show its strengths), this form of statistics was also taken up in official statistics in the last decade. This could be demonstrated, for example, in a corresponding survey on the use of machine learning in national statistical offices or on the basis of relevant conferences. German official statistics hardly differ from other statistical offices with regard to the areas of application, so that, in the author's opinion and according to the UNECE HLG-MOS machine learning project mentioned in Section 23.3, the following comments are valid for Germany. Machine learning is used to enable or support classification and coding, imputations (see Section 23.5.3 for examples of projects and research in Germany), estimates (for Germany an example has been shown in Section 23.5.2) or editing (see Section 23.5.3), or – if qualitatively justifiable – to perform them fully automated. In doing so, the tasks are often not just implemented using machine learning alone, but also supplemented by other methods. Projects in the editing domain, for example, ideally include four components in the future: (i) a machine learning component, e.g. an isolation forest (Liu et al. 2008, Hariri et al. 2020) that dynamically identifies outlier and implausible candidates in an unsupervised manner; (ii) a set of edit rules created by subject matter experts and updated over time, statically serving the same goal; (iii) a data set of before-and-after comparison cases that is as complete as possible (and can be kept up to date); and (iv) the expertise and experience of subject matter experts, possibly complemented by useful external information, cf. van der Loo (2020) for the latter. Apart from the editing domain, another focus for the use of machine learning is the task of assigning free text input to a code of a classification system. Automated classification of aerial or satellite images using machine learning is already or will at least be an important task in official statistics in the future, e.g. in order to validate official registers for statistical purposes.

Finally, the use of automation and "new" methods in statistical processes raises questions about quality and appropriate quality measurement. This concerns general quality aspects, as laid down in the Quality Framework for Statistical Algorithms (Yung et al. 2020), and detailed questions, e.g. how quality assurance can take place for training data and test sets or – as with any statistical model – how long a model or a predictor is valid and when it has to be learned again on the basis of new training material.

Machine learning approaches should be used if they offer quality-assured added value compared to previous approaches. This requires a fair comparison between previous approaches and machine learning, fair in terms of test data, labor, and time requirements, and statistical quality indicators to judge their performance. Furthermore, machine learning does not have to completely replace existing approaches. Also when machine learning supports or supplements an existing procedure, it represents already an increase in value if thereby time or manpower is saved or an otherwise better (e.g. more consistent or less faulty) processing of the task is made possible. Direct added value arises, of course, when machine learning is used for tasks that could not be processed without it. This includes, for example, tasks in not only the field of image recognition but also the example from Section 23.5.3.2.

Nevertheless, it must be stated that machine learning, despite all its successes, is not a panacea in official statistics. Not every task can be automated with machine learning in a quality-assured way. This is often because the sources do not contain enough information or the number of training examples is too small. Machine learning cannot show its advantages in this case and does not perform better than benchmark methods such as – in the case of classification – logistic regression. Furthermore, rapidly changing conditions (such as the addition or removal of features in surveys) are a problem, as previously learned models may no longer be applicable. It is also conceivable that the training of a machine learning model, which may be necessary, for example, every month, simply takes too long to be of interest for productive operation. In this case, a model that is – within reasonable limits – less accurate but can be calculated much more quickly should be determined and used in order to achieve a balance of the various quality dimensions, see Section 23.3.

Further research is required on the question of which factors are decisive for the fact that individual statistical (machine learning) methods perform better – whereby "better" must be specified for each individual use case – than others (other machine learning approaches but also compared to "traditional" methods), especially in the area of editing and imputation. It also seems unclear so far which steps of the otherwise usual preprocessing of data can be omitted when machine learning is applied and which should rather be retained or even extended. With regard to automated classification, the question often arises of how to best deal with a large number of classes, possibly imbalanced classes, and hierarchical systems. With respect to sampling, the combination of sampling theory, machine learning, and inferential statistics is a largely uncharted field and requires further engagement.

References

Beck, M., Dumpert, F. and Feuerhake, J. (2018). Proof of concept machine learning – Abschlussbericht. https://www.destatis.de/GPStatistik/receive/DEMonografie_monografie_00004835 (in German). Shorter English version available on arXiv: https://arxiv.org/abs/1812.10422 (accessed 23 April 2021).

Bischl, B., Binder, M., Lang, M., Pielok, T., Richter, J., Coors, S., Thomas, J., Ullmann, T., Becker, M. and Boulesteix, A.-L. (2021). Hyperparameter optimization: foundations, algorithms, best practices and open challenges. https://arxiv.org/abs/2107.05847 (accessed 03 March 2022).

Breiman, L. (2001). Statistical modeling: the two cultures (with comments and a rejoinder by the author). *Statistical Science* 16 (3): 199–231.

Breiman, L., Cutler, A., Liaw, A. and Wiener, M. (2021). randomForest. https://CRAN.R-project.org/package=randomForest (accessed 23 April 2021).

Chambers, R. (2006). Evaluation criteria for editing and imputation in Euredit. In: *Statistical Data Editing, Volume 3*, 17–27. New York and Geneva: United Nations Statistical Commission and United Nations Economic Commission for Europe, UNECE.

Chawla, N.V., Bowyer, K.W., Hall, L.O., and Kegelmeyer, W.P. (2002). Smote: synthetic minority over-sampling technique. *Journal of Artificial Intelligence Research* 16: 321–357.

Christmann, A., Dumpert, F., and Xiang, D.-H. (2016). On extension theorems and their connection to universal consistency in machine learning. *Analysis and Applications* 14 (6): 795–808.

Coronado, A. and Juárez, J. (2020). UNECE – HLG-MOS machine learning project: imagery theme report. https://statswiki.unece.org/display/ML/WP1+-+Theme+3+Imagery+Analysis+Report (accessed 23 April 2021).

Cover, T. and Thomas, J. (2006). *Elements of Information Theory*, 2e. New York: Wiley.

De Waal, T., Pannekoek, J., and Scholtus, S. (2011). *Statistical Data Editing and Imputation*. Hoboken: Wiley.

Dumpert, F. (2020a). Machine learning methods for imputation. https://statswiki.unece.org/download/attachments/285216428/ML_WP1_EI_Germany.pdf (accessed 23 April 2021).

Dumpert, F. (2020b). UNECE – HLG-MOS machine learning project: edit and imputation theme report. https://statswiki.unece.org/display/ML/WP1+-+Theme+2+Edit+and+Imputation+Report (accessed 23 April 2021).

Dumpert, F. and Beck, M. (2021). Weniger als 8.50 EUR? – Eine Machbarkeitsstudie auf Basis der Verdienststrukturerhebung. Destatis internal working paper.

Efron, B. (2020). Prediction, estimation, and attribution. *Journal of the American Statistical Association* 115 (530): 636–655.

Eurostat (2018). European statistics code of practice – revised edition 2017. https://ec.europa.eu/eurostat/documents/portlet_file_entry/4031688/KS-02-18-142-EN-N.pdf/e7f85f07-91db-4312-8118-f729c75878c7 (accessed 23 April 2021).

Friedrich, S., Antes, G., Behr, S., Binder, H., Brannath, W., Dumpert, F., Ickstadt, K., Kestler, H., Lederer, J., Leitgöb, H., Pauly, M., Steland, A., Wilhelm, A. and Friede, T. (2021). Is there a role for statistics in artificial intelligence? *Advances in Data Analysis and Classification*. Online first: https://doi.org/10.1007/s11634-021-00455-6 (accessed 03 March 2022).

Guertin, L., Bureau, M. and Morel, J. (2014). Editing the 2011 Census data with CANCEIS and options considered for 2016. https://unece.org/fileadmin/DAM/stats/documents/ece/ces/ge.44/2014/mtg1/Topic_4_Canada_Guertin.pdf (accessed 23 April 2021).

Hariri, S., Kind, M. C. and Brunner, R. J. (2020). Extended isolation forest. https://arxiv.org/abs/1811.02141 (accessed 23 April 2021).

Hessisches Statistisches Landesamt (2020). Einsatz maschineller Lernverfahren zur Plausibilisierung. https://statistik.hessen.de/zahlen-fakten/experimentelle-statistik/einsatz-maschineller-lernverfahren-zur-plausibilisierung (accessed 23 April 2021).

Honaker, J., King, G., and Blackwell, M. (2011). Amelia II: a program for missing data. *Journal of Statistical Software* 45 (7): 1–47.

Institut für Arbeitsmarkt- und Berufsforschung (2021). Integrierte Erwerbsbiografien (IEB). https://www.iab-forum.de/glossar/integrierte-erwerbsbiographien-ieb/ (accessed 23 April 2021).

James, G., Witten, D., Hastie, T., and Tibshirani, R. (2013). *An Introduction to Statistical Learning*. New York: Springer.

Julien, C. (2020). Machine learning project report. https://statswiki.unece.org/display/ML/Machine+Learning+Project+Report (accessed 23 April 2021).

Kaukal, M. and Peters, N. (2019). Vom Wort zur Zahl: Wie mit Hilfe automatisierter Verfahren Produktbeschreibungen in der Verbraucherpreisstatistik für das Forschungsdatenzentrum effizient bereitgestellt werden können – Ein Werkstattbericht. https://statistikhessen-blog.de/vom-wort-zur-zahl-wie-mit-hilfe-automatisierter-verfahren-produktbeschreibungen-in-der-verbraucherpreisstatistik-fuer-das-forschungsdatenzentrum-effizient-bereitgestellt-werden-koennen/ (accessed 23 April 2021).

Levina, E. and Bickel, P. (2001). The Earth Mover's distance is the Mallows distance: some insights from statistics. In: *Proceedings of the Eighth IEEE International Conference on Computer Vision. ICCV 2001*, vol. 2, 251–256.

Liu, F.T., Ting, K.M., and Zhou, Z.-H. (2008). Isolation forest. In: *ICDM'08 Eighth IEEE International Conference on Data Mining*, 413–422.

Lunardon, N., Menardi, G., and Torelli, N. (2014). ROSE: a package for binary imbalanced learning. *The R Journal* 6: 82–92.

Mayer, M. (2019). missRanger: fast imputation of missing values. https://cran.r-project.org/package=missRanger (accessed 23 April 2021).

Measure, A. (2020). UNECE – HLG-MOS machine learning project: machine learning integration. https://statswiki.unece.org/display/ML/WP3+-+Integration (accessed 23 April 2021).

Pech, B. (2019). Maschinelles Lernen: Classification and regression trees (CART) für die Imputation nutzbar machen. *Zeitschrift für amtliche Statistik Berlin-Brandenburg* 2019 (3): 12–21.

Rekatsinas, T., Chu, X., Ilyas, I., and Ré, C. (2017). HoloClean: holistic data repairs with probabilistic inference. *Proceedings of the VLDB Endowment* 10 (11): 1190–1201.

Russell, S. and Norvig, P. (2010). *Artificial Intelligence. A Modern Approach*, 3e. Upper Saddle River: Pearson.

Samuel, A.L. (1959). Some studies in machine learning using the game of checkers. *IBM Journal of Research and Development* 3 (3): 210–229.

Schierholz, M. and Ghani, R. (2020). Machine learning. In: *Big Data and Social Science*, 2e (ed. I. Foster, R. Ghani, R.S. Jarmin, F. Kreuter, and J. Lane), 143–192. Boca Raton: Chapman and Hall/CRC.

Schmidt, E. (2020). Korrektur des Tätigkeitsschlüssels der Bundesagentur für Arbeit mithilfe maschineller Lernverfahren. *WISTA – Wirtschaft und Statistik* 6 (2020): 37–47.

Schömann, A. and Rohde, J. (2021). Anomaliedetektion in der Beherbergungsstatistik mittels isolation forests. IT.NRW internal working paper.

Schrittwieser, J., Antonoglou, I., Hubert, T., Simonyan, K., Sifre, L., Schmitt, S., Guez, A., Lockhart, E., Hassabis, D., Graepel, T., Lillicrap, T., and Silver, D. (2020). Mastering Atari, Go, chess and shogi by planning with a learned model. *Nature* 588: 604–609.

Shalev-Shwartz, S. and Ben-David, S. (2014). *Understanding Machine Learning: From Theory to Algorithms*. Cambridge: Cambridge University Press.

Shmueli, G. (2010). To explain or to predict? *Statistical Science* 25 (3): 289–310.

Shorack, G.R. and Wellner, J.A. (2009). *Empirical Processes With Applications to Statistics*. Philadelphia: SIAM.

Silver, D., Hubert, T., Schrittwieser, J., Antonoglou, I., Lai, M., Guez, A., Lanctot, M., Sifre, L., Kumaran, D., Graepel, T., Lillicrap, T., Simonyan, K., and Hassabis, D. (2018). A general reinforcement learning algorithm that masters chess, shogi, and Go through self-play. *Science* 362 (6419): 1140–1144.

Spies, L. and Lange, K. (2018). Implementation of artificial intelligence and machine learning methods within the Federal Statistical Office of Germany. https://www.unece.org/fileadmin/DAM/stats/ documents/ece/ces/ge.44/2018/T4_Germany_LANGE_Paper.pdf (accessed 23 April 2021)

Statistisches Bundesamt (2016). Qualitätsbericht zur Verdienststrukturerhebung. https://www.destatis .de/DE/Methoden/Qualitaet/Qualitaetsberichte/Verdienste/verdienststrukturerhebung-2014 .pdf?__blob=publicationFile&v=3 (accessed 23 April 2021).

Steinwart, I. and Christmann, A. (2008). *Support Vector Machines*. New York: Springer.

Stekhoven, D.J. and Buehlmann, P. (2012). MissForest – non-parametric missing value imputation for mixed-type data. *Bioinformatics* 28 (1): 112–118.

Sthamer, C. (2020). UNECE – HLG-MOS machine learning project: classification and coding theme report. https://statswiki.unece.org/display/ML/WP1+-+Theme+1+Coding+and+Classification+ Report (accessed 23 April 2021).

Suthaharan, S. (2014). Big data classification: problems and challenges in network intrusion prediction with machine learning. *Performance Evaluation Review* 41 (4): 70–73.

Tejedor, M., Woldaregay, A.Z., and Godtliebsen, F. (2020). Reinforcement learning application in diabetes blood glucose control: a systematic review. *Artificial Intelligence in Medicine* 104: 101836.

Thurow, M., Dumpert, F., Ramosaj, B. and Pauly, M. (2021a). Goodness (of fit) of imputation accuracy: the good impact analysis. https://arxiv.org/abs/2101.07532 (accessed 23 April 2021).

Thurow, M., Dumpert, F., Ramosaj, B., and Pauly, M. (2021b). Imputing missings in official statistics for general tasks – our vote for distributional accuracy. *Statistical Journal of the IAOS* 37 (4): 1379–1390.

UNECE (2021). Generic statistical business process model. https://statswiki.unece.org/display/ GSBPM/Generic+Statistical+Business+Process+Model (accessed 23 April 2021).

UNSTATS (2021). Classification of individual consumption according to purpose (COICOP) 2018. https://unstats.un.org/unsd/class/revisions/coicop_revision.asp (accessed 23 April 2021).

van Buuren, S. (2012). *Flexible Imputation of Missing Data*. Boca Raton: CRC Press.

van Buuren, S. and Groothuis-Oudshoorn, K. (2011). Mice: multivariate imputation by chained equations in R. *Journal of Statistical Software* 45 (3): 1–67.

van der Loo, M. (2020). Machine learning for edit and imputation procedures in official statistics – A brief discussion on the occasion of the virtual workshop on ML in E&I under the HLG-MOS on 15 October 2020. https://statswiki.unece.org/download/attachments/285216428/E%26I%20discussion %20paper.pdf (accessed 23 April 2021).

van Engelen, J.E. and Hoos, H.H. (2020). A survey on semi-supervised learning. *Machine Learning* 109: 373–440.

Yung, W. and Turmelle, C. (2019). The use of machine learning in economic statistics programs at Statistics Canada. Short paper for EESW19.

Yung, W., Tam, S.-M., Buelens, B., Dumpert, F., Ascari, G., Rocci, F., Burger, J., Chipman, H. and Choi, I. (2020). A quality framework for statistical algorithms. https://statswiki.unece.org/display/ ML/WP2+-+Quality (accessed 23 April 2021).

24

Six Years of Machine Learning in the Bureau of Labor Statistics

Alexander Measure

U.S. Bureau of Labor Statistics, Washington, D.C., USA

24.1   Introduction

The past 10 years have seen dramatic advances in the computer's ability to process and understand human language. In a thoroughly publicized 2011 event, a computer beat the world's best human players at the trivia game of Jeopardy by extracting answers from massive collections of written text (Markoff 2011). The following years have brought many related advances that now impact our lives in countless ways. Computers accurately translate between dozens of languages, consumers regularly issue verbal commands to devices that respond intelligently, and anyone can get answers to millions of questions by simply typing them into a search engine.

These and many other advances have been made possible by rapid progress in the fields of machine learning (teaching computers to learn from data) and natural language processing (using computers to understand language). Increasingly, these topics are also of interest in official statistics. In 2019, for example, the UN Group for the Modernization of Official Statistics launched a Machine Learning project which attracted more than 120 participants from 33 national and 4 international organizations (Julien 2021). New venues such as the BigSurv conference have also emerged to address this growing interest. Nonetheless, there is relatively little information about how statistical organizations integrate and use such systems in production processes. This is an important gap because, as the UN's Machine Learning project report notes, "the integration [of machine learning] into production processes remains a challenge" (Julien 2021). Indeed the report notes that among participants, "only one application in the project had been in production long enough to have extensive experience in how to update the ML algorithms." We hope to help address this gap by sharing how this project, from the US Bureau of Labor Statistics (BLS), evaluated and ultimately used modern machine learning and natural language processing techniques to transform a complicated manual production process into one that is now mostly automated at better than human accuracy.

24.2   Why Official Statistics?

Language is the primary means by which humans communicate so it is perhaps unsurprising that it shows up almost everywhere. In official statistics, it frequently occurs in the form of text responses to survey questions. Much of our statistical information about worker occupations, business

Advances in Business Statistics, Methods and Data Collection. Edited by Ger Snijkers, Mojca Bavdaž, Stefan Bender, Jacqui Jones, Steve MacFeely, Joseph W. Sakshaug, Katherine J. Thompson, and Arnout van Delden.
© 2023 John Wiley & Sons, Inc. Published 2023 by John Wiley & Sons, Inc.

Table 24.1 SOII case coding example.

Collected narrative	Assigned codes	
Job title	*Type*	*Code (Description)*
Sanitation worker	Occupation	37-2011 (Janitor)
What was the employee doing just before the incident?	Nature	111 (Fracture)
Mopping floor in gym	Part	420 (Arm)
What happened?	Event	422 (Fall, slipping)
Slipped on water on floor and fell.	Source	6620 (Floor)
What part of body was affected?	Secondary source	9521 (Water)
Fractured right arm		
What object directly harmed the employee?		
Wet floor		

activities, and products and services is initially collected in this way, for example. Unfortunately, language is not easily analyzed for statistical purposes. To enable aggregation, we typically start by classifying the language according to a standardized system, a process sometimes known as "coding."

Among the many coding tasks performed in the BLS is the coding of the Survey of Occupational Injuries and Illnesses (SOII), an annual survey of US establishments that collects written descriptions of approximately 300,000 workplace injuries and illnesses each year. Each description (i.e. case) includes five text narratives describing different aspects of the worker and their incident. BLS uses this information to assign six codes to indicate the occupation of the worker, the nature of the injury, the part of body affected, the event that caused the injury, and the primary and secondary objects or substances (i.e. sources) involved. Occupation codes are assigned according to the Standard Occupational Classification (SOC) system (Office of Management and Budget n.d.). The others are assigned according to version 2 of the Occupational Injuries and Illnesses Classification system (US Bureau of Labor Statistics n.d.) (Table 24.1).

Until 2014, SOII case coding was entirely manual, incurring significant expense. The process required an estimated 25,000 hours of human labor each year, equivalent to approximately 12.5 full-time employees. The need for multiple human coders in turn results in another challenge; it is surprisingly difficult to get different people to code these cases in consistent ways. In one experiment in which 1000 cases were independently coded by multiple human experts, any two experts only assigned the same codes to the same case 70.4% of the time. This is at least partly a reflection of the difficulty of the task. The collected information is often ambiguous, and the coding systems are very detailed; source alone has 1400 possible codes and occupation more than 800. Although such issues are not unique to SOII, see for example Conrad et al. (2016) and Massing et al. (2019), they are nonetheless not ideal. In light of these challenges and the growing evidence that computers could handle such tasks, BLS launched an effort to investigate modern automation techniques in 2012.

24.3 How Should We Do It?

Automated coding is neither new nor unique to official statistics. In the broader natural language processing and machine-learning communities this task is more commonly known as text classification. This is an important connection because it allows us to draw from the vast research already conducted in this area. The Anthology of the Association for Computational Linguistics, for example, contains more than 10,000 papers mentioning the topic, and tens of thousands more dealing with closely related issues (Association for Computational Linguistics 2021).

Automated coding efforts in official statistics date back at least as far as the 1960s. In "The Use Of Computers in Coding Free Responses" (Frisbie and Sudman 1968), for example, the authors experiment with dictionary based approaches in which keywords and phrases are first mapped to codes. New texts are then coded by using the dictionary to map the words and phrases in these texts to associated codes. Such systems are often combined with simple rules and heuristics in an approach sometimes called "knowledge-engineering." But while the broader natural language processing community began moving away from such approaches in the 1990s (Sebastiani 2001), knowledge-engineering and dictionary-based approaches remain popular in official statistics. For example, the industry and occupation coding system from the US Census (Thompson et al. 2012), G-Code from Statistics Canada (Statistics Canada 2021), and the EU-supported CASCOT (Elias et al. 2014) all rely heavily on matching to dictionary-like structures, although in some cases, they provide automated mechanisms for constructing these.

The key drawback of the knowledge-engineering approach is that it is difficult to manually create effective knowledge representations because of the extraordinary complexity of human language. To take just one example, consider trying to automatically assign the Standard Occupation Classification code 37-2011, which translates roughly to "Janitors and Cleaners." One might start by creating a dictionary that links job titles containing "janitor" or "cleaner" to the code. But, in the 2011 SOII for example, of the 10,325 "Janitor and Cleaner" cases ultimately assigned this code, more than 80% contained neither "janitor" nor "cleaner." In fact, more than 2000 distinct job titles were used to describe this single code (Measure 2014). Complicating matters further, many of the keywords used in these job titles are not unique to this code and can refer to other codes depending on complicated factors like the job titling practices of individual companies and industries. To achieve strong performance even on this seemingly simple task, in other words, requires a large and complicated mix of keywords and rules. And all this for just one of the more than 800 occupation codes in the classification system.

The increasingly popular alternative is to use machine learning to acquire nearly all of the relevant knowledge directly from the data itself. Experiments by Creecy et al. (1992) provide an early example of the potential benefits. They compared knowledge-engineering and machine-learning-based systems for occupation and industry coding for the US Census and found the knowledge-engineering approach required significantly more resources to build (192 person-months compared to 4-person months), and also produced worse results (Creecy et al. 1992). Although the computational requirements of their machine learning approach posed a major obstacle to adoption at the time, such constraints have changed dramatically in the intervening decades.

Our first task, therefore, was to figure out which approach we should take. To answer this, we evaluated three pilot projects; a knowledge-engineering system developed by a widely used statistical software company, a machine learning system developed by a researcher working on a similar task, and a machine learning system developed using the tools and techniques popular among the natural language processing community at the time, specifically a bag-of-words model built using scikit-learn, a free and open source library for the Python programming language (Pedregosa et al. 2011). We found the latter option was cheaper, performed significantly better, and was simple to implement. Simple enough, in fact, that a complete program resembling the first SOII machine learning models used in production appears below:

```python
import pandas as pd
from sklearn.feature_extraction.text import CountVectorizer
from sklearn.linear_model import LogisticRegression

# Read in data
df_train = pd.read_excel('cases_2011.xlsx')
df_valid = pd.read_excel('cases_2012.xlsx')

# Create bag-of-words representation of text narrative
vectorizer = CountVectorizer()
X_train = vectorizer.fit_transform(df_train['NARRATIVE'])

# Fit regularized multinomial logistic regression model to data
model = LogisticRegression()
model.fit(X_train, df_train['INJ_BODY_PART'])

# Code uncoded narratives using model
X_uncoded = vectorizer.transform(df_uncoded['NARRATIVE'])
df_uncoded['ML_PART_CODE'] = model.predict(X_uncoded)
```

In this example, we fit (i.e. train) a regularized multinomial logistic regression model to predict injured body part codes from bag-of-words inputs. Multinomial means our model estimates the probability of each possible body part code (of which there are more than 180). Bag-of-words means the model inputs consist of variables indicating the occurrence of words in the narratives. The model expects an input for every distinct word found in the training data, which typically numbers in the tens or hundreds of thousands. To limit the overfitting issues associated with such a large model, the training procedure uses L2-regularization, i.e. it penalizes the model for learning large parameters. See Measure (2014) for additional details and experiments.

24.4 Is It Good Enough?

Our initial assumption was that automated coding would inevitably require some trade-off between quality and efficiency. Added efficiency could ultimately make-up for quality losses by allowing greater review, but the exact extent of this tradeoff is critical for determining whether such a process is worthwhile. To resolve this, we selected a simple random sample of 1000 cases coded by our manual process for the 2011 survey, hid the codes that had been assigned, and then had each re-coded from scratch by three separate experts with a fourth resolving disagreements. We call the result our gold-standard. Crucially, it allows us to calculate quality metrics for both the manual coding process as it existed in 2011, and any alternate process we might wish to evaluate, by comparing the codes assigned by these processes to the "expert" codes. Since machine learning models can often memorize the data they are trained on we never use the gold standard data to train our models, only to conduct evaluation.

We calculate two quality metrics popular in the text classification literature, accuracy, and macro F1-score. Accuracy is the portion of assigned codes matching expert codes when coding all cases. It

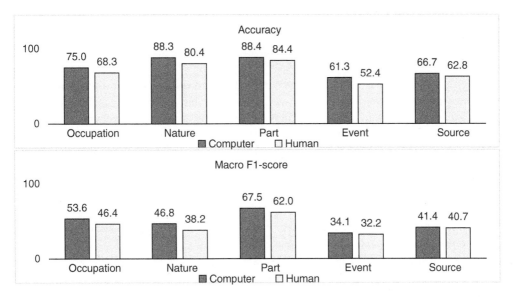

Figure 24.1 Coding quality comparison between machine learning and human coders.

captures the intuition that a classifier that assigns a higher portion of correct codes is better. Macro F1-score is the equally weighted average, across each possible code, of a code-specific quality metric called the F1-score. Macro F1-score reflects the intuition that we want our classifier to perform well at assigning different types of codes, regardless of their frequency in the data (see Appendix 24.A for details of the calculation).

Surprisingly, we find no tradeoff between coding quality and efficiency using either metric on our five primary coding tasks. For each task, the logistic-regression based models (see Figure 24.1) produced codes more consistent with the gold standard than the existing manual process, which had the added benefit of the multiple rounds of review that normally accompany our collection process.

The "Computer" coders in this chart consist of five separate multinomial logistic regression models, one for each coding task, each trained on approximately 1.3 million SOII cases collected, coded, and deemed usable for estimation between 2011 and 2015, with all gold standard cases excluded. See Measure (2014, 2017) for details of these models and the results of earlier related experiments.

24.5 How Should We Use It?

Improved accuracy and macro F1-score are obviously desirable, but is this the best we can do? After all, these are only aggregate measures of coding quality. They do not tell us whether there are pockets of cases where, for example, human judgment is still far superior. In fact, we have many reasons to believe these exist. For example, the model learns only from data that has been previously coded so new words and new uses of words are likely to cause problems. Bag-of-words models are also known to have other limitations such as difficulty distinguishing between the context-specific meanings of words like "back" in the phrases "injured his back," "back of hand" and "called for back up." We also know that for some cases we simply receive insufficient information to assign a code. In such a scenario, the appropriate response is not to code the case at all but rather to collect additional information, something our machine learning models cannot currently do. Ideally, therefore, we would like some reliable mechanism for routing work to the most appropriate coder, i.e. an autocoder or a human coder.

With appropriate training data we might even train another model to help identify the best coder for each case (in fact we have research underway in this area), but so far we have relied on a much more accessible mechanism. When the multinomial logistic regression model codes a case it starts by estimating the probability that each possible code is correct. These probabilities can be recovered from the model and, if they tend to be closely associated with the actual probability the code is correct, provide a reasonable mechanism for making these decisions.

One way we check the usefulness of the probabilities is by constructing a calibration plot. Specifically,

1. For each case in our gold standard dataset, we use the model to assign its highest probability code and the probability associated with that code.
2. We sort the data by these predicted probabilities and form contiguous bins of a pre-specified size (we use 50 in the example below).
3. For each bin, we calculate the mean predicted probability and the mean accuracy and plot the results.

A plot showing high correlation between mean predicted probability and mean accuracy indicates the probabilities are useful on average. In Figure 24.2, we show a calibration plot for a SOII event-coding model. The red line indicates perfect calibration, and the gray dots indicate the mean accuracy and predicted probability in each prediction bin.

All of our SOII models showed reasonable agreement between mean predicted probability and accuracy, suggesting the usefulness of this mechanism. The natural way to use it is by setting a threshold, for example 85%, and only allowing automatic code assignment when the predicted probability exceeds the threshold. This still leaves the question of where to set the threshold however.

To answer this, we used simulation on our gold standard data. Recall that the gold standard data already has two sets of codes, the codes that were assigned by our human staff when the

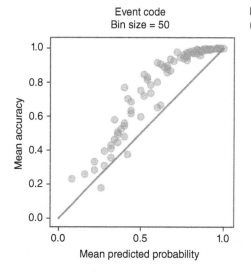

Event code
Bin size = 50

Figure 24.2 Calibration plot for SOII event coding model.

Figure 24.3   Quality versus efficiency plot for an event autocoder.

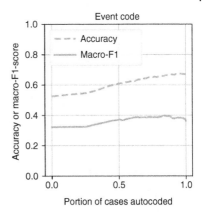

data were initially manually coded and the gold standard codes that were later assigned by a panel of experts. To this, we can easily add the codes from the machine-learning model along with its predicted probabilities. We then use these three sets of codes to simulate the coding produced by a given threshold by assuming that every case that can be automatically coded with a predicted probability above the threshold receives the machine code and all other cases receive the human code. The overall quality of the coding is then estimated by comparing the resulting codes to the expert codes and calculating standard quality metrics such as accuracy and macro F1-score. An estimate of coding efficiency, the portion of cases expected to be automatically coded, can also be calculated as the number of machine-assigned codes divided by the total number of codes.

By repeating this process for every threshold (in intervals of 1%), we produce plots like Figure 24.3, which shows the tradeoff between overall coding quality (as measured by accuracy and macro F1-score on the vertical-axis) and coding efficiency (as measured by the portion of codes automatically assigned on the horizontal-axis).

Since our primary goal is to maximize quality and our preferred quality metric is the macro-F1 score, this plot tells us we should set our event coding threshold at a level that is expected to code approximately 80% of cases.

24.6   How Do We Integrate It?

Simulations help us understand the quality tradeoffs between different mixes of automated and human coding, but they do not address another important issue. Transitioning from a purely manual process involving thousands of hours of labor to a largely automated one is a massive undertaking. Among the many challenges, we must figure out how to manage the resources affected by the transition. We must also guard against unforeseen challenges that might emerge from such a dramatically new process.

We decided, therefor, to move more gradually than our simulations suggested. For the first two years we did not use machine-learning models to assign codes at all. Instead, they were used solely to support data review. Cases were manually coded as normal, then the machine learning models estimated probabilities both for its preferred codes and the human selected codes. Large discrepancies in these probabilities suggested coding error (although not necessarily on the human side) and were prioritized for manual review.

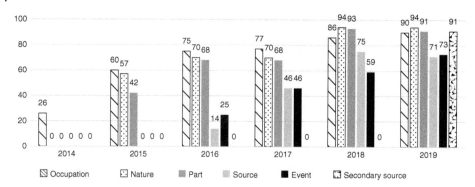

Figure 24.4 Percentage of SOII codes assigned automatically (2014–2019).

This proved effective in two ways. First, many of the discrepancies were in fact human coding errors, thus greatly improving our ability to target review effort on errors. Second, the resulting reviews allowed staff to gain first-hand experience with the strengths and weaknesses of the machine learning models.

By 2014, the implementation details had been worked out and comfort in the usefulness of machine learning was sufficient to begin automatically assigning codes. We started by targeting approximately 25% of occupation codes. This worked well so we expanded the next year, and then again and again (see Figure 24.4). By 2019, we were automatically assigning nearly 85% of all codes, achieving, approximately, the quality (i.e. macro F1-score) maximizing mix of human and automated coding according to our simulations.

24.7 How Do We Maintain It?

Although we found our initial machine learning systems surprisingly easy to build, maintenance is a far more complicated matter as others have observed. See, for example, "Machine Learning: The High Interest Credit Card of Technical Debt" (Sculley et al. 2014).

The main challenge is that machine learning models exhibit complex behavior. In the case of our initial logistic regression models, this behavior was determined by the hundreds of thousands of parameters learned from hundreds of thousands of training examples. Errors can occur because the model is not including appropriate inputs, the inputs and parameters are not allowed to interact in appropriate ways, or the training data and/or learning algorithm are causing the model to learn incorrect values of the parameters. In other words, there are many ways things can go wrong, and it is often difficult to identify and correct the underlying source of the problem.

So far, our primary mechanism for guarding against these problems has been increased manual review. Staff that used to assign many of the codes themselves are now responsible for additional review activities, including reviewing automatically assigned codes. One unexpected result was that human review resulted in far fewer changes than we expected from the blinded agreement rate on our evaluation data. When unable to see the machine assigned code humans choose a different code about 30–40% of the time, but this falls to only about 5% when the code is visible. The exact reason for the discrepancy is unclear, but several human coders have remarked that there are often multiple "acceptable" codes due to the high level of ambiguity frequently present in collected data.

To help monitor this issue we added a blinded review process. For a sample of cases that would otherwise be automatically coded, we instead hold back the machine codes forcing manual coding of the case. This allows us to monitor the blinded agreement rates (which are much more consistent with our original expectations). Importantly, it also provides us with a sample of data which, after blind expert recoding, can be used to update both our gold standard evaluations and our simulations for determining the optimal mix of human and computer coding.

Although manual monitoring has not yet identified any major unanticipated problems, there have been other more predictable maintenance challenges. For example, BLS periodically updates the classification systems it uses resulting, occasionally, in changes either to our models' inputs or outputs. Since the model only learns from what it has seen these changes require additional modification.

So far classification system changes have impacted the SOII machine learning project on three occasions, twice due to changes to the North American Industry Classification System (NAICS) which is an important input for occupation coding, and once to accommodate an update to the latest version of the SOC system, which is an important model output.

Each of these changes was addressed in the same basic way, by updating the training data to the new classification systems and retraining the affected models. This was relatively easy for NAICS changes as virtually all of the data could be cross-walked directly from the official crosswalks or by using other BLS data that had already been cross-walked. It was far more difficult for the SOC changes however, as they included many that could not be easily cross-walked. We built rule-based systems to convert most of these leaving a relatively small fraction requiring manual recoding.

Over time, other less predictable changes are also known to occur. Language gradually evolves, new words emerge or alter meaning, new workplace hazards emerge. Until recently, the pace of this change in worker injury narratives has been fairly slow. Our main process for adapting to these is to retrain our models at the end of each collection year using all the coded data available. The sudden emergence of COVID-19 however brought a dramatic challenge to this approach.

Since many of the terms used to describe COVID-19 had never occurred in SOII narratives previously, we suspected our machine learning models would not interpret them correctly resulting in coding errors. To prevent this we created a simple rule-based system to filter incoming data. Cases mentioning any variation of "corona" or "covid" would be coded only by humans until sufficient manually coded data could be collected to appropriately train and evaluate our models. Additional information about how the SOII is handling COVID-19 is available at https://www .bls.gov/covid19/effects-of-covid-19-on-workplace-injuries-and-illnesses-compensation-and-occupational-requirements.htm.

One last maintenance challenge has been the rapid pace of progress in the machine learning and natural language processing fields. When we first started, bag-of-words regularized logistic regression models were widely considered among the state-of-the-art approaches available in the computational linguistics community. This has dramatically changed in the intervening years, driven largely by rapid advances in a class of machine learning models known as deep neural networks.

A full discussion of deep neural networks is well beyond the scope of this paper, but at a verify simplified level, they can be thought of as networks of logistic regression-like models connected together so that the inputs to some become the outputs of others. Although it has taken decades to demonstrate, it is increasingly clear that properly designed neural networks provide major advantages over bag-of-words style models. For example, variations such as the long short term memory (LSTM) network (Hochreiter and Schmidhuber 1997) and the more recent Transformer (Vaswani et al. 2017) have demonstrated remarkable success at capturing the context-sensitive meaning of language. Furthermore, it is increasingly clear that neural networks can also provide powerful mechanisms for acquiring linguistic knowledge from unclassified text, and transferring learned knowledge across tasks, greatly reducing the amount of coded data required to train a model to equivalent performance on a new language task (Peters et al. 2018; Devlin et al. 2019). In fact, variations of transformer neural networks pretrained on large collections of unclassified text are used in all of the best performing systems on the widely adopted and highly competitive natural language understanding benchmarks of SuperGLUE (Wang et al. 2021) and SQuAD 2.0 (Rajpurkar et al. 2021).

We have found deep neural networks useful for our tasks as well. When evaluated against our gold standard, for example, our LSTM-based deep neural network models make about 24% fewer coding errors than our already very successful logistic regression models (Measure 2017). As a result, we replaced our logistic regression models with a single deep neural network starting in 2018. Unfortunately, effectively using these modern neural network techniques is far more challenging than our previous approach. Whereas our logistic regression models were easily trained on standard laptops with just a few lines of code, our deep neural networks required substantially more design and research effort and access to high-end graphical processing units (GPUs) to make the computations tractable. Our current production neural network was built using the Tensorflow (Abadi et al. 2015) and Keras (Chollet 2015) libraries and source code is available at https://github.com/USDepartmentofLabor/soii_neural_autocoder, but recent research has increasingly used the PyTorch (Paszke et al. 2019) and Transformers (Wolf et al. 2020) libraries. We have so far been unable to achieve significant additional improvements by using the now popular pretrained transformer neural networks, perhaps because we already have a lot of training data and the data typically used to pretrain these models is substantially different from what we collect, but we continue to pursue research in this area.

24.8 Conclusion

Our experiences transitioning the SOII from entirely manual coding to now mostly automated coding demonstrate that although modern machine learning and natural language processing techniques introduce new maintenance challenges, these challenges are surmountable and the benefits can be significant. We described how BLS addressed many of these challenges, demonstrated that modern tools make it surprisingly easy to use these techniques to automatically assign codes more accurately than trained humans on a wide variety of extremely difficult coding tasks, and showed that further quality improvements are possible by adopting newer neural-network based techniques.

As a result of these and other experiences, BLS is increasingly applying machine learning and natural language processing techniques to a wide variety of tasks including not just other coding tasks but also record matching, information extraction, and error detection. We are excited to see increased interest in these techniques in the official statistics community and hope our experiences are useful to other organizations pursuing similar efforts.

References

Abadi, M., Agarwal, A., Barham, P., Brevdo, E., Chen, Z., Citro, C., Corrado, G.S., Davis, A., Dean, J., Devin, M., and Ghemawat, S. (2015). *TensorfFlow: Large-Scale Machine Learning on Heterogeneous Systems*. tensorflow.org (accessed 21 June 2021).

Association for Computational Linguistics (2021). *ACL Anthology*. https://www.aclweb.org/anthology/search/?q=%22text+classification%22 (accessed 5 June 2021).

Chollet, F. (2015). *Keras.* https://keras.io (accessed 21 June 2021).

Conrad, F.G., Couper, M.P., and Sakshaug, J.W. (2016). Classifying open-ended reports: factors affecting the reliability of occupation codes. *Journal of Official Statistics* 32: 75–92.

Creecy, R.H., Brij, M.M., Smith, S.J., and Waltz, D.L. (1992). Trading MIPS and memory for knowledge engineering. *Communications of the ACM* 35 (8): 48–64.

Devlin, J., Chang, M.-W., Lee, K., and Toutanova, K. (2019). *BERT: Pre-training of Deep Bidirectional Transformers for Language Understanding.* https://arxiv.org/abs/1810.04805 (accessed 9 June 2021).

Elias, P., Birth, M., and Ellison, R. (2014). *CASCOT International version 5 User Guide.* https://warwick.ac.uk/fac/soc/ier/software/cascot/internat/ (accessed 7 June 2021).

Frisbie, B. and Sudman, S. (1968). The use of computers in coding free responses. *The Public Opinion Quarterly* 32 (2): 216–232.

Hochreiter, S. and Schmidhuber, J. (1997). Long short-term memory. *Neural Computation*, 15 November, 9 (8): 1735–1780.

Julien, C. (2021). *Machine Learning Project Report.* https://statswiki.unece.org/display/ML/Machine+Learning+Project+Report (accessed 21 June 2021).

Markoff, J. (2011). *Computer Wins on 'Jeopardy!': Trivial, It's Not.* https://www.nytimes.com/2011/02/17/science/17jeopardy-watson.html (accessed 21 June 2021).

Massing, N., Wasmer, M., Wolf, C., and Züll, C. (2019). How standardized is occupational coding? a comparison of results from different coding agencies in Germany. *Journal of Official Statistics* 35: 167–187.

Measure, A. (2014). *Automated coding of worker injury narratives.* https://www.bls.gov/osmr/research-papers/2014/pdf/st140040.pdf (accessed 21 June 2021).

Measure, A. (2017). *Deep neural networks for worker injury autocoding.* https://www.bls.gov/iif/deep-neural-networks.pdf (accessed 21 June 2021).

Office of Management and Budget (n.d.) *Standard Occupational Classification.* https://www.bls.gov/soc/ (accessed 21 June 2021).

Paszke, A., Gross, S., Massa, F., Lerer, A., Bradbury, J., Chanan, G., Killeen, T., Lin, Z., Gimelshein, N., Antiga, L., and Desmaison, A. (2019). PyTorch: An imperative style, high-performance deep learning library. *Advances in Neural Information Processing Systems* 32. http://papers.neurips.cc/paper/9015-pytorch-an-imperative-style-high-performance-deep-learning-library.pdf (accessed 21 June 2021).

Pedregosa, F., Varoquaux, G., Gramfort, A., Michel, V., Thirion, B., Grisel, O., Blondel, M., Prettenhofer, P., Weiss, R., Dubourg, V., and Vanderplas, J. (2011). Scikit-learn: machine Learning in Python. *Journal of Machine Learning Research* 12: 2825–2830. https://www.jmlr.org/papers/volume12/pedregosa11a/pedregosa11a.pdf (accessed 21 June 2021).

Peters, M.E., Neumann, M., Iyyer, M., Gardner, M., Clark, C., Lee, K., and Zettlemoyer, L. (2018). Deep contextualized word representations. *Proceedings of NAACL-HLT 2018*, pp. 2227–2237. https://www.aclweb.org/anthology/N18-1202.pdf (accessed 21 June 2021).

Rajpurkar, P., Jia, R., and Liang, P. (2021). *SQuAD 2.0 Leaderboard.* https://rajpurkar.github.io/SQuAD-explorer/ (accessed 21 June 2021).

Sculley, D., Holt, G., Golovin, D., Davydov, E., Phillips, T., Ebner, D., Chaudhary, V., and Young, M. (2014). *Machine Learning: The Highest Interest Credit Card of Technical Debt.* https://storage.googleapis.com/pub-tools-public-publication-data/pdf/43146.pdf (accessed 21 June 2021).

Sebastiani, F. (2001). *Machine Learning in Automated Text Categorization.* https://arxiv.org/abs/cs/0110053 (accessed 21 June 2021).

Statistics Canada (2021). *G-Code (Automated and Interactive Coding - Genealarized System.* https://www150.statcan.gc.ca/n1/en/catalogue/10H0033 (accessed 7 June 2021).

Thompson, M., Kornbau, M.E., and Vesely, J. (2012). *Creating an Automated Industry and Occupation Coding Process for the American Community Survey.* https://www.census.gov/content/dam/Census/library/working-papers/2012/demo/2012-io-coding-asa-paper-final.pdf (accessed 21 June 2021).

U.S. Bureau of Labor Statistics (n.d.) *Occupational Injury and Illness Classification Manual.* https://www.bls.gov/iif/oshoiics.htm (accessed 3 February 2021).

Vaswani, A., Shazeer, N., Parmar, N., Uszkoreit, J., Jones, L., Gomez, A.N., Kaiser, Ł., and Polosukhin, I. (2017). Attention is All You Need. *Advances in Neural Information Processing Systems* 30. https://arxiv.org/abs/1706.03762 (accessed 21 June 2021).

Wang, A. et al. (2021). *SuperGLUE Leaderboard Version 2.0.* https://super.gluebenchmark.com/leaderboard (accessed 21 June 2021).

Wolf, T., Debut, L., Sanh, V., Chaumond, J., Delangue, C., Moi, A., Cistac, P., Rault, T., Louf, R., Funtowicz, M., Davison, J., Shleifer, S., von Platen, P., Ma, C., Jernite, Y., Plu, J., Xu, C., Le Scao, T., and Gugger, S. (2020). Transformers: state-of-the-art natural language processing. *Proceedings of the 2020 Conference on Empirical Methods in Natural Language Processing: System Demonstrations.* Association for Computational Linguistics., pp. 38–45. https://www.aclweb.org/anthology/2020.emnlp-demos.6/ (accessed 21 June 2021).

Appendix: F1-score and Macro F1-score

The F1-score is an accuracy-like measure of class-specific classification performance. Let C denote a code in our classification system, for example 31-1014. The F1-score for code C is calculated as follows:

$$\text{F1 score} = 2 \cdot \frac{\text{precision} \cdot \text{recall}}{\text{precision} + \text{recall}}$$

where

$$\text{precision} = \frac{\text{number of times code C is correctly assigned by the coder}}{\text{number of times code C is assigned by the coder}}$$

$$\text{recall} = \frac{\text{number of times code C is correctly assigned by the coder}}{\text{number of times code C is the correct code}}$$

The macro F1-score is the simple arithmetic mean of the F1 scores. We adopt the default settings used in scikit-learn. Specifically, when calculating the macro F1-score for each coder, we average only over the F1-scores for unique codes appearing in the combination of predicted and true codes. If any of these F1-scores is undefined, we treat it as 0 when calculating the macro F1-score.

25

Using Machine Learning to Classify Products for the Commodity Flow Survey

Christian Moscardi[1] and Benjamin Schultz[2]

[1]*U.S. Census Bureau, Economic Reimbursable Surveys Division, Business Development Staff, Washington, DC, USA*
[2]*U.S. Census Bureau, Economic Management Division, Washington, DC, USA*

25.1 Background

25.1.1 Commodity Flow Survey (CFS) Background

The Commodity Flow Survey (CFS) is a joint effort between the U.S. Census Bureau and the Bureau of Transportation Statistics (BTS) within the U.S. Department of Transportation (USDOT). Policymakers at the national and local levels use these estimates to make infrastructure planning decisions. The survey's most widely used estimates are the domestic movement of goods by origin geography, destination geography, the product shipped, and mode of transportation. More information can be found on the Census Bureau and BTS websites (Bureau of Transportation Statistics 2021; U.S. Census Bureau 2020).

To collect data, every five years (most recently in 2017), the CFS surveys business establishments across the country and asks those businesses for a sampling of their shipment records throughout the year. This work will focus on two fields about product information that survey respondents were asked to provide for each shipment record they reported to the Census Bureau. The first was a free-text description of the product being shipped – an example response might be "steel beams." The second field asked respondents to provide the best-fitting Standard Classification of Transported Goods (SCTG) product code for the shipment. The SCTG product coding scheme is used by Census and BTS for various freight data products and focuses on transportation applications (Bureau of Transportation Statistics 2012). For each product shipped, there were 514 unique SCTG codes that respondents were asked to choose from.

25.1.2 CFS Data Collection Challenges

During the most recent collection, we identified the following challenges with the CFS data collection: nonresponse, problems with data quality, and heavy respondent burden. We will discuss each in turn.

25.1.2.1 Nonrespose

Our first challenge related to item-level nonresponse in the survey. Item-level nonresponse means that respondents would not answer a particular survey question. In this case, we focus on nonresponse to the SCTG code data item. As described in more detail in the data section, roughly

Advances in Business Statistics, Methods and Data Collection. Edited by Ger Snijkers, Mojca Bavdaž, Stefan Bender, Jacqui Jones, Steve MacFeely, Joseph W. Sakshaug, Katherine J. Thompson, and Arnout van Delden.
© 2023 John Wiley & Sons, Inc. Published 2023 by John Wiley & Sons, Inc.

7% of the 6 million shipment records that respondents reported in 2017 lacked an SCTG code. However, respondents did provide a free-text description with most of these records. Resource constraints meant that CFS subject matter experts (SMEs) were not able to spend time researching these descriptions to find a best-fitting product code themselves. As such, we sought to find an automated way to leverage these product descriptions to impute missing SCTG codes. It is also worth noting that this issue gave us a specific potential application to work toward that would have immediate and tangible benefit to 2017 CFS estimates.

25.1.2.2 Data Quality

Second, we identified significant data quality issues attributable to these respondent-provided codes. For example, respondents who used the SCTG online search tool to look up the keyword "fasteners" would find 2 codes: 24229, referring to plastic fasteners, and 40994, referring to sewing supplies. The search tool was missing another key code: 33310, referring to metal fasteners. Upon seeing an unexpectedly high quantity of records classified as sewing supplies, further investigation and validation of a random sample of records labeled as sewing supplies revealed that roughly 50% of records reported as 40994 by respondents had been misclassified. Within this sample, most of those records would correctly have been classified as metal fasteners (33310). We assume that this error was due to the fact that companies were unable to find the correct product code in the search tool.

25.1.2.3 Respondent Burden

The SCTG product coding system is used almost exclusively by the Census Bureau/USDOT on the CFS and related data products. In other words, respondents would not have SCTG codes for their products on file unless they had previously reported to CFS. Therefore, respondents had two options for determining the SCTG code:

(1) Look through a 21-page booklet/PDF describing each of the 514 SCTG commodity codes (U.S. Census Bureau 2017a).
(2) Use an online search tool. This tool was essentially equivalent to keyword-searching through the aforementioned booklet (U.S. Census Bureau 2017b).

After identifying these codes, respondents reported their shipment records either electronically via filling out a template spreadsheet, electronically via a form-like web interface, or via a paper form.

Through debriefing interviews, communications between respondents and Census staff, and written feedback provided during the survey response process (example shown below), it became clear that this code assignment process was particularly burdensome and frustrating for companies, see Figure 25.1. For example, a large company shipping a wide variety of products may have had to report 320 shipment records for the 2017 reference year. If each of those shipments was a different product, a respondent would have had to look through the codebook 320 times to find the best-fitting product code for each shipment.

```
'VERY ONEROUS AND CUMBERSOME TO COMPLETE. HAVE TO COMPLETE IN BITES FOR
ALL SECTIONS, OR BOUNCE BETWEEN MULTIPLE SCREENS.

YOUR ONLINE SCTG COMMODITY CODE REFERENCE IS USELESS […]'

- Respondent
```

Figure 25.1 Direct quote provided by respondent as feedback on the 2017 CFS.

Respondents also indicated that providing a free-text product description was less burdensome because companies commonly keep an English-language product description in their own records. This implied that asking respondents for only a product description, without requiring SCTG code lookup, would help reduce burden.

While not immediately applicable to the 2017 CFS, this issue has significant implications for the amount of data that the CFS can collect. The 2017 CFS estimates that approximately 16 billion shipments occurred within the United States in 2017 (U.S. Census Bureau 2020). The 6 million shipments that CFS collected represent a tiny fraction of that number. The primary constraint on the number of shipments CFS can collect is respondent burden – the marginal cost to Census of asking for more data is negligible. Therefore, by reducing respondent burden, the CFS program would be able to collect more shipment records and better represent the universe of US shipment activity.

25.1.2.4   Related Work

Other Census Bureau data collections, such as the American Community Survey, assign codes based on free-text descriptions as well (e.g. occupation codes). Typically, these programs do so via a combination of a dictionary-based autocoder and expert human coders (U.S. Census Bureau 2014). A dictionary-based autocoder typically takes literal text keywords and maps them to the appropriate code via a lookup table.

Findings from the Census Bureau and Bureau of Labor Statistics (BLS) highlighted the benefits of developing more advanced, ML-based autocoders to improve data quality (Dumbacher and Hanna 2017), suggesting that performance from ML-based models may exceed human coding by SMEs (Measure 2017; see also Chapter 23 of this volume). These findings implied that an ML-based process might also outperform CFS respondents, who are not experts in the SCTG coding scheme, in terms of coding accuracy.

Beyond government applications, industry has used ML to automate product coding for commercial applications. An example of using text descriptions to map to product codes – a technically identical use case to the CFS – can be found in the 2018 SIGIR eCom data challenge sponsored by the e-commerce site Rakuten (Yui-Chang et al. 2018).

In terms of technical approach, both the government and industry applications applied a supervised machine learning approach to the problem of autocoding and found success. More specifically, they have not only applied a variety of sophisticated ML models and methods but also demonstrated the production benefit that can be gained from even simple and straightforward classification algorithms such as multiclass logistic regression (Measure 2017; see also Chapter 23 of this volume).

25.2   Data

The 2017 CFS surveyed roughly 100,000 establishments and collected 6.4 million shipment records. This chapter focuses on the free-text product descriptions and SCTG codes that most respondents had provided. To give a sense of these descriptions and the SCTG coding scheme, the below table includes examples of free-text product descriptions provided by respondents, and the best-fitting SCTG code that would be associated. Typically, descriptions are 100 characters or fewer, and respondents provided varying levels of detail with respect to the product shipped. For example, as shown in Table 25.1, some respondents provided the description "Books," while others may have provided the title of the specific book being shipped.

Table 25.1 Example product descriptions provided by respondents, and accompanying SCTG codes.

Respondent-provided description	Associated SCTG code
BEER	**08100** Beer (malt beer) (excludes non-alcoholic beer, see 07899)
BOOKS	**29100** Printed books, brochures, leaflets, and similar printed products (except advertising materials including catalogs, see 29300; atlases and music books, see 29999)
TEXTILE CLOTHING	**30200** Textile clothing and accessories, clothing and headgear made of artificial fur (excludes clothing and accessories of plastics, see 24229; of rubber, see 24399; of leather or fur, see 30503; of asbestos, see 31994; of paper, see 28010, except safety headgear, see 40999)
#2 HEATING OIL	**18100** Fuel oils including diesel, distillate heating oil, Bunker C (excluding biodiesel, see below)
ENGINE PARTS	**34130** Parts of internal combustion piston engines (except pumps for liquids, see 34310; filters, see 34999; crankshafts and camshafts, see 34972; and bearings, see 3497x)
CONTACT LENSES	**38101** Eyewear including contact lenses and other lenses, goggles, and frames
DVD	**35629** Other pre-recorded media, not elsewhere classified (includes records, tapes, and compact disks, but excludes software, see 35621, and photographic film, see 23400)

Table 25.2 Approximate item-level response counts from 2017 CFS on the SCTG and product description fields.

Response type	Rounded number of shipment records in 2017 CFS
Both valid SCTG and product description	5,650,000
Product description, no or numerically invalid SCTG	400,000
No product description or product description from paper response not keyed, SCTG valid or invalid	395,000

Source: U.S. Census Bureau (2017a). Commodity Flow Survey.

In order to train a model, we needed a labeled set of free-text descriptions matching correct SCTG product codes. Given the fact that respondents had reported both product description and the best fitting SCTG code, we had a natural corpus of training data to use. In particular, as shown in Table 25.2, about 5.7 million records had both a respondent-provided product description and an SCTG product code label.

With production applications in mind, it is also worth noting the approximately 400,000 records in the original CFS data where respondents had provided a free-text product description, but had not provided an SCTG code. These records presented a natural set of data to pilot an initial, small-scale production application, as they had the necessary free-text information but lacked the target label (SCTG code) necessary to make the record usable for final estimates.

Last, roughly 395,000 lacked a product description entirely, or that product description had not been keyed in from a paper-based response. Regardless of whether or not the record included a valid

SCTG code, they are out-of-scope to both model development and unsuitable for model application. This is because they lack the key variable (text description) that this approach uses to ultimately classify product codes.

25.3 Methods

We now describe the process used to develop and evaluate a model given this source of training data. First, we discuss the filtering and text cleansing. Next, we describe variables developed from the text data, then discuss the functional form of the model itself. Last, we describe the process of model fitting (training) and evaluation metrics used.

25.3.1 Filtering and Text Cleansing

Table 25.3 gives an overview of the steps involved in our filtering and cleansing process, from beginning to end. Each step is described in the subsection listed in the table.

25.3.1.1 Filtering CFS Response Data

As discussed above, the first requirement for the training data set was that each record included had both a product description and an SCTG code, reducing our dataset size from 6.4 million records to 5.7 million records.

As a next filtering step, we removed all records labeled with the SCTGs corresponding to "miscellaneous manufactured products" and "miscellaneous mixed freight" (SCTGs 40999 and 43999). When responding, many respondents picked these two codes rather than finding a more specific product code, though the product descriptions imply a more specific code would be a better fit. In addition, some shipment records appeared otherwise valid except for the omission of an SCTG product code; without an SCTG code, the record could not be used in tabulation for final estimates. Survey SMEs at Census applied these codes in bulk to such records in order to make those records usable in tabulation. While we removed these records from our training set, we later used the model to recode many of these records into a better-fitting code. This is described later in the results and applications section. This reduced our training set by 200,000 records, from 5.7 to 5.5 million.

Table 25.3 Cleansing and filtering steps described in this section.

Filtering/cleansing step taken	Subsection	Rounded number of records after step
Original dataset	*Filtering CFS response data*	6.4 million
Remove all records without **both** SCTG code and product description	*Filtering CFS response data*	5.7 million
Remove all records coded as miscellaneous products	*Filtering CFS response data*	5.5 million
Cleanse text by removing data entry artifacts, spell-checking, stemming	*Text preprocessing*	5.5 million
Combined de-duplication and disambiguation	Algorithm #1 in *De-duplication and disambiguation*	400,000

Source: U.S. Census Bureau (2017a). Commodity Flow Survey.

25.3.1.2 Text Preprocessing

Given these descriptions and codes, we explored a few text cleansing steps to standardize respondent-provided descriptions. We explored these steps due to their prevalence in the text classification literature (Camacho-Collados and Pilehvar 2018).

1. Lower-case and remove artifacts of data entry, e.g. a significant number of shipments in the 2017 CFS had the description "#REF!" as the result of issues with the template spreadsheet that most respondents used to provide shipment data.
2. Spell-check descriptions.
3. Stem descriptions.

Stemming refers to the process of removing suffixes to reduce a word to its semantic basis. For example, we may not want to consider "Pencil" and "Pencils" to be separate words simply because one is singular and the other plural. Stemming is the general term for the systematic process that removes the "s" suffix from the latter description to ensure consistency (Manning et al. 2018).

Many algorithms and software packages exist to perform these steps – in our case, we used the popular C-based library hunspell to spell-check, and the python package nltk to stem (Németh 2021; Bird et al. 2009).

As we will share in the results, we identified a performance benefit from **minimizing** preprocessing. To evaluate the benefits of pre-processing, we developed three datasets that incrementally cleansed the text up to step 1, 2, or 3 above. These three datasets are described in more detail in Table 25.4.

25.3.1.3 De-duplication and Disambiguation

Next, we disambiguated descriptions reported with multiple codes. This issue is caused by multiple survey respondents in the same industry using identical product descriptions but finding different codes in the codebook for that description. This occurs for three reasons.

1. Respondents reporting a given product description selected an incorrect code. In some cases, this may be a minority of respondents. In other cases, the correct SCTG code can be hard to find and a majority of respondents selected an incorrect code. For example, none of the approximately 50 shipments labeled as "TAHINI" in the 2017 CFS were properly coded to 07231 ("fruit or nut pastes").
2. The given product description is not specific enough. For example, in the coal mining industry, many respondents labeled their shipments as "Coal." However, there are four possible SCTG codes for "Coal," depending on the specific type of coal. It is not clear even to an expert coder with full context – including potentially the origin location, value, weight, and destination of the shipment record – which type of coal such a shipment record is referring to.

Table 25.4 Names of three datasets created to evaluate relative benefits of text cleansing on model performance.

Data processing steps performed	Detailed cleansing steps
Minimal cleaning	Remove data entry artifacts
Spell checking	Remove data entry artifacts, spell check
Stemming + spell checking	Remove data entry artifacts, spell check, stem

3. There is ambiguity or confusion in the SCTG coding scheme itself. For example, a shipment of apples may qualify as "Apples, fresh or chilled" (SCTG code 03324) or "Items (including food) for grocery and convenience stores" (SCTG code 43991) depending on where the apples are going.

To ameliorate these issues, we selected the modal product code within an industry – that is, the product code that occurred most frequently within that industry for the given product description text. This approach is preferable for the following reasons.

In the case of the first reason above, provided that respondents in aggregate selected the correct code, this approach helps remove some erroneous classifications. In both the first case when respondents in aggregate chose the wrong code as well as the second case, this approach may not select a "correct" code for a shipment record. However, for our planned applications, SCTG is a hierarchical product coding scheme, and the CFS does not publish any estimates at the full five-digit level. In the case of "TAHINI," the most frequently reported code was 07232 ("processed fruit or nuts") – one digit from the correct five-digit code (07231, "seed or nut pastes"). Thus, we believe this approach typically determines a suitable code for the purposes of published CFS estimates. To further validate this assumption and with production applications in mind, we routinely perform expert review of the model's classification output, described below.

Finally, in the case of the third reason, disambiguating between two equally plausible codes may not accurately reflect how respondents in aggregate selected codes. This could lead to the model – when applied in aggregate – determining shares of SCTGs that vary widely from respondent-given distributions. The CFS staff is working on both clarifying the SCTG coding scheme and considering probabilistic assignment of SCTGs based on observed shares of codes in the microdata – described in the future work section below.

In addition, we de-duplicated records that were identical on the combination of the following three variables:

1. North American Industry Classification System (NAICS) code of establishment reporting the shipment record U.S. Census Bureau (n.d.).
2. Product description (in cleansed form as described above).
3. SCTG product code.

We disambiguated and de-duplicated in a combined process described in Algorithm 1.

Algorithm 1: Disambiguating and De-duplicating SCTG Codes

Input: All shipment records with same NAICS, (cleansed) product descriptions
Output: Product Description, NAICS code, SCTG code for training data
Steps:

1. For each (product description, SCTG) combination reported, compute the sum of how many **unique respondents** reported that combination at least once.
2. For each product description, select the SCTG that was most frequently reported according to the sums computed in #1.
3. For each product description, return (product description, SCTG selected in step #2).

Sometimes an establishment reports shipping multiple items of the same product description and SCTG code. We do not assume that a larger volume of shipping makes the establishment's coding of the product description more correct. Therefore, we only count unique combinations of establishment, product description, and SCTG code.

After these cleaning steps, we were left with about 400,000 training records – a significant reduction from the 6,400,000 shipment records received during 2017 CFS data collection. The most dramatic reduction in the number of records is from the combined de-duplication and disambiguation step. As implied above, many CFS respondents provide the same product description for all shipment records they report. For example, an establishment that ships different varieties of plastic pipes may have reported "Plastic Pipes" as the description for all shipment records they reported for the year (up to 320) and given the same SCTG product code for each of those records.

25.3.2 Deriving Variables (Features) from Text Data

An important step to using text data for classification modeling involves deriving variables to be used from the initially given free-text information. Typically, this is called "feature extraction" in ML literature; additionally, note that the terms "variable" and "feature" can be used interchangeably (Leskovec et al. 2020; Hastie et al. 2017). We tried extracting both word-level and character-level features from the free-text product description data. In the results section, we will share performance metrics from models that incorporated different subsets of the variable types described below.

Our simplest and first approach to converting text into variables for a model was to simply convert each word (i.e. a character string delimited by whitespace or beginning/end-of-line) into a binary indicator variable. This process is known as one-hot encoding in machine learning and natural language processing literature, and single-word variables are often called "unigrams" (Brownlee 2020). In the 2017 CFS and after the preprocessing described above, respondents used about 130,000 unique words; thus, our initial model trained on only 2017 CFS response data had about 130,000 variables.

Next, we derived word-level bigram variables. Specifically, this means creating a variable for *every two-word phrase* which occurs. Table 25.5 provides an example. For the 2017 CFS training data, this led to about 700,000 variables.

Finally, we derived character-level variables. This means that we took every subsequence of characters from within each description for certain subsequence lengths. We found the most success by extracting subsequences of length 3, 4, and 5, including spaces. These variables are separate from the full-word variables; in the below example, the subsequence of three characters "EEL" would not correspond to the unigram word "EEL" token. Using only 2017 CFS response data for scale, this led to roughly 800,000 variables.

After developing these features, we performed one extra preprocessing step common in NLP applications: weighting features based on term frequency – inverse document frequency (TF-IDF). TF-IDF is well described in other literature; at a high level, the more frequently a word appears across different product descriptions, the less important that word presumably is, so that variable should be weighted less than uncommon words that appear across fewer product descriptions (Leskovec et al. 2020).

25.3.3 Other Features Incorporated into Model – NAICS Code

Finally, after investigating what other features may be predictive of the type of product being shipped, we incorporated the NAICS code as another binary variable into our model to improve prediction (U.S. Census Bureau 2021). NAICS code is a variable on the CFS sample frame – every

Table 25.5 Example of extracting different types of features (variables) from a sample description.

Description	Feature extraction approach	Resultant binary indicator variables	Approximate # of variables created from 2017 CFS text
FIVE STEEL BEAMS	Unigrams (1-word tokens)	FIVE, STEEL, BEAMS	130,000
FIVE STEEL BEAMS	Bigrams (2-word tokens)	FIVE STEEL, STEEL BEAMS	700,000
FIVE STEEL BEAMS	Character-level 3-grams	FIV, IVE, VE_, E_S, _ST, STE, TEE, EEL, EL_, L_B, _BE, BEA, EAM, AMS	100,000
FIVE STEEL BEAMS	Character-level 4-grams	FIVE, IVE_, VE_S, E_ST, _STE, STEE, TEEL, EEL_, EL_B, L_BE, _BEA, BEAM, EAMS	300,000
FIVE STEEL BEAMS	Character-level 5-grams	FIVE_, IVE_S, VE_ST, E_STE, _STEE, STEEL, TEEL_, EEL_B, EL_BE, L_BEA, _BEAM, BEAMS	400,000

Source: U.S. Census Bureau (2017a). Commodity Flow Survey.

establishment is assigned a NAICS. In particular, we found that contextual information about the industry of the item being shipped helps the model differentiate between multiple possible codes for a given description. The example of "fasteners" mentioned previously is a good example of this. The sewing supplies industry ships a very different type of "fastener" (SCTG 40994) than the construction supplies industry (SCTG 33310).

To map an establishment-level NAICS to a shipment, we used the NAICS of the establishment that reported the shipment record. To then use NAICS in the model, we converted each NAICS, at the full six-digit level, into a binary variable (i.e. one-hot encoded). NAICS added about 500 more variables to our model: 1 binary variable for each NAICS code in-scope for CFS.

We also experimented with models incorporating other features, such as word-level trigrams and the value-to-weight ratio of the product being shipped, but found limited- to no-performance improvements in testing. We omit further detail and results for brevity.

25.3.4 Resolving Previously Unseen Variables during Prediction

It is worth noting, during the prediction process, how we resolve instances where a NAICS code, or a word is not seen in the training set. In that case, the word or NAICS is ignored. In the case of NAICS, all binary variables relating to NAICS will be set to zero, and in the case of a word, that token is likewise ignored by the model. The open-source package we use to develop the features and model, scikit-learn, implements this functionality (Pedregosa et al. 2011).

25.3.5 Model

Our initial model simply feeds these features into a set of L2-regularized logistic regression classifiers where each classifier is trained via a "one-vs.-rest" approach (Pedregosa et al. 2011). Other work in the space has found that logistic regression makes a strong baseline classifier, which our own work has confirmed (Measure 2017; see also Chapter 23 of this volume). The goal of regularization is to avoid allowing the model to weight any particular feature too heavily, as doing so may limit the model's ability to extrapolate to previously unseen records (Hastie et al. 2017). "One-vs-rest" refers to the means by which the model makes a decision among all 512 possible codes in our application: we train 512 binary classifiers to make a decision about the likelihood that a given record belongs to SCTG category. We chose this approach primarily due to its improved computational efficiency vis-a-vis alternatives such as one-versus-one and multinomial logistic regression, and comparable classification performance (Pedregosa et al. 2011).

In particular, for each of the 512 SCTG codes the model classified, indexed by j below, we seek to find weights and a bias term to minimize the following function (regularized log loss) over all input records x_i:

$$E(w_j, b_j) = \frac{1}{n} \sum_{i=1}^{n} \log\left(1 + \exp\left(-y_{ij}\left(w_j^T x_i + b_j\right)\right)\right) + \alpha \|w_j\|_2^2$$

w_j is the weight vector for SCTG j.
b_j is the bias term for SCTG j.
x_i is each input record, converted into a vector of features as described above.
y_{ij} is 1 when the SCTG code j is the correct code for record i, and 0 for all other SCTG codes.
α is a regularization term (typically called a hyperparameter in ML literature) that we can adjust depending on how strong we want weight regularization to be. In the next section, we discuss our strategy for finding an optimal value for α.

Then, after minimizing these functions to develop weights, we select the best fitting code on a given input record x_i by computing the following scores:

$$p_j(x_i) = \frac{1}{1 + e^{-w_j \cdot x_i + b_j}}$$

and selecting the maximum $p_j(x_i)$.

Because each classifier is independently trained, the $p_j(x_i)$ scores may not sum to 1. To normalize these scores to multiclass probabilities, we use the following normalization formula (Pedregosa et al. 2011):

$$\widehat{p}_j(x_i) = \frac{p_j(x_i)}{\sum_j p_j(x_i)}$$

We will heavily utilize these normalized probabilities to identify where the model is performing well.

All of these formulas – and a highly efficient minimization strategy for our log-loss function (Stochastic Gradient Descent) – are implemented in scikit-learn, the open-source python package we used to develop these models (Pedregosa et al. 2011).

We also explored other models and classification approaches such as Support Vector Machines, Random Forests, and Naïve Bayes, but found Logistic Regression to consistently provide equivalent or better classification performance. For brevity's sake, we do not include those models or their results.

25.3.6 Training and Evaluation

To fit and evaluate our parameters, we first split our 400,000 record cleansed, de-duplicated, and disambiguated dataset into a training set and a small held-out test set. This approach is typical in ML applications. The model is developed ("trained") on the training set, and then evaluated on the test set of records that it has not encountered before.

In particular, we chose a test set size of 10%, randomly selecting records from our 400,000 record dataset stratified by shares of SCTG in the dataset. As is typical in machine learning applications, we performed fivefold stratified cross-validation of our 90% training set to find an optimal value for our hyperparameter α (Hastie et al. 2017). We repeated this process for each of the three training datasets we created.

In the process of evaluation, we used a few different metrics, but accuracy is our main barometer of model performance. In this case, we define accuracy as the number of correct predictions over the total number of predictions.

This choice of metric makes sense given the wide multiclass nature of our problem – it gives an overall picture of how often the model selects the correct code for a given record. In addition, this notion of correctness is key to our applications, described below.

We also validated the model's performance on heretofore unlabeled records by having survey SMEs mark their agreement or disagreement with the model's output on a sampling of records. Given the previously mentioned issues with the quality of 2017 CFS response data, having a human-in-the-loop validation process was especially important to ensure our model was producing quality labels.

Given the applied nature of our work, we designed validation experiments with specific 2017 CFS data quality needs in mind. Our first validation exercise took a simple random sampling of 300 out of 100,000 records where the model's reported probability ($\hat{p}$) was greater than 50%. After this validation, we performed a second validation on another 300 records. In this second validation, we took a simple random sampling of 60 records from each $\hat{p}$ interval [0–10%], [10–20%], … , [40–50%] – in other words, bands of probabilities where model confidence was below 50%. Despite these being separate experiments, we present the results from these two validations together for clarity's sake.

When reviewing records, SMEs marked whether (i) they agreed with the model's labeling, (ii) disagreed with the model's labeling or more information was needed, or (iii) if the code was one of multiple possible correct codes. When presenting results below, we consider the label to be correct if SMEs reported option (i) or (iii) – the third response option was helpful for understanding ambiguities in the SCTG coding scheme itself. When marking their agreement, SMEs looked at all possible contextual information they could about the shipment record, including the company reporting the shipment, other shipments the company had reported, and any information they could find via other research methods (e.g. Google search or company website).

Subsequent applications included similar validation exercises before any corrections or imputations were made. In these cases, we took a simple random sample of records to be corrected or imputed, and SMEs validated the correctness of that sample as described above.

It is worth noting that this design carries the risk of introducing confirmation bias, as SMEs may be predisposed to confirm the model's output presented to them. We discuss solutions in the "future work" section below.

25.3.7 Imputing and Correcting Data – Edit Rule Agreement

We now briefly describe the CFS data quality-assurance processes that were key to our applications and ensuring the quality of our ML applications. These checks, developed by SMEs, help combine statistical pattern-matching with domain expertise to help improve data quality.

As is the case with many survey programs, CFS SMEs have developed rule-based edit checks ("edits" or "edit rules") to ensure data quality and flag anomalous records for SME review (U.S. Census Bureau 2020). We will use these edit rules to ensure our ML-based labels are as high quality as possible.

These edits typically compare the reported product code with other reported shipment information, such as the value-to-weight ratio of the shipment, mode of transportation used by the

Table 25.6 Shipment-level edit rules for the 2017 edits that used SCTG in their logic.

Edit name	Description	Example edit failure
SCTG/mode of transportation	Checks for invalid SCTG/mode of transport combinations.	**SCTG**: 01002 (live pigs) **Mode of transportation**: pipeline
SCTG value-to-weight ratio	Checks that the value-to-weight ratio for the provided SCTG code is within acceptable boundaries.	**SCTG**: 40941 (precious metal forms and shapes) **Value**: US$100 **Weight**: 10000 pounds
HAZMAT/SCTG	Checks inconsistencies between SCTG and reported HAZMAT information.	**SCTG**: 20221 (hydrochloric acid) **Reported Hazmat**: gasoline
NAICS/SCTG	Checks for unusual industry/product (NAICS/SCTG) combinations.	**SCTG**: pharmaceutical products **NAICS**: kiwi fruit farming
Temp control/SCTG	Checks for invalid temperature control/SCTG combinations.	**SCTG**: frozen poultry **Temp control**: no

shipment, or whether the shipment was temperature controlled. If subject-matter experts would be concerned that the particular combination of SCTG and the auxiliary variable in question is not valid, the edit rule fails and that record is flagged for review. Table 25.6 describes the product-related edit rules that we used as part of the ML correction and imputation process in 2017 CFS.

We used these edit rules for our applications in two ways: first, to validate the model's corrections and imputations, and second, to target records to correct and impute. By incorporating the expert knowledge that developed these rules in addition to the statistical pattern-matching encapsulated in the model, we produced higher-quality product code labels in our production application setting.

In the first use of these edits – validating the correctness of the models' labels – we ensured that any records we updated with model-based labels would not fail any edit rules.

Then, in the second use, we identified CFS records that were failing one or more of the above edits. From there, we checked whether (i) the model had made a suitably high-confidence prediction, and (ii) the model's predicted code would lead to that record passing *all* of the above edits. If both of these conditions were true, we updated that record.

25.4 Results

The results are divided into two sections. The first covers results from the modeling process itself. The second covers how we applied the model to improve 2017 CFS data quality, and the impact of those applications on the 2017 CFS. In many ways, this distinction is arbitrary – understanding potential applications was key to developing the model, and an understanding of the model was key to ensuring successful and high-quality applications.

25.4.1 Model Results

First, we present results from the models trained on a variety of different input features as well as different levels of text cleaning. The results can be seen in Table 25.7.

Table 25.7 Model results based on a variety of datasets input features.

Features	Data processing steps performed	Accuracy
Unigrams (1-word tokens) only	Minimal cleaning	0.49
Unigrams only	Spell checking	0.36
Unigrams only	Stemming + spell checking	0.44
Unigrams and bigrams (one-word tokens and two-word tokens)	Minimal cleaning (all word tokens)	0.55
Unigrams and bigrams	Spell checking	0.40
Unigrams and bigrams	Stemming + spell checking	0.46
Unigrams and bigrams, NAICS	Minimal cleaning (all word tokens)	0.64†
Unigrams and bigrams, NAICS	Spell checking	0.52
Unigrams and bigrams, NAICS	Stemming + spell checking	0.55
Unigrams, 3–5 character *n*-grams, NAICS	Minimal cleaning (all word tokens)	0.67*
Unigrams, 3–5 character *n*-grams, NAICS	Spell checking	0.58*
Unigrams, 3–5 character *n*-grams, NAICS	Stemming + spell checking	0.55*
Unigrams, bigrams, 3–5 character *n*-grams, NAICS	Minimal cleaning (all word tokens)	0.82*

Asterisk indicates that model was developed after 2017 CFS applications. † indicates the model was used in those applications.
Source: U.S. Census Bureau (2017a). Commodity Flow Survey.

With respect to features used, we were initially concerned that a model incorporating unigram and bigram word features as well as character-level features would suffer from the "curse of dimensionality" – that is, we would have more variables than sample records, and the model would overfit (Bishop 2006). However, results on our held-out test set of 10% of records showed that in the case of the problem of classification based on sparse textual data such as product descriptions, enabling the model to fit itself to these sparse features produced a model that can better extrapolate on product descriptions it has not seen before. We believe the reason for this has to do with the fact that our engineered features enable the model to capture various different types of natural language interactions, such as the word "steel" modifying "beam" in the description "steel beam."

In addition, as can be seen in the table below, incorporating NAICS indicator variables provides a significant performance boost for any given model. Models incorporating NAICS see roughly 10% accuracy improvement as compared with a model using similar text features, but not using NAICS. In this case, our results validate the intuition that capturing the industry context about a product helps improve the model's ability to classify products shipped within that industry.

With respect to the type of data processing used (i.e. level of text cleansing performed before modeling), no matter the features used, the dataset with minimal text cleaning consistently outperforms the models with comparable features trained on a dataset with more cleansing. We suspect that this somewhat counterintuitive result may be because our text descriptions are quite sparse compared with other natural language data. As a result, maintaining as much variation as possible within the input descriptions themselves helps the model. Our best model, trained on a dataset with minimal text cleansing and using all features that we generated, performs at 82% accuracy.

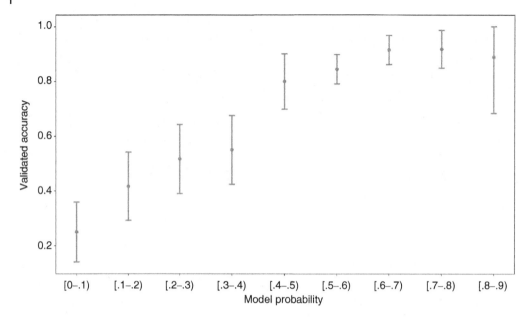

Figure 25.2 Model prediction accuracy as validated by the CFS SME team. Source: U.S. Census Bureau (2017a). Commodity Flow Survey.

Although we have since developed a model performing at a higher level of overall accuracy, our applications during the 2017 CFS cycle leveraged an earlier version of the model. In particular, the model we used did not incorporate character level features – only unigram and bigram word-level features. The model used in applications is indicated in the above table by the † symbol. In other words, the remainder of the results shown here, from validation results to applications to the 2017 CFS, are based on this model.

Next, we show the results from the first evaluation and validation exercises we conducted with the CFS SME team. In Figure 25.2, we show the combined results from both sampling designs (300 records with reported model probability [$\hat{p}$] 50% or higher, and 60 records within each of the probability bands below 50%). The model's probability is reported on the *x*-axis, while SME validated accuracy is reported on the *y*-axis. The error bars represent a 95% Bernoulli confidence interval. A clear increase in validated accuracy can be seen at the 40% $\hat{p}$ threshold, with the accuracies in probability bins below the 40% threshold consistently below accuracies in bins above the 40% threshold.

25.4.2 Applications to 2017 CFS and Impact of ML

Upon seeing early success with the model's high-confidence predictions, we successfully applied the model to several use cases in the production of the 2017 CFS.

25.4.2.1 Applications
25.4.2.1.1 Imputing 100,000 SCTG Codes
Our first use case was shipment records where respondents had provided a description but had either not included an SCTG code or had given an invalid code. Originally, roughly 400,000 records met these criteria. By the time, we began applying ML in the production setting, about 230,000 (58% of total) of these records had been coded by SMEs. For 100,000 of the remaining records (25% of total), the model predicted a code with high probability (50% $\hat{p}$ or above). After validating a sample

of 300 of these and determining the model was predicting correctly with 90% accuracy, we used these predictions to impute the SCTG code. In addition, that record was then only used in final 2017 CFS estimates if the model's SCTG label passed the survey's edit flags, as described above.

25.4.2.1.2   *ML Followed by Hot-Deck Imputation of 50,000 SCTG Codes*

For another 50,000 of these same records where respondents had provided a product description but no associated SCTG code, we developed a second process to impute a code that combined machine learning with a more traditional hot-deck imputation. In particular, the SCTG product coding scheme is hierarchical, and the first level of the hierarchy is the first two digits of the product code. We developed a separate model that was able to predict just the first two digits of the SCTG, and then used a hot-deck imputation process to assign the final three digits to have a complete five-digit code.

In other words, the first two digits of the SCTG code became the first level of our imputation cells, and we selected donors exclusively within that two-digit SCTG cell. We will omit further details of this process, but it is worth noting that during this hot-deck process, we ensured that the final donor SCTG code would pass all of the survey's rule-based edit checks, and we performed a separate validation exercise to confirm the quality of the two-digit model's predictions. This serves as another example of how ML can be combined with more traditional statistical correction and imputation methods to improve the baseline quality of those corrections.

25.4.2.1.3   *Relabeling 90,000 Miscellaneous SCTG Codes*

In the 2017 CFS, respondents labeled about 400,000 records as "miscellaneous" (either mixed freight or miscellaneous goods). However, in many cases, the description and other contextual factors clearly indicated to SMEs that the shipment could be labeled more specifically. Via another validation exercise, the CFS SME team was able to determine that approximately 90% of the time, when the model predicted an alternative label with high probability, the model's predicted code was the correct choice. We thus were able to relabel about 90,000 records previously labeled as miscellaneous.

25.4.2.1.4   *Targeting 15,000 Records Failing Edit Rules*

One of our final uses of ML involved targeting records that were failing one or more of the product-related edit rules. Because they were failing edit rules, these records would not have been used in final estimates. However, by relabeling with the SCTG code assigned by the model, we were able to use these records in our final estimates. Furthermore, as reported above, SME validation demonstrated these were remarkably high-quality corrections (93% accuracy). This example highlights the benefits of combining rule-based edit checks with the statistical knowledge encoded in a ML model.

25.4.2.2   Impact of ML

Last, though we have validated the correctness of the model's predictions as described above, we wanted to make sure we understood the impact of this process, in aggregate, on our final data products. This was especially important given our use of the model's reported prediction probability, as it could be possible that the model is able to correctly classify only certain types of products but not others. To do so, we investigated how ML-based processes impacted the distributions of SCTG codes in both microdata and macrodata (i.e. published estimates).

First, we will show results from investigating impacts on microdata. Figure 25.3 compares shares of high-level product categories before and after applying the variety of ML-based corrections

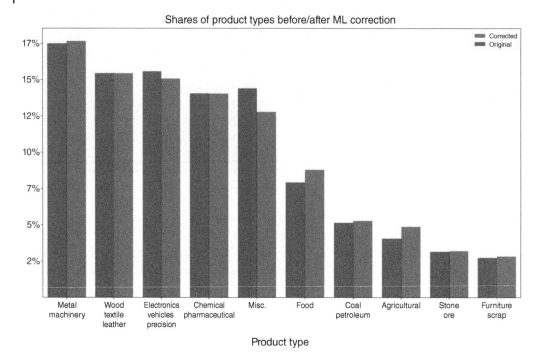

Figure 25.3 Impact of the ML correction and imputation processes on the (normalized) frequency distribution of high-level product categories in CFS microdata. Source: U.S. Census Bureau (2017a). Commodity Flow Survey.

described above. As you can see, the largest change was a reduction in the share of "miscellaneous" products from approximately 15% to 13% share. Food and agricultural products also gained roughly 1% point share each. In the case of the reduction of miscellaneous products, this reduction was by design: we recoded 90,000 miscellaneous records to more specific categories as described above. In the case of the food and agricultural products, we discovered that of the 150,000 records whose labels we imputed, a significant majority came from companies in food or agricultural product industries. As such, we would expect the shares of these two product types to increase.

Next, we discuss further implications of using ML. By coding or recoding roughly 250,000 records – roughly 4% of all CFS response data – we were able to produce approximately 2% more estimates that would have otherwise been suppressed or nonexistent due to lack of data – another boon for the quality and usefulness of CFS data.

Given these results, we are comfortable making the claim that ML improved 2017 CFS estimate data quality, if modestly. As described below, we are continuing to evaluate the impacts of ML as we look toward using these methods on a larger scale in future CFS cycles.

25.5 Conclusion and Future Work

We have determined that ML, applied correctly, can be a valuable method to improve data quality and automatically categorize text descriptions into codes ("autocode"). Furthermore, in our application, combining statistical learning with rules-based expert knowledge yields better results than statistical learning could alone. Next, we learned that in the case of short-length product description text, minimal text preprocessing and extracting character-level features helps improve model performance; additionally, context about the industry shipping the product is particularly helpful. Finally, while the impacts of ML on the 2017 CFS were modest, we used these applications as a means to validate the efficacy and benefits of using ML in preparation for larger-scale uses in future CFS efforts.

With respect to the model itself, we are currently seeking to improve the model's quality by improving the quality of the underlying training data. We are utilizing Amazon's Mechanical Turk (MTurk) "crowdsourcing" platform to develop a higher-quality set of labeled (and publicly available) data. We expect to improve model performance and the proportion of records it can automatically code. Furthermore, we are working with international trade experts at the Census Bureau to acquire the free-text product descriptions and Harmonized System product codes that shippers exporting goods from the United States are required to declare. Finally, we are also interested in improving the model's quality based on related work in the space that has shown alternative modeling approaches, such as LSTM neural networks, can boost classification performance (Measure 2017; see also Chapter 23 of this volume).

Introducing ML into data production processes requires careful evaluation of the impacts. As such, we are working to develop an even more detailed understanding of the impacts of ML on 2017 CFS estimates, despite the relatively small scale of changes (fewer than 5% of records modified). In particular, we are developing a system that enables us to rerun the entirety of the CFS estimation process – from initial edit checks, to statistical weighting, to final tabulation – so that we can run experiments where we compare how estimates would look under different conditions (such as having ML code all records in 2017 CFS, or recomputing 2017 CFS estimates without the corrections that we actually made).

Furthermore, continuous validation and quality assurance is key – for future applications of ML to CFS processes, we plan to continue with human-in-the-loop validation processes to ensure that our model provides high-quality labels even with changes in products in the marketplace over time. One noteworthy change to our process is that we have modified our validation design to avoid confirmation bias issues associated with verifying an output from the model. Instead, we plan to have SMEs find labels for a sampling of codes *a priori*, and evaluate how closely the model compares with this "gold standard." Our validation processes have been largely inspired by other, mature ML implementations (such as the one described by Measure in Chapter 23 of this volume), adapted to the needs of CFS.

Last, we are considering different strategies for assigning codes to records, such as multiple imputation or probabilistic assignment – i.e. selecting codes for a given record from the model's probability distribution. An approach like this would better mirror the reality of how respondents have historically determined these codes and would also help capture some of the ambiguity within the SCTG coding scheme itself for certain products. Relatedly, we continue to explore the benefits and potential ways of combining rule-based edit checks with an ML-based classification approach to ensure that subject-matter expertise continues to help inform product classification.

Going forward with the CFS in 2022 and beyond, we plan to use this process to obviate the need for respondents to provide an SCTG code, instead of simply requiring a product description. Because assigning SCTG codes was a major source of respondent burden during previous CFS data collections, this change also unlocks the ability to ask respondents to provide substantially more shipment records. Furthermore, we have begun to explore methods of data ingestion, such as an application programming interface (API)-based "dump" of shipment data from a company's database, avoiding the need for respondents to fill out a form. This enables the possibility of CFS estimates being published more frequently and at higher geographic granularity, without asking respondents for significantly more of their valuable time.

More broadly, it is possible to apply ML to many similar problems in which text descriptions are used to map to standardized codes of some form. At the very least, similar efforts are underway within other areas of the Census Bureau and at other US statistical agencies, such as the Bureau of Labor Statistics (Dumbacher and Hanna 2017; Measure 2017; see also Chapter 23 of this volume). We hope this work can help others realize the benefits associated with introducing ML into statistical data creation processes.

Disclaimer

Any opinions and conclusions expressed herein are those of the author(s) and do not represent the views of the U.S. Census Bureau or the Bureau of Transportation Statistics. All results have been reviewed to ensure that no confidential information is disclosed.

The Census Bureau has reviewed this work for unauthorized disclosure of confidential information and has approved the disclosure avoidance practices applied (Approval ID: CBDRB-FY21-ESMD002-018).

References

Bird, S., Loper, E., and Klein, E. (2009). *Natural Language Processing with Python*. O'Reilly Media Inc.

Bishop, C. (2006). The curse of dimensionality. In: *Pattern Recognition and Machine Learning*. Springer Verlag.

Brownlee, J. (2020). Why one-hot encode data in machine learning? https://machinelearningmastery.com/why-one-hot-encode-data-in-machine-learning/ (accessed 7 March 2022).

Bureau of Transportation Statistics (2012). Standard Classification of Transported Goods (SCTG) Codes. https://www.bts.gov/archive/publications/commodity_flow_survey/classification (accessed 7 March 2022).

Bureau of Transportation Statistics (2021). Commodity Flow Survey. https://www.bts.gov/cfs (accessed 7 March 2022).

Camacho-Collados, J. and Pilehvar, M.T. (2018). On the role of text preprocessing in neural network architectures: an evaluation study on text categorization and sentiment analysis. *Proceedings of the 2018 EMNLP Workshop BlackboxNLP: Analyzing and Interpreting Neural Networks for NLP*. https://doi.org/10.18653/v1/w18-5406.

Dumbacher, B. and Hanna, D. (2017). Using Passive Data Collection, System-to-System Data Collection, and Machine Learning to Improve Economic Surveys. https://www.census.gov/content/dam/Census/newsroom/press-kits/2017/jsm/jsm-presentation-dumbacher-hanna.pdf (accessed 7 March 2022).

Hastie, T., Friedman, J., and Tisbshirani, R. (2017). *The Elements of Statistical Learning: Data Mining, Inference, and Prediction*. New York: Springer.

Leskovec, J., Rajaraman, A., and Ullman, J.D. (2020). *Mining of Massive Datasets*. Cambridge, UK: Cambridge University Press.

Manning, C.D., Raghavan, P., and Schütze, H. (2018). Stemming and lemmatization. In: *Introduction to Information Retrieval*. Cambridge, UK: Cambridge University Press. https://nlp.stanford.edu/IR-book/html/htmledition/stemming-and-lemmatization-1.html.

Measure, A. (2017). Deep neural networks for worker injury autocoding. https://www.bls.gov/iif/deep-neural-networks.pdf (accessed 7 March 2022).

Németh, L. (2021). Hunspell: About. http://hunspell.github.io/ (accessed 7 March 2022).

Pedregosa, F., Varoquaux, G., Gramfort, A., Michel, V., Thirion, B., Grisel, O., Blondel, M., Prettenhofer, P., Weiss, R., Dubourg, V., Vanderplas, J., Passos, A., Cournapeau, D., Brucher, M., Perrot, M., and Duchesnay, É (2011). Scikit-learn: machine learning in python. *Journal of Machine Learning Research* 12: 2825–2830.

U.S. Census Bureau (2014). American Community Survey Design and Methodology (January 2014) Chapter 10: Data Preparation and Processing for Housing Units and Group Quarters, p. 9. https://www2.census.gov/programs-surveys/acs/methodology/design_and_methodology/acs_design_methodology_ch10_2014.pdf (accessed 7 March 2022).

U.S. Census Bureau (2017a). Commodity Code Search Tool. https://bhs.econ.census.gov/bhsphpext/brdsearch/survey_code_search.php?code=CFS (accessed 7 March 2022).

U.S. Census Bureau (2017b). SCTG Commodity Codes. https://www2.census.gov/programs-surveys/cfs/technical-documentation/code-list/CFS-1200_17.pdf (accessed 7 March 2022).

U.S. Census Bureau (2020). Commodity flow Survey (CFS). https://www.census.gov/programs-surveys/cfs.html (accessed 7 March 2022).

U.S. Census Bureau (2020). 2017 Commodity Flow Survey methodology. https://www.census.gov/programs-surveys/cfs/technical-documentation/methodology/methodology-2017.html (accessed 7 March 2022).

U.S. Census Bureau (n.d.). North American Industry classification system - NAICS. https://www.census.gov/naics/ (accessed 7 March 2022).

Yui-Chang, L., Das, P., and Datta, A. (2018). Overview of the SIGIR 2018 eCom Rakuten Data Challenge. http://ceur-ws.org/Vol-2319/ecom18DC_paper_13.pdf (accessed 7 March 2022).

26

Alternative Data Sources in the Census Bureau's Monthly State Retail Sales Data Product

Rebecca Hutchinson, Scott Scheleur, and Deanna Weidenhamer

US Census Bureau, Washington, DC, USA

26.1   Introduction/Overview

The US Census Bureau strives to provide timely and relevant data its data users. The COVID-19 pandemic surfaced an urgent need for more timely data on the state of the economy at more granular geographies. This was particularly important for the retail trade sector. Pandemic-related shutdowns and closures impacted retailers across the country with over 40% of retail store surfaces were closed during March 2020 (Wahba 2020). Retail analysts predict that over 20,000 retail stores will permanently close postpandemic (Richter 2020). In response to the urgent need for more timely data at the state level, the Census Bureau prioritized the creation of the Monthly State Retail Sales (MSRS) experimental data product.[1] The MSRS was created without any new data collections and without any additional respondent burden; thus, the focus was on using available survey and administrative data as well as available alternative data sources. The resulting MSRS is a blended data product that uses existing survey data, administrative data, and alternative data sources in a composite estimator. The MSRS is now published monthly with data available for each state and the District of Columbia[2] for all retail subsectors excluding nonstore retailers and food services.

Alternative data sources play a key role in the MSRS both as inputs to the composite estimator and as sources for validating the MSRS data. This chapter provides an overview of the MSRS data and highlights how this unique data product makes use of alternative data sources. Section 26.2 provides a history of Census Bureau work on MSRS data. Section 26.3 provides an overview of the MSRS data product. Section 26.4 summarizes the methodology used to create the MSRS estimates. Section 26.5 provides details on how alternative data sources were used both in the creation of the MSRS estimates and in the validation of the MSRS estimates. Section 26.6 summarizes next steps for the MSRS.

1 Census Bureau experimental data products are statistical products that were created using new data sources or methodologies to benefit our data users that may not meet all of the Census Bureau's data quality standards. Experimental data products are clearly identified as such and the Census Bureau encourages data users to submit feedback on the data products. Experimental data products may or may not become official statistical products depending upon demand and data quality. More information on experimental data products is available at What are Experimental Data Products? (https://www.census.gov/data/experimental-data-products.html).
2 For the purposes of this chapter, the word "state" will represent all 50 states as well as the District of Columbia.

Advances in Business Statistics, Methods and Data Collection. Edited by Ger Snijkers, Mojca Bavdaž, Stefan Bender, Jacqui Jones, Steve MacFeely, Joseph W. Sakshaug, Katherine J. Thompson, and Arnout van Delden.

26.2 History of State-Level Retail Sales at Census

The Census Bureau comprehensively measures the retail sector through the Economic Census, the Annual Retail Trade Survey (ARTS), the Monthly Retail Trade Survey (MRTS), and the Advance Monthly Retail Trade Survey (MARTS). Every five years, the Census Bureau produces retail sales by state, county, metro area, places, and zip codes as part of the Economic Census. The Economic Census sales figure is an annual sales figure for only the Economic Census year (e.g. the 2017 Economic Census collected and published annual retail sales for only the year of 2017). More timely retail sales estimates in the MRTS and the ARTS are collected but are published at only the national level. Prior to its discontinuation in December 1996, state and metro areas were published for a subset of retail industries as part of the MRTS.

Since the end of that publication in 1996, the Census Bureau has explored ways to resume publishing retail sales at more granular geographies. One of the exploratory efforts involved using point-of-sale data. A large body of work on point-of-sale data—also known as scanner data—has been done by official statistical agencies but that work has mostly focused on the price features of point-of-sale data. The product and pricing attributes of point-of-sale data are particularly useful in the development of price indices (Bird et al. 2014). The Census Bureau work with point-of-sale data used both price and quantity to find total sales. In 2015, the Census Bureau began exploring point-of-sale data from The NPD Group, Inc. (NPD). NPD is a private market research company that collects point-of-sale data from retailers across the country. These data include sales by detailed product types and are generally available at each establishment or physical location a retailer operates as well as online sales.[3] Because the data can be available at the individual establishment level and include a postal code, a state-level geography could be assigned and sales could be tabulated by state and potentially used to create state-level retail estimates.[4]

However, several features of the NPD data did not allow for the data to scale to a full state-level retail sales data product; NPD's business model only covers certain portions of the retail economy and has no coverage or limited coverage of grocery stores, pharmacies, or gasoline stations (US Census Bureau 2015). Additionally, for other portions of the retail sector, coverage is limited in scope. For example, NPD captures sales for automobile parts but not sales for automobiles themselves. Additionally, the retailer composition of NPD data tends to skew toward larger firms and may introduce bias in any estimates when used in the aggregate. Because of these limitations in the data, no attempts were made to create state-level retail sales estimates solely from this NPD data. While the NPD data were not useful in this effort, different cuts of the NPD data were useful in the new MSRS data product and their use will be discussed in Section 26.5.

Another exploratory effort to create state retail sales estimates used payment processor data. Payment processors serve as intermediaries between retailers and financial institutions, processing credit or debit card transactions. The Census Bureau purchased data from Fiserv,[5] a payment processor, to examine if the data could be used in small area estimates at the state level (Dumbacher et al. 2019). Like the NPD data, the Fiserv data has varying coverage across the retail sector. Unlike the NPD data, Fiserv provides no information about which retailers or which types of retailers are included in its data. Due to Fiserv's proprietary data disclosure rules, data are suppressed when

---

3 For the purposes of this chapter, an establishment will refer to each specific establishment or online operation that a retailer operates.
4 Some retailer data from NPD are only available at the national total and/or only available for brick-and-mortar sales.
5 Fiserv was formerly known as FirstData.

there are not enough retailers in a retail subsector or state. Additionally, Fiserv cannot disclose which retailers are included in the data. Using quality metrics that included suppression rates, coverage rates, and trends, this effort was able to create small area estimates at the state level for only five of the 12 retail subsectors, including grocery stores and gasoline stations.

One challenge that the Fiserv exploratory effort faced was the lack of external sources to validate the data against. Data produced by the Census Bureau are often considered the benchmark against which other measures are compared. When the Census Bureau creates a new data product, there are obviously no existing Census Bureau estimates to compare against. The only state-level retail sales data available are the annual figures produced as part of the Census Bureau's Economic Census every five years. The Fiserv data exploratory team recommended that more work needed to be done to find external data sources to validate state-level retail sales data.

There are other limitations to the Fiserv data that would inhibit creating a state retail sales estimates based solely on the Fiserv data. First, payment processor data only capture transactions made with a credit card, a debit card, an Electronic Benefit Transfer (EBT) card, or a gift card. Unlike point-of-sale data, payment processor data does not capture cash transactions. Second, the Fiserv data is limited to those retailers who contract Fiserv to serve as their payment processor, so Fiserv does not have coverage of the entire retail sector. Related, retailers can start and stop using Fiserv as their payment processor at any point in time, so creating a consistent time series in the raw data would be impossible. Consistent time series from alternative data sources are critical to establishing a stable data product.

Both the NPD and Fiserv efforts highlight additional critical issues that must be considered when using alternative data sources to create a Census Bureau data product. First, there is the risk that the data provider could cease operations which would stop the flow of data to the Census Bureau. Second, reliance on a single data source increases the risk that a third-party data provider could create a competing product to the Census Bureau's. Additionally, individual data sources often do not provide coverage of the entire retail sector or of all retail transactions; a diverse pool of sources provides the best path to covering the entire retail sector. This diverse pool is also critical when one provider's coverage deteriorates over time. And last, third-party data can be expensive. The Census Bureau is subject to a budget appropriated by the US Congress; if the data become too expensive or if the budget is cut, the data may no longer be purchased placing the continuation of a data product based on these data in jeopardy.

26.3 Overview of the MSRS

The new MSRS data product builds upon the lessons learned of the previous efforts detailed in Section 26.2 with a focus on both using multiple data sources as well as making use of the rich data that the Census Bureau already has. To that end, MSRS is a blended data product that combines previously collected MRTS data, administrative data, and third-party data sources. This section provides an overview of the MSRS as well as details of the MSRS methodology and the data sources included in the MSRS data.

The MSRS data product is published each month and includes year-over-year percentage changes for each state back to January 2019 to coincide with the start of the newest sample revision to the MRTS. The state-level data are not adjusted for seasonal variation, trading-day differences, moving holidays, or price changes.

The MSRS data are provided for Total Retail Sales excluding Nonstore Retailers as well as for 11 three-digit retail subsectors as classified by the North American Industry Classification System

(NAICS) (US Office of Management and Budget 2017). These 11 retail subsectors include the following:

- Motor vehicle and parts dealers (NAICS code 441)
- Furniture and Home Furnishing (NAICS code 442)
- Electronics and Appliances (NAICS code 443)
- Building Materials and Supplies Dealers (NAICS code 444)
- Food and Beverage (NAICS code 445)
- Health and Personal Care (NAICS code 446)
- Gasoline Stations (NAICS code 447)
- Clothing and Clothing Accessories (NAICS code 448)
- Sporting Goods and Hobby (NAICS code 451)
- General Merchandise (NAICS code 452)
- Miscellaneous Store Retailers (NAICS code 453)

We currently do not create MSRS estimates for Food Services (NAICS code 722) but hope to include these data in the future. Nonstore retailers (NAICS code 454) are also currently excluded from the MSRS. Nonstore retailers are often e-commerce type retailers. Allocating e-commerce sales to a state is challenging as a decision needs to be made on which state the sale should be attributed to: the state were the retailer is based, the state where the shipment originates, or the state where the purchaser resides. Even if that decision can be made, obtaining the data to make the appropriate allocation can be difficult. The Bureau of Economic Analysis has explored using

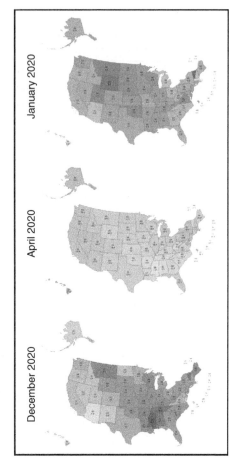

Figure 26.1 Year-over-year percentage changes for Total Retail Sales Excluding Nonstore Retailers (NAICS 454) MSRS data months January 2020, April 2020, and December 2020 (* Indicates that the 90% confidence interval includes zero. There is insufficient statistical evidence to conclude that the actual change is different from zero. MSRS retail sales data are not adjusted for seasonal variation, trading-day differences, moving holidays, or price changes.) Source: January 2020, April 2020, and December 2020 MSRS data.

the home location of a credit or debit card user as the geography where consumption expenditures are allocated (Dunn and Gholizadeh 2020).

The MSRS has provided data users a more localized view of retail sales as well as the ability to see how retail sales change over time. Figure 26.1 shows MSRS Total Retail Sales Excluding Nonstore Retailers (NAICS 454) data across the United States for January 2020, April 2020, and December 2020. States in blue had positive year-over-year percentages changes while states in orange had negative year-over-over changes. In April 2020, when shutdown orders impacted retail across the country, 48 states had negative and statistically significant year-over-year percentage changes.

26.4   Methodology

Most economic data products published by the Census Bureau produce estimates either using data collected by a survey designed specifically for the data product or using data from administrative sources. The MSRS is different from these data products in that it uses administrative data, third-party data, and data collected for another survey—the MRTS—to produce its estimates. Thus, its methodology required the development of a new composite estimator that could incorporate these data sources in a statistically sound manner.[6] The key components of the methodology include the survey and third-party data inputs, the frame creation, estimation and imputation, and creation of quality metrics. This section provides an overview of these components and highlights any challenges or limitations.

26.4.1   Directly Collected Data Inputs

Data that is most useful to the MSRS is data that captures retail activity at the state-level. Without any new data collection, we made use of two types of state-level data that we refer to as directly collected throughout this chapter: (i) data reported to the MRTS that can be associated with a single state, and (ii) third-party data that also can be associated with a single state. These data can be used as inputs to the MSRS estimation process. Some of these data can also be used as an input to the imputation process.

The MRTS is a national data product with a sample that was not designed to produce geographic estimates; however, some of the data that retailers report to the MRTS can be used in the MSRS estimation process if the data meet one of two criteria. First, retailers that are included in the MRTS that operate only one establishment are considered usable for estimation since the sales from that retailer can be tied to a physical location in a specific state. For the purposes of the methodology explanation in this chapter, we refer to the retailers that meet this criterion as single units (SU). Second, retailers that are report to the MRTS that operate more than one establishment and all of those establishments are operated in the same state can also be used in MSRS estimation. For the purposes of the methodology, we refer to these retailers that meet this second criteria as multiunits (MU). Any reported MU in MRTS is also eligible for use in the MSRS imputation process.

For third-party data sources, data also need to meet one of two criteria, but these criteria are different than those for the MRTS data. The first criterion is that the third-party data contains total monthly sales data by individual retail establishment for a retailer and a geographic identifier is included. For these data, we receive a dataset where we can derive the total monthly sales for Retailer X's store number Y, where Y is located in zip code 12345. Alternatively, the data set can include the state rather than the zip code; the inclusion of store number ensures that we can still identify unique establishments when a zip code is not provided. These data can be used in both the MSRS imputation and estimation process.

---

6 The complete technical documentation for the MSRS is available at: https://www.census.gov/retail/mrts/www/statedata/msrs_technical_documentation.pdf.

When working with third-party data providers, it can be difficult and expensive to obtain permission from individual retailers to provide the detailed data described in criterion one. During the creation of the MSRS, we brainstormed other datasets that could be used for MSRS estimation and established a second type of useful data: aggregated state-level sales data for a curated list of retailers. In this scenario, we can provide a third-party data provider with a list of retailers for each retail subsector and ask the data provider to deliver a dataset containing one total monthly sales figure for each state for each grouping of retailers. For example, we would provide a list of retailers in retail NAICS subsector 444 that includes Retailer A, Retailer B, and Retailer C. This approach work bests as a collaboration with the third-party data provider as the third-party data provider could also come back and let us know that we need to add more retailers to that group to ensure the grouping meets any internal disclosure rules held by the data provider. The third-party data provider could also tell us that legal agreements prevent it from sharing a specific retailer's data and the list of retailers will need to be edited. The benefit to this approach is that the third-party data provider is able to provide a dataset useful to the MSRS without disclosing information about any one retailer and is often able to provide aggregations without obtaining the retailer permissions needed for the data in requirement one. These aggregated groupings are used in the MSRS estimation process but not the imputation process.

When working with third-party data providers, they often have privacy protections in place that prohibit them from revealing information about the composition of their data. There may be the potential to use other third-party data where we don't know the specific retailer composition but that would be a long-term improvement to the MSRS.

26.4.2 Frame Creation

Frames for retail measurement at the Census Bureau are extracted from the Census Bureau's Business Register (BR). The BR provides the most complete, current, and consistent source of establishment-based information about US businesses (DeSalvo et al. 2016). It is a relational database with multiple tables to consolidate and link administrative, Census, and survey data. Records from multiple sources are loaded as received and used to add to or update tables containing records of enterprises, tax reporting entities based on Internal Revenue Service (IRS) Employer Identification Numbers (EINs), and establishments with the best available classification, size, address, and company affiliation information. Information for single establishments and EINs is updated continuously, including employment and payroll data based on payroll tax records, and receipts data based on income tax records from the IRS. Information from the BR is used to establish the different types of units needed for retail measurement (Van Delden et al. 2018). For example, national sampling units are needed for our survey-based MRTS estimates. For the MSRS, the important BR unit is the establishment level record. The frame of retail establishments used for MSRS is extracted from the BR. For retailers, we consider one establishment as defined by the BR to be one physical store location.[7]

The primary identifier of a multiunit firm is a unique alpha number. The Census Bureau assigns the alpha number to the multiunit firm and assigns a unique establishment identification number to each establishment within a multiunit firm. All establishments owned or controlled by the same multiunit firm have the same alpha number. If a retailer has more than one establishment, that retailer is assigned an alpha number and all establishments operated by that retailer are linked in the BR through that alpha number. If a retailer operates only one establishment, it generally does not have an alpha number and instead is identified by its EIN.

---

7 For retailers, an e-commerce operation captured by NAICS code 454 would also be considered an establishment. However, NAICS code 454 is currently not in scope to MSRS.

To create the frame for the MSRS, the associated EIN and/or alpha, NAICS classification, activity status, address and zip code, and annual payroll for 2018 for each individual retail establishment are extracted from the BR. Establishments had to be in scope to retail—NAICS codes beginning with either "44" or "45," have positive annual payroll for the reference year, be located in one of the 50 states or the District of Columbia, and be active. Each month, the MSRS frame is merged with directly collected MRTS sample data and/third-party data to identify companies with useable information in that month. To avoid duplication, if a company has data from both third-party data sources and MRTS survey collection, the third-party data will be used for estimation purposes; third-party data is provided at levels which can be attributed to a specific state, while MRTS data for MUs is collected at a national level. Reported MRTS sales for MUs are distributed to all active establishments in the frame based on the ratio of the establishment's annual payroll to the total annual payroll for the company. One limitation of the current frame creation is the timeliness of the payroll data. MSRS uses administrative data from the IRS for payroll and to determine activity status. There is a lag in the availability of the payroll data and the MSRS model may be using payroll data that is no longer reflective of the retailer's current status and payroll levels of the individual establishments. For example, the current MSRS includes data for 2021 but payroll is based on 2018 annual data. This is especially problematic given the number of known store closures and disruptions caused by the COVID-19 pandemic. Research is planned to investigate an update to the frame with the most current payroll available and to develop a more consistent method of updating the frame to reflect changes closer to real time than the current methodology allows.

26.4.3 Estimation and Imputation

The state-level retail sales estimates in the MSRS data product are composite estimates that combine synthetic estimates and hybrid estimates. Figure 26.2 provides a graphical depiction of both how the composite estimates as well as how the synthetic and hybrid components of the composite estimator are calculated.[8]

26.4.3.1 Composite Estimator

For a given month and for each state and retail subsector NAICS code combination in-scope to MSRS and identified in Section 26.3, a compositing factor is calculated based on the proportion of the variance of the synthetic estimate to the total variance of both the synthetic and hybrid estimates. The compositing factor is based on the variance rather than on the mean squared errors because a reliable estimate of the bias of the estimators is not available. This composite factor is the proportion of the hybrid estimator used for the composite estimator and the composite factor minimizes the variance of the composite estimator. The complement to the composite factor is the proportion of the synthetic estimate used.

For a given retail subsector NAICS code, a final adjustment factor is applied to ensure the sum of the states add to the final published national MRTS estimate for that retail subsector NAICS code. Then for each state and retail subsector NAICS code combination, year-over-year percent changes are calculated for publication.

One limitation of composite estimation is that the state sales estimates in each retail subsector are calculated independently each month. The published year-over-year percentage changes may

---

8 For more detailed descriptions of the methodology and formulas used to calculate the estimates and associated variances, see the technical documentation available at https://www.census.gov/retail/mrts/www/statedata/msrs_technical_documentation.pdf.

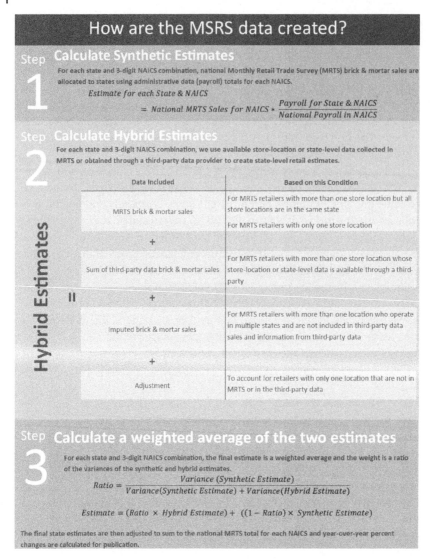

Figure 26.2 Overview of MSRS methodology. Source: MSRS Technical Documentation. Available at https://www.census.gov/retail/mrts/www/statedata/msrs_technical_documentation.pdf.

exhibit more variation if the coverage changes or if the portion of the composite estimator coming from the hybrid model changes between the years.

26.4.3.2 Synthetic Estimator

The synthetic estimator uses administrative annual payroll and MRTS national level estimates to estimate state level sales. For a given month, for each state and retail subsector NAICS code combination, national MRTS sales are allocated to each state using administrative data (payroll) totals. This is done by creating a ratio of payroll for all establishments on the frame in a given state and retail subsector NAICS code and dividing by all establishments in that retail subsector NAICS code. The resulting ratio can then be applied to the national MRTS total for the retail subsector NAICS code to get that month's estimate for each state retail subsector NAICS code combination.

This synthetic estimator provides computationally simple state-level estimates of monthly retail sales within an industry that add exactly to the survey total. However, it has the following limitations:

- The synthetic estimator requires very strong assumptions about the relationship between payroll (annual) and monthly sales for all states.
- The synthetic estimator ensures that year-to-year change estimates for each state are equivalent to the corresponding industry total estimates.
- The synthetic estimator fails to capture regional or state seasonal patterns; and
- The reliability of the synthetic estimator is dependent on the MRTS sample design and response. Recall that the MRTS sample was not designed on geography.

26.4.3.3 Hybrid Estimator

The hybrid estimator uses directly collected data identified in Section 26.4.1. For a given month and for each state and retail subsector NAICS code combination, the directly collected data from the MRTS (that meets the requirements specified in Section 26.4.1), the store-level, and aggregated data from third-party data sources are combined with imputed estimates for all remaining multiunit establishments on the frame. An industry-level adjustment factor is applied to ensure the state-level estimates add to the MRTS national estimate. This adjustment factor is based both on the MRTS national estimate. The directly usable data from MRTS and the third-party data as well as on the proportion of imputed multiunit establishments that fall in each state are removed from the adjustment factor. The adjustment accounts for establishments that are not eligible for imputation; these ineligible locations include single unit establishments, MRTS sampling units that did not match to the frame, and births of new retail firms that do not have business register payroll data.

The imputation models used to impute multiunit establishments are a Bayesian formulation of a linear mixed model that uses regression and random effects parameters to predict monthly retail sales given administrative payroll, state, and NAICS code. Multiple imputations from the predictive posterior distribution estimate the missing MU establishment data. Model parameters are estimated using MU establishment data based on reported MRTS data or third-party data provided at store level.

The hybrid estimator has several advantages in terms of statistical properties over the synthetic estimator presented. Because it maximizes use of auxiliary and directly collected data, it could yield theoretically unbiased estimates if data for of all of the retail trade establishments in the industry and state were available. As additional auxiliary or directly collected data are available and are incorporated, the accuracy and precision will improve. Variance can also be reduced by improving the imputation models. However, the estimator does have the following disadvantages:

- The hybrid estimator assumes there is no measurement error from auxiliary and directly collected data.
- The hybrid estimator is a poor estimator for the single unit component, as single units are imputed for indirectly through the national industry-level ratio adjustment. The overall effect of this poor imputation is minimized when third-party data total is close to corresponding MRTS industry total. The hybrid estimator can be extremely variable.[9]

---

9 This variability can be caused by a variety of things including but not limited to state and NAICS random effects and how much usable data is available in each state.

26.4.4 Quality Metrics

The MSRS data product is designated as an experimental data product by the Census Bureau. This means that the data may not meet all of quality metrics that official statistical data products are subjected to. To convey to data users that this is an experimental product and allow data users to make their own assessment of the data quality, we provide two quality metrics in each MSRS publication. First, we provide the standard errors for each month, state, and retail subsector combination. Among others, these standard errors capture the effect of sampling errors and non-response errors (of the hybrid estimate) and imputation errors (of both the hybrid and synthetic estimate). Second, we provide a coverage metric that provides an indication of how much directly collected data either from MRTS or from a third party is included in the estimates. As mentioned in Section 26.4.3.3, the quality of the MSRS model improves with better coverage.

26.5   Use of Alternative Data Sources in MSRS

In the methodology section, the use of third-party data is highlighted as a critical input to the hybrid estimator. Alternative data sources are not only critical to the creation of the MSRS estimates but also to the validation of the MSRS estimates. This section summarizes the alternative data sources that are currently being used in the MSRS estimation and in the MSRS validation work.

26.5.1   Input to MSRS Model

At this time, we currently use one third-party data source – data from NPD – for the MSRS estimates; however, this one NPD source provides two different types of datasets that we use in the MSRS estimation and imputation processes.

While the data from NPD mentioned in Section 26.2 did not prove useful as the singular source for creating the retail sales estimates by state, other NPD data have been useful in other ways. In 2019, the Census Bureau began using retailer data from NPD to assist with nonresponse in the MRTS (US Census Bureau 2019). When these NPD data are summed up across product types and establishments by retailers, they often tightly align with data reported by the retailers to the MRTS and the Economic Census (Hutchinson 2020). The data are used in MRTS for retailers who do not report to the survey by reporting deadlines and are also used to validate data reported to the survey by other retailers.

These NPD data are provided to the Census Bureau at both the national-level and the store-level. The store-level NPD datasets include a postal code that allows for the assignment of state-level geographies. The store-level NPD datasets also include a store number variable that corresponds to the store number often provided by retailers during the Economic Census and the Census Bureau's Company Organization Survey and can be found in the BR. These two features – the state-level geography and the store number – along with sales at the individual establishment make this data valuable to the MSRS composite estimator for imputation and estimation purposes.

While these store-level data are the ideal input to the MSRS model, they are also harder to obtain for a variety of reasons. The process the Census Bureau must follow to obtain the store-level data depends upon retailers' willingness to allow NPD to share sales data with the Census Bureau. As part of the effort to use the NPD data to assist with MRTS nonresponse mentioned earlier, NPD provided the Census Bureau with the universe of retailers that NPD has data for. From that, the Census Bureau provided NPD a list of retailers whose data would be useful and asked NPD to seek approval from the retailers.[10] Retailers must agree to allow NPD to share the data with the Census Bureau and it can be difficult for NPD to obtain that permission; only a small number of retailers granted NPD the approval. Those that declined cited a variety of reasons including legal and privacy concerns for not allowing NPD to share their data with the Census Bureau (Hutchinson 2020). These granular data can also be expensive as recruiting retailers to share these data and creating the datasets for the Census Bureau requires substantial upfront costs for NPD.

The store-level data were reviewed before being used as an input to the MSRS data product. Before the store-level data were used in the MRTS for nonresponse and validation purposes, the data were reviewed and quality was assessed using visual, statistical, and regression analysis (Hutchinson 2020). Store-level data have the advantage of allowing direct comparison to the data retailers report to the monthly and annual retail surveys as well as the Economic Census. In general, the NPD data often have a tight alignment to the data retailers report to the MRTS. This holds for the subset of retailers whose store-level data is used in the MSRS.[11] Figure 26.3 is a plot of the year-over-year percentage changes for the retailers with NPD data used in MSRS. The solid line is the year-over-year percentages in the NPD data; the dash representing the year-over-year percentage in the MRTS data.

During the COVID-19 pandemic, the store-level data that Census received each month presented a variety of challenges. Shutdown orders impacted many retailers for which we have store-level data. While store sales of zero sales were expected in the month of April 2020 and even into May 2020, it became difficult to differentiate permanent store closures from temporary,

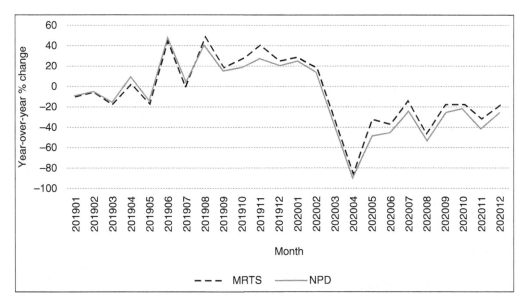

Figure 26.3 Year-over-year percentage changes in NPD and MRTS data for the retailers with NPD data used in MSRS. Source: January 2019–December 2020 MRTS data and NPD data.

---

10 Both to uphold the confidentiality and privacy laws that guide Census Bureau activities and also to facilitate productive work with specific retailers, a small number of NPD staff working on this project completed background investigations and were granted Special Sworn Status. With this Status, NPD staff are sworn to uphold the data stewardship practices and confidentiality laws put in place by United States Codes 13 and 26 for their lifetimes.
11 Some retailers only provide national-level retail sales data to NPD and had no store-level data that could be used in MSRS.

pandemic-related store closures. In the MSRS model, temporary, pandemic store closures with zero sales would be included in the imputation model, whereas permanent store closures would not. In real time, it was impossible to make this permanent versus temporary closure determination; thus, we decided to treat the closures as temporary through the end of 2020 when we would review all of the locations that still have zero sales. Any changes from temporary to permanent were reflected in the recent annual update of the data published in June 2021.

Another pandemic-related issue was several establishments that were likely closed reported negative sales. Whether these locations were accepting returns or other retail operations that resulted in negative sales is unknown; one drawback of using third-party data is we do not have a direct means of reaching out to the retailer with questions about the NPD data. For the purposes of the MSRS estimation and imputation, any retail establishment with negative sales was set to zero.

E-commerce sales were another challenge in the store-level data. The COVID-19 pandemic saw a large shift to shoppers making purchases online and either having purchases shipped to their homes or picked up at an establishment, also known "buy online, pick up in store" (Chodbury 2020). The retail industry has no standard reporting practices for whether "buy online, pick up in store" purchases should be tabulated as brick-and-mortar sales or as e-commerce sales. Some retailers will credit the sale to the establishment where the purchased was picked up and other retailers will credit the sales to their e-commerce sales and this allocation decision may change over time. This is an e-commerce measurement issue in general but during the retail store closures of the COVID-19 pandemic, we speculate that some retailers may have modified their accounting practices to have for "buy online, pick up in store" sales to count as brick-and-mortar sales. There is no way to determine this in the NPD data so we had no way to research, correct, or control for this; we do believe that this may have impacted the NPD data included in the MSRS estimates. It is also important to note that retailers may account for e-commerce sales differently in third-party data they give to companies like NPD than they do when they report to Census Bureau surveys.

One way to overcome the obstacle of obtaining retailers' consent to share their individual establishment data through a third-party is to have the third-party aggregate the sales data for retailers in similar NAICS codes by state. This aggregation ensures the privacy of any one retailer's data but still captures valuable state-level sales information.

From a list of all retailers that provide brick-and-mortar sales data to NPD, we provided lists of retailers by retail subsector NAICS code groupings. NPD researched each list of retailers to determine any disclosure issues in the aggregation; these disclosures issues were based upon NPD's internal data privacy rules. One example of a disclosure issue would be if within a three-digit NAICS code, a state only had data for one retailer on the list. By providing us with the data, NPD would be disclosing that retailer's sales; thus, NPD could not provide that state's data. This issue is common when selecting retailers who only operate establishments in certain regions of the country. To overcome these types of disclosure issues, two approaches were taken. The first approach was that data for that state and three-digit NAICS code combination were suppressed in the NPD-provided dataset. The second approach was adding retailers to the groupings that were not initially selected, targeting the selection of retailers who operated in the states where more retailer coverage was needed. The number of states covered in each retail grouping varies but ranges between 22 states and 49 states for the current groupings.[12]

---

12 NPD does not have data for retail establishments that operate in Alaska and Hawaii.

Before the aggregated groupings data could be included in the MSRS model, we needed to validate the data in the groupings. Because the MRTS collects data at the national level for retailers, we did not have an internal data source to check the state-level data in aggregated groupings against. Instead, we compared the aggregated groupings of the retailers at the national level against the aggregated national data for the same groupings of retailers in the MRTS. Figure 26.4 shows plots of this comparison for Clothing and Clothing Accessories Stores (NAICS 448), Sporting Goods, Hobby, Musical Instrument, and Book Stores (NAICS 451), and General Merchandise Store (NAICS 452).

We note there are some differences in the NPD and MRTS data shown in Figure 26.4, especially after the COVID-19 pandemic began. We attribute these differences to the pandemic-related challenges of measuring retail discussed earlier in this section. Overall, we find the state-level retail data from NPD to be highly correlated with MRTS (Table 26.1) and feel they are an excellent input to the MSRS model.

Each month, NPD provides a dataset for each retail subsector NAICS code grouping that includes the aggregated sales figures by states for the agreed-upon list of retailers. NPD also provides a list of which retailers are included in each grouping each month. During the early months of the COVID-19 pandemic, some retailers closed all establishments due to state mandated shutdowns, and there were no data for these retailers included in the aggregated groupings for some months. The retailers not in the data need to be accounted for in the model in another manner.

This aggregated data approach provided us with state-level sales data for retailers that we would not be able to have state-level data for through either MRTS or through the micro store-level data obtained from NPD. Additionally, the aggregated grouping data are less expensive than the store-level data. However, there are risks to the aggregated groupings as well. Retailers can stop providing data to NPD at any point. In some of the NPD retail subsector NAICS code aggregate groupings, a retailer dropping out may create disclosure issues that would prevent NPD from being able to share that grouping going forward. And while not as expensive as store-level data for an individual retailer, the aggregated groupings are purchased and subject to budget constraints.

26.5.2 Validation

Validating the state-level data output from the model was a critical step before the publication of the MSRS data. Previous state-level monthly retail sales work done at the Census Bureau found that validating any new state retail sales estimates was difficult as there were not enough external sources to validate against (Dumbacher et al. 2019). During the creation of MSRS, we were able to locate some external sources from public and private data sources that had useful state-level retail sales information for comparison. We compare the MSRS data to these sources each month but we also continue to seek other external data sources for validation but the comparisons detailed below provided insight into the precision of the MSRS data.

State revenue and taxation offices maintain records on sales tax collections for the state, including retail sales tax collection. Some states will also publish retail sales tax collections for the state by NAICS codes. While these retail sales tax collection levels will not align to retail sales levels, we can calculate the year-over-year percentage change of the retail sales tax collection data. These year-over-year percentage changes can be used to validate the MSRS data as changes in retail sales tax collection should move in a similar manner to retail sales themselves.

There do not appear to be standard guidelines for the frequency (e.g. monthly, quarterly, and annually) and level of industry detail provided on the state retail sales tax collection reports.

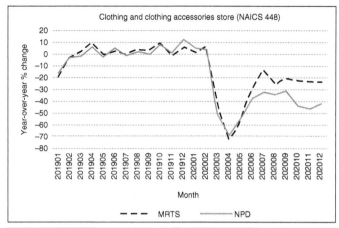

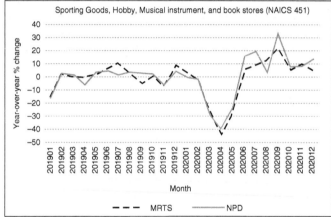

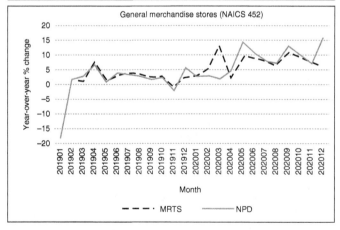

Figure 26.4 January 2019–December 2020 year-over-year percentage changes of the state-level retailers NPD data and MRTS data for NAICS 448, 451, and 452. Source: January 2019–December 2020 MRTS and NPD data.

Table 26.1 Pearson correlation coefficients for state-level retailers NPD data and MRTS data.

NAICS code	Description	Correlation coefficient
NAICS 441	Motor vehicle and parts dealers	0.845
NAICS 443	Electronics and Appliance Stores	0.925
NAICS 446	Health and Personal Care Stores	0.934
NAICS 448	Clothing and Clothing Accessories Stores	0.943
NAICS 451	Sporting Goods, Hobby, Musical Instrument, and Book Stores	0.991
NAICS 452	General Merchandise Stores	0.943
NAICS 453	Miscellaneous Store Retailers	0.949

Source: January 2019–December 2020 MRTS and NPD data.

Additionally, it does not appear that states are obligated to make these data publicly available on a structured schedule. Five states provide monthly retail sales at NAICS code levels comparable to the MSRS on their state revenue and tax department pages: Kansas,[13] Mississippi,[14] Nevada,[15] Oklahoma,[16] and Utah.[17,18] We calculated year-over-year percentage changes using the retail data by NAICS codes for these five states and compared to the year-over-year percentage chances in the MSRS. It is important to note that each state uses its own methodology to assign NAICS codes to the retailers included in its sales tax data. This assignment may vary from Census Bureau NAICS code assignments and can cause variability in the data. Figure 26.5 shows plots of the comparison between the MSRS state year-over-year percentage changes to the year-over-year percentage changes for retail sales tax data published by the states of Kansas, Mississippi, Nevada, Oklahoma, and Utah. State revenue data can be noisy (and sometimes negative) so we take that into account while reviewing these data.

Private companies have long produced state-level retail sales data products for customers and clients. Payment processors—including the aforementioned Fiserv—and credit card companies like MasterCard and VISA use the proprietary retail sales data they have to create for state-level retail sales data and estimates. Products created using third-party data sources are often available for purchase and are not a public good. While we do not have access to all of these third-party data sources, we do have access to some state-level retail sales data created by private firms with access to credit card transaction data. We conduct comparisons to this data each month, but assumptions made in the proprietary methodology used in the calculations for each of these data products can make it difficult to draw meaningful conclusions. Additionally, many of these data products include benchmarks to Census Bureau retail data which can cause our comparisons to be circular in nature.

---

13 Kansas data available at Kansas Department of Revenue https://www.ksrevenue.org/prsalesreports.html.

14 Mississippi data available at Sales Statewide by Industry Code (https://www.dor.ms.gov/statistics/sales-statewide-by-industry-code).

15 Nevada data available at Monthly Taxable Sales Statistics (https://tax.nv.gov/Publications/Monthly_Taxable_Sales_Statistics/).

16 Oklahoma data available at Oklahoma Tax Commission (https://oklahoma.gov/tax/reporting-resources/reports.html).

17 Utah data available at Sales Tax Statistics (https://tax.utah.gov/econstats/sales).

18 We are working with Census Bureau public sector survey staff to explore ways to obtain more monthly state-level tax data from other states.

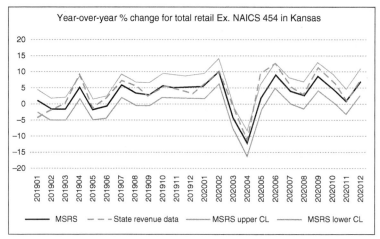

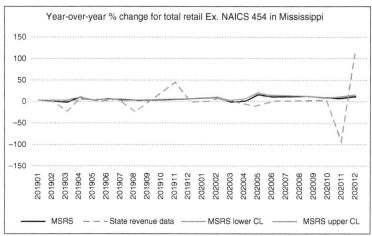

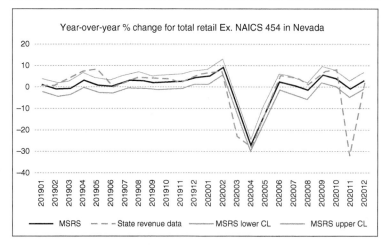

Figure 26.5 Comparison of the year-over-year percentage changes in Total Retail Sales Excluding Nonstore Retailers (NAICS 454) MSRS data and in retail sales data published by the states of Kansas, Mississippi, Nevada, Oklahoma, and Utah. Source: January 2019–December 2020 MSRS and State Revenue data from Kansas, Mississippi, Nevada, Oklahoma, and Utah.

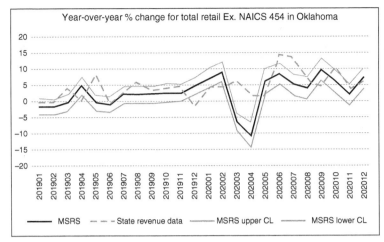

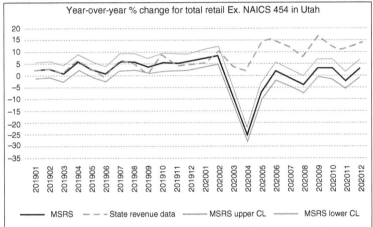

Figure 26.5 (*Continued*)

26.6 Conclusion

Using a composite estimator to create the state-level estimates was a critical innovation in economic data products. The use of alternative data sources and administrative data was especially important to the development of the MSRS, allowing it to be created without requiring a new data collection.

The MSRS data product is a key milestone in the Census Bureau's mission to provide more timely data at more granular geographies to data users. These types of data were even more important and useful during the COVID-19 pandemic when more granular data were critical to understanding impacts on more local economies. Using a composite estimator to create the state-level estimates was a critical innovation in economic data products. The use of alternative data sources and administrative data was especially important to the development of the MSRS, allowing it to be created without requiring a new data collection. Alternative data sources from private and public sources also allowed us to validate the MSRS data, an important step in the process of introducing a data product. Introducing a new data product during the pandemic posed some measurement challenges including identifying permanent and temporary store closures.

However, there is much work that remains to be done on the MSRS. First, we need to improve the quality of the estimates to allow us to publish state-level retail sales levels in addition to the year-over-year percentage changes currently being published. Since the first publication of the MSRS, data users have let us know that levels are critical to the usefulness of this data. The key to publishing levels is incorporating more store-location or state-level data that is directly collected either from a survey or third-party data; doing so is critical to improving the quality of the data. We are working to determine useful third-party data sets for inclusion to this effort. We would also like to publish nonstore retailer sales by state. Nonstore retailers are predominantly e-commerce operations and with the growing shift to online shopping, there is tremendous interest from our data users for these sales data.[19] The best method and data source needed to attribute e-commerce sales to state geographies is a bigger challenge that we still need to work through. Last, there may be applications of this MSRS methodology to other trade areas including the services sector.

Disclaimer

Any views expressed are those of the author and not necessarily those of the US Census Bureau. Census Bureau has reviewed Monthly State Retail Sales product for unauthorized disclosure of confidential information and has approved the disclosure avoidance practices applied. (Approval ID: CBDRB-FY21-ESMD002-033).

References

Bird, D., Breton, R., Payne, C., and Restieaux, A. (2014). Initial Report on Experiences with Scanner Data in ONS. https://www.ons.gov.uk/ons/guide-method/user-guidance/prices/cpi-and-rpi/initial-report-on-experiences-with-scanner-data-in-ons.pdf (accessed 21 August 2018).

Chodbury, S.R. (2020). More people are doing their holiday shopping online and this trend is here to stay. CNBC, December 14, 2020. Coronavirus pandemic has pushed shoppers to e-commerce sites (https://www.cnbc.com/2020/12/15/coronavirus-pandemic-has-pushed-shoppers-to-e-commerce-sites.html) (accessed 22 March 2021).

Desalvo, B., Limehouse, F., and Klimek, S. (2016) Documenting the Business Register and Related Economic Business Data. United States Census Bureau Center for Economic Studies Working Paper 16–17. March 2016. https://www2.census.gov/ces/wp/2016/CES-WP-16-17.pdf.

Dumbacher, B., Morris, D.S., and Hogue, C. (2019). Using electronic transaction data to add geographic granularity to official estimates of retail sales. *J Big Data* 6: 80. https://doi.org/10.1186/s40537-019-0242-z.

Dunn, A.C. and Gholizadeh, M. (2020). The Geography of Consumption and Local Economic Shocks: The Case of the Great Recession. United States Bureau of Economic Analysis Working Paper Series, WP2020-9. October 2020. The Geography of Consumption and Local Economic Shocks: The Case of the Great Recession. https://www.bea.gov/index.php/system/files/papers/bea-wp2020-9.pdf (bea .gov).

---

19 In addition to online and electronic shopping, the nonstore retailer subsector also includes establishments in this subsector include mail-order houses, vending machine operators, fuel dealers, home delivery sales, door-to-door sales, non-food street vendors, and direct-selling operations including but not limited to Christmas trees, office coffee supplies, and bottled water providers (US Census Bureau 2021).

Hutchinson, R. (2020). Investigating alternative data sources to reduce respondent burden in United States Census Bureau retail economic data products. In: *Big Data Meets Survey Science: A Collection of Innovative Methods* (ed. C.A. Hill, P.P. Biemer, T.D. Buskirk, L. Japec, A. Kirchner, S. Kolenikov, and L.E. Lyberg). Wiley.

Richter, F. (2020). Retailers Face Mass Extinction in Pandemic Fallout. Statista, August, 24, 2020. Chart: Retailers Face Mass Extinction in Pandemic Fallout | Statista on March 21, 2021. https://www.statista.com/chart/22672/number-of-retail-store-closures-in-the-united-states/.

US Census Bureau (2015). External report on the feasibility of using NPD data to supplement retail trade data. Internal Census Bureau Working Paper.

US Census Bureau (2019). U.S. Census Bureau Streamlines Reporting for Retailers U.S. Census Bureau Streamlines Reporting for Retailers. https://www.census.gov/newsroom/press-releases/2019/retailers.html (accessed 3 March 2021).

US Census Bureau (2021). North American Industry Classification System (NAICS) website. North American Industry Classification System (NAICS) U.S. Census Bureau. https://www.census.gov/naics/.

US Office of Management and Budget (2017). North American Industry Classification System: United States 2017. https://www.census.gov/naics/reference_files_tools/2017_NAICS_Manual.pdf.

Van Delden, A., Lorenc, B., Struijs, P., and Zhang, L.-C. (2018). Letter to the Editor. On statistical unit errors in business statistics. *Journal of Official Statistics* 34 (2): 1–9.

Wahba, P. (2020). It may be a while before many of America's stores open again as coronavirus crisis worsens. Fortune Magazine, March 26, 2020. Coronavirus store closings extended to April, May by many retail chains. When will they open? | Fortune on March 16, 2021. https://fortune.com/2020/03/26/coronavirus-stores-closed-extended-april-may-us-retail/.

Section 6

Topics in Sampling and Estimation

27

Introduction to Sampling and Estimation for Business Surveys

Paul A. Smith[1] and Wesley Yung[2]

[1] *S3RI & Department of Social Statistics & Demography, University of Southampton, Southampton, United Kingdom*
[2] *Statistics Canada, Ottawa, Canada*

27.1 Introduction

A lot has happened in the world of establishment statistics in the more than 25 years since the first International Conference on Establishment Surveys (ICES-I) and the seminal Business Survey Methods (BSM) book (Cox et al. 1995). Three out of the six sections of BSM covered topics of registers, sampling, and estimation, so we cannot hope to match that coverage in a single chapter. Fortunately, other chapters in this book cover some of the specific topics in detail. Here we aim to reflect the main methodologies for business surveys from the construction and use of business registers through designing and selecting samples to estimation to produce statistical outputs. We focus on the areas where there have been developments since BSM, providing enough of the general framework to set these in context.

One of those developments has been a way to describe survey processes, in the Generic Statistical Business Process Model (GSBPM; UNECE 2019). Figure 27.1 shows the top two levels of the GSBPM structure; in this chapter we focus on 2.4 (Design frame and sample), 4.1 (Create frame and select sample), 5.6 (Calculate weights), and 5.7 (Calculate aggregates). These areas contain the "traditional" elements of surveys where the use of sampling theory has provided the underpinning for techniques in practical survey-taking. This has been seen most obviously in design-based (randomization) inference, a strong preference for unbiased or asymptotically unbiased estimators in all instances, and therefore a focus on quality measured through sampling variances. However, many of the developments since ICES-I have been in areas away from this tradition – in Section 27.3, we review numerical approaches to stratification and allocation, and consider cut-off sampling which generally relies on models. We briefly mention other developments in sampling. Before this we give a summary of the operation of a statistical business register (Section 27.2). Section 27.4 presents an overview of estimation approaches, focusing on calibration estimation and with a review of developments in the treatment of outliers in this framework. Section 27.5 gives some examples of situations where model-based approaches are being used in establishment statistics.

27.2 Statistical Business Registers

Statistical Business Registers (SBR) play an essential role in the production of economic statistics. Traditionally, SBRs have been the source for sampling frames for economic surveys, but more

Advances in Business Statistics, Methods and Data Collection. Edited by Ger Snijkers, Mojca Bavdaž, Stefan Bender, Jacqui Jones, Steve MacFeely, Joseph W. Sakshaug, Katherine J. Thompson, and Arnout van Delden.

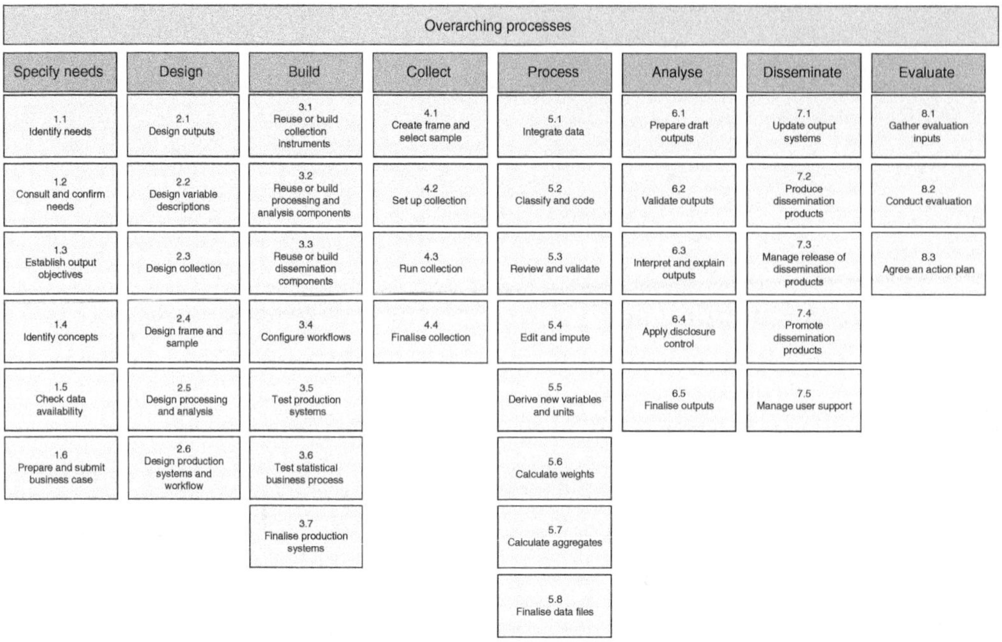

Figure 27.1 Levels 1 and 2 of the Generic Statistical Business Process Model (UNECE 2019). Source: UNECE (2019)/CC BY 4.0.

recently, they are also becoming the backbone for the integration of secondary data into economic statistics programs. In addition, they can be a source of economic statistics in their own right, for example for statistics on business demography. However, in this chapter, we will primarily restrict ourselves to their function as a source of frames for economic surveys and only mention a few outputs that have been produced from Business Registers. Readers interested in additional uses of SBRs are referred to UNECE (2015).

A statistical business register is a "regularly updated, structured database of economic units in a territorial area, maintained by a National Statistical Organization and used for statistical purposes" (UNECE 2015). Key terms in the definition include "regularly updated" as the value of an SBR as a source for survey frames, and other outputs, quickly diminishes if changes in the population of businesses are not captured. For survey results to be relevant, the survey frame must cover the entire population of interest or the results will be biased. A "structured database" is important to allow the representation of the relationships between the different economic units within a business. The concept of "economic unit" and the linkages among them are important for economic surveys as certain information is available only from certain types of units. The definitions of the different economic units will be discussed further in this chapter. SBRs are typically "maintained by a National Statistical Organization" (NSO) as access to administrative data required to build and maintain them is usually only available to NSOs. These data typically comprise those collected by national tax agencies.

Ideally, an SBR should cover all economic units involved in economic production within a territorial area. The term "economic production" is "a process carried out under the control and responsibility of an institutional unit that uses labor, capital, goods and services to produce outputs of goods and services" (2008 System of National Accounts (SNA), European Commission et al. 2009). Economic units are broken down into different types such as statistical units, collection or reporting units, and analysis units. Statistical units are those about which information is sought and for which statistics are compiled. Collection or reporting units are those where the required information can be obtained and analysis units are those which are constructed for particular interpretation or analysis (Smith 2013). In general, we need a units model, a model for the way that different units are defined and relate to each other (Colledge 1995).

The main statistical units used internationally are the following:

- Establishments or local kind-of-activity units
- Enterprises
- Enterprise groups.

According to the 2008 SNA, an enterprise is the "level of the statistical unit at which all information relating to transactions, including financial and balance sheet accounts, are maintained and from which international transactions, an international financial position, consolidated financial position and net worth can be derived." An establishment is "an enterprise or part of an enterprise, that is situated in a single location and in which only a single production activity is carried out or in which the principle production activity accounts for most of the value added" (European Commission et al. 2009). Finally, an enterprise group is a group of enterprises under the same ownership.

Based on these definitions, it is clear that an enterprise group may consist of multiple enterprises, which in turn can consist of multiple establishments, each of which could be carrying out economic production in different geographical areas and/or producing different outputs. In order to properly measure economic activity as required by the SNA, it is important to represent all of these units, and the relationships among them, on an SBR. Figure 27.2 illustrates a basic business structure that might be encountered in real life.

SBRs are typically constructed using administrative data from national taxation agencies as businesses are required to register for tax purposes. Once constructed, SBRs are commonly maintained using additional administrative data, feedback from survey collection and profiling. Profiling is the

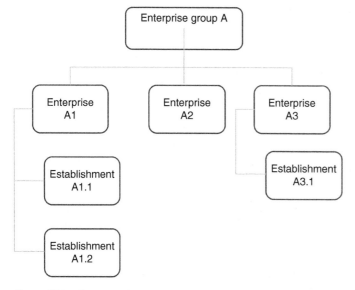

Figure 27.2 Example of a basic business structure showing the different types of units. Redrawn from Smith (2013, Figure 5.1).

practice of obtaining information about an enterprise to ensure that its structure on the SBR is up-to-date; it is usually done in collaboration with the enterprise. Profiling is especially important for enterprises with very complex structures which span multiple production outputs and geographical regions. For the largest, most important enterprises, profiling must be done in cooperation with the business in order to ensure that all of the relationships between the different statistical units are correct. While some mergers, acquisitions, and divestitures can be identified through administrative sources, profiling is another important source to identify these events. This approach has been extended to profiling of multinational enterprises in the Eurogroups Register compiled by Eurostat (Eurostat 2021), which presents a better view of the activity of these important businesses. The choice of unit for any particular study or analysis can have an impact on the results obtained, and this sensitivity to the unit definition has become known as "the unit problem" – see van Delden et al. (2018) and Lorenc et al. (2018) for more information.

Up to now, the discussion has been centered on ensuring that the SBR covers all economic activity. In order for the SBR to be used for survey frames, certain characteristics for each unit are required. First and foremost, every unit on the SBR must have a unique identifier. This identifier should also be used throughout the economic statistics program of the NSO to facilitate coherence across the program. Going one step further, many countries assign a unique identifier which can be used by all government departments with which the business may interact. The legal name and address for the business should also be on the SBR. This information is useful for linking businesses to the SBR from sources of data which do not have the unique identifier, for example lists of members from business associations. By being able to link to a unit on the SBR, the business' unique identifier can be used to further link that business to all parts of the economic statistics program. In this context, the SBR plays the role of a backbone to integrate many different data sources. The status of the units, that is whether they are active or inactive, is also important to allow surveys to target the units which are trading at the time of the survey, thus ensuring that collection efforts are not expended on inactive businesses. Information on seasonal businesses is also useful for surveys to be able to target the correct population of businesses.

Business populations are known to be highly skewed with a small number of businesses accounting for a large portion of the economic activity (e.g. Sigman and Monsour 1995, p. 133). To ensure efficient survey estimates, stratified sampling is commonly used in economic surveys. Typical variables used for stratification include geography, industry, and some measure of size. According to the 2008 SNA, "an industry consists of a group of establishments engaged in the same or similar kinds of activity" (European Commission et al. 2009, p. 87). The United Nations has developed the International Standard Industrial Classification (ISIC) of all Economic Activities, Revision 4 (United Nations 2008), which provides a global high-level classification. There are regional variants providing more detailed breakdowns consistent with ISIC, such as the North American Industrial Classification System (NAICS) (Statistics Canada 2018) and the Nomenclature statistique des Activités économiques dans la Communauté Européenne (NACE) (Eurostat 2008). Given the importance of the industrial dimension in the SNA, surveys typically target specific industries and are thus stratified by them. Thus, all units on an SBR must be classified into an industry according to the standard classification being used. When complex enterprises have activities in different industries, they are commonly classified to the industry from which the majority of their revenue is generated. This is known as the dominance rule.

In addition to industry stratification, due to the skewed populations, business survey samples are commonly stratified by size, and therefore SBRs should contain information such as revenue and the number of employees for all units, as these are commonly used for stratification purposes. Stratifying a survey frame by size can lead to more precise estimates or smaller sample sizes for a fixed level of precision in comparison to nonstratified sample designs – see Section 27.3.1.

In the time since ICES-I, there has been substantial development of businesses surveys targeting certain activities, for example research and development, so an SBR should be capable of storing information specific to a particular survey or activity. At Statistics Canada, the SBR contains survey-specific fields for just this purpose. These fields should be maintained by subject matter experts. Other activities that might be of interest include, but are not limited to, use of clean technology, production of a particular agricultural product and sale and purchase of environmental protection items. Surveys which are targeting particular activities can then use these fields as stratification variables to increase efficiency, although there is usually a need for some sampling of businesses without this identifier to estimate activity where it has not yet been identified on the frame.

With the wealth of information contained in an SBR, it makes sense to produce outputs from it. At Statistics Canada, the SBR is used to produce the Canadian Business Counts (Statistics Canada 2020a) product twice a year. This product consists of counts of enterprises within industries and geographical regions for both employer and nonemployer businesses. This is an example of business demographics which many NSOs produce. In addition to producing direct outputs, SBRs play an integral role in many additional business demographic outputs. For instance, Statistics Canada uses their SBR as the backbone to link 12 administrative data sources with data from 14 surveys to create an environment to support longitudinal and cross-sectional analysis of Canadian businesses. The environment is called the Linkable File Environment (Statistics Canada 2020b) and allows the creation of research datasets containing the variable of interest from the appropriate linkable files. The Linkable File Environment leverages the SBR and its unique identifier to define the population of interest, and to follow a unit through time allowing a longitudinal aspect. Without the SBR, the quality of the linkages and resulting research datasets would be much less. Additionally, SBR information has been combined with additional administrative or survey data to produce outputs on current topics such as entrepreneurship (BLS 2020), special populations (e.g. Jafri and Alasia 2019), and the impact that the COVID 19 pandemic has had on businesses (Lafrance-Cooke et al. 2020).

27.3 Sampling

We have already noted that establishment surveys are characterized by skewed populations, with a few large units having a disproportionate contribution to statistics, and a large number of smaller units. They also typically have good auxiliary data, derived from a business register (or an equivalent structured list covering other types of establishments), which can be used for efficient sampling and estimation. These two features are behind many of the differences in the methods used in establishment surveys compared with social surveys (Cox and Chinnappa 1995, Rivière 2002). The skewed population generally means that sampling has an important effect on estimates, and therefore design-based methods have been strongly preferred as a basis for objective statistics within NSOs.

Stratified designs in establishment populations typically generate some strata where all the units in the population are selected – completely enumerated (CE), certainty, or take-all strata. The numerical approaches described in Section 27.3.1 produce some CE strata as the optimal solutions and do not require special processing.

27.3.1 Stratified Sampling

The staple approach to sampling in skewed populations is stratification, and the underlying method was worked out long ago by Neyman (1934), but the challenges of applying the procedure in establishment surveys have led to a steady stream of research. Smith (2013) gives an overview of the procedures applied to business surveys. In fact, stratification can be used for a number of reasons (Lohr 2019, p. 74):

- to protect against selecting a poor sample by chance
- to ensure adequate sample sizes for subpopulations of interest; these subpopulations should generally form the strata
- for convenience or administrative costs purposes because of differences between parts of the population
- to produce estimates with better precision (or lower cost for the same precision).

While the last of these is often the driver, typically all of them influence a decision on a stratified design. There are four principal stages in designing a stratified sample: first, we need to decide which variables to use in a stratification; second, we have to work out how many strata to use; third, we have to define the boundaries of strata or substrata (when they are defined with continuous variables); and fourth, we must allocate the total sample among the strata. Traditional design processes are being challenged by numerical and machine learning approaches, which may combine some of these stages.

Deciding which variables to use as stratifiers is a neglected step, in part because the range of variables available (e.g. from a business register) might be quite restricted, or because there are standards associated with coordinated sampling (see Chapter 28) which limit the freedom to choose. The availability of alternative data sources (see Chapter 12), however, has made a wider range of variables available and increased the need for analysis at this step. We would want to develop models for one or a small number of the key outcome variables in a survey and to include the auxiliary variables that are their best predictors. Where the model fits well, stratification can be expected to have a very large impact in reducing the variance of the estimates relative to a simple random sample (SRS), and where it does not fit so well, the reduction in the variance will be smaller – but may still be a substantial improvement over SRS.

Parsimony is important, because we need the models to fit well over multiple time periods and datasets, but standard regression approaches may be inflexible, and tree-based approaches may uncover more complex relationships which are valuable in stratification. Fabrizi and Trivisano (2007) show that this only works in situations where there are enough pilot or previous data – 100 observations were too few, whereas 1000 was enough. Fabrizi and Trivisano (2007) also considered using flexible models to predict the outcome variable, and then designing with this predicted variable using the Dalenius–Hodges approach (Dalenius and Hodges 1957, 1959) which has been commonly used in business survey design. Benedetti et al. (2008) use a binary tree to partition a population (using many small strata called atoms which are taken to be indivisible) into strata and meet a range of constraints. Ballin and Barcaroli (2008) use a similar approach but with a different rule for the partitions.

Once we have decided which variables to use as stratifiers, we then need to determine the number of strata to use and their boundaries if they are defined on continuous variables. These stages often need to be done together, as the variance under a design with k strata can only be estimated if the boundaries are determined. So the design process is repeated for a small number of values of k and the number with the best trade-off of variance and number of strata is chosen (see, for example Smith 2013, Figure 5.3). As the number of strata increases, the sample size in each stratum becomes smaller, and the complexity of administering the survey becomes greater, so there is an incentive to keep the number of size strata relatively small.

Lavallée and Hidiroglou (1988) introduced an iterative approach to determine stratum boundaries to meet a target coefficient of variation (CV) under a specific allocation rule. They describe the approaches for power allocation and Neyman allocation, but the method can be extended to use other allocations. The Lavallée–Hidiroglou algorithm is widely used in Canada and the United States, but there are issues of convergence and the algorithm does not necessarily reach a global minimum, potentially getting trapped at local minima or a saddle point (Slanta and Krenzke 1996). Rivest (2002) extends this approach to the situation where the design (stratification) variable and survey (target) variable are different. A range of approximate methods is also available for determining the boundaries of strata on numeric variables, but Hidiroglou and Kozak (2018) advocate the use of numerical optimization approaches for stratification (and these, together with the standard approaches, are implemented in the `stratification` package in R (Baillargeon and Rivest 2009)), as these generally achieve smaller samples sizes for fixed variances, or equivalently smaller variances for a fixed sample size. The numeric approach of Kozak (2004) is both simple and effective, though the algorithm can get stuck in local minima. Hidiroglou and Kozak's principle could be extended to choosing the stratification giving the best estimated variance within each industry, by allowing the number of strata to vary by industry classification. The drive for standardization (often connected with sample coordination, see Chapter 28) has generally led National Statistical Organizations away from this approach, but there are potentially savings to be made.

Keskintürk and Er (2007) proposed a genetic algorithm to find the optimum stratification and allocation together for a single variable; a genetic algorithm is a simulation approach which evolves new candidate solutions at each step by "breeding" (combining parts of) the best solutions from the previous stage.

In practical survey situations, however, it is rare to be dealing with a single auxiliary variable, and rarer still to have a single outcome variable. Most surveys ask a range of questions, and structural business surveys may have hundreds of outcome variables; it is not practical to optimize over so many variables, and some key variables must again be chosen. Approximate solutions have included using principal components of the auxiliary variables, and using averages of sample sizes from allocations for different variables within a set of fixed strata. However, multivariate optimization is possible using numerical approaches. The tree-based approaches of Benedetti et al. (2008) and Ballin and Barcaroli (2008) are designed to deal with multivariate stratification and allocation. They rely on the Bethel–Chromy function (Bethel 1989, Barcaroli 2014), which is used to estimate the minimum sample size to achieve the variance constraints for a fixed stratification.

An alternative approach extends the genetic algorithm to deal with the optimization, again using the Bethel–Chromy function as the target of the optimization, with constraints on the total number of strata and the minimum sample size in each stratum (Ballin and Barcaroli 2008, 2013, O'Luing et al. 2018). This approach works with discrete-valued stratifiers, which requires some approximation by binning for continuous variables. These implementations require a starting number of strata, which can be a hard constraint, but they also include a parameter which allows the algorithm to explore larger numbers of strata at each step, up to a fixed maximum, if these improve the stratification as measured by the Bethel–Chromy function. The output is the stratification and allocation which achieves the constraints for the smallest sample size. This approach is implemented in the `SamplingStrata` package in R.

Lisic et al. (2018) use simulated annealing in the spirit of Kozak (2004), involving switching units between strata in the search for a better solution. In particular, they deal with continuous stratification variables, and their algorithm is suitable for optimum allocation of a fixed sample size with constraints on the coefficient of variation (rather than determining a smallest sample size meeting those constraints) – a situation quite common in establishment surveys where the sample size (and therefore cost) is fixed.

Many stratification algorithms produce optimal solutions on the stratification variables and rely on a strong correlation with the survey variables for this to be useful. Baillargeon and Rivest (2009) discuss how stratification can be done with anticipated moments, moments calculated under the sample design and a superpopulation model (a more coherent approach than that of Fabrizi and Trivisano (2007) mentioned above). When the superpopulation model is correctly specified, or suitably robust, then the outcome variables will (on average) meet their quality constraints. Lisic et al. (2018)'s approach also allows design with these anticipated moments.

27.3.2 Cut-off Sampling

The use of cut-off sampling, where a part of the population is not covered (and in establishment surveys this is often the smallest (micro-)businesses) has been known and used in establishment surveys for a long time (at least since Hansen et al. 1953, pp. 486–490), but there has been a surge in academic interest in the last decade. As Benedetti et al. (2010) say, "This strategy is employed so commonly in business surveys that its use is 'implicit' and 'uncritical', so that the inferential consequences of the restrictions caused to the archive by this procedure are mostly ignored." Yorgason et al. (2011) give an overview of uses in the US statistical system, some of which bear out this quote. Therefore, the development of some principled approaches to the design of cut-off samples is important.

Benedetti et al. (2010) adopt an approach very similar to that used in stratification in Section 27.3.1, using an iterative algorithm based on simulated annealing to allocate units to one of three strata – a completely enumerated stratum, a sampled stratum, and an excluded (take-none) stratum. The numerical approach allows them to deal with a cut-off type design based on multiple auxiliary variables (whereas the classical cut-off design is defined on a single auxiliary variable). They require good auxiliary information for the evaluation of the bias caused by excluding part of the population. There seems no particular reason why these strata should be connected (that is, form a single area within the space of the auxiliary variables), but in their example Benedetti et al. find that they are (Figure 27.3).

Haziza et al. (2010) focus on using models to reduce the bias caused by cut-off sampling, and use these in both balanced sampling and calibration approaches. Their general strategy is to use instrumental variables that are related to the probability of being cut off, leading to a "doubly robust" procedure which is unbiased if either the model for being in the cut-off or the model relating the response to auxiliary information are correctly specified. (However, using the perfect instrumental variable, defined as the one that determines whether a unit is cut off or not, does not work as it gives zero probability of inclusion to the cut-off units, and this value appears in the denominator). At the sampling stage, fewer variables are available, so an optimal strategy would be to use balanced sampling at this stage and then a further calibration in estimation.

Polanec et al. (2022, in press) adopt a different approach and seek to include the burden of responding in the optimization of the cut-off, through a cost–benefit trade-off. This opens up an alternative metric for sample optimization which accounts for costs as well as the contribution to quality.

27.3.3 Probability Proportional to Size Sampling

Sampling with Probability Proportional to Size (PPS) is another technique to deal with different unit sizes, but it is not widely applied in establishment surveys. It involves defining a probability

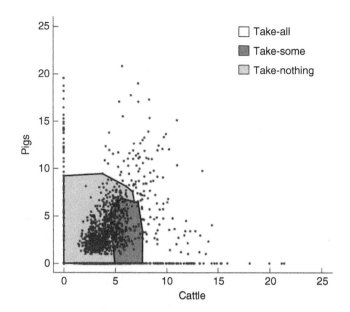

Figure 27.3 Example of a numerical partition of a farm population on two auxiliary variables (each axis shows the 4th root of the variable). Reproduced from Benedetti et al. (2010, Figure 5) by kind permission of the editors of the *Journal of Official Statistics.*

of selection for each unit in the population proportional to a chosen size measure, and then using a suitable procedure to realize a sample with approximately or exactly these selection probabilities. Poisson sampling can be used and has the advantage that Poisson samples are very easy to coordinate (see Chapter 28) and variance estimation is greatly simplified over PPS methods. However, Poisson samples have variable size, which potentially leads to larger estimation variances, and fixed size approaches are often preferred. The main procedure is systematic PPS, which is easily implemented and approximately respects the inclusion probabilities. The units are sorted in random order, and selection is done systematically on their size variables.

The main applications of PPS are in specialized surveys such as those which provide the input data for price indices. For example, the UK Consumer Prices Index (CPI) has five sampling stages, the first two of which use PPS (O'Neill et al. 2017, Box 8.1). The United States has probability selection at all stages, but only some of these utilize PPS (BLS 2015).

27.3.4 Indirect Sampling

There has been a long development of methods for sampling population units using a different but related unit for which there is better information or easier access. Much of this was pulled together and extended in Lavallée (2007) to present methods for sampling, and for estimation using the Generalized Weight Share Methods (GWSM). One of the main uses of indirect sampling is to survey hard to reach populations, and the availability of a business register and the information it provides has generally made this less of a challenge for business surveys. In recent times, however, indirect sampling has been used in France as a way to move from a sampling strategy based on legal units to outputs based on enterprises, as required for reporting in Europe. Details are given in Gros and Le Gleut (2018).

27.3.5 Balanced Sampling

Another big development in sampling since ICES-I is the availability of a practical method for selecting approximately balanced samples known as the cube method in the survey research methods literature (Deville and Tillé 2004). Balancing was already advocated as a protection against nonignorability in model-based sampling (Brewer 1995), and this approach is now made more practical. Balanced sampling can also be useful in cases where the number of domains and/or strata is large relative to the survey sample size, a kind of situation found often in small area estimation (see Section 27.5.1 and Chapter 30), and its use for designing business surveys with these kinds of objectives is proposed in Falorsi and Righi (2008), among others.

27.4 Estimation

With the availability of auxiliary information from registers and administrative data, calibration estimators are a natural choice for establishment surveys. Simple calibration estimates such as the ratio estimator are commonly used but nothing precludes the use of more complex estimators such as the generalized regression estimator. While the design-based approach is the most frequently used in establishment surveys, model-based and Bayesian estimation are becoming more popular in establishment surveys due to the availability of auxiliary data. Examples of some model-based estimation methods include small area estimation and time series models. Regardless of which estimator is chosen, establishment surveys must consider methods for dealing with outlying and unusual observations with large effects on estimates, and the ways in which bias and variance are traded off in these estimates.

27.4.1 Model-assisted and Calibration Estimation

The main goal of any survey is to produce estimates of parameters of the population of interest. In economic surveys, this usually means the population of all businesses in the territory or industry of interest. If a census of businesses is available (e.g. Parker 2014, National Bureau of Statistics of China 2019), one would simply sum up the information collected, assuming that all units report. However, censuses are extremely expensive and time consuming so most National Statistics Offices use sample surveys where a sample of units is selected from the population of interest. However, with the increased availability of administrative data, NSOs are investigating methods other than sample surveys – see Chapter 12. For the remainder of this section, we consider sample surveys. Probabilistic methods, such as those described earlier in the chapter, allow the statistician to control the sample selection mechanism and to calculate a probability of selection, π_i, for each unit i in the population. These probabilities of selection are used to produce a basic design weight defined as the inverse of the selection probability, $d_i = 1/\pi_i$ which can be interpreted as the number of units the selected ones represent in the population. For instance, if the probability of being selected in a SRS is 1 in 10, $\pi_i = 1/10$, then the design weight is simply $d_i = 10$ and each sampled unit represents 10 units in the population (itself, and nine others). Nonprobabilistic samples do not have selection probabilities, thus design weights are not produced and model based estimation methods are typically used. Unfortunately, these methods are beyond the scope of this chapter (for more details, see Chapter 29).

Armed with the design weight, the Horvitz–Thompson (HT) estimator (Narain 1951, Horvitz and Thompson 1952) of the population total Y is

$$\hat{Y}_{HT} = \sum_{i \in s} d_i y_i \tag{27.1}$$

where d_i is the design weight, y_i is the observed variable of interest for the ith unit, and $\sum_{i \in s}$ denotes the summation over all units in the sample s. Note that we have assumed that the observed values y_i exist for all units and that outliers have been treated (see Section 27.4.2). The HT estimator is what is called "design unbiased" in the sense that if all possible samples are drawn and $\widehat{Y}_{HT}$ is estimated for each one, then the average of the HT estimators would be equal to the true population total, Y. More rigorously, we have

$$E_p(\widehat{Y}_{HT}) = E_p \left(\sum_{i \in s} d_i y_i \right)$$

$$= E_p \left(\sum_{i \in U} d_i y_i \delta_i \right)$$

$$= \sum_{i \in U} d_i y_i E_p(\delta_i)$$

$$= \sum_{i \in U} \frac{1}{\pi_i} y_i \pi_i = Y$$

where δ_i is a sample indicator variable (1 if the unit is in sample and 0 otherwise), E_p is the expectation with respect to the repeated sampling, and $E_p(\delta_i) = \pi_i$ is the probability of selection of unit i.

In economic surveys, it is common that estimates are required for domains below the population level. For instance, one may be interested in estimates of revenue (or turnover) for a geographical region from a national survey. If we define a domain indicator variable as

$$\gamma_{di} = \begin{cases} 1 & \text{if unit } i \text{ is in domain } d \\ 0 & \text{otherwise,} \end{cases}$$

the HT estimator for domain d is simply

$$\widehat{Y}_{HT,d} = \sum_{i \in s} d_i \gamma_{di} y_i.$$

Under a stratified sample design, as commonly used in business surveys, the HT estimator of a total is

$$\widehat{Y}_{ST} = \sum_{h=1}^{L} \sum_{i \in s_h} d_{hi} y_{hi}$$

where $h = 1, \ldots, L$ label the strata, and d_{hi} is the inverse of the selection probability for unit i in stratum h, usually with $d_{hi} = N_h / n_h$. Domain estimates under a stratified design are calculated similarly as above by defining a domain indicator variable. Note that if the domain of interest is not controlled for during stratification, then the number of units in the sample is a random variable. This has implications for the ability to estimate for the domain, as there may be no units selected in the sample from the domain. Even if there are sample units in the domain the number may be small, and thus the accuracy of the resulting estimate may be poor. In addition if the domain cuts across strata, units may have significantly different weights which could lead to uneven contribution from sample units to the domain total. The take away from this is that if high-quality estimates for the domain of interest are required, then the domain should be defined as a stratum.

The HT estimator uses the design weights, $d_i = 1/\pi_i$, but there are multiple reasons why these might be adjusted. For instance, they are often adjusted for unit nonresponse (see Särndal and

Lundström 2005) and/or to incorporate auxiliary data. Nonresponse adjustment is not discussed in this chapter, but we will further discuss adjustments based on auxiliary data.

Auxiliary data are commonly used in economic surveys for two reasons:

(1) to improve the efficiency (that is, reduce the variance) of estimates; and
(2) to ensure consistency between outputs produced by the NSO. Chambers et al. (1999) point out that when many variables are involved there is a possible loss of efficiency by enforcing this consistency.

Auxiliary data can come from many different sources such as government departments, censuses performed by the NSO and administrative programs or registers. We note that auxiliary data do not have to be perfect but do have to cover the population of interest and should be correlated with the variable(s) of interest if the main goal is to improve efficiency of the estimates. For economic surveys, tax information, annual or subannual, is a common source of auxiliary data as it is typically available for all businesses and is highly correlated with the main variable of interest, revenue, or turnover. Additional data sources include private sector businesses offering data for purchase, web-scraped data, monitoring data, social media, and satellite images. However, careful evaluation of these data sources should be performed before their use.

For ease of notation, we will assume a simple random sample design and that we observe y_i for all units in the sample. Given the design weights, d_i, one can calculate the unbiased HT estimators given by Eq. (27.1). Now, suppose auxiliary data, x_i, exist and are available for all units in the population. If x_i is not available for all units in the population, then it must be available for all units in the sample and the total for the population, X, has to be known. The simplest estimator that uses these auxiliary data in estimation is the ratio estimator defined as

$$\widehat{Y}_{\text{RAT}} = \frac{\widehat{Y}}{\widehat{X}} X$$

where $\widehat{Y}$ and $\widehat{X}$ are the HT estimators of Y and X, respectively, and X is the known population total. The ratio estimator can be interpreted in a couple of ways. One may look at it as the ratio of $\widehat{Y}$ over $\widehat{X}$ applied to the known total X or as the HT estimator of Y adjusted for the difference that the sample has induced in the estimation of X (that is, the ratio between X and $\widehat{X}$). Clearly if Y and X are related (correlated), then the ratio estimator should be a "better" estimator of Y than the HT estimator as it uses more information.

When using a ratio estimator one implicitly assumes a ratio regression model, $y_i = \beta x_i + \varepsilon_i$ with $\varepsilon_i \sim N(0, \sigma^2 x_i)$ (Cochran 1977, Section 6.7, Lohr 2019, p. 133). Note that the ratio regression model does not include an intercept. Although the ratio estimator has an underlying model, it is still asymptotically design unbiased as it is a model-assisted estimator and not a model-based estimator (Särndal et al. 1992). Some model-based estimators are discussed in Section 27.5. The ratio estimator belongs to a family of estimators called calibration estimators which have become very popular since the 1990s. Calibration estimators use calibration weights, w_i, which are defined such that the w_i's are as close as possible, for some distance metric, to the design weights, d_i, while fulfilling the benchmark equation defined as

$$\sum_{i \varepsilon s} w_i x_i = X$$

where X is the known population total (Deville and Särndal 1992). For more on the different distance functions and the corresponding estimators, we refer the reader to Deville and Särndal (1992).

Returning to the ratio estimator, it can be written as

$$\hat{Y}_{RAT} = \frac{\hat{Y}}{\hat{X}} X$$

$$= \frac{\sum_{i\varepsilon s} d_i y_i}{\sum_{i\varepsilon s} d_i x_i} X$$

$$= \sum_{i\varepsilon s} w_i y_i$$

where $w_i = d_i X / \hat{X}$ is known as the calibration weight. If one uses the calibration weights to estimate X,

$$\hat{X}_{RAT} = \sum_{i\varepsilon s} w_i x_i$$

$$= \frac{\sum_{i\varepsilon s} d_i x_i}{\sum_{i\varepsilon s} d_i x_i} X$$

$$= X.$$

Thus, the ratio estimator is in fact a calibration estimator.

Calibration estimators are popular because this benchmarking property allows NSOs to ensure consistency between estimates of the same parameter across statistical programs. For instance, Statistics Canada uses a calibration estimator with tax information as auxiliary data to ensure that survey estimates are consistent with tax totals. In addition to the benchmarking property, if the auxiliary data are correlated with the variable of interest, significant gains in efficiency can be obtained. To see this, under a simple random sample design, the variance of $\hat{Y}_{HT}$ is

$$v(\hat{Y}_{HT}) = N^2(1-f)\left(\frac{n-1}{n}\right)\sum_{i\varepsilon s}(y_i - \bar{y})^2.$$

If auxiliary data are available, one can show that that variance of $\hat{Y}_{RAT}$ is

$$v(\hat{Y}_{RAT}) = N^2(1-f)\left(\frac{n-1}{n}\right)\sum_{i\varepsilon s}(e_i - \bar{e})^2$$

where $e_i = y_i - (\hat{Y}/\hat{X})x_i$. Thus, if Y is linearly related to X, the variance reduction can be significant.

Returning to our stratified simple random sample case, an easy implementation of the ratio estimator is to produce a ratio estimator for each stratum and then sum them over the strata. Given that the strata are independent, variance estimation is straightforward. This gives,

$$\hat{Y}_{ST,RAT} = \sum_{h=1}^{L} \frac{X_h}{\hat{X}_h} \sum_{i\in s_h} d_{hi} y_{hi}$$

$$= \sum_{h=1}^{L} \sum_{i\in s_h} w_{hi} y_{hi}$$

where $w_{hi} = d_{hi} X_h / \hat{X}_h$, $\hat{X}_h = \sum_{i\varepsilon s_h} d_{hi} x_{hi}$ and X_h is the known population total of X for the h-th stratum. Note that the X_h are needed for all strata. Calculating this ratio at the stratum level assumes that the ratio regression model holds for each stratum, and the model or calibration group is said to be the stratum. The model could be different in different strata, or could hold across strata, in which case the model group would be at a more aggregate level than stratum. Calibration groups should be defined such that the relationship $y_i = \beta x_i + \varepsilon_i$ is similar for all units in the group. Thus, calibration groups may not coincide with the strata. If the calibration groups cut across the strata, the theory still holds but the notation does become messier as well as variance estimation. However, the practitioner should consider this possibility when implementing a ratio, or any calibration, estimator in practice. The choice of calibration groups should depend on the relationship between the variable of interest and the auxiliary data and not the convenience of notation or variance estimation.

This section provides a very high-level overview of calibration methods, and there are many examples of specific applications and extensions. A good review of calibration methods in surveys can be found in Haziza and Beaumont (2017).

27.4.2 Outliers

Establishment surveys are regularly affected by outliers – observations which are correct, but unusual, often (but not necessarily) as a consequence of the skewed distributions of variables as mentioned in Section 27.3. Over repeated sampling, design-based estimators remain unbiased in the presence of outliers; the challenge is that when a survey is run only a single sample is observed, and one must use the information from it in the best way possible to make estimates. When a survey repeats regularly with overlapping samples, there may be longitudinal information which allows some assessment of whether an outlier is sufficiently unusual to need treatment (see Smith and Yung (2019) for a more general discussion of the use of longitudinal approaches in establishment surveys).

For a specific survey occasion, there is a need for some objective approach to dealing with possible outliers, and this involves some application of models (and we deal further with model-based approaches in Section 27.5). Lee (1995) presented the state-of-the-art at the time of ICES-I, and distinguished two situations based on winsorisation and M-estimation (using Huber functions). These are still the principal approaches, but Beaumont et al. (2013) have shown that these approaches all sit under a single unifying conditional bias framework.

The basic idea is that in estimating a population total we sum the responses from the sample values, and then predict the nonsample values using a suitable regression model $E(y_k) = \boldsymbol{\beta}^T \mathbf{x}_k$ with unknown parameters $\boldsymbol{\beta}$ estimated by $\widehat{\boldsymbol{\beta}}$:

$$\widehat{t}_y = \sum_{k \in s} y_k + \widehat{\boldsymbol{\beta}}^T \sum_{k \in U \backslash s} \mathbf{x}_k.$$

There are several equivalent ways to estimate $\widehat{\boldsymbol{\beta}}$, one of which is as the solution to the estimating equation:

$$\sum_{k \in s} c_k(y_k - \boldsymbol{\beta}^T \mathbf{x}_k)\mathbf{x}_k = 0 \tag{27.2}$$

which clearly shows the dependence of the estimated values on the model residuals $y_k - \boldsymbol{\beta}^T \mathbf{x}_k$. There are different choices for c_k which govern the weight of different units in the estimating equation. To deal with the impact of outliers, which have large residuals, we use a Huber function ψ_k which bounds the influence of large residuals in (27.2):

$$\sum_{k \in s} c_k \psi_k(y_k - \boldsymbol{\beta}^{*T} \mathbf{x}_k)\mathbf{x}_k = 0. \tag{27.3}$$

Both one-sided and two-sided Huber functions have been used for ψ_k, generally the type II Huber function which does not allow the estimate to be smaller than the sum of the sample responses, which are

$$\psi_k(y_k - \boldsymbol{\beta}^{*T}\mathbf{x}_k) = \begin{cases} \frac{1}{w_i}(y_k - \boldsymbol{\beta}^{*T}\mathbf{x}_k) + \frac{w_i-1}{w_i}\varphi & \text{if} \quad y_k - \boldsymbol{\beta}^{*T}\mathbf{x}_k > \varphi \\ y_k - \boldsymbol{\beta}^{*T}\mathbf{x}_k & \text{otherwise} \end{cases}$$

$$\psi_k|y_k - \boldsymbol{\beta}^{*T}\mathbf{x}_k| = \begin{cases} sign(y_k - \boldsymbol{\beta}^{*T}\mathbf{x}_k)\left[\frac{1}{w_i}|y_k - \boldsymbol{\beta}^{*T}\mathbf{x}_k| + \frac{w_i-1}{w_i}\varphi\right] & \text{if} \quad |y_k - \boldsymbol{\beta}^{*T}\mathbf{x}_k| > \varphi \\ y_k - \boldsymbol{\beta}^{*T}\mathbf{x}_k & \text{otherwise} \end{cases}$$

respectively. Because the residuals depend on the regression parameters $\boldsymbol{\beta}^*$, (27.3) needs to be solved iteratively. Winsorisation is a specific approach which uses a one-sided function and allows the approximate estimation of the tuning parameters in the Huber function through using past (or current) data in a one-step procedure (see Kokic and Bell 1994, Chambers et al. 2001, Clark et al. 2017). Mulry et al. (2016) show that under some conditions winsorisation can mask outliers where there is more than one (it is not completely clear how the threshold values have been calculated in their set-up); in principle some masking may be expected using Huber functions too. Using the Huber function and iterative fitting are becoming more widespread, with several studies in Canada and the United States investigating their properties (Beaumont and Alavi 2004, Beaumont et al. 2013, Mulry et al. 2018). Although the concept of robustness to outliers with large positive *and* negative residuals is attractive, masking can also affect the estimation of the tuning constant of the two-sided Huber function and cause convergence problems. Therefore, it seems that a one-sided Huber function is currently the best of the available techniques.

Huber functions deal with outliers in one variable at a time, and for one estimate at a time. Lee (1995) outlined the challenges of dealing with multivariate outliers to manage the influence of outliers on the relationships between variables, and on the difficulties of choosing an outlier treatment that controls the mean squared error in a good way in both a set of domains and the population total that they constitute. These remain open questions in dealing with outliers in surveys.

27.5 Model-based Estimation

The heated debate around whether design-based or model-based approaches are best has reduced in recent years, to be replaced by a more pragmatic approach making use of the best available methods in any particular situation. Prime examples of this are the acceptance of using model-based estimation methods when a survey sample cannot support the level of granularity desired (e.g. small area estimation methods) and the use of models to increase the timeliness of estimates (e.g. nowcasts).

27.5.1 Small Area Estimation

Small Area Estimation (SAE) has been a very hot topic over the past 10–20 years as NSOs have been asked to produce more granular data while also being asked to reduce sample sizes. In the context of business surveys, the small area may represent a geographical area or a detailed industry. While an explanation of the full theory behind SAE is beyond the scope of this chapter, we give a high-level overview of SAE and an example of how the technique can be used in business surveys. For more details on SAE, we refer the reader to Rao and Molina (2015) in general and to Chapter 30 for establishment surveys.

SAE uses linear mixed models to model the relationship between survey data and auxiliary data. There are two main classes of SAE depending on the unit used in the model. In situations where auxiliary data are available at the unit level (e.g. the business level), a unit level model can be used. Battese et al. (1988) proposed a nested error model given as

$$y_{ij} = \mathbf{z}_{ij}^T \beta + v_i + e_{ij} \text{ for } i = 1, \ldots, m \text{ and } j \in U_i$$

where $\mathbf{z}_i$ is the vector of auxiliary data, U_i is the set of units in small area i, $v_i \overset{ind}{\sim} N(0, \sigma_v^2)$ are the random effects and are independent of the random errors, e_{ij}, with $e_{ij} \overset{ind}{\sim} N(0, \sigma^2)$. If the auxiliary data is not available at the unit level, then an area level model as proposed by Fay and Herriot (1979) is commonly used. The Fay–Harriot (FH) model is given by

$$\widehat{Y}_i = \mathbf{z}_i^T \beta + b_i v_i + e_i$$

where $\widehat{Y}_i$ is the survey estimate of area i, $\mathbf{z}_i$ is the vector of auxiliary data, $v_i \overset{ind}{\sim} N(0, \sigma_v^2)$ are the random effects and are independent of the random errors, e_i, with $e_i \overset{ind}{\sim} N(0, \sigma_i^2)$ where σ_i^2 are assumed known.

SAE requires good auxiliary information from which to build models, and business surveys are in the advantageous position of commonly having tax data available which is highly correlated with revenue, or turnover, the usual variable of interest. Statistics Canada uses monthly tax data with a FH model to produce small area estimates for 12 census metropolitan areas (CMA) in Canada in its Monthly Survey of Manufacturers (MSM). A census metropolitan area is an urban area with a total population of more than 100,000 and at least 50,000 residing within an urban core. With the existing sample size, the MSM does not have enough sample in the 12 CMAs to produce estimates directly from the survey. However, by using small area estimation techniques, reliable estimates for the 12 CMAs can be produced, meeting the needs of data users. For more information on the use of small area estimation in Statistics Canada's MSM, see Landry (2020). Another example of the development of small areas estimation for use with establishment (in this case agriculture) surveys is given in Erciulescu et al. (2019), who proposed the use of a hierarchical Bayesian sub-area level model for estimating county-level crops estimates, though this seems not yet to be fully implemented. Other authors have investigated small area estimation for business surveys, but this research has translated into remarkably few regular outputs.

With the availability of tax data at the business level, one would natually think that unit-level small area models would perform well. Statistics Canada did investigate such a model for their Annual Survey of Research and Development in Canadian Industry (RDCI); however, the model did not perform as well as expected. Upon further investigation, it was noted that there were significant discrepancies between the observed values and the auxiliary data for some units. These outliers had such a large influence on the model, that they adversely affected the model fit and resulted in a mean squared error larger than the estimated variance from the survey estimator, and this seems to be a general challenge in establishment surveys. By fitting an area level model, the influence on the model of these outliers is reduced.

Recently, Smith et al. (2021) have investigated the performance of different approaches to dealing with outliers in unit-level SAE models, using M-quantile methods in a business survey example, and found that they out-perform competing methods, although the synthetic estimator remains relatively competitive without the additional complexity.

27.5.2 Nowcasting

One the most common complaints about survey based estimates is the time lag between the end of a reference period and the release of information. Reasons for this lag include, but are not limited to, the time required for data collection, processing of the data, validating the data, and finally compiling and analyzing the outputs. In response to this complaint, many NSOs are investigating ways to produce near real time estimates using either flash estimates or time series models. Flash estimates are produced using the subset of collected data received by a certain time after the reference period. These flash estimates can be thought of as very preliminary estimates which will be revised as more data come in.

An alternate approach would be to use time series models to produce either forecasts or nowcasts. The difference between forecasts and nowcasts is that forecasts do not use data related to the reference period, while nowcasts do. In general, NSOs do not like to produce forecasts as they tend to have large prediction errors, in particular in times of uncertainty. By using exogenous or auxiliary variables from the reference period in time series models, the outputs of nowcasts should be more accurate. While there are many different time series models available, not all have been fully developed to include auxiliary variables. Two families of time series models currently being investigated to produce nowcasts are the ARIMA-X and state space models. The ARIMA-X models are the classical Autoregressive Integrated Moving Average (ARIMA) models which have been augmented to include exogenous variables. State space models, described in Durbin and Koopman (2012), provide a general framework for time series models. The model is specified through two sets of equations, the first equation referred to as the measurement equation describes how the unobserved components relate to the variable of interest and generally includes a random error term (assumed to be normally distributed). A second set of equations, referred to as transition equations, describes how each state or component of the model evolves over time, often as a linear function of previous states with an error term. Readers interested in ARIMA-X and state space models are referred to Box and Jenkins (1970) and Durbin and Koopman (2012), respectively, as these details are beyond the scope of this chapter. Fröhlich (2018) investigated the properties of nowcast estimates of Austrian short-term statistics, finding that multivariate models reacted better at turning points than univariate ones. Early responders were used as an indicator of later behavior.

27.5.3 Model-based Estimators

There are some situations where the use of model-based estimators allows for more accurate estimation of certain parameters, accounting for more complex data structures. For example, there are surveys which collect variables for which a large number of the observations is zero – for example product surveys, where only a minority of the products is produced by any particular business. This can be treated in a design-based framework, but this typically results in estimates with large variances. An alternative approach is to use a model-based estimator, where the model can be split into two parts – one to estimate the probability of a nonzero response, and one to estimate the response conditional on it being positive. Karlberg (2000) investigated this approach using a logistic model for the nonzero response probability and a lognormal model for the values, and found it to be competitive. A similar model has been applied in the PRODCOM product survey in the United Kingdom (see Smith et al. 2003, Section 3.8), using a simple proportion estimator, and a cross-stratum ratio estimator for the positive values. But in general, the production of the main survey estimates from a model-based procedure is unusual. It does require periodic checking to ensure that the model continues to fit the data. A more general exposition of model-based survey estimation can be found in Chambers and Clarke (2012).

27.6 Conclusion

Since the first International Conference on Establishment Surveys, the survey basis of many establishment statistics has continued to develop, both by extensions to traditional sampling and estimation approaches and by the investigation and implementation of innovative approaches which have provided additional benefits. In particular, numerical methods have made substantial changes possible, in making sample designs more efficient, and in making it practical to fit and use more complex models in other parts of the survey process. Nonetheless, some of the hard problems that were already widely acknowledged by ICES-I, such as how to deal with multivariate outliers, continue to be challenging.

References

Baillargeon, S. and Rivest, L.-P. (2009). A general algorithm for univariate stratification. *International Statistical Review* 77 (3): 331–344. https://doi.org/10.1111/j.1751-5823.2009.00093.x.

Ballin, M. and Barcaroli, G. (2008). Optimal stratification of sampling frames in a multivariate and multidomain sample design. *Contributi ISTAT* 10/2008.

Ballin, M. and Barcaroli, G. (2013). Joint determination of optimal stratification and sample allocation using genetic algorithm. *Survey Methodology* 39: 369–393.

Barcaroli, G. (2014). SamplingStrata: an R package for the optimization of stratified sampling. *Journal of Statistical Software* 614.

Battese, G.E., Harter, R.M., and Fuller, W.A. (1988). An error-components model for prediction of crop areas using survey and satellite data. *Journal of the American Statistical Association* 83: 28–36.

Beaumont, J.-F. and Alavi, A. (2004). Robust generalized regression estimation. *Survey Methodology* 30: 195–208.

Beaumont, J.F., Haziza, D., and Ruiz-Gazen, A. (2013). A unified approach to robust estimation in finite population sampling. *Biometrika* 100 (3): 555–569.

Benedetti, R., Bee, M., and Espa, G. (2010). A framework for cut-off sampling in business survey design. *Journal of Official Statistics* 26: 651–671.

Benedetti, R., Espa, G., and Lafratta, G. (2008). A tree-based approach to forming strata in multipurpose business surveys. *Survey Methodology* 34: 195–203.

Bethel, J. (1989). Sample allocation in multivariate surveys. *Survey Methodology* 15: 47–57.

BLS (2015). BLS handbook of methods, chapter 17, consumer price indexes. https://www.bls.gov/opub/hom/pdf/homch17.pdf (accessed 4 April 2021).

BLS (2020). Entrepreneurship and the US Economy. https://www.bls.gov/bdm/entrepreneurship/entrepreneurship.htm (accessed 4 April 2021).

Box, G.E.P. and Jenkins, G.M. (1970). *Time Series Analysis: Forecasting and Control.* San Francisco: Holden-Day.

Brewer, K.R.W. (1995). Combining design-based and model-based inference. In: *Business Survey Methods* (ed. B.G. Cox, D.A. Binder, B.N. Chinnappa, A. Christianson, M.J. Colledge, and P.S. Kott), 589–606. NewYork: Wiley.

Chambers, R. and Clark, R. (2012). *An Introduction to Model-Based Survey Sampling with Applications.* Oxford: Oxford University Press.

Chambers, R., Kokic, P., Smith, P., and Cruddas, M. (2001). Winsorization for identifying and treating outliers in economic surveys. In: *ICES-II: Proceedings of the Second International Conference on Establishment Surveys. Invited Papers*, 717–726. Virginia: American Statistical Association.

Chambers, R.L., Skinner, C., and Wang, S. (1999). Intelligent calibration. *Bulletin of the International Statistical Institute* 58 (2): 321–324.

Clark, R.G., Kokic, P., and Smith, P.A. (2017). A comparison of two robust estimation methods for business surveys. *International Statistical Review* 85: 270–289. https://doi.org/10.1111/insr.12177.

Cochran, W.G. (1977). *Sampling Techniques*, 3e. New York: Wiley.

Colledge, M.J. (1995). Frames and business registers: an overview. In: *Business Survey Methods* (ed. B.G. Cox, D.A. Binder, B.N. Chinnappa, A. Christianson, M.J. Colledge, and P.S. Kott), 21–47. New York: Wiley.

Cox, B.G., Binder, D.A., Chinnappa, B.N., Christianson, A., Colledge, M.J., and Kott, P.S. (ed.) (1995). *Business Survey Methods*. New York: Wiley.

Cox, B.G. and Chinnappa, B.N. (1995). Unique features of business surveys. In: *Business Survey Methods* (ed. B.G. Cox, D.A. Binder, B.N. Chinnappa, A. Christianson, M.J. Colledge, and P.S. Kott), 1–17. New York: Wiley.

Dalenius, T. and Hodges, J.L. Jr. (1957). The choice of stratification points. *Scandinavian Actuarial Journal* 1957 (3-4): 198–203.

Dalenius, T. and Hodges, J.L. Jr. (1959). Minimum variance stratification. *Journal of the American Statistical Association* 54 (285): 88–101.

Deville, J.C. and Särndal, C.-E. (1992). Calibration estimators in survey sampling. *Journal of the American Statistical Association* 87 (418): 376–382.

Deville, J.-C. and Tillé, Y. (2004). Efficient balanced sampling: the cube method. *Biometrika* 91: 893–912.

Durbin, J. and Koopman, S.J. (2012). *Time Series Analysis by State Space Methods*, 2e. Oxford: Oxford University Press.

European Commission, International Monetary Fund, Organisation for Economic Co-operation and Development, United Nations and World Bank (2009). *System of National Accounts 2008*. New York: United Nations https://unstats.un.org/unsd/nationalaccount/docs/sna2008.pdf (accessed 4 April 2021).

Eurostat (2008). NACE Rev. 2. Statistical classification of economic activites in the European Community. Luxembourg: Office for Official Publications of the European Communities. https://ec.europa.eu/eurostat/documents/3859598/5902521/KS-RA-07-015-EN.PDF (accessed 4 April 2021).

Eurostat (2021). EuroGroups register. https://ec.europa.eu/eurostat/statistics-explained/index.php/EuroGroups_register (accessed 4 April 2021).

Erciulescu, A.L., Cruze, N.B., and Nandram, B. (2019). Model-based county level crop estimates incorporating auxiliary sources of information. *Journal of the Royal Statistical Society, Series A* 182: 283–303.

Fabrizi, E. and Trivisano, C. (2007). Efficient stratification based on nonparametric regression methods. *Journal of Official Statistics* 23 (1): 35–50.

Falorsi, P.D. and Righi, P. (2008). A balanced sampling approach for multi-way stratification designs for small area estimation. *Survey Methodology* 34 (2): 223–234.

Fay, R.E. III and Herriot, R.A. (1979). Estimation of income for small places: an application of James-Stein procedures to Census data. *Journal of the American Statistical Association* 74: 269–277.

Fröhlich, M. (2018). Nowcasting Austrian short term statistics. *Journal of Official Statistics* 34: 502–522. https://doi.org/10.2478/jos-2018-0023.

Gros, E. and Le Gleut, R. (2018). The impact of profiling on sampling: how to optimise sample design when statistical units differ from data collection units. In: *The Unit Problem and Other Current Topics in Business Survey Methodology* (ed. B. Lorenc, P.A. Smith, M. Bavdaž, G. Haraldsen, D. Nedyalkova, L.-C. Zhang, and T. Zimmermann), 91–105. Newcastle upon Tyne: Cambridge Scholars.

Hansen, M.H., Hurwitz, W.N., and Madow, W.G. (1953). *Sample Survey Methods and Theory, Methods and Applications*, vol. 1. New York: Wiley.

Haziza, D. and Beaumont, J.F. (2017). Construction of weights in surveys: a review. *Statistical Science* 32: 206–226.

Haziza, D., Chauvet, G., and Deville, J.-C. (2010). Sampling and estimation in the presence of cut-off sampling. *Australian & New Zealand Journal of Statistics* 52: 303–319.

Hidiroglou, M.A. and Kozak, M. (2018). Stratification of skewed populations: a comparison of optimisation-based versus approximate methods. *International Statistical Review* 86: 87–105.

Horvitz, D.G. and Thompson, D.J. (1952). A generalization of sampling without replacement from a finite universe. *Journal of the American Statistical Association* 47 (260): 663–685.

Jafri, H. and Alasia, A. (2019). A profile of businesses in indigenous communities in Canada. Ottawa: Statistics Canada. https://www150.statcan.gc.ca/n1/pub/18-001-x/18-001-x2019002-eng.htm (accessed 4 April 2021).

Karlberg, F. (2000). Survey estimation for highly skewed populations in the presence of zeroes. *Journal of Official Statistics* 16 (3): 229–241.

Keskintürk, T. and Er, Ş. (2007). A genetic algorithm approach to determine stratum boundaries and sample sizes of each stratum in stratified sampling. *Computational Statistics & Data Analysis* 52 (1): 53–67.

Kokic, P.N. and Bell, P.A. (1994). Optimal winsorising cut-offs for a stratified finite population estimator. *Journal of Official Statistics* 10: 419–435.

Kozak, M. (2004). Optimal stratification using random search method in agricultural surveys. *Statistics in Transition* 6: 797–806.

Lafrance-Cooke, A., Macdonald, R., and Willox, M. (2020). Monthly openings and closings: experimental series for Canada, the provinces, territories, and census metropolitan areas. https://www150.statcan.gc.ca/n1/pub/11-626-x/11-626-x2020014-eng.htm (accessed 4 April 2021).

Landry, S. (2020). Implementation of small area estimation techniques in an economic survey: the experience of the Monthly Survey of Manufacturing in Canada. *Proceedings of the Joint Statistical Meetings 2020*. American Statistical Association.

Lavallée, P. (2007). *Indirect Sampling*. New York: Springer.

Lavallée, P. and Hidiroglou, M.A. (1988). On the stratification of skewed populations. *Survey Methodology* 14: 33–43.

Lee, H. (1995). Outliers in business surveys. In: *Business Survey Methods* (ed. B.G. Cox, D.A. Binder, B.N. Chinnappa, A. Christianson, M.J. Colledge, and P.S. Kott), 503–526. New York: Wiley.

Lisic, J., Sang, H., Zhu, Z., and Zimmer, S. (2018). Optimal stratification and allocation for the June agricultural survey. *Journal of Official Statistics* 34 (1): 121–148.

Lohr, S.R. (2019). *Sampling Design and Analysis*, 2e. Boca Raton: CRC Press/Chapman & Hall.

Lorenc, B., Smith, P.A., Bavdaž, M., Haraldsen, G., Nedyalkova, D., Zhang, L.-C., and Zimmermann, T. (ed.) (2018). *The Unit Problem and Other Current Topics in Business Survey Methodology*. Newcastle upon Tyne: Cambridge Scholars.

Mulry, M.H., Oliver, B.E., Kaputa, S.J., and Thompson, K.J. (2016). A cautionary note on Clark Winsorization. *Survey Methodology* 42: 297–305.

Mulry, M.H., Kaputa, S., and Thompson, K.J. (2018). Setting M-estimation parameters for detection and treatment of influential values. *Journal of Official Statistics* 34 (2): 483–501.

Narain, R. (1951). On sampling without replacement with varying probabilities. *Journal of the Indian Society of Agricultural Statistics* 3: 169–175.

National Bureau of Statistics of China (2019). http://www.stats.gov.cn/english/PressRelease/201911/t20191120_1710326.html (accessed 4 April 2021).

Neyman, J. (1934). On the two different aspects of the representative method: the method of stratified sampling and the method of purposive selection (with discussion). *Journal of the Royal Statistical Society* 97: 558–625.

O'Luing, M., Prestwich, S. and Tarim, S.A. (2018). A grouping genetic algorithm for joint stratification and sample allocation designs. arXiv:1709.03076v2.

O'Neill, R., Ralph, J., and Smith, P.A. (2017). *Inflation – History and Measurement*. Basingstoke: Palgrave MacMillan https://doi.org/10.1007/978-3-319-64125-6.

Parker, R.P. (2014). Initial results of the 2012 economic census. *Business Economics* 49: 127–135.

Polanec, S., Smith, P.A. and Bavdaž, M. (2022, in press). Determination of the threshold in cutoff sampling using response burden with an application to Intrastat. *Journal of Official Statistics*.

Rao, J.N.K. and Molina, I. (2015). *Small Area Estimation*. New York: Wiley.

Rivest, L.-P. (2002). A generalization of the Lavallée and Hidiroglou algorithm for stratification in business surveys. *Survey Methodology* 28: 191–198.

Rivière, P. (2002). What makes business statistics special? *International Statistical Review* 70 (1): 145–159.

Särndal, C.E. and Lundström, S. (2005). *Estimation in Surveys with Nonresponse*. Chichester: Wiley.

Särndal, C.-E., Swensson, B., and Wretman, J. (1992). *Model Assisted Survey Sampling*. New York: Springer.

Sigman, R.S. and Monsour, N.J. (1995). Selecting samples from list frames of businesses. In: *Business Survey Methods* (ed. B.G. Cox, D.A. Binder, B.N. Chinnappa, A. Christianson, M.J. Colledge, and P.S. Kott), 133–152. New York: Wiley.

Slanta, J.G. and Krenzke, T.R. (1996). Applying the Lavallée and Hidiroglou method to obtain stratification boundaries for the Census Bureau's annual Capital Expenditure Survey. *Survey Methodology* 22: 65–75.

Smith, P. (2013). Sampling and estimation for business surveys. In: *Designing and Conducting Business Surveys* (ed. G. Snijkers, G. Haraldsen, J. Jones and D. Willimack), 165–218. Hoboken: Wiley.

Smith, P.A., Bocci, C., Tzavidis, N., Krieg, S. and Smeets, M.J.E. (2021). Robust estimation for small domains in business surveys. *Journal of the Royal Statistical Society, Series C* 70: 312–334.

Smith, P., Pont, M., and Jones, T. (2003). Developments in business survey methodology in the Office for National Statistics, 1994–2000 (with discussion). *Journal of the Royal Statistical Society, Series D* 52: 257–295.

Smith, P.A. and Yung, W. (2019). A review and evaluation of the use of longitudinal approaches in business surveys. *Longitudinal and Life Course Studies* 10: 491–511.

Statistics Canada (2018). North American Industry Classification System (NAICS) Canada 2017 Version 3.0. Ottawa: Statistics Canada. https://www150.statcan.gc.ca/n1/en/pub/12-501-x/12-501-x2016003-eng.pdf?st=t6aJe0Xs (accessed 4 April 2021).

Statistics Canada (2020a). Table 33-10-0267-01 Canadian Business Counts, with employees, June 2020. www.doi.org/10.25318/3310026701-eng (accessed 4 April 2021).

Statistics Canada (2020b). Linkable File Environment (LFE). https://www23.statcan.gc.ca/imdb/p2SV.pl?Function=getSurvey&SDDS=6000 (accessed 4 April 2021).

UNECE (2015). Guidelines on statistical business registers. United Nations: New York and Geneva. https://unece.org/fileadmin/DAM/stats/publications/2015/ECE_CES_39_WEB.pdf (accessed 4 April 2021).

UNECE (2019). Generic Statistical Business Process Model GSBPM, Version 5.1. https://statswiki.unece.org/display/GSBPM/GSBPM+v5.1 (accessed 4 April 2021).

United Nations (2008). International standard industrial classification of all economic activities, revision 4. United Nations: New York. Available from https://unstats.un.org/unsd/publication/seriesm/seriesm_4rev4e.pdf (accessed 4 April 2021).

van Delden, A., Lorenc, B., Struijs, P., and Zhang, L.-C. (2018). Letter to the editor: on statistical unit errors in business statistics. *Journal of Official Statistics* 34: 573–580. https://doi.org/10.2478/jos-2018-0027.

Yorgason, D., Bridgman, B., Cheng, Y., Dorfman, A.H., Lent, J., Liu, Y.K., Miranda, J., and Rumburg, S. (2011). Cutoff sampling in federal surveys: an inter-agency review. *Proceedings of the American Statistical Association, Section on Government Statistics* 2011: 76–90.

28

Sample Coordination Methods and Systems for Establishment Surveys

Alina Matei[1] and Paul A. Smith[2]

[1] *Institute of Statistics, University of Neuchâtel, Neuchâtel, Switzerland*
[2] *S3RI and Department of Social Statistics & Demography, University of Southampton, Southampton, United Kingdom*

28.1 Introduction

Establishment statistics are important tools for economic management, and the need to obtain information as the basis for such statistics has led to legislation in many countries making response to establishment surveys compulsory. The converse of this requirement has been the management of survey burdens, a concept articulated by Bradburn (1978) so that the information requirement from government is limited. Burden management has manifested in two ways. First, through the reduction of numbers of surveys, sample sizes, and numbers of questions, all aiming to reduce the overall burden; and second, through procedures to spread the burden so that any individual establishment is selected in as few surveys as possible at a given moment. A major tool in this second approach has been the use of sample coordination approaches.

Sample coordination refers to methods used to optimize the overlap of two or more samples. The samples can be selected on different occasions in a repeated survey, or over different surveys. If a survey's objective is to estimate change across time, or to reduce the costs associated with recruiting a new sample unit, the overlap between samples should be maximized. Sometimes one would like to reduce the probability of having the same sampling unit selected across different samples, and therefore to limit its response burden. In such cases, the objective is to minimize the overlap between samples selected over time or over different surveys. In the first case, one advocates *positive sample coordination*, while in the second one, *negative sample coordination*.

Sample coordination started with the pioneer works of Keyfitz (1951) and Raj (1956). As Ernst (1999) underlined, different names have been used in the literature such as "overlapping maps" (Raj, 1956), "optimal integration of surveys" (see for instance Pathak and Fahimi, 1992), and more recently "sample coordination," "sampling coordination," or "coordinated sampling."

Various procedures have been proposed for sample coordination (such as permanent random number procedures, methods based on mathematical programming, etc.), and these have given rise to several implementations in different countries. The national statistical offices of different countries currently use so-called "sample coordination systems." "Sample coordination methods" and "sample coordination systems" represent, in our opinion, two different concepts. The existing literature does not distinguish between them. Moreover, a definition of a sample coordination system has not yet been provided, while the term is widely used. This chapter aims to review these two concepts and to underline the similarities and distinction between them. To do this, we proceed

Advances in Business Statistics, Methods and Data Collection. Edited by Ger Snijkers, Mojca Bavdaž, Stefan Bender, Jacqui Jones, Steve MacFeely, Joseph W. Sakshaug, Katherine J. Thompson, and Arnout van Delden.
© 2023 John Wiley & Sons, Inc. Published 2023 by John Wiley & Sons, Inc.

as follows. In Sections 28.2 and 28.3, we review the main existing methods for sample coordination, and highlight their strengths and weaknesses. Section 28.4 provides the components of a sample coordination system; we review some of them currently being used in different countries in Section 28.5. In Section 28.6, we distinguish "sample coordination methods" and "sample coordination systems." In Section 28.7, we provide our conclusions.

28.2 Sample Coordination

28.2.1 Notation and Definitions

Establishment survey frames define the populations to be surveyed. These populations change over time: some units disappear from the populations (they are called "deaths"), other units appear ("births"), still others are split into several other units ("splits"), merge, or are taken over ("acquisitions"). Probability samples are selected from these frames as the basis for collecting information, and some businesses are included repeatedly in surveys because they are large enough that their contribution is vital (these are completely enumerated), or because including the same units increases period to period correlation of the estimates and reduces the variance of estimates of change. Sometimes, to reduce the response burden, some units are rotated out of the sample at each transition, and replaced with new units.

Let us consider a simple case of two overlapping finite populations of units denoted by U_1 and U_2, of sizes N_1 and N_2 respectively. From U_1, one selects a sample s_1, and from U_2, a sample s_2, using the sampling designs p_1 and p_2, respectively. The expected sample sizes for s_1 and s_2 are denoted, respectively, by n_1 and n_2. A bivariate sample $s = (s_1, s_2)$ is selected from $U_1 \times U_2$, using a joint sampling design p, with marginal sampling designs p_1 and p_2. The samples s_1 and s_2 are said to be *coordinated* if

$$p(s_1, s_2) \neq p_1(s_1)p_2(s_2)$$

that is, the samples are not drawn independently (see Cotton and Hesse, 1992b; Mach et al., 2006). The main goal of sample coordination methods is to optimize the overlap between samples.

The size of the *overlap* between s_1 and s_2, denoted by c, represents the number of units common to s_1 and s_2. It is in general a random variable having expectation

$$E(c) = \sum_{k \in U} \pi_{k,12}$$

with $\pi_{k,12} = P(k \in s_1, k \in s_2) = \sum_{\substack{(s_1,s_2) \\ k \in s_1, k \in s_2}} p(s_1, s_2), \forall k \in U$ and $U = U_1 \cup U_2$ is the so-called "overall population." In positive coordination, the goal is to maximize $E(c)$, while in negative coordination, it is to minimize it. In negative coordination, it is expected that minimization of $E(c)$ will reduce the perceived response burden incurred by units which are potentially selected in both samples, by minimizing the probability to be selected in both samples, with a concomitant reduction in the probability to be selected in neither sample.

Let $\pi_{k1} = P(k \in s_1)$ and $\pi_{k2} = P(k \in s_2)$ be the first-order inclusion probabilities of unit $k \in U$ in the first and second samples, respectively. In order to manage the births in $U \setminus U_1$ and the deaths in $U \setminus U_2$, we assume that $\pi_{k1} = 0$ if $k \notin U_1$ and $\pi_{k2} = 0$ if $k \notin U_2$.

28.2.2 Methods for Sample Coordination

Various sample coordination methods have been proposed in the literature. For an overview on sample coordination methods, one can see, for instance, Ernst (1999), Mach et al. (2006), and the references therein. See also Nedyalkova et al. (2008), Nedyalkova et al. (2009), and Grafström and Matei (2015). The extensive literature on sample coordination covers a wide range of sampling designs, from coordination for simple random samples without replacement to coordination for balanced samples (Tillé and Favre, 2004), and spatially balanced samples (Grafström and Matei, 2018).

An important approach in sample coordination is the use of *permanent random numbers* (PRNs). PRNs were introduced by Brewer et al. (1972) to coordinate Poisson samples and have been widely used afterward in other, different methods (Ohlsson, 1995). Brewer et al. (1972) provided the following method: one associates a uniform random number u_k drawn independently from the $U(0, 1)$ distribution to each unit $k \in U$, which is used in the selection process for samples across all surveys or different time occasions. The numbers u_k are called "permanent random numbers" since they are kept over time and over surveys for units which persist in the population. For a "birth," a new PRN is assigned; for a "death," the unit and its associated PRN are deleted from the corresponding survey frame.

One can roughly divide sample coordination methods into two categories: methods using PRNs, and methods that do not use PRNs. The main methods based on PRNs and some non-PRN methods are reviewed below. In their descriptions, we consider that s_1 and s_2 are selected with the same sampling method. However, one can also provide sample coordination using two different sampling schemes for s_1 and s_2.

28.2.3 Methods Based on PRNs

Methods based on PRNs are divided below in two categories (*Poisson sampling with PRNs and its extensions* and *fixed-ordered procedures with PRNs*) to overview the most important. Other PRN methods have also been developed in the literature; for instance, spatially balanced sampling with PRNs (Grafström and Matei, 2018).

a. Poisson sampling with PRNs and its extensions:
- In *Poisson sampling with PRNs* (Brewer et al., 1972), a unit $k \in U_1$ is selected in the sample s_1 if $u_k < \pi_{k1}$; for a positive coordination between s_1 and s_2, $k \in U_2$ is selected in s_2 if $u_k < \pi_{k2}$. To achieve negative coordination between s_1 and s_2, $k \in U_2$ is selected in s_2 if $1 - u_k < \pi_{k2}$. Using Poisson sampling with PRNs gives a high degree of coordination, as the bounds on the expected overlap size are reached; see Section 28.3.1. However, Monte Carlo studies showed that the variance of the sample overlap can be large in positive coordination (see, for instance, Grafström and Matei, 2015, 2018). The main drawback of the method is that it provides samples of random size that increase the variance of the estimators compared to simple random sampling without replacement (SRS-WOR). Null sample sizes are also possible. If the inclusion probabilities are equal ($\pi_{k1} = n_1/N_1, \forall k \in U_1, \pi_{\ell 2} = n_2/N_2, \forall \ell \in U_2$), one obtains *Bernoulli sampling with PRNs*.
- *Collocated sampling* (Brewer et al., 1972, 1984) is a variant of Poisson sampling with PRNs, used to reduce the sample size variability and to avoid null sample sizes. For the first sample s_1, a random permutation $R = (R_k)'$ of the units in U_1 is provided, where R_k is the rank of unit k in the permutation. A single random number $\varepsilon \sim U(0, 1)$ is generated. To each unit $k \in U_1$, the random number $t_k = (R_k - \varepsilon)/N_1$ is associated, where N_1 is the size of U_1. If $t_k < \pi_{k1}$, unit k is selected in s_1. Thus, t_k replaces u_k in the original Poisson with PRNs scheme. This modification allows a uniform spread of the population units, removing any potential clustering of u_k that can occur in small populations. The sample size becomes

almost not random because the R_k are equally spaced in $[0, 1]$. If $U_1 = U_2$, in positive coordination, selection of the second sample uses the same t_k, with updated probabilities $\pi_{k2}, k \in U_2$; for negative coordination, k is selected in s_2 if $1 - t_k < \pi_{k2}, k \in U_2$. Hesse (1999) pointed out that "it is difficult to use this technique for several samples at the same time, unless they adopt the same stratification and the same definition of scope." Brewer et al. (1984) discussed how to manage births and deaths that can occur between the two sample selections.

Ohlsson (1995, p. 161) introduced *PRN collocated sampling*. The PRNs u_k are sorted in ascending order, and the rank is addressed to each one of them. As before, a single random number $\varepsilon \sim U(0, 1)$ is generated. For each unit $k \in U_1$, the random number $t_k = (\text{Rank}(u_k) - \varepsilon)/N_1$ is associated. If $t_k < \pi_{k1}$, unit k is selected in s_1 (t_k replaces u_k in Poisson with PRNs). For a positive coordination, the second sample is drawn using the same u_k and ε but with updated ranks and probabilities π_{k2} (for a negative coordination, $1 - u_k$ and ε with updated ranks and probabilities π_{k2}). The coverage of births and deaths with PRN collocated sampling is discussed by Ernst et al. (2000).

– *Poisson mixture (PoMix) sampling* is a mixture of Bernoulli and Poisson sampling introduced by Kröger et al. (1999). The authors noted that it is "suitable for business surveys with its [sic] often highly skewed populations." Let $a \in [0, n_1/N_1]$ be a starting point. The PoMix inclusion probabilities are defined as

$$\widetilde{\pi}_{k1} = a + \left(1 - a\frac{N_1}{n_1}\right)\pi_{k1}, \quad k \in U_1 \tag{28.1}$$

A unit $k \in U_1$ is selected in s_1 if one of the following conditions is fulfilled:

a. $0 < u_k \leq a$;
b. $a < u_k \leq 1$ and $\widetilde{\pi}_{k1} \geq (u_k - a)/(1 - a)$.

The quantities $\widetilde{\pi}_{k1}$ are greater than a to avoid small $\widetilde{\pi}_{k1}$ values. If $a = 0$, one obtains Poisson sampling; if $a = n_1/N_1$, one obtains Bernoulli sampling. Other values of a yield a Poisson–Bernoulli sampling mixture, that is in fact Poisson sampling obtained by using the probabilities $\widetilde{\pi}_{k1}$ instead of π_{k1}. As in the case of Poisson/Bernoulli sampling, the drawback of this method is its random sample size. Kröger et al. (1999) conducted Monte Carlo simulation studies and showed that such mixtures provide estimates with smaller variance than Poisson sampling. The next sample s_2 is drawn as in Poisson sampling with PRNs, using the same u_k in positive coordination ($1 - u_k$ in negative coordination) and the same value of a, but with updated $\pi_{k2}, k \in U_2$, n_2, and N_2 (the size of U_2).

– *Conditional Poisson sampling* (Hájek, 1964) is a fixed-size sampling design having important theoretical properties, such as maximizing the entropy in the class of sampling designs with given first-order inclusion probabilities and fixed sample size.

The entropy of a sampling design $\tilde{p}(.)$ is defined as $-\sum_{\tilde{s}}\tilde{p}(\tilde{s})\log(\tilde{p}(\tilde{s}))$, with the convention that $0\log(0) = 0$, and $\tilde{s}$ being a possible sample (Hájek, 1981). A sampling design with high entropy speeds up the convergence of the Horvitz–Thompson estimator of the population total toward the normal distribution (and allows the construction of confidence intervals as usual; Berger, 1998). Furthermore, high-entropy sampling designs allow the second-order inclusion probabilities to be approximated by the first-order inclusion probabilities, thus greatly simplifying the variance of the Horvitz–Thompson estimator.

Grafström and Matei (2015) introduced two methods to coordinate Conditional Poisson (CP) samples. The first method uses PRNs and a sequential implementation of CP sampling. The second method is a non-PRN method that uses a CP sample in the first selection and provides an approximate one in the second selection because the prescribed inclusion probabilities are not exactly respected. On the simulations performed by Grafström and Matei (2015), the second method provided results similar to Poisson sampling with PRNs for $E(c)$, but a smaller variance of c in positive coordination.

b. Fixed-ordered procedures with PRNs refer to procedures using ordered quantities depending on PRNs, that draw samples of fixed size. We include in this category: SRS-WOR with PRNs, synchronized sampling, order sampling, fixed size PoMix sampling, and Ohlsson's exponential sampling.

- In *sequential simple random sampling* or *simple random sampling without replacement* (SRS-WOR) with PRNs the list of units is sorted in ascending or descending order of $u_k, k \in U_1$. The first sample is composed by the first or the last n_1 units in the ordered list. This method is described by Fan et al. (1962). A proof that this method generates a simple random sample without replacement is given for instance in Sunter (1977b) and in Ohlsson (1992). For positive coordination, the second sample is drawn using the same u_k, and sample size n_2; for negative coordination, the second sample is drawn using $1 - u_k$ and n_2.

- *Synchronized sampling* (Hinde and Young, 1984) assigns a PRN independently to each unit and selects units whose associated PRNs lie in an interval. The first sample of size n_1 is selected using SRS-WOR with PRNs. The used PRNs (in ascending order) lie in an interval $[b, e]$ (with b for "beginning" and e for "end"). For the next sample and positive coordination, the same interval is kept if the population doesn't change. If births or deaths occur, or the sample size changes for s_2, the interval is adjusted: e is increased, extending the interval to the right to include more units, or b is increased to reduce the interval from the left to exclude units, until the desired sample size is obtained. This process can increase survey rotation rates, and the increase can be substantial if births and deaths are frequent. Negative coordination is achieved by giving samples fixed, disjoint selection intervals within the range of the PRNs, and the selections of the samples take place wholly within these intervals (so the population must be sufficiently large to support the required sample sizes within these intervals). Brewer et al. (2000) comment that if the two surveys have different stratification, "positive coordination can only be achieved by a manual choice of the selection intervals."

- *Order sampling* (Rosén, 1997a,b) is a class of sampling designs with fixed sample size. Let $\lambda_{k1}, k \in U_1$ be the target inclusion probabilities, usually proportional to a size measure. To each unit $k \in U_1$ a continuous random variable $X_k = H^{-1}(u_k)/H^{-1}(\lambda_{k1})$ is associated, where $H(.)$ is a cumulative distribution function (cdf) defined on $[0, \infty)$. The first n_1 units in increased order of X-values form the first sample. The random variables $X_1, \ldots, X_k, \ldots, X_N$ each follow the same type of distribution, but are not necessarily identically distributed. Order sampling yields SRS-WOR samples when X_k are identically distributed.

  Various types of order sampling arise when the X_k follow different distributions:

  1. Uniform order sampling or sequential Poisson sampling (Ohlsson, 1990, 1998), where $X_k = u_k/\lambda_{k1}$, and H is the cdf of the $U(0, 1)$ distribution.

  2. Exponential order sampling or successive sampling (Hájek, 1964; Rosén, 1997b), where $X_k = \ln(1 - u_k)/\ln(1 - \lambda_{k1})$, and H is the cdf of the exponential distribution with parameter 1.

  3. Pareto order sampling (Saavedra, 1995; Rosén, 1997a,b), where

$$X_k = \frac{u_k/(1 - u_k)}{\lambda_{k1}/(1 - \lambda_{k1})}$$

  and H is the cdf of the Pareto distribution with shape parameter 2, and scale parameters u_k in the numerator and λ_{k1} in the denominator.

Note that the inclusion probabilities π_{k1} are not equal to the quantities λ_{k1}. If λ_{k1} are proportional to a size measure known for all units $k \in U_1$, the resulting order sampling is only asymptotically πps sampling, with a faster convergence for Pareto sampling (Rosén, 1997a). For all types of order sampling, positive coordination uses the same u_k, but $\lambda_{k2}, k \in U_2$ instead of λ_{k1} in the X_k definition to select s_2; in negative coordination, u_k is replaced by $1 - u_k$. For an application of Pareto sampling with PRNs, see Scholtus and van Delden (2016).

– *Fixed size PoMix sampling* (Kröger et al., 2003) is a mixture between order sampling and PoMix sampling. It was introduced to obtain a fixed sample size and to preserve the good properties of the PoMix sampling concerning the variance in skewed populations compared to Poisson sampling. The PoMix inclusion probabilities are defined as in (28.1). The method to obtain a sample is similar to order sampling. Different types of sampling arise by changing the parameter a and the values, depending on u_k, to be ordered. Ordered values of $u_k / \widetilde{\pi}_{k1}, k \in U_1$ and $a = 0$ gives sequential Poisson sampling; the same ordered values and $a = n_1 / N_1$, gives SRS-WOR with PRNs. Finally, ordered values of

$$\frac{u_k / (1 - u_k)}{\widetilde{\pi}_{k1} / (1 - \widetilde{\pi}_{k1})}, \quad k \in U_1$$

and any $a \in [0, 1]$, gives Pareto sampling. Note that the quantities $\widetilde{\pi}_{k1}$ are not equal to the inclusion probabilities π_{k1}.

The second sample is drawn using the same u_k for positive coordination ($1 - u_k$ for negative coordination), and $\pi_{k2}, k \in U_2$.

– *Ohlsson's exponential sampling* (Ohlsson, 1996) is a procedure that follows the same idea of ordering values depending on the PRNs. It is a method to select only one unit in a sample. It is assumed that $\sum_{k \in U_1} \pi_{k1} = \sum_{k \in U_2} \pi_{k2} = 1$. The quantities $\xi_k = -\log(1 - u_k) / \pi_{k1}, k \in U_1$ are computed. The first unit in the sorted order of ξ_k is selected in s_1. The name of the procedure is given by the distribution of the ξ_k, which is exponential with parameter $1 / \pi_{k1}$; see also Ernst (2001). For positive coordination, s_2 is selected using u_k ($1 - u_k$ for negative coordination) and $\pi_{k2}, k \in U_2$.

28.2.4 Non-PRN Methods

The non-PRN methods can be divided into *methods using mathematical programming* and *other methods*. Among methods based on mathematical programming, one can include the approaches of Raj (1956, 1968), Arthnari and Dodge (1981), Causey et al. (1985), Ernst and Ikeda (1995), Ernst (1996), Ernst (1998), Ernst and Paben (2002), Mach et al. (2006), Matei and Skinner (2009), Tiwari and Sud (2012), and Șchiopu-Kratina et al. (2014). In general, methods based on mathematical programming try to optimize the overlap between samples, under some constraints. Mathematical programming was also used to minimize the expected respondent burden as in Perry et al. (1993). Among the methods using mathematical programming for sample coordination, the transportation problem (TP) offers an attractive framework (Causey et al., 1985). *Other methods* include the approaches of Keyfitz (1951), Kish and Scott (1971), Sunter (1989), Tillé and Favre (2004), Matei and Tillé (2005), and Grafström and Matei (2015, method II).

Some non-PRN methods are reviewed below:

– *Keyfitz's method*: The method of Keyfitz (1951) can be applied for positive coordination when one unit per sample (or per stratum) is selected. It is assumed that $\sum_{k \in U} \pi_{k1} = \sum_{k \in U} \pi_{k2} = 1$, and $U_1 = U_2 = U$. A unit $\in U$ is selected in s_1 with probability π_{k1}. Let $I = \{k \in U | \pi_{k1} \leq \pi_{k2}\}$ be the set of "increasing" units, and let $D = \{k \in U | \pi_{k1} > \pi_{k2}\}$ be the set of "decreasing" units. Assume that unit k was selected in s_1 with probability π_{k1}. If $k \in I$, it is selected in s_2 with probability 1, else with probability π_{k2}/π_{k1}. If k was not selected in s_2, a new unit $\ell \in I$ is selected in s_2 with probability proportional to $\pi_{\ell 2} - \pi_{\ell 1}$. The method can be applied for two sampling designs with the same stratification. Kish and Scott (1971) extended Keyfitz's method to the case where units change strata in the second selection.

- *Sunter's method*: Sunter (1989) introduced a method for positive coordination of two general samples, inspired by Keyfitz's method. This method uses the selection probabilities of samples (that is, sets of selected units), that need to be computed under both the original and new designs. There are two time occasions: a sample s is selected on the first occasion with probability $p_1(s)$ and the probability that the same sample is realized on the second occasion is $p_2(s)$. If s_1 is selected on the first occasion, it is retained with probability 1 on the second occasion if $p_2(s_1) > p_1(s_1)$, and with probability $p_2(s_1)/p_1(s_1)$, otherwise. If s_1 was retained on the second occasion, the procedure ends. If not, it repetitively continues until a new sample is retained as follows: a new sample s_2 is selected with probability $p_2(s_2)$. If $p_2(s_2) < p_1(s_2)$, s_2 is rejected, else it is retained with probability $1 - p_1(s_2)/p_2(s_2)$.

- *Transportation problem*: Let $\mathcal{S}_1$ and $\mathcal{S}_2$ denote the sets of all possible samples on the first and second time occasion/survey, respectively, with $m = |\mathcal{S}_1|$, $q = |\mathcal{S}_2|$, and $|.|$ denoting the cardinality of a set. Let $s_{i1} \in \mathcal{S}_1$ and $s_{j2} \in \mathcal{S}_2$. It is assumed that $c_{ij} = |s_{i1} \cap s_{j2}|$, $p_{i1} = p_1(s_{i1})$, $p_{j2} = p_2(s_{j2})$, $i = 1, \ldots, m, j = 1, \ldots, q$ are known. Given that s_{i1} was already selected, the goal is to draw s_{j2}, conditionally on s_{i1}, by optimizing their overlap size as much as possible. Causey et al. (1985) optimized $E(c) = \sum_{k \in U} \pi_{k,12} = \sum_{i=1}^{m} \sum_{j=1}^{q} c_{ij} p_{ij}$ in positive coordination as a transportation problem (a well-known linear programming problem) given as

$$\max \sum_{i=1}^{m} \sum_{j=1}^{q} c_{ij} p_{ij} \qquad (28.2)$$

subject to the constraints

$$\left| \begin{array}{l} \sum_{j=1}^{q} p_{ij} = p_{i1}, \quad i = 1, \ldots, m \\[2mm] \sum_{i=1}^{m} p_{ij} = p_{j2}, \quad j = 1, \ldots, q \\[2mm] p_{ij} \geq 0, i = 1, \ldots, m, \quad j = 1, \ldots, q \end{array} \right.$$

where $p_{ij} = p(s_{i1}, s_{j2})$. Once the solution p_{ij} is obtained, a sample s_{j2} is selected with the conditional probability $p(s_{j2}|s_{i1}) = p_{ij}/p_{i1}$, noting that $p_{i1} > 0$, $i = 1, \ldots, m$, since $\mathcal{S}_1$ contains only *possible* samples. Since the marginal constraints are fulfilled by solving Problem (28.2), $p_{j2} = \sum_{i=1}^{m} p(s_{j2}|s_{i1})p(s_{i1})$ is respected and thus also $\pi_{k2}, \forall k \in U_2$.

To optimize $E(c)$ in negative coordination, use min $\sum_{i=1}^{m} \sum_{j=1}^{q} c_{ij} p_{ij}$ instead of max $\sum_{i=1}^{m} \sum_{j=1}^{q} c_{ij} p_{ij}$ as the objective function in (28.2), and keep the same constraints. When $c_{kk} = 1$ and $c_{k\ell} = 0, \forall k \neq \ell, k, \ell \in U$, with $U_1 = U_2 = U$, the problem reduces to the method of Raj (1956, 1968), where a sample is formed by a single unit.

The TP is limited to samples s_{i1} and s_{j2} that are selected sequentially. The use of a TP is computationally intensive since all possible samples on the two occasions/surveys must be enumerated, and their selection probabilities known. The method is impractical if U is large. For stratified designs, it can be solved, however, separately in each stratum. The method can be directly applied to consecutive stratified SRS-WOR designs. If the stratifications differ, then the approximate solution might use the stratum intersections. When both samples are selected by SRS-WOR,

Mach et al. (2006) showed how to reduce the dimension of the initial TP to a much smaller TP. The main advantage of using a TP is to provide the best solution in terms of optimizing $E(c)$, for given p_{i1} and $p_{j2}, i = 1, \ldots, m, j = 1, \ldots, q$.

28.3   Comparing Sample Coordination Methods

28.3.1   Measures Used in Sample Coordination

Different measures can be used to check the quality of a coordination method. The main ones are based on the bounds of the expected overlap size and on the response burden associated with a unit $k \in U$.

1. *Bounds of the expected sample overlap*: Any $\pi_{k,12}, k \in U$ has associated limits provided by the Fréchet bounds on the joint probabilities:

$$\max (0, \pi_{k1} + \pi_{k2} - 1) \leq \pi_{k,12} \leq \min (\pi_{k1}, \pi_{k2}) \tag{28.3}$$

By taking the sum over U in both sides of (28.3), one obtains bounds for $E(c)$:

$$\sum_{k \in U} \max (0, \pi_{k1} + \pi_{k2} - 1) \leq E(c) = \sum_{k \in U} \pi_{k,12} \leq \sum_{k \in U} \min (\pi_{k1}, \pi_{k2}) \tag{28.4}$$

These bounds are used to quantify the performance of sample coordination methods when the overlap optimization is considered as the main criterion. Yet, there are few methods in the literature able to reach these bounds; only Poisson sampling with PRNs, SRS-WOR with PRNs, and Keyfitz's method reach them among the methods presented in Section 28.2.2. For more details, see also Matei and Tillé (2005). Note that the solution to (28.2) does not necessarily meet the bounds in (28.4) because of the constraints on p_{i1} and p_{j2}.

Conditions to reach the bounds in (28.4) for given marginal sampling designs p_1 and p_2 have been provided by Matei and Tillé (2005). These conditions are, however, very restrictive and hard to fulfill if the given sampling designs p_1 and p_2 are, for instance, unequal probability sampling designs with fixed sample sizes.

2. *Measuring the response burden*: We point out that the reduction of the response load of a unit is a consequence of minimizing overlap size between samples, rather than a direct objective of sample coordination.

Response burden is a complex concept that is difficult to quantify (Haraldsen et al., 2013). Response burden influences nonresponse in surveys, and thus the quality of data collection. An easy definition of response burden is considered in Sunter (1977a). Let us use a general framework, where a unit i is exposed to several surveys $j = 1, 2, \ldots, M$ having associated $U_1, U_2, \ldots, U_M$ populations of units, and $U = \cup_{j=1}^{M} U_j$ represents the overall population corresponding to all the surveys. Each survey questionnaire is assessed for its response "load." Sunter (1977a) emphasized about the response load that "this would be expressed conveniently as a money equivalent to the time and effort required to complete the questionnaire." Let β_j be the response load imposed by the jth survey for all units selected to participate in this survey. The *response burden* of unit i in M surveys is a random variable $\mathrm{RB}_i = \sum_{j=1}^{M} \beta_j \times I_{ij}$, with $I_{ij} = 1$ if $i \in s_j$ and 0, otherwise (Sunter, 1977a). Its expectation is given by

$$E(\mathrm{RB}_i) = \sum_{j=1}^{M} \beta_j \pi_{ij}, \quad i \in U$$

where $\pi_{ij} = P(i \in s_j)$, and s_j is the jth survey sample, $j = 1, \ldots, M$. The response burden is usually associated with a negative coordination of samples: it is expected that RB_i is reduced if unit i is less often selected to answer the survey questionnaires, so when the overlap size is minimized. Haraldsen et al. (2013, p. 251), comments that "sample coordination does not affect the expected response burden, but is rather intended to control for excessive burdens and to allocate burdens in a fair way."

28.3.2 Criteria for Sample Coordination

It is possible to use different criteria to measure the quality of a coordination procedure. For example, Tillé (2020, p. 175) advocates the following four criteria:

1. "the procedure provides a controllable overlap rate,
2. the sampling design is satisfied for each sample,
3. for each unit, a period out of a sample is satisfied,
4. the procedure is easy to implement."

The first criterion in the list of Tillé (2020) is obviously less strong than the criterion related to the optimality of a coordination method, where the bounds in (28.4) are reached. The third criterion refers to the rotation of units in repeating surveys.

We use the following list of criteria inspired by Ernst (1999) to characterize each coordination method reviewed in this chapter:

1. uses PRNs/mathematical programming/other methods;
2. maximizes or minimizes the overlap size, or both;
3. the bounds given in Expression (28.4) can be reached (the method is optimal from this point of view);
4. allows sequential or simultaneous selection of samples, or both (sequential selection is useful for sample coordination over time, while simultaneous selection is more for sample coordination over surveys);
5. any constraint on the number of units to be selected in a sample (or stratum, in the case of stratified designs);
6. allows restratification, in the case of stratified designs;
7. allows independence of sampling from stratum to stratum (on each occasion, all strata are sampled independently of each other; for a single sample s this means that $P(i \in s, j \in s) = P(i \in s)P(j \in s)$ whenever units i and j are in different strata; this is important for variance estimation);
8. number of surveys to be coordinated;
9. allows the creation of a coordination system;
10. the main drawback of the method.

The criterion "the method allows the creation of a coordination system" is a result of the "number of surveys that can be coordinated." In some cases, a method allows only two samples to be coordinated, and thus its use over time is excluded. Many methods for sample coordination control the sample overlap; however, optimality (in the sense that the bounds on $E(c)$ given in Expression (28.4) are reached) is not always achieved. Table 28.1 provides an overview of the sample coordination methods presented in Section 28.2.2, on the basis of the above criteria.

We introduce below our own features of a coordination system, distinguishing between *sample coordination methods* and *sample coordination systems*.

Table 28.1 Properties of sample coordination methods described in Section 28.2.2.

Method	1	2	3	4	5	6	7	8	9	10
Poisson with PRNs	PRNs	Both	Yes	Both	No limit	Yes	Yes	No limit	Yes	Random sample size
Collocated	PRNs	Both	No	Both	No limit	No	Yes	No limit	Yes	Doesn't allow restratification or redesign of the survey
Pomix	PRNs	Both	No	Both	No limit	Yes	Yes	No limit	Yes	Random sample size
CP sampling										
Method I	PRNs	Both	No	Both	No limit	Yes	Yes	No limit	Yes	Less good coordination degree than Poisson with PRNs
Method II	Other	Both	No	Sequential	No limit	Yes	Not yet evaluated	2	No	Only the first sample is CP
SRS-WOR with PRNs	PRNs	Both	Yes	Both	No limit	Yes	Yes	No limit	Yes	Only equal inclusion probabilities of units
Synchronized sampling	PRNs	Both	No	Both	No limit	Yes	Yes	No limit	Yes	For different stratifications, positive coordination must be done "manually"
Ordered sampling (uniform, Pareto, exponential)	PRNs	Both	No	Both	No limit	Yes	Yes	No limit	Yes	Nearly πps sampling
Fixed size PoMix	PRNs	Both	No	Both	No limit	Yes	Yes	No limit	Yes	Nearly πps sampling for Pareto
Ohlsson	PRNs	Both	No	Both	1	Yes	Yes	No limit	Yes	Select only 1 unit
Keyfitz	Other	Maximizes	Yes	Sequential	1	No	Yes	2	No	Select only 1 unit
Sunter	Other	Maximizes	No	Sequential	No limit	No	Yes	2	No	Only for 2 samples
Causey, Cox, and Ernst	Mathematical programming	Both	No	Sequential	No limit	Yes	Yes	No limit	No	Unpractical for large U/large stratum

For the definitions of the columns, see the text.

28.4 Sample Coordination Systems

A range of procedures has been proposed for sample coordination, as summarized in Section 28.2.2. These methodological approaches do not, however, provide enough structure to deal with a range of different surveys with various designs and rotation patterns, and with the resulting range of positive and negative coordination characteristics. In order to manage this wider problem, we need a *sample coordination system*, and there has been a range of implementations, based on several of the available sample coordination methods, in different countries. A general system must deal with longitudinal surveys (including rotating panels); Nedyalkova et al. (2009), based on Cotton and Hesse (1992b), used the framework of longitudinal designs within a coordinating system as follows. For M surveys, a unit $k \in U$ has an associated probability vector $\pi_k = (\pi_{k,j})', j = 1, 2, \ldots, M$. A longitudinal sample associated with unit $k \in U$ is given by $(I_1, I_2, \ldots, I_M)$, where $I_j = 1$, if $k \in s_j$ or 0, otherwise, s_j being the jth sample, $j = 1, 2, \ldots, M$. Sample coordination itself generally has well-defined targets for optimization, but there are two incompatible strategies in a system which develops longitudinally (Nedyalkova et al., 2009):

- "to choose the cross sectional design and try to get the best coordination
- to choose a longitudinal systematic design and accept a progressive loss of control over the cross-sectional design."

To produce an implementation of a sample coordination system suitable for use in a national statistical institute generally means deciding on one of these strategies, and on one or more corresponding methods of sample coordination, and then developing the data requirements, procedures, and software which support the use of these methods. The sample coordination system includes the implementation and the data requirements together with the messy practical details.

It is challenging to define precisely what a sample coordination system consists of, but here is an attempt to enumerate its components:

a. One or more methods for sample coordination with defined goals (it will generally be most practical to use a single sample coordination method);
b. The system must be sequential to deal with changes in the survey portfolio (the set of surveys whose samples are to be coordinated using the system), and changes in sample design/stratification etc.;
c. The target measures to be optimized; in particular the burden should be spread as evenly as possible over the sample units with specific total selection probabilities;
d. Deals satisfactorily with many surveys and potentially many successive periods for each survey;
e. Allows both positive and negative coordination.

In addition, there are features which are not *required* for a sample coordination system, but which simplify its implementation:

f. Common stratification variables and common stratum boundaries;
g. (Under the assumption that control of either the designs or the coordination gradually breaks down as described above) allows the system to be updated to a new baseline, preserving as many of the coordination and control properties as possible at the time of updating. Or allows for gradual updating (via a moving time window) so that control of the target measures holds within the window but not outside it.

28.4.1   Optimization Measures in Sample Coordination Systems

In support of item c., Qualité (2009) points out that there are different ways in which positive and negative coordination can be defined, and we find it convenient to produce a typology so that we are able to discuss the different approaches. We therefore define:

p-coordination as a criterion based on the joint inclusion probability (named because it is defined with the inclusion **p**robabilities). If a unit k has inclusion probabilities π_{k1} and π_{k2} in two surveys (or, equally, two occasions of the same survey), respectively, then under independent selection its probability of being jointly included in both surveys is $\pi_k^{12} = \pi_{k1}\pi_{k2}$. If the achieved joint inclusion probability is $< \pi_{k1}\pi_{k2}$, then there is negative p-coordination, and if it is $> \pi_{k1}\pi_{k2}$, then there is positive p-coordination. We move therefore from the *coordination of samples* as underlined in Section 28.2.1 to *coordination of units* (see also Cotton and Hesse, 1992b, p. 27).

s-coordination as a criterion based on the units in the intersection of two designs (and named after the **s**ample size in the intersection). So if there are fewer units in the intersection than expected under independent sampling, that is $< \sum_{U_c} \pi_{k1}\pi_{k2}$, where U_c is the population of units common to both surveys, we say that there is negative s-coordination, and if there are more units than expected there is positive s-coordination.

b-coordination is a criterion based on equalizing the survey burden (and named after the **b**urden), which may vary between or within surveys, and possibly between survey occasions. If the variability of the burden across units is lower than expected under independent sampling, there is negative b-coordination, and if the variability is greater, then there is positive b-coordination. b-coordination could be implemented as a weighted p- or s-coordination.

28.5   Overview of Sample Coordination Systems

Systems for sample coordination have been of interest since the first developments in Australia and Sweden in the 1970s. Hesse (1999) reviewed sample coordination systems as part of an EU project, covering in detail Sweden, Australia, the Netherlands and France, where the methods and approaches were well documented, and with some comments on the coordination systems in Canada, Finland, New Zealand, UK, and USA. The only coordination methods which are suitable for generalization to a system of surveys are those based on PRNs (Hesse, 1999), but even here several approaches have been used, and we give an overview of the main methods and their uses below. Brewer et al. (2000) also include a small comparison covering the same countries.

28.5.1   Coordinated Poisson Sampling/Conditional Selection

Brewer et al. (1972) put forward a coordinated sampling approach based on PRNs in which the cross-sectional sample designs are Poisson, and therefore have variable sample sizes – Poisson sampling with PRNs from Section 28.2.2. Qualité (2009) notes that using Poisson designs makes coordination substantially easier to handle, particularly because

- the selection of any particular unit is not influenced by whether other units are selected or not;
- a substantial proportion of the loss in efficiency which arises from having a random sample size can be recovered by suitable calibration in the estimation phase.

However, the variable sample size has some undesirable features, since the probability of achieving a sample of size zero may be nonnegligible when target sample sizes are small. The sample size may be substantially smaller than desired even if it is not zero, leading to increased variances. The risk of both zero and small sample sizes are compounded when the survey is subject to substantial nonresponse. This potentially restricts the usefulness of coordinated Poisson sampling in highly constrained designs, or where optimization requires very specific sample sizes (for example, consider the interaction with numerical allocation for stratified sampling, in Chapter 27 Smith and Yung [2023]).

Qualité suggests algorithms for coordinated Poisson sampling that meet many of the requirements for a system, and this is the basis of the system implemented in Switzerland (see Qualité, 2019), for both business and household surveys. The process has essentially worked, providing a lot of flexibility, though there are still some challenges in the practical details. For business surveys, after 127 selections (including the waves of rotating panels) the system still functions well for a business population of 600,000 units. For household surveys with around 8.5 million units, the procedures slowed and became unusable after around 200 selections, eventually being restricted to only negative coordination. The size of the calculations grows at least with the square of the number of surveys in the case where both positive and negative coordination are implemented, so even with very efficient programming cannot be used for a very long time. The same method was developed independently in Australia (Bell, 2011) under the name of *conditional selection*, and is in use in Australia and New Zealand for coordination of the system of household surveys. The storage and processing requirements for a system based on this approach are substantial. Periodic resets of the system may therefore be needed to control them, and this has been done already in Switzerland.

The method of Qualité (2009) and Bell (2011) follows Poisson sampling with PRNs for the first two surveys/occasions in a system, and therefore achieves the optimum coordination for these surveys. Third and subsequent surveys/occasions are added conditional on the outcomes for earlier selections; so in these cases, coordination is not in general so good. It is therefore necessary to specify an ordering to selections to give the best control in the outcome, and although Bell (2011) explores the challenges of specifying the priority order of surveys in a coordination system, both he and Qualité suggest this as a topic for further research. This requirement for a priority of coordination rules contributes to making this approach practical (as it is clear what action to take when not all of the constraints can be met simultaneously), but also means that not all the constraints in the system are met. Therefore, there needs to be some assessment and reporting of the cases where, despite the sample coordination, some units are selected in more surveys and/or on more occasions than expected. Situations where few or no unsampled units remain may also be problematic for survey selections later in a sequence, and especially where some guarantee about the number or frequency of selection is given to businesses. Such evaluation and monitoring are particularly not only important in this system but also valuable monitoring tools to ensure that the implementation of other coordination systems does not produce unexpected results because of the conjunction of different designs. Bell (2011) also proposes a systematic selection approach within the same system, which induces a correlation between units which is not present in Poisson sampling with PRNs; Bell says, "In our simulations this correlation has no discern[i]ble effect on the selection probabilities for later surveys."

Sample coordination systems based on Coordinated Poisson sampling/conditional sampling are based on the joint inclusion probabilities and use p-coordination. They therefore do not explicitly take account of the realized burdens (although these could be used in the prioritization of surveys/occasions), and rely on the control of the joint inclusion probabilities to spread the burden more equally. In an evaluation of the Swiss system applied to business surveys, Qualité (2019) suggests that this makes relatively little difference for the largest (most frequently selected) and smallest (least frequently selected) units (which is intuitively true in general for coordination systems, Guggemos and Sautory, 2012), but does spread the burden for medium-sized units.

The variable sample size has been seen as a substantial drawback, so considerable research in sample coordination has gone into generating approaches which give fixed-size cross-sectional designs, and these form the basis of the other sample coordination systems discussed below.

28.5.2 SAMU

The *SAMordnade Urval* (SAMU) system has been used in Statistics Sweden for a long time (Ohlsson, 1992; Lindblom, 2003, 2014). It was instituted in the 1970s and is based on coordinating groups of surveys by allocating them suitable starts within the PRN range and a direction for selection (that is, whether it should use u_k or $1 - u_k$ as described in Section 28.2.2). Each survey within the group uses the same starting point for all the strata. This is (stratified) sequential random sampling with PRNs and is an s-coordination system seeking to control the size of the overlap between surveys. The SAMU system also includes (stratified) Pareto πps sampling as an option (an extension since Lindblom, 2003). Roughly half of the business surveys at Statistics Sweden used this system in 2017 (Lindblom, 2019).

There are different ways to implement rotation within this system, but SAMU employs five rotation groups in strata with a sampling fraction < 0.1, where the PRNs in the rotation groups are shifted each year. This ensures a constant rate of rotation within strata and is more easily managed in SAMU, which maintains the same starting values for survey groups, than the main alternative which involves updating the start values.

The stratification of surveys is based on a "frozen" version of the business register; there are four versions during a year, based on an initial frozen register, with updates for births and deaths, and some reclassification.

28.5.3 Synchronized Sampling

The system for coordination of business surveys in Australia is based on synchronized sampling (although conditional sampling – Section 28.5.1 – has been proposed, it has not yet been implemented for business surveys). The process works as described in Section 28.2.2 for positive coordination of panel samples and rotation can be straightforwardly introduced by making the starting points of selection intervals increase according to expected or achieved rates, depending on which is the faster (see McKenzie and Gross, 2001, for details). In order to achieve negative coordination, different surveys use disjoint intervals, and control over this coordination is increased if the surveys use common stratification.

Essentially, the same approach is used in the UK (the system is sketched in Smith et al., 2003), but their surveys are not confined to mutually exclusive intervals of PRN range, and therefore, occasional intervention is needed to prevent selections for surveys overlapping instead of being negatively coordinated. Statistics Canada has also implemented synchronized sampling (along with Poisson sampling with PRNs) in its generalized system *generalized SAMpling* (G-SAM), but here again, it is necessary to set the start points of selection ranges manually to achieve negative coordination.

In both Australia and UK, a unit starts afresh when it changes to a different stratum (that is, it is treated as death in the old stratum and birth in the new one) so that control of coordination is lost in these cases. The UK updates the stratification variables annually (except in exceptional cases where this makes a large difference to the survey estimates), as in the Swedish system, to avoid a lack of control during a year. The loss of coordination when units change strata is a challenge when the sample design must be updated, but some limited control can be exerted by an appropriate choice of start point for the new selection interval, as described by McKenzie and Gross (2001). Having found the start point that maximizes the required coordination (using positive indicators for positive coordination and negative indicators for negative coordination), the *next* element is chosen as the start, to reduce a bias in selection. More complex situations require an examination of the whole range of PRNs to identify a suitable range of values to start the redesigned survey from.

28.5.4 Burden-Based Coordination

The Netherlands sampling system was originally described (as *EnquêteDrukSysteem* [EDS]) by Van Huis et al. (1994) (although it had been developed earlier). EDS formed the basis for the development of a new system implemented in 2014 (Smeets and Boonstra, 2018) for coordination among groups of surveys. It is assumed that the surveys have common stratification, with some minor exceptions which allow division of strata into substrata. The basis of the method is to keep a PRN, an indicator of whether a unit was selected in each sample, and the cumulated burden for each unit. For a negative coordination, units are ordered at each selection by increasing cumulative burden, then by PRN to break ties in burden values. Then the first units in the resulting ordered list form the sample of units to be selected. For a positive coordination, units are ordered by the sample indicator for the survey with which positive coordination is desired; if necessary an adjustment can be made at this stage to induce a panel rotation by removing those units which have been in the survey the longest. Then the first units in the resulting ordered list again form the sample of units to be selected.

Some additional steps are needed to deal appropriately with births; when they join the population, they have no accumulated burden, and would be preferentially selected, leading to a sample containing too many recent births. To avoid this, the burden and the sample inclusion indicators should be imputed for a birth so that it has a typical value for the stratum. This is done by taking the values from the unit with nearest PRN within the stratum; then it will be treated appropriately in sampling.

A similar process occurs for stratum movers. First, the position in the old stratum is calculated, with respect to a user-defined ordering of burden, indicators and PRN, as $r/(N_h + 1)$, where r is the rank with respect to this order in stratum h, and N_h is the size of stratum h. This position is maintained in the new stratum, and new cumulated burden and inclusion indicators are imputed from the unit with the nearest position in the new stratum. Finally, the moving unit is assigned a new PRN (so in fact PRNs are not permanent in this system).

The Netherlands system therefore uses b-coordination explicitly, but within burden totals effectively uses sequential SRS-WOR with PRNs.

28.5.5 Coordination Functions

The outline of the approach seems to have been developed by Frank Cotton at *Institut National de la statistique et des études économiques, France* (INSEE) (France) in the late 1980s. It began with the idea of swapping PRNs between units so that previously selected units were not reselected (negative coordination), and the method was already implemented at this stage in software called OCEAN, for a single year. The paradigm of this approach is different from most other PRN methods (with the exception of the way rotation is implemented in the SAMU system) in that the PRNs are changed through a permutation of the random number line, while the selection interval remains fixed, always beginning from 0 and extending as far as is needed to achieve the required sample size for the survey being selected. The approach was extended to more general coordination functions which allowed different permutations of PRNs within different ranges in a series of papers. The full details were worked out in Cotton and Hesse (1992b) and summarized in Cotton and Hesse (1992a), then extended by Cotton and Hesse (1997) and Hesse (2001). This approach was implemented in two software packages, SALOMON and MICROSTRAT (Rivière, 2002) designed for use in EU member states. Despite this software availability, the method does not seem to have been used in earnest in France until the 2010s.

Notwithstanding the different selection paradigm, the approach is basically an implementation of sequential SRS-WOR with PRNs (Section 28.2.2), but the ability to permute the PRNs provides additional flexibility because it is not restricted to a single ordering. This also makes it more flexible for use in the case where the surveys within the system do not share the same stratification. By using a fixed end point for the selected PRN range, it can also be used for Poisson sampling designs.

The approach through permutation of PRNs in particular allows some measure(s) of the accumulated burden to be taken into account. The permutations are defined by sorting the population elements according to a small number of variables, with ties in the first variable being broken according to the order of the second variable, and so on, so sorting can be done by accumulated burden (for negative coordination), though of course this must be ignored for positive coordination. Ties in burden are broken by sorting by the PRNs within burden. Coordination is strongest with the variable at the first level of the sort and becomes weaker at lower levels; so it is important to define a hierarchy of coordinations, as in conditional selection (see Section 28.5.1). Because the coordination is based on the accumulated burden values, there is no control over the time in sample in rotating panels.

The method has been gradually extended and Guggemos and Sautory (2012) described a system based on coordination functions which allows positive and negative coordination over a wider range of surveys; they set out the theory in detail, including the challenges of approximating the burden functions with step functions and examine the effectiveness of the system through simulation. Gros and Le Gleut (2018) undertake a more extensive simulation based on the real designs of a range of surveys constituting 20 selections corresponding to a two-year period, and including both negative and positive coordination. The negative coordination is very effective, increasing the number of businesses selected in only one survey, and dramatically decreasing those in more than one compared with independent selections. The positive coordination is more effective than the previous approach described in Demoly et al. (2014).

A system based on coordination functions is basically an s-coordination, aiming to control the sample overlap, but it can be viewed at least partly as a b-coordination system when the accumulated burden values are specified as the sorting variables. This means that an extra process to calculate and update accumulated burden measures for all units is needed as part of the system.

28.6 Discussion

28.6.1 Distinguishing Sample Coordination Methods and Sample Coordination Systems

From these descriptions of sample coordination systems, we can deduce two properties that make a *system* distinct from a *sample coordination method*. The first is that coordination systems are much more concerned with *units* than with *samples*. Sample coordination aims to ensure maximum or minimum overlap between two samples, but a system focuses on whether a single unit is included in a disproportionate number of surveys, and the time in and out of a sample through rotation. Poisson sampling with PRNs is the sole member of the category of sample coordination methods that achieves unit coordination. This property makes this sample coordination method particularly easy to use as the basis of a system, which is why it has been introduced in Switzerland and (partially) in Australia.

The second difference is the explicit use of a measure of *survey burden* as part of the sample coordination system. None of the methods for sample coordination presented in Section 28.2.2 takes account of the accumulated burden that a unit has already expended in responding to surveys, but systems do. In some cases, this process is implicit, through control of the number of surveys or using sample coordination methods to exert control indirectly, but some systems use burden measures explicitly. In this way, they manage the process of spreading a fixed total burden more fairly across the units in the population. The corollary of this is that units will be reselected more quickly than under independent selections, but in many cases (particularly for the smallest businesses with small inclusion probabilities), the effect will not be noticeable to businesses, and therefore, their perceived burden will be lower.

28.6.2 Further Challenges

There are several other challenges which present themselves in operating a sample coordination system. One particular issue is that businesses have hierarchical structures, and surveys may use more than one unit in the hierarchy for sampling. Several authors of systems have addressed this, most by making the PRN for a higher-level unit and its largest lower-level unit the same. This means that there is dependence between surveys at the two levels, but that some coordination between levels is possible. While this is not as well controlled as for surveys at the same level, there is evidence that it manages the burden better than independent selections in Lindblom (2003) and Gros and Le Gleut (2018).

28.7 Conclusion

Sample coordination methods aim to maximize or minimize the overlap between samples. While the PRN methods are easier to use and thus more popular, theoretical properties of the expected overlap size $E(c)$ are in general difficult to establish. The performance of such methods are usually studied by Monte Carlo simulation. On the other hand, some non-PRN methods also offer good solutions to optimize $E(c)$, such as methods based on mathematical programming. Nevertheless, they are hard to use if the population size (or stratum size) is large, but can be applied, for instance, for surveys that employ a multistage design where samples of primary sample units have to be coordinated over time.

Coordination systems use coordination methods. Sometimes, different goals have to be reached, so that *optimization of the overlap* becomes less important, and it is replaced only by a *control of the overlap* between samples.

The landscape of sample coordination systems for business surveys has been remarkably stable in the last 20 years. The same four countries (Sweden, Australia, the Netherlands, and France) have continued as the principal proponents of systems and have continued to operate systems based on the methods that were in use at the time of Hesse (1999)'s review. France has moved to a full implementation of the methods based on coordination functions and Australia has considered but not implemented a change to conditional selection. The main development in sample coordination systems has been in Switzerland, where a system based on coordinated Poisson sampling has been introduced and run successfully.

Acknowledgments

We are grateful to the participants of the European Network for Better Establishment Statistics (ENBES) workshop on coordinated sampling, March 2019 in The Hague, which brought together information on many of the methods and systems described. We also thank Katherine Jenny Thompson, Joe Sakshaug, and Lionel Qualité for their helpful comments and suggestions on an earlier version of this chapter that allowed us to improve it. The research of Alina Matei was supported by the Swiss Federal Statistical Office.

References

Arthnari, T.S. and Dodge, Y. (1981). *Mathematical Programming in Statistics*. New York: Wiley.

Bell, P.A. (2011). Conditional selection for business and household surveys. Methodology advisory committee paper, Australian Bureau of Statistics.

Berger, Y.G. (1998). Rate of convergence for asymptotic variance for the Horvitz–Thompson estimator. *Journal of Statistical Planning and Inference* 74: 149–168.

Bradburn, N. (1978). Respondent burden. *Proceedings of the Survey Research Methods Section of the American Statistical Association*, Volume 35, pp. 35–40. Alexandria, VA: American Statistical Association.

Brewer, K.R.W., Early, L.J., and Joyce, S.F. (1972). Selecting several samples from a single population. *Australian Journal of Statistics* 3: 231–239.

Brewer, K.R.W., Early, L.J., and Hanif, M. (1984). Poisson, modified Poisson and collocated sampling. *Journal of Statistical Planning and Inference* 10: 15–30.

Brewer, K.R.W., Gross, W.F., and Lee, G.F. (2000). PRN sampling: the Australian experience. *Bulletin of the International Statistical Institute, 52nd Session, Tome LVIII*, pp. 155–163. International Statistical Institute, 2000. Invited paper at the 52nd Session of the ISI World Statistics Congress, Helsinki (10–18 August 1999).

Causey, B.D., Cox, L.H., and Ernst, L.R. (1985). Application of transportation theory to statistical problems. *Journal of the American Statistical Association* 80: 903–909.

Cotton, F. and Hesse, C. (1992a). Co-ordinated selection of stratified samples. *Proceedings of Statistics Canada Symposium 92*, pp. 47–54. Ottawa: Statistics Canada.

Cotton, F. and Hesse, C. (1992b). Tirages coordonnés d'échantillons. *Technical Report E9206*. Paris, France: Direction des Statistiques Économiques, INSEE.

Cotton, F. and Hesse, C. (1997). Sampling and maintenance of a stratified panel of fixed size. *Survey Methodology* 23: 109–117.

Demoly, E.E., Fizzala, A., and Gros, E. (2014). Méthodes et pratiques des enquêtes entreprises à l'Insee. *Journal de la Société Française de Statistique* 155 (4): 134–159.

Ernst, L.R. (1996). Maximizing the overlap of sample units for two designs with simultaneous selection. *Journal of Official Statistics* 12: 33–45.

Ernst, L.R. (1998). Maximizing and minimizing overlap when selecting a large number of units per stratum simultaneously for two designs. *Journal of Official Statistics* 14: 297–314.

Ernst, L.R. (1999). The maximization and minimization of sample overlap problems: a half century of results. *Proceedings of the International Statistical Institute, 52nd Session*, pp. 168–182. Helsinki, Finland.

Ernst, L.R. (2001). Retrospective Assignment of Permanent Random Numbers for Ohlsson's Exponential Sampling Overlap Maximization Procedure for Designs with More Than One Sample Unit Per Stratum. *Technical report*. U.S. Department of Labor, Bureau of Labor Statistics.

Ernst, L.R. and Ikeda, M.M. (1995). A reduced-size transportation algorithm for maximizing the overlap between surveys. *Survey Methodology* 21: 147–157.

Ernst, L.R. and Paben, S.P. (2002). Maximizing and minimizing overlap when selecting any number of units per stratum simultaneously for two designs with different stratifications. *Journal of Official Statistics* 18: 185–202.

Ernst, L.R., Valliant, R., and Casady, R.J. (2000). Permanent and collocated random number sampling and the coverage of births and deaths. *Journal of Official Statistics* 16: 211–228.

Fan, C.T., Muller, M.E., and Rezucha, I. (1962). Development of sampling plans by using sequential (item by item) selection techniques and digital computer. *Journal of the American Statistical Association* 57: 387–402.

Grafström, A. and Matei, A. (2015). Coordination of Conditional Poisson samples. *Journal of Official Statistics* 31 (4): 1–24.

Grafström, A. and Matei, A. (2018). Coordination of spatially balanced samples. *Survey Methodology* 44 (2): 215–238.

Gros, E. and Le Gleut, R. (2018). Sample coordination and response burden for business surveys: methodology and practice of the procedure implemented at INSEE. In: *The Unit Problem and Other Current Topics in Business Survey Methodology* (ed. B. Lorenc, P.A. Smith, M. Bavdaž, G. Haraldsen, D. Nedyalkova, L.C. Zhang, and T. Zimmerman), 141–156. Newcastle-upon-Tyne: Cambridge Scholars.

Guggemos, F. and Sautory, O. (2012). Sampling coordination of business surveys conducted by INSEE. *Proceedings of the International Conference on Establishment Surveys ICES-IV*. Alexandria, VA: American Statistical Association.

Hájek, J. (1964). Asymptotic theory of rejective sampling with varying probabilities from a finite population. *Annals of Mathematical Statistics* 35: 1491–1523.

Hájek, J. (1981). *Sampling from a Finite Population*. New York: Marcel Dekker.

Haraldsen, G., Jones, J., Giesen, D., and Zhang, L.-C. (2013). Understanding and coping with response burden. In: *Designing and Conducting Business Surveys* (ed. G. Snijkers, G. Haraldsen, J., Jones, and D.K. Willimack), 219–251. Hoboken, New Jersey: Wiley.

Hesse, C. (1999). Sampling Co-Ordination: A Review by Country. *Technical Report E9908*. Paris: Direction des Statistique d'Entreprises, INSEE.

Hesse, C. (2001). Generalisation des tirages a numéros aleatoires permanents ou la methode Jales+. *Technical Report 01*. Paris: Direction des Statistique d'Entreprises, INSEE.

Hinde, R. and Young, D. (1984). Synchronised sampling and overlap control manual. *Methodology report*. Canberra, Australia: Australian Bureau of Statistics.

Keyfitz, N. (1951). Sampling with probabilities proportional to size: adjustment for changes in the probabilities. *Journal of American Statistics Association* 46: 105–109.

Kish, L. and Scott, A. (1971). Retaining units after changing strata and probabilites. *Journal of the American Statistical Association* 66: 461–470.

Kröger, H., Särndal, C.E., and Teikari, I. (1999). Poisson mixture sampling: a family of designs for coordinated selection using permanent random numbers. *Survey Methodology* 25: 3–11.

Kröger, H., Särndal, C.E., and Teikari, I. (2003). Poisson mixture sampling combined with order sampling. *Journal of Official Statistics* 19: 59–70.

Lindblom, A. (2003). SAMU: The system for coordination of frame populations and samples from the business register at Statistics Sweden. Background facts on economic statistics, 2003: 3, Statistics Sweden, Örebro. http://share.scb.se/ov9993/data/publikationer/statistik/ov/aa9999/2003m00/x100st0303.pdf (accessed 16 March 2022).

Lindblom, A. (2014). On precision in estimates of change over time where samples are positively coordinated by permanent random numbers. *Journal of Official Statistics* 30 (4): 773–785.

Lindblom, A. (2019). Coordinated sampling for business surveys – theory, method and application at Statistics Sweden. *Presentation, ENBES workshop on Coordinated Sampling for Business Surveys.* https://statswiki.unece.org/display/ENBES/ENBES+Workshop+2019+%28The+Hague%29+-+Workshop+on+Coordinated+Sampling?preview=/234225830/244092342/Slides_Lindblom_2019.pdf (accessed 16 March 2022).

Mach, L., Reiss, P.T., and Șchiopu-Kratina, I. (2006). Optimizing the expected overlap of survey samples via the northwest corner rule. *Journal of the American Statistical Association* 101 (476): 1671–1679.

Matei, A. and Skinner, C. (2009). Optimal sample coordination using controlled selection. *Journal of Statistical Planning and Inference* 139 (9): 3112–3121.

Matei, A. and Tillé, Y. (2005). Maximal and minimal sample co-ordination. *Sankhyā* 67 (3): 590–612.

McKenzie, R. and Gross, B. (2001). Synchronised sampling. *ICES II: The 2nd International Conference on Establishment Surveys. Invited Papers*, pp. 237–243. American Statistical Association.

Nedyalkova, D., Pea, J., and Tillé, Y. (2008). Sampling procedures for coordinating stratified samples: methods based on microstrata. *International Statistical Review* 76 (3): 368–386.

Nedyalkova, D., Qualité, L., and Tillé, Y. (2009). General framework for the rotation of units in repeated survey sampling. *Statistica Neerlandica* 63 (3): 269–293.

Ohlsson, E. (1990). Sequential Poisson Sampling from a Business Register and its Application to the Swedish Consumer Price Index. *R&D Report 1990:6*. Statistics Sweden.

Ohlsson, E. (1992). The System for Co-ordination of Samples from the Business Register at Statistics Sweden. *R&D report 1992:18*. Statistics Sweden.

Ohlsson, E. (1995). Coordination of samples using permanent random numbers. In: *Business Survey Methods*, Chapter 9 (ed. B.G. Cox, D.A. Binder, B.N. Chinnappa, A. Christianson, M.J. Colledge, and P.S. Kott), 153–169. New York: Wiley.

Ohlsson, E. (1996). Methods for PPS Size One Sample Coordination. *Research report 194*. Sweden: Stockholm University, December 1996.

Ohlsson, E. (1998). Sequential Poisson sampling. *Journal of Official Statistics* 14: 149–162.

Pathak, P.K. and Fahimi, M. (1992). Optimal integration of surveys. In: *Current Issues in Statistical Inference: Essays in Honor of D. Basu* (ed. M. Ghosh and P.K. Pathak), 208–224. Hayward, CA: Institute of Mathematical Statistics.

Perry, C.R., Burt, J.C., and Iwig, W.C. (1993). Methods of selecting samples in multiple surveys to reduce respondent burden. *Proceedings of the International Conference on Establishment Surveys.* Alexandria, American Statistical Association, pp. 345–351.

Qualité, L. (2009). Unequal probability sampling and repeated surveys. Chapter 6: Coordinated Poisson sampling. Doctoral thesis. Neuchâtel, Switzerland: Université de Neuchââel. https://doc.rero.ch/record/12284/files/ (accessed 16 March 2022).

Qualité, L. (2019). Coordinated sampling: theory, method and application at SFSO. *Presentation, ENBES Workshop on Coordinated Sampling for Business Surveys.* https://statswiki.unece.org/display/ENBES/ENBES+Workshop+2019+%28The+Hague%29+-+Workshop+on+Coordinated+Sampling?preview=/234225830/244092344/Slides_Qualite_2019.pdf (accessed 16 March 2022).

Raj, D. (1956). On the method of overlapping maps in sample surveys. *Sankhyā* 17: 89–98.

Raj, D. (1968). *Sampling Theory*. New York: McGraw-Hill.

Rivière, P. (2002). Coordinating sampling using the microstrata methodology. *Proceedings of Statistics Canada Symposium 2001*.

Rosén, B. (1997a). Asymptotic theory for order sampling. *Journal of Statistical Planning and Inference* 62: 135–158.

Rosén, B. (1997b). On sampling with probability proportional to size. *Journal of Statistical Planning and Inference* 62: 159–191.

Saavedra, P.J. (1995). Fixed sample size PPS approximations with a permanent random number. *Proceedings of the Section on Survey Research Methods*, pp. 697–700. American Statistical Association.

Șchiopu-Kratina, I., Fillion, J.-M., Mach, L., and Reiss, P.T. (2014). Maximizing the conditional overlap in business surveys. *Journal of Statistical Planning and Inference* 149: 98–115.

Scholtus, S. and van Delden, A. (2016). PPS sampling with panel rotation for estimating price indices on services. Discussion paper, No. 18. Statistics Netherlands.

Smeets, M. and Boonstra, H.J. (2018). Sampling coordination of business surveys at Statistics Netherlands. In: *The Unit Problem and Other Current Topics in Business Survey Methodology* (ed. B. Lorenc, P.A. Smith, M. Bavdaž G. Haraldsen, D. Nedyalkova, L.C. Zhang, and T. Zimmerman), 127–137. Newcastle-upon-Tyne: Cambridge Scholars.

Smith, P.A. and Yung, W. (2023). Introduction to sampling and estimation for business surveys. In: *Advances in Business Statistics, Methods and Data Collection*, Chapter 27 (ed. G. Snijkers, M. Bavdaž, S. Bender, J. Jones, S. MacFeely, J.W. Sakshaug, K.J. Thompson, and A. van Delden). Hoboken: Wiley.

Smith, P., Pont, M., and Jones, T. (2003). Developments in business survey methodology in the Office for National Statistics, 1994–2000. *Journal of the Royal Statistical Society: Series D* 52 (3): 257–286.

Sunter, A. (1989). Updating size measures in a ppswor design. *Survey Methodology* 15 (2): 253–260.

Sunter, A.B. (1977a). Response burden, sample rotation, and classification renewal in economic surveys. *International Statistical Review* 45: 209–222.

Sunter, A.B. (1977b). List sequential sampling with equal or unequal probabilities without replacement. *Applied Statistics* 26: 261–268.

Tillé, Y. (2020). *Sampling and Estimation from Finite Populations*. Wiley.

Tillé, Y. and Favre, A.-C. (2004). Co-ordination, combination and extension of optimal balanced samples. *Biometrika* 91: 913–927.

Tiwari, N. and Sud, U.C. (2012). An optimal procedure for sample coordination using multiple objective functions and nearest proportional to IPPS size sampling designs. *Communications in Statistics, Theory and Methods* 41: 2014–2033.

Van Huis, L.T., Koeijers, C.A.J., and de Ree, S.J.M. (1994). EDS, Sampling system for the central business register at Statistics Netherlands. Internal paper, Statistics Netherlands. https://statswiki .unece.org/download/attachments/117774189/EDS%20EN.PDF (accessed 16 March 2022).

29

Variance Estimation for Probability and Nonprobability Establishment Surveys: An Overview

Jill A. Dever and Dan Liao

RTI International, Washington, DC, USA

The goal of variance estimation for finite population inference is to capture the variability in the characteristics of interest within the inferential population *and* the random attributes associated with the sample data. The sample attributes can include the mechanism by which sample members are "captured" for the study and random adjustments applied to create the final analysis weights (e.g. weight adjustments made to limit nonresponse bias), if weights are developed for analyses. Additionally, the analytic data file may contain imputed values for missing data arising from item nonresponse within an otherwise complete information set, or possibly unit nonresponse linked to nonparticipating sample members. Proper specification of these attributes is key to quantifying the precision of the survey estimates used for statistical tests, confidence intervals, and the like.

A sampling design specifies how participants are identified for a study. Probability sampling uses sourced information that (ideally) covers the entire population of interest with prespecified sample inclusion probabilities. For example, Dun & Bradstreet maintains a database of US businesses with many characteristics available for tailored sampling. However, when this approach is infeasible or inefficient for a study (e.g. a high-quality sampling frame does not already exist), researchers instead may collect data from an easily accessed set of establishments using convenient methods that lack a defined link to the population via random sampling (i.e. nonprobability sampling).

Survey weights and other analytic adjustments are made with the intent to mitigate certain biases present in the data (Valliant and Dever 2018). For example, bias linked to coverage may stem from an incomplete sampling frame or from a set of study participants that are not representative of the target population. When these techniques are inadequate, confidence intervals, statistical tests, and other metrics suffer, potentially producing a misrepresentation of the population and incorrect decisions based on the analytic results. Such is the charge for researchers to make the most from the data at hand.

Survey weight adjustments may be inefficient or infeasible if data are lacking for all or a large portion of an important population subgroup. For example, survey unit and item nonresponse may be high for small businesses that lack infrastructure to easily answer survey questions. At the extreme, small business respondent records may not be available for such an adjustment; alternatively, the adjustment may produce population estimates of poor quality that are never published. Loss of data reduces the power of statistical tests along with lowered estimated precision. Statistical imputation alone or in concert with weight adjustments may address these challenges, though this effort introduces additional random variability into the population estimates.

Advances in Business Statistics, Methods and Data Collection. Edited by Ger Snijkers, Mojca Bavdaž, Stefan Bender, Jacqui Jones, Steve MacFeely, Joseph W. Sakshaug, Katherine J. Thompson, and Arnout van Delden.
© 2023 John Wiley & Sons, Inc. Published 2023 by John Wiley & Sons, Inc.

Methodological differences in probability and nonprobability sampling designs and treatment of the collected data are important considerations for any study. This chapter discusses such decisions using techniques currently employed for establishment surveys or those applicable for future research. Section 29.1 provides background on variance estimation for probability surveys including a review of key aspects for design-based theory that underpins these methods. Section 29.2 expands the discussion to nonprobability surveys, noting how techniques developed with sampling theory are borrowed for use and the important assumptions at play. We conclude this chapter with a few overarching comments on variance estimation in general and for probability and nonprobability sampling designs.

29.1 Estimation for Probability Business Survey Data

This section focuses on statistical inference for probability surveys of establishments. We discuss different inferential approaches first and then focus on variance estimation methods for design-based inference. An extensive discussion is provided at the end to illustrate critical components in establishment surveys that need to be accounted for in the variance estimation procedure. Examples of variance estimation practices in real establishment surveys are listed as references.

29.1.1 Probability Sampling in Practice

Probability surveys utilize a random method to select sample units from their intended finite target population. A sample is considered probability based only when all the units in the target population can be enumerated (if only theoretically) and every enumerated unit has a known nonzero probability of selection. These characteristics permit design-unbiased estimation of population parameters out of the probability sample, such as totals, means, or proportions (Särndal et al. 1992).

The random selection method chosen for a survey is always intended to maximize the precision of estimators under practical constraints, including costs, time, and ease of implementation in the field. Many sampling textbooks (e.g. Cochran 1977; Särndal et al. 1992; Lohr 2010; Fuller 2009; Valliant et al. 2018) detail the theoretical and practical considerations for various sampling methods. For establishment surveys, the sampling scheme may be even more complex than household or person-level surveys, especially when a survey attempts to produce estimates at multiple levels of the data (e.g. both for schools and students). In some cases, the establishments (e.g. parent company, schools, hospitals) are randomly selected from a population frame list first and then individuals (e.g. subsidiary, students, patients) are randomly chosen within the selected establishments. Furthermore, other types of units (e.g. student's parent or patient's doctor) associated with the sampled individuals may be recruited for interview. In each of these steps, complex sampling schemes, such as stratification, clustering or multiphases, may be implemented. Table 29.1 presents some examples of probability establishment surveys and their sampling designs.

29.1.2 Theories of Population Inference

As a statistical framework to make inference with survey data, three approaches – design based, model based, and model assisted – have been developed considering different sources of randomness used to structure the inference (Särndal et al. 1978; Chambers and Skinner 2003; Lohr 2010). The distribution used for design-based inference relies on repeated random samples

Table 29.1 Examples of probability establishment surveys and their sampling designs.

Establishment survey	Sampling design
Current Employment Statistics Survey (US)	Stratified, single-stage design with equal sampling probability within strata
Unified Enterprise Survey (Canada)	Stratified, single-stage design with equal sampling probability within strata
Annual Business Survey (UK)	Stratified, single-stage design with equal sampling probability within strata
Community Innovation Survey (EU)	Stratified, single-stage design with equal sampling probability within strata
Annual Survey of Manufactures (US)	Stratified single-stage design with Poisson sampling within strata
National Compensation Survey (US)	Stratified, multistage design with geographic PSUs
National Assessment of Educational Progress (US)	Stratified, multistage design; schools selected at the first stage via a stratified systematic sampling scheme; students randomly selected at the second stage; groups of assessment items randomly assigned to a subsample of students
Agricultural Resources and Management Survey (US)	Unstratified and single-stage design using the Sequential Interval Poisson sampling method
Programme for International Student Assessment (OECD)	Three-stage design with stratification at each stage, selecting the area-level (geographic) PSUs first, then schools, and last students; stratification variables vary across different countries

US: the United States; EU: European Union; OECD: Organization for Economic Co-operation and Development; PSU: primary sampling unit.

from a finite population. In consequence, the random sampling methodology forms the basis to make design-based inference possible with probability surveys, a trait not directly applicable to nonprobability surveys. The design-based point estimator for a total can be expressed as follows: $\hat{T} = \sum_{i \in S} d_i y_i$, where S indicates the entire sample set, d_i is the base weight of sample unit i calculated as the inverse probability of selection, and y_i is the variable to estimate the total.

In the model-based approach, the distribution for inference is based on a "superpopulation" defined by a model under frequentist inference (Valliant et al. 2000) or on posterior distribution under Bayesian inference (Little 2006). A simple example of a model-based estimate of a total is $\hat{T} = \sum_{i \in S} y_i + \sum_{j \in \overline{S}} \hat{y}_j$, where $\overline{S}$ stands for the set of units in the population that are not in the sample, and $\hat{y}_j$ is the predicted y-value for unit j from a prediction model developed from the responding sample members. Model-based inference is particularly relevant to nonprobability surveys as discussed in Section 29.2.

The design-based approach is commonly used for probability surveys to evaluate the properties of estimators like bias and variance because it is considered free from any failure of model assumptions (model-free). However, it is often unrealistic to obtain data for all the units selected in the initial sample due to nonresponse. Therefore, a model-assisted methodology (Särndal et al. 1992) has been developed as a hybrid approach that incorporates auxiliary data via a "working" model to improve the accuracy of the estimators, while maintaining the desirable design-based properties. For instance, the generalized regression estimator (GREG; Deville and Särndal 1992; Särndal et al. 1992) is a well-known class of model-assisted estimators that can incorporate categorical and continuous covariates. Under the model-assisted approach, the auxiliary data are typically external to the survey and are available for the entire target population. In establishment surveys, the auxiliary data may include various size measures (e.g. the number of employees) or other information (e.g. establishment type) known for every establishment in the target population; or they may be the aggregated total of size measures (e.g. the total number of employees) or other aggregated information known for the entire population.

29.1.3 Basic Weighting Steps

To make design-based inference with design-based or model-assisted approaches, there are usually four basic steps to create the final survey weights for a probability survey (see, e.g. Valliant and Dever, 2018):

(1) base weights, which are the inverse of selection probabilities for sample units;
(2) unknown eligibility adjustment to address any units with unknown eligibility status (e.g. countries where information is not readily available to confirm if a business is still in operation);
(3) nonresponse adjustment to address sample units that did not respond to the survey; and
(4) calibration (e.g. poststratification) to align select estimated total to their external reference totals.

The first step is fundamental for making design-based inference and usually straightforward with a well-defined sampling design. Once the sample is selected, the selection probability for each sample unit should be stored so that its base weight can be easily computed. The unknown eligibility adjustment is only necessary when the eligibility status of some units on the sampling frame are unknown. Weighting class adjustments are usually used for unknown eligibility adjustments to account for the probability of units being eligible in each subgroup (class) of the sample. The third and fourth steps use the weighting class or more complicated methods, such as response propensity models or weight calibration models – see, e.g. SUDAAN's WTADJUST procedure (Research Triangle Institute 2012, Chapter 24). Each of the four steps can affect the distribution of the estimators and thus should be considered in the variance estimation procedure.

29.1.4 Variance Estimation for Probability Surveys

Once a population estimate is derived with data obtained from a probability sample, the associated variance or standard error (SE) must be computed to reflect the magnitude of uncertainty introduced by the randomness associated with this sample estimate. Variance estimation should consider the type of the estimator (e.g. whether it is a mean or a regression parameter) and the approach used for population inference. It should also account for variability introduced by the compound effects of sample design, weighting adjustment, and item imputation procedures. In this section, we will focus on variance estimation for probability surveys under design-based (including model-assisted) inference.

In general, there are three alternative methods commonly used to compute variances and SEs for probability sample estimates from the design-based perspective: exact (theoretical) formulas, linearization, and replication. Below, we illustrate these methods and summarize their strengths and weaknesses. Valliant et al. (2018), Särndal et al. (1992), and Wolter (2007) provide more mathematical details and discussions about these methods.

29.1.4.1 Exact Formulas

Under a particular sample design, the exact (theoretical) formula can be derived for a design-based variance provided that the estimator takes a linear form (e.g. totals of the form $\sum a_k y_k$). Since many estimators using survey data are nonlinear (e.g. ratio means, percentiles), they are not often used to compute variance estimates in the practical world. However, exact formulas are broadly used for two distinct purposes in survey statistics. First, they are frequently mentioned in sampling text-books to demonstrate how different sampling methods can affect the variance of estimates. For example, in comparison to simple random samples stratification with stratifiers that are associated with the variable of interest can reduce the variance while clustering may increase the variance. Second, as will be discussed next, exact formulas are used as a component within linearization. For illustration purposes, we present exact variance formulas for a population mean estimate under two example sampling designs used for establishment surveys. Lohr (2010) provides exact formulas for variance estimation under a variety of different sample designs.

29.1.4.1.1 Stratified Simple Random Sampling Without Replacement (STSRSWOR)

As shown in Table 29.1, Stratified Simple Random Sampling without Replacement (STSRSWOR) is a commonly used sampling design for establishment surveys. Under a STSRSWOR design, suppose that there are H strata in the population with N_h units in stratum h, and n_h units are selected from stratum h using SRSWOR. The mean for a population of size N is estimated as follows:

$$\hat{\bar{y}} = \sum_{h=1}^{H} W_h \hat{\bar{y}}_h$$

where $W_h = N_h/N$ is the known proportion of units in the population in stratum h with N_h representing the number of stratum-specific population units, and $\hat{\bar{y}}_h = \sum_{i \in S_h} y_{hi}/n_h$ is the estimated mean in stratum h with n_h specifying the number of sample members selected in that stratum.

The exact formula to estimate its variance can then be expressed as follows:

$$\text{var}(\hat{\bar{y}}) = \sum_{h=1}^{H} \frac{1 - f_h}{n_h} \hat{S}_h^2 \tag{29.1}$$

where $\hat{S}_h^2$ is the estimated population variance of y in stratum h, and $f_h = n_h/N_h$ is the sampling fraction in stratum h. As can be seen from this formula, the variance of the mean estimate will decrease when the sample size n_h increases or $\hat{S}_h^2$ decreases. In addition to the estimate of the population mean, this variance estimation formula can also be used for the estimate of proportion, considering that a proportion can be expressed as a mean of a binary variable.

29.1.4.1.2 Poisson Sampling with Unequal Selection Probability

Another example approach used for establishment surveys is Poisson sampling with unequal selection probabilities. With this approach, researchers can make the selection probability for each establishment in the population proportional to its size. This methodology also has the well-known property that the joint selection probability of two sample units is equal to the product of their individual selection probabilities. This property makes the variance estimation easier than many competing without-replacement sampling approaches. In addition, this approach can be implemented when the entire sampling frame is not readily available. For example, Poisson sampling can be used as business tax returns are submitted for auditing purposes. A disadvantage of this approach is that the overall (achieved) sample size is not fixed; this random sample size increases the expected variance over other fixed-sample unequal selection probability schemes. In practice,

Poisson sample sizes are very likely close to the expected number selected. The Poisson sampling approach can be used in conjunction with stratification or clustering designs.

In this example, assume the sample data are drawn using an unstratified single-stage Poisson sampling scheme. If the selection probability for unit i is π_i, the population mean can be estimated using $\hat{\bar{y}} = \sum_{i \in S} y_i/(N\pi_i)$. The exact formula to estimate its variance is

$$v(\hat{\bar{y}}) = \sum_{i \in S} \left(\frac{y_i}{N\pi_i} \right)^2 (1 - \pi_i).$$

Besides the estimated means, exact formulas can also apply for variances of other linear estimators, such as estimated totals or their linear combinations (e.g. the estimated sum of totals of multiple variables). The exact formulas not only can account for complex sampling features, like stratification and clustering, but also can account for joint selection probabilities when two units are selected for the same sample. When the sampling design is more complex, like multistage or multiphase designs, the exact formulas are very complicated.

29.1.4.2 Linearization Methods

As mentioned earlier, most estimators using survey data are nonlinear. Even when estimating a mean, one often uses a nonlinear estimator, $\hat{\bar{y}} = \frac{\sum_{i \in S} w_i y_i}{\sum_{i \in S} w_i}$, which is a ratio of two linear estimators. Nonlinear estimators often used in establishment surveys include ratio estimators (e.g. wage per employee, inventories to sales, and students to teachers), time series measures (e.g. month-to-month change estimate), weighted estimators with adjusted survey weights, and estimated regression coefficients (e.g. the estimated effect of classroom size on student's test scores). The idea of the linearization method, also known as the *Taylor series* or *delta* method, is to approximate a nonlinear estimator by a linear function, in plain language, converting a nonlinear estimator into its linear approximation (format). Then, the variance of its linear approximation can be estimated using exact design-based formulas. Suppose that an estimator $\hat{\theta}$ of a parameter θ can be written as a nonlinear function f of estimated totals,

$$\hat{\theta} = f(\hat{t}) = f(\hat{t}_1, \hat{t}_2, \cdots, \hat{t}_p),$$

where $\hat{t} = (\hat{t}_1, \hat{t}_2, \cdots, \hat{t}_p)^T$ and each estimated total, $\hat{t}_j$, must be a linear estimator. The first step is to convert the function of $\hat{\theta}$ into its linear approximation using the Taylor series expansion formula:

$$\hat{\theta} \cong \theta + \sum_{j=1}^{p} \frac{\partial f(t)}{\partial \hat{t}_j}(\hat{t}_j - t_j),$$

and then we have

$$\hat{\theta} - \theta \cong \sum_{j=1}^{p} \frac{\partial f(t)}{\partial \hat{t}_j}(\hat{t}_j - t_j) \tag{29.2}$$

where $\partial f(\hat{t})/\partial \hat{t}_j$ is the partial derivative of $f(\hat{t})$ with respect to its jth parameter $\hat{t}_j$ and t_j is the "true" population total value corresponding to the estimated total value of $\hat{t}_j$.

Because $V(\hat{\theta}) = E_\pi[(\hat{\theta} - \theta)^2]$, where E_π stands for the expectation with respect to the sample design, if we square both sides of Eq. (29.2) and evaluate their expectation to the sample design, we can obtain

$$V(\hat{\theta}) = E_\pi (\hat{\theta} - \theta)^2 \cong \sum_{j=1}^{p} \left[\frac{\partial f(t)}{\partial \hat{t}_j} \right]^2 V(\hat{t}_j) + \sum_{j=1}^{p} \sum_{k \neq j}^{p} \frac{\partial f(t)}{\partial \hat{t}_j} \frac{\partial f(t)}{\partial \hat{t}_k} Cov(\hat{t}_j, \hat{t}_k) \tag{29.3}$$

For more details, see Chapter 5.5 in Särndal et al. (1992) or Chapter 6 in Wolter (2007).

Linear Substitute Method The variances and covariances on the right side of Eq. (29.3) can be obtained through exact formulas for a particular sample design, under which the survey data used to estimate $\hat{\theta}$ are collected. However, estimating these variances and covariances for many components can be cumbersome. An alternative, called the *linear substitute* (Wolter 2007), simplifies this computation. To illustrate the idea of the linear substitute, suppose the survey data are collected from a stratified multistage design and each estimated total can be expressed as $\hat{t}_j = \sum_{h=1}^{H} \sum_{i=1}^{m_h} \sum_{k=1}^{m_{hi}} d_{hik} y_{hikj}$, where d_{hik} is the base weight for unit k in primary sampling unit (PSU) i in stratum h and y_{hikj} is its value in the jth analysis variable. Then, Eq. (29.2) can be expanded as follows:

$$\hat{\theta} - \theta \cong \sum_{j=1}^{p} \frac{\partial f(\hat{t})}{\partial \hat{t}_j}(\hat{t}_j - t_j) = \sum_{h=1}^{H} \sum_{i=1}^{m_h} \sum_{k=1}^{m_{hi}} d_{hik} z_{hik} + \text{constants}$$

with $z_{hik} = \sum_{j=1}^{p} \frac{\partial f(\hat{t})}{\partial \hat{t}_j} y_{hikj}$ and the constants depend on the population totals and derivatives, neither of which contribute to variability in estimation. The term z_{hik} is known as the "linear substitute," "linearized variable," or "score variable." Because the sum $z_j = \sum_{h=1}^{H} \sum_{i=1}^{m_h} \sum_{k=1}^{m_{hi}} d_{hik} z_{hik}$ is the estimated total of the z_{hik}, the variance estimation problem for the nonlinear estimator $\hat{\theta}$ is then reduced to a simpler problem for estimating the variance of a single estimated total.

The linear substitute method is generally the linearization approach used in commercial software like SAS®, SPSS®, Stata® and SUDAAN®. West et al. (2018) performed a comprehensive review of current software tools that can account for complex survey design in the estimation. Like exact formulas, the linearization method can be complicated especially when the sample design is complex and contains multistage or multiphase features, certainty units, or nonnegligible sampling rates, and when the sample data are treated with additional weighting adjustments or imputation procedures. In addition, the underlying theory of the approximation shown in Eq. (29.3) assumes that the partial derivatives $\frac{\partial f(\hat{t})}{\partial \hat{t}_j}$ can be derived and are evaluated at the population values. For example, when $\hat{\theta}$ is an estimator for a median or quantile, $f(\hat{t})$ is no longer differentiable. Deville (1999) extended the usual linearization methods to accommodate quantiles and other nondifferential statistics. Users of commercial software are limited to a fixed number of sample designs and estimators, for which the linear substitute variance estimators have been programmed. Users will need to derive and program their own variance estimation function for more complex estimators that are not available in the software.

29.1.4.3 Replication Methods

The general idea of replication methods for variance estimation is to divide the full sample (respondents and nonrespondents) into subsamples (i.e. replicates) first, then estimate the same parameter with each replicate, and lastly compute the variance based on all the replicate estimates. For design-based inference, the division of the full sample should ensure that the replicates are representative of the full sample. The linearization and replicate-based variance estimators are asymptotically design-consistent for differentiable estimators with a very large number of PSUs and other assumptions (Wolter, 2007; Shao and Tu, 1995). Nevertheless, in comparison to the linearization methods, the replication methods have a great advantage to reflect the effects on variances of nonresponse and calibration adjustments. If a weighting adjustment procedure is used for the full sample, the same procedure should be applied to create adjusted replicate weights for each replicate (Valliant 2004). With examples from establishment surveys, Shao and Thompson (2009) and Haziza et al. (2010) showed that without properly accounting for nonresponse adjustment the variance estimates will be biased. Another advantage of this approach is that it does not require theoretical derivation of variance estimation formulas that sometimes might be extremely complicated or even underivable when the function of the estimated parameter $\hat{\theta} = f(\hat{t})$ is very complex or not differentiable. Instead, replication uses a unified recipe for a variety of problems. Furthermore, the replication methods can be extended to account for uncertainties introduced by statistical imputation in variance estimation. Section 29.1.5 contains a review of the literature particular in this area.

There are several alternative replication methods that are often used for survey data: random group, jackknife, balanced repeated replication (BRR), and bootstrap. We will illustrate these methods in the subsequent sections and will use a stratified single-stage sample design as an example to illustrate each method, because this is a commonly used sampling design in establishment surveys. We will suppose that there are H strata, m_h PSUs in stratum h in this design, yielding $m = \sum_{h=1}^{H} m_h$ PSUs in total. Unit j in this sample has a base weight, denoted as d_j.

29.1.4.3.1 Random Group

The random group method was one of the oldest techniques developed to simplify variance estimation for complex surveys. Wolter (2007) classified the random group method into two fundamental variations: independent random groups by selecting K subsamples with replacement, and nonindependent random groups by randomly dividing the full sample into K subgroups (replicates). The latter variation is often used in practice for establishment surveys. For example, the Annual Retail Trade Survey in the United States used the random group method with 16 nonindependent random groups for variance estimation.[1]

The random group method requires that each subgroup has the same sampling design as the full sample. When the K replicates have the same or nearly the same sizes, the random group replicate base weight for unit j in replicate k is

$$d_{j(k)} = \begin{cases} Kd_j & \text{if unit } j \text{ is selected in replicate } k \\ 0 & \text{if unit } j \text{ is not selected in replicate } k' \end{cases}$$

where d_j is the base weight of unit j.

If the base weights went through one or more weighting adjustment procedures to derive the estimate of the full sample, the same weighting adjustment procedures should be applied within each replicate when deriving its estimate. The random group variance formula is

$$v_{RG}(\hat{\theta}) = \frac{1}{K(K-1)} \sum_{k=1}^{K} (\hat{\theta}_k - \hat{\theta})^2$$

where $\hat{\theta}_k$ is the estimate based on replicate k with the adjusted replicate weights and $\hat{\theta}$ is the full sample estimate. Mathematically, this formula estimates the mean squared error (MSE) of the estimate, which is the sum of the squared bias and variance of the estimate. Although this formula is commonly used in variance estimation, an alternative version of the random group variance formula centers around $\bar{\hat{\theta}}$, the average of $\hat{\theta}_k$ across all replicates, in place of $\hat{\theta}$ shown above.

29.1.4.3.2 Jackknife

The basic jackknife method, also known as the delete-1 jackknife, creates replicates by dropping one PSU from the full sample at a time and then reweighting each replicate to represent the full population. Under the example design, m jackknife replicates will be created, in each of which all

---

1 For more details, see:
https://www.census.gov/programs-surveys/arts/technical-documentation/methodology.html

units in one PSU are dropped from the full sample. (Note that for single-stage designs where the establishment is the only responding unit, the "PSU" referenced is the establishment.) When PSU i in stratum h is dropped, the base weights for units in the hth stratum are adjusted in the following manner to create the jackknife replicate base weights for replicate hi:

$$d_{j(hi)} = \begin{cases} 0 & \text{if unit } j \text{ is in stratum } h \text{ and PSU } i \\ \alpha_h d_j & \text{if unit } j \text{ is in stratum } h \text{ but not in PSU } i \\ d_j & \text{if unit } j \text{ is not in stratum } h \end{cases}$$

where $\alpha_h = \frac{m_h}{m_h - 1}$ is known as the *jackknife coefficient* and d_j is the base weight of unit j. In this way, units in PSU i within stratum h are dropped while the base weights of the units in the retained PSUs in stratum h are inflated by α_h times to represent the full stratum h. The base weights of units in the other strata remain intact. The jackknife replicate base weights are then adjusted using the same weighting procedures as applied to the full sample base weights. The jackknife variance formula for this design is

$$v_J(\widehat{\theta}) = \sum_{h=1}^{H} \frac{(1 - f_h)}{\alpha_h} \sum_{i=1}^{m_h} (\widehat{\theta}_{(hi)} - \widehat{\theta})^2 \tag{29.4}$$

where $f_h = n_h/N_h$ is the sampling fraction in stratum h, $\widehat{\theta}_{(hi)}$ is the estimate from replicate hi with the adjusted replicate weights, $\widehat{\theta}$ is the full sample estimate when estimating MSE, and $\widehat{\theta}$ is replaced with the average value of $\widehat{\theta}_{(hi)}$ across all replicates when estimating the variance solely.

Although jackknife variance estimation is available in most of the commercial software, one must pay attention to the default variance formula programmed in the software and check whether special options need to be specified. For example, in SAS PROC SURVEYMEANS, the default jackknife variance formula is unstratified: $v_J(\widehat{\theta}) = \sum_{r=1}^{R} \alpha_r (\widehat{\theta}_r - \widehat{\theta})^2$, where $\alpha_r = \frac{R-1}{R}$ is the default jackknife coefficient, R is the total number of replicates, and $\widehat{\theta}_r$ is the estimate based on replicate r. One must provide the jackknife coefficient in the JKCOEFS= or REPCOEFS= option to implement the proper variance formula as shown in Eq. (29.4) for a stratified single-stage sample design, which is also known as a stratified jackknife variance estimator.

Delete-A-Group (Grouped) Jackknife The delete-a-group jackknife (DAGJK) is a variation of the delete-1 jackknife method. Although there is no theoretical advantage of using DAGJK over the traditional delete-1 jackknife method, it offers computational advantages when there could be hundreds and even thousands of PSUs. Rust (1985), Kott (2001a, 2006), Lu et al. (2006), Wolter (2007) and Kott and Liao (2021) have studied the statistical properties of the DAGJK method extensively.

Many researchers select their establishment survey samples from frame lists that contain their population members of interest and often these establishments can vary greatly by their sizes. Therefore, it is common to stratify the frame list based on establishment size (and maybe other characteristics) prior to sampling for establishment surveys. This sampling method can lead to the number of sampled establishments and PSUs varying widely across different strata. The idea behind DAGJK is to group multiple PSUs together and then drop a group of PSUs rather than 1 PSU per jackknife replicate. This way can reduce the number of replicates, which can increase computational efficiency. In addition, jackknife replicate weights are often provided in public use data files for users to calculate variances by themselves without the need for sampling design information that may disclose participant identities. If there are thousands of PSUs in the design, it will be cumbersome to provide thousands of replicate weights in the data file. Hence, the DAGJK method, rather than the basic delete-1 jackknife method, is often used for establishment surveys, such as the Agriculture Resources and Management Study conducted by the U.S. National Agricultural Statistics Service (Kott 2001a, 2001b).

The jackknife replicate base weights under the DAGJK method can be created in a similar manner as the ones created under the delete-1-jackknife method. As per Kott (2001a), in the replicate *hi* when the *g*th group of PSUs in stratum *h* is dropped, its jackknife replicate base weights are

$$
d_{j(hg)} = \begin{cases} 0 & \text{if unit } j \text{ is in stratum } h \text{ and PSU Group } g \\ \alpha_{hg} d_j & \text{if unit } j \text{ is in stratum } h \text{ but not in PSU Group } g \\ d_j & \text{if unit } j \text{ is not in stratum } h \end{cases}
$$

where $\alpha_{hg} = \frac{m_h}{m_h - m_{hg}}$ and m_{hg} is the number of PSUs in the *g*th group of PSUs in stratum *h*.

The jackknife variance formula for DAGJK is also similar to the delete-1-jackknife method that can be expressed as follows:

$$
v_J(\hat{\theta}) = \sum_{h=1}^{H} \frac{(1 - f_h)}{\alpha_{hg}} \sum_{i=1}^{m_h} (\hat{\theta}_{(hg)} - \hat{\theta})^2
$$

A practical issue to consider is how to group PSUs together. In general, one should consider how each replicate can be a representative sample from the population after dropping the grouped PSUs together. For example, grouping all the PSUs from the same stratum and dropping this entire group in a replicate will not be appropriate because the replicate will no longer be representative of the population without having any unit from a particular stratum. Another issue to note is that the DAGJK method requires the number of PSUs per stratum be sufficiently large in all strata. This condition can be met in same establishment surveys, but not for all. Kott (2001a) proposed an extension of the DAGJK method to deal with the situation when the number of PSUs per stratum is less than the desired number of jackknife replicates.

29.1.4.3.3 Balanced Repeated Replication (BRR)

BRR or balanced half-sampling works by forming balanced replicates or half-samples from the whole sample, recomputing the survey estimate $\hat{\theta}$ on each replicate, and calculating the mean squared deviations of replicate estimates as the variance. The BRR method is developed particularly for sample designs where two PSUs are selected from each stratum. In practice, to apply BRR method to a design that is different than a 2-PSU-per-stratum design, researchers can adopt the collapse method to construct variance PSUs and strata first. If there are more than two PSUs in a stratum, the PSUs in the same stratum can be grouped together to form two "variance PSUs" (also called pseudo-cluster) within the stratum or they can be furtherly divided into different "variance strata" (also called pseudo-strata) so that each variance stratum contains 2 PSUs. For a 1-PSU-per-stratum sample design, the strata each with one PSU can be paired to form variance strata so that each variance stratum contains two PSUs. After the variance PSUs and strata are formed, the BRR method can then be applied. How to construct the variance strata and PSUs, however, should be carefully planned. For instance, Rust and Kalton (1987) examined the effect of collapsing strata in pairs, triples, and larger groups on the quality of the variance estimator for sample designs with one PSU per stratum.

Standard BRR The standard BRR method creates half-sample replicates by deleting one PSU per stratum according to a Hadamard matrix and doubling the original weights of the remaining units. A Hadamard matrix, named after the French mathematician Jacques Hadamard, is a square matrix with 2^h (e.g. 2, 4, 8...) dimensions whose entries are either +1 or −1 and whose rows and columns are orthogonal. If there are H strata (or variance strata) in the design of the sample data, the total number of BRR replicates is the smallest 2^h that is greater than H to achieve full orthogonal balance. For example, if $H = 12$, then $2^4 = 16$ BRR replicates should be created because $2^3 < 12 < 2^4$. Similarly, when a sample design has 4 strata, 4 BRR replicates should be created with a 4×4 ($h = 2$) Hadamard matrix H_4, which can be expressed as follows:

	BRR Replicate 1	BRR Replicate 2	BRR Replicate 3	BRR Replicate 4
Stratum 1	1	1	1	1
Stratum 2	1	−1	1	−1
Stratum 3	1	1	−1	−1
Stratum 4	1	−1	−1	1

Note that the value in each cell above (for each combination of stratum and replicate) is defined based on the Hadamard matrix. When the value equals to 1, then the first PSU in the corresponding stratum should be selected in the corresponding replicate while the other PSU will be dropped. Reversely, when the value equals −1, then the first PSU in the corresponding stratum should be dropped while the other PSU will be selected.

With the standard BRR method, the original base weights of the retained units in a half-sample replicate will be doubled so that each replicate can be considered as a representative sample for population inference. In the kth replicate, the BRR replicate base weights are the following:

$$d_j^k = \begin{cases} 0 & \text{if unit } i \text{ is in the PSU that is dropped in stratum } h \\ 2d_j & \text{if unit } i \text{ is in the PSU that is retained in stratum } h \end{cases}$$

Analogous to the random group and Jackknife methods, if one or more weighting adjustment procedures are used to derive the estimate of the full sample, the same weighting adjustment procedures should be applied within each BRR replicate when deriving its estimate. The BRR variance formula is the following:

$$v_{BRR}(\widehat{\theta}) = K^{-1} \sum_{k=1}^{K} (\widehat{\theta}_k - \widehat{\theta})^2$$

where $\widehat{\theta}_k$ is the estimate based on replicate k, $\widehat{\theta}$ is the full sample estimate when estimating MSE, and is the average value of $\widehat{\theta}_k$ across all replicates when estimating the variance solely.

Fay's BRR Because the standard BRR method removes half of the sample in each replicate, it was found that units in some small domains could be completely or largely removed from some replicates. This situation will lead to instability in estimating variances for these small domains and will yield the variance of the variance estimator to be quite high. To solve this problem, the Fay's BRR method (Fay 1984; Judkins 1990; Rao and Shao 1999) has been developed, in which the weights of the units within the selected PSUs will be inflated while the weights of the units in other PSUs will be deflated rather than becoming zero in the replicate (i.e. completely removed from the replicate). The Fay's BRR replicates are formed in the same manner as the standard BRR replicates using a Hadamard matrix. In the kth replicate, Fay's BRR replicate base weights can be computed as follows:

$$d_j^k = \begin{cases} \alpha d_j & \text{if unit } j \text{ is in the PSU that is dropped in stratum } h \\ (2 - \alpha)d_j & \text{if unit } j \text{ is in the PSU that is retained in stratum } h \end{cases}$$

where $0 \leq \alpha \leq 1$. When $\alpha = 0$, the Fay's BBR method is equivalent to the standard BRR method and thus it is also called the "generalized" BRR method. Judkins (1990) recommends setting the α value between 0.5 and 0.7 and most establishment surveys set it at 0.5. The Fay's BRR variance formula is the following:

$$v_{F-BRR}(\widehat{\theta}) = \frac{1}{K(1-\alpha)^2} \sum_{k=1}^{K} (\widehat{\theta}_k - \widehat{\theta})^2$$

Both the BRR and Fay's BRR are suitable for nonsmooth estimators (Rao and Wu 1985; Rao and Shao, 1999), such as quantiles or median values, while jackknife (Martin, 1990) and linearization methods require the estimators to be differentiable.

29.1.4.3.4 Bootstrap

Bootstrap is a resampling procedure that repeatedly selects subsamples (replicates) with replacement from the full sample data and then generates the sampling distribution of a statistic across the subsamples. Unlike nonindependent random groups, jackknife and BRR methods have rules to select replicates, there are many different ways to manipulate the full sample data and select replicates in the bootstrap method, which makes it the most versatile approach among the four. Mashreghi et al. (2016) reviewed a variety of bootstrap methods developed under the context of analyzing survey data and classified them in three classes: pseudo-population, direct, and survey weights methods. The most commonly used bootstrap method that is available in most statistical software is known as Rao–Wu bootstrap (Rao et al. 1992), which is one of the survey weights methods. This method usually takes the following steps for each replicate, supposing that there are B bootstrap replicates in total.

(1) From each stratum with m_h PSUs in the full sample, a bootstrap sample of m_h^* PSUs is drawn using a simple random sample with replacement sampling scheme.
(2) For each sample unit j within PSU hi, the base weight is adjusted to create an initial bootstrap weight as follows:

$$d_j^* = d_j \left\{ \left(1 - \sqrt{\frac{m_h^*}{m_h - 1}}\right) + \sqrt{\frac{m_h^*}{m_h - 1}} \cdot \frac{m_h}{m_h^*} \cdot \sum_{i=1}^{m_h} m_h^* \right\}$$

(3) The initial bootstrap weights are then adjusted using the same weighting adjustment procedures as applied to the full sample (to obtain the final survey weights).
(4) The estimate $\widehat{\theta}_b$ is calculated based on the bth bootstrap replicate using the adjusted bootstrap weights from the previous step.

With B bootstrap replicates, the bootstrap variance formula is the following:

$$v_{boot}(\widehat{\theta}) = B^{-1} \sum_{b=1}^{B} (\widehat{\theta}_b - \widehat{\theta})^2$$

In practice, m_h^* is often set as $m_h^* = m_h - 1$, which were found to perform well for smooth $\widehat{\theta}$ in empirical studies by Kovar et al. (1988). In this case, the weighting adjustment in step (2) can be simplified as follows:

$$d_j^* = d_j \frac{m_h}{m_h - 1} \sum_{i=1}^{m_h} m_h^*$$

One advantage of the bootstrap method is that it does not require collapsing strata or PSUs to form replicates as needed for DAGJK and BRR methods. Valliant et al. (2018, Section 15.4.3) also discuss the advantages of bootstrap over other replicate methods when estimating variables with a skewed distribution. Similar to the BRR methods, the bootstrap method can also estimate variance for nonsmooth estimators.

29.1.5 Variance Estimation with Imputed Values

Statistical imputation is commonly employed to treat item nonresponse and sometimes also for unit nonresponse in establishment surveys. When using imputed variables in estimation, the uncertainty introduced by the imputation procedure should also be accounted for in variance estimation, especially when a relatively large proportion of values are imputed. An extensive literature exists regarding variance estimation for establishment surveys under imputation procedures. Shao and Steel (1999), for example, proposed a variance estimation method based on a variance decomposition for Horvitz–Thompson type estimated totals based on survey data under imputation using a composite of multiple imputation methods (e.g. cold deck and ratio type). Their method only requires single imputation and can incorporate either linearization or replication variance estimation method. For their study, the Transportation Annual Survey conducted by the US Census Bureau was used as an example and motivation. Shao and Butani (2002) proposed a grouped Fay's BRR method with re-imputation within replicates to account for imputation in the variance estimation for the Current Employment Survey in the United States. Andridge et al. (2021) used the approximate Bayesian bootstrap (ABB), a multiple imputation approach (Rubin and Schenker 1986; Rubin 1987; Rubin 1996), for variance estimation when exploring hot-deck imputation method for multinomial data and applied this approach to the 2012 Economic Census as an empirical study. Furthermore, Andridge et al. (Chapter 31, 2023) compared the design-based variance estimation approach derived under the reverse-framework proposed in Shao and Steel (1999) with an approximate Bayesian Bootstrap under nearest neighbor ratio hot-deck imputation (Andridge and Little 2010) for unit and item nonresponse for selected industries surveyed by the US Census Bureau's Service Annual Survey.

29.1.6 Variance Estimation Applications Among Probability Establishment Surveys

As described in the previous section, variance estimation should account for most if not all sources of variability in estimation to properly measure the width of the confidence interval for the estimate of interest and to support statistical hypothesis tests. For many probability surveys of establishments, this means the variance estimator used for their estimation must account for the complex sample design, weighting adjustments, and if relevant, imputed values. Nevertheless, the secondary analyst is sometimes not familiar with variance estimation methods associated with survey data and could unintentionally ignore these factors. West and Sakshaug (2018) reviewed ten highly cited, peer-reviewed journal articles presenting secondary analyses of establishment survey data. Surprisingly, they found that only two out of the ten articles mentioned using survey weights in the analyses that are design-based, while the other eight articles did not incorporate the survey weights in their analyses that are model based. None of the ten articles reported that they accounted for sampling design features in their variance estimation. Furthermore, they performed alternative analyses to compare the analytical results before and after incorporating sampling design features and weights using the 2013 Business Research and Development and Innovation Survey (BRDIS) and showed that failing to properly account for these features can lead to substantial differences.

Variance estimation is further complicated by sampling designs with many stages of selection as used for some establishment surveys. Kalton (1979) discussed the ultimate clustering sampling approach that approximates the multistage design using only the variability of the estimated total across the first stage units (i.e. between-cluster variance component). Consequently, the within-cluster variance component is deemed negligible in this simplified form.

Many large surveys also adopt weighting adjustments for their initial base weights to mitigate errors introduced by coverage or nonresponse. It is also important to account for these adjustments in variance estimation. Siegel et al. (2007) compared variance estimates for schools and students when using the standard BRR method versus the linearization method, with data from the Education Longitudinal Study of 2002 (ELS:2002). Because the survey had a stratified multistage design and survey weights with both nonresponse and poststratification adjustments, they accounted for these adjustments in their BRR method but did not consider them in the linearization method for comparison. Their results showed that failing to account for nonresponse adjustment can underestimate the variance while failing to account for poststratification to known population totals can overestimate the variance.

Biemer (2010) and West et al. (2017) categorized the failure of incorporating critical survey features in variance estimation as *analytic error* under the Total Survey Error framework. To ensure proper inference, data producers and disseminators of establishment surveys should provide more information to the secondary users on how to conduct variance estimation when analyzing their data. Replicate weights can be provided to data users if the specific sample design information (e.g. stratum and cluster identifiers) are too sensitive to be released, or when the base weights are adjusted. For references, Table 29.2 lists a series of establishment surveys and their variance estimation methods.

Table 29.2 Examples of probability establishment surveys and their variance estimation methods.

Establishment survey	Variance estimation method	Reference
Agricultural Resources and Management Survey (US)	Delete-A-Group Jackknife (DAGJK)	Kott (2001a, 2001b); Kott (2007)
Annual Capital Expenditures Survey (US)	Delete-a-group Jackknife (DAGJK)	Thompson et al. (2003)
Annual Retail Trade Survey (US)	Random Groups	Annual Retail Trade Survey – Methodology[a]
Education Longitudinal Study of 2002 (US)	Standard Balanced Repeated Replication (BRR)	Siegel et al. (2007); Pratt, et al. (2014)
Annual Survey of Public Employment and Payroll (US)	Bootstrap	Cheng et al. (2010)
National Compensation Survey (US)	Fay's BRR	Lisic and Ojo (2008)
Survey of Construction (US)	Fay's BRR	Thompson and Sigman (2000)
Canadian Participation and Activity Limitations Survey (Canada)	Bootstrap	Langlet et al. (2003)
Programme for International Student Assessment (PISA) (OECD)[b]	Fay's BRR	PISA (2015)

US: the United States; OECD: Organization for Economic Co-operation and Development.
a)   See: https://www.census.gov/programs-surveys/arts/technical-documentation/methodology.html.
b)   A report on their sample design is available at: https://www.oecd.org/pisa/sitedocument/PISA-2015-Technical-Report-Chapter-4-Sample-Design.pdf.

29.2   Estimation with Nonprobability Establishment Survey Data

Section 29.1 focused on probability-based survey sampling where the sampling mechanism is defined by the statistician. In this section, we discuss nonprobability sampling with the goal of producing population estimates. Nonprobability sampling used for activities other than population inference – for example, to identify participants for a cognitive evaluation of questionnaire items – are well known and not considered further.

29.2.1   Nonprobability Sampling in Practice

Several general definitions exist in the literature for nonprobability-based surveys (e.g. Valliant 2020; Elliott and Valliant 2017; Baker et al. 2013). In summary, the investigator does not (or cannot) implement a repeatable, random selection mechanism to choose population units for a study. Consequently, the study selection probabilities and the base weights (inverse selection probabilities) are unknown, and randomization-based theory discussed in the prior section of this chapter does not apply. Choosing between the two "sampling" approaches may not be straightforward and instead may be influenced by several factors associated with the intended study.

Development of a study begins by defining the essential components (e.g. analytic objectives) that lend to methods for estimation. Statistics Canada's Quality Assurance Framework (2017) contains six study attributes – timeliness, accessibility, relevance, interpretability, accuracy, and coherence – that may guide such decisions for a survey (Dever et al. 2020). For example, the desire to collect data quickly (timeliness) from establishments without an existing, high-quality sampling frame (accessibility) could suggest a nonprobability approach. Moreover, some researchers may feel that declining response to survey requests have reduced the generalizability from probability sample estimates (relevance, accuracy). Reasons for the various design decisions such as choosing nonprobability over probability sampling generally are not stated in published works.

A few examples of nonprobability sampling for establishment surveys are available, but to our knowledge, this methodology has not been widely adopted for population inference (Table 29.3). Other examples include the development of registries, and hence potential sampling frames, using nonsampled administrative information and other sources such as the Global Group Register (GGR) of the United Nations Statistics Division, the Euro Groups Register (EGR) of Eurostat, and the Analytical Database on Individual Multinationals and Affiliates (ADIMA) of OECD to contain at least the largest multinational enterprises within and across many sectors of the world (Bavdaž et al. 2020).

Nonetheless, we discuss in the next two sections estimation methods that are employed with data from nonprobability samples across a variety of subject areas. These techniques may be applicable to specific conditions for current and future establishment surveys.

29.2.2   Analytic Objectives

The analytic objective is the extrapolation of information contained within a sample, however obtained, to the larger inferential population. How we treat the data to make the estimates generalizable is directly related to the representativeness of the participating sample units (e.g. establishments). In other words, are units missing from the sample meaningfully different from those who do not respond to threaten the external validity of the estimates? Little and Rubin (2002) coined

Table 29.3 Establishment surveys employing nonprobability sampling.

Study goal	Study design	Variance estimators
Test a model on the association of big data analytics capabilities for businesses with improved performance (Wamba et al. 2017)	Simple random sample from list provided by a market research firm with 10,000+ IT managers and business analysts	Model based
Understand impact of corruption on business health (Maruichi and Abe 2019)	Purposive sampling of participants at 3 conferences	Simple random sampling
Understand best practice for business process changes related to smart city development (Javidroozi et al. 2019)	Purposive sampling of employees with information job affiliation and role within the organization	Qualitative estimates only
Evaluate a model on a business's big data analytic capabilities on innovation performance (Ghasemaghaei and Calic 2020)	(Undefined) Sample of middle- and upper-level US managers with data collected from a market research firm	Model based
Assess factors influencing the promotion of the business as family owned (Motoc 2020)	Purposive sampling of 11 business	Qualitative estimates only
Determine correlates of the birth and maintenance of immigrant-owned small businesses (Welsh et al. 2021)	Purposive sampling	Model based
Provide broad-based monthly statistical data on current economic conditions and indications of future production commitments in the manufacturing sector (see https://www.census.gov/manufacturing/m3/about_the_surveys/index.html)	Purposive sampling	N/A

labels for the three distinct "missing data mechanisms" that may simultaneously exist within a study depending on the estimate of interest (see also Valliant et al. 2018; Valliant and Dever 2018):

(1) missing completely at random (MCAR) as with a stratified simple random sample where all sample units participate;
(2) missing at random (MAR), where MCAR is justified only with weighting or other analytic models that account for key population-level auxiliary variables; and
(3) not missing at random (NMAR), where MAR is not feasible using known characteristics or survey responses.

Probability surveys rely on MAR to justify population inference alone and especially in light of nonresponse and calibration adjustments applied via models to the base weights that are inherent to most surveys. Nonresponse bias analysis (see, e.g. Valliant et al. 2018: Chapter 13), for example, may suggest NMAR for some characteristics but generally not the key estimates from the survey; consequently, MCAR is assumed for generalizing the estimates. Probability surveys with a low response rate have been labeled nonprobability with the premise that nonignorable nonresponse bias exists in the estimates even though weight adjustments may have some benefits (Dutwin and Buskirk 2017).

By comparison, models used for nonprobability surveys not only need to address bias linked to nonresponse but also the undefined "sampling mechanism," collectively known as selection bias (Lee and Valliant 2009). Consequently, the model specification and especially, the available model covariates are extremely important (Mercer et al. 2018). Moreover, if the sample obtained through probability or nonprobability sampling is missing a key subpopulation, say family-owned businesses established in the past year, then estimation for this domain is not feasible and estimation for the full population possibly suspect. And the estimated confidence intervals may fall short of the desired coverage (e.g. 95%) because of the biased point estimate.

The literature contains several examples of estimation methods for nonprobability surveys that depend on available data and assumptions confirmed or otherwise about the underlying sampling mechanism. Below, we summarize techniques to generate population estimates from nonprobability survey data alone, followed by those used for nonprobability data combined with responses from a corresponding probability survey (hybrid estimation).

29.2.2.1 Methods for Nonprobability Estimation

Commonly used estimation methods for nonprobability survey data can employ general-purpose survey weights, where one set of analysis weights are used for all estimates or estimate-specific procedures newly implemented for every estimate. Estimate-specific survey weights are briefly mentioned for completeness.

29.2.2.1.1 Quasi-randomization Weighting

The premise behind quasi-randomization weighting is to generate survey weights as a base weight multiplied by a nonresponse adjustment, both estimated simultaneously as if the survey was probability based. As discussed in, for example, Valliant and Dever (2018) and Valliant (2020), this method relies on information available from a probability-based reference survey conducted on the same target population using a set of items common across both surveys. Additional assumptions are discussed in Valliant and Dever (2011). One approach is to use a weighted binary regression (e.g. logistic), with dependent variable coded as 1 for the nonprobability units and 0 for the probability units and covariates common to both, that results in a predicted propensity. The final analytic weights are incorporated for the probability units; either a weight of one or weights poststratified to population counts are used for the nonprobability cases. The inverted propensity serves as the "selection" weight directly or to form weighting classes where a common weight, say average, is adopted by all members of the class. In a second less-common approach, the estimated propensity serves to match units across the two surveys where the probability weight is then adopted by its twin (Elliott and Valliant 2017; Baker, et al. 2013; Ho, et al. 2007). A third method modifies the predicted propensities using Bayes' Rule to produce the nonprobability weight (Elliott and Valliant 2017; Robbins et al. 2020). Several sources mention the importance of using covariates that are strongly related to patterns of participation and ideally key estimates of interest; however, a large list of covariates from which to choose is seldom available in practice so that models may contain all commonly available items.

29.2.2.1.2 Quasi-randomization Model-assisted Weighting

Calibration weighting can reduce bias associated with nonresponse and coverage (Kott and Liao 2018, 2017; Deville and Särndal 1992) that may prove useful in reducing selection bias for nonprobability-based estimates (Valliant and Dever 2011). With relatively small nonprobability samples of size n, input weights are set to N/n, where N is the finite population size as for a simple random sample. Alternatively, researchers may use quasi-randomization weights for calibration adjustment.

29.2.2.1.3 Superpopulation Weighting

With superpopulation estimates, also known as the prediction approach (Valliant et al. 2000), sample member responses are used to predict all or a portion of the population not in the sample. For example, an estimated total for characteristic y is defined as $\widehat{t}_y = \boldsymbol{w}'\boldsymbol{y}$, where $\boldsymbol{w}$ is the transposed vector of survey weights, and $\boldsymbol{y}$ is a vector of y responses both of length n, the sample size. The survey weights in $\boldsymbol{w}$, borrowing notation from Valliant (2020), are calculated either as $w_i = \boldsymbol{t}'_U \left(\boldsymbol{X}'_s \boldsymbol{X}_s \right)^{-1} \boldsymbol{x}_i$ or $w_i = 1 + (\boldsymbol{t}_U - \boldsymbol{t}_{sx})' \left(\boldsymbol{X}'_s \boldsymbol{X}_s \right)^{-1} \boldsymbol{x}_i$, where $\boldsymbol{t}_U$ is a p-length vector of population totals like those used with weight calibration; $\boldsymbol{t}_{sx}$ is the corresponding vector of population totals calculated directly from the sample s; and $\boldsymbol{X}_s$ is an $n \times p$ matrix of x-values from the sample with $\boldsymbol{x}_i$ the vector associated with sample member i. The weights are similar if the sample is a relatively small portion of the population.

29.2.2.1.4 Multilevel Regression and Poststratification

The "Mr. P" method (Gelman 2007) is similar to the superpopulation technique in that the sample is used for prediction. Here, sample estimates are calculated within a set of mutually exclusive "poststrata" defined with important predictors for the desired construct. The poststratum estimates are weighted by their respective proportions in the population, either known or estimated. Note that MRP is estimate specific and does not lend to general purpose weights.

29.2.2.1.5 Model-based Methods

Population inference is not only relegated to descriptive statistics but also includes covariate-adjusted estimates obtained from a statistical model. If the model covariates account for selection into the nonprobability sample, then survey weights do not provide additional information for population inference. Pfeffermann and Sverchkov (2009) discuss a method to test whether survey weights are ignorable in model-based population inference with probability surveys. Applied to nonprobability surveys, this test could indicate if the weights were adding unnecessary noise to the estimates that would decrease the estimated precision.

29.2.2.2 Methods for Hybrid Estimation

Study benefits are noted for probability sampling and nonprobability sampling given a study's fit for purpose. Hybrid estimation, a general phrase used by Dever (2018), combines information from both sources ideally to yield MSE estimates with smaller values than those generated from each source individually. Many examples in the literature focus on combining data from a relatively small set of participants from a probability survey with a large set of respondents obtained from a less resource-intense nonprobability survey. This task can be accomplished with two general approaches: composite estimation and simultaneous estimation.

29.2.2.2.1 Composite Hybrid Estimation

Composite estimation has been applied to probability surveys since at least the 1960s to address frame undercoverage (Hartley 1962; Lohr and Raghunathan 2017). For example, a dual-frame estimator for a population total t_y with two sources is expressed as follows:

$$\widehat{t}_y = \lambda_g \widehat{t}_{1y} + (1 - \lambda_g) \widehat{t}_{2y} \tag{29.5}$$

where $\widehat{t}_{*y}$ is the population estimate from each survey, and $\lambda_g \leq 1$ is the composite factor defined within $g \geq 1$ mutually exclusive analysis groups that is applied to the input weights. For probability surveys, where $\widehat{t}_{*y}$ is considered design unbiased, the estimate with the smaller standard error, say $\widehat{t}_{1y}$, may be assigned $\lambda_g > (1 - \lambda_g)$ so that $\text{var}(\widehat{t}_y) < \text{var}(\widehat{t}_{2y})$. Studies requiring general purpose weights might have $\lambda = n_1/(n_1 + n_2)$ with $\hat{t}_{*y}$ generated from n_* participant records to align with this relative contribution to precision; though less-common, estimate-specific weights could be generated with λ as a function of the relative precision from $\hat{t}_{*y}$. Naturally, the number of composite factors increases with the number of population frames, but they must sum to 1.

Composite hybrid estimation is a quasi-randomization method to combine probability and nonprobability surveys that mirrors the traditional approach except that the composite factor should be higher for the source with the smallest MSE for at least a core set of estimates instead of the variance (see, e.g. Elliott and Haviland 2007). Fully adjusted randomization-based weights are used to generate $\hat{t}_{1y}$, the population total generated from the probability survey. A weighted estimate for $\hat{t}_{2y}$ could include any of the above-mentioned nonprobability weighting methodologies or possibly a "disjoint weight" proposed by Robbins et al. (2020), a modified propensity score weight based on Bayes' Rule.

Bayesian model-based methods have been proposed for composite hybrid estimation as well. One such approach was suggested by Sakshaug et al. (2019), where data from the nonprobability survey was used to construct the priors that was informed by the probability survey data through the posterior distribution.

These composite methods, regardless of the sampling mechanism and estimation approach, assume that each source yields an estimate of the *same* population parameter, i.e. $E(\hat{t}_{1y}) = E(\hat{t}_{2y})$, where E is the expectation defined for the design or model used for estimation. However, many critics of nonprobability sampling point to undercoverage bias as a major flaw in this requirement so that $E(\hat{t}_{1y}) \neq E(\hat{t}_{2y})$, also referred to as a violation of the common support criterion (Mercer et al. 2017). Research is ongoing on methods to parse the inferential universe for each survey to identify common subpopulations as well as those unique to each source (see, e.g. Dever 2018).

29.2.2.2.2 Simultaneous Estimation

Without common support, some researchers have turned to simultaneous estimation where the data are combined much like they were collected from a single survey. For example, Robbins et al. (2020) adapted propensity scores to estimate a sample members probability of being in the "blended sample."

29.2.3 Variance Estimators

Historically, some have taken the position that sampling errors were not appropriate for samples obtained without a defined random sampling mechanism (AAPOR 2015). Opinions have changed so now the question is not "if" standard errors should be calculated but by which method with appropriately documented assumptions behind their use.

Section 1 emphasized the importance of accounting for the sampling design in the calculation of variance estimates. Without explicit control over the design, a single-stage simple random with-replacement sample is the preferred choice. Additionally, researchers must align the choice of variance estimator with assumptions used for the point estimate.

29.2.3.1 Quasi-randomization Methods

Quasi-randomization methods, whether single source or hybrid, rely on linearization or replication variance estimation. A linearization variance estimator for the population total is defined as follows:

$$\text{var}(\hat{t}_y) = \frac{n}{(n-1)} \sum_{i \in s} (z_i - \bar{z})^2$$

where z_i is the weighted value for establishment i and $\bar{z}$ is the weighted mean. By comparison, Valliant (2020) notes that replication methods – such as (grouped) Jackknife or bootstrap – are preferred as they can account for adjustments applied in the construction of the survey weights (see also Valliant 2004).

29.2.3.2 Superpopulation and Model-based Methods

Superpopulation and other model-based methods rely on model residuals for variance estimation. For example,

$$\mathrm{var}(\hat{t}_y) = \sum_{i \in s}(w_i - 1)^2 v_i$$

with w_i defined for full or partial prediction of the target population, and $v_i = y_i - \boldsymbol{x}' \boldsymbol{\beta}_s$, the residual from ordinary least squares.

29.3 Concluding Remarks

Population inference – the extrapolation of information from a sample to the target population – is a critical task for surveys of establishments and other units of observation. Researchers employ multiple methods to enhance the generalizability of the estimates. Said another way, various tools are used before and after data collection with the goal of limiting MSE for a set of key estimates overall and within important subgroups.

Survey design begins with intensions for the data specified in an analysis plan considering available resources and other such constraints. This plan may detail analyses at various entity levels such as the parent company and subsidiary, which dictates the sampling design for the establishment survey. Additionally, one or more of the key estimates may focus on population quantities that are heavily skewed resulting in a highly stratified design. Using the six attributes within Statistics Canada's Quality Assurance Framework (2017) as a guide, either a probability or nonprobability sampling methodology may fit the purpose of the study given the study constraints. For example, a sampling frame may not exist to identify establishments with specific characteristics such as family-owned businesses founded since the onset of the COVID-19 pandemic for a certain set of countries, and creation of such a list frame may be time and cost-prohibitive.

Postdata collection activities are also important. For example, weight adjustments such as calibration to population totals may serve to lower bias in the estimates linked to nonresponse and frame undercoverage. In addition to lower bias, imputation can improve power for statistical tests that would be impacted by item and possibly unit nonresponse. Model covariates used in model-based estimation or in combination with weighting and imputation as with model-assisted estimation can further align the sample with the population of interest. Each method requires availability of high-quality information that limits unnecessary noise in the estimates.

Population inference is not complete without measures of precision (e.g. standard errors) to accompany the point estimates. The variance estimates should capture the key random attributes of the participating sample so that confidence intervals have the intended level of coverage and statistical tests are powered appropriately. Theory and methods for linearization and replication variance estimates with probability sampling designs is well established (Section 29.1). For example, replication methods account for random adjustments applied to the weights in addition to calibration. Additionally, ultimate cluster variance formula, available in survey analysis software, simplify the calculation for complex designs for a study of establishments.

Standard theory and methods do not exist, however, for nonprobability surveys because the sampling mechanism is not repeatable, and coverage of the inferential population may not be consistent. In response, researchers have adapted probability-based procedures for population inference to these data with some but inconsistent success (Section 29.2). For example, estimated propensity scores may be used in the creation of survey weights for analyses. Researchers must make assumptions to justify and then defend the analytic approaches with establishment data obtain from a nonprobability survey. Use of multiple estimation procedures (i.e. sensitivity analysis) may lend credibility to the results.

This chapter summarized many but not all considerations for producing variance estimates with data collected from probability and nonprobability establishment surveys. Instead, the materials are intended to provide a framework to choose an appropriate methodology. Future research and associated considerations are anticipated as we strive to produce accurate population estimates with precision that accurately reflects the uncertainties in the sample data.

References

AAPOR (2015). AAPOR Guidance on Reporting Precision for Nonprobability Samples. American Association for Public Opinion Research. https://www.aapor.org/getattachment/Education-Resources/For-Researchers/AAPOR_Guidance_Nonprob_Precision_042216.pdf.aspx (accessed 8 May 2021).

Andridge, R.R. and Little, R.J.A. (2010). A review of hot deck imputation for survey non-response. *International Statistical Review* 78 (1): 40–64.

Andridge, R., Bechtel, L., and Thompson, K.J. (2021). Finding a flexible hot-deck imputation method for multinomial data. *Journal of Survey Statistics and Methodology* 9 (4): 789–809. https://doi.org/10.1093/jssam/smaa005.

Andridge, R., Kim, J.K., and Thompson, K.J. (2023). Variance estimation under nearest neighbor ratio hot deck imputation for multinomial data: two approaches applied to the US Service Annual Survey (SAS). In: *Advances in Business Statistics, Methods and Data Collection*, Chapter 31 (ed. G. Snijkers, M. Bavdaž, S. Bender, J. Jones, S. MacFeely, J.W. Sakshaug, K.J. Thompson, and A. van Delden). Hoboken: Wiley.

Baker, R., Brick, J.M., Bates, N.A. et al. (2013). Summary report of the AAPOR task force on non-probability sampling. *Journal of Survey Statistics and Methodology* 1: 90–143.

Bavdaž, M., Snijker, G., Sakshaug, J.W., Brand, T., Haraldsen, G., Kurban, B., Saraiva, P., and Willimack, D.K. (2020). Business data collection methodology: current state and future outlook. *Statistical Journal of the IAOS* 36: 741–756. https://content.iospress.com/articles/statistical-journal-of-the-iaos/sji200623.

Biemer, P.P. (2010). Total survey error: design, implementation, and evaluation. *Public Opinion Quarterly* 74: 817–848.

Chambers, R.L. and Skinner, C.J. (2003). *Analysis of Survey Data*, Wiley Series in Survey Methodology. New York: Wiley.

Cheng, Y., Slud, E., and Hogue, C. (2010). Variance Estimation for Decision-Based Estimators with Application to the Annual Survey of Public Employment and Payroll. Governments Division Report Series, Research Report #2010-3.

Cochran, W.G. (1977). *Sampling Techniques*, 3rde. New York: Wiley.

Dever, J. (2018). Combining probability and nonprobability samples to form efficient hybrid estimates: an evaluation of the common support assumption. *Proceedings of the Federal Committee on Statistical*

Methodology Conference, Washington, DC. https://copafs.org/wp-content/uploads/2020/05/COPAFS-A4_Dever_2018FCSM.pdf.

Dever, J.A., Amaya, A., Srivastav, A. et al. (2020). Fit for purpose in action: design, implementation, and evaluation of the National Internet Flu Survey. *Journal of Survey Statistics and Methodology* 9 (3): 449–476. https://doi.org/10.1093/jssam/smz050.

Deville, J. (1999). Variance estimation for complex statistics and estimators: linearization and residual techniques. *Survey Methodology* 25 (2): 193–203.

Deville, J.C. and Särndal, C. (1992). Calibration estimators in survey sampling. *Journal of the American Statistical Association* 87: 376–382.

Dutwin, D. and Buskirk, T.D. (2017). Apples to oranges or gala versus golden delicious: comparing data quality of nonprobability internet samples to low response rate probability samples. *Public Opinion Quarterly* 81: 213–239.

Elliott, M.N. and Haviland, A. (2007). Use of a web-based convenience sample to supplement a probability sample. *Survey Methodology* 33: 211–215.

Elliott, M.R. and Valliant, R. (2017). Inference for non-probability samples. *Statistical Science* 32: 249–264.

Fay, R.E. (1984). Some properties of estimates of variance based on replication methods. In: *Proceedings of the Survey Research Methods Section*, 495–500. *American Statistical Association*.

Fuller, W. (2009). *Sampling Statistics*. Hoboken, NJ: Wiley.

Gelman, A. (2007). Struggles with survey weighting and regression modeling. *Statistical Science* 22 (2): 153–164.

Ghasemaghaei, M. and Calic, G. (2020). Assessing the impact of big data on firm innovation performance: big data is not always better data. *Journal of Business Research* 108: 147–162. https://www.sciencedirect.com/science/article/pii/S0148296319305740.

Hartley, H.O. (1962). Multiple frame surveys. In: *Proceedings of the Social Statistics Section, American Statistical Association*, 203–206.

Haziza, D., Thompson, K.J., and Yung, W. (2010). The effect of nonresponse adjustments on variance estimation. *Survey Methodology* 36: 35–43.

Ho, D., Imai, K., King, G., and Stuart, E. (2007). Matching as nonparametric preprocessing for reducing model dependence in parametric causal inference. *Political Analysis* 15: 199–236.

Javidroozi, V., Shah, H., and Feldman, G. (2019). Urban computing and smart cities: towards changing city processes by applying enterprise systems integration practices. *IEEE Access* 7: 108023–108034. https://ieeexplore.ieee.org/abstract/document/8787780.

Judkins, D.R. (1990). Fay's method for variance estimation. *Journal of Official Statistics* 6 (3): 223–239.

Kalton, G. (1979). Ultimate cluster sampling. *Journal of the Royal Statistical Society. Series A (General)*, 142(2), 210-222. doi:https://doi.org/10.2307/2345081.

Kott, P.S. (2001a). The delete-a-group jackknife. *Journal of Official Statistics* 17: 521–526.

Kott, P. (2001b). Using the delete-a-group jackknife variance estimator in NASS Surveys, Research Division, National Agricultural Statistics Service, U.S. Department of Agriculture, Washington, DC, March 1998, NASS Research Report, RD-98-01 (Revised July 2001). Retrieved from: https://www.nass.usda.gov/Education_and_Outreach/Reports,_Presentations_and_Conferences/allreports/Using_the_Delete-a-Group_Jackknife_Estimator_in_NASS_Surveys.pdf.

Kott, P.S. (2006). Delete-a-group variance estimation for the general regression estimator under poisson sampling. *Journal of Official Statistics* 22: 759–767.

Kott, P. (2007) Building a better delete-a-group jackknife for a calibration estimator (like that based on data from the ARMS III), Research Division, National Agricultural Statistics Service, U.S. Department of Agriculture, Washington, DC, NASS Research Report. Retrieved from: https://www

.nass.usda.gov/Education_and_Outreach/Reports,_Presentations_and_Conferences/reports/wces%20for%20website%20v2.pdf.

Kott, P.S. and Liao, D. (2017). Calibration weighting for nonresponse that is not missing at random: allowing more calibration than response-model variables. *Journal of Survey Statistics and Methodology* 5: 159–174.

Kott, P.S. and Liao, D. (2018). Calibration weighting for nonresponse with proxy frame variables (so that unit nonresponse can be not missing at random). *Journal of Official Statistics* 34: 107–120.

Kott and Liao (2021). An alternative jackknife variance estimator when calibrating weights to adjust for unit nonresponse in a complex survey. *Survey Methodology* 47 (2): 349–359.

Kovar, J.G., Rao, J.N.K., and Wu, C.F.J. (1988). Bootstrap and other methods to measure errors in survey estimates. *Canadian Journal Statistics* 16: 25–45.

Langlet, E., Faucher, D., and Lesage, E. (2003). An application of the bootstrap variance estimation method to the Canadian Participation and Activity Limitations Survey. In: *Proceedings of the Section on Survey Research Methods*. American Statistical Association.

Lee, S. and Valliant, R. (2009). Estimation for volunteer panel web Surveys using propensity score adjustment and calibration adjustment. *Sociological Methods and Research* 37: 319–343.

Lisic, J.J. and Ojo, O.E. (2008). *Application of Fay's Method for Variance Estimation in the National Compensation Survey Benefits Products*. Bureau of Labor Statistics: Office of Survey Methods Research Publication https://www.bls.gov/osmr/research-papers/2008/st080070.htm.

Little, R. (2006). Calibrated bayes: a bayes/frequentist roadmap. *The American Statistician* 60 (3): 213–223. Retrieved from 12 June 2021 http://www.jstor.org/stable/27643780.

Little, R.J.A. and Rubin, D.B. (2002). *Statistical Analysis with Missing Data*. New Jersey: Wiley.

Lohr, S.L. (2010). *Sampling: Design and Analysis*, Seconde. Cengage Learning: Brooks/Cole.

Lohr, S.L. and Raghunathan, T.E. (2017). Combining survey data with other data sources. *Statistical Science* 32: 293–312.

Lu, W.W., Brick, M.J. and Sitter, R.R. (2006) Algorithms for constructing combined strata variance estimators, *Journal of the American Statistical Association*, 101:476, 1680-1692, DOI: https://doi.org/10.1198/016214506000000267

Martin, M. (1990). On using the jackknife to estimate quantile variance. *The Canadian Journal of Statistics/La Revue Canadienne De Statistique*, 18(2), 149-153. doi:https://doi.org/10.2307/3315563

Maruichi, D. and Abe, M. (2019). Corruption and the business environment in Vietnam: implications from an empirical study. *Asia and The Pacific Policy Studies* 6: 222–245. https://onlinelibrary.wiley.com/doi/epdf/10.1002/app5.275.

Mashreghi, Z., Haziza, D., and Léger, C. (2016). A survey of bootstrap methods in finite population sampling. *Statistics Surveys*. 10: 1–52. https://doi.org/10.1214/16-SS113.

Mercer, A.W., Kreuter, F., Keeter, S., and Stuart, E.A. (2017). Theory and practice in nonprobability surveys: parallels between causal inference and survey inference. *Public Opinion Quarterly* 81: 250–279. https://academic.oup.com/poq/article-abstract/81/S1/250/3749176.

Mercer, A., Lau, A. and Kennedy, C. (2018). For weighting online opt-in samples, what matters most? Technical Report, Pew Research Center, Washington, DC. http://www.pewresearch.org/2018/01/26/for-weighting-online-opt-in-samples-what-matters-most/ (accessed 8 May 2021).

Motoc, A. (2020). Romanian family business branding: contextual factors of influence of decisional processes. *Proceedings of the International Conference on Business Excellence, Sciendo* 14: 607–616.

Pfeffermann, D. and Sverchkov, M. (2009). Inference under informative sampling. In: *Handbook of Statistics, Volume 29B Sample Surveys: Inference and Analysis* (ed. D. Pfeffermann and C. Rao), 455–488. Amsterdam, chap 39: Elsevier.

Programme for International Student Assessment (PISA) (2015) Chapter 8, Survey weighting and the calculation of sampling variance. PISA 2015 Technical Report. https://www.oecd.org/pisa/sitedocument/PISA-2015-Technical-Report-Chapter-8-Survey-Weighting.pdf.

Rao, J.N.K. and Shao, J. (1999). Modified balanced repeated replication for complex survey data. *Biometrika* 86: 403–415.

Rao, J.N.K. and Wu, C.F.J. (1985). Inference from stratified samples: second-order analysis of three methods for nonlinear statistics. *Journal of the American Statistical Association* 80: 620–630.

Rao, J.N.K., Wu, C.F.J., and Yue, K. (1992). Some recent work on resampling methods for complex surveys. *Survey Methodology* 18 (2): 209–217.

Research Triangle Institute (2012). SUDAAN Language Manual, Volumes 1 and 2, Release 11. Research Triangle Park, NC: Research Triangle Institute.

Robbins, M.W., Ghosh-Dastidar, B., and Ramchand, R. (2020). Blending probability and nonprobability samples with applications to a survey of military caregivers. *Journal of Survey Statistics and Methodology* smaa037: https://doi.org/10.1093/jssam/smaa037.

Rubin, D.B. (1987). *Multiple Imputation for Nonresponse in Surveys*. New York: Wiley.

Rubin, D. (1996). Multiple imputation after 18 years. *Journal of the American Statistical Association*, 91(434), 473-489. doi:https://doi.org/10.2307/2291635.

Rubin, D.B. and Schenker, N. (1986). Multiple imputation for interval estimation from simple random samples with ignorable nonresponse. *Journal of the American Statistical Association* 81: 366–374.

Rust, K. (1985). Variance estimation for complex estimators in sample surveys. *Journal of Official Statistics* 1: 381–397.

Rust, K. and Kalton, G. (1987). Strategies for collapsing strata for variance estimation. *Journal of Official Statistics* 3: 69–81.

Sakshaug, J.W., Wiśniowski, A., Ruiz, D.A.P., and Blom, A.G. (2019). Supplementing small probability samples with nonprobability samples: a Bayesian approach. *Journal of Official Statistics* 35: 653–681. http://dx.doi.org/10.2478/JOS-2019-002.

Särndal, C.E., Thomsen, I., Hoem, J. et al. (1978). Design-based and model-based inference in survey sampling [with discussion and reply]. *Scandinavian Journal of Statistics* 5 (1): 27–52. Retrieved from 21 May 2021 http://www.jstor.org/stable/4615682.

Särndal, C.E., Swensson, B., and Wretman, J.H. (1992). *Model Assisted Survey Sampling*. New York: Springer-Verlag.

Shao, J. and Butani, S. (2002). Variance estimation for the current employment survey. *Survey Methodology* 28 (1): 87–95.

Shao, J., and Steel, P. (1999). Variance estimation for survey data with composite imputation and nonnegligible sampling fractions. *Journal of the American Statistical Association*, 94(445), 254–265. doi:https://doi.org/10.2307/2669700

Shao, J. and Thompson, K.J. (2009). Variance estimation in the presence of nonrespondents and certainty strata. *Survey Methodology* 35: 215–225.

Shao, J. and Tu, D. (1995). *The Jackknife and Bootstrap*. New York: Springer.

Siegel, P.H., Chromy, J. and Scheib, E. (2007). A comparison of variance estimates for schools and students using taylor series and replicate weighting. Papers presented at the ICES-III, Montreal, Quebec, Canada (18–21 June 2007). Retrieved from: https://ww2.amstat.org/meetings/ices/2007/proceedings/ICES2007-000216.PDF.

Statistics Canada (2017). Statistics Canada's Quality Assurance Framework (3rd ed.). https://www150.statcan.gc.ca/n1/en/pub/12-586-x/12-586-x2017001-eng.pdf?st¼ZBVUvHOe (accessed 5 May 2021).

Thompson, K.J. and Sigman, R.S. (2000). Estimation and replicate variance estimation of median sales prices of sold houses. *Survey Methodology* 26: 153–162.

Thompson, K.J., Sigman, R.S., and Goodwin, R.L. (2003). Investigation of replicate variance estimators for the annual capital expenditure survey. In: *Proceedings of the Section on Survey Research Methods*, 4226–4233. American Statistical Association.

Valliant, R. (2004). The effect of multiple weight adjustments on variance estimation. *Journal of Official Statistics* 20: 1–18.

Valliant, R. (2020). Comparing alternatives for estimation from nonprobability samples. *Journal of Survey Statistics and Methodology* 8: 231–263.

Valliant, R. and Dever, J.A. (2011). Estimating propensity adjustments for volunteer web surveys. *Sociological Methods and Research* 40: 105–137.

Valliant, R. and Dever, J.A. (2018). *Survey Weights: A Step-by-Step Guide to Calculation*, Firste. College Station, TX: Stata Press.

Valliant, R., Dorfman, A., and Royall, R. (2000). *Finite Population Sampling and Inference: A Prediction Approach*. New York: Wiley.

Valliant, R., Dever, J., and Kreuter, F. (2018). *Practical Tools for Designing and Weighting Survey Samples*, Statistics for Social and Behavioral Sciences, 2nde. Springer https://doi.org/10.1007/978-3-319-93632-1.

Wamba, S.F., Gunasekaran, A., Akter, S. et al. (2017). Big data analytics and firm performance: effects of dynamic capabilities. *Journal of Business Research* 70: 356–365. https://www.sciencedirect.com/science/article/pii/S0148296316304969.

Welsh, D.H.B., Llanos-Contreras, O., Alonso-Dos-Santos, M., and Kaciak, E. (2021). How much do network support and managerial skills affect women's entrepreneurial success? The overlooked role of country economic development. *Entrepreneurship and Regional Development* 33: 287–308.

West, B.T. and Sakshaug, J.W. (2018). The need to account for complex sampling features when analyzing establishment survey sata: an illustration using the 2013 Business Research and Development and Innovation Survey (BRDIS), *Survey Methods: Insights from the Field*. Retrieved from https://surveyinsights.org/?p=9435

West, B.T., Sakshaug, J.W., and Guy, A.S. (2018). Accounting for complex sampling in survey estimation: a review of current software tools. *Journal of Official Statistics* 34 (3): 721–752.

West, B.T., Sakshaug, J., and Kim, Y. (2017). Analytic error as an important component of total survey error: results from a meta-analysis. In: *Total Survey Error in Practice* (ed. P.P. Biemer, E. de Leeuw, S. Eckman, B. Edwards, F. Kreuter, L.E. Lyberg, N.C. Tucker, and B.T. West). New York, NY: Wiley.

Wolter, K.M. (2007). *Introduction to Variance Estimation*, 2nde. New York: Springer.

30

Bayesian Methods Applied to Small Area Estimation for Establishment Statistics

Paul A. Parker[1], Ryan Janicki[2], and Scott H. Holan[1,3]

[1] *Department of Statistics, University of Missouri, Columbia, MO, USA*
[2] *Center for Statistical Research and Methodology, U.S. Census Bureau, Washington, DC, USA*
[3] *Office of the Associate Director for Research and Methodology, U.S. Census Bureau, Washington, DC, USA*

30.1 Introduction

Much of the literature on small area estimation (SAE) has been focused on analysis of data collected from household surveys or surveys of individuals. In principle, many of the same methods used to analyze household or individual survey data can be applied to the analysis of establishment-level survey data, although there are some fundamental differences in the characteristics of the data, as well as the survey design used to collect the data (Burgard et al., 2014). In establishment surveys, stratified sampling designs are typically used, where the strata are determined using cross classifications of business registry variables, such as employment size variables and industry classifications, as well as geographic variables (Hidiroglou and Lavallée, 2009). These stratified sampling designs, which are stratified with respect to industry and/or business size class, result in highly variable selection probabilities and sampling weights (Zimmerman and Münnich, 2018). The size variables that are used to stratify the population in establishment surveys are typically correlated with an outcome variable of interest, which itself is often highly variable, positive, and highly skewed. In particular, in many industries, the universe of "large" establishments is relatively small, but these large establishments dominate the industry, causing the distribution of the finite population characteristics to be skewed and possibly heavy tailed (Riviére, 2002). The positivity and skewness of the response data needs to be carefully accounted for, usually through some sort of transformation and/or use of a non-Gaussian distribution, in small area modeling to avoid bias in the predictions.

In the SAE of establishment statistics, the terminology *establishment* can be used to mean a survey of organizations or the physical locations associated with a specific business. In the former case, establishment surveys also sample companies, farms, schools, and hospitals, among others. In the latter case of establishment surveys, the sampling unit is typically a particular business location (e.g. store). When referring to establishments of large firms, the small area modeling can become increasingly more complex, as large firms can have multiple establishments in more than one industry and/or state. Throughout this chapter, we typically refer to establishment in the context of a specific business location. When this is not the case, the meaning should be clear from the context.

The overall sample size of many establishment surveys is large, guaranteeing high precision of survey estimates for certain characteristics of interest for large domains, such as at the state or

Advances in Business Statistics, Methods and Data Collection. Edited by Ger Snijkers, Mojca Bavdaž, Stefan Bender, Jacqui Jones, Steve MacFeely, Joseph W. Sakshaug, Katherine J. Thompson, and Arnout van Delden.
© 2023 John Wiley & Sons, Inc. Published 2023 by John Wiley & Sons, Inc.

national level for a specific industry classification sector. However, there may be additional demand for estimates of characteristics at finer cross classifications or for smaller geographic domains than the survey was designed. The uncertainty associated with the direct estimates at these lower levels is often too large, due to small area/industry-specific sample sizes, which can be exacerbated by the highly variable survey weights inherent to establishment surveys. In such situations, it becomes necessary to introduce statistical models to produce estimates with adequate precision. SAE models have been proven effective in increasing the effective sample size in small areas of interest, by introducing auxiliary predictors from administrative records or other outside data sources, and linking the different small areas through use of area-specific random effects (Rao and Molina, 2015). Models used for SAE problems generally rely on strong auxiliary predictors to produce precise estimates. However, many business registers do not include strong auxiliary information, which is an additional complication in applying SAE methods to establishment data (Burgard et al., 2014). Throughout this chapter, we use the terminology small area estimation to refer to both small areas and small domains, where the latter may refer to the tabulation level of a specific industry classification sector.

There are two general small area strategies that can be applied to survey data: area-level small area modeling, which models survey-weighted data aggregated to each small area of interest (i.e. direct estimates), and unit-level small area modeling, which models the individual record-level response data, i.e. individual person, household, or establishment data. Area-level small area estimates in which the underlying establishment is a farm, has been an area of ongoing research with several examples throughout the literature, including Wang et al. (2012), Erciulescu et al. (2019), and Erciulescu et al. (2020), among others. In the context of establishment survey data, Gershunskaya and Savitsky (2017) considered a variety of area-level small area models for estimation of employment, using Current Employment Statistics (CES) survey data. Their work builds on the popular Fay–Herriot small area model (Fay and Herriot, 1979), which assumes linearity, as well as normality and independence of sampling and model errors. Gershunskaya and Savitsky (2017) investigated the relaxation of these model assumptions by systematically increasing model complexity by accounting for spatial dependence, temporal dependence, and clustering in the data.

Perhaps the biggest challenge in area-level modeling of aggregated establishment survey data is accounting for the positive skewness in the distribution of the outcomes, which makes the usual assumptions of a linear model with Gaussian errors questionable. One solution to this problem is to transform the response data and the predictors so that linearity is more reasonable (Slud and Maiti, 2006; Sugasawa and Kubokawa, 2017; Chandra et al., 2018). The inferential goal in this situation is prediction of the inverse transformation of the linear predictor. An advantage of transforming the direct estimates to achieve linearity is that standard methods for inference using the theory of linear mixed models can be used.

Alternatively, the distribution of the error terms can be modified to account for skewness. Ferrante and Pacei (2017) proposed accounting for the skewness in the data by relaxing the assumption of normality in the classic normal–normal small area model, by instead using the skew-normal distribution for the distribution of both the sampling errors and the model errors. Instead of the skew-normal distribution, Fabrizi et al. (2017) considered the lognormal error distribution as an extension of the Fay–Herriot model.

Area-level small area models are popular, as they are effective in producing model-based predictions that are more precise, on average, than the corresponding direct estimates. Area-level models are also advantageous in that they are usually relatively easy to fit using standard software packages and often use publicly available data as the model inputs. However, there are some practical limitation in using area-level models. For one, it is difficult to make estimates at finer demographic or geographic levels than the level of the aggregated direct estimates. Second, if one or more of the direct estimates is based on a very small sample size, the distributional assumptions may be difficult to verify, and the design-based variance estimates of the direct estimates may be unstable. Finally, it is often necessary in practice to ensure that model-based predictions aggregate to some known total, so that, for example estimates of counts at a low geographic level add up to the corresponding estimate at a national level (Bell et al., 2013). In other words, tabulations produced at lower disaggregated levels are additively consistent with corresponding tabulations released at higher levels of aggregation.

In contrast, unit-level models use individual survey responses (i.e. record-level data), design variables, and survey weights as model inputs, and constitute a "bottom-up" approach, as they utilize the survey data at its finest resolution. Because the model inputs are at the unit level, predictions can be made at the same level as the inputs, and can be aggregated up to any desired level. The main difficulty with using unit-level models for survey data is that it can be difficult to account for the survey design, which is especially important when modeling establishment data due to the heterogeneity of the survey weights, and the correlation of the inclusion probabilities to the response variable.

Recent work on unit-level modeling of establishment survey data includes (Chandra and Chambers, 2011), which modeled the log transformed unit-level data, and Berg and Chandra (2014) and Molina and Martin (2018), which assumed a lognormal distribution on the unit-level response variables. Their work is an extension of the nested error regression model of Battese et al. (1988), which is a linear, mixed effects model. They assumed an *ignorable* survey design, that is, that the probability of selection in the establishment survey is uncorrelated with the variable of interest. Under the assumption of ignorability, the same model which holds for the units in the finite population also holds for the units in the sampled population. This allows model-based predictions of nonsampled units to be made based on a model fitted from sampled survey data, without adjusting for the survey design.

Due to the unique nature of establishment surveys, and the fact that a unit size variable is typically used in the survey design, the assumption of ignorability may be violated. With *nonignorable* survey designs, in which inclusion probabilities are correlated with response variables, it is critical to account for the survey design in the unit-level small area model by either including design variables (Little, 2012) or survey weights (Pfeffermann and Sverchkov, 2007) to avoid biased predictions (Nathan and Holt, 1980). Zimmerman and Münnich (2018) considered an extension of the model in Berg and Chandra (2014), which accounts for an informative survey design. Their approach is to solve a system of survey-weighted estimating equations (You and Rao, 2002). Smith et al. (In Press) considered outlier-robust unit-level SAE methods to reduce the impact of influential data points in establishment surveys. More generally, the survey design can be incorporated into a small area model by exponentially weighting the likelihood function by the survey weights (Savitsky and Toth, 2016; Parker et al., 2020b). This *pseudo-likelihood* approach (Skinner, 1989) is advantageous in the context of establishment survey data, in that nonstandard small area model likelihoods, such as the lognormal distribution, can be used to account for positive, skewed data.

In this work, we compare unit-level small area modeling with area-level modeling strategies when applied to positive and positively skewed data obtained from establishment surveys. We also examine the benefit of incorporating spatial dependence in the modeling framework. Importantly, we compare and contrast the differences in small area modeling for household and establishment surveys. Throughout this paper, hierarchical Bayesian versions of small area models are given, and in the examples and data analyses presented, point estimates and uncertainty estimates are made using posterior inference. The remainder of this chapter is organized as follows: In Section 30.2, background information and notation is introduced, and the Bayesian framework for modeling establishment survey data and incorporating various dependencies is discussed.

In Section 30.3, the basic area-level small area model is introduced, as well as its extensions for use with establishment data. Different strategies for modeling unit-level establishment data collected under informative and noninformative survey designs are discussed in Section 30.4. In Section 30.5, we present results of an empirical simulation study comparing different area-level and unit-level small area models using 2007 Survey of Business Owners (SBO) public-use micro-data, available at https://www.census.gov/data/datasets/2007/econ/sbo/2007-sbo-pums.html. A data analysis comparing model-based predictions using an area-level small area model with survey-based direct estimates is done in Section 30.6. Concluding remarks are given in Section 30.7. All relevant code is available at https://github.com/paparker/Bayesian_SAE_ES.

30.2 Bayesian Hierarchical Modeling for Dependent Data

Let $\mathcal{U} = \{1, \dots, N\}$ represent an enumeration of the finite population of interest. Let $d = 1, \dots, m$ index the disjoint small areas, and let $j = 1, \dots, N_d$ index the N_d establishments within area d. Associated with each Establishment, we observe a characteristic, Z_{jd}, and the usual inferential goal is estimation of either the finite population mean, $\overline{Z}_d = \sum_{j=1}^{N_d} Z_{jd}/N_d$, or the finite population total, $Z_d = \sum_{j=1}^{N_d} Z_{jd}$, for each area d. Typically, in the small-area literature, Y is used to denote the observations. However, in keeping with the hierarchical Bayesian literature, we denote the observed values by Z and reserve Y for the underlying latent process.

A random sample, $S \subset \mathcal{U}$, of size n is drawn according to a complex survey design. Let n_d be the area-specific sample size for area d. Associated to each sampled unit is a survey weight, w_{jd}, and either a vector of area-level covariates, x_d, or a vector of establishment-level covariates, x_{dj}. A design-consistent estimator of the small area means is given by the Horvitz–Thompson (HT) estimator (Horvitz and Thompson, 1952),

$$\hat{\overline{Z}}_d = \frac{1}{N_d} \sum_{j=1}^{n_d} w_{jd} Z_{jd} \tag{30.1}$$

Design consistency guarantees high precision of the HT estimator, so long as the area-specific sample size, n_d, is large. However, despite the large overall sample size that is typically achieved with a national survey, there will often be one or more areas where n_d is too small for adequate precision of the direct estimate. In such situations, it becomes necessary to introduce statistical models which incorporate auxiliary data and introduce random effects which link different areas and describe dependencies in the response data. Small area models effectively increase effective sample size in areas with small survey sample, and produce model-based predictions which are more precise than the corresponding direct estimates.

One important component of SAE, both in general and specifically for establishment statistics, is the incorporation of dependence structures. For example, businesses within the same industry may tend to have more similar survey responses than those of businesses from unrelated industries. In many other cases, survey units may exhibit geographic dependence. Inclusion of these dependence structures within a SAE model can yield more precise estimates.

A natural and popular framework for capturing various dependence structures (i.e. spatial, temporal, spatio-temporal, multivariate, network, etc.) is that of Bayesian hierarchical modeling (Cressie and Wikle, 2011). In a general sense, Bayesian hierarchical modeling can be thought of in three stages. The data stage of the model is the distribution of the observed data (i.e. the likelihood) after conditioning on a latent process and any model parameters. In practice, data are often modeled using a conditional likelihood from the exponential family (Bradley et al., 2020). This allows for many common types of survey data, including binary, categorical, Gaussian, and count data. The process model is used to capture any dependence structures. By integrating out the process stage of the model, the marginal likelihood can be revealed. However, in cases of non-Gaussian data, the marginal likelihood is often intractable, thus, working in the hierarchical setting simplifies computation considerably. Finally, the prior stage of the model is used to specify the prior distribution of any model parameters, coming from both the data and process stages.

Consider a vector of data, Z, and a latent process Y. Also consider a vector of model parameters $\theta = (\theta_D, \theta_P)$, where θ_D and θ_P correspond to the parameters used in the data and process models, respectively. Then, assuming conditional independence between θ_D and θ_P, we can write the joint distribution of the data and the process conditioned on the model parameters as

$$p(Z, Y|, \theta) = p(Z|Y, \theta_D)p(Y|\theta_P)$$

Using this representation, the three stages can be written

Data Model: $p(Z|Y, \theta_D)$

Process Model: $p(Y|\theta_P)$

Prior: $p(\theta)$

After full specification of a model, the usual task is to estimate both the process and the parameters after observing some data. Following Bayes Theorem, this is written as

$$p(Y, \theta \mid Z) \propto p(Z \mid Y, \theta_D)p(Y \mid \theta_P)p(\theta) \tag{30.2}$$

Sampling from this posterior distribution is often done using Markov chain Monte Carlo methods (see (Gelman et al., 1995) for a more in depth view of Bayesian methodology in practice).

Fundamental to (30.2) is the flexibility that this conditional way of thinking facilitates in complicated applications. In addition, the right hand side of (30.2) can be further decomposed into several submodels. For example, assuming conditional independence given the true underlying latent process provides a convenient path forward to modeling multiple area-level datasets with different spatial and/or temporal supports. Using hierarchical notation where $[Z|Y]$ and $[Y]$ are used denote the conditional distribution of Z given Y and the marginal distribution of Y, respectively, this can be achieved through the following specification

$$\left[Z^{(1)}, Z^{(2)}|Y, \theta_Z^{(1)}, \theta_Z^{(2)}\right] = \left[Z^{(1)}|Y, \theta_Z^{(2)}\right]\left[Z^{(2)}|Y, \theta_Z^{(2)}\right]$$

where $Z^{(j)}$ and $\theta_Z^{(j)}$ ($j = 1, 2$) correspond to the observations from the jth dataset, respectively, (Holan and Wikle, 2016). Importantly, in the multivariate setting, the process model can also be conveniently decomposed using a conditional specification. That is, letting $[Y] = [Y^{(1)}, Y^{(2)}]$, the process model can be specified as $[Y] = [Y^{(2)}|Y^{(1)}][Y^{(1)}]$. In this case, the order of conditioning is usually application specific and guided by the goals of the analysis (Royle and Berliner, 1999).

As previously mentioned, the use of Bayesian hierarchical modeling has important advantages for modeling dependent data. Without using a hierarchical approach, one would need to specify complex multivariate distributions for the likelihood. This can be extremely difficult, if not infeasible, especially in the case of non-Gaussian data. However, using a hierarchical approach, the dependence can be modeled at the process stage using a latent Gaussian process (LGP) model, while assuming conditional independence at the data stage (Gelfand and Schliep, 2016).

Another advantage of Bayesian hierarchical modeling is that it provides a natural framework for uncertainty quantification. We can use the entire posterior distribution to develop point estimates that minimize a desired loss function (e.g. the posterior mean for squared error loss), while also using the full posterior distribution to characterize any uncertainty around our estimates or predictions. Paramount to this approach is that sources of uncertainty coming from either the parameters or the process are properly propagated through the model.

One final advantage of Bayesian hierarchical modeling is the ability to provide regularization (Gelman et al., 2012). Many SAE models involve a high-dimensional parameter space. For example, with area-level models that use spatial random effects, there are typically at least as many random effects as there are observations. In these high-dimensional settings, it is critical to add a regularization component in order to be able to fit the model and avoid overfitting of the observed data. The use of Bayesian hierarchical modeling does this naturally, in a framework similar to Bayesian ridge regression.

30.3 Area-Level Models

The Fay–Herriot model (Fay and Herriot, 1979) is the foundation for most area-level modeling approaches to SAE. This model can be written

$$\hat{Z}_d = Y_d + \varepsilon_d$$
$$Y_d = x_d^T \beta + \eta_d \tag{30.3}$$

where the sampling errors, ε_d, are independent, mean-zero random variables with known sampling variances V_d, and the model errors, η_d, are mean zero random variables with common model error variance σ^2, independent of the sampling errors. The first equation in (30.3) is the *sampling model*, and the second equation is the *linking model*. The errors ε_d and η_d are often assumed to be Gaussian, but inference on Y_d can be done without this distributional assumption (Rao and Molina, 2015; Bradley et al., 2020). Inference can be based on the posterior distribution, after specifying a prior on the unknown model parameters β and σ^2. A common choice for a noninformative prior distribution is $\pi\left(\beta, \sigma^2\right) \propto \left(\sigma^2\right)^{-a-1} e^{-b/\sigma^2}$, where a and b are chosen to be small, positive values.

When the domain-specific sample sizes are large, the central limit theorem makes the assumption of normality of the sampling errors reasonable. However, when one or more of the n_d are small, there is no theoretical guarantee of this assumption. In addition, one of the main difficulties with modeling establishment survey data, compared to household survey data, is that the establishment survey data is often positive and highly skewed. For this reason, a small area model which assumes linearity with Gaussian errors may not be appropriate. For example, Steel and Fay (1995) studied a set of 1992 economic census industries (an establishment program) and found that the distribution of payroll appeared to be lognormal or a mixture of lognormals in almost all cases.

One solution to this problem is to make a data transformation which makes the assumptions of linearity and normality more reasonable (Slud and Maiti, 2006). For example, rather than modeling the direct estimates, $\hat{Z}_d$, in (30.3), a nonlinear transformation, $g\left(\hat{Z}_d\right)$, can be used as the response variable. In this situation, it may make sense to transform the predictors, x_d, as well. When using transformed response data in the Fay–Herriot model (30.3), the inferential goal becomes prediction of the inverse-transformed linear predictor, $g^{-1}\left(Y_d\right)$.

A common choice for g is the log transformation, particularly when modeling skewed, positive direct estimates (Chandra and Chambers, 2011). An important practical consideration when using transformed data, is that an estimate of the sampling variance, V_d^*, of $g(\hat{Z}_d)$, is needed in (30.3). If the analyst has access to the unit-level data file which includes the survey weights, the direct variance estimate V_d^* can be constructed in the same manner in which V_d was constructed. However, in practice, the analyst may not have access to this data. In this case, the delta method can be used to get an approximate sampling variance estimate for $g(\hat{Z}_d)$ to use in (30.3).

An alternative to using a data transformation when modeling skewed, positive survey data, is to keep the response data on the original scale, but modify the distributional assumptions of the error terms, ε_d and η_d, in (30.3). Fabrizi et al. (2017) used a lognormal distribution for both the sampling errors, ε_d, and the model errors, η_d. In their model specification, the sampling model in Eq. (30.3) is no longer linear, and instead can be written

$$\hat{Z}_d \mid Y_d, V_d \sim \text{LN}\left(Y_d^*, V_d^*\right)$$

where LN denotes the lognormal distribution. The linking model is then given by $Y_d = \exp\left\{x_d^T \beta + \eta_d\right\}$, where $\eta_d \sim N\left(0, \sigma_d^2\right)$. The parameters Y_d^* and V_d^* are related to Y_d and V_d using properties of the lognormal distribution, and the assumption that the direct estimates are unbiased on the original scale, that is, $E\left(\hat{Z}_d \mid Y_d\right) = Y_d$. Other distributions, such as the skew-normal distribution (Ferrante and Pacei, 2017), can be used to account for the skewness in the response data.

The Fay–Herriot model (30.3) links the various direct estimates through the random effect η_d and the covariates x_d which are both indexed by the small areas d. There are potentially additional sources of correlation which can be exploited to further increase precision of predictions. For example, in the case of establishment surveys, businesses belonging to the same industry may be more similar than businesses in another industry. A simple extension of the linking model in (30.3) which can be used to capture this relationship is

$$\hat{Z}_{id} = Y_{id} + \varepsilon_{id}$$
$$Y_{id} = x_{id}^T \beta + \eta_d + \xi_i \tag{30.4}$$

where d indexes the geographic areas, i indexes the industries, and ξ_i is an additional random effect which links the industries.

Incorporating various sources of dependence is a topic of wide-spread interest in the modeling of small area data. Often, direct estimates which are linked to a geographic region are similar to direct estimates linked to neighboring geographic regions. In this case, the small area model should include random effects with a distribution which incorporates this spatial dependence. Porter et al. (2014) extend the Fay–Herriot model to allow for spatial dependence as well as functional covariates. In addition, surveys are often conducted at regular intervals, such as monthly or annually, and there may be an underlying time trend in the data. The Fay–Herriot model can be extended to incorporate dependence over time by including temporal or spatiotemporal dependence in the distribution of the random effects (Bradley et al., 2015). Moving away from the Gaussian assumption, Bradley et al. (2020) develop a spatiotemporal framework that can be used for non-Gaussian data in the natural exponential family.

As with any Bayesian modeling exercise, it is important to assess convergence of the estimation algorithm and consider goodness-of-fit. There are several approaches to assessing convergence, including the Geweke diagnostic based on a test for equality of the means of the first and last part of a sample Markov chain (Geweke, 1992), the Gelman–Rubin diagnostic based on a comparison of within-chain and between-chain variance of the sample Markov chain Monte Carlo chains (Gelman et al., 1992), visual inspection of the trace plots of the sample Markov chain Monte Carlo chains, and several others. Regarding goodness-of-fit, in the area of SAE, there are several options. For example, one can consider the Bayesian p-value based on the posterior predictive distribution

(Gelman and Meng, 1996), which provides a method of checking the fit of the model to data while also improving on meaningful parameters. Alternatively, one can evaluate model performance, based on specified metric, using out of sample cross-validation. There are several other approaches to assessing convergence and goodness-of-fit. For an overview of different methods, see Gelman et al. (2013) and the references therein.

30.4 Unit-Level Models

Unlike area-level models, which treat the design-based direct estimates as response values, unit-level models instead model the survey responses directly. As a consequence of this, unit-level modeling strategies typically require some way to account for the survey design. Specifically, many survey designs result in unit probabilities of selection that are correlated or dependent on the response of interest. This is termed *informative sampling*, and failure to account for the design in such cases can introduce model biases.

Accounting for sample design is only one of the challenges presented by unit-level modeling approaches. In addition, unit-level models can be computationally challenging. One major reason for this is the massive increase in the size of the data under consideration. Area-level models have implicit dimension reduction by using the aggregated direct estimates. The full survey datasets that are used in unit-level modeling are often orders of magnitude larger. In addition to data size, unit-level responses are typically non-Gaussian (i.e. binary or categorical) which can introduce further computational challenges.

Despite the challenges associated with unit-level modeling, they are accompanied by some important benefits as well. First, unit-level models have been shown to have potential for more precise estimates (Hidiroglou and You, 2016). They also eliminate the need for imposing any benchmarking, which can be difficult in some circumstances. Finally, for many problems, distributional assumptions can be challenging at the area level, but may be simplified considerably at the unit level.

30.4.1 Basic Unit-Level Model

The basic unit-level model, given by Battese et al. (1988), is the foundation for many unit-level models. The model can be written hierarchically as

$$Z_{jd} | \boldsymbol{\beta}, \eta_d \overset{ind}{\sim} \mathrm{N}(\boldsymbol{x}_{jd}\boldsymbol{\beta} + \eta_d, \sigma_\epsilon^2)$$
$$\eta_d \overset{iid}{\sim} \mathrm{N}(0, \sigma_\eta^2)$$

where Z_{jd} represents the response value for unit j in small domain d. A unit specific vector of covariates is denoted by $\boldsymbol{x}_{jd}$, whereas η_d represents a domain-specific random effect. These domains can represent geographic areas such as states or counties, or perhaps in the case of establishment statistics, industries. Additional random effects can be added to account for different dependencies, or to link the different small areas by finer levels, such as geography by industry classification. This model can be fit in a Bayesian fashion after placing a prior distribution over $\boldsymbol{\beta}$, σ_ϵ^2, and σ_η^2.

In general, with unit-level modeling strategies, the model can be fit using the sample data and then predictions can be made for every unit in the population. In the case where only categorical covariates are used, this can be seen as a type of poststratification (Gelman and Little, 1997; Park et al., 2006). Often, population sizes within certain categorical groups are known based on the census or other data sources, whereas full population knowledge for continuous covariates can be difficult to attain. Once predictions have been made for all population units, it is straightforward to aggregate the "synthetic" population as necessary to construct any desired small domain estimates. In a Bayesian setting, this can be done for every draw from the posterior distribution, giving rise to a posterior distribution of any estimates that can be used to quantify uncertainty.

One drawback of the basic unit-level model is that it assumes the sample model holds for the entire population. That is, there is no adjustment for sample design, meaning the model is not appropriate under informative sampling scenarios. Nonetheless, this mixed regression framework can act as a building block for more complex models that do account for survey design. Similar to area-level models, when modeling at the unit level, it is important to assess convergence and consider goodness-of-fit (see Section 30.3).

30.4.2 Accounting for Survey Design

One extremely popular approach to accounting for informative sampling is to use a pseudo-likelihood within a unit-level model. Introduced by Binder (1983) and Skinner (1989), the pseudo-likelihood approach exponentially weights each unit's likelihood contribution by its associated sampling weight,

$$\prod_{j \in S} p(Z_{jd}|\theta)^{w_{jd}}$$

For frequentist estimation, this pseudo-likelihood may be maximized to yield a point estimate of model parameters.

Zhang et al. (2014) provide a basic example of pseudo-likelihood usage applied to small area estimation. They fit a survey weighted mixed effects logistic regression framework to estimate chronic obstructive pulmonary disease prevalence by county. After fitting the weighted model, which adjust for the informative sampling design, they use poststratification to create predictions for the entire population and then aggregate as necessary to construct their small area estimates.

As an alternative to frequentist use of the pseudo-likelihood, Savitsky and Toth (2016) justify the use of a pseudo-likelihood, in general, for Bayesian modeling under complex sampling designs (i.e. cluster sampling, multistage samples, etc.). They show that under suitable conditions, the pseudo-posterior distribution that results from the use of a Bayesian pseudo-likelihood,

$$\hat{\pi}(\theta|\mathbf{Z}, \tilde{\mathbf{w}}) \propto \left\{ \prod_{j \in S} p(Z_{jd}|\theta)^{\tilde{w}_{jd}} \right\} \pi(\theta)$$

converges to the population posterior distribution. In this case, $\tilde{w}_{jd}$ represents the weights after scaling to sum to the sample size, which is done to yield correct uncertainty estimation.

The Bayesian pseudo-likelihood approach is fairly general and not beholden to a specific model. In fact, it is straightforward to augment an existing model, such as the basic unit-level model, with a pseudo-likelihood through the use of the reported survey weights. Doing so adjusts for the informative sampling mechanism and thus reduces potential bias. In addition, the Bayesian paradigm provides a natural source of uncertainty quantification. This is particularly important for SAE, as federal agencies are often keenly interested in the quality of the disseminated estimates and any uncertainty associated with them.

The primary challenge with these Bayesian pseudo-likelihood models is often computational rather than specification of an appropriate model. In the case of Gaussian response data, the posterior distribution may be computationally tractable allowing for straightforward Gibbs sampling. However, in the case of non-Gaussian data with a LGP, the posterior distribution is generally not tractable. In these cases, other techniques may be necessary to sample from the posterior distribution.

30.4.3 Models for Non-Gaussian Data

One type of non-Gaussian data that shows up in various surveys is count data. For example, the SBO includes a count variable for the number of employees. Count data are often modeled using a Poisson data model; however, the use of a Poisson data model with a LGP model does not yield conjugacy. The resulting posterior distribution can be difficult to sample from in a Bayesian setting. As an alternative, Parker et al. (2020b) construct a count data model for surveys using a Poisson pseudo-likelihood as well as prior distributions based on the multivariate log-Gamma (MLG) distribution, introduced by Bradley et al. (2020). This density is denoted $\text{MLG}(\boldsymbol{\mu}, \boldsymbol{V}, \boldsymbol{\alpha}, \boldsymbol{\kappa})$. Importantly, the distribution of $\text{MLG}(\mathbf{c}, \alpha^{1/2}\mathbf{V}, \alpha\mathbf{1}, \alpha\mathbf{1})$ converges in distribution to a multivariate Normal distribution with mean $\mathbf{c}$ and covariance matrix $\mathbf{V}$ as the value of α approaches infinity. This allows one to effectively use a Gaussian prior while maintaining the computational benefits that arise from the use of the MLG prior. The full pseudo-likelihood Poisson multivariate log-Gamma (PL-PMLG) model is given as

$$\mathbf{Z}|\boldsymbol{\beta}, \boldsymbol{\eta} \propto \prod_{j \in S} \text{Pois}\left(Z_j | \lambda = \lambda_j\right)^{\tilde{w}_j}$$

$$\log(\lambda_j) = \boldsymbol{x}_j'\boldsymbol{\beta} + \boldsymbol{\phi}_j'\boldsymbol{\eta}, \quad j \in S$$

$$\boldsymbol{\eta}|\sigma_k \sim \text{MLG}(\mathbf{0}_r, \alpha^{1/2}\sigma_k\mathbf{I}_r, \alpha\mathbf{1}_r, \alpha\mathbf{1}_r) \tag{30.5}$$

$$\boldsymbol{\beta} \sim \text{MLG}(\mathbf{0}_p, \alpha^{1/2}\sigma_\beta\mathbf{I}_p, \alpha\mathbf{1}_p, \alpha\mathbf{1}_p)$$

$$\frac{1}{\sigma_k} \sim \text{Log-Gamma}^+(\omega, \rho), \quad \sigma_\beta, \alpha, \omega, \rho > 0$$

where Z_j represents the response value for unit j in the sample with size n. The p-dimensional vector $\boldsymbol{x}_j$ represents a vector of covariates and the r-dimensional vector $\boldsymbol{\phi}_j$ represents a set of spatial basis functions or domain incidence vectors. With this setup, $\boldsymbol{\eta}$ can be interpreted as a random effect. If desired, an additional individual level random effect can be added to the model to incorporate fine-scale variation and/or over-dispersion.

Binary and categorical variables are also very common in survey data at the unit level. For example, the SBO indicates whether or not a sampled establishment conducts e-commerce. For establishments, these variables tend to reflect characteristics of the establishment other than size, which is what is typically estimated, but can be used to estimate the prevalence of establishments with certain characteristics (i.e. businesses that conduct e-commerce, or that are veteran owned, etc.). Parker et al. (2020a) construct a SAE for Binomial unit-level data, written as,

$$\mathbf{Z}|\boldsymbol{\beta}, \boldsymbol{\eta} \propto \prod_{j \in S} \text{Bin}\left(Z_j | n_j, p_j\right)^{\tilde{w}_j}$$

$$\text{logit}(p_j) = \boldsymbol{x}_j'\boldsymbol{\beta} + \boldsymbol{\phi}_j'\boldsymbol{\eta}$$

$$\boldsymbol{\eta}|\sigma_\eta^2 \sim \text{N}_r(\mathbf{0}_r, \sigma_\eta^2\mathbf{I}_r) \tag{30.6}$$

$$\boldsymbol{\beta} \sim \text{N}_q(\mathbf{0}_q, \sigma_\beta^2\mathbf{I}_q)$$

$$\sigma_\eta^2 \sim \text{IG}(a, b)$$

$$\sigma_\beta, a, b > 0$$

where n_j and p_j represent the size and probability of occurrence, respectively, for unit j. By setting $n_j = 1$, the model can be used for binary variables. In order to produce conjugate full-conditional distributions, Pólya-Gamma data augmentation is used, as outlined by Polson et al. (2013). The model can be extended to handle Multinomial/categorical data by using a stick-breaking representation of the Multinomial distribution (Linderman et al., 2015). In the extremely high-dimensional case (e.g. when modeling data for the entire United States) (Parker et al., 2020a) provide a Variational Bayes approximation for efficient computation.

30.5 Empirical Simulation Study

To illustrate and compare various Bayesian approaches to SAE for establishment statistics, we develop an empirical simulation study using the public-use microdata sample from the 2007 SBO conducted by the US Census Bureau (U.S. Census Bureau, 2012). This survey contains responses from roughly 2 million business owners across the United States. By using microdata rather than tabulated data, we are able to illustrate and compare both area-level and unit-level methodology. Note that with this public-use data, certain measures have been taken for the purpose of disclosure avoidance, including combining samples from sparsely populated states such as Alaska and Wyoming, as well as adding a small amount of noise to continuous variables. From here on, when we refer to the state, we are referring to the grouped state variable, for which there are 47 total states or groups of states, which we index by $s = 1, \ldots, 47$. We index the industry sectors by $i = 1, \ldots, 20$.

We begin by treating the existing SBO sample data as the true finite population for which we wish to make estimates. We then take a further subsample in an informative manner, which we use to construct estimates and then compare to the truth. Specifically, we sample in two stages. In the first stage, we divide the population into strata based on unique combinations of industry sector and state. Within each strata, we take a simple random sample of two individuals. These individuals are included in the final sample with probability one. This is done to create estimates at the industry by state level while avoiding the complexities that arise from having no sample in some domains. In the second stage, for the remaining individuals in the population, we take a probability proportional to size sample using the Poisson method (Brewer et al., 1984), with an expected sample size of 20,000. We use the inverse of the reported survey weights as the size variable in this stage. This results in a final sample that is roughly 1% of the population.

Using the sample data, we construct estimates of the population mean receipts by sector and state, $\overline{Z}_{is}$. We first construct a direct HT estimate (using Eq. (30.1)), $\hat{Z}_{is}$. The sampling scheme is informative by design, which is why we use the weighted HT estimator rather than an unweighted estimator. The direct estimate of the population mean is accompanied by a direct estimate of the standard error, $\hat{\sigma}_{is}$, using the Hansen–Hurwitz estimator (Hansen and Hurwitz, 1943) from the mase package in R (McConville et al., 2018). In addition to the direct estimates, we construct three model-based estimates. Exploratory analysis indicates that the log-Normal distribution is a reasonable choice for this data, thus Model 1 is a Fay–Herriot model using the log transformed data. It is written as

$$\tilde{Z}_{is} | \beta, \eta \overset{ind}{\sim} N(Y_{is}, \tilde{\sigma}_{is}^2)$$

$$Y_{is} = \beta_0 + x_{1is}\beta_1 + x_{2is}\beta_2 + \eta_{is}$$

$$\eta_{is} | \sigma_\eta^2 \overset{iid}{\sim} N(0, \sigma_\eta^2)$$

$$\sigma_\eta^2 \sim \text{Inv. Gamma}(a, b)$$

$$\beta \sim N(\mathbf{0}, \sigma_\beta^2 \mathbf{I})$$

$$a, b, \sigma_\beta^2 > 0$$

where $\tilde{Z}_{is} = \log(\hat{\bar{Z}}_{is} + 1)$. We add one to the direct estimates to allow the log transformation to be used even when the direct estimate is zero. After transforming the direct estimates, we use the delta method to obtain the appropriate plug-in variance estimates, $\tilde{\sigma}_{is}^2$. Our first covariate, x_{1is}, is the log transformed average number of employees for businesses in sector i and state s. We let x_{2is} be the percentage of businesses that conduct e-commerce. Finally, we have a domain-level random effect, η_{is}. We use conjugate prior distributions in this model, and set the hyperparameters $a = b = 0.5$ and $\sigma_\beta^2 = 100$ to be uninformative, although stronger priors may be desired in cases where prior information is known.

Model 2 is similar to Model 1, although we use separate sector and state-level random effects,

$$\tilde{Z}_{is} | \boldsymbol{\beta}, \boldsymbol{\eta}, \boldsymbol{\xi} \overset{ind}{\sim} N(Y_{is}, \tilde{\sigma}_{is}^2)$$
$$Y_{is} = \beta_0 + x_{1is}\beta_1 + x_{2is}\beta_2 + \eta_s + \xi_i$$
$$\eta_s | \sigma_\eta^2 \overset{iid}{\sim} N(0, \sigma_\eta^2)$$
$$\xi_i | \sigma_\xi^2 \overset{iid}{\sim} N(0, \sigma_\xi^2)$$
$$\sigma_\eta^2 \sim \text{Inv. Gamma}(a, b)$$
$$\sigma_\xi^2 \sim \text{Inv. Gamma}(a, b)$$
$$\boldsymbol{\beta} \sim N(\mathbf{0}, \sigma_\beta^2 \boldsymbol{I})$$
$$a, b, \sigma_\beta^2 > 0$$

By using separate random effects for sector and state, this model is able to borrow strength across sectors and states when creating estimates. Note that this model is a Bayesian equivalent to the extension of the Fay–Herriot model explored in (30.4).

Finally, unlike the first two models, Model 3 is a unit-level model,

$$\tilde{Z} | \boldsymbol{\beta}, \boldsymbol{\eta}, \boldsymbol{\xi}, \sigma^2 \propto \prod_{j \in S} N(\tilde{Z}_{jis} | Y_{jis}, \sigma^2)^{\tilde{w}_{jis}}$$
$$Y_{jis} = \beta_0 + x_{1jis}\beta_1 + x_{2jis}\beta_2 + \eta_s + \xi_i$$
$$\eta_s | \sigma_\eta^2 \overset{iid}{\sim} N(0, \sigma_\eta^2)$$
$$\xi_i | \sigma_\xi^2 \overset{iid}{\sim} N(0, \sigma_\xi^2)$$
$$\sigma_\eta^2 \sim \text{Inv. Gamma}(a, b)$$
$$\sigma_\xi^2 \sim \text{Inv. Gamma}(a, b)$$
$$\sigma^2 \sim \text{Inv. Gamma}(a, b)$$
$$\boldsymbol{\beta} \sim N(\mathbf{0}, \sigma_\beta^2 \boldsymbol{I})$$
$$a, b, \sigma_\beta^2 > 0$$

where $\tilde{Z}_{jis}$ is the log transformed receipts (plus one) for business j in sector i and state s. This model takes a pseudo-likelihood approach via the scaled survey weights, $\tilde{w}_{jis}$. The covariate x_{1jis} is the log of the number of employees at the business plus one, and x_{2jis} is a binary indicator of whether or not the establishment conducts e-commerce. At the unit level, the data-level variance, σ^2, must be

Table 30.1 Simulation results: RMSE and absolute bias over 100 simulations using the 2007 Survey of Business Owners Public Use Microdata.

Estimator	RMSE	Absolute bias
HT Direct	1.10×10^4	4.64×10^2
Model 1	3.39×10^3	4.57×10^2
Model 2	2.20×10^3	9.38×10^2
Model 3	4.13×10^3	2.43×10^3

Estimators include a weighted direct estimate (HT Direct), a basic Fay–Herriot model (Model 1), an area-level model with separate sector and state random effects (Model 2), and a unit-level model (Model 3).

modeled rather than plugged in. The unit-level data appear to violate the log-Normal assumption; however, we still present this model to illustrate how unit-level SAE might be done in principle. In practice, it may be beneficial to construct a more complicated model, possibly using a mixture of log-Normal distributions and/or heteroskedastic variance.

We repeat the subsampling and estimation procedure 100 times. For all models, we use Gibbs sampling for 1000 iterations, and discard the first 500 iterations as burn-in. Convergence was assessed via visual inspection of the trace-plots of the sample chains, where no lack of convergence was detected. For the area-level model estimates, we use the posterior mean of $\exp(Y_{is}) - 1$ as our point estimate of the population mean receipts in sector i and state s. For the unit-level model, we use poststratification to predict receipts for every unit in the population, and then aggregate to obtain a synthetic population mean for sector i and state s. We use the posterior mean of this synthetic population mean as our point estimate. We compare the root mean-squared error (RMSE) and the absolute bias of each of the estimators in Table 30.1. RMSE is calculated as

$$\text{RMSE} = \sqrt{\frac{1}{20 \times 47 \times 100} \sum_{i=1}^{20} \sum_{s=1}^{47} \sum_{r=1}^{100} \left(\hat{Y}_{isr} - Y_{is}\right)^2}$$

and absolute bias as

$$\text{Abs. Bias} = \frac{1}{20 \times 47} \sum_{i=1}^{20} \sum_{s=1}^{47} \left| \frac{1}{100} \sum_{r=1}^{100} \hat{Y}_{isr} - Y_{is} \right|$$

where $\hat{Y}_{isr}$ is an estimate for industry i in state s for replications r of the simulation. All three model-based estimators are able to reduce the RMSE by a considerable amount compared to the direct HT estimate. Of the two area-level models, Model 2 seems to perform better in terms of RMSE, likely from the effect of borrowing strength across domains. In this case, Model 3 performs slightly worse than the area-level models, which is most likely due to bias from model mis-specification. Interestingly, comparing the results in terms of absolute bias and RMSE, it appears that reduction in variance appears to be the main contributor to the reduction in RMSE. A more flexible unit-level distributional assumption would likely give much better results than the log-Gaussian assumption used here.

30.6   Data Analysis

We illustrate the utility of SAE models by analyzing the complete microdata sample from the 2007 SBO. We exclude industry Sectors 21 and 55, as they include variance estimates of zero, as well as Sector 99, which is used to classify establishments that do not fit into other sectors. Although more complex methods may be available to construct estimates in these cases, we omit them for the purposes of illustration. We begin by creating direct HT estimates of the total receipts by sector and state. This is done for 17 sectors within 47 states, giving a total of 799 direct estimates. These direct estimates are accompanied by estimates of the standard error using the random group methodology outlined in the data users guide at https://www.census.gov/content/dam/Census/programs-surveys/sbo/guidance/2007_sbo_pums_users_guide.pdf.

The associated standard errors can be quite high due to small sample sizes within the sector and state, motivating the need for SAE approaches. Thus, we use Model 2 from Section 30.5 to improve upon the direct estimates. That is, we treat the log transformed direct estimate as our response, $\tilde{Z}_{is}$, and plug in the associated direct estimate of the variance, $\tilde{\sigma}^2_{is}$, after using the delta method. We use the log transformed HT estimate of total employment in the sector as well as the HT estimate of the proportion of businesses conducting e-commerce as covariates.

After fitting the model, we create scatterplots of the direct estimates compared to the model based estimates by sector in Figure 30.1. In general, both approaches result in similar estimates. A few sectors, such as 11 and 22, have some model-based estimates that deviate more from the direct estimates. These are the sectors with the smallest sample sizes. In cases with very little data, the model-based approach is able to borrow strength from covariates and data in other groups to yield better estimates. Sectors 54 and 44 have the most data points, and correspondingly, see little difference between the model-based and direct estimates.

We also plot the distribution of the ratio of model-based standard errors to direct standard errors by sector in Figure 30.2. In almost every sector, we see substantial reduction in standard errors through the use of model-based estimates rather than direct estimates. However, a few sectors, most noticeably Sector 22, contain some estimates where the model-based standard errors are greater. We also construct a scatterplot of the direct to model-based standard errors for all sectors in Figure 30.3. This shows that the few cases with greater model-based standard errors are near the origin, where the estimates are most precise anyway. In every other case, the model-based standard errors are an improvement, with the relative reduction increasing as the direct standard errors increase.

This analysis demonstrates how model-based approaches to SAE for establishment statistics can improve estimates for domains with small sample sizes. The use of covariates, as well as random effects that allow for borrowing of strength across domains, can provide leverage to adjust direct estimates appropriately. Even in cases with moderate sample size, where model-based estimates do not differ much from the direct estimates, the use of a model can provide a dramatic reduction in the uncertainty around the estimates. The methodology used here is powerful, yet relatively

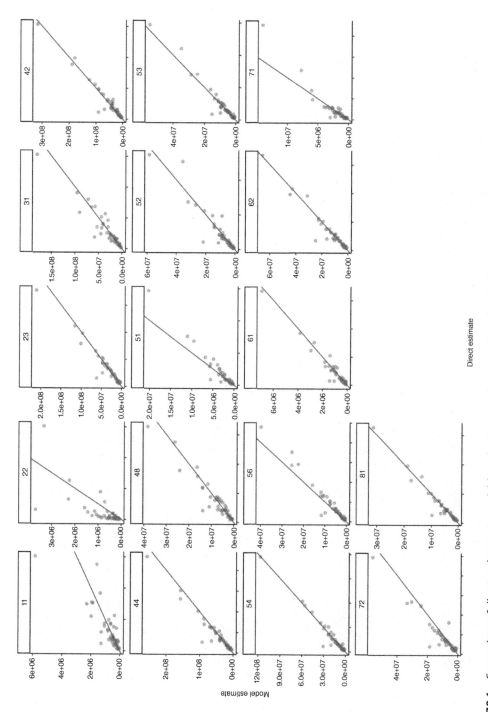

Figure 30.1 Comparison of direct estimates to model-based estimates of state total receipts by industry sector. The line indicates identical estimates. Data for direct estimates obtained from the 2007 SBO public use microdata sample, excluding Sectors 21, 55, and 99.

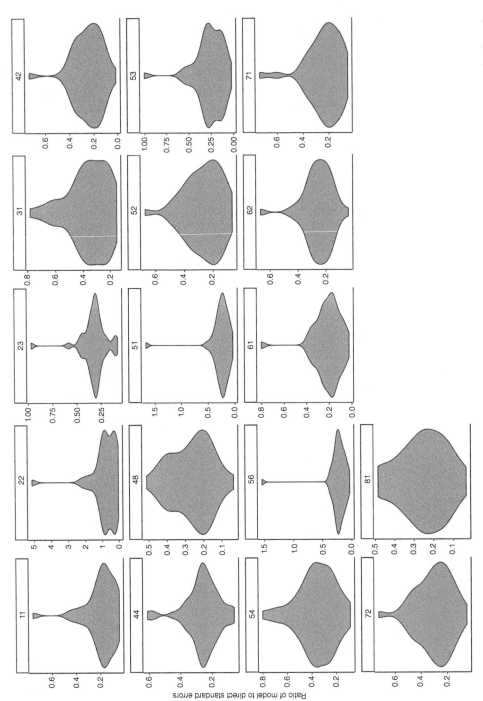

Figure 30.2 Distribution of ratio of model-based to direct standard errors by industry sector for estimates of state total receipts, where a value less than one indicates a reduction in estimate variability through the use of small area estimation. Data for direct estimates obtained from the 2007 SBO public use microdata sample, excluding sectors 21, 55, and 99.

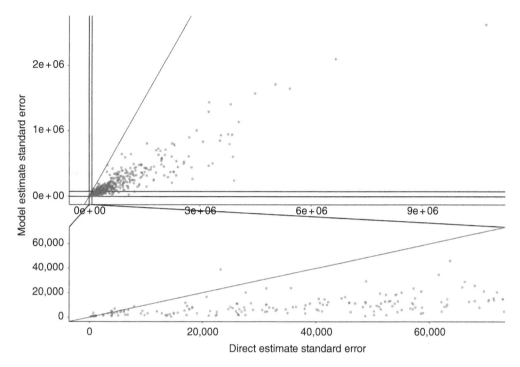

Figure 30.3 Scatterplot of direct standard errors to model-based standard errors for estimates of state by sector total receipts. The line corresponds to equivalent standard errors under both approaches. The lower subplot zooms in to the area near the origin to highlight the few cases with greater model-based standard errors. Data for direct estimates obtained from the 2007 SBO public use microdata sample, excluding Sectors 21, 55, and 99.

basic. The use of more complex dependence modeling, perhaps through spatial correlation structures, or time-based dependence with previous surveys, could lead to even more precise estimates.

30.7 Discussion

Creating small area/domain estimates for establishment surveys is a subject of ongoing and widespread interest. In this chapter, we have described several methods for small area estimation for establishment surveys, including both area- and unit-level model specifications. Importantly, we have provided a general overview of Bayesian hierarchical modeling and described its usage in this context.

In practice, the distinction between area- and unit-level models is important, with the choice of model often depending on the modeling goal and data availability. Data users outside an official statistical agency often only have access to area/industry-level tabulations and, thus, an area-level model seems to be the most natural choice, rather than modeling the public-use microdata. In contrast, official statistical agencies have access to the record-level data and, therefore, the modeling choice may depend on the specific use. Here, we have described both approaches and provided a comparison of some of the modeling strategies from each. Lastly, there are many aspects of the modeling frameworks that remain underdeveloped and, hence, provide a rich class of open problems for future research.

Acknowledgments

Support for this research through the Census Bureau Dissertation Fellowship program is gratefully acknowledged. This research was partially supported by the US National Science Foundation (NSF) under NSF grant SES-1853096. This article is released to inform interested parties of ongoing research and to encourage discussion. The views expressed on statistical issues are those of the authors and not those of the NSF or US Census Bureau.

References

Battese, G.E., Harter, R.M., and Fuller, W.A. (1988). An error-components model for prediction of county crop areas using survey and satellite data. *Journal of the American Statistical Association* 83 (401): 28–36.

Bell, W.R., Datta, G.S., and Ghosh, M. (2013). Benchmarking small area estimators. *Biometrika* 100: 189–202.

Berg, E. and Chandra, H. (2014). Small area prediction for a unit-level lognormal model. *Computational Statistics and Data Analysis* 78: 159–175.

Binder, D.A. (1983). On the variances of asymptotically normal estimators from complex surveys. *International Statistical Review* 51 (3): 279–292.

Bradley, J.R., Holan, S.H., Wikle, C.K. (2015). Multivariate spatio-temporal models for high-dimensional areal data with application to longitudinal employer-household dynamics. *The Annals of Applied Statistics* 9 (4): 1761–1791.

Bradley, J.R., Holan, S.H., and Wikle, C.K. (2020). Bayesian hierarchical models with conjugate full-conditional distributions for dependent data from the natural exponential family. *Journal of the American Statistical Association* 115 (532): 2037–2052.

Brewer, K.R.W., Early, L.J., and Hanif, M. (1984). Poisson, modified Poisson and collocated sampling. *Journal of Statistical Planning and Inference* 10 (1): 15–30.

Burgard, J.P., Münnich, R., and Zimmerman, T. (2014). The impact of sampling designs on small area estimates for business data. *Journal of Official Statistics* 30: 749–771.

Chandra, H. and Chambers, R. (2011). Small area estimation under transformation to linearity. *Survey Methodology* 37: 39–51.

Chandra, H., Aditya, K., and Kumar, S. (2018). Small-area estimation under a log-transformed area-level model. *Journal of Statistical Theory and Practice* 12: 497–505.

Cressie, N. and Wikle, C.K. (2011). *Statistics for Spatio-Temporal Data*. Wiley.

Erciulescu, A.L., Cruze, N.B., Nandram, B. (2019). Model-based county level crop estimates incorporating auxiliary sources of information. *Journal of the Royal Statistical Society: Series A (Statistics in Society)* 182 (1): 283–303.

Erciulescu, A.L., Cruze, N.B., and Nandram, B. (2020). Statistical challenges in combining survey and auxiliary data to produce official statistics. *Journal of Official Statistics* 36 (1): 63–88.

Fabrizi, E., Ferrante, M.R., and Trivisano, C. (2017). Bayesian small area estimation for skewed business survey variables. *Journal of the Royal Statistical Society, Series C* 67: 861–879.

Fay, R.E. and Herriot, R.A. (1979). Estimates of income for small places: an application of James–Stein procedures to census data. *Journal of the American Statistical Association* 74 (366A): 269–277.

Ferrante, M.R. and Pacei, S. (2017). Small domain estimation of business statistics by using mulitvariate skew Normal models. *Journal of the Royal Statistical Society, Series A* 180: 1057–1088.

Gelfand, A.E. and Schliep, E.M. (2016). Spatial statistics and Gaussian processes: a beautiful marriage. *Spatial Statistics* 18: 86–104.

Gelman, A. and Little, T.C. (1997). Poststratification into many categories using hierarchical logistic regression. *Survey Methodology* 23: 127–135.

Gelman, A. and Meng, X.-L. (1996). Model checking and model improvement. In: *Markov Chain Monte Carlo in Practice* (eds. W.R. Gilks, S. Richardson and D.J. Spiegelhalter), 189–201. Springer.

Gelman, A. and Rubin, D.B. (1992). Inference from iterative simulation using multiple sequences. *Statistical Science* 7 (4): 457–472.

Gelman, A., Carlin, J.B., Stern, H.S., and Rubin, D.B. (1995). *Bayesian Data Analysis*. London: Chapman and Hall.

Gelman, A., Hill, J., and Yajima, M. (2012). Why we (usually) don't have to worry about multiple comparisons. *Journal of Research on Educational Effectiveness* 5 (2): 189–211.

Gelman, A., Carlin, J.B., Stern, H.S., and Rubin, D.B. (2013). *Bayesian Data Analysis*. CRC Press.

Gershunskaya, J. and Savitsky, T. (2017). Dependent latent effects modeling for survey estimation with application to the current employment statistics survey. *Journal of Survey Statistics and Methodology* 5: 433–453.

Geweke, J. (1992). Evaluating the accuracy of sampling-based approaches to the calculations of posterior moments. *Bayesian Statistics* 4: 641–649.

Hansen, M.H. and Hurwitz, W.N. (1943). On the theory of sampling from finite populations. *The Annals of Mathematical Statistics* 14 (4): 333–362.

Hidiroglou, M.A. and Lavallée, P. (2009). Sampling and estimation in business surveys. In: *Sample Surveys: Design, Methods and Applications*, Chapter 17, vol. 29A (ed. D. Pfeffermann and C.R. Rao), 441–470. Amsterdam: Elsevier.

Hidiroglou, M.A. and You, Y. (2016). Comparison of unit level and area level small area estimators. *Survey Methodology* 42: 41–61.

Holan, S.H. and Wikle, C.K. (2016). *Hierarchical Dynamic Generalized Linear Mixed Models for Discrete-Valued Spatio-Temporal Data* (eds. R.A. Davis, S.H. Holan, R. Lund and N. Ravishanker), Handbook of Discrete-Valued Time Series, 327–348.

Horvitz, D.G. and Thompson, D.J. (1952). A generalization of sampling without replacement from a finite universe. *Journal of the American Statistical Association* 47: 663–685.

Linderman, S., Johnson, M.J., and Adams, R.P. (2015). Dependent multinomial models made easy: stick-breaking with the Pólya-Gamma augmentation. *Advances in Neural Information Processing Systems*, pp. 3456–3464.

Little, R.J. (2012). Calibrated Bayes, an alternative inferential paradigm for official statistics. *Journal of Official Statistics* 28 (3): 309.

McConville, K., Tang, B., Zhu, G., Cheung, S., and Li, S. (2018). mase: *Model-Assisted Survey Estimation*. https://cran.r-project.org/package=mase (accessed 16 March 2022).

Molina, I. and Martin, N. (2018). Empirical best prediction under a nested error regression model with log transformation. *Annals of Statistics* 46: 1961–1993.

Nathan, G. and Holt, D. (1980). The effect of survey design on regression analysis. *Journal of the Royal Statistical Society: Series B (Statistical Methodology)* 42 (3): 377–386.

Park, D.K., Gelman, A., and Bafumi, J. (2006). State-level opinions from national surveys: poststratification using multilevel logistic regression. *Public Opinion in State Politics*. 209–228. Stanford University Press.

Parker, P.A., Holan, S.H., and Janicki, R. (2020a). Computationally efficient Bayesian unit-level models for non-Gaussian data under informative sampling. *arXiv preprint arXiv:2009.05642*.

Parker, P.A., Holan, S.H., and Janicki, R. (2020b). Conjugate Bayesian unit-level modelling of count data under informative sampling designs. *Stat* 9 (1): e267.

Pfeffermann, D. and Sverchkov, M. (2007). Small-area estimation under informative probability sampling of areas and within the selected areas. *Journal of the American Statistical Association* 102 (480): 1427–1439.

Polson, N.G., Scott, J.G., and Windle, J. (2013). Bayesian inference for logistic models using Pólya–Gamma latent variables. *Journal of the American Statistical Association* 108 (504): 1339–1349.

Porter, A.T., Holan, S.H., Wikle, C.K., and Cressie, N. (2014). Spatial Fay–Herriot models for small area estimation with functional covariates. *Spatial Statistics* 10: 27–42.

Rao, J.N.K. and Molina, I. (2015). *Small Area Estimation*. Hoboken, NJ.: Wiley.

Riviére, P. (2002). What makes business statistics special? *International Statistical Review* 70: 145–159.

Royle, J.A. and Berliner, L.M. (1999). A hierarchical approach to multivariate spatial modeling and prediction. *Journal of Agricultural, Biological, and Environmental Statistics* 4 (1): 29–56.

Savitsky, T.D. and Toth, D. (2016). Bayesian estimation under informative sampling. *Electronic Journal of Statistics* 10 (1): 1677–1708.

Skinner, C.J. (1989). Domain means, regression and multivariate analysis. In: *Analysis of Complex Surveys*, Chapter 2 (ed. C.J. Skinner, D. Holt, and T.M.F. Smith), 80–84. Chichester: Wiley.

Slud, E. and Maiti, T. (2006). Mean-squared error estimation in transformed Fay–Herriot models. *Journal of the Royal Statistical Society, Series B* 68: 239–257.

Smith, P.A., Bocci, C., Tzavidis, N., Krieg, S., and Smeets, M.J.E. (2021) Robust estimation for small domains in business surveys. *Journal of the Royal Statistical Society, Series C*, 70: 312–334.

Steel, P. and Fay, R.E. (1995). Variance estimation for finite populations with imputed data. *Proceedings of the Section on Survey Research Methods, American Statistical Association*, CiteSeer.

Sugasawa, S. and Kubokawa, T. (2017). Transforming response variables in small area prediction. *Computational Statistics and Data Analysis* 114: 47–60.

U.S. Census Bureau (2012). 2007 survey of business owners public use microdata sample. https://www.census.gov/data/datasets/2007/econ/sbo/2007-sbo-pums.html (accessed 16 January 2021).

Wang, J.C., Holan, S.H., Nandram, B., Barboza, W., Toto, C., and Anderson, E. (2012). A Bayesian approach to estimating agricultural yield based on multiple repeated surveys. *Journal of Agricultural, Biological, and Environmental Statistics* 17 (1): 84–106.

You, Y. and Rao, J.N.K. (2002). A pseudo-empirical best linear unbiased prediction approach to small area estimation using survey weights. *The Canadian Journal of Statistics* 30: 431–439.

Zhang, X., Holt, J.B., Lu, H., Wheaton, A.G., Ford, E.S., Greenlund, K.J., and Croft, J.B. (2014). Multilevel regression and poststratification for small-area estimation of population health outcomes: a case study of chronic obstructive pulmonary disease prevalence using the behavioral risk factor surveillance system. *American Journal of Epidemiology* 179 (8): 1025–1033.

Zimmerman, T. and Münnich, R.T. (2018). Small area estimation with a lognormal mixed model under informative sampling. *Journal of Official Statistics* 34: 523–542.

31

Variance Estimation Under Nearest Neighbor Ratio Hot Deck Imputation for Multinomial Data: Two Approaches Applied to the Service Annual Survey (SAS)

Rebecca Andridge[1], Jae Kwang Kim[2], and Katherine J. Thompson[3]

[1]*Division of Biostatistics, The Ohio State University, Columbus, OH, USA*
[2]*Department of Statistics, Iowa State University, Ames, IA, USA*
[3]*Associate Directorate of Economic Programs, U.S. Census Bureau, Washington, DC, USA*

31.1   Introduction

Sample surveys are often designed to estimate totals (e.g. revenue, earnings). In addition, many surveys request sets of compositional variables (details) that sum to a total, such as a breakdown of total expenditures by type of expenditure or a breakdown of total income by source. The detail proportions can vary greatly by sample unit, and their multinomial distributions may be related to a different set of predictors than those associated with the total. All survey participants are asked to provide values for the total items (hereafter referred to as "totals"), whereas the type of requested details can vary. This creates two separate but related missing data challenges: (i) to develop viable imputation models for the total; and (ii) to develop viable imputation models for the set of associated detail items.

For business – or many establishment – surveys, the primary missing data challenge is the treatment of the details. With totals, reliable auxiliary data from the same unit are often available for direct substitution (e.g. administrative data); if not, business surveys can use ratio imputation models that rely on strong (verifiable) linear relationships between survey items. So it is reasonable to assume that a valid reported or imputed total item would be available for all units in a business survey. This contrasts with the requested detail data items, which may not be available from all respondents, especially small businesses that might not track the requested data items (Willimack and Nichols, 2010). Furthermore, the rate of missingness for the sets of detail items can be quite high, in part due to the perceived response burden (Bavdaž, 2010). Determining a viable imputation method for a set of detail items is crucial, given the high incidence of complete nonresponse for the set of details and the lack of alternative data sources outside of the survey itself available for imputation.

Consider the Service Annual Survey (SAS) conducted by the US Census Bureau, a business survey that uses imputation to account for unit and item nonresponse. The SAS is a mandatory survey of approximately 78,000 employer businesses having one or more establishments located in the United States that provide services to individuals, businesses, and governments. The SAS collects aggregate and detailed revenues and expenses, revenue from electronic sources, exports, and inventories data from a stratified sample of business firms with paid employees in selected industries in the services sector. The key items collected by the SAS are total revenue and total

Advances in Business Statistics, Methods and Data Collection. Edited by Ger Snijkers, Mojca Bavdaž, Stefan Bender, Jacqui Jones, Steve MacFeely, Joseph W. Sakshaug, Katherine J. Thompson, and Arnout van Delden.
© 2023 John Wiley & Sons, Inc. Published 2023 by John Wiley & Sons, Inc.

expenses, which along with the associated detail items are referred to as "balance complexes" (Sigman and Wagner, 1997). The revenue detail items vary by industry within sector. Expense detail items are primarily the same for all sectors, with an occasional additional expense detail or two collected for select industries. Complete information on the SAS methodology is available at https://www.census.gov/programs-surveys/sas/technical-documentation/methodology.html.

Figure 31.1 presents the balance complex for expenses included on the SAS questionnaire for businesses that operate in the full-service restaurant industry. The information requested in lines 1 (a–c), 2, 3, and 4 (a and b) are individual components of the total operating expenses reported in line 5. Of the seven items included in this set of details items, only gross annual payroll can be potentially verified using auxiliary administrative data (as can be inferred by the reference to Internal Revenue Service (IRS) form 941 and IRS form 944). The remaining items are only available from the survey response data, either collected from the sampled unit in the current or prior collection year. When available, administrative data can be substituted for missing or invalid total expenses. Otherwise, the SAS uses ratio imputation to account for missing or invalid values, constructing imputation parameters from valid respondent data.

The SAS imputation models fall into two broad categories:

- Auxiliary variable imputation, which imputes the missing variable in the current period from industry-average ratios of two variables from the same units and collection period (e.g. imputing the current year expenses value for a business as the unit's revenue value multiplied by the industry-average ratio of total expenses to total revenue);
- Historic trend imputation, which imputes the missing variable in the current period from industry-average ratios of the same variable in the current and prior period (e.g. imputing the current year expenses value for a business as the prior reported value multiplied by the industry-average ratio of total expenses in the current period to the total expenses in the prior period).

Thompson and Washington (2013) evaluated these imputation models in two of the sectors included in the SAS, explicitly fitting weighted no-intercept linear regression models using respondent data to assess model fit. For the totals, the ratio imputation models were appropriate. However, the results for the details items were far less convincing, with adjusted-R^2 values often well below 75% and nonsignificant slopes ($\alpha = 0.10$). Intuitively, this makes sense. Consider the detailed expenses requested in Figure 31.1. It seems reasonable that gross payroll (item 1a) would be a strong predictor of a business' total expenses. On the other hand, obtaining an accurate prediction of total expenses from temporary or leased employees (item 1c) seems tenuous. Moreover, it is quite common to have large fractions of complete sets of missing detail items, bringing the "representativeness" of the respondent-based ratios into question. This phenomena will be exacerbated in the 2020 data collection year, as many businesses were closed or had business limited due to the COVID-19 pandemic. Furthermore, the economic effects of COVID-19 in 2020 on services industries totals might lead to very different industry average ratios and trends than in previous years. This in turn makes ratio imputation less appealing for these detail items, which are historically less frequently and reliably reported than their associated totals and whose imputed values are generally more difficult to independently validate.

Developing good predictive models for each individual detail item collected by the SAS is perhaps infeasible. That said, there are verifiable predictors of the *set* of detail items (i.e. the multinomial distribution) such as industry or unit size. Returning to the example presented in Figure 31.1, a finance business will often report high proportions of total expenses in all three personnel cost categories, a scientific business is unlikely to report costs from temporary or leased employees, and a full-service restaurant would likely report the majority of its expenses from gross payroll and

	Mark "X" if None	2019 $ Bil.	Mil.	Thou.	Dol.

1. Personnel Costs

  a. Gross annual payroll - Total annual Medicare salaries and wages for all employees as reported on this firm's IRS Form 941, Employer's Quarterly Federal Tax Return, line 5(c) for the four quarters that correspond to the survey period or IRS Form 944 Employer's Annual Federal Tax Return, line 4(c). **Include** the spread on stock options that are taxable to employees as wages   1821 ☐

  b. Employer's cost for fringe benefits - Employer's cost for legally required programs and programs not required by law. **Include** insurance premiums for hospital plans, medical plans, and single service plans (e.g., dental, vision, prescription drugs); premium equivalents for self-insured plans and fees paid to third-party administrators (TPAs); defined benefit pension plans; defined contribution plans (e.g., profit sharing, 401K, stock option plans); and other fringe benefits (e.g., Social Security, workers' compensation insurance, unemployment tax, state disability insurance programs, life insurance benefits, Medicare). **Exclude** employee contributions. . . . . 1822 ☐

  c. Temporary staff and leased employee expense - Total costs paid to Professional Employer Organizations (PEOs) and staffing agencies for personnel. **Include** all charges for payroll, benefits, and services · 1823 ☐

2. Expensed equipment, materials, parts, and supplies (not for resale) - Include expensed computer hardware and other equipment (e.g., copiers, fax machines, telephones, shop and lab equipment, CPUs, monitors). **Include** materials and supplies used in providing services to others; materials and parts used in repairs; office and janitorial supplies; small tools; containers and other packaging materials, and motor fuels. Report packaged software in line **3** and leased and rented equipment in line **4b**. . . . . 1860 ☐

3. Expensed purchases of software - Purchases of prepackaged, custom coded, or vendor customized software. **Include** software developed or customized by others, web-design services and purchases, licensing agreements, upgrades of software, and maintenance fees related to software upgrades and alterations . . . . 1826 ☐

4. Other Operating Expenses

  a. Depreciation and amortization charges - Include depreciation charges taken against tangible assets owned and used by this firm, tangible assets and improvements owned by this firm within leaseholds, tangible assets obtained through capital lease agreements, and amortization charges against intangible assets (e.g., patents, copyrights). **Exclude** impairment . . . . 1831 ☐

  b. All other operating expenses - All other operating expenses not reported above, unless specifically excluded in the general instructions. Include office postage paid and package delivery. **Exclude** purchases of merchandise for resale and non-operating expenses. **If this item is greater than 20% of the total operating expenses, specify the primary source of the expenses below** ↗

     1879 ☐

5. TOTAL OPERATING EXPENSES
*Sum of lines **1a** through **4b*** · 1900

Figure 31.1 Expenses data (Total and Details) collected from businesses sampled from the full-service restaurants industry in the Service Annual Survey.

expensed equipment, materials, costs, or supplies. In a similar vein, a larger business might be more likely to expense costs and track depreciation than a smaller business.

Given the deficiencies of the item-by-item ratio imputation approach, the SAS methodologists were open to exploring using some form of hot deck imputation to impute the complete set of detail items for expenses. Hot deck imputation matches donor (respondent) and recipient (nonrespondent) records to impute the donor's complete set of proportions (Andridge et al., 2020). The recipient receives the donor's vector of proportions, and imputed dollar values for each expenses component are obtained by multiplying the (donated) proportion by the recipient's total. Hot deck imputation ensures plausible imputed values, as the donated values are obtained from reported values. Moreover, because hot deck imputation relies entirely on current data, it does not enforce historical patterns in the data that may no longer be true. Using the same donor record to impute a group of missing values prevents inconsistencies in the imputed data, thus preserving existing relationships between items in the imputed microdata; this objective is best achieved when the donor records are internally consistent with respect to the variables being imputed (Nordholt, 1998). Finally, hot deck imputation eliminates a major deficiency of the currently used SAS ratio-imputation procedure, which specifically enforces observably weak linear relationships between detail items and their corresponding total. Even so, hot deck imputation is not a perfect solution to the SAS missing data problem(s) for detail complexes if it is used to impute sets of detail items in "out of balance" complexes (details *not* summing to the total), as possibly valid reported data items will be replaced by entirely imputed values.

Perhaps the most important choice in implementing hot deck imputation is the donor selection method. Random hot deck imputation allows all responding units within an imputation cell to be eligible donors for any nonrespondent, selecting one donor per nonrespondent with equal probability from the entire donor pool. An underlying assumption of random hot deck imputation is that donors and recipients are exchangeable within an imputation cell. The imputation cells for SAS are industry-based (usually six digit North American Industry Classification System [NAICS] industry) cross-classified by tax-exempt status. The assumption of exchangeability seems shaky for the SAS, as the type and number of expenses reported within these subdomains are likely related to the business size (total revenue).

An alternative donor selection method that incorporates a predictor into the hot deck donor selection process is nearest neighbor imputation (Chen and Shao, 2000). This variation of hot deck imputation uses auxiliary variable(s) available for both donors and recipients to identify the "nearest" donor. Ideally, these variables should be highly correlated with the variables that are being imputed. A distance function determines the distance of each donor from each recipient. There are several different distance functions used in practice, and the selection generally depends on factors such as the number of available variables, the number and type of items to be imputed, and the form of the predictive relationship. The donor that is the smallest distance from the recipient is selected for imputation. In our application, all records have a valid value of total expenses. We use the Euclidian distance (absolute value of the difference) between donor and recipient total expenses as the distance measure; other distance functions are not discussed further. Since the distance function uses a single variable available for all sampled units, the resulting estimators are asymptotically unbiased (Yang and Kim, 2019). Nearest neighbor ratio imputation (NNRI) is useful when the set of proportions is correlated with unit size as in this example (size = total revenue or total expenses).

In short, using NNRI to impute expenses detail items in the SAS appears to be justified. Even so, there are data features that must be addressed. First, many categories of expenses have very small proportions. Using a single-donor record for imputation can artificially increase the probability of a zero imputed value for a rarely reported item. Second, there may be different multinomial distributions within the same industry for businesses with different tax-exempt status. Consequently, donors and recipients need to be matched within imputation cell to obtain reasonable imputations. If the sample size or the number of respondents in an imputation cell is small, then NNRI can create very inefficient estimates, as the same donors may be used multiple times. The effect of donor overuse in imputation cells with small proportions of donor records can be especially pronounced with unrestricted NNRI since a single donor can be used several times rather than using a "more distant" neighbor. In practice, potential donor overuse is overcome by collapsing imputation cells using "ad hoc" methods (Fang et al., 2009), which can induce bias in the imputed estimates.

Point estimation from NNRI data is straightforward. Variance estimation is less so, in part because the donor selection procedure is deterministic. Additionally, the SAS has a stratified design, with companies stratified by their major industry, then further substratified by estimated total receipts. All companies with total receipts above applicable size cutoffs are included in the survey as part of the certainty stratum. A simple random sampling without replacement (SRS-WOR) sample of firms (i.e., either single- or multi-establishment firms) is selected within each noncertainty size stratum. Sampling fractions can be quite large. The initial sample is updated quarterly to reflect births and deaths. In summary, the variance estimator for the NNRI SAS items must account for the stratified sampling design as well as the imputation procedure.

In this chapter, we consider a single and a multiple imputation (MI) approach to the same variance estimation problem. Section 31.2 introduces the notation, providing a basic set up. The single imputation (SI) approach outlined in Section 31.3 applies a replication variance estimator derived under the Shao and Steel (1999) framework, originally presented in Gao et al. (2021). The multiple imputation approach outlined in Section 31.4 presents a variation of nearest neighbor hot deck using multiple imputation with the approximate Bayesian bootstrap (ABB) originally presented in Andridge et al. (2020) and Andridge and Thompson (In press). Section 31.5 compares the properties of both variance estimation approaches over repeated samples under a uniform response mechanism via a simulation study. Section 31.6 applies both methods to empirical data from five industries in the 2018 SAS. We conclude in Section 31.7 with some general observations.

31.2 Basic Setup

Let Y_i be the study variable of business unit i in a particular industry. In what follows, we assume a single imputation cell; extension to more than one imputation cell is straightforward. Assume that a probability sample S is taken and let $\widehat{Y}_{HT} = \sum_{i \in S} w_i y_i$ be the Horvitz–Thompson estimator of $Y = \sum_{i \in U} y_i$, where w_i is the sampling weight of unit i. We assume that some of y_i are subject to missingness, and let $\delta_i = 1$ if y_i is observed and $\delta_i = 0$, otherwise.

To justify the NNRI, Y_i is assumed to satisfy the following model,

$$Y_i = m(x_i) + e_i \tag{31.1}$$

where $E(e_i \mid x_i) = 0$ and

$$m(x_i) = x_i R(x_i)$$

for some smooth function $R(\cdot)$ satisfying

$$|R(x_i) - R(x_i')| \le C |x_i - x_i'| \tag{31.2}$$

for some $C > 0$.

Let y_i^* be the imputed value of y_i using NNRI, given by,

$$y_i^* = x_i R_{i(1)} \tag{31.3}$$

where $R_{i(1)}$ is the value of $R_j = y_j / x_j$ for $j = i(1)$ and $i(1)$ is the index of the nearest neighbor of unit i. The nearest neighbor is determined by the value of x_i. Once y_i^* are obtained by NNRI, the imputed estimator of Y is given by

$$\widehat{Y}_I = \sum_{i \in S} w_i \left\{ \delta_i y_i + (1 - \delta_i) y_i^* \right\} \tag{31.4}$$

Note that,

$$\widehat{Y}_I - \widehat{Y}_{HT} = -\sum_{i \in S} w_i \left(1 - \delta_i \right) x_i \left(R_i - R_{i(1)} \right) \tag{31.5}$$

Thus, under assumption (31.2) and some regularity conditions, we can obtain that

$$\max_i \left| R(x_i) - R(x_{i(1)}) \right| = O_p(n^{-1})$$

and establish the asymptotic unbiasedness of $\widehat{Y}_I$.

31.3 Single Imputation Variance Estimation

We now discuss variance estimation of the imputed estimator in (31.4). If we define

$$d_{ij} = \begin{cases} 1 & \text{if unit } i \text{ is used as a donor for unit } j \\ 0 & \text{otherwise} \end{cases}$$

then we can express

$$y_j^* = x_j R_{j(1)} = \sum_{i \in S} \delta_i d_{ij} x_j R_i = \sum_{i \in S} \delta_i d_{ij} \left(x_j / x_i \right) y_i$$

Thus, the imputed estimator in (31.4) can be written as

$$\widehat{Y}_I = \sum_{j \in S} w_j \left\{ \delta_j y_j + (1 - \delta_j) \sum_{i \in S} \delta_i d_{ij} \left(x_j / x_i \right) y_i \right\}$$

$$= \sum_{i \in S} \delta_i w_i (1 + \kappa_i) y_i \tag{31.6}$$

where

$$\kappa_i = \sum_{j \in S} \frac{w_j x_j}{w_i x_i} (1 - \delta_j) d_{ij}$$

Note that κ_i satisfies

$$\sum_{i \in S} \delta_i w_i (1 + \kappa_i) x_i = \sum_{i \in S} w_i x_i \tag{31.7}$$

Under some regularity conditions, Gao et al. (2021) proved that

$$\sum_{i \in S} \delta_i w_i (1 + \kappa_i) x_i R(x_i) \cong \sum_{i \in S} w_i x_i R(x_i) \tag{31.8}$$

Combining (31.6) with (31.8), we have

$$\widehat{Y}_I \cong \sum_{i \in S} w_i \left[x_i R(x_i) + \delta_i (1 + \kappa_i) \{ y_i - x_i R(x_i) \} \right] \tag{31.9}$$

Using (31.1), we can express (31.9) as

$$\widehat{Y}_I \cong \sum_{i \in S} w_i \left\{ m_i + \delta_i (1 + \kappa_i) e_i \right\} \tag{31.10}$$

where $m_i = x_i R(x_i)$ and $e_i = y_i - m_i$. Thus, the asymptotic variance can be written as

$$V(\widehat{Y}_I - Y) \cong V \left(\sum_{i \in S} w_i m_i \right) + E \left[\sum_{i \in U} \{ I_i \delta_i w_i (1 + \kappa_i) - 1 \}^2 e_i^2 \right] := V^m + V^e$$

where $I_i = 1$ if $i \in S$ and $I_i = 0$, otherwise. The first term can be estimated by applying the standard variance estimator to $\widehat{m}_i$ in the sample and the second term can be estimated by

$$\widehat{V}^e = \frac{n}{N^2} \sum_{i \in S} \{ w_i^2 \delta_i (1 + \kappa_i)^2 + w_i - 2 w_i \delta_i (1 + \kappa_i) \} \widehat{\sigma}_e^2(x_i)$$

where $\widehat{\sigma}_e^2(x_i)$ is a model-based estimator of $\sigma_e^2(x_i) = E(e_i^2 \mid x_i)$. Gao et al. (2021) discussed several approaches to estimating $\sigma_e^2(x_i)$.

31.4 Multiple Imputation Variance Estimation

Multiple imputation (MI) is a commonly used technique for imputing missing data whereby missing data values are replaced multiple times, creating D multiple completed datasets. Inference is then performed by analyzing each imputed dataset separately and combining the results using the so-called Rubin's combining rules (Rubin, 1987). A distinct advantage of MI is that the postimputation combining rules are functions of standard complete data estimators of point estimates and variances, which are usually straightforward. Once the multiple imputations have been generated, each imputed dataset is analyzed separately, resulting in D point estimates and D variance estimates, that vary across d due to the imputed values varying across completed datasets. Suppose $\hat{\theta}_d$ is the estimate of the population parameter of interest in the dth imputed dataset, and W_d is the corresponding variance estimate. The overall MI estimate, $\hat{\theta}$, is then the average of the D individual estimates:

$$\hat{\theta} = \frac{1}{D} \sum_{d=1}^{D} \hat{\theta}_d \qquad (31.11)$$

The MI variance estimate is a combination of the average within-imputation variance, $\overline{W} = \frac{1}{D} \sum_{d=1}^{D} W_d$, and the between-imputation variance, $B = \frac{1}{D-1} \sum_{d=1}^{D} \left(\hat{\theta}_d - \hat{\theta} \right)^2$:

$$\hat{V}(\hat{\theta}) = \overline{W} + \left(1 + \frac{1}{D} \right) B \qquad (31.12)$$

Confidence intervals and significance tests using (31.12) can be constructed using a t-distribution, with degrees of freedom based on $\overline{W}$, B, and the number of imputations, D (see (Little and Rubin, 2019)). If degrees of freedom are small for the complete data analysis, as might occur in survey sampling, a small-sample correction to the degrees of freedom is available (Barnard and Rubin, 1999).

NNRI cannot be used for MI without modification, since it is a deterministic imputation method; the same (one closest) donor would be selected on each multiple imputation, resulting in $B = 0$. Instead, one option is to use the ABB, which is a non-Bayesian MI method that approximates a Bayesian MI method (Rubin and Schenker, 1986; Rubin, 1987). To combine NNRI with ABB, we first draw a random sample with replacement from the nonmissing y_i and then apply NNRI to obtain a single completed (imputed) dataset. This procedure is repeated independently D times. The resampling ensures that the one closest unit is not always selected, thus allowing for variability across imputations. In fact, assuming no ties in x_i, the nearest neighbor $i(1)$ for unit i will appear in the ABB sample 63% of the time ($1 - e^{-1} = 0.63$).

As an alternative to identifying the single closest neighbor with NNRI, another strategy is to identify a set of the k closest neighbors ("donor pool") and randomly select a single donor from this set. Typical values of k are 5, 10, and 20 (Morris et al., 2014). These k-NN imputation approaches can be used for multiple imputation, and with $k > 1$ the issue of always imputing the same donor is avoided. Despite no longer being deterministic, in order to properly mimic draws from a posterior distribution, k-NN methods should be combined with the ABB. In increasing the size of the donor pool from $k = 1$ to $k > 1$, we expect not only an increase in variability across MI datasets and a reduction in the overuse of a single donor but also a slight increase in bias from selecting a less close donor. We note that what we call k-NN imputation differs from the k-NN algorithms often used in machine learning (supervised learning) (Hastie et al., 2013). For k-NN with NNRI, we select a single donor (with equal probability) from the k donors and impute that unit's ratio as in (31.3); in supervised learning algorithms, commonly a consensus approach is taken where values from all k closest neighbors are used for classification (e.g. by averaging the k y_i values).

Prior work has shown that, when combined with the ABB, NNRI using the one closest neighbor (i.e. $k = 1$) results in underestimation of variance when using the standard combining rules (Andridge et al., 2020; Andridge and Thompson, In press). Using a donor pool of size $k = 5$ appears to remedy the problem, providing near-unbiased variance estimates with only a small increase in bias under combinations of sampling designs and missingness mechanisms (e.g. probability proportional to size [PPS] with large fractions of strongly missing-at-random data). Thus, in this chapter, we only consider multiple imputation using NNRI with a pool of $k = 5$ donors, which we refer to as NN5.

31.5 Simulation Study

31.5.1 Data Generation

We conducted a simulation study to evaluate the finite-sample performance of the NNRI single and multiple imputation variance estimators. The data generation is largely patterned after the realistic procedures described in Andridge et al. (2020), incorporating important features observed in several of the economic programs conducted by the US Census Bureau.

First, we generated $B = 2000$ finite populations of size N by drawing the size (auxiliary) variable x_i from $x_i \sim$ Lognormal$(12, 1.7^2)$. Then, we stratified each finite population on x_i using the stratum boundaries defined in Table 31.1.

For each unit $i = 1, \ldots, N$, we generated associated sets of detail items $y_i = (y_{i1}, y_{i2}, y_{i3}, y_{i4}, y_{i5})^\mathsf{T}$ such that all units have nonzero values assigned to (y_{i1}, y_{i2}) but can have zero values in (y_{i3}, y_{i4}, y_{i5}). To ensure that the number of nonzero detail items is related to unit size, we generated C_i (the number of nonzero *detail* items for unit i from a discrete distribution of $\{2,3,4,5\}$ with selection probability $P(C_i = c \mid x_i) = p(x_i)$, where $p(x) = (\pi_2, \pi_3, \pi_4, \pi_5)$ are given by

$$(\pi_1, \pi_2, \pi_3, \pi_4, \pi_5) = \begin{cases} (0, 0.91, 0.03, 0.03, 0.03) & \text{in Stratum 1} \\ (0, 0.50, 0.40, 0.05, 0.05) & \text{in Stratum 2} \\ (0, 0.20, 0.20, 0.30, 0.30) & \text{in Stratum 3} \\ (0, 0.05, 0.15, 0.40, 0.40) & \text{in Stratum 4} \end{cases}$$

Figure 31.2 presents bubble plots of the number of nonzero details (C_i) from a single simulated population, with the size of the bubble proportional to the percentage of units in the stratum with c nonzero details. As the unit size (x_i) increases, the number of nonzero detail items reported by each unit tends to likewise increase: for example, in the smallest unit size stratum (1), the majority of units provide two nonzero values, whereas in the largest unit size stratum (4), the majority of units provide four or five nonzero values.

Table 31.1 Specification for stratum boundaries in terms of X (the total item).

Stratum S	Total size X
1:	$<40,000$
2:	$40,000 \leq X < 150,000$
3:	$150,000 \leq X < 500,000$
4:	$\geq 500,000$

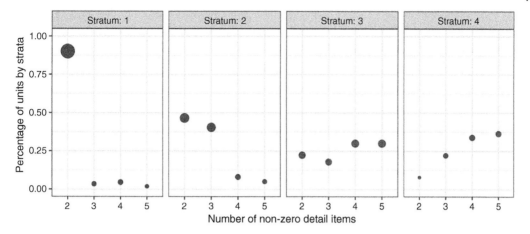

Figure 31.2 Distribution of realized nonzero detail items c in a single simulated finite population by sampling stratum. Sampling stratum 1 contains the smallest units; sampling stratum 4 contains the largest units.

Then, conditioning on the assigned c_i and x_i, we drew the R_i for each unit i from a multinomial distribution.

$$R_i \mid (x_i, c_i) \sim \text{Multinomial}\{x_i, (p_1, p_2, p_3, p_4, p_5)\}$$

with probabilities

$$(p_1, p_2, p_3, p_4, p_5) = \begin{cases} (0.60, 0.40, 0.00, 0.00, 0.00) & \text{if } c = 2 \\ (0.60, 0.30, 0.10, 0.00, 0.00) & \text{if } c = 3 \\ (0.60, 0.25, 0.10, 0.05, 0.00) & \text{if } c = 4 \\ (0.60, 0.20, 0.10, 0.05, 0.05) & \text{if } c = 5 \end{cases}$$

By design, $p_1 = 0.60$ for all units regardless of its stratum, ensuring that each unit reports this detail item as about 60% of its total (x_i). Figure 31.3 illustrates the subtle change in multinomial distributions as unit size (sampling strata) increases. By design, the largest proportion of the total is always reported in item Y_1, with item Y_2 following. The remaining three items are more rarely reported, with the probability of a reported nonzero value being strongly related to unit size. This mimics patterns that were observed by Andridge et al. (2020) in several economic census datasets.

Lastly, using these R_i, compute each unit's set of detail items

$$y_i = (y_{i1}, y_{i2}, y_{i3}, y_{i4}, y_{i5}) = x_i(R_{i1}, R_{i2}, R_{i3}, R_{i4}, R_{i5})$$

By definition, $x_i = \sum_{t=1}^{5} y_{it}$.

Next, we selected a (single) stratified SRS-WOR sample from each finite population. Table 31.2 provides the finite population size (N), the average stratum sizes N_h, the sampling fractions f_h, and average sample sizes n_h. As typically done in establishment survey designs, the largest units are grouped into a certainty stratum, and a high proportion of the medium-sized units are sampled at a very high rate. The overall sampling fraction (f) in the $N = 1000$ population is $302/1000$ and is $152/500$ in the $N = 500$ population; these sampling fractions are nonnegligible.

Last, we generate unit response indicators as $\delta_i \sim \text{Bernoulli}(\pi)$, with $\pi = 75\%$ and 50%, inducing a uniform response mechanism (missing completely at random).

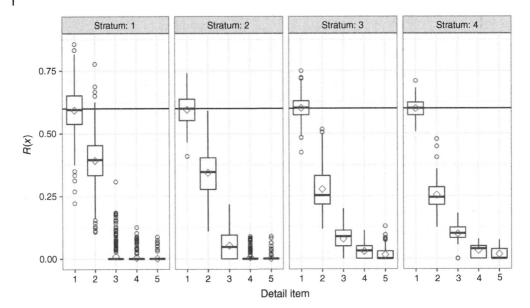

Figure 31.3 Distribution of detail item ratios $R(x)$ by sampling strata in a single simulated finite population. The horizontal asymptote is $R(x) = 0.60$.

Table 31.2 Stratum size and sample allocations averaged across the 2000 independent simulations; sampling fractions $(f_h = n_h/N_h)$ fixed in all simulations.

	N = 1000				N = 500			
Stratum S	1	2	3	4	1	2	3	4
N_h	442	255	219	83	221	128	110	42
f_h	1/10	1/4	1/2	1	1/10	1/4	1/2	1
n_h	45	64	110	83	23	32	55	42

31.5.2 Imputation Methods Implemented

Imputation and estimation are performed separately within each stratum, with x_i as the matching variable for the NNRI of $y_i = (y_{i1}, \ldots, y_{iT})$ as outlined in Section 31.2. Multiple imputation using 5NN is implemented as described in Section 31.4, using a number of imputations equal to the (expected) percentage of missing data (e.g. 25 imputed datasets for 75% response rate) as has been recommended as a rule of thumb (White et al., 2011). Variance estimation is conducted using the standard combining rules.

The proposed single imputation variance estimator requires a smooth estimator of $R(x)$ that can be used for *all* sampled units to estimate m_i. We consider the following estimators of $R(x)$:

1. *PLUG*: A parametric ratio estimator with $\widehat{R}(x_i) = \widehat{\beta} = \sum_{i \in S} w_i \delta_i y_i / \sum_{i \in S} w_i \delta_i x_i$, the best linear unbiased estimator of the weighted simple linear no-intercept regression model $y_i w_i^{-1/2} = \beta x_i w_i^{-1/2} + \epsilon_i w_i^{-1/2}$, $\epsilon_i \sim (0, x_i \sigma^2)$;
2. *OLS*: A similar parametric ratio estimator with $\widehat{R}(x_i) = \widehat{\beta}_h$, where $\widehat{\beta}_h$ is estimated separately within each sampling stratum h; and

3. *GAM*: A nonparametric generalized additive model (GAM) estimator (Hastie and Tibshirani, 1990) approximating the unknown smooth function of $R(x_i)$.

The first two estimators are frequently employed in the survey research methods literature (e.g. (Beaumont and Bocci, 2009; Magee, 1998), among others). These estimators assume strong linear relationships between the independent and auxiliary variables; this strong association is less likely to hold for rarely reported independent detail items. Furthermore, the parametric approximations develop *separate* regression models for each detail item component in y_i.

The nonparametric approach fits GAMs to approximate the *unknown* smooth function $f(x) = \hat{R}(x_i)$ (Wood et al., 2016). We use $\hat{R}(x_i) = \left\{ \sum_{k=1}^{K^{(1)}} \beta_k^{(1)} b_k^{(1)}(x_i), \sum_{k=1}^{K^{(2)}} \beta_k^{(2)} b_k^{(2)}(x_i), \dots, 1 - \sum_{t=1}^{T-1} \sum_{k=1}^{K^{(t)}} \beta_k^{(t)} b_k^{(t)}(x_i) \right\}$ for $i = 1, \dots, n$, where the $\{\beta_k^{(t)}\}_{k=1}^{K^{(t)}}, t = 1, 2, \dots, T-1$ are the coefficients for the t-th detail item and $\{b_k^{(t)}(x_i)\}_{k=1}^{K^{(t)}}, t = 1, 2, \dots, T-1$ are the known $K^{(t)}$ basis functions, obtained with the *thin plate regression splines* since they are the optimal smoother of any given basis rank in a defined sense (Wood, 2003). We also impose a model penalty during model fitting to control the number of basis functions K to improve the model performance.

To estimate $\hat{V}^m$, we use an approximate sampling-formula variance estimator, computed as

$$\hat{V}_m = \sum_h n_h \cdot \left(1 - \frac{n_h}{N_h}\right) \frac{N_h^2}{n_h} \frac{1}{n_h - 1} \sum_{i \in S} (\hat{m}_{hi} - \hat{\bar{m}}_h)^2 = \sum_h N_h^2 \left(1 - \frac{n_h}{N_h}\right) \widehat{var}(m_{hi})$$

This estimator easily incorporates the stratum sampling fractions. For more complex sampling designs, a replicate variance estimator might be preferred.

The $\hat{V}^e$ component requires $\hat{\sigma}_e^2(x_i)$ to estimate the variation of the residuals ($e_i = y_i - \hat{m}_i$). We consider three different estimators:

1. a plug-in variance estimator as $\hat{\sigma}_e^2(x_i) = x_i \hat{\beta}(1 - \hat{\beta})$, specified by the multinomial distribution of y_i, where $\hat{\beta}$ is the (*PLUG*) parametric WLS regression estimator. The complete variance estimate is denoted as $\hat{V}_{y,\text{PLUG}}$;
2. a parametric linear estimator of $\hat{\sigma}_e^2(x_i) = \hat{\alpha}_{0,h} + \hat{\alpha}_{1,h} x_i$ obtained by the OLS regression of $e_i^2 = (y_i - \hat{\beta}_h x_i)^2 = \alpha_{0,h} + \alpha_{1,h} x_i + \epsilon_i$ for $\delta_i = 1$ within each stratum, where $\hat{\beta}_h$ is the (*OLS*) stratum specific WLS regression parameter. The complete variance estimator is denoted as $\hat{V}_{y,\text{OLS}}$
3. a nonparametric estimator of $\hat{\sigma}_e^2(x_i) = \sum_{k=1}^K \hat{\beta}_k b_k(x_i)$ obtained by fitting a GAM of $e_i^2 = \delta_i(y_i - \hat{m}_i)^2 = \sum_{k=1}^K \beta_k b_k(x_i)$ for all strata, where $\hat{m}_i$ are obtained via the *GAM* procedure. The complete variance estimator is denoted as $\hat{V}_{y,\text{GAM}}$.

31.5.3 Evaluation of Performance

To evaluate the statistical properties of the considered NNRI estimates and variance estimates over repeated samples we calculated

- the *relative bias* (RB) of each estimator given by $\text{RB}(\hat{\theta}) = \frac{1}{B} \sum_{b=1}^{B} (\hat{\theta}^{(b)} - \theta)/\theta$, where $\hat{\theta}^{(b)}$ is the estimate from the bth sample and θ is the corresponding true value; and
- the *coverage rate* (CR), computed as the empirical proportion of approximate 95% approximate confidence intervals that contain the true population total.

Table 31.3 provides the population totals and empirical variances used as "truth" (θ) for RB and coverage rates. Population totals are averaged across the 2000 independent replicates; empirical variances are computed as the variance of the singly or multiply imputed NNRI estimates across the 2000 independent replicates for response propensities $\pi = 0.75$ and $\pi = 0.50$. Caution should

Table 31.3 Population totals (Y) and empirical variances ($V_{y(s)}$, single imputation; $V_{y(m)}$, multiple imputation) from the 2000 independent simulations.

			Y_1	Y_2	Y_3	Y_4	Y_5
$N = 1000$	$Y(\times 10^2)$		450.00	230.00	46.30	15.70	7.84
	$V_{y(s)}(\times 10^3)$	$\pi = 0.75$	321.00	271.00	46.60	10.90	7.90
	$V_{y(m)}(\times 10^3)$	$\pi = 0.75$	310.18	224.41	38.36	8.54	5.98
	$V_{y(s)}(\times 10^3)$	$\pi = 0.50$	390.00	394.00	86.90	21.10	16.30
	$V_{y(m)}(\times 10^3)$	$\pi = 0.50$	344.89	322.61	65.08	14.98	11.82
$N = 500$	$Y(\times 10^2)$		225.00	115.00	23.20	7.86	3.91
	$V_{y(s)}(\times 10^3)$	$\pi = 0.75$	155.00	128.00	23.30	5.17	4.00
	$V_{y(m)}(\times 10^3)$	$\pi = 0.75$	153.46	118.10	19.26	4.12	2.85
	$V_{y(s)}(\times 10^3)$	$\pi = 0.50$	193.00	193.00	41.80	10.7	7.87
	$V_{y(m)}(\times 10^3)$	$\pi = 0.50$	178.43	165.05	33.40	7.68	5.86

be exercised in over-generalizing the presented results, as the simulation utilizes a very specific multinomial distribution, a single sampling design, and a single-response mechanism.

31.5.4 Results

The NNRI *totals* are unbiased for all detail items, for both single and multiple imputation, regardless of population size and response propensity (data not shown). Of note, the use of a donor pool of size $k = 5$ for multiple imputation did not, in the simulation scenarios considered, result in any observable bias in the estimated totals. These results are partially an artifact of the simulation design, which ensured appropriate conditions for the distance function used to select the nearest neighbor and used a uniform response mechanism.

Table 31.4 reports the relative biases of the NNRI variance estimates for all the five detailed items for each population size and response propensity. As expected, the single imputation naïve variance estimator consistently underestimates the true variance, with the degree of underestimation increasing as the response propensity decreases. Except for Y_1, the single imputation estimator $\hat{V}_{y,\text{PLUG}}$ consistently underestimates the variances as well; this is likely due to the underestimation of $\hat{\sigma}_e^2$. On the other hand, nearly all of the single imputation variance estimates with $\hat{V}_{y,\text{OLS}}$ are nearly unbiased, with trivial underestimation. The performance of the single imputation estimator $\hat{V}_{y,\text{GAM}}$ is inconsistent, although greatly improved over the corresponding $\hat{V}_{y,\text{naïve}}$ and $\hat{V}_{y,\text{PLUG}}$ values. In contrast to the other proposed methods, this approach tends to overestimate the variances.

The multiple imputation variance estimator, $\hat{V}_{y,\text{NN5}}$, is approximately unbiased for Y_1, but shows some evidence of variance underestimation for the remaining detail items.

Figure 31.4 plots the 95% confidence interval coverage rates for all five detail items for each population size and response propensity. Not surprisingly, using $\hat{V}_{y,\text{naïve}}$ with single imputation almost invariably results in severe undercoverage, regardless of finite population size or response rate. Similar underperformance is seen with $\hat{V}_{y,\text{PLUG}}$. However, the confidence intervals constructed with $\hat{V}_{y,\text{OLS}}$ yield nominal coverage for all five detail items in *all* scenarios, and the confidence intervals constructed with $\hat{V}_{y,\text{GAM}}$ are either nominal or slightly larger than nominal.

Table 31.4 Relative biases of variance estimators from single imputation (SI) and multiple imputation (MI) for NNRI estimates of the total.

				Y_1	Y_2	Y_3	Y_4	Y_5
$N = 1000$	$\pi = 0.75$	SI	$\widehat{V}_{y,\text{naïve}}$	−0.13	−0.36	−0.49	−0.57	−0.62
		SI	$\widehat{V}_{y,\text{PLUG}}$	0.00	−0.47	−0.46	−0.23	−0.47
		SI	$\widehat{V}_{y,\text{OLS}}$	−0.01	−0.06	−0.01	−0.03	−0.02
		SI	$\widehat{V}_{y,\text{GAM}}$	0.01	−0.06	0.40	0.13	0.15
		MI	$\widehat{V}_{y,\text{NN5}}$	−0.04	−0.04	−0.08	−0.10	−0.10
	$\pi = 0.50$	SI	$\widehat{V}_{y,\text{naïve}}$	−0.39	−0.57	−0.73	−0.78	−0.82
		SI	$\widehat{V}_{y,\text{PLUG}}$	0.02	−0.47	−0.50	−0.30	−0.55
		SI	$\widehat{V}_{y,\text{OLS}}$	0.00	−0.01	−0.02	0.00	−0.01
		SI	$\widehat{V}_{y,\text{GAM}}$	0.04	0.04	0.36	0.13	0.10
		MI	$\widehat{V}_{y,\text{NN5}}$	0.00	−0.07	−0.08	−0.06	−0.11
$N = 500$	$\pi = 0.75$	SI	$\widehat{V}_{y,\text{naïve}}$	−0.12	−0.33	−0.50	−0.56	−0.64
		SI	$\widehat{V}_{y,\text{PLUG}}$	0.03	−0.45	−0.47	0.02	−0.49
		SI	$\widehat{V}_{y,\text{OLS}}$	0.01	−0.04	−0.04	0.00	−0.06
		SI	$\widehat{V}_{y,\text{GAM}}$	0.05	−0.01	0.40	0.20	0.12
		MI	$\widehat{V}_{y,\text{NN5}}$	−0.04	−0.10	−0.10	−0.10	−0.07
	$\pi = 0.50$	SI	$\widehat{V}_{y,\text{naïve}}$	−0.30	−0.57	−0.72	−0.79	−0.82
		SI	$\widehat{V}_{y,\text{PLUG}}$	0.01	−0.46	−0.48	−0.31	−0.53
		SI	$\widehat{V}_{y,\text{OLS}}$	−0.02	−0.03	−0.02	−0.04	0.00
		SI	$\widehat{V}_{y,\text{GAM}}$	0.06	0.08	0.44	0.12	0.11
		MI	$\widehat{V}_{y,\text{NN5}}$	−0.04	−0.09	−0.11	−0.09	−0.10

Results over 2000 replicates.

The confidence intervals constructed using multiple imputation ($\widehat{V}_{y,\text{NN5}}$) obtain nominal or just slightly below nominal coverage for all items. The slight undercoverage for MI occurs for the rarely reported detail items (Y_4, Y_5) which is a challenging imputation scenario; with smaller sample sizes and sparse reporting of these items, a large fraction of potential donors will have $R(x) = 0$ for these products, and thus the pool of $k = 5$ donors may be overrepresented by these zero ratio values.

Ultimately, both single and multiple imputation provided promising results with at least some of the considered variance estimators. For single imputation, the results obtained with $\widehat{V}_{y,\text{OLS}}$ are encouraging, especially given that the data generation model was not congenial to the *WLS* regression used to obtain $\hat{m}_i$. The nonparametric method used in the $\widehat{V}_{y,\text{GAM}}$ approach is also appealing due to its flexibility, especially given the reasonable coverage; it is possible that the model fit and estimation might be improved with a different choice of basis functions. For multiple imputation, despite some evidence of variance underestimation, $\widehat{V}_{y,\text{NN5}}$ provided near-nominal coverage, and its ease of implementation is a benefit. Given its poor performance over repeated samples, we dropped the single imputation variance estimator $\widehat{V}_{y,\text{PLUG}}$ from further consideration.

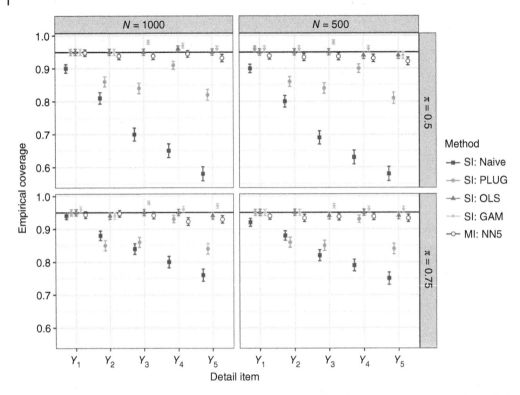

Figure 31.4 Coverage rates for single and multiply imputed NNRI estimates. Error bars show Monte Carlo 95% confidence intervals. Results over 2000 replicates.

31.6 Empirical Application

31.6.1 Background

This section presents an application to empirical expenditures data from five industries in the 2018 SAS collection. These industries represent a cross-section of expenses data collection and the sampling design features of the survey. Tables 31.5 and 31.6 provide important features of the study industries. The input data for this application study consists of the sampled companies in the selected industries that tabulated a *positive* (nonzero) total expenses value; companies reporting zero-valued expenses were dropped. We selected these five industries from a list of candidate industries provided by subject matter experts, validating the NNRI model assumptions and ensuring that all of their sampling strata contained at least three companies. Consequently, these industries are *not* representative of the larger survey. Furthermore, as discussed in Section 31.1, the SAS uses industry-average ratio imputation for missing and invalid expenses items and implements a naive random group variance estimator. For these reasons, in addition to the others discussed below, our estimates and variance estimates will be different from the official published values. For confidentiality protection, all data shown in the tables and figures in this section have been rounded (e.g. sample sizes, response rates, and coefficients of variation).

Table 31.5 Number of collected detail items and unweighted response rates of expenses details by certainty and noncertainty status.

Industry	Description	Number of details	Response rates		
			Total	Certainty	Noncertainty.
221122	Electric power distribution	7	74	64	97
517210	Wireless telecommunications carriers	9	32	62	27
541211	Offices of certified public accountants	7	82	74	84
621410	Family planning centers	9	84	78	89
713110	Amusement and theme parks	7	60	60	60

Source: Service Annual Survey (2018), U.S. Census Bureau.

Table 31.6 Sample design characteristics of SAS study industries.

NAICS	Overall	Sample size (*n*)		Number of strata	Strata sampling rates (n_h/N_h)	
	Overall *n/N*	Certainty	Noncertainty		Minimum	Maximum
221122	0.0785	80	30	7	0.0061	0.3448
517210	0.0620	60	350	15	0.0140	0.5000
541211	0.0035	40	150	13	0.0020	0.0894
621410	0.1055	50	50	7	0.0122	0.4468
713110	0.0709	40	30	4	0.0160	0.1125

Source: The range of strata sampling rates excludes the certainty stratum.

The unweighted response rates presented in Table 31.5 represent the proportion of sampled units that provided *a complete donor record* and do not therefore correspond to the official unit response rates. On inspection, the response patterns displayed in Table 31.5 appear to be atypical of business surveys, in which generally the larger businesses (e.g. the certainty companies) respond at higher rates. However, for NNRI, *all* detail items are imputed if either the company was a nonrespondent or if the reported set of expenses details did not add to the total, reducing the number of sampled units that are treated as respondents.

Figure 31.5 plots the percentage distribution of the detail items by industry. Percentages are computed as $\hat{R}_y = \hat{T}_y/\hat{T}_x$, where y is the NNRI HT estimate of the considered detail item and x is the HT estimate of the associated total (expenses). To simplify presentation, estimates are presented without error bounds. For confidentiality protection, the estimated percentage values are not provided. Each industry distribution includes a vertical reference line at $\hat{R}_y = 0.10$. In all industries, items Y_1 (gross annual payroll) and Y_7 (other expenses) each contribute more than 10% to the total, whereas the other items are less consistently reported.

Table 31.6 provides sample design characteristics of the study industries. Notice that the overall sampling rate (n/N) is nonnegligible in four of the five study industries. All industries utilize an entirely certainty stratum. The sampling rates for the noncertainty industry strata vary greatly, with at least one stratum in each industry having a nonnegligible sampling rate.

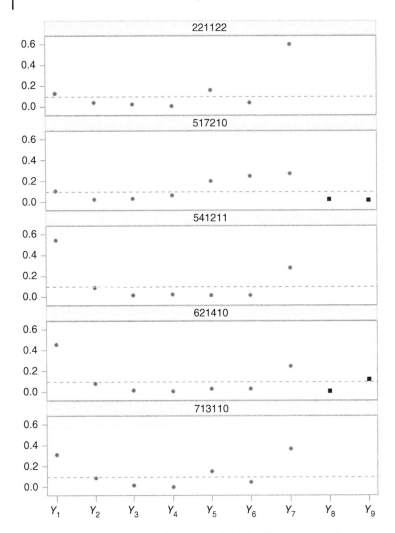

Figure 31.5 Percentage distribution of (NNRI) detail items to total expenses within industry. Vertical reference lines provided at $\hat{R}_y = 0.10$. Common items are indicated by circles; industry-specific detail items are indicated by squares. For all industries, the detail items are $Y_1 =$ gross annual payroll; $Y_2 =$ fringe benefits; $Y_3 =$ temporary staff payroll; $Y_4 =$ expensed software; $Y_5 =$ depreciation costs; $Y_6 =$ expensed equipment; and $Y_7 =$ other expenses. In industry 517210, $Y_8 =$ access charges, and $Y_9 =$ universal service and similar charges. In industry 621410, $Y_8 =$ professional liability insurance and $Y_9 =$ medical supply costs. Source: Service Annual Survey (2018), U.S. Census Bureau.

31.6.2 Results

Table 31.7 presents the coefficients of variation (c.v.) of each item for each considered variance estimator in percentages.

Consistent with the simulation results presented in Section 31.5.4, variance underestimation appears unlikely with the $\hat{V}_{\text{OLS}}$ and $\hat{V}_{\text{GAM}}$ estimators. In many cases, however, the differences between their corresponding c.v. statistics are striking. These large differences could be due to

Table 31.7 Coefficients of variation (c.v.) for the singly (SI) and multiply (MI) imputed NNRI detail items (HT Totals) in percentages.

Industry	Method	Y_1	Y_2	Y_3	Y_4	Y_5	Y_6	Y_7	Y_8	Y_9
221122	SI-OLS	5.4	6.6	34.1	27.0	6.8	30.2	5.4		
	SI-GAM	8.0	9.5	111.1[a]	68.5[a]	10.0	109.6[a]	6.1		
	MI-NN5	4.3	5.0	20.6	26.0	3.4	19.6	4.7		
517210	SI-OLS	34.1[a]	19.9	49.8	0.4	54.3	46.7	0.6	9.6	0.4
	SI-GAM	27.0	24.9	8.0	4.1	5.8	5.0	5.0	62.4[a]	14.5
	MI-NN5	1.6	1.5	0.7	0.5	0.4	0.4	0.8	4.2	0.3
541211	SI-OLS	3.5	5.5	18.7	7.7	9.1	28.8	4.7		
	SI-GAM	3.6	40.2	24.1	7.8	59.4[a]	1001.4[a]	7.6		
	MI-NN5	3.4	3.9	7.0	7.3	10.1	24.2	3.2		
621410	SI-OLS	4.1	3.8	11.8	16.0	7.3	13.4	7.1	12.4	4.5
	SI-GAM	17.6	3.9	25.5	61.9[a]	14.2	82.3[a]	56.4[a]	116.5[a]	4.1
	MI-NN5	3.2	3	8.9	11.2	4.0	13.4	6.1	10.4	4.1
713110	SI-OLS	93.9[a]	15.8	24.2	15.5	12.8	167.7[a]	11.9		
	SI-GAM	1.4	1.5	7.0	194.9[a]	24.8	40.7	2.0		
	MI-NN5	1.8	2.6	3.6	9.5	2.3	6.3	1.8		

[a]c.v. greater than 51% (= 1/1.96), not significantly different from zero at $\alpha = 0.05$.

Source: Service Annual Survey (2018), U.S. Census Bureau.

model misspecification; for example, the large c.v.s obtained with $\widehat{V}_{GAM}$ would be expected if the nonparametric models provided poor fits in industries 221122, 541211, and 713110. That said, most of the detail items represent a very small percentage of their total so that variance estimation method effects could be confounded with sample size effects. The c.v.s obtained via the multiple imputation NN5 method tend to be the smallest of the three and display similar patterns as the corresponding *OLS* statistics in three industries (221122, 541211, and 621410).

From a practical perspective, the choice of variance estimator can have a profound effect on inference. Figure 31.6 plots 95% confidence intervals for Y_1, Y_5, and Y_7, the three detail items that generally represent more than 10% apiece of their respective industry totals. Confidence intervals for Y_5 in industries 541211 and 621410 are not presented, as that item represents less than 10 % of the total in those industries.

Although the values of the bounds are suppressed for confidentiality protection, the visual contrasts for the same item within industry are often stark. Inference is most clearly affected in industry 517210 for Y_5, in industry 621410 for Y_7, and industry 713110 for Y_1. In the first and third case, the confidence interval constructed with the $\widehat{V}_{OLS}$ contains zero, whereas the other confidence intervals do not. In the second case, the confidence interval constructed with the $\widehat{V}_{GAM}$ contains zero, in contrast to the others.

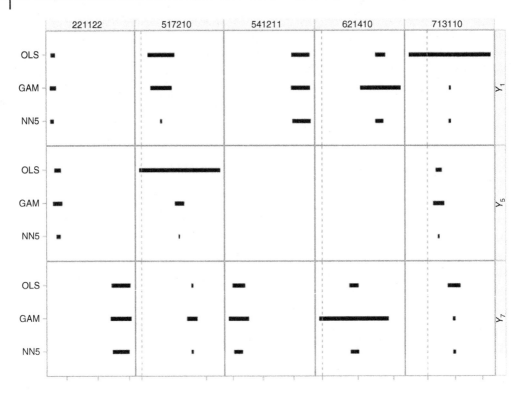

Figure 31.6 Empirical 95% confidence intervals for Y_1 (gross annual payroll), Y_5 (depreciation costs), and Y_7 (other expenses). A vertical reference line is provided at $x = 0$. Source: Service Annual Survey (2018), U.S. Census Bureau.

31.7 General Conclusion

Surveys that collect both totals and component details need to make an a priori decision about imputation, specifically which side of the equation to change when the additivity requirement is not satisfied (i.e. when details do not sum to the total). If both sides are reported, a methodologist might decide to automatically replace the reported totals with the summed details or to test both candidate values against a set of edit rules and select the value that fails fewer edits. As long as there are some reported detail items, the latter approach seems – at first glance – prudent. After all, it does retain reported data without relying on possibly tenuous model assumptions. On the other hand, the survey research methods literature posits that the reliability of such multinomial (detail items) data is questionable, especially for breakdowns that do not correspond to common financial or accounting practices. Furthermore, there are rarely independent sources of auxiliary data for validation, and of course, missing data rates for compositional details tend to be much higher than for totals, so there needs to be an imputation procedure in place for the set of details when none are reported.

That said, the totals requested by business surveys are often validated with reliable auxiliary data and can generally rely on strong ratio imputation models between survey items. In other words, more "detective work" can be implemented, and a methodologist would likely attribute a high degree of reliability to an imputed total. Thus, preserving a reported or imputed total over a set of compositional details is usually justified in practice. In this case, using hot deck imputation to impute entire sets of detail items is especially appealing. In this chapter, we consider NNRI. Instead of directly imputing the set of detail item values from the donor, NNRI imputes the proportions of donor ratios, which are in turn multiplied by the recipient's available total to derive imputed values for all items. Not only does this method guarantee a plausible set of imputed detail items while preserving multivariate relationships, it accommodates subtle distributional shifts in unit-level distributions and avoids inadvertently imposing possibly outdated historical patterns in the imputed data, as it is entirely restricted to current data (Andridge et al., 2020).

The introduction outlines many of the potential benefits of using NNRI on the Services Annual Survey expenditures data, especially in the COVID-19 reference year (2020). From an estimation-accuracy perspective, the potential gain is large (over existing practices). The implementation challenge lies in the variance estimation, as the NNRI procedure does not yield a smooth estimator.

In this chapter, we present two viable approaches to variance estimation with NNRI: (i) a single imputation variance estimator that requires a model (either parametric or nonparametric) to obtain smooth estimators for a set of ratios and (ii) a multiple imputation estimator and variance estimator that replicates the donor selection procedure within a cluster of "nearest neighbor" donor records. As with the choice of imputation method itself, both approaches require careful analysis before implementation. Neither method should be blindly applied without ensuring that it has been tailored to the data set at hand.

With the single imputation method, selecting an appropriate model for the data set at hand is essential. Compromise may be required; the most frequently reported detail items can tend toward strong associations with the total, whereas the relationship between rarely reported detail items and the total is less obvious. The simulation study results demonstrate the effect of model misspecification on variance estimate bias, as seen with the overestimation of the rare items when using the GAM to approximate a smooth multivariate ratio function. In the empirical application, neither the OLS or GAM approaches was uniformly the best; these methods were applied in all five industries without additional care to validate the underlying models. Customizing the model to fit the specific data set appears to be especially important for these variance estimation methods.

The multiple imputation approach requires a choice of k to create the donor pool. Selecting $k = 1$ leads to variance underestimation (Andridge et al., 2020), but as k approaches the imputation cell's sample size, the association between unit size and multinomial distribution is degraded and the imputation becomes a random hot deck (which ignores unit size in selecting a donor). In the simulation study and the empirical analysis, $k = 5$ is determined arbitrarily, and this may not be the appropriate value for all data sets. In particular, ensuring that imputation cells have enough responding units to support the choice of k is imperative, and with deep stratification and small sample sizes or response rates this may result in collapsing across imputation cells. Additionally, we observed slight (but consistent) variance underestimation when using NN5. That said, the confidence interval coverage in the simulation is generally nominal with only slight undercoverage for the rarely reported items.

Our results must be interpreted with some caution. While overall, both the single and multiple imputation approaches for NNRI appear promising, we only considered a single-design (stratified random sample) and a single-response mechanism. Our simulation study, while patterned off real data, only considered a single data generation mechanism and assumed a uniform response mechanism. Additionally, though nearest neighbor methods are preferred in situations where nonresponse is related to size, i.e. missing at random, we did not consider this in our simulation.

Acknowledgments

We thank Noah Bassel, Carol Caldwell, William Davie Jr., Matthew Thompson, and Katrina Washington for their helpful comments on earlier versions of this manuscript, and Chenyin Gao, Stephen Kaputa, and Shu Yang for their contributions to the research, methods, and analyses.

Disclaimer

Any views expressed here are those of the authors and not those of the US Census Bureau. The Census Bureau has reviewed this data product for unauthorized disclosure of confidential information and has approved the disclosure avoidance practices applied (Approval ID: CBDRB-FY21-ESMD002-032).

References

Andridge, R. and Thompson, K. Adapting nearest neighbor for multiple imputation: advantages, challenges, and drawbacks. *Journal of Survey Statistics and Methodology*, In press.

Andridge, R., Bechtel, L., and Thompson, K. (2020). Finding a flexible hot-deck imputation method for multinomial data. *Journal of Survey Statistics and Methodology*, In Press. https://doi.org/10.1093/jssam/smaa005.

Barnard, J. and Rubin, D.B. (1999). Small-sample degrees of freedom with multiple imputation. *Biometrika* 86: 948–955.

Bavdaž, M. (2010). The multidimensional integral business survey response model. *Survey Methodology* 36 (1): 81–93.

Beaumont, J.-F. and Bocci, C. (2009). Variance estimation when donor imputation is used to fill in missing values. *The Canadian Journal of Statistics* 37 (3): 400–416.

Chen, J. and Shao, J. (2000). Nearest neighbor imputation for survey data. *Journal of Official Statistics* 16 (2): 113–131.

Fang, F., Hong, Q., and Shao, J. (2009). A pseudo empirical likelihood approach for stratified samples with nonresponse. *Annals of Statistics* 37 (1): 371–393. https://doi.org/10.1214/07-AOS578.

Gao, C., Thompson, K.J., Kim, J.K., and Yang, S. (2021). Nearest neighbor ratio imputation with incomplete multinomial outcome in survey sampling, *Journal of the Royal Statistical Society: Series A (Statistics in Society).* In Press. https://doi.org/10.1111/rssa.12841.

Hastie, T.J. and Tibshirani, R.J. (1990). *Generalized Additive Models*, vol. 43. CRC Press.

Hastie, T., Friedman, J., and Tibshirani, R. (2013). *The Elements of Statistical Learning: Data Mining, Inference, and Prediction.* Germany, New York: Springer.

Little, R.J.A. and Rubin, D.B. (2019). *Statistical Analysis with Missing Data*, 3e. Wiley.

Magee, L. (1998). Improving survey-weighted least squares regression. *Journal of the Royal Statistical Society, Series B (Statistical Methodology)* 60 (1): 115–126.

Morris, T.P., White, I.R., and Royston, P. (2014). Tuning multiple imputation by predictive mean matching and local residual draws. *BMC Medical Research Methodology* 14: 75.

Nordholt, E.S. (1998). Imputation: methods, simulation experiments and practical examples. *International Statistical Review* 66 (2): 157–180.

Rubin, D.J. (1987). *Multiple Imputation for Nonresponse in Surveys.* New York: Wiley.

Rubin, D.J. and Schenker, N. (1986). Multiple imputation for interval estimation from simple random samples with ignorable nonresponse. *Journal of the American Statistical Association* 86: 366–374.

Shao, J. and Steel, P. (1999). Variance estimation for survey data with composite imputation and nonnegligible sampling fractions. *Journal of the American Statistical Association* 94 (445): 254–265.

Sigman, R. and Wagner, D. (1997). Algorithms for adjusting survey data that fail balance edits. *Proceedings of the Section on Survey Research Methods.*

Thompson, K.J. and Washington, K.T. (2013). Challenges in the treatment of unit nonresponse for selected business surveys: a case study. *Survey Methods: Insights from the Field.* Retrieved from http://surveyinsights.org/?p=2991.

White, I.R., Royston, P., and Wood, A.M. (2011). Multiple imputation using chained equations: issues and guidance for practice. *Statistics in Medicine* 30: 377–399.

Willimack, D. and Nichols, E. (2010). A hybrid response process model for business surveys. *Journal of Official Statistics* 26 (1): 3–24.

Wood, S.N. (2003). Thin plate regression splines. *Journal of the Royal Statistical Society: Series B (Statistical Methodology)* 65 (1): 95–114.

Wood, S.N., Pya, N., and Säfken, B. (2016). Smoothing parameter and model selection for general smooth models. *Journal of the American Statistical Association* 111 (516): 1548–1563.

Yang, S. and Kim, J.K. (2019). Nearest neighbor imputation for general parameter estimation in survey sampling. In: *The Econometrics of Complex Survey Data: Theory and Applications* (ed. K.P. Huynh, D.T. Jacho-Chavez, and G. Tripath). Bingley, West Yorkshire, England: Emerald Publishing Limited. 209–234.

32

Minimizing Revisions for a Monthly Economic Indicator

Nicole Czaplicki, Stephen Kaputa, and Laura Bechtel

Economic Statistical Methods Division, US Census Bureau, Washington, DC, USA

32.1 Introduction

National Statistical Institutes (NSIs) provide trusted measures of the social, demographic, and economic environment of the nation at a given point in time. Economic indicators are among the signature data products released by NSIs and are inputs into notable economic measures including price indices, gross domestic product (GDP), and national accounts. These statistics become headline news, especially in times of economic uncertainty. Financial markets shift upon their release. Policymakers, business leaders, and economists use today's indicators in decisions that shape the economic realities of tomorrow. In other words, the importance of economic indicators cannot be overstated.

Indicator programs are characterized by a high-frequency data collection (monthly or quarterly) of a small number of variables. For data users, timely data is prized, as the utility of these statistics diminishes as more time elapses between the end of the reference period and the data release. To meet this need, it is common for NSIs to release *advance* estimates of key data items ("early indicators") soon after the reference period ends, with revised estimates released when more data becomes available. The media reports on changes between these early indicators and their prior period estimates, and data users monitor the direction of any change and act accordingly. Revisions between these early releases and subsequent estimates are inevitable, but nonetheless highly scrutinized, especially if the revision reverses the direction of period-to-period change estimates.

With highly skewed economic data, nonignorable nonresponse can substantively contribute to differences in corresponding early and revised estimates; for example, if larger companies tend to report later in the collection cycle. To avoid this, a compromise approach is to construct the preliminary estimate from a probability subsample of the larger survey, i.e. a reversed two-phase sample approach, as done by the US Census Bureau for the Advance Monthly Retail Trade Survey (MARTS) and the Monthly Retail Trade and Food Services Survey (MRTS). The MARTS publishes estimates of total monthly sales in the retail trade and food service industries in the United States approximately two working weeks after the reference month. The MARTS is a probability sample of companies, subsampled from the MRTS. Approximately one month later, these *advance* estimates

Advances in Business Statistics, Methods and Data Collection. Edited by Ger Snijkers, Mojca Bavdaž, Stefan Bender, Jacqui Jones, Steve MacFeely, Joseph W. Sakshaug, Katherine J. Thompson, and Arnout van Delden.

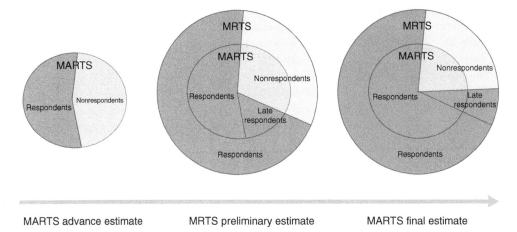

| MARTS advance estimate | MRTS preliminary estimate | MARTS final estimate |

Figure 32.1   Illustration of data available at each stage of Monthly Retail Trade production cycle (not to scale). The MARTS is a probability subsample of the MRTS.

are superseded by *preliminary* estimates from the MRTS. The following month, approximately two and a half months after the reference month, the estimates are revised again with the final MRTS estimates. Figure 32.1 illustrates the data used at each stage of the monthly retail trade production cycle. The difference between the advance indicator and subsequent estimates is often primarily due to changes in the data, such as from late or amended reports, but in the case of MRTS and MARTS, is also attributable to differences in methodology and processing.

The estimates of total sales released by these surveys are inputs into quarterly GDP published by the Bureau of Economic Analysis. Revisions to the advance totals are generally within the published confidence intervals. However, the *economic indicator* is the ratio of the two most recent estimates, the current month advance total from MARTS and the prior month preliminary total from MRTS (hereafter called the advance month-to-month change); the revised month-to-month change estimate is available from MRTS approximately four weeks later. Even when neither the advance nor the preliminary month-to-month change estimate is significantly different from zero, large revisions are scrutinized by expert data users, especially when the advance indicators are cited in policy decisions.

In 2016, the US Census Bureau authorized an extensive investigation of methodological enhancements to the current MARTS estimation and imputation procedures. This focus of the research is twofold: (i) align the MARTS totals to the corresponding preliminary MRTS totals thus reducing revisions; and (ii) replace subjective analyst review and imputation procedures with statistically defensible automated procedures. In Section 32.2, we present survey background and highlight key differences between the surveys that are known to contribute to revisions, motivating the research presented in Sections 32.3 through 32.5. Technical documentation and published estimates for MARTS, MRTS, and the Annual Retail Trade Survey (ARTS) are available from https://www.census .gov/retail/about_the_surveys.html. The remaining sections describe our research into modifications of the MARTS missing data treatment and estimation procedures. Section 32.3 describes an investigation into alternative estimators. Section 32.4 presents a (semi-) objective approach for selecting "high priority" MARTS units for additional interventions (nonresponse follow-up or analyst imputation as described in Section 32.2.5). Section 32.5 highlights our work-to-date on developing new automated imputation procedures. Section 32.6 presents our general conclusions and suggestions for future research.

Table 32.1 Differences between MARTS and MRTS.

SOURCE	MARTS	MRTS	Sections
Sample design	Stratified PPS from MRTS (36 strata)	Stratified SRS without replacement (79 strata)	32.2.1
Sample redesign cycle	Approximately every 2.5 years	Approximately every 5 years	32.2.1
Tabulation units	Directly modeled from reporting unit	Indirectly modeled from reporting unit	32.2.2
Tabulation industries	30 tabulation industries	83 tabulation industries	32.2.2
Time to respond	Approximately 7 business days	Approximately 5 weeks	32.2.3
Estimation	Link relative estimator	Horvitz–Thompson estimator	32.2.4
Imputation	Analyst impute for selected companies	Analyst imputes and ratio imputation	32.2.5

32.2 MARTS and MRTS Background and Motivation

A single cause contributing to a large revision is impossible to pinpoint due to the many design, processing, and estimation differences between MARTS and MRTS; see Table 32.1.

32.2.1 Sample Design

The MRTS collects national sales and inventory data for the retail trade and food services sectors as defined by the North American Industry Classification System (NAICS). The MRTS samples approximately 13,000 companies every five years from the ARTS using a stratified simple random sample without replacement (SRS-WOR) design.

For sampling, the MRTS is stratified into 79 retail trade industries that are further substratified using a measure of size (MOS) based on sales. The largest companies in each sampling industry are selected with a probability of one and are retained from sample to sample (certainty units). The remaining companies are substratified within industry using the cum-root-f rule (Dalenius and Hodges Jr 1959), with stratum sample sizes determined by Neyman allocation.

The MARTS collects only sales data for the same sectors covered by MRTS. The frame for MARTS is the most recent (updated) MRTS sample; every 2.5 years, approximately 5000 companies are sub-sampled via a stratified probability proportional to size (PPS) sample design. A new MARTS sample is introduced at the beginning and middle of the MRTS sample cycle.

The MARTS sampling industry strata are created by aggregating the MRTS sampling indus-try strata into 36 new (super) strata. Within each MARTS sampling industry, units that exceed a MARTS-specific sales-based size cutoff are sampled with a probability of one. Certainty units in MARTS will always be certainty units in MRTS, but a certainty unit in MRTS may be sam-pled with probability less than one for MARTS. The remaining MRTS units are grouped into sub-strata based on sales using the cum-root-f rule and PPS without replacement subsampling rates are determined using Neyman allocation. MARTS selection probabilities are determined using the MRTS sampling weights as the MOS, resulting in a self-weighting subsample and reducing the variance due to unequal weighting. However, this increases the probability of a company with a large weight within substratum being selected with a subsampling probability of one. [Note: Thompson et al. (2019) presents a simulation study comparing MARTS estimates using the current PPS subsampling procedure to corresponding estimates obtained using a stratified SRS-WOR subsample, finding no consistent improvements with the latter – more conventional – design.] The final MARTS design weight is the product of the MRTS sampling weight and the inverse of the MARTS sampling probability. For MARTS, we consider units with a final design weight of one to be certainty units and all others noncertainty units.

32.2.2 Unit Definitions

The Census Bureau's economic surveys typically distinguish between a sampling unit, reporting unit, and tabulation unit. Sampling units are selected from the sampling frame, defined at the company level. The reporting unit is an entity from which data are collected and are voluntarily established by the sampling unit(s) for their convenience, whereas a tabulation unit houses the data used in estimation.

In the simplest case, these three units are equivalent, but this is often not true for the largest companies that operate in more than one industry. The Census Bureau will request response by industry within sampling unit. Ideally, the company provides this disaggregated data by industry, creating a one-to-one match between reporting unit and tabulation unit. When a company that operates in more than one industry reports at a consolidated level, the Census Bureau must allocate the reporting unit data to the component industries, thus creating tabulation unit-level data.

32.2.3 Response Rates

With MARTS estimates published approximately two weeks after the reference month, companies have approximately seven business days to respond to the survey. Given that respondents have an additional month to respond to MRTS, many MARTS sample units miss the deadline for the advance data collection but provide their response for the same reference month in time for MRTS.

In many business surveys, it is generally observed that larger units respond more often than smaller units, in part due to the prioritization of larger units in nonresponse follow-up procedures (Thompson and Oliver 2012; Thompson et al. 2015). To gain insight into the composition of the respondent samples, we separated the units by broad size categories, with certainty status serving as a proxy for large units in Figure 32.2a,b. These figures present the unweighted unit response rates (number of respondent sampling units divided by the number of sampled units) for MRTS and MARTS, respectively, using data from May 2010 through December 2016 collections.

Figure 32.2a,b also illustrate the declining response rates over time that are indicative of a combination of sample fatigue and a general decline in response during this period. The introduction of a new sample typically results in an increase in response. This pattern is illustrated in 2013 in Figure 32.2a and 2015 in Figure 32.2b. The sharp increase in MARTS response in late 2013 corresponds to the partial shutdowns of the US federal government which resulted in delayed data releases and gave sampled units more time to respond to the survey.

32.2.4 Estimation Methodology

Although MARTS and MRTS estimate total sales across the retail trade and food services sectors, the larger sample size of MRTS allows for estimation at levels that are often more disaggregated than in MARTS. These sectors of the economy are divided into 83 disjoint tabulation industries for MRTS but only 30 disjoint tabulation industries for MARTS, with each MARTS tabulation industry

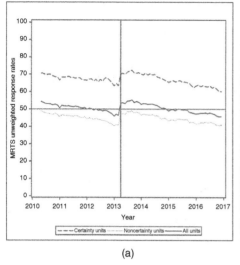 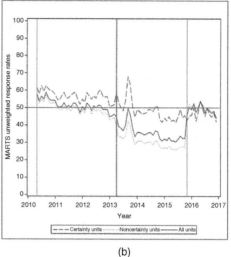

(a) (b)

Figure 32.2 (a and b) Unit Response Rates for MRTS (left) and MARTS (right) from May 2010 through December 2016. Response rates for all units are a solid line, certainty units are a dashed line and noncertainty units are a dotted line. Vertical lines indicate new samples, with thick vertical lines indicating MARTS samples occurring at the same time as new MRTS samples. Source: U.S. Census Bureau.

corresponding to one or more MRTS tabulation industries. A subset of the MRTS and MARTS tabulation industries have changed due to updates in the NAICS classification system since the presented research was conducted.

For both surveys, estimation and imputation are performed within their respective tabulation industries. Therefore, when comparing estimates from the two surveys, we are often comparing one tabulation industry estimate from MARTS to the sum of several tabulation industry estimates from MRTS. For the remainder of this chapter, we index the MRTS tabulation industries by j ($j = 1$, 2, ..., 83) and the MARTS tabulation industries by k ($k = 1$, 2, ..., 30). Furthermore, tabulation industry-level estimates are often not published on their own, but rather are aggregated to produce estimates at the publication industry level.

MARTS and MRTS use different estimators to calculate the estimated totals at the tabulation industry level. MRTS uses a Horvitz–Thompson estimator (Horvitz and Thompson 1952):

$$\hat{Y}_{\text{MRTS},j,t} = \sum_{i \in j} d_{i,t} y_{i,t} \tag{32.1}$$

where $d_{i,t}$ is the MRTS design weight assigned to unit i for month t, and $y_{i,t}$ is the MRTS value of sales for month t. As mentioned in Section 32.2.3, MARTS suffers from low response rates and a probable nonignorable pattern of nonresponse, making a similar estimate of the total from the survey likely to be biased. Instead, MARTS uses a link relative estimator (Madow and Madow 1978), a synthetic estimator that multiplies a benchmark total from the prior month by an estimate of the month-to-month change, known as the link relative ratio ($\hat{\Lambda}_{k,t}$), computed as follows:

$$\hat{Y}_{\text{LR},k,t} = \hat{Y}_{\text{MRTS},k,t-1} \left[\frac{\sum\limits_{i \in C_{\text{LR},k}} w_{i,t} \tilde{y}_{i,t}}{\sum\limits_{i \in C_{\text{LR},k}} w_{i,t} \tilde{y}_{i,t-1}} \right] = \hat{Y}_{\text{MRTS},k,t-1} \hat{\Lambda}_{k,t} \tag{32.2}$$

where

$\widehat{Y}_{\text{MRTS},k,t-1}$ = the MRTS preliminary estimate of MARTS tabulation industry k sales at period $t-1$

$C_{\text{LR},k}$ = set of MARTS sample units with valid values for both periods t and $t-1$ that are included in the calculation of the link relative ratio for industry k

$w_{i,t}$ = the MARTS design weight for unit i at period t

$\widetilde{y}_{i,t}$ = the MARTS value of sales for unit i at period t

$\widetilde{y}_{i,t-1}$ = the MARTS value of sales for unit i at period $t-1$

Notice that the benchmark total is the preliminary MRTS estimate for the prior month, not an independently obtained total.

The link relative estimator serves two purposes. First, it ensures that the level of the MARTS estimate remains approximately consistent with the MRTS estimate level. Second, it accounts for unit nonresponse, under the strong assumption that the nonrespondents' expected month-to-month change is the same as the estimated link relative ratio. This assumption must be empirically evaluated to justify the use of this estimator as described in Czaplicki et al. (2018).

32.2.5 Imputation Methodology and Procedures

MRTS tabulation units are imputed by multiplying the prior month value for each tabulation unit by its corresponding tabulation industry rate-of-change-ratio, computed as $\widehat{\Delta}_{j,t} = \dfrac{\sum\limits_{i \in j} d_{i,t} I_i y_{i,t}}{\sum\limits_{i \in j} d_{i,t} I_i y_{i,t-1}}$, where j indexes the MRTS tabulation industry, d_i is the MRTS design weight assigned to unit i, I_i is an MRTS indicator of current and prior month response (1 when unit i responds with valid values in months t and $t-1$, 0 otherwise), and $y_{i,t}$ and $y_{i,t-1}$ are the reported value of sales for months t and $t-1$. This ratio model is commonly used for business survey data because the previous period values are often very good predictors of the current period value and the intercept term is usually not significant (Lohr, Chapter 4; Andridge and Thompson 2015; Huang 1984, 1986).

MARTS does not have a generalized imputation procedure for all nonresponding units. Rather, unit nonresponse is primarily accounted for by the link relative estimator. The MARTS link relative estimation procedure is mathematically equivalent to a ratio imputation procedure that imputes missing values with the link relative ratio and then adjusts the imputed totals to a benchmark estimate. However, certain "high priority" nonresponding units are imputed by analysts using a combination of past company data, calendar effects, and subject matter knowledge (hereafter referred to as analyst imputes). The rate of analyst imputation differs by industry, with some industries receiving little or no analyst imputation.

The procedures for obtaining an imputed value may differ by company, industry, and analyst, but do have common elements. Historic company-level month-to-month changes are reviewed for the current calendar month (e.g. several years of December to January changes would be reviewed when imputing for January). Analysts typically select the *company-level* historic month-to-month change from the most recent year with a matching trading day pattern to the current year (same number of Sundays, Mondays, etc.). Applying this historic month-to-month change to the unit's prior period value (reported or imputed) results in an imputed value that accounts for both seasonality and trading day effects. However, finding a matching trading day pattern may require going several years into the past, making it questionable whether that historic month-to-month change is relevant to current economic conditions. For example, the matching year for *March 2020–February 2021* is ***2015–2016***; the matching year for *March 2021–February 2022* is ***2010–2011***.

An analyst-imputed value from MARTS is retained in MRTS unless the unit provides a reported value (late reporter), the analyst-imputed value is visibly different from the estimated industry trend, or the analyst-imputed value fails a MRTS edit test. Consequently, the imputed values in MARTS not only affect the MARTS estimates but also the MRTS estimates as well, although to a much lesser degree. Analyst-imputed values in MARTS are reviewed by more than one subject matter expert to promote consistency across the survey. However, the procedure is subjective, as is the determination of high priority units within an industry. This is discussed further in Section 32.4.

32.3 Estimation Evaluation

In this section, we present our research into alternative estimators for MARTS. Ratio-synthetic estimators such as the link relative estimator are severely biased unless the survey estimated ratio is close to the true industry population ratio (Rao 2003, Chapter 4.2, p. 37). Consequently, the first major phase of the research project focused on the role of the current estimation procedure in preventing revisions in monthly totals, with an eye toward potentially replacing the "unconventional" synthetic estimator. Estimates were computed for the 30 MARTS tabulation industries and evaluated at the tabulation level and at the various aggregated publication levels.

32.3.1 Estimation Methods Considered

The estimators considered in this research fall into two broad categories: link relative estimators and adjustment weighting estimators. The first category of estimator is designed to correct nonignorable nonresponse, whereas the second category assumes ignorable nonresponse. As discussed in Section 32.2.3, the anecdotal evidence indicates that the MARTS nonresponse mechanism is not missing at random (nonignorable), in turn providing anecdotal evidence against using the more conventional adjustment class weighting estimators proposed in Section 32.3.1.3. However, the ratio adjustment estimator proposed in Section 32.3.1.4 is fairly robust to deviations from ignorable response with a sufficiently strong prediction model. For all considered estimators, we considered two sets of adjustment cells: (A) MARTS tabulation industry and (B) certainty status (certainty/noncertainty) within MARTS tabulation industry.

32.3.1.1 Link Relative Estimation
Link relative estimation is used by the US Census Bureau to produce estimates of totals from two surveys: MARTS and the Manufacturers' Shipments, Inventories, and Orders Survey (M3). MARTS uses the traditional link relative estimator (see (32.2) in Section 32.2.4), whereas M3 uses the modified version of the estimator described in Section 32.3.1.2.

The link relative estimator for monthly data requires two data sources: (i) an (independent) estimate of the prior month total from a reliable source that will serve as the benchmark; and (ii) data from an ongoing survey from the same units for the current and prior month. The benchmark value provides an estimate of the level of the time series and the ongoing survey provides an estimate of the month-to-month change.

The link relative estimator assumes that all of the units within an estimation cell have the same expected rate of change from the prior month to the current month, $E[\tilde{y}_{i,t} \mid t-1] = \Phi_{k,t}\tilde{y}_{i,t-1}$. In other words, the data in an estimation cell are assumed to follow the model,

$$\tilde{y}_{i,t} = \Phi_{k,t}\tilde{y}_{i,t-1} + \varepsilon_{i,t}, \varepsilon_{i,t} \sim \left(0, \tilde{y}_{i,t-1}\sigma_{k,t}^2\right) \tag{32.3}$$

As a "quick and dirty" check, we fit this model using ordinary least squares estimation for each of the MARTS tabulation industries for each month from May 2010 to May 2016, then examined the R^2 statistics to evaluate the model fit (Note: adjusted-R^2 would have been more appropriate, but model fits were extremely good in the majority of cases). This was verified in Czaplicki et al. (2018).

In almost all industries, the majority of the variability in the current month was "explained" by the prior month value, with some variation in fit statistics by month, providing evidence for the usage of the link relative estimator.

32.3.1.2 Modified Link Relative Estimator

Although the assumed model for the link relative estimator is appropriate for most industries, there are units with outlying rates of change (identified by analysts) that are excluded from the link relative ratio in the MARTS implementation of the link relative estimator. The modified link relative estimator includes these units in the final estimates as follows:

$$
\widehat{Y}_{MLR,k,t} = \left[\widehat{Y}_{MRTS,k,t-1} - \sum_{i \in H_k} d_{i,t-1} \widetilde{y}_{i,t-1} \right] \left[\frac{\sum\limits_{i \in C_{MLR,k}} w_{i,t} \widetilde{y}_{i,t}}{\sum\limits_{i \in C_{MLR,k}} w_{i,t} \widetilde{y}_{i,t-1}} \right] + \sum_{i \in H_k} d_{i,t} \widetilde{y}_{i,t}
$$

where

$C_{MLR,k}$ = set of units with usable data for both periods t and $t-1$ that are included in the modified link relative ratio for MARTS tabulation industry k

H_k = set of units with usable data for both periods t and $t-1$ that are excluded from the modified link relative ratio for MARTS tabulation industry k, referred to in-house as "estimate separately" units.

We considered two sets of "estimate separately" units (i.e. units in H_k). The first (ES group 1) contains a set of companies that were identified as outliers during the MARTS production process and excluded from the link relative ratio. The second (ES group 2) augments this set of companies with the analyst-imputed companies.

32.3.1.3 Weighting Class Estimator

In the presence of nonresponse, the weighted total for the respondents is a negatively biased estimator of the total, Y_t. Adjustment cell weighting is a commonly used treatment for unit nonresponse, yielding unbiased estimates under an assumed (ignorable) response model. In this framework, response is a second phase of sampling:

Design phase: $N \rightarrow n$ where each unit i in the population has known probability of inclusion, determined by the sampling design

Response phase: $n \rightarrow r$, where each unit i in the sample has an unknown probability of response, estimated under an assumed response mechanism

The weighting class estimator assumes that the sample can be divided into mutually exclusive weighting cells, with homogeneous (equal) probability of response within adjustment cells, and heterogeneous (differing) probabilities of response across the cells. The sampling literature refers to this response mechanism as the within-weighting-cell uniform response mechanism, and estimators that can be justified under this response mechanism are referred to as "quasi-randomization" estimators (Oh and Scheuren 1983). Weighting cells may be strata, unions of strata (strata that are collapsed when they have insufficient respondents), or may cut across strata.

Little and Vartivarian (2005), among others, proposed estimating the second-phase probability as the unit response rate within the weighting cell, yielding the weighting class estimator:

$$\hat{Y}_{\text{WC},k,t} = \sum_{P \in k} \sum_{p=1}^{P} w_{i,t} \frac{n_{p,t}}{r_{p,t}} \tilde{y}_{i,t} R_{i,t}$$

$n_{p,t}$ = MARTS sample size in adjustment weighting cell p at time t

$R_{i,t}$ = 1 if unit i responded to MARTS at time t, 0 otherwise

$r_{p,t} = \sum_{i \in p} R_{i,t}$ = number of MARTS respondents in adjustment weighting cell p at time t

We also considered the weighting class estimator that includes the design weights in the response propensity estimate:

$$\hat{Y}_{\text{WC},k,t} = \hat{Y}_{\text{WC}(W),k,t} = \sum_{p \in k} \sum_{p=1}^{P} w_{i,t} \frac{\sum_{i \in S_{p,t}} w_{i,t}}{\sum_{i \in S_{p,t}} w_{i,t} R_{i,t}} \tilde{y}_{i,t} R_{i,t} = \sum_{p \in k} \sum_{p=1}^{P} w_{i,t} \frac{\hat{N}_{S_{p,t}}}{\hat{N}_{r_{p,t}}} \tilde{y}_{i,t} R_{i,t}$$

where $S_{p,t}$ = the set of sampled units for cell p at time t. This is the weighting class estimator presented in Särndal and Lundström (2005, p. 70) but is also discussed in Oh and Scheuren (1983), Kalton and Kasprzyk (1986), and Little (1986).

32.3.1.4 Ratio Estimator

Auxiliary variables can also be used to create a nonresponse weighting adjustment. Särndal and Lundström (2005, pp. 71–73) describe the ratio estimator (one weighting cell) and the separate ratio estimator (multiple weighting cells), that we refer to jointly as the ratio estimator and distinguish them by adjustment levels A or B, respectively. This estimator is valid under a covariate-dependent response mechanism or under a prediction regression model, like the model shown in Eq. (32.3). Let u_i be an auxiliary variable that is observed for all units in the sample. Then the ratio estimator for the total is

$$\hat{Y}_{\text{ratio},k,t} = \sum_{p \in k} \sum_{p=1}^{P} w_{i,t} \frac{\sum_{i \in S_{p,t}} w_{i,t} u_i}{\sum_{i \in R_{p,t}} w_{i,t} u_i} \tilde{y}_{i,t} R_{i,t}$$

We considered other adjustment-weighting estimators, such as generalized regression estimators and calibration estimators. However, for MARTS, auxiliary variables are scarce and sampling variables such as MOS can quickly become out of date. We used the most timely variable available for all sampled units, prior period sales obtained from MRTS ($y_{i,t-1}$), for the auxiliary variable in the ratio estimator. Issues arising from the limited sources of auxiliary data are discussed in detail in Section 32.5.

32.3.2 Estimation Evaluation Criteria

With minimal revisions from the MARTS advance total sales estimate to the corresponding MRTS preliminary total sales estimate, we would expect an intercept of zero and a ***slope*** (β_k) of one in the following no-intercept simple linear regression model:

$$\hat{Y}_{k,\text{MRTS Prelim},t} = \beta_k \hat{Y}^m_{k,\text{MARTS},t} + \varepsilon_t, \varepsilon_t \sim \left(0, \sigma_k^2\right)$$

After fitting this model for each tabulation industry k with each MARTS candidate estimator m, we examined the distribution of the estimated slope parameters across all tabulation industries for each estimator.

The revision error of the month-to-month percent change receives the most attention and scrutiny from expert data users. Therefore, we calculated the ***absolute revision error*** of the *month-to-month percent changes* over the study period to evaluate each considered estimator.

The MARTS month-to-month percent change estimate for estimator m is defined as

$$\widehat{M}^m_{\text{MARTS},k,t} = 100 * \frac{\widehat{Y}^m_{\text{MARTS},k,t} - \widehat{Y}_{\text{MRTS Prelim},k,t-1}}{\widehat{Y}_{\text{MRTS Prelim},k,t-1}}$$

The MRTS month-to-month percent change estimate is defined as

$$\widehat{M}_{\text{MRTS},k,t} = 100 * \frac{\widehat{Y}_{\text{MRTS Prelim},k,t} - \widehat{Y}_{\text{MRTS Final},k,t-1}}{\widehat{Y}_{\text{MRTS Final},k,t-1}}$$

The absolute revision error for estimator m is defined as

$$\left| \widehat{RM}^m_t \right| = \left| \widehat{M}_{\text{MRTS},k,t} - \widehat{M}^m_{\text{MARTS},k,t} \right|$$

Note that the MRTS month-to-month percent change does not include any MARTS estimates and is therefore a constant value for comparison.

32.3.3 Estimation Empirical Results

Using data from MARTS and MRTS from May 2010 through May 2016 (the most recent data available at the time), we computed MARTS estimates with and without analyst-imputed cases. The estimates without the analyst imputes ignore the analyst-imputed values and treat the companies as nonrespondents. Due to data reconstruction limitations, the estimates used in the research may not correspond exactly to the published estimates.

Table 32.2 presents summary statistics of the estimated slope parameters by estimator with and without analyst-imputed cases for the total retail trade and food services sales estimates. The link

Table 32.2 Summary statistics for slope parameters by estimator for total retail trade and food services sales estimates with two sets of adjustment cells: (A) MARTS tabulation industry and (B) certainty status (certainty/noncertainty) within MARTS tabulation industry.

Estimator	Adjustment cells	Without analyst imputes				With analyst imputes			
		Min	Median	Mean	Max	Min	Median	Mean	Max
Link relative	A	0.97	1.00	1.00	1.01	0.98	1.00	1.00	1.01
Link relative	B	0.96	1.00	1.00	1.01	0.95	1.00	1.00	1.01
Modified link relative ES 1	A	0.97	1.00	1.00	1.01	0.99	1.00	1.00	1.01
Modified link relative ES 1	B	0.96	1.00	1.00	1.01	0.95	1.00	1.00	1.01
Modified link relative ES 2	A	n/a	n/a	n/a	n/a	0.99	1.00	1.00	1.01
Modified link relative ES 2	B	n/a	n/a	n/a	n/a	0.96	1.00	1.00	1.01
Ratio	A	0.27	1.05	1.03	1.31	0.27	1.05	1.04	1.32
Ratio	B	0.22	1.05	1.03	1.27	0.22	1.05	1.03	1.26
Weighting class unweighted	A	0.27	0.90	0.88	1.69	0.27	0.75	0.75	1.25
Weighting class unweighted	B	0.29	0.92	0.91	1.69	0.29	0.82	0.80	1.18
Weighting class weighted	A	0.17	0.58	0.63	1.69	0.08	0.48	0.51	0.96
Weighting class weighted	B	0.31	0.82	0.82	1.69	0.31	0.76	0.72	0.96

Source: MARTS and MRTS May 2010–May 2016.

Table 32.3 Summary statistics for month-to-month change absolute revision error by estimator for total retail trade and food services sales estimates with two sets of adjustment cells: (A) MARTS tabulation industry and (B) certainty status (certainty/noncertainty) within MARTS tabulation industry.

Estimator	Adjustment cells	Without analyst imputes				With analyst imputes			
		Min	Median	Mean	Max	Min	Median	Mean	Max
Link relative	A	0.01	0.31	0.37	1.29	0.00	0.29	0.31	0.82
Link relative	B	0.01	0.31	0.35	1.37	0.00	0.25	0.28	0.80
Modified link relative ES 1	A	0.00	0.31	0.38	1.33	0.01	0.27	0.31	0.90
Modified link relative ES 1	B	0.02	0.30	0.36	1.34	0.00	0.27	0.28	0.77
Modified link relative ES 2	A	n/a	n/a	n/a	n/a	0.00	0.27	0.31	0.97
Modified link relative ES 2	B	n/a	n/a	n/a	n/a	0.01	0.24	0.28	1.03
Ratio	A	0.09	6.46	6.15	10.7	0.65	6.98	6.40	11.0
Ratio	B	0.05	6.26	6.00	10.8	0.19	6.97	6.20	11.2
Weighting class unweighted	A	0.04	4.64	0.96	18.9	6.31	20.9	24.6	55.9
Weighting class unweighted	B	0.11	3.29	3.91	13.3	4.72	16.6	17.8	39.6
Weighting class weighted	A	6.62	36.0	45.0	106	25.9	53.0	75.9	183.0
Weighting class weighted	B	0.82	11.1	12.2	25.8	14.5	27.1	29.4	56.2

Source: MARTS and MRTS May 2010–May 2016.

relative and modified link relative estimators have a very tight distribution around the target value of one. The four variations on the ratio estimator are also centered close to one but have more variability. The weighting class estimator variations show the greatest deviation from the target of one, indicating these MARTS estimates are poor predictors of the corresponding MRTS estimates.

Table 32.3 provides summary statistics for the absolute revision error of month-to-month changes for the total retail trade and food services sales estimates. The link relative and modified link relative estimators have much smaller revision errors than the many variations of weighting class and ratio estimators. Mean absolute revision errors are smaller when analyst imputes are included for the link relative and modified link relative estimators but larger when they are included in the ratio and weighting class estimators. This provides anecdotal evidence of nonignorable nonresponse which is augmented by the addition of the analyst imputes that are typically the largest units in the industry.

Given the poor performance of the ratio and weighting class estimators, we excluded these estimators from further consideration. It is important to note that the weighting class estimators and ratio estimators assume ignorable response mechanisms. However, the industry-level rates of change in MARTS computed without the analyst-imputed values were very dissimilar, providing evidence against the missing at random- or covariate-dependent response mechanisms (and by extension, evidence for using the link-relative estimator). Furthermore, among the variations of the link relative and modified link relative estimators considered, improvements over the currently used link relative estimator with analyst imputes and adjustment cells defined at the industry level are marginal.

32.3.4 Estimation Discussion

Our analysis provides strong evidence that changing the MARTS estimator will not reduce the revision error between the advance estimates from MARTS and the preliminary estimates from MRTS.

Indeed, many of the results provide supporting evidence for the currently used link relative estimator in MARTS, if minimizing revisions between the two releases is the objective. This objective is not unreasonable, given that the two programs are estimating the same parameter.

Although the alternative link relative and modified link relative estimators considered performed almost as well and at times even slightly better than the currently used link relative estimator, we do not find enough evidence to motivate a change in estimator at this time. Given that no change for our estimation procedures is warranted at this time, we next chose to address the subjectivity of selecting units for analyst imputation.

32.4 Automating the Detection of High-Priority Units for Imputation

Recall that MARTS does not currently employ an automated imputation procedure. Instead, a small set of nonresponding units are subjectively selected from output listings for imputation by analysts. Analyst imputes reduce the mean absolute revision error of the link relative estimates, as shown in Table 32.3, and will continue to be used until an automated imputation procedure is recommended. However, the subjective nature of both the selection of the units for analyst imputation and the imputed values themselves add an unmeasurable error component to the final estimates and limit the reproducibility and transparency of the survey's methodology.

To address the first issue, we developed an automated, repeatable procedure for selecting units for analyst imputation, with the objective of preselecting units whose nonresponse could unduly affect the link relative ratio estimate ($\widehat{\Lambda}_{k,t}$). These units may be prioritized for analyst imputation because of their sheer size or because, historically they have substantively changed the estimated industry month-to-month change. This is distinct from the practice of excluding outlying units from the link relative ratio during estimation as mentioned in Section 32.3.1.2.

For MARTS industries comprised of a very small number of companies, all companies in the industry are included in the MARTS sample with a probability of one. For these certainty-only industries, all units are considered high priority and were, therefore, excluded from this analysis.

This section describes the methodology developed to identify high-priority units for analyst imputation in MARTS.

32.4.1 Methods for Identifying Units for Analyst Imputation

Our objective is to identify high-priority units *before* data collection, thus providing the analysts with as much time as possible to compute analyst-imputed values in anticipation of unit nonresponse. However, some of the units flagged for imputation will respond to MARTS during the seven-day collection period. In this case, the reported values replace the analyst-imputed values for these units.

32.4.1.1 Influence Measure Method (Month-to-Month Change)

We began by seeking to identify units that will have a "large" influence on the link relative ratio ($\widehat{\Lambda}_{k,t}$). The measure used to identify high-priority units follows from a method used in the Economic Census' Outlier Review Tool (Sigman 2005; Czaplicki and Thompson 2013). This method compares the ratio of a given month's total to the prior month's total for a MARTS tabulation industry to the same ratio with a single unit's weighted value removed. This provides a measure of the influence of the individual unit on the estimated month-to-month change for the industry.

Prior to data collection, we cannot know which units will have a large effect on the estimate of the month-to-month change. Therefore, we use the units that have a large effect in the prior month (lag 1), to capture recent patterns, or prior year (lag 12), to capture seasonal patterns, to identify potentially influential units in the current month estimates. We define the influence of unit i in industry k at time $t-a$, where a is either 1 or 12 for all units in the current MARTS sample, as follows:

$$\text{Influence}_{i,k,t-a} = \frac{\widehat{Y}_{\text{HT},k,t-a}}{\widehat{Y}_{\text{HT},k,t-a-1}} - \frac{\widehat{Y}_{\text{HT}(i),k,t-a}}{\widehat{Y}_{\text{HT}(i),k,t-a-1}}$$

where

$$\widehat{Y}_{\text{HT},k,t-a} = \sum w_{i,t-a} y_{i,t-a}$$
$$\widehat{Y}_{\text{HT}(i),k,t-a} = \widehat{Y}_{\text{HT},k,t-a} - w_{i,t-a} y_{i,t-a}$$
$$\widehat{Y}_{\text{HT}(i),k,t-a-1} = \widehat{Y}_{\text{HT},k,t-a-1} - w_{i,t-a} y_{i,t-a-1}$$

Note that $y_{i,t-a}$ is obtained from MRTS in order to have a nonmissing value for all units and can be reported, machine-imputed, or analyst imputed.

Sigman (2005) sorts the entire set of sampled units by descending influence measure; starting at the top, analysts review as many units as time allows. The MARTS analysts wanted the method to provide a complete list of units for review and potential imputation that could be completed during the seven-day MARTS collection period. Certainty units, which have sufficient historic data to produce a "good" imputed value according to the method described in Section 32.2.5, were prioritized over noncertainty units, which often have limited historic data for producing an imputed value. Furthermore, even with the very limited production timeline, analysts were very concerned with missing a large, potentially high-priority unit which led us to focus on minimizing Type II error rather than Type I error.

To create the list of units for analyst imputation, we developed a cutoff value for the influence measure; units were flagged for imputation if the absolute value of the influence measure exceeded the cutoff value. The cutoff value was calculated by multiplying a standard normal critical value (z) at the 5% significance level by the standard error of the estimated month-to-month change ratio $\left(\frac{\widehat{Y}_{\text{HT},k,t-a}}{\widehat{Y}_{\text{HT},k,t-a-1}} \right)$, with separate cutoff values for the lag 1 ($a = 1$) and lag 12 ($a = 12$) ratios. The standard error was obtained using the SAS® procedure PROC SURVEYMEANS, thus accounting for the complex sampling design under 100% response (certainty units excluded from the sampling variance computations).

The cutoff values were often so large that no units were flagged in several industries, which raised a concern about missing large, potentially high-priority units. Subject matter experts provided alternative industry-specific thresholds based on their expert knowledge. These alternative thresholds were used when they were less than the calculated industry cutoff values to identify additional *certainty units* for imputation. Noncertainty units were still subject to the calculated industry cutoff values. Figure 32.3 summarizes this process for the case where the calculated cutoff value exceeds the alternative threshold.

32.4.1.2 Size Identification Method

The influence measure described above is unlikely to flag even a very large unit for imputation if the historic month-to-month change for the unit is very close to the historic month-to-month change for the rest of the industry. This was observed on several instances during the research. In some industries, these very large units can comprise 30% or more of the total industry's sales, making

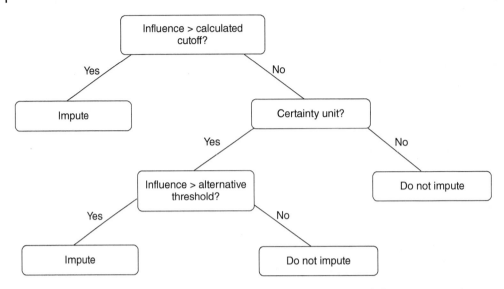

Figure 32.3 Decision tree depicting when a unit will be imputed based its influence measure in comparison to the cutoff values appropriate for the unit's size (certainty or noncertainty) when the calculated cutoff exceeds the alternative threshold.

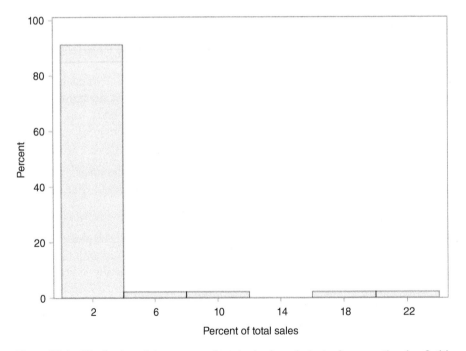

Figure 32.4 Distribution of the percent of total sales in an industry for a month using fictitious data.

them a priority for analyst imputation by their sheer size alone. Therefore, we developed a second method (**size identification method**) to identify units for analyst imputation based on a unit's weighted contribution to historic totals, with the objective of consistently flagging exceptionally large – and possibly outlying – units in the industry for analyst imputation.

Upon examination of industry-level histograms of the percentage of total sales, we observed that industries with large units (the target of this method) often had a clear break in the distribution between the large units and the rest of the units in the industry. Figure 32.4 illustrates this pattern using fictitious data. Industries without notably large units did not exhibit this stark break.

We developed a simple outlier detection method to identify units that fall above the natural break in the distribution if it exists. We calculated the weighted contribution to historic total sales attributable to each unit. Then we applied the natural log transformation to the percentage of the total sales for each unit $(q_{i,t-a})$. We calculated the mean $(\bar{q}_{t-a})$ and standard deviation (sd_{t-a}) for the transformed distribution without design weights because this analysis was specific to the current sample and not used for inference for the larger population. Finally, z-scores $\left(\frac{q_{i,t-a}-\bar{q}_{t-a}}{\mathrm{sd}_{t-a}}\right)$ were calculated for each unit in the transformed distribution. Units with z-scores that exceed the z-critical value at the 5% significance level were identified as high-priority units. Like the influence measure method, the size identification method was performed with data from the prior month $(a = 1)$ and the prior year $(a = 12)$.

32.4.1.3 Prioritization

High-priority units for imputation were first identified within tabulation industries, using both the influence measure method and the size identification method. Recall from Section 32.2.4 that many of the published industry estimates from MARTS are aggregates of several MARTS tabulation industries. Thus, units that affect estimates at the publication level are of particularly high priority for analyst imputation. We used the influence measure method with cells defined by the most disaggregated level of publication to further prioritize *certainty* units for potential imputation. Finally, a global score is created for each unit equal to the number of times the unit was flagged for imputation. The identified units are sorted in descending order to prioritize units with the highest score. Certainty units can be flagged up to six times in a given time period. Noncertainty units can be flagged up to four times. Table 32.4 summarizes the methods applicable to certainty and noncertainty units.

Table 32.4 Summary of methods applied to certainty and noncertainty units.

Method	Certainty	Noncertainty
Tabulation level		
$\text{Influence}_{\text{tab},t-1}$	X	X
$\text{Influence}_{\text{tab},t-12}$	X	X
$\text{Size}_{\text{tab},t-1}$	X	X
$\text{Size}_{\text{tab},t-12}$	X	X
Lowest publication level		
$\text{Influence}_{\text{pub},t-1}$	X	
$\text{Influence}_{\text{pub},t-12}$	X	

Table 32.5 Measures of classification performance used in the confusion matrix evaluation of the high priority units for analyst imputation identification method.

Statistic	Description
TP	Number of true positives
TN	Number of true negatives
FP	Number of false positives
FN	Number of false negatives
True positive rate	$\dfrac{TP}{TP + FN}$
True negative rate	$\dfrac{TN}{TN + FP}$
Precision	$\dfrac{TP}{TP + FP}$
Type I error rate	$1 - \dfrac{TN}{TN + FP}$
Type II error rate	$1 - \dfrac{TP}{TP + FN}$

32.4.2 Identifying High-Priority Units for Analyst Imputation Evaluation

Using the proposed methodology, we obtained a set of "true" high priority units based upon the influence measure and size identification procedure in the *current* month ($\text{Influence}_{\text{tab},t}$, $\text{Influence}_{\text{pub},t}$ and $\text{Size}_{\text{tab},t}$). Borrowing from the machine learning evaluation literature, we produced a confusion matrix for each month in the study period to compare the predicted set of high-priority units to the "true" set (Tan et al. 2018). Table 32.5 provides descriptions of the statistics used in the evaluation.

We tested the proposed methodology using data from January 2016 to December 2016. The number of high priority units flagged for imputation varied between 216 and 246 out of a sample of approximately 5000 units. The evaluation of the proposed method for identifying high-priority units for imputation is summarized in Table 32.6.

Over the study period, 95% to nearly 99% of the "true high priority units" were flagged for analyst imputation using the proposed method (True Positive Rate). Conversely, between 1% and 7% of high priority units in the current month were not identified as high priority units with the proposed method; therefore, the Type II error rate was at acceptable levels, at negligible cost to the Type I error rate. Examining the efficiency of the proposed method, between 77% and 86% of flagged high priority units were "true high priority units" (Precision), which translates to between 14% and 23% erroneously flagged units. In practical terms, this translates to time spent by an analyst to develop an imputed value for a unit that may not have needed to be imputed.

32.4.3 Identifying High-Priority Units for Analyst Imputation Discussion

In this section, we described an automated, repeatable method to identify companies for analyst imputation, removing one source of subjectivity from the analyst imputation procedure. Invaluable subject matter expertise is still employed in selecting some of the method parameters, such as the

Table 32.6 Evaluation statistics from confusion matrix evaluation of the high-priority units for analyst imputation identification method.

Month	True positive rate	True negative rate	Precision	Type I error rate	Type II error rate
January 2016	95.1	98.9	79.3	1.1	4.9
February 2016	92.7	99.1	81.2	0.9	7.3
March 2016	97.3	98.9	77.8	1.1	2.7
April 2016	97.3	99.2	82.9	0.8	2.7
May 2016	97.3	99.3	84.7	0.7	2.7
June 2016	95.2	99.2	82.9	0.8	4.8
July 2016	97.4	99.3	84.9	0.7	2.6
August 2016	98.0	99.2	83.8	0.8	2.0
September 2016	98.9	99.2	82.7	0.8	1.1
October 2016	96.3	99.2	82.3	0.8	3.7
November 2016	95.2	99.1	80.9	0.9	4.8
December 2016	96.2	99.3	86.1	0.7	3.8
Mean	96.4	99.2	82.5	0.9	3.6

alternative cutoff levels for the influence measure, but once the parameters are set, the method is objective and replicable. Parallel testing is currently underway to compare the current MARTS tabulations to those computed with analyst-imputed values only for those companies that were flagged for imputation by the proposed methodology. This testing will allow us to determine if adjustments are needed to the influence and size detection parameters, given the more recent data.

32.5 Automating Imputation Procedures

In this section, we introduce two different imputation models designed to replace the subjective analyst imputation procedures and present results from a simulation study, comparing the statistical properties of each method using the current MARTS link relative estimator. Of the many considered methods, we eliminated other models early due to their relative poor performance coupled with restrictive demands on modeling data; this included but was not limited to nearest neighbor hot deck imputation, propensity score matching, support vector regression, regression trees, and vector autoregression.

32.5.1 Imputation Model

Retail sales at the national level typically follow a very predicable seasonal pattern, including calendar effects such as trading day, leap year, and holidays. Unfortunately, as alluded to in Section 32.3, there are very limited auxiliary company level (unit level) data that is available for use in imputation models. The available data are the following:

- Current month MARTS respondents
- Historic MRTS data (reported or imputed)

Table 32.7 Imputation models.

Method	Imputation cell	Imputation unit	Software	Stochastic	Sections
RegARIMA forecast	MARTS tabulation industry	Tabulation	SAS	No	32.5.1.1
Hierarchical Bayesian regression	MARTS tabulation industry	Tabulation	rStan	Yes	32.5.1.2

- Frame MOS
- Industry codes (NAICS)
- Sample design parameters

Table 32.7 outlines two imputation models that make use of the above auxiliary data to impute missing values in the current month. Each model is discussed in greater detail below.

32.5.1.1 RegARIMA Time Series Model

Time series can often be modeled as a regression model with ARIMA errors, i.e. a RegARIMA model. The regression component may contain predefined regressors, such as trading day effects, moving holiday effects (Bell and Hillmer 1983), and outliers, with the errors following an ARIMA process (Box and Jenkins 1970). For this imputation method, we fit a RegARIMA model for each MARTS industry using estimates beginning January 2006 and ending the month prior to the month being imputed, then apply the ARIMA model parameters and estimated calendar adjustment factors to the *tabulation* unit data to produce a one-step ahead unit-level forecast as the imputed value.

We used X-13ARIMA-SEATS (X-13A-S), the seasonal adjustment software used at the Census Bureau, to identify the RegARIMA models, following closely to the model selection procedures used by MARTS in the seasonal adjustment process. Each industry series was log transformed and included either the six-coefficient trading day regressor (Bell and Hillmer 1983) or the one-coefficient trading day regressor (Gómez and Maravall 1996). Significant moving holiday regressors for Easter, Labor Day, or Thanksgiving were included in the model if the corresponding t-statistic of the model parameter was greater than 1.96 in absolute value (US Census Bureau 2017, p. 71). We did not explicitly identify outliers for the model beyond the automatically identified-level shift and additive outliers from X-13A-S. However, identified outliers were used for model estimation but were excluded from the calculation of the unit-level forecasts. Since the parameters estimated from the model are applied to tabulation unit-level data to produce a forecast, we only considered autoregressive models. The final ARIMA model selected for every industry was (1 1 0)(1 0 0); that is, order 1 nonseasonal and seasonal components and a nonseasonal first difference. This maximized the number of eligible tabulation units for imputation, as the forecasts only require unit-level values from $t-1$, $t-2$, $t-12$, $t-13$, and $t-14$. For more details on the RegARIMA forecast procedure, see Czaplicki and González (2019).

The calculation of the imputed value for MARTS unit i in time t, $\widetilde{y}_{i,t}'$, begins with the calendar adjustment and transformation of the unit's historic values. Let $\widetilde{x}_{i,t-1} = \ln(\widetilde{y}_{i,t-1}/l_{k,t-1})$ be the calendar-adjusted, transformed value for unit i in time $t-1$, where $l_{k,t-1}$ is the calendar adjustment factor in month $t-1$ for industry k and let other months be similarly defined. The calendar adjusted, transformed forecast for unit i in time t, $\widetilde{x}_{i,t}'$ is given below, where $\varphi_{k,1}$ and $\varphi_{k,12}$ are the industry k parameter estimates for the lag 1 and lag 12 autoregressive components, respectively. The imputed value, $\widetilde{y}'_{i,t}$, is obtained by simply exponentiating the transformed forecast and multiplying by the current month calendar adjustment factor.

$$\widetilde{x}'_{i,t} = (1 + \varphi_{k,1})\widetilde{x}_{i,t-1} - \varphi_{k,1}\widetilde{x}_{i,t-2} + \varphi_{k,12}\widetilde{x}_{i,t-12} - (\varphi_{k,1}\varphi_{k,12} + \varphi_{k,12})\widetilde{x}_{i,t-13} + \varphi_{k,1}\varphi_{k,12}\widetilde{x}_{i,t-14}$$

$$\widetilde{y}'_{i,t} = l_{k,t}e^{\widetilde{x}'_{i,t}}$$

This method assumes that the trading day effects, moving holiday effects, and historic data patterns estimated at the industry level are also applicable at the unit level.

32.5.1.2 Hierarchical Bayesian Regression (HBR) Model

Hierarchical (or multilevel) regression models incorporate covariate information at different levels of variation. There are two levels of variation with the MARTS data: industry across time and tabulation unit within industry. We fit the following hierarchical regression model to obtain a single-month prediction:

$$\ln(\widetilde{y}_{i,k,t}) = \alpha_{k,t} + \beta_{k,t} \ln(\widetilde{y}_{i,k,t-1}) + \delta_{j,k} + \varepsilon_{i,k,t}$$

$\varepsilon_{i,k,t} \sim N\left(0, \sigma_k^2\right)$ Error term for tabulation unit i in MARTS industry k at time t

$\alpha_{k,t} \sim N\left(\mu_{\alpha_k}, \sigma_{\alpha_k}^2\right)$ Intercept for MARTS industry k at time t

$\beta_{k,t} \sim N\left(\mu_{\beta_k}, \sigma_{\beta_k}^2\right)$ Slope for MARTS industry k at time t

$\delta_{i,k} \sim N\left(0, \sigma_{\delta_k}^2\right)$ Random intercept for tabulation unit i in MARTS industry k

where $\widetilde{y}_{i,k,t}$ is the sales value for unit i in industry k at time t ($t = 0, -12, -24,$ and -36, where 0 is the current month). This formulation borrows strength across time within industry, assuming that parameters follow a similar distribution. Current month data are modeled using a current-to-prior month regression (addressing seasonality), but incorporate more complete data from the past samples with higher response rates. Note that we model current-to-prior month change for the current month ($t = 0$) and the corresponding current-to-prior month change in prior years, not the full time series from $t = 0$ to $t = -36$. The model includes a random effect to account for a unit's deviation from the industry trend. All priors that are not defined are uniform over their constrained values. Model parameters are estimated using the open-source probabilistic programming language Stan (https:// mc-stan.org) in *R*. Stan uses the No-U-Turn sampler, which is a variation of Hamiltonian Monte Carlo. This efficient sampler converges quickly when compared to other samplers, like Gibbs samplers (Hoffman and Gelman 2011, 2014). Imputed values of sales use an estimate (median) from the posterior distribution of each unit, transformed back to the original scale. A variational inference algorithm was used to approximate the posterior distribution in the simulation study to reduce runtime but should not be used for any official statistics (Kucukelbir et al. 2015).

32.5.2 Simulation Study

The model-building stage for each of the proposed methods listed in Section 32.5.1 was conducted independently, using different test decks. Furthermore, to eliminate confounding of imputation model and estimator, there was limited assessment of interaction with the link relative estimator. To compare the performance of the candidate imputation methods in a pseudo-production setting, we conducted a coordinated simulation study using the same test decks for both imputation methods and including assessment of interaction with the link relative estimator. The simulation study used frame data from historic MRTS respondents, from which we selected repeated samples, mimicking key features of the MARTS design. This allowed us to evaluate the models on reported data, which can contain highly irregular distributions and varying seasonal and nonseasonal components and eliminated potential cofounding from the currently used MRTS imputation model. This approach also created real time-series from which to impute, avoiding artificially inducing conditions more appropriate for one of the considered approaches.

32.5.2.1 Simulation Study Design

For each month in 2016, we independently constructed a frame from MRTS respondents. Constructing a single frame for 2016 was infeasible because it requires a unit to respond in all 12 months, which reduced the eligible frame units to an insufficient level. We then merged up to an additional three years of historic unit level MRTS data onto each frame. Only the current month was limited to reported data; the source of the historic data was either reported or imputed.

For the results of the simulation study to be generalizable to the production survey, it is important that the time series properties of the study dataset closely resemble the time series properties of the complete data. Consequently, we dropped seven MARTS industries from the study, after comparing the autocorrelation functions (ACFs) for MARTS tabulation industries constructed using only MRTS reported values against those constructed from the full MRTS data (reported and imputed units). Accordingly, the simulation study results cannot be used to make inferences for the complete MARTS.

We determined new strata boundaries in each MARTS industry using the method introduced by Lavallée and Hidiroglou (1988) with the current month sales as the MOS and Neyman allocation to determine sampling rates. We lowered the targeted industry coefficient of variation until the achieved sample sizes were proportional in size to the production ratio of MARTS sample size to the MRTS sample size within industry. For each month (frame), we independently selected 500 PPS samples using the MRTS sampling weight as the MOS, mirroring the production design.

We used historic unit response rates to estimate response propensities for MARTS, assuming a missing at random response mechanism. Certainty units within a MARTS tabulation industry were split into two categories using cum-root-f rules using sales as the MOS for response propensity estimation, whereas all noncertainty units within a MARTS tabulation industry were placed into a single group (Czaplicki and González 2019, showed differences in response among certainty units of differing sizes, motivating this choice). Any estimated response propensities of zero or one were replaced by 0.05 and 0.95, respectively, and any units with missing response propensities were assigned a response propensity of 0.50. Finally, for each sample, nonresponse was randomly induced within the tabulation industry size categories defined above. Thus, the simulation study implements a missing-at-random (ignorable) response mechanism, although earlier research indicates a nonignorable response mechanism for MARTS.

32.5.2.2 Evaluation Statistics

A "true" MRTS total was estimated for each monthly respondent frame using the Horvitz–Thompson estimator, (i). This "true" MRTS total was compared to a MARTS link relative (ii) total estimated for each sample and imputation method. Specific to our research, we screened imputations for unrealistic values by comparing current-to-prior month change at the unit level. The resistant fences outlier detection method presented in Hoaglin et al. (1986) was applied to the ratio of the current-to-prior month $\left(\widetilde{y}^{j}_{i,t} / \widetilde{y}_{i,t-1} \right)$ within each industry to exclude unreasonably large- or small-imputed values. Outlier detection was only applied in industries that had 10 or more responding units available to calculate the industry-level tolerances.

To assess performance of each imputation model (when combined with link relative estimation) over repeated samples, we computed a conditional relative bias estimates at the tabulation level for each imputation model and for the No Imputation method (conditional on the MRTS realized sample of respondents). The No Imputation estimates serves as baseline for comparison.

$$
\mathrm{RB}\left(\hat{\overline{Y}}^{m}_{\mathrm{LR},k,t}\right) = 100 * \frac{\left(\hat{\overline{Y}}^{m}_{\mathrm{LR},k,t} - \hat{Y}_{\mathrm{MRTS},k,t}\right)}{\hat{Y}_{\mathrm{MRTS},k,t}}
$$

where

$\hat{Y}_{\mathrm{MRTS},k,t}$ = MRTS Horvitz–Thompson estimate of sales for industry k, and month t

$\hat{\overline{Y}}'_{\mathrm{LR},k,t} = \sum_{s}\hat{Y}'_{\mathrm{LR},k,t,s}/500$ = Average link relative estimate over s = 500 repeated samples for industry k, month t, and imputation model m

32.5.2.3 Simulation Results

Simulation results were compiled for each of the considered imputation methods across the 23 MARTS tabulation industries in the simulation for the 12-month study period, resulting in 828 estimates. To summarize results, for each month and industry, we score a method as one if it is the least biased and zero otherwise, then sum within industry and method to create the contingency table (Table 32.8). The method that performed the "best" for an industry is marked by double asterisks; this does not indicate a significant difference. All contingency table tests for independence use a 5% significance level. The marginal totals between methods are not significantly different (X-squared = 3.739, df = 2, p-value = 0.1542). Table 32.8 does provide evidence of an association between industry and imputation method (p-value < 0.0001) using the Fisher's Exact Test with simulated p-value.

However, these count analyses do not capture large or small differences in the magnitude of bias for a single month within industry. In some cases, all methods could have practically the same relative bias (minimal differences); in other cases, one method could outperform the others. To assess this visually, we examined box plots to compare the distribution of the relative bias estimates for each method for the 12 months in the study. Figure 32.5 presents boxplots for select industries where the No Imputation method yields the least biased estimates. The referenced magnitude problem is visible with industry 443120; although the No Imputation method had the least biased estimates 6 out of the 12 months, it also exhibits a single month with relative bias near 60%. This large bias was reduced by either imputation model, while producing comparable estimates in other months. So while the No Imputation method had the smallest bias in 6 out of the 12 months, one of the alternative methods may be preferable. Industry 441300 shows the reverse, with all methods producing approximate the same relative bias except for a single month with relative biases with either imputation method approximately 10% larger than the corresponding No Imputation estimates.

To summarize, there are clear improvements in relative bias for a subset of study industries with automatic imputation. However, neither proposed automatic imputation model consistently improved relative bias in these industries. Each imputation model incorporates features of the tabulation industry time series: the RegARIMA and HBR methods attempt to incorporate seasonal effects in the imputations by including year-to-year data (lag 12) and No Imputation method incorporates current-to-prior month data (lag 1) via the link relative estimator.

Figure 32.6 investigates the relationship between imputation method and industry time series characteristics. Using a similar procedure as in Table 32.8, we count the number of months in which

Table 32.8 Number of months with the least biased estimates by industry and method (**Best).

	Method		
NAICS	**No imputation**	**RegARIMA**	**HBR**
441100	**9	0	3
441200	**4	**4	**4
441300	**6	3	3
443120	**6	4	2
443X00	1	**8	3
444100	2	**7	3
444200	**6	1	5
447000	**8	1	3
448110	1	5	**6
448120	*6	2	4
4481L0	1	5	**6
448200	3	3	**6
448310	**5	2	**5
4511X0	3	**5	4
451XX0	4	1	**7
452110	**5	**5	2
452120	1	3	**8
452910	**6	4	2
453210	2	**9	1
454100	**6	4	2
454310	**6	0	**6
454X00	**6	2	4
722000	**7	0	5
Total	104	78	94

Fisher's Exact Test with simulated p-value <0.0001.

each *missing data approach* (automated imputation via RegARIMA or HBR versus No Imputation) yielded the lowest relative bias, with a tie indicating a count of six for both automated imputation and No Imputation. Figure 32.6 presents the ACF Lag 1 and ACF Lag 12 coefficients for each studied MARTS tabulation industry. A triangle represents improved performance using either automated imputation method in a majority of months, a star indicates improved performance using the No Imputation method in a majority of months, and a solid circle indicates a tie.

The industries in the lower right quadrant have a strong lag 1 correlation and a weak lag 12 correlation, corresponding to the regression model assumptions specified for the link relative estimator. The industries in the upper left quadrant have a strong lag 12 correlation and a weak lag 1 correlation, indicating a stronger seasonal pattern. Consequently, the imputation methods that directly utilize the lag 12 data yield substantive improvements for these industries.

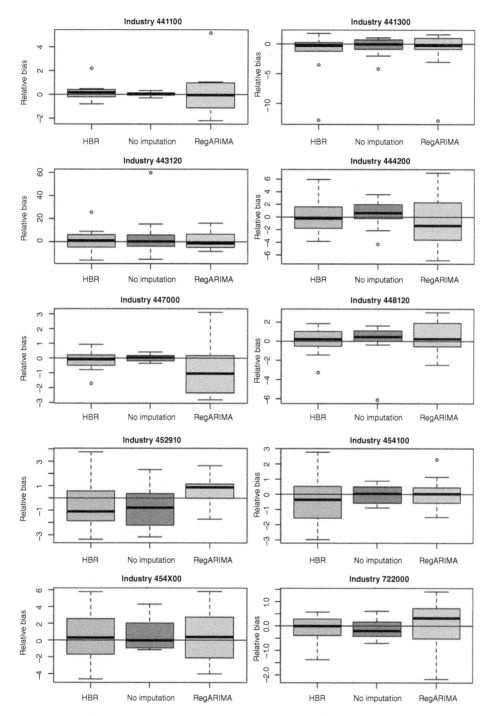

Figure 32.5 Relative bias for select NAICS industries. Please note, each plot has a different scale on the vertical axis.

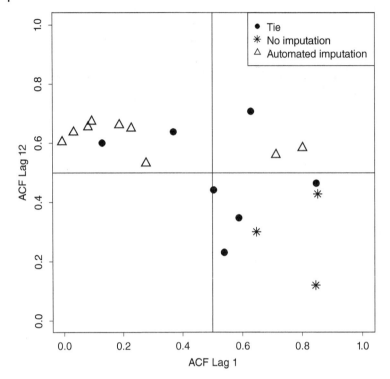

Figure 32.6 Best performing missing data approach (No Imputation versus Automated Imputation) by industry plotted against the values of the Lag 1 and Lag 12 autocorrelation functions.

32.5.3 Imputation Discussion

To assess the relative performance of the considered imputation methods, we conducted a simulation study by selecting repeated samples from a frame of empirical reported MRTS data, matching historic data from the same units to create real time series. In doing so, we had to drop selected industries, so the simulation results are not generalizable to the entire survey. Additionally, the results are dependent on the MARTS stratified PPS without replacement design. Remaining consistent with the objective to minimize revisions between corresponding MARTS and MRTS totals, the relative bias measures deviation from the MRTS estimates, not the corresponding population variables. Furthermore, the simulation study included varying response propensities across size categories resulting in a missing-at-random response mechanism, whereas it is likely that the MARTS response mechanism is nonignorable.

Regardless, the simulation study gave us a better understanding of the strengths and weaknesses of each imputation model in conjunction with the link relative estimator for the advance survey. With the two automatic imputation methods, we saw improved performance over No Imputation with industries with strong seasonal patterns in the time series, and we saw degraded performance when the seasonal pattern is weak. The latter pattern occurs in industries with weak seasonal trends, changing economic conditions, or unexpected price shocks.

The COVID-19 pandemic that began in 2020 has – at least temporarily – changed the seasonal patterns of many retail trade industries. In that case, the best predictor of the current value is likely to be from the most recent past. For now, we are conducting parallel testing with the RegARIMA and HBR models on 2019 and 2020 data. This will allow us to compare our modeled imputations with current analyst imputations to analyze how each approach affects production estimates.

32.6 Conclusion

Thompson et al. (2018) open the Special Issue from the Fifth International Conference on Establishment Surveys in the *Journal of Official Statistics* by stating

> Establishment surveys provide economic measures that change economies…Economic indicators move markets. Interest rate hikes and decreases follow the release of economic statistics. Definitions change as economies mature or become global. Data users include policymakers, business communities, and economists. The demand for timely, relevant, and accurate economic measures continues to increase, even as establishment surveys are plagued by the same decreasing response rates and budget challenges as their household counterparts.

The demand for quick turnaround in economic indicators is not a new phenomenon, nor is the understanding that this demand can have a large accuracy cost – at least among expert users and methodologists. Indeed, more than 25 years ago, Cox and Chinnappa (1995, Chapter 1, p. 15) stated, "Research is needed to identify methods that produce preliminary estimates that are good predictors of the final revised estimates."

Issues of estimate precision and bias are augmented in business surveys, whose populations are highly skewed. Program managers are especially cognizant of the important contribution that the largest businesses make to survey totals, and survey operation procedures are designed to increase the likelihood of obtaining valid responses from these large units. Even so, the priorities for receiving and giving timely and complete data differ for the sampled businesses that provide the data and the NSI that publishes the indicators. Certainly, the unit response rates for the *same* reference month in MARTS and MRTS are quite different, with differences attributable to a variety of factors including length of collection period and number of sampled units.

In this chapter, we present an evaluation of nearly all methodological facets of an economic indicator. Although the formulations considered are very specific to the advance indicator survey, the research approaches are not. The estimator evaluation compares alternative estimators using the same respondent data as advocated in Groves and Brick (2005). The high priority unit detection evaluation uses well-known outlier detection methods presented in numerous business data evaluations (Thompson and Sigman 1999; Bechtel 2011; Czaplicki and Thompson 2013), as well as in the machine learning evaluation literature (Tan et al. 2018). Finally, the imputation procedures introduce innovative approaches to modeling time-series data with irregular features.

That said, the studied methods are highly dependent on stationary time series, assuming a regularity in the autoregressive (prior to current) component as well as a strong seasonal pattern (high-priority unit detection and imputation methods). Sudden economic shocks, like the COVID-19 pandemic of 2020, disrupt the existing seasonal patterns. The pandemic also made what was previously a relatively rare occurrence more commonplace: reported sales of zero dollars. At present, it is unclear how these changes should be addressed, or whether it is necessary to address them at all once the retail trade economy stabilizes.

Of course, statistics produced from a reduced sample size can be imprecise. At best, nonresponse increases the sampling variance. At worst, it introduces nonresponse bias. By design, the MARTS subsample is less than half the size of MRTS. MARTS response rates are often well below 50%. In a business survey setting, the contention that the realized respondent set remains a probability sample is debatable given the (traditional) emphasis on obtaining responses from the larger sampled units. In this setting, one could argue that sampled smaller units "opt in" to respond; with MARTS, one could make a similar argument for the late reporting larger units. In fact, several discussions of the summary report of the AAPOR Task Force on nonprobability sampling (Baker et al. 2013) specifically question whether "a probability sample with less than full coverage and high nonresponse should still be considered a probability sample." Viewed from this perspective, it may be overly optimistic to assume that an automated imputation method for MARTS can overcome both the bias and variance obstacles caused by unit nonresponse. This optimism is further damaged by the disruption caused by the COVID-19 pandemic.

That said, optimistic does not mean impossible. The demand for more timely economic indicators has increased in light of the pandemic and is unlikely to decrease. Producing precise and accurate short-term statistics is challenging, especially with the public scrutiny placed on revisions. In essence, this chapter presents a framework for this necessary research while laying out the limitations created by other factors imposed by the advanced publication. We remain hopeful that our research will lead to large improvements in survey operations and data quality. At the same time, we are also realists, recognizing that ultimately other – perhaps more radical – changes may be needed to completely and consistently align corresponding MARTS and MRTS measures.

Acknowledgments

The authors would like to thank Katherine Jenny Thompson, Jim Hunt, Joseph Barth, and Scott Scheleur for their careful review and comments on earlier version of this manuscript. The authors would also like to thank Brian Dumbacher, Adam Smeltz, Scott Holan, Yarissa González, Michael Farina, Artaud Hourticolon Retzler, and Yeng Xiong for their contributions to this research.

Disclaimer

Any views expressed are those of the authors and not those of the Census Bureau. The Census Bureau has reviewed this data product for unauthorized disclosure of confidential information and has approved the disclosure avoidance practices applied. (Approval ID: CBDRB-FY21-ESMD001-012).

References

Andridge, R. and Thompson, K.J. (2015). Assessing nonresponse bias in a business survey: proxy pattern-mixture analysis for skewed data. *The Annals of Applied Statistics* 9 (4): 2237–2265.

Baker, R., Brick, J.K., Bates, N.A., Battaglia, M., Couper, M.P., Dever, J.A., Gile, K.J., and Tourangeau, R. (2013). Summary report of the AAPOR task force on non-probability sampling. *Journal of Survey Statistics and Methodology* 1 (2): 90–137.

Bechtel, L.T. (2011). Retro-fitting a simpler outlier detection procedure into a complex generalized system. *Proceedings of Statistics Canada Symposium*, Statistics Canada, Ottawa, Ontario, Canada.

Bell, W.R. and Hillmer, S.C. (1983). Modeling time series with calendar variation. *Journal of the American Statistical Association* 78: 526–534.

Box, G.E.P. and Jenkins, G.M. (1970). *Time Series Analysis, Forecasting and Control*. San Francisco, CA: Holden-Day.

Cox, B.G. and Chinnappa, B.N. (1995). Unique features of business surveys. In: *Business Survey Methods* (ed. B.G. Cox, D.A. Binder, B.N. Chinnappa, A. Christianson, M.J. Colledge, and P.S. Kott), 1–17. New York: Wiley.

Czaplicki, N. and González, Y. (2019). Imputing seasonal data in an advanced indicator with forecasts from X-13ARIMA-SEATS. *Proceedings of the Government Statistics Section*, American Statistical Association, Denver, Colorado, USA.

Czaplicki, N. and Thompson, K.J. (2013). Outlier detection for the manufacturing, mining, and construction sectors in the 2012 Economic Census. *Proceedings of the Survey Research Methods Section*, American Statistical Association, Montreal, Quebec, Canada.

Czaplicki, N., Gonzalez, Y., and Bechtel, L. (2018). Finding an estimator that minimizes revisions in a monthly indicator survey. *Proceedings of the 2018 Federal Committee on Statistical Methodology Research Conference*, Washington, DC, USA.

Dalenius, T. and Hodges, J.L. Jr., (1959). Minimum variance stratification. *Journal of the American Statistical Association* 54: 88–101.

Gómez, V. and Maravall, A. (1996). Programs TRAMO and SEATS, Instructions for the User (Beta Version: September 1996), Banco de España – Servicio de Estudios, Documento de Trabajo no. 9628 (English version).

Groves, R.M. and Brick, M. (2005). *Practical Tools for Nonresponse Bias Studies. Joint Program in Survey Methodology Short Course*. Maryland, USA: Bethesda.

Hoaglin, D.C., Iglewicz, B., and Tukey, J.W. (1986). Performance of some resistant rules for outlier labeling. *Journal of the American Statistical Association* 81 (396): 991–999.

Hoffman, M.D., and Gelman, A. (2011). The No-U-Turn sampler: adaptively setting path lengths in Hamiltonian Monte Carlo. arXiv 1111.4246. http://arxiv.org/abs/1111.4246.

Hoffman, M.D. and Gelman, A. (2014). The No-U-Turn sampler: adaptively setting path lengths in Hamiltonian Monte Carlo. *Journal of Machine Learning Research* 15: 1593–1623. http://jmlr.org/papers/v15/hoffman14a.html.

Horvitz, D.G. and Thompson, D.J. (1952). A generalization of sampling without replacement from a finite universe. *Journal of the American Statistical Association* 47: 663–685.

Huang, E.T. (1984). An imputation study for the Monthly Retail Trade Survey. In: *Proceedings of the Section on Survey Research Methods*, 610–615. American Statistical Association.

Huang, E.T. (1986). Report on the imputation research for the Monthly Retail Trade Survey. *Statistical Research Report Series No. CENSUS/SRD/RR-86-09*. Washington, DC: U.S. Census Bureau. https://www.census.gov/srd/papers/pdf/rr86-09.pdf (accessed 31 March 2021).

Kalton, G. and Kasprzyk, D. (1986). The treatment of missing survey data. *Survey Methodology* 12 (1): 1–16.

Kucukelbir, A., Ranganath, R., Gelman, A., and Blei, D.M. (2015). Automatic variational inference in Stan. arXiv 1506.03431. http://arxiv.org/abs/1506.03431.

Lavallée, P. and Hidiroglou, M. (1988). On the stratification of skewed populations. *Survey Methodology* 14: 33–43.

Little, R.J.A. (1986). Survey nonresponse adjustments for estimates of means. *International Statistical Review* 54: 139–157.

Little, R.J. and Vartivarian, S. (2005). Does weighting for nonresponse increase the variance of survey means. *Survey Methodology* 31 (2): 161–168.

Madow, L.H. and Madow, W.G. (1978). On link relative estimators. In: *Proceedings of the Section on Survey Research Methods*, 534–539. American Statistical Association.

Oh, H.L. and Scheuren, F.J. (1983). Weighting adjustments for unit nonresponse. In: *Incomplete Data in Sample Surveys*, vol. 2 (ed. W.G. Madow, I. Olkin and D.B. Rubin), 143–184. New York: Academic Press.

Rao, J.N.K. (2003). *Small Area Estimation*. New York: Wiley.

Särndal, C. and Lundström, S. (2005). *Estimation in Surveys with Nonresponse*. Hoboken, NJ: Wiley.

Sigman, R.S. (2005). Statistical methods used to detect cell-level and respondent-level outliers in the 2002 Economic Census of the Services Sector. *Proceedings of the Section on Survey Research Methods*, American Statistical Association, Minneapolis, Minnesota, USA.

Tan, P.N., Steinbach, M., Karpatne, A., and Kumar, V. (2018). *Introduction to Data Mining*. New York: Pearson.

Thompson, K.J. and Oliver, B. (2012). Response rates in business surveys: going beyond the usual performance measure. *Journal of Official Statistics* 28 (2): 221–237.

Thompson, K.J. and Sigman, R. (1999). Statistical methods for developing ratio edit tolerances for economic data. *Journal of Official Statistics* 15 (4): 517–535.

Thompson, K.J., Oliver, B., and Beck, J. (2015). An analysis of the mixed collection modes for two business surveys conducted By the U.S. Census Bureau. *Public Opinion Quarterly* 79 (3): 769–789.

Thompson, K.J., Phipps, P., Miller, D., and Snijkers, G. (2018). Overview of the special issue from the Fifth International Conference on Establishment Surveys. *Journal of Official Statistics* 34 (2): 303–307.

Thompson, K.J., Czaplicki, N., Dumbacher, B., and Kaputa, S. (2019). Developing imputation models for the Advance Monthly Retail Trade and Food Services Survey: a subsampled survey with seasonal data, low unit response, and high profile. *Proceedings from the Section on Survey Research Methods*, Statistical Society of Canada, Calgary, Alberta, Canada.

US Census Bureau (2017). *X-13ARIMA-SEATS Reference Manual*, Version 1.1, Time Series Research Staff, Center for Statistical Research and Methodology, U. S. Census Bureau, U. S. Department of Commerce. www.census.gov/ts/x13as/docX13AS.pdf (accessed 3 June 2020).

Section 7

Topics in Data Integration, Linking and Matching

33

Record Linkage for Establishments: Background, Challenges, and an Example

Michael D. Larsen[1] and Alan Herning[2]

[1] *Department of Mathematics and Statistics, Saint Michael's College, Colchester, VT, USA*
[2] *Data Strategy, Integration and Services Division, Australian Bureau of Statistics, Canberra, Australia*

33.1 Introduction

The goal of record linkage is to identify singular entities across two or more databases. Even when unique and error-free identification numbers do not exist in all the databases, it can be possible to identify multiple representations of a single entity with low probability of error. Discerning correct linkages relies on the comparison of variables in the separate files that strongly suggest that representations in the files pertain to the same entity.

Record linkage is applied in many contexts. Many examples can be found in Kilss and Alvey (1985), Alvey and Jamerson (1997), Herzog et al. (2007), Christen (2012), and Chun et al. (2021). Possibly the most common application is linking people across databases. See, for example, CDC (2020) and US Census Bureau (2021). Increasingly, surveys are designed and implemented with the idea in mind that survey respondents, and possibly nonrespondents as well, will be linked to another source. The second source could be a census or population register, administrative files collected for other purposes, or another survey. Establishments might seek to link internal records on their members or constituent units to other sources. Financial institutions and businesses, for example, might link applicants and inactive customers to public death records (CDC 2021) in one attempt to thwart fraudulent activity and remain current.

Record linkage also can be applied to records for establishments themselves. Governments maintain lists of businesses, farms, schools, and medical service providers, among other things. For example, Winkler (1995) reports on record linkage used to create mailing lists for the US Census of Agriculture. As establishments file required reports or respond to official surveys their responses must be associated with the proper record, accurately linking together responses over time. Suppose one source contains information on employees, wages, and taxes but another contains information on capital expenditures, revenue, and other expenses. Bringing together such information would make many interesting analyses possible. Several examples can be found on the page of Statistics Canada (2020).

Record linkage in the public and private spheres occurs and has occurred for many years in countries around the world. It is beyond the scope of this overview to describe the extent and variety of examples.

Advances in Business Statistics, Methods and Data Collection. Edited by Ger Snijkers, Mojca Bavdaž, Stefan Bender, Jacqui Jones, Steve MacFeely, Joseph W. Sakshaug, Katherine J. Thompson, and Arnout van Delden.
© 2023 John Wiley & Sons, Inc. Published 2023 by John Wiley & Sons, Inc.

Successful record linkage can occur when most entities are represented across files by detailed, accurate, and stable information that nearly uniquely identifies them in all files. The importance of the quality of the information going into record linkage cannot be overemphasized (Winkler 1995, 2021). Usually, variables present on the files must be preprocessed before use in linkage efforts to limit error and extract greater detail. One also must clearly understand the sampling and data generation processes to implement and realistically interpret results of record linkage. Statistical models and decision rules can be useful when aspects of the record linkage algorithm must be estimated from the data. For a survey statistician, record linkage has many interesting challenges and opportunities.

Section 33.2 discusses variables used in record linkage. Section 33.3 compares and contrasts exact, deterministic, and probabilistic matching methods. Section 33.4 presents additional considerations involving data structures, one-to-one matching, analysis of linked files, and confidentiality and computing. Section 33.5 provides an example of business data linkage in a longitudinal environment from the Australian Bureau of Statistics (ABS), followed by a detailed description of the linking methodology (Section 33.6) and data access model (Section 33.7). A concluding summary is provided in Section 33.8.

33.2 Variables for Linking Records

The best variables for linking persons and establishments across databases are unique identification numbers. In Australia, for example, most businesses are allocated an Australian Business Number (ABN) and when people commence paying personal income tax, they are assigned a unique Tax File Number (TFN). Examples of such numbers issued by the US government include the Social Security Number (SSN), the Taxpayer Identification Number (TIN), and the Employer Identification Number (EIN). Data Universal Numbering System (DUNS) numbers are numeric identifiers assigned by the company Dun & Bradstreet to business locations. There can be challenges to using these numbers for record linkage. SSNs, for example, are not completely unique and can be recorded with error or missing. Many studies, due to privacy and response rate concerns, no longer collect SSNs from individuals. The mapping between EINs and DUNS is complicated by several factors. Not every business needs an EIN. A company with multiple locations can have more than one DUNS number. EIN and DUNS numbers for an establishment can change over time. It is possible that these numbers, like SSNs, can be recorded incorrectly or are not collected in some instances. Other types of identification numbers, such as account numbers, are specific within a company or for a given purpose, sensitive, and generally not available for linkage purposes. In many applications, it is likely that other variables will be needed to link records across databases or at least to confirm hypothesized linkages.

Specific variables for linking persons include components of names, components of addresses, parts of ID numbers, phone numbers, geography, birth date and age, gender, race/ethnicity, marital status, relations to other people, and possibly other variables. Dividing a field of information into constituent parts is called parsing (Winkler 1995; Newcombe 1988). Name components can include first name, middle name, last name, extensions such as Jr., nick names, and maiden names. Some people use a middle name or nickname in place of their legal first name. Address and geography components can include house number, apartment number, street name, alternative street names, city, county, ZIP code, and state. Instead of using the full SSN, one could use the last four digits. The last four digits are not just so sensitive but also not unique. Misspellings and typographical errors are possible. Many of these variables, such as relations to others in the household, change over time. It also is possible for self-reporting of race, ethnicity, and gender/gender identification to vary by instance of response. Some individuals have multiple addresses and phones or change them over time.

Variables for linking establishments have some of the same issues as for linking persons, but new possibilities and challenges arise. Some establishments have many formal and informal names, exist at multiple locations and have more than one operational division, and use more than one address and phone number. The people running an establishment and providing data in studies change over time and can be different individuals.

It would be possible to consider variables pertaining to characteristics of the individuals and establishments for further linkage assessment. Such efforts implicitly involve some degree of modeling of relationships among variables. Establishments have a size dimension that relates to many variables simultaneously. A creative approach could conceivably use size-related variables to refine linkage decisions: an inconsistency among number of employees, revenue and expenditures, and payroll might alert one to a possible mismatch across files. Medical studies of individuals, for example, might be able to make use of medical status, treatment and expenditure categories, and dates of diagnosis and treatment to rule out some unlikely matches.

In preparation for record linkage of individuals and establishments, one must carefully consider the available variables. Variables that are available and recorded accurately for all or nearly all units, have numerous or even unique values, and remain stable over a long horizon are the most desirable.

33.3 Exact, Deterministic, and Probabilistic Matching

Once one has variables recorded on entities in two or more files, one must decide how to use the information to identify linkages of entities across the files. The process involves four steps: deciding which pairs of records to compare, comparing values of variables on the pairs of units in the files, evaluating or scoring the level of agreement as far as it is evidence about a pair being a match, and deciding which pairs to call matches. The description of methods below will assume that there are two files on a population with some members of the population represented on both files. The goal is to identify pairs of records, one from each file, that correspond to unique population units.

It will be assumed as well that each file contains only one record per individual or establishment. When this is the case, it makes sense to consider one-to-one matching, or the scenario in which only one record on a file is chosen to match to a record on the other file, and vice versa. The implementation of one-to-one matching in algorithms for record linkage often is a component of the matching decision process. One-to-one matching is discussed further in Section 33.4.2.

Files sometimes contain duplicate records for some units. Record linkage methods could be used to de-duplicate files before linking to other files. Other methods have been suggested for allowing many-to-one and many-to-many matches, which might be particularly relevant for linkage of companies with multiple locations or comprised of multiple businesses.

33.3.1 Exact Matching and Deterministic Matching with Multiple Passes

In exact matching, one selects key variables and declares pairs to links when they agree exactly on all the key variables. The combination of key variables ideally uniquely identifies entities in the databases. If not, then other information or manual review is required to clarify matches. The US Census Bureau uses the term "Protected Identification Key (PIK)" in its Person Identification

Validation System (PVS) to refer to a code string of values on key matching variables (Mulrow et al. 2011). In an establishment application, exact matching could be accomplished by requiring variables such as establishment name, address, and possibly other information to be identical on records in two files. Business matches might require equal 2017 North American Industrial Classification System (NAICS) six-digit codes across files.

An advantage of exact matching is it likely has a low false-positive rate, especially if agreement on multiple detailed variables is required. A disadvantage is that the rate of false negatives might be high. Exact matches can be missed due to typographical errors, missing values, and slight variations in information. Processing of files before linkage might avoid some missed matches. For example, businesses called *My Business, My Business Inc, and My Business Incorporated* at the same address might all be the same but judged different without appropriate consideration. If all words such as Inc, INC, or incorporated are removed before comparison, or if only the first eight characters of the name are used, then these similar business titles would not be considered different. Of course, relaxing the required level of agreement to reduce false negatives could possibly increase false positives. In matching of individuals, some applications have used SOUNDEX (National Archives 2020) or other sounds systems for names to deal with alternative spellings.

A variation on exact matching is deterministic matching. In deterministic matching, pairs considered to be matches need to agree on some key variables, but rules are given so that some disagreements are allowed. Some companies that exist in local communities as franchises adopt unique names. Two Ace Hardware stores in a part of Vermont send advertising as "Bibens Ace" and "Jerihill Ace Hardware." It is not hard to imagine that they might be recorded in some databases as "Bibens Ace Hardware," "Biben's Ace," "Jerihill Ace," "Ace Hardware," or simply "Ace." Even if names do not match, records might still agree on street name and number, phone number, and owner and manager names. On the other hand, names of businesses might agree across files, but alternate phone numbers, mailing address, or names of key people might exist, thereby leading to disagreements. Typographical errors also do occur. Deterministic matching might allow a match to be declared based on agreement on, for example, four out of five key variables.

Deterministic matching, as opposed to more strict exact matching, could reduce the number of false negatives, thereby finding more actual matches, but it does raise the possibility of an elevated false positive rate.

In practice, one can attempt to increase performance by a multipass approach. A pass through the data files uses one criterion to declare pairs across the files to be probable matches. The first pass might be exact matching. The second and subsequent passes might be different versions of exact matching or deterministic matching and utilize different sets of variables in different ways, thereby seeking matches while attempting to avoid nonmatches. At each pass, some records are declared to be matched pairs.

One must judge whether results coming out of a pass are clean enough for incorporation into the database of matches. A record linkage pass could be applied to all records or to only those records that have not already been assigned links. The latter option seems easier to implement, but the former should generate more information for review. Suppose five passes are completed. Should a pair of records not identified as a link in passes one and two, as unique links to each other in passes three and four, and as possible links to many records in pass five be considered a matching pair? With time and resources available, a decision could be based on study of the detailed information in the records. It is more likely that a sample of pairs are studied at each pass and records identified as matches at a pass receive the same treatment. Perhaps the fifth pass did not use a sufficiently restrictive criterion for results to be considered accurate. If the hypothetical record pair had been removed from further processing after the third pass, then results of latter comparisons would not have been known, affecting both the evaluation of the specific pair and the overall performance of subsequent passes.

33.3.2 Probabilistic Matching

Another approach to record linkage is probabilistic matching (Fellegi and Sunter 1969). In probabilistic matching, values of the variables for the records on two files are compared in terms of their level of agreement with each other. Agreement can be defined to be exact or partial agreement. In linkage of individuals, agreement on names often is defined to be agreement on sound-coded versions of names or substrings of names (Winkler 1995). Long and complex names are more likely to have errors, especially if not self-reported by the individual. Establishment names might be handled similarly, or closeness of names might be based on a string-comparator metric (Jaro 1989; Winkler 1990), which accounts for partial similarities of names. Agreement on age for adults often is defined as agreement within a caliper of, say, minus or plus three years. Agreements on size reported by establishments, such as number of employees, might also be judged within calipers. As with exact and deterministic record linkage, preprocessing of variables is an important step for reducing missed matches.

Once agreements and disagreements on variables are determined, the agreement pattern is given a score, which is sometimes referred to as a weight. Agreements add to the weight, whereas disagreements decrease the weight. When weights are high enough, pairs are declared to be matches. Determining weights to use for single and multiple variables and corresponding weight cut-off values for decisions are two critical components of probabilistic linkage algorithms.

Usually, only a subset of possible pairs is used in probabilistic linkage. For example, the National Center for Health Statistics (NCHS 2019) survey records on individuals are linked to the National Death Index (NDI) using ten items plus SSN, which can be recorded as all nine or the last four digits. Pairs are only considered linkage eligible if they agree on some key subsets of these variables. Pairs that pass linkage eligibility then are scored in terms of agreement on the several variables. Linkage of establishments, such as schools or businesses, might only compare pairs of records within states or counties. These restrictions are sometimes referred to as blocking, which is discussed in Section 33.4.1.

There are a couple of methods that have been used to compute weights. Typically, weighting methods assume that agreements on variables are independent of each other conditional on true match status. The probability of agreements and disagreements among either matches or nonmatches on several variables then is computed as the product of probabilities of the agreement outcomes on those variables. The log odds of agreements and disagreements among either matches or nonmatches are then the sum across variables of the log odds of the agreement outcome on a variable. The log odds will be positive if the outcome for a variable (typically agreement) is more likely among matches than among nonmatches. The log odds will be negative if the outcome for a variable (typically disagreement) is more likely among nonmatches than among matches. Newcombe et al. (1959) used log base two weights and called them binit weights.

In correspondence to the multiplicative conditional probability structure, weighting schemes in record linkage typically are additive. Points are awarded for agreement and subtracted for disagreement. Fellegi and Sunter (1969) and others have discussed using agreement rates on variables for pairs of records known to be matches to estimate appropriate weights for matches. If most pairs are nonmatches, then rates of agreement in randomly associated pairs could be used to estimate agreement–disagreement weights among nonmatches (Fellegi and Sunter 1969). Of course, weights can be adjusted based on past performance. As in all record linkage, the goal is to identify matching pairs of records while excluding record pairs corresponding to different entities. The more that the calculated weight distribution among true links and true nonlinks are separated, the easier it will be to correctly classify pairs.

Three points are worth considering. First, the impact on weights for agreement and disagreement do not have to be symmetric. Suppose two farm records are being compared. Being in the same county probably adds little weight to the impression that the records are for the same entity, unless sample sizes in a county are rather small and the two databases used the same samples. Being in a different county, however, adds substantial weight to the case that the records are for different entities. Second, it is possible to include interactions among variables by including an extra weight contribution based on comparisons simultaneously on two variables. Agreement on variables within match class likely is not independent across variables (Smith and Newcombe 1975; Winkler 1989b, 1995; Larsen and Rubin 2001). Suppose farms records on two files indicate that the farms are in the same county and the owner has the same last name. The positive impact on the weight could be specified to be larger than the sum of the impacts of the two agreements separately. Third, advantages might be had by adjusting weights based on values of the two variables instead of only on whether they agree. Agreement on long, uncommon names likely is stronger evidence of being a match than agreement on more common names (Winkler 1989c). Names and sequences of numbers can partially agree as well. Measures of partial agreement, such as string comparator metrics, can be used to moderate the impact of weights (Jaro 1989; Winkler 1995).

Once weights are determined, one must turn weights into decisions about match status. Sufficiently large weights indicate likely matches, whereas small weights indicate likely nonmatches. Between two cutoffs, one could consider a clerical review effort involving human judgment about uncertain pairs. In a large application, it might not be possible to review all pairs with intermediate weights. Instead, a sample of pairs with weights near the cutoff could be reviewed. Based on this review, the cutoff could be raised to reduce false-match errors or lowered to reduce false-nonmatch errors.

Fellegi and Sunter (1969) framed the record linkage as a dual hypothesis-testing problem. They showed that if one has probabilities of agreement–disagreement patterns for matches and for non-matches and one sorts record pairs according to estimated probabilities of matching (or, equivalently, the log odds of matching), then assigning pairs sequentially to nonmatches (with low match probabilities) and matches (with high match probabilities) until given error rates are reached produces the optimal result of minimizing unassigned pairs in the middle. Many applied articles and applications of record linkage that mention Fellegi and Sunter (1969) seem to primarily mean that they add weights together and then find a suitable cutoff above which pairs are declared to be matches.

In practice, one does not know probabilities of the agreement–disagreement patterns for matches and nonmatches. In some circumstances, they can be estimated, as described above, using empirical estimates. In other applications, weights are determined and adjusted in less formal ways. Using data from a different record linkage application or past experiences to determine weights and cutoffs is one possibility but doing so works only if the record linkage applications are similar enough to one another in important ways. A review effort still is needed to ensure that error rates are low.

Another alternative is to estimate probabilities through use of a statistical model. Larsen and Rubin (2001), Winkler (1988, 1989a), and others have fit a latent class model to counts of agreement patterns in a US Census Bureau application linking individuals. Latent class models have been used in other contexts as well. The method is applicable in some situations, but each application must be evaluated carefully as the model estimates do not always produce good separation between pairs that are matches and those that are not. For example, fitting three latent classes to counts of agreement patterns in the US Census application produced one class with high probabilities of being matches. The latent class model estimates can be used to produce weights and to set decision cutoffs for matches and nonmatches. Belin and Rubin (1995) also fit mixture models, but to transformed weights distributions. They estimated a Box–Cox transformation of distributions of weights among matches and nonmatches from data with known match status in another study location as part of the mixture model specification. Their use of mixture models focused on finding decision cutoffs. Discussion of details of these approaches and others is beyond the scope of this article.

A further approach to probabilistic record linkage could be multiple-pass probabilistic matching. As in exact or deterministic matching, in probabilistic record linkage one must select and process variables for use in record linkage. In probabilistic record linkage, different choices would lead to different weights distributions and different cutoffs. Pairs that are declared to be matches across multiple passes are more likely than to be true matches than pairs that are declared to be matches only with certain combinations of variables.

33.3.3 Combining Deterministic and Probabilistic Linkage

Many presentations of record linkage emphasize either deterministic or probabilistic record linkage. This is a false dichotomy. The goal of both approaches is to identify links across databases. In common implementations, one first examines possible links according to a strict standard. Once those links are decided, then one examines possible links according to a relaxed standard. This incremental approach defines an algorithm. Good practice in record linkage carefully defines the steps in a record linkage process. There is no principle that says one cannot combine the best of both approaches. If it is possible to use exact or deterministic linkage with a strict criterion to decide linkage status for some records, then doing so can be executed before probabilistic linkage. Probabilistic linkage is more likely to identify links when direct evidence is weak; probabilistic linkage adds evidence across many variables. In some implementations of probabilistic linkage, the matches identified using exact and deterministic methods can be used to help estimate weights. Larsen and Rubin (2001) explored an iterative algorithm for estimating mixture model parameters in record linkage.

33.4 Additional Considerations in Record Linkage

Record linkage of individuals and establishments has many additional dimensions to consider. Section 33.4.1 discusses some data structural issues. Section 33.4.2 extends the discussion of Section 33.4.1 to consider one-to-one matching, including a comment on Bayesian record linkage. Section 33.4.3 summarizes some issues in the analysis of files created through record linkage. Section 33.4.4 mentions confidentiality and computing.

33.4.1 Structural Considerations in Record Linkage

In record linkage of individuals or establishments, the structure of the data files, in terms of the units represented in the files, being linked impacts the process of making linkage decisions. First, not all pairs of records are compared as possible matches. Many pairs disagree on key variables and therefore are not reasonable to consider. When units are grouped into homogeneous groups and linkages among units are only contemplated between corresponding groups, it is called blocking (Winkler 1995). Blocking can greatly reduce the amount of computing necessary by reducing the number of pairs considered. Suppose two files each have a million records. All combinations of records are $10^{6*}10^6 = 10^{12}$ pairs. If each file has 10,000 blocks of 100 each, then there are $10^{4*}100^*100 = 10^8$ pairs; not a small number but 1/10,000 of the original. Smaller blocks produce a greater reduction in numbers of pairs. A disadvantage of blocking is that it can cause false nonmatches if a unit belongs to different blocks in different files. If the blocks are stable across databases and units do not switch blocks, then this source of error should be small. Linkage of establishments might use county or ZIP code as a blocking variable. Nine-digit ZIP code (ZIP + four) would be a more specific blocking variable.

Some files contain duplicate records. The duplicate records might not contain identical information on all variables. In a census of persons, there can be more than one opportunity to respond, and it might be challenging operationally to prevent multiple entries per household. One approach in such a situation would be to link each database to itself to locate as many duplicates as possible. A question then arises, what should one do with different entries on the same entity? Rules that attempt to choose the best value for a field of information when more than one value is available could either help, by removing erroneous information, or harm, by removing accurate information that would hurt chances of linkages to another database. One might consider a multipass approach, using different versions of information on each pass, and then integrating results of the different pass. Another option would be to make a database with duplicates, see how they link to another database, and then resolve the possible matches for cases with multiple instances in a file. In practice with limited resources and time, record linkage algorithms choose a way to handle discrepant information and move forward in locating as many matches as possible.

In dealing with establishments, some establishments can have more than one legitimate representation in a database. One person can own multiple businesses or have one business that operates in multiple locations. This complicates the issue of linkage. If one merges multiple records into a single record at some stage of the record linkage process, one wants to avoid choices that limit the performance of record linkage at later stages or in the future.

33.4.2 One-to-One Matching

Even without the issue of duplicates, it is possible that an entry on one file will have two or more plausible matches on another file. If exact linkage uses few highly discriminating variables or deterministic linkage defines agreement on fields with loose enough calipers, then multiple records could qualify as a match to a single record on the other file. If the goal is one-to-one linkage between files, then multiple linkages must be resolved using additional information or discarded. Sometimes the set of possible matches taken together can satisfactorily resolve some linkages. If record A on File 1 matches both records Y and Z on File 2, but record Z alone matches record B on File 1, then one might assign A–Y and B–Z as matches. An algorithm with the goal of assigning only correct links would declare none of them to be links, or perhaps take B–Z as the sole declared match. Refining linkage criteria might also resolve the issue.

In probabilistic linkage, a record in File 1 can have high weights when paired with many records in File 2. Those records in File 2 can similarly have high weights when paired with many records in File 1. A greedy search algorithm proceeds through a file or pairs of matches sequentially. It declares the records on File 1 and File 2 with the highest matching weight to be links and then removes those records from further possible linkages. This approach might assign a moderately likely link early in the process that then eliminates the possibility of assignment to a better choice later. In the abstract example of the previous paragraph, if the weight for the A–Z link is slightly higher than the weight for the A–Y link, a greedy algorithm would assign A–Z even if both A links have moderate but acceptable weights and the B–Z link has a high weight.

Alternative assignment algorithms consider all pairs of records together. Algorithms of this sort have been developed to solve the linear sum assignment problem (LSAP); see also Stable Marriage Problem (Gusfield and Irving 1989). They have been used in record linkage problems at the US Census Bureau. If weight for the A–Z link is slightly higher than the weight for the A–Y link, but both are moderate and the B–Z link has a high weight, a nongreedy algorithm could choose the A–Y and B–Z links to maximize total probable links.

The one-to-one assignment problem arises in the statistical representation of record linkage in probability models. Typical representations of the latent class, or mixture model, approach to record linkage use a concept of the complete data being the comparison vectors created by comparing fields of information on pairs of records and a set of dichotomous variables that indicate which records are matches. These indicators are useful in calculating the probability that a record pair is a match given its comparison outcomes and in computational approaches such as the expectation-maximization (EM) algorithm (Dempster et al. 1977). As usually formulated, however, the set of indicators for all record pairs typically is not employed with restrictions that enforce one-to-one matching. Computationally this is expedient, but it does mean that postprocessing estimate probabilities and weights to make linkage decisions, through LSAP algorithms and the like, is necessary.

Some authors have considered alternatives to one-to-one assignment. A few authors have proposed theory of record linkage involving the complete matrix of linkage indicators with one-to-one restrictions. Sometimes this has been done in a Bayesian framework. In Bayesian estimation of model parameters, iterative algorithms might sample values of indicators, including values of the entire linkage matrix with its restrictions.

Even if most record linkage work does not explicitly use Bayesian probability modeling record linkage incorporates prior information and experience in the many decisions that must be made during implementation. Using data from past experiences and other operations to estimate weights, for example, is akin to giving prior distributions for probabilities. In a latent class model approach, actual prior distributions could be used (e.g. Larsen 2002, 2004, 2010).

33.4.3 Using Linked Files in Analysis

Once a file has been created through record linkage, it is used in statistical analysis, such as estimating the size of a population or the relationships among variables. Errors in linkage impact results. Ideally, a report of an analysis should include a description of the success of the record linkage effort. Such a report could take many forms, but likely would describe the files being linked, the number of links found, the variables being used, and the quality of the matches. The quality of the matches might be characterized by the percent of certain matches, the percent of matches with some moderate discrepancies in variables or with possible alternative links, and specified error rates for false matches and nonmatches.

One way of reflecting uncertainty due to record linkage is a sensitivity analysis that presents results by certainties of linkage. Say a multipass has four passes that identify matches, with the first two passes producing near-certain matches, but the other two yielding strong candidates for linkage but with less certainty. Reporting results run on three data sets (matches from passes one and two, matches from passes one, two, and three, and matches from all four passes) could be informative.

Some authors have developed methods of incorporating probabilities of linkage for pairs directly into analyses. See, for example, Neter et al. (1965), Scheuren and Winkler (1993, 1997), and Lahiri and Larsen (2005). A number of more recent articles in this area are described in Winkler (2021).

Another approach has adapted ideas from survey sampling approaches to missing data. Suppose a survey of businesses is conducted with the respondents linked to a public database. Some businesses cannot be linked to the database and therefore are missing variables associated with the public database. Poststratification weighting based on stratification variables could be used to adjust survey weights for nonresponse due to nonlinkage. Further, as respondents have many variables reported on the survey, more extensive poststratification, including methods incorporating estimated propensity scores for the probability of linkage, could be considered. Methods of these sort have been studied for linkage of individuals at the National Center for Health Statistics (Judson et al. 2013; Golden and Mirel 2021).

An idea from the literature on statistical analysis with missing data that can be considered is multiple imputation (Kohnen and Reiter 2009; Reiter 2009, 2021). Multiple possible realizations of the linkages and combined values across databases, if provided to the user, could usefully indicate uncertainty due to linkage. Multiple imputations might also be useful in addressing confidentiality concerns, as described in Section 33.4.4.

33.4.4 Confidentiality and Computing

Confidentiality and computing impact the ability to link individuals and establishments. These broad topics are beyond the scope of this overview article, but that does not mean they are not important.

Data in many contexts are collected with explicit guarantees of confidentiality and promises that they will be used for specific purposes. Even before record linkage is attempted one must ensure that data are stored in a secure manner. Details that involve names, dates, and fine-level geographical information are particularly sensitive. Strict protocols for data collection, handling, and storage are needed to ensure that rules are followed.

To perform record linkage, it must be possible to compare detailed information in two or more files. In one arrangement, two organizations each possess one file to be used in linkage. If they can agree on a protocol and variables to be used in linkage, then one of them could perform the linkage and then share the results with the other. Sensitive information that is shared for the linkage process could be completely removed after linkage. Another alternative is to employ a third party to receive data files for linkage and then report linkage results to the two organizations desiring the linkage. Memoranda of understanding among all parties covering transferring, handling, and disposing of data are needed. Limits on the use of linked data sets also must be clearly specified.

A third alternative is referred to as privacy preserving record linkage (e.g. Hall and Fienberg 2010; Vatsalan et al. 2014; Schnell 2015; Christen et al. 2020). In this version of record linkage, two entities do not share actual values of records, but rather they share coded versions of the records. These techniques make use of developments in computer science as well as statistics. The method eliminates the possibility of sensitive information being discovered by the other party. Once records are linked, the two entities can share values of variables used in analysis, or possibly summary information (e.g. Karr et al. 2009). Businesses might consent to be linked to government databases under such terms.

Increasingly surveys of individuals that plan to link responses to other sources ask for permission to do the linkage and collect variables to enable said linkage. Consent for linkage in business surveys also is becoming more common (Sakshaug and Vicari 2018). In Europe, General Data Protection Regulation (GDPR) was passed in the European Union in 2016 with the aim of protecting the use and transfer of personal data.

When respondents refuse permission or do not provide sufficient information for linkage, there could be a bias in results due to nonlinkage. Methods useful for addressing missing data in statistical analyses could be used to adjust results. Sakshaug (2021) discussing how to measure and control for nonconsent bias in studies utilizing linked data sets.

Another dimension of confidentiality arises if one plans to make databases created through linkage available for researchers or in public use files. The enhanced databases contain a richer set of variables than any single source. If someone of nefarious purpose obtains a database, will the enhanced data enable identification of respondents? As with any data released to the public or summarized in detail, one needs to think about confidentiality.

Record linkage aims to identify individuals across databases. Confidentiality protection, disclosure limitation, and disclosure control seek to prevent linkages to individuals. Methods have been developed for measuring disclosure risk. These include, but are not limited to, differential privacy (Abowd et al. 2021) and model-based methods (Reiter 2005; Kim et al. 2015). This broad area of research will be increasingly relevant for record linkage as linkage projects expand in scope and data available on the web continue to grow exponentially.

One method for protecting entities and individuals who are covered by records in a file created by linkage is to require analysts to use the data only within the confines of a data center. The data center rules could prevent unauthorized searching of records or publishing of results that might reveal identities. Although effective, data centers are expense to maintain and use and restricted in geographical location. A second method would require analysts to submit desired analyses via Internet to a data center. Employees of the data center then would perform requested analyses and check them for disclosure risk. This approach could enable a broader group of individuals to engage in research, but it too comes with costs and limitations. One challenge is checking for unintended compromises of identities. A third method of enabling analysis while protecting confidentiality is to release public use data files from the linked data files that have had disclosure limitation methods applied. Such files typically have less detail on variables (e.g. age ranges rather than age, broad income and revenue categories, coarse geography indications) than in the original, random subsampling of records, and possibly noise added to the values (e.g. data swapping, random perturbations). Such efforts reduce the possibility of correctly identifying entities in the released databases. Another possibility is to release multiply imputed synthetic data files (e.g. Reiter 2002; Raghunathan et al. 2003).

In Section 33.7, the Australian example of Business Data Linking presents the access model that has been implemented by the ABS for granting researchers access to detailed microdata while maintaining the confidentiality and security of the data.

Record linkage is being contemplated for databases of ever-increasing size and complexity. Increases in computing power and memory and in efficiency of algorithms make this possible. Despite these changes, big applications require intelligent programming in appropriate computing languages. To consider multiple passes, weighting strategies, choices in processing variables, and decision rules in operational implementations, programs need to handle megabyte plus data files (reading, indexing, sorting, searching, comparing, and storing) with as little unnecessary work as possible.

33.5 A Practical Example of Business Data Linking: The Business Longitudinal Analysis Data Environment

There is a wealth of information about businesses held by all levels of governments. Some of this information can be found in administrative and directly collected survey datasets. Combining these high-value data sources provides a solid evidence base for research, productivity analysis, policy development, and evaluation. Discussed below is an Australian example of the application of the linkage concepts and issues discussed in the earlier sections.

33.5.1 Overview

The Business Longitudinal Analysis Data Environment (BLADE) integrates directly collected ABS business surveys data, administrative data from the Australian Taxation Office (ATO) and other sources to an integrating frame sourced from the Australian Bureau of Statistics Business Register (ABSBR) to produce a statistical asset. BLADE is maintained by the ABS.

BLADE was established in 2014 as a joint project between the ABS and the then Department of Industry and Science to enable Australia's participation in the OECD's Dynemp project on employment dynamics. BLADE included business taxation data and selected ABS survey data for all active businesses in the Australian economy from the 2001–2002 financial year to 2012–2013.

Over the last few years, the data available as part of the BLADE asset has been regularly updated and new data sets added. The standard BLADE asset now includes three taxation data sets from the ATO, seven ABS Business Surveys, data on international merchandise imports and exports, and data on intellectual property applications within Australia. In late 2020, the ABS also introduced an experimental business activity locations data set to further enable regional analysis. The ABS, in consultation with BLADE stakeholders and other government departments, is continually examining new data sources to ensure that BLADE remains relevant and a strategic statistical asset.

33.6 BLADE Linking Methodology

The BLADE integration methods have remained relatively consistent since their initial development. The majority of ABS Survey data and administrative data can be linked using exact matching, as presented in Section 33.3, using the ABN, a unique number that identifies businesses to government and the community; however, the reporting structures of ABS Survey data units and ABNs can differ over time, particularly for large and complex businesses which is discussed further in Section 33.6.1. To enable the integration and analysis of these data, they are linked via an Integrating Frame which identifies the relationships between ABS Statistical Units and ABNs (Figure 33.1).

33.6.1 BLADE Integrating Frame

The integrating frame for BLADE is sourced from the ABSBR, which provides the frame for most ABS Business Surveys to enable a consistent, coherent, point-in-time picture of the Australian economy. The scope of the ABSBR is that all organizations with an active ABN undertake productive activity in Australia's economic territory. The relatively insignificant economic activity of organizations which fall below the threshold for needing to register for an ABN (annual turnover of less

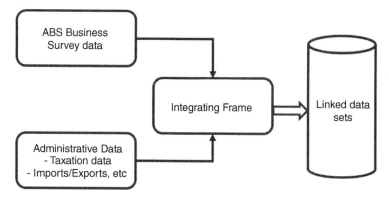

Figure 33.1 BLADE Integrating model.

than AU\$ 75,000 or AU\$ 150,000 for nonprofit organizations) and have chosen not to apply for an ABN remain outside the conceptual scope of the ABS Business Register.

The ABSBR uses an economic statistics model to describe the characteristics and the structural relationships between related businesses which are separated into two populations. The main distinctions between businesses in these two populations are the complexity of the business structure and the degree of the intervention required to reflect the business structure for statistical purposes. Most of the businesses in Australia are regarded as single legal entities that have a simple structure, and the ABN is suitable for ABS statistical purposes. This population of businesses is known as the "nonprofiled population."

For a small number of businesses, the ABS maintains its own economic unit structure (Figure 33.2) through direct contact with the businesses. These businesses constitute the "profiled population" with the production and the statistical units represented by Type of Activity Unit (TAU). TAUs are producing units comprising one or more legal entities, subentities, or branches of a legal entity that can report productive and employment activities via a minimum set of data items.

Ideally, all TAUs are constructed so that some level of industry homogeneity is observed. This ensures that good-quality industry estimates can be calculated by the ABS at that level. However, not all businesses are able to supply a complete set of accounts for every industry classification in

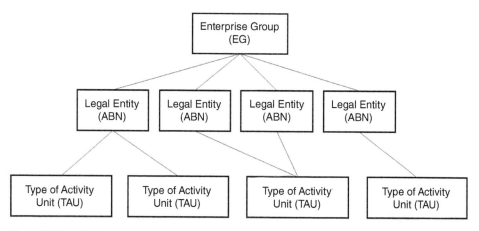

Figure 33.2 ABS Economics Units model.

which they have activity. The relationship between TAUs and the associated Legal Entities (ABN) may be one-to-one, many-to-one, or one-to-many and can change over time.

Although the profiled population is a small proportion of the active businesses, they account for the majority of economic activity within the Australian economy. The profiled population is regularly reviewed through contact with the business (ABS profiling) with structures and relationships between ABNs and TAUs updated to reflect real-world changes. The profiling process can result in TAUs and ABNs entering and exiting the profiled population on a regular basis.

The BLADE Integrating Frame is updated on an annual basis using a snapshot of the ABSBR taken in June of each year. The update identifies businesses that have ceased operating, new businesses and applies any changes to structures of active businesses.

33.6.2 Linking Data to BLADE

The BLADE consists of a series of modules that can be linked together via the BLADE Frame. Each data set linked is de-identified with a common linkage key enabling each data set to be directly linked with other data sets. The methods for linking data to the BLADE Frame have evolved over time and are dependent on which data sets are being used and the specific objectives of the project using the data (Figure 33.3).

33.6.2.1 ABS Survey Data
For ABS Business survey data, linking to the BLADE Frame is a direct linking process as the ABS Business Surveys are selected frame based on the ABSBR and are at the same ABS economic statistical units as the BLADE Frame.

33.6.2.2 BLADE Core
The BLADE Core consists of the business characteristics information from the BLADE Frame, such as industry classification and main location of operations, along with the various business income and taxation data sets from the ATO. The income and taxation data sets are provided to the ABS at the ABN level. For units in the nonprofiled population, there is a direct one-to-one match between the units on the taxation data sets and the BLADE Frame. Recent changes to the profiling process for the complex population is providing more information in regard to the links between the ABN and TAU as highlighted in Figure 33.2; however, when BLADE was established, there was limited information available on the direct links between ABNs and TAUs in the profiled

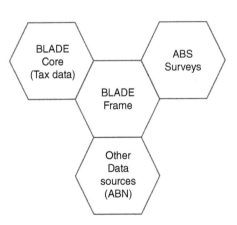

Figure 33.3 BLADE Linkage model.

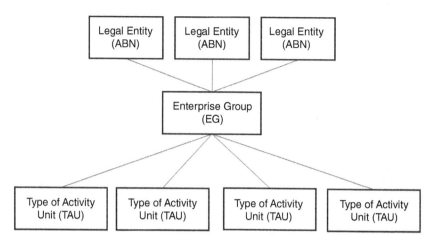

Figure 33.4 Historical ABN-TAU links.

population. For a significant period of the BLADE time series, it was only known which ABNs were linked to enterprise groups (EGs) and the TAUs associated with the EGs (Figure 33.4).

To apply a consistent linking methodology of taxation data to TAUs over the entire time series, for each financial year, ABNs associated with an EG are aggregated then proportioned to each TAU within the EG based on its employment ratio to the total employment for the EG. This methodology was initially developed to enable analysis of ABS Survey data directly with taxation data. From 2021 onwards, the BLADE Core will be made available to researchers at either the ABN or TAU level dependent on their research requirements.

33.6.2.3   Linkage of Other Administrative Data

For administrative data sources, such Merchandise Imports and Exports, data are generally available at the ABN level. In the first few years of BLADE being made available to researchers, administrative data was linked to the BLADE Frame and provided to users at the ABS Economic Units model level. This resulted in some of the granular information in the administrative data sets being lost due to the multiple links that can exist between ABNs and TAUs, that is, only characteristics of the TAU information, not the ABN, being provided to the researcher. This issue has been resolved in recent years by keeping the administrative data sets being integrated to BLADE at the ABN level and providing a concordance file between the de-identified ABN level data set and the BLADE Frame. This retains the detailed data in the administrative data set, allowing the researcher to best determine how the BLADE Core and ABS Business Survey data should be used with the administrative data (Figure 33.5).

To create the concordance file between the ABN and BLADE Frame, the industry code (Australian New Zealand Standard Industry Classification – ANZSIC) information from both the administrative data set and the BLADE Frame are used.

For ABNs associated with units in the nonprofiled population of BLADE, the linking is a direct one-to-one match. For units in the profiled population, an ABN can potentially link to multiple TAUs on the BLADE Frame. For EGs that only have one TAU, any ABN associated with the EG is linked to the TAU. Where the EG has multiple TAUs, the best match based on the industry code of the ABN, and the TAU is determined through a cascading matching process. First a link on four-digit ANZSIC class is sought, that being the most accurate match. Those that don't match via this step are matched on ANZSIC group (three digit), then ANZSIC subdivision (two digit), and

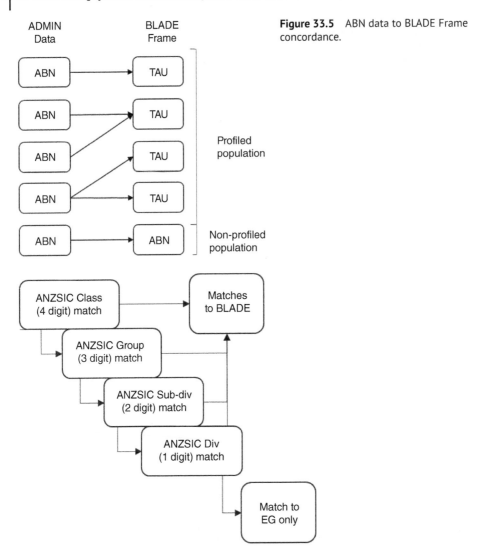

ADMIN Data — BLADE Frame

Figure 33.5 ABN data to BLADE Frame concordance.

Profiled population

Non-profiled population

Figure 33.6 BLADE Industry Linkage process.

lastly ANZSIC division (one digit) as presented in Figure 33.6. Where an ABN doesn't match to a TAU based on any level of ANZSIC a link to the EG is provided in the concordance file.

When an administrative data set is provided without industry coding information, the ABN level information on the ABSBR is used to supplement the industry information. There may also be instances where an ABN on the administrative data set doesn't exist on the ABSBR, due to either differences in scope or some businesses on the administrative data set being so new that they are yet to appear on the ABSBR. In these situations, the nonmatched units are retained on the administrative data set with a flag indicating that they did not match to the BLADE Frame.

33.6.3 Maintaining BLADE

One of the main issues encountered when maintaining and updating BLADE is that the majority of the data linked was collected by or reported to other government agencies for regulatory purposes, such as taxation purposes, and not for statistical or research purposes. As a result, data provided to the ABS can be regularly revised by the business or holding agency and variables available can change due to changes in regulatory reporting. This presents several challenges for maintaining BLADE.

To account for the historical updating of some data sources, the ABS produces annual versions of BLADE and its associated data sets. Each version of BLADE is based on an annual frame and the linked data that was available at the time of production. This enables researchers to undertake research on a static version of BLADE and allows for research to be repeated if required. Detailed explanatory notes are also provided with every version of BLADE to keep researchers informed of any major revisions to variables or changes to availability of variables due to regulatory changes at the data source. The explanatory notes also provide links to the data custodian's details on the data sets and information on the integration processes including quality indicators and match rates.

Minimal editing of the various data sets included in BLADE are undertaken to provide researchers with as close to source information as possible. In some administrative data sets, obvious outlier values are removed or edited; however, no imputation is undertaken for missing values or records.

33.6.3.1 Static and Dynamic BLADE

The annual versions of BLADE produced over the last few years have been found to be extremely useful in undertaking analysis of business performance over time and to analyze the impact of various government programs and identify new sectors of the economy that could benefit from support. However, recent national and international events, such as the 2019–2020 Australian Bushfires and COVID-19, have shown that closer to real time data rather than static data is required to measure the rapid impacts major events have on the economy and business performance and also to monitor the effect of government support and economic recovery.

To meet this emerging demand for more real-time linked data, in 2021 the ABS will be implementing and evaluating a dynamic version of BLADE as well as the regular static version. For key data sets that are available on a subannual basis, such as some of the taxation data and Merchandise Imports and Exports data, regular updates to BLADE data will be made available to some researchers alongside the static version of BLADE.

For example, where businesses report taxation information on a quarterly basis, this information will be made available as close to possible after the reference period. Updates to past quarters will also be revised, where available, to ensure that the data set is up to date as possible. This will enable researchers to quickly analyze the impact of major economic events and more rapidly examine the effect of government support and economic recovery. New and existing businesses will also be better identified.

33.7 BLADE Access Model

BLADE and other ABS integrated data products are available to researchers from other government departments, government contractors, and individuals sponsored by government, academics, and researchers from public policy institutes.

In 2017, the Australian government established the Data Integration Partnership for Australia (DIPA), a whole-of-government collaboration between over 20 Commonwealth agencies with a three-year investment to maximize the use and value of the government's data assets, data infrastructure, and data integration capabilities including the development, maintenance, and access to BLADE.

Prior to any data set being integrated to BLADE, or other ABS Integrated Asset, an endorsement from the data custodian is required to allow the information to be integrated and made available at the microdata level. From October 2020, accessing ABS integrated data assets has incurred a cost and is dependent on the type of integrated product requested and the funding arrangements already in place with the researcher's organization. To gain access to BLADE, researchers must first submit an Integrated Data project proposal. Project proposals are assessed against the Five Safes Framework to ensure safe and secure data access for projects that benefit the public. The five elements of the framework are the following:

- Safe People
- Safe Projects
- Safe Settings
- Safe Data
- Safe Outputs

The framework poses specific questions to help assess and describe each risk aspect in a qualitative way. This allows data custodians to place appropriate controls not only on the data itself but also in the way in which data are accessed and outputs released.

Researchers must satisfy specific criteria to meet the Safe People element, including being located in Australia, have quantitative research experience or have a referral from a researcher working on or overseeing the same project. Prior to accessing microdata all users must also complete the ABS Safe Researcher training and sign an individual undertaking and declaration of compliance. A Responsible Officer Undertaking must also be signed by the organization's CEO (or equivalent) to ensure that the researcher's organization is legally accountable for the safe use of the microdata.

To be approved as a Safe Project, researchers must show that the project has a statistical purpose, a public benefit, and no capacity to be used for compliance or regulatory purposes. Safe Setting can be considered in terms of both the IT and physical environment. Access to ABS Integrated microdata is through the ABS DataLab, which allows for virtual access to files that remain in the secure ABS environment. When accessing DataLab, researchers must also be aware of, and ensure that their physical environment is secure and data privacy is maintained.

To ensure that Safe Data is used, all data sets are de-identified (at a minimum) and further disclosure controls may be put in place by the ABS to minimize the risk such as confidentiality of unique units, removal, or treatment of certain variables.

The Safe Output element is assessed at the project evaluation stage, where expected outputs are defined in the project proposal. All analytical outputs that are required to be taken outside of the DataLab are also thoroughly checked by the ABS before release to minimize disclosure. Prior to any data set being integrated to BLADE, or other ABS Integrated Assets, an endorsement from all data custodians, both within and external to the ABS, is required. In some instances, data custodians also request to be consulted for any integrated data research projects that their data sets have been requested, or to approve any outputs or reports using their integrated data prior to being released or presented. This is an additional level of assurance to ensure that data are used correctly and that the privacy of the data is maintained.

33.7.1 Accessing BLADE

Once a project is approved, and the researchers have undertaken the required training and signed the appropriate undertakings, access to the de-identified BLADE microdata is provided through the secure ABS DataLab. DataLab is an analysis solution for high-end users who want to undertake real time complex analysis of microdata. The key feature of DataLab is the ability to view and analyze unit record information, via virtual access to data sets that remain in the secure ABS environment. Recent versions of analytical software including R, SAS, SPSS, and Python are also made available within the DataLab.

At the commencement of the project, researchers are provided with a project workspace with access to the requested data sets within DataLab. As discussed previously, all analytical outputs must be cleared by the ABS before they can be removed from the DataLab environment. Outputs that haven't been cleared can only be discussed or shown to other approved DataLab users listed on the project proposal.

33.7.2 Customized BLADE Products

The ABS also provides a data integration service, where the standard integrated asset doesn't meet project needs. This service includes the development of customized integrated data products and, the integration of data held by researchers or other government departments to ABS integrated assets. The ABS charges for access to standard microdata products and for custom data integration services on a cost-recovery basis. For the custom services, the cost will depend on the complexity of the required data product, level of curation required, and number of new linkages.

33.7.3 How BLADE Is Being Used

The number of analysts and researchers accessing BLADE has increased significantly over the last few years. In 2016, there were 26 government researchers accessing BLADE for four projects. In 2020, this has increased to 202 researchers from 31 government departments and 13 universities for 81 projects. Some examples of the how researchers are currently using BLADE are the following:

- Track the performance of actively trading businesses in Australia, including turnover, employment, and labor productivity.
- Provide insight into the size and industry distribution of government program participants, and the impact that these programs have on business performance and innovation.
- Exploring business characteristics such as Export status and Innovation status.

As part of the ABS policy on transparency of use of data all projects using BLADE are listed on the ABS BLADE Research Projects page on the ABS website.

At present, the only official ABS publication that the uses BLADE is the "Jobs in Australia" publication. The Jobs in Australia statistics are sourced from the linked employer-employee dataset (LEED) and presents information about the number and nature of filled jobs, the people who hold them and their employers. The employer component of the LEED is sourced from BLADE.

Most of the data sets that are included in BLADE are used to produce or supplement survey responses in ABS statistics. Apart from the Jobs in Australia, BLADE is not directly used in ABS Statistics. There are currently plans to undertake research projects to determine if BLADE can be used to replace current sources for several publications.

33.8 Conclusion

Record linkage of establishments and individuals as described above and illustrated in the BLADE example has the potential to create enhanced databases for many purposes and to address many important problems which can be accessed by a wide range of researchers while still protecting the confidentiality and privacy of establishments and individuals. Successful record linkage requires knowledge in the application area, statistical insight, and computer expertise (Winkler 1996). In record linkage, one must select and process variables, determine which pairs of records are to be compared to each other, compare values of variables for eligible pairs, score the strength of evidence that a pair is a link, and specify decision rules for declaring pairs to be matches and nonmatches. The interpretation of statistical results from analysis of data created through record linkage should consider the impact of possible errors. In general, accurate and complete data collection will not only make data useful for its original purpose but also for record linkage. The linkage of establishments and individuals are similar in many ways, but linkage of establishments can magnify some record linkage challenges. Establishments can be interrelated in complex ways. Establishments often have multiple, legitimate representations in databases. Record linkage of establishments and persons is happening and yielding useful insights and products. Improving data quality, advancing methods and algorithms for record linkage, and addressing challenges and concerns including confidentiality will enable record linkage to provide the greatest benefit to society.

References

Abowd, J.M., Schmutte, I.M., and Vilhuber, L. (2021). Disclosure limitation and confidentiality protection in linked data. In: *Administrative Records for Survey Methodology* (ed. A.Y. Chun, M.D. Larsen, G. Durrant and J.P. Reiter), 25–59. Hoboken, NJ: John Wiley and Sons.

Alvey, W. and Jamerson, B. (1997). Record linkage techniques – 1997. *Proceedings of an International Workshop and Exposition*, Arlington VA (20–21 March 1997). Washington, DC: Federal Committee on Statistical Methodology, Office of Management and Budget. https://nces.ed.gov/FCSM/pdf/RLT97.pdf.

Belin, T.R. and Rubin, D.B. (1995). A method for calibrating false- match rates in record linkage. *Journal of the American Statistical Association* 90: 694–707.

CDC/National Center for Health Statistics (2020). NCHS Data Linkage Activities. Page last reviewed: 24 November 2020, 09:50 AM. https://www.cdc.gov/nchs/data-linkage/ (accessed 19 March 2021).

CDC/National Center for Health Statistics (2021). NCHS Data Linked to Mortality Files. Page last reviewed 4 January 2021, 03:15 PM. https://www.cdc.gov/nchs/data-linkage/mortality.htm (accessed 19 March 2021).

Christen, P. (2012). *Data Matching: Concepts and Techniques for Record Linkage, Entity Resolution, and Duplicate Detection*. Berlin, Heidelberg: Springer-Verlag.

Christen, P., Ranbaduge, T., and Schnell, R. (2020). *Linking Sensitive Data: Methods and Techniques for Practical Privacy-Preserving Information Sharing*. Switzerland: Springer Nature.

Chun, A.Y., Larsen, M.D., Durrant, G., and Reiter, J.P. (ed.) (2021). *Administrative Records for Survey Methodology*. Hoboken, NJ: Wiley.

Dempster, A.P., Laird, N.M., and Rubin, D.B. (1977). Maximum likelihood from incomplete data via the EM algorithm. *Journal of the Royal Statistical Society B* 39: 1–38.

Fellegi, I.P. and Sunter, A.B. (1969). A theory for record linkage. *Journal of the American Statistical Association* 64: 1183–1210.

Golden, C. and Mirel, L.B. (2021). Enhancement of health surveys with data linkage. In: *Administrative Records for Survey Methodology* (ed. A.Y. Chun, M.D. Larsen, G. Durrant and J.P. Reiter), 271–296. Hoboken, NJ: Wiley.

Gusfield, D. and Irving, R.W. (1989). *The Stable Marriage Problem: Structure and Algorithms.* Cambridge, MA; London, England: The MIT Press.

Hall, R. and Fienberg, S. (2010). Privacy-preserving record linkage. In: *Privacy in Statistical Databases. PSD 2010. Lecture Notes in Computer Science*, vol. 6344 (ed. J. Domingo-Ferrer and E. Magkos), 269–283. Berlin, Heidelberg: Springer.

Herzog, T.N., Scheuren, F., and Winkler, W.E. (2007). *Data Quality and Record Linkage Techniques.* New York, NY: Springer.

Jaro, M.A. (1989). Advances in record-linkage methodology as applied to matching the 1985 Census of Tampa, Florida. *Journal of the American Statistical Association* 84: 414–420.

Judson, D.H., Parker, J.D., and Larsen, M.D. (2013 May). *Adjusting Sample Weights for Linkage-Eligibility Using SUDAAN.* Hyattsville Maryland: National Center for Health Statistics. https://www.cdc.gov/nchs/data/datalinkage/adjusting_sample_weights_for_linkage_eligibility_using_sudaan.pdf.

Karr, A.F., Lin, X., Reiter, J.P., and Sanil, A.P. (2009). Privacy preserving analysis of vertically partitioned data using secure matrix protocols. *Journal of Official Statistics* 25: 125–138.

Kilss, B. and Alvey, W. (1985). Record linkage techniques – 1985. *Proceedings of the Workshop on Exact Matching Methodologies*, Arlington, Virginia (9–10 May 1985). Washington, DC: Department of the Treasury. https://nces.ed.gov/FCSM/pdf/RLT85.pdf.

Kim, H.J., Karr, A.F., and Reiter, J.P. (2015). Statistical disclosure limitation in the presence of edit rules. *Journal of Official Statistics* 31: 121–138.

Kohnen, C.N. and Reiter, J.P. (2009). Multiple imputation for combining confidential data owned by two agencies. *Journal of the Royal Statistical Society Series A* 172: 511–528.

Lahiri, P. and Larsen, M.D. (2005). Regression analysis with linked data. *Journal of the American Statistical Association* 100: 222–230.

Larsen, M.D. (2002). Comments on hierarchical Bayesian record linkage. *JSM Proceedings, Section on Bayesian Statistical Science*, Alexandria, VA. pp. 1995–2000.

Larsen, M.D. (2004). Record linkage using finite mixture models. In: *Applied Bayesian Modeling and Causal Inference from Incomplete-Data Perspectives* (ed. A. Gelman and X.-L. Meng), 309–318.

Larsen, M.D. (2010). Record linkage modeling in federal statistical databases. *Proceedings of the 2009 Federal Committee on Statistical Methodology (FCSM) Research Conference*, Washington, DC. https://nces.ed.gov/FCSM/pdf/2009FCSM_Larsen_II-C.pdf.

Larsen, M.D. and Rubin, D.B. (2001). Iterative automated record linkage using mixture models. *Journal of the American Statistical Association* 79: 32–41.

Mulrow, E., Mushtaq, A., Pramanik, S., and Fontes, A. (2011). *Assessment of the U.S. Census Bureau's Personal Identification Validation System.* Bethesda, MD: NORC at the University of Chicago. https://www.norc.org/PDFs/May%202011%20Personal%20Validation%20and%20Entity%20Resolution%20Conference/PVS%20Assessment%20Report%20FINAL%20JULY%202011.pdf.

National Archives (2020). The Soundex Indexing System. Last reviewed on 27 February 2020. https://www.archives.gov/research/census/soundex (accessed 19 March 2021).

NCHS (2019). *The Linkage of National Center for Health Statistics Survey Data to the National Death Index — 2015 Linked Mortality File (LMF): Methodology Overview and Analytic Considerations.* Hyattsville, MD: National Center for Health Statistics. Office of Analysis and Epidemiology. https://www.cdc.gov/nchs/data-linkage/mortality-methods.htm.

Neter, J., Maynes, E.S., and Ramanathan, R. (1965). The effect of mismatching on the measurement of response errors. *Journal of the American Statistical Association* 60: 1005–1027.

Newcombe, H.B. (1988). *Handbook of Record Linkage: Methods for Health and Statistical Studies, Administration, and Business.* Oxford: Oxford University Press.

Newcombe, H.B., Kennedy, J.M., Axford, S.J., and James, A.P. (1959). Automatic linkage of vital records. *Science* 130: 954–959.

Raghunathan, T.E., Reiter, J.P., and Rubin, D.B. (2003). Multiple imputation for statistical disclosure limitation. *Journal of Official Statistics* 19: 1–16.

Reiter, J.P. (2002). Satisfying disclosure restrictions with synthetic data sets. *Journal of Official Statistics* 18: 531–544.

Reiter, J.P. (2005). Releasing multiply-imputed, synthetic public use microdata: an illustration and empirical study. *Journal of the Royal Statistical Society, Series A* 168: 185–205.

Reiter, J.P. (2009). Using multiple imputation to integrate and disseminate confidential microdata. *International Statistical Review* 77: 179–195.

Reiter, J.P. (2021). Assessing uncertainty when using linked administrative records. In: *Administrative Records for Survey Methodology* (ed. A.Y. Chun, M.D. Larsen, G. Durrant and J.P. Reiter), 139–153. Hoboken, NJ: Wiley.

Sakshaug, J.W. (2021). Measuring and controlling for non-consent bias in linked survey and administrative data. In: *Administrative Records for Survey Methodology* (ed. A.Y. Chun, M.D. Larsen, G. Durrant and J.P. Reiter), 155–174. Hoboken, NJ: Wiley.

Sakshaug, J.W. and Vicari, B.J. (2018). Obtaining record linkage consent from establishments: the impact of question placement on consent rates and bias. *Journal of Survey Statistics and Methodology* 6 (1): 46–71. https://doi.org/10.1093/jssam/smx009.

Scheuren, F. and Winkler, W.E. (1993). Regression analysis of data files that are computer matched. *Survey Methodology* 19: 39–58.

Scheuren, F. and Winkler, W.E. (1997). Regression analysis of data files that are computer matched, II. *Survey Methodology* 23: 157–165.

Schnell, R. (2015). Privacy-preserving record linkage. In: *Methodological Developments in Data Linkage* (ed. K. Harron, H. Goldstein and C. Dibben), 201–225. UK: Wiley. ISBN 1118745876.

Smith, M.E. and Newcombe, H.B. (1975). Methods for computer linkage of hospital admission-separation records into cumulative health histories. *Methods of Information in Medicine* 14 (3): 118–125.

Statistics Canada (2020). Microdata Linkage at Statistics Canada. Date modified: 2020-11-16. https://www.statcan.gc.ca/eng/record/gen (accessed 19 March 2021).

U.S. Census Bureau (2021). Data Linkage Infrastructure. https://www.census.gov/about/adrm/linkage.html (accessed 19 March 2021).

Vatsalan, D., Christen, P., O'Keefe, C.M., and Verykios, V.S. (2014). An evaluation framework for privacy-preserving record linkage. *Journal of Privacy and Confidentiality* 6 (1): https://doi.org/10.29012/jpc.v6i1.636.

Winkler, W.E. (1988). Using the EM algorithm for weight computation in the Fellegi-Sunter model of record linkage. In: *JSM Proceedings, Survey Research Methods Section*, 667–671. Alexandria, VA: American Statistical Association. Retrieved from http://www.asasrms.org/Proceedings/papers/1988_124.pdf.

Winkler, W.E. (1989a). Near automatic weight computation in the Fellegi-Sunter model of record linkage. *Proceedings of the Fifth Census Bureau Annual Research Conference.* pp. 145–155.

Winkler, W.E. (1989b). Methods for adjusting for lack of independence in an application of the Fellegi-Sunter model of record linkage. *Survey Methodology* 15: 101–117.

Winkler, W.E. (1989c). Frequency-based matching in the Fellegi-Sunter model of record linkage. In: *JSM Proceedings, Survey Research Methods Section*, 778–783. Alexandria, VA: American Statistical Association. http://www.asasrms.org/Proceedings/papers/1989_144.pdf.

Winkler, W.E. (1990). String comparator metrics and enhanced decision rules in the Fellegi-Sunter model of record linkage. In: *JSM Proceedings, Survey Research Methods Section*, 354–359. Alexandria, VA: American Statistical Association. http://www.asasrms.org/Proceedings/y1990f.html.

Winkler, W.E. (1995). Matching and record linkage. In: *Business Survey Methods* (ed. B.G. Cox, D.A. Binder, B.N. Chinnappa, A. Christianson, M.A. Colledge, and P.S. Kott), 355–384. New York: Wiley. https://www.census.gov/srd/papers/pdf/rr93-8.pdf.

Winkler, W.E. (1996). Overview of Record Linkage and Current Research Directions. Research Report Series, Statistics #2006-2, Statistical Research Division, U.S. Census Bureau, Washington, D.C. https://www.census.gov/srd/papers/pdf/rrs2006-02.pdf.

Winkler, W.E. (2021). Cleaning and using administrative lists: enhanced practices and computational algorithms for record linkage and modeling/editing/imputation. In: *Administrative Records for Survey Methodology* (ed. A.Y. Chun, M.D. Larsen, G. Durrant and J.P. Reiter), 105–138. Hoboken, NJ: Wiley.

34

Methods for Estimating the Quality of Multisource Statistics

Arnout van Delden[1], Sander Scholtus[1], Ton de Waal[1,2], and Irene Csorba[3]

[1]*Statistics Netherlands, The Hague, The Netherlands*
[2]*Tilburg University, Tilburg, The Netherlands*
[3]*Vrije Universiteit Amsterdam, Amsterdam, The Netherlands*

34.1 Introduction

With the increasing availability of data, official business statistics are more often based on multiple data sources. Evaluating the accuracy of outputs based on multiple sources has therefore become an important topic. With accuracy, we mean the bias and the variance of the output, as affected by error sources in the input data, processing of the data, or due to the estimation of the targeted output. Output accuracy of multisource statistics tends to be significantly affected by a greater variety of error sources than single source statistics. A first reason for this is that often more processing steps are involved such as linkage and standardization of the data. Another reason is that some sources that are used were originally not intended to be used for statistical purposes; we refer to this as secondary use. These first two reasons underline a greater variety of errors sources that come along with multisource statistics. In situations where sampling error or nonresponse error are not dominating (as is regularly assumed to be the case with single-source surveys), these other error sources also need to be accounted for when estimating the output accuracy.

Quantification of output accuracy of multisource statistics is relevant for various reasons. First of all, estimates of output accuracy of multisource statistics can be used directly to inform users about output quality. Second, in the long run, such estimates might be used to gradually improve output accuracy of statistics that are published regularly. For instance, measures about the effect of linkage errors on output accuracy can be used to judge whether the linkage step is of sufficient quality and whether improvements are needed. Furthermore, in some cases, there are different options for combining or processing the data and adjustments could be made if needed.

Various studies on estimation of output accuracy of multisource statistics are available. The European project KOMUSO, which ran from 2016 until 2019, produced an inventory of quality measures and computational methods to estimate output quality (Ascari et al. 2020; ESSnet Quality of Multisource Statistics – Komuso 2019). Based on that inventory, de Waal et al. (2021) distinguish three main groups of methods to estimate output accuracy: scoring methods, methods based on (re)sampling, and methods based on parametric modeling.

Many publications concern the effect of a specific error type on output quality, see examples in de Waal et al. (2020) and de Waal et al. (2021). Recently however, Meng (2018) proposed a general framework to estimate the accuracy of a total or a mean as affected by representation

Advances in Business Statistics, Methods and Data Collection. Edited by Ger Snijkers, Mojca Bavdaž, Stefan Bender, Jacqui Jones, Steve MacFeely, Joseph W. Sakshaug, Katherine J. Thompson, and Arnout van Delden.
© 2023 John Wiley & Sons, Inc. Published 2023 by John Wiley & Sons, Inc.

errors for different data source types. We define a representation error as the difference between the population of units for which observations are obtained and the (intended) target population. The effect of such representation errors on the bias of a quantitative output variable will be treated in the current chapter.

The framework by Meng (2018) has been extended by Biemer and Amaya (2018) to estimate the accuracy of a total or a mean as affected by both representation errors and by errors made on "the measurement side." We define an error on the measurement side as the difference between the obtained value for a variable in the data source and the true value according to the targeted concept, for the variable to be analyzed. In the remainder of this chapter, we will use the term "measurement error" for any error on the measurement side. In case of secondary data use, this measurement error can be further decomposed into reporting differences in the data set at hand between the obtained and the true value (according to the definition used within the data source), and in value differences that can be attributed to definitional differences between the variable within the data source and the targeted concept. In some cases, one can adjust the data for these definitional differences, see Scholtus et al. (2015) for an example.

In the current chapter, the definitions for representation and measurement errors are broad: they can be further subdivided in all kinds of underlying, more specific, error types. Examples of error frameworks that distinguish among multiple error types along the representation side and along the measurement side are Groves et al. (2004), who focus on total survey error, Zhang (2012) who focuses on integration of administrative data, and Reid et al. (2017) who added to the framework of Zhang (2012) an estimation and output quality evaluation step. Finally, we mention Amaya et al. (2020) who developed an error framework for secondary use of big data sources.

One of the forms of multisource statistics concerns the construction of an integrated microdata set. This may require data linkage of overlapping units in different data sets, which may result in linkage errors. On the microlevel, we consider as a linkage error any difference between the actual links that are made between the records of two data sets and correct links (matches). Unit-level linkage errors can be divided further into mislinks (where the wrong units are linked to each other) and missed links (where units are erroneously not matched). On the level of statistical outputs, these linkage errors can introduce both bias and variance. Bias can arise, for instance, when missed links are more likely to occur for certain subgroups in the population (similar to selective nonresponse). Bias in subpopulation estimates can also occur as a result of wrong values that are linked to units (due to mislinks). As will be shown in Section 34.3, mislinks can also lead to bias in estimated statistical outputs. Random linkage errors will tend to inflate the variance of statistical outputs.

Besides representation error, measurement error and linkage error, other kinds of errors may occur in multisource statistics. For instance, the population size may be unknown due to undercoverage error. In situations where a business register is lacking, population size can be estimated with methods such as capture–recapture. That is often treated in a separate estimation step and is therefore left out of the scope of this chapter.

Although a general framework for output accuracy has been developed with respect to representation and measurement errors, the contributions by Biemer and Amaya (2018) and by Meng (2018) do not answer the question how to actually *estimate* the components of their framework. For instance, Meng (2018) shows that the bias of an estimated population mean based on a nonprobability sample depends on the correlation between the target variable and an inclusion variable describing whether the unit responded or not (see Section 34.2.1.1); it is however not clear in general how to obtain an accurate estimator for that correlation.

The aim of the current chapter is to present a number of methods to estimate output accuracy as affected by representation errors, linkage errors, and measurement errors, and to illustrate these methods by case studies in business statistics. To limit the length of this chapter, we do not attempt to give a complete overview of such methods, but focus on a number of recent methods that seem promising to us and that have been examined at Statistics Netherlands itself.

For each of these three error types, the general aim of how to estimate their effect on output quality can be split further into three basic research questions. The first question concerns how to model and quantify the distribution of the error type at hand; for instance, what percentage of units is affected by linkage errors? Concerning the quantification of the size of the errors, one might take a sample of units and manually check them for errors but that is usually a very costly process. Can this be done more efficiently? The second question concerns how to estimate the effect of the error type on the accuracy of a given estimator. Numerical or analytical approaches may be used for this. The third question concerns: what is the best, i.e. most accurate, way to reduce the effects of the error and improve the accuracy of a given estimator? For instance if the error leads to biased estimates, can we correct for such a bias? Of course, the second and third questions are closely related, but they may require different methodologies. Under some conditions, it is easier to estimate the bias than to improve the estimator by correcting for this bias. We aim to look into these research questions in the current chapter. We note that the notation used in this chapter varies slightly for the different (sub)sections due to the wide variety of different methods considered.

The remainder of this chapter is organized as follows. We will introduce recently developed methods to estimate bias and variance of outputs affected by representation error (Section 34.2), linkage error (Section 34.3), and measurement error (Section 34.4). We illustrate the methods with practical examples, mostly from Statistics Netherlands. We do not aim to give a complete overview of the currently used types of methods; for such an overview, the reader is referred to de Waal et al. (2021). The chapter ends with some conclusions in Section 34.5.

34.2   Representation Error

This section focuses on representation error, i.e. the difference between the population of units for which observations are obtained and the (intended) target population.

Whereas traditional sample surveys are based on probability samples, the units in big data are mostly obtained from nonprobability samples, and in this section, we will assume that this is the case for our big data examples. For instance, Daas and Van der Doef (2020) derived whether businesses are innovative or not using website information. Since not all businesses have a (known) website, representation errors may occur, which may lead to selectivity. Selectivity occurs when the missingness is correlated with the target variables. In this section, we first briefly discuss estimation of the effect of selectivity on data quality and the correction of selectivity in Section 34.2.1, and then briefly describe two case studies for both kinds of problems in Sections 34.2.2 and 34.2.3.

34.2.1   Estimating and Correcting Selectivity

34.2.1.1   Estimating Output Accuracy with Respect to Representation Errors

In a seminal paper, Meng (2018) gives a simple expression for selection error when estimating the population mean $\overline{Y}$ of a target variable Y, using some data set, for instance a nonprobability sample. The selection error stands for the difference between the actual estimate based on the respondents versus the true population value. We denote the selection indicator by S, i.e. $S_i = 1$ if unit i of the target population is selected into the data set under consideration and $S_i = 0$ if unit i is not selected into the data set. The approach given by Meng (2018) holds for any nonprobability sample, the mechanism of responding or recording can either be entirely fixed or there can be some (unknown) probability mechanism underlying S. We denote the population size by N, the size of the data set under consideration as n, and the sample mean of Y in this data set by $\overline{y}^{(1)}$. The superscript "(1)" refers to the fact that the units that are selected in the data set under consideration, i.e. the units for which S equals one, are used to calculate the sample mean of Y. According to Meng (2018) the selection error $\mathcal{S} = \overline{y}^{(1)} - \overline{Y}$ is given by

$$\mathcal{S} = \overline{y}^{(1)} - \overline{Y} = \frac{\sigma_{SY}}{\overline{S}} \tag{34.1}$$

where $\sigma_{SY} = N^{-1} \sum_{i=1}^{N}(S_i - \overline{S})(Y_i - \overline{Y})$ is the covariance between the target variable Y and the selection variable S in the population and $\overline{S} = N^{-1} \sum_{i=1}^{N} S_i$. Interestingly, an expression of this form has already been given in Bethlehem (1988, expression (3.5)) which expressed the bias of a Horvitz–Thompson estimator affected by survey nonresponse. Meng (2018) rewrites (34.1) as a product of three terms:

$$\overline{y}^{(1)} - \overline{Y} = \rho_{SY} \times \sigma_Y \times \sqrt{\frac{N-n}{n}} \equiv \mathcal{S}_{\text{Meng}} \tag{34.2}$$

Meng (2018) refers to the first term ρ_{SY} on the right-hand side as *data quality*, to the second term σ_Y as *problem difficulty*, and to the third term as *data quantity*. Data quality $\rho_{SY} = \sigma_{SY}/(\sigma_S \sigma_Y)$ is the correlation between the selection mechanism S and the target variable Y and measures how S and Y are related to each other. *Problem difficulty* σ_Y is the standard deviation of target variable Y in the population, and measures the variability of target variable Y in the population. *Data quantity* $\sqrt{\frac{N-n}{n}}$ is the root of the ratio of the size of the unselected part of the population to the sample size n, so it measures the sample size in terms of the population size. Meng's formula explains why for a sample survey drawn by means of simple random sampling, the bias under the sampling design is zero, since we have $E[\rho_{SY}] = 0$, where the expectation is taken with respect to the sampling design.

The work by Meng (2018) is strongly related to work by Andridge and Little (2011) and Little et al. (2020). Whereas Meng (2018) considers a situation where population values are known and we have to account for some possibly selective selection mechanism S, Andridge and Little (2011) and Little et al. (2020) consider a situation where population values have to be estimated from the available nonprobability sample and an auxiliary variable Z is available. Andridge and Little (2011) and Little et al. (2020) then model the selection mechanism as

$$P(S = 1 | Y, Z, \phi) = g(\phi Y + (1 - \phi)Z)$$

where g is an arbitrary function and ϕ is an unknown scalar parameter, both assumed to be ranging between [0,1]. The parameter ϕ expresses the degree of nonrandom selection after conditioning on Z (Little et al. 2020). Under various model assumptions, Andridge and Little (2011) find the following maximum likelihood estimate for $\overline{Y}$:

$$\overline{Y}(\phi) = \overline{y}^{(1)} - \frac{\phi + (1 - \phi)r_{ZY}^{(1)}}{\phi r_{ZY}^{(1)} + (1 - \phi)} \frac{\sqrt{\sigma_Y^{2(1)}}}{\sqrt{\sigma_Z^{2(1)}}} (\overline{z}^{(1)} - \overline{Z})$$

$$S_{\text{MUB}} = \overline{y}^{(1)} - \overline{Y}(\phi) \tag{34.3}$$

where $\overline{Z}$ represents the population mean of the auxiliary variable Z. Conditioned on the selected units $(S = 1)$, $\overline{y}^{(1)}$ and $\overline{z}^{(1)}$ are the respective sample means, $\sigma_Y^{2(1)}$ and $\sigma_Z^{2(1)}$ are the respective sample variances, and $r_{ZY}^{(1)}$ represents the sample correlation between Z and Y. Little et al. (2020) refer to "$\overline{y}^{(1)} - \overline{Y}(\phi)$" as a measure of unadjusted bias (MUB). Little et al. (2020) transform $r_{ZY}^{(1)}$ in such a way that it ranges between [0,1]. Under certain conditions, (34.2) may be seen as a special case of (34.3), where instead of a general auxiliary variable Z the selection indicator S is used in (34.3).

34.2.1.2 Correcting for Representation Errors

In existing literature, there are two main approaches for correcting for selectivity due to representation errors: a pseudo-design based approach and a model-based approach (see, for instance, Elliott 2009; Elliott and Valliant 2017; Rafei et al. 2020). In the first approach, one tries to derive approximate inclusion probabilities for the nonprobability sample. In the second approach, one tries to fit a model to the target variable Y, using auxiliary variables X, and one assumes that the fitted model also holds for the nonobserved population. Both approaches can be combined to yield a so-called "doubly robust approach" (see, for instance, Chen et al. 2020). In Section 34.2.3, we briefly discuss a case study using a pseudo-design based approach.

34.2.2 Case Study on Estimating Bias Due to Selectivity

We examined the methods proposed by Meng (2018) and Little et al. (2020) for estimating selection error. We focused on the situation where a statistic is to be produced repeatedly, say, every quarter, and the data that are used to estimate this statistic are gradually filled over time. Such a situation occurs for the short term statistics (STS) at Statistics Netherlands. In the STS, the total turnover in the population is to be estimated for different industries (groupings of Nomenclature statistique des Activités économiques dans la Communauté Européenne [NACE] codes). For many industries, the estimation is largely done on value added tax (VAT) data obtained from the tax office. These VAT data are gradually filled over time. In particular, the enterprises that report their turnover early to the tax office form a selective group in the population, which implies that early estimates for the total turnover are likely to be biased.

We applied the methods to the economic sectors Manufacturing, Retail trade, and Employment activities for quarter 1 of 2014 until quarter 4 of 2016. We only show some preliminary results for quarter 4 of 2014, other periods gave similar results. We estimated the selection error of early estimates, 25 days after the end of the quarter, compared to late estimates when all turnover data are available. A few extremely large and complex enterprises were left out of the data set because the turnover of those enterprises is always requested (if missing) before output is published since their values dominate the results. If we would have kept those enterprises in the data set but considered their turnover to be always present, then we would have obtained a much smaller range of true selection errors. We also dropped enterprises with zero VAT turnover from the data set, since these are inactive and probably do not belong to the target population. Finally, we found a limited number of enterprises whose turnover varied more than a factor 1000 over the periods, probably because they did not report their complete turnover yet. We also dropped those enterprises from our data. We estimated the quarterly selection error for output industries, which are groupings of NACE codes that are used in the STS output at Statistics Netherlands: 24 industries (groups of NACE codes) for Manufacturing, 37 industries for Retail trade. For Employment activities, only the total is published, for that sector we used a more detailed grouping with six groups.

The quarterly turnover derived from the VAT data was taken as the target variable Y and the quarterly turnover of the previous quarter was used as auxiliary variable Z. In order to estimate expression (34.2) of Meng (2018), we need an estimate for ρ_{SY} and for σ_Y. We estimated σ_Y as $\hat{\sigma}_Y = \sigma_Z \bar{y}^{(1)} / \bar{z}^{(1)}$. For ρ_{SY}, we compared two estimates: (i) ρ_{SY} based on the previous period, and (ii) using $\hat{\rho}_{SY} = \rho_{SZ}$. Little et al. (2020) suggest to calculate $\mathcal{S}_{\mathrm{MUB}}$ with ϕ values of 0, 0.5, and 1 to get an interval for the possible selection error, but in the current study, the ϕ values were estimated from the previous period, using the expression $\phi = \left(\Delta_Y - r_{ZY}^{(1)}\Delta_Z\right) / \left(1 - r_{ZY}^{(1)}\right)(\Delta_Y + \Delta_Z)$, with $\Delta_Y = (\overline{y}^{(1)} - \overline{Y})/\sigma_Y$ and $\Delta_Z = (\overline{z}^{(1)} - \overline{Z})/\sigma_Z$ and $r_{ZY}^{(1)}$, Δ_Y and Δ_Z based on the previous period. For a robust estimation of ϕ, denoted by $\hat{\phi}_r$, we replaced the sample means $\overline{y}^{(1)}$ and $\overline{z}^{(1)}$ by their corresponding sample medians to estimate Δ_Y and Δ_Z. Because some estimated $\hat{\phi}_r$ values (a hat stands for an estimate) exceeded the [0,1] interval, these values were transformed to either 0 if $\hat{\phi}_r < 0$ or 1 if $\hat{\phi}_r > 1$.

For each industry, we are interested to estimate the relative selection error, denoted as $R\mathcal{S}$, defined as follows:

$$R\mathcal{S} = \frac{\overline{y}^{(1)} - \overline{Y}}{\overline{Y}} = \frac{N\overline{y}^{(1)} - Y}{Y}$$

Note that the relative selection error of a stratum total or of a mean for a certain period is the same, since its numerator and denominator are multiplied by the same population size N. In our data set, where the true relative selection error is known, we aim to compare this true relative selection error with a real-time measure of the relative selection error, i.e. when the true population mean $\overline{Y}$ is not yet known. The relative selection error was therefore estimated by replacing the population mean $\overline{Y}$ by its estimate $\hat{\overline{Y}} = \overline{y}^{(1)} - \mathcal{S}_{\text{MENG}}$ for the method by Meng (2018) and by $\hat{\overline{Y}} = \overline{y}^{(1)} - \mathcal{S}_{\text{MUB}}$ for the method by Little et al. (2020). These estimates are referred to as $\widehat{R\mathcal{S}}_{\text{MENG}}$ and $\widehat{R\mathcal{S}}_{\text{MUB}}$.

In Figure 34.1, the results are displayed for the sectors employment activities, retail trade, and manufacturing. It can be seen that Meng's (2018) method with $\hat{\rho}_{SY} = \rho_{SZ}$ and MUB with ϕ estimated from the previous period performed nearly equally well. However, Meng's (2018) method with ρ_{SY} estimated from a previous period clearly resulted in estimated relative selection error that could differ greatly from the true selection error. The reason for this poorer estimate is that it

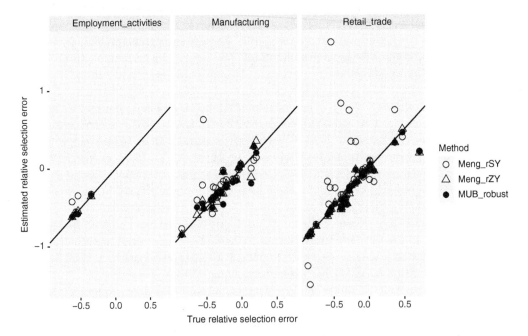

Figure 34.1 The true relative selection error ($R\mathcal{S}$) versus the estimated $R\mathcal{S}$ according to (34.2) by Meng (2018) and the robust MUB for three economic sectors. (Figure made by the authors.)

varied considerably which units actually responded in a certain period. Combined with a skewed turnover distribution, the correlation ρ_{SY} varied considerably from quarter to quarter. The correlation between selection indicator S from the current quarter and the auxiliary variable Z provided a far more accurate estimate of the correlation ρ_{SY} than using ρ_{SY} of the previous period.

In conclusion, in our application, both the method of Meng (2018) as well as the method of Little et al. (2020) resulted in quite good estimates of the true relative selection error, when the turnover of the previous period was used as an auxiliary variable. This auxiliary variable is already highly correlated with the target variable. In future work, we aim to derive an auxiliary variable that is even more closely related to the target variable, in order to improve the estimate of the relative selection error.

34.2.3 Case Study on Correcting Output for Selectivity

Huijskens (2020) studied the use of a pseudo-design based approach, namely sample matching (see Rivers 2006, 2007; Rivers and Bailey 2009), as a correction method for selectivity in nonprobability samples by means of a simulation study. Sample matching can be applied when one has a nonprobability sample of, say, size n with observed values for a variable of interest Y and a vector of auxiliary variables X, which may also be known from administrative data or population registers. Since we are dealing with a nonprobability sample that is not obtained by means of a predefined sampling design, the probabilities of being selected into the nonprobability sample are unknown. Huijskens (2020) examined the situation where one wants to estimate the population mean $\overline{Y}$, using the data in the nonprobability sample. For instance, one could think of a situation in which quarterly turnover is obtained from administrative data for smaller units and from a survey for the large units. The turnover in the administrative data is gradually filling over time. As already discussed in Section 34.2.2, for early estimates, the response in the quarterly data is incomplete and direct estimates based on early respondents may result in biased population estimates. Since the inclusion probabilities are unknown, one cannot use a weighted sample mean directly. In sample matching, one therefore first draws a probability sample of, say, size m (where $m \leq n$) by means of a well-defined sampling design, including the auxiliary variables X for each unit. Returning to the example above, one might use the data of the smaller units from the Structural Business Statistics for sample matching with auxiliary variables NACE code, number of employees, enterprise complexity, and yearly turnover of two years before. Obviously, this probability sample will not include the target variable Y; otherwise, one could simply use the probability sample to base population estimates for Y upon. Next, one matches each unit in the probability sample to a similar unit in the nonprobability sample. Generally, "similarity" is defined in terms of a distance function based on the values for the auxiliary variables X of a unit in the nonprobability sample and a unit in the probability sample. The value observed for target variable Y in the nonprobability sample is then donated to the matched unit in the probability sample. This procedure yields a matched sample of size m with known inclusion probabilities and (donated) values for target variable Y for all units. The final step in sample matching is to use the inverse of the inclusion probabilities to weight the values of the target variable Y and thus obtain a population estimate for, say, the population mean $\overline{Y}$.

The sample matching procedure relies on some rather strong modeling assumptions, such as the common support assumption and the ignorability assumption. The common support assumption says that the distributions of the auxiliary variables observed in the nonprobability sample should cover the same ranges as the distributions observed in the entire population. The ignorability assumption says that the event of being selected into the nonprobability sample is independent of the target variable Y conditional on the auxiliary variables X.

The simulation study by Huijskens (2020) showed, for instance, that, when the common support and ignorability assumptions are met, proximity-matching methods, where a distance function is used to measure the similarity between units from the probability sample and nonprobability sample, perform well in terms of bias reduction. Proximity-matching methods performed better in terms of bias reduction compared to exact matching, where units are matched only if their values on all (categorical) auxiliary variables are identical, and poststratification, where the nonprobability data are poststratified and then calibrated to known population totals. The performance of inverse propensity score weighting, where propensity scores for units to be included into the nonprobability sample are estimated based on both the probability sample and the nonprobability sample utilizing the sample weights in the probability sample, did equally well as proximity matching in some situations. However, as Huijskens (2020) showed, inverse propensity score weighting is more likely to become unstable in practical applications.

34.3 Linkage Error

Often, the production of statistical outputs requires that data from multiple sources is linked at the microlevel. As noted in the introduction, we consider as a linkage error on the microlevel any difference between the actual links that are made between the records of two data sets and correct links (matches). If a common unique identifier is available in all data sources, then linking data on the same units is relatively straightforward and can be done virtually without error. Although this situation occurs relatively often in business statistics, as compared to social statistics, still sometimes it is necessary to link data from different sources that lack a reliable common unique identifier. When a common unique identifier is not available, data sources have to be linked on the basis of indirect identifying variables such as business name, address, phone number, name of owner, and so on. Since these variables may contain measurement errors and missing values – and, even in the absence of such errors, may contain insufficient information to distinguish individual units in all cases – linkage errors can occur. Linkage errors concern both missed links (false negatives; identical units that erroneously have not been linked) as well as mislinks (false positives; two units that are linked incorrectly).

For a discussion of different techniques for deterministic and probabilistic linkage based on indirect identifying variables, see Larsen and Herning (Chapter 33 in this volume). In this section, we will first review some methods to quantify the prevalence of linkage errors and their effects on statistical outputs. We will then discuss different ways to correct statistical outputs for linkage errors and present findings from a simulation study on contingency tables.

34.3.1 Estimating the Effect of Linkage Errors on Outputs

The presence of linkage errors in combined data may lead to biased estimates (Sakshaug and Antoni 2017). It is therefore important to analyze the quality of the linkages (Harron et al. 2017; Moore et al. 2018). Harron et al. (2017) mention four approaches to evaluate linkage quality and to identify potential sources of bias. First, a gold standard data set can be used to estimate linkage error rates, for instance by clerical inspection of a subsample. An example can be found in Ravindra (2019) that describes linkage of three data sets to a frame (per province) concerning owners of real estate. A sample was taken to assess false positive and false negative linkage rates for each of the three data sets (see Table 34.1 for two provinces). Second, a sensitivity analysis can be used to assess the effect of varying the linkage conditions on the estimates. Third, characteristics of linked and unlinked

Table 34.1 Evaluating the linkage quality of real estate estimates.

Province	Files linked to property assessment file	Linkage rate (%)	False positive error rate (%)	False negative error rate (%)
Ontario	Census	93.3	<1.0	<0.5
	Tax and social insurance	98.0	<0.5	<0.5
	Business register	97.8	<2.0	n.a.
Nova Scotia	Census	86.6	<1.5	<1.0
	Tax and social insurance	93.3	<1.5	<1.0
	Business register	96.0	<8.0	<2.0

Source: Ravindra 2019.

data can be compared, for instance to investigate whether there are specific subgroups which are not linked. Fourth, in some situations, plausibility of the linked data can be evaluated (postlinkage evaluation). When the variables that come from different sources have logical relations to each other, those relations can be checked.

Information about the quality of linkage at the microlevel can be used to gain insights into the effects of linkage errors on the accuracy of statistical outputs. For missed links (false negative errors), there is a clear relation to the general problem of missing data. Thus, information about differences in the rate of nonlinkage between different subgroups as mentioned above can be used to assess the magnitude of bias due to missed links (Sakshaug and Kreuter 2012). Under the assumption that the missed links are "missing at random" in the terminology of Little and Rubin (2002), traditional survey methods could be used to correct for bias due to missed links, such as weighting (Yang et al. 2019) or imputation (Gessendorfer et al. 2018).

Note that, in general, two data sets that are to be linked may not contain the exact same set of units and it may therefore in fact be desirable that not all records are linked. Thus, the presence of records that remain unlinked is in itself not necessarily an indicator of missed links. Differences in population coverage between data sources that are to be linked, and potential selectivity issues that these may cause in the resulting linked data, can be regarded as representation errors as discussed in Section 34.2. Note that these issues may be relevant even in the absence of linkage errors (perfect linkage).

To illustrate the potential biasing effects of mislinks (false positive errors) on statistical outputs, we consider the following situation. There are two data files, A and B, containing, respectively, the variables $(x_1, \ldots, x_M, z_1, \ldots, z_K)$ and $(x_1, \ldots, x_M, y)$. The common variables $x_1, \ldots, x_M$ are used for record linkage. We suppose, for simplicity, that linkage is one-to-one and the two files contain exactly the same units, say $i = 1, \ldots, N$. Thus, the ideal linkage result would be to link every record in A to its (uniquely defined) corresponding record in B, and vice versa. Let $\mathbf{X}_A$, $\mathbf{X}_B$, $\mathbf{Z}_A$, and $\mathbf{y}_B$ denote the $N \times M$, $N \times M$, and $N \times K$ matrices and N-vector, respectively, of values that would be observed if the two files were sorted in such a way that the record in position i in file A belongs to the same unit as the record in position i in file B, for every $i = 1, \ldots, N$. The statistic of interest is some function of $\mathbf{Z}_A$ and $\mathbf{y}_B$, say $\theta = f(\mathbf{Z}_A, \mathbf{y}_B)$. As an example, we take the vector of ordinary least squares (OLS) regression coefficients of y on $z_1, \ldots, z_K$: $\boldsymbol{\beta} = \left(\mathbf{Z}_A'\mathbf{Z}_A\right)^{-1}\mathbf{Z}_A'\mathbf{y}_B$. An important special case for business statistics occurs when $z_1, \ldots, z_K$ are dummy variables that represent an assignment of units to domains (e.g. classified by economic activity code, size class, or region) and y represents a numerical variable (e.g. turnover or energy use); the regression coefficients in $\boldsymbol{\beta}$ then correspond to domain means of this numerical variable.

In practice, we do not observe $\mathbf{Z}_A$ and $\mathbf{y}_B$ simultaneously; otherwise, the linkage problem would be trivial. Even under the simplifying assumption that all records are linked, after record linkage we observe $\mathbf{Z}_A$ and $\mathbf{y}_B^*$, where $\mathbf{y}_B^*$ is some (unknown) permutation of $\mathbf{y}_B$. Thus, we can write $\mathbf{y}_B^* = \mathbf{C}\mathbf{y}_B$, for some (unknown) permutation matrix $\mathbf{C} = (c_{ij})$, i.e. a matrix of zeros and ones where each row and column sums to one. Any off-diagonal element $c_{ij} = 1$ $(i \neq j)$ corresponds to a mislink. From the combined file, we can compute the observed statistic $\theta^* = f\left(\mathbf{Z}_A, \mathbf{y}_B^*\right) = f(\mathbf{Z}_A, \mathbf{C}\mathbf{y}_B)$. For instance, for the above regression coefficients, we obtain $\boldsymbol{\beta}^* = \left(\mathbf{Z}_A'\mathbf{Z}_A\right)^{-1}\mathbf{Z}_A'\mathbf{y}_B^* = \left(\mathbf{Z}_A'\mathbf{Z}_A\right)^{-1}\mathbf{Z}_A'\mathbf{C}\mathbf{y}_B$. It is clear that we should expect that $\boldsymbol{\beta}^* \neq \boldsymbol{\beta}$ (and, more generally, $\theta^* \neq \theta$) unless $\mathbf{C}$ happens to be equal to the identity matrix, which means that no linkage errors occur.

To assess the bias in $\boldsymbol{\beta}^*$, a commonly made assumption is that linkage errors occur by a random mechanism which is *noninformative* in the sense that $E(\mathbf{C}\mathbf{y}_B \mid \mathbf{Z}_A) = E(\mathbf{C} \mid \mathbf{Z}_A)E(\mathbf{y}_B \mid \mathbf{Z}_A)$ (e.g. Chambers 2009). Let $\mathbf{Q} = E(\mathbf{C} \mid \mathbf{Z}_A)$. Under the assumed linear regression model it holds that $E(\mathbf{y}_B \mid \mathbf{Z}_A) = \mathbf{Z}_A\boldsymbol{\beta}$, so we find that

$$E(\boldsymbol{\beta}^* \mid \mathbf{Z}_A) = \left(\mathbf{Z}_A'\mathbf{Z}_A\right)^{-1}\mathbf{Z}_A'E(\mathbf{C}\mathbf{y}_B \mid \mathbf{Z}_A) = \left(\mathbf{Z}_A'\mathbf{Z}_A\right)^{-1}\mathbf{Z}_A'\mathbf{Q}\mathbf{Z}_A\boldsymbol{\beta} \tag{34.4}$$

which is generally not equal to $\boldsymbol{\beta}$ unless $\mathbf{Q}$ is the identity matrix. Thus, in general, mislinks cause bias in the estimated statistical outputs based on a combined file.

In practice of course, the matrix $\mathbf{Q}$ is not known and has to be estimated. Gold standard data for a subsample could be used for this, but some simplifying model assumptions are necessary in practice. A very simple model that is commonly used is the so-called "exchangeable linkage errors model" (Neter et al. 1965; Chambers 2009). For the exchangeable linkage model, $E(\mathbf{C} \mid \mathbf{Z}_A) = E(\mathbf{C}) = \mathbf{Q} = (q_{ij})$, where

$$q_{ij} = \begin{cases} q & \text{if } i = j \\ \frac{1-q}{N-1} & \text{if } i \neq j \end{cases} \tag{34.5}$$

Under this model, $P(c_{ii} = 1) = q$ for all i and $P(c_{ij} = 1) = (1-q)/(N-1)$ for all pairs of units with $i \neq j$. Thus, we have to estimate just one parameter: q, the true positive linkage rate. In practice, this model can be made slightly more realistic by applying it within blocks of units based on a blocking variable (Chambers 2009), under the assumption that no linkage errors occur between different blocks.

Alternatively, Chipperfield and Chambers (2015) proposed a parametric bootstrap method to estimate $\mathbf{Q}$ without assuming an explicit form for this matrix. This method may be more generally applicable than the simple exchangeable linkage errors model. It does require that probabilistic linkage is used according to the framework of Fellegi and Sunter (1969) and that it is feasible to repeat the linkage procedure many times.

If linkage errors are random, in addition to bias they also cause additional variance in statistical outputs. We return to the question of how to estimate this variance at the end of Section 34.3.2.

34.3.2 Adjusting Outputs to Correct for Linkage Errors

One field of research in handling potential bias due to linkage errors is to apply alternative linkage methods that try to minimize the bias. For instance, there are approaches that consider linkage as a missing data problem in which some target variable is missing. Rather than linking a unique record, a posterior distribution is estimated for the variable of interest making use of a set of records that may potentially match the recipient unit. Subsequently, multiple draws (imputations) are taken from this posterior distribution and statistical outputs are estimated using the standard rules for multiple imputation (Goldstein et al. 2012; Harron et al. 2014).

Another field of research in handling potential bias is to try to correct for this bias after the data set has been linked. As an example, consider again the estimated regression coefficient $\boldsymbol{\beta}^*$ discussed above. Under the assumption that $\mathbf{Q}$ is known and provided that $\mathbf{Z}_A'\mathbf{Q}\mathbf{Z}_A$ is an invertible matrix, it is clear from (34.4) that an unbiased estimator of $\boldsymbol{\beta}$ could be obtained as follows:

$$\boldsymbol{\beta}_{BC}^* = \left[(\mathbf{Z}_A'\mathbf{Z}_A)^{-1}\mathbf{Z}_A'\mathbf{Q}\mathbf{Z}_A\right]^{-1}\boldsymbol{\beta}^* = (\mathbf{Z}_A'\mathbf{Q}\mathbf{Z}_A)^{-1}\mathbf{Z}_A'\mathbf{Z}_A\boldsymbol{\beta}^* = (\mathbf{Z}_A'\mathbf{Q}\mathbf{Z}_A)^{-1}\mathbf{Z}_A'\mathbf{y}_B^* \tag{34.6}$$

Given an estimate of $\mathbf{Q}$, this provides a way to estimate $\boldsymbol{\beta}$ consistently from the combined data. Chambers (2009) discussed this type of estimator in the more general context of generalized linear models. He also proposed extensions to situations where the two files contain different numbers of units; see also Chambers and Da Silva (2020).

A different method to correct the bias in $\boldsymbol{\beta}^*$ was proposed by Lahiri and Larsen (2005). They noted that provided that the assumed linear model for $\mathbf{y}_B$ holds true, under noninformative linkage errors, the observed vector $\mathbf{y}_B^*$ also follows a linear model but with predicted mean $E\left(\mathbf{y}_B^*|\mathbf{Z}_A\right) = \mathbf{Q}\mathbf{Z}_A\boldsymbol{\beta}$. Hence, given $\mathbf{Q}$ a consistent estimator for $\boldsymbol{\beta}$ can be found from this model by OLS:

$$\boldsymbol{\beta}_{LL}^* = \left[(\mathbf{Q}\mathbf{Z}_A)'\mathbf{Q}\mathbf{Z}_A\right]^{-1}(\mathbf{Q}\mathbf{Z}_A)'\mathbf{y}_B^* = (\mathbf{Z}_A'\mathbf{Q}'\mathbf{Q}\mathbf{Z}_A)^{-1}\mathbf{Z}_A'\mathbf{Q}'\mathbf{y}_B^* \tag{34.7}$$

Again, in practice $\mathbf{Q}$ has to be estimated first. Chambers (2009) and Chambers and Da Silva (2020) noted that this OLS estimator is theoretically suboptimal, because linkage errors introduce heteroskedasticity into the linear model for $\mathbf{y}_B^*$ even when the original model for $\mathbf{y}_B$ has homoskedastic disturbances. It is possible to construct a weighted least squares estimator for $\boldsymbol{\beta}$ that is more efficient in theory. However, this requires an estimate of the additional variance in $\mathbf{y}_B^*$ (given $\mathbf{Z}_A$) due to linkage errors and could also make the correction method less robust to model misspecification.

As a different type of application, we consider the estimation of a contingency table. This could for instance concern the situation of the linkage of a data set A on court decisions on bankruptcies to a data set B with a population of enterprises, where one is interested to tabulate numbers of bankruptcies by economic activity code or by size class. In the same context as the above regression example, now let $\mathbf{Z}_A$ and $\mathbf{Y}_B$ denote matrices of dummy variables that encode two categorical variables. The target statistic is a contingency table given by $\mathbf{T} = \mathbf{Z}_A'\mathbf{Y}_B$ with elements $t_{kl} = \sum_{i=1}^N z_{ik}y_{il}$. Under linkage errors, instead of $\mathbf{Y}_B$, we observe $\mathbf{Y}_B^* = \mathbf{C}\mathbf{Y}_B$. The naive estimated contingency table after record linkage is

$$\mathbf{T}^* = \mathbf{Z}_A'\mathbf{Y}_B^* = \mathbf{Z}_A'\mathbf{C}\mathbf{Y}_B \tag{34.8}$$

with elements $t_{kl}^* = \sum_{i=1}^N z_{ik}\sum_{j=1}^N c_{ij}y_{jl}$. Again, it is clear that in general $\mathbf{T}^* \neq \mathbf{T}$ and, under noninformative linkage errors, $E(\mathbf{T}^*|\mathbf{Z}_A) = \mathbf{Z}_A'\mathbf{Q}\mathbf{Y}_B \neq \mathbf{T}$. In this case, if $\mathbf{Q}$ were known an obvious bias-corrected estimator would be given by

$$\mathbf{T}_{BC}^* = \mathbf{Z}_A'\mathbf{Q}^{-1}\mathbf{Y}_B^* \tag{34.9}$$

In practice, an estimate for $\mathbf{Q}$ can be substituted in this expression. Alternatively, the following adjustment is suggested by the right-most term in the Lahiri–Larsen estimator (34.7):

$$\mathbf{T}_Q^* = (\mathbf{Q}\mathbf{Z}_A)'\mathbf{Y}_B^* = \mathbf{Z}_A'\mathbf{Q}'\mathbf{Y}_B^* \tag{34.10}$$

It is easy to show that $\mathbf{T}_Q^*$ is biased as an estimator for $\mathbf{T}$, since in general $\mathbf{Q}'\mathbf{Q}$ is not equal to the identity matrix. In fact, Scholtus et al. (2022) show that under exchangeable linkage errors the relative bias of $\mathbf{T}_Q^*$ is *larger* than that of the naive estimator $\mathbf{T}^*$. Nevertheless, this estimator turns out to have some merit in certain situations due to its reduced variance; see Section 34.3.3.

Chipperfield and Chambers (2015) developed an alternative bias-correction approach for contingency tables, yielding an estimate of the form

$$\mathbf{T}_{CC}^{*} = \mathbf{T}^{*} + \mathbf{Z}_{A}'(\mathbf{I} - \mathbf{Q})\mathbf{Z}_{A}\mathbf{\Pi}_{CC} \tag{34.11}$$

where $\mathbf{I}$ denotes the identity matrix of order N and $\mathbf{\Pi}_{CC}$ denotes an estimate of the matrix of conditional probabilities $\pi_{kl} = P(y = l \mid z = k)$. The latter estimate is obtained by an iterative algorithm, which uses the naïve estimate based on $\mathbf{T}^{*}$ as a starting point and repeatedly applies the additive adjustment from (34.11) until the estimates converge, fixing estimated conditional probabilities at 0 or 1 if necessary if these bounds are exceeded. In Scholtus et al. (2022), it is proved that in the special case of exchangeable linkage errors, $\mathbf{T}_{CC}^{*}$ converges exactly to $\mathbf{T}_{BC}^{*}$ from (34.9) if no conditional probabilities have to be fixed at any point in the algorithm.

In practice, a relevant question is how to evaluate the variance of either a naive estimator or a bias-corrected estimator under linkage errors. Zhang (2019) noted that a limitation of the exchangeable linkage errors model is that it only describes the first moment of the distribution of $\mathbf{C}$, so that variances (as well as all higher-order moments) are undefined under this model. Chambers (2009) proposed a possible second-order extension of the exchangeable linkage errors model and used this to derive the variance due to linkage errors of various regression-based estimators.

For contingency tables, Chipperfield and Chambers (2015) proposed a bootstrap procedure to estimate the variance of $\mathbf{T}^{*}$ due to random linkage errors. They also proposed a double bootstrap procedure to estimate the additional variance in bias-corrected estimators such as $\mathbf{T}_{CC}^{*}$, $\mathbf{T}_{BC}^{*}$, or $\mathbf{T}_{Q}^{*}$ due to the fact that $\mathbf{Q}$ has to be estimated. Finally, users that are not interested in finite-population statistics but in the parameters of an underlying super-population model should also account for an additional variance component in all these estimators due to sampling from a multinomial model for y and z (Chipperfield and Chambers 2015).

An entirely different approach to bias-correction and inference under linkage errors is proposed by Zhang (2019). As before, assume that record linkage is one-to-one and complete, and let $\mathbf{C}_{0}$ denote the (unknown) permutation matrix that puts the records in file B in the same order as those in file A. Let $\mathbf{G}_{AB} = G(\mathbf{X}_{A}, \mathbf{X}_{B})$ denote the comparison information that is available as a basis for record linkage (e.g. probabilistic linkage under the Fellegi–Sunter framework). Zhang (2019) proposed to define a posterior probability distribution for $\mathbf{C}_{0}$ by

$$f(\mathbf{C}_{0} \mid \mathbf{G}_{AB}) = \frac{f(\mathbf{G}_{AB} \mid \mathbf{C}_{0})}{\sum_{\mathbf{C}} f(\mathbf{G}_{AB} \mid \mathbf{C})} \tag{34.12}$$

where the summation in the denominator is over all possible permutation matrices of order N. Note that in (34.12) a uniform prior distribution is assumed for $\mathbf{C}_{0}$, so that $f(\mathbf{C}_{0}) = f(\mathbf{C})$ can be omitted from the numerator and denominator. A model for $f(\mathbf{G}_{AB} \mid \mathbf{C}_{0})$ can now be assumed which directly accounts for the modeling assumptions made during record linkage (e.g. independence over different comparison variables in the Fellegi–Sunter framework). Although conceptually appealing, a practical problem with this approach may be that the number of possible permutation matrices can become prohibitively large. Unless the number of records to link is quite small, evaluating – or even deriving a numerical approximation to – the right-hand side of (34.12) seems to be computationally challenging (Zhang 2019).

34.3.3 Simulation Study on Correcting Contingency Tables for Linkage Errors

In a recent project, Statistics Netherlands compared the accuracy (bias and variance) of different approaches to estimate a contingency table from a linked file in the presence of random linkage errors. The study focused on one-to-one, complete linkage of two data files of the same size. First, two sets of true target statistics were generated by simulating two microdata sets of $N = 300$ records, each containing two categorical variables z and y with five categories. In the first data set, these attributes could be called "dependent," in the sense that the true 5×5 contingency table $\mathbf{T}$ does not pass a statistical test of independence at conventional significance levels ($\chi^2 = 96.57$, $p < 0.0001$). In the second data set, the attributes could be called "independent" ($\chi^2 = 7.32$, $p = 0.9666$). We refer to Scholtus et al. (2022) for more details on how these data sets were generated.

Next, for both data sets, the effects of combining the two target variables under nonperfect record linkage were simulated. The exchangeable linkage errors model was assumed, and two matrices $\mathbf{Q}$ were defined by (34.5) with $q = 0.90$ or $q = 0.80$. To simulate random linkage errors, in both cases 1000 random permutation matrices $\mathbf{C}$ were drawn with $E(\mathbf{C}) = \mathbf{Q}$, by applying the procedure of Cox (1987) for controlled random rounding to $\mathbf{Q}$.

For the 1000 simulated linked data sets defined by these permutation matrices, the following estimators were computed and compared: (i) the naive estimator $\mathbf{T}^*$ from (34.8); (ii) the bias-corrected estimator $\mathbf{T}^*_{BC}$ from (34.9); (iii) the adjusted estimator $\mathbf{T}^*_Q$ from (34.10); and (iv) the estimator $\mathbf{T}^*_{CC}$ from (34.11) proposed by Chipperfield and Chambers (2015). The empirical bias, variance, and mean squared error (MSE) of each entry in these estimated contingency tables were evaluated. In addition, for each entry, it was examined in what percentage of the 1000 cases each of the adjusted estimators (ii)–(iv) improved on the naive estimator, in the sense that the estimated value was closer to the corresponding value in the true contingency table.

The main findings of this study were as follows (for detailed results, see Scholtus et al. 2022):

- As expected from the theory, the results for $\mathbf{T}^*_{CC}$ were very close to the results for $\mathbf{T}^*_{BC}$.
- For the table with "dependent" attributes, even with $q = 0.80$ the naïve estimator $\mathbf{T}^*$ often outperformed the adjusted estimators in terms of MSE. Although $\mathbf{T}^*_{BC}$ and $\mathbf{T}^*_{CC}$ were able to reduce the bias, this was offset by a relatively large increase in variance, in particular for $q = 0.80$. Conversely, using $\mathbf{T}^*_Q$ reduced the variance but increased the bias, making this the worst performing estimator in this case in terms of MSE.
- For the table with "independent" attributes, the estimator $\mathbf{T}^*_Q$ had the lowest MSE. Here, the bias of the naive estimator is small. Consequently, the bias-corrected estimators $\mathbf{T}^*_{BC}$ and $\mathbf{T}^*_{CC}$ often had the largest MSE in this case due to their inflated variances.
- The results in terms of the percentage of cases where an adjusted estimate yielded a value closer to the true value than the naive estimate were in line with the above results in terms of MSE. Notably – and perhaps counterintuitively – it is by no means guaranteed that an adjusted estimate by either method is closer to the true value than the original naïve estimate in all instances, even for the best estimator in terms of MSE in a particular scenario.

Overall, the conclusion of this simulation study was that the effect of the various correction methods for linkage errors on the accuracy of the estimated output was rather limited and not always beneficial. Moreover, which method provided the best results depended strongly on properties of the target table that would be unknown in practice. There is no reason to assume that these methods would perform better under more challenging conditions, e.g. with a more complicated linkage error model. Thus, there still appears to be room for improved solutions to the problem of correcting statistical outputs for the effect of linkage errors.

34.4 Measurement Error

Recall that measurement error is defined as the difference between the obtained value for a variable in the source and the true value according to the targeted concept, for the variable to be analyzed.

When one has just a single source for a variable in business statistics, one usually detects measurement errors by looking into the logical relations between variables of the same units – in the form of logical edit rules – or by looking into the distribution of variables within a subpopulation of similar units. With multisource statistics, one sometimes has multiple measurements of the same variable for the same units from different sources, or with (nearly) the same variable that comes from different sources for different subpopulations. That may result in additional information about measurement errors in the variables that are used to make outputs. In the current section, we first briefly discuss how the size of measurement errors may be quantified in Section 34.4.1.

The next step is to estimate the effect of measurement errors – given their size – on the accuracy of a given estimator. de Waal et al. (2021) distinguish between two main groups of methods to do so: methods based on (re)sampling and methods based on parametric modeling. In the case of resampling methods, one samples from the data or from a distribution. This is explained in Section 34.4.2, followed by two case studies in Sections 34.4.3 and 34.4.4. Furthermore, we are interested to obtain a bias-corrected estimator for classification errors which is treated in Section 34.4.5 and illustrated in Section 34.4.6.

34.4.1 Quantifying Measurement Error

To estimate the extent of measurement errors in a data set, one might aim to determine the true (target) value of the variables that one is interested in for a subset of the units in the data set (an audit sample). In this way, a gold standard set can be created. Manually creating such a gold standard set is often very time-consuming. Moreover, there may be situations where it is nearly impossible to determine the correct values of variables in business statistics, just by clerical review. In that case, one may try to find additional sources, such as yearly reports, or information on the Internet, or one might contact or even visit the enterprises. The information about the different variables may have to come from different persons within an enterprise, making it more difficult to obtain the correct values (Snijkers 2016). All in all, usually one tries to limit the work by restricting the gold standard set to a small sample which is easier to handle for clerical review. One of the situations in which clerical reviews are used is in the maintenance of a statistical business register concerning the units and their properties, such as economic activity codes (UNECE 2015).

The availability of multiple sources for the same variable can be very helpful for estimating measurement errors: for instance data from different surveys, or observations from administrative and survey data. In such cases, one approach that is sometimes used is to consider one of the sources as the gold standard set. However, such an assumption is usually not very realistic, since nearly all sources are prone to measurement errors. Alternatively, one may apply a model-based approach to estimate the size of measurement errors. Examples of such models are latent class models (Hagenaars and McCutcheon 2002; Biemer 2011) in the case of categorical data and structural equation models with latent variables (Oberski et al. 2017) in the case of continuous variables. These models assume that the observations in the different data sources are indicators of a common, latent (or "hidden") concept. In terms of measurement error, it is often assumed that the latent concept concerns the true values that one is interested in but cannot observe, and the observations are indicators that have random and/or systematic deviations from those true values. An example of the use of structural equation modeling to estimate error size, and output quality, can be found in Scholtus et al. (2015). Results of that study can also be found in van Delden and Lewis (Chapter 11 in this volume). In that study, two surveys, an administrative source and a small gold standard set (from clerical review) are used to estimate errors in turnover, and correct for bias in the output.

A slightly different modeling approach for continuous variables is given by so-called "contamination models": there one assumes that the values for a subset of all units are erroneous, while those of the others are correct, see for instance Di Zio and Guarnera (2013). The idea behind the contamination models is that the population consists of two groups of units, each with their own distribution of the values of the target variable(s), and it is not known beforehand to which group each unit belongs. This approach can be extended, assuming that the population is a mixture of multiple groups each with their own error distribution. Such an approach has been applied when trying to understand differences in quarterly turnover of enterprises based on VAT data versus survey data, see van Delden et al. (2018). Some results of that study can be found in van Delden and Lewis (Chapter 11 of this volume).

34.4.2 Estimating the Effect of Measurement Error on Outputs

In situations where estimates are based on multiple sources that together cover nearly the complete population, and when those data sets are linked using unique identification keys, representation nor linkage error hardly affects output accuracy. However, in these cases, output accuracy may still be affected by measurement error. In this section, we focus on a particular type of measurement error, namely errors in an observed classification variable that is used for output stratification. Well-known examples of such stratifications are size class and economic activity (NACE code); this situation is illustrated in Section 34.4.3. Sometimes, the classification variable is not directly observed for the complete population, but it is (partly) predicted from a supervised machine learning classifier. Examples are whether enterprises have a web shop or not, or whether they are innovative or not; this is illustrated in Section 34.4.4.

The effects of classification errors on the estimation of contingency tables have been derived previously in various disciplines; see Buonaccorsi (2010) for an excellent review of the literature. In business statistics, one is often interested in the totals or growth rates of a continuous target variable, such as profit, turnover, or costs. van Delden et al. (2016) derived an approach to estimate the effect of classification errors on level estimates of a continuous variable and van Delden et al. (2022) extended the approach to the estimation of ratios, such as a growth rate. Both approaches assume that only classification errors occur and that the target variable is observed error-free.

Let $i = 1, \ldots, N^t$ denote the units, say enterprises, of the target population for period t. Given the classification of interest, for instance their NACE code, each enterprise has an unknown true code $s_i^t \in \{1, \ldots, H\}$, where H is the total number of possible codes. For each enterprise, we have an observed code $\hat{s}_i^t \in \{1, \ldots, H\}$, which may differ from the true code. We assume that random classification errors occur, independently across units, according to a (possibly unit-specific) level transition matrix $\mathbf{P}_{Li}^t = \left(p_{ghi}^t\right)$, with $p_{ghi}^t = P\left(\hat{s}_i^t = h | s_i^t = g\right)$. The true codes are considered fixed. Furthermore, classification errors may change over time. We define the change transition matrix, $\mathbf{P}_{Ci}^{t,u} = \left(p_{gkhli}^{t,u}\right)$, with $p_{gkhli}^{t,u} = P\left(\hat{s}_i^t = h | s_i^u = g, s_i^t = k, \hat{s}_i^u = l\right)$, where $u < t$ denote different time points.

We are interested in a target parameter for period t, denoted by θ^t, for a numerical target variable, denoted by y_i^t, for instance, turnover for enterprise i. The target parameter follows as a function of the target variable and the classification variable in the population: $\theta^t = f\left(y_1^t, \ldots, y_N^t; s_1^t, \ldots, s_N^t\right)$. A natural way to estimate this target parameter from the observed data is by $\hat{\theta}^t = f\left(y_1^t, \ldots, y_N^t; \hat{s}_1^t, \ldots, \hat{s}_N^t\right)$, where, as usual, a hat refers to an estimate. In the current example, we limit ourselves to domain totals. This domain total can now be written as $Y_h^t = \sum_{i=1}^{N^t} y_i^t I\left\{s_i^t = h\right\}$, where $I\{.\}$ is an indicator variable that equals 1 if its argument is true and 0 otherwise. The natural estimator for this domain total is $\hat{Y}_h^t = \sum_{i=1}^{N^t} y_i^t I\left\{\hat{s}_i^t = h\right\}$.

Likewise, we are interested in a ratio of a domain, denoted by $Q_h^{t,u}$, with $Q_h^{t,u} = Y_h^t/Y_h^u = \sum_{i=1}^{N^t} y_i^t I\{s_i^t = h\} / \sum_{i=1}^{N^u} y_i^u I\{s_i^u = h\}$. The ratio $Q_h^{t,u}$ is estimated by replacing the true codes s_i by their observed counterparts. We are now interested in the bias and variance of $\widehat{Y}_h^t$ and $\widehat{Q}_h^{t,u}$. Using the transition matrix $\mathbf{P}_{Li}^t$, analytical expressions were derived for the bias and variance of $\widehat{Y}_h^t$; see van Delden et al. (2016). Likewise, for the transition matrices $\mathbf{P}_{Li}^t$ and $\mathbf{P}_{Ci}^{t,u}$, analytical expressions were derived for the bias and variance of $\widehat{Q}_h^{t,u}$; see van Delden et al. (2022).

In practice, the transition matrices $\mathbf{P}_{Li}^t$ and $\mathbf{P}_{Ci}^{t,u}$ have to be estimated. We do not estimate separate matrices for each unit i, but we define groups of units which we assume to have the same transition matrix. We refer to those groups as probability classes k. Probability classes are formed by units that share certain background variables.

Making use of the estimated transition matrices, van Delden et al. (2016) also derived a bootstrap procedure for level estimates and van Delden et al. (2022) derived a bootstrap procedure for the estimation of ratios. For the level estimate $\widehat{\theta}^t$ this procedure works as follows. Within one bootstrap replicate r (with $r = 1, \ldots, R$), draw a new code $\widehat{s}_{ir}^{*t}$ given the original observed code $\widehat{s}_i^t$ for each enterprise in the population. The new codes are drawn using probabilities that mimic (our best estimate of) the original process by which $\widehat{s}_i^t$ was generated from s_i^t:

$$P\left(\widehat{s}_{ir}^{*t} = h|\widehat{s}_i^t = g\right) \equiv \widehat{P}\left(\widehat{s}_i^t = h|s_i^t = g\right) = \widehat{P}_{ghi}^t$$

Based on the obtained values $\widehat{s}_{1r}^{*t}, \ldots, \widehat{s}_{Nr}^{*t}$, we compute the bootstrap replicate $\widehat{\theta}_r^{*t} = f\left(y_1^t, \ldots, y_N^t; \widehat{s}_{1r}^{*t}, \ldots, \widehat{s}_{Nr}^{*t}\right)$. This procedure is repeated R times, yielding replicates $\widehat{\theta}_1^{*t}, \ldots, \widehat{\theta}_R^{*t}$. From these replicates, the bias and variance of $\widehat{\theta}^t$ are estimated as follows (see also Efron and Tibshirani 1993):

$$\widehat{B}_R^*(\widehat{\theta}^t) = m_R(\widehat{\theta}^{*t}) - \widehat{\theta}^t \tag{34.13}$$

$$\widehat{V}_R^*(\widehat{\theta}^t) = \frac{1}{R-1} \sum_{r=1}^{R} \left\{\widehat{\theta}_r^{*t} - m_R(\widehat{\theta}^{*t})\right\}^2 \tag{34.14}$$

with $m_R(\widehat{\theta}^{*t}) = R^{-1}\sum_{r=1}^{R}\widehat{\theta}_r^{*t}$. In the bootstrap literature, it is often recommended to take $R \geq 200$ for variance estimates and $R \geq 1000$ for bias estimates. An extension of this bootstrap procedure for ratio estimates can be found in van Delden et al. (2022).

34.4.3 Case Study on Turnover Growth Rates by Economic Activity

Scholtus et al. (2019) and van Delden et al. (2022) estimated the effect of classification errors on growth rates of quarterly turnover in 2014 and 2015 of enterprises in nine economic activities within the economic sector car trade. Turnover values were obtained from VAT data for the small- and medium-sized enterprises and from survey data for the large enterprises. Error probabilities were estimated from clerical review of an audit sample of 225 enterprises in 2014 and of 270 enterprises in 2015. The error probabilities were estimated as a function of the background variables of the units. To estimate the transition probabilities between economic activities, the observed yearly changes in the business register were also used as inputs. Details of the estimation procedure can be found in Scholtus et al. (2019) and references therein.

Estimated bias and standard deviation of quarter-on-quarter growth rates are shown in Figure 34.2. The original computations were done for nine, detailed, industries, see Scholtus et al. (2019) or van Delden et al. (2022). The output of the car trade sector is stratified into six industries, which consist of one or two of those more detailed industries. These six output industries are

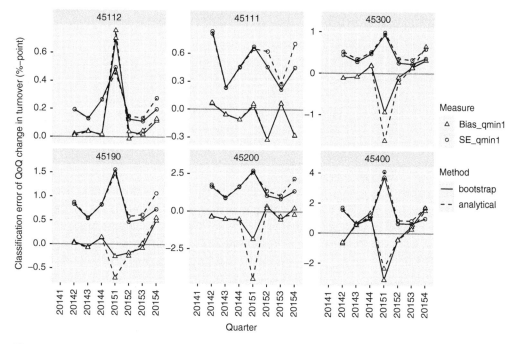

Figure 34.2 Comparison of bias (triangles) and standard errors (circles) of quarter-on-quarter turnover growth rates for six industries in the car trade, based on bootstrap simulation (solid lines), and analytical formulas (dashed lines).

shown from upper left to bottom right ordered from large to small average quarterly turnover. Results show that bias and variance of growth rates are larger for the smaller industries. Results based on bootstrap (using $R = 10,000$ replicates) and analytical formulas generally agreed reasonably well, with some exceptions. Analysis of results showed that differences were due to the skewness of the numerical variable (quarterly turnover). With skewness of the data, some of the assumptions of the analytical approximations no longer (completely) hold.

34.4.4 Case Study on Internet Purchases

Meertens (2021) applied the presented methodology of Section 34.4.2 to estimates of total annual turnover from foreign companies established in the EU obtained from Internet sales in the Netherlands. A register with foreign companies in the EU who filed tax returns in the Netherlands was classified as having a web shop or not. A training set of 180 companies was labeled manually via clerical review; all other enterprises were classified with a trained machine learning algorithm, using website texts as input. The errors made by the machine learning classifier were estimated using a fivefold cross-validation on the training set data and were used to estimate $\mathbf{P}_{Li}^t$. A bias-corrected total turnover of enterprises with a web shop was given by

$$\widehat{Y}_{\text{corr}}^t = Y_L^t + \left\{ \widehat{Y}_{ML}^t - \widehat{B}\left(\widehat{Y}_{ML}^t\right) \right\}$$

where Y_L^t stands for the total turnover of the labeled enterprises (with a webshop), $\widehat{Y}_{ML}^t$ is the turnover of enterprises that were predicted to have a webshop according to the machine learning algorithm, and $\widehat{B}\left(\widehat{Y}_{ML}^t\right)$ is an estimate for the bias of $\widehat{Y}_{ML}^t$. Furthermore, they also estimated the

Table 34.2 Estimated total annual turnover (in millions of euros) of cross-border internet purchases.

Year	Y_L^t	$\widehat{Y}_{ML}^t$	$\widehat{B}\left(\widehat{Y}_{ML}^t\right)$	$\widehat{Y}_{corr}^t$	$\widehat{Sd}\left(\widehat{Y}_{corr}^t\right)$
2014	405	495	63	837	97
2015	565	586	21	1132	101
2016	725	667	19	1372	110

Source: Meertens (2021).

standard deviation, $Sd\left(\widehat{Y}_{corr}^t\right)$. All estimates, including the standard deviation of $\widehat{Y}_{corr}^t$ were computed with analytical formulas given in van Delden et al. (2016) and Meertens (2021). Details on the estimation of a bias-corrected estimator that Meertens (2021) minimizes the MSE of the bias estimate can be found in van Delden et al. (2016, formula 25).

Meertens (2021) found that, in 2014, the estimated bias $\widehat{B}\left(\widehat{Y}_{ML}^t\right)$ was considerable relative to the total: 63 on a total of 495 (in millions of euros), see Table 34.2. The estimated standard deviation of $\widehat{Y}_{corr}^t$ was approximately 10% of the value of $\widehat{Y}_{corr}^t$ which is a considerable uncertainty.

34.4.5 Obtaining a Bias-corrected Estimator for Measurement Errors

In Sections 34.4.2 and 34.4.3, we were interested in assessing the quality of a given, possibly already published, estimator as affected by classification errors. In the current section, we are interested in *correcting* an estimator for the bias to produce an unbiased estimator. This method can be applied to single source statistics but is also relevant for multisource statistics. For instance, the classification variable itself may be derived from multiple sources.

In the example of Section 34.4.4, we already presented such a *bias-corrected* estimator. It is an example of a "subtracted-bias estimator." That estimator was not optimal, in the sense that this estimate was biased itself, because the estimation procedure starts from observed data that is contaminated with a certain level of error. An alternative is to use the misclassification probabilities to correct for this initial bias. The disadvantage of that approach is that it can lead to a bias-corrected estimator that has a much larger variance than the subtracted-bias estimator. Both issues are explained in more detail in van Delden et al. (2016). Li (2020) has proposed an alternative method that results in a bias estimate which is very close to the true bias, but this method has only been worked out for a binary variable. The method by Li (2020) is based on the estimation of a mixture of normal distributions (McLachlan and Peel 2000).

Kloos et al. (2020) have compared the MSE of three bias-corrected estimators for the case of frequency counts. This is for instance relevant for output on the number of enterprises in a country by NACE code, the number of family businesses by size class, or the number of innovative enterprises by region.

Assume that we are interested in estimating the number of units in class 1 of a binary classifier: $N_1 = \sum_{i=1}^{N} I\{s_i = 1\} = N\alpha_1$, where N stands for the population size, α_1 stands for the proportion of units in class 1, while $I\{s_i = 1\}$ is an indicator variable that is 1 when a unit belongs to stratum 1 and 0, otherwise. For the remainder, we limit ourselves to estimating α_1 as affected by misclassifications. The naive estimator is given by $\widehat{\alpha}_1 = \sum_{i=1}^{N} I\{\widehat{s}_i = 1\}$ which is referred to in Kloos et al. (2020) as the classify-and-count estimator. This estimator, $\widehat{\alpha}_1$, is biased in general, as noted before. The bias is given by $B(\widehat{\alpha}_1) = E(\widehat{\alpha}_1) - \alpha_1 = \alpha_1 p_{11} + (1 - \alpha_1)(1 - p_{00}) - \alpha_1$. The probability p_{00}

is defined as $p_{00} = P(\hat{s}_i = 0 | s_i = 0)$, so p_{00} stands for the probability to estimate class 0 for a unit given its true class is 0. Likewise $p_{11} = P(\hat{s}_i = 1 | s_i = 1)$ stands for the probability to estimate class 1 given the true class is 1. Kloos et al. (2020) compared three ways to reduce misclassification bias:

1. Subtracted-bias estimator: subtract the estimated bias from the original estimator.
2. Misclassification estimator: correct the estimator using the misclassification matrix $\mathbf{P}_L$.
3. Calibration estimator: correct the estimator using a calibration probability matrix.

Ad 1. The bias $B(\hat{\alpha}_1)$ is estimated by $\hat{B}(\hat{\alpha}_1) = \hat{\alpha}_1(\hat{p}_{00} + \hat{p}_{11} - 2) + (1 - \hat{p}_{00})$, where the estimated probabilities $\hat{p}_{00}$ and $\hat{p}_{11}$ are computed based on a sample of labeled data of size n. Let $n_{uv} = \sum_{i=1}^{n} I\{s_i = u\}I\{\hat{s}_i = v\}$, with $u, v \in \{0, 1\}$, denote counts from this labeled data set. Then $\hat{p}_{00} = n_{00}/(n_{00} + n_{01})$ and $\hat{p}_{11} = n_{11}/(n_{10} + n_{11})$. Let $\hat{\alpha}_{1,b}$ denote the subtracted-bias estimator, given by

$$\hat{\alpha}_{1,b} = \hat{\alpha}_1 - \hat{B}(\hat{\alpha}_1) = \hat{\alpha}_1(3 - \hat{p}_{00} - \hat{p}_{11}) - (1 - \hat{p}_{00})$$

Ad 2. The expected value of $\hat{\alpha} = (\hat{\alpha}_0, \hat{\alpha}_1)^T$ in terms of the transition matrix based on misclassifications, $\mathbf{P}_L$, is given by $E(\hat{\alpha}) = \mathbf{P}_L^T \alpha$. Let $\hat{\alpha}_{1,p}$ denote the misclassification estimator: a bias-corrected estimator based on misclassification probabilities. This estimator is given by

$$\hat{\alpha}_p = \left(\mathbf{P}_L^T\right)^{-1} \hat{\alpha}$$

Using a plug-in estimator $\hat{\mathbf{P}}_L^T$ for $\mathbf{P}_L^T$, yields

$$\hat{\alpha}_{1,p} = \frac{\hat{\alpha}_1 + \hat{p}_{00} - 1}{\hat{p}_{00} + \hat{p}_{11} - 1}$$

Ad 3. Recall that the matrix $\mathbf{P}_L$ is normalized on the true class memberships (row-normalized) with probabilities $p_{gh} = P(\hat{s}_i = h | s_i = g)$. Similarly, let $\mathbf{C}_L$ be the matrix normalized on the observed class memberships (column-normalized), with probabilities $c_{gh} = P(s_i = g | \hat{s}_i = h)$. The estimator $\hat{\alpha}_c = \mathbf{C}_L \hat{\alpha}$ is an unbiased estimator for α, referred to as the calibration estimator. Using a plug-in estimator $\hat{\mathbf{C}}_L$ for $\mathbf{C}_L$, one obtains

$$\hat{\alpha}_{1,c} = (1 - \hat{\alpha}_1)\hat{c}_{10} + \hat{\alpha}_1\hat{c}_{11} = (1 - \hat{\alpha}_1)\frac{n_{10}}{n_{00} + n_{10}} + \hat{\alpha}_1\frac{n_{11}}{n_{01} + n_{11}}$$

Kloos et al. (2020) derived bias and variance expressions for the three bias-corrected estimators given above.

34.4.6 Simulation Study Comparing the Bias-corrected Estimators

Kloos et al. (2020) performed a simulation study in which the classification error probabilities were varied to compare the relative accuracies: bias, variance, and MSE of the classify-and-count estimator and the three bias-corrected estimators. Results are given in Table 3 and Figures 2 and 3 in Kloos et al. (2020). They concluded that the calibration estimator based on the plug-in estimator $\hat{\mathbf{C}}_L$ has the smallest MSE under most conditions. Moreover, the calibration estimator is unbiased, as long as the plug-in estimator $\hat{\mathbf{C}}_L$ is an unbiased estimator for $\mathbf{C}_L$. When the estimated error-probabilities are based on historical data for instance, then this might no longer be the case. An interesting point for future work is to extend the formulas by Kloos et al. (2020) to a multiclass situation.

34.5 Conclusion

Multisource business statistics cover a very wide field of estimators in which different types of data can be combined in many ways (de Waal et al. 2020). The data integration process tends to be more complex than is needed for single-source statistics which makes the estimation of output quality of multisource statistics rather difficult.

We have shown some first approaches and results of how the selection error of a given estimator as a result of representation errors can be estimated from historical data. We used the framework that has been developed by Meng (2018) and compared it with the estimator by Little et al. (2020). In our case study, we had strong correlations between the target variable and the selection indicator and between the target variable and an auxiliary variable. Under those conditions, both the approach by Meng (2018), when estimated by $\hat{\rho}_{SY} = \rho_{SZ}$, as well as the estimator by Little et al. (2020) yielded reliable estimates of the selection error. It will be interesting to investigate how strong these correlations have to be exactly in order for the results to be sufficiently accurate. With respect to a bias-corrected estimator, Huijskens (2020) compared various pseudo design-based methods. He found that, when the common support and ignorability assumptions are met, proximity matching methods perform well in terms of bias reduction and better than exact matching. Huijskens (2020) showed that inverse propensity score weighting also performs well in bias reduction, but the results can become unstable in practical applications. For one set of conditions, Valliant (2020) compared the performance of pseudo design-based estimators, superpopulation model-based estimators, doubly robust estimators, and poststratum estimators to correct for bias. He found that a doubly robust estimator led to the smallest relative bias. A topic for future research is to find out which bias-correction methods for representation errors work best under which conditions.

With respect to the bias correction for linkage errors of frequency estimates, Scholtus et al. (2022) performed a simulation study in which three methods were compared. Unfortunately, they found that the effect of the various correction methods for linkage errors on the accuracy of the estimated outputs was rather limited, and under some conditions, the uncorrected estimator had the smallest estimation error. Which method performed best in a given situation depended on properties of the target variables that would be unknown in practice. So the challenge remains to develop an effective bias-corrected estimator in case of linkage errors, not only for frequency estimates but also for other statistics.

Recently, we developed methods to estimate the bias and variance for a given level or ratio statistic due to classification errors and showed their use in case studies. A point of improvement is that the bias estimates – and to a lesser extent the variance estimates – are biased themselves. The subsequently developed method by Li (2020) for continuous variables and the method used by Kloos et al. (2020) for frequency tables yield more accurate bias estimates, but both methods are currently limited to binary classifications. A point for future research is to extend them to a multiclass situation. Except for Li (2020), the developed methods also assume that the extent of the misclassifications is known. Since the use of audit samples to estimate the amount of misclassifications is generally very time-consuming, there is a need to develop automated methods. Besides classification errors, also some work has been done in estimating the effect of measurement errors in continuous variables on output accuracy, which is treated by van Delden and Lewis (Chapter 11 in this volume).

With respect to the methods that have been developed in the literature on representation, linkage, and measurement errors, it is worthwhile to gain more insight into the consequences of violating the assumptions underlying the approaches and to learn which methods are most suitable under which conditions. Also new methods may be developed with higher accuracy or in which certain assumptions may be alleviated.

We conclude this chapter by mentioning two additional points of ongoing research. The first point of research is what is the net effect of multiple error types on output accuracy? The answer to this question starts with understanding and quantifying interactions between error types. An increase in the number of incorrect links may for instance lead to an increase in measurement errors – when variables of different units are combined. Likewise, missed links may lead to missing data or to missing units. The second point of research relates to bias-corrected estimators. For some conditions, we might work out a method to obtain a good bias-corrected estimator. As Valliant (2020) remarked: one cannot be sure what the quality is of a bias-corrected estimator. The question then arises whether we can also quantify the accuracy of that final, bias-corrected estimator.

References

Andridge, R. and Little, R. (2011). Proxy pattern-mixture analysis for survey nonresponse. *Journal of Official Statistics* 27 (2): 153–180.

Ascari, G., Blix, K., Brancato, G., Burg, T., McCourt, A., Delden, A., van Krapavickaitė, D., Ploug, N., Scholtus, S., Stoltze, P., de Waal, T., and Zhang, L.-C. (2020). Quality of multisource statistics – the KOMUSO project. *The Survey Statistician* 81: 36–51.

Amaya, A., Biemer, P.P., and Kinyon, D. (2020). Total error in a Big Data world: adapting the TSE framework to Big Data. *Journal of Survey Statistics and Methodology* 8: 89–119.

Bethlehem, J.G. (1988). Reduction of nonresponse bias through regression estimation. *Journal of Official Statistics* 4 (3): 251–260.

Biemer, P.P. (2011). *Latent Class Analysis of Survey Error*. Hoboken, NJ: Wiley.

Biemer, P.P. and Amaya, A. (2018). A total error framework for hybrid estimation. *Presentation given at BIGSURV18*, Barcelona, Spain (26 October 2018).

Buonaccorsi, J.P. (2010). *Measurement Error: Models, Methods and Applications*. Boca Raton, FL: Chapman and Hall/CRC Press.

Chambers, R. (2009). Regression analysis of probability-linked data. *Official Statistics Research Series* 4, Wellington, New Zealand.: 1–72.

Chambers, R.L. and da Silva, A.D. (2020). Improved secondary analysis of linked data: a framework and an illustration. *Journal of the Royal Statistical Society Series A* 183 (1): 37–59.

Chen, Y., Li, P., and Wu, C. (2020). Doubly robust inference with nonprobability survey samples. *Journal of the American Statistical Association* 115: 2011–2021.

Chipperfield, J.O. and Chambers, R. (2015). Using the bootstrap to account for linkage errors when analysing probabilistically linked categorical data. *Journal of Official Statistics* 31 (3): 397–414.

Cox, L.H. (1987). A constructive procedure for unbiased controlled rounding. *Journal of the American Statistical Association* 82: 520–524.

Daas, P.J.H. and van der Doef, S. (2020). Detecting innovative companies via their website. *Statistical Journal of the IAOS* 36: 1239–1251.

van Delden, A., Scholtus, S., and Burger, J. (2016). Accuracy of mixed-source statistics as affected by classification errors. *Journal of Official Statistics* 32: 619–642.

van Delden, A., Scholtus, S., and Ostlund, N. (2018). Modelling measurement errors to enable consistency between monthly and quarterly turnover growth rates. *Proceedings of Statistics Canada Symposium 2018*, Ottawa, Canada.

van Delden, A., Scholtus, S., Burger, J., and Meertens, Q. (2022). Accuracy of Estimated Ratios as Affected by Dynamic Classification Errors. *Journal of Survey Statistics and Methodology*: pre-print published online, 25 May 2022.

https://academic.oup.com/jssam/advance-article/doi/10.1093/jssam/smac015/6592179 (Accessed November 2022).

van Delden, A. and Lewis, D. (2023). Methodology for the use of administrative data in business statistics. In: *Advances in Establishment Statistics, Methods and Data Collection*, Chapter 12 (ed. G. Snijkers, M. Bavdaž, S. Bender, J. Jones, S. MacFeely, J.W. Sakshaug, K.J. Thompson, and A. van Delden). Hoboken: Wiley.

Di Zio, M. and Guarnera, U. (2013). A contamination model for selective editing. *Journal of Official Statistics* 29: 539–555.

Efron, B. and Tibshirani, R.J. (1993). *An Introduction to the Bootstrap.* Boca Raton, FL: Chapman & Hall/CRC.

Elliott, M.R. (2009). Combining data from probability and non-probability samples using pseudo-weights. *Survey Practice* 2 (6): 1–7.

Elliott, M.R. and Valliant, R. (2017). Inference for nonprobability samples. *Statistical Science* 32 (2): 249–264.

ESSnet Quality of Multisource Statistics – Komuso (2019). Quality Guidelines for Multisource Statistics (QGMSS). https://ec.europa.eu/eurostat/cros/content/quality-guidelines-multisource-statistics-qgmss_en (accessed March 2021).

Fellegi, I.P. and Sunter, A.B. (1969). A theory for record linkage. *Journal of the American Statistical Association* 64: 1183–1210.

Gessendorfer, J., Beste, J., Drechsler, J., and Sakshaug, J.W. (2018). Statistical matching as a supplement to record linkage: a valuable method to tackle nonconsent bias? *Journal of Official Statistics* 34: 909–933.

Goldstein, H., Harron, K., and Wade, A. (2012). The analysis of record-linked data using multiple imputation with data value priors. *Statistics in Medicine* 31: 3481–3493.

Groves, R.M., Fowler, F.J. Jr., Couper, M., Lepkowski, J.M., Singer, E., and Tourrangeau, R. (2004). *Survey Methodology.* New York: Wiley.

Hagenaars, J.A. and McCutcheon, A.L. (ed.) (2002). *Applied Latent Class Analysis.* New York: Cambridge University Press.

Harron, K., Dibben, C., Boyd, J., Hjern, A., Azimaee, M., Barreto, M.L., and Goldstein, H. (2017). Challenges in administrative data linkage for research. *Big Data & Society* 4 (2): 1–12.

Harron, K., Wade, A., Gilbert, R., Muller-Pebody, B., and Goldstein, H. (2014). Evaluating bias due to data linkage error in electronic health records. *BMC Medical Research Methodology* 14: 36.

Huijskens, R.C.A. (2020). Correcting selectivity of non-probability samples by means of sample matching. Master thesis, Utrecht University, the Netherlands (available from the authors upon request).

Kloos, K., Meertens, Q.A., Scholtus, S., and Karch, J. (2020). Comparing correction methods to reduce misclassification bias. *Proceedings of the BNAIC/Benelearn Conference*, Leiden, The Netherlands (19 and 20 November 2020).

Lahiri, P. and Larsen, M.D. (2005). Regression analysis with linked data. *Journal of the American Statistical Association* 100: 222–230.

Larsen, M.D. and Herning, A. (2023). Record linkage for establishments: background, challenges, and an example. In: *Advances in Establishment Statistics, Methods and Data Collection*, Chapter 33 (ed. G. Snijkers, M. Bavdaž, S. Bender, J. Jones, S. MacFeely, J.W. Sakshaug, K.J. Thompson, and A. van Delden). Hoboken: Wiley.

Li, Y. (2020). Estimating the effect of classification errors on domain statistics. Master thesis, Leiden University, the Netherlands (available from the authors upon request).

Little, R.J.A. and Rubin, D.B. (2002). *Statistical Analysis with Missing Data*, 2e. New York: Wiley.

Little, R., West, B., Boonstra, P., and Hu, J. (2020). Measures of the degree of departure from ignorable sample selection. *Journal of Survey Statistics and Methodology* 5 (8): 932–964. https://doi.org/10.1093/jssam/smz023.

McLachlan, G. and Peel, D. (2000). *Finite Mixture Models*. New York: Wiley.

Meertens, Q.A.. (2021). Cross-border internet purchases. Chapter 5 in: Misclassification bias in statistical learning, PhD thesis, Q.A. Meertens. SIKS Dissertation Series No 2021-10. https://dare.uva.nl/search?identifier=4b031bbd-5a46-4181-b0f1-52b38a3b63a6 (Accessed November 2022).

Meng, X.-L. (2018). Statistical paradises and paradoxes in Big Data (I): law of large populations, Big Data paradox, and the 2016 US Presidential Election. *The Annals of Applied Statistics* 12 (2): 685–726. https://doi.org/10.1214/18-AOAS1161SF.

Moore, J.C., Smith, P.W.F., and Durrant, G.B. (2018). Correlates of record linkage and estimating risks of non-linkage biases in business data sets. *Journal of the Royal Statistical Society Series A* 181: 1211–1230.

Neter, J., Maynes, E.S., and Ramanathan, R. (1965). The effect of mismatching on the measurement of response error. *Journal of the American Statistical Association* 60: 1005–1027.

Oberski, D.L., Kirchner, A., Eckman, S., and Kreuter, F. (2017). Evaluating the quality of survey and administrative data with generalized multitrait-multimethod models. *Journal of the American Statistical Association* 112: 1477–1489.

Rafei, A., Flannagan, C.A., and Elliott, M.R. (2020). Big Data for finite population inference: applying quasi-random approaches to naturalistic driving data using Bayesian additive regression trees. *Journal of Survey Statistics and Methodology* 8 (1): 148–180.

Ravindra, D. (2019). Making the best use of administrative and alternative data at Statistics Canada. *Paper presented at the European Establishment Statistics Workshop 2019*, Bilbao, Spain (24–27 September 2019).

Reid, G., Zabala, F., and Holmberg, A. (2017). Extending TSE to administrative data: a quality framework and case studies from Stats NZ. *Journal of Official Statistics* 33: 477–511.

Rivers, D. (2006). Sample matching: representative sampling from internet panels. Polimetrix White Paper Series, Palo Alto, CA. http://www.websm.org/uploadi/editor/1368187057Rivers_2006_Sample_matching_Representative_sampling_from_Internet_panels.pdf (accessed 26 March 2021).

Rivers, D. (2007). Sampling for web surveys. *Proceedings of the Joint Statistical Meetings*, 627–639.

Rivers, D., and Bailey, D. (2009). Inference from matched samples in the 2008 U.S. National Elections. *Paper presented at the 64th Annual Conference of the American Association for Public Opinion Research*, Hollywood, FL.

Sakshaug, J. W., and Antoni, M. (2017). Errors in linking survey and administrative data. In: *Total Survey Error in Practice* (ed. P. P. Biemer, E. de Leeuw, S. Eckman, B. Edwards, F. Kreuter, L. E. Lyberg, N. C. Tucker, and B. T. West). https://doi.org/10.1002/9781119041702.ch25

Sakshaug, J.W. and Kreuter, F. (2012). Assessing the magnitude of non-consent biases in linked survey and administrative data. *Survey Research Methods* 6: 113–122.

Scholtus, S., Bakker, B.F.M., and van Delden, A. (2015). Modelling measurement error to estimate bias in administrative and survey variables. Discussion Paper, The Hague: Statistics Netherlands. https://www.cbs.nl/nl-nl/achtergrond/2015/46/modelling-measurement-error-to-estimate-bias-in-administrative-and-survey-variables (accessed 26 March 2021).

Scholtus, S., van Delden, A., and Burger, J. (2019). Evaluating the accuracy of growth rates in the presence of classification errors. Discussion Paper, The Hague and Heerlen: Statistics Netherlands. https://www.cbs.nl/en-gb/background/2019/44/the-accuracy-of-growth-rates-with-classification-errors (accessed 26 March 2021).

Scholtus, S., Shlomo, N., and de Waal, T. (2022). Correcting for linkage errors in contingency tables – a cautionary tale. *Journal of Statistical Planning and Inference* 218: 122–137.

Snijkers, G. (2016). Achieving quality in organizational surveys: a holistic approach. In: *Methodische Probleme in der empirischen Organisationsforschung* (ed. S. Liebig and W. Matiaske), 33–59. Wiesbaden: Springer-Gabler.

UNECE (2015). *Guidelines on Statistical Business Registers*. New York and Geneva: United Nations Economic Commission of Europe, United Nations.

Valliant, R. (2020). Comparing alternatives for estimation from nonprobability samples. *Journal of Survey Statistics and Methodology* 8: 231–263.

de Waal, T., van Delden, A., and Scholtus, S. (2020). Multi-source statistics: basic situations and methods. *International Statistical Review* 88 (1): 203–228.

de Waal, T., van Delden, A., and Scholtus, S. (2021). Commonly used methods for measuring output quality of multisource statistics. *Spanish Journal of Statistics* 2: 79–107.

Yang, D., Fricker, S., and Eltinge, J. (2019). Methods for exploratory assessment of consent-to-link in a household survey. *Journal of Survey Statistics and Methodology* 7: 118–155.

Zhang, L.-C. (2012). Topics of statistical theory for register-based statistics and data integration. *Statistica Neerlandica* 66 (1): 41–63.

Zhang, L.-C. (2019). On secondary analysis of datasets that cannot be linked without errors. In: *Analysis of Integrated Data* (ed. L.-C. Zhang and R. L. Chambers), Chapter 2. Boca Raton, FL: CRC Press.

35

Adopting Previously Reported Data into the 2022 Census of Agriculture: Lessons Learned from the 2020 September Agricultural Survey

Linda J. Young[1], Joseph B. Rodhouse[1], Zachary Terner[1,2], and Gavin Corral[1]

[1] USDA National Agricultural Statistics Service, Washington, DC, USA
[2] National Institute of Statistical Sciences, Washington, DC, USA

35.1 Introduction

Each year the US Department of Agriculture's National Agricultural Statistics Service (NASS) conducts more than 100 surveys and produces more than 500 reports on all facets of US agriculture. As the agricultural industry has become increasingly concentrated, precise estimates of agricultural production require participation of the large producers. Consequently, the burden on these large producers has been increasing with some being asked to respond to more than 20 surveys each calendar year. This has contributed to increased nonresponse. In addition to surveys, NASS conducts the Census of Agriculture in years ending in two and seven. Although producers are required by law to complete the Census questionnaire, the penalty for failure to do so is small and seldom enforced. The response rate for the Census has been declining, falling from 78.2% in 2007 to 74.6% in 2012 to 71.8% in 2017. To reduce respondent burden, mitigate the rise in nonresponse, and improve data quality, NASS has begun exploring the use of previously reported data (PRD).

NASS has been reluctant to use PRD, or its methodological cousin-dependent interviewing (DI), until recently. These methodologies typically describe the use of information from previous surveys, administrative records, or other sources that are "fed forward" (Jäckle 2006, p. 1) to aid in the conduct of a current survey. Although the literature has shown that using PRD or DI can be beneficial, there is also evidence that these methodologies may have unintended negative impacts. For example, an experiment using DI in an interviewer-administered NASS survey found that respondents were more likely to "satisfice" (Krosnick 1991) when their PRD were given to them than respondents who were not made aware of their PRD (Stanley and Safer 1997). Stanley and Safer (1997) concluded that cattle ranchers were likely satisficing when reporting that their inventories were no different from their PRD, as the number of respondents reporting their current inventory to be equal to their previous quarter's inventory significantly increased despite the cattle industry's propensity for variability in inventory on a day-to-day basis. Furthermore, using PRD or DI may not make as much of a difference in the burden of the response task for smaller establishments compared to larger establishments. As businesses get larger, the burden of the survey response task becomes increasingly complex (Tomaskovic-Devey et al. 1994). Smaller establishments may have less complexity, and therefore respondents may be more likely to be able to retrieve their answer directly from memory without having to rely on cognitive heuristics (such as anchoring and adjustment when PRD are used) or internal records (Ridolfo and Edgar 2015, Stanley and Safer 1997).

Advances in Business Statistics, Methods and Data Collection. Edited by Ger Snijkers, Mojca Bavdaž, Stefan Bender, Jacqui Jones, Steve MacFeely, Joseph W. Sakshaug, Katherine J. Thompson, and Arnout van Delden.
© 2023 John Wiley & Sons, Inc. Published 2023 by John Wiley & Sons, Inc.

In a study of web surveys, respondents to the DI instrument completed the survey 10 percent faster than those without DI. However, both respondents with DI and those without perceived the burden of the response task to be the same, though it is believed that DI saved frustrated respondents from breaking off and becoming nonrespondents (Hoogendoorn 2004). Lastly, using PRD has not been shown to increase response rates but, on several indicators of data quality, questionnaires with PRD outperform those without PRD (Holmberg 2004). For example, in a repeated measurement study designed to capture changes of just a few percent, Holmberg (2004) found that preprinting PRD resulted in smaller response variability, and fewer and smaller extreme values compared to a control group with no preprinted PRD. In Holmberg's analysis, preprinting PRD decreased measurement errors (p. 349). The benefits of DI and PRD are evident to researchers, and they may also be evident to respondents who are sampled in multiple surveys each year. NASS has conducted a series of focus groups to determine in what areas producers would like for NASS to improve; providing PRD for their use when responding to surveys and censuses was consistently suggested.

Based on this feedback, NASS is committed to providing PRD in its 2022 Census of Agriculture. A series of tests are being conducted to understand the impacts of PRD on the quality of the data and the resulting estimates. The results from an experiment embedded in the 2020 September Agricultural Survey provide insights into the effect of PRD use on response rates and data quality and are the focus of this paper. In Section 35.2, the Agricultural Production Survey and its sources of previously reported data are described. The design and results of the study are presented in Section 35.3 and Section 35.4, respectively. In the final section, insights gained from the study as well as future avenues of research are discussed.

35.2   Agricultural Survey and Previously Reported Data (PRD)

The Agricultural Survey is a quarterly survey conducted in all states. Based on producer responses, national estimates of crop acreage, yields, and production and quantities of grain and oilseeds stored on farms are published; state estimates are also provided for the states with the largest production. The crops for which data are collected depend on the crops being grown within a state and the amount of acreage devoted to those crops. Thus, the survey questionnaire is unique to each state. Questions about all crops do not appear on the Agricultural Survey each quarter. The presence of a particular crop for a given quarter's survey depends upon the crop's growing season. For instance, data for a small grain, such as winter wheat, are obtained in December, March, and June to determine acreage and in September to determine production. In contrast, data for row crops, such as corn, are collected in March and June for acreage determination and in December after the majority of the crop has been harvested and the production determined.

The Agricultural Survey sample is stratified by state and drawn using Maximal Brewer Selection with Poisson Permanent-Random-Number (PRN) sampling (Brewer 1963, Kott and Bailey 2000), which is sometimes referred to as multivariate probability proportional to size (mpps) sampling. The sample is drawn early in the calendar year for the upcoming growing season. Thus, surveys are sent to all producers selected in the portion of the sample representing row crops in March, June, and December. In contrast, survey information is collected from producers in the portion of the sample representing small grains in December of the year in which the sample is drawn and in March, June, and September of the following year. (See Bailey and Kott (1997) for a detailed discussion of mpps applied to the Agricultural Survey.)

The September Agricultural Survey, which is the focus of this study, targets small grains: winter wheat, spring wheat, Durum wheat, oats, rye, and barley. The survey is conducted after most of the crop has been harvested, and it is the fourth and final time that producers in that particular sample are surveyed during the small grain growing season.

NASS has historically stored the final edited data used to produce reports, not the PRD. Therefore, the only PRD available for the 2020 September Agricultural Survey were obtained from responses collected via computer-assisted self-interviewing (CASI) using a web questionnaire or computer-assisted personal interviewing (CAPI). A new CASI/CAPI system was established for the 2017 Census of Agriculture, and all surveys were in the system by late 2019. This system is the source of PRD for this study. A challenge is that the proportion of CASI/CAPI responders to a survey tends to be low, generally less than 5%.

Beginning in late 2019, NASS began making a concerted effort to increase the availability of PRD for use in dependent interviewing. In addition to CASI and CAPI, NASS collects data through computer-assisted telephone interviewing (CATI) and the mail. CATI data are collected in Blaise, a computer-assisted interviewing system and survey processing tool designed for use in official statistics and complex surveys (Statistics Netherlands 2020). Some processing changes had to be made before PRD could be saved within Blaise. These changes were completed in mid-2020 after the last PRD for the 2020 September Agricultural Survey were collected. Because over half of the survey responses are collected via CATI, this is a rich source of PRD, which will be available in the future. NASS generally collects 10–15% of the responses to a survey via the mail. The responses are keyed-in and stored. Prior to mid-2020, it could not be determined with certainty whether the data that were keyed-in from those surveys had been edited; therefore, they were not used for dependent interviewing. The processing of mail responses has been changed so that these will also be a source of PRD.

In summary, for this study, all relevant CASI and CAPI responses are available for PRD, but they constitute a small portion of the respondents. Although the processing of CATI and mail responses have transitioned so that these responses can be used as PRD, they were not available for this study. As a consequence, less than 3% of the records in the 2020 September Agricultural Survey had PRD associated with them.

35.3 Study Design

A study was conducted within the 2020 September Agricultural Survey to assess the impact of using PRD on response rates, question completion times, and data quality. Because declining response rates have been a major concern, NASS wanted to determine whether PRD had any effect on response rates even though none was anticipated. The question completion times were expected to decrease with the use of PRD. The concern that respondents will satisfice, potentially resulting in biased estimates, was evaluated by comparing the update rates, defined as the proportion of times that the reported value differed from the PRD. A significantly lower update rate could be an indication of satisficing. Because high edit rates could be an indication of lower data quality, the proportion of responses that were edited was also compared between the two treatment groups. The choice of survey questions for PRD, choice of PRD, presentation of PRD, the study design, data collection, and analyses conducted are now discussed.

35.3.1 Survey Questions and PRD Included in the Study

The study did not involve changing question wordings or routing respondents around certain questions where PRD were used, as might be found in DI data collections. Rather, this study was more akin to Holmberg's (2004) "pre-printing" study, where the decision was made to keep the questionnaires unchanged, and simply preprint respondents' PRD into their unique web survey links, which they could edit and change as they went through the survey. For a given farm, crops and the acreage devoted to those crops may, and often do, change from one growing season to the next. However, within the same growing season, many farms' circumstances may not have changed much (or at all) in the time between the Agricultural Surveys conducted in two consecutive quarters for some of the questions. Among respondents who are included in multiple surveys, such as panel surveys, a common complaint is having to answer the same questions over and over again even though their circumstances have not changed from one survey to the next (Phillips et al. 2002).

At NASS, some respondents sampled in multiple surveys have made similar complaints. Research has shown that these respondent concerns can be alleviated when using PRD for questions that are inherently stable over time (Jäckle 2006). Therefore, for the 2020 September Agricultural Survey, only those questions that were not anticipated to change during the growing season were considered for study inclusion. After a review of the survey questionnaire, 15 questions were identified for PRD: the acreage planted to all crops, total farm acreage, on-farm grain storage capacity, and the acres planted and harvested (or to be harvested) to each of the small grains. (See the online repository for the full September Agricultural Survey questionnaire.) These questions are asked each quarter, and the responses are not likely to, and often do not, change during the growing season.

For each question, the most recent PRD available were presented to the producer; the order in which PRD were selected was as follows: (i) 2020 June response, (ii) 2020 March response, and (iii) 2019 December response. Due to item nonresponse, the PRD presented to a producer could have been pulled from different questionnaires. Further, PRD were not always available for all questions. Because the types of small grains a producer has varies with location and individual farming practices, the number of responses to the 15 questions with PRD naturally varied.

Historically, NASS has archived the edited responses to its questionnaires, but not its producer reported data (the PRD). Holmberg (2004) found that, if respondents do not recognize the PRD given to them, it negatively affects their confidence, goodwill, and cooperation with the survey. As a result, only the exact producer-provided PRD were shown to respondents, and not the NASS-edited version of the PRD.

35.3.2 Design of the Study

Of the 62 534 records in the 2020 September Agricultural Survey *sample*, 1657 had PRD from their responses to at least one earlier Agricultural Survey during the growing season (December, March, June). Due to security concerns, it was decided not to use PRD in the mail questionnaire; PRD were targeted for use in the CASI (web) instrument. Although NASS is making efforts to increase web response, the proportion of responses provided through the web is still low; in June, 3.1% of those in the survey sample, which is 5.6% of the responders, answered the questions online. To increase the likelihood of including producers who would respond via the web in the study, a propensity model predicting the likelihood that a producer would submit a web response was developed. Only the 1453 producers with a probability of at least 0.5 of responding on the web were eligible for the study.

The sample was stratified using two variables: region and farm size. Originally, the regions were to be the 12 NASS regions, which are based on within-region homogeneity of agriculture. However, this led to small numbers of available survey records in some regions. Thus, to form the strata for regions, states with similar farming practices with respect to small grain production, the focus of the September Agricultural Survey, were grouped together until a substantial number of survey

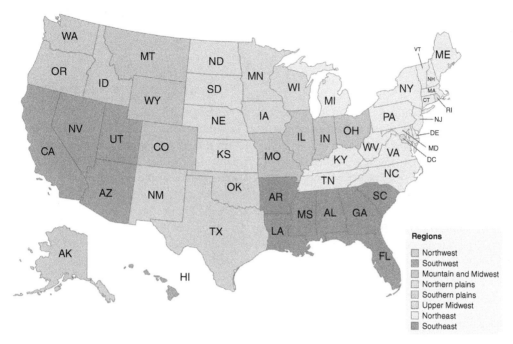

Figure 35.1 Regions of the United States used to stratify the study sample.

sample records were present in each regional stratum, resulting in eight strata: Northwest, Southwest, Mountain and Midwest, Northern Plains, Southern Plains, Upper Midwest, Northeast, and Southeast (see Figure 35.1 (Mapchart.net 2021)).

Farm size, the other stratification variable, had two strata: large and small. To define the strata, the median number of cropland acres of the 1657 farms in the survey sample with PRD was determined to be 831. Farms with cropland acres at or above 831 acres are denoted as large, and farms with fewer than 831 acres are described as small. Thirty-nine (39) of the 1453 records with a propensity of at least 0.5 of responding on the web did not have a positive value for cropland acreage, an indication that they had no cropland, and were excluded from the study. Thus, 1417 records had PRD, a propensity of at least 0.5 of providing a web response, and a positive value of cropland acreage; these constituted the *study population*.

The study was embedded in the 2020 September Agricultural Survey, which is a production survey used to produce a Principal Federal Economic Indicator for wheat, one of the indicators in a series describing the current condition of the US economy. Out of concern for potential loss of data quality and the subsequent impact on the official estimates, it was decided to restrict the study sample size to 1000 and to ensure that the sample was distributed across the nation. The sample of 1000 was drawn from the study population stratified by region (eight regions) and farm size (large or small). The *study sample* was drawn with probability proportional to size from the stratified study population. Within each sample stratum, producers were randomly assigned to the treatment group (PRD) with probability of 0.5, and the remaining records were assigned to the control group (No PRD). Of the 1000 sample records, 498 and 502 were in the No-PRD and PRD groups, respectively. During processing in preparation for the survey, some identified to be in the study sample could not be positively confirmed to be in the 2020 September Agricultural Survey sample of 62 534 records. As a consequence, they were not included in the processing associated with loading the PRD into the questionnaires; all of these records (both those identified for PRD and those that were not to receive PRD) were deleted from the study prior to its initiation, leaving 428 in the PRD group and 432 in the No-PRD group. See Table S.1 in the supplementary materials for details on the study population and sample size by stratum.

35.3.3 Data Collection

The survey was conducted between August 25 and September 7. The study sample was processed with all other records in the 2020 September Agricultural Survey sample. The survey letter for the treatment group had an additional sentence noting that they would be shown their PRD when responding on the web; otherwise, the letter was the same as that of the No-PRD group and the remaining survey sample. It was hoped that the sentence about the presence of PRD in the pre-notification letter would increase response rates. After one to two weeks of self-administered data collection via the mail or web, the records were sent for telephone follow-up. Once the data were collected, the study sample records were sent through the editing and summarization processes with all other records. Those records without a CASI response were sent for CAPI follow-up. However, only the CASI responses are in scope for this study.

35.3.4 Analysis of the Study

After data collection, editing, and imputation, the records were summarized to produce official estimates. The analysis of the study began after the official estimates were published on September 11 due to security concerns. For the No-PRD and PRD groups, response rates were calculated using AAPOR RR1 from the American Association of Public Opinion Research Response Rate Standard Definitions manual (AAPOR 2016) and compared. The times to complete the questionnaire were evaluated for the No-PRD and PRD groups. To assess potential satisficing, the rates at which producers in the No-PRD and PRD groups updated a response to be different from the PRD (the update rates) were compared. For the PRD group, this meant that producers were provided the PRD response value and decided to update it. For the No-PRD group, the PRD values were *not* provided to the producer; however, each producer's responses were compared to the corresponding PRD values in NASS's records. In addition, the sizes of the updates from the PRD to the currently reported data were compared. Based on the 15 questions for which PRD were available, the postsurvey edit rates, the proportions of a record's survey responses changed during the editing and imputation processes, were also compared.

The analysis of each response variable reflected the 8×2^2 factorial design of the study. The factors were region (8), farm size (large and small), and treatment (PRD and No PRD). All main effects, two-factor interactions, and three-factor interaction were included unless the data were sparse. When data sparseness prevented fitting the full model, the three-factor interaction was dropped and, if needed, two factor interactions involving region were excluded from the model. For each, a generalized linear model was fit in Proc GLIMMIX in SAS 9.4 (SAS 2021), with the response variable distribution and the link function depending on the response being analyzed. The reported estimated proportions and means of the response variables are the least squares means, which adjust for the means of other factors (region and size when considering treatment) in the model.

35.4 Study Results

The 2020 September Agricultural Survey response rate of those in the study sample was 65.2%. Of those in the survey sample, 3.1% responded using the web questionnaire, which was 4.7% of the

Table 35.1 Number of item-level responses to each question.

Response of interest	PRD	No PRD
Acres of cropland	215	211
Total acres of land	216	212
On-farm grain capacity	156	131
Barley planted	22	27
Barley harvested	17	18
Durum wheat planted	4	5
Durum wheat harvested	4	3
Oats planted	39	40
Oats harvested	15	20
Rye planted	11	18
Rye harvested	4	7
Spring wheat planted	25	25
Spring wheat harvested	24	23
Winter wheat planted	108	102
Winter wheat harvested	93	84

respondents. A questionnaire was considered complete if at least one section was completed with a nonnegative response (a valid zero or a positive value). All of the web questionnaires opened by a respondent were completed; that is, there were no break-offs in the midst of completing the web questionnaire. This is likely due to the familiarity of the respondents with the questionnaire and the limited time required to complete it.

Producers only respond to those questions that are germane to their operation. Thus, the number of item-level responses varies (see Table 35.1). Five questions had at least 84 responses for each treatment: acres of cropland, total acres of land, acres planted to winter wheat, acres of winter wheat harvested, and on-farm capacity for grain storage. Where appropriate, individual analyses were conducted for these questions; the other 10 questions had no more than 40 responses per treatment and were only considered in the overall analyses.

35.4.1 Comparison of Response Rates

The use of propensity models to identify those more likely to respond via the web led to the study sample having a larger proportion of web responses (49.8%) than was observed in the survey sample (3.1%) based on the AAPOR RR1. For the study sample, 50.2% (216) of the PRD group and 49.1% (212) of the No-PRD group responded via the web (see Table 35.2), which is not a significant difference ($z = 0.41$; $p = 0.68$).

For the analysis of response based on the study design, the response variable was a Bernoulli random variable indicating whether a person responded. None of the main effects (farm size, region, and treatment), two-factor interactions (region by farm size, farm size by treatment), or the three-factor interaction (region by farm size by treatment) were significant ($p > 0.4$). The estimated proportions responding are 0.50 for the PRD group and 0.52 for the No-PRD group; the *p*-value for

Table 35.2 Number of the study sample records by response and treatment.

	PRD	No PRD
CASI response	216 (50.5%)	212 (49.1%)
No CASI response	212 (49.5%)	220 (50.9%)
Total	428 (100.0%)	432 (100.0%)

the main effect of treatment is 0.53. (See the online supplementary materials for more details of the response rate analysis.) If informing respondents of the presence of PRD prior to taking the survey can impact response rates, the single sentence included in the study's prenotification letter to the PRD group was not sufficient given the conditions of this data collection. However, these results are consistent with earlier studies that found the use of PRD did not increase response rates (Hoogendoorn 2004).

35.4.2 Comparison of Completion Times

The completion time, the time required for a respondent to complete a questionnaire, was compared for the respondents (with completed questionnaires) in the PRD and the No-PRD treatment groups to assess whether PRD reduced that aspect of burden. During exploratory data analysis, a small number of extremely long completion times was observed for both groups. This could occur if a respondent decided to take a break in the midst of completing the questionnaire. In an effort to reduce the impact of these breaks, all records that had an item-level completion time greater than an hour (60 minutes), which results in a completion time of well over an hour, were removed from the analysis. In a few cases, a negative response time was recorded by the survey system; these too were removed from the analysis. After eliminating the records with at least *one item* response time exceeding an hour and those with negative response times, 188 of the original 215 responding records remained in the PRD treatment group, and 185 of the original 212 responding records were in the No-PRD group.

The distribution of completion times, the response variable, is highly skewed. Thus, a generalized linear model assuming a lognormal distribution with an identity link function was fit. The study design was fully reflected by the model factors, including the main effects (region, farm size, and treatment), the two-factor interactions (region by farm size, region by treatment, and farm size by treatment), and the three-factor interaction (region by farm size by treatment). The estimates and their standard errors were back-transformed to the original scale (SAS 2013, p. 3168, Zeng and Tang 2011, Baskerville 1972). The estimated mean completion times of 7.6 (standard error of 3.4 minutes) and 8.1 minutes (standard error of 3.7 minutes) for the PRD and No-PRD groups, respectively, were not significantly different ($p = 0.28$), though this observed decrease of 7.0% is similar to the 10% savings in time previously reported by Hoogendoorn (2004). The three-factor interaction was significant ($p = 0.03$), which implies that the interaction of region and farm size depends on the treatment group (see Figure 35.2). The presence of PRD appears to result in less fluctuation in completion times across regions. (See the online supplementary materials for more details of the completion time analysis.)

As discussed earlier, five questions had at least 84 responses for each treatment: acres of cropland, total acres of land, acres planted to winter wheat, acres of winter wheat harvested, and on-farm

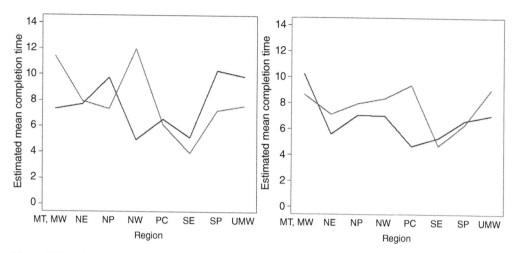

Figure 35.2 Mean completion times: Interaction between Farm Size (Small = black, Large = grey) and region for the No-PRD (left) and PRD (right) treatment groups.

capacity for grain storage. Individual analyses were conducted for these response variables. For each question, the time to complete that question was the response variable. The analysis was the same as that for the total completion time reported above, except for acres of winter wheat harvested. The data were too sparse to fit the full model when including any interaction involving region. Thus, only the main effects and the interaction between treatment group and farm size were considered.

The mean completion times were significantly greater for the PRD group than for the No-PRD group when reporting on-farm grain storage capacity ($p < 0.0001$), but significantly less for acres of cropland ($p = 0.0223$, see Table 35.3). For the other three questions, the observed mean completion time was greater for the PRD group than for the No-PRD group for one (total acres of land) and lower for the other two questions (acres planted to winter wheat and acres of winter wheat harvested), though none of these differences were significant. This could indicate that the presence of PRD allows responders to move more rapidly through some questions, such as cropland, but require them to pause and consider their responses more carefully in other cases. Further study is needed to assess the reasons for these differing results. For some questions, the main effects for

Table 35.3 Estimated mean completion times by treatment group with associated p-value for Test of Their Equality for Five Survey Questions.

	Estimated mean completion times and standard errors				
	PRD		**No PRD**		
Response of interest	**Mean**	**Standard error**	**Mean**	**Standard error**	**p-value for test of equality of means**
Acres of cropland	0.74	0.0507	0.93	0.0672	0.0223
Total acres of land	1.65	0.1084	1.54	0.1038	0.4761
On-farm capacity for grain storage	0.47	0.0110	0.35	0.0084	<0.0001
Acres planted to winter wheat	0.77	0.0488	0.84	0.0540	0.3537
Acres of winter wheat harvested	0.23	0.0307	0.25	0.0335	0.7541

p-value for test of their equality for five survey questions.

region and farm size were significant. The two-factor interaction of region and treatment group and the three-factor interaction were significant for on-farm grain capacity; no other interaction terms were significant for the five questions.

35.4.3 Analysis of Update Rates

One of NASS's primary concerns, and the primary reason that PRD have not been used earlier, is that respondents may satisfice, which could bias official estimates. One approach to evaluating whether satisficing is likely with PRD is to compare how often responses differ from the PRD when it is available versus when it is not. Of the 1879 questions with positive responses (responses with values that are greater than zero) across all questionnaires in the study sample, the PRD were updated for 1003 of them. The PRD group could view their PRD and updated 505 of their responses to the 953 questions with positive responses. The No-PRD group had PRD available but was not shown the PRD on the questionnaire. That group updated 498 responses to the 926 questions with positive responses.

The number of questions with positive responses varied from 1 to 11, depending on the grain crops being grown and whether on-farm grain storage was present. For a more in-depth analysis, the update rate, the proportion of times a respondent reported a value that was different from the PRD, was the response variable for analysis. Only those questions with at least one positive value for the PRD, the currently reported value, or the final edited value were considered. The generalized linear model was based on the assumption of the response being binomially distributed with a logit link function.

The estimated proportions of positive-response updates between the PRD and reported values were 0.53 for the PRD group and 0.55 for the No-PRD group; these are not significantly different ($p = 0.38$). The interaction between region and treatment is significant ($p = 0.003$, see Figure 35.3). The proportion of times the PRD were updated for a small farm is 0.51 compared to 0.56 for large

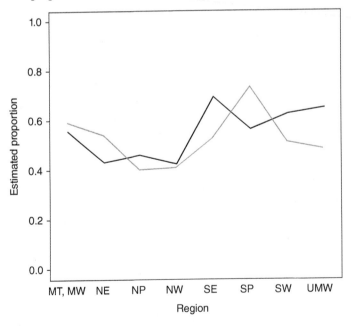

Figure 35.3 Region by treatment interaction for Estimated Update Rate to PRD (No-PRD = black, PRD = grey).

farms, leading to the main effect of farm size being marginally significant ($p = 0.05$). This is likely due to the increased diversity that is often seen with large farms, resulting in more in-season updates. Thus, because the rate at which responses were updated did not differ significantly between the two treatment groups, the concern that the respondents might not make needed changes to their PRD (satisfice) is largely not supported by this study.

As with completion times, the five questions having at least 84 responses for each treatment (acres of cropland, total acres of land, acres planted to winter wheat, acres of winter wheat harvested, and on-farm capacity for grain storage) were analyzed individually. For each question, the response variable was an indicator of whether or not the PRD were updated to a new value in the September Agricultural Survey; thus, the distribution was assumed to be Bernoulli with a logit link function. The study's design was fully reflected in the analysis of acres of cropland and total acres of land. Due to sparseness of the data, the model with all factors and interactions could not be fit for on-farm grain capacity, acres planted to winter wheat, or harvested acres of winter wheat, and reduced models were considered. For on-farm grain storage capacity, the main effects and two-factor interactions were included, but the region by size by treatment interaction was omitted. The model of the update rate for the acres planted to wheat included the main effects of region, farm size, and treatment as well as the two-factor interaction between size and treatment. The update-rate model for the acres of harvested wheat had only the three main effects.

For four of the five questions, the estimated proportions of response updates are smaller for the PRD group than for the No-PRD group, but none of the four are significantly different (Table 35.4). The update rate of acres devoted to cropland (0.54) is significantly lower ($p = 0.03$) for the PRD group (0.54) than for the No-PRD group (0.66). (See the online supplementary materials for more details of the update rate analysis by question.)

The size of the updates could also be affected by whether or not the respondent was able to view their PRD. Using the same analysis methods described above, the differences in the reported value and the PRD were compared for the five questions that had at least 84 responses for each treatment. The observed mean size of the updates did not differ significantly between the PRD and No-PRD groups for any of the questions nor were any interactions with treatment significant. The median and mode for both the groups were zero for all five questions. Further, the range in the changes did not appear smaller for either treatment. For example, when considering nonzero differences in the reported value and PRD for total acres of land, the PRD group made updates that ranged from 1 to

Table 35.4 Estimated proportion of response updates by treatment group with associated.

	Estimated proportions and standard errors				
	PRD		**No PRD**		**p-value for test of equality of proportions**
Response of interest	**Proportion**	**Standard error**	**Proportion**	**Standard error**	
Acres of cropland	0.54	0.04	0.66	0.04	0.03
Total acres of land	0.56	0.04	0.54	0.04	0.69
On-farm capacity for grain storage	0.55	0.04	0.44	0.05	0.08
Acres planted to winter wheat	0.58	0.05	0.57	0.05	0.94
Acres of winter wheat harvested	0.50	0.07	0.45	0.07	0.59

p-value for test of their equality for five survey questions.

15 209, and the differences for the no-PRD group ranged from 1 to 7000. In contrast, for cropland, the PRD group made updates that ranged from 1 to 4500 compared to the No-PRD group that had reported differences ranging from 1 to 31 010. In summary, the size of the update from the PRD does not appear to depend on whether or not the respondent was able to view the PRD.

35.4.4 Analysis of Edit Rates

All records, including those in both the PRD and No-PRD treatment groups, were sent through the editing process with all other survey records that were not in the study sample. Some editing is automated, and other edits are made by data analysts in the regional field offices. In either case, there was no indication on a record to indicate whether it was part of the study sample; thus, the editing process was blind with respect to treatment.

As with the analysis of the update rates, only those questions with at least one positive value for the PRD, the currently reported value, or the final edited value was considered. Of the 1879 questions from the study sample questionnaires with PRD, edits were made to 63 of these. Twenty-four (24) edits were made to the 876 responses that had no update to the PRD, and 39 edits were made to the 1003 responses that differed from the PRD, which is not significantly different ($p < 0.17$ for the Cochran–Mantel–Haenszel Test).

Given the sparseness of the data, a full model reflecting the study design could not be fit. The response variable was an indicator of whether the reported value was updated during the editing process. The distribution was assumed to be Bernoulli with a logit link. The main effects of region, farm size, and treatment were incorporated into the model. The only significant effect was farm size ($p = 0.04$). The edit rate for small farms (0.04) is significantly greater than that for large farms (0.02).

Sufficient data were present to analyze five questions separately: acres in cropland, total acres of land, acres planted to wheat, harvested acres of wheat, and the on-farm grain storage capacity. As in the earlier analyses, not all aspects of the study design could be incorporated due to sparseness of the data. In each case, there was no significant effect due to treatment.

35.5 Discussion

Increasing undercoverage for most list frames and decreasing survey response rates are occurring as the public's demand for more data, often at finer temporal and spatial scales, is increasing. At the same time, the public is expressing concerns about the increasing response burden from the surveys being used to gather this information. One response to these challenges has been to explore the use of nonsurvey data, such as administrative or remotely sensed data, in the estimation process. Progress is certainly being made in that effort. Yet, survey data provide a firm statistical foundation for evaluating other data sources and remain an important tool in the production of official statistics. The integration of all data, including survey and nonsurvey data, has the potential to improve the quality of reported statistics and to allow federal statistical agencies to provide more timely reports. To do this, every effort must be made to reduce survey response burden. Using PRD is one approach and, although it is useful for reducing real response burden (i.e. reducing response times), it may not always result in a reduction in the respondent's perceived burden (Hoogendoorn 2004). However, NASS is currently conducting research to examine respondents' perceived burden when presented PRD in the Census of Agriculture, and additional insights on this area are, therefore, forthcoming. Furthermore, it could make some parts of the survey less burdensome, while simultaneously making other parts more burdensome, if the accuracy of the PRD, or the respondents' recognition and recall of the PRD, varies from section to section, or question to question.

Some federal statistical agencies have been using PRD in their surveys for an extended period of time. The Census Bureau, for example, has used PRD and DI for several decades in some, but not all, of its surveys (Bailar 1987). Examples are the Survey of Income and Program Participation (SIPP)(Doyle et al. 2000) and the Current Population Survey (Fallick and Fleischman 2001). Others, including NASS, have been slow to adopt it.

The reasons for not incorporating PRD into data collection vary. As an illustration, NASS is responsible for six Principal Federal Economic Indicators. Because of the importance of these estimates and the potential bias that can occur with PRD (Mergerson and O'Connor 1992, Stanley and Safer 1997), the Agency has been hesitant to adopt the use of PRD on a large scale, though it has incorporated PRD into smaller, relatively stable surveys. Gottschall (2009) showed that, for some NASS surveys, only a limited number of data items can even be used as PRD in future surveys, indicating that the utility of PRD may be quite limited. In the September Agricultural Survey, only 15 of the roughly 60 potential responses were candidates for PRD. Furthermore, an experiment using PRD in an interviewer-administered NASS survey found that respondents were more likely to "satisfice" (Krosnick 1991) when their PRD were given to them than respondents who were not made aware of their PRD (Stanley and Safer 1997).

Yet, producers have increasingly called for NASS to begin using more PRD and, in response, NASS will provide it for the 2022 Census of Agriculture, which is conducted every five years. The Agency is now focused on ensuring that the quality of the data is at least as good with PRD as without it. The 2020 September Agricultural Survey is the first study leading up to that major effort and provided numerous lessons.

The questions on acres of cropland and on-farm capacity for grain storage highlight the challenge of drawing firm conclusions on the impact of PRD use on data quality. These were the two questions that had a significant difference in completion time, and the rate with which PRD was updated was also significant for on-farm capacity for grain storage. Both acres of cropland and on-farm capacity for grain tend to be stable during a growing season. The sizes of the response updates for the PRD and No-PRD groups were not significantly different. When asked about the acres of cropland, a higher, but not a significantly higher, proportion of producers who had PRD updated their responses (56%) than those without it (54%); the response time was significantly shorter for the PRD group than for the No-PRD group. Thus, for this question, the presence of PRD may have reduced burden without introducing satisficing. When responding to the question asking about on-farm capacity for grain storage, a significantly smaller proportion of producers who were shown their PRD (54%) updated the PRD value compared to those who were not shown their PRD (66%); however, those in the PRD group had significantly longer response times than the No-PRD group. In this case, when presented with PRD, producers may spend more time considering the response if their initial thoughts on how to respond differ from the data provided, increasing response burden but potentially reducing spurious changes. Together these results appear to represent an instance in which providing PRD has more likely resulted in a reduction of spurious changes than an increase in satisficing. Further study is needed to determine under what circumstances this is a valid conclusion.

When determining whether to incorporate PRD into a survey or census data collection process, it is important to assess its availability. For this study, only 2.6% of the survey sample records had PRD because the only confirmed nonedited data available were collected via CASI or CAPI. Once processing updates are made so that PRD are saved, it takes time to accumulate the PRD. For surveys taken annually, at least a year is needed. Thus, the decision to use PRD often requires a substantial lead time for implementation.

For this study, all PRD had to be manually identified, collected, and uploaded into the web instrument. This took weeks to accomplish, and it became evident that using PRD is only a viable production process if its use is automated. NASS has now established a contract to automate pulling PRD into a database and uploading it. Such updates are costly and, as with acquiring PRD, take time.

Administrative data are another source of PRD. Each year producers who participate in a United States Department of Agriculture (USDA) program complete the USDA Farm Service Agency's (FSA's) FSA-578 form. Data collected include the type of crop planted to each field, the acres in the field, and some information on farming practices, such as whether the field is irrigated. By mid-season, these data are available and could serve as a rich source of PRD. In fact, many producers expect NASS to use that information because they have already provided it to one of the USDA agencies. Currently, NASS pulls these data manually as needed under a Memorandum of Understanding with FSA. Although efforts are underway to automate this process, another barrier to their use is the need to link the survey responses to the FSA data. NASS and FSA currently have different definitions of a farm, making this a major challenge. The accuracy with which administrative data can serve as PRD is an important consideration.

The steps taken to inform responders of the availability of PRD may have an impact on response. For this study, a single sentence informing the respondent that PRD would be available to them was added to the presurvey letter, and a message appeared on the screen preceding the start of the questionnaire that the respondent's PRD would be shown and that it could be updated. For this study, the sentence did not increase the response rate. The message alone may encourage completion of the questionnaire, but is unlikely to affect response. Perhaps highlighting that PRD will be available in the presurvey letter could lead to a greater response. To test this hypothesis, a study of the impact of providing this information in presurvey letters is being conducted as part of the 2021 Census of Agriculture Content Test.

In summary, the study conducted within the 2020 September Agricultural Survey identified challenges, such as availability of PRD and automation of processing, that must be addressed for PRD to be used routinely in surveys and censuses. Potential opportunities to increase response rates, such as informing sampled producers that PRD are available, were identified. Finally, and most importantly, no negative impacts on data quality were found. In fact, for on-farm capacity for grain storage, it appears that the use of PRD reduced spurious changes, a positive impact on data quality. As a consequence, NASS continues to move aggressively to implement the use of PRD in the 2022 Census of Agriculture while continuing to assess the effects it has on data quality.

Acknowledgments

The authors are deeply appreciative of the efforts made by NASS's full Non-Edited Reported Data (NERD) Team without whose efforts this study could not have been conducted. The following members played especially substantive roles: Ramonia Davis (implemented changes to web survey instrument), Goshko Georgiev (populated the survey instrument with NERD), Jay Johnson (identification of regions), Troy Joshua (identification of regions), Greg Lemmons (led PRD sourcing and ranking effort), Jared Pratt (developed the NERD dataset), Ty Tolbert (project management), and Tyler Wilson (led team formation).

References

Bailar, B.A. (1987). Nonsampling errors. *Journal of Official Statistics* 3 (4): 323–325. https://www.scb
.se/contentassets/ca21efb41fee47d293bbee5bf7be7fb3/nonsampling-errors.pdf.

Baskerville, G.L. (1972). Use of logarithmic regression in the estimation of plant biomass. *Canadian Journal of Forest Research* 2 (1): 49–53. https://doi.org/10.1139/x72-009.

Bailey, J.T. and Kott, P.S. (1997). An application of multiple list frame sampling for multi-purpose surveys. In: *Proceedings of the Section on Survey Research Methods*, 496–500. Washington, DC: American Statistical Association http://www.asasrms.org/Proceedings/papers/1997_084.pdf.

Brewer, K.R.W. (1963). Ratio estimation and finite populations: some results deducible from the assumption of an underlying stochastic process. *Australian Journal of Statistics* 5: 93–105. https://doi
.org/10.1111/j.1467-842X.1963.tb00288.x.

Doyle, P., Martin, E., and Moore, J. (2000). Methods panel to improve income measurement in the survey of income and program participation. In: *Proceedings of the Section on Survey Research Methods*, 953–958. Washington, DC: American Statistical Association http://www.asasrms.org/Proceedings/papers/2000_163.pdf.

Fallick, B. and Fleischman, C.A. (2001). The importance of employer-to-employer flows in the U.S. labor market. *Finance and Economics Discussion Series* #2001-18, Board of Governors of the Federal Reserve System, April 2001. https://papers.ssrn.com/sol3/papers.cfm?abstract_id=268852 (accessed 16 April 2001).

Gottschall, C. (2009). Previously reported data usage in NASS field offices. CSD Staff Report DCB-09-01. Washington DC: National Agricultural Statistics Service. https://www.nass.usda.gov/Education_and_Outreach/Reports,_Presentations_and_Conferences/reports/gottch_prd-final.pdf (accessed 16 April 2021).

Hoogendoorn, A.W. (2004). A questionnaire design for dependent interviewing that addresses the problem of cognitive satisficing. *Journal of Official Statistics* 20 (2): 219–232. https://www.scb.se/contentassets/ca21efb41fee47d293bbee5bf7be7fb3/a-questionnaire-design-for-dependent-interviewing-that-addresses-the-problem-of-cognitive-satisficing.pdf.

Holmberg, A. (2004). Pre-printing effects in official statistics: an experimental study. *Journal of Official Statistics* 20 (2): 341–355. https://www.scb.se/contentassets/ca21efb41fee47d293bbee5bf7be7fb3/pre-printing-effects-in-official-statistics-an-experimental-study.pdf.

Jäckle, A. (2006). Dependent interviewing: a framework and application to current research. *ISER Working Paper Series No. 2006-32*, Institute for Social and Economic Research (ISER), University of Essexhttps://www.econstor.eu/handle/10419/92099 (accessed 16 April 2021).

Kott, P. S. and Bailey, J. T. (2000). The theory and practice of Maximal Brewer Selection with Poisson PRN sampling. *Proceedings of the 2000 International Conference on Establishment Surveys*, https://ww2.amstat.org/meetings/ices/2000/proceedings/S04.pdf.

Krosnick, J.A. (1991). Response strategies for coping with the cognitive demands of attitude measures in surveys. *Applied Cognitive Psychology* 5 (3): 213–236. https://doi.org/10.1002/acp.2350050305.

Mapchart.net (2021). https://mapchart.net/usa.html (accessed 16 April 2021).

Mergerson, J.W. and O'Connor, T.P. (1992). The effect of using historical data in CATI grain stocks enumeration in the March 1988 agricultural survey. *SRB Research Report* 92-01. Washington DC: National Agricultural Statistics Service. https://www.nass.usda.gov/Education_and_Outreach/Reports,_Presentations_and_Conferences/Survey_Reports/The%20Effect%20of%20Using%20Historical%20Data%20in%20CATI%20Grain%20Stocks%20Enumeration%20in%20the%20March%201988%20Agricultural%20Survey.pdf (accessed 16 April, 2021).

Phillips, M., Woodward, C., Collins, D., and O'Connor, W. (2002). Encouraging and maintaining participation in the families and children survey: understanding why people take part, department for work and pensions research working paper number 6 https://webarchive.nationalarchives.gov .uk/20050816120000/http://www.dwp.gov.uk/asd/asd5/wp2002.html (accessed 16 April 2021).

Ridolfo, H. and Edgar, J. (2015). *Let Me Tell You What You Told Me: Dependent Interviewing in Establishment Surveys*. Washington DC: Bureau of Labor Statistics, Office of Survey Methods Research http://www.asasrms.org/Proceedings/papers/1997_084.pdf.

SAS Institute Inc. (2013). *SAS/STAT® 13.1 User's Guide*. Cary, NC: SAS Institute Inc.

SAS Institute Inc. (2021). *SAS/STAT® User's Guide: The GLIMMIX Procedure*. Cary, NC: SAS Institute Inc. SAS Help Center: The GLIMMIX Procedure.

Stanley, J. and Safer, M. (1997). Last time you had 78, how many do you have now? The effect of providing reports on current reports of cattle inventories. *Proceedings of the American Statistical Association, Section on Survey Research Methods* 875–879. http://www.asasrms.org/Proceedings/papers/1997_151.pdf.

Statistics Netherlands (2020). https://blaise.com/support/documention (accessed 16 April 2021).

The American Association for Public Opinion Research (2016). *Standard Definitions: Final Dispositions of Case Codes and Outcome Rates for Surveys*, 9th edition, AAPOR, Standard Definitions (aapor.org).

Tomaskovic-Devey, D., Leiter, J., and Thompson, S. (1994). Organizational survey nonresponse. *Administrative Science Quarterly* 39 (3): 439–457. https://doi.org/10.2307/2393298.

Zeng, W.S. and Tang, S.Z. (2011). Bias correction in logarithmic regression and comparison with weighted regression for nonlinear models. *Nature Precedings* https://doi.org/10.1038/npre.2011.6708.1.

36

Integrating Alternative and Administrative Data into the Monthly Business Statistics: Some Applications from Statistics Canada
Marie-Claude Duval, Richard Laroche, and Sébastien Landry

Statistics Canada, Ottawa, ON, Canada

36.1   Context for Integrating Alternative and Administrative Data

In recent years, similar to other National Statistical Offices (NSO), Statistics Canada is modernizing its statistical programs to respond to a rapidly changing and increasingly complex economy and society, a proliferation of data and providers, and increased user expectations for "real-time" and detailed information. Statistics Canada's modernization includes an administrative and alternative-data-first agenda, an environment where data and insights already present in the data ecosystem are leveraged before surveys or other collection methods are used (Statistics Canada, 2019). Unsurprisingly, many monthly business programs at Statistics Canada such as manufacturing, retail, and food services and drinking places started integrating alternative data and/or expanding the use of administrative data. These new approaches have many advantages. As described in Statistics Canada (2016, Chapter 3.5), the use of administrative or alternative data can potentially allow NSOs to

- improve the quality of statistical products (e.g. reduce sampling or nonsampling errors);
- improve the relevance of statistical products (e.g. produce more detailed or more frequent estimates);
- fill data gaps;
- reduce the costs of statistical products; and
- reduce response burden.

The expansion in the use of administrative or alternative data in monthly business programs has been a success and it has brought improvements in the different programs where they were applied, either in cost reduction, less response burden, or more granular data while improving or maintaining quality. One important element to this success was the evaluation of their use before implementing it. These evaluations allowed the assessment of the methods, the appropriateness of the data, and indicated some improvements that were needed before integrating them in the production process.

This chapter will present applications in the use of alternative or administrative data in three monthly economic programs. The first application is the replacement of survey data by the Goods and Services Tax and the Harmonized Sales Tax (GST) data in the Monthly Survey of Food Services and Drinking Places (MSFSDP). The second is the use of scanner data to replace survey commodity

Advances in Business Statistics, Methods and Data Collection. Edited by Ger Snijkers, Mojca Bavdaž, Stefan Bender, Jacqui Jones, Steve MacFeely, Joseph W. Sakshaug, Katherine J. Thompson, and Arnout van Delden.

data in the Retail Commodity Survey (RCS). The last application is the use of small area estimation (SAE) techniques that integrate survey data and administrative data in the Monthly Survey of Manufacturing (MSM). For each project, a description of the context, the methodology, the assessment, and results will be provided. Lastly, the impact of the pandemic and future initiatives for the monthly business statistics programs will be discussed briefly.

36.2 Replacement of Survey Data by Tax Data in the Monthly Survey of Food Services and Drinking Places

The Tax replacement project in the Monthly Survey of Food Services and Drinking Places (MSFSDP) was undertaken in late 2018. The main goal was to reduce the collection cost and response burden by using as much data as possible from the Goods and Services Tax and the Harmonized Sales Tax (GST) file provided to Statistics Canada every month by the Canada Revenue Agency (CRA).

The MSFSDP provides estimates of the value of sales of restaurants, caterers, and drinking places by province and territory and by four subsectors under the North American Industry Classification System (NAICS) 722. The subsectors are at a four or six-digit level as described in Table 36.1.

These data are used by federal and provincial governments, private associations, and food service businesses for consulting, marketing, and planning purposes. The provincial and federal governments use the information to estimate provincial taxation shares. Approximately 100,000 establishments are identified each month as being in-scope for the MSFSDP from the Statistics Canada Business Register (Statistics Canada, 2020).

The first subsection will describe the previous methodology under a survey design, the second subsection will provide a brief overview of the GST administrative file, and the third subsection will explain the new methodology proposed to replace survey data with administrative data. The remaining subsections will describe the assessment of the requirements before its implementation, the implementation itself, conclusions, and future work.

36.2.1 Previous Methodology Under a Survey Design

Before October 2020, a survey was conducted each month to collect data from a sample. The sample was selected through a stratified design by NAICS, geography, and size with take-all (TA), take-some (TS), and take-none (TN) strata. The take-none portion covered the smallest establishments that as a whole make up at most 10% of the total revenue in each NAICS and geography combination. They are not subject to sampling.

Table 36.1 NAICS code description covered by the Monthly Survey of Food Services and Drinking Places.

NAICS code	Description
7223	Special food services
7224	Drinking places (alcoholic beverages)
722511	Full-service restaurants
722512	Limited-service restaurants

The sampling unit for the MSFSDP was clusters of establishments that are defined as all in-scope establishments that belong to the same enterprise or establishments that belongs to a restaurant chain agreement within the same NAICS and same geography. The same sample was kept over five years with a sample of births added every month. A restratification process was performed every five years and a new sample was then selected. This included a six-month parallel run for which the two samples were collected. While this process allowed for data linkage with the historical series, it was costly and time- and resource-consuming.

The restaurant chain agreement is an important element of that survey. For many years, the MSFSDP has negotiated reporting arrangements with several major restaurant chains to collect data for all of its outlets through the head office of these chains. This means that the head office becomes the collection entity, rather than the individual outlets. This approach decreases response burden since outlets belonging to the chain are not subject to collection; it also frees some of the MSFSDP's fixed sample size for assignment elsewhere and improves data quality (it is a census with no sampling error of the outlets belonging to the head office). In terms of sampling units, the chains represent 8500 clusters that represent around 35% of total sales in that industry. With the collection agreements, less than 100 questionnaires are needed to get data for these clusters.

A total of around 2600 questionnaires were sent to collection every month. Most of the MSFSDP respondents were surveyed through an electronic questionnaire (EQ), but some questionnaires were mailed or faxed to accommodate respondents. E-mail or telephone reminders occurred during the month of collection.

Every month, nonrespondents were imputed within imputation classes and using historical survey data, current data, or administrative data through trend or ratio methods. There was a sequential process to use the best method and according to the information available. The imputation rate is around 25% each month. Also, a calendarization process was performed on data that do not cover periods corresponding perfectly to calendar months.

Ratio estimation was used for the MSFSDP, with the take-none portion incorporated into the ratio estimation process. The sales from the previous month from the GST processed file were used as the auxiliary variable for the ratio estimation since the GST sales for the current month were not yet available by the time the estimates had to be produced. Quality indicators were also derived accounting for the coefficients of variation (CV) and the imputation rates. Finally, this survey provides preliminary estimates, followed by two revised estimates as well as an annual revision.

In late 2018, the tax replacement project in the MSFSDP was undertaken with the availability and the stability of the GST administrative file, as described in the next subsection. The survey measures sales, which is available on the GST administrative file. The expectation was that the GST replacement data would significantly decrease collection costs and response burden. Also, with almost a census of businesses, it would allow the production of more granular estimates.

36.2.2 The GST Administrative File

The Goods and Services Tax and the Harmonized Sales Tax (GST) file is an administrative file provided to Statistics Canada every month by the CRA for many years. GST, sometimes referred as the value added tax, is collected by individual businesses and the sales amount is reported periodically to the CRA, along with the period covered. Reporting frequency to the CRA is determined by the business size in terms of their annual gross business income (GBI)[1]:

---

1 The reporting frequency is technically determined based on the annual taxable sales of the business. For most businesses in this industry, the annual taxable sales is very close to or the same as the GBI.

- Businesses with GBI greater than C$ 6 million must report monthly;
- Businesses with GBI between C$ 1.5 and C$ 6 million are asked to report at least quarterly;
- Small businesses with a GBI of less than C$ 1.5 million are asked to report at least annually;
- Very small businesses with GBI less than C$ 30,000 do not have to collect and report GST data to CRA.

In the Food Services and Drinking Places industry, the monthly reporters represent around 60% of the GBI, the quarterly 30%, and the annual 5%. The businesses that do not report GST data have sales estimated at less than 5%.

The data received are processed at Statistics Canada and monthly microdata files are made available to internal users. First, an edit and imputation process, including outlier detection, are applied to correct or impute for incorrect data or late reporters. Then, a calendarization process is performed on data that do not cover periods corresponding perfectly to calendar months. This happens when a business's reporting period is a year, quarter, or month different from the calendar month. Finally, an allocation process is done to redistribute the information available at the business level to a finer industry-provincial level (establishment or location) for each complex structured business. For consistency with other economic data, the allocation factors from the Business Register at Statistics Canada are used (Glikofridis, 2017). For more information on the processing of GST data, refer to Kirkland (2016a, b).

36.2.3 The New Methodology Proposed to Replace Survey Data with Administrative Data

In the first phase of this project, it was decided to continue to collect sales for chains and franchises, as for these complex businesses, often operating in different provinces and subsectors, the GST data allocated to the establishment level are not as accurate as the data collected for each industry and each province. Also, these businesses required less than 100 questionnaires to be sent as special collection arrangements exist with them. They represent around 35% of the annual GBI. For quality purposes, it has been decided to continue the survey collection for them.

For the remaining establishments with annual GBI greater than C$ 30,000, sales data from the GST processed file are used. They represent around 60% of the total sales. The very small establishments with less than C$ 30,000 that do not report GST data have their monthly sales modeled using their annual GBI and the proportion of the GST that comes from the reference month compared to the total annual GST (for establishments with GST data in the last 12 months), as shown in the following formula.

$$
\text{GST}_{i,m} = \text{Annual Revenue}_i * \frac{\sum\limits_{j \in R} \text{GST}_{j,m}}{\sum\limits_{j \in R} \sum\limits_{t=m-11}^{m} \text{GST}_{j,t}} \tag{36.1}
$$

R denotes the set of establishments with GST data for the last 12 months, m the month for which the value is calculated, and i and j denote establishments. The modeled establishments represent less than 5% of the total sales.

The new estimates can be expressed by the three components:

$$
\hat{\theta}_d = \hat{\theta}_{d,\text{CHAIN}}^{\text{SURVEY}} + \hat{\theta}_{d,\text{REPORTERS}}^{\text{GST}} + \hat{\theta}_{d,\text{MODELED}}^{\text{GST}} \tag{36.2}
$$

where d is the domain (NAICS and geography).

Variance due to imputation is also derived for each component and aggregated to the total. Figure 36.1 compares the old and the new design.

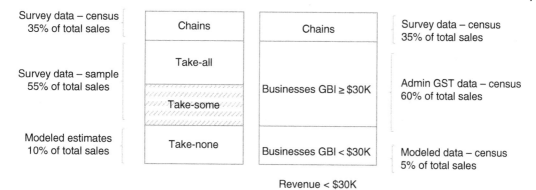

Figure 36.1 Comparison between the old and the new design.

36.2.4 Assessment and Requirements Before the Implementation

Many assessments were carried out before the implementation of the extensive use of administrative data. They included comparisons of the estimates (level, trend, and their revised values), the impact and the quality of the monthly sales data for quarterly and annual reporters, the impact of the allocation process, the impact due to not having updates from collection about the business operation (inactivity, change of industry classification), and comparison with the annual data and differences in concept. These assessments showed that there were no important issues. The trend estimates were comparable most of the time and in the few areas with differences, they could be explained by erroneous data on one file or the other. Concerning the level estimates, it seems that there is a difference in level for some domains between GST and survey data. GST tends to report sometimes larger values and can be explained by other sales revenue generated by the sale of items such as clothing or other novelty items. Respondents can provide estimates of their monthly sales through the survey while they report actual revenue to the CRA. These differences were explained and considered acceptable. Also, the estimates from the new method summed over 12 months were closer to the sales estimates from the Annual Food Survey. For more information on the assessment, refer to Laroche and Caruso (2020).

A major requirement before going ahead with the replacement of survey data with GST data was to get the GST data file processed one week earlier than usual to meet the official releases which are around the 22nd day of each month. A study was carried out to evaluate the impact. The results of the study showed that even though the percentage of reported GST sales would drop by about 7%, the impact on the estimates after imputation was negligible: it was of the order of less than 0.5% for most industries. It is important to mention that the impact is only on the preliminary estimates. There was no impact on the revised estimates since the revised GST file, which contains more reported data, is used for the revisions. Consultations with the users were held and with their agreement, a formal request to CRA was made to receive the GST data the second working day of the month instead of the 9th working day, which was accepted.

36.2.5 Implementation

The application of the new approach in production was preceded by a six-month parallel run. The objective of the parallel run was to monitor the new estimates based on the tax replacement approach and to allow for the linkage of the historical series due to some shifts in level in some

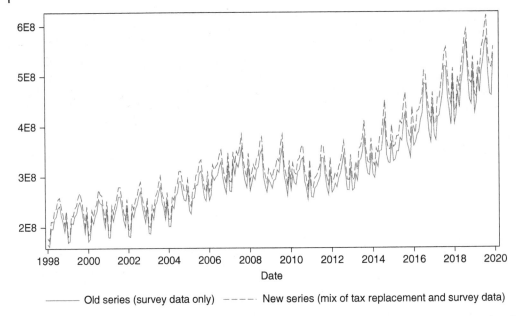

Graph 36.1 Example of the difference in sales estimates between the previous method (survey data) and the new method (tax replacement and survey data): Province of British Columbia in the industry 722511 (Full-service restaurants).

domains between the two methods. The method consisted of using the new approach retroactively to replace the estimates of the reference period beginning January 2016 and proceeding with a linking exercise to revise estimates before January 2016 (Verret, 2021). Graph 36.1 provides an example of the differences between the sales estimates from the previous method (survey data) and the new method (tax replacement and survey data, including the linkage exercise before January 2016) in a specific province and industry. The solid line represents the series from the previous method and the dotted line the series from the new method including the linkage exercise. In this specific example, the trend of the estimates is very close between the methods which are desired with a slight upward change in the level. This is usually the case for other domains of interest (NAICS and geography). The series was analyzed for each domain of interest and corrected if necessary, but most of the time the differences were accepted and explainable as previously mentioned under Section 2.4.

The six-month parallel run was originally scheduled to end in the spring 2020, but due to the pandemic, it was decided to continue the parallel run for a few additional months. The tax replacement project was then launched in production for the reference month of August 2020. Since then, the estimates continue to be monitored closely, especially during the pandemic. For more details on the new methodology, refer to Landry et al. (2021).

36.2.6 Conclusion and Future Work

The tax replacement project in the MSFSDP was a success, both in terms of cost savings (the new process allowed for a collection cost reduction of 80%) and response burden reduction. Since the survey is now a census, there is no need for stratification, a parallel run, and a data linkage process every five years. This also contributes to an additional cost reduction. In terms of response burden, less than 100 questionnaires are sent to collection (for the chains) as compared to 2600 questionnaires under the old design. Another advantage with the census is the possibility to provide more granular detailed estimates: this is part of future work and described in more detail below. Also, the precision of the estimates improved as the only source of variability comes from the imputation models for the nonresponse. There is no more variability due to sampling under the new approach.

However, a possible weakness, as often mentioned in the literature related to the use of administrative data, is that obtaining these data relies entirely on the supplier (CRA). It is for this reason that Statistics Canada is in close collaboration with CRA for many years, so any issues, changes in the legislation, or other changes that could affect the delivery of the file or the data are communicated to Statistics Canada in a timely manner. Another consideration with the project is the use of a census instead of a sample, which means a larger data set. It may require more effort and time when unexpected estimates arise. Diagnostics are very important to provide support in the analysis of the data to detect and correct as quickly as possible for any erroneous or suspicious estimates.

As mentioned above, future work for the MSFSDP includes the production of more granular data at the sub-provincial level for nine large census metropolitan areas (CMAs) by industry group. The CMA is an area consisting of one or more neighboring municipalities located around a major urban core with a population of at least 100,000 inhabitants of which 50,000 or more live in the urban core. Since the survey is now a census, the publication of the data could include more CMA's as well as smaller areas. Data are currently being allocated at the location level instead of the establishment level using allocation factors on Statistics Canada's Business Register (Statistics Canada, 2020) to make this possible. More assessments are needed to evaluate the accuracy of the allocation process that distributes the sales of collected and GST data to the location level.

36.3 Replacement of Survey Data by Scanner Data in the Retail Commodity Survey

The replacement of survey data by scanner data in the RCS was undertaken in 2017. The main objective was to decrease the response burden, and a secondary objective was to improve the quality of the data. The scanner data from a large retailer was assessed to determine the feasibility of this approach. This included the coding of each product description to the North American Product Classification System (NAPCS).

The first part of this section will provide information on the RCS, followed by a description of the scanner data file, and the coding process and then the methodology used to replace survey data by scanner data. The remainder of this section will describe the quality assurance process put in place followed by future work and a conclusion.

36.3.1 The Retail Commodity Survey

The RCS collects detailed information about retail commodity sales in Canada. The objective is to produce estimates of the sales of various commodities at the national level for different types of retail outlets in Canada. The survey is a complement to the Monthly Retail Trade Survey (MRTS). MRTS gathers total monthly retail sales, while RCS collects a breakdown of these sales by commodity type.

The information provided by RCS can be used to track commodity sales within and across various types of retail stores, as well as to calculate commodity market share, and to gain a better understanding of the rapidly changing retail industry. The data show the type of outlets, where consumers prefer to buy certain commodities, and the shifts in the different types of commodities retailers decide to sell. Analysis of these data assists in establishing trends in commodity sales over time. The RCS data are used by Statistics Canada's System of National Accounts in their estimates of personal expenditures. Other users of the data include federal and provincial government departments, retail analysts, market researchers, industry experts, and independent consultants.

Sales estimates are produced quarterly for 12 retail subsectors in Canada and up to 140 commodities defined by the NAPCS. Monthly estimates are also produced at a less-detailed level, i.e. by commodity at the national level, not by subsector. The survey uses a sampling design with take-all, takes-some, and takes-none strata based on revenue size within NAICS and geography. The target population consists of all establishments on Statistics Canada's Business Register (Statistics Canada, 2020) that are classified to the retail sector using the NAICS code (ranging from 441100 to 454110). A new design and sample selection are performed every five years. The same sample is kept over five years with a sample of births added every month. The data on sales are collected every month by commodity (at national level) through the MRTS under the same sample. Before the implementation of scanner data, sales by commodity were collected via 6500 questionnaires.

36.3.2 Scanner Data File and Coding by Commodity

The scanner data file from a large retailer has been received every week for a few years now and contains detailed information about products and sales for each location of that business. Each file received contains more than 10 million observations. The transactions are grouped by product and store. The following table uses fictitious examples to illustrate the content of the file for some selected variables (Table 36.2).

The NAPCS code for each product is not available on this scanner data file, as may often be the case for scanner data. An automated coding approach was developed using machine learning (ML) techniques to assign a NAPCS code to all the product descriptions found on the scanner data files. To assess the performance of the automated coding, a quality framework was developed that includes the assessment of the ML model for the coding to NAPCS and a quality assurance process that is applied periodically to evaluate the quality of the model through time.

To derive and assess the model, the scanner data file was split into subsets to act as training, validation, and testing datasets. First, for each description, a NAPCS was derived based on a concordance table as well as manual coding and validation. Data from 42 months were used to ensure that seasonal products were included in the training data. The library XGBoost (with linear regression as the underlying method) of the open-source software R was used to develop a model to code product descriptions to NAPCS. The testing dataset showed an overall accuracy of 99%, which is excellent. The accuracy is defined as the ratio of the number of descriptions correctly coded by

Table 36.2 Partial layout of the scanner data file with a fictitious example.

Product description	Quantity sold	Total sales	Address	City	Internal classification code	Desc. 1	Desc. 2	Desc. 3
Salt and vinegar chips	50	C$ 200	123 AAA Street	Guelph	11111	Snacks	Chips	Reg.
Soft drink	60	C$ 120	456 ZZ Blvd.	Ajax	22222	Drinks	Soft drinks	Reg.
...	...	...	...	...	...	...	...	...

the model over the total number of descriptions. The fact that this scanner file contained an extra variable to describe the products that were close to the NAPCS level contributed to the high accuracy. This might not be the case with other scanner data files.

36.3.3 Methodology to Replace Survey Data with Scanner Data

Being confident with the derived model, the next step was to reconcile the locations on this scanner data file to all establishments on the frame. The scanner data file covered hundreds of establishments on the frame with 60% of them already in the sample and collected via more than 50 questionnaires.[2] All of the establishments represented in the scanner data file were included in the sample to capitalize on the richness of these data. They were assigned a weight of one. Adjustments had to be made on the weights of the remaining sample. Few sampling units, less than 10, were added to the sample to ensure a minimum sample size within each stratum. The new and old estimates by commodity and NAICS were compared to ensure they were similar and consistent.

36.3.4 Quality Assurance Process

A quality assurance process has been put in place to ensure that the model is still valid through time, especially for new products. A sample of 1000 product descriptions is selected periodically to assess the quality of the model. The sample design is stratified by recurrent and new products as well as by the confidence score (this variable is an output from the algorithm on the confidence in the coding, which takes a value between 0 and 1; generally the higher the score, the greater the confidence in the prediction). In each stratum, the products are sorted by NAPCS and sales, and a systematic sample is selected in each stratum.

The quality assessment process is as follows: For each description selected, the NAPCS code is manually assigned. The NAPCS codes obtained through the manual coding are then compared to the NAPCS codes obtained by the model. Table 36.3 gives a summary of the average accuracy from eight samples. Up to now, the model is quite stable and still reliable. The overall accuracy rate is 84%, i.e. the model can correctly code 84% of the products. When the products are weighted by the sales, the accuracy rate goes up to 93%. In other words, 93% of the sales of the retailer are well classified. As expected, the algorithm is not as accurate when the confidence score is lower than 0.9 but quite good for new descriptions. Important to note is that out of more than 100,000 different descriptions, less than 10% have a confidence score lower than 0.9, and less than 4% a confidence score lower than 0.8, which is considered very good.

In addition to the accuracy, other quality indicators are also derived to measure the reliability of the model: sensitivity, precision, F1 score as well as the Matthews correlation coefficient. For more information on these measures, refer to Laroche and Tremblay (2020) and Boughorbel et al. (2017).

Different options are available when the quality is not met. One option is to retrain the model with the manual coding results in the training set. Another option is to use an exception file that allows the results of the automated coding to be overwritten for some specific descriptions. Lastly, problematic NAPCS or descriptions can be identified and revised manually. These have not been applied yet based on the results which are still satisfactory.

---

2 The difference between the number of establishments in the sample and the number of questionnaires sent is mainly due to the use of clusters of establishments as sampling units. A cluster is defined as all in-scope establishments that belong to the same enterprise within the same NAICS and same geography.

Table 36.3 Accuracy rates (average of eight samples).

		Weighted accuracy (%)	Economically weighted accuracy (total sales) (%)
Product description	Recurring	84	93
	New	80	85
Confidence score	≥0.9	87	95
	<0.9	63	75
Overall		84	93

Another assessment is on the file itself. It is important to ensure that every scanner data file that is received corresponds to what is expected in terms of format and contents before applying the machine learning model. Basic checks related to the size of the file, the number of observations, and the numbers of variables are done every time a new file is received. More elaborate checks are also made to make sure that the number of products sold, the number of points of sale as well as total sales (by product and by point of sale) for a given week are consistent with what was observed in the past. Depending on the issue, some corrections can be resolved internally; otherwise, the data provider can be asked for explanations or an updated file. This happened only once for that retailer. The files received so far have been of high quality.

For more information on assessing the quality of this project, refer to Laroche and Tremblay (2020).

36.3.5 Future Work and Conclusion

Scanner data from another retailer is expected to be used in the next few months. The plan is to use the same model since it is in the same sector, and fine-tune the model or retrain it with additional data if higher accuracy is required. If the current model does not hold, a new model will have to be assessed specifically for that retailer. The same reconciliation process with the frame and the sample will have to be performed once a model is considered sufficiently accurate. The impact of that new retailer will be more important in terms of the number of establishments it represents and consequently in the reduction of the response burden. Preliminary results showed that this retailer represents more than 100 questionnaires that are currently sent each month. Some adjustments might be required on the methodology adopted with the first retailer.

The replacement of survey data by scanner data in the RCS for one retailer was an important accomplishment. First, it decreased the response burden for that retailer. Second, it improved the quality and the precision of the estimates because of the quality of the file received in terms of data and coverage, as well as more units being added to the sample. This will continue to improve as more scanner data are added. More scanner data will also allow the production of more granular estimates, for example at the subprovincial level. Finally, scanner data benefit other programs at Statistics Canada. For example, the Consumer Price Index uses it to get prices for a selected list of products. However, it is important to remember that there is a cost associated with the use of these scanner data such as the storage of these large files and the time and resources dedicated to evaluate and process them. The benefits are in the richness of these data and their use in different programs to improve their capacity to provide information, including the analytical capacity with the use of many different data sources. Also, there is a potential gain in timeliness with these data usually coming in on a weekly basis.

36.4   Integration of Survey Data with Administrative Data in the Monthly Survey of Manufacturing Using Small Area Estimation Techniques

Requests have been made to Statistics Canada to produce monthly subprovincial estimates of sales of goods manufactured for 12 large CMA by industry group from its MSM. The use of SAE techniques was evaluated to produce these subprovincial monthly estimates without increasing the sample size.

The MSM publishes the values (in current Canadian dollars) of sales of goods manufactured, inventories, orders as well as the values of capacity utilization rates and inventory to sale ratios by geography and subsectors under the NAICS codes 31, 32, and 33. Results from this survey are used by both the private and public sectors including federal and provincial government departments, the Bank of Canada, the System of National Accounts, the manufacturing community, consultants and research organizations in Canada, the United States and abroad, and the business press. Data collected by the MSM provides a current "snapshot" of sales of goods manufactured values by the Canadian manufacturing sector, enabling analysis of the state of the Canadian economy, as well as the health of specific industries in the short- to medium-term.

The first subsection will briefly describe the MSM methodology. The second one will explain the SAE method used, and how it was implemented. The third subsection will give a short explanation of the confidentiality strategy adopted, followed by a conclusion and future work.

36.4.1   Methodology of the Monthly Survey of Manufacturing (MSM)

Approximately 120,000 establishments are identified each month as being in-scope for the MSM from the Statistics Canada Business Register (Statistics Canada, 2020). The sampling frame is stratified by industry (27 subsectors NAICS 3–4 level), by province and territories, and size (the size variable is the business' annual revenue from the business register). Each industry-geography cell is divided according to the businesses size, into one take-all (TA) stratum, which contains the largest businesses, up to two take-some (TS) strata, which contain medium-size businesses, and one take-none (TN) stratum, which contains the smallest businesses that globally account for at the most 10% of total revenue for each industry-geography cell. The take-none units are not subject to sampling. Overall, a sample of around 6500 establishments is contacted every month: around 3500 from the take-all strata and around 3000 in the take-some strata.

The MSM is currently designed to provide estimates at the provincial level, not at the CMA level which is subprovincial. The effective sample size for CMA domains may not be large enough to produce reliable estimates on its own. Methods that have become very popular to improve the quality of estimates from small sample sizes are the SAE techniques. One SAE method was evaluated in the context of this project.

36.4.2   Small Area Estimation (SAE) Method and Implementation

The SAE model chosen is the Fay–Herriot area-level model (Fay and Herriot 1979). This model assumes a linear relationship between the domain estimates coming from the survey and the auxiliary information. For this project, the total monthly sales from the Goods and Services Tax and the Harmonized Sales Tax (GST) file provided to Statistics Canada every month by the CRA were used as the auxiliary information. The total monthly sales from the GST file are highly correlated to the monthly sales collected from the survey.

The Fay–Herriot area-level model has two components: a sampling model and a linking model. The final SAE estimate for domain i is then a linear combination of the estimate coming from the survey and the synthetic estimate coming from the SAE model:

$$\widehat{\theta}_d^{SAE} = \gamma_d \widehat{\theta}_d^{SURVEY} + (1 - \gamma_d) \widehat{\theta}_d^{SYNTHETIC} \tag{36.3}$$

with

$$\gamma_d = \frac{\widehat{V}(v_d)}{\widehat{V}(e_d) + \widehat{V}(v_d)} \text{ and } \widehat{\theta}_d^{SYNTHETIC} = z_d'\widehat{\beta} \tag{36.4}$$

where d is a domain, $\widehat{V}(e_d)$ is the estimated sampling variance, $\widehat{V}(v_d)$ is the estimated model variance, $\widehat{\theta}_d^{SURVEY}$ is the survey estimate, $\widehat{\theta}_d^{SYNTHETIC}$ is the modeled estimate, z_d' is the auxiliary information,[3] and $\widehat{\beta}$ is the estimated regression model coefficient.

Since the take-all units represent themselves, there is no need or advantage to include them in the model. They do not have sampling errors associated with them and also, the data for the large complex businesses will not be as reliable on the GST file due to the allocation process that is not as precise as the data collected at a lower level (industry and province). The take-none units were also excluded since they do not have any estimates from the survey sample. They will be estimated from the SAE model using the synthetic portion only. Therefore, only the take-some portion is used in the SAE model.

There was a possibility of 324 domain estimates (12 CMAs by 27 industries [mainly three-digit NAICS code]). The model was tested for many months to evaluate the stability of the model through time. Based on the preliminary results, some adjustments were made to improve the model fit such as the following:

- No intercept was used in the SAE model to avoid the possibility of negative SAE estimates.
- The model was better with the use of the mean of the sales instead of the total sales. This implies that after the model parameters had been estimated, the resulting SAE estimates and mean square error (MSE) were rescaled to obtain estimates of totals.
- The variance of the domain estimates of totals (means) obtained from the survey can be quite unstable when the associated sample size is small. They were smoothed using a variance smoothing model.
- Outlier detection was carried out on the results obtained from the variance smoothing model and the Fay–Herriot area-level model to improve the model. These outliers were excluded from the final model.

Various diagnostics were carried out to assess the validity of the SAE model. In general, the precision of the SAE estimates improved significantly. The following graph (Graph 36.2) that compares the relative root mean square error (RRMSE) from the SAE estimates with the smoothed direct coefficient of variations (CV) from the survey estimates reflects this point. Each point corresponds to a CMA take-some domain with sampled units for a given month. We can see that the points are below the line and this implies better precision.

The final estimate for a domain is the sum of the TA subdomain estimate, the TS subdomain estimate, and the TN subdomain estimate. As stated earlier, the TA subdomain estimate is obtained

---

3 The auxiliary information is the monthly sales from the GST file. For the preliminary estimates, it uses the GST data from the previous reference month since the GST file is not processed on time for the MSM production. For the revised estimates, the GST data for the same reference month is available and used.

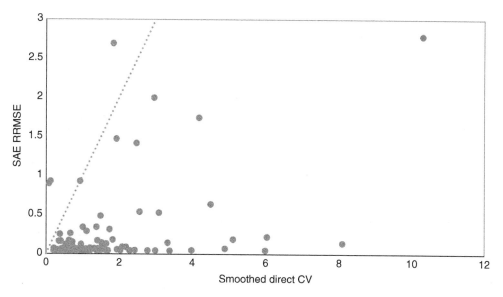

Graph 36.2 Comparison between the smoothed direct CV coming from the survey and the SAE relative root mean square error (RRMSE) for the CMA take-some subdomains: an example from the reference period November 2020.

directly from the survey. The TS subdomain estimate will be the SAE estimate. The TN subdomain estimate will be a synthetic estimate. The following formula summarizes this:

$$\widehat{\theta}_d^{\text{SAE}} = \widehat{\theta}_{d,\text{TA}}^{\text{SURVEY}} + \widehat{\theta}_{d,\text{TS}}^{\text{SAE}} + \widehat{\theta}_{d,\text{TN}}^{\text{SYNTHETIC}} \tag{36.5}$$

Since the TA subdomain estimate is assumed to be free of bias, the MSE of the domain estimate is computed as the sum of the variance of the TA subdomain estimate, the MSE of the TS subdomain estimate, and the MSE of the TN subdomain estimate. Note that the variance for the take-all strata occurs because some of the data have been imputed:

$$\widehat{\text{MSE}}\left(\widehat{\theta}_d^{\text{SAE}}\right) = \widehat{V}\left(\widehat{\theta}_{d,\text{TA}}^{\text{SURVEY}}\right) + \widehat{\text{MSE}}\left(\widehat{\theta}_{d,\text{TS}}^{\text{SAE}}\right) + \widehat{\text{MSE}}\left(\widehat{\theta}_{d,\text{TN}}^{\text{SYNTHETIC}}\right) \tag{36.6}$$

The final estimates were subject to editing and adjustments to ensure that the total CMA estimates within a province did not exceed the estimate of the province for each industry. Although this occurrence should be rare it is possible. If this occurs, the SAE estimates from the take-some and the take-none portion are adjusted so that the sum is equal to the take-some and take-none portions of the provincial and industry estimate.

36.4.3 Confidentiality Strategy for the SAE Estimates

Finally, a confidentiality strategy for the SAE estimates had to be put in place to protect confidential data. According to Canada's Statistics Act, Statistics Canada must protect data to ensure that no published estimate reveals information about an entity (person, business, etc.). In our case, since the estimates come from different sources (survey and model estimates), in consultation with our confidentiality experts at Statistics Canada, it was decided to account for both sources, using the population data file, and by first protecting reported data obtained from the survey. Thereby, for the businesses in the sample, the data used in the confidentiality pattern are their reported sales from the collection. For businesses in the population but not in the sample, the data are the synthetic sales value derived from the SAE model ($z_j' \widehat{\beta}$, where j is a business). This synthetic data is considered a good proxy for sales for a business. Primary suppressions were applied on domains with very small populations or where one business is dominant within its domain. Secondary suppressions were also performed to ensure the primary suppressions could not be derived and also to account for the confidentiality pattern at the provincial and industry level already determined. The generalized system G-CONFID from Statistics Canada (Statistics Canada, 2021) has been used. As a result, around 60% of the CMA-industry domains, representing around 85% of the total sales is published every month.

Refer to Landry (2020) for more information on this project.

36.4.4 Conclusion and Future Work

The production of subprovincial monthly estimates of sales of goods manufactured for 12 large CMA by industry group was a success. These estimates have been published monthly since September 2019. Historical SAE estimates from January 2009 were also provided. The use of SAE techniques allowed to produce more and good quality estimates at the subprovincial level without increasing the sample, thus no increase in the collection cost and the response burden. However, as a new product, it is important to remember that more time is required each month to validate the model and to analyze these new estimates before disseminating them.

In terms of ongoing and future work, seasonal adjustment is currently being performed on the CMA estimates and will be published in the near future, and additional CMAs are expected to be added to the scope of this project.

36.5 Impact of the COVID-19 Pandemic in the Monthly Business Programs and the Administrative and Alternative Data Sources Used

Once the COVID-19 pandemic started to impact the country in March 2020, questions and concerns were raised in the monthly business programs at Statistics Canada in the manufacturing, wholesale, retail, and food and drinking places sectors such as the following:

- Will businesses continue to answer our surveys?
- Are the current imputation methods appropriate in the current context?
- Will administrative and alternative data used in our programs still be available, complete, of good quality, and received on time?
- Could the programs provide more timely data and could they collect additional indicators of the impact?

36.5.1 Survey Responses

In terms of the response rate of these surveys, different avenues were examined and applied to help to obtain responses. Note that these surveys are mainly conducted via EQ questionnaires with e-mails and phone follow-ups. First, increased monitoring and follow-ups were done. For example, different collection codes were added, one to identify temporary closure due to the pandemic and another one to identify open businesses that reported they were too busy to answer. This was considered by the analysts when looking at the estimates and the imputed data. Second, a list of businesses was created each month to prioritize the follow-ups. The list considered the importance of a unit in a domain and the importance of the domain. Third, efforts were made to maintain good respondent relations and to demonstrate our support and appreciation by adapting the introductory letters, the reminders, and the interviewers' interventions to the current context. The response rate decreased during the pandemic, but was considered satisfactory given the context. While it was around 95% before the pandemic for the critical monthly programs (manufacturing, wholesale and retail), it dropped to around 85% during the pandemic. Having the same sample each month (with some births added) surely has helped the response rate; most businesses sampled are accustomed to the surveys. For births, some surveys decided to exclude them from the collection for the first months to avoid imposing an additional burden on these businesses. The hope and expectation is for the response rates to return to previous levels. Extra collection measures have been put in place to achieve it, for examples by doing more research from different sources to get other contact information and to help identifying temporary closures.

36.5.2 Imputation Methods

Early in the pandemic, the existing imputation methods were reviewed and modified when necessary. One challenge was to ensure that the proposed changes would be operationally feasible within a short period. In addition, we wanted imputation methods that reflected the current context (the pandemic). The use of only historical data would not have been accurate in industries impacted by the pandemic. Each survey uses a sequential approach to impute data, ordered by the best imputation method given the available data. Given this, the simplest and most appropriate strategy was to not use the methods based only on historical information. The imputation classes were also adjusted as needed to have more homogeneous groups to take into account specific behaviors or rules in certain industries and certain provinces. Given the consistently high response rate, around 85%, we were confident with the few implemented changes to the imputation methods. They reflected the current context and were simple to implement.

36.5.3 Scanner Data and Administrative GST Data

The scanner data and the administrative GST data used in the monthly business programs continued to be provided during the pandemic. The scanner data continued to be available weekly with the same coverage and quality as expected.

However, for the administrative GST tax data, fewer businesses reported to the CRA in the first three months of the crisis. For example, the number of monthly reporters weighted by revenue decreased from 82% in March 2019 to 59% in March 2020; and from 85% in April 2019 to 71% in April 2020. It was therefore important to ensure that the imputation methods were appropriate. The imputation methods of the GST data were reviewed, and some adjustments have been made to better reflect the current context. Among the changes, the use of the time series approach to assign quarterly and annual values to monthly values was replaced by monthly distributions derived from current monthly filers; the extrapolation method using previous values to impute monthly nonfilers was replaced by a trend method using historical and current data, and imputation classes were adjusted to add the province in the original imputation classes which included only NAICS and sales class. As a result, the changes have been quite significant in some industries affected by the pandemic. For example, in the Food Services and Drinking Places industry, a drop of 13% was observed in the sales estimates between the estimates derived under the old imputation methods versus the new imputation methods for March 2020. A more important drop of 37% was observed in April 2020. The sales estimates derived from GST data under the new imputation methods were also closer to the sales estimated from the survey. On a positive note, although fewer businesses reported their GST information in the first month, they tended to do so later. For example, for the reference month of March 2020, the number of monthly reporters' businesses weighted by their sales increased from 59% to 89% between the preliminary and the revised files.

36.5.4 Advance Estimates and Supplementary Questions

Starting with the first COVID months, the monthly surveys on Manufacturing, Retail, and Wholesale are providing information earlier, referred to as advance estimates. In view of the rapidly changing economic situation, preliminary estimates are quite relevant. While estimates from monthly surveys are typically released six to seven weeks after the end of the reference month, advance estimates are provided approximately two to three weeks after the end of the reference month. For retail and wholesale, they are included in their usual publication; for manufacturing, they are provided one week after their main release. For example, estimates for the retail sector for November were released on 22 January, and they included the estimate of anticipated sales for December. To date, only aggregate sales figures are provided, and they are based on responses received so far for that month. The response rate for this advance estimate is around 50%, as compared to around 85% with the regular release. Further research has been undertaken to improve and extend the use of these advanced estimates, for example by providing more detail with acceptable quality.

Finally, the monthly surveys on Manufacturing, Retail, Wholesale, and Food and Drinking Places added up to nine supplementary questions to their questionnaire during the months of the pandemic to assess its impact. These questions have been developed a few years ago at Statistics Canada to assess the impact of a shock on the activities in the economy on different industries and provinces. They are used as needed, and they go through an edit, imputation, and estimation process. These questions are referred to as the fast track module (FTM). Some questions are provided below as examples:

- Were your business or organization activities for reference month xxx impacted by the pandemic? (yes/no)
- How did it impact your business or organization (select all that apply)? (Shortage of labor, shortage of raw materials, shortage of working capital, disruption in energy supply, disruption in transport, others)
- Was your business or organization shut down due to the pandemic? (yes/no). If yes, for how many days?
- Please estimate the impact on your sales, in dollars or in percentages.
- Please estimate the impact on your inventories, in dollars or in percentages.

36.6 Future Initiatives for the Monthly Business Programs

Lately, there has been a strong interest in providing estimates earlier. With the pandemic, the monthly business surveys in retail, wholesale, and manufacturing began to produce these estimates, referred to as advance estimates. As described above, these estimates are provided approximately two to three weeks after the end of the reference month as compared to regular estimates that are released six to seven weeks after the end of the reference month. The method consists of producing estimates with the early collected data (received by a given date) and with the same methodology used in the usual process. Studies using historical data have shown that these sales estimates are reliable enough to be used. So far, only an advanced estimate of overall sales has been provided. Further analysis needs to be done on other variables and by domain. In addition, other methods and studies will be explored to provide more reliable and granular estimates, which could include the use of administrative or alternative data or model-based methods.

Further modeling should improve the efficiency of the surveys. Although the GST file is a very good source of sales data, it is the only available variable. Since most monthly surveys also collect inventory information, studies have begun that assess the feasibility of modeling inventories based on administrative data or other alternative sources.

Finally, monthly business programs will go through a review of their confidentiality strategy and methods, to publish more estimates.

36.7   Conclusion

As many other NSO, Statistics Canada has to adapt its statistical programs to respond to a rapidly changing economy and society, a proliferation of data and expectations for "real-time" and detailed information. This includes an extensive use of administrative and alternative data to provide statistics, these data being leveraged before surveys or other traditional collection methods. It has been shown in the literature that the use of administrative or alternative data could have many advantages for NSO such as the improvement in quality, the improvement in relevance with more detailed or more frequent estimates, filling data gaps, and the reduction of cost and response burden.

This chapter has provided three successful examples of the expansion of the use of administrative and alternative data in monthly business statistics programs at Statistics Canada. Replacing survey data with the Goods and Services Tax and the Harmonized Sales Tax data in the Monthly Food Services and Drinking Places Survey reduces collection costs and response burden, as well as improves the precision of the estimates. It will also allow for more granular data with its census design. Using scanner data to replace sales survey data in the RCS reduced the response burden while providing more data and better precision. This impact will increase by integrating more scanner data. The SAE Techniques project that integrates survey and administrative data into the MSM provides more granular estimates of high quality at no additional collection costs and no additional response burden.

As mentioned in this document, evaluations of these methods were essential before their implementation and directly incorporated refinements and improvements. In addition, monitoring of this data, such as coding quality or model validation, should be done regularly to maintain standard quality and improve where necessary. Finally, while the use of administrative and alternative data increases the wealth of information that can be provided and the analytical capacity, there is a cost associated with the processing and maintenance of these files, as well as a cost to validate and analyze this new information before releasing them. These costs need to be considered when assessing the fitness of use of administrative and alternative data sources.

Acknowledgments

The authors thank Jean-Francois Beaumont, Cynthia Bocci, Michelle Caruso, Kenneth Chu, Jessica Mulligan, Robert Philips, and Pier-Olivier Tremblay for their specific contribution and their thoughtful comments and assistance in the development of these different projects.

The authors thank also Michel Hidiroglou, Normand Laniel, Dave MacNeil, Steve Matthews, and Wesley Yung for their thoughtful comments in the revision of this chapter.

References

Boughorbel, S., Jarray, F., and El-Anbari, M. (2017). Optimal classifier for imbalanced data using Matthews Correlation Coefficient metric. *PLoS One* https://doi.org/10.1371/journal.pone.0177678.

Glikofridis, C. (2017). Factor Allocation Overview and User Guide. Internal document, Statistics Canada.

Fay, R.E. and Herriot, R.A. (1979). Estimation of income from small places: an application of James-Stein procedures to census data. *Journal of the American Statistical Association* 74: 269–277.

Kirkland, T. (2016a). Calendarization Strategy for the GST Project. Internal document, Statistics Canada.

Kirkland, T. (2016b). GST Imputation Strategy. Internal document, Statistics Canada.

Landry, S., Laroche, R., and Mulligan, J. (2021). New methodology of the Monthly Survey of Food Services and Drinking Places. Internal document, Statistics Canada.

Landry, S. (2020). Implementation of small area estimation techniques in an economic survey: the experience of the monthly survey of manufacturing in Canada. In: *JSM Proceedings, Survey Research Methods Section*, 1544–1553. Alexandria, VA: American Statistical Association.

Laroche, R. and Caruso, M. (2020). Replacing survey data with GST data in the Monthly Survey of Food Services and Drinking Places: an Assessment. Internal document, Statistics Canada.

Laroche, R. and Tremblay, P.-O. (2020). Assessing the quality of a coding process generated by a machine learning algorithm. In: *JSM Proceedings, Government Statistics Section*, 1112–1120. American Statistical Association: Alexandria, VA.

Statistics Canada (2016). Compendium of Management Practices for Statistical Organizations from Statistics Canada's International Statistical Fellowship Program, Catalogue 11-634-X2016001, ISBN 978-0-660-05813-9.

Statistics Canada (2021). G-Confid (Disclosure Avoidance – Generalized System). https://www150 .statcan.gc.ca/n1/en/catalogue/10H0109.

Statistics Canada (2020). Business Register. https://www23.statcan.gc.ca/imdb/p2SV.pl? Function=getSurvey&SDDS=1105.

Statistics Canada (2019). Statistics Canada Data Strategy. Catalogue no. 89-26-00032020001.

Verret, F. (2021). Linking the Monthly Survey of Food Services and Drinking Places (MSFSDP) for the switch from survey data to GST data. Internal presentation, Statistics Canada

Index

Advances in Business Statistics, Methods and Data Collection. Edited by Ger Snijkers, Mojca Bavdaž, Stefan Bender,
Jacqui Jones, Steve MacFeely, Joseph W. Sakshaug, Katherine J. Thompson, and Arnout van Delden.
© 2023 John Wiley & Sons, Inc. Published 2023 by John Wiley & Sons, Inc.